THE PLACES WHERE MEN PRAY TOGETHER

Minaret of the Mosque of Ibn Ṭūlūn, Cairo, completed in A.D. 878 to the order of the founder of the Ṭūlūnid state. Courtesy of the Egyptian Tourism Authority.

PAUL WHEATLEY

THE PLACES WHERE MEN PRAY TOGETHER

CITIES IN ISLAMIC LANDS

SEVENTH THROUGH THE TENTH CENTURIES

THE UNIVERSITY OF CHICAGO PRESS
CHICAGO & LONDON

Paul Wheatley (1921–99) was the Irving B. Harris Professor Emeritus of Comparative Urban Studies at the University of Chicago. He was the author of, among others, *The Pivot of the Four Quarters: A Preliminary Inquiry into the Origins and Character of the Ancient Chinese City* and *Nagara & Commandery: Origins of the Southeast Asian Urban Tradition.*

The University of Chicago Press, Chicago 60637
The University of Chicago Press, Ltd., London

Printed in the United States of America

10 09 08 07 06 05 04 03 02 01 1 2 3 4 5
ISBN: 0-226-89428-2 (cloth)

Library of Congress Cataloging-in-Publication Data

Wheatley, Paul.
The places where men pray together : cities in Islamic lands, seventh through the tenth centuries / Paul Wheatley.
p. cm.
Includes bibliographical references and index.
ISBN 0-226-89428-2 (alk. paper)
1. Urbanization—Islamic countries. 2. Cities and towns—Islamic countries. I. Title.

HT384.I67.W44 2001
307.76′0917′671—dc21 99-049896

∞ The paper used in this publication meets the minimum requirements of the American National Standard for Information Sciences—Permanence of Paper for Printed Library Materials, ANSI Z39.48-1992.

For the two Elsies

Contents

Illustrations

Figures

Tables

Preface

This is not a history of Islamic urban architecture, nor is it a study of art-historical motifs traditionally associated with Islamic cities; still less is it a historical gazetteer of city names and locations. Rather, it is an attempt to elicit from not always ekistically forthcoming sources the faded lineaments of thirteen settlement systems that agglomerative and accessibility factors had molded into pyramidal urban hierarchies by the tenth century. *Urbanism* in this context is defined as a primarily centripetalizing societal process in which spatial and locational strategies are employed to structure social and economic integration. In a very real sense an *urban hierarchy* is the cumulative summation of the functional roles that its constituent cities collectively perform while yet serving as the rationalizing principle mandating those very roles.

Data for reconstructing such hierarchies in the first four Islamic centuries are almost invariably fragmented, often ambivalent, and never—by modern standards—adequate for meaningful demographic analysis. There is, for example, no systematized information on even crude rates of natural population change; and even if there were, demographic deductions therefrom could only be speculative unless supported by age-specific fertility and mortality rates and a well-founded understanding of nuptiality—information that is not available and unlikely to be in the foreseeable future. Such fragments of data as can be salvaged have to be acquired from incidental and anecdotal references in what may be categorized as entertainment literature and, to a lesser extent, in the descriptive topographies of the time. Clearly the best that can be hoped for in these circumstances is the recognition of simplified urban hierarchies as they were perceived by their inhabitants and interpreted by contemporary outsiders. That is what most of this book (chapters 4 through 16) is about, although I have also exercised the option of maintaining, however imperfectly, the external explanatory perspective of a twentieth-century urbanist. In this endeavor I have had the good fortune to be able to rely on a tenth-century author who, uncharacteristically for his time, gathered precisely these data types and interpreted them in a manner meaningful to himself and his fellows. This paragon among pioneer urbanists was Shams al-Dīn Abū ʿAbd Allāh Muḥammad ibn Aḥmad ibn Abī Bakr al-Bannāʾ al-Maqdisī. He deployed, in fourteen structured systems of hierarchically ordered urban forms, the vast amount of information he collected about Islamic cities during the travels of a lifetime (for reasons given below, I have excluded one of these systems—that of India—from discussion). Within each of these systems, which in the aggregate reached from the Atlantic Ocean to the Indus River and from the Caspian Sea to the Sūdānese lands, he consistently discriminated four ranks of urban centers culminating ideally in a single metropolis.

Although al-Maqdisī's resulting work, the *Aḥsan*

al-Taqāsīm fī Maʿrifat al-Aqālīm, must rank as one of the most ambitious studies of human organization ever attempted in the medieval world, it has to be acknowledged that the author was not innately omniscient. What is more, in the tenth century the systematic collection and collation of information from a region stretching one-fifth of the way around the world was a task virtually impossible to achieve. Inevitably al-Maqdisī incurred errors of both fact and interpretation, although many fewer than might have been expected; and not infrequently he himself noted and apologized for a shortcoming of coverage or understanding. Moreover, he was not entirely free of the prevalent medieval proclivity that historian al-Masʿūdī characterized as woodcutting by might: he sometimes reported a plurality of authoritatively approved, though not necessarily wholly conformable, versions of events rather than distilling from them a single constructed account believed to approximate the truth.

To compensate for these imperfections I have combed the roadbooks, topographies, histories, *adab* literature, and gazetteers of the time for relevant and comparative material, always cognizant of the important distinction between an author's authenticity and his veracity; in so doing I have not hesitated to adapt, elaborate, and expand al-Maqdisī's seminal exposition. I have, though, excluded from discussion five districts (*kūrah*) in al-Sind on which al-Maqdisī reported but did not visit. To that extent this book can be construed as a twentieth-century update of al-Maqdisī's depiction of a fundamental aspect of medieval society; or if that is too presumptuous a claim, at least as sustained gloss on the *Aḥsan*.

The role of a particular settlement within an urban hierarchy is determined almost exclusively by its function, hardly at all by its form—in simple terms, by what it does rather than by what it is. To incorporate this dimension in the following discussions, I have apportioned the urban centers comprising the thirteen systems among three conventionally recognized, analytically distinct, but by no means mutually exclusive functional categories, namely

1. A relatively uniform spread of settlements, each of which offers a range of goods and services to a surrounding territory of a magnitude appropriate to its ranking in the hierarchy. Here I must warn central-place aficionados that this settlement categorization as used in this context implies nothing as to its origin; merely that at the time specified it served as an exchange mart for a surrounding district that in modern times would be called its city trade area.
2. A lineally deployed component providing freight-handling and allied services strung along transportation routes.
3. A clustered component comprising urban centers engaged in specialized activities tied to particular resources.

In chapters 4–16 these urban functions are evaluated for each *iqlīm* in the order that they are mentioned here.

Thus far this exposition has focused almost exclusively on urban systems, which in the aggregate have not previously received much attention. However, some readers by this time may have become curious about the physical and sociocultural milieus exemplified by individual nucleated components of the hierarchies. Accordingly, chapter 17 offers an overview of the epiphenomenal manifestations of certain institutional classes affecting a city's ranking in its hierarchy; it also describes their spatial deployment within the settlement. This description of urban internal structure, however, treats institutions generically—for example, as a mosque, not as a particular, architecturally distinctive mosque, as an architect or art historian would probably do. I have also occasionally alluded to the city as a macroscopic role system, a social environment promoting a distinctive style of life and thought. These aspects of medieval Islamic urbanism have been studied intensively in recent times. Nonetheless, I briefly discuss some of them in this book, mainly to shed more light on intrinsically important topics that, while peripheral to my main thesis, complement the preceding narrative; I also do so because many previous studies have concentrated on the later Middle Ages at the expense of the much less richly documented earlier Islamic centuries. Moreover, I have permitted myself a minor amount of duplication between chapters so that, after familiarizing themselves with chapter 3, readers will be able to tackle a series of more or less self-contained essays.

In collecting materials for both the external (hierarchical) and internal (structural) organization of cities in the first four centuries of Islam, I have relied on the classes of primary sources I specified earlier, explicating them whenever possible with contemporary commentary. The result is a series of functional urban regions integrated around metropoleis exceptionally expressive of regional capacity and sentiment, thereby substantially preserving the prevailing perceptions of the tenth century. The hierarchies devised by al-Maqdisī were relatively simple systems based on an array of political and administrative functions. His method turned out to be not such a bad thing: in the tenth century, functional economic regions prevalently reflected the reach of political power and authority. One indication of al-Maqdisī's achievement is that it was not repeated anywhere in the world for almost a millennium.

Perhaps I should also forestall possible misunderstandings about my database sources. One might assume that any contemporary representation of urban distributions in the early Islamic world would owe a great deal to Georgette Cornu's *Atlas du Monde Arabo-Islamique à l'Époque Classique IXe-Xe Siècles,* issued at Leiden in 1985. Actually, figure 2 in this book, which is the principal underpinning of my analysis, was first published in paper (in *Ekistics* 42 [1976]: 360) and subsequently reproduced by Dale F. Eickelman in his *Middle East: An Anthropological Approach* (Englewood Cliffs, N.J., 1981, p. 264)—on both occasions on a relatively small scale. It has not been significantly altered in the intervening decades, although it appears here on a larger scale. Such discrepancies as exist between Dr. Cornu's representation and mine stem mainly from our different purposes: she was plotting place-names in response to *la nécessité de situer visuellement sur une carte les nombreux toponymes rencontrés* (*Atlas,* p. vii), whereas I was selecting from the same sources only those settlements that according to my canons could be considered urban—admittedly a procedure fraught with judgmental perils. A second work that was published too late to benefit me is Basil A. Collins's meticulous, but unfortunately unannotated, English translation of al-Maqdisī's great survey. My book was virtually completed when *Al-Muqaddasi: The Best Divisions for Knowledge of the Regions* appeared in 1994 (compare with my paper in *al-ʿUṣūr al-Wusṭā* 5 [1993]: 4–6). Needless to say, I would have benefited proportionately had these works been available when I was compiling the main body of this book.

During the protracted preparation of this volume I have incurred innumerable debts, both intellectual and organizational. Clearly, in tackling a topic of this magnitude I have stood on the shoulders of generations of my predecessors who systematized materials and made hitherto neglected texts accessible. I believe that I have acknowledged my indebtedness to these scholars appropriately in text or supplementary note. To those who lacked a name or whom I overlooked I apologize, as I do to all those past colleagues who either formally or informally, and perhaps unwittingly, helped to shape my understanding of Islam's early centuries. Particularly influential in this respect were the Oriental Institute's biweekly seminars on early Middle Eastern urbanism under the direction of Dr. Donald Whitcomb. The seminars ran continuously from 1991 through 1995 and brought together in animated discussion not only faculty and students at the University of Chicago but also a schedule of visitors constituting a veritable who's who of scholars in the field.

Dr. Whitcomb also deserves recognition at a more personal level. Not only has he instructed me in the mysteries of processual archaeology, the results of which I have incorporated in my analysis to the best of my ability, but he has also alerted me to recondite references and spent countless hours debating both the nature of early Islamic urbanism and competing methodologies for its understanding. Not that he and I are always in agreement in our interpretations. Some of these disparities reflect the lack of a necessary congruence between conclusions resulting from respectively inductive and deductive reasoning, especially in regions and periods for which data are sparse. Whereas I am not unsympathetic to the medieval topographers' desire to gather up every scrap of relevant information and cover all possibilities (a stance not unknown to Lucretius and vigorously advocated by, among others, Isidore of Seville), and have not scrupled to proceed, when it seemed advantageous to do so, on fundamentally inductivist principles, Dr. Whitcomb's primary aim is to construct a deductive model of a class of settlement relationships that will enable him to predict the locations where his excavations will be most effective. It has to be said, though, that when I disagree with him I do so with trepidation, in keen anticipation of his archaeological expertise, the ultimate arbiter in such matters, eventually pronouncing against me. This should not surprise anyone: a hypothetico-deductive methodology is directed avowedly toward discovery, whereas inductive systematization is concerned at least as much with verification and confirmation; and, where the database is too meager to sustain the deductive process, may be made to yield nascent interpretative structures.

Two scholarly institutions are especially deserving of

my gratitude: The Lynde and Harry Bradley Foundation for underwriting a year of secretarial assistance in a late phase of the work, and the Department of Near Eastern Languages and Civilizations at the University of Chicago for providing me with a congenial environment within which to write chapter 17—a gracious gesture without which the book would probably never have been finished. Professors Fred M. Donner and Norman Golb are owed a special debt of gratitude for their help at that time. I also extend my thanks to Dale F. Eickelman, who critiqued the whole work and provided a dossier of persuasive, indeed sometimes mandatory, suggestions, almost all of which I have adopted. Finally, I must pay tribute to those members of the University of Chicago Press who transformed a monstrous typescript into a handsome volume: Penelope Kaiserlian, who watched over the whole complicated operation; Robert Williams, whose design skills are apparent on every page; and especially Sandy Hazel, my copyeditor, who not only tightened up my discursive prose but also probed inconsistencies in the text, notes, and bibliography to the point where she made the whole enterprise her own.

Of course, none of the numerous friends and associates who have helped me over the years are responsible for the way in which I have used that assistance. What I hope to have achieved is the construction of a tenth-century foundation for studying the urban hierarchies that were to be the principal bearers of Islamic civilization in subsequent eras, for which a greater abundance and variety of available data will mandate the use of more sophisticated techniques of analysis.

Center for Middle Eastern Studies
University of Chicago
Al-ʿĪd al-Aḍḥa A.H. 1418

Publisher's note: Paul Wheatley worked on this manuscript over two decades but did not live to see the book in print. He died on 30 October 1999, while the manuscript was still in editing. He had painstakingly checked the editing through chapter 16. We are indebted to Margaret Wheatley and Davíd Carrasco for overseeing the final stages of editing and seeing the book through to publication. Davíd Carrasco and Donald Whitcomb read and commented on part III, which remains to a large extent as the author wrote it. We also acknowledge with thanks the help of Joel Kraemer and John Woods, who checked the Arabic transliterations; Katharine W. Hannaford, who worked with the author in the preparation of many of the maps; and Mohamed Zakariya, who provided calligraphy on page 337.

Explanatory Notes

Matters of Definition

City in this volume is used generically to denote any urban form and carries none of the ancillary connotations of size, status, or origin implicit in contemporary American and English usage. *Urbanism* denotes the operation of that particular set of functionally integrated institutions which evolved some five thousand years ago to mediate the transformation of relatively egalitarian, ascriptive, kin-structured groups into socially stratified, politically organized, territorially based societies. These institutions have, since their origin, progressively extended both the scope and autonomy of their spheres so that today they mold the actions and aspirations of the majority of humankind. *Urbanization* refers to the ratio of urban dwellers to total population. It follows that the distribution of urbanization is not necessarily congruent with the distribution of urbanism (measured as the number and size of cities) or the distribution of urban dwellers.

As for the Arabic terms in the text, I have made every effort to define them at their first occurrence whenever practicable. All but the most common terms may be found in the glossary at the back of the book.

Orthographical and Related Matters

Whereas the transliteration of Arabic, Berber, and Persian—the three languages from which the majority of names and terms mentioned in this book are derived—challenges the ingenuity of linguistic specialists on their own ground, to students of Islamic society whose interest lies in the attributes of the reality behind the name, it is simply a vexing preliminary to their main work. Yet it is a task that the canons of scholarship require that they perform scientifically, accurately, and systematically. The transliteration problem is exacerbated by the amount of borrowing that has occurred between Arabic and each of the other languages, so that a particular term may exhibit two or perhaps three vocalizations. A special case of such borrowing is the rendering into medieval Arabic texts of contemporary Berber and Persian place-names, so that, say, a Persian settlement of the period may be known to us in both Persian and Arabic forms; only in its Arabicized form; or, in a fair number of instances, by a totally distinct Arabic name. Such, for instance, was the case with Bāb al-Abwāb, the Arab designation of the city called Darband by the Persians. Moreover, in North Africa and the northern fringes of the Middle East, where Islam had assumed control of sectors of the classical world, it was not uncommon for a place-name to be reported by the respective texts in both classical and Arabicized forms (e.g., Mopsuestia/al-Maṣṣīṣah or Theveste/Tabassā) or even as two etymologically unrelated names (e.g., Theodosiopolis/Qālīqalā, modern Erzurum). I have tended to retain in the text the Arabic version (often, more accurately, one of the Arabic versions) as preserved in the numerically predominant Arabic topographies of the time. However, I have not been entirely consistent in this. In any case, variant versions are often included in the relevant chapter notes. Additionally, the present-day versions of place-names are given at their first mention in each chapter and in Appendix B.

In the matter of transliteration I have not been overly ambitious. With one major exception, I have broadly adopted the systems proposed by the Royal Asiatic Society (Arabic and Persian) and, for the small number of cases where it is relevant, the Latin alphabet promulgated officially by the Turkish Republic. Fortunately, these systems do not differ too radically from that employed in the second edition of *The Encyclopaedia of Islam,* the main difference being that I, in company with most English-speaking Arabists, substitute *q* for *ḳ* and *j* for *dj*. I have used neither the ligature that is sometimes employed to signify that two consonants denote a single sound, nor the apostrophe favored in the Edinburgh *Islamic Surveys* to show when adjacent consonants are to be sounded separately. So far as Arabic, the language that furnishes most of the names mentioned in this book, is concerned, I have retained a final *h* as written even when it is not pronounced. I have also transcribed one of the two diphthongs as *ay* (not *ai*), and more or less arbitrarily rendered the ending variously written *-iya, -iyya, -iyyah,* and so forth as *-īyah.*

Proper names in the form of genitive compounds are transliterated on the model of, for example, ʿAbd al-Majīd, even though a strict rendering of the classical Arabic would require the "possessor" to take a final vowel dependent on case. This name is frequently transcribed as ʿAbduʾ l-Majīd, but, in such instances of the *hamzat al-waṣl* I have usually retained the definite article in unelided form, so that I have written Abū al-Fidāʾ rather than Abūʾ l-Fidāʾ. At the same time, I have transcribed the *al-* of the Arabic script instead of assimilating it to an immediately following *sun* letter, as occurs in speech: thus al-Shām, not ash-Shām; al-Raḥbah, not ar-Raḥbah; al-Nawūsah, not an-Nawūsah. Structurally discrete words joined together by conventions of the Arabic script have been hyphenated in transliteration and *ibn* has been written throughout even when *b* or *bin* might have seemed more natural. In transliterations from Persian the *majhūl* vowels have been ignored, and the *izāfat* rendered as *i*.

The prefixing of the article *al-* to Arabic toponyms in medieval and later texts is hardly better than arbitrary. Although the formal grammatical rule would appear to require that it be prefixed to Arabic but not to foreign names, exceptions abound. Although the rivers Tigris and Euphrates went under non-Arabic names, the first was invariably written simply Dijlah, and the second equally regularly as al-Furāt. Al-Ubullah, from Greek Ἀπόλογος, was always written with the article. Purely Arabic names can be found both with and without articles: for example, al-Kūfah, but Wāsiṭ. Whereas Makkah never takes the definite article, al-Madīnah invariably does so. In many instances the article was variously prefixed to a name or not according to the caprice of the author, so that, for example, both Juddah and al-Juddah can be found in early topographies. In the Īrānian provinces the Arabic article tended to be omitted in the course of time, so that, for example, al-Qarnīn became Qarnīn, and al-Sīrajān Sirjān. In the following pages, whenever a personal name included an article, I have retained it in the text. However, in the notes and references from chapter 3 onward, the definite article has usually been omitted so that, for instance, al-Maqdisī becomes Maqdisī, al-Masʿūdī becomes Masʿūdī, and al-Iṣṭakhrī plain Iṣṭakhrī.

The main and consistent exception to these rules is the transliteration of Arabic and Berber names in al-Maghrib, which have usually been rendered according to the system customarily employed by French scholars in this region. To have maintained the system of transliteration used for the rest of the Islamic world would have made it unduly difficult for the lay reader unfamiliar with the dialectal peculiarities of Maghribī Arabic to have related my versions to those of French or French-trained writers who for a century or so have virtually monopolized scholarly investigation in this part of the world. Thus, a French system of transliteration combined with the distinctive Maghribī persistence of a free accent uncontrolled by long vowels or double closure has given rise to such French orthographies as *oued* for *wādī*, *bled* for *balad*, *el-Kairouan* for *al-Qayrawān*, or Tlemcen for Tilimsān.

Generally speaking, I have used the above systems of transliteration consistently, even extending them to names that have earned a widely accepted conventional spelling. In this I have pursued the "foolish consistency" that so troubled R. W. Emerson. Makkah for Mecca may seem a gratuitous obfuscation to some readers, but in despair at discerning the line dividing recondite from familiar, I have opted for consistency.

The Islamic Date

Dates in original sources emanating from the Islamic cultural realm refer to the Hijrī calendar, which takes its origin from Muḥammad's migration from Makkah to al-Madīnah on a day corresponding to the Western date of 16 July 622.* Hijrī dates are more convenient for the specialist historian to work with, but, because the Muslim lunar year is somewhat shorter than the Christian year, they are liable to mislead the Western reader, including the comparative urbanist, who is likely to be among the principal users of this book. The rather clumsy expedient of citing dates according to both calendars is made even more awkward by the fact that the Christian equivalent of a Hijrī date inevitably encompasses parts of two years, as when, say, A.H. 900 began on 2 October 1494 of the Christian era and ran until 21 September 1495. A reasonably accurate conversion from one calender to the other is provided by the following formula:

$$\left(\mathrm{H} - \frac{3H}{100}\right) + 622 = C,$$

where H = the Hijrī year and C the Christian equivalent.

* Strictly speaking, the Hijrī era begins not with the date on which Muḥammad left Makkah for al-Madīnah but with the date of the same day of the week in the year in which the caliph ʿUmar inaugurated the new calendar.

Conversion tables are to be found in F. Wüstenfeld, *Vergleichungstabellen der muhammedanischen und christlichen Zeitrechnung* (2d ed., rev. under E. Mahler [Leipzig, 1926]); W. Haig, *Comparative Tables of Muhammedan and Christian Dates* (London, 1932); and C. H. Philips, ed., *Handbook of Oriental History* (London, 1951), 33–40.

Bibliographical Matters

References for sources mentioned in the text, both primary and secondary, as well as informational and explicatory materials, are provided in full in the bibliographies at the end of the book. I give my rationale for the ordering of Arabic and Persian sources on page 517. As I am writing as much for comparative urbanists as for Middle Eastern specialists, I have deemed it necessary to provide the former with a good deal of background information that the latter will no doubt find otiose. I hope that by doing so I shall alert urbanists unfamiliar with the region to the complexities of cultural relations in the early Islamic period as well as enable them to acquire some understanding of the nature and reliability of the sources on which we erect our edifice. Much of this ancillary material has been relegated to the chapter notes and references at the back of the book, where full citations have been furnished for all references on first mention. When references are repeated they are usually given in abbreviated form. Some contemporary Middle Eastern scholars writing in European languages transpose the order of their names and/or transcribe them in nonconforming ways; in such instances I have preserved the preferred Western form, sometimes with the original version in parentheses.

In a few instances page references will appear as follows: 153 [57]–154 [58]. Such references typically are to texts in which an author's papers have been compiled from other sources but not reprinted. Consequently, the bracketed folios refer to the original pagination; the other folios, the revised pagination. Depending on the publisher, however, the converse of this arrangement may be true.

In Qur'ānic citations, verse numberings follow those of the standard Egyptian edition, *Al-Maṣḥaf al-Sharīf*, as authorized by King Fu'ad I in A.H. 1344/A.D. 1924.

PART I

Introduction

Chapter One
The Roots of Islamic Society

And so We have revealed to thee an Arabic Lectionary *[Qur'ān]*, that thou mayest warn the Mother of Settlements *[Umm al-Qurā]* and those who dwell about it, and thou mayest warn them of the Day of the Gathering.

—Qur'ān 42 *(al-Shūrā)*:7

Arabia of the *Jāhilīyah*[1]

The imprint of Islam on urban life and form in the Middle East can be traced to events that took place in the seventh century on the fringe of one of the most highly urbanized regions of the ancient world. During the three and a half millennia since city life first appeared in Lower Mesopotamia, urban society had diffused through virtually all the habitable terrain of southwestern Asia, into Mediterranean and Balkan Europe, and through much of North Africa. In the early decades of the seventh century A.D. the territories collectively known today as the Middle East were effectively partitioned between the empires of Byzantium and Sāsānid Persia. In the northern part of the region these polities faced each other across a common frontier running from the eastern shore of the Black Sea to the upper Euphrates River, but farther south they were separated by a group of quasi-independent kingdoms of uncertain allegiance. It was on the southern edge of this theater of power politics, in al-Ḥijāz, a region beyond the effective control of either empire, that the ideology of Islamic urbanism had its roots.

It seems that the earliest cities on the Arabian Peninsula proper had arisen among the uplands of the southwest, where proto-urban development appears to have followed a pattern common not only to other parts of the Middle East but also to realms of nuclear urbanism elsewhere in Asia and the New World. In the kingdom of Sabā', which existed from about the eighth to the second century B.C., the first capital, at Ṣirwāḥ, apparently took the form of a ceremonial center similar in function to the religio-administrative cities of early Mesopotamia. At the head of the polity was a personage with a title recorded epigraphically as either *MKRB*[2] or *malik* or both. Subsequently, after the enlargement of the kingdom and the transference of its capital late in the seventh century B.C. to Ma'rib, some sixty miles east of present-day Ṣan'ā', the rulers appeared under the dynastic style *Mulūk Sabā'*, signifying "Kings of Sabā'."

Generally similar polities also existed in early times under the names Ma'īn, with its capital at Qarnāw in southern al-Jawf (eighth to third century B.C.);[3] Qatabān, with its capital at Tamna', usually identified with modern Timna' in Wādī Ḥarīb (fifth to first century B.C.); 'Awsān, seemingly a kingdom that gained temporary independence from Qatabān; Ḥaḍramawt, with its capital at Shabwah (ancient Sabbatha), the classical Sabota (middle of the fifth century B.C. to the end of the first century A.D.); and Sam'ay and 'Arba', about which little is known. The religious and ceremonial nature of Shabwah is reflected in the traditions that attributed to it more than sixty temples. However, its extant ruins imply that most of these temples—and the number may well have been exaggerated—were located outside the city walls.[4]

Toward the close of the second century B.C., all or most of the southwestern angle of the peninsula was dominated by the so-called tribe of Ḥimyar (the *Homeritae [Ὁμηρῖται]* of the *Periplus of the Erythraean Sea* and of Pliny), who established their capital at Ẓafār (perhaps the Sephar of Genesis 10:30 and certainly the Sapphar of classical authors), some ten miles or so southwest of Yarīm.[5] The royal title that has been preserved in Arabic literature is *tubba*ʿ (pl. *tabābiʿah*), but epigraphy attests that by the beginning of the fourth century A.D. the style of the Ḥimyarite dynasts included the attributions "King of Sabāʾ, Dhū-Raydān,[6] Ḥa[ḍramaw]t and Yamanāt,"[7] to which was subsequently added "and of their *Aʿrāb* on the plateau and in the Tihāmat."[8] By the fifth century, South Arabian sources bear witness to Ḥimyarite control over the greater part of Central Arabia.[9]

Government, as implied by a fairly substantial corpus of inscriptions, seems in both the Sabaean and Ḥimyarite periods to have taken a patrimonial form: essentially the ruler extended his patriarchical control over his family to his subjects. As a result, state affairs and court administration were highly coincidental, while beneficelike privileges were bestowed on subordinate rulers *(ashrāf,* sing. *sharīf)* in return for services rendered to the court in a context of duty and formalized respect.[10] It is also evident that the kin-based groupings characteristic of such societies had not been entirely replaced by specialized political institutions but retained a good deal of their ability to generate social and political power. As developing technological ability began to stimulate competition for available resources between urbanized groups and induce a progressive differentiation between sedentary peasants and migratory *badū* (nomads of the desert)—a state of affairs that probably was being exacerbated as the patrimonial mode of government proved increasingly inadequate for administering extensive and diverse territories—so fortifications came to assume an important role in settlement layout. They were especially prominent in the palace precincts, several of which were veritable fortresses. The most celebrated was the citadel of Ghumdān, built on the site of present-day Ṣanʿāʾ by the ruler Īlsharcḥ Yaḥḍub[11] in the first century A.D.

Apart from a brief period of Abyssinian rule from about A.D. 340 to 378,[12] the Ḥimyarites remained in power until 525, when the last *tubba*ʿ, a Jew, was deposed by a second Abyssinian (Aksūmite) invasion, which, according to the Tradition, was instigated by Emperor Justin I of Byzantium in retaliation for Ḥimyarite persecution of Yamanī Christian converts.[13] For the next fifty years the Aksūmite rulers sought to make of Ṣanʿāʾ, now the capital of southwestern Arabia, a Christian rival to the pagan shrine at Makkah (Mecca), and in so doing imposed a largely Christian aspect on the morphology of the city. Prominent among such features was the magnificent cathedral built at the command of the Aksūmite viceroy Abrahah and known to Arab authors as al-Qalīs.[14] In 575 the Christian period of Yamanī history came to an abrupt end when the Mazdean Sāsānids reduced the country to the status of a Persian satrapy.

These kingdoms of southwestern Arabia were based on a fairly advanced paleotechnic ecotype in which sedentary agriculture, supplemented by *petit bétail* stock raising, was made possible by a developed irrigation technology, of which the most impressive example was the celebrated Sadd Maʾrib. Tradition in the Arab world ascribed the building of this great dam to the mythical Luqmān ibn ʿĀd,[15] but inscriptions at the site make it clear that the scheme was originally carried through by the *tubba*ʿ Sumhuʿalay Yanuf and his son Yathaʿ-amar Bayyin, probably in the middle of the seventh century B.C. Restorations and additions were subsequently undertaken in the fifth century B.C. and the sixth century A.D.[16] During the second half of the fifth century A.D. and the first half of the sixth, however, the irrigation system appears to have deteriorated, probably because silt deposition had raised the level of the fields above that of the distribution channels—a process that Islamic literature archetyped into a single catastrophe known as "the bursting of the [Maʾrib] dam" (compare Qurʾān 34 *[Sabāʾ]:*16). In any event, the resulting desiccation of Yamanī agricultural land induced the migration of numerous tribes to more northerly latitudes—supposedly including the Banū-Ghassān to the Ḥawrān, the Banū-Lakhm to the neighborhood of al-Ḥīrah, and the Banū-Ṭayyiʾ and the Kindah to Central Arabia—with far-reaching implications for the future of those regions.

But if agriculture provided the staples of life, in the earlier periods it was trade, chiefly in spices and aromatics, that brought wealth and prosperity to the cities of the region known to the classical world as Arabia Eudaemon or Arabia Felix.[17] Situated in the strategic angle where Red Sea shipping entered the Indian Ocean, the Sabaeans were early able to control the trade route from Bāb al-Mandab to Wādī al-Ḥammāmāt and thence to the Nile River valley. Subsequently they avoided the hazards of Red Sea navigation by developing a caravan route overland from al-Yaman to Syria along the upland rim of the peninsula. Along this route for many centuries passed the "perfumes of Arabia," as well as those from East Africa and India. According to Strabo, the journey from Minaea (Maʿīn) to Ælana (al-ʿAqabah) took seventy days,[18] and Ḥimyarite trading stations were strung along it at easy stages.[19] In the early centuries of the Christian era, however, both Romans and Greeks managed to establish themselves in the spice trade and subvert the Arabian monopoly. In the fourth century A.D. the diversion of the main channel of trade from western Arabia to other routes was a powerful factor contributing to the decline of the Ḥimyarite kingdom.[20]

These agriculturally and commercially based cities of South Arabia had emerged through an internally generated process of societal transformation. In contrast, the cities in the northern part of the peninsula generally had arisen in response to Hellenistic and Roman influences from Syria permeating through societies whose dominant mode of life was that of nomadic, seminomadic, and sedentary tribalism. Although ethnically Arab originally, by the beginning of the Christian era these cities had been strongly impregnated with Hellenized Aramaic culture, and were characterized by heterogeneous populations drawn from a wide range of territories. The earliest of these states was probably that of the Nabataeans (Arabic al-Anbāṭ), who, by the beginning of the second century B.C., had established a polity which at its zenith reached from the Gulf of ʿAqabah northward to the Dead Sea and included part of the northern Ḥijāz. In other words it comprised substantially the territories, other than Sinai, known to classical authors as Arabia Petraea.[21] The capital of this kingdom for most of its history was the partially rock-hewn city of Petra,[22] situated in the only locality between the Jordan River and central Arabia where water was both abundant and pure, and consequently an important node on the caravan route from Sabāʾ to the Mediterranean (see fig. 1). The city was also distinguished by its shrine to the god Dūshara,[23] who was worshipped in the form of a rectangular black stone.

The rest of the Nabataean kingdom consisted essentially of trading stations strung along caravan routes radiating north, south, and west from the capital. Under Ḥārithath IV[24] (r. 9 B.C.–A.D. 40) it included both the already ancient city of Damascus in the north and the important center of al-Ḥijr, present-day Madāʾin Ṣāliḥ, in al-Ḥijāz. From the middle of the first century B.C. to the end of the first century A.D., the Nabataean kingdom acted as a more or less willing ally of the Romans, serving as a screen between the settled eastern territories of the empire and the shifting *badū* coalitions of Northern Arabia; but in A.D. 105 Trajan formally annexed it as a Roman province. The capital was transferred to Bostra (Arabic Buṣrah) in Ḥawrān, which was then enlarged to such an extent that it deserves to be regarded as a new foundation.[25] The other important Nabataean caravan cities were reconstituted as nominally autonomous district capitals.

In any case, by this time a realignment of Northern Arabian trade routes consequent on the Parthian conquest of Mesopotamia came at a cost to Petra: Palmyra was usurping its place in the skeletal urban hierarchy of the region. By the opening of the Christian era this latter city, which had already had a long history under its ancient Semitic name of Tadmor,[26] was beginning to draw dividends from its position as a trading mart in neutral territory between the empires of Rome and Persia. In the time of Hadrian (r. A.D. 117–38) Palmyra became a vassal of Rome and received the honorific title of Hadriana Palmyra. At the beginning of the third century it was constituted as a Roman colony and the inhabitants began to adopt Roman names, but it seems still to have enjoyed a high degree of autonomy. It attained the apogee of its prosperity between A.D. 130 and 270, when its trade relations extended throughout the Middle East and far into Asia. In 262, as a reward for assistance in Rome's protracted struggle with the Persians, Odaynath,[27] the ruler of Palmyra, was appointed *Dux Orientis,* vice-emperor of the East; three years later he was accorded the title of *Imperator* and given control of the Roman legions in the East. When Odaynath was assassinated in 267, his widow,

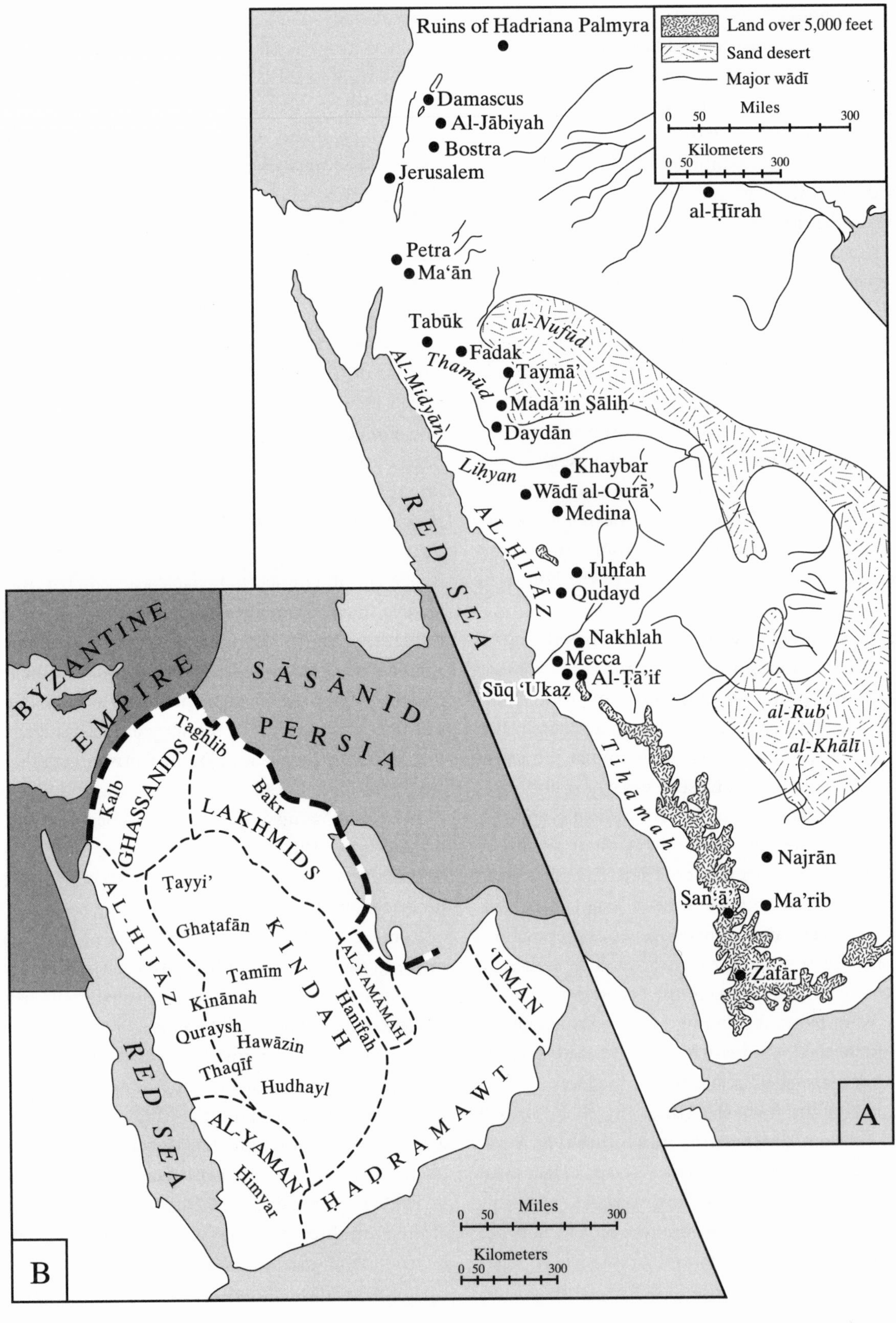

Land over 5,000 feet
Sand desert
Major wādī
Miles
0 50 300
Kilometers
0 50 300
Ruins of Hadriana Palmyra
Damascus
Al-Jābiyah
Bostra
Jerusalem
al-Ḥīrah
Petra
Ma'ān
Tabūk
al-Nufūd
Fadak
Thamūd
Taymā'
Al-Midyān
Madā'in Ṣāliḥ
Daydān
Liḥyan
Khaybar
Wādī al-Qurā'
Medina
RED SEA
AL-ḤIJĀZ
Juḥfah
Qudayd
Nakhlah
Mecca
Al-Ṭā'if
Sūq 'Ukaẓ
al-Rub'
al-Khālī
Tihāmah
Najrān
Ṣan'ā'
Ma'rib
Ẓafār
A
BYZANTINE EMPIRE
SĀSĀNID PERSIA
Taghlib
GHASSANIDS
Kalb
Bakr
LAKHMIDS
Ṭayyi'
Ghaṭafān
KINDAH
AL-ḤIJĀZ
AL-YAMĀMAH
Tamīm
Ḥanīfah
Kinānah
Quraysh
Hawāzin
Thaqīf
Hudhayl
'UMĀN
RED SEA
AL-YAMAN
Ḥimyar
ḤAḌRAMAWT
Miles
0 50 300
Kilometers
0 50 300
B

the famous Zenobia,[28] arrogated to herself the style of queen of the East and proclaimed her son, known to the classical world as Athenodorus,[29] as Caesar Augustus. After some initial successes, including the occupation of Alexandria in 270, the troops of Palmyra were eventually defeated in 273 by a Roman army under Aurelian. The walls of the city were razed and its kingdom dissolved.

The trade that had formerly focused on Palmyra was now diverted to Bostra and other towns in the Ghassān chiefdom. The early history of this confederacy is known only from archetyped Arab traditions that have its rulers migrating to al-Ḥawrān from Yaman toward the end of the third century A.D.[30] Certainly by the end of the fifth century the Banū-Ghassān had displaced the Salīḥ from their Syrian territories and adopted both a Syrian form of Monophysite Christianity and the Aramaic language.[31] In recognition of his defeat of certain Persian vassals, the Ghassānid ruler al-Ḥārith ibn Jabalah (ca. 529–69)[32] was made a *patricius* and phylarch[33] of the Byzantine Empire, and appointed ruler of all the Arab tribes of Syria. At first the Ghassān chiefs ruled from a migratory camp, which subsequently seems to have been stabilized at al-Jābiyah in the Jawlān. At another period it was located at Jilliq in the valley of the Yarmūk River.[34] Under al-Ḥārith's successors, relations with Byzantium deteriorated into open hostility, culminating in the deportation of two rulers and the virtual disintegration of the kingdom. It is uncertain for how long it survived in vestigial form, but the raid of 613–14, in which the Sāsānian Khusraw Parwīz captured Jerusalem and Damascus, signaled its formal demise. When the levies of Islam swept northward in 634 they encountered no resistance from the levies of Ghassān.

While the Ghassānids ruled a substantial tract of territory within the western arc of the Fertile Crescent mainly in the interests of Byzantium, the Naṣrid or Lakhmid dynasty controlled the eastern parts of the Syrian Desert. During the disturbed conditions associated with the transference of power from the Arsacids to the Sāsānians, a group of tribes—presumably a confederacy like the northern ʿAnazah who until recently controlled most of the Syrian Desert—calling themselves Tanūkh and claiming a Yamanī origin,[35] established a tented camp not far from the site of ancient Babylon. When, in the second half of the third century, this settlement developed into the permanent capital of Persian Arabia, it retained the name of al-Ḥīrah, derived from the Syriac *ḥirtā*, meaning "camp." The population was predominantly Christian of the East Syrian (subsequently Nestorian) Church. Its rulers, except for the last of the Lakhmid house, remained pagan, however. The kingdom achieved its highest degree of autonomy under al-Mundhir III[36] (ca. 505–54), who raided as far west as Antioch until he was defeated by al-Ḥārith of Ghassān. The Lakhmid dynasty was finally exterminated after an abortive rebellion against the Persian emperor Khusraw II. In M. J. Kister's interpretation, it was abolished because it proved incapable of securing the borders of the Persian Empire against raids by Arab tribes and consequently failed to protect some of the most important Persian commercial routes.[37] In any case, Sāsānian governors ruled through Arab puppets until the arrival of the Muslim army in 633.

Figure 1. Arabia at the time of Muḥammad. *A* denotes principal settlements; *B*, tribal territories.

In contrast to the Ghassānids, in Arabian tradition al-Ḥīrah was always regarded as an integral part of the Arab cultural world. Its relations with the rest of the peninsula were more direct than were those of the Syro-Hellenistic states. As a result, although it never attained the degree of cultural sophistication reached by the Nabataean, Palmyrene, and Ghassānid courts, its influence on peninsular society was stronger and more lasting. According to Ibn Rustah, it was from al-Ḥīrah that Muḥammad's tribe acquired its script and its false belief,[38] and it has been claimed that Christianity was brought to Najrān by members of the Syrian Church at al-Ḥīrah. The closeness of Lakhmid ties with the peninsula was well illustrated during the reign of ʿAmr (554–69), when three of the seven reputed authors of the *Muʿallaqāt* resided at his court.

The histories of the polities that arose within Arabia in pre-Islamic times are very inadequately documented. The most ancient name—probably that of a tribe or confederacy rather than of a group with legitimate title to statehood—is Tamud, which figures in the cuneiform annals of Sargon II of Assyria (721–705 B.C.) and which is usually identified with the Thamūd of later Ḥawrān epigraphy and the Qurʾān.[39] The language of the inscriptions is Northern Arabic, but the script in which it is written uses a by-form of the South Arabic alphabet.[40] Similar inscriptions attest the existence of a kingdom of Liḥyān,[41] with its capital at Daydān,[42] modern al-ʿUlah, in northern al-Ḥijāz. The relationship between the Thamūdic and Liḥyānī peoples is still obscure, but there is reason to think that the latter may have constituted a subgroup within a Thamūdic confederacy. During Ptolemaic times the Liḥyānī contested control of the desert trade routes with the Nabataeans and, after the Roman annexation of that kingdom, were apparently left in control of the city of al-Ḥijr, itself believed to have once been in Thamūdic hands. The Qurʾānic tale (7 *[al-Aʿrāf]*:73 and 9 *[al-Tawbah]*:70) of the destruction by earthquake of the Thamūd capital whose inhabitants, after rejecting a prophet sent by Allāh, "were found prostrate in their dwellings" hewn out of the mountainside, may preserve an archetyped remembrance of some natural calamity at a settlement of rock-hewn habitations similar to those at Petra. In fact there is some evidence implying that the cities of Thamūd and Liḥyān were both under Nabataean suzerainty at one point. Another powerful confederation, also claiming a South Arabian origin, was that of the Banū-Ṭayyiʾ. Although it entered only briefly into pre-Islamic history, it provided a ruler of al-Ḥīrah, under Persian tutelage, after the fall of the Lakhmid dynasty.

One of the more interesting of the early Arabian tribal confederations was that of the Banū-Kindah. According to Arab tradition, in A.D. 480 a Kindah chief was appointed ruler over several Central Arabian tribes by the Ḥimyarite Ḥassān ibn Tubbaʿ.[43] So powerful did this confederacy become that by the time of its third ruler, al-Ḥārith ibn ʿAmr, it was able to mount an invasion of the ʿIrāqī lowlands and occupy al-Ḥīrah. Driven from the city in about 529, and with some fifty of its leaders put to death by the resurgent Lakhmids, the Kindah confederacy reverted to a congeries of more or less independent tribal groups.[44] Although as a polity it had failed to develop adequate institutional solutions to the problems that accompanied increasing political and social differentiation, it is important in pre-Islamic Arabian history for foreshadowing the subsequent formation of a more enduring Islamic state in al-Ḥijāz.

Al-Ḥijāz

Islam was born in the northern sector of the raised western edge of the Arabian Peninsula. The term *Ḥijāz,* from a root connoting separation and obstruction, appropriately reflects the manner in which these severely dissected highlands separate the narrow lowland bordering the Red Sea from the interior plateau of Najd. In the more northerly tracts, known as al-Midyān, the highest peaks exceed eight thousand feet; southward both elevation and relief tend to decline, allowing relatively easy access to the interior at the point where one can effect the shortest crossing of the peninsula. Over the entire Ḥijāz, rainfall is exiguous, often averaging less than five inches a year, so that vegetation is almost wholly xerophytic. Extensive stretches of steppe and desert scrub are diversified only occasionally by clumps of cactiform euphorbias, acacias, and tamarisks. Cultivation is possible only in a few specially favored *wādī*s and depressions where the water table approaches the surface during certain seasons of the year.

Aʿrāb and *Ḥaḍarī*

In this austere environment the traditional basis of life has been pastoralism in one or another of its several forms, ranging from true nomadism to sedentary herding, supplemented in especially favored oases by cereal and date cultivation. In recent as doubtless in pre-Islamic times, the distinction among these modes of ecological adaptation has not been sharply defined; rather, a gradation exists from one pattern of life to the other. The fundamental contrast, of course, has been that between *aʿrāb* (sing. *ʿarab*), dwellers in portable tents, and *ḥaḍarī,*[45] or inhabitants of permanent houses—that is, cultivators living continuously on tilled land. But the *aʿrāb* might be either *badū,* nomads of the *bādīyah* ("desert") and dependent mainly if not exclusively on camels—in the Ḥijāz the Muzaynah, Ghifār, and Fazārah were of this type, in the neighboring Najd the Ṭayyiʾ and the Asad—or *shwāyah* (also *shūyān*), who, as they owned flocks of goats and sheep, were restricted to the desert borderlands. The *ḥaḍarī* in turn were by no means homogeneous. Among them the *qarawīyūn* (sing. *qarwanī*) never ventured far from established dwellings, whereas the *rāʿīyah* (sing. *rāʿi* or *rāʿu*), although possessing permanent houses and raising crops, became tent dwellers when they followed their flocks of sheep and goats into the steppe during the rainier winter season. In any case, these terms denote mutable categories. In fact it is scarcely an exaggeration to say that traditional modes of ecological adaptation have been as inconstant as the desert sands to which they were a response. It is known, for example, that the semisedentary Tanūkh, Iyād, al-Namir ibn Qāsiṭ, and Taghlib, who in the sixth century A.D. were pasturing flocks of sheep in the Euphrates valley, had roamed the Najd and Eastern Arabia as true nomads, presumably *grands bédouins chameliers,*[46] before their displacement by the Tamīm, Asad, Ṭayyiʾ, and the Bakr ibn Wāʾil confederacy.

Tribal Organization

Among the nomadic, seminomadic, and sedentary peoples of the Ḥijāz during the *Jāhilīyah,* the most highly integrated level of society was that of the confederacy, an ideological framework within which wider political alliances were believed to be potentially possible. Within these confederacies tribal organization, at once structurally decentralized and functionally generalized, was still very much in evidence, with descent and community groups hierarchically arranged.[47] Through the instrument of patrilineally organized, ranked common-descent groups, an incipient political structure had become established over and above the level of simple tribal community. At the base of this society was the patrilocal extended family occupying either one or, more often, a group of tents. Such a camping cluster formed what in present-day Arabia would be called a *ḥayy* or, among the Āl Murra, a *dār.* A varying but substantial number of such groups acknowledging certain blood relationships constituted what in classical Arabic was often termed an *ʿimārah,* a grouping today often known as a *qawm,* a word that unfortunately is customarily, but misleadingly, translated as "clan." A number of these kindred so-called clans together formed a *qabīlah* or tribe. Within this framework a man's kin *(ahl)* were probably then, as now, recognized as his paternal ancestors to the third, or sometimes fifth, generation; other descendants of those ancestors to the third generation; and his own descendants in the male line to the third generation.[48]

It follows that the kin of two kinsmen were not necessarily identical. For example, the lists of kinfolk for a boy and for his patrilineal great-uncle respectively would have overlapped to only a limited extent. It was upon this paternal blood relationship *(ʿamām)* that much of tribal custom was founded. In particular it was the duty of a tribesman's *ahl* to avenge his murder.[49] In the morality of the time blood could be paid only in blood, and there are numerous examples of a blood feud *(thaʾr)* being pursued for years and ultimately involving whole tribes. The blood feud that allegedly precipitated the forty-year Basūs War between the Banū-Bakr and the Banū-Taghlib during the sixth century A.D. is a classic, although certainly archetyped, example. Conversely, a tribesman could rely on his kin, as understood in this restricted sense, for protection and support. Furthermore, it was possible under certain circumstances for an outsider from a totally unrelated clan or tribe to acquire rights of blood relationship *(ḥaqq al-banī-ʿamm),* upon which he was obligated to protect the neighbor *(qasīr),* guest *(ḍayf),* and companion *(khawī)* of his new kin. Similar protection was also accorded to clients *(mawālī;* sing. *mawlā)* of the kin group. In extreme instances a whole clan might seek the protection of, and finally be absorbed by, a more powerful clan or tribe.

In a broader sense members of a clan or even a tribe regarded themselves as descended from the same paternal ancestor. They customarily occupied either the whole or a discrete part of a camp, prefixed their shared name with the word *banū,* signifying "offspring of," and recognized the authority and titular headship of a *shaykh,*[50] who was a member of the dominant lineage, the *ahl al-bayt.* As prestige derived primarily from proximity to the main line of descent, so the construction of genealogies had an important function in society, and the *shaykh*s of the *Jāhilīyah* took great pride in recording their noble ancestry. "No people, other than the Arabians," writes Philip Hitti with pardonable exaggeration, "have ever raised genealogy to the dignity of a science."[51] Although the *shaykh* exercised a true authority, his power was limited. He was elected based on his genealogical standing, the wisdom of his counsel, his courage, and his generosity, and his opportunities for coercion and exploitation were severely restricted. His chieftainship was not a class society but what Marshall Sahlins terms "a structure of degrees of interest rather than conflicts of interest; of graded familial priorities in the control of wealth and force, in claims to others' services, in access to divine power, and in material styles of life."[52] The *shaykh*'s function was essentially that of arbitration rather than command. And in judicial, military, and other affairs of public concern his authority was by no means absolute, for he was constrained to take the advice of a council of elders, the *majlis,* made up of the heads of families and representatives of clans.

To some extent the tribal structure was a political arrangement induced by tactical considerations. This was even more true of the tribal confederacies or chiefdoms that occasionally arose, notably that of the Banū-Kindah, whose rulers were the only true Arabians ever to assume the style of *malik* ("king"). Most such supratribal formations were no more than shifting patterns of alliances and coalitions engendered by threat of external force, and were soon subverted by the segmentary divisions of their tribal infrastructures and the divisive manner in which the constituent groups perceived their economic interests.

The Role of Reciprocity

In many ways it is misleading to speak of a tribal economy—or indeed of tribal politics, tribal religion, and so forth. Tribal organization is generalized in such a way that its religious activities are conducted not by institutions designed specifically for the purpose but incidentally by lineage and clan segments, households, and villages (even encampments in the case of the *badū*). It lacks an autonomous economic sector, a specialized political organization, and independent religious institutions. "In a tribe, these are not so much different institutions as they are different *functions* of the institutions. . . . Holding an estate in land, the lineage appears as an economic entity; feuding, it is a political group; sacrificing to the ancestors, a ritual congregation."[53] From this point of view, then, the economy of the Ḥijāzi tribes in immediately pre-Islamic times is properly to be regarded as a particular arrangement of generalized social groups and relations that also exercised a range of other functions. Basically it assumed the character of a network of instrumental exchanges grounded in tribal morality, a reciprocative mode of economic integration designed to promote group solidarity. But tribal morality was then, as now, contextual rather than absolute, so that the type of reciprocity practiced involved situational norms that were sectorally organized. As Sahlins succinctly puts it, "Reciprocity marched in character with segmentary distance."[54] In other words, each sector of tribal life was characterized by a distinct mode of exchange.[55] Among close kin this took the form of generalized reciprocity, as manifested in family sharing and mutual aid, activities in which the obligation to reciprocate was diffuse, and the expectation of a quid pro quo unspecified as to time, quantity and quality.

In the matter of hospitality *(ḍiyāfah),* considerable elasticity seems to have been evident in the extension of canons of generalized reciprocity beyond the kin group. Arabian tribesmen viewed hospitality as a sacred duty; the pagan poets of the *Jāhilīyah* praised it as a cardinal virtue and archetyped it in the celebrated legend of Ḥātim al-Ṭāʾī.[56] Elaborate rules governed the granting and termination of hospitality to persons outside the lineage, doubtless in response to the functional significance of the traveller in a society of highly dispersed, and often nomadic, encampments. The guest was a welcome diversion during the long, monotonous months of winter migration and a source of news from other encampments, even the outside world. Moreover, provision of protection and safe conduct for him was believed to display the host's authority, to attest the reality of his control over his territory. In an age when raiding was endemic and a man without the protection of his tribe was no better than an outlaw, it was the institution of the *ḍiyāfah* that enabled travel through tribal territories.

The *Ghazū*

In those sectors of tribal life beyond the influence of the lineage the preferred mode of exchange took place within the context of balanced reciprocity. Exchanges tended to be direct and to approximate transactions that today are denoted by the terms *trade* or *barter.* Generally speaking, this relatively fair and immediate exchange predominated among distant kin and was extended to traders visiting villages and encampments. At a still greater social distance—beyond, say, the tribe—forms of negative reciprocity prevailed.[57] These comprised activities for acquiring commodities at less than their full value and might include anything from sharp bargaining to various types of chicanery; but they received their most dramatic expression in the institution of the *ghazū,* or raid.[58] For the herdsman there was always a strong temptation to augment his wealth from the flocks and herds of those "other peoples" beyond the compass of even fictive kinship, tribesmen from whose friendship he had little or nothing to gain. In years of severe drought, however, when pastures failed, water holes dried up, and flocks were stricken, raiding had a real economic basis. Although it did not increase the total available resources, the *ghazū* did serve as an instrument for the redistribution of wealth and, under certain circumstances, could be used to drive a tribe from coveted pastures. Blood was shed only in extremis, so that the raid did little to reduce the pressure of population on the exiguous resources of desert and steppe, particularly as weaker tribes or settlements often chose to buy protection rather than resist.

That such raiding was endemic during the century preceding the *Hijrah* is amply attested by early Arabic literature, which preserves archetyped records of a series of intertribal conflicts known as the Battle Days of the Arabs *(Ayyām al-ʿArab)*.[59] Usually these stemmed from relatively petty disputes over the ownership of animals, access to pastures or springs, or the infliction of comparatively minor personal slights and injustices; but from small beginnings the quarrels often escalated to absorb the energies of whole tribes, and occasionally confederacies, sometimes for decades. Notable among these struggles were the Day of Buʿāth fought between the Aws and Khazraj tribes of Yathrib;[60] the Days of al-Fijār, in which the Quraysh and the Kinānah opposed the Hawāzin and in which the young Muḥammad is said to have participated;[61] the Harb al-Basūs between the Banū-Bakr and—somewhat unusually—their putative kinsmen, the Banū-Taghlib;[62] and the Day of Dāḥis and al-Ghabrā' fought by the tribes of ʿAbs and Dhubyān.[63] Glorified in later Arabic literature, the values and terminology of the *ghazū* were carried over into the period of the Islamic conquests, and the ideal of *al-kāmil,* "the exemplary man," owed not a few traits to the warrior *shaykh*s of the Days, notably chiefs such as Kulayb ibn Rabībʿah, his brother the poet Muhalhil, and Jassās ibn Murrah, all of whom took part in the Basūs War. Early in the Umayyad period the poet al-Quṭāmī wrote, "Our business is to make raids on the enemy, on our neighbour and on our own brother, in the event we find none to raid but a brother."[64] Clearly in this author's mind the segmentary system of reciprocities had developed marked cleavages at its lower levels such that the group of kinsmen was envisaged as hardly exceeding a single tent. This sustained hostility to all but very close kin is even more graphically reflected in a *badawī* prayer quoted by Abū Dā'ūd in the thirteenth century: "O Lord, have mercy upon me and upon Muḥammad, but upon no one else besides."[65]

External Trade

Running through these patterns of tribal reciprocity like colored threads through a *badawī* blanket were tough strands of external trade that had been spun originally by the ancient kingdoms of South Arabia in conjunction with the Aramaicized states of the north. During the fourth century A.D. the trade routes that for nearly one thousand years had run along the eastern flank of the western Arabian highlands seem to have been superseded by routes through the Persian Gulf and the Euphrates valley and through the Red Sea to the Nile. In the second half of the sixth century, however, trade along both these routes was severely impeded by conflicts between Byzantine and Persian satellites in Northern Arabia and Syria and by internal disorders in Egypt. Consequently traders reverted to the overland route from al-Yaman to the Mediterranean coastlands. As their predecessors had done for centuries, they avoided the hot and humid Tihāmah in favor of the eastern slope of the western uplands, following a route leading from Shabwah in the Ḥaḍramawt by way of Ma'rib to Najrān, and thence north to al-Ṭā'if, Makkah, Madīnah, al-ʿUlah, al-Ḥijr, Maʿān, and Petra, whence one route led across the Wādī al-ʿArabah to al-Ghazzah while another struck northward to Bostra and Damascus.[66] From Najrān a branch route traversed al-Yamāmah to al-Ḥīrah.

Apart from providing equal opportunities for raiding and escorting, this caravan trade had little effect on the *badū* of al-Ḥijāz. Rather, it was the oasis settlements that controlled and profited from it. As Aksūmite rule oriented al-Yaman politically to East Africa rather than to the northern tracts of the peninsula, and as the Palmyrene and Nabataean kingdoms faded from the stage of history, so mastery of the trade route passed to the settled societies of al-Ḥijāz. At this time the main Ḥijāzī settlements were at Makkah, al-Ṭā'if, and Yathrib, with subsidiary communities established in scattered oases chiefly in the northern parts of the region, notably at Khaybar, Juḥfah,[67] Fadak,[68] Tabūk, Taymā', and strung along the Wādī al-Qurā running north from Yathrib toward Syria.[69] The basic livelihood of all these communities was precariously dependent on the resources of the local environment, but in addition each strove—in its own way and with varying degrees of success—to squeeze what it could from the trade that came its way.

"The Mother of Settlements"[70]

The most prestigious of the settlements of al-Ḥijāz during the early seventh century was Makkah, situated in an alluvium-filled *wādī* in the Tihāmah. Searingly hot, intensely arid, and devoid of all but scanty, stunted plant life, this inhospitable valley had little to offer in the way of resources other than a well of sweet water, the Zamzam, which tradition avers—if Robert Serjeant's understanding of a phrase in Ibn Isḥāq's *Sīrah* is correct—was made available to all, irrespective of tribal affiliation.[71] Even Ibrāhīm, while imploring Allāh to cause the hearts of men to yearn toward it, was—according to Qur'ān 14 *(Ibrāhīm):*37—constrained to admit that the valley was unfit for cultivation.[72] In the tenth century A.D. the topographer al-Maqdisī summarized conditions in the *wādī* as "suffocating heat, a pestilential wind, and clouds of flies,"[73] and a twentieth-century author writes, "On eût difficilement imaginé un paysage plus désolé, un site plus austère, dans cette âpre contrée du Ḥiǵāz."[74]

In fact the initial significance of the site derived not from its natural resources but from the presence of a shrine that apparently antedated the teaching of the Prophet. In the Ptolemaic corpus it appeared under the orthography *Makoraba,*[75] surely a Greek rendering of Sabaean *MKRB,* here to be vocalized as *makurabah* and signifying "sanctuary."[76] Muslim tradition holds that the shrine was originally under the control of the South Arabian tribe of Jurhum, after which it passed first to the Khuzāʿah and the Banū-Bakr ibn ʿAbd Manāt ibn Kinānah, and subsequently by conquest to the Quraysh in the person of Quṣayy, the grandfather of Muḥammad's great-grandfather.[77] Serjeant, who has interpreted events in Makkah at this time in the light of the organization of shrines in the Ḥaḍramawt of the recent past, believes this sequence of archetyped events implies that Quṣayy had come to be regarded as the founder and first guardian of the sacred enclave *(ḥaram)* at Makkah.[78] Al-Nuwayrī (d. 1332) preserves a not implausible tradition that the sanctuary was set amid scrub thickets *(ghayḍah)* subject to freshet floods in the *wādī* bottom. During the pilgrimage season this stunted vegetation was supposed to have been beaten down near the shrine by the feet of the pious, only to revive when they had departed.[79] The Tradition also holds that it was Quṣayy who first cleared the brush permanently, raised a roof over the shrine, assigned camping grounds to the different *qawm*s, built a council chamber *(dār al-nadwah),* and organized the pilgrimage. Dubious though this particular piece of information may be, such shrines were not rare in pre-Muslim al-Ḥijāz and took a variety of forms reflecting not only indigenous Arabian beliefs but also Christian, Gnostic, Jewish, and Persian influences.[80]

Religion of the *Badū*

Like all tribal religions, that of the *badū* was organized at several discrete levels paralleling the structural organization of the tribe.[81] At the family and lineage level was a stratum of animistically conceived spirits inhabiting natural features such as trees, wells, caves, rocks, and suchlike. Perhaps the most famous of these was the well of Zamzam mentioned earlier, from which Hagar and Ishmael were said to have drunk in later times.[82] At least one other well, that of ʿUrwah, seems to have shared a similar holiness.[83] In Nakhlah was the cave of Ghabghab,[84] and in Najrān a sacred palm to which were offered weapons, garments, and cloths.[85] The Dhātu-Anwāṭ ("that on which things are hung"),[86] to which the Makkans made an annual pilgrimage, was presumably also a tree or palm. When spirits of natural features were hostile rather than benign they were known as *jinn,* and these countless demons lurked in every untrodden corner of the wilderness. At the tribal level were both totemic gods, about which little is known,[87] and others that often appear to have been symbolized in a rock or stone, and were carried with the tribe on its migrations—and even into battle—housed in a red tent somewhat analogous to the Hebrew Ark of the Covenant. Of these deities Bernard Lewis writes, "God and cult were the badge of tribal identity and the sole ideological expression of the sense of unity and cohesion of the tribe. Conformity to the tribal cult expressed political loyalty. Apostasy was the equivalent of treason."[88]

Third, in accordance with the precept that the sphere of immanence of a spirit or deity is commensurate with the compass of the social group serving it,[89] there was a stratum of high gods whose influence transcended the confines of the tribe, drawing adherents from large sectors of Arabia. As supernatural forces tend to decrease in materiality and particularity as they increase in social range,[90] so these high gods were more generalized, more pervasive, and less susceptible to precise definition than the lower spirits. Nevertheless, some of them had become associated with natural features that had originally been the abodes of animistic souls. Perhaps the most prominent among these high gods were the so-called three daughters of Allāh,[91] al-ʿUzzā, al-Lāt, and Manāh.

Al-ʿUzzā, identified with Venus, the "morning star," was the most venerated idol among the Quraysh.[92] Her cult, which involved human sacrifice, was celebrated in a sanctuary of three trees at Nakhlah, east of Makkah, but her favors were sought almost throughout Arabia. In Sabaean epigraphy she is featured as the recipient of a golden image offered on behalf of a sick girl with the sobriquet of Amat ʿUzzay-an ("The Maid of al-ʿUzzā"),[93] while in the far north of the peninsula in about A.D. 544 al-Mundhir III of al-Ḥīrah sacrificed a son of the Ghassānid ruler to the same goddess. Al-Lāt (from *al-Ilāhah,* "the goddess")[94] was mistress of a *ḥaram* near al-Ṭāʾif, within which all life was accorded the inviolability of the goddess herself. Within its confines no plant could be gathered, no tree felled, no animal killed, no human blood shed. Manāh, the goddess of destiny,[95] was especially popular with the Aws and Khazraj tribes of Yathrib. Her chief shrine was a black stone in Qudayd, between Yathrib and Makkah,[96] but her name also occurs in Nabataean inscriptions from al-Ḥijr.[97]

Other high gods who had places in the Arabian pantheon during the *Jāhilīyah* included Hubal, probably of Aramaean origin; Jalsad and Kahl, who appear to have had special relations with the Banū-Kindah; Shums, who was venerated by the Ḍabbah, Tamīm, ʿUkl, ʿAdiyy, and Thawr; Dhū al-Khalaṣah and Yaghūth, who were worshipped in al-Yaman;[98] and Allāh, who possessed at least some of the attributes of a supreme deity. This last name was already ancient, occurring in at least two South Arabic inscriptions, one Sabaean and the other Minaean from al-ʿŪlah, and fairly commonly in the form *HLH* in Liḥyānī epigraphy of the fifth century B.C.[99] Apparently of Syrian provenance, this god figures as Hallāh both in the al-Ṣafah inscriptions from Ḥawrān at the beginning of the second century A.D. and in a Christian Arabic inscription, dated to the sixth century A.D., from Umm al-Jimāl.

Mention must also be made of a small group known to later Muslim scholars as *ḥunafāʾ* (sing. *ḥanīf*),[100] who were professing "the pure religion of Ibrāhīm," presumably a form of monotheism; but at the beginning of the seventh century they played only a small part in the segmentary religious hierarchy of al-Ḥijāz. Finally, there were individuals who laid claim to the role of prophet. Such a one was Hūd in the Ḥaḍramawt,[101] but the best known are those who, because of their opposition to the nascent Islamic polity, figure in the Tradition as false prophets: namely al-Aswad in the Yaman, Ṭulayḥah ibn Khuwaylid of the Banū-Asad, Sajāḥ of the Banū-Tamīm, and—apparently the most powerful—he who became known as Musaylimah ibn Ḥabīb in al-Yamāmah.[102]

In Makkah, the locality of primary concern in the present instance, each of these levels of religious activity was represented at the end of the sixth century. Near the head of the pantheon was Allāh, in which connection it is certainly significant that the name of the prophet Muḥammad's father was ʿAbd Allāh, signifying "servant of Allāh." The chief shrine at Makkah was a simple cube-shaped structure—hence its name of al-Kaʿbah—allegedly built by an Abyssinian in 608 from the timbers of a Greek ship wrecked near Shuʿaybah on the Red Sea coast.[103] Inside was the famous Black Stone, a meteorite venerated as a fetish, together with other stones and idols. The chief deity of al-Kaʿbah, though, was apparently Hubal, who was represented in human form[104] and whose soothsayer *(kāhin)* undertook divination by means of ritual arrows (belomancy). In Muslim tradition, which often reflects earlier pagan belief, the Kaʿbah was originally built by Ādam according to a heavenly prototype, and after the Deluge rebuilt by Ibrāhīm and Ismāʿīl:

> And when We appointed the House to be a place of visitation for the people and a sanctuary, [saying] "Take as your place of prayer the place where Ibrāhīm stood [to pray]." And we covenanted with Ibrāhīm and Ismāʿīl: "Purify My House for those who will circle round it, and for those who will cleave to it, and for those who will bow down and prostrate themselves."
>
> ....
>
> And when Ibrāhīm, and Ismāʿīl with him, were raising up the foundations of the House [and praying], "Our Lord, accept [this] from us. Thou art the All-hearing, the All-knowing."[105]

Around the shrine stretched its sanctified *ḥaram,* the inviolable refuge where feuds were abated and where no blood was shed.[106] At certain seasons of the year pilgrims from the length and breadth of al-Ḥijāz, and perhaps even further afield, converged on the Kaʿbah. During the period that subsequently became the eleventh, twelfth, and first months of the Islamic calendar, the Tradition states that pilgrims focused entirely on religious observances; during what later became the month of Rajab, however, the gathering was concerned mainly with trade.[107] *Ḥarams* of this type were not uncommon in pre-Islamic Arabia. Sanctuaries dedicated to the god Dhū-Samāwī at Timnaʿ, the capital of Qatabān, and at al-Hazm in Jawf of al-Yaman were set within a similarly sacred enclave, referred to in inscriptions as a *maḥram.* And both epigraphy and the Tradition point to other *ḥarams.*[108]

The Quraysh

By the end of the sixth century, as we have seen, the *shaykhs* of the Quraysh had established themselves as guardians of the Kaʿbah.[109] By this time, though, the authority that probably inhered originally in the person of the guardian had been distributed among a variety of offices and functions, notably the guardianship itself *(al-ḥijābah),* responsibility for provisioning pilgrims *(al-rifādah),* superintendence of the water supply *(al-siqāyah),* the right of presiding over assemblies *(al-nadwah),* the obligation of deciding when intercalations *(al-nasīʾ)* should be introduced into the lunar calendar, and responsibility for the tribal standard *(al-liwāʾ)* during raids. In addition to the prestige and privileges associated with these offices, certain of them were also revenue producing. The *rifādah,* for instance, was described as a "contribution" *(al-kharj)* made by Quraysh to the guardian of the Kaʿbah at every festival,[110] while a charge was also levied on pilgrims drawing from the well of Zamzam. The Tradition further implies that taxes were imposed on merchants and pilgrims, but the means of their collection and the rationale behind their disbursement are not at all clear.

In connection with the governance of the *ḥaram* at Makkah, the anonymous *Nihāyat al-Arab fī Akhbār al-Furs wa-l-ʿArab*[111] emphasizes the role of ʿAbd al-Muṭṭalib, Muḥammad's grandfather, as the officer in charge of the *siqāyah.* When the inhabitants of Makkah fled into the hills at the approach of the army of Abrahah, the Abyssinian viceroy, ʿAbd al-Muṭṭalib, together with Shaybah ibn ʿUthmān ibn ʿAbd al-Dār, who held the office of *ḥijābah,* remained in the city to ensure the provisioning of the *ḥaram.*[112] Apocryphal though this tale may be, it nicely depicts the manner in which the *ḥaram* was subsequently perceived as having stood aloof from tribal conflicts. The same work, on no better grounds, also credits ʿAbd al-Muṭṭalib with purchasing the wells called al-Ajbāb from the Banū-Naṣr ibn Muʿāwiyah in order to supplement the water from Zamzam.

At the same time, the Quraysh had profited from the resurgence of the overland trade routes between al-Yaman and the Levant after the decline of the client kingdoms of the Byzantine and Sāsānid Empires; some of them even renounced the migratory life of the true *badū.*[113] As one pre-Islamic poet puts it, "They lived in cities when only the shaykhs of the Banū-ʿAmr did so, and when others still followed the *badū* way of life,"[114] while another lamented that, had he remained with the Quraysh, he would not then be roaming the desert and spending the night in an evil lodging with brackish water.[115] From small beginnings when they sold protection to caravans, the Quraysh had begun to trade on their own account. In the *Nihāyat al-ʿArab* they are remembered in archetyped phrases as growing wealthy on the profits from trading in those territories: "Thus the Arabs overcame the ʿAjam [foreigners in the sense of those who spoke a language other than Arabic, i.e., *barbaroi*] by the abundance of their wealth, generosity, and excellence. [The Quraysh] were men of mind, reason, dignity, generosity, excellence, staid behavior, and nobility. They are the chosen people of God's servants, the best of His creatures and noblest of His peoples."[116] The words of Wellhausen are a fair representation of the way in which Islamic tradition has depicted this trade:

> Die Mekkaner verstanden es aus ihren heiligen Ressourcen weltlichen Gewinn zu ziehen. Das Wichtigste ist, dass sie auch die auswärtigen Märkte ringsum für sich zu fruktificiren wussten. Von den Messen der Nachbarorte schöpften sie das Fett ab. Mina (Minā'), Maganna (Majannah), Dhū'l Magâz (Dhū al-Majāz), und nicht zum wenigsten Ukâtz (ʿUkāẓ) waren gleichsam Aussenstationen des Handels von Mekka. An allen diesen Orten finden wir die Quraischiten, sie hatten das Geschäft in der Hand. Welches Ansehen sie genossen, ersieht man daraus, dass die Waffen, die Während der Märkte und des Hagg *(ḥajj)* abgelegt werden mussten, bei einem Quraischiten deponirt zu werden pflegten.[117]

Prominent among the commodities allegedly transported northward by Qurashī caravans were leather, especially camel, cattle, and gazelle hides from al-Yaman; dried raisins; incense; and precious metals, in return for which cereals, oil, wine, mule skins, silk, and sundry luxury goods were imported into Makkah.[118] More than a century ago Sprenger estimated the volume of trade supposedly handled by the Quraysh:

> Dem Gesagten zufolge müssen wir annehmen, dass die Makkaner jährlich über 12000 Zentner Waaren nach Syrien schickten und ebenso viele von dort bezogen. Wir dürfen aber den Werth nur zu 10 Mithḳâl *(mithqāl)* per Zentner veranschlagen, denn sie handelten auch mit Korn. Der Export und Import in jener Richtung belief sich etwa auf eine Viertel Million Mithḳâl [the equivalent of 11,250 kg. of gold]. Wenn der Handel nach Süden ebenso bedeutend war, so setzten sie jährlich für eine halbe Million Waaren um. Der Profit war wohl selten unter 50 Procent und sie erzielten somit ein Benefice von wenigstens 250000 Mithḳâl.[119]

Reconstructions of this type, which accept the Tradition more or less at its face value, are almost certainly projections into the sixth or seventh centuries of conditions during the eighth or later centuries; but it is by no means improbable that, as will be explained later, the Quraysh did negotiate safe passage for their caravans with *badū shaykh*s. And it is not impossible that, as in later times, they made arrangements with *khafīr*s, persons of substance who, in return for shares in the profits of an expedition, acted as guarantors of its safety; underwriters who, though they supplied a small escort, relied primarily on their own prestige and the blood bond with their tribe to deter raiders, and whose share in the proceeds amounted to an insurance premium. The Quraysh may well also have engaged *dalīl*s, guides who not only supervised the organization of the caravans but also possessed an intimate knowledge of currently usable trails and water holes. As safety lay largely in numbers, there was an incentive to make caravans as large as possible, but the tradition that some comprised as many as twenty-five hundred camels and were valued at up to fifty thousand *mithqāl*[120] is surely an exaggeration.

The Tradition would further have us believe that, to concentrate the capital necessary for such undertakings, the Quraysh had devised credit institutions capable of utilizing the resources of a considerable section of the Makkan populace; and that by these means even the most humble sums could be converted into capital, down to a *dīnār* or gold piece, or even a gold half-ducat.[121] Al-Wāqidī's account of the Makkan caravan that was attacked by Muslim Madīnese at Badr in 624, archetyped as it is into a heroic encounter, gives full expression to the way in which a fairly representative ninth-century author viewed the Qurashī caravan trade. This particular caravan was held to have numbered one thousand camels, and

> almost every man of Quraysh had a stake in it, even if it was only a small amount. It is said that 50,000 *dīnār*s were invested [in the expedition], mostly contributed by the Umayyad family of Ṣāʿid ibn al-ʿAṣī, either [in the form of] his own resources or of others borrowed in return for a half-share in the profits. The Banū-Makhzūm are said to have contributed 200 camels and 4–5,000 *mithqāl* of gold, al-Ḥārith ibn ʿAmir ibn Nawfal and Umayyah ibn Khalaf each 1,000 *mithqāl.* Several caravans belonging to individual Makkan families had joined together to form this one expedition, whose destination was the Ghazzah market.[122]

It is uncertain what role money played in the conduct of Ḥijāzī trade at the turn of the seventh century. Certainly it had not attained the status of a universal commodity, perhaps because of the absence in Arabia of a central political authority whose effigy and imprint might have standardized the value of the divers Byzantine and Persian coins that were in circulation. Even in later centuries coins were still weighed rather than counted; that is, they were treated as bullion.[123] The Tradition also implies that food, milk and wine, clothing, camels, and slaves were sold for money in the markets of the towns; that camels were hired out for caravan duty, and on occasion even ransoms were calculated, in monetary terms; and that certain occupations such as shepherding, guiding caravans, building, and leeching were at least sometimes rewarded with monetary wages.[124] Although the information is almost certainly a retrojection from a later age, it is not inherently unreasonable that bread prices should have risen after bad harvests.[125] What is more surprising, perhaps, is to find a poet of the *Jāhilīyah* implying that the cost of horses fluctuated according to market conditions.[126] Al-Wāqidī's report of a house worth four hundred *dīnārs* being sold for a down-payment of one hundred *dīnārs*, with the balance paid in installments, is probably an anachronism in the sixth or early seventh centuries.[127]

Makkan Commerce

Muslim tradition ascribes a very early, although unspecified, date to the development of Makkan international commerce; as a result, those modern scholars who have relied principally on Arab sources (i.e., all but a handful) have sought its origins far back in the *Jāhilīyah.* Leone Caetani, for instance, assumed that the Makkan trade tentacles reached into Egypt at least as early as the time of Quṣayy, whom the received genealogy places five generations before the Prophet.[128] A subsequent Italian scholar, Francesco Gabrieli, adopted essentially the same point of view,[129] as did A. J. Wensinck.[130] Father Lammens believed that the Quraysh had commandeered a flourishing long-distance trade when they had ousted the Banū-Khuzāʿah from the sanctuary at Makkah.[131] Harris Birkeland concluded that the Quraysh had gained control of western Arabian trade "about a hundred years before the Prophet,"[132] and A. J. Kister explicitly extended that conclusion to include the trade of Eastern Arabia.[133] W. Montgomery Watt, who was probably the most prominent scholar to treat commerce as a dependent variable in the rise of Islam, postulated that the Quraysh developed their trade on a large scale immediately after the conquest of al-Yaman by the Abyssinians.[134] Eric Wolf, an anthropologist seeking to elicit the structural dimensions of the developmental process, made the rise of Makkan commerce contingent on the dissolution of the Kindah confederacy.[135]

The predominantly Muslim Arab historians have naturally been constrained by the dictates of their faith to accept the traditional versions of the origins of Makkan commerce more or less at their face value.[136] In outline, these accounts attribute the establishment ex nihilo of a long-distance, Makkah-focused trading network to Hāshim, the great-grandfather of Muḥammad, more often than not with the assistance of his three brothers. According to tradition, these sons of ʿAbd Manāf concluded commercial treaties with the rulers of Byzantium, Sāsānid Persia, al-Yaman, and Abyssinia, as well as pacts of security *(al-īlāf)* with the *badū shaykhs* through whose territories the caravan routes passed.[137] The institution of the *īlāf* is defined by Muslim historians and commentators with a variety of subtly differing nuances,[138] but the best opinion today holds that it was a bilateral contract guaranteeing the safe passage of Qurashī caravans through tribal territories along the trade routes leading north, east, and south from Makkah.[139] It must be emphasized that an *īlāf* was not merely an alliance *(ḥilf)* for mutual help and protection but rather an arrangement whereby the *shaykhs* of the tribes involved shared in the profits of the expedition and furnished escorts from among their tribesmen. Based on the evidence available, it may have been primarily an instrument for dealing with tribes who, although strategically positioned to advance and protect Qurashī commerce, did not perform the pilgrimage to Makkah or respect its sacred months and who, as often as not, were situated within the sphere of influence of kingdoms client to the great empires.

As transmitted in the traditions, the tale of the sons of ʿAbd Manāf exhibits all the characteristics of an archetyped version of events in which a developmental process has been fathered on a real or fictive ancestor. In the first place, scholars agree that the four treaties were concluded not with emperors and kings but with local functionaries in border territories.[140] In the second, Simon has shown that the wider political situation in the Middle East would have prevented the simultaneous initiation of these agreements, as the Tradition asserts.[141] Even after the fall of the Ḥimyarite kingdom, the Quraysh were not immediately able to engross Yamanī trade with the Levant, control over which in fact passed into the hands of Abyssinians and Lakhmids during the fifth decade of the sixth century A.D. Moreover, a passage in al-Balādhurī's *Ansāb al-Ashrāf* implies that even then Yamanī merchants played an important part in the trade passing along the incense route.[142] According to Simon, it was not until some time toward the end of the sixth century that the Quraysh could dispatch their own caravans to the Yaman on commercial ventures that eventually became a virtual monopoly of the Banū-Makhzūm clan.[143] The archetyped symbol of this consummation was—in Simon's view, at any rate—the formation of the alliance known to traditionists as the Ḥilf al-Fuḍūl.[144]

To the north, Qurashī trade with Syria on a substantial scale had to await the extinction of the Ghassān chiefdom, long a Byzantine satellite, early in the 580s. Simon finds this determination confirmed by certain details in the story of ʿUthmān ibn al-Huwayrith, an apparently Christian Qurashī who, during the late sixth century, aspired to become ruler of Makkah under Byzantine auspices.[145] In short, although there are indications that the Quraysh may not have been entirely excluded from the Syrian trade perhaps a couple of decades earlier, it is unlikely that they were sending their own caravans to Syria before about 560.

Similarly, it can be argued that the sending of Qurashī caravans to ʿIrāq would have been impracticable as long as the Lakhmids and their client Qays ʿAylān tribesmen controlled the western approaches to the lower Euphrates valley. It was only after the Quraysh and the Kinānah, in the celebrated Ḥarb al-Fijār, had soundly defeated the Banū-Hawāzin and the Thaqīf who protected Lakhmid commerce that Qurashī caravans could be sent to ʿIrāq with any chance of success.[146] According to a tradition given literary expression in the *Kitāb al-Aghānī*, even as late as Muḥammad's time Qurashī commerce with ʿIrāq was an uncertain venture—so much so that Abū Sufyān ibn Ḥarb, at the head of a group of Quraysh and Thaqīf, was said to have halted his caravan three stages outside Makkah and warned his companions that they faced great danger "because we shall be entering the realm of a despotic ruler who has not authorized our venture and whose territories are not a locus of trade for us."[147] Altogether the evidence is pretty conclusive that Qurashī participation in trade between the Ḥijāz and al-ʿIrāq barely antedated the advent of Islam.

As for the supposed commercial treaty between the Quraysh and the Najāshī of Abyssinia, all that we know of the Middle East in the sixth and seventh centuries A.D. militates against the conclusion of such an agreement. At that period the trade passing through the Red Sea was the exclusive preserve of the Abyssinians and the Byzantines,[148] and Ḥijāzī tribesmen had little or nothing to do with the sea in any case. Indeed, Arab maritime commerce did not develop until the time of the Umayyads. Clearly the venture of ʿAbd Shams ibn ʿAbd Manāf to Abyssinia must be deemed a fabrication by later traditionists.

Fairs

All in all, Simon's general conclusion seems to be sound: Makkan long-distance commerce could not, as the Tradition claims, have been developed by an individual. Rather, it was forged hesitatingly and uncertainly, beginning in the middle of the sixth century and culminating only in the time of the Prophet.[149] Prior to about A.D. 550 the only economic exchanges in which the Quraysh shared had been barter transactions during the fair that took place during the pilgrimage month.[150] Although fairs such as this, including those at Majannah, Dhū al-Majāz, and the celebrated ʿUkāẓ, were regulated by the *shaykhs* of the territories in which they occurred, the bulk of the commodities traded—if al-Qālī is to be believed—were brought to Makkah by foreign merchants and merely redistributed by the Quraysh among neighboring tribes.[151] Al-Thaʿālibī (A.D. 961–1038) in his *Thimār al-Qulūb* also noted the tradition that the Quraysh traded only with merchants who visited Makkah on their way to or from the fairs at Dhū al-Majāz and ʿUkāẓ. The reason that al-Thaʿālibī offered for this was that the Quraysh were devoted to their religion *(dīn)* and clove to their sacred enclave *(ḥaram)* and their shrine *(bayt)*.[152] The same distributive function was also attributed to the Quraysh by al-Azraqī, who reported that wares arriving in Makkah from Egypt were stored in the so-called Egyptian Compound *(Dār Miṣr)* belonging to a certain Ṣafwān ibn Umayyah al-Jumaḥī. Tribesmen would then come to that establishment, located in the lower part of Makkah, to purchase the goods.[153]

Simon, relying on a passage in al-Marzūqī's *Kitāb al-Azminah wa-l-Amkinah*, emphasizes the role of the rulers of the satellite kingdoms of the great empires in promoting and exploiting the fairs. The passage in question runs as follows: "And the Arab nobles were accustomed to frequent the fairs in the company of merchants, because the kings [of the satellite kingdoms] used always to give the nobles—each noble—a share of the profit. And the nobles of each region customarily repaired to the fair in their own territory, except in the case of ʿUkāẓ, whither they came from all parts."[154] In any event, Qurashī trade before the middle of the sixth century could have been of only local importance, mainly distributive in character, and similar to that associated with any of the other pilgrimage centers in Arabia.

For the rest, the Quraysh were still *badū* herdsmen, many of them probably fully nomadic. Of this the Tradition, despite a legendary overlay, may have provided indirect confirmation. It will be recalled that in the story of ʿAbd al-Muṭṭalib's meeting with Abrahah, the leader of invading Yamanī forces, the only restitution demanded by "the Lord of the Quraysh and Master of the Makkan Well" was the return of the two hundred camels that Abrahah's raiders had lifted from him—a characteristic *badū* response.[155] Solicitousness for the welfare of his camels is characteristic of the *badawī:* in truth they are the only possessions he really values, the very "gift of Allāh," as he calls them; he will endure greatly to recover them when stolen or, indeed, to raid the herds of neighboring tribes.[156] The fact that the events referred to in this vignette allegedly took place about A.D. 547[157] implies that the old *badū* ways were still strong among the Quraysh of Makkah less than twenty-five years before the supposed birth of the Prophet. And there is evidence that most of them probably continued this manner of existence throughout the lifetime of Muḥammad and even later. Their familiarity with the desert wastes was essential to their roles as caravan guides and escorts. And these roles in no way diminished, in fact they multiplied, as the Quraysh established themselves in the network of Arabian trade exchanges in the half century or so before Muḥammad began to preach.

In his study of Makkah on the eve of the *Hijrah,* Father Lammens has mentioned, in addition to the various pagan Arabians and Jewish inhabitants, Syrian caravanners, travelling monks and itinerant healers, Syrian merchants, foreign smiths, Coptic carpenters, black-skinned sculptors of idols, Christian doctors, surgeons, dentists, scribes, Christian women married into a Qurashī clan, and Abyssinian sailors and mercenaries, as well as Abyssinian, Mesopotamian, Egyptian, Syrian, and Byzantine slaves offered for sale in the markets.[158] For reasons we have already advanced, this is almost certainly a picture of Makkah in perhaps the eighth century, although some of the groups mentioned were certainly to be found there in the time of the Prophet. Montgomery Watt has estimated that there were then a thousand or so men capable of bearing arms in the settlement, from which he infers a total population of "rather more than 5,000 people in all."[159] I am inclined to believe that the resident population was a good deal less than this during much of the year. There is no reason, though, to dissent from the Qur'ānic assessment that, at the beginning of the seventh century, Makkah was "a settlement *(qaryah)* secure and at peace."[160] *Sūrah* 106 *(Quraysh)* of the Qur'ān, traditionally believed to have been revealed early in Muḥammad's ministry, is an appeal to the Quraysh to worship "the Lord of this House [the Kaʿbah]" to ensure the continuation of this relative prosperity.

> In the Name of God, the Merciful, the Compassionate.
> For the protection *(li-'īlāfi)* of the Quraysh,
> For the protection of the winter and summer journeys *(riḥlāt)* [i.e., the annual caravans to the south and north respectively],
>
> Let them serve the Lord of this House
> Who hath afforded them provision against famine
> And secured them against fear.[161]

The Quraysh best able to profit from these economic developments were those *shaykhs* with seniority in the religious hierarchy, particularly those of the Umayyad clan. By the beginning of the seventh century there was already apparent among the Quraysh a differentiation based on wealth not only between clans but also between clan members. Tradition relates that, whereas the powerful Umayyad and Makhzūm clans occupied those sectors of the settlement adjoining the Kaʿbah and were designated Quraysh of the Center *(Quraysh al-Baṭāʿiḥ),* the eight other less wealthy clans, known as Quraysh of the Outskirts *(Quraysh al-Ẓawāhir),* were relegated to the fringes of Makkah and even beyond.[162] Moreover, it seems that by the time of Muḥammad new functional units were beginning to appear in Makkan society side by side with the so-called clans, namely clusters of prosperous merchants, together with their dependents, including clients (p. 9 above) who were linked to the possessors of social power not by birth but by ties of ritual kinship.[163] According to the Tradition, there were thirteen major groups of clients in Makkah, each affiliated to a patron lineage. Eric Wolf, who has analyzed the composition of these groups, concludes that they were composed of freed slaves, outlaws from other tribes seeking refuge, individuals who had entered into lineage protection through matrilocal marriage, and some who were simply adopted persons.[164]

During this same period the *ḥaram,* the sanctified enclave surrounding the Kaʿbah, was constituted as the focus of Qurashī territory. Also, the Quraysh were ensuring safe passage for merchants and pilgrims to the shrine through various pacts with other tribal groups (pp. 9–10 above), an expedient earning them the scorn of some of the *badū* in other parts of the peninsula. "No one has yet lived through a terror (raid) by them," sneers a Hudhayl poet,[165] and another poet characterizes them as "good only for appearing in the ranks of processions."[166] Moreover, whereas the relation of god to worshipper had previously been seen, in terms of the ancient Arabian social system, as a bond between patron and client, henceforward was the gradual ascendancy of that particular god, Allāh, who was especially concerned with relationships lying outside the ethical motivations of the kin community. As Julius Wellhausen puts it,

> Allah ist der Zeus Xenios, der Schützer von Gâr *(jār)* und Daif *(ḍayf)*, von Klient und Gast. Innerhalb des Geschlechtes und im minderen Masse innerhalb des Stammes schützt die Rahim *(raḥīm)*, die verwandtschaftliche Pietät, die Heiligkeit des Blutes. Wenn es aber über das Geschlecht hinaus Rechte und Pflichten gibt, so ist Allah derjenige, welcher sie auflegt und verbürgt. Er ist der Hüter des Givâr (*jiwār:* the patron-client relationship), wodurch der natürliche Gemeinschaftskreis eine Erweiterung und Ergänzung erfährt, die vor allem dem Klienten und dem Gaste zu gute kommt.[167]

In Makkah the locus of political power had come to coincide fairly closely with that of economic power.[168] Power theoretically resided in a council drawn from the *majlis*es of the clans known as the *Mala'*. In practice, however, this council was dominated by the same *shaykh*s, mainly from the Qurashī clans of Banū-Umayyah and Makhzūm, who both controlled the trade of the settlement and virtually monopolized the chief religious offices. It was they who concluded agreements of *ḥilf* and *īlāf*, ensured the inviolability of the *ḥaram*, and—so the Tradition would have us believe—commanded a sort of praetorian guard, possibly inspired by those at the courts of the Banū-Kindah[169] and the Persian satellite al-Ḥīrah.[170] Despite its economic and religious standing, the council commanded no legislative power. Its only effective instrument of social control was the sanction of the blood feud, for potential transgressors of customary norms were disinclined to risk an encounter with the powerful Quraysh of the Center. Indeed, the inhabitants of Makkah, like those of all other Ḥijāzī settlements, were still subservient in many respects to the norms of the nomadic *badū* and *shwāyah*, particularly in their political organization, ethics, and intellectuality.[171]

Muḥammad's Message

It was in this milieu that, according to the Tradition, in about 610 Muḥammad, son of ʿAbd Allāh, who was the son of ʿAbd al-Muṭṭalib, of the *qawm* of Hāshim and the *qabīlah* of Quraysh, began to preach publicly. He claimed that he had been designated as Allāh's messenger[172] and deputed to warn the Makkans that they could escape the fires of hell only by worshipping Him.[173] In a rational, almost technical, manner that may be epitomized as the exclusive service *(islām)* of the One God,[174] Muḥammad declared that Allāh, through the last, the Seal *(Khātam)*, of his prophets, was showing men the path to Paradise.[175] The precise content of the earliest form of his message is not entirely clear.[176] The *sūrah*s of the Qur'ān are not arranged chronologically, but analysis of those passages that recent authorities have agreed to assign an early date[177] leads to the conclusion that Muḥammad's original message fell broadly within the already ancient tradition of Judeo-Christian monotheism—even though its style was that of the traditional soothsayer *(kāhin)*, being cast in short, paratactic, rhymed phrases and sprinkled with oaths invoking objects of the Arab natural world: the heavens, water, air, wind, light, and darkness, as al-Najīramī specified them.[178] As the revelation developed, its main themes became the immanence of the One and Only God's goodness and power; the ineluctable and essential justice of a resurrection to judgment followed by reward or punishment; acknowledgment of man's dependence on God and expression of gratitude for His goodness by acts of worship; the necessity of following a way of life consonant with these circumstances; and the vocation of Muḥammad as God's envoy.

Watt argues that in its early form the message was an attempt to offer a satisfying alternative to the "presumption" *(ṭaghā)* and "pride in wealth" *(istaghnā)* that recur in the Qur'ān almost as technical terms.[179] If that were indeed so, the alternative was prescribed within the old kin-structured social framework of *badū* Arabia. It was to a tribe, at most to the tribes actually or potentially in alliance with Makkah, that the Prophet was sent, so that in effect Muḥammad was attempting to link a lower-order segment of the social hierarchy to a higher-order segment of the divine hierarchy. On this ground alone it is not surprising that his teaching was rejected by the leaders of Makkan society, including the oligarchs, the "Union of the Quraysh." Muslim tradition has advanced a variety of reasons of its own for this rejection, but all bear the imprint of traditionist bias.

In more recent times Professor Watt has suggested that the influential merchants of Makkah feared that Muḥammad, by castigating their attitude toward the accumulation of wealth, was undermining their whole way of life.[180] This is an overly simplistic reading of the situation, for it fails to take into account certain important aspects of Ḥijāzī culture in the seventh century. It should be noted, too, that this interpretation of events derives from Professor Watt's more comprehensive theory that the transition from a nomadic to a settled, commercial lifestyle had induced a malaise in Makkan society that required a totally new approach to the relationship between God and man.[181] This interpretation can be countered on two grounds. First, the *badū* ethic had by no means been superseded in Makkah at the time of the Prophet (compare with p. 18 above). Indeed, it has been questioned whether seasonal trading alone could have supported a sizable sedentary population in a locale where agriculture was impracticable.[182] And second, Muḥammad was not advocating innovation *(bidʿah):* by and large he accepted the ethical code and social organization of his time. He fit into the system of law and custom into which he had been born,[183] and did not try to restructure Makkan, let alone Ḥijāzī or Arabian, society.

Consolidation of Quraysh Authority

Certain attempts at monistic or near-monistic interpretations of events at Makkah in the first half of the seventh century are subject to criticisms of a kind different from those levelled at Watt's work. Caetani's reliance on population pressure as a dependent variable in the formation of the Islamic state,[184] Becker's emphasis on exclusively economic motivations,[185] Belyaev's preoccupation with a postulated class struggle in Makkah,[186] Grimme's attempt to characterize Islam as a movement of social reform,[187] Bendelī Jawzī's Marxist interpretation of Muḥammad's life and actions,[188] Aswad's focus on ecological disequilibria in al-Madīnah as favoring sociopolitical integration,[189] and Wolf's concern with the internal evolution of Makkan urban society,[190] all undervalue—sometimes virtually ignore—that Makkah was a shrine before it became a commercial center.

Of course, traditionally the emergence of the Islamic state has been considered a purely religious phenomenon mediated through the powerful personality of Muḥammad, and not a few authors are still wedded to that belief, particularly Muslim writers.[191] At the other extreme, from at latest Voltaire there have been those who have regarded Muḥammad as at best deluded, at worst an imposter exploiting religion to further both personal and tribal ambition.[192] Works of this type are of no concern to us in the present context, but it is noteworthy that the actions of the Prophet and his supporters on the one hand and those who opposed him on the other were at an early date confused, in some cases totally obscured, when the *Ḥadīth* (record of an action, utterance, or decision of the Prophet and his followers, or Companions) was corrupted in the interests of factional conflict during the centuries following Muḥammad's death.[193] It appears, though, that for a while the dissensions may have followed lines of contention within the Qurashī tribe itself.[194]

In attempting to probe behind the semitransparent, sometimes even opaque, veils that the traditionists have drawn between us and the age of the Prophet, it is most profitable to begin with the religious role of Makkah to discern in eighth-century and later accounts the lineaments of a seventh-century reality. The mythology incorporated in the Qurʾān attributes the founding of the sanctuary to Ādam, and its subsequent rebuilding to Ibrāhīm and Ismāʿīl,[195] an ascription entirely in accord with the ancient cosmo-magical symbolism of the Western Semites that was imposed on Makkah by later traditionists.[196] Although few non-Muslims would accept this dating, the sanctuary would have been in existence some centuries before Muḥammad if—as many believe—it did indeed figure in Ptolemy's schedule of Arabian toponyms as a Greek transcription of a Sabaean term signifying "shrine" (p. 12 above). Although the *Geographia* is to an undetermined extent a cumulative text, its depiction of the Arabian Peninsula is in fairly close accord with the information that can be gleaned from other contemporary sources. In addition, there is no prima facie cause to doubt that the designation *Makurabah,* which Ptolemy must have acquired from a predecessor or a contemporary informant, was at least as early as the second century A.D., when the first version of the *Geographia* was compiled.[197]

Muslim Tradition asserts that the city of Makkah was established by Quṣayy, a Qurashī *shaykh* living five generations before Muḥammad, but this tale bears the unmistakable stamp of an archetyped legend crystallized around a heroized tribal figure.[198] However, the truth or otherwise of the tradition in this matter is not an issue here, nor is it in the case of the various contributions to the prosperity of the shrine allegedly made by Quṣayy, his grandson Hāshim, and his great-grandson ʿAbd al-Muṭṭalib.[199] What is pertinent to our discussion is that sometime before the start of the seventh century the Quraysh had acquired control over the shrine at Makkah, together with the *ḥaram* surrounding it. The lord of such a shrine, as in South Arabia in recent times, was held to be in receipt of spiritual power that as often as not inhered in the family as a whole and, regarding the Makkan sanctuary, perhaps to a certain degree in the entire tribe of Quraysh, which was in fact categorized by Ibn Durayd as *Ahl Allāh.*[200] In ancient times persons of such spiritual distinction were often accorded the title of *sayyid* or *sharīf.* As Father Lammens states, "Rien de plus ordinaire dans l'antiquité au temps de la préhistoire islamique (al-Jāhilīyah) que la réunion des dignités de Kāhin [soothsayer] et Saiyid."[201] Commenting on this remark, Serjeant adds that some *kāhins* were also judge-arbiters *(ḥukkām;* sing. *ḥakam),* and some *sayyids* were guardians (sing. *sādin*) of temples of the goddess al-Lāt, while a certain Hishām ibn Mughīrah was described as a *sayyid miṭʿām,* that is, one who entertained the guest, probably defraying the cost from shrine revenues.[202]

Within the Makkan *ḥaram,* all feuds were abated and the shedding of blood strictly forbidden, whether of men or beasts.[203] The Tradition also records that the cutting of trees was prohibited until Quṣayy abrogated the taboo so that houses could be built.[204] In a milieu in which tribes were embroiled in a perpetual round of wars, truces, and transient alliances, all governed by the rigid prescriptions of tribal custom *(ʿādah),* the inviolability of the *ḥaram* guaranteed a physically secure locale within which tribesmen from opposing factions could meet to arrange truces or the payment of blood money, seek favors from the local deity, or conduct an economic exchange. Mediating these transactions between hostile parties was a member of a holy family, combining within a single person the mutually supportive roles of soothsayer and *sayyid,* backed by the authority of the patron deity of the shrine. According to the Tradition, in Makkah this office had been a prerogative of the Quraysh for five generations, although not without internal dissensions between kinsmen.[205]

The taxes allegedly imposed on tribal chiefs by Hāshim[206] were probably not too different from the *khums* until recently exacted by guardians (*manṣabs*) from inhabitants of Ḥaḍramī *ḥawṭahs*, and, as in these latter, were very likely supplemented by votive offerings and perhaps fines levied on tribesmen for infractions of *ḥaram* custom. In any event, by the beginning of the seventh century the authority originally inhering in the guardian of the shrine, as we have seen (p. 14 above), had been distributed among a number of offices and functions. And it was into one of these Quraysh families, the Sayyid house of Hāshim, both noble and holy, that Muḥammad was born. His aristocratic status among the tribes is amply attested in the *Sīrah* by the use of technical terms signifying that he was held in honor and protection *(manʿah),* while his uncle Ḥamzah is characterized in a poem attributed to Kaʿb ibn Malik as "A noble prince, strong in the high-born line of Hāshim / Whence come prophecy, generosity, and lordship."[207]

Security for person and property encourages economic exchange, and we have already examined the role of the *ḥarams* surrounding pilgrimage sites in pre-Islamic Arabia as distribution centers (p. 17 and note 150) where commodities brought in by foreign merchants were traded to local tribesmen. To the extent that the tribesmen were, or eventually became, dependent for these commodities on the dwellers within the *ḥaram,* particularly on the holy family believed to have access to the divinity in the shrine, the lord or guardian of the sanctuary was converting authority into a very real power. Serjeant has recorded the manner in which the *manṣab* of a Ḥaḍramī *ḥawṭah* during the first half of the present century influenced surrounding tribesmen through his control of the market (mainly by punishing a misdemeanor by interdiction from the market *[sūq]*),[208] and the Quraysh may have employed similar forms of persuasion in the seventh century; but the main instrument contributing to the development of Qurashī trade in western Arabia (as opposed to the longer-distance commerce conducted under *īlāf* agreements: p. 16 above) was the institution of the *Ḥums.*

The *Ḥums*

The *Ḥums* constituted an amphictyony focused on the Kaʿbah at Makkah and uniting, in adherence to certain religious rites, those tribes whose alliance was important for Qurashī trade. It also ensured the inviolability of the *ḥaram* at Makkah not only for the duration of the pilgrimage but throughout the year.[209] According to al-Azraqī, the *qawms* and tribes included in the *Ḥums* were the Quraysh, Kinānah, Khuzāʿah, al-Aws, al-Khazraj, Jusham, ʿĀmir ibn Ṣaʿṣaʿah, Ghaṭafān, al-Ghawth, ʿUdwān, ʿIlāf, and Quḍāʿah, but other traditionists furnish substantially different lists.[210] However, it is clear that for the traditionists generally the designation *Ḥums* included the Quraysh, other inhabitants of Makkah, and certain peoples outside Makkah; that is, it subsumed groups from diverse tribal divisions. The *ʿāmir* ibn Ṣaʿṣaʿah, for instance, belonged to the tribe of Muḍar, Kalb (which figured in Ibn Ḥabīb's list) to that of Quḍāʿah, and Thaqīf (Ibn Ḥabīb's list) probably to the Qays ʿAylān, while the Khuzāʿah were of South Arabian origin. Moreover, these various groups were not clustered in one sector of the peninsula but scattered wherever Qurashī caravans passed: Thaqīf to the southeast of Makkah and Kinānah to the south guarding the trails to al-Yaman; ʿĀmir ibn Ṣaʿṣaʿah to the northeast and Quḍāʿah to the north watching over the route to Syria; and Yarbūʿ and Māzin (Ibn Ḥabīb's list) protecting caravans en route to al-Ḥīrah and Persia. All were bound by their recognition of the sanctity of the Kaʿbah and their acknowledgment of the ritual authority of its guardians, the holy tribe of Quraysh. It is likely that the confederacy came into being in about the middle of the sixth century.[211]

Tradition recounts that during the pilgrimage, members of the *Ḥums* imposed special hardships on themselves. For instance, they allegedly performed the *Wuqūf* at al-Muzdalifah instead of at ʿArafah, they stayed within the boundaries of the *ḥaram* during the whole of the sacred months, abstained from meat and curd, avoided the shade of a dwelling, and did not enter through the door.[212] It is further reported that the Quraysh married their daughters only into tribes that had entered into the *Ḥums* confederacy.[213] Ritual restrictions were also said to have been imposed on tribesmen entering the *ḥaram* who were not members of the confederacy; they were, for instance, obliged to leave their provisions outside the sacred enclave and to don special clothing.[214] Tribes *(qabāʾil)* who did not belong to the *Ḥums* yet respected the sanctity of the Makkan *ḥaram* were known as *Ḥillah.*[215] But there were other tribes who refused to observe either the sacred months or the inviolability of Makkah,[216] and it was against their depredations that the Quraysh are said to have organized a sort of praetorian guard—designated by Kister as "an inter-tribal militia"[217]—to defend their *ḥaram* and its markets.[218]

The amphictyony of the *Ḥums* as depicted in the Tradition was a delicately balanced network of fragile loyalties founded on common interests and sanctified by its association with the Kaʿbah. Rituals performed in the *ḥaram,* especially those of the *Ḥajj* (major pilgrimage), facilitated information exchanges between the disparate societal systems of economy and religion. By means of the *Ḥums,* the sanctity of the Kaʿbah was extended to a series of propositions, customs, and actions not usually touched by religion, and the arbitrary thereby transformed into the necessary through substantial sectors of Makkan society.[219] Even so, the system could quickly be rendered unstable by either external pressures generated by the great empires and transmitted through their satellite kingdoms or by fortuitously induced shifts in power among the tribes of the Arabian Peninsula. This instability was by no means eliminated even when the *Ḥums* was conjoined with the security pacts known as *īlāf* (discussed earlier), the institution of the holy months *(ashhur ḥurum)* during which caravans could travel unmolested throughout Arabia except the territories of the *Muḥillūn* (compare with note 214),[220] and the privilege of arranging intercalations in the lunar calendar so that these months would coincide with the seasons. This last prerogative, exercised by the *mālik* ibn Kinānah under Quraysh control,[221] may well have enabled the holy months to be timed for the advantage of Qurashī commerce. In any case the confederacy appears to have functioned as an effective instrument for the consolidation of Qurashī trade relations. Not for nothing did a *kāhin* of the Lihb refer to Makkah as *al-Dār al-Ḥums.*[222]

It may be that, as the Tradition asserts, the Quraysh were incurring the scorn of the Muḥillūn because they no longer raided the tribes within the amphictyony or with whom they had concluded *īlāf* pacts. Even so, their caravans were now passing safely through the territories of their traditional tribal enemies, while the inviolable security of the *ḥaram* was both attracting merchants and promoting local distributive exchanges with *badū* from much of northwest Arabia.[223] Whereas the pyramidal political polities of the Banū-Kindah and the Lakhmids had relied on ties of kinship and military supremacy to control peoples rather than territory, the Quraysh were relying primarily on sanctity—the sanctity of the Kaʿbah and their own privileged religious status—as a functional equivalent of political power. And loyalties within the confederacy were focused on a shrine, on a place, rather than on a people.

Muḥammad's Opposition

But it was the ritualistic underpinnings of the Qurashī trading network that Muḥammad's insistence on the exclusivity of the One God was most likely to undermine. The *sayyids* of Makkah viewed his message as subverting a system of peaceful transactions that had been established with difficulty over half a century or so. Consequently Muḥammad was perceived—in contrast to Quṣayy, the Uniter *(Mujammiʿ)* of the *qawms* of Quraysh[224]—as a Divider of the Association *(Mufarriq al-Jamāʿah),* as a threat to the whole sacro-economic edifice of Qurashī diplomatic and trade relations. The exclusivity of Muḥammad's community of believers, which threatened to absolve them of certain traditional lineage responsibilities, was also perceived as a threat to the solidarity *(ʿaṣabīyah)* of the tribe, as is implied in the story of Nuʿaym ibn ʿAbd Allāh of the ʿUwayj, whose father was known to have fed the poor of the ʿAdiyy. When Nuʿaym embraced Islam, he was upbraided by al-Walīd ibn al-Mughīrah of the Makhzūm with the following words: "Son of ʿAbd Allāh, you pulled down what your father built, and you severed what he joined [by his care for the indigent] when you followed Muḥammad."[225]

Moreover, although Muḥammad came from a noble religious family associated with the Kaʿbah for five generations—according to the Tradition, at any rate—there are hints here and there in the Tradition that he was excluded, either temporarily by reason of age or permanently by descent, from religious office. In one of those passages that seem to have survived the excisions of traditionists because their import was not fully understood, Ibn Isḥāq relates that al-Walīd ibn al-Mughīrah (mentioned above), on hearing of Muḥammad's claim to revelation, expostulated, "Is revelation given to Muḥammad while I am ignored, even though I am the Kabīr[226] of Quraysh and their *Sayyid,* to say nothing of Abū Masʿūd ʿAmr ibn ʿUmar al-Thaqafī, the *Sayyid* of Thaqīf, we being the important persons in the two towns?"[227] Evidently, the *Sayyid* class of the Ḥijāz did not regard Muḥammad as a proper candidate for high office in the religious hierarchy. Furthermore, after he had left Makkah for al-Madīnah (Medina), Muḥammad showed little respect for the truce that the Makkan confederacy observed during the holy months. As al-Ṭabarī reports the Qurashī view of events, "Muḥammad claims he is obeying God . . . but he was the first to profane the sacred month and has killed our comrade during Rajab."[228] The impious act referred to was the waylaying of a Qurashī caravan near al-Nakhlah on the road from al-Ṭāʾif to Makkah during a period of truce, a violation of a ritually sanctioned covenant subsequently justified by a revelation asserting that "persecution [by the Quraysh] is more serious than killing [by the Muhājirūn of al-Madīnah]."[229] Although al-Ṭabarī's account of the ambush is clearly an archetyped version of events, it nevertheless seems to preserve fairly realistically the Qurashī view of Muḥammad as a dissident. His substitution of religiopolitical loyalties to the Muslim community *(Ummah)* for the traditional bonds of the lineage was regarded by the Makkans as equally impious and probably even more subversive of their social order, as witness the reported bitter cry of Abū Jahl, leader of the Makkan relief force at the battle of Badr: "O God, destroy this morning him who more than any of us has severed the ties of kinship and wrought what is not permitted."[230]

At any event, the opposition to Muḥammad's preaching was sufficiently strong and sustained to cause him to look beyond Makkah for a receptive audience. He also sought protection for his followers, particularly those outside the Hāshimite lineage, who were vulnerable to attacks and retaliation from members of their own descent groups and who were therefore virtually without protection. It is said that at one time the Quraysh declared a total interdiction of social and economic relations with the two ʿAbd Manāf clans, namely the Banū-Hāshim and the Banū-Muṭṭalib.[231] The upshot was that in 622 Muḥammad migrated with a small group of followers to Yathrib, or al-Madīnah, as it came to be known.

Characteristics of Makkah

The settlement from which Muḥammad fled was a town more in name than substance. Essentially it was a shrine surrounded by a *ḥaram,* the sanctity of which had been exploited by its guardians to undergird a confederacy in the interests of local trade and longer distance commerce. Even during the lifetime of Muḥammad—despite the building that the Tradition attributes to Quṣayy and his successors—most of the structures in Makkah were of palm fronds and similar light materials, and were clustered on the *wādī* floor near the Kaʿbah and the well of Zamzam. At higher levels were encampments of *badū:* some more or less permanent to enable lineage representatives to watch over their stakes in the confederacy, others merely transitory halts in the endless *badū* search for water and pasture, perhaps combined with paltry trade exchanges. During the *Ḥajj,* we can imagine the number of tents multiplying dramatically, blackening the adust slopes of the surrounding hills; and when the winter and summer caravans returned there was doubtless a centripetal surge of tribesmen from outlying districts toward the *ḥaram.*[232] But this was no merchant republic in the later European sense of that term, nor indeed in the sense in which Father Lammens uses it. The Qurʾān has got it just right when it epitomizes Makkah as "a settlement secure and at peace."[233] M. J. Kister has already drawn attention to two passages from al-Balādhurī's *Ansab al-Ashrāf* that express in verse precisely these two salient characteristics of the settlement. In the first a *sayyid* of Makkah nicely captures the aura of security pervading the *ḥaram,* and in the second a *badawī* who cannot accustom himself to the tranquillity within its bounds hankers after the harsh regimen of the desert and the constant nervous alertness that it engenders.[234]

There is no hint in these passages of the social malaise that Montgomery Watt thought he discerned: of tribesmen caught in a rapidly changing world that they could not comprehend, of a yearning for a new value system more consonant with the times (p. 20 above). In fact *badū* values and norms still prevailed in Makkah; metaphorically, and to a noticeable extent in actuality, the desert intruded into the heart of the settlement. What the *badawī* prized were security and peace, conditions rarely occurring in the normal course of events but that existed within the *ḥaram* and while travelling through the territories of the *Ḥums.* But it was the sacred basis of the institutions maintaining this security that Muḥammad's teaching was threatening to subvert, and with it the trade and commerce that it enabled.

Yathrib (al-Madīnah)

The locality to which Muḥammad came was an oasis slightly less than three hundred miles northeast of Makkah across a tract of particularly barren volcanic terrain *(ḥarrah).* It had originally been settled by Jewish tribes, of whom the most powerful in Muḥammad's time were the Qurayẓah, the Naḍīr, and the Qaynuqāʿ. The nucleus of these tribes may have been Israelites who had fled from Palestine after the Roman conquest in the first century A.D., but their names and their technical farming vocabulary indicate that many of them were Judaized Arabians and Aramaeans.[235] It has, in fact, been suggested that it was Aramaic-speaking Jews who were responsible for the name of the settlement changing from Arabic Yathrib to Aramaic Medīntā, whence al-Madīnah, the name by which it was known in Muslim times.[236] Subsequently Arabs of the tribes of Aws and Khazraj had settled among the Jewish pioneers, first as their clients but from the earlier decades of the sixth century as the dominant ethnic group. However, even at the beginning of the next century the Jewish clans of al-Naḍīr and Qurayẓah still retained some of the best agricultural land in the oasis.

The cultivation of dates and cereals, no doubt combined with the raising of goats and sheep on the fringes of the desert, formed the basis of subsistence for Jews and Arabs alike. Additionally, the clans of the Jewish tribe of Qaynuqāʿ were not only traders, with a profitable market under their control, but also silversmiths and armorers. The Tradition implies that in pre-Islamic times Yathrib lacked a distinctively urban focus, instead consisting of fairly discrete clan settlements set amid palm groves and fields. A century of bitter feuding between the Madīnese tribes, particularly between the Aws and the Khazraj, had resulted in the inhabitants of these settlements building themselves refuges in the form of groups of fortified tower houses *(uṭūm;* pl. *āṭām),* perhaps as many as two hundred at any one time. Originally designed to be occupied only in emergencies, there are indications that during the decades of chronic insecurity immediately preceding Muḥammad's arrival, these tower houses often served as permanent residences.

According to the Tradition, it was as a judge and arbiter of their internal disputes that the Madīnese, or at least some of them, had invited Muḥammad to their settlement; that is, they recognized him as an authority on tribal custom *(al-maradd),* a status evidently deriving from his membership in the holy family of Makkah. Underneath the overlay of mythical, archetyped, and heroized events retailed by Ibn Isḥāq and other traditionists[237] is the basic idea that Muḥammad was behaving—as Robert Serjeant has demonstrated in a series of articles—very much like the *manṣab* of a Ḥaḍramī *ḥawṭah* as recently as the twentieth century; he was undertaking to act as a mediator *(ḥakam)* between feuding tribes.[238] Prior to his negotiation with *shaykhs* of the Aws and Khazraj in Yathrib, Muḥammad is said to have unsuccessfully solicited protection, and probably recognition as an arbiter, from several *badū* tribes, in particular the Banū-Kindah, Banū-Kalb, Banū-ʿĀmir ibn Ṣaʿṣaʿah, and the Banū-Ḥanīfah,[239] as well as from the Thaqīf in al-Ṭāʾif.[240] When finally he induced a faction of the Aws and Khazraj in Yathrib to accord him protection, the agreement was ratified at the ʿAqabah in Makkah in two pacts. The first, known to the Tradition as the Pledge of Women *(Bayʿāt al-Nisāʾ),* committed the guarantors to certain standards of personal morality; the second, known as the Pledge of War *(Bayʿāt al-Ḥarb),* committed the parties to mutual support.[241] By participating in this second pact, Muḥammad transferred responsibility for his protection from his lineage in Makkah to his supporters *(al-Anṣār)* in Yathrib.

The result of these negotiations was that Muḥammad, accompanied by some of his followers, made the journey *(al-hijrah)* to Yathrib in 622, the date which, seventeen years later, the caliph ʿUmar would designate as the official beginning of the Islamic era. From this point Muḥammad's teaching increasingly emphasized the importance of the community of Muslim converts versus the bloodline of *qabīlah* and *qawm.* The term ultimately used to denote this community of believers was *al-Ummah,* which, during Muḥammad's ministry, evolved from a general concept of shared community interests applicable to Arab and non-Arab groups alike into the notion of a specifically and totally monotheistic Muslim community, exclusive of and apart from all unbelievers for all time.[242] By insisting on the spiritual equality of all men before the absolute majesty of Allāh, Muḥammad in effect established believers in the role of clients of the God of Clients. "And warn therewith those who dread being gathered to their Lord," says the Qurʾān 6 *(al-Anʿām):*51, "that patron or intercessor they shall have none but Allāh, so that they may guard against evil." And again in *Sūrah* 2 *(al-Baqarah):*257: "Allāh is the patron of those who have believed; He brings them out of darkness into light." The induction of a believer into the *Ummah* was largely equivalent to emancipating him from the hitherto all-pervasive bonds of kin. Henceforward, not he of the most powerful lineage but "he who fears Allāh the most is most worthy of honor in the sight of God."[243] Al-Wāqidī has Muḥammad declaring as he entered Makkah in 630: "Allāh has put an end to pride in noble ancestry. You are all descended from Ādam, and Ādam from dust. The noblest among you is he who is most pious."[244]

The Constitution of Madīnah

The principal source illustrative of these changes in the nature of the Muslim community at al-Madīnah is a document commonly, but misleadingly, known among European scholars as the Constitution of Madīnah. It is in no manner of speaking a constitution but rather a collection of treaties drafted according to the tribal customs *(maʿrūf)* prevailing at Yathrib during the seventh century. It is preserved in two recensions, the fuller in the *Sīrah* of Ibn Isḥāq (d. 768)[245] and an abbreviated version in Abū ʿUbayd's *Kitāb al-Amwāl* of the ninth century.[246] Certain clauses from the treaties survive as elements in a few *ḥadīths* and some of the provisions are almost certainly alluded to in the Qurʾān itself, most notably in *Sūrah* 3 *(Āl-ʿImrān):*101: "For protection have resort to the pact *(ḥabl)* of God as a group *(jamīʿ-an)* and do not split apart." Abū ʿUbayd's recension is, as Patricia Crone has observed,[247] a typical product of written transmission, replete with copyists' errors, interpolations, and omissions of unintelligible clauses; and in accordance with ninth-century practice it has been furnished with an uninterrupted chain of authorities *(isnād),* in this case going back to al-Zuhrī (ca. 671–742), doyen of the Madīnan historical school.[248] Serjeant also identifies two provisions of the document with the *Sunnat al-Jāmiʿah* that would subsequently be included in the arbitration agreement between ʿAlī and Muʿāwīyah at Ṣiffīn in 657.[249]

Despite a lack of information about the origin of the document beyond the *ḥadīth*s that it was once in ʿAlī's possession, virtually all scholars who have studied it have concluded that it is at least in part an authentic relic of Muḥammad's sojourn in Yathrib.[250] Even Crone and Cook, two of the severest critics of the reliability of the *ḥadīth*s, characterize it as "a plausibly archaic element of the Islamic tradition."[251] Its precise date, however, is uncertain, and attributions in any case depend on the manner in which the document is interpreted. Moshe Gil, for instance, who regards it as a unitary text exhibiting a "strong connection between its elements" and focusing on "a limited number of ideas, representing the immediate political aims of the Prophet," accepts the traditions that place the drafting a few months after Muḥammad's arrival in Yathrib, approximately five months according to al-Diyārbakrī.[252] On the other hand Serjeant, who treats the so-called Constitution as comprising eight discrete documents, perforce has to date each one separately. He concludes that they were spread over the first seven years or so of Muḥammad's Madīnan period.[253] In my opinion, Serjeant's interpretation is to be preferred, not least because the language of the document itself, with its recurring terminating formulae, dictates such a division; and it is this exposition that I shall follow in the ensuing discussion.

The treaties are introduced by Ibn Isḥāq with an exordium that succinctly states their purpose:

> And the Apostle of Allāh prepared a document [lit., wrote a writing *(kitāb)*] between the *Muhājirūn* (those Qurashī tribesmen who had undertaken the Hijrah, that is, accompanied Muḥammad to Yathrib[254]) and the *Anṣār* (lit., "The Helpers," that is, Muḥammad's Medīnan supporters from the Aws and Khazraj tribes) in which he made a peace *(wādaʿah)* with the Jews and a covenant *(ʿāhadah)* with them; and he confirmed them in their religion *(ʿalā dīni-him)* and properties, specified the obligations owed to them, and imposed obligations upon them [as follows].

The documents recognized by Serjeant and rearranged by him in a postulated historically logical order are as follows:

- ***Document A:*** a treaty of confederation *(Ummah).* At this time the term still denoted a theocratically based confederation; only later would it come to signify the Muslim community). The treaty begins: "This is a writing from Muḥammad the Prophet, Allāh bless and honour him, between the Believers *(Muʾminūn)*[255] and Muslims *(Muslimūn)* of Quraysh and Yathrib, and those who follow them, and join with them, and strive *(jāhadū)* along with them. They constitute a single confederacy *(ummah)* and are not [to be regarded as members of] individual groups [any more]."[256] The remaining clauses deal with such matters as the payment of bloodwit, the ransoming of captives, and the obligations of *Muʾminūn* to the *Ummah.* Whereas the payment of blood money was to be the responsibility of each clan, the ransoming of captives was to be a collective concern of the *Ummah* "in the customary manner" *(ʿalā ribʿati-him).*
- ***Document B:*** a supplement to Document A. It deals principally with the internal security of the *Ummah,* but the final clause establishes Muḥammad unequivocally as the supreme arbiter in the affairs of the various settlement groups: "Over whatever thing you differ, its reference back *(moradd)* is to Allāh, Great and Glorious, and to Muḥammad, may Allāh bless and honour him."

These two articles formed the basis of the confederacy that Muḥammad established in Yathrib. Serjeant tentatively identifies them as the two pacts of alliance *(ḥilf)* that the Tradition asserts were drawn up in the house of Anas ibn Mālik, a Khazrajī of the Banū-al-Najjār, to which, incidentally, Muḥammad was related through a female ancestor. The same author assigns both articles to Muḥammad's first year in Yathrib.[257]

- ***Documents C, D, and E*** are articles defining the status of the Jewish tribes included in the confederacy; Serjeant relates the articles one to another as an initial agreement (C), a codicil refining the definitions of certain client relationships specified in Document C (D), and a reaffirmation of the original treaty (E). Serjeant dates Document C to the first year after the *Hijrah,* Document D soon afterward, and Document E to year 3, following the murder by a Ḥārithī tribesman of his Jewish client.[258] A succession of clauses records by name each tribe responsible for Jewish client groups on the pattern "The Jews of

Banū-ʿAwf are a confederacy *(ummah)* with the *Muʾminūn,* the Jews having their religiously sanctioned custom *(dīn)* and the *Muslimūn* having theirs, their clients *(mawālī)* and their persons, excepting anyone who acts wrongfully *(ẓalama)* or treacherously, for he only slays himself and the people of his house."[259] Another clause prescribes that, like the *Muʾminūn,* the Jews should pay the levy known as *nafaqah*[260] in time of war. It is also stated categorically in Document D that the tribal affiliations set forth therein can be dissolved only by the Prophet himself: "No one will dissociate himself from *(kharaja)* them except by permission of Muḥammad, Allāh bless and honour him."

- ***Document F:*** the proclamation of the establishment of a *ḥaram* at Yathrib. It is to be dated to the year 607. Because of its importance in the present context, I shall quote Serjeant's rendering of this article (slightly modified) in full:

  "The Jawf of Yathrib[261] is [constituted as] a *ḥaram* for the people of this document *(ṣaḥīfah).* The protected person *(jār)* is as [one's] self, neither liable to molestation nor committing an unlawful act. A woman *(ḥurmah)* shall not be accorded protection except by permission of her people (i.e., the near male members of her lineage). Whatever aggression *(ḥadāth)* or quarrel occurs between the people of this sheet (that is, the signatories to the document), which it is feared may cause dissension *(fasād),* will be referred *(maraddu-hu)* to Allāh, Great and Glorious, and to Muḥammad the Apostle of Allāh,[262] Allāh bless and honour him. Allāh is [surety] for what is most avoided of covenent breaking and what is most honoured in the observance of what is conveyed by this sheet."

- ***Document G:*** a treaty binding the Muʾminūn and the Qurayẓah, the only Jewish tribe remaining in the oasis,[263] to defend Yathrib against the Quraysh of Makkah and their allies. It is to be dated shortly before the siege of Yathrib by the Makkans that has come to be known as the Battle of the Trench *(Khandaq),*[264] that is, according to discrepant traditions, either year 4 or year 5 after the *Hijrah.*

Professor Serjeant suggests that this article is the *kitāb* that was torn up by the Naḍīrī, Ḥuyayy ibn Akhṭab, after he had persuaded the Qurayẓah chief to renege on his pact *(ʿaqd)* with the Apostle of Allāh.[265] According to Ibn Kathīr, the Banū-Saʿnah, Asad, Usayd, and Thaʿlabah dissociated themselves *(kharajū)* from the rest of the Qurayẓah in this matter and remained firm supporters of Muḥammad.[266] Serjeant also suggests, plausibly enough, that this article has been misplaced, and should properly precede Document F.

- ***Document H:*** a codicil to Document F, which constituted the Jawf of Yathrib as a *ḥaram,* and ought, therefore, presumably to be dated to about year 7 after the *Hijrah.* In Serjeant's translation it reads as follows:

  This writing does not intervene between a wrongdoer and one committing a criminal act. He who goes out is secure and he who stays is secure in al-Madīnah, except one who does wrong or commits a criminal act. Allāh is a protector for him who observes undertakings and keeps free of dishonourable acts and offences, and Muḥammad, Allāh bless and honour him, is the Apostle of Allāh.[267]

If the eight documents are even partially authentic in their essentials—there can be no doubt of their archaic character—it is evident that by migrating to Yathrib Muḥammad had capitalized on his status as a member of one of Arabia's holy families to establish himself as an arbiter among belligerent factions. As Serjeant has been reminding us for more than thirty years, this was precisely the principal function of the *manṣab* in a Ḥaḍramī *ḥawṭah* in the very recent past. In fact the following verbatim extract from this author's field notes would not have been anomalous in the sequence of articles that we have been discussing:

> The *aḥbāṭ* is land surrounding the *ḥawṭah,* occupied by sundry tribes who make agreements *(wuthūr)* with the *Manṣab* [the lord of the *ḥawṭah*] to respect and venerate the *ḥawṭah.* They agree also that if there is any quarrel between them they will go and submit the matter to his judgement—(perhaps I should say arbitration here). When a *ḥawṭah* is well organized, the various tribes of the *aḥbāṭ* are bound to the *Manṣab* by *wuthūr* to assist him, and to help him to use the threat of force to execute a judgement.[268]

According to the Tradition, within a year of his arrival in Yathrib, Muḥammad was beginning to translate this sacrally based authority into political power by entering into agreements with the tribes to establish a confederacy under his aegis. It is noteworthy that, despite Ibn Isḥāq's description of the treaty (p. 26 above), Document A does not refer to either the *Muhājirun* or the *Anṣār,* but instead to the *Mu'minūn* and *Muslimūn.* Here is the seed of that exclusivity that ultimately caused the transmutation of the confederacy into a religious community. There is no reason to suppose that Muḥammad set out to abolish the old tribal framework of Madīnan, let alone Ḥijāzī or Arabian, society. His initial concern was not to subvert the lineage as the basis of social organization but to devise a functionally more adaptable form of kinship. The *Muhājirūn,* for example, were to sever ties with their kinfolk in Makkah and regard the Anṣār as their brethren and mutual heritors. "Verily, those who believed and migrated [to al-Madīnah] and who staked their wherewithal and their lives in the cause of Allāh (i.e., the Muhājirūn), and those who took them in and helped them (i.e., the Anṣār), these are close kin one to another."[269]

The Madīnan Confederacy

During the early years after the *Hijrah,* Muḥammad expelled the Jews from al-Madīnah. From the beginning most of the Jews refused to accept the validity of his revelations and to acknowledge him as the culmination of the prophetic line from Adam through Mūsā (Moses) and ʿĪsā (Jesus). What they heard as the rambling distortions of their own Scriptures did nothing to convince them that it was indeed God speaking through the mouth of the tribal judge-arbiter. Their own rabbis were the repositories of monotheistic lore, and they, from their intimate knowledge of the sacred books, rejected the scion of the Makkan house of Hāshim as an imposter. As one of Muḥammad's own revelations summed it up: "They say, 'No one but Jews or Christians will enter the Garden'? Such are their wishful fancies. Say, 'Give us proof if what you say is true.' No, whosoever commits himself exclusively to Allāh and does what is right shall have his reward with his Lord."[270]

It must have been galling to the Seal of the Prophets, who alone had been vouchsafed the final and most comprehensive revelation until the end of earthly time, that those most familiar with monotheistic doctrine (even if, as he believed, not in its final form) ignored his warning. Moreover, the Tradition hints that the Jews of al-Madīnah may have been intriguing with the Quraysh of Makkah during the difficult times between Badr and Uḥud.[271] At any rate, soon after arriving in al-Madīnah (most traditions specify the second year), Muḥammad changed the Muslim *qiblah,* the direction in which believers should face during ritual prayers, from Jerusalem, for centuries past the premier cosmological center of the Western Semites,[272] to Makkah. Allegedly he effected this change in response to a series of revelations, of which the following is probably the most explicit:

> We have seen thee turning thy face about in the heaven, so now we shall bestow on thee a *qiblah* that will satisfy thee. Turn thy face in the direction of the Inviolable Place of Worship, and, wherever ye may be, turn your faces toward it. Those to whom the Book has been vouchsafed know that it is the truth from their Lord. And Allāh is not unaware of what they do.[273]

At about the same time, Muḥammad reportedly substituted the fast in Ramaḍān, the month in which the engagement at Badr had been fought, for that of the ʿAshūrā, which had been modelled on the Jewish Yōm Kippūr observed on the tenth day of the month of Tishri.[274]

Finally, Muḥammad came to reject not only Jewish customs and observances but also the Jews themselves. The first of their tribes to be expelled from al-Madīnah was the Banū-Qaynuqāʿ, allegedly not long after Muḥammad had returned from the Badr raid in 624.[275] A year later the al-Naḍīr were forced to leave and their dwellings and palm groves given to the Muhājirūn so that these latter would no longer be dependent on the generosity of the Anṣār.[276] In 627 it was the turn of the Qurayẓah, who, although they had remained formally neutral during the siege of al-Madīnah, were suspected of negotiating secretly with the Makkans. According to the Tradition, their punishment was proportionately more severe, the men being beheaded in the main *sūq* of the settlement and the women and children sold as slaves.[277]

It is difficult to evaluate the reliability of the traditions that seek to justify the excision of the Jews from the social fabric of al-Madīnah. Most of them are only too obviously later justifications and rationalizations, and not very effective ones at that, for the overlay of pious vindication and divine intervention fails to obscure the fundamental fact that the whole wretched episode was simply the application by the embattled Muslim sect of the old tribal sanctions of the *Jāhilīyah.*[278] This interpretation of events goes a good way toward explaining why the Arab confederates did little or nothing to protect their client tribes. According to the Tradition, ʿAbd Allāh ibn Ubayy, a chief of the Khazrajite clan of ʿAwf, was powerless to honor his obligations to either the Qaynuqāʿ or al-Naḍīr, but ʿUbādah ibn al-Ṣāmit, also of the Banū-ʿAwf, simply abjured his alliance with the Qaynuqāʿ, declaring, "O Apostle of God, I take God and His Apostle and the Believers as my friends, and I renounce *(abraʾu)* my alliance *(ḥilf)* and friendship with the unbelievers."[279] The sentiment among the Aws in favor of honoring the obligations of Qurayẓah clientage was circumvented by Muḥammad's manipulation of the old tribal institution of the judge-arbiter.[280] What few of the participants could have realized at all clearly—and certainly not those like the Khazrajī Ibn Ubayy or those of the Aws who tried to preserve the sacred bonds between patron and client—was that a new system of social relationships was evolving in al-Madīnah based not on ties of blood and obligations of ritual kinship but on shared monotheistic beliefs, backed when both necessary and practicable by the focused force of a political confederacy. At any event, the expulsion of the main Jewish *communities* from al-Madīnah (a sizable number of *individuals* remained) marked a significant advance toward an exclusively Islamic community. This process was to all intents and purposes completed in 628, when Muḥammad subdued the predominantly Jewish oasis of Khaybar and imposed treaties on the colonies of Jews at Fadak, Wādī al-Qurā, and Taymāʾ.

The confederacy that Muḥammad engineered, and which was validated in the misnamed "constitution," was at this time inferior in both power and extent to the Kaʿbah-focused amphictyony of the *Ḥums,* further strengthened and extended as that was by the *īlāf* pacts and the sacred months. Founded on a subsistence basis of date and cereal cultivation symbiotically integrated with the raising of sheep, goats, and camels, and supplemented by sporadic raiding of neighboring settlements[281] and Makkan caravans,[282] the Madīnan confederacy offered no promise of prosperity comparable with that achieved by the Quraysh of Makkah. Moreover, it was held together by fortuitous conjunctions of common interest and respect for a religious leader whose authority derived originally from a *ḥaram* in a rival settlement.[283] Indeed, Muḥammad had brought an aura of Qurashī sanctity with him to al-Madīnah and had gone a good way toward rendering Islam acceptable to all Arabs, not just the Quraysh and their allies. Yet the basis of the confederacy that he established was—as the documents described above make clear—one of secular pragmatism, and consequently vulnerable to changing interests and perceptions among its constituent groups.

This latter weakness was partially remedied when, in the sixth or seventh year of the *Hijrah,* Muḥammad constituted Yathrib as a *ḥaram.* By this action he not only complemented loyalty to a sacred person with loyalty to a sanctified territory (as was true of the amphictyony of the *Ḥums*) but also established a physically secure locale (on the pattern of the Makkan *ḥaram*) where intertribal intercourse of all types could take place, including what had never become accepted in Makkah: the collective worship of the One God. And the agreements that have been designated *B* and *F* on pages 26–27 constituted Muḥammad, in his capacity as the spokesman of Allāh, as supreme judge-arbiter among the groups in al-Madīnah.

Ultimate political authority had thereby been transferred from the hands of tribal *shaykh*s to Allāh Himself, who had delegated it to Muḥammad as His vicegerent. Muḥammad had been denied the authority of prophethood in Makkah and debarred from political power, yet in al-Madīnah he had parlayed an attenuated, Quraysh-derived, sacral authority into a base of confederate power, from which he was able to promote his role as prophet.[284] Or, as it might be put rather more succinctly, his recognition as a prophet had to wait on his success as a tribal politician. Eventually, by effecting a fusion of monotheism with tribal politics, Muḥammad was in fact able to lay the foundation of an incipient state structure.[285]

The organization of this developing theocracy was haphazard and, of the machinery for carrying out governmental functions, only the executive was adequately provided for, and that only so long as Muḥammad remained alive. Nevertheless, it signified the first, crucial steps along the path of political evolution that would lead eventually to the empire of the Caliphate.

Muḥammad's years in al-Madīnah were characterized

by almost continuous hostilities between the Muslim confederacy based on that settlement and the Makkan amphictyony. During this time both parties achieved successes and suffered reverses, but in 630 the Makkan oligarchy finally submitted to a Muslim force from al-Madīnah that occupied the settlement and destroyed the pagan idols in both the Kaʿbah and private dwellings.[286] In words attributed to Faḍālah ibn al-Mulawwiḥ al-Laythī, a supposed witness of the event, "God's light became manifest / And darkness covered the face of idolatry."[287] It is reported in a tradition that Muḥammad, standing at the door of the Kaʿbah, declared, "All claims of privilege or blood or property are abolished except custody of the temple and the provision of water for pilgrims." It was probably at this time, too, that verse 28 of *Sūrah* 9 *(al-Tawbah)* of the Qurʾān, which has subsequently been interpreted as prohibiting non-Muslims from approaching the *ḥaram* at Makkah, was revealed:

> O ye who believe, the polytheists are indeed unclean, so let them not come near the Inviolable Place of Worship after this present year. If ye fear poverty [resulting from the loss of their trade], Allāh will in the end enrich you from his bounty if He so wills. Allāh is knowing and wise.

The last lines of this *sūrah* were presumably intended to reassure Makkan traders that they would somehow be compensated for the expected diminution in trade and revenues after polytheistic worshippers were barred from the Kaʿbah precincts.

After about 625 the term *Ummah* was replaced in the Qurʾānic record of Muḥammad's revelations by the word *Jamāʿah* (assembly; company; totality) or by the phrase *Ḥizb Allāh* ("The Party of God"). At the same time, the use of force to settle disputes became an attribute of the state. The family or lineage retained the right to resolve civil disputes among the faithful of the *Jamāʿah,* but the blood feud was taken largely out of their hands and elevated to an instrument of state policy in which, in Procksch's words, "Die Gläubigen sind einer des andern Bluträcher auf dem Kriegspfade Gottes."[288] A revelation usually reckoned to be early Madīnan leaves no doubt that family blood revenge was to be subordinated to the power of the incipient state and clearly distinguished from war, which henceforth would be undertaken only by the *Ummah,* as Qurʾān 4 *(al-Nisāʾ):*92–93 states:

> It is not for a believer to kill a believer, except it be in error. If anyone should kill a believer by mistake, let him set free a believing slave and pay the blood-money to the slain's relatives, unless they forgo it as an alms offering. If the slain belongs to a people at enmity with you and is a believer, then a believing slave is to be set free; [but] if he belong to a people allied with you by compact, then the blood-money is to be paid to his relatives and a believing slave set free. Whosoever cannot find the means [to pay these penalties] shall fast for two successive months. . . .
>
> Whoso intentionally slays a believer, his recompence will be Jahannam (Gehenna), wherein he will abide. Allāh will be wroth with him, will damn him, and visit him with awful punishment.

After the encounter at Badr, the *badū* custom of assigning one-fifth of all booty to the *shaykh*[289] for paying bloodwits, entertaining guests, and caring for widows and orphans was also elevated to the rank of a state institution; Muḥammad, as Shaykh of the Muslim Confederacy, assumed custody of these spoils. Similarly, the institutionalization of the alms tax *(zakāh)* as one of the five pillars *(arkān;* sing. *rukn)* of Islam transposed to the state level. This tax was akin to a graduated income tax, a financial mechanism formerly a lineage responsibility. This effective taxing power, together with booty and voluntary donations of alms, afforded a reasonably firm financial basis for the emergent Islamic state, especially after Muḥammad established a system of agents *(ʿummāl)* to supervise tax collection in several parts of the peninsula, more particularly the Ḥijāz.[290]

Extending the *Ḥizb Allāh*

After the occupation of Makkah, Muḥammad focused his efforts on extending the sphere of the *Ḥizb Allāh* by expanding the confederacy. The coalescence of the hitherto separate *ḥarams* of Makkah and al-Madīnah into a single theocratic polity, the Ḥaramān, as it was sometimes called, provided both a more diversified base of political power and a superstructure of religious authority stronger than any that had previously emerged in al-Ḥijāz. The pattern of mutual security agreements concluded by the tribes in al-Madīnah under the aegis of the Prophet was extended to include an ever-widening circle of tribes on the Arabian Peninsula. Despite opposition from some of his followers,

Muḥammad pursued a policy of expansion with such vigor that by the time of his death in 632, extensive tracts of Arabia acknowledged his authority at least nominally. Most of the tribes in a broad zone adjacent to the cities of Makkah and al-Madīnah, and those whose grazing grounds lay along the Central Arabian route to al-ʿIrāq, had joined the confederacy through the profession of Islam.

It is not unlikely, however, that the decision to throw in their lot with the Muslims was sometimes caused by Muḥammad's control over the main settlements in the Ḥijāz, for he was consequently in a position to exclude the *badū* from access to the *sūqs* on which they depended for all that the desert could not provide. In al-Yaman, converts generally comprised only groups within tribes, but may have amounted to as many as half the total population. In al-ʿUmān and along the shores of the Persian Gulf the proportion was considerably less. In the north conversions had not been numerous, but Muḥammad had concluded peace treaties with the Christian *shaykh* of Aylah (al-ʿAqabah) and with the Jewish tribes inhabiting the oases of Maqnah, Uḍruḥ, and al-Jarbāʾ. In fact the continually expanding Muslim community *(dhimmat Allāh)* comprised both tribal and nontribal groups, including Jews and Christians, whose social status was deemed not inferior to that of Arab tribesmen. The year prior to Muḥammad's death (A.H. 9/A.D. 631–32) is known as the Year of Delegations *(Sanat al-Wufūd),* for it witnessed the arrival in al-Madīnah of a series of allegedly unsolicited deputations offering political allegiance to the ruler of the *Ḥizb Allāh.* The alliances that they contracted with him were purely political in character and personal to the Prophet, so that on his death, according to Arab custom, they lapsed automatically. Moreover, many among the *wufūd* appear to have been delegates not from tribes as such but from dissident minorities, who saw in an alliance with the ruler of al-Madīnah a source of support for their own aspirations. Generally speaking, Muḥammad forged his confederacy by means of persuasion, rewards of material goods or status, and the exercise of political pressure, although he was prepared to dispatch punitive expeditions against the obdurate or those who reneged on agreements. In any case, the form and principle of the security pacts he was at first offering, and then imposing, were already familiar to tribal Arabia and, apart from acceptance of the Muslim brand of monotheism, destruction of their idols, performance of certain outward rituals, and payment of either the purification tax of believers or that levied on associates, necessitated little change in tribal ways of life.

Some among the new recruits to the confederacy that was gradually becoming a community were no doubt truly converted, but the Qurʾān and *Ḥadīth* indicate that others accorded only expediential acquiescence, conceding perhaps that Allāh might be the most powerful deity while yet remaining more remote than their familiar tribal gods. Professor Maxime Rodinson gives this summation: "Tous les cas individuels se présentaient, de l'adhésion ferme à l'incrédulité affichée. Mais toutes ces tribus, en tant qu'entités politiques, étaient liées à Mohammad. C'était l'important."[291] If the extant versions of the Prophet's correspondence with the Arab tribes are authentic in form, even though not at all or only partly in substance,[292] then the treaties of mutual support and guarantees concluded between Muḥammad and leaders of groups entering the *Ummah* are clearly analogous to the articles subsumed within the so-called Constitution of al-Madīnah. If genuine, they point to the expansion of the *Ummah* to the very borders of—although not throughout—Arabia, even within the Prophet's lifetime. This expansion and its sequel far outside the bounds of the peninsula will be described in the next chapter.

Al-Ṭāʾif

While sociocultural changes were taking place in Makkah and al-Madīnah, al-Ṭāʾif, the third important settlement in al-Ḥijāz, remained something of a backwater. Some seventy miles (or from two to three days' journey)[293] to the southeast of Makkah, and some four thousand feet higher, then as now it afforded an attractive retreat from the rigors of the Makkan environment, "a piece of Syrian earth" or "a corner of al-Yaman," as it has been variously called.[294] Honey, watermelons, bananas, figs, grapes, almonds, peaches, and pomegranates were all products of its gardens and orchards, while its roses were famous for their scent throughout al-Ḥijāz. According to a tradition preserved in the *Kitāb al-Aghānī,*[295] the vine had been introduced into the locality by a Jew, perhaps a vague remembrance of the activities of Jewish farming immigrants at the end of the first century A.D. During the sixth century the al-Ṭāʾif settlement was a proven trade rival to Makkah, an outpost of Yamanī culture, and formerly a possible base for Sāsānian political maneuvers. However, after the Wars of the Fijār, in which the Hawāzin and some of the Thaqīf (the most prominent tribe of al-Ṭā'if) were leagued against the Quraysh and Kinānah,[296] control over much of its commerce appears to have fallen into the hands of the Quraysh, mainly through the machinations of a pro-Makkan party among the Thaqīf.

About the city itself—as opposed to its environs—in pre-Islamic times little is known, although the Tradition preserves several references to fortified dwellings (*uṭūm*, p. 24 above), presumably similar in form and function to those at al-Madīnah; and the settlement was apparently unique in al-Ḥijāz in being surrounded by a wall.[297] The chief shrine, located just outside the settlement, was a rough cube of granite representing the goddess al-Lāt. In Islamic tradition the inhabitants are, of course, notorious for having rejected Muḥammad's overtures immediately prior to the *Hijrah* and for having opposed, under Thaqīf leadership, the Muslim forces after the Battle of Ḥunayn in 630. The Thaqīf finally accepted Islam later in the same year but, according to the Prophet's correspondence with their leaders (which Serjeant regards as "clearly genuine"),[298] the agreement between Muḥammad and the Thaqīf was a compromise. While proscribing the practice of usury, it recognized the integrity of the *ḥimā* (a sanctified grazing reserve sharing some of the characteristics of the *ḥaram* at Makkah) that the Thaqīf had established in the Wādī Wajj.[299] Moreover, the Thaqīf may have been absolved from payment of the *zakāt* (legal alms): at any rate, they do not figure in the extant versions of Muḥammad's stipulations, and there is apparently no surviving record of an agent having been appointed to supervise its collection.[300]

After this brief involvement in the momentous events of the seventh century, al-Ṭā'if was never again in the forefront of the Islamic stage, although many of its tribesmen, including scholars of some distinction, did settle in the cities of ʿIrāq, particularly al-Baṣrah and al-Kūfah, during the great *tamṣīr* (see p. 39).

Urbanism in the Jāhilī Ḥijāz

In the non-Muslim world, understanding the structure of the Islamic *sīrah* tradition is in a state of flux. Opinion is especially divided regarding materials purportedly relating to the *Jāhilīyah* and the life of the Prophet, with the result that the form and function of the settlement at Makkah are subject to a wide range of interpretations. There is rather better agreement, however, as to the nature of the theocratic polity that developed during the seventh century in al-Madīnah. The conclusion reached in the preceding pages will not meet with universal approbation, especially among Muslims: briefly, at the beginning of the seventh century relatively little urban development existed in the Ḥijāz. Makkah qualified for at most proto-urban status with only weakly developed centralized leadership, social reinforcement, and mediatory functions, and consequently presented only an inchoate nexus of built forms within which lifestyles barely differed from those prevailing elsewhere in the Ḥijāz. Al-Madīnah, on the evidence available, appears to have comprised a relatively dispersed collection of farming settlements. It may be that the apparently more compact settlement at al-Ṭā'if, if we knew enough about it, would turn out to have been the most—but still not highly—urbanized settlement in al-Ḥijāz.[301]

The title of this chapter refers not to direct roots in the sense that subsequent cities in the Islamic world owed either form or function to Arabian cities of the *Jāhilīyah* or the early decades of the Islamic era. As will become apparent in succeeding chapters, the vast majority of the cities that came under Muslim rule had existed in pre-Islamic times, and those that were established de novo by Muslims were almost totally uninfluenced directly by remembrance of the proto-urban settlements of the Jāhilī Ḥijāz. What this corner of northwest Arabia did contribute was a paradigm for ordering institutional and group action at all levels of society. This paradigm consequently conditioned the way in which men comprehended their environment, including all levels of the settlement hierarchy, and prescribed the manner in which, within the fused framework of tribal *sābiqah* and Islam, they attempted to order that system and the nodal centers comprising it. As far as South Arabia was concerned, its direct contributions to this process—if any—remain to be elucidated.

Chapter Two
The Shaping of Urban Systems in the Islamic World

Make war against those who believe not in God and the Last Day . . . against those who are Scripturaries, until they render tribute *[al-jizyah]* out of hand and are humbled.

—Qur'ān 9 *(al-Tawbah)*:29

The Expansion of Islam

According to Arab custom, Muḥammad's death terminated the contracts of political allegiance that had been concluded between him and the tribes of Arabia, some of which had already become restive under Madīnese rule. Tribes near al-Madīnah (Medinah) had been fully absorbed into the *Ummah* and shared its interests, but others in more distant parts of the peninsula now repudiated the authority of the nascent Islamic state. Although in Muslim tradition this secession came to be represented as apostasy *(al-riddah)* on a grand scale, it is more accurately an automatic lapsing of treaty relations, with a consequent suspension of tribute, after one of the parties to an agreement dies. Abū Bakr, who acceded to the leadership of the *Ummah,* with the title—so it is said—of *Khalīfat Rasūl Allāh* ("Vicegerent of God's Messenger"),[1] successfully concluded new treaties with some of the nearer tribes, but those farther afield were reincorporated in the *Ummah* only after military subjugation. Campaigns were initiated more or less simultaneously against the secessionist tribes of Arabia and against others that had yet to submit, and raids were undertaken into the nominally Ghassānid territories of the north and the lowlands of Sāsānian ʿIrāq.[2]

Campaigns of Conquest

There has been a long, continuing debate as to how and why the *riddah* wars developed into the great campaigns of conquest that established Muslim rule over most of the Middle East and North Africa. Almost every possible cause, environmental and cultural, has been invoked at one time or another, either singly or in combination, to account for the subjugation of such vast territories and the ensuing outflow of sedentary and nomadic groups from the Arabian Peninsula into the conquered lands. And not always have the twin ideas of conquest and migration been kept conceptually distinct. A minority of scholars have emphasized mainly ecological factors, which they believe propelled tribesmen out of Arabia. Winckler[3] and Caetani,[4] for instance, postulated a deterioration in pasturage caused by a progressive desiccation of Arabia. For Butzer the operative factor was a shorter period of severe drought, which he believed occurred between A.D. 591 and 640.[5]

Most historians of the period, however, have adduced broadly cultural causes as the overriding attractions drawing tribesmen out of Arabia, regardless of whatever may have been happening within the peninsula. Sir William Muir, for example, wrote of the tribesmen's "love of rapine" luring them, like "locusts darkening the land," in search of booty in the old centers of Middle Eastern civilization.[6] In a similar vein, Lammens described the Muslim conquests as born of the Arabs' *irrésistible penchant à la razzia.*[7] Becker shifted the argument somewhat while retaining the same general conceptual framework by characterizing hunger and the hope of material reward as the principal stimuli to Arab expansion.[8] It must be noted, though, that both Lammens and Becker, unlike Muir and some other early European authors, discriminated between the causes of the conquests and the causes of the migrations. Lammens also was prepared to accord the Arabs a superior military organization, a conclusion subsequently challenged by Canard, who made a good case for the view that the Arab levies were inferior to their opponents in weaponry, organization, tactics, and numbers.[9]

The authors cited thus far appear to have regarded, either explicitly or implicitly, the initial conquests as largely fortuitous extensions of the traditional Arabian raiding patterns that the Muslim government had given centralized direction in al-Madīnah and to some extent had formalized during the *riddah* wars. Shaban, in a comparatively recent reinterpretation of early Islamic history, agrees with this conclusion. Yet he believes that the initially disorganized raids into the Fertile Crescent were a response to the Ḥurūb al-Riddah disrupting commerce; many tribes needed the profits from these transactions.[10]

The desire for material gain as a factor behind the raids was subsequently validated by its frequent mention by early (but not necessarily contemporary) Muslim authors. They carefully subordinated it, however, to a religious motivation in a primarily providential context. The Persian (but Arabic-writing) annalist Aḥmad ibn Yaḥyā al-Balādhurī was especially conscious of this aspect of the conquests. In a passage in his *Futūḥ al-Buldān,* for example, he relates that Abū Bakr "wrote to the inhabitants of Makkah, al-Ṭāʾif, al-Yaman, and all the Arabs in Najd and al-Ḥijāz, summoning them to sacrally sanctioned war against the infidel *(jihād),* and arousing their desire for battle and for the booty to be seized from the Greeks."[11] In another passage he has the Persian commander opposing the Arab armies address a Muslim envoy as follows: "I am aware that your deeds have been forced upon you solely by restricted means of livelihood and privation. We are ready to satisfy your desires and to see you leave with the things you want."[12] The same point is made with poetic force in the *Ḥamāsah* of Abū Tammām:

> No, not for Paradise didst thou the nomad life forsake;
> Rather, I believe, it was thy yearning after bread and dates.[13]

The Muslim community traditionally ascribes the phenomenal, totally unanticipated success of Arab arms to the converts' zeal for the new Faith and the divine favor that they enjoyed. While this extreme monistic interpretation has not been popular among non-Muslim scholars (although Georges H. Bousquet came quite close to it),[14] not a few have adduced religious commitment as a (or sometimes *the*) principal factor motivating the conquests. Prominent among those who have hewn to this line of thinking in one way or another are Maxime Rodinson,[15] John Saunders,[16] Francesco Gabrieli,[17] and Laura Veccia Vaglieri.[18] Claude Cahen[19] and Gustave von Grünebaum have relied somewhat more explicitly on multivariate approaches in which Islam is cast as but one—although an important one—in a nexus of interacting factors.[20] However, in the recent controversial book mentioned in note 70, page 353, Patricia Crone and Michael Cook attempt to reconstitute religious faith as a dependent variable, but in a manner quite different from that of earlier Western historians of Islam and as part of an argument assuredly unacceptable to even the most lukewarm of Muslims. For these authors, the *Hijrah* was not the Muslim exodus from Makkah (Mecca) to al-Madīnah but rather the migration of the Arabs (in their role as descendants of Ismāʿīl) northward to reclaim the Promised Land of the so-called Hagarites.[21] In this interpretation, it was the old Ibrāhīmic faith currently being elaborated in terms of Mosaic revelation as proto-Islam that drew the tribesmen northward toward the traditional, although locationally elusive, Hagarene cult shrine. Although this thesis has attracted few adherents, it is in accord with the initial thrust of the Arab armies into southern Syria.

The most comprehensive recent evaluation of these interpretations is incorporated in Professor Fred Donner's book *The Early Islamic Conquests.* Unlike some of his predecessors, Donner distinguishes rigorously between the causes of the Muslim conquests, the reasons for their success, and the causes of the Arab migrations that followed the conquests. After a shrewd but sympathetic appraisal of each principal theory that has been proposed to account for these phenomena, he is forced to conclude that "the true causes of the Islamic conquests—currents in the minds of men—will probably remain forever beyond the grasp of historical analysis."[22] On the reasons for the success of the conquests, he is more positive: they were "first and foremost the product of an organizational breakthrough . . . and it was the new religion of Islam . . . which provided the ideological underpinning for this remarkable breakthrough in social organization. . . . [It] was Islam—the set of religious beliefs preached by Muḥammad, with its social and political ramifications—that ultimately sparked the whole integration process and hence was the ultimate cause of the conquests' success."[23] On the causes of the Arab migrations into the Fertile Crescent, Professor Donner is equally assured: they can best be explained as "a result of the state's policy toward tribesmen . . . whom it recruited and settled in garrison towns, where they could more easily be controlled and could themselves serve as instruments of state control and state expansion."[24]

I am in general agreement with these conclusions, although—as is evident from chapter 1—Professor Donner and I differ substantially in our understandings of the nature of the "breakthrough in social organization" undergirding the success of the Arab conquests and of the role of Islam in that process. And perhaps he is a little too pessimistic about our ever being able to specify the causes of the conquests. If the Crone-Cook thesis should ever be substantiated, for instance, it may be that the causes of the conquests could eventually be brought within the grasp of historical analysis. Fortunately, it is not necessary for our present purpose to follow Professor Donner into these realms of hazardous speculation: it will suffice to outline the chronology of the conquests and migrations, note the form they assumed, and, primarily, assess their impact on the several urban hierarchies of the Middle East.

Continuing Expansion

Whatever may have been the nature of the motivations that led to the conquests, the centrifugal movements thus initiated generated their own momentum. An Arab victory at ʿAqrabāʾ in eastern Najd in 633, which demonstrated both the power of the Muslim levies and the capabilities of the government in al-Madīnah, signalled the effective beginning of the conquests. Shortly thereafter, apparently exploratory raids revealed the relative impotence of Ghassānid and Persian levies in the face of Arab onslaughts. Not only had the resources of the Sāsānian and Byzantine Empires been weakened by generations of internecine warfare and the loyalty of their subjects eroded by crippling levels of taxation, but the moral basis of their authority had also been undermined by heresies and schisms. This was particularly true of the Byzantine world, where the rise of Monophysite heresies in the fifth century had resulted in the Greek Orthodox Church persecuting both the Coptic communities of Egypt and the Aramaic population of Syria. In southern ʿIrāq and southern Syria, the first two regions outside Arabia to experience the incursions of Muslim armies, there were special reasons the populace should have been disaffected. The former was a Semitic province under the rule of a Persian military despotism, while the Arab feudatories of the latter resented the emperor Heraclius's withdrawal of subsidies once disbursed by the Byzantine treasury. To communities such as these, the tribute demanded by the Muslim conquerors was often perceived as a less onerous burden than the exactions of Byzantine or Sāsānian overlords, and the disdain accorded the status of *mawlā* (client) or *dhimmī* (a member of a tolerated religion) by Muslim Arabs was generally preferable to the persecution inflicted on heretics by the Greek church.

The Arabs for their part surged forth from the Arabian Peninsula as the armies of an ethnic theocracy geared to political expansion. From their faith they derived a sense of unity and communal purpose, while under the banner of Islam they possessed a talisman that, as the campaigns continued, seemed ever more surely to guarantee success. Actually, in the early years of the expansion the Arabs owed their victories less to religious zeal than to the military ability of two field commanders, Khālid ibn al-Walīd and ʿAmr ibn al-ʿĀṣ, both of whom proved to be supremely skillful strategists. Using the desert wastes bordering the Fertile Crescent as their recruiting grounds, inviolable lines of communication, and havens of refuge in adversity, time after time they routed surprised adversaries with tactical warfare adapted from nomadic raiding practice. It was probably fortunate for the Arab cause that Madīnese control, by virtue of the distances involved and the difficulty of communication, was restricted to the general direction of policy; the initiative in any particular situation remained with the army commanders or provincial governors.

During the exploratory raids that Abū Bakr sent against southern Syria, the tribesmen of Arabia came, presumably, to identify the cause of Islam with their own interests. From that point onward conquest followed conquest with all but incredible swiftness, the process reaching its apogee under the decade-long caliphate of ʿUmar ibn al-Khaṭṭāb (634–44). The first major success came when Syria was prized from the enervate grasp of Byzantium, with Jerusalem falling in 638.[25] Relatively unsuccessful raids against al-ʿIrāq undertaken simultaneously under tribal leadership reconciled the Arabs to the necessity of Madīnese direction of a subsequent campaign against the Sāsānian heartland.[26] In 641 effective large-scale Persian resistance ended with the Battle of Nihāwand, and the subjection of Makrān some two or three years later brought the Arab armies to the borders of India. Not for another decade, however, was the power of the Sāsānian dynasty entirely eliminated. Meanwhile Egypt was invaded in 640, and within two years was almost entirely under Arab control, although Alexandria was not finally subdued until 647.[27] Even before this happened, Arab columns had penetrated deep into al-Ifrīqiyah (Tunisia and western Libya), and Qarṭājannah (ancient Carthage) had been put under tribute; but Byzantine resistance and Arab preoccupations with events in Syria and al-ʿIrāq delayed the consolidation of Muslim power in this region. In 670 (or possibly a little earlier) the city of al-Qayrawān (Kairouan) was founded and used as a base for operations against the Berber tribes of al-Maghrib, but not until the early eighth century did Muslim forces completely control what is present-day Algeria and establish themselves as far west as the Atlantic coast of modern Morocco.[28]

In the early phases of Arab expansion the tribal levies doubtless regarded conquered territories as little more than providentially acquired pasture grounds for their herds. The Makkan and Madīnese leaders, by contrast, looked upon the vast lands that were falling into their hands as potential generators of commercial profit. Although they were for the most part unfamiliar with the technical operation of an agricultural economy, they quickly perceived its possibilities as a source of revenue—provided, that is, that the countryside was not ravaged by unruly tribesmen. To that end, early in the campaigns the tribal warriors were persuaded to relinquish their claims to the conquered lands in exchange for fixed shares of its revenues in the form of monetary stipends and produce. One result of this arrangement was that the tribesmen, when not campaigning, could be virtually confined to garrison settlements instead of diffusing through the territory in the manner to which many of them had been accustomed in their Arabian days. This in turn enabled the central government to exercise more effective control over its levies than would otherwise have been possible, but at the cost of constituting the Arabs as a subsidized military caste.

Evolution of Islamic Institutions

The backwardness of the Arabian Peninsula compared with neighboring countries inevitably rendered the early evolution of Islamic institutions as virtually a matter of adjustment to the cultural norms of older Middle Eastern civilizations. In the political sphere, this adjustment involved adapting largely uncodified ordinances, promulgated by Muḥammad and set in a matrix of tribal custom, to the needs of a cosmopolitan empire incorporating huge tracts of territory once administered by Byzantine and Sāsānian bureaucracies. Under the circumstances, the Arab conquerors had no alternative but to retain the vanquished people's existing machinery of provincial administration, together with their officials and, in some cases, their coinage. It followed that there was no unified law of the empire but rather variations in usage reflecting less Arabian customs than Latin, Greek, or Persian legal traditions.

Within the Arabian Peninsula no religion other than Islam was tolerated, and membership in the Muslim military commonwealth was denied to those not of Arabian birth. Moreover, ʿUmar, the second caliph, decreed that Arabian Muslims should not hold or cultivate land outside the peninsula. Byzantine and Sāsānian state lands, together with properties of enemies of the Islamic polity, were to be administered by the Arab government. Other landowners in those territories were granted freehold rights against payment of land and capitation taxes, and were absorbed into the *Ahl al-Dhimmah* ("Community of the Covenant"), a term used to denote members of officially tolerated religions.[29] Such communities were allowed to live under the jurisdiction of their own canon law as administered by their religious leaders in a manner established when Damascus (Dimashq) capitulated to the armies of Allāh in September 635. At that time the victorious commander had set terms that became the model for Arab dealings not only with other Syro-Palestinian cities but, suitably modified, with numerous communities located much farther afield:

> In the name of Allāh, the Compassionate, the Merciful. This is what Khālid [ibn al-Walīd] will grant

> to the inhabitants of Damascus if he enters therein. He promises to give them security for their lives, property, and churches. Their city wall shall not be demolished, nor shall any Muslims be quartered in their houses. Thereunto we give them the pact of Allāh and the protection of his Prophet, the caliphs and the believers. As long as they pay the poll-tax *(jizyah),* nothing but good shall befall them.[30]

For other than those who qualified for the status of *dhimmī,* the choice was restricted to conversion or the sword. Although theoretically entitled to the full rights of Islamic citizenship, in practice non-Arab Muslims were long excluded from certain privileges enjoyed by their Arab coreligionists. In the first place they could enter the Faith only by becoming clients *(mawālī)* of an Arab tribe and, even when inducted, were still generally ineligible to receive the stipends and pensions disbursed to Arab warriors by the Dīwān (governmental official).

It was in Damascus in 659 that the Arabs established the capital of their first centralized, secular state under the house of Umayyah. The apparent secularization of government under this dynasty, which stressed the political and economic basis of statehood rather than its religious validation, was largely an attempt to forge a new cohesion in the empire: the old theocratic bonds had been seriously weakened by the murder of ʿUthmān, the third caliph; by the war that ensued; and by the removal of the capital from the hallowed soil of al-Ḥijāz. ʿAbbāsid and later historians anxious to discredit the dynasty deposed by Abū al-ʿAbbās invoked this secularization of the state as an excuse to deny the title of caliph to all but one of the fourteen Umayyad rulers; each was designated a *malik* (king), a term abhorrent to the true Arab.[31] Certainly the authority exercised by the Umayyads differed markedly from that of their Rāshidūn predecessors, for it derived primarily from the loyalty accorded by the new Arab polity to its secular head rather than from the reverence felt by tribesmen for leaders once associated with the birth of Islam and for the administrative institutions devised by the Prophet.[32]

The looseness of the bureaucratic organization serving this patrimonial-style authority was reflected in the composition of the chief organ of executive government, the *Shūrā.* It took the form of a council of *shaykh*s summoned by the ruler and supported by the *wufūd,* or tribal delegations. In the provinces authority was exercised through nominated governors, each assisted by a *shūrā* patterned on that in Damascus. Provincial tributes were typically controlled by a special revenue officer, the *ṣāḥib al-kharāj,* who answered directly to the ruler. At lower levels of provincial administration, the staffs and procedures of the former Greek and Sāsānian bureaucracies were retained to such an extent that Bernard Lewis is able to write, "In its administration the Umayyad Caliphate was not so much an Arab state as a Persian and Byzantine succession state."[33] Not until the reign of ʿAbd al-Malik (685–705) were these administrative procedures replaced by an imperial system with Arabic as its official language. ʿAbd al-Malik was also responsible for initiating the process of fiscal rationalization that developed ultimately into a distinctively Islamic form of taxation.

The Umayyad state was based initially on the assumption that a hereditary minority caste of Arab Muslims would continue to rule over, and be heavily subsidized by, a massive majority of tax-paying *dhimmī*s. The Arabs paid no land tax *(kharāj),* only a personal religious tithe *(ʿushr).* Moreover, they constituted the majority of those entered in the registers of the Dīwān and therefore eligible for stipends provided from surplus booty and revenue. Further, from the beginning of Umayyad rule, Arabs were permitted to acquire land outside Arabia, both by purchase from *dhimmī*s and by grant from the central government. The domain lands of Byzantine and Sāsānian governments, estates abandoned by their Greek owners, together with waste and uncultivated terrain, constituted *mawāt* or "dead" lands, huge tracts of which were granted to members of the Umayyad royal family and other wealthy Arabs under leases known as *qaṭāʾiʿ* (sing. *qaṭīʿah*).[34] In time *qaṭāʾiʿ* properties became very numerous and, through continually being bought and sold, came to be regarded effectively as private property.

At the same time, converts to Islam with the status of *mawālī* soon outnumbered the Arabs. Although *mawālī* in principle were able to claim social and economic equality with Arab Muslims, in practice relatively few of them were exempt from *kharāj* and *jizyah* until the reforms of ʿUmar II (r. 717–20).[35] Under the later Umayyads, the tax structure was based on the fiction that the land (rather than the landowner) paid the full *kharāj,* regardless of the proprietor's religion. *ʿUshr* land continued to pay the lower-rating tithe, but it could not be added to. *Dhimmī*s continued to pay both *kharāj* and *jizyah.*

Extension of the Empire under the Umayyads

Already under the Rāshidūn caliphs the Arabs controlled territories stretching from Barqah in the west to Makrān in the east. Under the Umayyads Arab power was firmly established in Khurāsān and extended beyond the Jayḥūn (classical Oxus; modern Āmū Daryā) River, where Bukhārā and Samarqand were occupied. In 711–12 Sind was subdued by a Muslim army composed predominantly of Syrians, and in the next year the conquest was pushed as far north as Multān in the southern Panjāb.[36] At the other end of the Muslim ecumene, recently occupied territories in northern Morocco were used as a base from which to launch an invasion of the Iberian Peninsula, and in 711 the Visigothic kingdom collapsed with the final defeat of its army at Jerez de la Frontera.[37]

In 717 or 718 a composite Arab and Berber army crossed the Pyrenees onto what is today French soil; Muslims maintained themselves there for nearly half a century, but were ultimately forced to withdraw. Their last stronghold to withstand Frankish counterattacks was Narbonne, which they relinquished in 759. Their most decisive defeat, however, had occurred near Poitiers in 732 when Charles Martel, mayor of the palace at the Merovingian court, had thrown back the army of ʿAbd al-Raḥmān in what has become for Muslim historians a "pavement of martyrs" *(balāṭ al-shuhadā')*.[38] In the same year that the Muslims invaded Frankish territory, another of their armies invested Constantinople for a third time (previous sieges had been mounted in 669 and 674–80), but, like its predecessors, was ultimately forced to withdraw, this time owing to scarce provisions and Bulgar attacks. These failures in western and southeastern Europe defined the boundaries of the Islamic world in relation to Latin and Greek Christendom, with the exception of Muslim encroachments into Sicily and southern Italy during the ninth and tenth centuries.

The empire ruled by the later Umayyads was the most extensive unified polity ever to be controlled by an Arab—or indeed a Muslim—dynasty. By the centennial of Muḥammad's death a localized confederation in western Arabia, dependent on rudimentary political and economic institutions and with an apparently uncertain future, had developed into an empire. Its own distinctive mode of government enabled it to encompass a vast range of cultures and environments from the Atlantic Ocean to the Indus River and the borders of China, and from the Aral Sea to the lower cataracts of the Nile River. Throughout this enormous expanse of territory Arab military force had made the Muslim religion coextensive with Muslim political control.

For the ensuing seven centuries—that is, until the Muslim withdrawal from the Iberian Peninsula—only a few sizable Muslim communities existed in Christian states. But political, as opposed to cultural, unity was shorter lived. Concomitantly with the passing of dominion from the Umayyad to the ʿAbbāsid dynasty, the establishment of an independent state in Spain initiated a process of political fragmentation that continued until the Ottoman Turks reimposed a unity on the Arab world in the sixteenth century. By that time Spain had been permanently lost to Islam, but sword and Ṣūfī (mystics) had carried the worship of Allāh far afield in Asia and Africa.

Early in the eleventh century Maḥmūd of Ghaznah incorporated most of the Panjāb in an empire whose western frontiers marched with the Zagros and the Caspian.[39] With the rise of the Sulṭānate of Delhi in the early fourteenth century, Islam was spread throughout Hindustān and into most of the Dekkan, though only in the former did it maintain itself as an integral polity for more than a relatively short time.[40] From the ports of western India Ṣūfīs carried their religion along the trade routes to Southeast Asia. The ruler of Melaka was converted at the beginning of the fifteenth century, and a ruler in Java became a Muslim in succeeding decades. Ultimately Islam spread through the Malaysian world as far as the southern Philippines, establishing itself even among the Chams on the mainland.[41] By the eighth century Muslim communities had arisen in the cities of both North and South China, while under the Southern Sung dynasty Arab traders resident in ports such as Ch'üan-Chou and Hang-Chou enjoyed a degree of extraterritoriality. They were permitted to inhabit special quarters which, furnished with mosques and *sūq*s and under the authority of Muslim *qāḍī*s, constituted veritable cities within cities, enclaves of Islamic culture on the South China coast.[42]

In Africa Islam diffused early down the east coast. Then, from the eighth century onward, it spread through either persuasion or *jihād* across the Saharan trade routes: first into the Sūdān, and eventually into West Africa in the narrow sense, where it is still actively proselytizing.[43]

In what follows we shall focus our discussion on the

city as it developed, and is still developing, in that sector of the earth's surface stretching from the Atlantic to the Indus—land which was defined once and for all as the core region of Islamic culture while under Umayyad rule. By the mid-eighth century the Muslim communities within this realm had been constituted as vehicles of the living Faith, whose task it had become

> to evolve a comprehensive pattern for a life under God, covering every phase of human existence from conception to burial and eliminating any distinction between the sacred and the profane aspects of life by making every instant of it religiously relevant and requiring ritualistic perfection for the performance of any action whatsoever. In this manner behaviour was stereotyped to a point, but the whole of life, down to its most repulsive detail, was given the supreme dignity of religious significance.[44]

The duties and obligations laid upon the Muslim could be performed fully and correctly only within the ambiance of an organized community of Believers. And the social ideals inherent in the service of the One God could be realized only if that community of Believers were safeguarded against external threats and internal schisms, and generally ordered so as to afford conditions under which the prescriptions for the good life could be implemented—that is, if it were provided with a centralized government. This dual requirement of community and government meant that the Muslim's religious obligations could be discharged most fully only in a settlement of some size, ideally a town. These obligations, later summarily formalized as the *ḥisbah* duty "to prescribe what is approved and proscribe what is reproved" *(al-amr bi-l-maʿrūf wa-l-nahy ʿan al-munkar),*[45] were as wide as the *Ummah;* as a result, the broad swaths cut by the Muslim armies through Africa and Asia were delineated by cordons of cities manifesting an enormous range of responses to these needs.[46] Some such settlements were created wholly or essentially ex nihilo, as were al-Kūfah and al-Baṣrah in ʿIrāq, al-Fusṭāṭ in Miṣr, al-Qayrawān in the Ifrīqiyah, Fez (Fās) and Marrakesh (Marrākush) in the Maghrib, Almería (al-Marīyah) and Córdoba (Qurṭubah) in Spain, and Shīrāz and Iṣfahān in the old Sāsānian territories. The majority, however, typified by Damascus (Dimashq), Jerusalem (al-Quds, Bayt al-Maqdis),[47] Alexandria (al-Iskandarīyah), Palermo (Balarm), and Seville (Ishbīliyah), were adaptations of preexisting urban forms. Naturally cities of this latter type were for long greatly influenced in both form and function by the cultural traditions that had prevailed before the advent of Islam.

Within the Umayyad empire (excluding the Iberian Peninsula), it is possible to distinguish four traditions of urbanism: a Hellenistic tradition that had been continued in the former Byzantine territories; a Persian tradition, which subsumed an ʿIrāqī subtradition; a South Arabian tradition; and a North African tradition which, although compounded of Greek and Latin elements, was sufficiently distinctive to merit separate status.[48] Throughout the areal extent of these realms, Islam gradually imposed on originally distinctive urban forms certain structural similarities deriving from a community of purpose and shared habits of life. This is not to imply that the Middle Eastern city was everywhere the vehicle of a uniform lifestyle, but rather that it provided the framework within which diverse cultures to varying degrees absorbed and internalized the main duties *(ʿibādāt)* of the Faith as expressed in the five pillars *(arkān)* of Islam.

The Great *Tamṣīr*[49]

French Arabists typically discuss the urban forms resulting from the expansion of Islam under the categories *villes spontanées* and *villes créées,*[50] which is essentially the way that we viewed them in the preceding paragraph. "*La ville spontanée,*" writes Georges Marçais, "semble être le produit naturel du sol. Un groupe d'humanités anonymes qui s'accroissait au cours des années, est venu habiter tel point du pays, afin de profiter des avantages qu'il lui offrait pour se défendre contre les dangers extérieurs ou jouir des ressources dont il attendait sa subsistance." "*La ville créée,*" by contrast, "est l'oeuvre arbitraire d'un homme, qui en a choisi l'emplacement, tracé les limites, ébauché la physionomie future, dans un but qu'il juge utile à lui-même et à ses descendants, ou pour y établir une collectivité dont il veut assurer le bien-être."[51] Two perspectives are reflected in these definitions: both categorizations of urban forms apply only to cities emerging somehow under Muslim aegis, or, from the Arab point of view, preexisting cities are to be regarded as "spontaneous." In any case it is doubtful whether the urban forms taken over, as opposed to those created, by the Arab conquerors ever came to reflect Islamic urban ideology in anything like its totality.

One would presume to find the purest manifestations of the Islamic ideal of urban design and function in those cities that were laid out de novo by caliphs and princes on previously uninhabited terrain. But the concept of the created city has its limitations even in this context: a princely foundation, once established, inevitably developed its own evolutional dynamic, which often diverged markedly from its founder's intent. Moreover, in the absence of a vigorous and encompassing municipal organization—a situation characteristic of the Muslim world—a "created" city was likely to lose the ideological imprint of its founder relatively quickly and ultimately become indistinguishable from a spontaneously generated city. In fact not a few such foundations failed altogether to survive the vicissitudes of political and economic change. In ʿIrāq, for example, the lineaments of al-Kūfah, "la grande cité qui fut la plus *arabe* des métropoles musulmanes,"[52] today are barely discernible on the ground, while in North Africa even the name of al-Qalʿah, the ancient capital of the Banū-Ḥammād (1015–1152), is unknown to most Algerians. Other "created" cities survived but failed to fulfil the ambitions of their founders. Rabāṭ (Ribāṭ al-Fatḥ), for instance, did not expand to fill the extensive area enclosed within its walls by ʿAbd al-Mu'min, the first Muwaḥḥid *sulṭān* (1130–63), until French colonial times. Al-Qayrawān and al-Mahdīyah, both in the Ifrīqiyah, are other examples of "created" cities whose brief spans of glory were succeeded by long centuries of relative insignificance.[53]

It was these translations from power to impotence or extinction in the settlement patterns of the Muslim world that led Francisco Benet to epitomize the urbanization process in Islamic lands as "Penelope's handiwork."

> The earth in Islam is pock-marked with the skeletons of dead cities and those which passed the test of time have inherited, for a relatively limited tradition, large domains and undisputed gravitational fields. In our [Western] cities the process of decline and renewal goes on all the time; we build over the same decaying corpses and manage a mildly successful attempt at urban eternity. Islamic cities are short lived and their death is final so that every few generations there are kaleidoscopic rearrangements in the total urban landscape. It is the parallax as opposed to the palimpsest method.[54]

In some respects Benet perhaps overstates his case, for the number of foundations that have sustained a high rank in the urban hierarchy against all vicissitudes—cities such as Baghdād, Cairo, Marrākush, and Córdoba, to name but four—gives the lie to the Penelope metaphor with its implication of a recurrent ravelling of the tapestry in its totality at the end of an epoch. But Benet was right to emphasize the degree of mutability that formerly characterized the higher ranks of the Islamic urban hierarchy as compared with, say, those of Europe, Hindu India, or East Asia.

Amṣār

The early Muslim campaigns beyond the Arabian Peninsula were undertaken primarily by Arab tribesmen whose natural element—whether they were *qarawīyūn, rāʿīyah, shwāyah,* or true *badū*—was the desert or steppe or, at its most benign, the sand-enveloped oasis such as Taymā' or al-Madīnah. Yet it was these same tribesmen who were required to garrison the conquered provinces without totally despoiling them. The immediate solution was to settle them between campaigns in military camps strung along the desert fringe. Such camps were known to Arab historians as *amṣār.*[55] Some of the earliest were established in the vicinity of Syrian cities during the campaigns undertaken after the *riddah* wars, namely al-Jābiyah, Ḥimṣ, ʿAmwās, Ṭabarīyah (Tiberias), and al-Ludd. Within a decade after Muḥammad's death, al-Kūfah and al-Baṣrah had been established in ʿIrāq, and during the first century of the Islamic era what may be termed the *miṣr* mode of control was extended not only into former Sāsānian territories (e.g., ʿAskar Mukram in Khūzistān and Shīrāz in Fārs), but also on a smaller scale into the territories beyond the Jayḥūn River. In Egypt al-Fusṭāṭ was laid out in 641 near the Roman fortress of Bābalyūn, to be followed in 643 by Barqah and in 670 by al-Qayrawān,[56] both in the Ifrīqiyah, and by Tagrart[57] in the Maghrib as late as the eleventh century.

As represented in the Tradition, the settlement of Arabian tribesmen in the *amṣār* was not achieved easily. These parasites of the camel,[58] in the words of the caliph ʿUmar, furnished Islam with its raw material,[59] with natural warriors, but not with instinctive citizens. "Der Begriff des rechtlichen Zwanges," as Procksch puts it, "war den Arabern unbekannt; überall herschte in letzter Instanz das

Reservatrecht der persönlichen Entscheidung."[60] Muslim tradition has archetyped the anomie and personality disorientation experienced by tribesmen incarcerated in the *amṣār* at a heroic level. Trapped as they were in an environment alien to the *badū* or *shwāyah* way of life, they discovered that stipends and booty did nothing to assuage their nostalgia for the air of the desert, to diminish a yearning that tradition reified as an unassuageable thirst for camel's milk. It is related that when tribesmen fell ill with fever in al-Madīnah, Muḥammad sent them out as herdsmen so that they might restore their strength with doses of milk laced with camel's urine.[61] But this remedy exposed them to the temptation to revert to ancient tribal ways with the ensuing likelihood of apostasy *(irtidād)*, a sin that ranked as mortal *(kabīrah)*. The Prophet himself allegedly expostulated, "What I dread for my people is milk, where the devil slips 'twixt foam and teat. Their yearning for it will induce them to return to the desert, forsaking the places where men pray together."[62]

Muslim tradition also asserts that Muḥammad offered neophyte converts a choice between a full oath of allegiance *(bayʿat hijrah)* and a limited *badū* oath *(bayʿat ʿarabīyah)* consistent with a continued sojourn in the tribe.[63] Those who took the latter pledge were counted as allies and probably as members of the *Ummah*—certainly as having entered the service of Allāh—but were denied a share in the booty acquired on the warpath of God. Even if this distinction were only a myth foisted onto history by later traditionists, by the time the *amṣār* were being established, *hijrah,* the sundering of bonds of family and lineage for the sake of lodging in a permanent, Islamically governed settlement, was being exalted as the consummate symbol of submission to the will of the One God. When a fever-racked *badawī,* unable to bear any longer the deprivations of al-Madīnah, committed suicide, the Prophet allegedly said that Allāh would pardon him by virtue of his *hijrah.*[64] The very vigor with which sedentarization within the *amṣār* was urged on wavering tribesmen testifies to the magnitude of the *badū* anachorein[65] that threatened early Islamic leaders as they sought to institutionalize their faith and consolidate the foundations of empire in a realm where there had traditionally been a perpetual osmotic translation of men back and forth between city and countryside.[66]

The inaugural *khuṭbah* in 666 of Ziyād ibn Abīhi, newly appointed governor of al-Baṣrah, vividly reflects the preoccupations of authority with social instability in that city some thirty years after the founding of the original camp, when much of the populace—in Ziyād's words—still allowed the bonds of kinship to prevail over ties of religion: "Woe to those who shout the tribal rallying cry *(daʿwah)!* I shall have their tongues cut out. You have invented new crimes, but I shall devise fitting punishments: for him who throws his fellow into the water, drowning; for him who breaks through the wall of a house or sets it alight, burning or piercing of the chest; for him who desecrates a grave, burial alive."[67]

Ziyād goes on to assure his unruly townsmen-in-the-making that the tedium of their sojourn among the mud walls of al-Baṣrah would not only be relieved by opportunities to raid along the frontier but also rewarded with punctual payment of stipends and pensions from the Dīwān. Perhaps more significantly, he equivocates in his adherence to the fundamental tenet of the *Ummah,* namely that it constituted a community linked by faith rather than blood, and partially resuscitated the old order of kinship obligations. To induce a measure of peace in the turbulent settlement, he reinstituted the principle of group responsibility according to which the family answers for its members' transgressions. Even though this policy was in effect perpetuating the *ʿaṣabīyah,* the old lineage loyalties of the tribesmen, now they were being directed toward new aims. In fact Ziyād's regimen was only one manifestation of the general Sufyānī policy of substituting its own monopoly of force for the traditional private retaliation of the tribes. In other words, the irrevocable arbitraments of the blood feud were being replaced within the *Ummah* by the laws of a state. Penal and repressive though they were, they were still laws, norms of social conduct sanctioned by a relatively stable government. In any case, Ziyād's measures would appear to have achieved a degree of success and earned the approbation of several contemporary and later writers.[68]

For a few of the *amṣār,* notably al-Baṣrah and al-Kūfah—known familiarly to Arab authors as the ʿIrāqān—and al-Fusṭāṭ, early Muslim topographers and historians have left us with brief accounts of how the Arabian tribesmen disposed themselves in these new settlements. Unfortunately, the information provided by these sources is not uniform among the several *amṣār.*

Al-Baṣrah

Some of the material in these accounts relates to the early years of al-Baṣrah.[69] Al-Balādhurī's reconstruction of events is as follows:[70]

> When ʿUtbah ibn Ghazwān pitched his camp at al-Khuraybah (The Little Ruin), he wrote to ʿUmar ibn al-Khaṭṭāb, telling him of his sojourn there, and asserting that the Muslims needed a place in which they could pass the winter, and into which they could retire when they returned from a raid. ʿUmar replied to him, "Assemble thy followers in one place; let it be near water and pasture; and write me a description of it." So he wrote to him, "I have found a land abounding in reeds,[71] on the extremity of the desert over toward the river tract [the Shaṭṭ al-ʿArab], and below it are swamps with reeds." When ʿUmar read the letter, he said, "This land is verdant, near to watering and grazing places and firewood." So he wrote to him (ʿUtbah) to station the tribesmen there, which he did. They built huts of reeds, and ʿUtbah built a mosque of reeds. This was in the year 14 [i.e., A.D. 635/36].

On a preceding page[72] is the supplementary statement that

> [t]here were in the district of al-Baṣrah at that time seven settlements *(dasākir;* sing. *daskarah,* an Arabicized rendering of Pahlavi *dastkart),* two in al-Khuraybah, two in al-Zabūqah, and three in what is now the Dār al-Azd. ʿUtbah quartered his companions in these villages, he himself staying in al-Khuraybah. This had housed a garrison of the Persians that Khālid ibn al-Walīd had conquered, and that had then been abandoned by the Persians. ʿUtbah wrote to ʿUmar informing him of the place in which he and his companions were located, and ʿUmar replied, ordering him to transfer them to a location near water and pasture. So he changed to the site of al-Baṣrah. . . . They put up there booths and tents of leather and of coarse cloth, and did not have any real buildings.

Founding of the City

These passages present one of two apparently contradictory traditions relating to the founding of the city. The other assigns the origin to the initiative, in 637/38 or 638/39, of the Arab commander Saʿd ibn Abī-Waqqāṣ, one of the Companions whom Muḥammad had promised entry into Paradise after the battle of Badr, and who also established the settlement at al-Kūfah.[73] It has sometimes been assumed that these two traditions reflect the subsequent rivalry of al-Baṣrah and al-Kūfah: the Baṣrians advanced a date of the establishment of their city that coincided with that of al-Kūfah, and the Kūfans ascribed the origin of al-Baṣrah to a subordinate of their own founder. However, al-Masʿūdī, alone among ancient authors,[74] advanced a third version of events that incorporated elements from both mainstreams of tradition, namely that al-Baṣrah had been established *(muṣṣirat)* by ʿUtbah ibn Ghazwān in 637/38 or 638/39[75] on a site where he and his followers had already camped in 635/36. This version leads Charles Pellat to suggest that the conflicting traditions may have arisen through the genuine confusion of two separate occupations of the site rather than as a result of deliberate falsification of the chronology.[76] In any case, whatever the date or precise manner of its founding, the new cantonment could hardly have looked forward to a propitious future. Situated in an uncultivated tract of territory some four *parasangs*[77] west of present-day al-Baṣrah, it could have expected to derive few advantages either from its barren soil,[78] oppressive climate, and scarcity of fresh water,[79] or from its tribal inhabitants, who were preoccupied with war to the virtual exclusion of commerce and the arts.

According to the prevalent tradition, the Arab army camped in and around seven villages that had been abandoned by their former inhabitants. At first the tribesmen pitched tents and ran up temporary shacks, but within a year or two they were using reeds from the marshes north of al-Baṣrah to construct more substantial huts. Even these were temporary, for al-Balādhurī writes that

> [w]hen the inhabitants went on a raid, they used to take down these reeds, pack them up, and lay them away until they should return from the raid; and when they returned, they restored their buildings. This custom persisted for some time. Then the inhabitants demarcated boundaries and constructed regular dwellings.[80]

An Arab topographer tells us that the camp was originally laid out in the shape of a stole *(ṭaylasān)*[81] centered on the angle formed by the two waterways Nahr Maʿqil and Nahr al-Ubullah. Al-Yaʿqūbī reports that at its foundation the encampment covered an area of two *parasangs* by one.[82] Some thirty years later it had developed into at least a proto-city of considerably greater extent. Initially it was not provided with perimeter defenses, though at least once in extremis the inhabitants were constrained to excavate an enclosing ditch.[83] Not until 771/72, in the reign of the ʿAbbāsid caliph al-Manṣūr, was the settlement finally walled,[84] and even then the wall did not enclose the Mirbaḍ, the vast combined caravanserai and market lying on the western or desert approach to the city.[85] This suburb was linked to al-Baṣrah proper by the Sikkat al-Mirbaḍ, which, piercing the wall at the Bāb al-Bādīyah ("The Desert Gate"), continued east as the main thoroughfare of the city. The fact that al-Bādīyah was the sole gate in the entire wall is a powerful indication of the orientation of Baṣrian interests even a century and a half after the founding of the settlement. It was still toward the great terminal of western caravan trade that the city turned its face.[86]

The first mosque to be established in al-Baṣrah, which was also the first mosque to be set up as a freestanding structure in a territory conquered by the Arab armies, was simply an open space fenced round with reeds.[87] Subsequently the governor Abū Mūsā al-Ashʿarī replaced this primitive enclosure with a building of sun-dried brick *(labin)* having a thatch *(ʿushb)* roof.[88] At the same time the tribesmen began to build dwellings of brick, and Abū Mūsā erected a gubernatorial residence *(dār al-imārah)* of the same material which also housed the *dīwān* and a prison. But not until the governorship of Ziyād ibn Abīhī (666–73), when baked brick *(ājurr)* came into general use, and when Ziyād completely rebuilt both mosque and governor's residence,[89] did al-Baṣrah begin to assume the form and social characteristics of a securely established city—and even then the transformation was only beginning.

Tribal Groups

About the tribal affiliations of the warriors who first camped at al-Baṣrah, and about the sequence in which they established themselves, we are poorly informed, although it is clear that the core of the Muslim army that conquered ʿIrāq was recruited from the Ḥijāz. The seven *dasākir* preexisting on the site appear to have played little or no part in the organization of the cantonment, for it is recorded that by 660/61 at latest the settlement was divided into five tribal aggregations known as "fifths" *(akhmās;* sing. *khums).*[90] Although this arrangement could have stemmed from the initial settlement of tribesmen at al-Baṣrah, there is no detailed account of the system relating to a period before 686/87.[91] At that time the several tribal groups were disposed in *akhmās* as follows:[92]

- ***The Tamīm,*** whose tribe was scattered through the steppes, as well as the villages and towns, of northeastern Arabia,[93] may be regarded as the principal founders of the settlement. They occupied the southeastern sector with the Banū-Ḍabbah clan of the Zayd Manāt, a smaller group that had also established itself at al-Baṣrah at an early date. During the first century of the Islamic era it was the Tamīm who provided most of the intellectual, religious, and political élites within the city, and who in great measure determined its political and Sunnī orientations.
- ***The Azd,*** a tribe having lineages in both ʿAsīr (Azd Shanūʾah) and ʿUmān (Azd ʿUmān), are the only tribesmen whose settlement in al-Baṣrah can be dated with a degree of assurance. Small sections of this tribe, notably the Azd Sarat, lived in the cantonment from an early period, and al-Ṭabarī records the existence of several Azdī *masjids* in 670. The main settlement, however, in the northwestern sector, did not take place until the end of Muʿāwiyah's reign and the beginning of Yazīd's, that is, during the last quarter of the seventh century. Despite their late arrival, within a few years the Azd became the largest tribe. Leagued with other "Yamanī" tribes such as the Quḍāʿah, Kalb, Tanūkh, Ṭayyiʾ, ʿAdī, Kindah, and Hamdān, they became the chief proponents of the so-called southern Arab cause in its protracted conflict with the northern Arabs' aspirations.
- ***The Ahl al-ʿĀlīyah,*** *badū* of the highlands south of al-Madīnah, comprised tribesmen from the Quraysh, Kinānah, Bajilah, Qays ʿAylān (the largest group in this *khums*), Muzaynah, and Asad. They occupied the land to the west of al-Baṣrah proper, mainly between the Mirbaḍ and the *jāmiʿ*.
- ***The Bakr ibn Wāʾil,*** from the neighborhood of al-Ḥīrah, although less numerous than the Azd or Tamīm, played an important part in tribal conflicts

during the latter half of the seventh century. In particular, they were the principal representatives in al-Baṣrah of the purely pastoral mode of life, subsuming as they did the individual clans of Sadūs, Dhuhl, Shaybān, Yashkur, and Ḍubayʿah, together with the Lahāzim federation of clans. Their holdings were situated more or less centrally to the camp as a whole, and on the south adjoined those of their implacable opponents, the Tamīm.

- Although ***the ʿAbd al-Qays,*** the predominant tribe in al-Baḥrayn, formed the smallest *khums* in al-Baṣrah, they had demarcated their own district on the northeastern outskirts of the city by about the mid-seventh century.

Associated with the Arab tribes, and to be considered under the same heading, were the slaves and clients whom they brought into the camp with them. This latter group comprised both pure-blooded members of weak tribes who had accepted client status in return for the protection afforded by membership in a powerful tribe; and former slaves who had been freed and adopted as clients in pre-Muslim times, and who had subsequently been more or less assimilated into the Arab community. Both these classes of clients regarded themselves as superior to the *mawālī* newly, and often expediently, converted to Islam as a result of the Arab conquests. In addition to this numerically predominant category subsumed under the rubric *Aʿrāb,* several other culturally significant elements made up the population of al-Baṣrah during the first century or so of its existence.

- ***Indigenous groups.*** The mass of the population of the Sawād, the irrigated and cultivated "black land" of Lower Mesopotamia, were probably Aramaean speakers Īrānicized to a greater or lesser degree. To Arab authors they were often known as al-Anbāṭ, that is, Nabaṭaeans.[94] They played no part in the conquest and were incorporated in the Islamic state as a class of peasant farmers apart from, and inferior to, the Arab conquerors.
- ***Īrānians and Īrānicized subjects.*** Before the conquest, the Sawād had been administered primarily by minor members of the Persian nobility *(dahāqīn;* sing. *dihqān,* from the Middle Persian *dēhkān),* and the Arabs preserved most of this bureaucratic structure. Both al-Balādhurī and al-Ṭabarī affirm that *dahāqīn* came to be entrusted with collecting the *kharāj* when Arab officials proved corrupt.[95] Moreover, al-Masʿūdī noted that, even as late as the tenth century, "the majority of the descendants of the Persian kings . . . were still living in the Sawād, where they registered and preserved their genealogical qualifications with a respect equalling that of the Arabs of Qaḥṭān and Nizār."[96] Along with this cadre of civic officials of Īrānian and Īrānicized origin, a military contingent of two thousand men brought from Bukhārā by ʿUbayd Allāh ibn Ziyād was quartered in Sikkat al-Bukhārīyah.[97]
- ***Sindī and Indians.*** The Sindī, known to Arab writers as *Zuṭṭ,* appear to have reached Lower Mesopotamia from the Indus valley by two routes. One group, originally brought to the coasts of the Persian Gulf early in the fifth century, had accepted Islam at the time of the conquest. Soon afterwards a number of them were transferred by Abū Mūsā al-Ashʿarī to al-Baṣrah, where they became clients of the Banū-Ḥanẓalah of the Tamīm confederacy.[98] The other group members were brought into ʿIrāq by al-Ḥajjāj after his campaigns on the Indus, and were settled, together with their families and livestock, in the district of Kaskar.[99] It would seem also that certain mounted mercenaries, known to historians under the Arabicized name of *asāwirah* (sing. *uswārī*), who had deserted from the Persian army to join the Muslim cause, were also ultimately of Sindian origin.[100]
- ***Indonesians.*** Gabriel Ferrand has shown that the Sayābijah whom the chroniclers customarily mentioned in association with the Zuṭṭ were probably Sumatrans employed by the Sāsānians to combat piracy in the Persian Gulf.[101] In 656 they were being employed as treasury guards. According to al-Balādhurī, they had originally been "joined with" the *asāwirah,* but after the Muslim conquest they entered into clientage with the Banū-Ḥanẓalah, and were settled by Abū Mūsā at al-Baṣrah.[102] The Sayābijah were never a numerous community, though some historians mention as many as four hundred employed in the service of the Baṣrian treasury.[103]
- ***Zanj.*** These were blacks from the East African coast who had been brought to al-Baṣrah as slaves, and who were employed mainly as laborers in the swampy lands of the Baṭāʾih.[104] Al-Jāḥiẓ enumerated four subgroups, the Qunbulah, Lanjawīyah, Naml, and

Kilāb,[105] presumably distinguished by their tribal affiliation or provenance, although these names have not been identified as East African ethnonyms or toponyms.

The figures given by the several chroniclers for the population of al-Baṣrah are virtually all somewhat suspect. The troops of ʿUtbah ibn Ghazwān, who formed the original nucleus around which subsequent arrivals gathered, almost certainly numbered fewer than a thousand,[106] but Pellat estimates that less than twenty years later the settlement comprised more than fifty thousand people.[107] In about 670 some eighty thousand tribesmen figured on the rolls of the Dīwān,[108] while al-Ṭabarī claims that in 714/15 the Baṣrian contingent fighting in Khurāsān amounted to forty thousand men.[109] Pellat's estimate for the total population of al-Baṣrah at the end of the first Islamic century is on the order of two hundred thousand.[110]

Al-Kūfah

The two main sources for the Arab settlement of al-Kūfah are a chapter in al-Balādhurī's *Futūḥ al-Buldān* entitled "Tamṣīr al-Kūfah" and three pages in al-Yaʿqūbī's *Kitāb al-Buldān.*[111] In this latter work we find the following succinct account:

> When the conquest of al-ʿIrāq had been completed, [the Caliph] ʿUmar ibn al-Khaṭṭāb wrote to Saʿd ibn Abī-Waqqāṣ commanding him to establish his residence at al-Kūfah. Saʿd ordered his troops to dispose themselves in *khiṭaṭ* at that place. The shaykh of each tribe was allotted a defined space for the dwellings of his followers.[112]

Other sources, including Sayf ibn ʿUmar in al-Ṭabarī's history, furnish somewhat different accounts of the origins of the cantonment and make much of the fact that al-Kūfah was Saʿd's second choice for a garrison headquarters. Previously he had quartered his troops in the abandoned Sāsānian capital, known to the Arabs as al-Madāʾin. The sources are not in agreement as to the reasons for the move, but one version has ʿUmar instructing Saʿd to "Establish a permanent settlement *(dār al-hijrah)* for the nomadic tribesmen *(al-aʿrāb),*"[113] from which it may be inferred that the availability of pasture factored into the decision. The date of the foundation is specified variously as the fifteenth, sixteenth, seventeenth, or eighteenth year after the *Hijrah*—that is, in Gregorian reckoning, between 14 February 636 and 1 January 640.

The camp thus established was situated on a tongue of sandy terrain that intruded itself between the Euphrates River on the east and a tract of low-lying ground on the west. It was close to the point where the caravan trails linking al-Ḥijāz and al-Yaman to Persia and High Asia crossed the Euphrates, and in a locality that had already witnessed the rise of ancient Babylon and more recently the Lakhmid capital of al-Ḥīrah. Prior to the founding of the encampment, the site was apparently inhabited by a sparse population of Īrānicized, sedentary, Aramaean agriculturalists, among whom there circulated a sprinkling of Arab herdsmen.[114]

Khiṭāṭ

Into this essentially fluid population Saʿd introduced his camp for some thirty thousand veterans of the Battle of Qādisīyah, including a Madīnan contingent several thousand strong, about twelve thousand Yamanī Arabs who were settled on the east side of the cantonment, and an estimated eight thousand Nizārī Arabs who were assigned to the west side. For its first five years the settlement was simply an organized aggregation of reed huts. Then walls of sun-dried brick began to be built, and finally, as at al-Baṣrah, during the governorship of Ziyād ibn Abīhi baked brick came into use as the main construction material. The first dwellings to be raised in this type of brick were in the tribal sector *(khiṭṭah;* pl. *khiṭāṭ)* of the Kindah, among both the Murad and the Khazraj clans, the latter of whom had concluded a *ḥilf* pact with the Kindah.[115]

Initially the *khiṭāṭ* were disposed around a centrally situated congregational mosque and Saʿd's *dār al-imārah* according to the directions of a certain Abū al-Hayyāj ibn Malik al-Asadī,[116] but the influx of migrants that followed the conquest[117] seriously disrupted the original pattern of the settlement. Generally speaking, those tribes that had figured most prominently in the conquest maintained their positions close to the center of the cantonment while less prestigious groups, especially those with a large *rawādif* component, resigned themselves to the outskirts.[118]

Asbāʿ

Ultimately the flow into the settlement of immigrants, many absorbed from neighboring al-Hīrah and al-Qādisīyah, so disrupted the tribal organization that Saʿd sought permission to reconstitute the *khiṭāṭ* as roughly equal sevenths. For the ensuing three decades the camp consisted of seven sections *(asbāʿ;* sing. *subʿ),* organized primarily for military purposes but serving also as instruments for distributing booty and disbursing stipends. As systematized by Massignon,[119] these sevenths were constituted as follows:

- The Ahl al-ʿĀlīyah comprised Kinānah and Jadīlah (Banū-ʿĀmir ibn Qays ʿAylān). Although this group was never very numerous, during the period of the Rāshidūn caliphs (632–61) it was extremely influential: its *shaykh*s were the natural allies of the Qurashī governors of the settlement.
- Quḍāʿah, Ghassān ibn Shibām, Bajīlah, Khathʿam, Kindah, Ḥaḍramawt, and Azd together exerted a strong Yamanī influence. Generally speaking, within this sector power lay with the Kindah, whose destiny was in the hands of the powerful lineage that included the distinguished warrior and provincial governor al-Ashʿath ibn Qays,[120] and with the Bajīlah, whose *shaykh* was a close friend of the caliph ʿUmar's.
- Madhḥij, Ḥimyar, and Hamdān together constituted another powerful Yamanī sector, among whom the Hamdān were the most influential.
- Muḍarid elements were present: Tamīm[121] and al-Ribāb, Banū-Aʿṣur.
- Asad, Ghaṭafān, Muḥārib, Namir (of the Bakr confederacy), Ḍubayʿah, and Taghlib all generally upheld the Bakr interest.
- Of the Iyād, ʿAkk, ʿAbd al-Qays, Ahl Hajar, and al-Ḥamrāʾ, the Iyād and the ʿAkk were simply remnants of tribes that once pastured their herds in the vicinity of al-Ḥīrah. The ʿAbd al-Qays had migrated from al-Baḥrayn under the leadership of a Tamīm *shaykh* of the Saʿd clan, Zuhrah ibn Ḥawīyah, who had also brought into the settlement some four thousand Persian troops *(al-ḥamrāʾ),* with whom he had concluded a pact of *ḥilf.*[122]
- The ethnonym Ṭayyiʾ is lacking in the explicit sources. Massignon, however, on a variety of inferential grounds, has deduced the presence of members of the tribe from the very beginning of the settlement.

After the Battle of the Camel in 656, the caliph ʿAlī transferred his capital from al-Madīnah to al-Kūfah. As a result, he found it politically and militarily expedient to reorganize the *asbāʿ* of the latter city, this time modifying the tribal groupings as follows:

1. Hamdān and Ḥimyar;
2. Madhḥij, Ashʿar, and Ṭayyiʾ;
3. Qays (ʿAbs and Dhubyan) and ʿAbd al-Qays;
4. Kindah, Ḥaḍramawt, Quḍāʿah, and Mahrah;
5. Azd, Bajīlah, and Khathʿam;
6. Bakr, Taghlib, and the remainder of the Rabīʿah[123] (except the ʿAbd al-Qays); and
7. Quraysh, Kinānah, Asad, Tamīm, Ḍabbah, and Ribāb.[124]

That the integrity of the tribal groupings survived both these attempts at reorganization is ample testimony that two decades within the narrow confines of the *miṣr* had done little to subvert the kinship basis of Arab social organization; it was apparently still the only mode of administrative subdivision either envisaged by the government and/or acceptable to the migrants and their families.

At this time the *asbāʿ* of al-Kūfah still functioned essentially as tribal encampments, although they consisted of permanent, brick-walled dwellings arranged with some degree of regularity. According to Ibn al-Faqīh,[125] the total population of the settlement in about the middle of the seventh century was eighty thousand, half of whom were fighting men. Authority over the settlement as a whole, insofar as it was exercised by any group, was held by a small caucus of *shaykh*s from al-Ḥijāz. The bulk of the inhabitants comprised three groups of settlers. There was a pure *badū* component, "bédouins de grande tente" who had arrived as conquerors and now were experiencing sedentary life for the first time as pensioners of the Dīwān. Prominent among them were the Tamīm and the Ṭayyiʾ. There also were seminomadic pastoralists, both *shwāyah* and *rāʿīyah,* who were either dwellers in the area before the Muslim conquest (Asad and Bakr), or were more or less Īrānicized immigrants from various parts of Eastern Arabia (the ʿAbd al-Qays from Ḥajar). Further, there were substantial South Arabian elements from al-Yaman and Ḥaḍramawt, some of whom were semisedentary, in some cases *rāʿīyah* (Kindah and Bajīlah), and others of whom once lived in ancient cities (Madhḥij, Ḥimyar, and Hamdān). Massignon has already pointed out that it was this last, already urbanized component in al-Kūfah's population that—unlike the situation at al-Baṣrah, where such elements were numerically negligible—provided the milieu within which urban institutions began to crystallize out from a matrix of tribal customs.[126]

From Tribal to Urban Society

Despite this leaven working within the relatively heterogeneous society of al-Kūfah, the urbanization process appears to have operated more slowly than at al-Baṣrah. One reason that has been advanced in partial explanation of this seeming anomaly is that, although the four principal lineages *(buyūtāt)* of the tribal nobility all settled at al-Kūfah rather than at al-Baṣrah,[127] for several decades they resided in tented encampments outside the *miṣr* proper. As a result, they removed from the physical confines of the settlement important loci of power and authority and deprived it of some of the material structures most expressive of differentiating institutional spheres. A cantonment in which such institutions were located circumjacently was clearly likely to evolve more slowly than one in which, as at al-Baṣrah, they were at the heart of the settlement. Perhaps al-Baṣrah's close connection with the trade of the Persian Gulf was also a factor in the rapidity of its growth,[128] but chief significance almost certainly has to be accorded to the politico-religious role of the settlement as a focus for the maneuverings and aspirations of both principal parties in the conflict that preceded the establishment of the Umayyad kingdom.[129]

In any case the relatively slow transformation from tribal to urban society in al-Kūfah is evident enough: as late as 670 Ziyād ibn Abīhi,[130] in an attempt to contain the chronic intertribal conflict that continually threatened the stability of the settlement, was constrained to undertake yet another reconstitution of its tribal dispositions. He established four wards (*arbāᶜ*; sing. *rubᶜ*, literally, "quarter"), composed in each instance mainly of two of the principal tribes.[131] In some respects these *arbāᶜ* were analogous to the *akhmās* that had been created earlier in al-Baṣrah, but in the case of al-Kūfah the reorganization was administrative rather than territorial, and did not invariably entail a physical relocation of tribesmen. What it effectively achieved was the association, within common administrative units, of lineages and clans having long histories of conflict. The Rabīᶜah and the Kindah, both ultimately of South Arabian provenance, were brought together to form a single *rubᶜ*, while the remaining Yamanī tribes were dispersed between the *arbāᶜ* of the Banū-Asad and the Tamīm. Only the Ahl al-ᶜĀlīyah, relatively few in number but prestigious because they included elements of the Quraysh tribe, were the sole members of a *rubᶜ*. The schedule of *arbāᶜ* was

1. Ahl al-ᶜĀlīyah (Kinānah and Jadīlah),
2. Tamīm and Hamdān,
3. Rabīᶜah (Bakr) and Kindah, and
4. Madhḥij and Asad.

By means of this expedient, which juxtaposed tribal groups having potentially antagonistic interests, Ziyād was able to reduce the dimensions of intertribal conflict considerably and, perhaps more importantly, to render relatively harmless a good deal of anti-Umayyad sentiment. But this reduction in tribal autonomy was not the total extent of his reforms. Equally effective was the manner in which he diminished the power of the *shaykhs*, who were usually known collectively as *ashrāf al-qabā'il.* This he achieved by vesting authority within each *rubᶜ* in an official *(ᶜarīf)*[132] appointed, or at least agreed to, by the governor. In this way Ziyād intruded governmental authority into internal tribal affairs in the interests of a general policy of centralization.

Father Lammens appears to have regarded these measures of Ziyād as signalling the total dissolution of the old tribal framework and the immediate creation of urban wards.[133] If this were so, then it was in name only, for the sets of organically induced linkages that define life in a city ward or quarter are not conjured out of tribal segmentalism by governmental fiat: rather, they are generated by people living in close proximity over time. Possibly the transformation was achieved slightly more rapidly in the *rubᶜ* of the Hamdān and Tamīm—who, although hereditary enemies, had been forced as early as 657/58 to accept a joint military commander—than among the Bakr and Kindah, who, bound by a pact of *ḥilf,* would presumably not have found the new arrangements especially deleterious to the tribal basis of their society. In any case, the subsequent history of al-Kūfah affords abundant evidence that the old kin-based associations were not immediately disenfranchised, but persisted for at least a century in an increasingly urbanized and politicized environment. In fact, certain among them endured until the decline of the city in the tenth century.

Morphology

The morphology of al-Kūfah is better known than that of any of the other *amṣār*. Al-Ṭabarī has preserved, for example, the tribal composition of the fifteen rows of tents as they were assigned by Saʿd ibn Abī-Waqqāṣ at the founding of the encampment.[134] The locations of the *khiṭāṭ* assigned to the more prestigious tribes appear not to have changed greatly during the evolution of the settlement from camp to city, apart from the transference of the Tamīm *khiṭṭah* from an easterly to a westerly site sometime between 638 and 657, and the annexation of the ʿAbd al-Qays *khiṭṭah* by the Ḥamdān when the former group migrated to al-Baṣrah soon after 660.[135] In addition to these tribal holdings, there were also individual fiefs held under *qaṭāʾiʿ* leases, mainly by clan chieftains and *shaykhs* of the Madīnese contingent: al-Yaʿqūbī provides a list of twenty-five such lessees, of whom nineteen were Companions.[136]

In the center of the cantonment was an open square *(ṣaḥn);* the chief mosque of the settlement stood on its northeastern edge. Originally this structure was as primitive as the earliest mosque at al-Baṣrah. According to al-Balādhurī, it consisted solely of a square space, with each side two bow-shots long and demarcated only by a ditch.[137] The sole architectural feature was a covered colonnade *(zullah),* formed of marble columns purloined from buildings erected by the Lakhmid princes of al-Ḥīrah, which ran the whole length of the southern side of the mosque. The *zullah* was open on all sides, so that al-Ṭabarī was led to remark that a man praying there could see at one and the same time the convent of Dayr Hind and the Jiṣr Gate.[138] In 670 this primitive building was replaced by the grandest congregational mosque *(masjid al-jāmiʿ)* in Islam, with a roof structure based on that of an *apadāna,* or hall of columns, of the Persian kings. The masons employed at the site were "craftsmen of the Jāhilīyah," that is, non-Muslims, at least one of whom had worked on a construction for the great Khusraw.[139] Smaller, tribal *masjids* were dispersed through the *khiṭaṭ.* As early as 642, for instance, the tribe of ʿAbs had its own *masjid;* by 680 the Banū-Makhzūm were similarly provided for; by 685 the ʿAbd al-Qays; and by 686 the Banī-Jadhīmah. By the end of the century, virtually all tribal *khiṭāṭ* seem to have acquired their own *masjids.*

On the *qiblah* side of the primitive mosque, in strong contrast to it and contrary to the caliph ʿUmar's alleged preference for the old-fashioned simplicities of al-Ḥijāz at the time of the Prophet, Saʿd built for himself a residence *(dār al-imārah)* modelled on the royal palace at Ctesiphon (al-Madāʾin). Indeed, the gates of the old Persian capital were re-erected at the entrance to Saʿd's palace. The public treasury *(bayt al-māl)* was incorporated in the same building.

For nearly a century and a half al-Kūfah lacked a perimeter defense, but shortly after 762 the caliph al-Manṣūr enclosed the city by a ditch, into which he diverted water from the Euphrates. The resulting canal afforded access to the city gates for river travelers.[140] Surprisingly, the settlement had no potable well water during its first century, and, as Mughīrah ibn Saʿīd had pronounced cistern water unlawful for Muslims, supplies had to be brought in by carriers from the river.[141]

The main markets *(aswāq;* sing. *sūq)* of the cantonment stretched from the *maydān* north to the *khiṭṭah* of the Thaqīf and Ashjaʿ; Massignon has assembled extant references to the trades practiced there.[142] One of the more interesting of these references tells of two Chinese painters, Fan Shu and Liu Tzʿū, who resided in al-Kūfah during the years 751–62.[143] The Dār al-Rizq, the warehouse where booty awaiting distribution among the tribesmen was stored, was near the bridge leading from the camp across the Euphrates. A market quarter that also functioned as a caravanserai—in fact, the Kūfan analogue of al-Baṣrah's Mirbaḍ—was that known as the Kunāsah, toward the western edge of the encampment. Originally used as the night-soil depository of the Banū-Asad, this open space subsequently became a market for livestock and slaves, a loading and unloading depot for caravans trading across the western desert, the workplace of smiths, and finally, when al-Kūfah entered into its decline, an independent suburb.[144]

Prominent features in the Kūfan topography about which early authors have preserved some information were the tribal muster grounds-cum-assembly venues (sing. *jabbānah*). Each was located more or less centrally in its *khiṭṭah.* Those mentioned by al-Balādhurī[145] and Ibn al-Faqīh,[146] among others, are discussed in Hichem Djaït, *Al-Kūfa,* chapter 21.

The population estimates offered by the chroniclers

for al-Kūfah inspire no more confidence than do those for al-Baṣrah (p. 45 above). Al-Balādhurī, on the authority of al-Walīd ibn Hishām, whose grandfather had been in charge of the army registers in the years following 775, quoted figures of sixty thousand men and eighty thousand hearths.[147] However, the precise significance of the word *ʿiyālāt,* here translated as "hearth" (implying family), is by no means certain, and may indeed stand for an individual rather than a group, so that, even if al-Balādhurī's figures are reasonably accurate, it is still hazardous to attempt to calculate the total population of the city. It may be significant that al-Jahshiyārī advanced a total of only eighty thousand, including both warriors and their families.[148] In any case, Massignon's estimate of 400,000 inhabitants is excessive:[149] 150,000 might be a more realistic figure for a time toward the end of the first Islamic century.

Al-Fusṭāṭ

> After the conquest of Bābalyūn[150] by ʿAmr ibn al-ʿĀṣ in the year 20 (A.D. 641), during the caliphate of ʿUmar ibn al-Khaṭṭāb, the Arab tribes established their *khiṭāṭ* about the pavilion *(fusṭāṭ)*[151] of ʿAmr—whence the name al-Fusṭāṭ. Subsequently they were extended to the bank of the Nile. The *khiṭāṭ* took their names from the tribes that occupied them. ʿAmr ibn al-ʿĀṣ built there a congregational mosque, as well as a governor's residence, known as the *Dār al-Raml;* and he caused markets to be set up around the congregational mosque, situated on the east bank of the Nile. On his instructions each tribe deployed its defences,[152] and had at its head an *ʿarīf.*[153]

This is the account of the founding of al-Fusṭāṭ furnished by al-Yaʿqūbī; no other early author substantially improves on it, though some differ in their details.[154]

Founding of the Cantonment

The terrain on which the camp was pitched encompassed three low eminences, now known respectively as Jabal Yashkur, Sharaf Zayn al-ʿĀbīdīn, and Sharaf al-Raṣad,[155] on the east bank of the Nile River. In the seventh century the river channel was some two hundred fifty yards east of its present position, and the western *khiṭāṭ* of the encampment approached the water as closely as the declivity of the riverbank permitted. During the same period the islet of al-Rawḍah, which divides the waters of the Nile, was somewhat south of its present position, so that al-Maqrīzī was probably correct when he located the fortress of Bābalyūn opposite to it.[156] Prior to the conquest this fortress, known to the Arabs as Qaṣr al-Shamʿ, was the focus of settlement on this sector of the riverbank, but several convents and Coptic churches were also in the vicinity,[157] and possibly a Greco-Roman town at an unidentified location nearby.[158]

The precise site on which ʿAmr set up his pavilion is a matter of dispute among the chroniclers,[159] but all agree that it lay hundreds of yards to the north of the Qaṣr al-Shamʿ. It was here that he raised the first Muslim place of prayer in Africa, in the form of a simple quadrangle much like those erected more or less contemporaneously at al-Baṣrah and al-Kūfah. Around the mosque the kindred of ʿAmr and his close followers established the *khiṭṭah* that came to be known as Ahl al-Rāyah. The other tribal groups making up the army laid out their *khiṭāṭ* approximately on the sites that they had occupied before the investment of the fortress. The names of most of the individual tribal *khiṭāṭ,* together with some information about their boundaries, have been preserved in special chapters in the works of both al-Maqrīzī and Ibn Duqmāq; their locations were mapped in recent times by Rhuvon Guest, Paul Casanova, and Wladyslaw Kubiak.[160]

Generally speaking, however, a plot of ground seems to have been recognized as the property of its occupants as long as they continued to utilize it.[161] The whole site occupied an area roughly five thousand yards from north to south and some one thousand or so yards wide, so that its perimeter enclosed a tract of nearly three square miles. It was not walled, though there are references to a temporary breastwork *(zarībah)* of reeds southeast of the ʿAmr mosque, and to a moat being excavated on the east side of the camp when Marwān ibn al-Ḥakam invaded Egypt in 684.[162]

The settlement by *khiṭāṭ* did not necessarily constitute each tribe as an entirely separate entity. In fact there seems to have been a principle in operation according to which all *khiṭāṭ* tended to be assimilated to a mean size. Whereas it was apparently customary for a tribe to be settled in a single *khiṭṭah,* some large tribes, in conformity with this principle, were split into two or more divisions. What is more, certain groups were obliged to combine because individually they were too small to constitute an effective muster in the *dīwān*. The Khiṭṭah Ahl al-Ẓāhir was inhabited by late migrants who found spaces adjacent to their own kin already occupied and perforce had to combine in a separate *khiṭṭah*—all of which is reminiscent of somewhat contemporary developments in al-Kūfah. The case of the al-Lafīf is especially interesting, for it throws unusual light on the organization of a *khiṭṭah.* This group was formed by the voluntary union of individuals and detachments in the following of a particular *shaykh* whose desire to be constituted as a separate *khiṭṭah* had been frustrated by the objections of their kinsmen in neighboring *khiṭāṭ*. Instead it was arranged that they should each muster with their own kin while yet remaining spatially adjacent to one another in their dwellings.[163]

From these and other similar instances, it would seem reasonable to infer that the *khiṭāṭ* at their inception represented more or less faithfully the military organization of ʿAmr's army. Furthermore, the three *khiṭāṭ* situated farthest to the north were occupied by non-Arab groups. Known respectively as al-Ḥamrāʾ al-Dunyā, al-Ḥamrāʾ al-Wuṣṭā, and al-Ḥamrāʾ al-Quṣwā, they were inhabited mainly by Syrian Christians and Jews who had attached themselves to the Muslim armies, together with a variety of other *dhimmī*s. Finally, in addition to denoting these tribal allotments, the word *khiṭṭah* was also used for sites occupied by individual tribesmen or subordinate groups. Ibn Duqmāq refers to at least sixty such holdings. It would seem, therefore, that the term was applied to several levels of ownership, with the possibility of a tribal *khiṭṭah* incorporating a sectional *khiṭṭah,* which in turn could be made up of family *khiṭāṭ.*

Morphology

The only building from the early days of the cantonment to be described by the chroniclers was the congregational mosque, named after the commander Jāmiʿ ʿAmru. Even in a later improved form, it was by no means an impressive building. Measuring only seventy-five by thirty feet, it had a low roof, a pebble floor, no plaster on its walls, no minaret *(miʾdhanah),* no internal decoration other than a *miḥrab* and a pulpit, and was incorrectly oriented.[164] Like the congregational mosques in other *amṣār,* this one served a variety of purposes other than as a place of prayer, including council chamber, courtroom, post stage, and rest house. It appears that most, perhaps all, *khiṭāṭ* were served by *masjids,*[165] which were presumably even less pretentious buildings than the congregational mosque. Ibn Duqmāq observed that they were furnished with minarets by order of the governor from an undisclosed date, when a minaret was added to the Jāmiʿ ʿAmru.

In contrast to al-Baṣrah and al-Kūfah, each of which had its *dār al-imārah,* or house appointed for its governor, al-Fusṭāṭ may have lacked such a feature. Despite the assertion of al-Yaʿqūbī that ʿAmr erected a gubernatorial residence virtually at the founding of the settlement, al-Kindī, who spent part of his life in al-Fusṭāṭ, implied that Marwān ibn al-Ḥakam was the first to institute a regular dwelling of this kind, in 682 or soon after.[166]

Other features of the settlement that were mentioned by early chroniclers included a small public bath, the Ḥammām al-Fār, ascribed to the initiative of ʿAmr; and two others, Ḥammām Wardān and Ḥammām Buṣr ibn [Abī] Arṭah, which may have been built at any time during al-Fusṭāṭ's first twenty years. Al-Yaʿqūbī would seem to be in error when he states (p. 49 above) that ʿAmr grouped the *sūqs* of al-Fusṭāṭ round the congregational mosque (implying exclusivity), for Ibn Duqmāq mentions several scattered through the settlement whose names, such as Sūq Wardān, Sūq al-Wihāf, and Sūq Yaḥsub, imply that they dated from the inception of the camp. Perhaps al-Yaʿqūbī's statement should be taken to refer only to the main market of the settlement. Finally, as at al-Baṣrah and al-Kūfah, there were many open spaces within the confines of the encampment, notably one in front of the southeast door of the Jāmiʿ ʿAmru and another separating the al-Rāyah *khiṭāṭ* from those of the Tujīb. Others have been listed by Guest.[167]

Summarizing his investigations into the character of al-Fusṭāṭ in the time of ʿAmr, A. R. Guest writes,

> The busy commercial town described by Ibn Ḥawqal with its crowded markets and its blocks of buildings, some containing as many as two hundred people, belongs to the tenth century. This state must have been reached gradually. A long straggling colony of mean houses and hovels, or more likely of huts and booths, such as one may see nowadays attached to some town to which semi-nomad Arabs resort; arranged irregularly in groups in loose order concentrated to some extent

about the mosque of ʿAmr, as the focus formed by the centre of authority; the mosques in the various groups being practically the only constructions to be distinguished from the rest, but so insignificant as to be in no way remarkable—this is the picture that our account of al-Fusṭāṭ in the days of ʿAmr enables us to draw.[168]

The Process of Sedentarization

These words fail to take full account of the evidence for a preconceived layout of the cantonment, the real significance of the central square, and the role of principles of Arabo-Islamic precedence in the disposition of individual groups: otherwise they are not wholly inappropriate to al-Baṣrah or al-Kūfah, or, indeed, to any of the other large encampments established by the Arab armies. Nor has the urbanization process that they typified been restricted to the era of the Arab conquests. Numerous examples of similar transformations from a tribal to an urban level of sociocultural integration can be cited from later periods, and some from comparatively recent times. When, for example, Father Ohrwalder first saw the camp of the Mahdī at Omdurman in 1886, it consisted of an agglomeration of straw huts *(tokul)* surrounded by fences *(zarībah)* of jujube thorns and focusing on the mud houses of the *khalīfahs* and principal *amīrs*. The mosque consisted simply of a square enclosure surrounded by a hedge. Within two years the *tokuls* had been replaced almost entirely by mud dwellings, and the hedge round the mosque by a wall of sun-dried bricks.[169]

Still more recently H. St. J. B. Philby has described an analogous process initiated by Ibn Suʿūd in the heart of Arabia during the early twentieth century. In an attempt to induce the *badū* of Najd to abandon their nomadic ways for sedentary life, Ibn Suʿūd established a series of agrarian settlements at strategic points throughout the territory. Philby's account of these is worth quoting in extenso:

> The necessary spade-work was done by the priests and preachers sent forth by him [Ibn Suʿūd] and his father to warn the tribes of the dangers with which they were menaced by the Turks and other infidels, and to summon them to joint action in defence of their faith. Much of the seed fell on rocky ground and withered, and some fell by the wayside, with a like result; but some of it fell upon fertile soil, and the crop that grew from it was good if at first of small extent.
>
> Ibn Suʿūd was by no means discouraged by the small beginnings of a movement which might yet produce great results if it were properly husbanded; and in this year of 1912, when he had successfully countered the last menace to his immediate security, he was ready to garner in the first-fruits of his new policy. The desert wells of Arṭawiyah were selected for the honour of being the first "refuge" of the faithful, who were ready to leave their all—which was little enough, in all conscience—to follow the banner of religion. The choice of the site was probably due to the fact that the majority of the converts to the new idea were of the Muʿtayr tribe, in whose range it lay; but henceforth there was for them neither tribe nor kith nor kin, and they assumed the designation of *Ikhwān*, or "Brethren," to emphasise the link that bound them together and would extend, without distinction of tribe or class, to all who professed the same principles. The sacred law of the Sharīʿah was the sovereign authority in their community, superseding all the old customary laws of revenge and retaliation and blood-money and the rest of it, including hospitality and sanctuary. The outward and visible nucleus of the new colony was a little mosque built by the settlers themselves with the assistance of a small subsidy from Ibn Suʿūd's none too full treasury. Round this place of worship slowly and laboriously they built their little mud huts and marked out their tiny patches of ground for the equally laborious cultivation of grain for their immediate needs and young palms for the years to come, irrigating them from the neighbouring wells, which had never before been used for such a purpose. But perhaps the most attractive feature of the colony in the eyes of most of its first inhabitants was the free issue of arms and ammunition proportionate to the number of able-bodied citizens on the register of the mosque, which was also the local school, not only for the children, but primarily for the grown-ups determined to make amends for their misspent years by learning to read the Sacred Book. It was a strange hamlet, this little group of airless mud hovels housing a population which had never breathed anything but the pure desert air under the cover of the black-hair tabernacles; but slowly and steadily it grew into a village,

> and from a village to the dignity of a town, with a great circuit wall and a population reckoned now [1930] at 10,000 souls or more. Today Arṭawiyah is, as it were, the cathedral town of the Ikhwān movement, with a diocese comprising a hundred or more towns, villages and hamlets scattered over the vast desert spaces of Najd . . . the founding of Arṭawiyah may be regarded as the climax of a long and arduous process of political consolidation which ushered in an era of imperial expansion.[170]

The establishment of Arṭawiyah by Ibn Saʿūd, this latter-day Ziyād ibn Abīhi, was followed in succeeding years by the founding of similar settlements at other strategic points. At the end of 1927 Ameen (Amīn) Rihānī estimated that there were no less than seventy-three such colonies,[171] and by 1946 well over a hundred, with a total population of one hundred thousand.[172] Francisco Benet has correctly pointed out that this modern *tamṣīr,* like its ancient analogue, involved not so much the obliteration of tribal social structures as their adaptation to a new mode of life.[173]

It is evident that within the cantonments settled in the seventh century the tribal warriors involved in the conquests were allotted space based on their kinship ties and degree of Islamic precedence, the only principles of administrative subdivision practicable for the segmental communities of seventh-century Arabia. The tribal holdings were disposed irregularly, or with only partial regularity, about a religious and administrative core comprising a congregational mosque and the army commander's residence. The smallest holding was the *dār,* a plot occupied usually by one, but sometimes by several, households. It was normally of small size but in the case of *shaykhs* and other notables might amount to a large estate. The lowest self-sufficient unit within the *khiṭṭah* was the combined holdings of the so-called clan,[174] which was often provided with its own *masjid* and *sūq.* The *khiṭṭah* was mainly the holding of a tribe, and was often furnished with its own *jabbānah,* which served both as a place of assembly and a tethering ground for army mounts.

Despite the strong tribal basis of the *khiṭāṭ,* their relatively small size, coupled with their frequent inability to absorb the migrants of particular tribes that flooded into the *amṣār,* rendered them unsatisfactory as administrative units, and various attempts were made to modify their tribal structure. In al-Kūfah and al-Baṣrah these assumed the shape of formal reapportionments that combined tribal groups into roughly equal and more manageable units; in al-Fusṭāṭ the process of equalization of administrative units proceeded less formally, but the results seem to have been much the same. Perhaps the first real administrative inroad into the autonomy of the tribe was Ziyād ibn Abīhi's reorganization of the populace of al-Kūfah literally into "quarters" (p. 47 above), each of which encompassed tribal groups of opposing political persuasions; but even there tribal ties, as in the other *amṣar,* remained strong until they, and the *khiṭāṭ* with them, began seriously to erode in the Marwānid period.[175] The larger divisions, however—the "fifths," "sevenths," and "quarters"—persisted until the very end of the Umayyad period, not only as the barracks of army regiments but also as frameworks for factional loyalties.

After the *riddah* wars, Arabian society comprised, in descending order of precedence, a stratum of ruling *shaykhs*, most prominent among whom were the Quraysh; a stratum of tribesmen who had proved their devotion to Islam by joining with al-Madīnah in the conquest of Arabia;[176] and, at the bottom of the hierarchy, the Arabs who had accepted Islam reluctantly, typically after being subjugated in the *riddah* wars. All three strata ultimately came to be represented in one or other of the *amṣār.* Although old tribal privileges and prejudices died hard there, they were first softened and then, by the end of the 760s, began to be somewhat modified, perhaps in certain cases eroded.

Sedentarization had two principal effects on the structure of Arab society within the cantonments. In the first place, as we have seen, it tended in the long term to subvert tribal autonomy. In the second, it enhanced the power and prestige of the chiefly families, who not only maintained law and order in the *khiṭṭah* or quarter and commanded the tribesmen in war, but also—according to Arabian custom—participated in the informal council of tribal *shaykhs* that functioned as a channel of communication between governor and tribesmen. Membership in the *majlis* also entailed sharing in the traditional, indeed mandatory, display of generosity by the paramount *shaykh,* now installed as governor of a cantonment or a province. Such generosity typically took the form of special land grants, a largesse which over time did much to nurture an aristocracy of chiefly families, the *ashrāf* of the Umayyad period. In this way, the old customary role of *shaykhs* as *primi inter pares* was slowly being nudged toward becoming an aristocratic governing class. While individual *shaykhs* were losing political power—in al-Kūfah at any rate—under Ziyād ibn Abīhi's policy of centralization (p. 47 above), the *shaykh*ly class as a whole was accumulating economic power based on control of landed property.

Ribāṭs

A class of settlements that performed functions in some respects similar to those of the *amṣār* but on a reduced scale, and that sometimes developed into fully urban communities, were the *ribāṭs*.[177] In the context of the *tamṣīr,* this term usually connoted a fortified barracks where tribesmen in the holy war kept post for the defense of Islam and often occupied themselves with religious devotions between campaigns. Whereas those *ribāṭs* located toward the interior of conquered territories tended to emphasize their religious functions, most of those situated on the frontiers or the coast were invariably primarily military establishments. They were particularly numerous, for example, in the Ifrīqiyah, where they were established prior to the conquest of Sicily.[178] Sousse (Sūsah) was a former Byzantine city (Justinianopolis) fortified in this way by the Aghlabids in 827, and Monastir derived its name from a Christian monastery that was converted into a *ribāṭ* in the same century. Sfax and Tripoli were other cities that began as *ribāṭs* at much the same time. Another cluster of such settlements is found on the Atlantic coast of Morocco, where they served as defenses against Norman incursions. Rabāṭ (Ribāṭ al-Fatḥ) preserves in its name the memory of its origin as a fortified monastery, and Tāzah, in the northern foothills of the Middle Atlas, began as a frontier post supporting Muwaḥḥid raids into the Murābiṭ territories on the plains.

At the other end of the Islamic world, *ribāṭs* were being established until quite late times on the Jayḥūn frontier, among them Ribāṭ Afrighūn, probably founded under the earlier Sāmānids (ninth century); Ribāṭ al-Ājurr (the *ribāṭ* of baked brick) on the eastern frontier of Ṭabaristān; Ribāṭ Ḥafṣ in the same locality; Ribāṭ-i Karvān on the upper Harī Rūd; Ribāṭ-i Malik, built by Shams al-Mulk in 1078/79 on the Malik steppes, west of Karmīniyah; Ribāṭ-i Sarhang in Farghānah; Ribāṭ Ṭughānīn in the district of Bārchinlighkant; and Ribāṭ Farāv, on the frontier between Khurāsān and Dihistān.[179] The contributions of these and other *ribāṭs* to the structure of individual urban hierarchies in the Islamic world will be noted systematically in succeeding chapters and summarily in chapter 17.

Princely and Dynastic Foundations

Even though the Umayyad capital was established at Damascus (Dimashq), only Muʿāwiyah and ʿAbd al-Malik appear to have resided permanently and continuously in the city. Most of their line built relatively substantial dwellings on the fringes of the Syrian Desert whither they could retire during *rabīʿ*, the season of plenty when the steppe blossomed following the winter rains. In the beginning these desert retreats seem to have been little more than tented camps, which were subsequently replaced by palaces and even by palace complexes, some of which achieved at least proto-urban status. The majority of these structures were scattered along the southwestern edge of the Syrian Desert, and some were fortresses on the former Roman *limes* remodelled by Umayyad architects.

In al-Balqāʾ (ancient Moab), for instance, Yazīd II, son of ʿAbd al-Malik, either constructed or restored a pleasure palace known as Muwaqqar.[180] His son al-Walīd II transformed Qasṭal[181] and al-Azraq,[182] Roman fortified posts in Jordan, into desert châteaux, and built a palace known only by its modern name of al-Mshattā.[183] Other Umayyad desert complexes included Khirbat al-Mafjar, ʿAnjar, Khirbat al-Minyah, and two separate sites, both called Qaṣr al-Ḥayr; but best known of all the Umayyad desert palaces is the Quṣayr ʿAmrah, built between 712 and 715, probably by al-Walīd I, on a site east of the Jordan River at a point where it enters the Dead Sea.[184] When Yazīd III acceded to the caliphate in 744, the Umayyad treasury had been so depleted by the cost of these elaborate desert retreats that the new ruler was induced to promise that he would reside in Damascus and "lay neither stone on stone nor brick on brick . . . to build no palace."[185]

Subsequent dynasts often created entirely new capitals to symbolize the power of their kingdoms and project the glories of their achievements on a far grander scale while insulating their Arab troops from the threat of subversion by local populations. Established initially as palace complexes, these foundations often became foci for developed urban forms as populations were either attracted to the purlieus of the royal enceinte or were forcibly transported thither. Al-Saffāḥ, the first of the ʿAbbāsid caliphs (r. 749–54), set an example when he established his court successively at a series of places, each known as al-Hāshimīyah;[186] but his successor, al-Manṣūr (r. 754–75), abandoned the last of these sites for a governmental complex that he had built near a Persian village known as Baghdād.[187] This locality, on the west bank of the Tigris River near the ruins of the former Sāsānid capital of Ctesiphon (Arabic Ṭaysafūn), had already witnessed the rise and fall of that city and of the earlier metropolis of Babylon. Later authors would have us believe that when al-Manṣūr laid the foundation stone of his palace precinct in 762, he was fully prescient of the potentialities of the site. Here is the version of events preserved by al-Yaʿqūbī:

> This island, bounded on the east by the Tigris and on the west by the Euphrates, is the crossroads of the world. All the vessels that ascend the Tigris from Wāsiṭ, al-Baṣrah, al-Ubullah, al-Ahwāz, Fārs, ʿUmān, al-Yamāmah, al-Baḥrayn and beyond will anchor here. Merchandise brought down the Tigris by boat from al-Mawṣil, Diyār Rabīʿah, Ādharbayjān, and al-Armīniyah, and wares conveyed along the Euphrates from Diyār Muḍar, al-Raqqah, Syria and the marches [of Asia Minor], al-Miṣr and al-Maghrib will be unloaded here. This place will be a staging-post for the people of al-Jibāl, Iṣfahān, and the districts of Khurāsān. Praise be to Allāh who has reserved it for me and caused my predecessors to neglect it. By Allāh, I shall build here, and dwell here as long as I live, and my descendants shall dwell here after me. It will surely become the most prosperous city in the world.[188]

Baghdād

However that may be, the original precinct laid out at al-Manṣūr's command, and designated officially "The City of Peace" *(Madīnat al-Salām),* was constructed on a rigorously executed circular plan, whence it became known popularly as "The Round City" *(al-Mudawwarah).*[189] The whole complex consisted of concentric circles of double outer wall, moat, and inner wall enclosing the caliphal palace, known both as "The Golden Gate" *(Bāb al-Dhahab)* on account of its gilded entrance and as "The Green Dome" *(al-Qubbat al-Khaḍrāʾ),* from the roof structure that surmounted the audience chamber. Flanking the palace on the northeast was the great mosque. From this administrative and religious focus four highways radiated out to breach the encircling walls by means of elaborate gateways in their northeastern (Khurāsān), southeastern (al-Baṣrah), southwestern (al-Kūfah), and northwestern (Syrian) sectors. It is reported that the construction of this complex of buildings required the services of one hundred thousand craftsmen and laborers, took four years to complete, and cost 4,883,000 *dirhams*.[190] However, even before the Round City had been completed an agglomeration of artisans, laborers, and tradesmen was forming outside its walls, where, within a very few years, there developed a sprawling network of residential quarters, each with its own market, mosque, and cemetery, which ultimately reached the eastern bank of the Tigris. Shortly afterward the *sūq*s, originally housed in the outer arcades *(ṭāqāt)* of the Round City, were transferred to an extramural site in the southern suburb of al-Karkh,[191] thus further emphasizing the separation of the administrative enclave from the craft and commercial quarters of the city.

Baghdād remained the political and spiritual focus of the ʿAbbāsid Caliphate for all but a half century or so of its duration. During that period, specifically from 836 to 892, the official seat of the caliph was some sixty miles farther up the Tigris. In an attempt to escape from the threat of a popular revolt—and in recognition of the insurmountable supply and security problems posed by the juxtaposition of a Turkish army and a restless civil populace—al-Muʿtaṣim, eighth of the ʿAbbāsid caliphs, established a new capital at Sāmarrā, a site previously unoccupied except for a few monasteries and hamlets.[192] The city was extended and ornamented by his son al-Mutawakkil and seven succeeding caliphs, but abandoned in 892 when al-Muʿtaḍid restored the seat of government to Baghdād. Strictly speaking, the settlement briefly comprised two cities, for in 859/60 al-Mutawakkil extended the Shāriʿ al-Aʿẓam, the main axial thoroughfare of Sāmarrā, northward for some three *farsakh*s to reach a locality known as al-Maḥūzah, where he constructed another palace complex styled al-Jaʿfarīyah.[193] When al-Mutawakkil was murdered in his new palace in December 861, his successor "ordered the whole of the population [that had followed the Caliph thither] to leave al-Maḥūzah, to pull down the buildings and transport their materials back to Sāmarrā. . . . The palaces of al-Jaʿfarīyah, together with its houses, dwellings, and markets, rapidly fell into ruin, and the site lay waste, empty, uninhabited, as if it had never been otherwise."[194]

North Africa

With the transference of the focus of the Caliphate from Damascus east to Baghdād, the central government grew less concerned with the affairs of the western provinces, a tendency soon resulting in an inability to control powerful governors, and ultimately in a series of secessions from the empire. In the Ifrīqiyah in 800 Ibrāhīm ibn al-Aghlab established an effectively autonomous amīrate that he ruled from the palace complex of ʿAbbāsīyah, a bare two and one-half miles southeast of al-Qayrawān. In 876, however, the Aghlabids transferred the seat of government to another palace precinct in the same general locality, this time at Raqqādah, six miles from al-Qayrawān.

In the Maghrib the Idrīsids founded Fez (Fās), probably in the early ninth century,[195] at a point on the edge of the plain of Sāʾs where an easy route from the Mediterranean littoral opposite the Spanish coast to the Ṣaḥārā intersected the main latitudinal line of communication between the Atlantic Ocean and the central Maghrib. For almost two centuries the city comprised two sections, one on the right bank of the Oued Fès (Wādī Fās) and one on the left. In its early days the population of the bifurcated city was made up of Arabs attracted by the prestige of the Idrīsid lineage, Berbers drawn in from the surrounding region, and small groups of *dhimmī*s, predominantly Christians and Jews. Within a few years these were augmented by several hundred Berber families expelled from Córdoba (Qurṭubah) by al-Ḥakam I and by a substantial influx of Arabs fleeing from al-Qayrawān in the wake of popular revolts. Whereas the Andalusians installed themselves in the right-bank city, which henceforth became known as the Andalusian Bank *(ʿIdwat al-Andalus),* the Arab immigrants settled in the left-bank city, from which it gained the sobriquet of "Qarwānī Bank" *(ʿIdwat al-Qārawīyīn).*

When, during the third quarter of the tenth century, the Idrīsid state passed under the control of the Spanish Caliphate, the divided city on the Oued Fès continued to prosper. Population increased; new mosques, hostelries, and public baths were built; bridges were erected to join the two sectors; and construction extended beyond the city walls, but the two halves of the urban complex still functioned as separate entities within an at least partly integrated whole. Not until Yūsuf ibn Tāshfīn (r. 1061–1106) established the Murābiṭ (Almoravid) dynasty were the separate enclaves brought within a single unifying rampart. Under the Murābiṭ rulers and their successors of the Muwaḥḥid (Almohad) dynasty, the city received influxes of administrative functionaries, scholars, skilled craftsmen, and military officials from Spain; it was from this period that its reputation for scholarship and advanced technology derived.

When the Berber Marīnids occupied Fez in 1248, they took over, and designated as their seat of government, an already important administrative, commercial, and military node in the urban hierarchy of al-Maghrib. For a quarter of a century the Marīnid sovereigns ruled their kingdom from an administrative quarter designed for the needs of a province. In 1276, however, Abū Yūsuf laid out an entirely new governmental complex—known throughout the Marīnid period quasi-officially as "The White City" *(al-Madīnah al-Bayḍah)* but subsequently as New Fez *(Fās Jadīd)*—some 750 yards from the old city, which came to be designated colloquially as Old Fez *(Fās al-Bālī)* or, more simply, as "The City" *(al-Madīnah).* Again the capital of the state had come to comprise two separate enclaves of settlement but, whereas the ʿIdwat al-Andalus and the ʿIdwat al-Qārawīyīn had competed as rivals, Fās Jadīd and Fās al-Bālī exercised complementary functions. Old Fez remained the focus of commerce and science, and retained its former population. New Fez, by contrast, was a governmental enclave, wherein resided the sovereign and his family, dignitaries and state officials, and servitors and menials, along with two corps of the Marīnid army. Its architecture was that of palaces, mansions, mosques, and barracks, the whole complex being surrounded by a massive double rampart crowned with merlons and flanked by square towers.

Other New Foundations

As early as the mid-tenth century ʿAbd al-Raḥman III of al-Andalus (Islamic Spain) and his court moved four miles out of Córdoba to a new palace precinct at Madīnat al-Zahrā',[196] named for the caliph's favorite concubine. No effort was spared to make this new enceinte worthy of the power and prestige of the Spanish Umayyads. The walls were laid out in the Roman and Byzantine tradition, columns were brought from Rome, Carthage, and Constantinople, and it is said that a fountain decorated with human figures was also transported from this last city. But barely thirty years later, in 981, the Ḥājib al-Manṣūr bi-Allāh[197] abandoned Madīnat al-Zahrā', transferring both the court and the central secretariat, which had remained till then in the Umayyad palace at Córdoba, to yet another new governmental precinct situated to the east of that city and styled al-Madīnah al-Zāhirah ("The Brilliant City").[198] Both these administrative complexes were sacked during the Berber revolt that broke out in 1010, the latter being completely razed. Half a century later Marrākush was founded as the capital of a Murābiṭ kingdom that subsumed both al-Andalus and al-Maghrib.[199]

Meanwhile, farther east the Fāṭimid *imām* ʿUbaydullāh al-Mahdī abandoned the old Aghlabid governmental precinct of Raqqādah in 920 to reside in a new capital that he founded on the Tunisian coast, and which he styled al-Mahdīyah.[200] Then, in 948/49, the capital was transferred to a new governmental complex, on the outskirts of al-Qayrawān, which received the honorific title of al-Manṣūrīyah. In 969 the center of Fāṭimid power shifted to Egypt, where Jawhar al-Ṣiqillī laid out a governmental precinct some two miles outside al-Fusṭāṭ. He styled it al-Qāhirah ("The Triumphant"), and in 973 officially constituted it the capital of the Fāṭimids. But for long the new city was reserved for the caliph, his entourage, government officials, and troops. The Cairo Geniza documents reveal that the initial distinction between the stiff protocol of court conduct in the administrative city and the more expansive way of life of the middle classes in the old city of al-Fusṭāṭ was still evident in the twelfth century,[201] and the Maghribī traveller Ibn Saʿīd commented on the differing lifestyles of the two cities as late as the middle decades of the thirteenth century.

We shall have more to say about the manner in which these and other princely foundations were integrated into the urban systems of the Islamic world in subsequent chapters.

Spontaneously Generated Cities

Scattered among the camps and barracks and princely seats, many of which ultimately developed fully urban functions, and all encompassed within a preexisting hierarchy of urban forms often of great antiquity, was a smaller number of specifically Islamic cities that grew up under, but without the specific intervention of, authority. Most of these developed around sanctuaries of some sort. Although the veneration of saints has no Qur'ānic sanction, and indeed only received the approval of the *ʿulamā'* (sing. *ʿālim*) in the tenth century, the divine blessing *(barakah)* of a prophet's tomb or the shrine of a saint had, from pre-Islamic times, exercised a powerful attraction for popular piety. What the Maghribī *faqīh* Ibn al-Ḥājj advocated in the fourteenth century had been believed and practiced by innumerable Believers in earlier times:

> It is needful [for the believer] not to be remiss in visiting the saints and the pious elect *(al-awliyā' wa-l-ṣāliḥīn)*, by whose sight Allāh revives dead hearts even as He revives the earth through heavy rain. Through [the saints] hardened hearts come to be at ease and difficult matters become simple. For [the saints] are standing at the door of the Generous Benefactor *(al-Karīm al-Mannān)*. So none who seeks them out will be rejected, and none who keeps their company *(mujālisu-hum)*, or seeks their acquaintance *(muʿārifu-hum)*, or cleaves to them, will be disappointed, for they are the gateway to God that stands open to His servants. And he that is of this kind would go forth to see them and obtain their blessing for, by seeing some of them, he would acquire such understanding, vigilance, and like [gifts] as no one could describe.[202]

Prominent among the cities that crystallized around the nuclei of shrines were the two ʿIrāqī centers of Shīʿism, Karbalā' and al-Najaf. The first of these, situated on the edge of the Western Desert some fifty-five miles south-southwest of Baghdād, developed around the tomb of al-Ḥusayn, second son of the Rāshidūn caliph ʿAlī and arch-saint and martyr of the Shīʿah community. Although in 850 the caliph al-Mutawakkil destroyed the original shrine, it was resuscitated on a magnificent scale in 979 by the Buwayhid *amīr* ʿAḍud al-Dawlah. By the fourteenth century it had become the focus of a fully urban community some twenty-four hundred paces in circuit.

The second of these sacred cities, al-Najaf, developed around the tomb where ʿAlī himself, the unwitting founder of the Shīʿah movement, was interred. Tradition asserts that the precise location, an uninhabited spot not far from al-Kūfah, was kept secret until rediscovered by the caliph Hārūn al-Rashīd in 791.[203] However that may be, it was the Shīʿite Buwayhids who in the tenth century refurbished the shrine and accorded it such honor that a small urban community arose nearby. Under the Īl-Khāns of Persia in the thirteenth century, and during the revival of Persian influence in the Ottoman period, the town grew considerably and, despite frequent raids by Sunnī *badū*, has survived into the modern world as an important focus of Shīʿite Islam.

A shrine that eventually gave rise to the fourth-largest city of modern Īrān was that associated with the alleged martyrdom in 817 of ʿAlī al-Riḍā, son-in-law of the caliph al-Ma'mūn, in the village of Sanābādh. His tomb became an object of pilgrimage, and the city that grew up around it assumed the name of Mashhad ("Place of Martyrdom"). Although the shrine was damaged in the tenth century, by the Mongols in 1220, and subsequently by Turkoman and Uzbeg invaders, its *barakah* never diminished. In the seventeenth century the Ṣafawid *shāh* ʿAbbās (r. 1587–1629) enhanced its reputation in an effort to discourage pilgrimages to shrines under the control of Sunnī Turks. Subsequently Nādir Shāh (r. 1736–47) constituted the city, then reported to have a population of two hundred thousand or more, as his capital. During the second half of the eighteenth century Mashhad's population declined to a bare twenty thousand as a result of Uzbeg raids, but its fortunes were finally restored under the Qājār dynasty, especially during the reign of Fatḥ ʿAlī (1797–1834).

The role of shrine cities such as these in the Islamic urban hierarchies of the tenth century will be discussed in subsequent chapters.

Cities Modified by Muslim Occupation

The great majority of cities within the Middle East were neither "created" de novo nor generated spontaneously, but were preexisting urban forms adapted to, and progressively modified by, Muslim occupation. When the Arab armies surged out of Arabia into the Levant, they found themselves in one of the most highly urbanized areas of the medieval world. At first they avoided the large urban centers such as Damascus, Antioch, Ḥimṣ, and Jerusalem, which as a consequence remained predominantly Christian during the first century of the Islamic era. They settled instead in the smaller cities of the desert borderlands such as Tadmur (Palmyra), al-Ruṣāfah, Khunāṣirah, and Ḥūwārīn.[204] On the eastern flank of the Fertile Crescent and in North Africa the Arabs initially eschewed existing cities altogether, as we have seen, and congregated in camps. But ultimately they and their Muslim converts did come to comprise the majority of urban dwellers in most of the territories they conquered, and to impose on cities, new and old alike, a distinctively Islamic governmental imprint.[205]

In the former Greek and Roman territories the imposition of this imprint often involved the gradual transformation of an orthogonal grid layout into a centripetally organized aggregation of quarters, of "la ville antique romaine d'allure ouverte, régulière et bien dessinée" into "une ville musulmane aux voies tortueuses et compliquées à allure parfois de labyrinthes aux demeures claquemurées, qui se complaît aux culs de sac, aux replis d'ombre, aux coins secrets."[206] In the words of Gustave von Grünebaum,

> The ancient political interest in the community, the classical ideals of city-oneness and of the clarity of the architectural (and administrative) design have been replaced by . . . ideals of quarter or group loyalty, by the desire to shield the family group from dispersal and contamination, and by the concept of government as an outside agency with which one no longer identifies but which one rather wishes to keep at arm's length from the spheres of one's personal and familiar life.[207]

As a matter of fact the orthogonal design may not have been invariably of Hellenistic or Roman origin. Nikita Elisséeff suggests that the geometrical regularity of the plan of, for instance, Damascus may have had a pre-Hellenistic, Aramaean provenance.[208] In any case the dissolution of the Hellenistic grid pattern had begun in many cities during the Byzantine era, sometimes as early as the second century A.D. And it is probable that the quarters (sing. *ḥārah*) of the developed Islamic city may occasionally have owed something to parochial organizations in the Byzantine city.[209]

Nevertheless, it is generally true that the Hellenistic grid of numerous Middle Eastern cities, whether already rendered partially ineffective in Byzantine times, was essentially erased in Islamic times by the formation of economically and religiously autonomous quarters, each with its own mosque, public bath, water supply, bakery, and local market. Moreover, although the tolerance of Shāfiʿite and Ḥanafite legislation was a positive inducement to the private encroachments that at first dislocated, and ultimately obliterated, the clarity of the reticulate design (only Ḥanbalite custom stipulated that permission to encroach on the public way be obtained from an appropriate authority),[210] city walls usually continued to delimit effectively the same space as had previously been defined by orthogonal coordinates. Frequently there was, too, considerable continuity in the broader patterns of land use within the city, as manifested, for example, in the persistence of sanctuary sites,[211] rampart alignments, market installations, and craft localizations.

In the former Sāsānian territories the Arabs encountered urban layouts entirely different from those of the Greek world. In these realms the nucleus of the city comprised a walled enclosure, the *shahristān* ("place of power"), part of which typically was occupied by a citadel *(diz)*. Essentially the *shahristān* was a governmental enclave somewhat similar in function to the palace precincts of the princely seats founded by Arab rulers. Below its walls, in an area known as the *bīrūn*,[212] clustered the dwellings of the populace, interspersed with markets *(bāzār)*[213] and other service facilities, both economic and social. Not infrequently the *bīrūn* was enclosed within a second and outer wall, so that the city as a whole assumed a form commonly encountered in all the main realms of nuclear urbanism, namely that of a walled enceinte within which the offices of government and the dwellings of the élite were insulated from the activities and habitations of the populace by enclosure within an inner walled precinct.[214] Under Muslim occupation the exclusiveness of the *shahristān* tended to be broken down, and the focus of city life often migrated to the former suburbs, not least because the principal mosque was often sited on the main crossroads of the *bīrūn*. In these Persian and Turkestānian cities, quarters on the Islamic pattern already existed; these were simply adapted to Muslim purposes, with the *sūqs* tending to follow the lines of the main streets.

*

During the first three or four centuries after the *Hijrah* the urban hierarchies of southwest Asia and North Africa were both augmented by incorporation of the several classes of "created" cities described above and transmuted into systems of urban forms. These forms expressed in their political, social, and economic organization the norms and values of diverse modes of Islamic civilization. It is with a discussion of these systems of cities as they existed through the tenth century that chapters 4 through 16 will be principally concerned.

Chapter Three
Preliminaries

This chapter has been compiled for the especial benefit of those who would like to acquire a knowledge of the metropoleis *(amṣār)* of the Muslims and of the districts into which the several provinces are divided, and who wish to become acquainted with the number of the provincial capitals *(qaṣabāt)* and their [district] towns *(mudun)*. . . . I have in consequence . . . written it compendiously and in straightforward language, eschewing prolixity.

—Abū ʿAbd Allāh Muḥammad ibn Aḥmad al-Maqdisī, *Aḥsan al-Taqāsīm fī Maʿrifat al-Aqālīm* (985–86) (Berlin recension only), translated from M. J. de Goeje's edition in *Bibliotheca Geographorum Arabicorum,* vol. 3 (Lugduni Batavorum, 1906), 47.

The Concept of the Urban System

A city comprises a set of functionally interrelated social, political, administrative, economic, cultural, religious, and other institutions located in close proximity in order to exploit scale economies. A group of such institutional sets, together with their attributes and mutual relationships, constitutes an urban system, an arrangement in which the concurrent operation of agglomerative tendencies and accessibility factors tends to induce a hierarchical arrangement of the constituent parts. Although both the horizontal (or spatial) and the vertical (or organizational) components of this hierarchy have been the subject of much research during the past half century, a unitary theory capable of accommodating the generation and relative dispositions of all the constituent elements has yet to be devised. And if this is the situation in the modern world with its plenitude of data, it is even more true of the Islamic world in the tenth century, for which the available information is vastly more meager.

Many of the analytical techniques and models employed by scholars studying settlement hierarchies depend for their effectiveness on the deployment of large quantities of data that are almost invariably processed with the aid of digital computers. Certainly this is the case with the more sophisticated techniques of analysis, a circumstance that inevitably renders them inapplicable to the urban systems of the Middle East a millennium or more ago, for which the evidence is fragmented, far from uniform, and to be prized only with difficulty from texts that are intractable and invariably defective for the purpose at hand. This means, of course, that the following discussion can only be cast effectively in qualitative, as opposed to quantitative, terms.

The pattern of settlement in a region typically consists of three analytically, though not always functionally, distinct components:

1. A relatively uniform spread of settlements, each of which offers a range of goods and services to a surrounding territory, and which consequently is termed in the relevant literature as a "central place."
2. A lineally deployed component arising from the provision of freight-handling and allied services disposed along transportation routes. Not only does the transference of goods from one mode of transport to another afford convenient opportunities for processing of commodities to take place, but also such points of transshipment inevitably tend to generate auxiliary services such as repackaging, storing, and sorting. Such transport foci may be modally, and often centrally, situated within an almost entirely homogeneous region, or, equally frequently, may function as links between contrasting regions.
3. A clustered component comprising urban centers engaged in specialized activities that may range from

mining and manufacturing to the provision of recreational and religious facilities. As the principal localizing factor is a particular resource such as a mineral deposit, access to some form of industrial power or fuel, a favored stretch of coast, or the existence of a shrine, such cities may occur singly or in clusters, reflecting the spatial distribution of the resource. As in the case of the transport foci mentioned above, exploitation of a resource of whatever kind tends to induce the development of a constellation of satellite services and industries.[1]

The Spatial Expression of the Settlement System

As was pointed out earlier, no model constructed thus far comprehends satisfactorily both the causation and the relative locations of these three elements in settlement patterns. Considerable progress has been made, however, in elucidating the arrangement of one component, namely the central-place network, but only under certain rather restrictive conditions.

The foundations of Central-Place Theory were laid in 1933 by the German geographer Walter Christaller with the publication of his book *Die zentralen Orte in Süddeutschland.*[2] On the basis of the fundamental spatial concept of the range of a good, and using strictly economic arguments, Christaller was able to define an optimal spatial arrangement for a hierarchy of retail centers developed on a postulated isotropic surface.[3] Under these conditions settlements are, ideally, regularly spaced to form a triangular lattice, and, again ideally, centrally located within hexagonally shaped market areas—this shape requiring the least average travel distance to the central settlement.

The hierarchical dimension in this pattern arises from the assumption that higher-order central places supply all the goods and services offered by lower-order central places, together with a number of higher-order goods and services distinctive to themselves. Consequently, higher-order central places provide wider ranges of goods and services, are loci of larger clusters of retail and service establishments, house more people, serve more extensive market areas and larger populations, and engage in greater volumes of business than do lower-order central places. It follows that this hierarchical arrangement is expressed spatially in higher-order central places that are more widely spaced than lower-order central places, and in lower-order central places "nesting" within the market areas of higher-order central places according to a definite rule. The whole hierarchical system is then integrated with, and given coherence by, an interconnected set of regional and national *metropoleis.*[4]

The difficulty in applying Central-Place Theory to settlement patterns in the distant past—or even, in some instances, the not-so-distant past—is that it is derived from a theory of retail demand of an essentially modern type. Yet there is no doubt that something approaching contemporary, and even more so nineteenth-century, retailing and sevicing occurred widely in tenth-century Middle Eastern cities. Bazaar exchanges (as distinct from reciprocative, redistributive, mobilizative, and long-distance wholesaling transactions) were an integral part of both urban and rural life long before the advent of Islam and have continued down to the present. Traditionally, however, they have been so embedded in a distinctive cultural nexus of noneconomic institutions that they have constituted essentially an open system subject to pressures generated outside the sphere of demand, cost, and price. Under these conditions, in Karl Polanyi's succinct phrases of forty years ago, "In so far as exchange at a set rate is in question, the economy is integrated by the factors which fix that rate, not by the market mechanism."[5] In short, the prevailing system of market transactions in the early Islamic world often lacked the institutional autonomy assumed by Christaller and his successors; or, as central-place theorists are wont to phrase it, the location of tertiary economic activity in such circumstances is best regarded as an economic process to which certain noneconomic functions contribute a "noise" or "error-term" element.[6]

For these and other reasons, it is of more than passing interest that J. H. Kolb and E. de S. Brunner have proposed an alternative, though less thoroughly elaborated, model of market center distribution in which the influence of size on location induces a clustering of settlements.[7] In this model, major towns are located more or less centrally in relation to minor towns, which are spaced around the perimeters of their spheres of influence; villages are arrayed around the circumferences of the trade areas of minor towns. This cluster hypothesis is more flexible than the regular-lattice model in that it specifies neither distances nor directions. In addition, it is in accord with certain other models of spatial interaction, notably those known respectively as the Law of Retail Gravitation[8] and the Proportional Range of Influence,[9] both of which imply that smaller central places are likely to arise nearer to each other than to large clusters. Kolb and de Brunner recognized three main tributary zones surrounding the urban settlements that they studied: (1) a narrow primary zone of personal service (which, incidentally, was not distinguishable around the larger cities); (2) a secondary service zone, which served as the generalized trade area for most goods and services supplied by the town; and (3) a specialized service zone, which was not present in the smaller, unspecialized urban settlements. The urban centers associated with this hierarchy were apportioned among five main types according to population size.

Such testimony as empirical studies have provided for the validity of the cluster hypothesis is ambivalent, although a statistically significant relationship between city size and spacing clearly exists.[10] In the most sophisticated investigation of this problem undertaken so far, Leslie King could do little more than conclude that the relationship between city size and spacing in the United States is considerably more complex than that envisaged in the regular-cluster model. A multiple regression analysis of a sample of two hundred towns appeared to indicate that spacing is in fact a complex function of the sizes of cities, their occupational structures, and the physiographic character of the region in which they are situated—a conclusion neither unexpected nor particularly informative.[11] For the Islamic world in the tenth century, inadequate evidence prevents a thorough evaluation of the applicability of these competing models, although there are indications in the data from the Maghrib, al-Yaman, and the Sayḥūn Provinces that they might be more assimilable to the cluster hypothesis than to the regular-lattice formulation. In the following discussions of Islamic urban systems the term *central place* will be used to denote any component in a regional network of centers furnishing basic goods and services to surrounding areas without implying the precise nature of the urban system involved.

Parenthetically, it may be noted that a primitive notion of central-place hierarchy, and perhaps even more of a clustered arrangement of settlement units, have not been entirely alien to Islamic thought. As early as the tenth century the lexicographer Abū Manṣūr al-Azharī observed in his *Tahdhīb al-Lughah* that "Every city is the mother *(umm)* of the settlements around it."[12] However, this insight—if indeed it were that—remained an undeveloped maxim without theoretical implication. Of al-Maqdisī, who developed the notion of a hierarchical arrangement of Middle Eastern cities in the second half of the tenth century, much will be said later in this chapter.

The Vertical Organization of the Settlement Hierarchy

It is readily observable that the smaller urban centers in a region greatly outnumber the larger ones. Discussion of this topic has focused principally on the question as to whether the settlements are disposed in an orderly manner among size categories, as is implicit in Christaller's schema, or, alternatively, ranged along a continuum. The latter distribution, which can be adapted to various explanatory hypotheses, has been generalized by G. K. Zipf as the Rank-Size Rule.[13] Simply stated, this means that the size of the *n*th city in the hierarchy approximates one-*n*th the size of the largest city. The distribution underlying this rule can be regarded as lognormal and is often said to obey the Law of Proportionate Effect, according to which all cities of a given size are deemed to have an equal probability of growing at the same rate. Although the rule is essentially an empirical finding rather than a theoretical proposition, M. J. Beckmann has shown that, with the addition of a random variable, the discrete size categories of Christaller's hierarchy merge into a virtual rank-size distribution.[14]

The precise significance of the several modes of city-size distribution remains somewhat debatable, but H. A. Simon's suggestion that lognormal distributions are generated as limiting cases by some stochastic growth process has gained considerable favor.[15] In testing the hypothesis for the distribution of city sizes in the state of Washington, U.S.A., Berry and Garrison found a reasonably close agreement between observed and predicted frequency distributions.[16] Berry has subsequently argued that rank-size (lognormal) distributions are typical of territorially extensive countries with long traditions of urbanism in economically and politically complex contexts. By contrast, primate distributions, in which a deep stratum of small urban forms is dominated by one or more very large cities, are allegedly characteristic of recently urbanized small countries possessing relatively simple political and economic institutions.[17] And, as will become abundantly evident in succeeding sections of this work, metropolitan primacy, in which the largest city (usually the capital) was much larger than any other urban center in a regional hierarchy and exceptionally expressive of that region's capacity and sentiment, was by no means unknown to the Middle East in the tenth century.

Primary Sources for the Study of Tenth-Century Middle Eastern Urban Systems

By the tenth century the components of the Middle Eastern urban system had evolved into about a dozen more or less internally coherent hierarchies. Īrānian, Hellenistic, Latin, and other urban patterns had been transformed by the Arab occupation and augmented with new Arab foundations, and all had come to manifest to a greater or lesser degree the imprint of Islam. Yet before this transmutation had been effected, the unity of the Islamic world itself, ironically, no longer existed. Al-Andalus (Islamic Spain) had defected as early as 756, al-Maghrib in 788, al-Ifrīqīyah (Tunisia and western Libya) in 800, and Egypt in 868. In eastern Persia the Ṭāhirids ruled as hereditary governors from 822 to 873, to be followed by the Ṣaffārids (867–908) and the Sāmānids (892–999). In al-Yaman power was in the hands of the independent Zaydite dynasty, while in the northern Levant *badū* ideals had undergone an ephemeral but brilliant renaissance under the Ḥamdānids. In ʿIrāq the caliphs, already reduced to mere puppets of their ministers and military commanders, ceded political power to the Persian Buwayhids in 945, and the great office of Vicegerent of Allāh—the style that had supplanted the original, more modest Vicegerent of the Messenger of Allāh—survived only as a source of legal authority for the rule of a schismatic Commander of Commanders *(Amīr al-Umarāʾ)* in a capital located no longer at Baghdād but at Shīrāz in Fars.

After the ferment of the later Umayyad and earlier ʿAbbāsid periods, technological progress and economic development had practically ceased, so that the urban system had acquired a relatively static quality it had not possessed since the inauguration of the Arab *tamṣīr* in the seventh century. Consequently the second half of the tenth century affords a convenient opportunity to assess urban development at the close of its formative phase. This phase was, incidentally, midway through the course of the greatest of all Arab dynasties, during a period that Adam Mez once designated "the Renaissance of Islam,"[18] and just before the onset of the foreign invasions that, from the eleventh century onward, were progressively to transform the cultural and political bases of city life. In Europe the retreat of Islam before the forces of Christianity in Spain and Sicily was only part of a far-spreading wave of Western conquest that culminated in the twelfth century in the establishment of Crusader principalities in the Levant. At the same time, in the east the frontiers that had remained inviolate virtually since Umayyad times were crumbling before an invasion of more lasting moment than that of the Cross, namely the incursions of Saljūq Turks from Central Asia. First entering the territories of the caliphate in about 970, these warrior tribesmen soon overran the greater part of the Īrānian provinces. In 1055 they occupied Baghdād itself, thereby ushering in an era of Turkish dominance over the heartland of the Arab world that was to survive into the twentieth century.

Al-Maqdisī

The framework for the construction of the urban system depicted in figure 2 (see p. 74) is based on the great work of al-Maqdisī[19] entitled, in what is thought to be the oldest manuscript, *Aḥsan al-Taqāsīm fī Maʿrifat al-Aqālīm.*[20] This author was, as his *nisbah* implies, a native of Jerusalem, where he was born probably toward the middle of the tenth century; internal evidence in his book indicates that he lived until at least the last decade of that century. Al-Maqdisī's work testifies not only to a fairly thorough literary and legal training, but also to a continuing interest in the aesthetics (but not the technical engineering aspects) of architecture, possibly fostered by his paternal grandfather Abū Bakr, an architect who had constructed the maritime defenses of ʿAkkā for Ibn Ṭūlūn, at that time ruler of Egypt.[21]

M. J. de Goeje's standard edition of the text of the *Aḥsan*[22] is founded on two manuscripts preserved respectively in Berlin (MS. Sprenger 5: Ahlwardt. no. 6034) and Istanbul (Aya Sofia, no. 2971 [bis]). The latter, known conventionally as the C(onstantinopolitanum) recension, is slightly shorter than the B(erolinense) version, which inclined de Goeje to consider it the earlier document.[23] If this were indeed so, then certain internal orientations in the two manuscripts would seem to imply a shift in al-Maqdisī's political sympathies from the Sāmānids of Khurāsān and Mā Warā' al-Nahr (Transoxania) to the Fāṭimids of Egypt. Two other manuscripts, the Leyden (Cod. Or. 2063) and a second Berlin (Cat. Ahlwardt. no. 6033), are later than those used by de Goeje, the former being a relatively recent copy of the Constantinople, and the latter a poor copy of the Ahlwardt no. 6034. André Miquel suggests that the varying titles in different recensions and references (compare note 20) imply the previous circulation of abridged versions, contemporaneous with the master text and probably prepared by al-Maqdisī himself to serve as handy vade mecums for members of the governing class and administrators. He concludes, not unreasonably, that the Constantinople and Berlin recensions are probably different combinations of an original complete text and one or more abridgments.[24] These more ancient manuscripts, probably dating from the last two decades of the tenth century, incorporate maps of the "provinces" *(aqālīm)* into which al-Maqdisī divided the Islamic world, and to which he himself refers early in his book, but they are not reproduced in de Goeje's edition. A few of his maps are, however, readily accessible in Konrad Miller's compendium of Arab cartography.[25] It is evident in this work that the maps are derived almost exclusively from the Balkhī-Iṣṭakhrī corpus (Miller's "Islam-Atlas"), which we will discuss later in the chapter; schematic and without scale, they are simply sketches illustrating the written text.

The text itself continues a tradition already developed by al-Balkhī, al-Iṣṭakhrī, and Ibn Ḥawqal, but generally speaking expands the amount of detail comprehended within this conventional framework. Al-Maqdisī states it as his purpose to "focus on a branch of knowledge hitherto treated only imperfectly, namely the description of the provinces of the Islamic domain *(mamlakat al-Islam)*" (1).[26] According to his own exordium, he undertook rigorous and protracted preparations for this task:

> I did not undertake the task of compilation until I had travelled through the [various] Islāmic lands, roaming from country to country; had discoursed with the learned and waited on princes; had conversed with *qāḍīs* and studied under doctors of the law; had consorted with men of letters, reciters [of the *Qur'ān*], and transmitters of *aḥādīth;* had engaged in familiar intercourse with ascetics and mystics; and had listened in the audiences of popular story-tellers *(quṣṣāṣ)* and of public preachers *(mudhakkirūn)*. It was my custom, moreover, to engage in trade everywhere I went, and to associate with people of all classes. Everywhere I paid close attention to matters of commerce until I came to understand the principles of that art. I became thoroughly acquainted with the provinces by measuring them in *farsakhs;* I perambulated the frontiers and established their limits; I familiarized myself with military districts *(ajnād)* by visiting them; I investigated religious sects and came to know them well; I duly noted and classified both dialects and complexions; and I have reflected on the character of districts. I also examined revenue receipts and estimated their yields, and similarly inquired into the quality of the air [i.e., climate] and the water resources [i.e., hydrology]. To this end I necessarily endured severe privations and incurred great expense, pursuing always what was legitimate and avoiding what was sinful,[27] and exerting every effort to warn the Muslims of the Reckoning [to come], while reconciling myself to humiliation and absence from my country and friends, [yet] observing the laws of Allāh and standing in fear of Him.[28]

It is more than likely that in this passage al-Maqdisī was idealizing his experiences and ascribing a sustained intellectual purpose to what were in fact the random experiences of his life. But he had certainly travelled extensively—probably to all the Islamic territories except al-Andalus, East Africa, and al-Sind (now a province of Pakistan)—and acquired considerable erudition in his chosen field. Where his information can be checked against independently derived evidence, it usually proves to be substantially correct. Presumably he reports accurately when he writes that he did not venture to publish his book until "I had attained maturity, had visited all parts of the Islamic world, and had attended upon men of science and religion. It was completed in the metropolis *(miṣr)* of Fārs [that is, Shīrāz] in the reign of the Commander of the Faithful Abū Bakr ʿAbd al-Karīm al-Ṭā'iʿ li-llāh[29] and in that of Abū Manṣūr Nizār al-ʿAzīz bi-llāh,[30] Commander of the Faithful in the western realms, in the year 375 A.H. [A.D. 985]" (8–9).[31] If this were the case, then the text must have been occasionally amended and expanded, for both the Berlin and Constantinople recensions incorporate information datable to the close of the tenth century.

As mentioned earlier, al-Maqdisī worked within the framework of a preexisting geographical tradition. This was the so-called Balkhī school of Islamic geography and cartography, so designated after its earliest important figure, Abū Zayd Aḥmad ibn Sahl al-Balkhī (ca. 850–934).[32] Al-Balkhī's work has long been lost but appears to have taken the form of brief annotations to the twenty sections of a map depicting the Dār al-Islam, possibly a map similar to that compiled by the Khurāsānī astronomer Abū Jaʿfar al-Khāzin.[33] Writers of the Balkhī school gave what has been called "a positive Islamic colouring" to their topographical descriptions.[34] They not only restricted their coverage to the Dār al-Islam but also emphasized such topographical ideas as occurred in the Qur'ān or the Tradition. Furthermore, they rejected both the Īrānian *kishwar* and the strict Greek *klimata* systems of subdivisions, favoring derived territorial units *(aqālīm;* sing. *iqlīm)* that they generally treated as domains of autonomous political power influenced only slightly by physiographic constraints. Balkhī geographers also assigned Arabia, the "Peninsula of the Arabs," as they called it, the preeminent position within the Islamic world by virtue of its role in the working out of God's plan for humanity, and consequently placed it at the head of their expositions.

As we shall see, al-Maqdisī expanded the scope of the Balkhī approach and formalized its exposition, thereby constituting himself as the master geographer of his age.[35] But his extraordinary achievement in formulating a new human geography in which general propositions were sought in manifestations of local diversity is not our prime interest here. Rather, we are concerned with his treatment of the urban systems in the Islamic world. Of course, other authors, both within and without the Balkhī school, had described the principal settlements of whatever subdivisions they had employed. Ibn al-Faqīh, al-Yaʿqūbī, Ibn Khurradādhbih, Ibn Rustah, and al-Masʿūdī, all to be classed with the so-called ʿIrāqī school, had listed and commented on at least some aspects of the cities of Islam and occasionally some within the Dār al-Ḥarb. Al-Iṣṭakhrī, eminent in the Balkhī tradition, had emphasized the role of the more important cities in twenty *iqlīms* at the expense of addressing the physiographic features such as mountains, seas, and rivers that had figured prominently in earlier topographical treatises. Of this author Miquel writes, "Quand il annonce son intention de parler villes, c'est en réalité tout le chapitre de la géographie humaine qu'Iṣṭa<u>h</u>rī entame par ce mot, si grand, si ambitieux que l'ensemble de la description de la province vient se regrouper autour de lui."[36]

In the *Aḥsan,* al-Maqdisī carried this principle to the point where his fourteen *iqlīms* became functional (as opposed to formal) urban regions. More clearly than any other early Muslim geographer—indeed, more clearly than any other Muslim student of the city before Ibn Khaldūn—al-Maqdisī recognized the city as the locale in which the essential properties of larger systems of social relations are concentrated and intensified. With only three exceptions, his *iqlīms* comprised structured systems of hierarchically ordered spatial interaction focused on a metropolis. No writer before his time had treated the urban network consistently as a system. Al-Maqdisī's exposition of the spatial and hierarchical arrangement of urban forms in the culture realm of tenth-century Islam, a zone up to two thousand miles wide extending for nearly a quarter of the way around the earth, must rank as one of the most ambitious studies of human organization ever attempted in the medieval world. Nor was it to be repeated for almost a millennium. The topographers and scholars who worked within the Islamic geographical tradition right down to modern times never reached the level of abstraction represented by al-Maqdisī's discussion of the urban hierarchy. Even the incomparable Ibn Khaldūn (1332–1406), whose primary aim was to elicit from the flux of events the internal *(bāṭin)* rational structure that gave form and meaning to external *(ẓāhir)* manifestations, paid relatively little attention to the spatial expression of the institutions whose nature and evolution he was investigating.[37] We shall have more to say about al-Maqdisī's urban systems later in this chapter.

Al-Maqdisī's Sources

Direct Observation

Al-Maqdisī was quite explicit about the sources of information on which he based his constructions.[38] Most fundamental to his enterprise was direct personal observation *(ʿiyān),* and he had seen much. His own, no doubt idealized, summary of his experiences from one end of the Islamic world to the other runs as follows:

> I have had my share of all that commonly befalls a traveller, except for begging and falling into grievous sin. I have studied law and literature, practised asceticism and piety, taught [in my turn] law and literature, preached from pulpits, uttered the call to prayer from minarets, officiated as an *imām* in *masjids*, preached in cathedral-mosques, frequented schools, enunciated prayers in convocations, spoken in councils, supped on *harīsah*[39] with Ṣūfīs, on *tharīdah*[40] with monks, and on *ʿaṣīdah*[41] with seamen. I have been driven from mosques in the night, wandered in empty wastes, and lost my way in deserts. At times, I have been scrupulously pious, at others I have partaken of the forbidden foods. I have mixed with the devotees on the mountain of Lubnān[42] and not infrequently have associated with persons in authority. I have [both] owned slaves and [had to] carry things in a basket on my own head. On several occasions I came close to drowning and a number of times my caravan was waylaid. I have been in the service of *qāḍīs* and notables, have conversed with rulers and ministers, kept company on the road with rogues, chaffered in markets, been confined in prison and accused of spying. I have seen the warships of Rūm in battle and heard the sound of *nawāqīs*[43] in the night. I have earned my keep as a binder of books *(al-mujallid)*, bought my water with songs,[44] ridden in litters[45] and on horseback, and marched through *samūm*[46] and snow. I have lodged [both] among noblemen at the courts of royalty and among the vulgar in weavers' quarters.[47] Power and honour I have known, yet my death has been plotted more than once. I have undertaken the Greater Pilgrimage and relied on the hospitality of mosques. I have taken part in military forays and served in frontier posts (sing. = *ribāṭ*), have drunk *sawīq*[48] at the public drinking places in Makkah, have subsisted on bread and chick-peas in monasteries,[49] have had to rely on the hospitality of Ibrāhīm, the Friend [of God],[50] and on the eleemosynary sycamore figs of ʿAsqalān. I have been invested with robes of honour by kings, who conferred gifts upon me, [yet] on numerous occasions I have [also] been destitute and without [proper] clothes. I have corresponded with rulers, been reproved by members of the nobility, asked to administer religious endowments *(awqāf)*,[51] and humbled myself before the dissolute. I have been charged with innovation[52] and accused of greed, [yet] *amīrs* and *qāḍīs* have made me their confidential assistant.[53] I have been made an executor of wills and appointed a comptroller. I have encountered [both] cutpurses and *ʿayyārūn* fraternities,[54] have been persecuted by scoundrels, opposed by those who envied me, and slandered to the authorities. I have visited the baths of Ṭabarīyah[55] and the fortresses of Fārs *(al-qilāʿ al-Fārisīyah)*;[56] and I have seen the Festival of the Fountain *(al-Fawwārah)*[57] and the Feast of [Saint] Barbārah,[58] as well as the Well of Buḍāʿah[59] and the castle of Yaʿqūb and his lands[60] [Here the Constantinople MS adds: as well as the Mihrajān, the Sadhah, the Nayrūz (i.e., Nawrūz) and its marvels in ʿAdan, and the Feast of Mār Sarjah][61]. . . . It has been my custom when passing on the highway by a town no more than 10 *farsakhs* distant to leave the caravan and hasten toward that town so that I might familiarize myself with it. Not infrequently, I hired a party of men to accompany me and travelled by night so that, though vexed and out of pocket, I could yet rejoin my companions at the appointed time.[62]

Al-Maqdisī's passion for *ʿiyān,* the lived experience, manifests itself on page after page of the *Aḥsan* and is not wholly alien to the miscellanea of general information in the *adab* writings of earlier authors such as Ibn al-Faqīh and, of course, al-Jāḥiẓ. In addition, it was not only subordinated to the rational ordering principle of the *iqlīm,* but also supplemented by expediential devices adopted from the schools of jurisprudence, specifically *istiḥsān* (discretionary opinion, equitable preference), *qiyās* (analogical deduction), and *taʿāruf* (conventional usage). *Istiḥsān* was, and is, an important supplementary source of law in the legal theory of Abū Ḥanīfah, whom al-Maqdisī praises as "the prince of jurisconsults" *(faqīh al-fuqahāʾ)* (113)[63] and whose teaching, characterized by a relative freedom and flexibility, he clearly found the most congenial offered by any of the schools. *Qiyās* was invoked by al-Maqdisī only with circumspection; in fact, he states his attitude to it explicitly enough: "This branch of knowledge [geography] cannot depend wholly on analogical reasoning to achieve uniformity in its expositions" *(wa laysa huwa biʿilmin yaṭṭaridu bi-l-qiyāsī fayatasāwā)* (6).[64]

Taʿāruf, for al-Maqdisī at any rate, in the case of place-names was conventional usage (152),[65] but when applied to more theoretical matters amounted to little more than common sense.[66] He summarizes his practice in these matters in the following words:

> Take note that in this book uncertain questions are resolved in accordance with *taʿāruf* and *istiḥsan,* just as jurists decide in the case of written contracts and oaths. In arranging my materials I have chosen to follow the principles of the ʿIrāqī schools of jurisprudence, with which study has made me conversant. I have also had recourse to *qiyās* at appropriate points.[67]

Eyewitness Reports

Al-Maqdisī's second principal source of information was the testimony of trustworthy persons (43). He tells us that, when he wanted to find out about distant places that were impracticable for him to visit, he "consulted with men of intelligence whom he knew to be of shrewd and sound understanding." Only when their accounts agreed, however, did he accept their information as fact; otherwise he rejected it. When al-Maqdisī failed to grasp an idea or it seemed beyond reason, he either named his informant or simply stated, "It is said that . . ." (3, 43) When information was of doubtful authenticity or was "transmitted on the authority of a single individual *(ṭarīq al-āḥād),*" he duly recorded the name of the person from whom he had heard it (8).[68]

The *Aḥsan* provides abundant confirmation that al-Maqdisī did indeed rely mainly on these two sources of personal observation and cautious inquiry from reliable informants. His third source of information, however, authoritative writings by earlier authors, seems only too often to have been invoked simply to satisfy the tenth-century requirements of geographical writing, thereby forestalling much potential criticism.[69] He virtually says as much: "[In this book] we have adduced proofs that will establish its authority, incorporated tales drawn from authentic sources, made [occasional] use of rhymed prose to impart elegance [to the writing], and quoted traditions *(al-akhbār)*[70] in order to merit divine favour. . . . We have arranged our materials according to the system employed in the works of canon lawyers so that it may earn the approval of the learned who study it seriously; we have noted differences of opinion so as to give depth to [the discussion] and made our points with circumspection" (8).

Sacred and Secular Sources

For al-Maqdisī the most authoritative of written sources was, of course, the Qurʾān, the foundation of all knowledge, including the topographical. It was on the authority of *Surah* 55 *(al-Raḥmān):*19–20[71]—supported by a tradition based ultimately on the authority of ʿAbd Allāh ibn ʿAmr ibn al-ʿĀṣ,[72] for example—that he maintained the integrity of "the two seas" as opposed to, say, the three of al-Balkhī, al-Iṣṭakhrī, and Ibn Ḥawqal (who included the ocean surrounding the world), the four of Ibn al-Faqīh, or the five of al-Jayhānī and Qudāmah (six if the encircling ocean be included) (10–19).[73] He had difficulty with *Surah* 31 *(Luqmān):*27, which incorporates a somewhat equivocal reference to seven seas, but was eventually able to reconcile both Qurʾānic allusions with personal experience—to his satisfaction, at any rate—by an involved argument hinging on the double value, both generalizing and determinant, of the Arabic definite article.[74] He may have sensed that his reasoning was likely to prove unconvincing (actually it was false), for he eventually fell back on the position that Allāh had addressed the Arabs only on topics "with which they were familiar and which were always before their eyes, the better to impress the facts on their minds." And, had not all their voyages taken place over "that one sea which, under a variety of names, encompassed their country from al-Qulzum to ʿAbbādān" (17)?

Clearly al-Maqdisī was not entirely happy with his resolution of this apparent conflict between Qurʾānic authority and *ʿiyān,* but his own wide experience, commitment to the touchstone of firsthand observation, and respect for informed opinion compelled him to stretch the meaning of even the word of God to accord with reality. It is also evident that, whatever formal concessions he might have deemed it expedient to make to sacred authority, for practical purposes he relied on the testimony of certain "*shaykh*s born and bred on the sea,[75] ship's captains, supercargoes,[76] talleymen,[77] agents,[78] and merchants who possessed the most intimate knowledge of the [Arabian] Sea, its anchorages, winds, and islands."[79] In spite of his unfeigned devotion to Islam, al-Maqdisī clearly found the witness of the Qur'ān less impressive than the opinion of one such informant, *Shaykh* Abū ʿAlī ibn Ḥāzim, a prominent merchant and master navigator *(muʿallim)* who drew an outline of the great eastern sea in the sand with his finger as he sat with al-Maqdisī on the shore outside ʿAdan (11). Had our author not considered himself a follower of a Kūfan law school that did not scorn free inquiry, he might well have found himself even more embarrassed by contradictions between sacred and secular geography. As it is, it remains a problem with which we need not be unduly concerned, for the Qur'ān offers few specifics about cities, leaving al-Maqdisī free to describe urban systems as he perceived them.

Al-Maqdisī's secular written sources comprised whatever books and documents he could find in princely libraries and official archives (43; compare also pp. 4–5).[80] The topographies he consulted included those of al-Jayhānī,[81] al-Balkhī,[82] Ibn al-Faqīh,[83] and Ibn Khurradādhbih,[84] as well as the *adab* writings of al-Jāḥiẓ,[85] all of which he faulted on one ground or another: al-Jayhānī lacked an adequate conceptual structure and focused on routes and physiography to the exclusion of cities; al-Balkhī presented maps without adequate interpretation; and al-Faqīh included irrelevant literary material, while the works of Jāḥiẓ[86] and Ibn Khurradādhbih were too insubstantial to be of much use. Whenever possible, al-Maqdisī liked to furnish his account with a chain of authorities *(isnād)* on the pattern espoused by *ḥadīth* scholars.[87] When that proved impracticable he usually fell back on a formula such as "It is said that . . . ," or "I have heard that . . . ," thereby signifying the unverifiability of a particular piece of information.

Doctrinal Influences

We have already noted on page 63 that while he was collecting information for his book, al-Maqdisī appears to have transferred his sympathies, if not his political allegiance, from the Sāmānids to the Fāṭimids. Later we shall see that this shift in loyalties almost certainly colored his evaluation of the role of *metropoleis* in the eastern and western sectors of the Islamic world.[88] We have also observed al-Maqdisī's attachment to the teachings of Abū Ḥanīfah, which in no way discouraged his expression of discretionary opinions *(istiḥsan);*[89] but his doctrinal sympathies were broader than this and, indeed, sometimes appear to have been contradictory. He leaves us with the distinct impression, for instance, that he was not opposed to at least some of the doctrines of the Karrāmīyah, a Ṣūfī-inclined sect that originated in Khurāsān in the ninth century, and that by al-Maqdisī's time had spread widely through the eastern and central parts of the Islamic world.[90] He was also a frank admirer of the Muʿtazilites[91] and manifested more than a casual interest in Shīʿism.[92] Indeed, al-Maqdisī's Shīʿite affinities, coupled with his evident approbation of the Fāṭimid rulers of Egypt, have led André Miquel to discern in the peripatetic topographer an Ismāʿīlī agent *(dāʿī)*[93] in the service of the Fāṭimids.[94] Al-Maqdisī himself acknowledged his affinity with "ascetics and those given to religious exercises,"[95] and his adoption of the lifestyle of a *dāʿī* would help to explain the extent of his travels in the company of all types and conditions of men, as well as the humiliations, imprisonment, and threats against his life that he recounts in the passage quoted on page 65 above.[96]

What all this amounts to is that our principal source of information about the urban systems of the Islamic world (*qua* systems) at the end of the tenth century is a "Syrian" *(au sens large)* writing with a native's understanding of the Levant, having long personal and family acquaintance with much of the Eastern Caliphate and Egypt, but having increasingly superficial knowledge as he carried his descriptions westward into the Maghrib. Although his account incorporated virtually all current and previous modes of Islamic topographical description except the mathematical, its primary value for our purpose resides in the way its information is organized in terms of functional urban regions.

Al-Iṣṭakhrī and Ibn Ḥawqal

Although al-Maqdisī's *Aḥsan* is conceptually the most sophisticated of the topographies that treated of cities in the entire Islamic world, significant supplementary material is provided by several other tenth-century compendia. Two of these were, like the *Aḥsan,* in the tradition of al-Balkhī: namely the topographies of, respectively, Abū Isḥāq Ibrāhīm ibn Muḥammad al-Fārisī al-Iṣṭakhrī[97] and Abū al-Qāsim ibn ʿAlī al-Naṣībī, better known as Ibn Ḥawqal. For the first of these authors virtually no biographical details exist, but his topographical handbook entitled *al-Masālik wa-l-Mamālik* is clearly in the old tradition of the *Ṣūrat al-Maʾmūnīyah*,[98] with maps providing annotations to an extended independent text. As he met with Ibn Ḥawqal in 951/52, by which time his own book had been completed, it is certain that he had compiled it during the fourth and fifth decades of the tenth century. Parts of this work were first published by J. H. Möller (*Liber Climatum* [Gotha, 1839]) and translated by J. H. Mordtmann (*Das Buch der Länder* [Hamburg, 1845]). It was subsequently edited in its entirety by M. J. de Goeje as the first volume of his *Bibliotheca Geographorum Arabicorum*, and more recently by ʿAbd al-ʿĀl al-Ḥīnī.[99]

As would be expected of a follower of al-Balkhī's, al-Iṣṭakhrī organized his materials in terms of *iqlīms*, which for him, as for al-Maqdisī, were typically regions under the jurisdiction of a single political power. Although his descriptions of the *iqlīms* paid a good deal of attention to cities, his accounts of urban systems were less methodical, as well as less comprehensive, than those of al-Maqdisī. However, it is evident from numerous comments in his text that he shared this latter author's Shīʿite sympathies.

About Ibn Ḥawqal we are better informed. Born in Naṣībīn in al-Jazīrah (Upper Mesopotamia), he early conceived "a desire to understand clearly the location of cities and the situation of metropoleis, the limits of provinces and regions." In 943 he set out on an impressive series of journeys that took him, probably—based on incidental remarks in his work—in the roles of merchant and, parallelling al-Maqdisī, Fāṭimid political agent,[100] to places as far apart as Spain and Transoxania. His surviving work is a topography of the Islamic world that is today known under the titles *Kitāb al-Masālik wa-l-Mamālik* and *Kitāb Ṣūrat al-Arḍ*. Like the *Aḥsan al-Taqāsīm*, it relies for its information primarily on direct personal observation rather than on book learning. Although the history of this text cannot be elucidated in detail, it would appear that Ibn Ḥawqal originally intended only to revise the received cartographical corpus of the school of al-Balkhī. However, as the annotations increased in number and length, the scope of the enterprise broadened until the commentary developed into an independent compendium. The *Kitāb* seems to have appeared in several redactions, the first of which can be shown to have antedated the year 967;[101] the second can be assigned to about 977, and the third, definitive version to about 988.

The cumulative character of the *Kitāb*, together with the author's adoption of al-Iṣṭakhrī's *Masālik wa-l-Mamālik* as a framework within which to structure his own book, have introduced certain obscurities into the text. Nonetheless, Ibn Ḥawqal's work exhibits a more logical arrangement of information and a vastly greater amount of detail than anything that had gone before—excepting, of course, in the matter of urban hierarchies the *Aḥsan* of al-Maqdisī. It was undoubtedly his commercial interests that led him to focus on modes of production and to attempt to relate his statements to particular times and conditions. His work proved most useful to the present inquiry in connection with the urban forms of the Maghrib and of the Sāmānid territories in the northeastern part of the Islamic world, although even there it was not always possible to discriminate the author's original contributions from those of the Balkhī tradition in general and those of al-Iṣṭakhrī in particular. An edition of the text published by de Goeje in 1873[102] has now been superseded by that of J. H. Kramers.[103]

Ḥudūd al-ʿĀlam

Almost contemporary with al-Maqdisī's *Aḥsan al-Taqāsīm* and the third redaction of Ibn Ḥawqal's compendium was the schedule of general geographical information entitled *Ḥudūd al-ʿĀlam*, which was compiled by an anonymous author in A.H. 372/A.D. 982–83 and dedicated to Amīr Abū al-Ḥārith Muḥammad ibn Aḥmad of the Farīghūnid dynasty ruling in Gūzgānān. In 1258 this unique manuscript was copied by Abū al-Muʾayyad ʿAbd al-Qayyūm ibn al-Ḥusayn ibn ʿAlī al-Fārisī. It was this copy that was discovered in Bukhārā in 1892 by Mīrzā Abū al-Faḍl Gulpāyagānī; brought to the attention of Russian orientalists by Major-General A. G. Tumansky; published under the posthumous editorship of V. V. Barthold in 1930[104] and again by Manūchihr Sūtūdah in 1962;[105] printed by Sayyid Jalāl al-Dīn Ṭihrānī as an annex to his Calendary for the Persian year 1314 (A.H. 1353–4/A.D. 1935);[106] and translated into English with exhaustive annotation by V. Minorsky.[107]

Like the *Aḥsan*, the *Ḥudūd* purports to be a description of the world as known to Muslims of the tenth century, but it is much less detailed than the former work. And unlike al-Maqdisī, its author was not a traveller but what Minorsky calls "a cabinet scholar." In that writer's opinion, only in the section on Gūzgānān, the author's homeland, and less certainly in that on Gīlān, does the text reflect some personal experience (xlviii).[108] For the rest the information is derived from two classes of secondary records, namely "books of the predecessors" (*kitāb-hā-yi pīshīnagān:* fols. $2a_1$ and $13b_3$) and a miscellaneous category subsuming "memories of the sages" (*yādhkird-i ḥakīmān:* fol. $2a_2$), "information [heard]" (*akhbār:* fol. $13b_3$), and "mention" (*dhikr:* fol. $12a_2$) (xlviii). Minorsky had endorsed Abū al-Faḍl Gulpāyagānī's intuitive assumption that the text of the *Ḥudūd* was originally conceived as a preface to a map *(muqaddama-yi naqsha būda).*[109] In fact the anonymous author occasionally mentions a map that he had prepared (fols. $5b_{11}$, $8b_{10}$, $25b_{13}$, $33b_{16}$, and $37a_{15}$) and that seems to have been something more than a simple illustration of the text.[110] If the map was indeed compiled before the text, then it is not unlikely that the author based his work on some previous cartographic source, which Minorsky suggests may have been the maps, perhaps in amended form, of Abū Jaʿfar al-Khāzin (xlix).[111]

As far as literary sources were concerned, the anonymous compiler relied principally on the work of al-Iṣṭakhrī (compare p. 67 above). In Minorsky's opinion the chapters on the countries between the Mediterranean Sea and the Indus River "are practically a mere abridgement of al-Iṣṭakhrī, sometimes with a verbatim translation of details," although the Īrānicized form of Khurāsānian and Caucasian toponymy would imply that al-Iṣṭakhrī was known to the author of the *Ḥudūd* only in Persian translation (lii). Another source that the compiler used fairly systematically was an unspecified work that was also drawn on by Ibn Rustah, al-Bakrī, Gardīzī, ʿAwfī, and others, and which is usually considered to have been the lost *Kitāb al-Mamālik wa-l-Masālik* of Abū ʿAbd Allāh Muḥammad ibn Aḥmad Jayhānī. As Sāmānid *wazīr* from 914 to 922, and again from 938 to 941, Jayhānī was afforded excellent opportunities for collecting and organizing geographical intelligence. Al-Maqdisī, who was sometimes unjustly critical of his predecessors, writes that Jayhānī "assembled foreigners and interrogated them about their kingdoms, their revenues, the state of the roads leading to them, the altitudes of the stars above their horizons, and the length of the shadows [when the sun was on the meridian]."[112] Minorsky ascribes some information in the *Ḥudūd* relating to the Turko-Īrānian frontier districts ultimately to the writings of al-Jayhānī.[113] He further concludes that the author of the *Ḥudūd* was indebted for a few items to an otherwise unknown source of which Masʿūdī possessed only an abstract, and possibly for a few snippets of Arabian material to al-Hamdānī's *Ṣifat Jazīrat al-ʿArab.* In the present study it is in the elucidation of the urban hierarchies in al-Daylam, Khurāsān, and Transoxania that the *Ḥudūd al-ʿĀlam* has proved of most value.

Al-Hamdānī

The aforementioned *Ṣifat Jazīrat al-ʿArab* is the most comprehensive extant account of the Arabian Peninsula in the tenth century, but it also incorporates a great deal of information about earlier periods, much of it well documented by the standards of the time. Abū Muḥammad al-Ḥasan ibn Aḥmad ibn Yaʿqūb ibn Yūsuf ibn Dāwūd al-Hamdānī, also known as Ibn al-Ḥāʾik, was born in Ṣanʿāʾ, spent a large part of his life in Raydah under the protection of Abū Jaʿfar al-Ḍaḥḥak (Sayyid Hamdān), became involved in political controversy that led to his imprisonment in Ṣaʿdah, and died in Ṣanʿāʾ in 945. Miquel epitomizes his scholarly standing in the following words: "il se montre un incontestable savant, par son sens critique, le sérieux de sa documentation et la souci de confronter un sujet traditionnel aux acquisitions de la science de son temps."[114]

The *Ṣifat Jazīrat al-ʿArab* may have been compiled as a supplement to an otherwise unknown *Kitāb al-Masālik wa-l-Mamālik.* Another work in which al-Hamdānī displayed his unrivalled knowledge of Arabia was *al-Iklīl min Akhbār al-Yaman.* A careful account of the antiquities and genealogies of the peoples of the southwestern corner of the peninsula, the *Iklīl* was based on information furnished by Abū Naṣr Muḥammad ibn ʿAbd Allāh ibn Saʿīd (also called al-Yaharī and al-Ḥanbaṣī), genealogical records of the Khawlān tribe in Ṣaʿdah, and other local sources both oral and literary.[115] Although only four of its original ten books remain, they are fundamental for our understanding of the dispositions and attitudes of the South Arabian tribes in early times. Because of the variety of his literary works, al-Hamdānī has been rightly favored with the sobriquet "Tongue of the Yaman" *(Lisān al-Yaman).*

Al-Masʿūdī and His Contemporaries

Most of the material utilized in this chapter has been extracted from the works of the topographers discussed in the preceding pages; but other, including earlier, authors have been laid under tribute whenever they have proferred information likely to throw light on the evolution of the settlement hierarchy. One such author whose work occasionally proved useful in this connection was the analist and topographer Abū al-Ḥasan ʿAlī ibn al-Ḥusayn al-Masʿūdī. Not a great deal is known about this author, as his style of learning found little favor among orthodox schoolmen. It is evident, however, that he spent a great deal of his life in travel, that he was genuinely interested in topographical matters, and that he was writing at much the same time as al-Iṣṭakhrī. In particular, al-Masʿūdī regarded the physical environment as exerting a preponderant influence on animal and human life, whence stemmed his view of geography as a prologue to history.

In the organization of his topographical material he followed the Īrānian *kishwar* (or equal circles) system,[116] which was already of venerable antiquity in the Persian cultural realm. Although he was prepared on occasion to challenge orthodox interpretations when they conflicted with his own observations or with information he had read or heard, al-Masʿūdī was generally content to accept the testimony of secondary, sometimes dubious, sources at their face value. Only seldom did he investigate primary written sources. Like the topographers of the so-called ʿIrāqī persuasion,[117] though, he was prepared to extend his interests beyond the borders of the Dār al-Islam. Indeed, his sympathetic recording of other than Islamic customs, institutions, and religions has been a subject of frequent comment by modern commentators. Al-Masʿūdī's Shīʿite predilection is not in doubt,[118] and Miquel goes so far as to argue that, like al-Maqdisī and Ibn Ḥawqal, al-Masʿūdī was an Ismāʿīlī missionary. Miquel sustains this argument, however, only by postulating a generous use of legal dissimulation (compare note 96) in al-Masʿūdī's works.[119]

The work of al-Masʿūdī that has proved most useful in the compilation of this volume has been the *Murūj al-Dhahab wa-Maʿādin al-Jawhar* (A.D. 943),[120] an encyclopedic mélange of history and geography laced with incidental and episodic information of all sorts, which was itself an epitome of a much larger compendium in thirty volumes, now lost. Only very occasionally has resort been had to Masʿūdī's *Kitāb al-Tanbīh wa-l-Ishrāf*,[121] a summary survey and supplementation of almost all he had written previously, which he completed shortly before his death in 956.[122]

A contemporary of al-Masʿūdī's who has furnished a limited amount of information for the construction of figure 2 is Ibn Sarābiyūn, compiler of the *Kitāb ʿAjāʾib al-Aqālīm al-Sabʿah* during the first half of the tenth century.[123] This work, of which only fragments remain, was a general geography modelled on that of al-Khwārizmī. In Miquel's opinion it "représente incontestablement une mise en forme littéraire de données arithmétiques."[124] It was probably never completed, as certain sections proposed, including one on cities (fol. 67a), are lacking in the only extant manuscript. However, although there is no formal discussion of urban networks, numerous cities are mentioned incidentally during descriptions of the river and canal systems constituting the substantive part of the book as it has survived. In the present instance, the main value of the work resides in its accounts of Baghdād and the waterways of Mesopotamia, together with mentions of the cities along their banks.[125]

Another contemporary of al-Masʿūdī's, as indeed of al-Iṣṭakhrī's, who provided information about one particular region was Abū Bakr Aḥmad ibn Muḥammad al-Rāzī. In addition to a description of Córdoba *(Ṣifat Qurṭubah)* that has not survived, this author compiled a work in roadbook style in which he reported on the routes, ports, cities, and administrative divisions of the Iberian Peninsula. This work has been preserved only in a Portuguese version subsequently translated into Spanish.[126]

Other Sources

From the ninth century comes a group of sources that provide a framework for reconstructing the urban hierarchy at that time—a framework almost as extensive as, though less detailed than, that derived from the systematic topographies of the tenth century—namely the roadbooks of Ibn Khurradādhbih, al-Yaʿqūbī, and Ibn Rustah. The first of these, in some ways the prototype for all medieval Islamic roadbooks, was compiled by Abū al-Qāsim ʿUbayd Allāh ibn ʿAbd Allāh (var. Aḥmad) ibn Khurradādhbih, grandson of a Zoroastrian convert to Islam.[127] Born in Khurāsān probably during the third decade of the ninth century, this author received a sound literary education. Relatively early in his career he held the position of director of posts and intelligence *(Ṣāḥib al-Barīd wa-l-Khabar)* in Jibāl Province, subsequently being promoted to the rank of director-general of similar departments successively in Baghdād and Sāmarrā. During this time he became a familiar and confidant of the caliph al-Muʿtamid, so al-Maqdisī is almost certainly correct in asserting that Ibn Khurradādhbih was permitted access to government archives.[128]

He was the author of a corpus of works of both a learned and an *adab* character, but his reputation as a scholar has traditionally rested on his roadbook entitled *Kitāb al-Masālik wa-l-Mamālik*, the first draft of which was prepared in 846/47 and the second in 885/86. This work, arranged according to the four cardinal compass directions, with al-ʿIrāq in the center, was often drawn on by later topographers. In the following pages I have found it useful in verifying readings and identifying urban forms whose names and locations are not immediately evident from the accounts of tenth-century topographers.[129]

The second ninth-century topographer who structured his work on a modified *kishwar* principle and, equating al-ʿIrāq with Īrānshahr, began his description with that province, was al-Yaʿqūbī.[130] This author spent his youth in Baghdād and Armenia, and subsequently entered the service of the Ṭāhirids in Khurāsān. On the fall of that dynasty, he migrated to Egypt, where in 891 he completed his *Kitāb al-Buldān*, a topographical compendium based on fairly protracted personal and literary investigations. The sections on India (which he visited), China, Byzantium, and—what is especially unfortunate for the present inquiry—those relating to al-Baṣrah and Central Arabia, have been lost. The work as a whole, which might be described as a functional and unadorned handbook for administrators, provides brief descriptions of important territories and cities, the distances between them, and the revenues derived from them. Like his successors Ibn Ḥawqal and al-Maqdisī, al-Yaʿqūbī was at his best when recording his personal observations *(ʿiyān)*, and he seems also to have shared their Shīʿite sympathies.[131] The *Kitāb al-Buldān* was published by T. G. J. Juynboll in 1861,[132] and again by M. J. de Goeje in 1892.[133] A French translation was produced by Gaston Wiet.[134]

Kitāb al-Aʿlāq al-Nafīsah, compiled soon after A.D. 903 by Abū ʿAlī Aḥmad ibn ʿUmar ibn Rustah, a native of Iṣfahān,[135] has been consulted by me occasionally, but it has not contributed greatly to the present study: although the seventh (and only surviving) section of this work addresses topographical matters, the information is usually elaborated elsewhere. However, Ibn Rustah's descriptions of the sanctuaries of Makkah (Mecca) and al-Madīnah (Medina) are more detailed than those of any other early author. What is more, his schedule of major cities is not wholly valueless, even though he admitted that his descriptions of all except Iṣfahān were at second hand, "sometimes accurate, sometimes of dubious reliability, or derived from accounts on which I had to depend even though I knew that they were of less than perfect truthfulness."[136]

Although the presentation and arrangement of the geographical (including urban) material shows an affinity with the ʿIrāqī style of topographical writing, the *Aʿlaq* belongs to those productions of that school which accord precedence to Makkah and Arabia rather than to Īrānshahr. It also manifests unmistakable Shīʿite tendencies, as well as a desire to reconcile the results of objective inquiry into the nature of the world—a world conceived as capable of disclosing to believers the power and majesty of God—with the testimony of the divine word as enshrined in the Qurʾān. André Miquel's conclusion, arrived at after close study of the *Aʿlaq,* is that it, or at any rate its extant portion, "ne peut ainsi s'expliquer que dans le contexte d'ensemble d'une oeuvre qui est elle-même le produit des conflits d'idées dans l'Ispahan des années 900. Il s'agit pour elle moins d'exposer une connaissance, selon les principes signalés, que d'utiliser lesdits principes à une revendication: celle d'un Islam composite, héritier de plusiers cultures et ensemble de nations diverses."[137]

Qudāmah ibn Jaʿfar, a convert from Christianity to Islam who held office as a revenue accountant in the central administration at Baghdād, also left a work on which I have drawn occasionally. This was the *Kitāb al-Kharāj,* completed soon after 928.[138] The complete work in nine books, of which only 5, 6, 7, and part of 8 have survived, was conceived as a comprehensive guide to the administration of the Islamic Empire,[139] with special emphasis on the role of the civil official *(kātib).* The extant books, however, deal only with the provincial boundaries of the Caliphate, the organization of the postal service, and the apportionment of taxation. Such information about cities as they contain is incidental to discussions of these topics, and even then pertains almost exclusively to location rather than structure.

Occasional reference has also been made to the *Kitāb al-Buldān* compiled by Abū Bakr Aḥmad ibn Muḥammad ibn al-Faqīh al-Hamadhānī in about 903, but now known only in an abridged version *(mukhtaṣar)* prepared by Abū al-Ḥasan ʿAlī ibn Jaʿfar al-Shayzārī in 1022. However, despite its title, this work is less a topography or a geography than an anthology of *curiosa.* Blachère characterizes it succinctly as "un livre d'*adab* qui se propose d'instruire en amusant."[140] As al-Maqdisī points out, al-Faqīh mentioned only the most important cities and treated districts and military establishments in cavalier fashion, if at all;[141] but the numerous digressions in *adab* style[142] do provide valuable information about the cultural context within which cities flourished during the second half of the ninth century A.D., mainly in the territories of the Eastern Caliphate. In any case, al-Maqdisī did not scruple to appropriate information from the *Kitāb al-Buldān* when it suited his purpose, and Yāqūt made it one of his main quarries. No epitomization of Ibn al-Faqīh's *humanisme géographique*[143] is more apt than Miquel's conclusion to his study of the *Kitāb al-Buldān:* "d'une part, il renforcera la tendance, manifestée très tôt, mais de façon velléitaire, par la géographie technique sous toutes ses formes, vers une ouverture aux thèmes de l'*adab,* d'autre part, il contribuera à fixer au monde de l'Islam la curiosité des écrivains. En ces deux sens, il déterminera, de façon décisive, les options prises par des genres aussi essentiels que la géographie administrative avec Qudāma et la *ṣūrat al-arḍ* avec Balḫī, dont la conjonction sera une des bases du genre des *Masālik wa-l-Mamālik.*"[144]

Furthermore, I have made some use of authors who, although writing after the close of the tenth century, provided material that projected back to that period. The most valuable of these has proved to be Abū ʿUbayd ʿAbd Allāh ibn ʿAbd al-ʿAzīz al-Bakrī, an erudite, although armchair, topographer writing in Qurṭubah (Córdoba) in the second half of the eleventh century. All that remains of his *Kitāb al-Masālik wa-l-Mamālik,* a description of the entire Islamic world, are fragments relating to al-ʿIrāq and Spain, the section on Egypt, and a detailed review of conditions in North Africa and the Sūdān.[145] This last section was highly valuable in the construction of figures 2 and 16 in the present text.

Some of the information in this section of al-Bakrī's work appears to have derived from the first half of the eleventh century and, by implication, not infrequently to refer to the tenth century. But a good deal of it is derived explicitly from the now-lost *Kitāb al-Masālik wa-l-Mamālik* of Muḥammad ibn Yūsuf al-Qarawī al-Warrāq, a Spanish topographer who, after a lengthy residence in al-Qayrawān (Kairouan), returned to Córdoba in the reign of the Umayyad caliph al-Ḥakam II (961–76).[146] In this case there can be no doubt that materials drawn from al-Warrāq's personal observations or recorded by him on the testimony of trustworthy informants refer to the second half of the tenth century. Another source on which al-Bakrī relied was the *Niẓām al-Marjān,*[147] compiled in predominantly *adab* style by Aḥmad ibn ʿUmar al-ʿUdhrī, a native of Dalias (Dalāyah), in the second half of the eleventh century, but incorporating some material from the tenth. Al-Bakrī's style is dry and precise, as befitted a work destined for the instruction of chancellery officials. Although the material is arranged in the form of itineraries, it is interspersed with digressions of capital importance for the student of North African cultures and societies in the tenth and eleventh centuries.

Other post-tenth-century topographers and encylopedists whose works I have scanned for information relevant to urban developments in the period under consideration include Nāṣir-i Khusraw, an Ismāʿīlī poet and philosopher who, just after the mid-eleventh century, published a diary of his pilgrimage from Khurāsān to Makkah, which he combined with visits to Egypt, Syria, and Arabia;[148] the author of an account of the Province of Fārs, published in 1107;[149] Abū ʿAbd Allāh Muḥammad ibn Muḥammad al-Idrīsī, who, while at the court of Roger II of Sicily, in 1154 published the *Nuzhat al-Mushtāq fī Ikhtirāq al-Afāq,* a description of the known world organized in (what is for present purposes) an inconvenient system of *klimata;*[150] Ibn Jubayr, a Spanish Arab who published his diary of a pilgrimage to Makkah, undertaken in 1183, and of an additional journey as far east as Baghdād;[151] Yāqūt, compiler of a voluminous topographical dictionary completed in 1225;[152] and Ḥamdallāh Mustawfī, who wrote (in Persian) in 1340 a description of Mesopotamia and Persia under the Mongols.[153]

In addition to the use made of these works, which were conceived purely as topographies and geographies of one sort or another, I have derived a not negligible increment of relevant material from certain general chronicles, local histories, biographical dictionaries, and *adab* writings (*belles-lettres,* with an emphasis on mores, etiquette, and spiritual refinement). Perhaps the most useful of these categories was that of the local histories, a genre of literature that flourished particularly vigorously in the eastern sectors of the Dār al-Islam.[154] Included within it were histories of individual cities, at one time so numerous as to give the impression that almost every urban center of note had produced one. The majority of these works are now either lost or have not been accessible to me. Moreover, most of those that I have been able to consult, in addition to focusing on a period after the tenth century, have seldom done more than expatiate on the merits *(faḍā'il)* of the city in question and on the exemplary lives of eminent worthies who hailed from there (often to the extent of being virtually biographical dictionaries).

A few, however, provided material of greater relevance to the present investigation. One of these was the *Ta'rīkh Baghdād* by Abū Bakr Aḥmad ibn ʿAlī ibn Thābit ibn Aḥmad ibn Mahdi al-Shāfiʿī, known more commonly as al-Khaṭīb al-Baghdādī (d. 1071), which incorporates a substantial topographical introduction.[155] Another was a twelfth-century Persian epitome of an Arabic history of Bukhārā compiled by Abū Bakr Muḥammad Narshakhī for presentation to the Sāmānid *amīr* Nūḥ ibn Naṣr in 943 or 944. The twelfth-century translator is accurate enough when, in his introduction to this work, he describes it as "containing an account of Bukhārā, its qualities and excellencies, all the amenities of life that are to be found in the city and its environs, and of general matters relating to it. It also includes *ḥadīths* on the superiority of the city that have derived from the Prophet (May God bless him and give him peace)."[156] But its value for our present purposes stems very largely from the fact that, unlike most local histories, it is more concerned with topography and political events than with biography. Another compilation of patrician biographies focussed on a particular city to which I have referred occasionally now exists only in derivative texts. It is the *Ta'rīkh Naysābūr,* in six, eight, or twelve volumes (depending on the authority consulted), by the traditionist Muḥammad ibn ʿAbd Allāh al-Ḥākim al-Nīsābūrī, known as Ibn al-Bayyiʿ (933–1014).[157]

Many local chronicles of this type remain unpublished. Among the fairly readily available ones furnishing information about prominent inhabitants in cities of the Eastern Caliphate are the *Ta'rīkh Wāsiṭ,* compiled by Aslam ibn Sahl Baḥshāl in about 900;[158] a history of Iṣfahān written by Abū Nuʿaym Aḥmad al-Iṣfahānī (946 or 948–1038);[159] the *Tārīkh-i Qumm,* written in Arabic by Ḥasan ibn Muḥammad ibn Ḥasan Qummī in A.H. 378/A.D. 988–89 but now surviving only as five (out of the original twenty) chapters in a Persian translation made by Ḥasan ibn ʿAlī ibn Ḥasan ibn ʿAbd al-Malik Qummī in 1402–3;[160] the *Shīrāz-Nāmah,* composed by Ibn Zarkūb Shīrāzī as late as 1342–43 but incorporating considerable information from earlier times;[161] a political and annalistic history of al-Mawṣil, extant only for the years 719–838, compiled by al-Azdī, who died in 945;[162] an early eleventh-century history of Samarqand by Abū Saʿīd ʿAbd al-Raḥmān ibn Muḥammad al-Idrīsī, which was continued down to the twelfth century by the celebrated theologian al-Nasafī, epitomized by al-Samarqandī, and which has survived only in the form of a Persian translation of this abridgment;[163] a twelfth-century history of Bayhaq by Ẓahīr al-Dīn Abū al-Ḥasan ʿAlī ibn Zayd ibn Fundūq al-Bayhaqī;[164] a history of Ṣanʿā' by Aḥmad ibn ʿAbd Allāh al-Rāzī written just prior to the mid-eleventh century;[165] from the Levant a well-known history of Dimashq (Damascus) composed by Ibn ʿAsākir in the second half of the twelfth century;[166] and from al-Andalus a history of the *qāḍīs* of Qurṭubah by Abū ʿAbd Allāh Muḥammad ibn al-Ḥārith al-Khushanī, who died in either 971 or 981.[167] Incidentally, it is greatly to be regretted that al-Warrāq's tenth-century studies of Maghribī towns such as Ṭāhart, Wahrān, Sijilmāsah, and Nākūr are no longer extant.

These, then, are the main works used in the construction of figure 2. None—even the *Aḥsan,* which provided the framework for the urban systems depicted therein—can be used without discretion. Such caution implies not simply acceptance or rejection of an item of information, but rather selection according to circumstance. Topographers and geographers, historians and encyclopedists, bureaucrats and *adab* writers were all capable of misperception and misunderstanding; not a few, including some of the intellectually most gifted, showed themselves prone to prejudice and distortion in support of strongly held beliefs. Many, perhaps most, drew upon local traditions that were sometimes of dubious reliability. And in cases in which an original text was at some point translated, abridged, or elaborated, it is often difficult to discriminate between the contributions of the original author and those of subsequent translators or redactors. In other words, the content of these medieval texts must be evaluated both skeptically and contextually, chapter by chapter, line by line, even word by word if necessary. Unfortunately, imposing such restrictions on the acceptance of already scanty evidence can sometimes result in rather meager returns to generous expenditures of energy and time.

In the following discussions, references to the major topographies on which figure 2 is based (such as those of al-Maqdisī, Ibn Ḥawqal, al-Bakrī, or Yāqūt) will be in the form of the author's name followed by the abbreviated title of his work and the page of the principal edition cited in the paragraphs of this section. Works mentioned only incidentally will be accorded a full bibliographical reference.

The Urban Systems

Figure 2 depicts the urban systems in the Middle East during the second half of the tenth century insofar as it has proved possible to reconstruct them from the sources just described. As is to be expected of any distribution deriving from the tenth century, the evidence on which these urban systems are based is inadequate in several respects. In the first place the spatial coverage is by no means comprehensive. Even al-Maqdisī, whose ekistic schedules are the most detailed of any provided by the early topographers, in accordance with the practice of the Balkhī school deliberately restricted his account to territories controlled by Muslim governments. "We did not trouble ourselves," he writes, "with the countries of the infidels, as we have never entered them, and have not thought it worthwhile to describe them."[168] He did, however, occasionally mention in passing infidel lands where colonies of Muslims had settled. His most notable omission, and one that remains uncorrected by any other medieval Arab or Persian geographer, was his failure to provide a systematic account of Muslim settlements in the Indus valley. Nor did he discuss the Muslim communities of the Upper Nile, such as that at Meroë, which was mentioned in Chinese sources dating from the ninth century,[169] or those that were establishing themselves in the ports of East Africa during the same century.[170] Similarly he has little to say about Muslim colonies in Khazarīyah, although he did include Itil[171] in his list of provincial *metropoleis.*[172]

Within the vast culture realm of medieval Islam, al-Maqdisī's coverage was, not unexpectedly, uneven—a fact he readily acknowledged. On page 57 of his account,

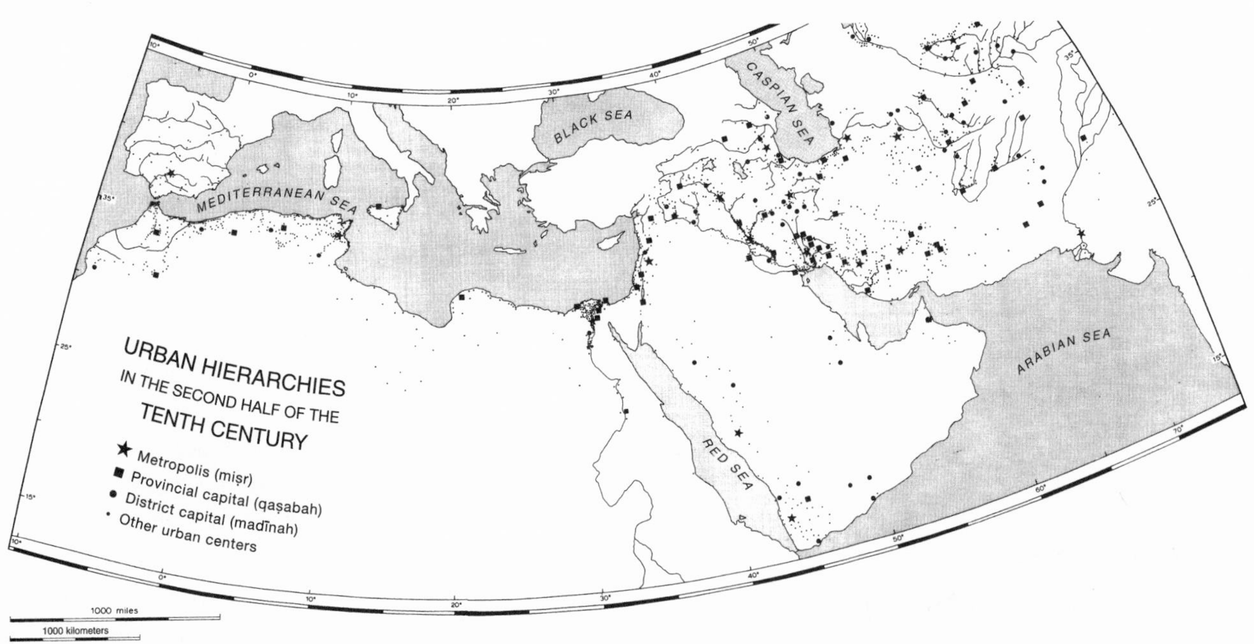

Figure 2. Hierarchical urban systems in the Islamic world in the second half of the tenth century constructed according to principles enunciated by al-Maqdisī.

for example, he admits that "A few of the cities of Islam have been totally omitted from this account because we are unacquainted with them"; and on page 230 he remarks with engaging candor that "Between Fās and Ṣaʿin the *rustāq* of Miknāsat al-Ṣāghah there is a large and pleasant city, abounding in trees and rivulets, the name of which I have forgotten." This unnamed city was probably Safrū (Sefrou). When describing Qulzum and its district he observes that, as it was an unattractive locality, he saw "no advantage in giving an account of the remaining towns in it" (196); of the Sarawāt locality he remarks, "I do not know if it contains towns or only villages, as I have not entered it" (86). Like other Arab geographers, al-Maqdisī found little to say about the cities, other than the capital, of Bardasīr District, on the edge of the Persian desert" (461). Moreover, he occasionally concluded a schedule of cities in a district or region with some such phrase as "and others." In the Tihāmah of al-Yaman, for instance, he listed nineteen urban centers by name, together with an unspecified number of "others" (70). In the district of Diyār Muḍar in al-Jazīrah, eleven cities were named out of an again unspecified total; in Diyār Rabīʿah and Diyār Bakr, respectively, fifteen and six out of unstated totals, with the balances being indicated by the phrase "and others" (137).

Yet, on the whole, the consistency with which al-Maqdisī recorded the cities of an extensive tract of the earth's surface stretching from the Atlantic Ocean to the Indus River is worthy of the highest praise, and represents one of the great achievements of medieval geography. Even his occasional admissions of inadequacy incline the reader, perhaps too readily, to place greater confidence in the rest of the information contained in the *Aḥsan*. In any case, its deficiencies are sometimes made good by one or the other of the topographical accounts discussed above.

Al-Maqdisi's Criteria for Urban Status

Al-Maqdisī nowhere explicitly specified any general criteria for urban status, but it is implicit in his descriptions that he regarded a congregational mosque *(masjid al-jāmiʿ)* and a permanent market *(sūq)* as essential attributes of the mature urban form (figure 3 delimits his functional urban regions). Indeed, this was the customary practice of medieval Muslim topographers. The emphasis on the congregational mosque is important for present purposes because, until the end of the tenth century, such buildings were restricted to reasonably substantial settlements. In fact some small centers made efforts to enhance their status precisely by obtaining the right to support a *jāmiʿ*. This task was often difficult, for the number of congregational mosques in an administrative district was controlled by law, and in practice limited to one building in each lowest-order administrative division. In this matter Shāfiʿite doctrine was stricter than Ḥanafite. Whereas the former stipulated both an independently compelling reason for the building of a second *jāmiʿ* in a settlement and caliphal permission, Ḥanafite law required only the caliph's consent.[173]

An example of the difficulties that even this latter, less stringent requirement might cause is preserved in al-Maqdisī's record of a minor civil war that broke out in Isbījāb in the tenth century when the Ḥanafī *ʿulamāʾ* of the district capital of Bārāb (Fārāb) sought to prevent the hitherto dependent settlement of Kadar from enhancing its status with a *jāmiʿ*.[174] In the case of Egypt, insistence on the presence of a *jāmiʿ* led al-Maqdisī to underrecord substantially the degree of urbanization obtaining there. "The reason why there are not many cities in Egypt," he declares, "is that while the majority of the people of the Sawād are Copts [i.e., Christians], according to our principle of analogical reasoning *(qiyās)* we cannot recognize as a city any settlement which does not possess a *minbar* (sc. mosque)" (193).[175] In actual fact, Lower Egypt by any objective standard was one of the more highly urbanized provinces of the Islamic world.

It is evident that al-Maqdisī's criteria for urban status also took some account of population size, for he dismisses the towns *(madāʾin)* of the Ḥulwān District as "not worthy of mention, being small and ruinous" (123). In describing the urban pattern in al-Shām (Syria), he excuses the pedantry that induced him to exclude some substantial settlements from consideration: "It must be admitted that there are villages in this province larger and more noteworthy than many of the chief towns in the Arabian Peninsula. Such [for example] are Dārayyā, Bayt Liḥyā [both in the Ghūṭah of Damascus], Kafar-sallām, and Kafar-sābā; but they exhibit the characteristics of villages, and, in accordance with conventional usage *(taʿāruf)*, are here reckoned as such" (155).[176] For similar reasons al-Maqdisī was unhappy when his classificatory

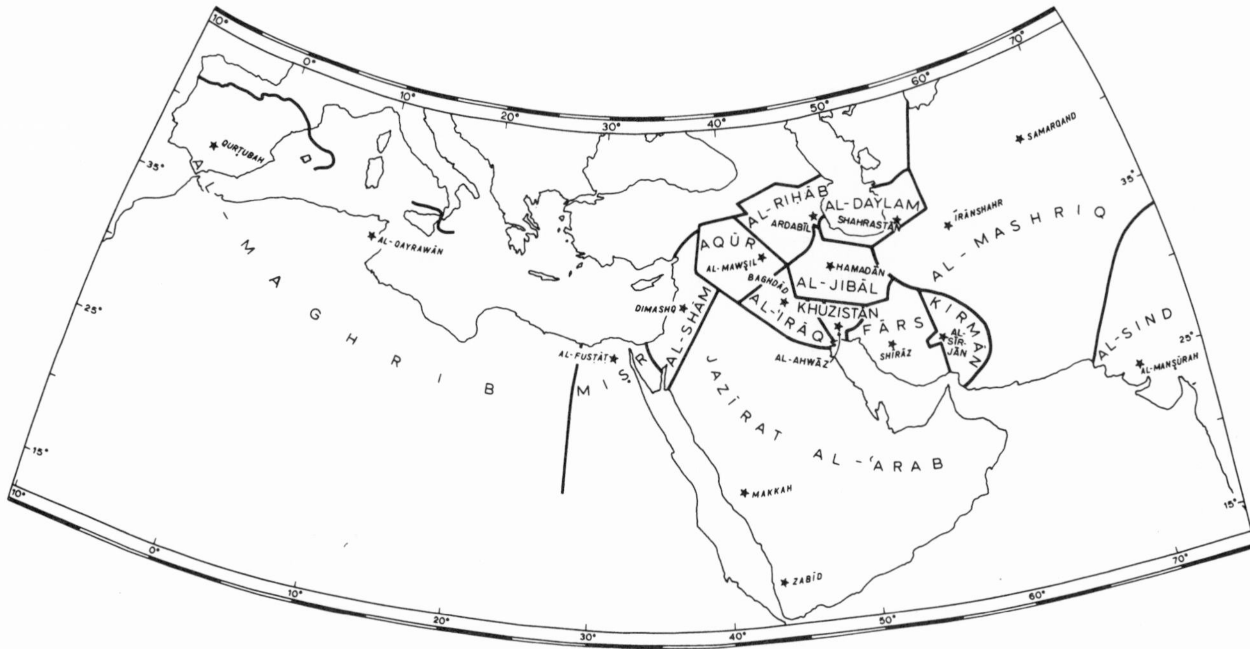

Figure 3. Al-Maqdisī's functional urban regions (*aqālīm*) and their *amṣār.*

principles forced him to omit from his account "many villages in Khurāsān which are larger than most of the towns [surrounding Baghdād]." He also felt it appropriate to offer a fairly lengthy apology for not including the unimpressive settlement (in Islamic times) of Bābil (Babylon) among the *mudun* of al-ʿIrāq, despite its illustrious antecedents (122, 115).[177]

Some three-quarters of a century later al-Bakrī notes that the Maghribian settlement of Tanaguelalt was "well populated and in a prosperous state," but it lacked a congregational mosque.[178] In fact this latter place affords a good example of a settlement that, although appearing to meet the requirements of the twentieth-century investigator, would have been denied urban status by the medieval Muslim. Izmāmah was precisely such another, for, despite its fortress, *sūq,* and several caravanserais, al-Bakrī, writing in the eleventh century, felt compelled to comment on its lack of a *jāmiʿ* (143). Tamaghīlt, with its brick-built citadel, *sūq,* and suburb below the castle walls, would appear on social and economic grounds to have possessed an even stronger claim to urban status, yet there is no mention of a congregational mosque within the settlement (143). It is curious, too, that as late as the eleventh century Tamedalt, yet another North African city, although provided with two public baths and a much frequented *sūq,* all enclosed within a wall of stone and brick furnished with four gates, apparently still lacked a mosque—even though the number of *jāmiʿ*s had increased rapidly throughout the Islamic world after the tenth century (163).

However, these last examples raise the question as to whether certain crucial indices of societal differentiation may not occasionally have been omitted from topographical descriptions as being too obvious to require mention. This question is particularly pertinent in the case of a settlement possessing two public baths but no *recorded* mosque, for the *ḥammām* was institutionally an adjunct of the *jāmiʿ*. Barvān in al-Daylam was an example of an undistinguished, although administratively important, town that lacked a congregational mosque, and Biyār ("The Wells") in Qūmis of a reasonably prosperous one with the same deficiency. Finally, al-Aḥsāʾ, capital of Hajar, deserves mention as a seat of district government, "large . . . flourishing and populous," yet in which the congregational mosque, because of Qarmiṭī aversion to prayer, had been abandoned.[179] Nevertheless,

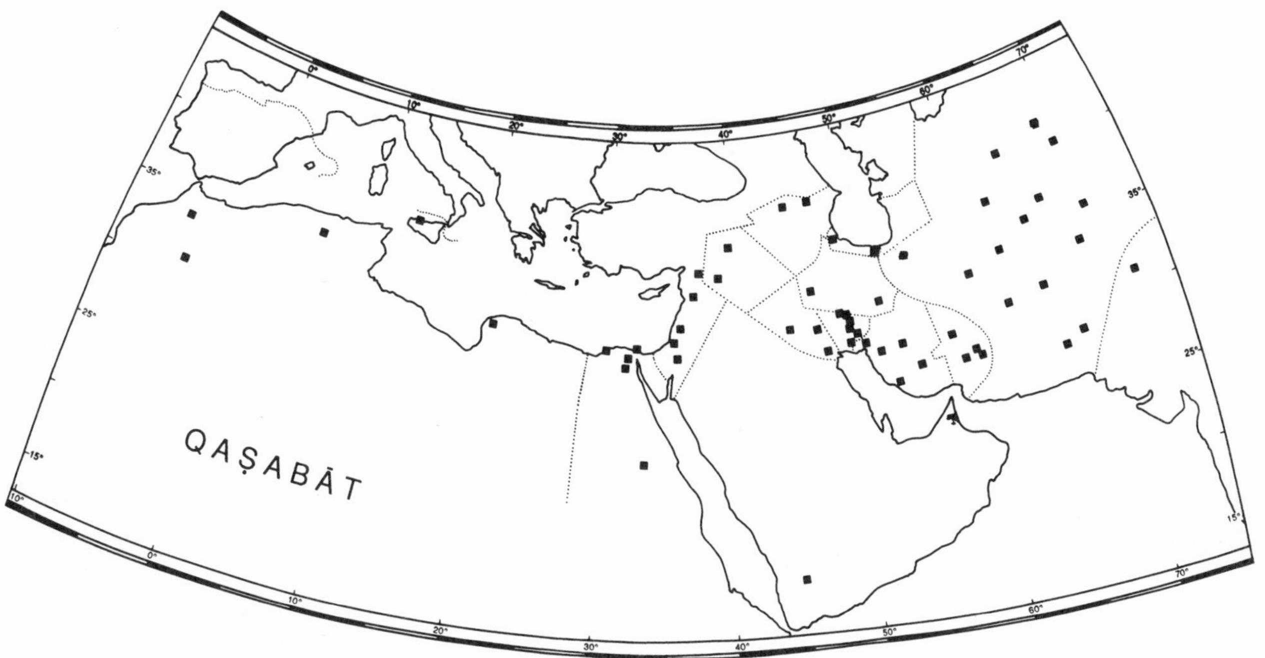

Figure 4. Distribution of *qaṣabāt* among al-Maqdisī's urban regions.

al-Maqdisī assigned it to the third rank of his urban hierarchy.

Al-Maqdisī's Urban Hierarchies

In the *Aḥsan,* al-Maqdisī distinguished four ranks of urban centers distributed through fourteen regions (sing. *iqlīm*). Generally (but not invariably) these regions comprised structured systems of spatial interaction oriented to a metropolis; that is, they constituted functional urban regions. In only three of them did the urban hierarchy subsume two *metropoleis,* and there were never more than two. In some instances, such as Miṣr or Khūzistān, the regions coincided fairly closely with political or administrative units of the time, but others were made up of several such formal divisions. For example, *Iqlīm* al-Riḥāb, literally "The Region of the High Plains," encompassed the Provinces of Ādharbayjān (Azerbaijan), Arrān, and Armīnīyah, and the Maghrib comprised not only the territory proper of that name but also al-Ifrīqīyah and al-Andalus. Even when al-Maqdisī did adopt an administrative division as the basis of a region, he did not necessarily retain its customary designation. Al-Jazīrah, for instance, he recorded as *Iqlīm* Aqūr, a name of uncertain origin.

The highest-ranking city in each of al-Maqdisī's hierarchies was the metropolis *(miṣr),* defined as "the locale *(balad)* where the supreme ruler of a territory resides, where the departments of state concerned with fiscal administration *(aʿmāl)* are located, and which exerts a dominant influence over all other urban centers in an *iqlīm*" (47).[180] They were seventeen in number, in the order in which al-Maqdisī lists them: Samarqand in Transoxania, Īrānshahr (Naysābūr) in Khurāsān, Shahristān in Gurgān (Jurjān), Ardabīl in Ādharbayjān, Hamahān in al-Jibāl, al-Ahwāz in Khūzistān, Shīrāz in Fārs, al-Sīrjān in Kirmān, al-Manṣūrah in Sind, Zabīd in al-Yaman, Makkah in al-Ḥijāz, Baghdād in al-ʿIrāq, al-Mawṣil (Mosul) in al-Jazīrah (Aqūr), Dimashq in al-Shām, al-Fusṭāṭ in Miṣr, al-Qayrawān in al-Ifrīqiyah, and Qurṭubah in al-Andalus (47).

The second-ranking cities in the hierarchies were the provincial capitals *(qaṣabāt;* sing. *qaṣabah)* (fig. 4). Curiously enough, in his epitome of their distribution (48), al-Maqdisī recorded the total number as seventy-seven but listed only sixty-two names (47–48). His schedule, with the occasionally unusual orthographies he adopted, was as follows (table 1):

Table 1. Al-Maqdisī's Second-Ranking Cities

al-ʿAbbāsīyah	al-Faramā	al-Raqqah
Āmid	Fās	al-Rayy
Āmul	Ghaznīn	Sāmarrā
Ardashīr	Ḥalab	Ṣanʿāʾ
Arrajān	Harāt	Shahristān (Shapur)
al-ʿAskar (ʿAskar Mukram)	Ḥimṣ	Sijilmāsah
	Ḥulwān	Sīrāf
Balarm	Iskandarīyah	Ṣughar
Balkh	Iṣṭakhr	al-Sūs
Bamm	Itil	Ṭabarīyah
Bannajbūr	Jīruft	Tāhart
Bardha ʿah*	Junday-Sābūr	Ṭarfānah/Ṭarfālah
Barqah	al-Kūfah	Tustar
Barvān	Marv	Uswān
al-Baṣrah	al-Multān	Wāsiṭ
Bilbays	Narmāsīr	Wayhind
Būnjikath	Numūjkat	al-Yahūdīyah (Iṣfahān)
Bust	Qannauj	
Dabīl	Qāyin	al-Yahūdīyah (Maymanah)
al-Dāmghān	Quzdār	
Dārābjird	Rāmhurmuz	Zaranj
al-Dawraq	al-Ramlah	

*Amended from the Marāghah of the text. Although not impossible as a copyist's mislection, this is more likely to have been an instance of Homer nodding and al-Maqdisī's memory playing him false.

Eleven cities that al-Maqdisī omitted from this list but subsequently treated as *qaṣabāt* in his text were Akhsīkath, Binkath (Tashkent), Hulbuk, Isbījāb, Jurjānīyah, Kāth, and Tūnkath in Transoxania; Abshīn in Gharjistān; and Qurḥ, Ṣuḥār, and al-Aḥsāʾ in Arabia. The reasons for this discrepancy are wholly obscure: not improbably simple authorial error, perhaps legitimate revisions of ekistic status over a period of time, conceivably even changes in al-Maqdisī's classificatory criteria. Because of the author's ambivalence in the matter and the historical and hierarchical contexts in which these cities are cited, in figures 2 and 4 I have plotted only four as *qaṣabāt,* namely Akhsīkath, Binkath, Isbījāb, and Ṣuḥār; the rest I have treated as *mudun,* a seemingly more appropriate classification. It is worthy of record, though, that the *qaṣabah* statuses of four additional settlements could possibly be masked by al-Maqdisī's sometimes paratactic descriptive style, which would bring the total to the seventy-seven he claimed. In any case, of the cities that al-Maqdisī did enumerate, two lay outside the sphere of Islamic political control, namely Itil in Khazarīyah, where Muslim traders figured prominently among the inhabitants; and Qannawj on the Ganges, between 836 and 1037 the seat of the powerful Gurjara-Pratīhāra kings. The name Ṭarfānah, for reasons discussed below, has been amended to read Ṭarfālah. In the Arabic script the change required to produce this reading is graphically very minor.

The third-ranking cities in al-Maqdisī's hierarchies were the district capitals *(mudun;* sing. *madīnah)* (fig. 5). They appear to have constituted a somewhat heterogeneous class of urban forms, with an uneven distribution through the Islamic culture realm. There were, moreover, only about fifty of them,[181] so that they were considerably fewer than the *qaṣabāt.* The reason for the unexpectedly meager development of this rank in the urban hierarchy would seem to be that the *mudun* were primarily associated with Muslim settlement in politically—and often ecologically—marginal zones, where they functioned as capitals of what al-Maqdisī called "dependencies." They were sparse, for example, in core areas of old-established and long-consolidated political authority such as Fārs (without a single *madīnah* but with no less than five *qaṣabāt*) or Miṣr, al-Shām, al-ʿIrāq, and Khūzistān (each with one *madīnah* compared with, respectively, five, five, four, and six *qaṣabāt*), but were relatively more numerous on the desert borders of Arabia, al-Jibāl, Khurāsān, and Transoxania.

The fourth, and lowest, distinguishable rank in the hierarchies comprised a very broad band of urban centers ranging in size from, say, Ṭāliqān in Khurāsān, with its populous markets and magnificent congregational mosque, a city as large as its district capital Marw al-Rūdh;[182] to Marand, a small fortress in Ādharbayjān with a mosque and *sūq* as twin foci of an incipient suburb below its walls.[183] Clearly a category subsuming urban forms as disparate in size and range of functions as those represented by these two settlements must have been a composite of several ranks. The quality of the available evidence is, however, unfortunately inadequate for their discrimination.

Plotting of Place-Names

Plotting the lowest discernible rank in the urban hierarchy in figure 2 also introduced difficulties and uncertainties that generally were not encountered when dealing

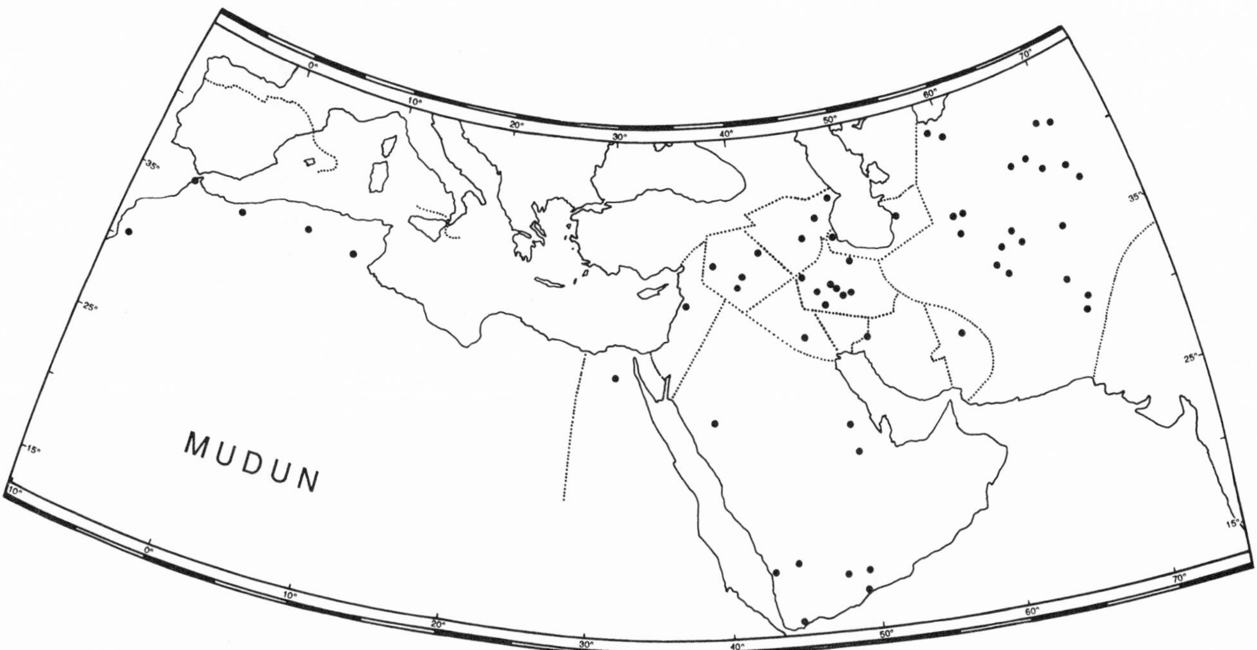

Figure 5. Distribution of *mudun* among al-Maqdisī's urban regions.

with the higher ranks. Whereas information relevant to the *amṣār, qaṣabāt,* and *mudun* was derived in compendious and mainly unequivocal form from the *Aḥsan,* the fourth rank had to be abstracted from virtually the whole range of Islamic topographical writing discussed in the preceding section, a great deal of which could be made to yield only intractable and ambivalent testimony. A persistent difficulty at all times concerned the identification of urban sites,[184] though this problem was not entirely absent in the plotting of the higher levels of the hierarchy. Barvān, the provincial capital of Daylam, for instance, no longer exists, and none of the medieval itineraries provide its exact position.[185] The location of Wayhind, *qaṣabah* of Sind, can only be approximated, and that of al-ʿAbbāsīyah in the Egyptian delta is far from certain.

In the case of numerous low-order central places, however, the difficulty is greatly exacerbated. Ultimately I have frequently had to settle for a reasonable degree of probability. In fact, perhaps about 10 percent of the lowest-order urban centers in figure 2 could be assigned only an approximate location. They were recorded as having been in the vicinity of, close to, or not far from, an established location. Or a center may have been described as roughly midway between two known points. Or, occasionally, it may have been implied that it was in a particular part of a district. Nevertheless, all such circumstantial identifications were worth plotting, as the reduced scale on which figure 2 has been printed goes a long way toward eliminating errors deriving from subjective locational judgments. In any case, errors surviving this transformation of scale are unlikely to seriously affect the generalized *pattern* of urban distribution with which we are primarily concerned in this work.[186]

There are several areas in which locating place-names is especially difficult. One of the most notorious is the mountainous region known to Arab geographers as Ghūristān, extending from Harāt to Bāmiyan and Kābul. Al-Yaʿqūbī describes it as "a land of arid mountains, laborious trails, valleys difficult of access, and strong fortresses."[187] According to Ibn Ḥawqal, in the tenth century it was predominantly infidel territory, although many Muslims lived there; but the *Ḥudūd* asserts that, although the province was formerly pagan *(kāfir),* "actually most of the inhabitants are [now] Muslim."[188] Certainly al-Maqdisī, al-Iṣṭakhrī, and Ibn Ḥawqal refer to a number of urban centers in the area, but only a handful are now identifiable. Even in less forbidding realms it is sometimes difficult to locate a proportion of the towns that are mentioned by tenth-century authors. This is particularly true of the Provinces of Sughd and Shāsh in the east, and of the districts of Sijilmāsah and Sūs al-Aqṣā in the west.

Subjectiveness was not restricted to the plotting of place-names: it also pervaded numerous decisions as to what constituted an urban settlement. In the higher levels of the hierarchy this problem did not arise, and even in lowest rank by far the larger proportion of urban forms could be discriminated without difficulty. Muslim topographers set the imprimatur of urban status on a settlement when they recorded that it possessed a congregational mosque beside its marketplace, perhaps adding a remark or two on its public baths and fortifications, and, less frequently, appending a comment implying some degree of societal and economic differentiation. A representative paragraph dealing with a substantial but, in the present context, lower-order urban settlement, runs as follows:

> *Naṣībīn.* This city is more pleasant, but smaller . . . than al-Mawṣil. It abounds in fruits, and has good baths and stately palaces. Its people possess both wealth and intelligence. The *sūq* stretches from gate to gate, and a citadel constructed of stone and cement dominates the city. The congregational mosque is centrally situated. May Heaven protect us from the scorpions of Naṣībīn![189]

This type of statement attesting urban status was repeatedly applied by medieval topographers to settlements throughout the Islamic world. Ambivalences arise only when some of the material features expressive of differentiated institutional spheres are lacking. Medieval authors were conscious of these difficulties, and al-Maqdisī himself confronted such a problem when he sought to categorize Minā, a settlement situated a *farsakh* or so from Makkah, where certain rites associated with the *Ḥajj* were, And are, performed. His general description of Minā' reads as follows:[190]

> Minā' extends over two valleys through which run the streets of the town. The Masjid [al-Khayf][191] is situated on the right-hand road, and the Masjid al-Kabsh[192] in the vicinity of al-ʿAqabah (the Pass).[193] In Mina' there are wells and cisterns, trading houses and shops. The town is well built of stone and Indian teak, and lies between two hills that rise above and overlook it.

The question of urban status posed by al-Maqdisī was that

> Minā' is populous in the pilgrimage season, but for the rest of the year is devoid of inhabitants except for those who are stationed in it as guards. Abū al-Ḥasan al-Karkhī[194] supports Abū Ḥanīfah[195] in permitting the Friday prayers to be held there as it constitutes with Makkah a single urban centre *(miṣr)*. But when Abū Bakr al-Jaṣṣāṣ on his pilgrimage saw how far apart those settlements were [specified as 1 *farsakh* three lines previously on the same page], he considered that argument untenable, asserting instead that Minā' is a particular Islamic city *[miṣr]* that is inhabited at one season of the year and evacuated at another. Its [seasonal] abandonment does not exclude it from the category of *miṣr*. Qāḍī Abū al-Ḥasan al-Qazwīnī holds the same opinion. When he asked me how many people lived in Mina' throughout the year, I replied that there were twenty or thirty men, and additionally in almost every tent a woman to take care of it. Upon which he said, "Abū Bakr is right, and what he taught you is correct." But when I met with the *faqīh* Abū Ḥāmid al-Baghūlanī[196] at Naysābūr and repeated all this to him he replied, "The true reason is that given by Abū al-Ḥasan. Do you not recall that the Most High hath said, 'Thereafter the lawful sacrifice is by the Ancient House,'[197] and hath referred to '. . . an offering to be delivered at the Kaʿbah'?[198] Now it is in Mina' that sacrifices are performed."[199]

Modern scholars, furnished with a much wider range of models of urban function than that available to medieval authors, would probably accord Minā' urban status on other grounds than those adduced by the learned doctors, and might be inclined to lean less heavily on Authority; but they still have to face the same types of problems as confronted al-Maqdisī. How, for instance, should they treat the "settlement" of Bandanījān, a reasonably important place near the border between al-ʿIrāq and Jibāl Provinces? According to Yāqūt, who was writing in a later period than that with which we are concerned here,

Bandanījān was the name applied to a group of four villages: Buwayqiyā, Sūq Jamīl, Filisht, and Bāquṭnāyā, "separate one from another and each invisible from the others." Bāquṭnāyā was the site of a *sūq* and of the residences of the governor and the *qāḍī*, and apparently there was, or at least had been, another market at Sūq Jamīl. Is it to be concluded that these four settlements functioned compositely as a low-order central place with enough specialized collectivities and roles to justify it being regarded as urban?[200] Or were there simply four villages, of which one was in the course of developing supra-village functions consequent on its selection as a seat of secular and religious authority?

A similar classificatory problem was presented by the caravanserai of Dayr al-Jiṣṣ, situated on the desert road about halfway between what are today the Kargas and Siyāh hills in Jibāl Province. It was described as a strong place, built of burnt brick and provided with iron gates, where guides for the desert trails were stationed by order of the *ṣultān.* Its large water tanks were never allowed to fall into disrepair, and there were shops selling provisions to travellers about to undertake the desert crossing.[201] Should this settlement be regarded simply as a staging post, or would it be more appropriately categorized as proto-urban, a town in the making?

An essentially similar problem is posed by the aggregation of population at Kharā'ib Abī Ḥalīmah on the Libyan coast. The nucleus of this settlement was a fortress enclosing a *sūq* and five wells,[202] but the precise manner in which the population was disposed around the citadel is unknown. North Africa and the mountainous territories of Ādharbayjān and Alburz were especially prodigal of situations of this sort, in which, typically, fortresses established for purely military reasons were being transformed into incipient urban nuclei. A topographer's account occasionally hints that this was being achieved through the socially consolidatory mechanism of markets set up below the walls of the citadel. At other times it appears to have come about through the development of a mutual interdependence, as when Arab garrisons needed to augment their labor force for construction work within the fortress, at the same time the indigenous folk sought to obtain goods imported to, or manufactured within, the citadel. To be classified as urban for inclusion in figure 2, a settlement had to appear to be something more than an aggregation of peasants working adjacent fields. It had to provide evidence of its functioning as an instrument for the organization of surrounding territories, not merely as the locus of a labor force. Confirming this classification has required evaluating the relevant passages in the general context of the nature of the sources concerned and the events being described.

Below the lowest-ranking urban forms in the hierarchy were one or more strata of rural settlements that cannot now be reconstructed, even though frequent general references to them exist in topographical writings of the time. Sometimes these references were vague statements about "many" or "numerous" villages in such-and-such a locality. Representative examples occur in al-Maqdisī's account of Ghubayrā in the Bardasīr district of Kirmān,[203] al-Bakrī's discussion of Jamūnah al-Sabūn in the Ifrīqīyah,[204] and Ibn Ḥawqal's description of the country around Jizah in Sijistān.[205]

At other times such references are incidental to an account of a journey, as when al-Maqdisī mentions that he passed through villages and palm groves for the distance of a day's journey outside Ṭabas al-Tamr in Qūhistān.[206] In addition, several topographers attested that in the tenth century a line of populous villages extended for more than a day's march along the road from Harāt to Sijistān.[207] In North Africa, al-Bakrī related that Copt villages stretched along the high road both east and west of Tripoli for a total distance of three days' journey and south for two days' march;[208] "a cluster of villages resembling towns" occupied the Warghah valley in al-Maghrib;[209] and the banks of the Wādī Sabū in the neighborhood of Fās (Fez) provided sites for numerous villages.[210] Occasionally some or all of a series of villages referred to in this way are enumerated individually. Iṣṭakhrī, for example, named numerous villages in the Kāmfīrūz district of Fārs,[211] and al-Bakrī did the same for Berber villages in the vicinity of Jarawah in al-Maghrib.[212]

Not infrequently a topographer recorded a precise figure for the number of villages in a district. When only small numbers were involved, as, for instance, in Ibn Ḥawqal's reference to seven villages on the plain surrounding Andakhud,[213] they can presumably be relied on as being fairly accurate, but the larger figures occasionally cited are certainly no more than gross estimates indicating a general order of populousness. Such must be the import

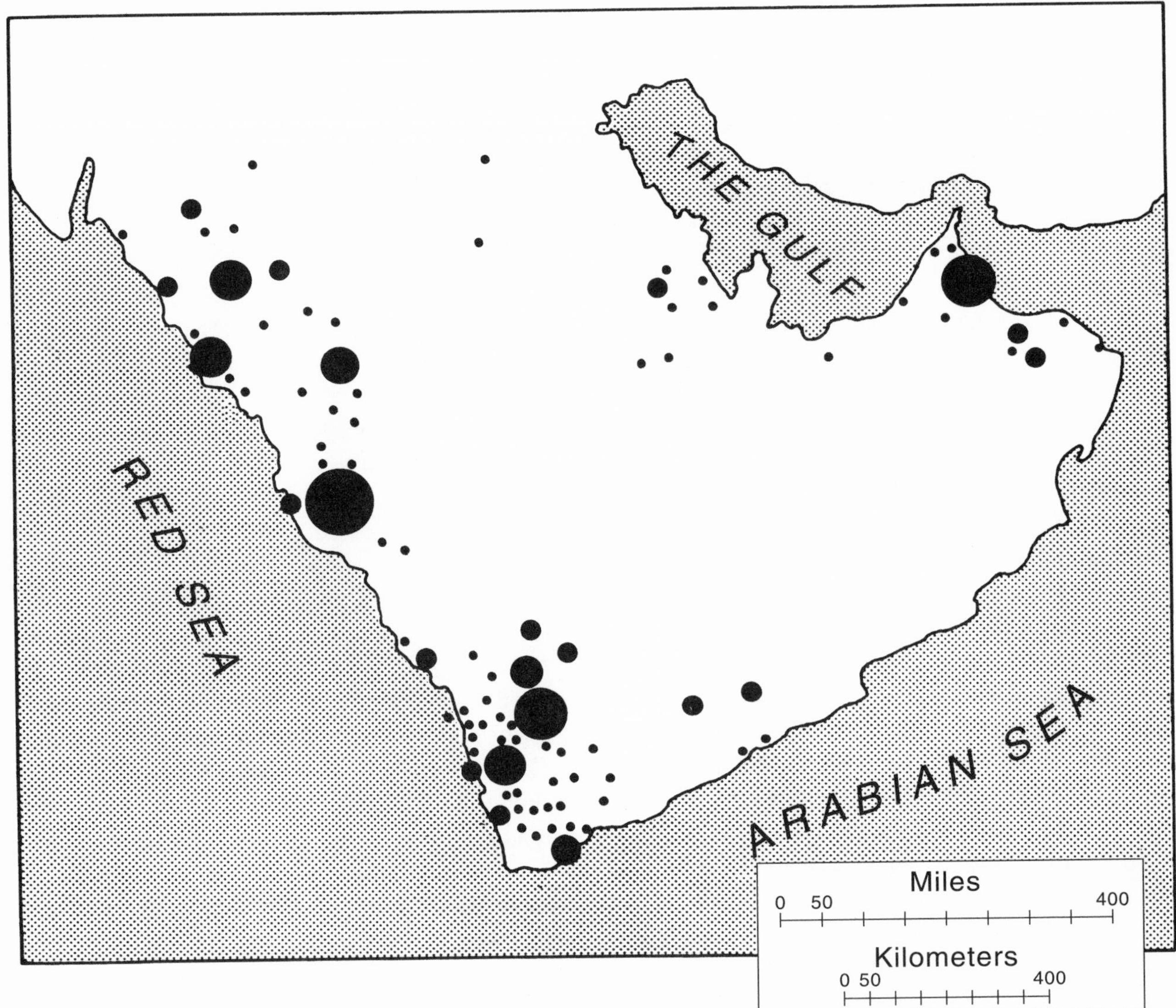

Figure 6. An impressionistic representation of the relative sizes of urban centers on the Arabian Peninsula in the second half of the tenth century as reported by al-Maqdisī. Jabalah and Mahāʾiʿ, both categorized as reasonably sized towns in the Ḥijāz, cannot be located and are therefore omitted from the map. The largest symbol represents the Holy City of Makkah, sanctified both cosmologically and soteriologically.

of, for example, al-Maqdisī's apparently precise estimate of 226 large villages in the neighborhood of Kundur in the Busht district of Qūhistān,[214] the estimate of 2,200 hamlets in Wālishtān,[215] and the 6,000 villages in the districts surrounding Ṣāghāniyān.[216]

Relative Sizes of Cities

Estimating the size of medieval cities is inevitably a hazardous undertaking, and the Islamic world affords no exception. Although Muslim topographers sometimes attached statements of area or population to their descriptions of cities, the assurance with which these statistics were advanced seldom disguises the fact that they were estimates, and often not very informed ones at that. At their crudest they were simple statements of relative size. Surt (Madīnat al-Sulṭān), for example, was characterized as a large city;[217] al-Rammādah, a small one.[218] More valuable are the accounts in which the relative sizes of a series of cities are estimated. The way in which such pieces of information can, in favorable circumstances, be combined to produce a graphic impression of relative urban-size distributions is illustrated in figure 6. This figure depicts the relative sizes of the cities of Arabia as estimated by al-Maqdisī.[219] Heading the hierarchy was Makkah, the cynosure of Islam, upon the size of which al-Maqdisī forebore to comment explicitly. Yet it was inferentially among the larger cities of the tenth century, if not the largest, on the peninsula. The second-largest city of Arabia was probably Ṣuḥār, capital of ʿUmān, which was "larger than [either] Zabīd [the metropolis *(miṣr)* of al-Yaman][220] or Ṣanʿāʾ [the capital of Najd al-Yaman]." Ṣanʿāʾ, in turn, was "larger than [either] Zabīd" or Ṣaʿdah, the seat of the ʿAlawīyah (a branch of the descendants of the caliph ʿAlī). In the northern tracts of the peninsula, al-Madīnah was described as occupying "rather less than half the area of Makkah." As Qurḥ (al-Qurah) was designated the largest city of al-Ḥijāz after Makkah, it is to be presumed that it was larger than al-Madīnah, perhaps two-thirds or three-quarters the size of Makkah. Yanbuʿ was also characterized as more prosperous, and by implication larger, than al-Madīnah.

At a lower level of the hierarchy al-Maqdisī categorized Jabalah, Mahāyiʿ,[221] ʿAdan, ʿAththar, Salūt, Nazwah, al-Ḥajr, and al-Aḥsāʾ as "large urban centres," al-Sirr as smaller than Nazwah, and Jurash and Najrān of middling size, a category that was particularized as being smaller than Ṣaʿdah. Juddah, Suqyā Yazīd, Badā Yaʿqūb, al-ʿAwnīd, Mukhā, Galāfiqah, and Ḥaly were each described as either "populous" and "flourishing" or both, or by some other epithet that appears to have distinguished them from the common run of towns. Qarn, al-Ṭāʾif, Amaj, Badr, al-ʿUshayrah, al-Ḥijr, Maʿqir, ʿAbrah, Ghārah, al-Makhnaq, al-Sirrayn, and Ḍank were discriminated unequivocally as "small towns." The sizes of the rest of Arabia's urban forms were not indicated specifically, but the information that al-Maqdisī provided about them more often than not bespoke a small center. In figure 6 they have been represented by the same symbol as that used for the towns designated specifically as small.[222]

Occasionally, and for regions of restricted extent, a relative size ranking of urban centers can be supplemented with a modicum of quantified information, usually of somewhat dubious authenticity. Figure 7 depicts

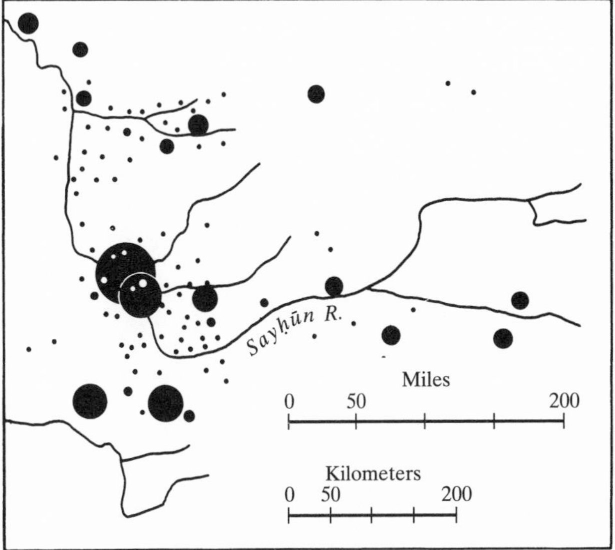

Figure 7. An impressionistic representation of the relative sizes of urban centers in the Sayḥūn provinces in the second half of the tenth century, based on sources listed in chapter 14. The largest symbol represents the district capital (*madīnah*) of Shāsh.

the relative sizes of the cities of the Sayḥūn provinces as compiled from the writings of Iṣṭakhrī, Ibn Ḥawqal, and al-Maqdisī, and to a minor extent from information in the *Ḥudūd al-ʿĀlam.*[223] During the tenth century the largest urban center in this region was Shāsh,[224] the ruins of which are now known as Old Tashkand. The city consisted of three notionally concentric walled enclaves. The innermost constituted a *shahristān* with a citadel standing adjacent to it. Outside its wall spread an almost completely built-up suburb, and beyond that an outer suburb less densely peopled and with much of its area in gardens and orchards. According to al-Maqdisī the city was one league in diameter.

The second-largest city in the Shāsh District was Banākath.[225] Tūnkath[226] was said to be half the size of Shāsh; Isbījāb,[227] with a perimeter of one league, one-third as large. Būnjikath,[228] provincial capital of Ushrūsanah, was only as large as the *shahristān* of Shāsh, and was allegedly inhabited by ten thousand (active) men, implying perhaps a total adult population of between twenty thousand and thirty thousand. Zāmīn was almost as large as Būnjikath. If Ibn Ḥawqal was correct in his statement that the *shahristān* of Akhsīkath was a mile across, then the city would have been about one-sixth the area of Būnjikath.

Qubā' was almost as large as Akhsīkath. Ūsh was described as a large urban center, and Ūzkand was two-thirds its size. Additionally, Rishtān, Jamūkat,[229] Bārāb,[230] Subānīkath,[231] Shāvaghar,[232] and Ṭarāz were categorized as large, and Sawrān[233] as very large. Sābāṭ, Marasmandah, and Khasht[234] were accorded the distinguishing epithet of "populous," and Marghīnān, Waynkard, and Wasīj were classified as small. For what it is worth, "large" in the case of Bārāb allegedly signified seventy thousand inhabitants.[235] The sizes of the remaining urban centers in the region were not specified, but in figure 7 have been assumed to have been small.

In the chapters that follow we shall examine in sequence the urban systems in each of al-Maqdisī's regions.

PART II

Urban Systems in the Islamic World, Seventh through the Tenth Centuries

Chapter Four
The Urban System in al-ʿIrāq

. . . the country of men of refinement, and the well-head of the learned.
—Al-Maqdisī, *Aḥsan al-Taqāsīm,* 113.

When al-Maqdisī was compiling the *Aḥsan,* al-ʿIrāq was still the metropolitan province of the ʿAbbāsid Empire. Baghdād remained the seat of the caliphate, even though that office commanded little more than formal allegiance beyond the lower Mesopotamian plain, since effective power had passed into the hands of Buwayhid *amīrs* ruling from Shīrāz. According to contemporary Arab authors, the province stretched from the upper end of the Persian Gulf along the courses of the Tigris (Arabic = Dijlah) and Euphrates (al-Furāt) Rivers to about the latitude of Takrīt. Arab writers customarily referred to this region of alternating marsh, mud plain, and sand, seamed throughout its length by a network of anastomozing stream channels, as al-Sawād, "The Black Ground."[1]

In the tenth century both of the great natural waterways of al-ʿIrāq followed courses significantly different from their present ones. The greater deviation was exhibited by the Tigris, which, since Sāsānian times, had flowed in a channel along what is today the Shaṭṭ al-Ḥayy, up to seventy miles west of its modern (and indeed its pre-Sāsānian) course. As a result, the southeastern sector of the province was left so desiccated as to be almost uninhabitable. The present channel of the Euphrates was at that time an extensive swamp curving in an arc against the desert edge from a few miles south of al-Kūfah to the neighborhood of al-Baṣrah.[2] What is today the Ḥillah branch of the river was defined by a large irrigation canal known as the Nahr Sūrā. In addition, the two main arteries of the Euphrates were linked by a network of canals, mostly inherited by the Arabs from the earlier Persian administration. The northernmost of these canals, the Nahr ʿĪsā, ran from al-Anbār on the Euphrates to the Tigris immediately below the point where the caliph al-Manṣūr had built the Round City, the nucleus of Baghdād. To the south of this latitude ran a succession of transverse canals, including the Nahr Ṣarṣar, the Nahr al-Mālik, the Nahr Kuthā, and the Great Ṣarāh. The Dujayl[3] was a loop canal that branched off from the Tigris below Sāmarrā to a point approximately one hundred miles below Baghdād.[4]

Marketing and Service Centers

Basic to the urban hierarchy in this region was a network of exchange and service centers that, on this plain where sedentary life was tied to permanent water sources, were inevitably disposed along the main rivers and canals. Although this network had originated deep in the past of Babylonia, the Arabs had made important contributions, chiefly through the founding of new military and administrative centers. A general decline in the intensity of urban settlement evidently occurred during the later Sāsānian period, and the Arabs seem not to have reversed this trend until the rise of the ʿAbbāsids brought the capital of the caliphate from Syria into the Sawād in the mid-eighth century. Representative of the lowest-order urban foci in the settlement pattern were such local service centers as Bābil (much reduced from its former greatness as the capital of Babylonia), ʿAbdas,[5] Bādhbīn, and al-Sīb, surrounded by olive groves,[6] all on the plain south of Baghdād. Of a somewhat higher order were al-Nuʿmānīyah, the chief town of the Upper Zāb District; al-Anbār on the Euphrates about ten *farsakh*s west of Baghdād;[7] al-Daskarah in the Diyālā valley; and ʿAbertā, "abounding in fruits and producing excellent grapes."[8] At a still higher level of the hierarchy were settlements such as al-Nahrawān (Sifwah), chief city of the Middle Nahrawān region,[9] al-Jāmiʿān,[10] and Dayr al-ʿĀqūl, which provided a range of goods and services almost as wide as that of the district capitals.

On this pre-Islamic hierarchy of exchange centers, the Arabs had superimposed a weighty superstructure of new cities, only some of which had been fully integrated into the urban system by the tenth century. Preeminent among these foundations was Baghdād, the imperial capital (in al-Maqdisī's parlance the *miṣr* of the *iqlīm*). Its size and prosperity were a reflex not so much of regional or provincial responsibilities as of the greatness and vitality of the whole ʿAbbāsid Empire. The establishment of this sprawling city of possibly one million inhabitants has been described in chapter 2 and will be analyzed more fully in chapter 17.

The founding of Sāmarrā, for fifty-six years and eight caliphs the capital of the ʿAbbāsid Empire, has been touched upon in a previous section and will also be discussed again in chapter 17. After the seat of the caliphate was restored to Baghdād in 892, large tracts of Sāmarrā fell into ruin. When al-Maqdisī was writing, "A traveller might walk for two or three miles without chancing upon an inhabited place,"[11] probably only a year or two previously al-Muhallabī had recounted the following: "Passing through Sāmarrā soon after the morning prayer, I walked down a street bordered on both sides by dwellings which appeared to have been abandoned very recently. They lacked only roofs and doors: the walls proper seemed newly built. We walked until just after midday before coming to a locality which, right in the centre of Sāmarrā, amounted to hardly more than a small village."[12] The congregational mosque, which al-Maqdisī says was architecturally superior to the great mosque of Dimashq (Damascus), still survived, but the center of population had moved to the far northerly suburb of al-Karkh.[13] Such prosperity as the former imperial capital still enjoyed derived mainly from its function as a center of Shīʿah pilgrimage, for within the neighborhood known as ʿAskar Muʿtaṣim were the tombs of the tenth and eleventh *imāms*, as well as the underground chamber whence the promised Mahdī had been translated to Paradise in 878.

The founding of the ʿIrāqān, al-Baṣrah and al-Kūfah, has already been discussed in some detail in chapter 2. Both subsequently flourished sequentially as army base camps and administrative centers (*qasabāt* in al-Maqdisī's schema), strategically located on the border between Sawād and desert, for an empire whose focus was first in al-Ḥijāz, subsequently in Syria, and finally in al-ʿIrāq. Even before the heyday of these two cities the Umayyad viceroy al-Ḥajjāj had been wont to say, "Al-Kūfah is a beautiful slave girl without wealth of her own, who is yet sought after for her beauty, whilst al-Baṣrah is an ugly old woman who is, nevertheless, rich and sought after for her money."[14] In coarser fashion Ziyād ibn Abīhi likened al-Kūfah to the uvula, "which is moistened by cool and sweet water, whereas al-Baṣrah resembles the bladder, which only receives the water after it has become changed and unsavory."[15] What impressed virtually all who observed the two cities in their prime was the contrast between the austere but often unorthodox character of Kūfan cultural life, an extreme intellectualization—some would say an overintellectualization—of the values popularly ascribed to the era of the Rāshidūn Caliphate; and the vibrant, polyglot, expediential mores of al-Baṣrah, which yet maintained schools of scholarship in some respects more creative than those of al-Kūfah.

When the Umayyads began to reorient their interests to take account of events in the eastern provinces—particularly after Wāsiṭ, developed as a seat of strong regional government midway between the two rebellious *amṣār* and garrisoned with Syrian troops, began to usurp the political power of the ʿIrāqān—the cultural and economic preeminence of these two cities was undermined. The decline was especially evident in the status of al-Kūfah. Al-Iṣṭakhrī, in the mid-tenth century, remarked that it exceeded al-Baṣrah in the excellence of its architecture and that its markets were second only to those of the latter city.[16] He might also have recalled that ever since ʿAlī ibn Abī-Ṭālib had moved his capital to al-Kūfah in 656, the city had been the generative center for the Shīʿite movement. In and around the city ʿAlī had mobilized his forces for the Battles of the Camel and Ṣiffīn; his son Ḥasan had been elected and had abdicated there; the uprising of Ḥujr ibn ʿAdī al-Kindī and the martyrdom of Ḥusayn had taken place there; and both the Tawwābūn movement and al-Mukhtār's revolt had begun there. Furthermore, in the same city in early Umayyad times, Shīʿī supporters had joined with the Khawārij in opposing the privileged position claimed by the traditional tribal leaders *(ashrāf al-qabāʾil).*

In its heyday al-Kūfah had been a city of predominantly Arabian culture, drawing for its sustenance on the resources of the Sawād and functioning as a reservoir of *muqātilah* destined for service on the Īrānian frontier. But from the middle of the seventh century onward, al-Baṣrah had been outdistancing al-Kūfah in the conquest of the Khurāsānian East. Near the end of the tenth century al-Maqdisī could still describe al-Kūfah as "a large and pleasant city, well built, its markets copiously supplied, and providing a habitation for numerous folk who are able to find in it an easy means of livelihood," but, he adds, "The city is declining and its suburbs are in ruins."[17]

The western suburbs of al-Baṣrah also were in ruins by this time, and the Mirbaḍ on its way to becoming the detached oasis that Yāqūt was to describe in the early years of the thirteenth century.[18] The commercial importance of al-Baṣrah at the close of the tenth century was still such that al-Maqdisī compared its areal extent with that of the imperial capital;[19] but the truth is surely that, despite their continuing cultural vitality, both the ʿIrāqān had by that time become little more than provincial towns: *qaṣabāt*, as al-Maqdisī justly categorized them. Nevertheless, Hichem Djaït, recalling their glorious pasts, very properly refers to them as having been "fundamental matrices which defined the general lines of the culture of Islam, each with its own genius: Kūfa excelled in the recovery of the Arab poetic patrimony, in the exegesis of the Ḳurʾān, in law and genealogy, whereas Baṣra, more rationalist and critical, invented Arabic grammar and was the great centre of Muʿtazilī speculation."[20]

Two other important administrative centers established by the Arabs in al-ʿIrāq included the mint city of Wāsiṭ, already mentioned, situated some fifty leagues up the Tigris from al-Baṣrah;[21] and al-Nīl, capital of the Sūrā District. Both were founded by the Umayyad viceroy al-Ḥajjāj, and for a time early in the eighth century Wāsiṭ was effectively the administrative capital for the entire eastern half of the Islamic Empire. In addition, not a few old Persian cities were virtually reconstituted when Arab rulers and commanders chose them as seats of government. Notable among such centers were Madīnat ibn Hubayrah and al-Anbār,[22] both sometime residences of the caliph al-Saffāḥ (r. 749–54); Ītākhīyah,[23] a small town on what is today called the Nahrawān Canal, the name of which was changed to al-Muḥammadīyah by the caliph al-Mutawakkil (r. 847–61) in honor of his son Muḥammad al-Muntaṣir; and al-Ṣalīq,[24] a city standing on the shore of a lagoon in the Great Swamps below Wāsiṭ. From 949 to 979 this last city was the seat of ʿImrān ibn Shāhīn, an independent ruler who made such strategic use of the swamps that the ʿAbbāsid armies were unable to oust him. In 983 one of ʿImrān's generals established a second period of independent rule in al-Salīq, which a year or two later al-Maqdisī described as a typical swamp settlement. He ranked it as the headquarters *(madīnah)* of a politically and ecologically marginal district:

> The fields [of Ṣalīq] extend right up to the outskirts of al-Kūfah, but the heat is very great, and the air foul and oppressive. The mosquitoes are a perfect pest, making life miserable. The food [of the inhabitants] is fish, their drink is warm water, and nights are a torture. [The populace] is boorish and its speech corrupt. There is a shortage of salt and great misery. However, [the district] is a source of abundant flour, has a benign government,[25] abundant water and considerable quantities of fish. The city has a great name, and the inhabitants are without exception good fighters, and knowledgeable about the river. One of their localities is reminiscent in its pleasantness of the canal of al-Ubullah.[26]

The way in which these higher-order administrative cities were integrated with the lower-order marketing centers that provided a framework for the expression of local identities is obscure and, at this point, likely to remain so, but it is beyond doubt that below the level of the district capital, bureaucratic controls were severely attenuated. It is equally certain, though, that the lower-order marketing center somehow not only generated a localized territorial identity but also linked the local level with district, provincial, and ultimately even state systems through exchanges and the provision of services.[27]

Transportation Foci

The at least notional symmetry inherent in this basic pattern of exchange and service centers was distorted to an extent by the institutional effects of long-distance (as opposed to city-region) trade. Although virtually all the cities of medieval al-ʿIrāq acted as centers for tertiary economic activity, supplying goods and services to their immediate environs, many of them also performed more specialized transportation functions for wider regional, and even imperial, markets. The more important of these transportation foci were situated in two environmentally distinctive, but functionally homologous, locations: along the great trade routes converging on Baghdād from all points of the compass,[28] and at the head of the Persian Gulf, where commodities carried over the Indian Ocean were transferred from seagoing vessels to riverboats or pack animals. Significantly, trade passing through the entrepôts of al-ʿIrāq consisted predominantly of imports, a clear reflection of the redistributive—or, perhaps more accurately, mobilizative—mode of economic integration underpinning the political structure of the ʿAbbāsid Empire. As al-Yaʿqūbī put it succinctly enough at the end of the ninth century, "Such a great volume of trade comes [to Baghdād] from Hind, Sind, 'China,' Tibet, the Turkish lands, al-Daylam, the Khazar territories, Abyssinia, and other countries that more articles of commerce are to be found in that city than in the countries of origin themselves."[29] And fed into these centripetal flows were the huge volumes of grain, meat, olive oil, sugar, and fuel (for bakeries and public baths) that were extorted from the *Jazīrah* (Upper Mesopotamia) and eastern al-Shām (Greater Syria) to meet the demands of a burgeoning and ever-restless urban populace.

The most celebrated of the trunk routes traversing the empire was undoubtedly the great Khurāsān road, which led from Baghdād northeast up the Diyālā valley toward Ḥulwān, the Persian highlands, and ultimately to the frontier towns of the Sayḥūn and the borders of China. The stages of the road within the limits of al-ʿIrāq were listed by al-Maqdisī as follows:

• from Baghdād to al-Nahrawān,	two *barīds* (one *barīd* here = six Arab miles[30]);
• thence to Dayr Bārimmah,[31]	two *barīds*;
• thence to al-Daskarah,	one stage *(marḥalah* = six or seven *farsakhs*);
• thence to Jalūlāʾ,	one stage;
• thence to Khāniqīn,	one stage.

Then, reversing direction,

• from Ḥulwān to Qaṣr Shīrīn,	one stage;
• thence to Khāniqīn,	one stage.[32]

Of these staging posts the most important was the provincial capital *(qaṣabah)* of Ḥulwān, usually reckoned as the sixth city of al-ʿIrāq in ʿAbbāsid times. A surrounding countryside of gardens, vineyards, and fig orchards[33] supported a flourishing *sūq* below the walls of a *quhandiz,*[34] within which was a congregational mosque; but the importance of the city derived primarily from its strategic location at the junction of no less than eight roads. Al-Maqdisī specifies these as Khurāsān, al-Bāqāt, al-Muṣallā, the Jews (because it led to a highly venerated Jewish temple), Barqīṭ, the Jewess, and Mājakān.[35] Daskarat al-Malik[36] (so called from the Persian king Hormuz I having resided there), Jalūlāʾ, and Dayr Bārimmah were smaller centers; al-Nahrawān and Khāniqīn were bridge towns where the Khurāsān road crossed respectively the Nahrawān Canal and the Diyālā River;[37] and Qaṣr Shīrīn was a settlement that had originally grown up around the palace of the Lady Shīrīn, a paramour of King Khusraw Parwīz, but which had subsequently benefited from its location on the Khurāsān road.[38]

By Qurʾānic prescription every Muslim must, once in his lifetime and at a specified season of the year, undertake the pilgrimage *(Ḥajj)* to the holy sites at Makkah (Mecca), ʿArafah, and Minā. It was probably three or four years after the *Hijrah* that the following *sūrah* was revealed:

The first House established for the people
was that at Bakkah [traditionally and invariably
assumed, for obscure reasons, to have been an
alternative designation for Makkah], a blessed
house providing guidance to the worlds.
Therein are unmistakable signs—the place where
Ibrāhīm stood to pray,
and security for him who enters it.
It is the duty of all men toward Allāh to come
to the House as pilgrims, if they are able to
make their way thither.
But if anyone disbelieve, Allāh is sufficient
beyond need of the worlds.[39]

In the course of time this injunction, together with prescriptions in *Sūrahs* 2 *(al-Baqarah):* 196–200 and 5 *(al-Māʾidah):* 1–2 and 95–96, were formalized as the fifth pillar of Islam, the obligatory pilgrimage. ʿ*Umrah,* the Lesser Pilgrimage to Makkah, was permitted individually and at any time. Compliance with these obligations was facilitated by the existence of an elaborate network of roads, mostly inherited from the Sāsānian Empire, which, under the ʿAbbāsids, was modified so as to radiate outward from Baghdād. The Khurāsān road was one such strand in this transportation system. Its westward extension led first south from Baghdād to al-Kūfah, then southwest across the Arabian wastes toward al-Ḥijāz, while an alternative route followed a more southerly course toward the Holy City via al-Baṣrah. Along these, and numerous other of the great post roads, tribute gravitated toward Baghdād, while each year during the weeks preceding Dhū al-Ḥijjah, the month when the *Ḥajj* proper began, a contrary flow of human bodies set in, carrying Believers toward the Holy House in Makkah.

One ʿIrāqī settlement whose annual regime was especially linked to the flow of pilgrim traffic was al-Qādisīyah,[40] on the desert border five leagues west of al-Kūfah. It comprised a walled enceinte defended by a mud-walled fortress, and its springs of tolerable water had been supplemented by the digging of a canal from the Euphrates to a reservoir at the Baghdād Gate. Another canal leading to the Desert Gate (Bāb al-Bādīyah) was supplied with water only during the season of pilgrimage. In fact that was the period when the settlement came alive, the time when, as al-Maqdisī writes, "It is populous and all sorts of desirable commodities are brought thither."[41] In front of the congregational mosque which stood, significantly, at the Desert Gate, a great market was set up, and the town, again in al-Maqdisī's words, "became one large *sūq.*" Then, as the pilgrims moved on to the west, the settlement reverted to its local-service function amid the palm groves marking the transition from Sawād to desert.

In addition to the major staging posts along the imperial highways, there were numerous small, now barely remembered, market towns that exploited their positions at river or canal crossings. Such, for example, were Ṣarṣar, where a pontoon bridge carried the highway from Baghdād to al-Kūfah over the canal of the same name; and Nahr al-Malik and Kūthā Rabbā, which performed the same function respectively five and eight *farsakh*s farther along the road.

A particularly prominent group of cities offering break-of-bulk and allied services was located at the head of the Persian Gulf. Among these cities were al-Ubullah, some distance up the Blind Tigris (Dijlah al-ʿAwrā, now the Shaṭṭ al-ʿArab), which had earned for itself the sobriquet "Gateway to India";[42] and ʿAbbādān, furnished with protective *ribāṭ*s, on the coast between this estuary and that of the Dujayl.[43] Smaller ports were Shiqq ʿUthmān, across the river from al-Ubullah, and Sulaymānān,[44] a few leagues east of ʿAbbādān. At the other end of the Sawād, al-Muḥawwal derived the prosperity manifested in its imposing architecture and well-stocked *sūq*s directly from its function as a break-of-bulk point, where the cargoes of river barges passing from the Euphrates to Baghdād along the ʿĪsā Canal were transferred to small boats able to pass under the bridges spanning that waterway in the suburb of al-Karkh.[45]

Industrial and Craft Centers

The third component in the settlement pattern comprised centers rendered distinctive by their performing specialized functions for regions, even states, larger than their own city trade areas. At one end of the spectrum of locational mobility were, theoretically, those cities concerned with the exploitation of particular natural resources. In other provinces these were often tied to mineral lodes, but mining was never an important activity in al-ʿIrāq, where most industrial enterprises migrated freely along the locational continuum between raw materials and markets. Under the conditions of craft manufacture that obtained in the medieval world, this meant that they enjoyed a high degree of locational autonomy.

With its huge population and consequent demand for consumer goods, Baghdād was certainly the largest manufacturing center in al-ʿIrāq in the tenth century; and, as al-Yaʿqūbī had noted at the end of the ninth century, skilled artisans from far and wide had flocked to the city so that "whatever could be manufactured in other countries could be produced in Baghdād."[46] Notable among its products were colored silks, in particular the famous *ʿattābī* cloths; crystals turned on a lathe; glazed ware; and sundry medicaments and electuaries.[47] Other textile centers were Takrīt, whose wool workers were commended by al-Maqdisī; Qaṣr ibn Hubayrah; al-Kūfah, which manufactured turbans of fine floss silk; al-Ubullah, producer of linen cloths after the manner of Egyptian *qaṣab;* and al-Nuʿmānīyah, which "made excellent mantles and cloths of wool of the colour of honey" and carpets like those of al-Ḥīrah.[48] Al-Baṣrah, like Baghdād, was a focus of diversified industrial activity ranging from textile manufacture, principally silks and linens, to the processing of minerals such as antimony *(rāsukht),* cinnabar *(zunjufr),* Mars saffron *(zinjār),* and litharge *(murdāsanj),* and the making of fine jewelry. According to Ibn Rustah, the small town of Jabbul, on the Tigris between Baghdād and Wāsiṭ, was the site of government bakeries.[49]

Among the horticultural products with more than local reputations were pomegranates and figs of unequalled quality from Ḥulwān (the latter earning the sobriquet *shah anjīr* ["King of Figs"]); sesame from Takrīt; essence of violets from al-Kūfah; lupins from Wāsiṭ; sugarcane from Shafāthā; and dates from ʿAyn al-Tamr, al-Kūfah, and especially al-Baṣrah, for which al-Maqdisī lists—perhaps with excessive imagination—no less than forty-nine varieties.[50]

Religious Centers

Within the class of cities performing specialist functions, one category requires separate mention, namely centers providing religious facilities. Apart from places of prayer of various types, these facilities were primarily shrines for the veneration of saints and other holy men. Al-Maqdisī has this to say about those in ʿIrāq:[51]

> Of holy places in this province there are many. At Kuthā Ibrāhīm was born and his fire set burning.[52] At al-Kūfah Nuḥ built his ark, and his oven poured forth its boiling water.[53] There likewise are the monuments of ʿAlī and his tomb,[54] as well as the tomb of al-Ḥusayn and his place of martyrdom.[55] At al-Baṣrah are the tombs of Ṭalḥah,[56] Zubayr,[57] the Prophet's brother,[58] al-Ḥasan al-Baṣri,[59] Anas ibn Mālik,[60] ʿImrān ibn Ḥusayn,[61] Sufyān al-Thawrī,[62] Malik ibn Dīnār,[63] ʿUtbah the Slave,[64] Muḥammad ibn Wāsiʿ,[65] Ṣāliḥ al-Murrī,[66] Ayyūb al-Sikhtiyānī,[67] Sahl al-Tustarī,[68] and Rābiʿah al-ʿAdawīyah.[69] There also is the tomb of Ibn Sālim.[70] At Baghdād is the tomb of Abū Ḥanīfah,[71] over which Abū Jaʿfar al-Zammām[72] has raised a monument. By the side of it, behind the *sūq* of Yaḥyā, is another tomb. That of Abū Yūsuf[73] is situated in the Qurashī cemetery, where also are to be found the tombs of Ibn Ḥanbal,[74] Maʿrūf al-Karkhī,[75] Bishr al-Ḥāfī,[76] and others. The tomb of Sālmān[77] is at al-Madāʾin.[78] At al-Kūfah there is also the tomb of a certain prophet whom I believe to be Yūnus—on whom be peace.

The Sacral Hierarchy

The all but invariable association of a congregational mosque with urban status in the early Islamic world tended to blur somewhat the distinction between sacred and secular cities. In practice, however, the medieval Muslim was intuitively aware that varying degrees of holiness attached to different urban forms. Gustave von Grünebaum has formalized this notion of the perceived holiness of Islamic cities in terms of a sacral hierarchy in many respects paralleling the economic and administrative rankings discussed above.[79] At the lowest level were the ordinary urban centers, which in no way aspired to be classed as especially sacred cities but which were yet held to offer a way of life devotionally more meritorious than was possible in a rural community. Of marginally greater religious significance were those towns on which devolved responsibility for the religious organization of a district, or those which served as foci of missionary activity. At a still higher level in the hierarchy were those cities possessed of "sanctity stemming from the *barakah,* or blessing, of a prophetic tomb or the sanctuary of a saint, from the presence . . . of an unusually high number of descendants of the Prophet Muḥammad or of another personage of high religious rank, or else, combined with this distinction, from the spiritual effect of accumulated religious learning."[80] The shrines listed by al-Maqdisī in the passage quoted above are entirely representative of the almost numberless sacred localities throughout the Islamic world, possession of which raised an urban center to the third level of sanctification. Of such concentrations of *barakah* von Grünebaum writes:

> By the eleventh century A.D. the consensus of the doctors had approved the popular devotion of the "friends of God," or saints, whose most important characteristic was seen in the fact that, with the permission of their Lord, they were able, on specific occasions and for specific purposes, to act contrary to the customary course of nature. Upon their death, their supernatural force would cling to their grave[a] and the realisation of this *baraka* by their disciples and the local population would give rise to a cult, generally well organised under the direction of their natural or spiritual descendants. As time wore on, popular piety came to be centered increasingly on the local saint and his sanctuary; not infrequently the sanctity of the place was seen as due to the remains of one of the countless prophetic harbingers of Muḥammad having found their last resting-place in that particular spot. Pilgrimages and festivals at the sanctuaries became the vogue. The well known *ḥadīth* which permits pilgrimages apart from *Ḥajj* (and *ʿUmra*) to Mecca only to the Mosques of Medina and Jerusalem reflects the earlier battle, long since abandoned, which the theologians fought against the cult of those minor sanctuaries.[81]

To assist the Believer in comprehending the virtues *(faḍāʾil)* of the multitude of shrines transmitting spiritual benefits to devout suppliants, pilgrim manuals and guides were developed. Typically these would justify the act of pilgrimage to a particular shrine in light of the prophetic tradition; provide information about the life of the incumbent saint or prophet, emphasizing his supernatural powers and exemplary conduct; and prescribe the most effective ritual to be observed in the holy place. Representative of such manuals relating to a particular shrine is the *catalogue raisonné* of the virtues of Ḥabrā (Hebron), deriving primarily from the presence of the tomb of Ibrāhīm, prepared by Abū al-Fidāʾ al-Tadmurī early in the fifteenth century.[82] Ibrāhīm, "The Friend of God" *(Khalīl al-Allāh),*[83] was associated with holy sites throughout the Fertile Crescent, one of the most important being his alleged birthplace at Kuthā in al-ʿIrāq, mentioned by al-Maqdisī in the passage cited on page 92. Of the type of pilgrim guide that provided a conspectus of sanctuaries over a broad area, the *Kitāb al-Ishārāt ilā Maʿrifat al-Ziyārāt*[84] is as good an example as any. Written by Abū al-Ḥasan ʿAlī ibn Abī Bakr al-Harawī near the turn of the thirteenth century, it lists literally hundreds of shrines and tombs spread throughout the entire Muslim world of the time, except for Mā Warāʾ al-Nahr (Transoxania) and India. On the other hand, an example of a work providing more restricted, but still regional, coverage is Yāqūt's schedule of *mashāhid* and *mazārāt* in Egypt.[85]

At the fourth level in the sacral hierarchy came those cities manifesting what von Grünebaum has called soteriological holiness: sanctity accruing by virtue of a specific role in some episode recognized as crucial to the divine economy.[86] Preeminent among such cities were al-Madīnah (Medina), Jerusalem, Dimashq, and Karbalāʾ (or Mashhad Ḥusayn). The first of these had welcomed Muḥammad when he had fled from Makkah, and ultimately provided the site for his tomb. Subsequently this tomb, together with those of the caliphs Abū Bakr and ʿUmar, were enclosed within the precincts of the Great Mosque, a structure of very high-order sanctity indeed. According to a prophetic saying, the space between the Prophet's tomb and his pulpit constituted "one of the gardens of Paradise." There were, too, numerous lesser, though still important, sanctuaries in the neighborhood, including the Masjid al-Taqwah, the mosque in Qubāʾ where, on the occasion of the *Hijrah,* Muḥammad had rested for a few days before entering the city proper. The inclusion of al-Madīnah in the pilgrimage to Makkah, although never obligatory, became a recommended custom.

Jerusalem, or Bayt al-Maqdis, ranked third in sanctity among the cities of the Islamic world, after Makkah and al-Madīnah. It figured in Muḥammad's miraculous "night journey" *(isrāʾ)* as the site of "The Farthest Mosque" *(al-Masjid al-Aqṣā),* whence the Prophet had ascended to Heaven on a celestial steed. Dimashq also enjoyed a reputation for great sanctity, having been chosen as the place where Allāh will manifest His glory and power on the last day of historical time. Karbalāʾ, which, as described previously, harbored the tomb of the Shīʿite martyr Ḥusayn, and al-Najaf, where one tradition locates the burial place of ʿAlī ibn Abī-Ṭālib, fourth of the Rāshidūn caliphs, were the only two sites in al-ʿIrāq to achieve this particular level of holiness.[87]

Makkah as the Epitome

The highest order in the hierarchy of sanctity was fully attained by only one urban center in the whole Islamic culture realm, namely Makkah—although vestiges of a former cosmologically induced sanctity still suffused perceptions of Jerusalem in the tenth century A.D. The conceptual framework within which the city was accorded this degree of supremacy pertained to a complex of ideas that René Berthelot has characterized as "astrobiological."[88] It was this mode of thought that afforded a paradigm for cosmological speculation during the long period between the phases of pre-urban folk society, with its intensely personal participant apprehension of phenomena; and modern industrial society, with its predilection for reducing particular events to types subject to universal laws. The basis of this conception was a structural parallelism between the mathematically expressible regimes of the heavens and the biologically determined rhythms of life on earth as manifested conjointly in the succession of the seasons and the annual cycle of plant regeneration. Some important components in this system, particularly those concerned with the definition of space, had been incorporated from a still earlier phase of intellectual speculation that Berthelot subsumes under the term *bio-astral.*[89]

In the astrobiological mode of thought the divine was, as Walter Otto phrases it, "neither a justifying explanation of the natural course of the world nor an interruption and abolition of it; it was itself the natural course of the world."[90] The natural world was, therefore, conceived as an extension of the human personality, and consequently apprehended in terms of human experience. The "real" world, by contrast, transcended the pragmatic realm of textures and geometrical space, and was perceived schematically in terms of an extramundane, sacred experience. Only the sacred was real, and the purely secular—insofar as it could be said to exist at all—was never more than trivial.

Through rites dramatizing the inception of universal order, ritual specialists sought to establish an ontological link between the realm of the sacred and that of the profane. Not infrequently these rites dramatized the cosmogony by reproducing on earth a reduced model of the cosmos. In other words, sacrality (which was synonymous with reality) was achieved by imitating a celestial archetype. This customarily involved the construction of a shrine or temple-city, into the architecture and design of which was incorporated a substantial element of cosmomagical symbolism. This central point, this focus of creative force, was the place where communication between cosmic planes was effected most expeditiously, and through this point of ontological transition passed the axis of the universe. The sacred space thus delimited within the continuum of profane space defined a sanctified—and therefore habitable—locale, within which could be conducted the rituals necessary for ensuring that intimate harmony between macrocosmos and microcosmos, without which there could be no prosperity in the human world.[91]

In the ancient Semitic world several places, at various times and in various traditions, were regarded as *axes mundi;*[92] but the really great cosmological center in later times was Jerusalem,[93] and this symbolism was subsequently transferred by Muslim *ḥadīth* to Makkah. Significantly, the early Islamic traditions regarding the sacred cities of Arabia and the Levant were thoroughly impregnated with ancient cosmomagical symbolism, yet none of these cities—in Islamic times, at any rate—exhibited the sanctified morphology that in the ancient Middle East and much of the rest of Asia constituted them as sacred enclaves within the continuum of profane space. In other words, the forms of a pre-Islamic urban symbolism were incorporated into Islamic ideology to endow a new urban hierarchy with prestige and authority, but without comprehension of the "performative" rites— in an Austinian sense[94]—required to activate the validatory process that was the raison d'être of the symbolic system in the first place.

Interestingly enough, as in the hierarchy of tertiary economic activities previously discussed, cities performing higher-order sacral functions customarily performed lower-order ones as well. For example, Makkah and Jerusalem, the two cities accorded cosmological significance, were also distinguished by their being the final resting places for many prominent religious personalities and by having been the scenes of soteriological events as well. The soteriologically endowed center of Damascus was similarly celebrated for the number of its *barakah*-engendering shrines. The lowest order of sanctity, by definition, was as widespread as Islam, and the *barakah* of the prophetic tomb scarcely less so; but soteriological holiness was distributed more sparingly. The highest-level sanctity, which derived from cosmological status as "The Navel of the Earth" *(Ṣurrat al-Arḍ),* the place from which the earth had been created and from which the order of nature was regulated, was necessarily restricted by its very uniqueness. It followed that urban centers partaking of the higher orders of sanctity were virtually restricted to the core region of the Islamic culture realm and, as one manifestation of a religion revealed specifically to the Arabs in their own language, to the Arab culture hearth.

Urban Centers on the Diyālā Plains

Available evidence has thus far restricted discussion of the urban centers of al-ʿIrāq to qualitative terms, but for one sector of the plain, material permits a minor degree of quantification. The Diyālā Basin Archaeological Project, undertaken jointly by the Oriental Institute of the University of Chicago and the Directorate-General of Antiquities of the Government of ʿIrāq, has employed techniques of topographic archaeology to reconstruct the settlement pattern on the Diyālā plains as it evolved from the earliest occupation about 4,000 B.C. down to Islamic times (fig. 8). Whenever possible, the purely archaeological findings have been supplemented by epigraphic and literary evidence. In his report summarizing these investigations, Robert McC. Adams distinguishes, on an areal basis, a five-tiered settlement hierarchy composed of the following somewhat arbitrarily discriminated ranks:

• Imperial Capital	—
• City	more than one hundred hectares in extent
• Small Urban Center	more than thirty hectares
• Large Town	more than ten hectares
• Town	more than four hectares
• Village or Hamlet	less than four hectares[95]

So far as the Islamic period is concerned, archaeological and literary evidence alike indicate a decline in the intensity of settlement on the Diyālā plains consequent upon the dissolution of Sāsānian authority. On the basis of Adams's data, Jacob Lassner has calculated that almost 60 percent of the aggregate settlement area was abandoned during or soon after the final phase of Sāsānian rule.[96] The aggregate area of the Cities was reduced by some 78 percent, of the Small Urban Centers by 25 percent, of the Large Towns by 70 percent, and of the remaining settlements by 67 percent. Most of the abandoned sites were not subsequently resettled. During the first century or so of Muslim occupation, the situation appears not to have changed significantly. It was a time when Islamic settlement was still tied to the pattern established in response to the needs of the conquest, with its foci in the garrison cities of al-Kūfah and al-Baṣrah. With the virtual elimination of the Persian imperial capital at Ctesiphon (al-Madā'in), for the first time in one thousand years there was no city of premier rank on the lower Diyālā plains; the imperial capital, except for a few years, was located in the Ḥijāz or Syria.

The founding of Baghdād as the ʿAbbāsid capital in the mid-eighth century initiated an intensification of settlement in the region that was ultimately to exceed that of any preceding period. The comparative areas of urban sites in the Parthian, Sāsānian, and Islamic periods are displayed in table 2, prepared by Lassner from data in Adams's book.[97]

In ʿAbbāsid times, even excluding the imperial capitals of Baghdād and Sāmarrā, Cities (in the sense in which Adams uses this term) accounted for about one-third of the total area of all settlements (fig. 9); but, more important, the capitals jointly occupied an area some seven times as large as the aggregate of all other settlements (and, incidentally, approximately four times as large as the combined areas of all settlements in Sāsānian times). Lassner has likened the ekistic structure of the Diyālā

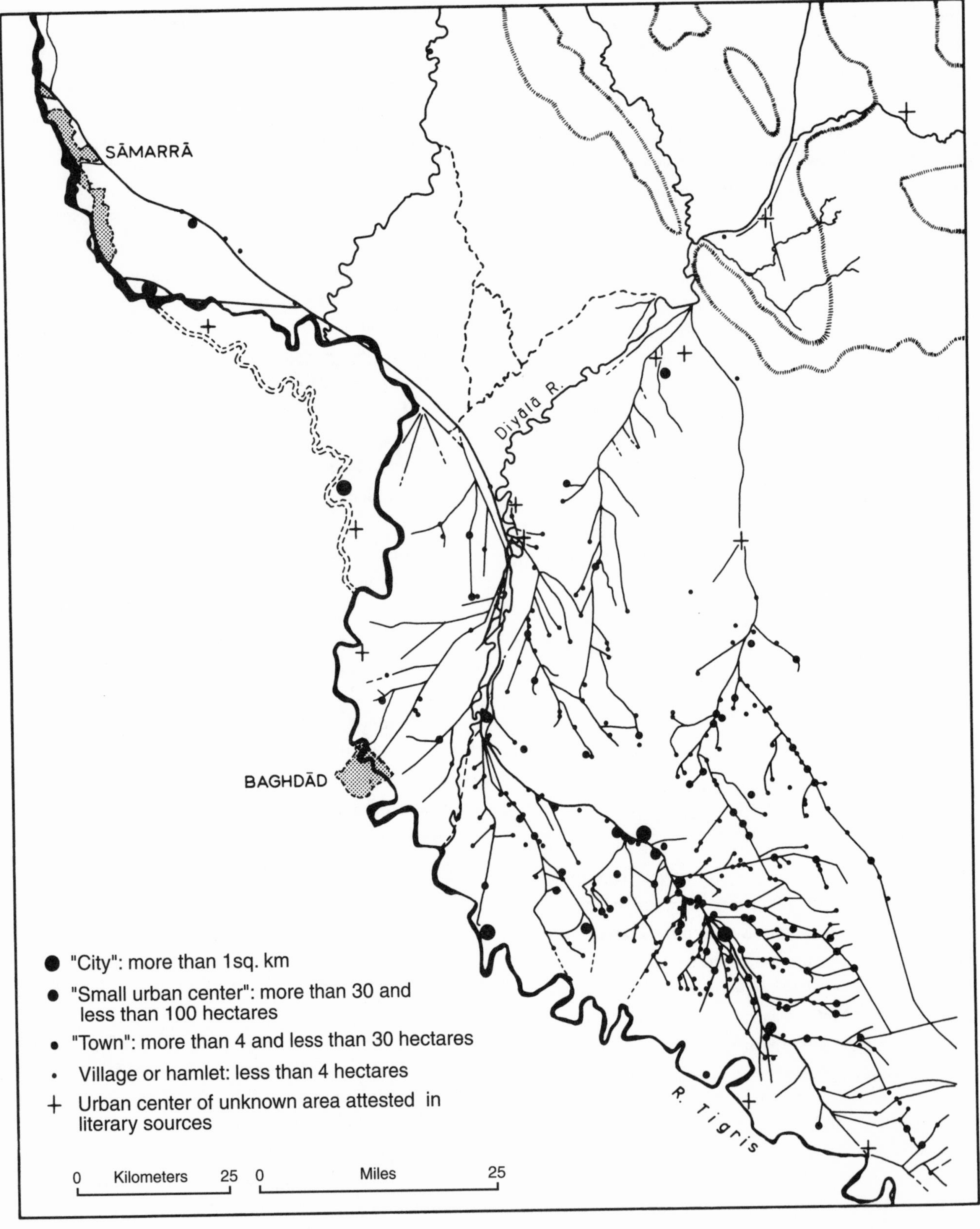
SĀMARRĀ
Diyālā R.
BAGHDĀD
R. Tigris
"City": more than 1sq. km
"Small urban center": more than 30 and less than 100 hectares
"Town": more than 4 and less than 30 hectares
Village or hamlet: less than 4 hectares
Urban center of unknown area attested in literary sources
0 Kilometers 25
0 Miles 25

Table 2. Areas of Urban Sites on the Diyālā Plains in Parthian, Sāsānian, and Islamic Times

	Parthian (140 B.C.–A.D. 224)		Sāsānian (A.D. 224–64)		Islamic (A.D. 637–1250)	
Rank in Hierarchy	Number of Sites	Average Area of Occupation (Hectares)	Number of Sites	Average Area of Occupation (Hectares)	Number of Sites	Average Area of Occupation (Hectares)
Imperial Capitals	0	—	1	540	2	7,000
Cities	4	110	8	162	4	182
Small Urban Centers	5	51	4	47	6	44
Large Towns	24	14	35	17	28	14
Towns	50	6	59	6	57	6
Villages	116	1.5	308	1.5	234	1.5

Source: Jacob Lassner, *The Topography of Baghdad in the Early Middle Ages* (Detroit, 1970), 164–68.

plains at this time to that of "a highly caricatured dwarf—a massive urban head surmounting a truncated rural body in a ratio of approximately 7:2."[98] This primate distribution of city sizes had arisen for much the same reason that it occurs today in many underdeveloped territories, namely the convenience, under relatively poorly differentiated socioeconomic conditions, of consolidating the instruments of state power in one center capable of providing a comprehensive range of urban institutions: political, administrative, financial, commercial, industrial, social, and religious.[99]

The growth and prosperity of Baghdād and Sāmarrā, in their role as imperial capitals, depended less on the various interactions generated on the Diyālā plains than on the general prosperity of the ʿAbbāsid Empire, a contingency accurately reflected in the parallel fortunes of city and kingdom. The toponymy of early Baghdād as recorded in literary sources confirms—what might well have been conjectured on other grounds—that the rapid population growth in the eighth and early ninth centuries stemmed not so much from a centripetal movement of people into the city from immediately surrounding rural areas as from immigration from outside the region. And as the caliphate lost its vigor and the larger part of its territory, so the "Madīnat al-Islam" shrank to the unremarkable urban center al-Maqdisī describes in slighting terms: "fast falling to ruin and decay, and shorn of all its [former] splendour. I did not find it . . . an attractive city, and any praise I might bestow upon it would be merely conventional."[100] The city that had once stood "like a master among slaves"[101] had become the client of the Daylamite in his Shīrāzī palace.

The settlement hierarchy on the Diyālā plains during the Early Islamic period, as reconstructed by Robert Adams, is depicted in figure 8. It was composed of the following components in addition to the imperial capital: sixteen important urban centers identified in contemporary Arabic sources;[102] eight Early Islamic-Sāmarrān *Large Towns* continuing into, or reoccupied during, the later ʿAbbāsid period;[103] twenty-eight *Small Towns* and eighty *Villages* having the same history; and four *Small Towns* and twenty-two *Villages* founded in the post-Sāmarrān period.[104] Adams himself warns against generalizing from the ekistic experience of a single region to that of al-ʿIrāq as a whole, particularly when, as in the case of the Diyālā plain, the region was spatially and culturally marginal to the alluvial heartland of Mesopotamia. His purpose, he reiterates, was not to determine the degree of deviation of the lower Diyālā plains from some norm of cultural evolution, but to demonstrate one means of studying general historical trends within a specific regional and cultural context.[105]

Figure 8. Archaeologically attested settlements on the lower Diyālā plains during the Early Islamic-Sāmarrān (ca. 637–883) and post-Sāmarrān ʿAbbāsid (ca. 883–1258) periods. Adapted from Robert McC. Adams, *Land Behind Baghdad: A History of Settlement on the Diyala Plains* (Chicago, 1965), fig. 6.

Commentary

Despite Adams's warning against generalizing from the course of events in the Diyālā basin, considerable evidence from historical sources indicates that the trajectory

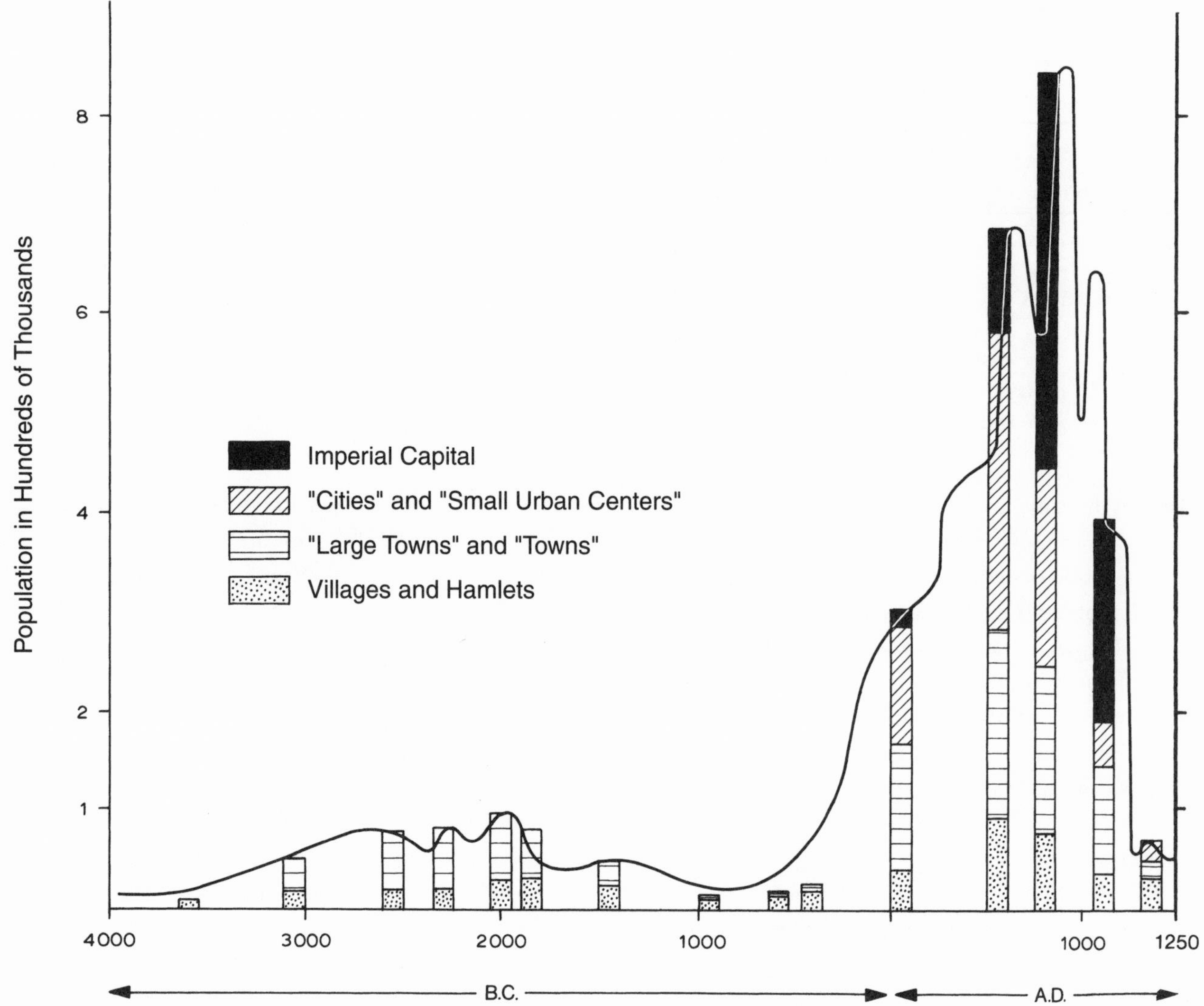

Figure 9. The emergence of urban primacy on the lower Diyālā plains during the Early Islamic-Sāmarrān period. Adapted from Robert McC. Adams, *Land Behind Baghdad: A History of Settlement on the Diyala Plains* (Chicago, 1965), table 25.

of urban development in ʿIrāq as a whole was not fundamentally different from that elicited by his study. The later decades of the Sāsānian imperium had witnessed a decline in economic prosperity, caused partly by the cumulative impact of the hydrological changes mentioned above (p. 87). Mainly these were a westward shift in the channel of the Tigris River, which subverted the agricultural potential of the southeastern sector of the province; and the formation of the Baṭā'iḥ, which functioned as a great sump absorbing the waters of the Euphrates (fig. 10). Into the already crumbling Sāsānian urban hierarchy[106] further dislocated when in 637 Muslim forces under the command of Saʿd ibn Abī-Waqqāṣ overran its metropolis of Ctesiphon—the Arabs injected new vigor in the form of urban foundations that ultimately revivified fairly extensive sectors of the system. Yet the Arab

Figure 10. The upper ranks of the urban hierarchy in *Iqlīm* al-ʿIrāq in the second half of the tenth century. Al-Balādhurī dates the formation of the Baṭā'iḥ to the end of the fifth century A.D. (*Futūḥ al-Buldān,* 292), which, according to Ibn Rustah, was also the period when the Tigris channel shifted westward (*al-Aʿlāq,* 94–96). The river system depicted approximates to that of the tenth century.

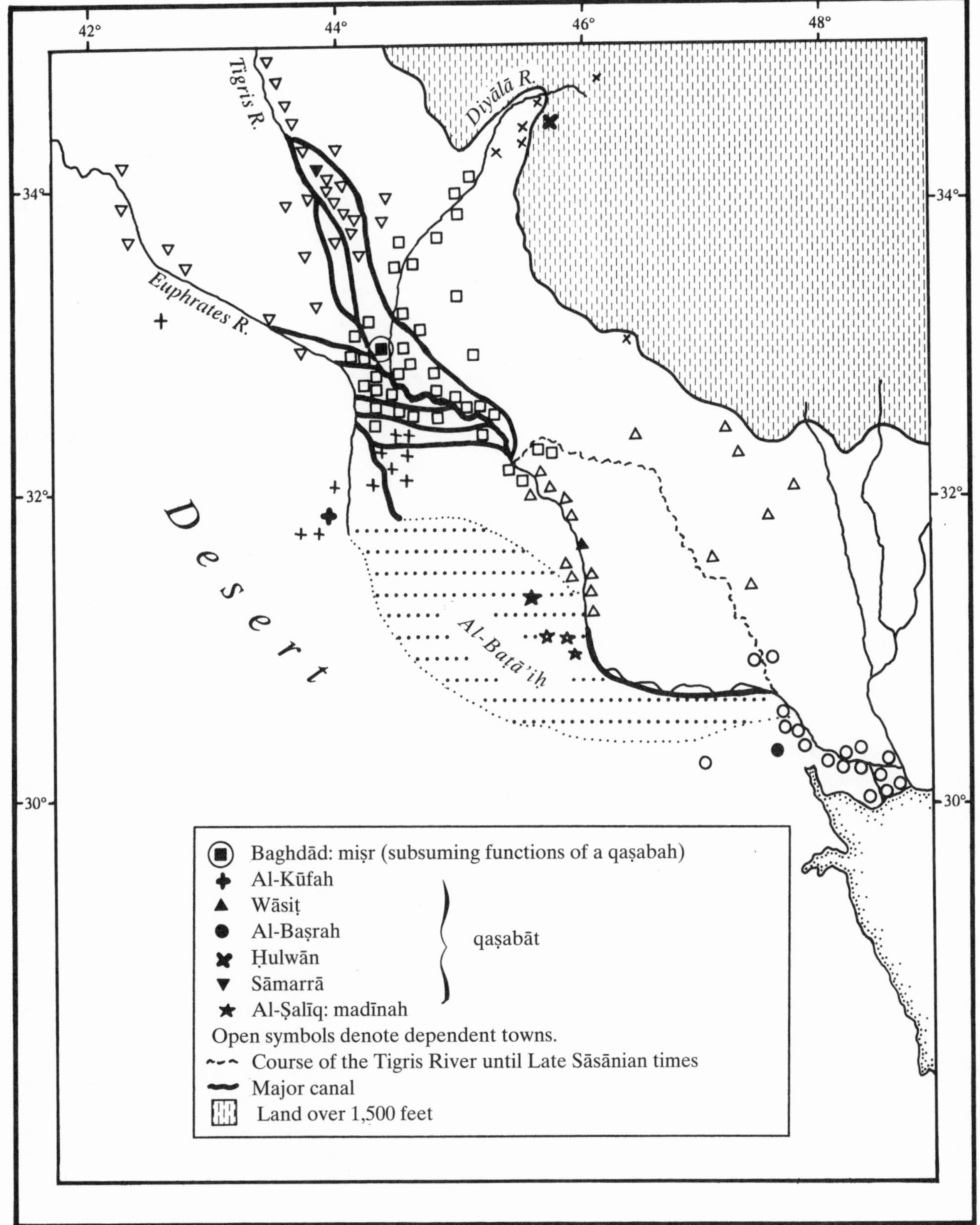
42°
44°
46°
48°
34°
32°
30°
Tigris R.
Diyālā R.
Euphrates R.
Desert
Al-Baṭā'iḥ
Baghdād: miṣr (subsuming functions of a qaṣabah)
Al-Kūfah
Wāsiṭ
Al-Baṣrah
Ḥulwān
Sāmarrā
qaṣabāt
Al-Ṣalīq: madīnah
Open symbols denote dependent towns.
Course of the Tigris River until Late Sāsānian times
Major canal
Land over 1,500 feet

conquest stimulated a *selective* process of urbanization, not a *general* intensification and extension of the settlement hierarchy.[107]

Arab Settlements

New Arab settlements in al-ʿIrāq were restricted mainly to garrison cantonments and administrative capitals, both not infrequently being attached to preexisting Sāsānian cities. The earliest of the cantonments were, of course, the *amṣār* at al-Baṣrah and al-Kūfah, but other garrison encampments soon followed. Saʿd ibn Abī-Waqqāṣ, for example, installed an Arab garrison in al-Anbār, which even in Sāsānian times had been a predominantly Arab city;[108] al-Madāʾin, the site of the old Persian capital, housed an Arab garrison by 637 at latest;[109] al-Ḥajjāj established both al-Nīl[110] and Wāsiṭ[111] during his governorship of al-ʿIrāq; and Ḥulwān was occupied in 685–86,[112] the Persian fortress of ʿAyn al-Tamr on the fringe of the western desert in 687–88,[113] and Jalūlāʾ[114] and Balās[115] at much the same time.

New administrative cities, which of necessity served also to a greater or lesser extent as garrison settlements, were preeminently a feature of the ʿAbbāsid era. When the new rulers took what must have been the carefully calculated risk of establishing their imperial administration in al-ʿIrāq,[116] they prudently avoided anything more than a temporary attachment to the ʿIrāqī *amṣār.* After a brief sojourn in al-Kūfah, which witnessed the new caliph's inaugural *khuṭbah,* the administration was removed to the first in a succession of provisional centers. This appears in the historical record under the elusive name Ḥammām Aʿyan, which seems to have denoted a locality close to the old Lakhmid capital of al-Ḥīrah.[117]

Here Abū Salāmah al-Khallāl, who assumed control over al-Kūfah at the outbreak of the ʿAbbāsid revolution, had already stationed a garrison of Khurāsānī troops.[118] By adscripting these troops of undoubted loyalty to the ʿAbbāsid cause, the caliph al-Saffāḥ could exploit the strategic potentialities of the middle Euphrates region in the military campaigns still to be fought in Syria and ʿIrāq while yet insulating his troops from the possibility of Kūfan-inspired sedition. However, after a few months the caliph completed and enlarged a palace complex in the vicinity of al-Kūfah that had been left unfinished by Yazīd ibn ʿUmar ibn Hubayrah, the last Umayyad governor of ʿIrāq. He soon transferred the administrative center of the empire first to an adjacent site *(bīḥiyālihā),* but then to al-Anbār, which remained the capital until his successor (and brother) restored it to Madīnat ibn Hubayrah. The reasons for these repeated shifts of the capital are still unexplained, although Jacob Lassner has offered some speculations;[119] but presumably they were undertaken to secure a site offering particular resources apparently not specified in any extant account.

The whole sequence of transfers is further confused by the circumstance that all four of these official capitals were designated by the honorific al-Hāshimīyah. From early ʿAbbāsid times this name was believed to have commemorated Hāshim ibn ʿAbd Manāf, in the Tradition the great-grandfather of the Prophet and progenitor of the *Ahl al-Bayt* that also included ʿAlī ibn Abī-Ṭālib and al-ʿAbbās, ancestor of the ʿAbbāsid caliphal line; that is, it signified the restoration of power to the Hāshimite lineage after the termination of the Umayyad usurpation. However, a century ago Gerlof van Vloten showed that in Umayyad times the term *Hāshimīyah* denoted a religio-political, proto-Shīʿite faction whose members believed that the imāmate had passed from the ʿAlid Muḥammad ibn al-Ḥanafīyah to his son Abū Hāshim.[120] The most important group among Abū Hāshim's followers held that the imāmate had then been transferred to Muḥammad ibn ʿAlī ibn ʿAbd Allāh ibn al-ʿAbbās, and so to the house of ʿAbbās. If the name of the capitals did indeed commemorate this group, the Hāshimīyah, which had done more than any other to promote the ʿAbbāsid revolution in Khurāsān, then the honorific would have focused attention on the legitimacy of ʿAbbāsid claims to rule as opposed to those of the Ḥusaynid party. Although this seems to be the more likely interpretation, it does not exclude the possibility that the new rulers welcomed an ambiguity involving such an eminent name as that of Hāshim ibn ʿAbd Manāf, even though that was not their primary intention. What is curious, though, is that the honorific was abandoned when in 762 the administrative center of the caliphate was reconstituted as Madīnat al-Salām in the vicinity of a village called Baghdād.[121] It was as though, for reasons that are today unknown, the ʿAbbāsids wished to disown their recent past and launch a new era to be symbolized by a much more grandiose scale of architectural design.

Even this was not the finale (except in scope) of the sequence of ʿAbbāsid capitals: Sāmarrā was laid out in 836 by al-Muʿtaṣim but functioned as an imperial capital for only just over half a century.[122] In addition, the ʿAbbāsid caliphs and their ministers adorned not a few small towns and villages with palaces that invariably changed the character of those settlements. A typical example was the palace called al-Jaʿfarīyah, built by Jaʿfar al-Mutawakkil some three *farsākh*s north of Karkh Fīrūz in 859. When al-Mutawakkil ran a branch of the Baghdād-Mawṣil (Mosul) road to the palace gates, a new town developed around it and assumed the name of al-Mutawakkilīyah or Qaṣr al-Jaʿfarī.[123] The palace itself was abandoned when al-Mutawakkil was assassinated only nine months and three days after he had occupied it.

Agricultural Development

These garrison cities and administrative capitals not only diversified the landscape with their architectural assemblages but also did much to transform the surrounding countrysides. In part this change was simply the development necessary to provide food for new and intrusive populations; often, however, the caliphs or their provincial governors sponsored essential infrastructural irrigation projects to increase the imperial tax revenues, or, less commonly, to reward officials and clients with *qaṭīʿah* grants.[124] These latter were particularly prominent in the neighborhood of al-Baṣrah; in fact this was the only region in all of al-ʿIrāq where *mawālī* and Arab notables participated significantly in the process of agricultural development. Elsewhere it was the caliphs and their governors, or sometimes members of the caliphal family, who initiated the reclamation of wastelands, particularly in the Baṭāʾiḥ and along the course of the Euphrates. Generally speaking, the Umayyads appear to have prosecuted these undertakings more consistently and with more vigor than did the ʿAbbāsids, focusing principally on the countrysides around al-Baṣrah, al-Nīl, parts of the Baṭāʾiḥ, and, most intensively of all, in the territories controlled from Wāsiṭ. After continuing certain developmental projects in these districts, the ʿAbbāsids—as far as the sources permit an opinion—seem to have restricted attempts at agricultural development to the vicinities of their often transient administrative capitals and palaces.[125]

Throughout this period, the rural economy of ʿIrāq remained essentially dependent on the hydraulic infrastructure that the Arabs had inherited from the Sāsānian Empire. Unfortunately, the relevant sources reveal very little about either official or unofficial investment in the maintenance of that infrastructure: their concern is almost exclusively with the extension of the system and the reclamation of wasteland *(mawāt)*. The impression to be gleaned from extant administrative and legal texts, however, is that the responsibility of the state for the upkeep of hydraulic structures was limited, not going much beyond maintaining the embankments of the main rivers, supervising the use of canals and dikes, and mediating disputes arising therefrom.[126] In fact some evidence indicates that, whatever the lawyers might rule in theory, the state did not invariably assume responsibility for maintaining even those irrigation facilities that it had itself initiated.[127]

Significant for our present inquiry is that this agricultural development was undertaken only in the vicinity of new Arab settlements, which were almost exclusively princely foundations or garrison towns; that is, centers ranking fairly high in the administrative hierarchy. At least three of them (al-Baṣrah, al-Kūfah, and Baghdād), in fact, eventually transcended the regional function of providing services for a clearly defined area and became subject to external forces generated within the Islamic world at large, and even beyond it. In some instances the expansion of these supraregional cities was achieved at the expense of lesser settlements, as when numerous towns on the Diyālā plains declined in competition with Baghdād. Moreover, as new Arab settlements stimulated local agricultural development, such development reciprocally contributed to the expansion and elaboration of the basic exchange functions of those cities (central-place-type functions, as some might claim). As a result, tertiary economic functions were under continual pressure to intensify to match the administrative rankings of the cities concerned.

But these developments were not spread equally throughout the *iqlīm*. Sites for administrative centers and garrison cantonments were chosen based on strategic considerations and those for palaces often on the whim of a caliph or a wealthy patrician. Consequently these settlements and the agricultural advances that they promoted were distributed irregularly through al-ʿIrāq, which came to be characterized by selective urbanization and localized rural development. There is no evidence that economic development in the favored areas generated significant flows of investment outward to the rest of the province. Furthermore, as the Arab foundations were almost invariably established in the upper ranks of the settlement hierarchy, in the case of Baghdād and Sāmarrā at the summit, their cumulative effect was to exacerbate its primate character. Baghdād was not merely exceptionally expressive of the cultural aspirations of ʿAbbāsid Islam and at least half as large again as either of the ʿIrāqān; it was also ten times the size of the old Persian capital of Seleucia-Ctesiphon, while Al-Baṣrah and al-Kūfah were both larger than any cities in pre-Islamic ʿIrāq.[128]

In the tenth century the general configurations of the lower levels in the ʿIrāqī urban hierarchy remained largely unchanged from Sāsānian times, although, as we have seen, some of their component settlements had declined in competition with new Arab foundations. But the upper levels in many sectors of the *iqlīm* had been wholly remodelled, and the cultural and economic influences of these upper levels were so pervasive as to justify us in regarding the reconstituted settlement system as primarily an Arabo-Islamic (as opposed to a Sāsānian) hierarchy. One aspect of the system had not changed, however: its ancient generalized spatial (as distinct from its hierarchical) patterning. The physiographic constraints of a parched land[129] still ensured that settlements were strung like beads on a string along rivers and other water courses (apart, that is, from the ports on the Persian Gulf), which generated an elongated network of urban centers in which the master strands were the Tigris and Euphrates Rivers. The Arabs had filled certain lacunae in this pattern and changed the character of not a few of its components, but, given the environmental technology of the time, they were no more able than the Sāsānians to free the ʿIrāqī settlement pattern from its bondage to the hydraulic works of both nature and human endeavor.

Chapter Five
The Urban System in Aqūr [al-Jazīrah]

. . . the province with the most dangerous roads, the best horses, and the most noble people.

—Al-Maqdisī, *Aḥsan al-Taqāsīm,* 33.

The Province of Aqūr, as defined by al-Maqdisī, comprised the undulating plains and mountain fringe tributary to the Tigris and Euphrates river systems from their sources as far south as the northern border of *Iqlīm* al-ʿIrāq. It was customarily divided into three districts known respectively as Diyār Rabīʿah, Diyār Muḍar, and Diyār Bakr, after the Arab tribes that had colonized the region. Also in this province was a northern zone of mountainous territory for control of which the armies of Islam contested bitterly with the forces of the Byzantine Empire.[1] Al-Maqdisī's depiction of Aqūr reflected the Balkhī school of topographers' predilection for territorial subdivisions based on spheres of political authority: during most of the tenth century, *Iqlīm* Aqūr comprised essentially the Eastern Amīrate of the Ḥamdānid kingdom. In 905 a member of the Arab *badū* tribe of Taghlib, Abū al-Hayjāʾ ʿAbd Allāh, was appointed to the governorship of al-Mawṣil. Before the end of the reign of the ʿAbbāsid caliph al-Muqtadir (908–32), ʿAbd Allāh's lineage had transformed a family principality into an effectively autonomous state. From 944 a branch of the same lineage was established in Ḥalab (Aleppo) in al-Shām (Greater Syria), with both families taking their regnal name from that of a ninth-century ancestral *badawī* (and Khārijī) chieftain, Ḥamdān ibn Ḥamdūn ibn al-Ḥārith.

In 978 the Eastern Amīrate passed under the control of the Buwayhids of Baghdād, which remained the situation when al-Maqdisī was compiling the *Aḥsan.* Almost immediately after its completion, however, and probably within that author's lifetime, the weakening of Buwayhid power allowed the partitioning of Aqūr (or al-Jazīrah, as it was more commonly known) between the Kurdish Marwānids on the one hand, who held sway over Diyār Bakr, and the ʿUqaylid line of the *badū* confederacy of ʿĀmir ibn Ṣaʿṣaʿah on the other, who eventually exercised dominion over most of the Diyār Rabīʿah and the Diyār Muḍar under the nominal suzerainty of the Buwayhids. Both dynasties were finally extinguished by the Saljūqs.[2]

Marketing and Service Centers

The basis of the urban hierarchy in Aqūr Province was a stratum of local exchange centers of great antiquity, represented by such settlements as Baʿashīqā,[3] Marj Juhaynah,[4] and Balad,[5] all in al-Mawṣil District; Naṣībīn, on the upper course of the Hirmās River;[6] Raʾs al-ʿAyn, near the source of the Khābūr;[7] and Mayyafāriqīn (Silvan), situated on a tributary of the Batmān Ṣu in Diyārbakir.[8] These centers seemingly functioned as close to the manner postulated by classical Central-Place Theory as is likely to have occurred in the tenth century. They were mostly fairly prosperous, serving as markets for the surplus products of surrounding agricultural communities. Ninth- and tenth-century topographers frequently referred to thriving markets, irrigated fields, and productive gardens.

Southern Aqūr in the tenth century was, as now, a region of steppe and desert, with cultivation restricted to the close proximity of the main rivers. However, the triangular tract of territory enclosed by the Armenian highlands on the north and the Jabal Sinjār and Jabal ʿAbd al-ʿAzīz on the south was, by Middle Eastern standards, a relatively productive farming area, contributing principally cereals, fruit, and livestock. Cultivation was also fairly extensive in the neighborhood of al-Mawṣil, as well as along the lengths of the Balīkh and Great Khābūr Rivers. Not surprisingly, it was in these more productive areas that the lower levels of the urban hierarchy were most fully developed. Only with the rise to power of the Ḥamdānid dynasty do we begin to detect signs of decline in certain sectors of the urban system (see p. 110 below).

At the summit of the urban hierarchy in Aqūr was al-Mawṣil (Mosul), metropolis *(miṣr)* of the province and at the same time district capital of Diyār Rabīʿah, a city that had succeeded to the locational advantages and utilities of ancient Nineveh (Arabic Nūnawā).[9] During the caliphate of ʿUmar (634–44), Harthamah ibn ʿArfajah al-Bāriqī had laid out a military camp adjacent to the Sāsānian city of Būdh Ardashir primarily as a forward garrison post for Kūfan troops, apportioned family holdings, and built a congregational mosque.[10] Subsequently Arabs from al-Baṣrah (though of South Arabian origin) settled in villages in the vicinity. The city was walled during the reign of ʿAbd al-Malik, provided with a new mosque by Marwān ibn Muḥammad, in 762–63 adorned with an impressive palace by the ʿAbbāsid governor Jaʿfar ibn Abī Jaʿfar, and shortly thereafter furnished with a permanent garrison for the express purpose of combatting Khārijīs.[11] The turbulent character of its predominantly Kurdish population during these centuries has led Ira Lapidus to categorize the city as the Kūfah of the province.[12] Under the later Umayyads, the settlement had prospered and, in the time of Marwān II, the last of the caliphs of that dynasty, was formally established as the chief city of Aqūr Province.

Under the later Umayyads and earlier ʿAbbāsids, however, al-Mawṣil, together with its dependent districts, was more often than not constituted as an administrative unit separate from the government of Aqūr *Iqlīm*. The governors of al-Mawṣil seem to have been appointed directly by the caliph in Baghdād and very seldom held the governorship of al-Jazīrah concurrently. The city's jurisdiction apparently embraced roughly the lower two-thirds of that part of the Tigris valley running through Aqūr Province.[13] In 969 Ibn Ḥawqal found a flourishing city,[14] and a decade and a half later al-Maqdisī wrote of "a great city, well built . . . with good markets and inns, and inhabited by many personages of distinction and learned men . . . never lacking a high authority on *ḥadīth* or a noted doctor of law." Most of its *sūqs* were roofed, and the Wednesday Market *(Sūq al-Arbaʿah)* was held within the precincts of its fortress, the Murabbaʿah. The Palace of the Caliph *(Qaṣr al-Khalīfah)* stood half a *farsakh* away on the opposite bank of the river.[15]

At the next-lower level in the administrative hierarchy were the two provincial capitals *(qaṣabāt)* of Āmid and al-Raqqah, seats of government for Diyār Bakr and Diyār Muḍar, respectively. Āmid, the Roman Amida, was described by al-Maqdisī as "an important frontier city of the Muslims and an impregnable stronghold."[16] Al-Raqqah had been close to the site of an important urban center on the Syrian frontier in pre-Muslim times,[17] and had retained some significance under the Umayyads; but on the accession of the ʿAbbāsids the caliph al-Manṣūr, doubting the loyalty of its inhabitants, in 771 built the city of al-Rāfiqah ("The Companion") nearby, and garrisoned it with Khurāsānian troops loyal to the new dynasty.

The historical record is clear that this new city was not established for the settlement of Arab tribesmen, as al-Mawṣil had been more than a century earlier. Rather, like Wāsiṭ, founded nearly seventy years previously, and Baghdād, established a decade earlier, al-Rāfiqah was built to secure the authority of central government as well as furnish a base for local administration. What is more, it was to defend northern Syria against *badū* marauders and serve as an advanced bastion in the recurring conflicts with Byzantium. It was reportedly laid out, on the plan of Baghdād, as a circular administrative precinct. Hārūn al-Rashīd extended the enceinte and constructed the Palace of Peace *(Qaṣr al-Salām)* as his refuge from the heat of the Baghdād summers. Whereas Ibn Ḥawqal writes of the twin cities of al-Raqqah and al-Rāfiqah, each with its own cathedral mosque, al-Maqdisī describes only a single city called al-Raqqah.[18] The reason for this apparent anomaly seems to be that, as the older city decayed, al-

Manṣūr's foundation usurped not only its functions but also its name.

In addition, the Arabs founded or profoundly modified a number of other cities, among which the following were the most important:

- ***ʿImādīyah,*** near the headwaters of the upper Zāb River, founded by the Daylamite prince ʿImād al-Dawlah in the first half of the tenth century.[19]
- ***Al-Raḥbah,*** established on the desert fringe some distance west of the confluence of the Great Khābūr and Euphrates Rivers during the reign of the caliph al-Maʾmūn (813–33). This city was often referred to as Raḥbat Mālik ibn Ṭawq, after its founder.[20]
- ***Ruṣāfah al-Shām,*** in the desert between al-Raḥbah and al-Raqqah. The site of this city had already been occupied by Ghassān princes in pre-Muslim times, but in the second quarter of the eighth century the Umayyad caliph Hishām added a palace precinct as a refuge from a plague sweeping through Syria. As late as the eleventh century the inhabitants were predominantly Christians, who made a livelihood by combining brigandage with the convoying of Ḥalabī caravans.[21]
- ***Al-Ḥadīthah,*** on the Tigris River one league above its confluence with the Great Zāb, had been the provincial capital under the Sāsānians. It was garrisoned by Harthamah ibn ʿArfajah soon after the establishment of al-Mawṣil, and reinforced early in the eighth century by migrants from Anbār fleeing the governorship of Ibn al-Rufayl. Much of the city was rebuilt by the last Umayyad caliph, Marwān II.[22]
- ***Jazīrat Ibn ʿUmar,*** a district capital on the Tigris about midway between al-Mawṣil and Āmid, had taken the name of its founder, al-Ḥasan ibn ʿUmar of the Taghlib tribe.[23]

Transportation Foci

Long-distance commerce (as distinct from localized, city-region trade) was poorly developed in Aqūr, and consequently few urban centers had elaborated their commercial institutions significantly. The main commodities that moved, and then only in restricted quantities, were the natural products of the land. Al-Maqdisī gets to the heart of the matter when, in the introduction to his section on Aqūr, he attributes to the province "the best breed of horses," "grain supplied to most parts of al-ʿIrāq," and "excellent fruits."[24] Neither this author nor his contemporaries say much about the distribution of livestock in the province, but what little evidence can be elicited from their accounts leaves the impression that enduring ecological constraints ensured that tenth-century patterns of livestock husbandry were not fundamentally different from those in more recent times: that is, camels in the desert tracts, sheep and goats on the steppes and the uplands, and cattle, donkeys, and horses on richer pastures bordering the main rivers.[25] It is perhaps noteworthy that the only references to stock raising that I have discovered in ninth- and tenth-century accounts of Aqūr relate to the Tigris valley above and below al-Mawṣil.

Cereals were grown widely in the Diyār Rabīʿah north of the Jabal Sinjār and Jabal ʿAbd al-ʿAzīz, as well as along the courses of the Balīkh and Great Khābūr Rivers; al-Mawṣil was the collecting point for grain shipped to the Baghdād market.[26] Fruit were grown in virtually all river valleys and other favored locations, and some were sufficiently distinctive to be exported from the province. Those from Qarqīsiyā and the Great Khābūr valley, for example, were winter exports to al-ʿIrāq; a particularly prized variety of pomegranate from Sinjār was sent to the great markets of the southern province; and especially luscious quinces from al-Raḥbah were sought throughout Aqūr.[27] Dates are recorded as a product of the northern reaches of the Wādī Tharthār, even though that locality is now beyond their normal latitudinal range;[28] cotton was grown fairly extensively in the Great Khābūr and Balīkh valleys, whence it was exported to al-Shām and elsewhere.[29]

From Jazīrat ibn ʿUmar boatloads of honey, cheese, walnuts, almonds, hazelnuts, raisins, figs, and other comestibles were sent downriver to be sold in the markets of al-Mawṣil;[30] from Ḥarrān were exported cotton, honey in wine jars, and a sweetmeat called *qubbayṭ,* which was compounded of carob sugar, almonds, and pistachio nuts. From Manbij raisins were dispatched across Syrian desert to the Ḥamdānid capital of Ḥalab and elsewhere; from al-Ḥasanīyah came cheese, partridges, chickens, curdled whey, and dried fruit; from Maʿlathāyā milk products, grapes, fruit, hemp and hemp seed, and dried meat; and from Balad beestings shipped in five-*manah* jars aboard riverboats.[31]

However, not all trade passed through these formal channels. At the Sūq al-Aḥad, situated on a tributary of the Greater Zāb River in the foothills of the Zagros Mountains, a periodic fair brought together Kurdish mountaineers and lowland peasants for the exchange of commodities from contrasting, yet complementary ecosystems.[32] Structurally similar transactions also took place among Arab *badū,* Kurdish highlanders, and prosperous Christian residents of the town of Kafr ʿAzzā in the valley of the Greater Zāb.[33]

Nonagricultural raw materials exported from the *iqlīm* were not numerous. Such as they were, they included pitch, iron, gypsum, and a carbonaceous earth, possibly a true coal, from al-Mawṣil (the latter two items presumably having been brought down the Tigris from farther north).[34] In addition, a siliceous earth *(jawāhir al-zajāj)* from Naṣībīn was eagerly sought for use in glass making throughout Aqūr and al-ʿIrāq, and even in the Byzantine territories.[35]

The post roads traversing Aqūr were in the main extensions of those radiating north from Baghdād and following the general course of the two great rivers, together with east–west links between al-Mawṣil and the upper Euphrates valley by way of Sinjār, Sukayr al-ʿAbbās, and Qarqīsiyā; between al-Mawṣil and al-Raqqah by way of Naṣībīn and Ra's al-ʿAyn; and between the towns of the upper Tigris valley and those of the Euphrates by way of Mayyāfāriqīn, Āmid (Diyarbakir), and Ruhā. Cities spaced along these routes, especially during ʿAbbāsid times, often developed break-of-bulk and ancillary services, notably so in the cases of Takrīt, Jabultā, Sinn, Hadīthah, Balad, Sinjār, Qarqīsiyā, Naṣībīn, Kafartūthā, Āmid, al-Raqqah, Jazīrat Ibn ʿUmar, Alūsah, ʿĀnah, al-Furḍah, Ruṣāfah, Ḥarrān, and Ruhā (Edessa).[36] Although al-Mawṣil could not compare with Baghdād as the hub of a road system, it was still an important center of communications and transshipment: in the words of Ibn Ḥawqal, "the meeting-place of merchants from Ādharbāyjān (Azerbaijan), Armīnīyah, al-ʿIrāq, and al-Shām."[37] Thirty *farsakhs* farther up the Tigris, Jazīrat Ibn ʿUmar played a similar role in mediating trade between Armīnīyah, Arrān, the town of Diyārbakir, and the Greek territories beyond.[38] Barqaʿīd, set amid extensive wheat and barley fields on the road from al-Mawṣil to Naṣībīn, had originally prospered as a caravan-provisioning town but had progressively declined as the Banū-Ḥabīb, in whose hands it lay, had acquired an evil reputation for raiding and thievery.[39]

Industrial and Craft Centers

Specialized manufacture was only meagerly developed in Aqūr Province, although there are sporadic references to the production of hardware and a flourishing weaving industry in al-Mawṣil; the export of inkstands and fulling bats from Naṣībīn; shoe manufacturing in Sinjār; the making of soap and the processing of olive oil in al-Raqqah, as well as the making of pens from reeds that abounded in neighboring swamps; and the weaving of linen and wool fabrics in Āmid. The floating flour mills known as *urūb,* which, so far as our sources are concerned, in Aqūr were found only in the vicinity of al-Mawṣil and Balad, were considered an impressive technological achievement. Often constructed of teakwood and anchored by iron chains in the middle of the full flow of the Tigris, each of these mills had four millstones, each pair of which could convert up to fifty mule loads of grain into flour in twenty-four hours.[40]

Fortified Settlements

A class of cities characterized by their developed defensive functions was found mainly in the northern and western parts of the province, that is, along the Syrian and Byzantine frontiers (fig. 19 in chapter 17). Such fortress cities became especially important when the Byzantines under Leo VI (r. 886–912) established an administrative enclave to the east of the upper Euphrates. The role of Āmid in this connection has already been touched upon; Ḥiṣn Hanāb[41] and Ḥiṣn Kayfā[42] were other citadel cities guarding the Tigris valley respectively above and below Āmid. In the far northwest the important city of Malaṭiyah (Malatya) controlled the bridge by which the high road crossed the Qubāqib River west into Greek territory.[43] The caliph al-Manṣūr rebuilt the city in 756 and provided it with a fine mosque, subsequent to which it changed hands several times before finally being accounted a Greek town by Yāqūt in the thirteenth century.[44] Other fortress cities on the frontier included Ḥiṣn Ziyād,[45] Ḥiṣn Manṣūr,[46] Ḥiṣn Maslamah,[47] Ṭarandah,[48] Zibaṭraḥ,[49] and al-Ḥadath.[50]

In the mountainous districts of eastern Anatolia—

which, although generally included by Arab authors among the dependencies of al-Jazīrah Province, in fact constituted a marchland between Muslim and Christian realms—the institutional responses to a state of chronic conflict rendered the categorization of fortress cities somewhat artificial. Scarcely an urban center in this region did not function as a foward bastion of Muslim arms. Furthermore, allegiances frequently were transferred between Muslims and Greeks, of which the best known is the defection of the Banū-Ḥabīb in about 930. To escape the repression of the Ḥamdānid rulers in al--Mawṣil, segments of this tribal group went over to the side of the Greeks, converted to Christianity, and promptly began to raid back into Diyār Muḍar and even farther east. After seizing the fortresses of Ḥiṣn Ziyād and Ḥiṣn Manṣūr, they went on to sack Kafartūthā and Dārā. So successful were the Banū-Ḥabīb in this raiding, it became for them, in Ibn Ḥawqal's phrase, "a habit and a custom" that they followed every year at harvesttime. Eventually their raiding parties would penetrate as far east as Jazīrat Ibn ʿUmar, whence they would turn back to the west, ravaging Arzan and Mayyāfāriqīn on the way.[51] Clearly, it was not only far out on the frontiers of Aqūr that cities, both large and small, had to ensure effective defenses: occasionally those within the very heart of the province and amid its most fertile territories also had to look to their ramparts.

Although Arab authors before Yāqūt are extremely sparing in their descriptions of cities in this region, it is evident that the representative urban form consisted of a citadel with a residential suburb extending below its walls. The chief cities in this frontier zone in the tenth century were Qālīqalā (Erzurum) on the Qārā Ṣū (Western Euphrates)[52] and Malāzkird on the Murād Ṣū (Eastern Euphrates).[53] The latter was described by al-Maqdisī as a heavily defended fortress with a congregational mosque in the middle of its *sūq*.[54]

Not all hostilities originated outside Aqūr Province. Within its boundaries *badū* raiding never entirely ceased. In fact, Ibn Ḥawqal reported that in the tenth century it was endemic along the Great Khābūr River. The towns of ʿArābān, ʿUbaydiyah, al-Tunānīr, Jaḥshīyah, and Ṭalabān, all in this wheat- and cotton-producing region, finding their ramparts ineffective, sought protection via payment of various imposts and in some cases clientage to a *badū* tribe. Nor was such raiding unknown in the very heart of the province, for Ibn Ḥawqal relates that the town of Bawāzīj, situated in the Lesser Zāb valley some four leagues above its confluence with the Tigris, and fewer than eighty miles from al-Mawṣil, was the market for loot from Banū-Shaybān raids and a refuge for the marauders. He also notes that nomadic raiding had driven the settled population from the plains between the Upper and Lower Zāb Rivers, which had become no more than winter pastureland for the Kurdish tribe of Hadhbāniyah and summer grazing for the Arab Banū-Shaybān.[55]

Religious Centers

Although foci of cosmological and soteriological sanctity were lacking in Aqūr, several cities disseminated the *barakah* of saintly and prophetic association. Chief among them were the sites at Nūnawā, supposedly connected with the prophet Yūnus. The Tall al-Tawbah had been furnished with a mosque and pilgrim quarters by Jamīlah, daughter of the Ḥamdānid prince Nāṣir al-Dawlah, governor of al-Mawṣil from about 926 to 967. Al-Maqdisī notes that seven visits to this shrine were regarded as equivalent to a *ḥajj*.[56] Jonah's Spring *(ʿAyn Yūnus)*, half a league distant, was also provided with a mosque, beside which was the Tree of the Gourd *(Shajarah al-Yaqṭīn)*, allegedly planted by the Prophet himself. Balad also boasted a spring from which it was said Yūnus had emerged.[57] At Qariyat al-Thamānīn ("The Village of the Eighty"), which al-Maqdisī describes as a good-sized town, Noah (Nūḥ) was supposed to have emerged from the ark and set up habitations for his eighty companions. Consequently it was popularly considered to have been the first urban center to be built in al-Jazīrah.[58]

In the more northerly and westerly territories of the province, this hierarchy of Islamic sanctity was matched by another of Christian sacredness. At al-Ruhā,[59] for instance, the celebrated relic known as "the napkin of Jesus" had been preserved until 944, when it was surrendered to the Byzantines to save the city from pillage. Ibn Ḥawqal estimates that as many as three hundred churches and monasteries were required to serve the predominantly Christian population of the city.[60] Whereas the congregational mosque was "a squalid building standing apart," the Christian cathedral, its vaulted ceiling covered with mosaics, was ranked even by the Muslim al-Maqdisī as one of the wonders of the world.[61] Al-Mawṣil contained the tomb of the prophet Jurjīs (Saint George). One *farsakh* outside Mayyāfāriqīn was the Monastery of St. Thomas *(Dayr Tūmā),* within which was kept the desiccated body of an alleged apostle of Jesus.[62]

In the Jewish quarter of the same city, what seems to have been a phylactery containing the blood of Joshua had the reputation of being a powerful apotropaion; while in a cave outside Abrīq, the chief fortress city of the Paulicians according to Qudāmah and al-Masʿūdī, the bodies of certain martyrs were preserved.[63] Perhaps more surprising is that at Ḥarrān, a town on the upper reaches of the Balīkh River no more than four hundred miles from the imperial capital, pagan cults persisted from the seventh through the tenth centuries. In fact, according to a perhaps not altogether trustworthy story current among the Christians of Ruhā, from 816/17 the pagans of Ḥarrān were permitted to perform their cultic rites in public. Whether this was strictly true, David bar Paul was more than justified in referring to the city as a "nest of paganism" whose inhabitants were "afflicted with the ulcers of idolatry."[64]

Commentary

Throughout the period with which we are here concerned, the urban system of Aqūr Province retained the basic hierarchical ordering that had been established in Sāsānian or even earlier times. The Arabs added a few new cities—al-Mawṣil, al-Rāfiqah, al-Raḥbah, Ruṣāfah al-Shām, Jazīrat ibn ʿUmar, and, near the end of our period, ʿImādīyah—but they were intruded into the system without fundamentally disturbing the structure of the preexisting hierarchy. In fact al-Mawṣil, al-Rāfiqah, and al-Ruṣāfah were simply substitutions for already existing settlements: the first for Sāsānian Nineveh, the second for Callinicum/al-Raqqah, and the third for a decayed, mainly Christian settlement formerly patronized by Ghassān chiefs. It is true, though, that at the end of the Sāsānian period the administrative headquarters of Nōdh-Ardashīrakan was divided between the town of Irbil and a satellite military and administrative enclave some twelve kilometers to the southwest.[65] In the hierarchical administrative structure, therefore, al-Mawṣil must be held to have been a replacement for Irbil and its satellite, even though in the spatial arrangement of the settlement pattern it was a successor to Nineveh. In addition to these new foundations, Arab garrisons were established at al-Ḥadīthah, Sinjār, Naṣībīn, Dārā, Mayyāfarīqīn, Raʾs al-ʿAyn, Bālis, and Ruhā, but these deployments of troops did little to change the relative standings of individual levels in the urban hierarchy. And they had scarcely more effect on the overall spatial distribution of urban forms, which appears not to have been altered significantly by the Islamic conquest.

In the south and far west of the province, settlements were, as in al-ʿIrāq, bound by an inescapable need for water to the major river courses. In the northern mountain tracts they were confined by physiography to predominantly latitudinal valleys in the fold-mountains of eastern Anatolia. But in the intervening regions of central Aqūr the physiographic constraints on location were considerably relaxed, so that the size and location of cities such as Ruhā or Naṣībīn were responses as much to the climatic and edaphic factors controlling agricultural development as to the irrigation or transport benefits of the far from impressive headwaters of a Balīkh tributary or the Hirmās River.

The Urban System

The organization of the urban system of Aqūr Province in the tenth century differed from that of al-ʿIrāq in three respects. First, the province was less intensively settled and its settlement pattern more dispersed. Second, Arab settlement had not been confined to garrison cantonments and administrative enclaves. Long before the Islamic conquest, Arab *badū* and *shwāyah, qarawīyūn* and *rāʿīyah,* and even townsmen, had been settling in northern Syria and the *Jazīrah* (the Aqūr Province of al-Maqdisī). These migrations were intensified when, late in the fifth century, the resumption of border warfare between Byzantium and Sāsānian Persia began to subvert established authority in the area. It was at this time that excessive desiccation of the Arabian territories of the Banū-Taghlib, already being encroached on by the Kindah confederacy, drove segments of the former group north to the inviting pastures between the Tigris and the Euphrates Rivers, particularly to the steppe between Sinjār and Naṣībīn. During the sixth century they were followed by other groups of Taghlib, elements of the Banū-Numayr, and subgroups of the Bakr ibn Wā'il, notably the Thaʿlabah, ʿIjl, and Dhuhl.

At the time of the Muslim conquests, Arab pastoralists of varying ecological adaptations, as well as husbandmen, were to be found all through the western two-thirds of Aqūr from the upper Tigris south to the Euphrates.[66] With the conquest, these spontaneous migrations in search of pasture and cropland became a directed, though still sporadic, flow. During the caliphate of ʿUthmān the Tamīm tribe was settled on unclaimed steppe in al-Rābīyah; Qays, Asad, and others in al-Māziḥīn and al-Mudaybir; and the Banū-Rabīʿah in the middle Tigris valley.[67] By the mid-seventh century, the population of Aqūr constituted a mosaic of tribal groups of varying degrees of assimilation, practicing diverse modes of subsistence, espousing different religions and cultural values, and all interspersed among indigenous, ethnically diverse, but often Christian towns and agricultural villages.

The third respect in which the urban hierarchy of Aqūr differed from that of al-ʿIrāq was in its lower level of systemic integration. Extensive tracts of mountainous territory along the upper Euphrates, although claimed by the Caliphate for the Dār al-Islam, were either de facto independent all or part of the time or were permanently or temporarily in Byzantine hands. This was a zone of predominantly small, fortified settlements controlling strategic river and road routes through eastern Anatolia. It had possessed this character in pre-Islamic times and continued to fill the same role long after the period with which we are here concerned.

Conditions in the western sectors of the *iqlīm* were rather different. Control of this territory was in more or less continual dispute not only between Muslim and Greek but also between rival Muslim factions, for it boasted reliable pastures and considerable—though localized—agricultural productivity in which a network of regional exchange centers managed to survive the vicissitudes of war and weather with surprising success. The experience of Ruhā is not atypical of the towns in this district of Diyār Muḍar, that is, essentially the land within the salient formed by the great westward-looping course of the middle Euphrates.[68] In the caliphate of ʿUmar (634–44), Muʿāwiyah ibn Abī-Sufyān had been instructed to settle tribes of the Muḍar confederacy between the Great Khābūr River and the Euphrates,[69] and as early as 644 Ruhā was used as a military base to repel a Byzantine advance into Aqūr. In the struggle between Umayyads and ʿAbbāsids the city was seized by Isḥāq ibn Muslim (a supporter of the Umayyads), besieged by Abū Jaʿfar (subsequently the caliph al-Manṣūr), and maintained its loyalty to the Umayyads for some years after the ʿAbbāsid victory, but was ultimately stormed by al-Manṣūr's forces. Its walls, like those of numerous other cities of Aqūr at this time (but not including Ḥarrān and Mayyāfarīqīn), were razed. In the civil war following the death of Hārūn al-Rashīd, the city favored the cause of al-Amīn, yet Naṣr ibn Shabath al-ʿUqayli, one of al-Amīn's Qaysite supporters, demanded a large payment from the citizens in return for sparing their famous cathedral. In about 814 the walls of Ruhā were rebuilt by a certain Abū Shaykh Janawayah, who charged the expenses to the "notables and rich men of the city." With the accession of the caliph al-Ma'mūn, the city was garrisoned by the mutinous troops of the governor al-Ṭāhir ibn Ḥusayn, which was scarcely more to be desired than an overt enemy occupation. In fact the greatest threat to the safety of the city in the early centuries of Islam may have been the lawlessness of Arab military leaders in times of civil unrest, a situation often exacerbated by the fact that most of the inhabitants of al-Ruhā were Christian.

Christian Communities

During the seventh through the tenth centuries, the Christians of al-Ruhā shared the disabilities imposed on People of the Book in all the cities of Aqūr. Generally speaking, their lives were secure on payment of the poll tax *(jizyah)* and, if they were landowners, the *kharāj.* Their existing churches were protected, but the construction of new places of worship was prohibited within specified distances of towns. These Christians were also subject to restrictions on dress, conduct, housing, and property that were promulgated from time to time by the caliph on the advice of his jurists. They were also forbidden to display the cross in public and to sound their *nawāqīs* at the hours of Muslim prayer.[70]

Precisely how heavily these restraints weighed upon the Christian population depended ultimately on the caprice or beneficence of a particular caliph or governor. The caliph al-Manṣūr (r. 754–75), for instance, decreed that all Christians should be branded, and Muḥammad ibn Marwān, governor of Mesopotamia, toward the end of the seventh century had prescribed death for anyone refusing to convert to Islam. The caliph al-Ma'mūn, by contrast, was by all accounts more kindly disposed toward his Christian subjects. When he passed through al-Ruhā on his way to campaign against Byzantium, according to a Christian author,

> he entered the Great Church and wondered at its beauty. He asked the Metropolitan how much was the revenue of this shrine. The Bishop replied, "Through your bounty, O King, its property is great. But, indeed, even though it is great, it is spent by the exaction of the *jizyah* which is based on its revenues." Then Ma'mūn commanded that the *jizyah* should not be taken by them on *khāns,* shops, baths, and mills—only on gardens and lands. For he affirmed that it is not right that anything that has a roof on it should pay the *jizyah.*[71]

Naturally, Christian communities in the towns of Diyār Muḍar would be regarded with even greater suspicion when the country was being ravaged by Byzantine armies, as happened in 915, 927, 942, 943, 952, 959–60, and 963. In 968 or 969 Byzantine forces again wasted the countryside around Ruhā, and yet again in 974–75, although on this occasion they spared the city itself "out of consideration for the monks who dwelt in the near-by hills." Little wonder that al-Maqdisī was moved to remark that, although the province was "full of Nature's blessings . . . the depredations of the Greeks had brought ruin to the fontiers."[72] He might also have noted that a few years previously the once flourishing town of Adhramah, on the plain between Naṣībīn and al-Mawṣil, had lost most of its inhabitants after being sacked by the Byzantines, while Kafartūthā "had been a beautiful city before the Byzantines had conquered it."[73]

Then in 993–94 a new enemy appeared from even farther west when Fāṭimid forces devastated the lands of Ruhā and "inflicted immense harm on the city." Moreover, these humanly inflicted disasters were interspersed with continually recurring natural hazards of floods,[74] droughts, and pests,[75] resulting in plagues and famine;[76] yet, despite these all-too-frequent reverses, most of the cities of Diyār Muḍar enjoyed fairly extended periods of prosperity at one time or another. That at the beginning of the fourth quarter of the eighth century was not atypical. Of al-Ruhā in 766–77 it was written,

> all the countryside . . . was beautiful with vineyards and fields and cattle in profusion. There was not a single wretched pauper in a village who did not possess a plough, donkeys, and goats, and there was not a place cultivable to a greater or lesser degree that was not planted with a vineyard. . . . Wheat and vines grew in abundance.[77]

Even the extortions of unscrupulous tax-farmers whose exactions were execrated in words bitter as gall in the Syriac chronicles of the time could not entirely subvert the resilience of the rural economy and the network of local exchange centers that it supported.[78]

Ḥamdānid Rule

For some three centuries the urban system of Diyār Rabīʿah, far removed from the threat of Byzantine incursions, was generally more stable than that of either Diyār Muḍar or Diyār Bakr. In the tenth century, however, it too, in company with the rest of the *iqlīm,* found its prosperity being undermined by the exactions and maladministration of the Ḥamdānid rulers. Arab authors have almost invariably bestowed high praise on this dynasty because of its patronage of poets and scholars, but Ibn Ḥawqal leaves us in no doubt as to the inordinate burdens that the Eastern Amīrate imposed on its subject peoples. Even in al-Mawṣil, its capital, governmental extortion had driven many noble families from the city.[79] In other parts of the province conditions were worse. Whereas "Naṣībīn had once been a city to which one went for recreation, amusement, and feasting," under the Ḥamdānids it had suffered "all sorts of affronts, afflictions, and refinements of arbitrary oppression," including the imposition of "taxes hitherto unheard of" and "unaccustomed exactions" so severe as to necessitate the forced sale of land and buildings (211).[80] The town of Balad had enjoyed a prosperity based on the export of its agricultural products until the moment when the *amīr* Nāṣir al-Dawlah (929–69) "brought it under his control and oppressed the inhabitants with all his might. . . . He spared neither ewe nor she-camel, disasters overwhelmed the citizens, and this bird of ill-omen inundated them with calamities" (220). Similarly, Jazīrat Ibn ʿUmar would have been a flourishing city "had it not been governed by devils and schismatics" (225).

In those parts of the *iqlīm* under the authority of the Western Ḥamdānid Amīrate, government appears to have borne no less heavily on the cities. The districts of Ṭūr ʿAbdīn and Dārā in the Diyār Muḍar, for instance, had been ruined and depopulated by the exactions of "that ruler [Sayf al-Dawlah, 945–67]—May God strike him down—whose injustice and oppression have been tolerated for too long" (214). The twin cities of al-Raqqah and al-Rāfiqah had also "suffered greatly from Sayf al-Dawlah's abuse of power in the form of taxes, imposts *(nawāʾib),* exactions, and confiscations that were inflicted one after another on the population" (225–26). Even the mighty fortress of Āmid had seen its fields wasted by the Greeks as Sayf al-Dawlah's grandiose but ill-conceived military ventures, fruitless against Byzantines and Ikhshīdids alike, drained the resources of the amīrate. "Of what use are walls without troops and arms? And now there are no fighting men," laments Ibn Ḥawqal, who adds, "The Ḥamdānids' only ambition is to hear their names invoked from the *minbar* and to solicit the blessing of God; but . . . prayers are a poor defence for a frontier city" (222–23).

Even though Ibn Ḥawqal may have had personal reasons for denigrating the rule of the Ḥamdānids and may have exaggerated the rapacity of their governors, much corroborative evidence indicates that until the very end of their hegemony they retained a characteristically *badū* inability to cope with the routine exigencies of government and administration. To judge from the *Ḥudūd,* al-Maqdisī, and retrospective comments by later topographers such as Yāqūt and al-Mustawfī, however, the establishment of Buwayhid authority over the Eastern Amīrate in 978 allowed, if not actively encouraged, a measure of recovery in the rural economy, and thereby in the cities of Diyār Rabīʿah and the eastern third of Diyār Muḍar.

In the western tracts of the province, though, Ḥamdānid ineptness and exactions continued through the end of the tenth century. In brief, the urban system of Aqūr *Iqlīm* encompassed a reasonably stable hierarchical network in Diyār Rabīʿah (essentially the lands tributary to the middle Tigris and upper Khābūr Rivers) that graded west into a fluctuating and ekisticly unstable zone of conflict between Greeks and Arabs (roughly coincident with the Diyār Muḍar). The north and northwest sectors of the *iqlīm* formed an arcuate, fractured network of urban centers strung along the upper Euphrates River and its tributaries, many components of which seem to have been independent of the main urban network centered on al-Mawṣil. During the tenth century, Ḥamdānid rapacity subverted the prosperity of the main urban system and aggravated the effects of nomadic raiding and Byzantine incursions in the fringe zones, although there is some evidence that during the last two decades of the century, Buwayhid rule permitted a limited degree of economic recovery.

Chapter Six
The Urban System in al-Shām

. . . the province most favoured with blessings, pious men, ascetics, and shrines.
—Al-Maqdisī, *Aḥsan al-Taqāsīm,* 33.

When the Arab levies penetrated the western flank of the Fertile Crescent, which was fairly coextensive with al-Maqdisī's *iqlīm* of al-Shām (Greater Syria), they found themselves in a highly urbanized region with numerous cities of great antiquity. They initially settled in military cantonments (notably al-Jābiyah in the Jawlān), in certain cities partly deserted by Christian inhabitants, and sometimes in smaller desert towns such as Tadmur (Palmyra, Tadmor),[1] al-Ruṣāfah,[2] al-Khunāṣirah,[3] and Ḥuwwārīn.[4] Nevertheless, they eventually came to constitute an important ethnic group in most of the old urban centers, but they established relatively few new foundations.

The configuration of the Province of al-Shām illustrates a feature common to several of al-Maqdisī's *aqālīm.* We have noted already that these subdivisions were typically based on a degree of political, or at least administrative, autonomy, modified in various ways to accommodate physiographic constraints.[5] However, in several instances the political framework of an *iqlīm* as defined by al-Maqdisī was not specifically that obtaining at the time when he was writing. Instead, it appears to have derived from an earlier period featuring the political ascendancy of a powerful and prestigious dynasty: "une sorte d'apogée politique," as André Miquel has put it.[6] This was particularly true of al-Shām, which had been a zone of conflict for more than a century before al-Maqdisī's compilation of the *Aḥsan.* From 878 to 905 the province had been under the control of the Egyptian Ṭūlūnids. By 941, after nearly four decades of precarious ʿAbbāsid rule, the southern half of the province had been incorporated in the Ikhshīdid kingdom, and from 969 in that of the more powerful and enduring Ismāʿīlī Fāṭimids. When al-Maqdisī was writing, the northern half of al-Shām was held by the Ḥamdānid *amīr* Saʿīd al-Dawlah Saʿīd (r. 967–91), who ruled as a tributary of the Byzantines from his capital at Ḥalab (Aleppo).[7] Nevertheless, al-Maqdisī, apparently harking back to the early decades of the tenth century when Syria and Palestine had been constituted as an integral province of the ʿAbbāsid Empire, treated al-Shām as a single functional urban region. It should be noted, though, that as far as can be determined, most of the actual elements of the urban system that he described pertained to the second half of the tenth century.

Marketing and Service Centers

The settlement that al-Maqdisī designated as the *miṣr* of this politically composite province was the ancient city of Dimashq (Damascus), which had undergone considerable architectural modification during the nearly ninety years that it had been the capital of the Umayyad Caliphate (661–750).[8] Set as it is in the heart of an oasis (known as the Ghūṭah) some sixteen miles long by ten wide where the Baradā and Aʿwaj Rivers provide irrigation for fruit and cereals in abundance, the subtle harmonies of the venerable city and the fertility of its environs have always exercised a powerful effect on Arab authors, and the comparison with Paradise has been a stock-in-trade of poets and prose writers alike.[9] But the city was not only a former dynastic capital and a center of agricultural production and textile manufacture: it was also a transportation node on the desert edge where an important longitudinal route running the length of the Levant intersected one of the main caravan trails linking al-ʿIrāq to the Mediterranean. What is more, Dimashq was a center for the exchange of commodities from contrasting (though neighboring) ecotypes. Yet by the tenth century the city had fallen from the high estate it had enjoyed as the capital of an empire more extensive than that of Rome at its apogee. The transference of the seat of the caliphate to Baghdād

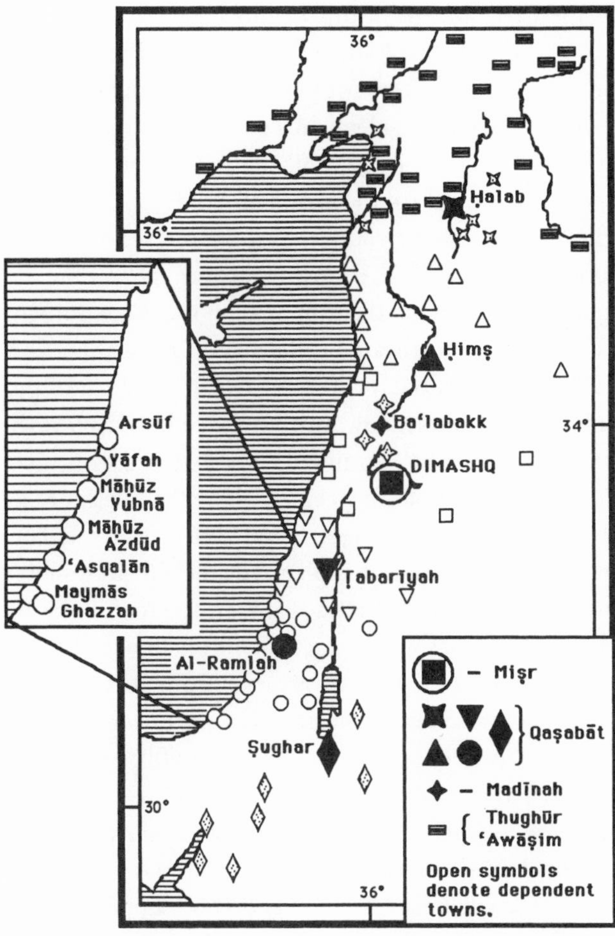

Figure 11. The upper ranks of the urban hierarchy in al-Shām, together with the frontier fortress of the north (*al-thughūr* and *al-ʿawāṣim*), as recorded by tenth-century authors generally. Inset: fortified posts *(ribāṭāt)* where exchanges between Muslims and Byzantines could be pursued, including the ransoming of Muslim captives.

under the ʿAbbāsids had stripped the city of those functions deriving directly from the status of imperial capital. As a result, it had become a seat of provincial government sustained mainly by manufacture and trade, and for much of the tenth century under Egyptian rule.

At the next-lower level of the urban hierarchy were the *qaṣabāt* of Ḥalab, Ḥimṣ, Ṭabarīyah, al-Ramlah, and Ṣughar (fig. 11). Ḥalab, the old city of Chalybon, which Seleucus Nicator had redesignated Beroia, had become the capital of the Ḥamdānid kingdom in 944/45. Toward the end of the tenth century al-Maqdisī remarked that the city was not large but was reaping the benefits that inevitably accrued to a seat of dynastic government.[10] However, that glory had been somewhat dimmed when in 962 the city was sacked, except for its citadel, by the Byzantines and the Hamdānid *amīr* became a vassal of the Greeks.

Ḥimṣ (Emesa), although designated early as the capital of a *jund* of the same name and in the tenth century "as large as any city in al-Shām," had in the interim lost some of the prosperity it had enjoyed as Byzantine Emesa, a decline shared by the other cities of the district.[11] Ṭabarīyah (Tiberias), situated on the western shore of Lake Tiberias, succeeded Skythopolis as capital of the Urdunn "province," consequently experiencing substantial growth during Umayyad times. It had been built by the tetrarch Herod Antipas sometime between A.D. 17 and 22 and named in honor of the Roman emperor Tiberius.[12]

Al-Ramlah (Ramleh), although founded in comparatively recent times by Sulaymān, the future caliph ʿAbd al-Malik (715–17) when he was governor of Filasṭīn, had become fully integrated into the urban hierarchy by the tenth century. Al-Maqdisī describes it as a "fine city . . . abounding in fruits and products of contrasting character." Situated as it was on the edge of the Shephelah, its trading area encompassed both the coastal tract and the uplands of Judaea; consequently, "Commerce was thriving and means of livelihood easy . . . It possessed attractive hostelries and pleasant baths . . . spacious houses, fine mosques, and broad streets." The congregational mosque, located in the *sūq*, was of an elegance that rivalled the great congregational mosque in Dimashq.[13] Ṣughar,[14] at the southern end of the Dead Sea, was afflicted with a pestilential climate.[15] Nevertheless, with the intensification of Egyptian-Levantine trade under the Egyptian dynasties, it had come to enjoy a commercial prosperity that made it "a little Baṣrah."[16]

The lower levels in the urban hierarchy of al-Shām subsumed a wide spectrum of city sizes and types, from small urban centers serving essentially agricultural trade areas—such as Nawā, "most rich in wheat and grain;"[17] Baysān, "abounding in palms and producing all the rice consumed in Filasṭīn and al-Urdunn;"[18] Kābul, surrounded by stands of sugarcane;[19] and al-Farādhiyah, with its vineyards[20]—through substantial cities such as Bāniyās[21] that offered a reasonably wide range of services, up to a district capital *(madīnah)* such as Baʿlabakk.[22] In northern al-Shām urban centers were generally disposed along the coast and in the valleys of the Orontes (al-ʿĀṣī) and Quwayq Rivers, with only a thin scattering on the more fertile tracts of the eastern steppes. In the south the coastal plain and the Shephelah were highly urbanized, with a scattering of centers among the Judaean hills; but on the uplands beyond the Jordan, the ancient land of Moab, cities were few.

Transportation Foci

Al-Shām had traditionally been a zone of passage, functioning as a land corridor between Asia and Africa while affording the shortest and easiest route from the Mediterranean region to inner Asia. Consequently, it is not surprising that any theoretical symmetry in the settlement hierarchy (such as would be implied by the operation of Central-Place principles, for instance, but which was in reality already distorted by the immediate juxtaposition and frequent interpenetration of benign and inhospitable environments) should have been further deformed by the development, at strategic nodes in the network of Middle Eastern trade, of cities performing specialized transportation services. The most prominent of these were strung along the coast: as al-Maqdisī phrases it, the Sea of Rūm "continuously brought thither commodities of commerce" *(al-ḥumūlāt fīhi ilayhi).*[23]

The sequence of ports stretched from Iskandarūnah[24] in the north to Yāfah (Jaffa) in the south, which, although only "a small town, was the emporium of Filasṭīn and the port of al-Ramlah."[25] Between these two extremes was a series of harbor towns of varying importance, among them al-Suwaydīyah, the outport of Anṭākiyah (Antiochia) at the mouth of the Orontes River;[26] al-Lādhiqīyah (Latakia);[27] Jabalah;[28] Bulunyās;[29] Anṭarṭūs;[30] Rafanīyah;[31] Aṭrābulus (Tripoli), called by al-Iṣṭakhrī and Ibn Ḥawqal "the port of Dimashq [Damascus]";[32] Bayrūt (Beirut);[33] Ṣaydā (Sidon);[34] Ṣūr (Tyre);[35] ʿAkkā (Acre);[36] and Qayṣārīyah (Caesarea), raised by Herod Antipas to the dignity of an imperial city and renamed in honor of his suzerain Caesar Augustus.[37] South of Yāfah were a few more tertiary ports, including ʿAsqalān (Ascalon)[38] and Mīmās, the outport of Ghazzah (Gaza).[39] In the far south, at the head of the Gulf of ʿAqabah (described by al-Maqdisī as "an arm of the China sea"), was Waylah (al-ʿAqabah), "a substantial and flourishing city . . . the port of Filasṭīn and the emporium of al-Ḥijāz."[40] Significant for the development of this commercially oriented port was that in late Umayyad and early ʿAbbāsid times it became a recognized center of Islamic legal studies, numbering among its residents at one time or another the distinguished traditionist Shihāb al-Zuhrī and several scholars who assumed the *nisbah* al-Aylī.[41]

Around the inner frontiers of al-Shām a series of cities along the desert fringe served as inland "ports" for the caravan trade, among them Buzāʿah in the Wādī Buṭnān, a day's march northeast of Ḥalab;[42] al-Khunāṣirah, on the desert edge two days' journey to the southeast of the same city;[43] Tadmur, now much decayed from its former grandeur;[44] Buṣrah;[45] ʿAmmān;[46] Maʾāb;[47] and Udhruḥ.[48] Maʿān was a provisioning center where the pilgrim road to Makkah (Mecca) entered the desert proper.[49] Urban centers in the interior of al-Shām that benefited from the caravan trade included Kafar Sābā on the road from al-Ramlah to Dimashq,[50] Kafar Sallām on the road from al-Ramlah north,[51] ʿĀqir on the road from al-Ramlah to Makkah,[52] and Ghazzah on the main road from al-Shām to Egypt.[53] In Judaea, Ḥabrā (Hebron) fulfilled the function of a pilgrim hostel on an impressive scale. Within the sanctuary thought to contain the tombs of the patriarchs Ibrāhīm, Isḥāq, and Yaʿqūb was a public guest house with a resident cook, baker, and servants, who supplied a dish a lentils and olive oil to indigent travellers—and, indeed, to those with means if they so desired. Rest houses had been constructed around the city mosque to accommodate the many pilgrims visiting the shrine.[54] Similar services had also been instituted at Baghrās "on the road to the frontier fortresses" (see below), where Zubaydah, wife of Hārūn al-Rashīd, had provided endowments *(awqāf)* so that "anybody visiting the town could be put up and entertained *(mīhmānī).*"[55]

Just as most of the urban centers listed here performed ranges of functions besides the transportation services that gave them their special character, so conversely numerous other cities incorporated break-of-bulk and transportation facilities to a certain extent among their more generalized services. Ḥalab was especially notable in this regard, occupying a nodal site[56] whence caravan routes led west to Anṭākiyah, southwest to al-Lādhiqīyah, south to Ḥimṣ, southeast to Tadmur, east to Bālis[57] and al-Raqqah, northeast to the towns of the upper Euphrates, and northwest by way of the Baylān pass to Cilicia.

Dimashq was clearly in a somewhat similar position, where routes following the interior lowlands from north to south intersected latitudinal routes leading from the Mediterranean to the interior.[58] Mention should also be made of Anṭākiyah's specialized role as a military staging post on the road to the Byzantine frontier.

Industrial and Craft Centers

By common consent, al-Shām in the tenth century was rated a fertile and agriculturally productive *iqlīm*. Ibn Ḥawqal and al-Maqdisī alike were lavish in their assertions to that effect. Ḥimṣ, for example, lay "in a fertile plain possessed of both an unusually benign climate and one of the richest soils in al-Shām";[59] Anṭākiyah was set in a "beautiful and fertile region";[60] and al-Ramlah, too, was situated "in the midst of fertile districts," which al-Maqdisī characterizes as "well favoured above all others."[61] On at least one occasion a whole province—in this instance Filasṭīn—was described as "the most fertile province in the *iqlīm*,"[62] and not for nothing was the Ghūṭah of Damascus included among the earthly paradises.[63] Nor was this reputation for productivity wholly undeserved, especially when the *iqlīm* is compared with its neighbors—even allowing for the Hierosolymite al-Maqdisī's tendency to enlarge on the advantages of his native country.

Agricultural practice was based essentially on the cultivation of various combinations of winter cereals and summer fruit, into which was integrated stock raising (chiefly sheep and goats) as environmental opportunity offered. Physiographic diversity and its accompanying agricultural opportunities ensured that the farming pattern of al-Shām was a mosaic of land uses, each typically of restricted extent, in which patches of intensive cultivation alternated with tracts of low productivity and even barren rock. Cereals (wheat and barley) were confined generally to the less accidented lands at lower elevations: the coastal lowlands (especially the Plain of Sharōn and the lands bordering the present-day Gulf of Iskanderūn);[64] interior valleys such as the northern sectors of the great rift depression; the Orontes valley and the Biqāʿ;[65] and certain favored areas east of the Jordan River, notably the vicinity of ʿAmmān,[66] Ḥawrān, and the Jawlān (Golan) heights, the last of which, according to al-Maqdisī, supplied Dimashq with most of its provisions.[67]

Fruit of different sorts were grown almost everywhere that either upland or lowland provided appropriate climatic and edaphic conditions. Those of al-Ramlah were considered by al-Maqdisī to be as fine as any grown in al-Shām,[68] while the quinces of Jerusalem—in the same author's eyes, at any rate—were unmatched anywhere.[69] Vines were grown successfully in warm corners among the uplands;[70] figs were recorded at Maʿarrat al-Nuʿmān,[71] al-Ramlah,[72] and Yubnā (Yavneh), those from this last locality being of the prized Damascene variety;[73] and the glaucous olive dotted hillsides wherever its roots could take hold.[74] At intermediate elevations, temperate-latitude fruit were occasionally grown alongside the prevailing Mediterranean species, notably apples at Ḥabrā, the environs of which appeared from a distance "as a continuous orchard of vines and fruit-trees."[75] Al-Maqdisī notes that a sizable part of the fruit crop was exported to Egypt and other neighboring countries.[76]

Sugarcane was reported from the coastal plain at Kābul[77] and Bayrūt, and from Ṭabarīyah in the upper Jordan valley where, al-Maqdisī says, the inhabitants spent two months of each year "playing on the reed," which he glosses as "sucking on the [sugar]cane" *(yamuṣṣūn al-qaṣab);*[78] while cotton was grown in the neighborhood of Ḥulah, immediately south of Bāniyās.[79] In the Jordan valley, particularly in its southern sector, known locally as al-Ghawr, hot summers permitted the growth of tropical crops such as the newly introduced banana,[80] dates,[81] and the indigo plant *(al-nīl),*[82] but east beyond the Jordan, farming and horticulture gradually yielded to pastoralism in one or another of its gradations. This progressive transformation was already evident on the desert border in Balqāʾ District where flocks were rated coequal with grain in the agricultural economy;[83] and a few miles beyond was completed with the virtual total ascendancy of pastoralism over agriculture. The traveller leaving ʿAmmān for the east would see few cultivated crops until reaching the irrigated lands along the Euphrates River.

Specialized manufacturing was as prominent in al-Shām as in any part of the Islamic world. Much of it was concerned with the processing of the agricultural products just mentioned: in Ṣughar indigo dyeing;[84] in Bayt al-Maqdis (Jerusalem) and Ḥalab the spinning of cotton; in Dimashq the preparation of olive oil, in Ḥalab of the red ochre called *al-mughrah*, in Baʿlabakk of the sweetmeat of dried figs called *malban*,[85] in al-Ramlah of omphacine oil, in Ṣūr and Kābul of sugar; and in Qadas the weaving of mats from the *ḥalfā* reed. Metalworking was of considerable importance in Bayt al-Maqdis (mirrors and needles) and Dimashq (brass vessels), and a glass industry flourished in Ṣūr. But the most developed of all manufactures was that concerned with textiles: carpets from Ṭabarīyah; cloths of the stuffs called *munayyar* and *baʿlīsī*[86] from Qadas; brocades and *maʿṣūr* and *baʿlīsī* cloths from Dimashq; various fabrics from Ḥalab; and veils from al-Ramlah that were superior to any in the Islamic world.[87] Equally renowned were the silk fabrics of ʿAsqalān.[88] The use of paper, introduced into al-ʿIrāq at the time of Hārūn al-Rashīd, had diffused as far west as Egypt by 800. In the tenth century it was being manufactured in al-Shām at Ṭabarīyah and Dimashq (180–81).

Maritime fishing was mentioned as a resource in connection with Waylah (178), and al-Maqdisī preserves the interesting information that the *bunnī* fish, believed to be a species of carp, had been introduced into the Ḥūlah Lake from ʿIrāqī Wāsiṭ (162).[89] Al-Shām was not minerologically well endowed, and the only references I have found to such resources are to marble quarries at Bayt Jibrīl (Bayt Jibrīn 174, 152)[90] and bitumen from the Dead Sea.[91]

Fortified Settlements

A class of specialized urban functions that was prominently represented in al-Shām was that of military defense. The cities within which these functions were most fully developed were located in two contrasting situations: on the northern and northeastern frontiers of the *iqlīm* and along the Mediterranean coast. Both, however, were directed to the same purposes, namely the containment of Byzantine incursions and the mounting of raids into Greek territory.

On the northern marches of al-Shām two categories of frontier fortresses were recognized by contemporary authors: forward strongholds known as *al-thughūr* (sing. *al-thaghr*) and supporting positions to the rear known as *al-ʿawāṣim* (sing. *al-ʿāṣimah:* "protectress"). The type locations for both classes of fortress were at the intersection of military roads or at the entrance to passes through the northern mountains. Under the Rāshidūn and early Umayyad caliphs the strongholds that would subsequently be considered *ʿawāṣim* were actually frontier posts strung between Manbij on the Euphrates and Anṭākiyah on the Orontes, while those destined to be *thughūr* were in a no-man's-land extending from Ḥalab and Anṭākiyah north to the foothills of the Taurus and Anti-Taurus ranges. Most were preexisting cities that had been refortified and garrisoned by the Muslims. Subsequently the Umayyads extended their control over much of this no-man's-land, particularly after ʿAbd al-Malik concluded a treaty with Justinian II by which the Byzantines virtually withdrew behind the Taurus Mountains.

Originally the whole of the frontier zone had, nominally at any rate, been dependent on the *Jund* of Ḥimṣ, but from about 680 had been constituted as the independent *Jund* of Qinnasrīn. In 786 Hārūn al-Rashīd regrouped the strongholds of Manbij, Dulūk, Raʿbān, Qūrus, Anṭākiyah, and Tīzīn into a single administrative unit designated the *ʿawāṣim,* allegedly signifying that they afforded the Muslims protection when they returned from raids into Greek territory.[92] Sometimes *ʿawaṣim* and *thughūr* were united into a single command; at other times the *thughūr* were established as a separate province. In either case, the topographers distinguished between a northeastern group of fortresses protecting the *Jazīrah* (*al-thughūr al-Jazarīyah,* already described in chapter 5) and a northwestern group guarding al-Shām *(al-thughūr al-Shāmīyah).* Individual fortresses in the *thughūr* and *ʿawāṣim* zones often changed hands several times between the seventh and tenth centuries as the fortunes of war favored now the Byzantines and now the Muslims. At the beginning of the tenth century the capital of the *ʿawāsim* was at Anṭākiyah,[93] but in 970 the amīrate of Ḥalab was forced to cede both *thughūr* and *ʿawāṣim* territories to the Byzantine emperor Nicephorus Phocas, and they remained tributary to the Greeks for the rest of the century. It appears that by the tenth century, and possibly a good deal earlier, the terms *al-thughūr* and *al-ʿawāṣim* had become virtually interchangeable, for the list of *thughūr* preserved in the *Ḥudūd*—Sumaysāṭ, Sanjah, Manbij, Ḥiṣn Manṣūr, Qūrus, Malaṭīyah (Malatya), Marʿash, Ḥadath, al-Hārūnīyah, Bayās, Kanīs, Kafarbayyā, Maṣṣīṣah, ʿAyn Zarbah, Adhanah, Ṭarsūs, and Awlas—overlapped substantially with the roster of cities elsewhere designated as *ʿawāṣim.*[94]

Finally, it should be recorded that, although in many of the frontier zones of al-Shām "the people lived in continual terror of the Greeks, who have driven many from their homes, ravaged the outlying districts, and attacked the frontier strongholds,"[95] yet not a few of the towns in these zones occasionally attained a modest degree of prosperity. For example, the *Ḥudūd*—probably drawing on information provided by al-Iṣṭakhrī[96]—characterized no less than ten of the towns listed above as "flourishing" or "prosperous," another (ʿAyn Zarbah) as having "well cultivated fields," and another (Adhanah) as having a "flourishing market." Nor is it without interest that Tīnāt, "the home of courageous warriors who know well the vulnerable points of the Greek territories, as well as the easy passes and dangerous spots," was also the center of a logging industry exporting coniferous lumber to all parts of al-Shām, the frontier districts, and even to Egypt.[97]

The second principal type of fortified city was found along the coast of al-Shām. From Iskandarūnah in the north to Ghazzah in the south, virtually all coastal cities were fortified against assault from the sea.[98] Anṭarṭūs, for example, was described as "a fortress on the sea";[99] Aṭrābulus, Bayrūt, and Ṣaydā (Sidon) as "strongly fortified towns";[100] and ʿAsqalān as "well defended."[101] Ṣūr, too, was "a fortified town on the sea, or rather in the sea, for it is entered through one gate only after crossing a single bridge, and the sea surrounds it."[102] The harbor was enclosed by triple walls except for a narrow entrance that was secured with a chain at night. A chain was also used as part of the harbor defenses constructed at ʿAkkā by al-Maqdisī's grandfather to the order of Ibn Ṭūlūn.[103]

Of special interest are the seven fortified posts *(ribāṭāt)* spaced along the southern reaches of the coast, namely—in order from north to south—Arsūf, Yāfah, Māḥūz Yubnā, Māḥūz Azdūd, ʿAsqalān, Mīmās, and Ghazzah;[104] for these were some of the relatively few points where institutionalized nonmilitary exchanges between Muslims and Byzantines could take place. In each port, for example, there were Greek-speaking traders who undertook missions into Byzantine territories in search of all types of provisions. Furthermore, each port was linked to al-Ramlah, the *qaṣabah* of Filasṭīn Province, by a chain of beacons capable of transmitting an alarm from the shore to the capital in hardly more than an hour by day or night. But not all confrontations between Muslims and Christians were totally hostile. Occasions of peaceful exchange occurred when the beacons signalled the arrival of Greek warships[105] bringing Muslim captives. "As drums were beaten on the city keep, calling the populace down to the *ribāṭ* on the shore, the people hurried out in force . . . and then ransoming began. One captive would be exchanged for another, or money and jewels would be offered, until eventually all the prisoners in the Greek ships had been freed."[106] The ransom asked by the Greeks in al-Maqdisī's experience was one hundred *dīnārs* for three captives.

Religious Centers

As for the sacral hierarchy, al-Shām was one of the only two provinces of Islam to include urban centers at all levels of sanctity. After referring to the province as "the land of prophets, the abode of righteous men, and the home of the Saints,"[107] al-Maqdisī continues:

> It is a centre of attraction for the virtuous. It contains the First Qiblah[108] (= Jerusalem: a reference to cosmological sanctity), and the places of the Gathering *(al-Ḥashr)* [on the day of Resurrection][109] and of the Night Journey[110] [two examples of soteriological holiness]. It is the Holy Land, with many fortified posts *(ribāṭāt),* marcher cities *(thughūr),* and noble hills. There are the places to which Ibrāhīm migrated *(muhājar),*[111] as well as his tomb;[112] and there are also the habitations of Ayyūb (Job) and his well,[113] the *Miḥrāb* of Dāwūd (David) and his gate,[114] the wonders of Sulaymān (Solomon) and his cities,[115] the burial-places of both Isḥāq (Isaac) and his mother,[116] the birth-place of the Messiah (al-Masīḥ) and his cradle,[117] the village of Ṭālūṭ (Saul) and his river,[118] the place where Jālūt (Goliath) was slain, together with his castle,[119] the well *(jubb)* of Jeremiah and his prison *(ḥabs),*[120] the place of prayer of Ūrīyā (Uriah) and his house,[121] the Dome of Muḥammad and his gate,[122] the rock of Mūsā (Moses),[123] the hill of ʿĪsā (Jesus),[124] the *miḥrāb* of Zakarīyāʾ (Zacharias),[125] the battle-ground of Yaḥyā (John),[126] the shrines of the prophets, the villages of Ayyūb[127] and the dwelling-places of Yaʿqūb (Jacob),[128] the Masjid al-Aqṣā,[129] the Mount of Olives *(Jabal Zaytā),*[130] the city of ʿAkkā, the shrine of Ṣiddīqā,[131] the sepulchre of Mūsā,[132] the resting-place of Ibrāhīm and his tomb,[133] the city of ʿAsqalān,[134] the spring of Siloam (Sulwān),[135] the country of Luqmān,[136] the Wādī of Kanʿān[137] and the cities of Lūṭ (Lot),[138] the Place of the Gardens (al-Jinān),[139] the mosques of ʿUmar[140] and ʿUthmān's endowment,[141] the gate named by the Two Men *(al-Rajulān)*[142] and the hall in which

> the Two Litigants *(al-Khaṣmān)* appeared,[143] the wall between torment and pardon[144] and the Near Place[145] [both conferring soteriological sanctity], the holy shrine at Baysān,[146] the noble and glorious gate of Ḥiṭṭah,[147] the Gate of the Trumpet *(al-Ṣūr)* [that will sound on the Judgment Day],[148] the place of *al-Yaqīn,*[149] the tombs of both Mary (Maryam) and Rachel (Rāḥīl),[150] the place of meeting of the two seas,[151] the dividing-place of the two worlds,[152] the Gate of the Sakīnah[153] and the Dome of the Chain *(Qubbat al-Silsilah),*[154] the final station of the Kaʿbah [*manzil al-Kaʿbah:* soteriological holiness again],[155] as well as other holy places without number.[156]

This encomium sufficiently attests the holiness that al-Maqdisī ascribed to the *iqlīm* of al-Shām, and within that *iqlīm* particularly to the Province of Filasṭīn. In fact a large corpus of literature addresses the *faḍāʾil al-Quds* (that is, the sacral significance of both the province and Jerusalem),[157] stemming ultimately from the Qurʾānic designation in *Surah* 5 *(al-Māʾidah)*:21: "My people, enter now into the Holy Land which God hath ordained for you." Yet there were also marked differences of opinion regarding the validity of much of the substance of these accounts. Muṭahhar ibn Ṭāhir al-Maqdisī, for instance, reported—with fairly evident approval—that the belief in the eventual quickening of the dead in Jerusalem was held by some to be based on a forged *ḥadīth (mawḍūʿ)* and that God would effect the Resurrection wherever it might please Him,[158] while Ibn Kathīr characterized the same belief as merely an invention propagated to attract visitors to the city.[159] In the thirteenth century the theologian Ibn Taymīyah devoted a whole treatise to refuting what he regarded as exaggerated claims for the sanctity of Filasṭīn.[160] And, in truth, as the late Professor Goitein put it, even a comparatively liberal man like Muṭahhar ibn Ṭāhir "could not but realize that most of the traditions about Jerusalem were local and largely of foreign origin and had no foundation in the old Muḥammedan stock."[161] The most vocal proponents of the especial sanctity of Jerusalem in particular and of Filasṭīn in general tended to be the ascetics and mystics who would subsequently come to be known as Ṣūfīs. Goitein very pertinently observes that virtually all the great early mystics—such as Sufyān al-Thawrī, Ibrāhīm ibn Adham, Bāyazīd Bisṭāmī, Bishr al-Ḥāfī, and Sarī al-Saqaṭī—made a point of visiting Jerusalem.[162] And as figure 12 makes clear, for such persons[163] Jerusalem was the focus of sanctity not only for the Province of Filasṭīn but for the whole of al-Shām.[164]

As early as the beginning of the second century of the *Hijrah* (soon after the beginning of the eighth century A.D.), there seems to have been a near consensus within the Muslim community that Jerusalem should be included among the three especially Holy Cities of the Faith, the others being, of course, Makkah (Mecca) and al-Madīnah (Medina). Actually, the sanctity of these cities was invariably specified in terms of their principal mosques, as in the *ḥadīth* that licensed pilgrimage to the three shrines just mentioned: "You shall saddle up for [travel to] only three mosques—the Sacred Mosque [in Makkah], my mosque [in al-Madīnah], and the Farthest (al-Aqṣā) Mosque [in Jerusalem]."[165] The mosque that bestowed this degree of sanctity on Jerusalem was the Masjid al-Aqṣā, so called in allusion to Qurʾānic *Surah* 17 *(al-Isrāʾ)*:1: "Glory to Him who transported His servant by night from the Masjid al-Ḥarām [in Makkah] to the Farthest Mosque, the precincts of which We have blessed."[166] According to the received account, it stood on the site of the ancient temple of Solomon. A primitive mosque seems to have been built at an undetermined date on the ruins of the Herodian Royal Stoa, which had been destroyed by Titus in A.D. 70. Certainly such a structure was described by the pilgrim Arculf in about 680,[167] but it was not until A.H. 72 (A.D. 691/92) that the Umayyad caliph ʿAbd al-Malik gave appropriate architectural significance to the site by raising nearby the oratory known as the Qubbat al-Ṣakhrā, or in English translation "The Dome of the Rock"—the rock being a natural outcrop on the summit of Mount Moriah, from which the Prophet had ascended to heaven and on which the angel Isrāfīl will sound the last trumpet on the Resurrection Day.[168] This magnificent structure, which is said to have consumed the revenue of Egypt for seven years,[169] became—and was intended to be—a worthy rival to the splendid churches of Jerusalem, Ludd, Dimashq, Edessa (Urfa), and other Christian centers.[170] Then in 709 the caliph al-Walīd rebuilt the Aqṣā Mosque itself in a style more worthy of its role in Islamic soteriology.[171]

Jerusalem further benefited from the custom of the *taʿrīf.* This had been instituted in the early days of Islam to permit Muslims whose duties in distant lands prevented them from undertaking the annual Great Pilgrimage to Makkah nevertheless to participate in certain rites of the *Ḥajj,* notably the most holy *Wuqūf,* in some of the provincial capitals.[172] It is not known how many Muslims attended these assemblies in Jerusalem during the tenth century, but in 1047 the Persian pilgrim Nāṣir-i Khusraw reported that more than twenty thousand persons performed the *Wuqūf* in the city[173]—by which he meant, as is clear from his use of this number elsewhere, simply a large gathering.[174]

All Filasṭīn Province was considered sacred by reason of its history of prophecy and revelation, but al-Maqdisī gives a more precise territorial expression to the "Land which God—may He be exalted—has called Blessed."[175] "The Holy Land," he writes, "is counted as the country lying within forty miles of Jerusalem *(Īliyāʾ),* including the *qaṣabah* [al-Ramlah] and its district centers, twelve miles of coastal territory, the towns of Ṣughar and Maʾāb, a distance of five miles into the steppe *(al-bādiyah),* in the direction of the *qiblah* (south) as far as al-Kusayfah and the land over against it, and in the north to the confines of Nābulus." The territory thus specified is shown in figure 12 as enclosed within the circle centered on Jerusalem.

Al-Maqdisī's own account (p. 117 above) and the combined testimony of other more or less contemporary authors abundantly confirm Jerusalem as the focus of sacrality in al-Shām; but holy sites and relics did occur elsewhere, notably in association with a secondary focus at al-Dimashq. In 714/15 this lesser sacral concentration was symbolized architecturally by the erection of a splendid congregational mosque that al-Maqdisī, although a devout Hierosolymite (Jerusalemite), could not forbear to describe as "the fairest of any in the Islamic world."[176] From these two foci, the degrees of sacrality declined rapidly outward so that even the coastal cities of Filasṭīn, which were formally within the "Holy Land" as defined by al-Maqdisī, could lay claim at most only to the *barakah* of association with a religious scholar. In the case of Ghazzah, though, that association was the dual circumstance of having been the birthplace, in 767, of none other than Muḥammad ibn Idrīs al-Shāfiʿī, founder of one of the four principal juridical schools *(madhāhib)* of Sunnī Islam and allegedly housing the tomb of Hāshim ibn ʿAbd Manāf, the Prophet's great-grandfather.[177]

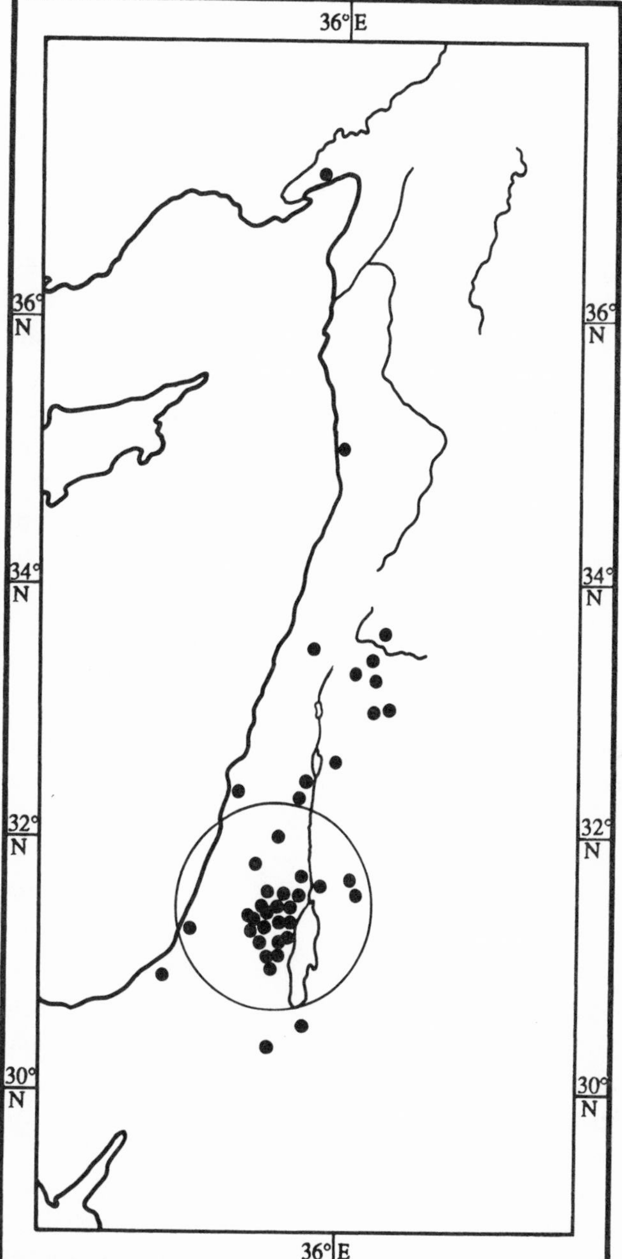

Figure 12. Muslim holy places in al-Shām in the second half of the tenth century. The circle centered on Jerusalem delimits al-Maqdisī's interpretation of the "Land which God has called Blessed" (Qurʾān 21 *[al-Anbiyāʾ]*:71).

As often as not, the *barakah* emanated from a relic of the Islamic past. Udhruḥ, a frontier town between al-Shām and the Ḥijāz, which in the second half of the tenth century seems to have been of small account, nevertheless enjoyed a certain renown for having both a mantle of the Prophet's and a treaty with him inscribed on parchment.[178] In the northern half of the *iqlīm* I have found a record of only two *barakah*-disseminating relics: one in Ḥiṣn Muthaqqab, a small frontier stronghold on the border between the ʿ*awāṣim* and the *thughūr,* where there was a second copy of a Qurʾān copied by the caliph ʿUmar ibn ʿAbd al-ʿAzīz (r. 717–20), who had established the fortress; and the other in the coastal town of Anṭarṭūs, where the caliph ʿUthmān's personal Qurʾān was preserved.[179]

Commentary

At the time of the Arab conquest al-Shām was already a highly urbanized province, and during the ensuing three centuries the Muslims added only a few new cities to the system. Chief among them was the *qaṣabah* of al-Ramlah, founded early in the eighth century. The others were mainly frontier fortresses in the north: for example, al-Hārūnīyah, built by Hārūn al-Rashīd in 799 on the western flank of the Jabal Lukkām; and ʿAyn Zarbah, also established by Hārūn, further fortified in 804, laid waste by Byzantine armies, rebuilt by the Ḥamdānid Sayf al-Dawlah at a cost of three million *dirhams*, but again captured by the Greeks in 962.[180] Others of these frontier strongholds were so strongly fortified as to have become virtually new cities, among which al-Ḥadath was fairly typical. Rebuilt by the caliph al-Mahdī in 779 after being razed by the Greeks, it changed hands several times before being refortified by the Ḥamdānids in 954, only to be lost to the Byzantines yet again.[181] However, these additions to the system had little effect on the overall pattern of urban distribution. Nor did shifts in the administrative ranking of individual cities seriously affect the hierarchical structure of the urban system in the southern two-thirds of the *iqlīm,* where, for example, al-Ramlah had replaced ancient Ludd and become the *qaṣabah* of Filastīn Province and Ṣughar had superseded Udruḥ in that role in al-Sharāʾ.

Northern Strongholds

In the far north, though, changes in the relative rankings had been more dramatic. Qinnasrīn, constituted as the *qaṣabah* of a *jund* by the caliph Yazīd ibn Muʿāwīyah, had declined precipitously in competition with Ḥalab when that city had become the capital of the Ḥamdānid amīrate and, by the time of al-Maqdisī, had lost most of its inhabitants. But in the frontier zone between Christian and Muslim, the urban system *qua* system had undergone the greatest degree of disintegration. Ibn Ḥawqal puts it succinctly enough: "The marches have no district capital so that each town is [virtually] independent."[182]

Thughūr strongholds often changed hands several times during the three and a half centuries with which we are concerned and in the ʿ*awāṣim* districts, some cities changed hands almost as frequently. As we have seen, Anṭākiyah, chief city of the ʿ*awāṣim,* fell before the armies of Nicephorus Phocas in 964; Qinnasrīn was left in ruins; even Ḥimṣ, far to the south in the upper Orontes valley, saw its lands ravaged by Byzantine soldiery;[183] and Ibn Ḥawqal sadly contrasts the prosperity of Ṭarsūs under the Muslims with its allegedly diminished state under the rule of the Byzantines (183–84).[184] When he passed through the city soon after the mid-tenth century, he thought the garrison must have amounted to nearly one hundred thousand horsemen, made up of volunteer contingents from virtually the whole of the Muslim world. Of all the great cities within the borders of Persia, Mesopotamia, Arabia, Syria, Egypt, and the Maghrib, he writes, "there is none that does not maintain here in Ṭarsūs a hostelry *(dār)* and a *ribāṭ* in which to house its warriors for the Faith *(ghāzī)*. . . . They are diligent in both prayer and worship. They receive rations and pay, together with large revenues and alms in quantity, as well as funds to which rulers commit themselves and the help of wealthy men motivated by piety and devotion" (184). The same author then goes on to say that throughout the Islamic world, persons of power and wealth were placing their property in *waqf* for support of warriors in the *ribāṭāt* of Ṭarsūs. But it was all in vain. In 965 the city fell to the Greeks. "The men perished and their possessions vanished. It was as though they had never been . . . had never inhabited these places" (184).[185]

The Emerging Urban System

Another prominent feature of the urban system of al-Shām was the dissonance between the administrative and sacral hierarchies. The peaks of these hierarchies culminated not only in different cities but in different levels of cities. Whereas the sacral hierarchy had assumed the form of a steep-sided, scalene cone with its base in the southern half of the *iqlīm,* the administrative hierarchy was more broadly based and pitched less steeply. While the former encompassed all levels of sanctity up to the cosmological holiness (albeit attenuated) of Jerusalem, the latter did not rise above the *miṣr* level of the regional metropolis of Dimashq. After the fall of the Umayyad dynasty, of course, there was no imperial capital in al-Shām to match the cosmological associations of Jerusalem. It is also noteworthy that the Islamic sacral hierarchy overlapped substantially with developed Jewish and Christian hierarchies, so that a sizable number of shrines were common to all three systems. In that limited respect, at least, the three main monotheistic religions of al-Shām were functionally supportive of one another.

The internal coherence of the urban system in al-Shām was further subverted during roughly the last quarter of the ninth century and the second half of the tenth, when the *iqlīm* had been divided between competing empires. Whereas the comparatively benign suzerainty of Ikhshīdids and Fāṭimids apparently did little to modify the structure of the urban hierarchy in the south of the *iqlīm,* Sayf al-Dawlah ʿAlī's establishment of the Western Ḥamdānid Amīrate in Ḥalab in 944 imposed a fairly strong centripetalizing administration on the urban system in the northern half; many of the economic and sacral ties forged during Umayyad and early ʿAbbāsid times seem to have persisted across the political boundary. But the cities of the north paid a high price for this limited hierarchical coherence. Sayf al-Dawlah's military forays against the Ikshīdids, the Turks, and especially the Byzantines not only failed to achieve any lasting successes but ultimately provoked a devastating Greek counteroffensive that would overrun many of the *thughūr* cities and reduce several of the *ʿawāṣim* to tribute-paying dependencies. And the price for these military adventures was not merely decline to subordinate status but extortions of all sorts directed against the cities still outside the reach of the Greeks.

Ibn Ḥawqal was as vehement in his denunciation of the Ḥamdānid rulers as in his execration of the Byzantine invaders. The predicament of Ḥalab was especially galling to him, for the inhabitants were—through "the baseness and greed of the Ḥamdānid ruler"—subject to double taxation, being forced to pay tribute to the Greeks at the same time as the Arab government exacted heavy imposts for its own purposes. Among other mobilizative instruments employed by the Arab *amīr* was the purchase of imported goods at low, fixed prices and their subsequent resale at inflated prices—as Ibn Ḥawqal phrases it, "in a most vile and ignoble manner." Moreover, the *amīr* had also established a monopoly of vinegar and soap manufacture. In short, concludes Ibn Ḥawqal, "There was no business transaction from which he did not skim a shameful profit."[186]

And it was oppressive measures of this kind, coupled with a progressive weakening of governmental control, as much as depredations by the Greeks, that were inducing merchants to follow the inland route from north to south along the desert edge in preference to the roads through the heart of the urban system. The brighter side to this situation was the rise to economic prominence of Khunāsirah as a provisioning center on the desert route (179). Ibn Ḥawqal also blamed the Ḥamdānids (probably quite properly) for the Byzantine capture of Anṭākiyah in 970. In a bitter tirade he castigates the potentates, lords, princes, and—somewhat incongrously in this company—*badū,* who, preoccupied with the advancement of their own affairs, had not lifted a finger to prevent the rape of the city (179–80). Generally speaking, history has vindicated Ibn Ḥawqal's views, prejudiced though they surely were.

It is evident, then, that the persistence of the pre-Islamic settlement pattern in its essentials through the first three and a half centuries of Muslim occupation does not imply total stasis in the hierarchical ordering of the urban system. In the southern two-thirds of the *iqlīm,* that situation probably came fairly close to the truth.[187] In the northern sectors, however, translations of cities between hierarchical levels were quite violent. The unrest began with the rise of Dimashq to replace Anṭākiyah at the summit of the system, it recurred with the elevation of Ḥalab to be the Ḥamdānid capital and the unravelling of the frontier fringe, which involved the destruction of some *ʿawāṣim* cities and the total loss to the Byzantines of some *thughūr* fortresses.

Eastern Cities

Most of the preceding discussion has concerned itself with cities lying to the west of the Jordan-Orontes rift or close to it, which was, of course, the more highly urbanized sector of the *iqlīm.* It is proper, though, to comment briefly on some of the cities to the east, notably those that had formerly constituted the famed Decapolis. This confederation of totally Hellenized cities had come into being, after Pompey's creation of the new Roman province of Syria in 64 B.C., as a means of curbing *badū* raids while discouraging expansion by neighboring Jewish princes and Nabataean monarchs. Like most Greek cities in the Levant, the individual members of the Decapolis enjoyed communal freedom, their own councils, minting privileges, rights of asylum and property, administration of surrounding territory (what today would be called the city trade area), and in their particular case the right of association for defense and possibly commerce. Although the confederation as a formal league of mature cities (if it had ever achieved that status) came to an end in A.D. 106, when Trajan instituted the Roman province of Arabia, the prestige of having been a Decapolitan city lingered into later times, as did, perhaps, some of the associational links.[188]

The only member of the league to the west of the Jordan River was Skythopolis. Located in the Vale of Jezreel, it commanded a main route from the Greek cities of the Mediterranean coast to the Jordan fords, and so eventually to Mesopotamia, while also participating actively in the traffic passing longitudinally along the Jordan valley. The other nine cities of the original Decapolis were deployed fanlike along three roads leading to the east: Hippos on a road trending north toward Damascus; Gadara, Raphana, and Canatha on the route leading northeastward toward the Ḥawrān; and Pella, Dion (if as seems most likely, this city is to be identified with present-day Tall al-Ḥuṣn), Gerasa, and Philadelphia on the main route southward. Damascus seems to have been an adjunct, or perhaps in some fashion honorary, member of the confederation, and eight more cities were admitted during its lifetime, mostly in the northern sectors in the direction of Damascus and including Abila and Kapitolias.[189]

Not all the cities of the Decapolis survived into the Muslim period, although late in the ninth century Baysān, Fiḥl (Pella), Jarash (Gerasa), Bayt Rās (Kapitolias), ʾĀbil (Abila), and Sūsīyah (Hippos) figured in Ibn Khurradādhbih's list of *kūrahs* in the *Jund* of Urdunn (ʿAmmān, the former Philadelphia, was included in the *Jund* of Dimashq).[190] The Muslim topographers were strangely reticent about the cities of Transjordania, but that deficiency has been partially remedied recently by considerable archaeological research.[191] We know, for instance, that Skythopolis, once a prominent member of the Decapolitan league (although lying to the west of the Jordan), as Muslim Baysān was much diminished from its heyday in the fifth century as metropolis of the province of Palaestina Secunda. Even before the close of the sixth century there were signs of decay in the urban fabric that could only have been exacerbated by the Persian conquest in 614. Under the Umayyads the decline was rendered permanent with the transfer of the capital of the *Jund* of Urdunn to Ṭabarīyah. In 749, as the Umayyad period came to its end, the city was destroyed by an earthquake that wrought havoc among numerous Palestinian and Jordanian settlements.[192] It was subsequently resettled by old or new inhabitants, probably both, but never again became anything more than a reasonably prosperous, local service center lacking any vestige of its former grandeur.[193]

Among other Decapolitan cities surviving into the Islamic era, Pella surrendered peacefully to a Muslim army in 635 and, with its name re-Semiticized to Fiḥl, became a *kūrah* headquarters in the *Jund* of Urdunn.[194] Writing in 891, al-Yaʿqūbī reported that the population was half Greek and half Arab,[195] but from then on the city appears to have declined rapidly and, despite a possible revival immediately following the earthquake of 749, was not mentioned at all by the tenth-century topographers.[196] ***Jarash*** apparently recovered from a late-Byzantine economic decline and, under Umayyad rule, enjoyed minting privileges while developing a ceramics industry that exported wares at least as far as neighboring cities. Although it escaped seismic damage in 749, archaeologists have yet to find evidence of occupation after the end of the eighth century.[197] ***Philadelphia*** had expanded from a locally important but modestly sized urban center into a major *polis* toward the end of the first century A.D. Three centuries later, however, signs of decline became only too apparent—fostered, in the opinion of Professor MacAdam, by reduced agricultural yields consequent on soil erosion, heavy taxation, earthquakes, and plagues.[198] Yet by the eighth century the city had resumed its ancient name in the Arabic guise of ʿAmmān and become the chief city of the Balqāʾ; nonetheless, the transference of imperial power from Dimashq to Baghdād in the mid-eighth century seems to have initiated a more lasting decline.[199]

At the site of ***Gadara*** (Umm Qays), founded as a military colony by the Ptolemies and granted the rights of a city by the Seleucids, the public baths had fallen into disuse during the first half of the seventh century, presumably the result of either the Persian or Islamic conquest, or of both. In any case, under the Umayyads the baths were converted to residential quarters, which in turn were levelled by the earthquake of 749 and thereafter abandoned. Whether the vicissitudes of this particular sector of the site are fairly representative of the city as a whole must await further archaeological exploration.[200] The occupational history of ***Abila*** in the late Byzantine and early Islamic periods has not been elicited in requisite detail. In fact the residential area of the city has not yet been identified, but occupation appears to have continued until the earthquake of 749, after which the city is believed to have been abandoned.[201] Similarly, excavation at Bayt Rās ***(Kapitolias)*** has not progressed far enough to allow any conclusions to be drawn about that settlement's development beyond the certainty that it was occupied as late as the eighth century.[202] For ***Hippos*** (Sūsīyah) the evidence is even less satisfactory, the exploratory work undertaken at the site by the Israeli Department of Antiquities having focused on the Iron Age and the Romano-Byzantine periods.[203] The other cities of the old Decapolitan league presumably failed to survive into the Islamic era.

Nor is it only former Decapolitan cities for which archaeology has either supplemented written records or in some instances substituted for them. ***Umm al-Jimāl*** in the southern Ḥawrān is a case in point. This was the site of a substantial settlement that achieved urban status as the result of a period of sustained growth between the fifth and seventh centuries A.D., especially after Justinian delegated control of Byzantium's Syrian frontier to Ghassān chiefs. The excavators of the settlement discerned evidence of a population decrease during the Umayyad period and a final abandonment of the site after intense seismic damage, most probably in 749.[204] As far as I have been able to determine, this town was not mentioned in literary records. ***Rihāb*** and ***Khirbat al-Samrā'*** are the sites of two towns whose importance in Byzantine times can be gauged from the fact that each boasted no fewer than eight churches. However, they differed markedly in their functions and history. Whereas Rihāb was a local service center that came into existence in Byzantine times and was abandoned at about the time of the Islamic conquest, Samrā' was apparently a Nabataean foundation that subsequently became a military strongpoint adjacent to a Roman highway. It continued to prosper throughout the Umayyad period but then, for reasons unknown, vanished from the landscape.[205] ***Ghurdan*** in the central Jordan valley, on present evidence, seems to have been established as a minor Umayyad administrative center that survived as late as the ʿAbbāsid period. ***Fadayn*** was transformed from a fortress to a palace complex with at least proto-urban functions under the Umayyads and served as an important stage on the pilgrim route to the Ḥijāz well into ʿAbbāsid times.[206]

Archaeological investigation in what is now the Hashemite Kingdom of Jordan has also furnished a good deal of information about the lower levels of the settlement hierarchy: the villages, small towns, and isolated settlements that are rarely mentioned in literary sources and that in most *aqālīm* are almost wholly irrecoverable. These included—in addition to agricultural villages—small military establishments, villas, so-called desert palaces, monasteries, and numerous sites whose precise functions have not been determined.[207] What archaeology is demonstrating increasingly clearly, and on both sides of the Jordan, is a prevailing continuity of settlement from Byzantine into Umayyad times.[208] Generally speaking, there is little evidence that the Muslim conquest inflicted immediate serious social dislocation on these southern tracts of the *iqlīm*, and a good deal to the contrary.[209]

Transformation of the Urban System

Clearly, many of the changes that supervened in the urban system of al-Shām during the earlier Islamic centuries stemmed directly from political or administrative action. This might take place at any level of the hierarchy, and might be either positive or negative in its effect. The cities here designated as *qaṣabāt* clearly benefited from their roles as Islamic administrative centers, and none more than the new foundation of al-Ramlah, which came completely to replace the old provincial capital of Ludd. An example of a city that survived severe vicissitudes to become the dominant settlement in the northern sector of al-Shām was Ḥalab. As Beroia it had functioned both as a metropolitanate and, under Emperor Maurice (r. 582–602), as a military base. Under the Umayyads, however, it lost its administrative preeminence, though not its political influence, for it eventually became the seat of a branch of the ʿAbbāsid family descendant from Ṣāliḥ ibn ʿAlī ibn ʿAbd Allāh, uncle to both al-Saffāḥ and al-Manṣūr, founders of the dynastic line. Finally, as the capital of a

Ḥamdānid Amīrate, in the second half of the tenth century it became a commercial and cultural center of renown throughout the Islamic world.

The fate of ancient Chalcis was the exact opposite of this success story. As Arabic Qinnasrīn, during the caliphate of Yazīd I (r. 680–83) it had been constituted as the administrative center of its own *jund,* only to decline later in competition with Ḥalab. In 964 the city was sacked by a Byzantine army, after which it seems never to have been repopulated. In a similar fashion, though on a reduced scale, Udhruḥ, at one time capital of the Sharā', had been supplanted by Ṣughar in its role as *qaṣabah* of the Ghawr. Ma'arrat al-Nu'mān, in the *Jund* of Ḥimṣ, was an example of a Byzantine village that grew through four Islamic centuries into an important regional service center. Bostra, by contrast, declined from being the Byzantine capital of Provincia Arabia to exercising only local authority in the Ḥawrān; while Ṭabarīyah, in its role as the administrative center of the *Jund* of Urdunn, completely eclipsed Skythopolis, the old capital of Palestina Secunda. Jābiyah, the great cantonment where the caliph 'Umar seems to have formalized the institution of the *dīwān* in 638 and that for a while served as the headquarters of the *Jund* of Dimashq, began to decline when the base of military operations was transferred to Dābiq, north of Ḥalab.

Maritime Cities

At the same time, two sets of forces were at work that were more distantly related to Muslim hegemony over the Levant and operated at supradistrict levels. The first of these was the transformation of the Mediterranean from a commercial seaway under Byzantine control to a frontier war zone bordering the Muslim domain. As a result, the administration and economy of al-Shām turned first inward upon itself and the caliphal capital of Dimashq, but later under the 'Abbāsids it turned east toward the metropolitan region of 'Irāq. Significantly, the *miṣr* of al-Maqdisī's *iqlīm,* together with its five *qaṣabāt* and single *madīnah,* were all situated inland despite the importance of some coastal cities in Byzantine and earlier times: Laodicea had been the administrative and religious center of the small province of Theodorias; Tyros, the capital of Phoenicia Maritima; Byblos, Botrys, Porphyrion, and Ace/Ptolemais, the seats of bishoprics; Sidon and Tripoli, important commercially; and Berytos, a center of legal studies. Under the Muslims the maritime cities of al-Shām collectively found their commercial *raisons d'être* undermined, so that only a minority prospered (Caesarea/Qayṣārīyah was the archetype, although its prosperity depended on its function as a regional service center rather than on its moribund port). A somewhat larger number survived as centers of small agricultural regions or for individually specific reasons (e.g., Yāfah because it was near al-Ramlah, and the other *ribāṭāt* strung along the coast of the *Jund* of Filasṭīn because they could handle informal exchanges with the Greeks), and some disappeared altogether (e.g., Jamnia [Yavneh], Diospolis, Paltos, and Arados, the last of which seems never to have recovered from its capture by the Muslims in 650).[210]

When these coastal towns did survive it was often as fortified strongpoints rather than as trading ports. Tyros/Ṣūr afforded a classic example of such a change of function, as both Umayyad and 'Abbāsid administrations developed it as a naval base. 'Akkā provided a comparable, although possibly more capricious, example. Although it was constituted as an important shipbuilding yard by the Umayyads, that function was soon transferred to Ṣūr by the caliph Hishām (r. 724–43). However, the 'Abbāsid al-Mutawakkil (r. 847–61) reestablished the port as a naval base, while the Egyptian ruler Ibn Ṭūlūn (r. 868–84), recognizing that his grasp on al-Shām could be maintained most effectively by means of sea power, reconstructed the city's harbor defenses. But not until the Egyptian Faṭimids seized control of the southern part of the *iqlīm* in the latter half of the tenth century did the coastal towns experience a partial revival of their commercial functions. It was not so much that trade with countries bordering the Mediterranean ceased completely in the early Islamic period, but rather that it was greatly diminished and, moreover, channelled through fewer ports. The restricted commercial dealings undertaken in the *ribāṭāt* in the *Jund* of Filasṭīn have already been mentioned. Of considerably greater importance was a trade route running from al-Baṣrah by way of Raqqah and Ḥalab to the Mediterranean that was opened up at the beginning of the ninth century and that served as a conduit for Asian spices, aromatics, and luxury articles bound for Constantinople itself. Certainly, these limited trading ventures in no way reversed the commercial decline of the Levantine coast following the Islamic conquest. For the next three and a half centuries the future of the coastal cities, such as it was to be, would lie with maritime defense rather than commerce. Peter Brown is not far off the mark in characterizing the Levantine coast of this period as "the numbed extremity of a great Eurasian Empire."[211]

Desert-Border Cities

The other set of primarily external forces working to modify the internal structure of the urban hierarchy of al-Shām was what appears to have been a beduinization of the desert borders, a process apparently encouraged (though not necessarily instigated) by the lapsing of treaty relationships between nomadic tribes and the competing powers of Byzantium and Sāsānian Persia and by the failure of the ʿAbbāsids from the second half of the ninth century onward to patrol adequately the Syrian and Arabian desert regions—all combined from the turn of the tenth century with incursions by Qarmaṭī raiders. A resulting decline in both agriculture and trade was reflected in a concomitant diminution in the vitality of urban life that in extreme cases could justifiably be characterized as de-urbanization.[212] Market towns on the fringes of the Ḥawrān were particularly severely affected: Philippopolis and Dionysias survived as scarcely more than villages, and Phaena disappeared altogether. This weakening of the urban system was evident even closer to the Jordan valley. Hugh Kennedy has already commented that by the tenth century no substantial urban center survived to the south and east of Galilee, the very region that had once supported the old episcopal cities of Gadara, Kapitolias, and Pella.[213] Even the once grand and flourishing city of Gerasa proved unworthy of mention by topographers or historians after a brief reference by al-Yaʿqūbī, writing in 891.[214] South of the Balqā there were no important urban centers, although Areopolis persisted in a depressed state as Arabic Maʿāb. In the southernmost tracts of al-Shām, the former Palestina Tertia, de-urbanization appears to have been all but complete, with even the one-time episcopal city of Elusa succumbing well before the tenth century.[215]

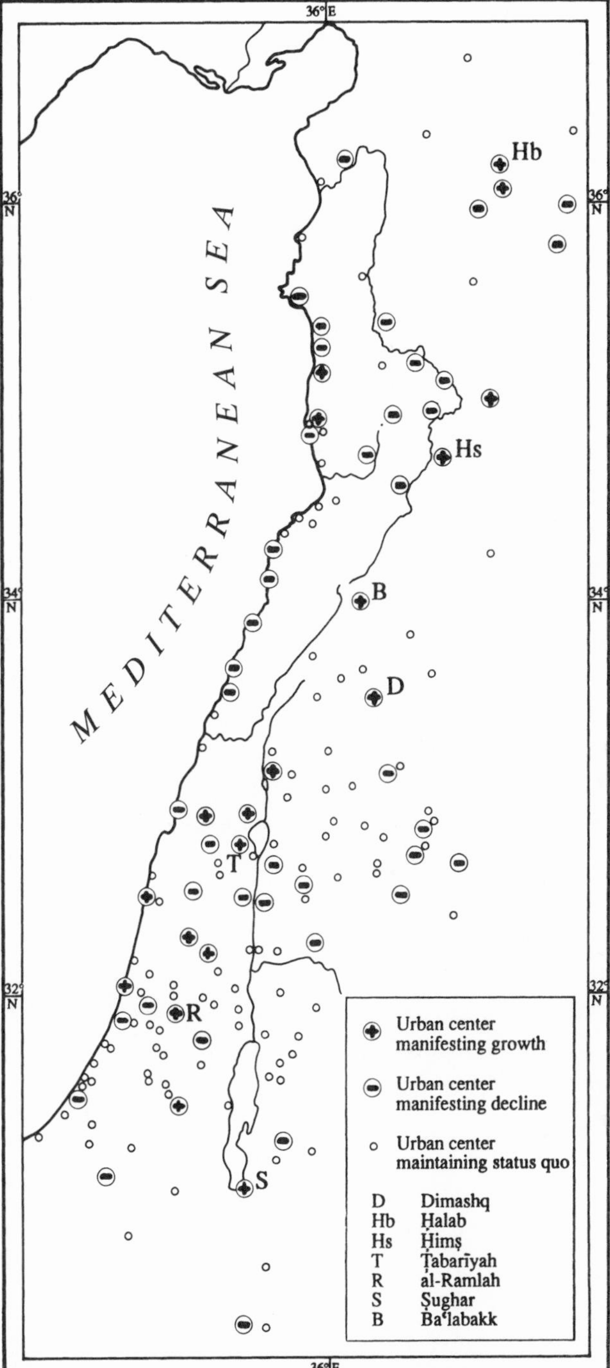

Figure 13. Recoverable changes in the urban system of al-Shām from the seventh to the tenth century. For limitations inherent in the distribution depicted on this map, see page 126.

Summary

Figure 13 offers a visual summation of such changes in the urban system of al-Shām between the seventh and tenth centuries that could be recovered from a variety of texts—few of which are explicit on these matters—and scattered archaeological excavations. The base distribution of urban centers in the *iqlīm* in Late Antiquity was abstracted from map 5 of *The Cities of the Eastern Roman Provinces,*[216] and the relative importance of the cities depicted thereon was assessed from a sporadic and often inconsistent archaeological record; such literary documents as were available, including valuable lists of bishoprics; and a range of secondary sources, not excluding Professor Jones's book cited above. The subsequent fate of those cities was determined from the type of Islamic historical, topographical, archaeological, and literary sources used throughout this book (see especially chapter 3). It is proper, though, to enter certain caveats concerning this map. In the first place, it depicts only a recoverable situation, validated by information that is either explicit or inferrable beyond reasonable doubt. Inferences from regional trends were not acceptable, with the result that tendencies of any kind could be elicited for only about half the cities of al-Shām. The remainder may have maintained something approaching a status quo, or, equally probably, a lack of information may be masking so far undiscovered, though not always unsuspected, changes.

Second, the map depicts only simple positive or negative change in the political, economic, or cultural fortunes of a city, either singly or in combination. It affords no indication of the degree of change involved.

Third, it must be noted that not all the changes recorded on the map resulted directly from the Islamic conquest: some of the discernible trends appear to have been initiated late in Byzantine times. There is some evidence, for example, that both Ḥalab (Beroia) and Ḥimṣ (Emesa) were already beginning to increase in wealth and prestige at that time. Apamea, by contrast, had never recovered from its sack by Persian forces in 573 and the Islamic conquest simply sealed its fate. Seleucia-in-Pieria was also in decline when the Arab armies arrived.

Finally, a fourth point to be borne in mind concerns the period during which the recorded changes took place. Although the symbols on the map refer to the first four Islamic centuries, they specify nothing as to rates or consistency of those changes. Jarash, for example, flourished as a mint city under the Umayyads but had virtually disappeared by the tenth century. Fiḥl initially became a *kūrah* headquarters in the *Jund* of Urdunn and appears to have survived the earthquake of 749, yet still followed Jarash into oblivion. Salamīyah also improved its prospects under both Umayyads and ʿAbbāsids, largely owing to the influence of the branch of the latter dynasty mentioned above in connection with Ḥalab, but was virtually destroyed by Qarmaṭī rebels in 902. In figure 13, whereas Jarash and Pella are recorded as overall declines by reason of their relatively rapid loss of vitality. Salamīyah is depicted as a growth center by virtue of its prosperity that continued until the beginning of the tenth century.

Despite these evident limitations, figure 13 does depict salient trends in the urban hierarchy of al-Shām during the early Islamic centuries, namely a collectively (although by no means always severally) prevailing decline of coastal towns, a decline of urban centers on the desert borders, and the concentration of the major cities inland.

Chapter Seven

The Urban System in the *Jazīrah* of the Arabs

> It is a country subject only to tithe (*ʿushr*),[1] by reason of which it has figured in the books of the pre-eminent doctors of law (*fuqahāʾ*). Teachers of the law (*sharīʿah*) must therefore acquire a good knowledge of it so as to be able to interpret their texts.
>
> —Al-Maqdisī, *Aḥsan al-Taqāsīm*, 67.

After the so-called *riddah* wars, virtually all the inhabitants of Arabia had accepted the faith of Islam. Henceforth no other religion was tolerated within the peninsula. The equating of Arab ethnicity with profession of the Islamic faith rendered unnecessary the instruments of conquest and pacification such as *amṣār* and *ribāṭāt* employed in non-Arab lands, while the intense sanctity of Makkah (Mecca) and al-Madīnah (Medina) inhibited the establishment of new princely foundations having pretensions to world superiority. It followed that in succeeding centuries, indeed down to modern times, the structure of the urban hierarchy of Arabia probably changed less than that in any other major province of the Islamic world.

Arabia was one of the three provinces in which al-Maqdisī recognized two *metropoleis (amṣār)*. In doing so he acknowledged two urban (and indeed political) traditions that had persisted in western Arabia since pre-Muslim times, namely those of al-Ḥijāz and al-Yaman. These traditions were characterized by markedly different modes of urban development. In al-Yaman the hierarchy had evolved from a reasonably dense scatter of essentially agricultural settlements organized around a number of ceremonial and administrative centers, and institutionally adapted to exploit the commercial opportunities presented by a strategic location in the southwestern angle of the Arabian Peninsula. In al-Ḥijāz, by contrast, where pastoralism in one form or another predominated over agriculture, the representative urban center had developed, sometimes under Hellenistic influence, from an oasis settlement shared by sedentary and nomadic herdsmen who also participated in the caravan trade as merchants, cameleers, guides, and negatively as raiders. As a matter of fact, al-Maqdisī could justifiably have designated a third urban system occupying the eastern fringe of the peninsula and focusing on Ṣuḥār, a city larger than either Zabīd or Ṣanʿāʾ. This region had traditionally turned its back on the heartland of Arabia and sought its economic fortunes on the sea (a characteristic it shared with the Ḥaḍramawt coast), while manifesting political and social affinities with the Īrānian cultural realm. When the ʿAbbāsids reconstituted the imperial capital in ʿIrāq, the ports of the Persian Gulf, including those of ʿUmān, benefited proportionately.

For much of the seventh through tenth centuries, the Arabian Peninsula was a mosaic of political entities often only nominally under the control of the central government. Umayyad governors were reasonably effective in maintaining order in the Ḥaramān, which, despite the establishment of a rival caliph in Makkah for a brief period after the death of Muʿāwiyah and a Khārijī occupation in the waning years of the dynasty, enjoyed a century or so of prosperity and repute. Under the ʿAbbāsids, however, the two Holy Cities constituted a reservoir of followers of the ʿAlid cause, hopeful of regaining the primacy lost first to Dimashq (Damascus) and subsequently to Baghdād, a circumstance of which several ʿAlid pretenders took advantage.[2] With the onset of the decline of the dynasty at the beginning of the ninth century, political anarchy prevailed in the Ḥijāz, and it was not uncommon for a number of claimants to suzerainty to plant their banners severally on the plain of ʿArafāt during the annual pilgrimage. But ʿAlids were not the only disruptive force in the region: Sulaymī *badū* raided in and around the Holy Cities toward the mid-ninth century and Qarmaṭī rebels[3] during the first half of the tenth, the latter going so far as to remove the sacred Black Stone from the Kaʿbah to al-Aḥsāʾ, whence it was returned only after a lapse of two decades. Conditions were somewhat stabilized only when, in about the mid-tenth century, a family of Ḥasanids under the style Mūsāwids established the Sharīfate of Makkah,[4] at much the same time as a Ḥusaynid line began ruling as *amīrs* of al-Madinah. Shortly thereafter the ʿAbbāsids entrusted the guardianship of the Ḥaramān to the Ikhshīdid dynasty of Egypt, who in turn passed on the responsibility to the Fāṭimids—to the evident satisfaction of al-Maqdisī.[5]

Farther south in the Yaman, political conditions were hardly more stable. In 820 a governor sent by the caliph al-Maʾmūn to quell an ʿAlid-inspired revolt on the Tihāmah plain established a Ziyādid dynasty that, although according nominal allegiance to the ʿAbbāsids, ruled virtually independently from its capital at Zabīd. After the death of al-Mutawakkil in 861 ʿAbbāsid authority in this southwestern corner of Arabia became even more attenuated. The Yuʿfirids, claiming descent from the *Tubbaʿ*s of ancient Ḥimyar, founded a state focused on Ṣanʿāʾ; Zaydī *imāms* in Ṣaʿdah laid the foundations of a future Rassid dynasty;[6] and the Ḥaḍramawt rejected all allegiance to the ʿAbbāsids. The eastern tracts of the peninsula were equally disturbed. In al-Yamāmah, for instance, an Ukhayḍirid line forged a transient unity among nomadic tribes pasturing in the vicinity of al-Ḥajr, but more important and longer lasting was the Qarmaṭī principality centered on al-Aḥsāʾ which emerged at the turn of the tenth century. The prosperity of this oligarchic republic was largely dependent on the labor of black slaves, yet it seems to have practiced an almost communistic mode of economic redistribution among its free subjects. It was also aggressively expansionist, raiding in turn al-Baṣrah (900), al-Kūfah (901), and Makkah itself (930), and soon after overrunning the Ibāḍī Imāmate of ʿUmān.

The early Islamic political history of this last region is complicated and far from clear, but the structural outline would seem to be something as follows. After a period of quasi-independence following the initial Arab conquest, a Julandā *imām* was elected in about 750, only to be deposed by a caliphal expedition some three years later and not restored until early in the 790s. In 893 the imāmate survived a temporary occupation by caliphal levies, after which it continued in power until a Qarmaṭī invasion in 930/31. In 943 yet another caliphal force reestablished ʿAbbāsid rule, which was reinforced in 965 or thereabouts by the Buwayhids, whose governors proved to be remarkably benevolent administrators for the rest of the century. When al-Maqdisī was collecting materials for his survey, Qarmaṭī influence was dominant throughout the eastern and interior tracts of Arabia, even though the Buwayhid *amīrs* had by then reestablished nominal authority over ʿUmān.

Marketing and Service Centers

This then was the "Peninsula of the Arabs," which, toward the end of the tenth century, al-Maqdisī chose to apportion within the spheres of influence of two *amṣār: metropoleis,* be it noted, that exhibited significant differences in both their forms and their functions. As we have seen in chapter 1, Makkah had begun as a cult center, which in turn had fostered distributive economic functions; but by the tenth century these had been largely superseded by its role in the unfolding of events of unique cosmological significance. Zabīd, on the other hand, had been established as a seat of government as recently as 820 by the founder of the Ziyādite dynasty.[7] Although Makkah had undergone certain architectural modifications—notably the elaboration of the precincts of the Masjid al-Ḥaram and the building of numerous *khāns* and hostelries to cater for the pilgrim traffic—it was still a cramped, elongated city confined by the walls of its *wādī* and manifesting all the characteristics of unplanned growth. Zabīd, in contrast, was "a splendid, well built city, commonly referred to as the Baghdād of al-Yaman . . . a noble city without peer in the whole of al-Yaman."[8] Al-Maqdisī asserted that it was "on the whole more thriving and busier, and of greater natural abundance, than Makkah."[9]

In al-Ḥijāz in the tenth century the distribution of urban centers had not changed greatly from what it had been in the time of Muḥammad. Essentially, urban forms were restricted to the Tihāmah and to a series of oases lying on the eastern slope of the uplands. In some of these, perhaps most, tribal institutions were strong and lineage a potent factor in the organization of urban life—as it would be right down to the present. Al-Juḥfah, for example, was "a flourishing settlement inhabited by the Banū-Jaʿfar," who, incidentally, also controlled al-Marwah.[10] Ḥādhah was "a pleasant town belonging to the descendants of Abū Bakr,"[11] and the lineage of al-Ḥasan, the eldest son of ʿAlī and Fāṭimah, dominated the important port of Yanbuʿ.[12] In fact it is difficult not to conclude that some of the Ḥijāzī settlements incorporated in figure 2 were actually clusters of clan fortresses under the domination of particular lineages, something after the pattern of Yathrib in pre-Islamic times (chapter 1) or, indeed, parts of the Ḥaḍramawt as recently as the twentieth century. Amaj, for instance, although described as a small settlement, had five forts grouped around a congregational mosque on the high road, al-Suwāriqīyah had "a large number of forts," and Ḥādhah "several."[13] One locality that had apparently changed somewhat more rapidly was the Wādī al-Qurā, "The Valley of the Habitations," where the pre-Islamic oasis settlement of al-Qurā had developed into the second-largest town in al-Ḥijāz, after Makkah, "as well as the most flourishing and populous, and the most abounding in merchants, commerce, and wealth . . . a Syrian, Egyptian, ʿIrāqī, and Ḥijāzī city all in one."[14] The inhabitants at this time were predominantly Jewish.

The third-largest city of al-Ḥijāz was probably Yanbuʿ,[15] which al-Maqdisī described as a lively market; and the fourth was al-Madīnah, rather less than half the size of Makkah and inhabited mainly by descendants of the Shīʿite martyr al-Ḥusayn. Like Makkah, al-Madīnah (Medina) had lost the old austerity that had been so greatly prized by the caliph ʿUmar. However, the early Islamic associations of the two cities had attracted to them scholars eager to salvage whatever could be learned of the climacteric events of the seventh century. In Makkah it was ʿAbd Allāh ibn al-ʿAbbās[16] who established the reputation of its school of Tradition; in al-Madīnah it was Anas ibn Mālik[17] and ʿAbd Allāh ibn ʿUmar ibn al-Khaṭṭāb.[18] Wealthy Arabs desirous of enjoying, undisturbed by political turmoil, fortunes newly acquired in the wars of conquest, and pilgrims from one end of the Muslim world to the other, brought material prosperity to the Holy Cities, together with a secularization typified by archetyped tales told of the salon of the Sayyidah Sukaynah, daughter of Ḥusayn and granddaughter of ʿAlī.[19] Not unnaturally al-Ṭāʾif, the summer resort of the Makkans, shared to some extent in these changing social fashions, as is witnessed by the numerous episodes in Arab literature featuring the incomparable ʿĀʾishah, daughter of the Companion Ṭalḥah and granddaughter of Abū Bakr.[20]

In al-Yaman, although Zabīd was the seat of the Ziyādite dynasty, Ṣanʿāʾ, the "provincial" capital *(qaṣabah)* of the upland territory of Najd al-Yaman, was apparently larger.[21] Probably in pre-Islamic times the site of a sacred enclave *(hajar, maḥram)* analogous to the *ḥaram* of Makkah, and for long the capital of all the Yaman, by the tenth century Ṣanʿāʾ had lost that status to Zabīd, and al-Maqdisī's account leaves the impression that its leaders were compensating for the loss of present political power by calling up the glories of the past. "There are in it [Ṣanʿāʾ]," he writes, "many learned men whose equals in dignity of appearance and power of intellect I have not found in the whole of al-Yaman."[22] In the mountains farther north, Ṣaʿdah functioned as a district capital ruled over by the ʿAlawīyah, who read the *khuṭbah* in the name of the Ziyādites.[23] ʿAththar, the port for both Ṣanʿāʾ and Ṣaʿdah, was a similar dependency under the government of the Tihāman prince Sulaymān ibn Ṭarf. Other district capitals specified by al-Maqdisī were Sabaʾ, Ḥaḍramawt, al-Shiḥr, and ʿAdan.[24]

On the eastern flank of the Arabian Peninsula were two other zones of urban settlement. In the district now known as al-Ḥasā, where artesian structures gave rise to perennial springs in otherwise waterless country, a group of settlements focused on al-Aḥsāʾ, the capital *(qaṣabah)* of Hajar, a city founded in 899 by Abū Saʿīd al-Ḥasan al-Jannābī, chief of the Qarāmiṭah of al-Baḥrayn. In 976/77 the line of Abū Saʿīd, which regarded itself as only a temporary custodian of power while awaiting the anticipated reappearance of the occulted *imām,* had been succeeded by a council of six *sayyids* whose rule of justice and order was praised by al-Maqdisī, Ibn Ḥawqal, and Nāṣir-i Khusraw, none of whom was of the Qarmaṭī persuasion. In accordance with Qarmaṭī rejection of the outward forms of orthodox Islam, the Friday mosque in the capital had been allowed to fall into decay, but a Persian pilgrim had financed the building of another for the use of his orthodox fellow travellers.[25] Farther south, al-Ḥajr was the district capital of al-Yamāmah.[26]

ʿUmān, the territory occupying the southeastern angle

of the Arabian Peninsula, has always been so remote from the centers of civilization bordering the Red Sea that it has inevitably formed its closest political, commercial, and even religious relationships with the Īrānian lands to the north. Under Qarmaṭī rule the seat of its *imāms* had been at Nazwah, on the southern flank of the Jabal al-Akhḍar;[27] but when the Buwayhids conquered the country in 966 they established the district capital at Ṣuḥār.[28] In al-Maqdisī's time this was "a city of wealth, with numerous merchants [mostly Persian] and excellent markets."[29] The other urban forms in ʿUmān were mostly either small central places among the uplands of the interior (e.g., Ḍank, Salūt, Samad) or ports to be discussed below.

Transportation Foci

The peripheral disposition of urban settlement around a subcontinental expanse of desert and steppe given over predominantly to one or another mode of pastoralism, so that east–west travel necessarily involved either a lengthy desert crossing or an even longer sea voyage, ensured that break-of-bulk services featured prominently among the institutional structures of numerous Arabian urban centers. The main caravan route was that leading from ʿAdan northward through either Zabīd or Ṣanʿāʾ to al-Ṭāʾif and Makkah, whence one branch followed the Tihāmah to Waylah and Egypt while another continued through the oases on the dipslope of the uplands to al-Shām (Greater Syria). Prominent among the "caravan cities" on this latter route were al-Juḥfah (where tribes of the Ṭayyiʾ confederation used to congregate during the searing heat of summer),[30] al-Madīnah, Khaybar, al-Qurā, al-Ḥijr (the old Madāʾ in Ṣāliḥ), and Taymāʾ, this last also serving as a supply center for surrounding *badū* tribes.[31] Affording passage to a smaller quantity of merchandise, but amply compensating by the volume of their human traffic, were the two routes bringing pilgrims from al-ʿIrāq and beyond, namely the caravan trails from Makkah to respectively al-Kūfah and al-Baṣrah. The Rubʿ al-Khālī has always proved an effective barrier to land communication between ʿUmān and western Arabia, forcing commerce on to the sea; but nevertheless one extremely arduous caravan trail was in occasional use. Al-Maqdisī's itinerary for it is as follows:

> If you travel to Makkah from ʿUmān, go from Ṣuḥār to Nazwah; thence to ʿAjlah 30 miles; thence to ʿAdhwah, which is a fortified post, 24 miles; thence to Biʾr al-Silāḥ 30 miles;[32] thence to Makkah 21 days, during which there are four stations with wells, while eight stages pass through a waste of sand.[33]

Although Makkan involvement in the long-distance caravan trade appears to have dwindled after the seat of government of the *Ummah* developed in al-Madīnah—a decline that was rendered permanent when the Muslim conquest of ʿIrāq diverted trade between the Indian Ocean and the Mediterranean into the old route by way of the Euphrates valley—pilgrim traffic increased steadily during the first four centuries of Islam. The majority of the caliphs, both Umayyad and early ʿAbbāsid, as well as their families were not only diligent in undertaking the Greater Pilgrimage, but also sought to encourage their subjects to do likewise by providing amenities along the pilgrim routes and in the vicinity of Makkah itself. At the very beginning of the Umayyad era, Muʿāwiyah had made unsuccessful attempts to grow cereals on the outskirts of the city. A century later Hārūn al-Rashīd built cisterns and guardhouses along the road between the Ḥaramān while his wife Zubaydah (known to her contemporaries as Umm Jaʿfar, the mother of Jaʿfar ibn al-Manṣūr) provided rest stations and drinking water throughout the environs of Makkah.[34] And the example of the caliphal families was emulated by ministers, officials, and even private individuals at virtually all levels of society. The Ziyādid *wazīr* of Yaman, Ḥusayn ibn Salāmah, is a fine representation of such a benefactor, who in the tenth century constructed a series of mosques, rest stations, wells, and milestones along the whole length of the caravan trail from Ḥaḍramawt to the Holy City. Another such exemplar was ʿAbd Allāh ibn Āmir, a Makkan who was twice appointed to the governorship of al-Baṣrah and who earned a reputation for extraordinarily generous support of public works, including a series of wells along the route from al-ʿIrāq to Makkah. He was reportedly heard to remark that, had it been left to him, a woman travelling to Makkah would have been able to alight every day at a place supplied with water and a market.[35]

With an interior featuring huge tracts inimical to sedentary occupation, and with a coastline exceeding four thousand miles in length, it is not surprising that traffic between the settled realms of Arabia should have taken to the sea whenever possible. Add to this a regional location at the southwestern angle of Asia where the commerce of the "Sea of China" met that from the "Sea of the Franks,"[36] and the development of Arabian port cities is readily comprehensible. Ports tended to be larger and generally more numerous in two types of location: where the settled hinterlands of al-Yaman and ʿUmān fronted onto the sea-lanes of the "Sea of China," and where the northern reaches of the Red Sea linked the settled tracts of al-Ḥijāz to the densely populated regions of Egypt. In the former category Ṣuḥār and ʿAdan were each separately epitomized by al-Maqdisī as "the antechamber of al-Ṣīn (China)."[37] Ṣuḥār was further categorized as "the emporium of the East and of al-ʿIrāq,"[38] whereas the smaller port of al-Masqaṭ, although sharing in the Indian and Īrānian trade, directed a greater proportion of its commercial activities toward western Arabia. It was, in fact, the landfall in ʿUmān for incoming Yamanī vessels.[39] Persian, rather than Arab, entrepreneurs dominated the merchant communities in number and status in both cities. In complementary fashion ʿAdan, although having a considerable stake in eastern commerce, functioned primarily as an entrepôt for the trade of the Red Sea, the Ḥaḍramawt, and the Horn of Africa.[40]

The two chief ports of al-Ḥijāz were Juddah and Yanbuʿ. The former, often said to have become the port of Makkah only in the time of ʿUthmān,[41] was, in the words of al-Maqdisī, "fortified, flourishing, and populous, inhabited chiefly by merchants and men of wealth [who were subsequently identified as primarily Persians], the granary of Makkah."[42] This last remark was a reference to the grain imports from Egypt on which Makkah (like Juddah itself), with no local agriculture, was entirely dependent. Yanbuʿ, "a large and splendid city," was described as more prosperous than al-Madīnah.[43] Today it functions as the port of al-Madīnah, but in the tenth century that role seems to have fallen to the smaller port of al-Jār.[44] Other ports of local importance on the coast of al-Ḥijāz were al-ʿAwnīd, the gateway to al-Qurā; al-Ḥawrāʾ, the port for Khaybar; and al-ʿUshayrah, blessed with an excellent *khān* that evoked al-Maqdisī's admiration.[45] Farther south, in the Tihāmah of al-Yaman, were al-Sirrayn, the port for the productive agricultural district of al-Sarawāt: Ḥaly; ʿAththar (where the public bath was in execrable condition);[46] al-Sharjah, al-Ḥirdah, and ʿAṭanah, all three of which shipped millet from their hinterlands to Juddah and ʿAdan; Ghalāfiqah, the port of Zabīd; and Mukhā.

Because of the relatively high level of urban development in the physiographically unpropitious environment of much of Arabia, imports predominated over exports. Among the commodities imported into ʿUmān, al-Maqdisī listed apothecaries' drugs, all kinds of aromatics including musk, saffron, sapanwood *(baqqam)*, teak, shisham-wood *(sāsam)*, sandalwood, ivory, pearls, brocades, onyx, rubies, ebony, coconut, sugar, sandarac,[47] aloes, iron, lead, canes, earthenware, glass, and pepper, to which were added in the case of ʿAdan ambergris, *shurūb* (fine linen cloths),[48] leather bucklers, Abyssinian slaves, eunuchs, tiger skins, and chinaware.[49] Evidently several of these imported items derived ultimately from South Asia and eastern Asia, probably by way of the elusive mart known to Arabo-Persian traders from the ninth century onward as Kalah, which Abū Zayd characterized as the principal emporium for such commerce. "It is thither," he observes, "that ʿUmānī trading ventures make their way."[50] Writing toward the middle of the tenth century, al-Masʿūdī confirmed that Kalah was "the rendezvous for Muslim ships from Sīrāf and ʿUmān, where they encounter vessels from 'China.'"[51] Although the precise location of this port is in dispute, there is fundamental agreement that it was somewhere on the west coast of the Siamo-Malay Peninsula.[52]

Industrial and Craft Centers

Such specialist manufacturing activities as were undertaken by the cities of Arabia were restricted overwhelmingly to the handling and processing of natural commodities: leather and an indigo *(nīl)* of the color of lapis lazuli in Zabīd; leather in al-Ṭāʾif; whetstones and henna in Yanbuʿ; *ṣayhānī* dates in al-Madīnah; *burdī* dates and bdellium in al-Marwah; copper from mines at Lasayl, the Wādī Andam, and Muṣfah; frankincense and myrrh in al-Shiḥr;[53] dried peaches[54] in Qurā; senna in Makkah; and *maṣīn* dates in the cities of ʿUmān. Apart from the production of water vessels in Ṣaʿdah, bowls in Ḥaly, and baskets in ʿAththar, each of which attained more than a local reputation, the only manufacture of significance was that of textiles, which achieved a level of excellence remarkable in a region not otherwise noted for its technical expertise. Among the cloths that enjoyed reputations outside Arabia were the *shurūb* of ʿAdan, which were sometimes held to be superior to the *qaṣab* (fine linens) of Egypt; the fibers called *līf* from al-Mahjarah; the *burūd* (striped cloaks) of Suḥūlā[55] and al-Jurayb; and the *saʿīdī* (striped stuffs) of Ṣanʿāʾ.[56] To these al-Hamdānī added valuable silk cloths *(ḥarīr)* fit for a king *(mulukī),* silk carpets from al-Rīḥ, and rainproof leather mats *(anṭāʿ)* from al-Ṣutt.[57]

Religious Centers

In the "Peninsula of the Arabs," the hierarchy of sacred cities achieved its fullest development, with the supremely sacred cosmological center of Makkah at its apex. When Muḥammad transferred the *qiblah* from Jerusalem to Makkah, he was introducing into Islam the key component in a set of concepts already of great antiquity in southwest Asia. Fundamental to this fragment of *Isrāʾilīyāt,* as it was elaborated in Muslim *Ḥadīth,* was the notion of Makkah as the navel of the earth *(ṣurrat al-arḍ),*[58] a point that had been in existence—according to a tradition preserved by al-Azraqī on the authority of Kaʿb al-Aḥbār—for forty years (signifying long) before Allāh created the heavens and the earth.[59] Another *ḥadīth* accorded the Kaʿbah a priority of two thousand years over the rest of creation, but the discrepancy is of little consequence. The important thing is that Makkah, or strictly speaking the Kaʿbah, was held to be the spot at which the cosmogony had been initiated; from which, in the words of the Qurʾān, the earth had been spread out.[60] And, in accordance with the cosmological lore of the Western Semites, Makkah, as the navel of the earth and the *axis mundi,* was the point of ontological transition between the worlds, the place where communication was effected most readily between heaven and earth.

It followed logically that it was the locale where prayer was likely to be most efficacious, a belief manifested in a tale told of the tribesmen of ʿĀd, who, in a time of drought, supposedly sent messengers all the way from the Ḥaḍramawt to Makkah to pray for rain in the place where their prayers were most likely to be heard.[61] A similar set of preconceptions was evident in the story of ʿAbd Allāh ibn ʿAbbās, who, fearing that even the "passing insinuations of the heart" *(khawāṭir al-qalb)* would be audible to Allāh from his home in Makkah, prudently transferred his residence to al-Ṭāʾif, where presumably he hoped to be held responsible only for his overt actions and speech.[62] This existential abrogation of distance was sometimes translated into material terms, so that al-Kisāʾī of Kūfah early in the ninth century could argue that the Kaʿbah constituted the culmination of terrestrial topography because, being directly below the Pole Star, it was consequently "over against the centre of Heaven."[63] This notional elevation of Makkah also accounts for the fact that, in one tradition, the waters of the Deluge failed to inundate the Kaʿbah, around which Nūḥ was able to perform a ritual circumambulation *(ṭawāf)* in the ark. Finally, the cosmological *omphalos* subsumed in an existential sense the whole extent of the *Ummah.* What transpired at the axis of the universe affected the whole order of nature, a belief exemplified by al-Qazwīnī when he writes, "When in any year rain beats against one side of the Kaʿbah, that year will witness fertility in the territory on that side; when it beats on all sides, then fertility will ensue on all sides."[64]

In addition to this cosmological holiness, a great deal of soteriological sanctity accrued to Makkah through its having been the locale of transcendental events connected with the revelation of Islam in the seventh century. In this second level of sanctity al-Madīnah also shared, for it was "the *ḥaram* of the Messenger of God,"[65] the city which had given him refuge and, above all, in which he was buried. As was to be expected of the country that had witnessed the birth of Islam, the *barakah* of holy tombs and shrines was widely diffused through western Arabia from Uḍruḥ in the north, where the Prophet's mantle was preserved,[66] to the tomb of Hūd in the Ḥaḍramawt.[67] In ʿUmān and Hajar, localities that had played little or no part in the great events of the seventh century, and that had traditionally been more influenced by Persia than by western Arabia, the sacral hierarchy was only poorly developed.

Commentary

The urban system of Arabia was the least thoroughly integrated of any in the *iqlīm*s discussed by al-Maqdisī, with the exception of al-Riḥāb and the Maghrib. The desert heart of the peninsula, with few exceptions, from time immemorial had repelled permanent settlement, thrusting it centrifugally outward to the fringes of the land mass. Politically and economically the urban system that developed in these peripheral zones was fragmented, its several regional components as often as not functioning independently of one another. Only the sacral hierarchy manifested an unquestioned integrity. The preeminence of the Ḥaramān was acknowledged in the Wādī Ḥaḍramawt and on the Bāṭinah coast of ʿUmān as readily as in al-Ḥijāz. And it was the most fully developed of all sacral hierarchies in the Islamic world, for it included all conceivable degrees of sanctity: from the merest intimation of *barakah* up to the supreme cosmological significance of Makkah as the navel of the earth, the generative source of terrestrial creation. True, the urban hierarchy of al-Shām similarly encompassed all levels of sacrality, but at its apex the cosmological holiness of Jerusalem fell far short of that of Makkah.

It is evident from the preceding discussion that the Arabs had effected little change in the spatial distribution of urban forms within their eponymous peninsula. Numerous cities had increased in size, but hardly any new ones had been founded. Even a caliphal contender like ʿAbd Allāh ibn al-Zubayr established himself in Makkah instead of building a new capital, and in an essentially Arab and Islamic land there was clearly no need for the various types of frontier fortresses that in other regions served as bastions against alien incursions. As a result, the overall spatial patterning of urban life remained structurally very much what it had been in the time of Muḥammad, with the enhanced density of urban settlements resulting from increases in the size of individual cities rather than from an increase in their total number.

The Ḥijāz

Although the Ḥijāz, as the birthplace and spiritual focus of Islam, was the quintessentially sacred territory of that faith, its urban development between the seventh and tenth centuries was by no means spectacular and often uneven. Comparatively slight changes in the run of a caravan trail, particularly when it involved pilgrim traffic, could either make or break a settlement. Suqyā ibn Ghifar, al-Sayyālah, Rawḥāʾ, and Nakhlah were examples of staging posts on the pilgrim route from al-Shām that developed into substantial settlements. Marwah, al-Ruḥbah, and Suqyāʾ al-Jazl even blossomed into fully fledged towns, while al-Juḥfah and Dhāt ʿIrq developed into permanent settlements by catering to the needs of pilgrims who were required to enter into ritual purity at those points. The obverse of the coin occurred when the diversion of a route brought about the decline of a settlement. A classic instance of such a decline occurred early in the tenth century, when the diversion of the caravan trail from Waylah to al-Madīnah subverted the principal economic support of a series of Ḥijāzī settlements, including Shaghb, Badāʾ, al-Bayḍāʾ, al-Marr Ẓahrān, and, ironically, the above-mentioned towns of Marwah and Suqyāʾ al-Jazl that some three centuries previously had owed their rise to an analogous shift of a caravan route.

The Ḥaramān

Although the Ḥaramān had benefited from the large sums lavished on their shrines by the Umayyad and earlier ʿAbbāsid caliphs—even though the former seem at times to have favored the claim of Jerusalem to equivalent rank in the sacral hierarchy—Makkah and al-Madīnah lacked the clarity of design that betokens planned development. Of the two, Makkah had grown the more, in the tenth century occupying about twice the area of al-Madīnah. Despite a dispute about the moral and legal propriety of constructing residential quarters in the city as opposed to preserving its original character, houses had climbed steadily up the sides of the *wādī*. Already by the beginning of the Umayyad dynasty they were overlooking the well of Jubayr ibn Muṭʿim and clustering on the hill of Abū Qubays. By the tenth century they filled the *wādī* and its bounding slopes, a development that would have proved impossible had not various caliphs and other public-spirited individuals taken measures, mainly the digging of wells and canals, to improve the water supply.

Al-Madīnah grew more slowly than Makkah and appears to have retained a good deal of its pre-Muslim open character, with palm groves and gardens interspersed among a variety of buildings, including the mosque designated in the Tradition as the Prophet's own, a lofty citadel, the mansions and villas of wealthy retirees, and the mud houses of tribesmen. Until 974, when the Buwayhid ʿAḍud al-Dawlah walled the central city in response to a perceived threat from the Fāṭimids of Egypt, the urban landscape merged gradually with that of the surrounding countryside. Even when al-Maqdisī was writing, crops and palm groves lapped against the periphery of the city.[68] And this archaic morphology was nicely matched by the political decline of the city after it ceased to be the capital of the caliphate. Despite harboring revolts against both Umayyads and ʿAbbāsids, most of the time it was a political backwater—"a bright and cheerful place," as al-Maqdisī characterizes it[69]—where those who wished to remain aloof from the political turmoil of the times could find a safe and agreeable haven. But the city's function as an administrative center for often large estates brought considerable prosperity, manifested as real-estate speculation within the city and a steep rise in land prices, especially in the vicinity of the mosque.[70]

It was the wealth that many of these individuals, particularly members of the Quraysh, brought with them that made al-Madīnah a byword for luxury in the Arab world. Al-Ṭabarī,[71] for instance, has Marwan II, last of the Umayyad caliphs, express surprise—mock surprise, perhaps—that a leader in a revolt in 745 could tear himself away from the wine and singing girls of the city. Outside the Ḥaramān, significant urban development in the Ḥijāz was restricted, first, to the primarily Jewish town of al-Qurā, whose merchants and traders had effectively exploited its location on the route between Makkah and Dimashq; and, second, to the Red Sea ports through which Egyptian grain was imported for the Holy Cities.

The Yaman

In the Yaman, urban life was rooted in an ancient tradition of ceremonial and administrative centers supported by an agricultural population that was fairly dense—by Arabian standards at any rate. To this tradition the Arabs added only one major new foundation, the southern *miṣr* of Zabīd; it is a moot question how far they advanced the level of urbanization by increasing the size of individual cities generally. In the tenth century, urban centers appear to have been distributed fairly evenly through four of the five physiographic zones of the Yaman, namely the Tihāmah, the middle slopes, the highlands, and the eastern plateau. The exception was the desert fringe of the interior, which was devoid of urban forms. However, at least two sizable towns were apparently prospering in the sands of Ḥaḍramawt.[72] When al-Maqdisī characterized their inhabitants as heretical, in the South Arabian context it almost certainly meant Ibāḍī, implying that the influence of the Sayyids who settled in Ḥaḍramawt in the mid-tenth century was still confined to the eastern sectors of the *wādī*. To a greater degree than the Ḥijāz, al-Yaman turned away from the harsh interior of the peninsula. For long it had close connections with the Horn of Africa (Abyssinians had ruled most of the Yaman from ca. 349–78 and 525–75), and in Islamic times had developed maritime contacts not only with other parts of Arabia but also with the farthest shores of the Indian Ocean. As a result, several of its ports had prospered, especially ʿAdan, which had become one of the leading entrepôts on the Arabian Sea.

ʿUmān

Certain characteristics of this Yamanī hierarchy reappear in the urban system of ʿUmān. In the first place, the latter system was of an antiquity long antedating Islam. Second, the region had forged long-standing ties with the Persian homeland and more recent ones with countries around the shores of the Indian Ocean. Ṣuḥār, in particular, had been an important commercial node in the Sāsānian maritime empire, and continued to be the principal port and economic center of ʿUmān even when Julandā[73] and Ibāḍī rulers successively established their seats of government at Nazwah,[74] in arid country on the southern skirts of the Jabal al-Akhḍar.[75] As such it afforded a fine example of regional primacy, being never less than four times the size of the next-largest urban center. The separation of the political and economic capitals during these years clearly reflects the contrast between the narrow, localized interests of the tribal society of the interior and the broader concerns of the cosmopolitan, partly foreign communities of the coast that was a persistent feature of ʿUmānī life. It was Ṣuḥār's links with ʿUmānī overseas communities in al-Baṣrah and Khurāsān that led to the city becoming an active center in the Ibāḍī movement. Where the ʿUmānī settlement system differed most strongly from that of the Yaman was in its lower overall level of urbanization.

*

Before concluding this chapter it is necessary to enter a caveat as to the completeness of the reconstruction of the urban systems upon which the preceding discussion is based. Generally speaking, Arabia was not well served by the topographers, who almost invariably lavished attention on the Holy Cities but had less to say about the rest of the peninsula. Al-Hamdānī, of course, is an exception, but his work is heavily historical in tone. Moreover, apart from al-Maqdisī, the topographers did not consistently structure their information around urban hierarchies, or even in terms of individual cities. And in the case of Arabia, al-Maqdisī, a central pillar of many of our reconstructions, twice admits to inadequacy: he was unable to provide information about the towns of al-Sarawāt district, as he had not visited it (86), and, with fetching modesty, "Although I (al-Maqdisī) passed a whole year visiting the towns [of al-Yaman] . . . a great deal no doubt escaped me" (88). In the Yaman the lacunae have probably been filled by other authors, but omissions possibly persist in other parts of figure 2: perhaps, for instance, in the schedule of ports serving the eastern end of the Wādī Ḥaḍramawt.

Chapter Eight
The Urban System in al-Jibāl

> ... the province with the finest milk and honey, the most appetizing bread, and the strongest saffron.
>
> —Al-Maqdisī, *Aḥsan al-Taqāsīm,* 33.

Al-Jibāl, "The Mountains,"[1] was the name of the province occupying what would today be described as the northern sector of the central Zagros, a zone of subparallel mountain ranges separated by deep but not infrequently broad valleys, with an eastward extension along the foothills of the Alburz mountain range to include the important nodal center of al-Rayy (Rey). Permanent settlements were disposed predominantly in lineal arrangements reflecting the directional trend of the valleys from northwest to southeast, with cluster patterns developing where valleys widened into relatively fertile, basinlike depressions.[2]

Marketing and Service Centers

At the apex of the urban hierarchy of al-Jibāl was the *miṣr* of Hamadān: the former Ekbatana,[3] ancient capital of the Medes, a winter resort of the Achaemenids, subsequently an important relay station between Mesopotamia and the East, and always the center of an agricultural region so productive in the tenth century as to support three streets of *sūqs* in that city.[4] In one of these *sūqs* stood the congregational mosque, a venerable structure dating nearly to the time of the conquest in 645. Hamadān had been almost entirely rebuilt since that period, and in the tenth century comprised a *shahristān* a *farsakh* square[5] and designated by the term *Sārūq,*[6] outside the walls of which there had developed a populous suburb. Although the inner precincts had become rather dilapidated,[7] not even a massacre of the inhabitants by the Daylamī condottiere Mardāwīj ibn Ziyār in 931,[8] a severe earthquake in 956, and religious dissension in 962[9] had prevented the city as a whole from achieving considerable prosperity as a commercial and agricultural center.

At the next-lower level of the hierarchy were three provincial capitals *(qaṣabāt):* Qirmīsīn in the west, al-Rayy in the northeast, and Iṣfahān in the southeast. Qirmīsīn,[10] a Sāsānian foundation,[11] was the seat of government for the region that since Saljūq times has been known as Kurdistān, "The Land of the Kurds." Ibn Ḥawqal in 978 described it as a pleasant city, with an abundance of commodities in its *sūqs.*[12] Hārūn al-Rashīd had sometimes held his summer court there, and al-Maqdisī noted that the Buwayhid ʿAḍud al-Dawlah (r. 949–83) had constructed an imposing palace on the main street.[13] Al-Rayy,[14] a city whose great antiquity earned it the popular sobriquet "Umm al-Bilād," was known officially during the ʿAbbāsid period as Muḥammidīyah in honor of Muḥammad, the future caliph al-Mahdī, who rebuilt a large part of the city while he resided there during his father's reign. During the reign of al-Mahdī himself, al-Rayy became the chief mint city of the province. In the tenth century it was a league[15] or a league and a half[16] square. An inner enclave, known as al-Madīnah, "The City" proper, contained the government offices and the congregational mosque, while an outer enceinte, to which the honorific Muḥammadīyah particularly applied, enclosed the hill on which the citadel had been erected.[17] Both Ibn Ḥawqal and al-Maqdisī observe that during the second half of the tenth century the focus of activity in the city had shifted from al-Madinah (the *shahristān*), much of which was falling into ruin, to Muḥammadīyah, though Ibn Ḥawqal still considers it "the finest city in the whole of the Orient, save for Baghdād."[18]

Iṣfahān (signifying "a mustering-place for troops"), among the eastern foothills of the Zagros in the southeastern angle of Jibāl Province, was the name given to a double city on the northern bank of the Zāyindah Rūd. The western of the two halves was al-Yahūdīyah, "The Jewish Town," popularly supposed to have been established as a settlement of Jews in the time of Nebuchadnessar.[19] Of approximately the same size as Hamadān, it may actually have been the largest and most populous city in Jibāl Province. Two miles to the southeast was the smaller fortified enceinte of Jayy, known colloquially as Shahristānah, "The [Capital] City."[20] As was the case in Hamadān, its citadel was called *Sārūq*. Each of the twin cities had its own congregational mosque. In the mid-eleventh century they were described by Nāṣir-i Khusraw as together constituting the largest urban center in all the Persian-speaking territories.[21]

At the third level of the administrative hierarchy were no less than seven district capitals *(mudun)*, namely the Kurdish city of Shahrazūr,[22] government seat of a district of the same name; Ṣaymarah, capital of the district of Mihrajānqudhaq; Nihāvand, often known as Māh al-Baṣrah[23] owing to its revenues having been allocated for the payment of pensions to the Baṣrians; Dīnawar, in the tenth century the capital of a local dynasty, the Ḥasanwayhids, which took its style from the name of the chief of the dominant Kurdish tribe in the vicinity;[24] Karaj, granted to the general and poet Abū Dulaf as a fief in perpetuity free of all imposts, save a fixed annual tribute *(īghār)*;[25] Burūjird, which became fairly important after Ḥamūlah, a *wazīr* of the Abū Dulaf family just mentioned, built a fine congregational mosque there;[26] and Qazwīn, which had long served as a frontier base for Arab punitive expeditions into the semiautonomous territories of Ṭāliqān and Daylam. Even in the tenth century the city retained many of the features associated with that role, notably the heavy fortifications that separated the inner enceinte from its adjacent suburb.[27] Although from the mid-ninth century the city had come under the control in turn of the ʿAlids of Ṭabaristān, the Ṭāhirids, the Ṣaffārids, and the Sāmānids, during the second half of the tenth century it remained firmly in Buwayhid hands.

The lower tiers of the urban hierarchy comprised several strata of service centers that, based on available evidence, are not distinguishable. Alānī, Ardistān, Darbīl, Fīrūzān, Khuftiyān, and Sujās were reasonably representative of this composite order of central places, which had grown up primarily to service surrounding agricultural districts, but which also often functioned as exchange marts for seminomadic and transhumant herdsmen in the surrounding hills.

Transportation Foci

The urban centers most closely geared to providing transportation and allied facilities were those strung along the great Khurāsān road, which crossed the province from west to east. After entering the foothills of the Zagros at Ḥulwān, the road looped southward toward Qirmīsīn, passing en route Mādharūstān, an old palace of the Sāsānian king Bahrām Gūr; the station of Marj al-Qalʿah ("The Meadow Castle"), set amid eponymous grasslands where the ʿAbbāsid caliphs pastured their stud horses; the market town of Ṭazar; and al-Zubaydīyah. Thence it wound through transverse cluses (known locally as *tangs*) in the Zagros ranges to Hamadān, on to the fortified city of Sāvah, and so to al-Rayy.[28] At intervals the Khurāsān road was crossed by others running more or less longitudinally through the province. From Sinn Sumayrah ("Sumayrah's Tooth"), near Qirmīsīn, a road turned off northward through Dīnavar and Sīsar to Marāghah in Ādharbāyjān (Azerbaijan); from Hamadān a road led southward to Nihāvand, Burūjird, and Sābūrkhwāst,[29] with a branch diverging from Burūjird to Karaj and ultimately to Iṣfahān. The trail from this last city to al-Rayy followed a course parallel to the desert edge through Qāshān and Qumm.[30] Sāvah was an important caravan city at a point where the trail from Karaj crossed the Khurāsān road en route to Qazwīn. Its camels and camel drivers were in demand not only within Jibāl Province but throughout the length of the Khurāsān road.[31] But the premier provider of pack camels for the whole region was Iṣfahān, which is not surprising if, as Ibn Ḥawqal claimed, the city was indeed the commercial center not only for Jibāl, but for Fārs, Khūzistān, and Khurāsān as well.

Industrial and Craft Centers

Within Jibāl Province the chief manufacturing center was al-Rayy, with textiles chief among its products—more particularly the silk stuffs known as *munayyar* and striped cotton mantles famous throughout the Islamic world.[32] Iṣfahān exported its *ʿattābī, washī, seqlāṭūn,* and other cloths throughout the territories from al-ʿIrāq to Khurāsān.[33] In addition, the workshops of al-Rayy produced various items of hardware and needles as well as china,[34] and combs and large bowls, both fashioned from a fine-grained hardwood known as *khalanj* from the forests of Ṭabaristān. Lesser, though by no means negligible, craft centers were Qazwīn (clothes, leather wallets, bows), Qumm (chairs, horse accoutrements, divers stuffs), Iṣfahān (overcloaks, salted meat, padlocks), Nihāvand (perfume), and Qāshān (lustrous blue-and-green tiles known from the name of their place of manufacture as *qāshī,* and a kind of dried date).[35] And, finally, food processing was an almost universal, though small-scale, industry, represented typically by the cheeses of Hamadān and Dīnawar. Qumm was a center of saffron production,[36] Iṣfahān exported its fruit to ʿIrāq, and Burūjird's fruit crop was in demand as far away as Hamadān and Dīnawar.[37]

Religious Centers

Cities exhibiting the higher orders of sanctity were entirely absent from Jibāl Province, and significant *barakah* was less pervasive than in the Arab-speaking provinces of southwest Asia. Mustawfī reports that the waters of an extensive lake near Sāvah had suddenly "sunk into the earth in joy at the good news" of the Prophet's birth, and that the tomb of Abū Dajānah al-Anṣārī, a Companion of the Prophet, was to be found in the village of Māshān, near Hamadān;[38] what is more, the alleged shrine of the prophet Samuel was situated four leagues to the west of the same city. Nonetheless, these localities never attained the degree of sanctity accorded numerous Islamic shrines in, say, al-Shām (Greater Syria). No medieval author mentions the tomb of Fāṭimah, sister of the eighth *imām* ʿAlī al-Riḍā, which now ranks second only to Mashhad as a Shīʿite sanctuary. In fact this shrine was practically unknown until early in the seventeenth century, when Shah ʿAbbās, in an attempt to discourage pilgrimages into the territories of the Sunnī Turks, raised a magnificent sanctuary on the spot. It should be noted, moreover, that Qumm was one of the principal centers of Shīʿism in Persia, while al-Rayy, after remaining predominantly Sunnite almost to the end of the ninth century, subsequently became a powerful focus of Shīʿite activity.[39]

Commentary

There is reason to suspect that the urban hierarchy in Jibāl Province *as reflected in available sources* is overweighted in its upper tiers. Roughly one-fourth of all identified urban settlements are incorporated in the three uppermost tiers, which is considerably above the average. That there was a strongly developed stratum of rural settlement below that of the lowest level of urban center is not in doubt, for it is frequently mentioned in the sources. Ibn Ḥawqal, for instance, refers to the villages in the countryside surrounding Iṣfahān as being "as numerous as the days of the year," and, interestingly enough, further specifies that a number of the dependent settlements in the vicinity of al-Rayy were actually larger and more important than some of the towns he had mentioned (one even having a population of more than ten thousand men), yet lacked the all-important facility of a mosque.[40] Ibn Muhalhal, writing in the tenth century, although surviving only in quotations by Yāqūt, described the many villages around Shahrazūr.[41] Al-Maqdisī noted the dense rural population of Mihrajānqudhak District, and the *Tārīkh-i Qumm,* written at about the same time, assigned—implausibly, unless a substantial proportion were very small—nine hundred villages *(dīh)* to Qumm District.[42] In the fourteenth century Mustawfī listed, for example, forty-six villages in Sāvah District, seventeen in Āvah District, twenty-five in Chahrūd District, forty-two in Būsīn District, and so on. And in each instance up to five or six of the largest villages were named.[43]

Would some of these more populous villages have qualified as urban centers, at least from the economic point of view, if they had been examined more closely by al-Maqdisī and the other topographers? I think it unlikely. However, the enhanced demand for services and exchange facilities generated by the strong development of the village level of the settlement hierarchy may have resulted in a somewhat larger average size of towns in the lowest strictly urban stratum. Such a conclusion could be supported, though admittedly only weakly, by reference to the comparatively few centers specifically designated as small in the records relating to Jibāl Province.

Fortified Settlements

The occupation and development of existing towns was an important component in the strategy of the Arab settlement of Jibāl, but the intention and the process differed considerably between Umayyad and ʿAbbāsid times.[44] As early as the fifth decade of the seventh century, Arab garrisons were established at a number of strategic locations, including Iṣfahān, Qazwīn, al-Rayy, Qumm, Nihāvand, Dīnawar, Sīrawān, and Ṣaymarah. At Iṣfahān, for example, ʿAbd Allāh ibn Budayl ibn Warqā al-Khuzāʿī razed the old city center and founded a new *miṣr* at Jayy. Shortly thereafter Thaqīf, Tamīm, Banū-Ḍabbah, Khuzāʿī, Banū-Ḥanīfah, and Banū-ʿAbd al-Qays tribesmen from al-Kūfah and al-Baṣrah settled in the *miṣr*,[45] which eventually evolved into the *shahristān* described on pages 136–137. At much the same time the governor al-Hudhayl ibn Qays al-ʿAnbarī brought the entire ʿAnbarī clan to settle in and around the city,[46] a precedent subsequently followed by other Arab officials with followings of land-hungry clients. It is known that after the initial occupation of the city, Arabs also settled successively in the surrounding localities of Badhānah, Fabizān,[47] Buzāʾān, Jarm Qāsān, and Taymarā, all of which had been furnished with centripetalizing mosques by the mid-eighth century, while the last mentioned acquired a mint in 745–46. The cumulative result of these garrison assignments, client settlement, and independent migration was a dispersed settlement focused on the first Friday mosque to have been built in the vicinity after the conquest, that at Khushīnān.[48]

Another city founded as a *miṣr* near an earlier Sāsānian settlement was Qazwīn. Established in 645 and garrisoned with a mere five hundred men,[49] almost immediately it began to attract immigrants from the ʿIrāqān and farther afield eager to participate in the frontier wars in Ṭabaristān. And the campaigns in their turn brought governors and other important officials to the city who contributed materially to its development, among them Rabī ibn Khuthaym, who built the first mosque. Many of the settlers, including the original Arab garrison, owned or occupied holdings outside the city, where they brought new land into cultivation and, according to Ira Lapidus, formed an incipient landowning class.[50] The outcome was that Qazwīn under the Umayyads became the hub of a ring of surrounding settlements bound tightly by administrative, cultural, and economic ties to the central city.[51]

Morphologically the development of the city of Qumm was similar to those of Iṣfahān and Qazwīn, but the generative factors were quite different. In 644 Talḥah ibn al-Aḥwaṣ al-Ashʿarī established an Arab garrison in a village not far removed from the old Persian city, thereby creating a focus for future Arab settlement. Among the groups availing themselves of the opportunity was a community of Kūfan ʿAlids, who appear to have appropriated certain Persian landholdings in the vicinity of the city.[52] In succeeding years there was frequent conflict, primarily between intrusive Arabs and indigenous Persians and secondarily between garrison Arabs and ʿAlid newcomers, with affiliates of each occupying their own walled enclaves. Eventually the ʿAlids seem to have gained the upper hand, and at some time in the first third of the eighth century, some of these fortified settlements were brought within a single containing wall. Equally important for the development of Qumm was the new farming technology that the Arabs brought to its harsh natural environment. Not only did they improve and extend the *kārīz* system of supplying water for irrigation by bringing it from Taymarā and Anār districts; they also introduced new crops. Before their arrival the only crops cultivated in that particular region had been barley, caraway seeds, and saffron. To these the Arabs added wheat, millet, rape, cotton, legumes, and an array of vegetables, fruit, and nuts.[53]

Although information about al-Rayy under the Umayyads is exiguous, the city appears, from what is said about it in later times, to have followed a developmental course not fundamentally different from that of the cities already mentioned. A new Arab enclave was established next to an already existing city and furnished with a mosque as early as the reign of ʿUthmān. Umayyad governors took up their quarters in a citadel known as al-Zanbadī.[54]

ʿAbbāsid Settlement

In brief, the Arab settlement process under the Umayyads as reflected in the principal cities of al-Jibāl was one in which competing communities settled in and around existing towns and contributed thereby to the emergence of dispersed urban settlement patterns. Under the ʿAbbāsids, by contrast, the characteristic urban process—again as reflected in the principal cities—became one of imperially sponsored synoecism, a consolidation of hitherto loosely integrated settlements designed to facilitate caliphal control. Iṣfahān affords an instructive example. When the ʿAbbāsids came to power it comprised a constellation of Persian and Arab settlements subordinate in varying degrees to the Muslim garrison at Jayy. Its planned development began in about 767, when the caliph al-Manṣūr announced his intention of making Iṣfahān his capital. Although this plan was never implemented, it did result in a great deal of rebuilding and development, including the reconstitution of Yahūdīyah as the administrative center, the construction of a palace *(qaṣr)* and mosque in Khushīnān, the relocation of the city's markets, and the building over of open spaces so that Yahūdīyah became an integral part of the city of Iṣfahān.[55]

Qazwīn also benefited from caliphal attentions at this time. After al-Hādī and his former slave Mubārak had settled the Madīnat Mubārak and the Madīnat Mūsā with Arab households,[56] Hārūn al-Rashīd initiated the construction of walls around the town. When the walls were eventually completed more than half a century later in 868, they enclosed no fewer than nine quarters, which were at least partly occupied by Arabs forcibly recruited from the surrounding countryside. But perhaps Hārūn's most important contribution to the development of Qazwīn was his incorporation of the city into his hierarchy of administrative centers, which entailed annexing several additional districts to its jurisdiction.

Hārūn also made a major contribution to the development of Qumm, which for the first half century of ʿAbbāsid rule persisted as an effectively independent ʿAlid settlement. In 800–801 he sent an army to enforce the collection of taxes and in 806–7 built a new mosque to symbolize the reality of caliphal authority. He also established the city as a regional capital by integrating it into the ʿAbbāsid administrative system. A series of rebellions over the ensuing two centuries did much to subvert the city's prestige and prosperity, and toward the end of the tenth century the author of the *Ḥudūd* remarked that it was in ruins[57]—which sufficiently explains why al-Maqdisī did not include this city long identified with regional government in his administrative hierarchy.

The strategic location of al-Rayy where the Khurāsān road along the southern slopes of the Alburz range intersected routes to Ādharbāyjān and Iṣfahān ensured that the ʿAbbāsid rulers, who were frequently involved in military campaigns to the north and east, would participate actively in the development of the city. From the mid-eighth century onward they added a sequence of new quarters to the old urban nucleus so that by the tenth century, the city bore the stamp of ʿAbbāsid administrative and military concern as strongly as did Iṣfahān, Qazwīn, Qumm, or any other city of al-Jibāl.

As much as any region other than the metropolitan heartland of Arabian ʿIrāq, al-Jibāl attracted ʿAbbāsid attention, which was manifested most clearly in the utilization of segments of the urban system to consolidate caliphal power. The ʿAbbāsids established a process of controlled synoecism—exemplified archetypically by Iṣfahān but equally evident in several other cities—and supplemented it by providing facilities such as mosques, markets, and streets, and assigning jural and fiscal responsibilities. As a result, they underpinned their military and administrative policies with no little success. In so doing they implemented what Ira Lapidus has characterized as "a regional urban development plan for Western Iran."[58] The urban hierarchy that had emerged by the end of the tenth century as a result of these policies was essentially a more tightly structured, Arabicized adaptation of the system that had obtained in Sāsānian times.

Hamadān was in some respects an unexpected choice by al-Maqdisī as the *miṣr* of this *iqlīm,* for, in contrast to its illustrious history under a succession of Persian dynasties, it had not played a conspicuously prominent administrative or military role in Islamic times. Ibn Ḥawqal's assertion that it was "a new city, built in Islamic times"[59] must be taken to mean only that it had been largely rebuilt, and probably consolidated in the manner of Iṣfahān or Qazwīn. Information about the development of the city in the decades following the conquest is meager, even Ibn al-Faqīh al-Hamadhānī recording few details about his birthplace; but it is known that Arabs from the tribes of Rabīʿah and ʿIjl were settled in the city at the end of the seventh century, alongside Christians and Jews.[60] To judge from the reports of tenth-century topographers and others, Hamadān at that time was less important as a cultural or intellectual center than either Iṣfahān or al-Rayy, and certainly lagged far behind the latter in the development of its industry. It was essentially the focus of a relatively productive agricultural region that also benefited from its situation astride the Khurāsān road.

Perhaps al-Maqdisī was influenced in his choice of a *miṣr* by the fact that the city had served as a capital for a few subordinate rulers effectively under Buwayhid suzerainty. At all levels of the hierarchy wholly new foundations were remarkably few; the chief example was Qāshān, which is usually said to have been founded by Zubaydah, wife of Hārūn al-Rashīd. The Arabs set their imprint on the urban system of al-Jibāl not by establishing new cities but by reconstituting the old. To that extent they intensified its internal interactions while leaving its spatial distribution largely unchanged.

Chapter Nine
The Urban System in Khūzistān

> . . . the province with, in all possible respects, the most degraded inhabitants.
> —Al-Maqdisī, *Aḥsan al-Taqāsīm,* 33.

Khūzistān, comprising the alluvial lands of the lower Kārūn River and its tributaries,[1] was essentially a southeastward extension of the Sawād of al-ʿIrāq. But its urban settlements were distributed more evenly over the landscape than in al-ʿIrāq, being tied less closely to the immediate vicinity of large rivers and canals.

Marketing and Service Centers

The lower levels of the urban hierarchy in this *iqlīm,* as in ʿIrāq, consisted of a system of local service centers: for example, Sūq al-Arbaʿā ("The Wednesday Market"), close to the inland edge of the estuarine swamps at the head of the Persian Gulf.[2] In fact the number of settlements incorporating the element *sūq* (= "market") in their name at all periods of history is eloquent testimony to the productivity of the clays and loams of Khūzistān, especially in its northern tracts, where drainage is better. Other centers performing similar functions included Baṣinnā, on the Karkhah River, where seven grain mills similarly attested the productivity of the fine fluvial silts of the surrounding plain;[3] Bayrūt (Beirut), a moderately large town among groves of date palms;[4] Dizfūl, among the pastures of the Lur River plain (Ṣaḥrāʾ Lur) in the extreme north of the *iqlīm* (408); Īdhaj, the chief market town of the Great Lur (414);[5] Karkhah (or Karkhā), a small center protected by a castle and holding its weekly market on Sundays (414); Sanbīl, on the opposite side of the Ṭāb (Zohreh) River from the Fārsī city of Arrajān;[6] and Masruqān, on the canal of the same name constructed to water the lands south of Tustar.[7]

The metropolis of Khūzistān was al-Ahwāz,[8] an old Persian district capital that, after the Arab occupation, suffered severely during the Zanj rebellion of the ninth century. In the following century it was largely rebuilt by the Buwayhid prince ʿAḍud al-Dawlah. In its numerous large warehouses, commodities from nearly all of Khūzistān were collected before being transshipped to al-Baṣrah,[9] leading the author of the *Ḥudūd* to laud al-Ahwāz as the most prosperous city in the whole *iqlīm.* [10]

At the next-lower level of the administrative hierarchy were five provincial capitals. Al-Sūs was the most northerly of these, situated near the bank of the Karkhah River in its middle course. In the tenth century this city functioned as a rural market center, but it occupied the site of the ancient Persian capital of Sūsa. When al-Maqdisī categorized it as a *qaṣabah* he was probably responding to its former glories and administrative responsibilities, for in the tenth century only its suburbs (sing. *rabaḍ*) were inhabited.[11] Thirty miles to the southeast was the city of Junday-Sābūr,[12] which under the Sāsānians had been the capital of Khūzistān. Its main claim to fame in ʿAbbāsid times was its medical school, founded under Nestorian auspices probably in the sixth century; from the time of Hārūn al-Rashīd (r. 786–809) the school was a center of diffusion of Islamic medical lore. More generally, Junday-Sābūr transmitted Greek learning from Nestorian centers such as Edessa (Urfa) and Nisibis to the ʿAbbāsid capital of Baghdād. Al-Maqdisī, however, states that in the tenth century most of the city was in ruins as a result of Kurdish assaults, a statement apparently confirmed by archaeological investigation.[13] Possibly the decline of the city had really begun with disturbances in Khūzistān associated with the Zanj rebellion and the campaigns of Yaʿqūb ibn Layth toward the end of the third century A.H.

Still farther to the southeast, where the Kārūn River bifurcated into two separate channels, was the important urban node of Tustar;[14] and due south, where today the channels of the river are reunited,[15] was ʿAskar Mukram. At the end of the seventh or the beginning of the eighth century Mukram ibn al-Fazr, sent by the viceroy of al-ʿIrāq to quell a rebellion in Khūzistān, had pitched his camp *(ʿaskar)* near the ruins of the old Persian city of Rustam Qawādh.[16] This settlement had subsequently evolved into an important urban center and, in the tenth century under the Buwayhid ruler Muʿizz al-Dawlah, a mint city in the manner already exemplified by Shīrāz, al-Baṣrah, al-Kūfah, and al-Fusṭāṭ. Some thirty miles below al-Ahwāz, in the agriculturally productive district of Surraq, was the city of Dawraq, on the pilgrim route from Fārs and Kirmān to the Ḥarāmān;[17] and three days' march east of the metropolis was Rāmhurmuz, the center of a grain-, cotton-, sugar-, and mulberry-producing region. In addition to commodious *sūqs* constructed by ʿAḍud al-Dawlah, this last city also boasted a celebrated library built and endowed by a certain Ibn Sawwār.[18] Finally, between the headwaters of the Ṭāb River and a tributary of the Kārūn, almost on the border between Khūzistān and Fārs, was Lurjān,[19] administrative headquarters *(madīnah)* of the District of Sardān and one of the few important centers of Khūzistān to be located off the alluvium.

Transportation Foci

In a province where most of the larger rivers and canals were navigable by boat, virtually all of the urban centers situated on these waterways provided transportation services for commodities moving from north to south or vice versa. Probably the most southerly of the specialist transportation centers and the nearest approach to a port of entry was Ḥiṣn Mahdī, located where the Aḍudī Canal, coming from the Shaṭṭ al-ʿArab at Bayān, joined the Kārūn.[20] Here several guardhouses (sing. *rabāṭ*) built by the caliph al-Mahdī controlled the flow of goods entering and leaving the province. Until the mid-tenth century there were also toll barriers higher up the river at Sūq Baḥr, where it was not unknown for unauthorized as well as legitimate duties to be exacted. These centers aside, transportation nodes were most fully developed where the principal land routes from west to east crossed the longitudinally aligned river arteries, most notably at al-Sūs, Tustar, ʿAskar Mukram, and Ahwāz. This last city benefited from a situation where the Kārūn River cut through the sandstone ridge of the Ahwāz Hills, creating thereby a series of rapids that necessitated the transshipment of goods between vessels on the upper and lower reaches of the river. Al-Maqdisī describes Ahwāz as the "storehouse *(khizānah)* of al-Baṣrah . . . an emporium and a meeting-place for merchants."[21] Dizfūl's transportation function was implicit in its name, Persian *dizpūl* signifying "castle bridge,"[22] while Yāqūt regarded the great stone bridge over the Kārūn at Īdhaj on the road from northern Fārs to ʿAskar Mukram as one of the wonders of the world.[23] The main exception to this type of location for a transportation focus was Rāmhurmuz, which functioned as a major nodal center on the eastern edge of the alluvium. Dawraq, we have seen, was a stage on the pilgrim route from Kirmān and Fārs to Makkah.

Industrial and Craft Centers

The chief primary product for which Khūzistān was distinguished was sugarcane, a plant that had been introduced into Persia from India in Sāsānian times. According to the Armenian historian Moses of Khorene, who was writing in the second half of the fifth century, the cane was then under cultivation in Elymais, near Junday-Sābūr;[24] and in the tenth century al-Maqdisī observed that the only sugar used throughout Persia, al-ʿIrāq, and Arabia was exported from Khūzistān.[25] Al-Thaʿālibī added that the extent of cane cultivation and the quantity of the product were unequalled elsewhere in the whole world.[26]

The dominant feature of craft industry in tenth-century Khūzistān was textile manufacture, and more particularly the network of *ṭirāz* factories supplying clothing and furnishings to the ʿAbbāsid court, the Buwayhid *sulṭāns*, and high officers of state.[27] Sundry comments by medieval and later authors attribute the expansion of this industry in Sāsānian times to the forced settlement in Khūzistān of weavers deported from Aqūr, al-Shām, and even the Roman territories.[28] However that may be, textile manufacture flourished under both Sāsānians and Arabs. Ibn Taghrībirdī reports that when a certain Aḥmad al-Rāsibī, governor of "the territory from Wāsiṭ to Junday-Sābūr and from Sūs to Shahrazūr," died in 913–14, he controlled no less than eighty *ṭirāz* factories.[29] Preeminent among the textile-producing cities of Khūzistān was Tustar, which manufactured splendidly embroidered and costly satins worthy to be mentioned in the same breath as those of Rūm,[30] together with other fine cloths and rugs. Al-Iṣṭakhrī notes that the *sulṭān* Muʿizz al-Dawlah owned a *ṭirāz* factory in the city,[31] while Ibn Ḥawqal claims that "at one time every king of al-ʿIrāq had had one there, with a representative *(ṣāḥib)* in attendance."[32] It was, therefore, eminently appropriate that the city's congregational mosque should have stood in the *sūq* of the cloth merchants.[33]

Other important textile-manufacturing centers were al-Sūs, from which came "expensive embroidered silks of regal quality";[34] Junday-Sābūr, which, al-Maqdisī notes, had many *ṭirāz* factories;[35] Baṣinnā and neighboring small towns and villages, which produced veils, curtains *(sutūr)*, carpets, and spun wool;[36] Qurqūb, where *ṭirāz* factories belonging to *sulṭān* Muʿizz al-Dawlah manufactured the famous *sūsanjird* embroideries;[37] and Dawraq, best known for its coarse tent cloth called *khaysh*.[38] Lesser textile centers included Rāmhurmuz, a producer of garments of *ibrīsm* silk,[39] and Nahr Tīrā, whose merchants habitually passed off their locally manufactured garments as products of Baghdād, even in the markets of that very city.[40] Ibn Ḥawqal additionally observes that these clothes were so well made that "no one suspected they were not made in Baghdād."[41]

Other industry in the *iqlīm* was restricted to the processing of agricultural products and was inevitably on a small scale, although as many as seven grain mills, mounted on barges anchored in the Karkhah River, were operating near Baṣinnā at the end of the tenth century, and raisin syrup *(dūshāb)* was exported from the small town of Asak.[42]

Religious Centers

The degree of sanctity achieved by the cities of Khūzistān nowhere rose above that of the prophetic tomb, though at this level *barakah* was fairly widely diffused. Among the better-known shrines were the tomb of Yaʿqūb ibn al-Layth, founder of the Ṣaffārid dynasty, who had made Junday-Sābūr his capital and eventually died there in 878, and a fine mosque commemorating the alleged discovery of the coffin *(tābūt)* of the prophet Daniel in al-Sūs.[43] There was also a Persian fire temple at Dawraq, a city that still attracted adherents of the old Persian religion even in the tenth century and that derived additional prestige from its warm sulphur springs, held to be particularly beneficial in treating skin diseases.

Commentary

Khūzistān was one of the more highly urbanized regions of the Eastern Caliphate, but there is reason to believe that, as in Jibāl, the lower orders of towns were not always adequately represented in contemporary sources. Certainly, individual cities were not described as fully as was customary in some provinces.[44] The urban hierarchy portrayed in this chapter was essentially the Sāsānian system as developed by the Arabs after they conquered the Īrānian culture world. They eliminated very few elements in the settlement pattern of Khūzistān, but when, as in the case of al-Sūs, large areas of the already declining city were razed, they were subsequently restored. Nor did the Arabs contribute many new foundations to the urban system. Even their premier addition, the newly built ʿAskar Mukram, merely embodied the site values and virtually duplicated the location of the old Persian city of Rustam Qawādh. Moreover, the shifting of the metropolis from Sūsa (al-Sūs) to al-Ahwāz had virtually no effect on the overall structure of the urban hierarchy. What the Arabs did achieve was the elaboration and consolidation of the system through the development of existing cities, particularly those involved in administration and textile manufacture or offering strategic transportation services.

Khūzistān, whether under that name or as Sūsiana, had traditionally been a prosperous province. By the tenth century it was benefiting from the agricultural revolution that followed the Arab conquest and that resulted in the introduction of new crops, new strains of already acclimatized crops, and new farming technologies.[45] Among these last were irrigation practices that the Arabs grafted onto already extensive systems of water control inherited from the Sāsānians. The great weirs on the Kārūn River a little below, respectively, al-Ahwāz and Tustar were already in place when the Arabs assumed control of the province; they made only minor adjustments to the irrigation networks dependent on these constructions. Generally speaking, the Arabs were responsible less for the extension of irrigation systems than for their intensification. Nevertheless, it was the revised cropping systems, signifying more intensive use of the land and facilitated by irrigation, that permitted the apparent increase in the size of market centers that seems to be reported in the texts. The author of the *Ḥudūd* sums up his opinion of Khūzistān with the assertion that "[i]t is more prosperous than any province adjoining it."[46]

Like so much else in the economy of Khūzistān, the textile industry that gave a distinctive industrial character to some of the components of the urban hierarchy—

particularly several of the provincial capitals and a group of smaller centers strung along the Karkhah valley—was a Sāsānian legacy. Despite the probable influence of weavers from farther west on the growth of this industry in certain cities, the *ṭirāz* as a functioning system seems here to have originated in the state factories of the Sāsānian kings.[47]

With prosperity came an enrichment of intellectual life, which in the tenth century was still dominated by Muʿtazilite thought—a Hellenistically inspired system of dogmatics that insisted on the claims of reason in matters of theology—even though the movement was by then losing ground in the Muslim world in general. And one of the principal centers of Muʿtazilī learning was the library at Rāmhurmuz mentioned above: the Dār al-ʿIlm, or "Abode of Learning," as it was called. According to al-Maqdisī this library ranked second only to that at al-Baṣrah (also founded by Ibn Sawwār) in the size and diversity of its collection.[48] Yet despite its prosperity and the vigor of its intellectual life, Khūzistān projected an unprepossessing image to the rest of the world. Scarcely a traveller failed to mention the agues and worse that afflicted the inhabitants of that hot, humid, and waterlogged region. Al-Ahwāz was often singled out for special comment. Al-Thaʿālibī, for example, writes of its "persistent clinging fevers" that killed off natives as quickly as outsiders,[49] a scourge readily intelligible in light of al-Maqdisī's complaint about "mosquitoes that bit like wolves"[50] and al-Jāḥiẓ's comment that sewage from privies and drainage from ablution facilities were allowed to flow directly into streams and swamps.[51] This last circumstance was by no means uncommon in the Middle East, but in the case of Khūzistān the tropical climate would have exacerbated the ill effects. However, the region retained its prosperity from generation to generation and from century to century, so that there can be no doubt but that love of gain triumphed over fear of morbidity in the urban system of the *iqlīm*.

Chapter Ten

The Urban System in Fārs

. . . the province with the most ingenious people and merchants, and the most widespread profligacy.

—Al-Maqdisī, *Aḥsan al-Taqāsīm,* 33.

The Province of Fārs in the tenth century comprised the southern tracts of the central Zagros Mountains roughly from the latitude of the head of the Persian Gulf as far as the Strait of Hurmuz. Physiographically this region was a continuation of the longitudinally oriented succession of ranges and valleys that constituted the salient morphological features of Jibāl Province, although in Fārs the ridges were somewhat lower, the valleys rather broader, and intermontane basins more extensive. It was a region of ancient settlement that had been the metropolitan territory of the Achaemenid and Sāsānian dynasties and that still preserved numerous relics of that glorious past. Not the least of these was the system of central place–like settlements inherited by the Arabs when they overran the province. In its lower echelons this system consisted essentially of fortified market towns serving agricultural districts of limited extent, virtually all of which had been in existence in pre-Islamic times. Kuvār,[1] al-Nawbandajān,[2] and Khiyār[3] were sufficiently representative of this class of urban center.

Marketing and Service Centers

One of the few cities that was for all intents and purposes an Arab foundation was Shīrāz, the metropolis *(miṣr)* of the province. True, a settlement had existed on the site in pre-Islamic times, but seems to have been relatively unimportant when, in 693, a certain Muḥammad, either a brother or a cousin of al-Ḥajjāj, viceroy of al-ʿIrāq, established an army camp there from which to conduct the siege of intransigent Iṣṭakhr.[4] By a process presumably similar to that already described in chapter 2 for al-Baṣrah, al-Kūfah, and al-Fusṭāṭ, the tribally organized camp evolved into an urban center; but it remained small, its sole claim to significance until the second half of the ninth century being the tomb of the Shīʿī martyr Aḥmad ibn Mūsā. Then the Ṣaffārid dynasty made it the capital of their semiautonomous principality. In 879 the second ruler of that dynasty built the first congregational mosque. In the tenth century the city acquired yet greater prestige when the Buwayhid *amīrs*, masters of the Caliphate itself, established it as their principal seat of government *(dār al-mulk),* the effective focus of secular administration for the rump of the ʿAbbāsid Empire. At this time Shīrāz was nearly a league in diameter, with eight gates in its perimeter[5] and busy, but narrow *sūqs*.[6] It was at this time that the Buwayhid ʿAḍud al-Dawlah (r. 949–83), by common consent the most illustrious of his line, half a league outside Shīrāz laid out a new palace precinct that he styled Gird Fānā Khusraw after his personal name. Al-Maqdisī, carried on wings of vaulting hyperbole, characterizes this palace as "reflecting the loveliness and the beauty of Paradise."[7] Wool weavers, brocade makers, and other craftsmen were brought, together with the ruler's military bodyguard, to dwell in the vicinity of the palace. Soon the precinct became the nucleus of an administrative and commercial center sufficiently prosperous for the taxes on its shops to yield an annual revenue of twenty thousand *dīnārs*. Small wonder that it became known popularly as "The *Amīr*'s Market" *(Sūq al-Amīr).* For a time it was designated a mint city, but its prosperity did not outlast the life of its founder and, by the close of the tenth century, it had fallen into ruin.

At the next-lower level of the urban hierarchy al-Maqdisī designated five cities. Four of these (together with Shīrāz) were capitals of the major districts (sing. *kūrah*)[8] into which Fārs had been divided in Sāsānian times, and which had been incorporated into the administrative structure of the Caliphate:

1. ***Shāpūr,*** commonly known as Shahristān, "The City,"[9] the center of a productive agricultural region occupying the basin of the upper Shāpūr River and its tributaries. Ibn Ḥawqal considered the city to be as extensive as Iṣṭakhr and more populous,[10] but al-Maqdisī in his day found whole sectors falling into ruin as the inhabitants migrated to neighboring Kāzirūn, which had replaced it as a more dynamic regional economic center.[11] However, this decline was not at all evident in the surrounding countryside, where the same author noted that

   > [i]t is possible to find in a single garden date palms, olives, oranges, carobs, walnuts, almonds, figs, grapes, jujubes, reeds, sugar-cane, violets, and jasmine. Brooks flow under overhanging fruit trees and villages stretch away into the far distance. As in Sogdia, one can walk for hours in the shade of trees, finding refreshment at any time of the day. (424)

2. ***Arrajān,***[12] a flourishing seat of "provincial" government on the southern bank of the Ṭāb River, at a point where it was able to control traffic over two bridges carrying high roads into Khūzistān. The city was said to have been founded by the Sāsānian king Kawādh I (r. A.D. 488–96, 499–531), who settled prisoners of war from Āmid, Diyārbakr, and Mayyāfāriqīn (Silvan) in the neighborhood. As Ibn Ḥawqal phrased it, Arrajān was a city that partook simultaneously of the milieus of sea (one stage distant), mountains, plain, and desert.[13]
3. ***Iṣṭakhr,*** on the river Pulvār a short distance above its confluence with the Kur, and scarcely an hour's journey to the north of the ruins of the ancient Persian capital known to the Greeks as Persepolis. It had been the seat of the Sāsānian kings; housed the dynastic fire, *Anāhid-ardashīr;* was a principal node in the irrigation system of the Marvdasht plain; and, at the time of the Muslim conquest, was one of the largest cities of Fārs. However, in the mid-tenth century even al-Iṣṭakhrī, who may have hailed from the city, was constrained to admit that it was only of middling size.[14] In fact four Fārsī cities—Shīrāz, Fasā, Sīrāf, and Arrajān—all surpassed Iṣṭakhr in size. It was, at that time, about a mile in diameter.[15]
4. ***Dārābjird,*** the capital of the easternmost *kūrah* of Fārs, was a roughly circular, walled city standing in the midst of the celebrated pasturelands *(marghzār)* of the noble Ismāʿīlī tribe of Shabānkārah. In the tenth century it was a league in diameter.[16]
5. The fifth *qaṣabah* mentioned by al-Maqdisī was the port of ***Sīrāf*** on the Zuhayr coast of Īrāhistān.[17] No documentary record of this port exists prior to the ninth century A.D., when it was already the principal entrepôt for the maritime commerce of Fārs; but recent archaeological investigations suggest that its origins go back at least to Sāsānian times.[18] Al-Iṣṭakhrī asserted that in about the mid-tenth century the city was almost equal to Shīrāz in size.[19] This estimate has been partially confirmed by archaeological excavation that has revealed a congested settlement squeezed for a distance of more than a mile and a half between a precipitous ridge and the waters of a shallow bay. The congregational mosque stood on the shore near the center of the settlement and at the western end of a bazaar some five hundred yards long, while the main residential quarter occupied rising ground at the foot of the ridge. Another residential sector was situated on level ground to the west of the congregational mosque. Al-Iṣṭakhrī's emphasis on the high quality of much of the housing—built to a height of several storeys, incorporating teakwood from the Zanj countries, and overlooking the sea—has recently been to some extent validated by the discovery of several streets of impressive courtyard houses in the first of these residential quarters.[20] One such house, which had a ground-floor area of 540 square meters, gives substance to al-Iṣṭakhrī's account of a merchant of his acquaintance in Sīrāf spending no less than thirty thousand *dīnārs* on his residence.[21] A complex of structures in one of the higher parts of the main residential sector is thought at the time of writing to have been the palace of the city governor.

Transportation Foci

Even in the absence of literary confirmation, it would be evident that the prosperity of Sīrāf, which al-Maqdisī speaks of as rivalling that of al-Baṣrah,[22] must have been based entirely on commerce, for aridity rendered the port's immediate hinterland almost totally unproductive. In fact the city was devoid even of gardens, and fruit and other produce had to be brought from the mountains of Jamm nearly twenty miles inland. The web of trade on which Sīrāf depended for its prosperity extended from the head of the Red Sea and the East African coast all the way to Southeast Asia. As early as the eighth century Ibāḍī merchants from Sīrāf were voyaging to this latter part of the world, and possibly beyond;[23] and in 943 al-Masʿūdī noted that Sīrāfī dhows were rendezvousing with "Chinese" merchantmen in a Southeast Asian harbor, the name of which he transcribed as Kalah.[24]

Cargoes arriving from the Orient were re-exported to East Africa and the countries bordering the Red Sea; dispatched by boat to al-Baṣrah and Baghdād; carried on pack animals to Fīrūzābād,[25] Shīrāz,[26] and other inland cities; and redistributed through a system of secondary and tertiary ports on the Fārsī coast. From north to south these included Mahrubān, which was the first port of call for Baṣrian vessels bound for India, and the gateway to Arrujān, whence its three large caravanserais, "each one as strong and tall as a fortress";[27] Sīnīz, half a league from the open sea on the creek now known as Bandar Daylam;[28] Jannābā, a not very secure anchorage in the estuary of a stream that Arab geographers called the Nahr al-Shadhkān;[29] Najīram, on the border between the Zuhayr and Muẓaffar coasts of Fārs;[30] Nāband, the port of Mīmand, at the head of a small creek *(khawr);*[31] Qays (Persian Kīsh), a walled city on the island of the same name, some four leagues off the ʿUmārah coast;[32] Huzū, on the mainland opposite Qays island, which had been heavily fortified by the Buwayhids when they made it their state prison;[33] Qalʿah al-Dīkdān,[34] a small but strongly fortified port; and Sūrū, where the caravan road from Ṭārum reached the ʿUmārah coast.[35]

During the last quarter of the tenth century a conjunction of natural disaster and political machination brought about a major restructuring of the port hierarchy along the Fārsī coast. In 977 a series of earthquakes disrupted life in Sīrāf, and, together with the weakening of Buwayhid power, afforded the *amīr* of Qays the opportunity to force shipping to make its landfall at his island rather than at Sīrāf.[36] By the beginning of the thirteenth century only the mosque of Sīrāf remained standing, and the harbor was so choked with silt that ships had to rely on Nāband to provide shelter on the Zuhayr coast. Although, as al-Qazwīnī puts it, the heat at Qays exceeded that of the hottest room in the bathhouse,[37] the city soon became the premier port of Fārs and exceedingly populous.

The inland cities of Fārs with developed break-of-bulk functions were strung along the caravan routes radiating out from Shīrāz to the borders of the province.[38] One of the most important of these was the road from Shīrāz to Sīrāf by way of Kavār, at the crossing of the Sakkān River, and Fīrūzābād. Another route led from Shīrāz to Jannābā, with intermediate staging posts at Kāzirūn and Tawwaj. This latter town was as large as the *qaṣabah* of Arrajān and inhabited mainly by Syrian Arabs transported thither by ʿAḍud al-Dawlah.[39] The most detailed information provided by the earlier topographers, however, relates to the road leading northward from Shīrāz to Khūzistān, which carried what for the time was heavy traffic. There were alternatives to some sectors of this route, but the main road in the tenth century was probably that from Shīrāz to Juwaym and Khullār (both to the north of the Dasht Arzin plain), Karkān, al-Nawbandajān, Khūbdhān, Darkhīd, Gunbad Mallaghān (which al-Maqdisī noted was in ruins toward the end of the tenth century),[40] and so to the bridges over the Ṭāb River at Arrajān. Three separate routes led from Shīrāz to Iṣfahān, of which the most direct turned off the Khūzistān road at Juwaym and proceeded by way of Bayḍā on the Marvdasht plain, Kūrad, Kallār, and Sumayram. In the cities situated on the routes to the more arid lands of the east, caravanserais tended to be more prominent in the spectrum of urban features than in the more densely settled regions of central Fārs, and particularly so in Yazd, Unās, Dārābjird, and Ṭārum. In the fourteenth century Mustawfī noted that some of the muleteers who travelled with Fārsī caravans hailed from the regions of Upper and Lower Khumāyijān, around and beyond the headwaters of the Shāpūr River;[41] and it is not unlikely that the same held true in the tenth century.

Industrial and Craft Centers

In virtually all the cities of Fārs except those of some of the Gulf ports and interior settlements on the desert fringe, where aridity prohibited agriculture, primary economic activities occupied a very high proportion of the labor force. By the standards of the time, the intermontane valleys of the Zagros were productive environments. In fact the impression that the *iqlīm* as a whole left with travellers was one of "fertility" or "fruitfulness." Particularly praised were the grain fields of the Marvdasht plain, which, close to the metropolitan heart of Sāsānian Persia, were fed copious irrigation water from dams on the Kur River; and those around the headwaters of the same river, which were served by the two market towns of Kūrad and Kallār. Still farther north were the arable lands of Dasht Run, which were said to yield four crops a year. Equally celebrated were the rich pastures *(marghzār)* of Dārābjird and the Dasht Arzin, and the "narcissus meads" *(marghzār narkis)* adjoining the city of Kāzirūn.

Nicely complementary to, and occasionally integrated symbiotically with, the settled farming communities were a variety of nomadic and transhumant tribes, all of which were rubricated by tenth-century topographers as "Kurds," the ethnic designation of the largest of such groups in the Īrānian cultural realm as a whole, although Kurds sensu stricto were but poorly represented in Fārs. According to al-Iṣṭakhrī, followed by Ibn Ḥawqal, in Fārs they numbered half a million tents,[42] each of which could furnish up to ten men, including herdsmen, hired men, and followers. This was surely an exaggeration, and one of which al-Iṣṭakhri was probably vaguely aware in conceding that an accurate count could be obtained only by examining the figures in the *ṣadaqah*[43] registers. Ibn Ḥawqal reports that the taxes on tribal districts were assessed by contract *(muqāṭaʿah),* estimation *(ʿibrah),* or a proportion of the annual yield *(muqāsamah)* in the case of transhumant shepherds migrating seasonally between upland and lowland.[44] The principal livestock raised by Fārsī nomads and transhumants were sheep and mares.[45] These groups certainly had little to do with towns, although some of their animal products found their way there, and some of their tribesmen played a part in the caravan trade that underpinned the urban system.

Some of the products of the countryside enjoyed more than a local reputation, particularly those providing a basis for the secondary crafts of perfume manufacture. Shāpūr, for instance, produced no less than ten different kinds of unguents prepared from the violet, nenuphar, narcissus, palm flower, lily, jasmine, myrtle, sweet marjoram, lemon, and orange flower, and distributed throughout the lands of the Eastern Caliphate. But preeminence among the perfumery of Fārs undoubtedly lay with the rosewater of Jūr (Fīrūzābād), made up from the petals of roses grown on the plain surrounding the city:

> How many slender [flasks], standing like doe-eyed virgins
> with their shifts wound round them, as if they were fragrantly scented wallflowers!
> Every maiden who has grown up in Jūr, who sways gracefully
> along in her short, silk-lined robe,
> Exhaling from herself a subtle odour of perfume like
> a breeze wafting pervasive fragrance,
> Induces desire that is stronger than that of a distant
> lover for the presence of his beloved.[46]

Fārs is not well endowed mineralogically, and several casual references to mining by topographers of the tenth and earlier centuries must be regarded as suspect. Well attested, though, was the production of the bituminous vulnerary known as *mūmiyāʾ*, which was mined under government monopoly in the neighborhood of Dārābjird and exported thence throughout the Middle East.[47]

A particular suite of epithets commonly employed by tenth-century authors writing about the cities of Fārs implied in one way or another a substantial measure of prosperity.[48] And, except for Sīrāf, whose wealth derived predominantly from foreign trade, the higher levels of prosperity were closely correlated with the presence of textile manufacturing. Preeminent among such cities were those possessing *ṭirāz* factories.[49] These fell into two groups: a northwestern group and a southeastern group. The former comprised the following cities:

- ***Sīnīz,*** whence came linens of the *qaṣab* type. Al-Maqdisī notes that the requisite flax *(kattān)* was sometimes imported from Egypt (not a difficult undertaking in view of the fact that Sīnīz was the premier port of Arrajān *kūrah*), although most was grown locally.[50]
- ***Jannābāʾ,*** the main port of Shāpūr *kūrah.* Ibn al-Faqīh cites Jannābī stuffs as one of the most famous products of Fārs.[51]
- ***Tawwaj,*** of which al-Maqdisī remarks that it enjoyed a great reputation because of the linen garments

manufactured there.[52] It is said that ʿAḍud al-Dawlah settled Syrian Arabs in the city, no doubt to the benefit of the textile industry.

To these should be added the following:

- ***Kāzirūn,*** which al-Maqdisī characterizes as the "Dimyāṭ of the Persians" because, he explains, "the linen garments which are made and sold there resemble in their manufacture the *qaṣab* from Shaṭā [a town in the Dimyāṭ-Tinnīs textile complex in the Nile Delta: pp. 194–95 below], even though they are of cotton *(ʿuṭb).*"[53] When al-Maqdisī was writing, *Sulṭān* ʿAḍud al-Dawlah had recently built a meetinghouse *(dār)* for the merchants engaged in the linen trade, the rooms in which yielded an annual rent of ten thousand *dirhams.* The same author also records that most of the so-called *tawwajī* textiles came not from Tawwaj but from Kāzirūn. However, he took care to add that the Tawwajī weavers produced a better quality cloth.[54] It is curious that no medieval author mentioned a *ṭirāz* factory in Kāzirūn and al-Iṣṭakhrī asserts explicitly that no such enterprise existed in the city.
- ***Ghundījān,*** the chief city of Dasht Bārīn District, which produced carpets *(busuṭ),* curtains *(sutūr),* and cushions *(maqʿad)* that the looms of Armīniyah could not match, and which were exported to destinations both within Fārs and farther afield.[55]

The southeastern group of *ṭirāz* cities included the following:

- ***Jahram,*** which was responsible for the manufacture of a variety of carpets, including a special *jahramī* type that could take the form of runners *(nakhkh),* high-quality prayer mats *(muṣallayāt),* and unusually large-sized rugs *(zullīyah;* pl. *zalālī).*[56]
- ***Ṭārum,*** which produced *susanjird*[57] and large fans (*mirwah:* assuming these to have incorporated some textile in their manufacture).[58] Al-Jāḥiẓ contributed the unexpected information that this city was one of the few places in Persia proper where the brilliant crimson *qirmiz* dye was obtainable.[59]
- ***Fasā,*** which possibly offered a wider range of textile manufactures than any other of the *ṭirāz* cities, including garments of *qazz* silk, robes *(aksiyah),* carpets *(anmāṭ* and *busuṭ),* wrappers *(fūṭah), munayyar*[60] in the style of Iṣfahān, *washī* figured cloth,[61] octagonal-patterned curtains *(sutūr muthammanah),* tents *(kharkāhāt),* and napkins *(mindīl)* of *Sharābīyah* cloth.[62]

Other towns producing textiles, often in quantity, even though they seem to have lacked *ṭirāz* factories included Arrajān (wrappers, coarse garments *[kundakī],* and Indian stuffs *[barbahār]*),[63] Yazd (cotton garments),[64] Rūdhān (garments resembling those made in Bamm),[65] Darīz (linens),[66] Iṣṭakhr (finely textured garments known as *al-abāʾī*),[67] Dārābjird (upholstery cloth *[thiyāb]* similar to the famous Ṭabarī stuffs, robes of all qualities, mats *[ḥuṣur]* of the ʿAbbadānī kind, carpets *[busuṭ]* and curtains *[sutūr]* of *susanjird*),[68] Furj (carpets, curtains, and linens),[69] and the port of Sīrāf (wrappers *[fūṭah]* and linen loincloths *[izār]*).[70]

Shīrāz deserves special mention in this connection (fig. 14). In its capacity as *miṣr* of the *iqlīm,* it had developed textile manufacture on a large scale, including the production of high-quality cloaks *(abrād)* and robes *(aksiyah), munayyar* stuffs, and brocades.[71] As the city was essentially a creation of the Arab conquest, these manufactures must have been attracted to its environs during Islamic times, presumably from already established centers of production. Serjeant has suggested that the *munayyar* stuffs, for example, could have been introduced from al-Rayy, the *qaṣabs* from other cities in Fārs and Khūzistān, and brocades from one of the districts in which Sāsānian kings had settled Greek prisoners.[72] Al-Maqdisī does, in fact, furnish an instance of textile workers being planted in Kard Fanā Khusraw, the palace complex established by ʿAḍud al-Dawlah virtually as a suburb of Shīrāz: "[He] transported thither workers in wool *(ṣūf)* and artificers *(ṣunnāʿ)* in *qazz* silk and brocade."[73] Although they were founded by the *sulṭān,* these Shīrāzī enterprises were never designated explicitly as *ṭirāz* factories by the tenth-century topographers. Contrariwise, not all textiles produced within the *ṭirāz* factories were for the exclusive use of the *sulṭān,* for Ibn Ḥawqal notes specifically that "[m]ore than one *ṭirāz* factory belonging to the Sulṭān *and merchants* is to be found [in Jahram]."[74] Whereas in Baghdād the *ṭirāz* had become an adjunct of the Buwayhid palace, in Fārs—as in Khūzistān[75]—it apparently came under more diversified ownership, and it is doubtful whether the caliphal court in Baghdād figured at all prominently in the enterprise.

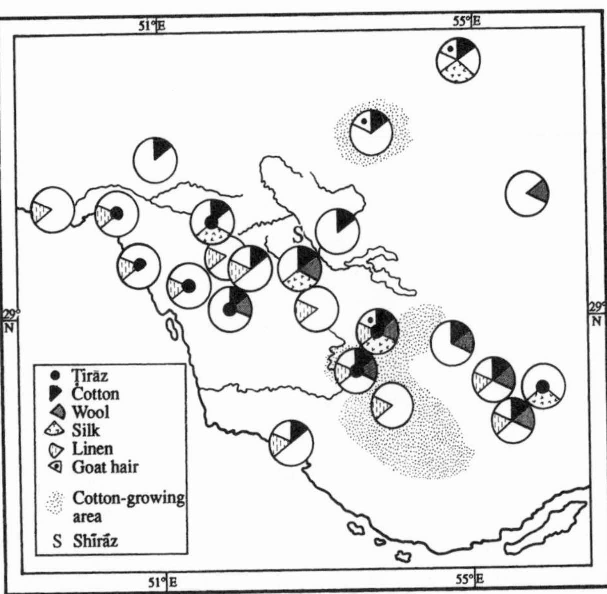

Figure 14. The Fārsī textile industry in the tenth century as recorded in medieval literature.

Fortified Settlements

Another distinctive feature of the settlement system of Fārs was the prevalence of fortifications; and here I speak not so much of the standard walls and citadels associated with the larger cities but rather of the castles that crowned numerous hills and crags throughout the province. I have counted more than forty—certain ambiguities in the texts prevent a more accurate determination—in the writings of tenth-century and earlier topographers, but Ibn Ḥawqal claims to have heard "knowledgeable men of sound judgment" who were familiar with the Fārsī terrain affirm that there were altogether some five thousand such castles.[76] These castles took a variety of forms and ranged widely in size, but all reflected a preoccupation with family and clan security and defined in unambiguous terms the limits of central-government power. Reflecting on the evolution of the Fārsī settlement pattern from his vantage point in the fourteenth century, Mustawfī attributed the decline of commerce and crafts in many towns of Arrajān to the depredations effected from the shelter of such castles, particularly by the Assassins.[77] But such raiding had been endemic long before the fourteenth century, sometimes extending on to the waters of the Gulf, as when the ʿUmārah branch of the Khārijite Julandids of ʿUmān tracked the movements of shipping from their Dīkbāyah *ḥiṣn* (fort) and permitted safe passage only on payment of an arbitrarily determined toll.[78] Many of these castles were veritable storehouses of provisions and furnished with cisterns for retaining rainwater so that they could withstand protracted sieges. The most impressive of these precautionary measures was surely the system of tanks, capable of holding enough water for a thousand men during a year's siege, that ʿAḍud al-Dawlah had constructed within the castle of Iṣṭakhr Yār, situated on a hill overlooking Iṣṭakhr proper.[79] Finally, it is noteworthy that at least one of these castles belonged to the group of so-called "Kurdish" tribes known as the Zamm al-Akrād.[80]

Religious Centers

Religious specialisms transcending those required of all Islamic cities, while not entirely lacking in Fārs, were scarcely more numerous than in Jibāl Province. Among the better-known shrines were the tomb of Saʿīd, brother of the theologian al-Ḥasan al-Baṣrī,[81] in the city of Khabr, and that of a certain *Shaykh* Gul Andām at Māyin, the principal urban center in the district of Rāmjird. On the road leading north from this latter city was the *mashhad* of Ismāʿīl, son of the seventh *imām* Mūsā al-Kāẓim. Abarqūh[82] was distinguished by its possession of the tomb of the greatly revered saint Ṭāʾūs al-Ḥaramayn, "The Peacock of the Two Sanctuaries" (that is, Makkah [Mecca] and al-Madīnah [Medina]).[83]

It is evident, too, that the Islamic sacral hierarchy in the tenth century had by no means wholly supplanted the old Zoroastrian order. Ibn Ḥawqal went so far to say that there were Zoroastrian temples in virtually every city and village in Fārs.[84] Among the most venerated was the temple in the town of Kāriyān, whence priests distributed the sacred fire throughout the province and far beyond. Moreover, not a few of the castles discussed in the preceding paragraph were actually in the hands of Zoroastrians. Al-Maqdisī tells us that adherents of that faith surpassed in numbers the combined total of Christians and Jews in the *iqlīm*.[85] Occasionally we encounter evidence of an apparent fusion of Islamic and older Persian beliefs, as when the mausoleum of Cyrus at Pasargadae was venerated by Muslims as the tomb of King Sulaymān's mother.[86]

Commentary

The urban system of Fārs Province, like that of Khūzistān previously described, was almost wholly a legacy from the Sāsānians, who had themselves inherited a good deal of it from their predecessors. The principal addition that the Arabs made to the system was the city of Shīrāz, although established near the site of a preexisting Sāsānian settlement, it was in all important respects a new foundation. Even so, it failed to develop significantly until selected as the Ṣaffārid capital in the second half of the ninth century and, more especially, after it became the seat of Buwayhid administration in the tenth. In this role it continued the old Persian tradition of maintaining a major focus of political power roughly in the geometrical center of the province—although not in the same *kūrah.*[87] And it was not only the structure of the urban hierarchy that was Persian: the vast majority of the population were Persian and gave a distinctive ambience to cities that were nominally Muslim. Nothing better illustrates the persistence of Sāsānian culture in Fārsī cities as late as the tenth century than the virtual omnipresence of Zoroastrians *(Gabr)* and their fire temples. Even in the Arab foundation of Shīrāz there were two such temples within the walls and another at one of the eight gates. At the same time, al-Maqdisī was castigating the Shīrāzī custom of decorating the *sūqs* on Zoroastrian festivals and denouncing infidels for not wearing the distinctive clothing *(ghiyār)* prescribed for *dhimmīs*. He also deplored the lack of respect accorded "Wearers of the Ṭaylasān," meaning the Muslim religious classes, and the prevailingly low moral tone of the province, which, he claimed, even countenanced prostitution in its cities.[88] Moreover, archaeological remains from the Persian empires were accessible without major excavation at more than forty sites in Fārs, of which the most extensive were at or near Iṣṭakhr, Fīrūzābād, and Bīshāpūr.[89] Arab and Persian alike, wherever they turned, could not escape the presence of the Persian past.

It is evident from the accounts of Mustawfī, the *Fārs-Nāmah,* and Yāqūt that after the tenth century the lower levels of the Fārsī urban hierarchy were reasonably strongly developed. There is little reason to doubt that this state of affairs was equally true of the tenth century, even though the topographers of the time furnish only faint intimations of such a development. In any case, this stratum of market towns depended primarily on the productivity of surrounding rural districts that were benefiting significantly from the agricultural revolution described in chapter 9. The majority of the irrigation systems underpinning these developments had been inherited from the Sāsānians, although some were extended in Islamic times and a few constructed de novo. Most of these latter stemmed from the initiatives of ʿAḍud al-Dawlah, including the famous Band-i ʿAḍudī dam, which al-Maqdisī praises as "one of the wonders of Fārs."[90] With the assistance of ten huge waterwheels, this dam raised the water level high enough to effect the irrigation of as many as three hundred villages.

At higher levels of the urban hierarchy the Arabs tended to increase the size of individual cities without bringing about major changes in the spatial organization of the system. And such increases in size, and sometimes in regional importance, were very often associated with the expansion of textile industries. These were deployed in two discrete and functionally specialized areas: a predominantly linen-manufacturing region in the northwest of the *iqlīm* and a predominantly cotton-manufacturing region in the southeast. Clearly, both specialisms owed something to the environment, for flax, although a climatically tolerant crop, does best in a reasonably firm and moist soil. The cotton plant, on the other hand, requires a long, frost-free summer and a considerable amount of moisture, which in southeastern Fārs could have been supplied generally in the form of rain or locally by irrigation water. But two other factors undoubtedly helped to establish the linen industry in the northwest. First, before it can be made into cloth, flax requires a good deal of preparatory labor in the field, a commodity more abundant in the relatively densely settled *kūrahs* of Ardashīr, Arrajān, and Sābūr than in the semiarid southeastern sector of the *iqlīm.* And second, although a preponderance of the flax consumed by the industry was grown locally, a proportion was imported from Egypt,[91] an expedient that may have drawn manufacture from upland valleys, where it was most strongly represented, to the coastal outposts at Sīnīz and Jannābā. This circumstance, together with the prevalence there of Egyptian-style manufactures such as *qaṣab, sharb,* and *dabīqī* cloths, also raises the interesting possibility that the linen industry had been introduced into Fārs directly from the Nile valley, but such a transmission has not been proven. That cotton was grown extensively in the southeastern sector of the province is attested by both the author of the *Fārs-Nāmah* and Mustawfī.[92]

The other component of the urban system that, generally speaking, appears to have developed fairly consistently under Muslim rule was the ports. It was true of those ports such as Sīnīz and Jannābā, which served the northwestern textile region and the metropolitan district around Shīrāz, but was especially evident in the case of Sīrāf, which al-Maqdisī perceived as rivalling al-Baṣrah in importance.

It was noted in chapter 3 that so-called district capitals *(mudun)* tended to be scarce in core regions of long-established settlement but more numerous in politically and/or ecologically marginal zones. Consequently it is not surprising that al-Maqdisī identified no cities in Fārs as belonging to this class.

Under the Buwayhids Fārs regained some of the prosperity it had known under pre-Muslim Persian dynasties. Shīrāz, especially under ʿAḍud al-Dawlah, ranked as one of the premier Islamic capitals and as an intellectual center of the first order. Other cities were expanded, industry developed, commerce facilitated, agricultural innovation encouraged, irrigation extended, roads constructed (especially to the holy places of Islam), caravanserais and hospitals founded, and in general the preexisting Sāsānian settlement pattern intensified within its already established framework. As for the renowned Fārsī vitality, let al-Iṣṭakhrī have the last word: "I have never known Fārsīs in any city by land or sea where they were not among the notables of that city."[93]

Chapter Eleven
The Urban System in Kirmān

. . . the province with the sweetest dates and the most servile inhabitants.
—Al-Maqdisī, *Aḥsan al-Taqasīm,* 33.

The Province of Kirmān encompassed territories intruding between Fārs on the west and the Dasht-i Kavīr (Great Desert) of central Persia on the east, and presenting a short coastline on the Strait of Hurmuz. As al-Iṣṭakhrī noted in his tenth-century description of its topography,[1] approximately one-fourth of the province was mountainous and consequently temperate in climate, and the rest desert,[2] so that for the most part urban centers were sparse on the ground and separated from one another by wide tracts of uncultivated (and as often as not uncultivable) land.

The position of Kirmān as a transitional zone between locally fertile and predominantly prosperous Fārs and one of the bleakest deserts on earth while straddling trade and pilgrim routes between the Persian Gulf and both India and Central Asia seems to have attracted dissidents and rebels throughout the first four centuries of Islam. Although the first Muslim Arabs arrived in the province in 638, it was not finally subdued until 649/50 and the control of the central government was never very secure. In 681/82 the countercaliph ʿAbd Allāh ibn Zubayr seized Kirmān and held it at least until 688/89.[3] In 691 the Khārijite ʿAṭīyah ibn al-Aswad usurped the governorship, which was not recovered for the caliphate until 695/96. Even then the province continued to be an attractive asylum for rebels in precarious circumstances, including Ḥamdān Qarmaṭ, founder of the Qarmaṭian movement, in 701/2 (702/3 in some sources). After the suppression of Yazīd ibn Muhallab's rebellion in about 720, however, the Umayyads were usually able to assert their control, most often through the agency of a governor of Khurāsān, an arrangement that was continued under the early ʿAbbāsids. In about 865, though, Kirmān was incorporated in the territories controlled by the Ṣaffārid brothers Yaʿqūb and ʿAmr ibn al-Layth; from a descendant of whom, in 907/8, it passed into the hands of the slave commander Subkarī. Although ʿAbbāsid rule was re-established at least nominally within three or four years, the Ṣaffārids collected revenue from the province as late as 929.

However, from the middle thirties of the tenth century until 968 Kirmān was governed by the Banū-Ilyās, who, although acknowledging the Sāmānids in the *khuṭbah,* acted as virtually independent rulers. Only in the latter year was the Buwayhid ʿAḍud al-Dawlah able to end Ilyāsid rule and bring Kirmān again under nominal ʿAbbāsid authority. Strangely enough, these vicissitudes in the history of the province seem to have had relatively little effect on its urban system until the disruptions consequent on ʿAḍud's campaign of reconquest—although the annual impost of half a million *dīnār*s exacted for several years by the Sāmānid Naṣr ibn Aḥmad must have proved an onerous drain on the province's resources.[4]

Marketing and Service Centers

Al-Maqdisī regarded al-Sīrjān[5] as the metropolis *(miṣr)* of Kirmān, a choice reflecting his persistent inclination to structure his urban hierarchies within what he perceived as politically stable, though not necessarily contemporary, frameworks.[6] In this instance he was harking back to the ninth century, when a governor *(wālī)* appointed from Baghdād had resided in the city, rather as if ʿAbbāsid rule were the normal state of affairs and the Buwayhids and Ilyāsids merely transient aberrations. Al-Sīrjān, located in a sleeve of territory (al-Iṣṭakhrī's phrase) projecting into central Fārs, had been the capital of the province in

Sāsānian times, and had continued as such under the Caliphate.[7] At the close of the ninth century al-Yaʿqūbī had considered it the most important city in Kirmān,[8] a point of view echoed by al-Iṣṭakhrī half a century later;[9] but in the mid-tenth century Muḥammad ibn Ilyās had transferred his government to Bardasīr, probably to distance his capital, and thereby his treasury, as far as possible from Buwayhid territory.[10] However, toward the end of the tenth century al-Maqdisī estimated that al-Sīrjān was still larger than Shīrāz in Fārs.[11] The city had two main *sūq*s, with the congregational mosque standing between them. Three centuries later Yāqūt asserted that, although al-Sīrjān was then only the second city of Kirmān, it possessed no less than forty-five mosques, both large and small.[12]

Below the metropolis were four *qaṣabāt,* each the chief city of a *kūrah* that the Arabs had adopted from the former Sāsānian administrative system. The most northerly was Bardasīr,[13] on the site of present-day Kirmān. Originally built by Ardashīr, founder of the Sāsānid dynasty, the city seems to have remained little more than a military cantonment until it was constituted as the seat of government of the semi-independent Ilyāsid dynasty in the tenth century. When al-Maqdisī was writing, it was still not a very large city,[14] but it was extremely strongly fortified.

The *kūrah* capital for the entire southern half of Kirmān Province was Jīruft,[15] on the only Kirmānī river that the medieval topographers mentioned by name, the Dīv Rūd (modern Khalīl Rūd). In the tenth century it was a large city, some two miles in diameter, set in the midst of an agricultural district producing crops of both lowland and upland types.[16] Bamm and Narmāsīr were farther east on the desert edge. The former was a regional service center with large *sūq*s within the fortified inner city and in the outer suburbs as well as on the Jarjān bridge, and three mosques: one in the citadel, one in the marketplace for Khārijites (who were by no means numerous but disproportionately wealthy), and one for Sunnīs in the textile *sūq.*[17] The citadel, standing close to the city proper, was considered to be impregnable. Narmāsīr, according to al-Maqdisī, was smaller than al-Sīrjān, but strongly fortified.[18] A third city on the desert fringe in the eastern sector of the province was the "district" capital *(madīnah)* of Khabīṣ, virtually an oasis surrounded by groves of date palms and mulberry gardens.[19] We have already had occasion to note that *mudun* were often situated in ecologically marginal zones such as this.

The lower levels of the urban hierarchy in Kirmān Province were unusually discontinuous, with vast extents of steppe and desert devoid of towns, sometimes of any form of permanent settlement at all. Al-Iṣṭakhrī observes that, whereas most deserts included tracts of pasturable terrain, the Wilderness of Khurāsān (Marfāzat Khurāsān)—the name by which Arab topographers subsumed both the Dasht-i Kavīr and the Dasht-i Lūṭ—repelled even nomadic incursions save on its fringes. Only caravan trails and post stations, al-Iṣṭakhrī notes, intruded on its solitude.[20] The smaller towns in the more arid sectors of Kirmān were essentially oases that were ringed, in climatically and edaphically suitable situations, by groves of date palms (note that al-Sīrjān and Bardasīr lay beyond the northern limit for reliable ripening of this fruit). Representative of those oasis towns whose date harvests deserved comment were Rikān,[21] Kurk,[22] and Bāhar[23] as well, of course, as the *qaṣabāt* of Bamm and Narmāsīr and the *madīnah* of Khabīṣ. Al-Maqdisī reports that at a particular season of the year, one hundred thousand camels converged on Narmāsīr to load up with dates for transport to various parts of Khurāsān.[24] Not altogether surprisingly, at that time the city became a stews of prostitution and profligacy.

On the slopes of the Jabal Bāriz and other uplands lying toward the center of the *iqlīm,* a modest increment of orographic precipitation permitted the cultivation of rain-fed crops to supplement those wholly dependent on *kāriz* irrigation.[25] Between al-Sīrjān and Bardasīr, for example, the *Ḥudūd* reports "260 villages, prosperous, pleasant, and populous."[26] The Jīruft District at the same time produced indigo, cardamom, and raisin syrup *(dūshāb),* as well as sweet melons and narcissi, from the last of which was extracted a celebrated perfume.[27] There is reason to think, though, that several parts of the province were better watered in the tenth century than at present, possibly as a result of a higher rainfall but more probably because of a more continuous forest cover helping to retain moisture in the soil. According to Ibn Ḥawqal, the Jabal Bāriz supported a forest canopy,[28] while al-Maqdisī records orchards as stretching uninterruptedly from Bardasīr to Māhān through what is now almost total desert; and Māhān itself was surrounded by gardens for a day's march in every direction.[29] In more-favored localities such as these, the network of lower-level service centers approached more closely that in, say, Fārs Province.

Transportation Foci

The situation of Kirmān as a transition zone between the relatively highly urbanized Province of Fārs and the vast desert over which caravan trails led to Khurāsān and Sijistān had induced in many of its cities the elaboration of break-of-bulk functions. The routes entering the province from the west without exception focused on al-Sīrjān and Bīmand, both situated in the salient of Kirmān territory that projected westward into Fārs. roads from Unās, Shahr-i Bābak, Iṣṭakhr, Shīrāz, and Dārābjird converged on this strip of land before radiating out again toward Bardasīr (itself a major node in the road system), Khabīṣ, Bamm, Narmāsīr, Rikān, Jīruft, and ultimately to Hurmuz.[30] Two cities offered particularly well-developed transport facilities and ancillary services. One of them, Narmāsīr, on the eastern frontier of Kirmān, was an important stage on the pilgrim road from Sijistān to Makkah (Mecca) as well as a distributing center for Indian goods brought by caravan over the Dasht-i Kavīr (Great Desert).[31] Khurāsānī merchants trading with ʿUmān were particularly prominent among its inhabitants. The other of these two caravan cities was Jīruft, situated where the road from India met the road from Hurmuz and epitomized by Ibn Ḥawqal as "the mart of Khurāsān and Sijistān."[32] Only slightly less important a node in the transportation network of the province was Maghūn, where roads from Rikān (and ultimately Sijistān) to the east and Jīruft to the north converged en route to Hurmuz. So prosperous was this city at the end of the tenth century that al-Maqdisī was moved to designate it—with some hyperbole, it is true—"the Baṣrah of Kirmān."[33]

Kirmān possessed only a short, but strategically positioned coastline around the eastern flank of the Gulf of Hurmuz. In the tenth century the port of Hurmuz, half a day's march (two post stages) along the bank of the creek called al-Jīr, was "the emporium of Kirmān."[34] Al-Iṣṭakhrī was much impressed by the size of the warehouses, where commodities of the Indian trade were stored, many of them being situated in outlying villages as much as two leagues from Hurmuz itself; most of the merchants lived in these same villages.[35] Nor was it only foreign goods that passed through the port, for al-Maqdisī notes that cereals grown in the Gulāshkird District were exported through Hurmuz.[36]

Industrial and Craft Centers

Specialist production in Kirmān was largely restricted to the processing of agricultural crops, notably dates in the oases of the east; *dhurrah,* cumin *(zirah),* and indigo farther west; sugarcane in the hinterland of Hurmuz; and sweet melons and narcissus flowers (for perfume) from Jīruft (p. 154 above).[37] In Kūhbanān and Bihābād, tutty *(tūtiyā),* an impure oxide of zinc used as an eye salve, was manufactured and exported to most parts of the Muslim world.[38] Although the presence of other minerals is mentioned by the topographers, including gold, silver, iron, copper, and sulfur, no urban developments seem to have been associated with their exploitation.[39]

Specialist craft industries having more than a local reputation were restricted to textile manufacturing, of which the *qaṣabah* Bamm was the principal center. Here were woven "magnificent, costly robes of great durability"; embroidered (?) *ṭaylasāns,* each of which might fetch as much as thirty *dīnār*s in the markets of ʿIrāq, Egypt, or Khurāsān; and turbans (pl. *ʿamāʾim*) greatly prized in those same countries. Bammī garments, adds Ibn Ḥawqal, were as durable as those of ʿAdan and Ṣanʿāʾ, and the robes manufactured in the city's workshops were "of the kind that kings acquire and hoard."[40] Al-Maqdisī, though, notes that Bammī-style textiles were also woven in the towns of Avārik and Mihrkird, and even as far afield as al-Sīrjān, while a majority of the garments reasonably attributable to Bamm itself were manufactured in the village of Jabal Kūd, a *farsakh* outside the city.[41] Al-Iṣṭakhrī also refers to a specialized production of linings (pl. *baṭāʾin*) in Zarand, whence they were exported to Fārs, ʿIrāq, Egypt, and the farthest parts of the Maghrib,[42] while Ibn Ḥawqal mentions that "the Sulṭān had formerly owned a *ṭirāz* factory in Bamm, but it had perished with him."[43] The *sulṭān* in question was presumably either the Buwayhid Rukn al-Dawlah or his father.

Fortified Settlements

In a province where tribal loyalties were still strong enough to compete with obligations to prince and polity, defensive structures were prominent features at all levels of the settlement hierarchy. Bardasīr, for example, although a relatively small city, was protected by three fortresses: one *qalʿah* (citadel) in the center of the city beside the congregational mosque, another on the summit of a hill outside the city whither Ibn Ilyās was wont to repair at night, and a *ḥiṣn* (fort) guarding one of the city's four gates.[44] But it was in the cities on the eastern, desert frontier that fortifications intruded most noticeably on urban morphology, for they were always likely to be raided by Balūṣ (Balūch) and Qufṣ tribesmen. Rāvar, on the edge of the Great Desert, was furnished with an unusually strong fortress specifically for the protection of this frontier.[45]

Religious Centers

The level of sanctity of Kirmān cities nowhere rose above that of the locally revered shrine.[46]

Commentary

Arab settlement in Kirmān at the time of the Muslim conquest was neither widespread nor intense, but those tribesmen who did put down roots in the new land appear to have been assimilated fairly rapidly—although, with the exceptions of the Gulf coast, the two successive *amṣār,* and a few smaller towns such as Māhān, they were rather widely dispersed.[47] The urban system that we have been able to reconstruct was essentially a modified version of that of Sāsānian times. The larger cities had all been pre-Muslim foundations, and al-Maqdisī's retention of al-Sīrjān as *miṣr* of the *iqlīm* did not significantly affect the overall structure of the urban hierarchy. The transference of the capital to Bardasīr, however, did establish the *miṣr* somewhat closer to the geometrical center of the province (although not to the center of its population distribution); but at the same time it capped the settlement hierarchy with a metropolis whose relatively small size betrayed the fact that political expediency rather than economic growth so constituted it.

No new towns of any size or importance were built during the seventh through tenth centuries, and neither ʿAbbāsids nor Buwayhids sponsored significant construction projects. However, the Ilyāsids, particularly Muḥammad ibn Ilyās, were responsible for a considerable number of buildings in the territories under their control. In his new *miṣr* of Bardasīr, for example, Muḥammad raised a mosque, rebuilt the citadel outside the walls and surrounded it with gardens, and constructed two new forts. The same ruler also built a citadel to protect the sizable textile-manufacturing city of Zarand, a fortress between the small towns of Avārik and Mihrjird, and additions to the defenses of Khabīṣ. At Ghubayrā he built a market below the walls, and his son Abū al-Muẓaffar Ilyasaʿ is credited with having constructed the Dār al-Imārah in Bardasīr.[48] None of this changed the basic lineaments of the urban system to any measurable degree, but four centuries of Arab rule did witness, even if it did not proximately cause, a perceptible increase in the size of some cities, notably al-Sīrjān and Bamm.

The harsh nature of much of the terrain and the discontinuous character of the settlement pattern rendered Kirmān Province an attractive refuge for dissidents and renegades, who not infrequently sought the support of turbulent tribal groups inhabiting the region. Prominent among these latter in early Islamic times were the Qufṣ and Jabal Bārizīs, upland agriculturalists and stock raisers; and the Balūṣ, herdsmen on the lower slopes of the Qufṣ Mountains. All were harried in turn by Muslim armies, by Ṣaffārids, Buwayhids, and Sāmānids, but none was ever permanently subdued. Ibn Ḥawqal reports that seven ridges in the Qufṣ chain each had its own chieftain, and that they collectively raided as far afield as Sijistān and Fārs.[49] The *Ḥudūd* adds that government tax collectors *(ʿāmil-i sulṭān)* did not venture into the Qufṣ strongholds but assessed their collections under a *muqāṭaʿah* arrangement and farmed them to the tribal chiefs.[50] The Qufṣ also joined with the Balūṣ in aiding Muḥammad ibn Ilyās in his unsuccessful attempt to prize Kirmān from the Buwayhid grasp. A combined tribal force was defeated by the Buwayhid army in 970 and the Balūṣ again in 972, after which the survivors were resettled elsewhere, their place in the mountains being taken by peasants who farmed the land as sharecroppers.[51] Shortly thereafter the Buwayhids mounted a successful campaign against the tribes of the hot coastal lowlands (Jurūmīyah).[52] Even more turbulent than the Qufṣ and Balūṣ—according to al-Iṣṭakhri at any rate—were the tribes of the Bāriz Mountains. They had adopted Islam as their faith only in ʿAbbāsid times and had submitted to Muslim rulers only under the Ṣaffārids.[53]

These and other tribes of the mountains and deserts were a perpetual threat to the caravan trade crossing Kirmān between Fārs and Khurāsān; and it was not unknown for a local ruler to aid and abet their banditry. It was rumored, for instance, and subsequently reported as fact by Miskawayh, that Muḥammad ibn Ilyās was no better than a bandit *(jarā majrā baʿḍ al-mutaṣaʿlikīn),* in league and sharing the spoils with Qufṣ and Balūṣ freebooters.[54] Ibn Ḥawqal was sure that ʿAḍud al-Dawlah's campaigns had broken the power of the Balūṣ once and for all,[55] and al-Maqdisī reports that caravans crossing the Great Desert were in his day tolerably safe from marauders if they had an escort provided by the Buwayhid *amīr* of Fārs.[56] However, these conditions did not last, and before the advent of the Saljūks the tribes had resumed their depredations. Although Ibn Ḥawqal attributes the decline in provincial revenues during the second half of the tenth century to disruptions consequent on Aḍud al-Dawlah's ousting of the Ilyāsids,[57] the prevalence of banditry along the caravan trails crossing the province must have done something to hinder urban development.

The final verdict on the urban system of Kirmān in the tenth century is that it was attenuated and discontinuous. Especially in the more arid parts of the province, central-place functions tended to be relatively less developed, and break-of-bulk services relatively more so, than in the more favored provinces previously discussed. The manufacturing component in the settlement hierarchy was hardly more than modest, the commercial component subject to disruption whenever the central government was weak, and the religious component negligible.

Chapter Twelve

The Urban System in al-Riḥāb

. . . the abode *(jāygāh)* of merchants, fighters for the Faith *(ghāziyān)*, and strangers from all parts.

—*Ḥudūd al-ʿĀlam*, 142.

Al-Riḥāb ("The Heights" or "High Plains") was the name that al-Maqdisī used to denote the violently fractured plateau country where the Pontic and Taurus ranges of Asia Minor meet the Zagros and Alburz (Elburz) ranges of Īran. Generally speaking, the plateau surfaces—often covered by geologically recent lava flows—no less than the peaks and volcanic cones, have repelled permanent settlement, which has concentrated in riverine tracts and in the basins of the three great lakes of the region. In the tenth century each of these lakes was the focus of an administratively defined province: Armīniyah, around Lake Vān; Arrān, in the angle between the Kur (Kura) and Aras Rivers[1] to the east of the Gukchah Lake (Lake Sevan); and Ādharbāyjān (Azerbaijan),[2] around Lake Urmīyah.[3] Of these provinces, even as late as the tenth century Arrān and Armīniyah were barely accounted part of the Dār al-Islam. Despite the presence of governors appointed by the caliphs and the early penetration of Muslim settlers into these areas, the majority of the population was still Christian, thereby preventing Arab topographers from according these regions more than perfunctory treatment. Ādharbāyjān too was less important than it was to become under the Mongols, being still essentially a frontier zone of Islam, with its urban centers mostly small.

The *iqlīm* in its totality as defined by al-Maqdisī corresponded fairly closely to the territories that, in the mid-tenth century, had been ruled by the Daylamī Musāfirid dynasty.[4] However, that correspondence at least partially masked a persistent disaggregation of political authority. At the time of the Arab conquest the region supported a mosaic of quasi-autonomous statelets and dependencies, and a similar pattern of power distribution held at the end of the tenth century. In Ādharbāyjān, after the caliph Muʿtaṣim quelled a revolt by the Khurramī rebel Bābak in 837, ʿAbbāsid control gradually weakened. Nevertheless, governors of the Sājid family maintained at least a nominal ʿAbbāsid presence in the region until the last of their line revolted in 929, after which the power vacuum was filled by native dynasties. After a brief subjection to the Arabo-Kurdish, Khārijī Daysam dynasty, in 941 Ādharbāyjān was conquered by the Daylamī *marzubān* ibn Muḥammad of the Bāṭinī (Ismāʿīlī) persuasion, whose family was eventually deposed by a line of Kurdicized Rawwādids that ruled the province from 984 to 1070.[5]

Meanwhile, in Armīniyah neither the Umayyads nor the ʿAbbāsids were able to establish secure authority despite the efforts of determined Arab governors and a mass deportation of the nobility in 852. A decade later the caliph al-Mutawakkil was constrained to recognize a member of the Bagratid family as the chief prince *(biṭrīq al-baṭāriqah)* of the province. Nearly a quarter of a century subsequently, the reigning caliph conferred on the same prince the style of king; and the family, through many and severe vicissitudes, held on to power in central and northern Armīniyah throughout the tenth century.[6] In southern Armīniyah the Ardzrunī family ruled over the kingdom of Vaspurakan, with the city of Vān as its capital.[7] In addition, there was a series of small, semi-independent statelets and several Arab amīrates, none of which acknowledged the dominion of the caliphate. And the whole unstable political congeries was further complicated by incursions of ʿAbbāsid, Byzantine, Sājid, Ḥamdānid, and Musāfirid forces, all maneuvering for control of the province.

Conditions in Arrān were no more stable.[8] In the seventh century the territory was occupied by a plethora of small kingdoms, some of which owed allegiance to the Khazars. Throughout the following century it became an almost permanent war zone between these predominantly nomadic people spilling out from the Volga steppe and the armies of the Caliphate. As early as 725, large Arab garrisons were established in the province, with their headquarters at Bardhāʿah (Barda); but not until the governorship of Marwān ibn Muḥammad (731–44)[9] were the Arabs able to assert their ascendancy over the Khazars. Henceforth local Arrānian, and sometimes Armīniyan, rulers laying claim to lands within the province would pay taxes and tribute to the ʿAbbāsids. From 941 to 957, most of Arrān (as well as Ādharbāyjān) was subject to the *marzubān* ibn Muḥammad ibn Musāfir, during which time Bardhaʿah was plundered by the Rūs.[10] Subsequently Arrān fell under the sway of the Shaddādids, probably of Kurdish origin, who in 941 succeeded in establishing their capital at Ganjah and, during the ensuing two centuries, earned a reputation throughout the Islamic world as doughty fighters for the Faith.

In short, in al-Riḥāb political fragmentation combined with a highly accidented relief and the vicissitudes of a frontier situation to inhibit the emergence of a coherent urban hierarchy. And al-Maqdisī's urban system *qua* system must have been largely a fiction even during the middle years of the tenth century, when the Musāfirids had imposed a rare political unity on much of the region.

Marketing and Service Centers

Al-Maqdisī designated Ardabīl,[11] capital of the Musāfirid family,[12] as the metropolis of the whole *iqlīm* of al-Riḥāb. In his time it was a reasonably large city, about two-thirds of a league in diameter, on the upper waters of a tributary of the Qārā Ṣū River, itself an affluent of the Aras. In its layout it incorporated the basic elements of urban design characteristic of the province, and, indeed, of the Īrānian cultural realm in general. At the heart of the city was an enceinte (walled for most of the period with which we are concerned) in which governmental edifices and private dwellings clustered about a citadel,[13] while an outer suburb was bisected both latitudinally and longitudinally by streets serving as the main *sūqs*. At the intersection of these streets, and therefore in the midst of the markets, stood the congregational mosque. However, in 943 the walls of the city were demolished by the *marzubān* ibn Muḥammad in reprisal for the inhabitants having extended more than a perfunctory welcome to the Daysamī conqueror Ibn Shadhalawayh.[14]

At the second level of the urban hierarchy were two "provincial" capitals *(qaṣabāt)*. Barda (Bardhāʿah; Armenian Partaw), the chief city of Arrān, stood on the bank of the Tharthūr (Terter) River at a point where that stream entered the plains of the lower Kur River. Built in the form of a square with sides a mile in length, it was much the largest city in those parts. In Ibn Ḥawqal's estimation, all of the cities between al-ʿIrāq and Tabaristān, only al-Rayy (Rey) and Iṣfahān were larger.[15] The produce of its environs (known as al-Andarāb), where gardens and orchards were continuous for a day's journey in every direction, was brought weekly into a great market held at the Kurdish Gate (Bāb al-Akrād) of the city. Because the market was held on Sundays (Greek Κυριακὴ = the Lord's Day) the district became known locally as al-Kurkī.[16] By reason of its productive environs and its strategic importance as a military base for raids into Khazar territory, by the tenth century Bardhāʿah had become a notably prosperous city that al-Maqdisī did not scruple to characterize as "the Baghdād of Arrān."[17] Despite this encomium, it does not appear to have developed its manufacturing sector to any significant degree.

Although Dabīl[18]—the second *qaṣabah* in al-Maqdisī's urban hierarchy, a persistent locus of provincial government, and for at least three centuries the principal urban center in Armīniyah—was also larger than Ardabīl, it received only cursory attention from Arab topographers, probably because its mainly Kurdish inhabitants were predominantly Christian. However, this deficiency was largely compensated for in the Armenian histories, which naturally focused attention on their own seat of government. In any case the congregational mosque, standing side by side with the church, was here deprived of the preeminence it enjoyed in a predominantly Islamic city.[19] Throughout the four centuries considered here, Dabīl had a troubled history. Direct Muslim administration began with the appointment of an *ostikan* (Arab governor) during the caliphate of Muʿāwiyah, as a result of which the city was furnished with a *dār al-imārah,* a mosque, a prison, and a mint; but for the ensuing three centuries there was seldom a lasting peace. Civil wars and foreign invasions followed one another in almost predictable succession. To mention only a few of the vicissitudes experienced by the city during the tenth century: in the 920s either one or two Greek expeditions invested the city; in 937 King Gagik of Vaspurakan compelled the inhabitants to pay tribute; in 941/42 Daysam ibn Ibrāhīm al-Kurdī of Ādharbāyjān was striking his coinage in the city; in about 951, after Daysam and a Musāfirid had contested the rulership of the city, both lost it to the founder of the Shaddādid dynasty; in about 953 a Musāfirid recaptured the city, but soon after 983 it passed into the hands of Abū Dulaf al-Shaybānī, *amīr* of Goghthn, who in turn was forced to surrender it to the Rawwādids in 987. A year or two later, however, Abū Dulaf reclaimed the city. Finally—so far as the tenth century was concerned—the Bagratunī king Gagik I defeated the *amīr* and presumably established himself in Dabīl. Nor were wars and conquest the only impediments to urban development, for in 893 the city was ravaged by a major earthquake that destroyed a large number of buildings, including the palace of the Catholicos.[20]

At the third level of the administrative hierarchy were three *mudun:* al-Shammākhīyah, Mūghān, and Tabrīz. The first of these, capital of the Sharvān District, was the focus of a productive agricultural region at the foot of the mountains on the opposite edge of the lower Kur plains from Bardhāʿah. As such it lay outside the conventional limits of Arrān but in the kind of administratively marginal zone typically governed from a *madīnah.*[21] The city had originally been named in honor of Shammākh ibn Shujāʿ, who was ruling over Sharvān toward the end of the eighth century.[22] This line of Sharvān *shāh*s maintained their control of the area certainly until some time in the mid-tenth century, and perhaps longer. However, in 919 the city was rebuilt by the Sharvān *shāh* Yazīd II and renamed Yazīdīyah.[23] Mūghān[24] was the regional center for the swampy plain that made up the southern half of the composite delta of the Kur and Aras Rivers. Its precise location cannot now be determined from the topographical information available, but nearly a century ago Le Strange advanced reasons for believing that it was identical with the city known to Mustawfī in the fourteenth century as Bajarvān.[25] The third of the *mudun* was Tabrīz, in the upper part of a broad valley leading down to Lake Urmīyah. Although a city on this site had, under the name of Tauris, become the capital of the Armenian king Tiridates III in the third century A.D., it had remained small until the mid-eighth century, when a certain al-Rawwād al-Azdī settled there. He and other members of his family constructed palaces and subsequently ringed the expanded settlement with a wall. Despite its virtual destruction by an earthquake in 858, it had developed into an impressive regional capital by the end of the tenth century.[26] The walls of the city had been built by ʿAlā ibn Aḥmad al-Azdī, an ʿAbbāsid financial agent for Armīniyah, in about 865.[27]

The lower ranks of the urban hierarchy were filled by cities disposed along the coastal plain bordering the Caspian Sea, along the river valleys leading into the mountainous heart of the *iqlīm,* and in the depressions containing the great lakes. The waters of both the Vān and Urmīyah Lakes are brackish, the latter especially so, and fluctuate considerably in extent, so that in summer the receding waters leave tracts of black, fetid mud exposed. For this reason settlements have traditionally tended to avoid the lakeshores in favor of sites on the valley slopes, particularly the banks of streams capable of supplying water for irrigation. In locations of this character around Lake Vān were the relatively populous city of Akhlāṭ;[28] Arjīsh,[29] the market center for a prosperous grain-producing region; Bārkīrī;[30] a town below the walls of the fortress of Vasṭān for which the topographers have bequeathed us no name[31] at a rather greater distance from the lake, Bitlis (Badlīs), which, in the thirteenth century when Yāqūt was compiling his dictionary, was the service center of an apple-exporting region;[32] and Vān, a town that two topographers mention but neglect to describe.[33] Within the basin of the Urmīyah Lake were also a good number of settlements occupying similar sites, several of them founded by Arab *shaykh*s and their followers. Among the more important were Ṭarūj,[34] Dākharraqān,[35] Laylān,[36] Urmīyah,[37] and the Kurdish city of Salmās.[38] Marāghah,[39] fortified as an Arab military base for operations against the Khazars by the caliph Marwān II

(r. 744–50), had served as the district capital until the government treasury and administration were transferred to Ardabīl. It occupied a situation analogous to that of Tabrīz, specifically in the broad Ṣāfī valley where that river broke out of the mountain fastnesses on its way down to Lake Urmīyah. The fortifications of the city, which had been rebuilt by Hārūn al-Rashīd and repaired by the caliph al-Maʾmūn, were razed in 908 by order of Yūsuf Abū al-Sāj Dīvdād, founder of the Sājid dynasty.

Other rural service centers that happen to have been listed by Ibn Ḥawqal included Mīyānij (Mianeh), Khūnaj, Khuy (Khawī, Khroy), Marand, Barzand, Warthān, Baylaqān, Sūq Jābrawān, Āhar, and Warzaqān. All were described by that author as small towns in districts bountifully endowed with agricultural and horticultural products and blessed with an abundant labor force that permitted intensive cultivation. "This region," he writes, "is fortunate in its harvests and much blessed. Fruits can be obtained for almost nothing and food is so cheap as to seem free."[40] And these views were echoed in other contemporary accounts. The *Ḥudūd,* for example, characterizes more than a score of towns as "prosperous," while sometimes fleshing out such generalized ascriptions with references to "flourishing gardens" *(marāghah),* "a flourishing countryside with many fields and a great deal of fruit (Bardāʿ, for Bardhāʿah), or simply "extensive fields" (Ganjah and Shamkūr [Mutawakkilīyah]). Ushnūh seems to have cultivated a profitable commercial relationship with transhumant Kurds who pastured their flocks outside the city in summer, which led to a series of fairs arising at different seasons of the year that attracted traders from considerable distances.[41] It should not be overlooked, though, that in many districts this prosperity was achieved through the medium of large, Arab-owned landholdings worked by a not always wholly pliant indigenous peasantry.

Transportation Foci

The chief transportation foci in al-Riḥāb were nearly all ranged along the high roads that continued northward from Jibāl Province. One of these, leaving the Khurāsān road at Qirmīsīn, entered Ādharbāyjān at Barzah, where it bifurcated into branches following the lines of settlements on respectively the western and eastern slopes above the Urmīyah Lake, thereby ensuring a caravan-servicing function for cities such as Urmīyah, Salmās, Laylān, Marāghah, Dih Khuwārqān, Tabrīz, and Marand. The two branches came together again at Khawī, whence the road continued northward to Dabīl in Arrān. Thence an important caravan trail wound its way northwestward through the eastern Pontic ranges to Ṭarābazandah (Trebizond, Trabzon) on the Black Sea, the principal port by which Byzantine goods found their way into the eastern Muslim lands. Although Armenians dominated the carrying trade, some Muslim merchants resided more or less permanently in Ṭarābazandah to organize commercial ventures into the Greek territories and to handle the import of commodities from Constantinople.[42]

A second route, which diverged from the Khurāsān road at Hamadhān, split into two at Zanjān in northern Jibāl, with one branch turning northwestward to Tabrīz along the line followed by the present-day highway from Tehran to Tabrīz, and the other running northward through Ardabīl to Mūghān, Baylaqān, Bardhāʿah, and so to Tiflīs (Tblisi) in Gurjistān (Georgia).[43] The most northerly outpost of Islam was Bāb al-Abwāb ("Gate of the Gates": entrances to the passes), a port on the Caspian Sea (Baḥr al-Khazar) a short distance north of the estuary of the Samūr River[44] and therefore deep in Khazar country. In the tenth century the city was larger than the metropolis of Ardabīl, and the principal center for trade with the infidels. The chief commodity handled by the port was slaves, who, as the *Ḥudūd* puts it, "were of every kind of infidel from that part of the world."[45] Its harbor was protected by two moles whose extremities were joined by a chain to prevent unauthorized entry.[46] Bākūyah (Baku) was a port on the Caspian Sea that seems to have been better known for its naphtha springs than for its trading functions, although al-Masʿūdī in the mid-tenth century reported that vessels were clearing the port for Gīlān, Daylam, and perhaps even for Itil, the Khazar capital in the Volga delta.[47]

Industrial and Craft Centers

The natural products of these northern lands were not numerous. The apples of Badlīs have already been mentioned, and to them should be added the perfumed melons of Marāghah; the horses and cattle traded by the Kurdish town of Ushnūh to al-Mawṣil (Mosul) in Aqūr Province; the saffron, mules, and slaves (obtained from the Khazar lands) of Bāb al-Abwāb; beaver pelts from Qabalah; and several types of fish from the lakes and rivers, notably the sturgeon *(surmāhī)*[48] of Bardhāʿah and Warthān and the *ṭirrīkh* (a kind of herring) from Lake Vān.[49] Mineral resources were restricted to borax from the margins of the same lake, which was exported to al-ʿIrāq and elsewhere for use in baking; certain arsenical rocks occurring south of that lake; and from Bākūyah the aforementioned naptha, "all that was used in the Daylamān country," according to the *Ḥudūd;*[50] to which Abū Dulaf adds that the lease *(qabālah)* of the main naphtha seepage was valued at one thousand *dirhams* a day and that of another yielding so-called white naphtha at an equal amount.[51]

Like its neighbors in the northern tier of provinces, al-Riḥāb contributed its share to the textile trade of the Caliphate, although it is sometimes difficult to discriminate between local manufactures and cloths imported from the Byzantine territories. This is particularly true in records relating to the period prior to the tenth century. Al-Jāḥiẓ, for instance, writing in the ninth century, treated both classes of textiles together: "The best quality and most expensive material," he noted, "is the crimson-dyed, Armenian mohair with a double woof *(al-marʿazzā al-qirmizī al-Armanī al-munayyar),* followed in descending order by the striped silk *(al-khazz al-raqm),* the Khusrawānī-style brocade of Rūmī [i.e., Byzantine] manufacture,[52] the khazz-silk brocaded in the manner of Maysānī cloth,[53] and the *buzyūn* silk[54]."[55] Altogether Jāḥiẓ listed felts *(lubūd),* cushions *(barādhiʿ),* upholstery cloth *(farsh),* fine-quality carpets *(busuṭ),* trouserbands *(tikkah),* and wool *(ṣūf)* among the exports from the region.[56] In the tenth century al-Iṣṭakhrī, Ibn Ḥawqal, al-Maqdisī, and the *Ḥudūd* jointly confirmed the importance of these manufactures,[57] and made particular reference to the provincial metropolis of Ardabīl and the Armenian *qaṣabah* of Dabīl, as well as to the cities of Marand, Bardhāʿah, Baylaqān, Khuwī, Badlīs, Arjīsh (Erciş), and Akhlāṭ. Bāb al-Abwāb was singled out by al-Iṣṭakhrī as the sole center in all Ādharbāyjān, Armīniyah, and Arrān in which linen was produced,[58] while several authors commented on the raising of silkworms in the neighborhood of Bardhāʿah and the resulting manufacture of *ibrīsm* silk, much of which was exported to Fārs and Khūzistān.[59]

Despite the volume and quality of textile manufactures in al-Riḥāb, the most distinctive feature of the industry was the use of two special dyes. We have already encountered the bright red coloring agent prepared from the *qirmiz* insect in Fārs Province,[60] but al-Riḥāb was the territory in which it was used most abundantly. Wool, mohair, and silk alike were treated with this dye and exported far beyond the boundaries of the *iqlim.* Particularly prominent in this process were the environs of Dabīl, Ardabīl, and Marand.[61] Al-Balādhurī notes that a settlement near Dabīl known as Azdisāṭ actually earned the sobriquet of "Qirmiz Village" *(Qaryat al-Qirmiz),* but he did not specify whether this was because of the settlement's importance in the production of the dye or in its use.[62]

The second of the distinctive dyes, also of a bright red color, was obtained from the root of the madder plant, *Rubia tinctorum,* Linn. Its use was restricted virtually to Arrān and Sharvān. Bardhāʿah, Warthān, and Bāb al-Abwāb were the cities particularly associated with this process,[63] although Ibn Ḥawqal reports that "Madder is found throughout the land of Arrān from the most distant parts of Bāb al-Abwāb to Tiflīs [in Gurjistān], and from the vicinity of the Nahr al-Rūs (the Volga) to the districts of Gurgān." The same author adds that the madder was carried across the Caspian Sea to Gurgān and thence by the land route to India.[64]

Fortified Settlements

Somewhat surprisingly in view of the frontier location of al-Riḥāb and the reputation of its inhabitants as *ghāziyān,* military constructions do not figure unduly prominently in the early descriptions of the towns of the *iqlīm.* Perhaps this situation reflected the fact that many of the Arab settlers resided in their own castles in rural areas. It is true, though, that many cities, probably most, were walled; castle keeps were sometimes mentioned; Hārūn al-Rashīd had further fortified Marāghah; and a great fortress *(qalʿah)* existed on the frontier between Armīniyah and Arrān.[65] However, the military function does not appear to have been the dominant, or even primary, role of any city in the *iqlīm,* even including Bardhāʿah, which was described explicitly enough as a frontier fortress.

Religious Centers

The Islamic sacral hierarchy in al-Riḥāb was poorly developed, and the two shrines of importance in the tenth century were in territories only partially Islamicized.

Muslim tradition, but not much else, connected Mūghān (Bajarvān) with the Fountain of Life allegedly discovered there by the prophet Khiḍr (Elias);[66] and al-Shammākhīyah (Yazīdīyah), conveniently remote in Sharvān, was often identified as the site of the Rock of Mūsā referred to in the Qurʾānic *Sūrah* of the Cave.[67]

Commentary

The urban system of al-Riḥāb was probably the least integrated of any province in the Islamic world. In other *iqlīm*s such as the Arabian Peninsula or the Maghrib, the system was often compartmentalized, but on a grander scale. In Arabia, for instance, although the Ḥijāzī, Yamanī, and ʿUmānī subsystems were functionally almost totally discrete and generated relatively little interaction among themselves, each constituted a reasonably well integrated urban hierarchy in its own right. And the same could be said of the North African, Andalusian, and Iṣqiliyan (Sicilian) subsystems in the *iqlīm* rubricated as al-Maghrib. But in al-Riḥāb the compartmentalization was often evident at the level of the individual city. The vicissitudes of political and economic fortune that were rehearsed for Dabīl on page 160 were by no means unique to that city: rather, they were the norm for many settlements. Under such circumstances systemic integration over a substantial extent of territory was inevitably rare and hardly ever enduring.

In fact the urban system of al-Riḥāb was hardly a system at all but rather, at any given time, a congeries of partially, quasi-, and fully autonomous political entities, each dependent on the integrative power of a principal city and its associated settlements. Despite the existence of a few more or less permanent centroids of power in especially fertile and/or strategic localities, political fragmentation, reinforced by dramatically dissected relief and ethnic diversity, ensured a prevailingly disjunctive urban system within the *iqlīm*. The principal exception was the period of Musāfirid dominance in the tenth century, which, as we have already noted, seems to have provided al-Maqdisī with the political basis for the *iqlīm*.

During the first four centuries of the Islamic era few new towns were established in al-Riḥāb and the urban system retained essentially its pre-Muslim lineaments. Marāghah had apparently been established as an Arab military camp either on the site of, or close to, Sāsānian Afrāzah Rūdh in the mid-eighth century; Tabrīz, although on the site of a pre-Muslim settlement, became fully urban only when it was constituted as the seat of the independent Rawwādī dynasty in the mid-ninth century; Narīr and Sūq Jābrawān were settled by Arab tribesmen who "ordered their own affairs as if the *ʿāmil* of Ādharbāyjān did not exist"; Mutawakkilīyah, formerly Shamkūr, was both rebuilt and renamed by the eponymous caliph in 854; and al-Shammākhīyah was named, and probably rebuilt, for one Sharvān-*shāh,* before being again rebuilt and renamed for another, this time as Yazīdīyah.

There were also less dramatic changes in certain of the cities of al-Riḥāb occasioned by shifts in population. In Armīniyah and Arrān particularly, the presence of Arab administrations attracted such a volume of Arab immigration into some cities that they eventually became for all intents and purposes Arab settlements. A prime example of this process working itself out is afforded by Dabīl. More generally, Joseph Marquart asserts—although on what evidence is uncertain—that Arab administrators ordered the evacuation of whole quarters in some cities in order to leave them open to Arab settlement.[68] In Ādharbāyjān, Barzah, al-Mayānij, and Khalbāthah were each settled (though probably not founded) by Arab tribesmen but were not permitted *minbar*s, the symbol of caliphal authority, until the mid-ninth century. Interestingly enough, in the case of Barzah, that privilege had to be imposed on the inhabitants against their will.

It is noteworthy, though, that the disaggregated nature of the urban system did not prevent the growth or subvert the prosperity of some of its component cities. The basis of this prosperity was the agricultural productivity of the valleys and lacustrine basins within the *iqlīm*. Writing in the second half of the tenth century, Ibn Ḥawqal commented on "the highly productive rural districts and prosperous regions where freehold estates yield abundant harvests and revenues. In all these mountains, districts, and towns and on these plains," he added, "one cannot but be impressed with the low cost of living, the fertility of the soils, the pastures dense with flocks and herds, the produce of the farms . . . the trees, watercourses, fruits of all sorts both fresh and dried, and timber of every kind."[69] And this agricultural productivity was reflected in the economic structures of cities at all levels of the hierarchy, from Bardhāʿah, with its fertile fields extending for a day's journey in every direction and its function as a regional service center underpinning its role as the administrative capital of Arrān; to Sarāt (for Sarāb), the center of a prosperous farming region astride the road from Ardabīl to Tabrīz which was almost entirely in the hands of large landowners; to the small town of Kalantar, set amid grain fields below Mount Sabalān.

Although the urban system—so called—of al-Riḥāb underwent no major structural changes during the first four centuries of the Islamic era, there are scattered but fairly conclusive indications that certain cities at each of its hierarchical levels grew in size and importance. Sometimes, as in the case of Dabīl, this was the result of Arab settlement in the city. In similar fashion Marand took a new lease on life when Abū al-Baʿīth Ḥalbas of the tribe of Rabīʿah and his followers settled there; Urmīyah, when Ṣadagah ibn ʿAlī, a client of Azd, took it over; and Miyānah, when ʿAbd Allāh ibn Jaʿfar of the tribe of Hamdān fortified it. The al-Awd clan occupied Barzah, Murr ibn ʿAmr al-Mawṣilī of the Ṭayy confederacy ruled in Nayrīz, and the lineage of al-Ashʿath ibn Qays of Kindah held Sarāb. At other times such a development was consequent on the assumption of administrative functions, as when al-Shammākhīyah became the seat of the Sharvān-*shāhs*. In still other instances, as at Bāb al-Abwāb, increases in prosperity and size were dependent on strategic trading locations; and in still others such growth was generated by industrial enterprises, which in virtually every case turned out to be involved in one way or another with textile manufacture. The cities that prospered most memorably were, not unexpectedly, usually those combining an important administrative role with one or more of the other above-mentioned functions.

In view of the political instability of the *iqlīm,* it is surprising that the cities of the region manifested the degree of prosperity that they did. It is true that Ibn Ḥawqal lamented the effects of the harsh rule of the Sallārids (the dynastic name by which he knew the Musāfirids) on Ardabīl, which he likened to an invalid in comparison with its former healthy condition, "when caravans had brought great quantities of merchandise to the city."[70] He also deplored a similar decline in the prosperity of Bardhāʿah, where, he claimed, only five bakers were at work in place of the twelve hundred of former times. Interestingly enough, though, he attributed this decline not to the Russian invasion of 943—which the city had apparently weathered rather well—but to misgovernment and excessive taxation, presumably by the Musāfirids. To Ibn Ḥawqal's litany of calamities, a twelfth-century redactor added incursions from "the neighbourhood of al-Kurj," which in this context can only have referred to raids instigated by the Shaddādids of Ganjah.[71] There is no doubt but that internal dissension and external aggression from time to time hindered the development of individual cities and perhaps even segments of the urban hierarchy much in the manner deplored by Ibn Ḥawqal—due allowance being made for the fact that he was something of a Jeremiah—but our final conclusion must be that the system, disaggregated though it was for most of the first four centuries of Islam, survived remarkably intact.

Chapter Thirteen
The Urban System in al-Daylam

> . . . the province producing the greatest quantity of wool and silk and, in proportion to its extent, yielding the highest revenue.
>
> —Al-Maqdisī, *Aḥsan al-Taqāsīm,* 33.

Al-Daylam—or, more commonly, the dual form *al-Daylamān*—originally denoted the mountainous districts lying between the territories of Gīlān, Qazwīn, and Zanjān. In the tenth century, following the success of certain Daylamī *amīrs* in reviving the old Īrānian national tradition and ultimately establishing their supremacy over the Baghdād caliphate, the term was often used to include all the lands bordering the southern shores of the Caspian Sea. Al-Maqdisī provides an extreme example of this usage, for he included not only Gīlān, Ṭabaristān, Gurgān, and Qūmis in his Province of al-Daylam, but also the Khazar territory to the north.[1]

With this last we are not here concerned, for it lay outside the Islamic political realm. The other provinces may be said to have comprised the Alburz Mountains and their environs. Ṭabaristān was the mountain chain proper together with the lowlands bordering the Caspian Sea; Qūmis, the narrow zone of oases strung along the southern edge of the Alburz between the foothills and the Dasht-i Kavīr (Great Desert of central Persia); Gīlān,[2] essentially the delta lands of the Safīd Rūd; and Gurgān[3] consisted of the plains of the Gurgān and Atrāk Rivers. The diversity of environments that al-Maqdisī subsumed within the single *iqlīm* of al-Daylam, ranging from mountain pastures above ten thousand feet to alluvial deltas below sea level, from malarial swamps to desert sands, from hardwood forests to open steppes, was reflected in the irregular distribution of central places. Basically these were disposed in two clusters, to the southwest (Gīlān) and southeast (Gurgān) of the Caspian, which were linked by zones of permanent settlement running along the northern and southern flanks of the Alburz.

At the close of the seventh century the territories that would eventually be subsumed within al-Maqdisī's *iqlīm* of al-Daylam were neither united among themselves nor fully integrated into the Sāsānian Empire. The prevailing political fragmentation is evident from the following schedule. Gurgān was a Sāsānian marcher benefice whose patrimonial-type Turkish ruler affected a style transcribed by later Muslim historians as *Ruzbān-i Ṣūl,* probably their rendering of *Marzubān Ṣūl.* Ṭabaristān was a mosaic of petty Zoroastrian fiefdoms whose princes laid highly suspect claims to Sāsānian royal blood, among them the Sukhrānids and their overlords the *gīlānshāh*s, known formally at the time of the Arab conquest as the supreme *iṣpahbads* (*iṣpahbad* of *iṣpahbads*) and residing in Āmul. Dunbāvand (Damāvand) was another Sāsānian benefice, governed in this instance by a dynasty affecting the style *maṣmughān* ("Great One of the Magi"). Gīlān appears to have consisted almost wholly of tribal territories, the paramount chief of which assumed the already mentioned title of *gīlānshāh.* Al-Daylam in its restricted sense was incorporated in the Sāsānian Empire only at the beginning of the sixth century A.D. Even then it enjoyed a considerable degree of independence under a Sāsānian-appointed governor who was in fact one of its own paramount chiefs, the supreme *wahrīz* (*wahrīz* of the *wahrīz*es). The poverty of their mountain homeland had long disposed the Daylamīs to raiding farmland down on the plains and entering service as mercenaries in the Sāsānian army. No less than four thousand of these tribesmen, for instance, are said to have taken part in the Battle of Qādisīyah in 637 and, after conversion to Islam, to have settled in al-Kūfah. Rūyān was regarded as a Daylamī dependency.

The Muslim conquest of these south Caspian provinces was spasmodic and uncertain. In the cases of Ṭabaristān, Gurgān, and Dunbāvand the Arab commanders were forced to settle for an annual tribute in return for virtual fiscal and administrative autonomy. Rarely did their peace terms encroach seriously on the prerogatives of the local chieftains *(dahāqīn)*. Al-Daylam and Gīlān remained firmly entrenched in the Dār al-Ḥarb. Only when Yazīd ibn al-Muhallab was appointed to the governorship of Khurāsān by the caliph Sulaymān (r. 715–17) did the Muslims, with the goal of protecting their rear during raids into Turkish territory, attempt a definitive conquest of the south Caspian provinces. The main result was the annexation in 717 of Gurgān to the Umayyad Empire and the clamping of harsher fiscal controls on Rūyān and Dunbāvand.

Al-Daylam and Gīlān, however, still proved to be beyond the Muslims' grasp. Only when the ʿAbbāsids perceived the northern principalities and tribes as a threat to the strategic route linking ʿIrāq to Khurāsān and Transoxania did al-Manṣūr order the annexation in 760–61 of Ṭabaristān, Rūyān, and Dunbāvand. And not until 816 did ʿAbd Allāh ibn Khurradādhbih incorporate Lāriz and Shirriz, domain lands of the *maṣmughān* of Dunbāvand, into his governorate of Ṭabaristān. Al-Daylam still preserved its independence while providing the base from which the Buwayhids in the tenth century launched their assault on the Caliphate, and Gīlān became the seat of the Ziyārid dynasty. Only the Bāwandids, the Qārinids, and the Pādūspānids, all holding sway over remote and mountainous territories, continued as tributaries, albeit on less favorable terms than had previously obtained.

In the annexed territories the old Sāsānian administrative system of provinces, districts, cantons, and villages was retained in its essentials, but administrative officials above the village level were henceforth almost exclusively Arabs or Irānian Muslims from Khurāsān or Ma Warāʾ al-Nahr (Transoxania). At the same time, military garrisons were established principally in the upper levels of the urban hierarchy but also at strategic points in the uplands. There is no evidence that the tax rates rose significantly as a result of the annexations, but there is no doubt that Arabo-Muslims replaced local chiefs as fiscal beneficiaries while the lands of the latter were redistributed either to sharecroppers or as *qaṭāʾiʿ* holdings to military and civil Muslim officials.

Marketing and Service Centers

At the apex of the composite urban hierarchy of al-Daylam, al-Maqdisī placed the city of Gurgān. Chosen as an army base by Yazīd ibn al-Muhallab in 716 after his defeat of the Chöl (Ṣūl) Turks, the city had a checkered history despite serving as the capital of the Muslim province and being, from A.D. 928 to 1042, the seat of the Daylamī Ziyārid dynasty. In 935, with the death of their founder, Mardāwīj, the Ziyārids had to acknowledge the supremacy of the Buwayhids. Consequently their capital lost most of its political importance while yet remaining one of the largest cities in the Caspian region. In the tenth century, although manifesting uncertain loyalties in the chronic conflicts between Sāmānids and Buwayhids, Gurgān was still a large settlement,[4] a dual city in fact, set astride the Ṭayfūrī River (the site of Gurgān of the present day). On the eastern bank was Gurgān proper, the seat of Ziyārid administration, which al-Maqdisī catalogued under the name Shahristān, that is, "The City"; on the western bank was Bakrābādh,[5] itself a sizable settlement. The whole aggregation apparently functioned as a dual city, with Bakrābādh in the role of a residential adjunct to the princely enclave of Shahristān.

Gurgān was a prosperous settlement situated in one of the agriculturally more productive of the Caspian borderlands, and was probably larger than any other urban center in al-Daylam; but the essentially artificial character of that *iqlīm* is betrayed by the eccentric location of this metropolis, constituting, as the *Ḥudūd al-ʿĀlam* phrases it, "the frontier between Daylamān and Khurāsān."[6] Clearly, what al-Maqdisī had in mind when he delimited this urban region was the territory controlled for much of the tenth century by the Ziyārids.[7] This included Gurgān, Ṭabaristān, and a good deal of Qūmis, to which al-Maqdisī appended the quasi-independent territories of Gīlān and al-Daylam. In this respect his judgment was almost certainly at fault, for at the time when he was writing, the settlements of these latter two regions were probably more closely integrated with the urban hierarchies of either al-Jibāl or Ādharbāyjān (Azerbaijan) than with that of the Ziyārid kingdom.

In contrast with the productivity of its environs, Gurgān was notorious throughout the Islamic world for its pestilential climate. Al-Thaʿālibī, for example, referred to it as "the graveyard of the people of Khurāsān,"[8] while the otherwise unknown Abū Turāb al-Nīshāpūrī is remembered only for his saying that when the realms of the world were apportioned among the angels, Gurgān fell to Abū Yaḥyā, the Angel of Death.[9]

At the next-lower level of the urban hierarchy were three *qaṣabāt:* al-Dāmghān, Barvān (Barwān), and Āmul, the provincial capitals respectively of Qūmis,[10] Daylam proper, and Ṭabaristān. Al-Dāmghān, situated in semi-arid steppe country at the southern foot of the eastern Alburz, lacked adequate water for irrigation, so it depended for its prosperity less on agricultural exploitation of its environs than on its manufactures and its location on the so-called Khurāsān road. At the time of the Arab conquest the eastern sectors of Qūmis were included among the territories of Khurāsān, and as late as the end of the ninth century al-Yaʿqūbī still regarded Dāmghān as pertaining to that province.[11] In any case, by the close of the tenth century the city was in decline and, although still strongly fortified, was beginning to exhibit a dilapidated appearance. Nevertheless, it still supported two *sūq*s, which al-Maqdisī termed the upper and the lower.[12]

Barvān, in backward Daylam proper, was something of an anomaly in the urban hierarchy. According to al-Maqdisī, the settlement lacked a congregational mosque and possessed neither fine dwellings nor good local markets; yet regional and long-distance trade flourished under the management of wealthy merchants who lived in a governmental enclave known as the *shahristān.* This description would seem to imply not so much a spontaneously generated urban form as a colonial-style foundation imposed on a predominantly tribal society as a means of securing political authority and trading privileges.[13]

Āmul, the third *qaṣabah* in the *iqlīm* of al-Daylam, was a prosperous administrative, industrial, and trading center at the point where the Harāz River, flowing from high Alburz, entered the narrow Caspian coastal plain. It maintained its position as the premier city of Ṭabaristān from the eighth century, when Arab governors were first stationed there, even during the decades when Ṭāhirids and ʿAlids reestablished the provincial capital at the traditional site of Sārīyah.[14] In the tenth century, in addition to a hospital, the city supported two congregational mosques, the older standing in the main *sūq,* the newer near the wall of its suburb. Incidentally, Āmul was the only city that I have come across in the Īrānian culture realm in which the inner city *(shahristān)* was unwalled, although even in this instance it was separated from its suburb by a moat.[15] According to Ibn Ḥawqal, in the second half of the tenth century the city was more extensive than Qazwīn and exceedingly populous.[16]

The only urban center in the whole of al-Daylam to which al-Maqdisī accorded the status of *madīnah* was Dūlāb, the administrative seat of Gīlān. Although it was a city finely built in stone and possessing a well-stocked market,[17] it was in a politically—and from the point of view of the Caliphate, economically—marginal situation characteristic of *mudun.*

The network of local service centers comprising the lowest tier of the urban hierarchy in al-Daylam encompassed wide disparities in size and spacing. Ṭabaristān, for instance, incorporated two juxtaposed but contrasting patterns: the Alburz chain, where even at the lower heights settlements were small and widely spaced; and the Caspian lowlands, which featured the closest network in all al-Daylam, and where even lower-order marketing centers attained a substantial size. Notable among these latter were Sārīyah, a former seat of Ṭāhirid governors and in the tenth century still a populous city;[18] Nātilah;[19] Shālūs;[20] Mīlah;[21] and Māmaṭīr.[22] On the broad plains of Gurgān this order of center was represented by Astarābād;[23] in Qūmis by Bisṭām, situated in a fertile stretch of the Shahrūd River valley that, as Ibn Ḥawqal notes, was the most productive part of the province,[24] and furnished with a congregational mosque that al-Maqdisī describes as "standing like a fortress in the market place";[25] Khuvār;[26] and Samnān.[27] In Daylam proper the lower-order marketing center was adequately represented by Baylamān.[28]

Transportation Foci

The pivotal position of al-Daylam (in the extended sense in which al-Maqdisī used the name) ensured that a relatively high proportion of its urban centers were stimulated to offer specialized transportation facilities. Particularly was this true of Qūmis, where the chief cities were strung along that sector of the Khurāsān road running from al-Rayy in Jibāl Province to Nīshāpūr in Khurāsān. Entering the province a day's march east of al-Rayy, the road passed successively through Khuvār, Qariyat al-Milḥ, Samnān, Dāmghān, Bisṭām, and so to Jājarm in Khurāsān. On the northern flank of the Alburz another road ran from Kalār on the mountainous western border of Ṭabaristān, through Shālūs, Nātilah, Āmul, Māmaṭīr, Sārīyah, Ṭāmisah, and Astarābād, to the metropolis of Gurgān. Transmontane links between these two high roads were few and difficult, although both al-Iṣṭakhrī (copied by Ibn Ḥawqal) and al-Maqdisī listed the stages along a road from al-Rayy (Rey) northward to Āmul by way of the Imāmzadeh Hāshim pass at eighty-seven hundred feet.[29] A city off these main lines of communication but providing break-of-bulk facilities on a considerable scale was Ābaskūn, a Caspian port serving Gurgān and Astarābād, from both of which it was a day's march distant. During the tenth century it was not only a focus of Caspian cabotage—where, incidentally, substantial dues were assessed on vessels using those waters—but also the border mart for the silk trade between Īrānians on the one side and Turks and Ghūzz on the other.[30] Al-Maqdisī refers to the city as "the great harbour of Gurgān,"[31] and its importance was reflected subsequently in Yāqūt's remark that the Caspian was often called the Sea of Ābaskūn[32]—although waters were slowly engulfing the port, even as he was writing, owing to a temporary deviation in the course of the Jayḥūn River.[33] Two other Caspian ports of lesser significance were ʿAyn al-Humm,[34] the harbor serving Āmul, and in later times at any rate, Shahrābād, sheltering behind the spit of Nīm Murdān.[35]

Industrial and Craft Centers

Generally speaking, specialized manufacture contributed less than commerce to the urban economies of al-Daylam. Apart from the processing of locally produced foodstuffs,[36] the carving of sundry utensils from *khalanj* wood, and the preparation of perfumed waters at Sārīyah,[37] virtually the only manufactured products of note were textiles of various sorts, among which silks and woollens predominated. That the textile industry had its roots deep in the Persian past is attested by Ibn Isfandiyār. Writing in 1216/17, he recalled from a source now lost that, after the Arab conquest, the semi-independent *iṣpahbad* ruler of Ṭabaristān had been assigned the same tax responsibility as in Sāsānian times. This impost had included three hundred bales of green silk carpets and quilts, three hundred bales of high-quality colored cotton, and three hundred bales of gold-embroidered garments of Rūyānī and Lafūrajī types.[38] Subsequently Ṭabarī stuffs came to enjoy a very high reputation throughout the ʿAbbāsid realm, a fashion created perhaps—so Professor Serjeant surmises[39]—when tribute was paid to the caliph al-Manṣūr in Ṭabarī carpets.[40] In the ninth century al-Jāḥiẓ rated the *ṭaylasāns*[41] from Rūyān District, amid the mountains on the western border of Ṭabaristān, as the finest in the world, followed in order of excellence by those from Āmul, the provincial capital of Ṭabaristān; Egypt; and Qūmis. That in ascribing a Daylamī manufacture to three of the four finest *taylasāns* al-Jāḥiẓ was not especially biased toward that *iqlīm* is evident from his ranking Ṭabarī woollen robes *(aksiyah)* below those of Fārs, Khūzistān, Shīrāz, and Iṣfahān.[42] Ibn Isfandiyār's account of the textile trade in Ṭabaristān in the last quarter of the tenth century is as follows:[43]

> In early times there used to be assembled in Ṭabaristān and thence exported to the most distant parts of the world satins *(aṭlas),* woven stuffs *(nasaj),* priceless *ʿattābī,*[44] different kinds of precious brocade, valuable *siqlāṭun . . . ibrashīm* curtains *(pardah)* and others of wool, high-quality women's cloaks *(miʾzar),* felts *(anmād)* superior to those of [the Fārsī *ṭirāz* city of] Jahramī,[45] and *qālī-hā-yi-maḥfūrī* (? sculptured carpets).[46]

Subsequently numerous topographers, historians, *adab* authors, and others praised the celebrated Ṭabarī cloths,[47] among them al-Maqdisī, who noted the great quantity of coarse, heavy stuffs *(khaysh)* exported abroad, particularly to Makkah.[48] The greater proportion of these Ṭabarī textiles were actually manufactured in the provincial capital of Āmul, for which the *Ḥudūd* records the following items: linen cloth, kerchiefs of a mixture of linen and cotton *(dastār-i khīsh),* Ṭabarī rugs *(farsh),* Ṭabarī mats . . . white Qūmis *gilīms* with gold thread *(zarbāft),* and various kerchiefs shot with gold *(dastārcha-yi zarbāft).*[49]

In the manufacture of various kinds of woollen goods, Qūmis was not far behind Ṭabaristān. Al-Yaʿqūbī, Ibn

Rustah, al-Iṣṭakhrī, and Ibn Ḥawqal all commented on this industry, which was directed chiefly to the production of *ṭaylasāns* and robes;[50] but al-Maqdisī was more specific in listing white cotton napkins (*mandīl:* cotton figured among the crops grown in the vicinity of Khuvār), of all sizes and both plain *(sādhij)* and hemmed *(muḥashshāt),* and with some of these kerchiefs fetching as much as two thousand *dirhams*, as well as robes, *ṭaylasāns*, and fine-quality woollen cloth *(thiyāb).*[51] To this schedule the *Ḥudūd* adds napkins of *sharāb* (a type of linen cloth) from Dāmghān.[52] Al-Jāḥiẓ was the only author to specify garments of goat and camel hair among the textiles produced in Qūmis.[53]

While the Gurgān District also produced some woollen goods, the distinctive feature of the province's textile manufacturing was its range of silk *(ḥarīr)* pieces, the principal production center being the capital of the same name. Chief among the products was the famed *ibrīsm* silk, which was made up into long veils *(viqāya)* exported as far as the Yaman, and brocades *(dībā),* the latter of which al-Maqdisī accounts of poor quality.[54] Astarābād, the second city of Gurgān, also shared in the silk industry to the extent that al-Maqdisī characterizes a majority of its inhabitants as skilled silk weavers[55] who, we learn from the *Ḥudūd,* produced cloths of *mubram* and *zaʿfurī* types.[56]

Fortified Settlements

Another prominent form of urban specialization was defense, particularly along the border between the Īrānians and the Turks. Here were to be found the *ribāṭs* in which *ghāzīs*, or warriors of the Faith, gathered from all over the Islamic world to fight the Turkish tribes of the steppes. Among the more important of such settlements was the city of Dihistān, which the author of the *Ḥudūd* describes as a frontier post *(thaghr)* against the Ghūzz. The same source noted that there was a *minbar* in the *ribāṭ.*[57] On the steppe to the east, at the beginning of the desert road to Khwārizm, was a settlement known simply as al-Ribāṭ;[58] and in a similar position to the southeast, on the frontier between Dihistān and Khurāsān, was the *ribāṭ* settlement of Farāvah, within which was a spring providing water for the garrison of volunteer *ghāzīs*.[59] According to Yāqūt, the original *ribāṭ* had been built by ʿAbd Allāh the Ṭāhirid during the reign of the caliph al-Maʾmūn.[60] In the mountain fastnesses of Ṭabaristān, moreover, were numerous fortresses with dependent settlements that might have been classified appropriately as proto-urban. Firrīm, the stronghold of the Sāsānian family of Qārin (who still ruled the mountain tracts behind Āmul even in Islamic times) was just such a fortress settlement,[61] as was Ṭāq in Rūyān District, last refuge of an *iṣpahbad* who had finally capitulated to Muslim arms only in the time of the caliph al-Manṣūr (r. 754–75).[62]

Religious Centers

The higher orders of sanctity were lacking in the cities of al-Daylam, but the *barakah* of sanctified tombs was encountered fairly commonly. Bisṭām, for example, was the burial place of the Ṣūfī *shaykh* Abū Yazīd, more generally referred to as Bāyazīd Bisṭāmī, who had died in 874;[63] and Dihistān attracted pilgrims to the shrine of ʿAlī ibn Sukkarī (Sagzī?).[64]

Commentary

The *iqlīm* of al-Daylam as defined by al-Maqdisī was an artificially conceived assemblage of political units encompassing an unusually contrastive range of ecotypes. It was, in effect, a region where diversified physiography and often highly accidented landscapes militated against unified control, and where a frontier location invited encroachment from beyond its borders, while terrain restrained its effectiveness. As al-Masʿūdī puts it with only pardonable exaggeration, "Never in the memory of man has an enemy penetrated thither; there is no record of such a happening in the history of the region."[65] In fact, caliphal hold on the region, whether directly in early Islamic times or subsequently through the agency of Buwayhids, Ṭāhirids, or Sāmānids, was seldom wholly secure and never complete. Consequently the urban system supporting this composite *iqlīm* could not have been anything other than disjointed. In fact, in order to ground his urban system in a firm Ziyārid political framework, al-Maqdisī was constrained to treat a series of essentially discrete and centrifugally inclined systems as a unitary urban hierarchy. In this endeavor it was impossible that he could achieve more than partial success. Gīlān, for example, was never incorporated fully in the caliphal dominions, and its skeletal urban system was almost certainly integrated—if at all—more closely with those of al-Rihāb and al-Jibāl than with the Ṭabaristān hierarchy; while in the eastern sector of the *iqlīm* the Ziyārids of Gurgān shifted their allegiance expedientially between Buwayhids and Sāmānids as now one, now the other, prevailed.

Although it was principally political fragmentation that subverted the development of an integrated urban hierarchy in al-Daylam, it was physiographic diversity that was primarily responsible for discontinuities and attenuations in the urban pattern. It was Ziyārid and Buwayhid involvement in the region that stimulated its handicraft and commercial development, but even in the tenth century there were no large towns in the steppe and semidesert tracts of Qūmis, although some settlements such as Samnān and Dāmghān achieved a modest prosperity from their function as staging posts on the Khurāsān road (supplemented in the case of the latter by a not negligible textile industry). Urban life on even a small scale was also lacking throughout most of the Alburz range. In its mountainous western tracts that comprised the district of Rūyān,[66] and which were not annexed to Ṭabaristān until about 770, Kajjah appears to have been the only urban settlement,[67] although the district also encompassed the town of Shālūs at a lower elevation nearer the Caspian Sea.[68] In Dunbāvand there were only two small, probably proto-urban, settlements in addition to the capital, namely Wīmah and Shalanbah.

Farther to the east, Sihmār was the only town in the Kūh-i Qārin, a forbidding sector of the Alburz whose inhabitants had yielded to the Arabs only in the ninth century and who, even then, maintained their own local dynasty ensconced in the great fortress of Firrīm.[69] Although the precise location of this stronghold has not been identified, it merits a brief description as representative of a fortress settlement that was beginning to manifest some of the functional diversity of an at least proto-urban center. In the tenth century the seat of the ruling Bāwandid *Iṣpahbad*s was a military cantonment *(lashkargāh)* situated half a *farsakh* from the main settlement.[70] Although the district—which allegedly, though more than dubiously, supported "more than ten thousand villages"[71]—was inhabited almost exclusively by Zoroastrian *(gabrakān)* "soldiers and husbandmen" (presumably a sort of yeomanry), many Muslim artisans *(pīshavar)* and merchants resided either in, or in close proximity to, the fortress. Possibly a tradition of Muslim settlement in the vicinity dated back to when a garrison of five hundred men was established in Firrīm in early ʿAbbāsid times;[72] and it was certainly sufficient to induce Māzyār ibn Qārin to raise a mosque there at some time during the fourth quarter of the ninth century.[73] But the principal integrative institution in this frontier settlement was undoubtedly the fortnightly market, which served not only exchange but also socially consolidatory functions, as "from all the region men, girls, and youths come there dressed up *(arasta)*, frolic *(mizāḥ kunand)*, organize games *(bāzī kunand)*, play on stringed instruments *(rūdh zanand)* and make friends *(dūstī gīrand)*."[74] Another upland region wholly devoid of urban life was the Jabal Fādūsbān (Pādūspān), where no settlement was of sufficient size to rate a Friday mosque. The seat of the paramount chief was the village of Uram.[75]

The continuities in the urban system of al-Daylam embodied a zone of substantial urban development running along the lowland between the Alburz and the interior desert; a cluster of cities where these two zones converged in Gurgān to the east; and an extremely attenuated development in Gīlān to the west. This system (or perhaps more accurately, *these systems*) had been inherited in its (or their) essentials from the Sāsānians, and the Arabs had added few new foundations. Generally speaking, their contribution was a reinforcement of existing components in the hierarchy, as when in about 763 Abū al-ʿAbbās al-Ṭūsī, third governor of Ṭabaristān, established garrisons *(masāliḥ)* of from two hundred to one thousand Arab and Persian troops in cities and strategic posts from Ṭamīsah in the east to Shālus and Kalār in the west.[76]

An instance of the founding of new settlements occurred when Khālid ibn Barmak, during his governorship of Ṭabaristān from 768 to 772, attempted to expand Islamic influence by building towns in certain highland territories that were under the de facto control of Vindādhhurmuzd of the house of Qārinvand; but these settlements lasted only until the departure of the governor, when they were razed by the Bāwandid Sharvīn.[77] Other towns established under Muslim auspices included two founded by the Arab general ʿUmar ibn al-ʿAlāʾ: Kajjah, designated the capital of Rūyān after the annexation of that territory in 760, and ʿUmarābād, together with Saʿīdābād, initiated by the governor Saʿīd ibn Daʿlaj. Still another, and more prominent, example was the New Town *(Madīnah Muḥaddathah)* where ibn al-ʿAlāʾ as governor settled Daylamīs who had submitted to him and adopted Islam.[78]

But the single instance of an Arab foundation developing into a major city was the *miṣr* itself, Gurgān, which was established by an Arab conqueror in 716/17.[79] An idea of the commercial interests of a prominent religious family in Gurgān toward the close of the tenth century has been rescued from oblivion by Professor Richard Bulliet. In his *Taʾrīkh Jurjān,* Ḥamzah al-Sahmī included among the business losses suffered by Abū Saʿd al-Ismāʿīlī in 1007 cotton sent to Darband but lost at sea, goods being transported from Iṣfahān that were looted by Kurds, wheat being shipped from Khurāsān that was plundered, and trees on an estate in Kuskarah village that were uprooted by order of the local ruler.[80] Losses though these transactions were, they convey a fair idea of the sources of income available to a resourceful businessman in Gurgān at the turn of the eleventh century.

The lower levels of the urban hierarchy were mainly service centers for agricultural districts, for, despite Ibn Ḥawqal's characterization of Ṭabaristān as a land given over to water, marsh, and forest, pockets of fertility existed in the province; they occurred as well as on the desert borders of Qūmis and along the Caspian coastlands, including the lower courses of the Safīd Rūd and the Gurgān River. At the turn of the tenth century Ibn al-Faqīh counted forty cantonal seats in Ṭabaristān.[81] At higher levels in the hierarchy, prosperity was associated principally with the textile industry, the products of which included cloths famous throughout the Islamic world, and, especially in Qūmis, with the provision of transportation facilities. Administrative responsibility also played a part in the development of Āmul, seat of the ʿAbbāsid governors, and of Gurgān prior to 935, when the Ziyārids were forced to yield precedence to the Buwayhids. In spite of al-Maqdisī's confident selection of Gurgān as the metropolis of al-Daylam, it seems likely that for much of the period subsequent to the Arab conquest it was a polynuclear hierarchy that structured urban life in the *iqlīm,* with the effective, as opposed to the formal, apex oscillating between Āmul and Gurgān as shifts in political authority dictated.

Somewhat more surprising, perhaps, is the perception of this region on the fringe of the Islamic world as a center of learning. It is, of course, widely known as the birthplace of the celebrated historian and Qurʾānic exegete Abū Jaʿfar Muḥammad ibn Jarīr al-Ṭabarī (838–923), and the town of Hawsam, on the Caspian coast in Gīlān, enjoyed a reputation as a center of Nāṣirīyah scholarship in early times. What is probably less widely appreciated is the existence of a Ṭabaristān school of astronomy, "a group of local people who make every effort to excel in astronomy," as Abū Dulaf phrases it.[82] Several of these scholars have been identified by Professor Minorsky, including five who used the *nisbah* "Ṭabarī": ʿUmar ibn al-Farrukhān, who died in about 815; his son Muḥammad ibn ʿUmar; the Christian Sahl Rabban (ca. 786–845), whom some credit with the first Arabic translation of Ptolemy's *Almagest,* and his son ʿAlī ibn Sahl, who was the teacher of none other than the great Abū Bakr al-Rāzi; and Vījān ibn Rustam al-Kūhī, who undertook a series of observations for the Buwayhid court in 988. In Gurgān the astronomer Abū Saʿīd al-Ḍarīr was active in the first half of the ninth century, and in Gīlān it was Kiyā Kūshyār ibn Labbān ibn Bashahrī al-Jīlī during the period 953–93.[83]

Chapter Fourteen
The Urban System in al-Mashriq

> . . . the province which is the most extensive, which produces the finest fruits, which has the greatest number of learned men and notable persons, and which has the coldest climate.
>
> —Al-Maqdisī, *Aḥsan al-Taqāsīm,* 33.

Al-Mashriq ("The Orient") was the term that al-Maqdisī used to denote the broad swath of Islamic territories lying between the Provinces of al-Daylam, al-Jibāl, and Kirmān on the west and al-Sind (now a province of Pakistan), Tibet, and the Turkish tribes of Central Asia on the east. Acknowledging the political basis of this *iqlīm,* he writes, "We have taken al-Mashriq as designating the territories of the House of Sāmān," that is, the dynasty that was ruling over Mā Warā' al-Nahr (Transoxania) and Khurāsān at the time when al-Maqdisī was composing his book.[1] However, the great extent and diversity of this *iqlīm* prevented it from being a truly functional urban region, so that al-Maqdisī was constrained to assign it two *metropoleis,* Īrānshahr (Nīshāpūr) and Samarqand. These two cities functioned, in fact, as the *amṣār* of, respectively, Khurāsān and Transoxania, regions that individually did exhibit a considerable degree of functional unity.

Khurāsān

Marketing and Service Centers

The name *Khurāsān* had various connotations during the Middle Ages, but, as an administrative province of the ʿAbbāsid Empire, it comprised four "quarters" *(arbāʿ; sing. = rubʿ),* focusing on respectively the four cities of Nīshāpūr, Marv, Harāt, and Balkh.[2] In the early days of the Muslim conquest the capital of Khurāsān had been established successively at Marv and Balkh; but under ʿAbd Allāh the Ṭāhirid (830–44) the seat of administration was transferred permanently to Nīshāpūr,[3] which then or at some subsequent date received the honorific Īrānshahr, "The City [namely Capital] of Īrān." The city retained its status as a district capital under the Ṣaffārids, and, even though the Sāmānids ruled from their capital at Bukhārā, the governor *(sipāhsālār)* of the territories south of the Āmū Daryā (Jayḥun; classical Oxus) River resided in Nīshāpūr. By the tenth century this city had grown up to a league in diameter (depending on the direction of measurement), with a population probably between fifty thousand and one hundred thousand persons,[4] distributed through no less than forty-two quarters. According to al-Maqdisī, some of these quarters were each half the size of Shīrāz.[5] At this time the city could have served as an exemplar of urban form in the Persian territories.

A citadel *(quhandiz)* with two gates adjoined the walled *shahristān,* or inner city; and both were enveloped by an extensive outer city *(bīrūn)*[6] that, by the tenth century, was fast becoming the main locus of urban life. The principal congregational mosque, built by ʿAmr the Ṣaffārid (879–901), was located in this *bīrūn* on a public square known as al-Muʿaskar ("The Parade Ground"). Adjacent to it, and facing onto another square called the Maydān al-Ḥusaynīyīn, was the governor's palace. Also in the *bīrūn* were the two main *sūqs,* known as the Great Square *(al-Murabbaʿah al-Kabīrah)* and the Lesser Square *(al-Murabbaʿah al-Ṣaghīrah).* As was the case in many cities in the Islamic world at the time, the larger of the markets was close to the main congregational mosque, while the Lesser Square in this instance was in the western sector of the outer city, in the vicinity of the governor's residence and the Maydān al-Ḥusaynīyīn.

In the tenth century Nīshāpūr was one of the wealthiest cities in the Islamic world, but al-Maqdisī writes harshly of its filthy streets, congested *khān*s, mean shops, and crumbling walls. Despite his claim to expertise in the conduct of trade (p. 63 above), this fastidious literatus clearly found the expediential mores of the bazaars in one of the foremost commercial centers of Islam little to his taste. Boorishness *(jafā')* was the word that came most readily to his mind when he sought to characterize the commercially minded inhabitants of this city.[7]

Nīshāpūr functioned both as metropolis of the administrative province of Khurāsān and as the capital *(qaṣabah)* of the western *rub*ʿ. The *qaṣabah* for the northern *rub*ʿ, which consisted essentially of the Murghāb River valley and adjoining districts, was Great Marv, often called Marv al-Shāhijān[8] to distinguish it from the smaller settlement of Marv al-Rūd higher up the Murghāb. Under both the later Sāsānid kings and early Arab governors the city had served as the seat of government for all Khurāsān. For most of the period with which we are here concerned, it exhibited a morphology reminiscent of that of Nīshāpūr, with its *quhandiz* as large as many another town.

In the tenth century Marv boasted no less than three congregational mosques: the Jāmiʿ of the Banū-Mahān, actually within the citadel; the so-called Old Mosque *(Masjid al-ʿAtīq)* just within the Bāb al-Madīnah where the Sarakhs road left the *shahristān;* and the New Mosque in the Mājān suburb. This suburb, laid out around the *maydān* below the walls of the *shahristān,* was the focus of both administrative and commercial activity in the city, for here were, in addition to the New Mosque, the government offices, the prison, and the principal markets.[9] In the tenth century, when the Sāmānids incorporated Khurāsān in a polity based in Transoxania, Marv inevitably lost a good deal of its military importance.[10]

In the eastern *rub*ʿ of Khurāsān the *qaṣabah* was the ancient city of Balkh, sometimes designated by Muslim writers as "The Mother of Countries" *(Umm al-Bilād).*[11] The city had been razed by the armies of Islam during the caliphate of ʿUthmān,[12] when the Arabs had established a military camp at Bārūqān, some two *farsakh*s (about eight miles) from Balkh. Subsequently, in 725, the governor Asad ibn ʿAbd Allāh al-Qasrī reconstructed the city on its former site and resettled there the Arab troops that had hitherto been quartered at Bārūqān,[13] thereby providing the only known instance of the Arabs abandoning a military camp that had already developed at least proto-urban functions in favor of a pre-Islamic foundation previously destroyed by them. Eleven years later Asad transferred the capital of Khurāsān from Marv to Balkh.

However, during the later ninth and early tenth centuries, the city was the seat of a line of Abū Dā'ūdids,[14] who contributed a number of imposing edifices to the townscape; then all were destroyed, together with numerous others, by Yaʿqūb, founder of the Ṣaffārid dynasty. Under the Ṭāhirids and Sāmānids, though, Balkh became one of the largest cities in Khurāsān, and according to al-Maqdisī rivalled even Bukhārā in size. In the tenth century the author of the *Ḥudūd* wrote of "a large and flourishing city . . . very pleasant and prosperous, the emporium *(bār-kadha)* of Hindūstān."[15] The topographers are not in complete agreement as to the layout of the city, but all confirm that it exhibited something like the tripartite arrangement described for Nīshāpūr and Marv.[16]

The *qaṣabah* of the southern *rub*ʿ was Harāt, a city that came as close as any to the ideal type of Khurāsānian urban form:[17] a citadel with four cardinally oriented gates opening onto the main urban axes, which led to four gates in the walls of the *shahristān,* itself a half league square. Inside each gate was a *sūq,* and outside it an extensive suburb.[18] The governor's residence was situated a mile or so outside the city in a locality known as Khurāsānābād. Although Harāt was never the seat of an independent ruler, and although it lay off the main trade routes (the most direct trail from Persia to Turkestān—the old Khurāsān road—ran from Nīshāpūr through Sarakhs and Marv to Bukhārā), the city prospered from the fertility of the Harī Rūd valley and commercial dealings extending through southern Persian to distant Fārs.

The symmetry of this quadripartite arrangement of *rub*ʿ capitals was somewhat disturbed by al-Maqdisī's attribution of *qaṣabah* status to al-Yahūdīyah,[19] the capital of Gūzgān (Arabic Jūzjān), a tract of territory lying along the northern foot of the Band-i Turkestān. Such meager information as is available for the tenth century implies that this city, in addition to its administrative functions, was the trading center for a reasonably productive agricultural district.[20] According to the *Ḥudūd,*[21] the ruler *(malik)* of Gūzgān resided in a military camp *(lashkargāh)* a *farsakh* and a half outside the city.

These were the *qaṣabāt* of Khurāsān proper, but the Provinces of Qūhistān and Sijistān (or Sīstān) were generally regarded by Arab topographers as dependencies of the Khurāsānian government. Qūhistān, "The Mountain Land," comprised the irregular upland country forming the eastern rim of the Persian plateau. The provincial capital was Qāyin, a strongly fortified city situated at an elevation only slightly below five thousand feet. Although water was brought to the environs by underground channels (*qanāts*), continental extremes of climate inhibited the growth of crops. However, the city possessed a considerable degree of nodality underpinning a commercial importance that justified al-Maqdisī's dubbing it "the [land]port for Khurāsān and the treasury of Kirmān" *(furḍat Khurāsān wa-khizānat Kirmān).*[22]

In Sijistān, essentially the lowland country lying around and to the east of the Hāmūn-i Hilmand,[23] the seat of government was located at Zaranj. Already when al-Yaʿqūbī was writing in the ninth century, this city was some four leagues in circumference,[24] and in the tenth century al-Maqdisī was impressed as much by the wealth and learning of its inhabitants as by the strength of its citadel *(qalʿah).*[25] In the southwestern quadrant of the inner city was a palace built by Yaʿqūb the Ṣaffārid that subsequently became the residence of the governor, and in the northeastern sector was a treasury erected by ʿAmr ibn Layth, second of the same line. The congregational mosque was also in the inner precinct, adjacent to the central *sūq*, but the offices of government, together with most other institutional foci, were located in the outer city. Here too were flourishing markets, including the Sūq ʿAmr, whose rents, exceeding a thousand dirhams daily, were apportioned between the congregational mosque of Zaranj, the city hospital, and the Kaʿbah at Makkah (Mecca).[26]

The *qaṣabah* for all the mountainous country of eastern Sijistān[27] was Bust, situated a league above the confluence of the Arghandāb and Helmand Rivers. A sizable proportion of its population were merchants trading with India,[28] but a productive countryside also contributed to the prosperity of the city. Half a league outside its walls was al-ʿAskar ("The Camp"), an administrative precinct where the local *sulṭān* had laid out a palace complex.[29] Still farther northeastward, deep in the mountain heart of present-day central Afghānistān, the *qaṣabah* for Zābulistān—that is, the territories around the headwaters of the Helmand and Qandahār Rivers—was Ghaznah,[30] one of the entrepôts *(furaḍ)* controlling trade between Khurāsān and India. During the seventh and eighth decades of the tenth century a succession of Turkish slave governors ruled there on behalf of the Sāmānids, causing the prosperity of the city to decline somewhat (at least according to Ibn Ḥawqal),[31] but during the closing years of the century the Ghaznavid *sulṭāns* began to transform the city from a trading post into the capital of an empire.

Also included in al-Maqdisī's Khurāsān were the peripheral territories of Makrān and the Dasht-i Kavīr (Great Desert of central Persia). Here the two *qaṣabāt* were Fannazbūr[32] and Quṣdār. The former of these was a relatively small, fortified settlement set amid palm groves in the Rakhshan River valley.[33] Al-Maqdisī remarks that the inhabitants were Muslim only in name, being in reality savage Balūṣīs (Balūchīs) speaking an unintelligible language.[34] Quṣdār, the seat of government for the district of Ṭūrān, exhibited an urban form by no means unknown elsewhere in the Muslim world. On one side of a *wādī* was an administrative enceinte enclosing a citadel and the palace of the *sulṭān,* who, incidentally, until 977/78 recognized no authority other than that of the caliph himself; in that year, however, he was forced to submit to the Ghaznavid Sebüktigin. On the other side of the *wādī*, which was sometimes called Būdīn, were the *sūqs* and residences of a relatively powerful merchant fraternity.[35]

As has been noted previously, *mudun* tended to arise most frequently in ecologically and politically marginal zones. One such group was to be found in and around the mountain country to the north of Nīshāpūr. Amid the lower slopes of the Kūh-i Hazār Masjid was Nisā, the regional focus for the broad lowland presently known as Darrah Gaz ("Vale of Manna").[36] Soon after 977, the Sāmānid Nuh ibn Manṣūr made a gift of the city to the ruler of the northern part of Khuwārazm, who held it until it was conquered by the Ghaznavids in 1017.[37] Eastward, on the very edge of the Marv desert, was Abīvard, which combined the role of a prosperous local service center with that of a node of long-distance trade.[38] But better known than either of these cities were the twin settlements of Nūqān and al-Ṭābarān, which together constituted Ṭūs, the second city of the Nīshāpūr *rubʿ*. In the ninth century Nūqān was the larger of the two halves,[39] but by the end of the tenth century Ṭābarān had surpassed it. The evident prosperity of the city derived from its combined roles as the focus of a fertile agricultural and mining locality, a craft center, and a place of pilgrimage.[40]

A similar constellation of district capitals had taken

shape in the southern or Harāt quarter of the province. A good day's march to the west of the city of Harāt, and a short distance to the south of the Harī Rūd, was Būshanj,[41] the native city of the founder of the Ṭāhirid dynasty. In fact the district was thoroughly Islamized only under that dynasty. According to Ibn Ḥawqal, the city was about half the size of Harāt.[42] To the south of this latter city, in the valley of the river now known as the Hārūd of Sīstan, was Asfuzār (Sabzivār).[43] Although this city was the eponymous capital of its district, some topographers noted that the largest settlement in the district was a city called (in Arabic) Kuwāshān. However, Asfuzār was sometimes accorded the alternative appellation of Khāstān, which Le Strange has suggested may have been another Arabic rendering of an original Persian form of which Kuwāshān was but one transcription;[44] in which case the names Asfuzār and Kuwāshān would have denoted the same city. In the mountainous terrain of Bādghīs to the north of Harāt the *madīnah* was Baban,[45] seat of the governor of Kanj Rustāq; but beyond observing that it was a prosperous city larger than Būshanj, the topographers devoted little attention to it.[46] Farther east, at a point where the Murghāb River flowed out of the Ghūr Mountains to the plains of Turkmenistān, stood Marv al-Rūd, district seat of a fertile and prosperous agricultural region.[47] Four marches farther upstream was Pīshīn,[48] chief city of the Gharj al-Shār, the mountainous district around the headwaters of the Murghāb;[49] but no topographer had much to say about it other than that it possessed a strong castle and a congregational mosque, and supplied Balkh with rice. Eastward from the upper Murghāb and Harī Rūd, the mountainous heart of present-day Afghānistān was known to Arab topographers as Ghūr or Ghūristān. Although colonies of Muslims had penetrated the fringes of this mountain fastness, in the tenth century its all but inaccessible heart was still almost entirely infidel territory, and even as late as the thirteenth century Yāqūt observed that it had no towns of note.[50] At its eastern end was the district of which the old Buddhist city of Bāmiyān was the capital. According to al-Iṣṭakhrī this city, although sited on a hill, was otherwise unfortified—a comparatively rare occurrence not only in Ghūristān but also in al-Mashriq more generally. The same author estimates that the city was half the size of Balkh, while al-Maqdisī characterizes it as "the emporium of Khurāsān and the treasure-house of Sind."[51]

In the southern dependencies of Khurāsān and the peripheral territories, *mudun* were noticeably few. In eastern Sijistān, Banjway was reported to be the capital of the fertile district of al-Rukhkhaj.[52] Farther south, Sībī was the administrative center for the Bālis region, although the governor customarily resided at al-Qaṣr ("The Castle"), a palace complex a league or so from Isfanjāy, two marches to the north of Sībī.[53] Finally, on the extreme eastern border of Makrān, on the edge of the Indus River plains, was Qandābīl, chief city of the district of al-Badahah.[54] It has been identified with present-day Gandava.

The lowest level of the Khurāsānian urban hierarchy as depicted in figure 2 (page 74) consisted of a stratum of local service centers varying considerably in size and spacing. In Khurāsān proper the inequalities in the pattern were less marked than in the peripheral territories, although even here the spread of settlements was by no means uniform. In the Nīshāpūr *rubʿ*, central places tended to be both larger and more numerous on the lower slopes of, and in the fertile and populous valleys between, the subparallel mountain ranges that constituted a southeasterly continuation of the Kopet Dagh. Here were market centers such as Rīvand;[55] Bushtaqān, where toward the end of the ninth century ʿAmr the Ṣaffārid had laid out a famous garden;[56] Sabzivār, characterized by the author of the *Ḥudūd* as "a small town" *(shahrakī-st khurd);*[57] Farhādān;[58] Isfanj;[59] Isfarāyin, whose fertile environs underpinned its role as the administrative seat of one of the rustāqs of Nīshāpūr;[60] and Jājarm, strategically situated on the western border of Khurāsān, so that its markets served not only parts of Nīshāpūr *rubʿ* but also substantial tracts of Gurgān and Qūmis.[61] The mountainous ridges of the northeast and the salt depressions *(kavīr)* in the southwest were the only areas of the *rubʿ* totally devoid of urban settlement.

In the Harāt quarter, settlements were distributed on similar principles, with urban centers avoiding both the uplands of Paropamisus and Ṣafīd Kūh and the steppe-deserts of the southwest in favor of the river valleys of Bādghīs and Asfuzār. In the Marv and Balkh quarters, by contrast, service centers tended to cluster in a few relatively favored zones. In many of them, moreover, local marketing appears to have been so poorly developed as to be hardly other than an adjunct of more specialized functions. In the *rubʿ* of Marv those urban centers with developed local marketing, as opposed to regional trading, functions were almost all situated on or close to the

Murghāb River: Dizak,[62] Marv al-Rūd,[63] Qaṣr Aḥnaf,[64] Panj-dīh,[65] Lawkarā,[66] al-Qarīnayn,[67] Zarq (which functioned as the distribution center for irrigation waters from the Murghāb,[68] Jīranj,[69] Sinj,[70] Sūsanqān,[71] and Hurmuzfarrah, on an important irrigation canal.[72] In the *rub'* of Balkh such centers were virtually confined to a cultivable zone along the northern foot of the Band-i Turkestān and its associated ranges: Ṭāliqān;[73] Jurzuwān, the summer retreat of the governor of Gūzgān District;[74] Kandaram;[75] al-Yahūdīyah;[76] al-Fāryāb;[77] Shubūrqān, set amid copiously irrigated fields of grain;[78] Anbār;[79] Siyāhjird;[80] Khulm;[81] Siminjān;[82] and Rūb.[83]

Southward in the arid Provinces of Sijistān and Makrān, urban forms were bound even more closely to permanent water sources than was the case in Khurāsān proper. In Sijistān the main cluster of local service centers was situated in the plains northeast of the Hāmūn-i Hilmand,[84] which were watered by the Farāh, Khāsh,[85] and Helmand Rivers. Prominent among them were Juwayn[86] and Farāh,[87] both on the Farāh River; Khāsh, famous for its dates;[88] and al-Qarnīn, a prosperous little town best known as the birthplace of the Ṣaffārid princes Ya'qūb and 'Amr Ibn Layth.[89] Secondary groupings occurred in the district of Zamīndāwar,[90] where the Khardarūy River (present-day Argandhāb) flowed into the broad Helmand valley (for instance, Baghnīn[91] and Sharvān);[92] and in Rukhkhaj District, particularly in the valleys of the Tarnak and Arghastān Rivers (for example, al-Qandahār[93] and Bakrābād).[94]

In Makrān the tendency for local service functions to decline as aridity increased was even more evident than in Sijistān. Although in the tenth century, and indeed later, topographers possessed little information about Makrān, often restricting their comments on urban development to a mere listing of names, tertiary economic activity clearly played only a minor role in the life of the cities. An exception must apparently be made in the case of Rāsk, the focus of a fertile district called al-Kharūj.[95] And somewhat surprisingly, the uplands of Qūhistān, despite the rigors of their climatic regime, supported a fairly regular network of moderately sized, though rather widely spaced, service centers. While the upper elevations were given over to transhumant, so-called Kurdish, shepherds,[96] the valleys and lower slopes often afforded agricultural bases for regional marketing centers. One such was Turshīz[97] in the northwestern district of Būsht. Its markets were in such flourishing condition that it became known popularly as "the storehouse of Khurāsān." Al-Maqdisī considered the congregational mosque in the city to rival that of Damascus in magnificence.[98] Another market center almost as large was Kundur, whose trading area once encompassed more than two hundred substantial villages.[99]

Transportation Foci

The main axis of trade and communication in Khurāsān was the road of the same name. When it entered the province from Bisṭām in Qūmis Province, this so-called road had already bifurcated into two separate routes: the caravan trail described in parts by al-Iṣṭakhrī and Ibn Ḥawqal and, too late for present purposes, in detail by Mustawfī; and the post road that featured in the roadbooks of the ninth century. The former route, over which passed the bulkier commodities of Khurāsān commerce, clove to the foothills of the Alburz and the ranges of the northeast, passing by way of Jājarm, through Azadhvār in the broad, elevated plain of Juvayn, to Nīshāpūr. The post road, used primarily for administrative and military purposes, was shorter and more direct. From Badhash in Qūmis it followed a track close to the desert edge to Asadābād, Khusrūjird, Sabzivār, and so to Nīshāpūr. Generally speaking, the towns strung along the caravan route tended to be both larger and more diversified, while those on the post road were smaller and more specialized—more highly geared to the provision of transportation facilities. From Nīshāpūr the Khurāsān road skirted the eastern end of the Kūh-i Bīnālūd to Ṭūs, Mazdarān, and Sarakhs at the crossing of the Tajand River, whence it struck across the desert to al-Dandanqān,[100] Marv al-Shāhijān, and Āmul on the Jayḥun (classical Oxus, present-day Āmū Daryā) River. At various points along this great trans-Islamic artery, branch roads diverged to the dependent territories of the south: from Asadābād to Turshīz and ultimately to Yazd; from Nīshāpūr to the pilgrim shrines at Būzjān, and so on to Harāt; from Marv al-Shāhijān to Marv al-Rūd, where the road joined another running northeastward from Harāt to Balkh.

Most of the urban centers spaced along these routes, whatever other functions they may have performed, had elaborated the break-of-bulk aspects of their economies to varying degrees as manifested in the presence of *khāns*, hostelries, warehouses, and relatively high proportions of their labor forces engaged in the caravan trade. But the true caravan cities—as exemplified by urban centers in which transportation services, together with satellite industries, had come to predominate—were found primarily in the arid southlands, particularly on the borders of the Great Desert, which tenth-century Arab topographers designated al-Mafāzah, "The Wilderness."[101] For travellers of the time, the desert was a place of fear and hardship, as was attested at first hand by Ibn Ḥawqal[102] and al-Maqdisī.[103] In fact the former author refers to it as the least inhabited of all the deserts of the known world, as well as being the most infested with brigands. The first characteristic, of course, stemmed directly from the prevalence of salt lakes *(namak)*, salt swamps *(sabkhah)*, and *kavīr*s seamed with streams of ooze *(shaṭṭ)* that made travel hazardous and settlement virtually impracticable; the second, Ibn Ḥawqal correctly discerns, stemmed from fragmented and incomplete control by adjacent administrations. Al-Maqdisī had once taken seventy days to make the passage across this desert, following a trail marked by domes constructed over water pits at intervals of a day's march. All the while he was terrorized by roving bands of Balūṣ or Qufṣ tribesmen, who would rather crush a man's head with a boulder than needlessly dull the fine edge of a sword.[104] Subsequently the Buwayhid ʿAḍud al-Dawlah succeeded in curbing Balūṣ rapine to the extent that, by the end of the tenth century, caravans were tolerably safe so long as they were escorted by his troops and carried his letters of protection. However, the raiding of Sāmānid caravans continued unabated.

These circumstances offered the few oasis cities in the desert, as well as those along its fringes, ample opportunities for the turning of monopoly profits. The author of the *Ḥudūd*, for instance, remarks on the important caravanserai *(manzil gāh)* just outside the city wall of Dandanqān, on the southwestern edge of the Marv oasis. In an analogous situation on the northeastern edge was Kushmayhan, where the traveller would find numerous hostelries, well-stocked markets, and commodious baths before setting out across the desert to Bukhārā. Beyond that point he would encounter no settlements other than post stations until he reached the Āmū Daryā at Āmul.[105] Ibn Ḥawqal similarly remarks on the number of hostelries in both the *shahristān* and the *rabaḍ* of Zaranj, the point where roads from Harāt in the north and Bust in the east joined prior to making the desert crossing by way of Sanīj to Narmāsīr in Kirmān.[106] At Ribāṭ Mīlah, where the road from Balkh crossed the Āmū Daryā into Transoxania, was an especially well appointed hostelry, established as a *waqf* by Abū al-Ḥasan Muḥammad ibn Ḥasan Mah, which Ibn Ḥawqal describes as "of imposing construction and large enough to accommodate an army."[107]

According to Ibn Ḥawqal, Sanīj, in the valley of Naṣratābād, was the only urban center in the entire Great Desert, and even there the waterless terrain of the wilderness extended right up to the dwellings.[108] The route upon which the settlement was situated was the shortest of the three most frequented desert crossings, taking rather less than two weeks from Narmāsīr to Zaranj. In the northern and broadest sector of the desert only a single trail threaded its way through sand, salt slime, and mud from Iṣfahān to Ṭabas[109] in Qūhistān by way of the oasis of Jarmaq, where more than a thousand families were settled in three villages.[110] The third trail led from Rāvar in Kirmān to Khūr in Qūhistān by way of the oasis of Nāband, which Ibn Ḥawqal describes as a score or so of dwellings clustered about a *ribāṭ*.[111]

In the territory of Makrān, Fannazbūr (Panjgūr)[112] was the focus for all routes, both those linking the Province of Sijistān to the Indian Ocean or the Province of Kirmān to the Indus valley. One of the most travelled was that between Fannazbūr and Tīz, a port on the east side of Chahbar Bay, which derived its importance from its being the last commodious harbor for eastbound vessels during the monsoon, and in winter the only sheltered anchorage for westbound ships beating up against northerly winds. Merchandise was carried inland on the backs of camels and donkeys, which made their way up the beds of watercourses *(kaurs)* that were invariably dry except after very infrequent heavy rains. Al-Maqdisī comments on both the size of the warehouses in Tīz and the cosmopolitan character of its population.[113]

Industrial and Craft Centers

Specialist manufacture in Khurāsān was restricted very largely to the four quarters of the province proper, but there it was fairly well developed. As was true throughout the Islamic world, the most important manufacture, whether measured in terms of numbers employed (including, of course, part-time workers) or value of output, was the production of textiles.[114] That the *ṭirāz* system was established at an early date is attested by the *Aghānī,* which mentions a liberated slave being appointed governor of those factories in Khurāsān about 767.[115] The two *ṭirāz* cities were Marv and Nīshāpūr, the textile industry in the former city being especially well documented. It is known, for example, that Nīshāpūrī cloths resembled those produced by the industry of Tīnnīs and Dimyāṭ in Egypt[116] and bore silk inscriptions. At the beginning of the tenth century Ibn al-Faqīh noted that the city produced *mulḥam* cloths that were "the finest of their kind."[117] Other fabrics manufactured there, in the tenth century at any rate, included *ibrīsm* silk and a great deal of *qazz* silk, and cotton was grown locally.[118] These and other Marvian stuffs were exported as far as Africa and Spain, for, in a tale about Miknāsah, al-Bakrī refers to "a beautiful saddle-cloth of Marvian manufacture,"[119] while Ibn ʿAbd Rabbihi, laureate for the Spanish Umayyad ʿAbd al-Raḥmān III, allows that he too knew of such cloths, at least by reputation.[120] In the heart of the ʿAbbāsid Caliphate, according to al-Thaʿālibī, al-Muktafī (r. 902–8) left at his death no less than "63,000 Khurāsānī, Marvazī, and Shuʿaybī garments," together with 13,000 Marvazī turbans *(ʿamāʾim),*[121] which, incidentally, Miskawayh categorizes as "Shāhijānī turbans."[122] However, in assessing these figures, we would do well to bear in mind al-Thaʿālibī's warning that the Arabs used to call any closely woven garment from Khurāsān *Marawī* and every finely woven garment *Shāhijānī.*[123]

The textile manufactures of Nīshāpūr were as famous as those of Marv and, if we can believe the tenth-century topographers, more diversified. Early in that century Ibn al-Faqīh listed *mulḥam* and Ṭāhirī cloths together with *tākhtanj* and *rākhtanj,* the latter two stuffs being unique to that city.[124] Later in the same century Ibn Ḥawqal observed that many countries were represented in the *funduqs* and warehouses *(khānbārāt)* of the clothmakers (sing. *bazzāz*), whence various kinds of cloth *(bazz)* and cotton and silk garments were exported throughout the Islamic world and beyond to satisfy a demand generated by uniqueness of product and high manufacturing standards.[125] Al-Maqdisī was a little more specific, noting that Nīshāpūr textiles included, in addition to those already mentioned, white *ḥaffī*[126] garments, *baybāfs,*[127] *ḥaffī* Shāhijānī-style turbans, *ʿattābī,* Saʿīdī,[128] *ẓarāʾifī,*[129] and *mushtī*[130] cloths, together with mohair robes *(thiyāb al-shaʿr).*[131] Within the Nīshāpūrī trade region was a group of towns that also competed effectively in the textile market, notably Ṭūs (trouser cords superior in quality even to those of Ṭīb in ʿIrāq, and striped cloaks), Khabūshān ("much cloth"), Nisā (*banbūzī*[132] garments and fox furs), and Abīward (*qazz* silk).[133] In subsequent centuries textiles were produced in Shahristān, Sarakhs, and Dandanqān,[134] but, although it is likely that some manufacture took place in these centers in the tenth century, corroborative evidence is lacking.

Both Marv and Harāt had long histories of textile production, and before the end of the seventh century the servants in the Qubbat al-Ṣakhrā ("The Dome of the Rock") in Jerusalem were wearing striped garments of cloth from these cities known as *ʿaṣb.*[135] At much the same time ʿUmar ibn Abī Rabīʿah was noting the wearing of expensive Harātī robes in Makkah.[136] In the tenth century al-Maqdisī listed the textile products of Harāt as "a great deal of cloth, cheap brocades, and taffeta *(khuldī).*"[137] Balkh does not seem to have been a major textile producer, but Gūzgān in the western sector of its *rubʿ* was a source of rugs *(zīlū)* and certain woollen garments worn by the poor *(palās).*[138] The felts of Ṭāliqān, in the same region, were ranked by al-Jāḥiẓ as third in the world, after the Chinese and Maghribī.[139] Although al-Iṣṭakhrī thought that expensive materials were not manufactured in Qūhistān,[140] the province did produce a cloth popularly known as *qūhī,* which was distributed widely throughout the Middle East.[141]

From the other dependent territories came mainly felts and carpets, such as those exported (together with saddle cloths and cushions) from Gharj al-Shār and the "stuffs used for carpets"[142] in Ṭabaristī style and *zīlū* rugs of Jahrumī type, both of which were produced in Sijistān.[143] However, Abū Dulaf does report that the Ṣaffārids had established a *ṭirāz* factory somewhere in Sijistān, inferredly in the capital city of Zaranj, but he says nothing about its products beyond a bare mention of costly robes of honor bestowed on visitors.[144] Bust, the second city of Sijistān, and Zāliqān[145] were also credited with significant textile industries, with—if al-Iṣṭakhrī is to be believed—weavers constituting a majority of the population in the latter city, although it is unlikely that all those so designated worked full time at that occupation.[146] Finally, mention must be made of the indigo *(al-nīl)* dye from Kābul, which was as important as the quality of the Kābulī cloths themselves in ensuring their distribution throughout Khurāsān and Sind, and even as far afield as China.[147]

Apart from textiles, the craft industries of Khurāsān were predominantly localized and derivative from agricultural practice. Yet some commodities became fairly widely known. Ṭā'ifī raisins *(mavīz),* for example, were exported from Mālin and "fine raisins" from Karukh, both in the Harāt *rub*ʿ; grape syrup *(dushāb)* from Baban; currants from Shurmīn in Gharj al-Shār; and myrobalans from Kābul;[148] while rice was sent from Abshīn in the upper Murghāb valley by caravan across the steppe to Balkh.

Mineral wealth was mentioned from time to time in the uplands of Khurāsān but often perfunctorily as if it were merely something mountain country was expected to have. There was substantial truth, though, underpinning the reputation of the mountainous heart of Badakhshan as a source of precious stones, particularly rubies and lapis-lazuli, rock crystal and bezoars, and of more mundane use, asbestos, known to the Arabs as "wick stone," or *ḥajar al-fatīlah.* But perhaps the most famous mineral resource in the whole province was the silver ores mined in the neighborhood of Banjahīr in Kābulistān. In the ninth century, under the Ṣaffārids, this settlement had been constituted as a mint city producing *dirhams* bearing the names of both Ṣaffārids and ʿAbbāsids, but in the second half of the tenth century Ibn Ḥawqal described it as inhabited by ten thousand unruly miners given to evil living. Other miscellaneous craft manufactures of Khurāsān included ironware from Nīshāpūr and Harāt (with some of the ore being imported from Sarandīb, that is, Sri Lanka), brass pots and cofusion-produced steel from Marv, jars of serpentine from Nūqān, whetstones from Ṭūs, and saddlebags *(ḥaqība)* and saddle girths *(tang-i asp)* from Gūzgānān. From the dependency of Ghūr came slaves, armor, *(zirih)* and coats of mail *(jaushan),* and from Sijistan date baskets known as *zanabīl.*[149]

Fortified Settlements

As virtually every city comprised a citadel at least partially surrounded by a walled *shahristān* and a walled *rabaḍ,* it is not always easy at this distance in time on morphology alone to distinguish those exercising specialist military functions from the general run of urban forms. Generally speaking, however, the centers in which institutions of defense predominated over those providing other services were located in the frontier zones, where Islamic political control was feeble. One such center was Durghush, a frontier fortress *(thaghr)* against the Ghūr,[150] in which defense was the *raison d'être* of the city and other urban functions were so attenuated as to be almost purely supportive. Somewhat less than twenty miles lower down the Helmand was Dartal,[151] also a fortress, garrisoned by cavalry posted to guard the road leading into the Ghūr highlands. But in this particular instance defense was only one of several urban functions, for the city was also the service center for a far from unproductive agricultural region. Fortress cities of the type described were not uncommon on the fringes of the mountainous regions of Ghūr and Gharj al-Shār; but in the desert marches of Turkmenistān they took a rather different form, as exemplified by Abīvard, a prosperous local service center that also exploited its position on the edge of the Marv desert to develop long-distance trading facilities. In addition, the city controlled a *ribāṭ* at Kufān, some six *farsakh*s distant, which had been built, complete with a mosque, by ʿAbd Allāh the Ṭāhirid toward the middle of the ninth century to police the frontier.[152]

Religious Centers

The higher levels of sanctity were not in evidence in Khurāsānian cities, but saintly *barakah* was not lacking. The most famous of such shrines were undoubtedly those at Sanābādh, two post stages distant from Ṭūs, where were the tombs of the caliph Hārūn al-Rashīd and of the eighth *imām* ʿAlī al-Riḍā, who was allegedly poisoned by al-Ma'mūn in 817. Ibn Ḥawqal reports that already in the tenth century these shrines were much frequented by pilgrims,[153] as a result of which a *sūq* had been instituted, numerous dwellings run up, the shrines walled, and a mosque built by the *amīr* ʿAmīd al-Dawlah that, according to al-Maqdisī, was the equal of any in Khurāsān.[154] At Bisṭam was the tomb of Abū Yazīd al-Bisṭamī, one of the most famous of the ecstatic mystics of Islam.

There was also a competing hierarchy of sacred shrines that only slowly yielded precedence to the religious power of Islamic *barakah.* These were the fire temples of the

Zoroastrians, one of the most impressive of which at the time of the Arab conquest had been the Naw Bahār, outside Balkh. Although the temple was destroyed by the Arab armies, its site was regarded as sacred by Zoroastrians at least as late as the eighth century.[155] In the tenth century one of the most venerated fire temples was that at Karkūyah in Sijistān, where the sacred fire had never been allowed to die. Around the great temple, believed to date from the time of the Persian ruler Rustam, lived not only Marians but also numerous Khārijī ascetics.[156]

Transoxania

The northern half of al-Maqdisī's *iqlīm* of Mashriq comprised the territories lying between the Jayḥūn River and the Aral Sea (Buḥayrah Khuwarizm). To the Arabs these lands, of predominantly Turkish *(au sens large)* population, were known either as *Mā Warā' al-Nahr* ("The [Lands] beyond the River") or as the territories of the Hayṭal, an ethnikon applied loosely to all Tūrānian people beyond the Jayḥūn.[157]

Marketing and Service Centers

The metropolis *(miṣr)* of this vast tract of steppe, desert, fertile valleys, and irrigated oases was Samarqand, situated on rising ground a short distance from the left bank of the Zarafshān River. The heart of the city was a *quhandiz,* far gone in dilapidation when Ibn Ḥawqal was writing in the second half of the tenth century, but apparently restored in later times. Surrounding this inner citadel, on the ruined site presently known as Afrāsiyab, was the *shahristān,* within which the congregational mosque and government offices stood in the immediate shadow of the citadel; and the main marketplace, the Rās al-Ṭāq,[158] toward the outer limit so that it functioned as a focus for the *sūq*s of the suburbs disposed along the riverbank. The wall enclosing these suburbs on their landward side was some twelve *farsakh*s long. According to al-Ṭabarī, it had been constructed by Abū Muslim in 752–53 when he was governor of Khurāsān,[159] and restored (or improved) by Hārūn al-Rashīd.[160] Barthold, influenced by a report of a Chinese traveller that just before the Mongol invasion the city had housed one hundred thousand families, estimates its population under the Sāmānids (819–1005) to have been in the neighborhood of half a million persons.[161]

Some 150 miles or so lower down the Zarafshān was Bukhārā, in al-Maqdisī's hierarchy technically a *qaṣabah* but in fact a city rivalling Samarqand in most secular respects and surpassing it in religious status. In the thirteenth century the Persian historian Juvayni would eulogize it as "the cupola of Islam in the eastern lands, and in those regions like unto Baghdād."[162] The same author also observed that at the time of its foundation the name of the city was Bumijkath (for *Numijkath, the correct form established by a Chinese pilgrim in the seventh century A.D.).[163] The name Bukhārā itself probably derived ultimately from Sanskrit *vihāra,*[164] meaning a monastery; and Richard Frye has recently found cause to suggest that, on the evidence of medieval Islamic maps, Bukhārā, the settlement around the monastery, was originally separated by a stream or canal from Numijkath, the citadel.[165] Only subsequently were the two halves of the city fused into a unitary urban center.

At the end of the ninth century Bukhārā became the capital of the Sāmānid kingdom, which comprised at its maximum extent the valleys of the middle Jayḥūn, the Zarafshān, and the middle Ṣayhūn (classical Jaxartes, present-day Sīr-Daryā) Rivers under direct control; Khurāsān as a dependency; and the Ṣaffārids of Sijistān, the Farīghūnids of Gūzgān, the Afrīghid Khwārizm-*shāhs,* and the rulers of the upper Jayḥūn principalities of Chaghāniyān and Khuttal as tributaries. Al-Iṣṭakhrī clearly discerns the nodal position of the capital in relation to these territories and its strategically advantageous situation for control of the Jayḥūn crossing at Āmul-i Shaṭṭ:

> The Sāmānid governors of Khurāsān established themselves at Bukhārā because it was the nearest of the Transoxanian cities to Khurāsān. When someone fixes himself there, he has Khurāsān in front of him and Transoxania behind him. It was their [*sc.* the people of Bukhārā] respectful behaviour towards their governors and the infrequency of their rebellions that persuaded the Sāmānids to settle among them.[166]

In the tenth century Bukhārā exhibited the tripartite division of *quhandiz, shahristān,* and *rabaḍ* customary in that part of the world. Close to the citadel were the congregational mosque and the Sāmānid palace, together with the departments of government,[167] the last two standing in the great square known as the Rīgistān. The city as a whole measured approximately a league in diameter.[168]

The only other *qaṣabah* in the whole of Mā Warāʾ al-Nahr was Būnjikath,[169] the provincial capital of Ushrūsanah, whence it was often referred to as Madīnat Ushrūsanah, the City (signifying the capital) of Ushrūsanah. Although the city consisted of the usual citadel, town proper, and suburb, in this instance the fortress was situated outside the *shahristān*. The congregational mosque was raised inside the *shahristān*, but the governor's palace stood on crown property in the *rabaḍ*. *Sūq*s were to be found in both the *shahristān* and the *rabaḍ*. In the tenth century the city as a whole was estimated to have as many as 10,000 male inhabitants,[170] probably implying a total population of from 20,000 to 30,000 adults.

At the next-lower level of the urban hierarchy were no less than eleven *mudun:*

1. ***Nasaf*** (Pers. Nakhshab) was on the Nahr al-Qaṣṣārīn (= "The Fullers' River"; the present-day Kushkah). The gubernatorial palace stood on the bank of the river at a point known as Rās al-Qanṭarah (= "The Bridge Head"). The congregational mosque stood near one of the gates of the *shahristān* (the Bāb Ghūbadhīn), and the main *sūq*s ran between it and the palace.[171]
2. ***Kish.*** According to Yaʿqūbī,[172] this *madīnah* had once been the most important city in Sughd, but by the tenth century its citadel and *shahristān* were in ruins, and the *rabaḍ* alone was still inhabited. However, a new city was being laid out at a short distance from the *rabaḍ*. The governor's palace, presumably because of the dilapidated state of the citadel and *shahristān*, was outside the city, in the vicinity of al-Muṣallā (= "The Place of Prayer"). Here too were most of the city's hostelries.[173]
3. ***Ṣaghāniyān*** was the seat of government for the district of the same name that, under the authority of an effectively independent *amīr*, occupied the valley of the Surkhān River. Al-Iṣṭakhrī[174] estimates that, in the tenth century, the city was larger than Tirmidh, and al-Maqdisī[175] likens it to al-Ramlah (Ramleh) in al-Shām (Greater Syria).[176] This latter author also reports that the district of Ṣaghāniyān as a whole comprised some sixteen thousand settlements (some of which must have been very small) capable of putting ten thousand warriors in the field.[177] Bread was cheap and meat available in large quantities.
4. ***Hulbuk,*** capital of the *amīr* of Khuttal, was the mountainous district lying between the Jayḥūn and the Wakhshāb (now known as the Surkhāb) Rivers. The city was sited on the left bank of the Kulāb-Daryā (known to al-Maqdisī as the Akhshawā) River, close to its confluence with the Kohi-Surkhāb.[178] According to the topographers, although Hulbuk was the administrative headquarters of the district, both Munk[179] and Halāward[180] were larger.
5. ***Badakhshān*** was the *madīnah* of the district of the same name that occupied the mountain country of what is today northeast Afghānistān. The topographers were unanimous in listing this district among the most prosperous of those on the upper Jayḥūn, with magnificent pastures, cultivated valleys, and mines of ruby and lapis lazuli; but none left an itinerary precise enough to identify the site of the capital.[181] Probably, given the difficult terrain of most of the district, the tenth-century city was located in the valley where the capitals, including present-day Fayzābād, have traditionally stood.
6. ***Shāsh***[182] was the largest of the Arab cities beyond the Sayḥūn River.[183] The city was an important assembly point for *ghāzī*s eager to wield their swords against the Turkish infidels.
7. ***Tūnkath*** was the chief city of the Īlāq locality, situated in the angle between the Īlāq River and the great bend of the Sayḥūn. It was only half the size of Shāsh. According to Ibn Ḥawqal, the capital stood on the bank of the Īlāq River at a distance of eight leagues from Shāsh. It exhibited the tripartite division customary in the cities of Transoxania.[184]
8. ***Akhsīkath*** was the capital of Farghānah and residence of the ruling *amīr* and his ministers *(ʿummāl).* This *madīnah,* situated on the right bank of the Sayḥūn River, was known to Ibn Khurradādhbih[185] as Farghānah City. The three subdivisions of the representative medieval Īrānian city were clearly distinguishable, but, whereas Ibn Ḥawqal located the *quhandiz* within the *shahristān,* al-Maqdisī assigned it to the *rabaḍ.*[186] *Sūq*s occupied a considerable amount of space

in both the *shahristān* and the *rabaḍ,* but particularly the former. Like Samarqand and Bukhārā, Akhsīkath also had a section of its riverbank reserved for festival prayers.[187]

9. ***Isbījāb***[188] was the administrative center for the extensive district of the same name that comprised a tract of cultivated land stretching eastward from the Sayḥūn River along the valleys of the Arīs River and its tributaries. Nuḥ ibn Asad, Arab conqueror of the city, built the first wall around it as a protection against Turkish raids. The city, on the site of present-day Sayrām, some eight miles east of Chimkant, was one of the chief rendezvous for *ghāzīs*, for whom—according to al-Maqdisī's presumably inflated estimate—seventeen hundred *ribāṭs* had been built; but when that author was writing, the citadel had already fallen into ruin. However, al-Maqdisī comments on the prosperity of the *sūqs* within both the *shahristan* and the *rabaḍ,* noting especially the Market of the Cotton Merchants *(Sūq al-Karābīs),* the shop rents from which, amounting to as much as seven thousand *dirhams* a month, were devoted to charitable purposes. A notable feature of the near environment of the city was the grazing grounds not only for the stock of its own inhabitants but also for those of other settlements within the Sayḥūn catchment area. On these pastures were to be found a thousand felt tents of trucial Turks who had converted to Islam.[189]
10. ***Kāth*** was capital-in-chief of the western or Persian territories of Khwārizm. From the sixth century A.D. small groups of Turkish Oghuz had been filtering into the lands of the upper Jayḥūn River and onto the Dihistān steppe. During the eighth century the confederation as a whole migrated from Mongolia westward to the Irtysh and Sayḥūn River valleys and into the neighborhood of the Aral Sea. Al-Masʿūdī and Ibn Ḥawqal reported in the tenth century that these Oghuz had rebuilt the old Hunno-Turkish settlement of Yängikänt,[190] situated two marches from the mouth of the Sayḥūn. Although it was infidel territory, a colony of Muslims had settled in the city, as they had also in the northern towns of Jand[191] and Khuwārah.[192] But the country between Jand and Fārāb, that is, the whole of the middle course of the Sayḥūn, was considered Dār al-Kufr until the end of the twelfth century.[193]

The lower reaches of the Jayḥūn, by contrast, were solidly Muslim. Kāth, the residence of the Khwārizm-*shāh,* was situated at some little distance from the right bank of the river at a point fairly central to the irrigated land of what was in effect an extensive oasis set amid the steppes. At the time of the Arab conquest in 712 the city was divided into three parts, within the innermost of which was a *quhandiz* bearing the name of Fīl or Fīr.[194] Subsequently this clay-and-brick fortress, together with a large sector of the *shahristān,* was undermined by the waters of the Jayḥūn River so that the inhabitants were forced to build new quarters to the east. According to al-Maqdisī, the new city, known to the Persians simply as Shahristān ("The Capital"), was about the same size as Nīshāpūr.[195] Even so, al-Maqdisī was scathing in his condemnation of the filthiness of the streets.[196]

11. ***Jurjānīyah,***[197] chief city of Khwārizm, was situated close to the great Wadhāk Canal,[198] which left the Jayḥūn somewhat above Kāth and watered the earth for a hundred miles westward. In the tenth century the city was already the chief trading center of Khwārizm, and al-Maqdisī remarked that—unlike Kāth—it was daily increasing in size.[199] In fact before the end of the century Abū ʿAlī Maʾmūn, *amīr* of Jurjānīyah, was to usurp the style of Khwārizm-*shāh,* hitherto a prerogative of the rulers of Kāth. It was this same ruler who built a splendid palace at the Bāb al-Ḥujjāj ("The Pilgrim's Gate"), while his son Abū al-Ḥasan ʿAlī constructed another fronting onto the same sandy square.

The lowest-order service centers of which the present study takes account were distributed very irregularly through Transoxania. On the one hand there were provinces with as dense a network of urban centers as occurred anywhere in the Islamic culture realm. Of Shāsh and Īlāq, for example, Ibn Ḥawqal writes that "In Khurāsān and Mā Warāʾ al-Nahr, no other tract of country of equivalent size has so many congregational mosques [i.e., urban settlements], so many rich and flourishing villages, and such extensive cultivation."[200] The same author compares "the Sughd of Samarqand" to the Ghūṭah of Dimashq and the Tigris River estuary in the vicinity of al-Ubullah,[201] traditionally listed among the earthly paradises. Equally densely settled were the valley of the Zarafshān River between Samarqand and Bukhārā (all the topographers who had anything to say about Bukhārā attested to the existence of a developed urban system in and around its oasis), and the lower Jayḥūn in the neighborhood of Kāth. Al-Maqdisī claims there were as many as twelve thousand settlements (some almost certainly individual farmsteads) in the District of Mazdakhqān, situated in the angle between the Jayḥūn River and the Kurdar Canal; and Ibn Ḥawqal adds that each village within the administrative orbit of Kurdar town was served by an irrigation canal drawing its water from the Jayḥūn.[202] In the Province of Isbījāb, al-Maqdisī reckons there were close to fifty towns,[203] while Ibn Ḥawqal ascribes a score or so of important urban centers to Tūnkath District, only a few of which can now be identified.[204]

In strong contrast to highly urbanized areas such as these were the mountainous fringes of Badakhshān and Tajikistān and the steppes and deserts of Turkmenistān, which were virtually devoid of urban life, or, indeed, often of any form of permanent settlement whatsoever. On the steppe pastures of Būrnamadh, for instance, there were no towns and only a very few small villages (499). In the whole of Nasaf territory, stretching along the lower reaches of the Qaṣṣārīn (Kushkah) River, there were only two towns with mosques, namely Bazdah (which incidentally was larger than Nasaf itself) and Kasbah (502–3). Other towns existed, but topographers tended to treat them with disdain as lacking the essential component of properly Muslim urban centers. Another area devoid of urban life was the swampy southern shore of the Aral Sea with a marshy extension southward along the course of the Jayḥūn as far as the neighborhood of Madhmīnīyah (480).[205]

And between these extreme situations stretched a whole spectrum of urban-density gradations, which themselves subsumed service centers at several levels of functional integration. They ranged from populous settlements such as Banākath,[206] the second city of Shāsh Province; or Darghān in Khwārizm, which al-Maqdisī describes as being almost as large as the *madīnah* of Jurjānīyah and surrounded by more than five hundred vineyards;[207] to small towns such as Madhyāmajkath,[208] Khudīmankan (489), and Kharghānkath (489) (all in Sughd), which were barely able to boast a *minbar*. The spectrum also included isolated towns serving basically agricultural enclaves in prevailingly inhospitable regions. Such, for example, were Khīvah, situated on the fringe of the steppe west of the Jayḥūn;[209] Nūkfāgh, in an ecological situation similar to that of Khīvah in that it was located on the desert fringe on the far side of the Jayḥūn but was also served by a network of canals;[210] and Sūkh, a town in the district of Upper Nasyā, whose location in the mountains bordering Farghānah guaranteed it a substantial degree of autonomy.[211]

Transportation Foci

Numerous cities in Transoxania performed specialized transportation functions not only for al-Mashriq but often for the entire Eastern Caliphate. Prominent among such cities were those strung along the easternmost extension of the Khurāsān road. Crossing the Jayḥūn between Āmul al-Shaṭṭ (Amūyah) and Firabr, the road followed the left bank of the Sughd River by way of Bukhārā and the "Royal road" *(Shāh-Rāh)* to Samarqand, whence it turned northeastward to Zāmīn in Ushrūsanah. Thence one branch went to Shāsh and the Turkish territories of the lower Sayḥūn. Another road carrying a good deal of traffic led from Balkh across the Jayḥūn to Tirmidh, where it bifurcated, so that one fork led northward through the defile in the Ḥiṣār Mountains known as the Iron Gate[212] to Kish and Samarqand, and another generally northeastward to Ṣaghāniyān and Wāshjird.

Along all these roads, as indeed along other less frequented routes, transportation facilities featured prominently among urban institutions. The *khān*s, baths, and *sūq*s of Samarqand were thronged by merchants from all the lands of Asian Islam.[213] Tirmidh's caravanserais catered to the trade between Khurāsān and the north,[214] as did those of Firabr, on the opposite side of the Jayḥūn from Āmul (p. 176 above). Outside this latter city, on the Bukhārā road, a *muṣallā* provided for both prayer and lodging, as well as alms for indigent travellers.[215] In Isbījāb, "there abounded merchants from all over the world *(maʿdan-i bāzurgānān)*."[216] Along the valley of the upper Sayḥūn the cities of Farghānah handled a good deal of the traffic in Turkish slaves.[217]

To the *sūq*s of Sawrān[218] came—in times of peace—Turkic tribes to barter with Muslim merchants; and out on the steppe some eighty miles northeast of Isbījāb the city of Ṭalās (Ṭarāz) was the chief commercial emporium for Muslim trade with the Qarluq (Kharlakhīyah) Turks.[219]

Other towns benefiting from the Turkish trade were Sutkand, an assembly center and trading post for Islamized Ghuzz and Qarluq pastoralists;[220] Ūzkand, the easternmost city of Farghānah;[221] and Jurjānīyah, where Ghuzz and Khazar caravans met those from Khurāsān. Especially prominent in the *sūq*s of this last city were furs brought from the Bulghār country of the Volga, of which al-Maqdisī provides a lengthy list. A few Muslim merchants penetrated even as far as Mirkī, a Khallukh settlement beyond the Ṭalās River.[222] But the principal beneficiaries of trade with both settled and nomadic peoples of the steppes were the merchants of Khwārizm,[223] who mediated the exchange of clothing and grain for livestock, hides, furs, and—particularly—slaves, who in the last decade of the tenth century were so numerous in Transoxania that they fetched no more than thirty *dirham*s a head, and often less.[224] And it was Khwārizmians who came to constitute the chief representatives of the trading class throughout al-Mashriq, whose tall fur caps were to be seen in the *sūq*s of every major city in Khurāsān.[225]

One of the least arduous routes travelled by merchants was that leading up the Zāmil River from Tirmidh to Ṣaghāniyān, which had been blessed by the generosity of the governor Abū al-Ḥasan ibn Ḥasan Māh. At Sarmanjī, two stages north of Ṣaghāniyān, this benefactor had built a hostel where a *dīnār*'s worth of bread was distributed daily to needy travellers. At Dārzanjī, a stage further on, Abū al-Ḥasan had built another hostel, and two stages beyond that, at Ṣaghāniyān, had established several more hostels and benevolent institutions for the benefit of the indigent.[226]

In later times the lands beyond the Jayḥūn River were celebrated for their great fairs, some of which already existed in the tenth century. Several, for instance, were held in the vicinity of Bukhārā at stated times each month. One, known as the Mākh fair, which was held for a single day twice a year, purveyed nothing but the very un-Islamic commodity of (presumably Buddhist) statuettes. It was said that more than fifty thousand *dirhams*' worth of these items were sold every day that the fair was open.[227] Another, held annually for ten days in the month of Tīr at al-Ṭawāīs, offered opportunities for the sale of defective goods such as curtains and covers on an "as is" understanding and without privilege of return. It attracted merchants from all over Khurāsān and beyond,[228] as did another fair at Marsamandah in Ushrūsanah that, during the single day in the year that it functioned, brought in business *(bāzargānī)* worth one hundred thousand *dīnārs*.[229]

Water transport was never of primary importance in Transoxania, but both the Jayḥūn and the Sayḥūn Rivers were navigable by medium-sized river craft. In fact the cities of Khujandah and Kand shipped grain along the Sayḥūn from eastern Farghānah and northern Ushrūsanah to supplement the inadequate yields of their own fields.[230] Numerous irrigation canals drawing water from the Jayḥūn were also navigable by small boats, among them the Hazārasp, Gāvkhwārah (Cattle Feeder), Nahr Khīvah, Wadhāk, and Nahr Buwwah, all in Khwārizm; two canals in the network enveloping Samarqand; and several of those in the neighborhood of Bukhārā city.[231] It should be noted, however, that for between two and five months both the Jayḥūn and the Sayḥūn froze over in their passage through the Khwārizm country so that even heavily laden camel and mule trains could cross on the ice.[232] The Aral Sea, shallow and reed ridden, was apparently not navigable, so that the journey from the Jayḥūn delta to the Sayḥūn estuary had to be a four-day overland trek through what was then called the Desert of the Ghuzz Turkomans.[233]

Industrial and Craft Centers

The third component in the settlement pattern, namely centers providing industrial products for substantial segments of the Islamic world, was reasonably highly developed in Transoxania. Least developed of all such settlements were the mining towns, mostly in the uplands of Farghānah, whence came gold and silver, turquoises, quicksilver, iron, copper, and millstones. One of the more important of these settlements was Khāsht,[234] a mint city close to the silver mines in the Īlāq hills. Another in the same locality was Kūhsaym *(*Kūh-i Sīm)*,[235] which also owed its existence to a silver mine. Qariyat Barātakīn, on the northeastern border of Khwārizm, was in the vicinity of quarries providing building stone used throughout that province.[236]

As far as manufacturing was concerned, the demand for consumer goods generated by the large populations of Samarquand and Bukhārā ensured that those two cities were the main craft centers of Transoxania. From the looms of Bukhārā came carpets *(busuṭ)*, prayer rugs *(muṣallayāt),* and fine cloths of various types, including the famed *zandanījī* stuffs, originally from the village of Zandanah.[237] At least from ʿAbbāsid times there was a *ṭirāz* workshop *(bayt al-ṭirāz)* in the city, in which were woven hazel-colored robes for the caliph. Of the quality of the cloths produced in this workshop, al-Narshakhī brags that the whole of the *kharāj* tax from Bukhārā could be spent on a single door hanging. (The *kharāj* was, in fact, paid in textiles selected by a special official *[ʿāmil]* sent from Baghdād.[238] Robert Serjeant has also drawn attention to the indirect nature of governmental control of the *ṭirāz* in Bukhārā, which contrasted markedly with Egyptian practice, and possibly with that prevailing in other cities.[239]) Al-Narshakhī goes on to lament the dismantling of this workshop and the dispersal of its workforce. It might be surmised that its closing was linked to the fall of the Ṭāhirids in 873, but the late Professor V. F. Minorsky made so bold as to suggest that the account of the workshop's ruined state might have been an anti-Arab interpolation by the Persian translator.[240] From the workshops of Samarqand poured forth cloth called *mumarjal* and cloth-of-silver, brocades, the celebrated Wadhārī textiles,[241] and raw-silk stuffs. Both Bukhārā and Samarqand also exported various classes of hardware. But the really distinctive product of Samarqand was paper, which, says the *Ḥudūd,* was "exported all over the world."[242]

Textile centers of note in Sughd were Karmīnīyah (kerchiefs),[243] Dabūsiyah (various kinds of cloth and brocade) (324), and Rabinjan (red felts and prayer carpets) (324). Generally speaking, in the provinces of the Sayḥūn manufacture was less developed, though Shāsh produced fine white cloths, swords, and other weaponry, together with brass- and ironwork (325). In Khwārizm also, commerce was relatively more important than craft activities, the main manufacture being carpets, coverlets, brocades of mixed cotton and silk, cloaks and veils, various colored cloths, Dabīqī fabrics,[244] and quilted garments *(qazhāgand).*[245]

Fortified Settlements

In the provinces that marched with, and even incorporated sectors of, the Dār al-Ḥarb, the elaboration of defensive functions was a feature common to a relatively high proportion of urban centers. Particularly was this true of the frontier districts proper, which were characterized by large numbers of *ribāṭāt,* whose construction costs were usually defrayed partly by the inhabitants of the larger cities and partly by gifts from the nobility.[246] In Isbījāb, no mean city, we read on the one hand of the *ribāṭāt* of the Nakhshabīs (Nasafians), Bukhārāns, and Samarqandīs, and on the other of the *ribāṭ* of Qarā-tagīn, governor of Balkh under Naṣr ibn Aḥmad.[247] Generally speaking, the closer to the frontier the *ribāṭ* was situated, the more pronounced its military character; and the farther from the frontier it lay, the more prominent its cloister connotation. Representative of the former type were those of Kālif,[248] which had *ribāṭāt* on both banks of the Jayḥūn River, that on the south being known as Ribāṭ Dhi'l-Kifl and attracting to itself significant suburban development, that on the north being given the sobriquet of Ribāṭ Dhi'l-Qarnayn.[249] Others were Firabr, also known as Ribāt Ṭāhir ibn ʿAlī, situated on the northern bank of the Jayḥūn opposite Āmul;[250] Shilāt, a frontier post *(thaghr)* on the watershed between the upper Sayḥūn and Jidghil Rivers;[251] Ūsh, with its *ribāṭ* high on the hills above the Sayḥūn, where "observers *(pāsbān)* and scouts *(dīdabān)* were posted to report on the movements of infidel Turks";[252] Sawrān, the chief frontier fortress against the Ghuzz;[253] and Barkī, the farthest Muslim settlement in the Turkic lands, where there had been built a heavily fortified *ribāṭ.*[254]

Religious Centers

Whatever military institutions these frontier territories may have encouraged, it is not to be expected that they would have generated a developed sacral urban hierarchy. In fact the highest level of sanctity attained by any settlement was the possession of a saintly tomb or other pious association. Khudīmankan, for example, was famous for several traditionists who had been born there; the *Ḥudūd* mentions the tomb *(turbat)* of Shaqīq Balkhī at Vayshagirt;[255] al-Maqdisī knew of the tomb of the prophet Ayyūb outside the village of Jalālābād;[256] the grave of the Prophet's cousin Qutham ibn ʿAbbās drew pilgrims to Samarqand at least from ʿAbbāsid times, and tombs of martyrs brought large numbers of pilgrims to Nūr, situated between Bukhārā and Samarqand; while word had got around Farghānah that certain Companions of the Prophet and their followers to the number of twenty-seven hundred lay awaiting the Judgment Day at Ispīd-bulān, in the neighborhood of Andījān.[257] More believable than this first tale was the attribution of the burial place of ʿAbd Allāh, grandson of the *imām* Ḥusayn, to Khuwāqand;[258] and no less an authority than al-Narshakhī attested the tomb of Qutaybah ibn Muslim, the Arab conqueror of Transoxania, in the village of Kākh in Farghānah.[259] Although not strictly a shrine, the house in the Mājān quarter of Marv al-Shāhijān where the first black ʿAbbāsid robes had been dyed was still a place of visitation as late as the first half of the tenth century.

Commentary

Al-Maqdisī's *iqlīm* of al-Mashriq, coterminous as he intended it to be with the Sāmānid kingdom, extended for a longitudinal distance of more than seven hundred miles through a tract of basin-and-range topography lying athwart a climatic zone characterized by summer drought and a prevailingly inadequate winter precipitation, as often as not of less than ten inches. Consequently a very substantial proportion of the territory was inarable by reason of elevation, dissection, or aridity; permanent settlement was of necessity dependent on the effects of orographic rainfall in the form of better watered upland valleys, spring lines at the mountain foot, and streams flowing out from the uplands into desert and steppe.

Nor was the northward extension of the *iqlīm* onto the plains of Turkmenistān physiographically better served. There river systems exerted an even greater restraining influence on the settlement pattern, creating oases of enormous productivity in the middle course of the Sīr Daryā (Sayḥūn), the lower reaches of the Āmū Daryā (Jayḥūn), and particularly the middle and lower sections of the Zarafshān River, which—as we have noted above—ranked among the terrestrial paradises. However, even a mighty river did not guarantee settlement along its course. The middle reaches of the Āmū Daryā River, for example, which were unsuitable for irrigation, were devoid of large settlements other than those serving as break-of-bulk points at strategically situated river crossings. The other principal towns of the region were sited on higher ground at a considerable distance from the river. Another locality without permanent settlements of any size or kind was the swampy southern margin of the Aral Sea, as well as its eastern border.

Al-Maqdisī was justified in assigning two *metropoleis* to the *iqlīm* of al-Mashriq not only on account of its vast size but also by reason of the differing ecotypes, histories, and ethnic compositions of the regions lying respectively to the south and north of the Āmū Daryā. Moreover, Khurāsān had been incorporated in the Arab Empire more than half a century earlier than Mā Warāʾ al-Nahr, which had subsequently developed an economy that was in many respects distinct from that in the more southerly territories.

Khurāsān

In Khurāsān, on the collapse of the central Sāsānian government, the *marzbāns* (district administrators with both civil and military authority) became effectively independent, so that the Arab conquest amounted to little more than concluding peace treaties with individual rulers. Moreover, the Arabs received the cooperation of the majority of the Īrānian nobility. It should also be borne in mind that the easternmost border of the Sāsānian Empire lay along the Murghāb River, beyond which the Arabs were to encounter a congeries of principalities, many nominally subject to the Jabghū of Ṭukhāristān, which militarily were often better organized than the Sāsānians. The selection of Marv as a base for the Arab armies, and subsequently as the seat of the Arab governors of Khurāsān, signified recognition of that fact. It is likely that caliphal government at first intended to follow Sāsānian practice and maintain its frontier on the Murghāb; but the necessity of pacifying the border, as well as the proclivities of local Arab communities for raiding, drew the Arab armies inexorably eastward and northward, first to the Āmū Daryā, but ultimately to the Zarafshān and the Sīr Daryā, where they incorporated into the empire territories that had previously constituted the Greco-Bactrian, Kushān, and Hephthalite kingdoms. There too the Arabs encountered a loose confederacy of small principalities that the late Sir Hamilton Gibb found "strikingly reminiscent of the Hellenic city-states."[260]

In both Khurāsān and Mā Warāʾ al-Nahr the Arabs inherited developed urban systems of considerable antiquity (fig. 15). In Khurāsān evidence for the precise structure of the system in late Sāsānian times is exiguous, but retrojection of data from the early Islamic era implies a hierarchy along the following lines. At the lowest level there was a stratum of fortified rural centers in a mix of agricultural villages and small towns. The exact proportions of these components are no longer recoverable, but suffice it to say that in agriculturally more productive localities such settlements were profuse on the ground. A phrase such as "with many dependent villages" is a common accompaniment to urban description in the writings of the topographers.[261] Sometimes actual numbers are provided, as in the case of Jājarm with 70 attached villages,[262] Bādhghīs in the *rubʿ* of Harāt with 300,[263] or Būzjān, chief city of the Zām district in Qūhistān, with 180;[264] while it is evident from the combined testimony of the topographers that in the tenth century there was more or less continuous settlement and cultivation along the Murghāb from Little Marv down to Great Marv.

A group of small towns with their dependent villages constituted a district (often termed a *kūrah*), a number of which were integrated into a canton *(nāḥiyah)*, several of which in turn formed a *rubʿ*. A Pahlavi text dating from ʿAbbāsid times specified twelve, presumably provincial, "capitals" of Khurāsān (under which was subsumed Transoxania), including Samarqand, Navārak, an unnamed city in Khwārizm, Marv [al-Shāhijān], Harāt, Būshanj (Pūshang), Ṭūs, Nīshāpūr, Qāyin, Jurjān, and Qūmis.[265] It is uncertain to what extent this catalog is an accurate representation of the upper levels of the urban hierarchy in Khurāsān in late Sāsānian times; but twelve is a cosmologically charged number, so the list may have served a purpose other than historical accuracy. Moreover, early Islamic records strongly imply that the schedule was both skewed and incomplete. In any case, the Arabs appear not to have drastically altered the structure of the Sāsānian settlement pattern, although they did adapt it to their own political and administrative imperatives and, in especially favored regions, intensified it.

Arab settlement in Khurāsān followed essentially the pattern that has already been demonstrated in the more westerly provinces of Īrān. Military garrisons established in, or in the vicinity of, cities such as Nisā, Abīvard, Harāt, Marv al-Rūd, Tirmidh, Zamm, Būshanj, Ṭāliqān, Ṭūs, Balkh, Nīshāpūr, and Marv al-Shāhijān were reinforced at intervals by influxes of new troops, who were followed in due course by the clients of Arab governors and other administrators—all of which prepared the way for the eventual immigration of independent Arab settlers.[266]

Nīshāpūr can serve as a representative example of such developments. The first mosque in the area was built in 651–52 by Arab tribesmen settled in the surrounding countryside, to be followed shortly by at least two more—one of which may have been within the *quhandiz*—erected by ʿAbd Allāh ibn ʿĀmir, Umayyad governor of al-Baṣrah and architect of the Arab conquest of Khurāsān. In 697 Azd clans settled in and around the city when their commander al-Muhallab ibn Abī Ṣufrah was appointed al-Ḥajjāj's deputy in Khurāsān; and early in the eighth century they are reported to have built a new minaret—though whether for a new mosque of their own or for one that they had appropriated is unclear. In 738 another governor, ʿAbd Allāh al-Qarī, laid out an entirely new suburb. In 754/55 no less a personage than Abū Muslim, leader of the revolutionary ʿAbbāsid movement, constructed a larger *jāmiʿ*. Subsequently both Asad ibn ʿAbd Allāh and ʿAbd Allāh ibn Ṭāhir, governors of Khurāsān, built palace enclaves, the latter's construction being known as al-Shadhiyākh. Manṣūr ibn Ṭāhir (r. 822–29) raised yet another minaret, presumably signifying the establishment of a new suburb or the Islamization of an old one.

This pattern of events whereby new suburbs and adjacent villages coalesced into an integrated city appears also to have held for Balkh. An Arab garrison of predominantly Azd, Bakr, and Tamīm (that is, Syrian) tribesmen was initially quartered in surrounding villages. In 725, however, the previously mentioned Asad rebuilt the city proper after it had been razed by Qutaybah ibn Muslim in reprisal for the revolt of Nēzak Ṭarkhān, and brought troops from neighboring Bārūqān into the *shahristān* itself. A new mosque was required in 742, and another, built by al-Faḍl ibn Barmak, soon after the ʿAbbāsids came to power.

Not all Khurāsānian cities developed in precisely this way, however. At Marv al-Shāhijān, for instance, the earliest Arab garrison was quartered within the city, so that the first mosque was built within the *shahristān*. In 672/73 this exclusively centralizing tendency was halted when as many as fifty thousand troops from al-Kūfah and al-Baṣrah, together with their dependents,[267] were settled in villages throughout the Marv oasis as a counterthreat to Hephthalite incursions. Subsequently, as the Arabs cast covetous eyes on the fair lands of Ṭukhāristān and beyond, additional troops were quartered in the oasis: six thousand, for instance, during the caliphate of Yazīd ibn

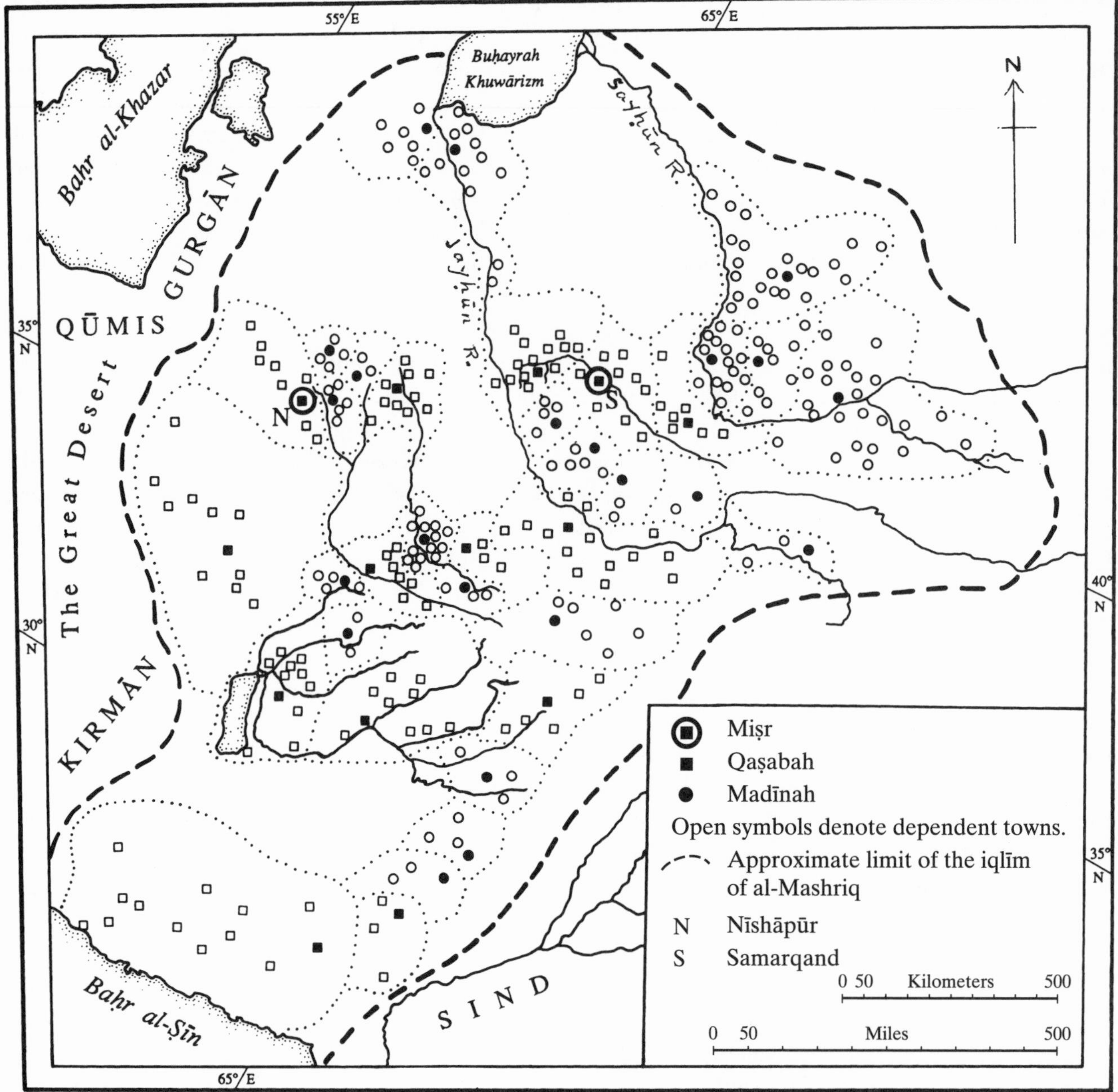

Figure 15. The middle and upper ranks of the settlement hierarchy in al-Mashriq in the second half of the tenth century. The circumstance that some of the settlements are positioned only approximately does not seriously subvert the purpose of this map at the scale at which it is here reproduced.

Muʿāwiyah (r. 680–83), while an additional twenty thousand from al-ʿIrāq arrived in Khurāsān during the reign of Hishām (r. 723/24–43)—at least some of whom would have ended up in the vicinity of Marv. Although Abū Muslim laid out a new *maydān* that became the focus of the extensive Mājān suburb and Ḥusayn ibn Ṭāhir added a whole new quarter to the city, the very scale of the Arab immigration prevented the quartering of more than a small proportion of these troops within Marv or its immediate environs. Consequently the city remained essentially an urban nucleus surrounded by satellite settlements, much on the pattern that we have observed among the principal cities of al-Jibāl in Umayyad times.

Transoxania

In the principal cities of Transoxania, Arab settlement proceeded in a manner similar to that just described, but it began later and the process of synoecism appears relatively seldom to have culminated in a completely integrated city—and certainly not in the great centers of Samarqand and Bukhārā. The former city was not occupied by Arabs until 711/12 and the latter not until 712/13, when an Umayyad garrison was stationed in the Faghsādrah quarter adjacent to the citadel.[268] The first mosque in Bukhārā, it should be noted, had been built by Qutaybah ibn Muslim in 713 within the citadel precincts. However, a substantial increase in the Muslim population is implied by the construction of a new mosque in the *quhandiz* in 770/71, a new cathedral mosque in 794/95, and another mosque by Abū Jaʿfar al-Barmakī at the end of the century when he was serving temporarily as governor of Khurāsān.

There was in fact no compelling incentive to concentrate Arab populations within the confines of the cities proper, since both were protected by walls that encompassed not only their built forms but also large proportions of their oases. At Samarqand a series of preexisting walls was restored by Abū Muslim at the beginning of the ʿAbbāsid period; at Bukhārā similar long walls were integrated into a powerful defensive system between 782 and 830, and elaborated in 850. Throughout the Mā Warāʾ al-Nahr Qutaybah appointed governors in important cities to supervise the collection of taxes and organize defensive strategies principally against Turkish marauders. But as often as not, local dynasts were permitted to retain a limited authority, as indeed did the Bukhār Khudāh dynasty in Bukhārā.

Both of the urban systems that al-Maqdisī subsumed within the *iqlīm* of al-Mashriq were fundamentally agriculturally based and, in response to the physiography of the province, discontinuous, often zoned along springlines and natural or artificial watercourses and not infrequently fragmented. In Khurāsān the Arabs did not significantly alter the basic structure of the urban hierarchy that they inherited from the Sāsānians, although they did interchange some of the components, particularly in the higher ranks of cities, and greatly amplified the system as a whole. Changes in the location of the *metropoleis*, established first at Marv al-Shāhijān, subsequently transferred to Balkh, and finally under the Ṭāhirids to Nīshāpūr, seem not to have had much effect on the general configuration of the hierarchy. Naturally the growth of each of these cities was stimulated by its role as a provincial capital, especially in the case of Balkh, which seems to have assumed considerably greater importance under the Arabs than it had enjoyed in late Sāsānian times.[269]

Throughout the tenth century Khurāsān was an integral part of the Sāmānid kingdom, whose *amīrs* were loyal to the caliph so long as that did not involve the payment of tribute or taxes. During the first half of the century the Khurāsānī economy—as indeed that of the whole state—was strong, with both indigenous Persian and some immigrant Arab cultivators reaping dividends from the old Sāsānian investment in various types of irrigation, supplemented locally by a number of public and private Arab initiatives. The textile industry, represented at its best by two *ṭirāz* workshops in Khurāsān proper and another in Sijistān, enjoyed a high reputation for quality throughout the Islamic world, and the province lay astride some of the major trade routes through southwest Asia.

But it was not primarily for reasons of productivity that the cities of Khurāsān increased in size during the tenth century, sometimes severalfold. One other reason was the growth of the bureaucracy in the centralized Sāmānid state. Another—and probably the most important—was the decline of the countryside, at least partly the result of a taxation system that in effect transferred peasant surpluses into the hands of predominantly urban elites. The *dihqāns*[270] lost most of their power and, together with their peasantry, migrated to the cities. Their place in the countryside was taken by a class of former tribesmen, officials, and army officers who, at a certain juncture in the acculturation process, had acquired landed estates. As exactions became ever more severe, still more peasants sought the only relief practicable in flight to the cities, with the result that during the second half of the tenth century, cities in virtually all ranks in the urban hierarchy increased in size. In particular, peasants migrated in substantial numbers to cities either founded or revitalized by Muslims.

Transoxania provides one of the few instances in which al-Maqdisī chose not to allow political or administrative circumstances to influence his choice of a *miṣr.* Although the Sāmānids maintained their capital at Bukhārā, he opted for Samarqand as the metropolis of the lands beyond the Āmū Daryā River. It was a correct choice, for Samarqand was always the most extensive and the most populous city not only in the Zarafshān valley but in the whole of the Mā Warā' al-Nahr. Between about the beginning of the eighth century and the second half of the ninth, this region had been transformed from a collection, sometimes a confederacy, of petty statelets into a relatively stable and integral part of the Sāmānid kingdom focused on the two great cities of the Zarafshān. At a somewhat later date Khwārizm developed from a region of farms grouped around fortified enclaves to a densely settled urbanized zone along the lower course of the Āmū Daryā.

An important source of revenue for both private merchants and the Sāmānid state was the trade in Turkish slaves,[271] which in turn was largely dependent for its human wares on Muslim raiding forays, particularly after the Muslims went on the offensive against the pagan Ghuzz and other nomadic peoples at the beginning of the tenth century. Although the motivation for Sāmānid expansion to the north and east was the acquisition of slaves rather than religious proselytizing, the dervishes and missionaries who followed the Arab armies did much to diffuse Islam over the steppes of Turkmenistān and through the headwaters of the Āmū Daryā and Sīr Daryā Rivers.[272] The effect of these frontier conditions on the settlement pattern was to stimulate the emergence of a zone of *ribāṭāt* and *thughūr* along the northern fringe of the Sāmānid state. Some of the posts, such as Isbījāb, attracted *ghāzīs* from all over the eastern Islamic world who were eager to fight the infidel. But with the eventual conversion of the Turks to Islam, the *ghāzīs* were no longer needed in Central Asia, and many moved westward to the Byzantine frontier in Anatolia. The scale of this migration is evident from Ibn Miskawayh's remarks that in 964 five thousand *ghāzīs* crossed from Khurāsān into Buwayhid territory, while two years later some twenty thousand sought permission to follow the same route in order to reach the Byzantine frontier.[273] It followed that the *ribāṭāt* and other fortified posts constructed as defensive bastions and forward bases in the wars against the infidel Turk were no longer required. As their *ghāzīs* left for more sanguinary fields, they were mostly abandoned; and insofar as the urban centers to which they were attached lacked alternative functional supports, they too declined.

*

The processes outlined in the preceding pages have been appositely epitomized by Ira Lapidus as selective urbanization.[274] The Arabs, generally speaking, stimulated agricultural production, mainly by reclaiming and irrigating land, only in those districts where they actually settled. The selection of those particular districts was a response less to considerations of potential productivity or the subsistence needs of the empire than to imperatives of imperial political policy, regional administration, and border defense, circumstances clearly reflected in the unusually large number of *mudun* that al-Maqdisī listed for al-Mashriq.

It has already been observed that *mudun* comprised that rank in the urban hierarchy most reliably indicative of political or economic marginality. Of the twenty-three such cities so designated by al-Maqdisī, some five or six were marginal by reason of elevation or aridity; the majority of the remainder were in localities the chief town of which merited a degree of recognition as the seat of government of a developing territory but was not yet constituted as a regional capital.[275] However, despite the segmented nature of urban development in al-Mashriq during the first four centuries of Islam, the Arabs did not fundamentally change the structure of the settlement hierarchy in the *iqlīm.* Intensification occurred here, elaboration there, and adaptation elsewhere, but the overall configuration of the system remained more or less constant.

Chapter Fifteen
The Urban System in Miṣr

. . . the province where there are most devotees, Readers [of the *Qur'ān*], riches, commerce, specialized production and grain.

—Al-Maqdisī, *Aḥsan al-Taqasīm,* 33.

Miṣr was the name customarily applied by Arab topographers to the country now known as Egypt—that is, essentially the Nile Delta and the floodplain of the river as far upstream as Uswān (Aswan) together with the western oases and a strip of coastal settlement running east from the Delta to al-ʿArīsh and west to Raʾs al-Qanays. For purposes of description al-Maqdisī divided this *iqlīm* into seven districts, namely al-Jifār, al-Ḥawf, al-Rīf, al-Iskandarīyah, Maqadūniyah, al-Ṣaʿīd, and al-Wāḥāt ("The Oases").[1]

Marketing and Service Centers

The metropolis of Miṣr and capital of the district of Maqadūniyah[2] in al-Maqdisī's ordering of the settlement hierarchy was al-Fusṭāṭ. (The establishment of a cantonment of this name in 641 has been traced in some detail in chapter 2 and will be further evaluated in chapter 17). Three centuries later this military camp laid out around the pavilion of ʿAmr ibn al-ʿĀṣ had by all accounts been transformed into one of the foremost *metropoleis* of Islam. However, the matter is not quite that simple, mainly because we are dealing with not one settlement but two in close proximity to each other. For earlier topographers such as al-Yaʿqūbī, Ibn Rustah, and al-Masʿūdī, "al-Fusṭāṭ" signified the city founded in 641.[3] It is true that in 751 the ʿAbbāsids had laid out a short-lived government enclave on the Jabal Yashkur in an attempt to escape an epidemic, but they soon removed to the Fusṭāṭ suburb of al-ʿAskar ("The Cantonment"), where they stimulated the building of fine houses, markets, and a large mosque. Moreover, in the ninth century Aḥmad ibn Ṭūlūn had established the military-administrative quarter of al-Qaṭāʾiʿ ("The Wards"), which included a *dār al-imārah,* a palace, the famous Jāmiʿ Ibn Ṭūlūn that still stands, *sūqs,* and reportedly magnificent gardens. But these and other similar developments had subsequently been incorporated in an organically expanding city of Fusṭāṭ.

When the Fāṭimids came to power,[4] by contrast, they established a new governmental precinct at *Miṣr* al-Qāhirah (Cairo), two miles outside al-Fusṭāṭ, which was officially designated the capital of the Fāṭimid kingdom in 973 and furnished with appropriate icons of power, notably a palace complex, army barracks, and the new congregational mosque of al-Azhar. The founding of this new capital did not at first seriously undermine the prosperity of al-Fusṭāṭ, which continued to be an exceedingly important commercial, industrial, and residential center well into the eleventh century, and even stretched its declining years into the twelfth century. There was through time a slow but steady movement of population northward to al-Qāhirah in response to the positive attractions of the capital acting in concert with the negative influence of a progressive westward shift in the course of the Nile River.

Superseded in the Miṣri administrative hierarchy though al-Fusṭāṭ was, the prestige of its name was such that it came to subsume the whole urban agglomeration comprising the original Fusṭāṭ and its suburban accretions, together with the rapidly urbanizing governmental enclave of al-Qāhirah; few authors in the tenth century and for most of the eleventh distinguished consistently between the two principal components. When Ibn Ḥawqal, for example, reported with evident approbation on his visit to al-Fusṭāṭ in the mid-940s, he was describing the city of ʿAmr ibn al-ʿĀṣ, which the vicissitudes of history had then brought to be the Ikhshīdid capital. When the same author described a second visit to al-Fusṭāṭ subsequent to 973, he still regarded the city of ʿAmr as the more important foundation, with al-Qāhirah merely "an administrative center *(madīnah)* established by the Maghribians outside al-Fusṭāṭ."[5] For al-Maqdisī, who, on internal evidence of the *Aḥsan al-Taqāsīm*, must have passed through Egypt in Fāṭimid times, al-Fusṭāṭ was the powerhouse economically, if not administratively, of the conurbation—more populous than Nīshāpūr, architecturally more impressive than al-Baṣrah, and more extensive than Dimashq (Damascus)—in sum, as al-Maqdisī phrases it, "the city that is today what Baghdād used to be."[6]

Al-Maqdisī, as was noted previously, may have had a political incentive to gild the lily when he describes Fusṭāṭ-Qāhirah as "the Cupola of Islam *(Qubbat al-Islam)* . . . the proudest possession of the Muslims" and "the treasure-house of the West and the emporium of the East,"[7] but even the sober author of the *Ḥudūd,* who could have known it only by repute, refers to it as "the wealthiest city in the world."[8] And despite the hyperbole that characterizes al-Maqdisī's account of al-Fusṭāṭ, that author was not outrageously inaccurate in characterizing it as "the centre of the world's commerce."[9] Not only was the city situated in the nodal area where converging routes running from north to south through the Nile Delta were fused into a single strand leading up the Nile valley; but it was also the point where the caravan trails linking the Maghrib to the Levant, Arabia, and the eastern territories of the Caliphate crossed this longitudinal artery as they skirted the apex of the Delta in order to avoid its transversely directed distributaries, drainage channels, and annual floods.

At the next level of the urban hierarchy were five *qaṣabāt.* Al-Faramā,[10] the chief city of al-Jifār District,[11] the desert eastern march of Egypt, was a fortified settlement one *farsakh* from the Greek Sea (the Mediterranean) at a point where several caravan trails converged. In former times it had played a key role in the defense of the Nile Delta against invaders from the east, but after Miṣr and al-Shām (Greater Syria) had been brought within the Caliphate, it had declined in importance. Al-ʿAbbāsīyah was the administrative center for al-Rīf, the district that al-Maqdisī believed "stretched along both banks of the Nile."[12] Despite this city's evident prosperity in the tenth century, its precise location is uncertain. De Goeje apparently identified it with the [Qaṣr] ʿAbbāsah that Yāqūt described as the first Egyptian city encountered, at a distance of fifteen *farsakhs*, on the route from al-Qāhirah to al-Shām.[13] The difficulty with this identification is that, whereas Yāqūt and Abū al-Fidāʾ bear witness that the settlement was founded as late as 893 by ʿAbbāsah, a daughter of Aḥmad ibn Ṭūlūn, al-Maqdisī categorizes it as "an ancient city."[14] Moreover, al-ʿAbbāsīyah, as the *qaṣabah* of al-Rīf, must have been located within the Delta, whereas the implication of all texts, as well as the site of present-day al-ʿAbbāsah, is that Qaṣr ʿAbbāsah lay farther to the east. The location of this *qaṣabah* in figure 2 (page 74), close to the Dimyāṭ distributary of the Nile in the heart of the Delta, is not based on precise textual evidence, but at the scale at which the map is reproduced is unlikely to be grossly misleading.

The third *qaṣabah* was Bilbays,[15] the seat of government for the district of al-Ḥawf.[16] The topographers did not say much about this city beyond testifying to its size and prosperity.[17] In the northwestern angle of the Delta was al-Iskandarīyah (Alexandria), capital of the district of the same name. The topographers were unanimous in representing it as an inordinately handsome city in the shadow of a seemingly impregnable fortress, but S. D. Goitein has drawn on documents in the Cairo Geniza to show that the city was not the major emporium of Miṣr. That was the prerogative of Fusṭāṭ-Qāhirah. Of the hierarchical relationship between these two cities—perhaps at a somewhat later date than that with which we are mainly concerned here—Goitein has written the following:

> The unmistakable testimony of hundreds of Geniza letters proves that Fusṭāṭ, although inland, was also the commercial and financial center on which Alexandria, the originally Greek maritime town, was economically dependent in every respect. Fusṭāṭ was the emporium of the region, where all goods were stored. Even commodities from Mediterranean countries, which were imported by way of Alexandria, had to be obtained from Fusṭāṭ when they became scarce in the former city. Foreign currency from places with which Alexandria entertained a lively commerce was regularly acquired by Alexandrians in Fusṭāṭ. Humdrum commodities,

such as shoes and clothing, instruments for silversmithing, or parchment were ordered from Alexandria in the capital, "for here, [namely in Alexandria, as several letters emphasize] nothing is to be had."[18]

The fifth *qaṣabah* was Uswān, capital of al-Ṣaʿīd (Upper Egypt). This city, which al-Maqdisī describes as large and flourishing, was situated just below the first cataract of the Nile.[19] In spite of a checkered history in the ninth century principally caused by Beja and Nubian raids, the city prospered from its functions as a mart for gold mined in the Wādī al-ʿAllāqī and as the premier trade center of the region. It was also the only city in Upper Egypt having a majority Muslim population. The sole *madīnah* mentioned by al-Maqdisī was al-Fayyūm, in the oasis of the same name: "an important place, with fields producing excellent rice and flax of middling quality."[20]

Not altogether surprisingly, those urban centers deriving their *raisons d'être* primarily from local service functions were restricted in Lower Egypt to the confines of the Nile Delta and in Upper Egypt to the floodplain of the Nile River. Representative of the former were al-Mashtūl, whose broad fields produced grain for numerous mills;[21] and ʿAyn-Shams,[22] both in the district of al-Ḥawf, together with Shubrū Abū Mīnah, set amid fields of grain and other crops some eight miles southeast of al-Iskandarīyah.[23] In Upper Egypt Ikhmīm, "a town abounding in palms . . . with many vines and extensive cultivation," was fairly typical of this class of settlement.[24] But it must be remembered that this level of the urban hierarchy was underrecorded by al-Maqdisī (and more than probably by the other topographers) owing to the absence of congregational mosques, criteria of urban status, from the settlements of the substantial Coptic element in the population.[25]

Transportation Foci

The pivotal position of Egypt between the Islamic lands of Africa and those of Asia had induced the elaboration in numerous cities of institutions concerned with transportation. One of the best examples was afforded by al-Faramā, "a rendezvous for merchants who arrived at all hours of the day and night . . . in caravans that filed into the city continuously," many having crossed the shifting sands of al-Jifār, which, drifted *(munʿaqidah)* by the wind, were liable to obscure the track, rendering necessary—or at least opportune—the provision of a hostelry *(ḥānūt)* at each post station.[26] Another such city was al-Jīzah (Giza), the starting point of the high road to al-Maghrib.[27] Some idea of the quantities of merchandise handled by such urban centers can be gathered from al-Maqdisī's remark that, in a single week, he had counted as many as three hundred camel loads of flour and cakes leaving al-Mashtūl for the Ḥijāz.[28]

Prominent among the ports of Miṣr were al-Iskandarīyah, Tinnīs, and al-Qulzum. The first of these provided transshipment facilities for Mediterranean commodities being imported into al-Fusṭāṭ, and probably served as the international bourse and entrepôt for the silk trade.[29] The port itself comprised eastern and western harbors on either side of the island of Pharos with its famous lighthouse, construction of which had been begun by Ptolemy Soter at the turn of the third century B.C. In later times, and probably in the tenth century, the western harbor was reserved for Muslim shipping while that from the Dār al-Ḥarb was directed into the eastern roads, which were notoriously difficult of access. Tinnīs was situated on an island in Lake Manzālah, so that it was unable to produce comestibles of its own and depended for its sustenance entirely on imports. The evident wealth of this predominantly Coptic city derived equally from its function as "the emporium of east and west"—al-Maqdisī's phrase[30]—and from its textile manufactures, which are discussed subsequently.

Al-Qulzum was the port of Miṣr that handled the bulk of the Red Sea trade. Positioned at the head of the waterway presently known as the Gulf of Suez, it was—again in al-Maqdisī's words—"a dreary and depressing place"; "arid, waterless, devoid of herbage or cultivation; nor is there found there any milk,[31] or fuel, or trees, nor grapes nor fruits. Water is brought [to the city] in ships, and also on the backs of camels from a place six miles away called Suways (Suez). It is drinkable water but of very poor quality."[32] Yet notwithstanding this unpropitious environment, the city was solidly, even impressively, constructed with what al-Maqdisī calls "palatial buildings" as the material expression of the wealth that its merchants accumulated from foreign trade and the provision of ancillary services. In particular they profited from the export of Egyptian grain to the Ḥijāz, at the same time as they made handsome supplementary profits from providing supplies for pilgrims to the two Holy Cities of Arabia.

Nor should the immense prestige of al-Fusṭāṭ as an administrative city and a former capital be allowed to obscure its function as a trading center where routes converged into a funnel at the apex of the Nile Delta. As al-Maqdisī wrote at the end of the tenth century: "Syrian and Maghribī fruits are available at all seasons, caravans from al-ʿIrāq and al-Mashriq are always arriving, and vessels from the Arabian Peninsula and the Byzantine territories make their way thither. Its commerce is extraordinary, its shops profitable, and its wealth abundant."[33]

Industrial and Craft Centers

Specialist manufacture was relatively highly developed in the urban centers of Miṣr. As was to be expected, the chief focus of craft industry other than textile manufacture was the metropolis of al-Fusṭāṭ, with al-Iskandarīyah running a poor second. But it was textiles that gave Miṣrī industry its characteristic configuration and supported a trade in high-quality cloth that extended virtually throughout the Islamic world. However, neither the manufacture nor the trade had originated with the Arabs, for Egypt had been one of the Middle East's principal producers of textiles for centuries before the Arab conquest. In any case, the Arabs were not slow to avail themselves of the finest Miṣrī textiles, with both Rāshidūn caliphs ʿUmar and ʿUthmān covering the Kaʿbah with Coptic cloths *(qubāṭī),* to be followed in due course by Muʿāwiyah, first of the Umayyad caliphs, who added to this covering another of brocade *(dībaj).*[34]

Robert Serjeant has suggested that the *qubāṭī* were furnished by the Tinnīs-Dimyāṭ group of factories, where weaving continued to be an exclusively Coptic occupation long after the Arab conquest.[35] This assumption is not unlikely, because the towns grouped around the Buḥayrat Tinnīs (present-day Lake Manzālah) together constituted the premier textile-producing region of Miṣr. Tinnīs and Dimyāṭ were preeminent in their roles as *ṭirāz*[36] cities, but also manufacturing the white-linen *qubāṭī* cloth were Shaṭā,[37] Dabīq,[38] Tūnah,[39] Dumayrah,[40] and Dīfū,[41] as well as smaller settlements that cannot now be identified. Serjeant's suggestion is given additional credence by al-Maqrīzī's mention of a *qubāṭī* covering for the Kaʿbah actually commissioned from the weavers of Shaṭā in the time of Hārūn al-Rashīd. It was these fine linen cloths that caught the popular imagination as exemplified in, for example, the Umayyad-era comparison of Egyptian cloths to the membrane enveloping an egg, as opposed to, say, Yamanī textiles that called up images of spring flowers.[42]

As was the case in most of the textile-manufacturing cities of Lower Egypt, the principal products of the Tinnīs-Dimyāṭ region were linen stuffs. Al-Jāḥiẓ's remark that "Whereas cotton cloths are characteristic of Khurāsān, it is linens *(kattān)* that are associated with Egypt"[43] is both accurate and well known. Al-Maqdisī contributes the additional information that the workforce in Dimyāṭ was more highly skilled than that in Tinnīs and its cloth consequently of higher quality, as well as the fact that the latter city produced colored garments in contradistinction to the white cloth from Dimyāṭ.[44] Also in the last quarter of the tenth century, al-Muhallabī characterized the workforce of the two cities in the following, not wholly complimentary, way:

> One of the curious things about Dimyāṭ and Tinnīs is that the weavers there who make these fine garments are the lowest, humblest and meanest of Copts in the manner of their eating and drinking. Although the larger part of their diet consists of salt or evil-smelling *ṣīr* fish, most of them do not wash their hands after eating, but return to those valuable and highly esteemed cloths and resume weaving. Then the garment is cut [from the loom] and the person who takes it has not the slightest doubt but that it has been perfumed with *nadd* scent.[45]

That these workmen were not invariably satisfied with their lot is evident from the comments of the Christian patriarch Dionysius, who visited Egypt in about 815:

> Although Tinnīs has a considerable population and numerous churches, we have never witnessed greater distress than that of its inhabitants. When we enquired into the cause of it, they replied: "Our town is encompassed by water. We neither look forward to a harvest nor maintain flocks. Our drinking water comes from afar and costs us 4 *dirhams* a pitcher. Our work is the manufacture of linen, which our women spin and we weave. We receive from the dealers half a *dirham* a day. Although our earnings are not sufficient to put bread

in our mouths, we are required to pay tribute and 5 *dīnārs* a head in taxes. We are beaten, imprisoned, and compelled to give our sons and daughters as securities. For every *dīnār* they have to work two years as slaves."[46]

Almost as celebrated a textile center as Tinnīs and Dimyāṭ was the city of Shaṭā, for which al-Maqdisī provides a succinct account of the government-controlled vertical organization of its industry:

> As for Shaṭawī cloth, the Copts are not allowed to weave it unless the stamp of the Sulṭān is placed on the finished article. Nor can it be sold except through the intermediacy of brokers entrusted with that task,[47] the transaction being entered in an official inventory of sales. Then the cloth passes [through several hands] as it is rolled up, placed in its wrapping *(qishr),* packed in frails (sing. *safaṭ*), and finally tied securely; and each operation is charged an official fee *(rasm).*[48] An [additional] tax is levied at the entrance to the harbour. Each participant in the packaging process puts his mark on the frails and the vessels are inspected at the time of sailing.[49]

What all the writers of the time agree on is that the cloths produced in the Tinnīs-Dimyāṭ textile region were of high quality, and consequently proportionately expensive. Ibn Ḥawqal, for instance, praised the

> striped cloaks *(ḥullah)* manufactured in Tinnīs which exceed anything else on earth in price and beauty, softness and luxury, thinness and fineness. Sometimes a single such cloak fetches 200 *dīnārs* when it contains gold thread, without the gold thread about 100 *dīnārs.*[50]

Al-Kindī implies much the same when he writes, "There is not a *ṭirāz* factory in the world a simple garment *(thawb sādhij)* from which, without any gold thread, fetches 100 *dīnārs* except those at Tinnīs and Dimyāṭ."[51] An especially expensive cloth was the *būqalamūn* manufactured exclusively in Tinnīs, which al-Jāḥiẓ describes (under the rubric *abū qalamūn*) as "one of the crimson-colored, imperial, Greek-style textiles *(zillīyah Khusrawānī Rūmī qirmizī)* with variously hued warp and woof, violet thread being crossed with red and green. It is said to change colour with the time of day and the brightness of the sun [meaning, presumably, that it was iridescent]. It is extremely costly to buy."[52] Half a century after the close of our period, Nāṣir-i Khusraw observed working conditions in the *ṭirāz* factory at Tinnīs which had apparently improved during the more than two centuries since the visit of the patriarch Dionysius. He remarked, "Because the full price is paid for all the linen *(qaṣab)* and *būqalamūn* woven for the Sulṭān, the workmen labour willingly, in contrast to [the situation in] some other countries, where they are subject to forced labour for vizier and sulṭān."[53] Or perhaps the improvement lay in the eye of the beholder.

Another locality in the vicinity of Lake Manzālah that produced a fine-quality, expensive cloth through much of the first four centuries of Islam was Dabīq, apparently a town in the hinterland of Dimyāṭ.[54] The *Aghānī* mentions a Dabīqī napkin in its biography of the celebrated musician Ishḥāq ibn Ibrāhīm al-Mawṣilī (767–850) and has the caliph al-Muʿtaṣim (r. 833–42) wearing a Dabīqī shirt *(qamīs)* "which looked as if it had been cut from the planet Venus."[55] Professor Serjeant has assembled numerous other references to the use of this cloth during ʿAbbāsid times, including all kinds of furnishings, among them—rather unexpectedly—awnings of gold-embroidered Dabīqī cloth *(aghshiyatuhā Dabīqī mudhhab)* on Baghdādī pleasure boats.[56]

The state of the textile industry in the Tinnīs-Dimyāṭ region as a whole in the last quarter of the tenth century is summarized by Ibn Ḥawqal as follows:

> Although Shaṭā, Dabquwā (Dabīq), Dumayrah, and Tūnah, together with adjoining islands, manufacture valuable cloths . . . yet they do not compare with the Tinnīsī, Dimyāṭī, and Shaṭawī [The repetition of this name was evidently an oversight on the part of Ibn Ḥawqal], a load of which for the ʿIrāqī trade currently fetches 20–30,000 *dīnārs.*

But the same author notes the following, presumably as an addendum to the later edition of his work:

> This production has now ceased because of exactions placed on it, and the person primarily responsible is the accursed Abū al-Faraj ibn Killīs, *wazīr* of al-ʿAzīz (975–996), who has destroyed the industry by his burdensome imposts and levies and his oppression of the labour force, including the

imposition of a tax on those entering and leaving Tinnīs.[57]

Outside the Tinnīs-Dimyāṭ region, there was also a *ṭirāz* factory in al-Iskandarīyah, but most of the available information about its production relates to a period subsequent to the tenth century. Al-Qalqashandī, after describing in some detail its *ṭirāz* cloths as they were being manufactured early in the fifteenth century and noting how their embroidery "drew attention to the status of the royal owner or that of the person so honoured by the investiture as a token of friendship, a means of payment or a gift," adds that both Umayyad and ʿAbbāsid caliphs in their day had followed the same custom.[58] Most of the other early mentions of Iskandarī cloth are incidental or connected with the foreign commerce of the city, including the trade in silk with the Byzantine territories, which had been inherited from pre-Muslim times.[59] However, the *Kitāb al-Muwashshā* did include Iskandarī among the clothes affected by the man of fashion in the third Hijrī century.[60] Information about the *ṭirāz* manufacture in Fāṭimid al-Qāhirah is nearly all of too late a date to be invoked in the present study, but about the Fayyūm, including Bahnasā and Qays, we are better informed. The fullest account is provided by Ibn Hawqal:

> In the Fayyūm there are large and flourishing towns and renowned *ṭirāz* factories,[61] as well as great estates belonging to both the government and private individuals. There are manufactured textiles too well known to require enumeration. In Bahnasā [for instance], curtains, brocade *(istabraqāt)*, awnings (or sails), tents, cloaks, veils (*satāʾir:* or perhaps covers of some sort), carpets *(busuṭ)*,[62] large *(miḍrab)* and very large pavilions *(fusṭāṭ)* are made of wool and linen, and dyed with colours that do not fade. . . . The managers of these factories are government servants who accept orders from caliphs, senior officials, and merchants from all parts of the world. There are made long curtains *(sutūr)* of great price, each about 30 *dhirāʿ* long and fetching some 300 *dīnārs* a pair.[63]

Other Fayyūmī towns manufacturing textiles were Qays and Ahnās,[64] while Būṣīr Qūrīdus was the service center for a district growing high-quality flax.[65]

Nor was Upper Egypt (al-Ṣaʿīd) without textile manufacture. *Ṭirāz* factories were reported at Ṭaḥā, "where woollen cloth of very high quality was woven";[66] at Akhmīm, which, toward the end of the ninth century and probably much later, was known for its "cut" carpets *(al-farsh al-quṭūʿ)*;[67] and at Asyūṭ,[68] about which Nāṣir-i Khusraw had this to say:

> In Asyūṭ sheep's wool is woven into a cloth *(dastār)* which has no equal anywhere in the world. The fine-quality woollens exported to Persia under the name Miṣrī all come from al-Ṣaʿīd, for wool is not woven in al-Qāhirah. In Asyūṭ, I myself saw a shawl *(fūṭah)* of sheep's wool the like of which I have seen neither in Lahāwar (Lahore) nor in Multān. It was so fine that it could have passed for silk.[69]

In addition to these *ṭirāz* cities, two others were listed as exporters of linen cloth, namely Ashmunayn, which sent its products "to al-Fusṭāṭ (Miṣr) and elsewhere"; and Uswān, the *qaṣabah* of Upper Egypt, which dispatched cloth and napkins *(mandīl)* to Fusṭāṭ and the Ḥijāz.[70]

Fortified Settlements

After the Arab conquest, specialized military functions in Miṣr were most in evidence along the Mediterranean coast and on the frontier of Upper Egypt. In the former area, virtually all cities were fortified after a devastating raid by the Byzantines on Dimyāṭ in 853. The earliest Arab settlement in al-Iskandarīyah was a garrison *(ribāṭ)* of tribesmen rotated from al-Fusṭāṭ at six-monthly intervals, while in Geniza letters of the eleventh and twelfth centuries, the city was often referred to as al-Thaghr, that is, "The Frontier Fortress";[71] al-Maqdisī notes numerous *ribāṭāt* in and around Dimyāṭ to which at a certain time of the year volunteer fighters for the Faith *(murābiṭūn)* flocked from all parts of the Islamic world.[72] At the opposite end of the country, Uswān was described in similar terms as a border fortress against the Nubians,[73] although Ibn Ḥawqal observed that in the second half of the tenth century the city's defensive role was in abeyance consequent on the pacification of the Nubians.[74]

Religious Centers

In a country having a substantial Coptic rural population, it is not surprising that Islamic shrines were relatively scarce. The tomb of al-Shāfiʿī, the great jurisconsult who died in 820, situated at the foot of the Muqaṭṭam outside al-Fusṭāṭ,[75] and the tomb of Jālīnūs (Galen) at al-Faramā[76] were among those mentioned by topographers, while in Upper Egypt the town of Ikhmīm enjoyed a transient fame as the birthplace of the ascetic Dhū al-Nūn.[77] There was, though, a sketchily developed level of soteriological holiness, within which the individual nodes were not always undisputed and sometimes contradictory. One of the most vaguely perceived of these holy sites *(mashāhid)* was the wilderness where the Israelites had dwelt after leaving Egypt, which was commonly believed to have been the inhospitable district between al-Jifār District and Sīnā'.[78] Other such identifications included a settlement named al-Amn, taken to be the place where the Banū-Isrā'īl crossed out of Egypt;[79] in the same locality the Qur'ānic olive tree "Neither of the East nor of the West";[80] the point in the vicinity of al-Qulzum where the Banū-Isrā'īl had entered the Red Sea;[81] at Fusṭāṭ-Qāhirah, the place where Yūsuf ibn Ya'qūb had been sold into slavery;[82] and either Egypt as a whole or the vicinity of its capital as "the lofty ground offering both lodging and a spring" to Maryam and the infant 'Īsā.[83] But all the indications are that this soteriological holiness was too diffuse and too poorly defined to have influenced significantly the development of the urban system.

Commentary

Al-Maqdisī's apology for understating the degree of urbanization in Miṣr has already been cited on page 193 and in chapter 3. Essentially it amounted to an awareness that the analogical principles *(qiyās)* espoused in the construction of his settlement hierarchies did not permit him to categorize as urban an aggregation of population which, whatever its size, lacked a mosque. As a sizable proportion of the Egyptian population was still Coptic Christian, churches substituted for mosques in many settlements, to which al-Maqdisī, in the interests of methodological consistency, consequently felt obliged to deny the status of town or city. As other topographers added few names to al-Maqdisī's schedule of Miṣrī cities, it is to be presumed that they too harbored the same reluctance to recognize predominantly Coptic settlements as fully fledged urban forms. All of which raises the issue as to the proportion of the population that had been converted to Islam by the tenth century. The question cannot be answered with certainty, as Arabic sources tend to be reticent on the matter and, when they do vouchsafe a comment, are not always in agreeement among themselves; but it is safe to infer that, during the first three Islamic centuries, a predominantly Christian *iqlīm* ruled by a small Arabo-Muslim minority was slowly transformed into a Muslim *iqlīm* having a substantial Christian minority.[84]

Initially the primary Arab goal was not conversion so much as the preservation of order among the populace, thereby maintaining the social stability necessary for the high level of economic productivity that had characterized the province under Byzantine rule, and which could now be taxed for support of the Arab armies. Not until the reign of 'Umar ibn 'Abd al-Azīz (717–20) did the Arabs actively encourage conversion to Islam, and their attitude toward the Coptic Church during this period was prevailingly paternalistic.[85] From the third decade of the eighth century, however, official policy was more encouraging of conversion at the same time as it became less protective of the Coptic Church. Nevertheless, the Muslim authorities continued to permit the building of new churches right through the eighth century, and in 735/36 the Christian quarter of al-Ḥamrah in al-Fusṭāṭ, originally settled by Syrian Christians in the train of 'Amr's armies, was completely rebuilt.[86]

It is apparent, though, that conversion was not invariably sufficient to guarantee full acceptance into the Arabo-Muslim community. Resentment at this ethnic discrimination remained latent, however, until excessive taxation incited a series of Coptic rebellions extending over a century or more. These in turn provoked various forms of retaliatory persecution that, culminating in total suppression during the reign of al-Ma'mūn, undermined the religious and communal solidarity of Coptic society, thereby opening the way for mass conversions to Islam. In fact al-Maqrīzī notes specifically that it was immediately following the last rebellion in 832 that the majority of Miṣrī villages became Muslim.[87] This author may have been guilty of some exaggeration, especially when he asserted that never before had a whole people undergone such rapid conversion; but there can be no doubt that the ninth century witnessed an enormous increase in the Islamization of the Coptic population. "Not the Arab conquest itself," writes Ira Lapidus, "but the ninth century was the great watershed in the history of Egypt."[88]

It is not to be expected that conversion would have proceeded uniformly throughout the *iqlīm*. One of the premier centers first of revolt and then of conversion was the Ḥawf, where some five thousand Qays households had settled in the neighborhood of Tinnīs late in Umayyad times.[89] Professor Lapidus has suggested that these sedentarizing *badū* may have "lent the local Coptic population a veneer of Arabic-Islamic and possibly bedouin identifications" so that the combined Qays-Coptic rebellion of 829–32 would have been expression of tensions arising from both sedentarization and conversion.[90] Incidentally, the Ḥawf is one of the regions within Miṣr where it has proved practicable to recover a reasonably high proportion of urban settlements for inclusion in figure 2. In Upper Egypt (al-Ṣaʿīd) it is likely that raiding of settled communities by Arab tribesmen, especially during the reigns of al-Mustaʿīn (862–66) and al-Muʿtazz (866–69), further undermined the morale of Coptic communities already strained by discriminatory taxation and repression. The persecution of Coptic clergy and the destruction of churches in the vicinity of Iskandarīyah probably contributed to a similar result. In any case, for one reason or another, by the tenth century a presently unspecifiable majority of the Egyptian populace seem to have become nominally Muslim.

Professor Lapidus summarizes the condition of the Christian communities at the time as follows:

> we cannot say that the minority of Christians was anything less than very substantial in the ninth and tenth centuries. The Coptic urban populations seem to have remained in vigor in the eighth, ninth and tenth centuries. Coptic was spoken in Fusṭāṭ in the eighth century. Alexandria remained strongly Coptic. Damietta retained a large Coptic population, for in the great Byzantine assault of 238/852–53 both Muslims and Copts were indiscriminately taken prisoners. Tinnīs remained largely Coptic into the tenth century as did Shaṭā.... The great importance of Coptic artisans and officials throughout the ʿAbbāsid period gives further, though indirect, evidence for the persistence of Christianity among the urban artisan and professional classes. Coptic shipbuilders prepared the Arab vessels for war against Byzantium. Coptic artisans staffed the cloth and *ṭirāz* factories of Egypt, and the administration of the country was then, as in almost all succeeding ages, staffed by Copts. Even the construction of the great mosque of Aḥmad ibn Ṭūlūn, of such manifest religious importance, was supervised by a Copt.
>
> In the rural areas of lower and upper Egypt important Coptic communities also remained in vigor late in the tenth century. From Ibn Ḥawqal [pp. 139–142] we can see, despite many mosques and Muslim communities, that churches were still to be found in many towns and villages in the *Rīf* or western delta. Ibn Ḥawqal found churches in Tarnūṭ, Barsīq, Ṣā, Babīj, Dayyāy, Ṣāfiyya, Sandīyūn, Maḥalla Marsūq, Sandabīs, Farnawa, and, of course, Alexandria. The *Rīf* seems to have retained an important Coptic population, though it was no longer exclusively Christian.
>
> Similarly, other parts of Egypt retained part of their Christian populations. Many villages in the Ṣaʿīd area continued to be Christian.... The oases of the western desert were also Christian in the tenth century, though Ibn Ḥawqal [pp. 155–156] reports that the oases, once entirely Christian, had a Muslim population as well.[91]

These remarks go a long way toward validating al-Maqdisī's reasons for omitting an unknown number of towns from the Miṣrī urban hierarchy—and, incidentally, implying that the number was not small. In the construction of figure 2 I have attempted to compensate for al-Maqdisī's omissions by drawing on non-Muslim sources, but with only limited success. In any case, there may be another reason for there being fewer Miṣrī cities in figure 2 than the *iqlīm's* pre-Islamic and post-tenth-century histories might have led us to expect. That is the circumstance that a large proportion of the predominantly farming population lived not in urban service centers (low-order central places, in some readings of the situation) but in villages, hamlets, and individual farms dispersed through the fields, and would not have been incorporated in al-Maqdisī's settlement hierarchy in any case.

It should also be remarked incidentally that this *iqlīm* represents a higher than usual proportion of unlocatable toponyms: settlements such as Anbūrīt,[92] Bīkhīt,[93] and Qabīshah,[94] which can be assigned nothing more precise than regional locations and whose functions in the settlement system are matters of uncertain inference. Nor were such problem settlements found only on the margins of the *iqlīm*. We have seen above that al-ʿAbbāsīyah, one of the Miṣrī *qaṣabāt* and situated within the Delta itself, has thus far resisted efforts to assign it a definite location.[95] But, in partial extenuation of what may be regarded as an insufficiently cautious attempt to reconstruct this settlement hierarchy, it must be pointed out that the scale at which figure 2 is reproduced allows considerable latitude in the spatial positioning of a cartographic symbol before seriously subverting the purpose of the map.

When toward the mid-seventh century the Arabs overran Egypt, they assumed control of what, by the standards of the time, was a highly developed urban system in the Delta lands, with a chain of settlements stretching southward along the Nile valley for upwards of five hundred miles. Clearly, physiography placed severe constraints on the level of integration attainable in this southern sector of the settlement hierarchy. There is no evidence that during the ensuing three and a half centuries the Arabs significantly changed either the fundamental character or the structure of this system. The basis of life in Upper and Lower Egypt was agriculture, and what might appropriately be termed the type city of these regions was a center of restricted local influence serving the needs of peasants in the surrounding countryside. Ascent to a higher level in the hierarchy was achieved by assumption of additional administrative, industrial, or commercial functions, with a military role making a minor contribution in certain localities.

It is true that the Arabs transferred the metropolis of the province from Iskandarīyah, which in 641 still retained more than a vestige of the grandeur that had invested it as the capital of the Ptolemaic empire,[96] to al-Fusṭāṭ. In so doing they exchanged a venerable capital long recognized as being next to, rather than of, Egypt for a new metropolis that, like Memphis in ancient times, lay in the very heart of the country at the point of articulation of its two halves. Whereas Iskandarīyah (as Alexandria) had turned its face to the Mediterranean and fostered ties to the Roman world, and indeed remained the seat of the Christian patriarchate as late as the eleventh century, al-Fusṭāṭ was above all an Arab capital owing allegiance to the Caliphate, first in al-Madīnah (Medina) and then in Dimashq. Whereas Iskandarīyah had shipped Egyptian grain to Byzantium, al-Fusṭāṭ's trade relations were principally with the Maghrib, the Ḥijāz, and the Levant. But this change in the location of the metropolis did not vitally affect the structure of the urban hierarchy, particularly in the earlier decades of the Arab hegemony, when al-Iskandarīyah still far outranked al-Fusṭāṭ in size, industry, commerce, learning, and, even among Muslims, in prestige.

Although the reorientation of cultural and commercial ties from the Mediterranean toward the caliphal metropolis consequent on the Muslim conquest seriously subverted the power and prestige of al-Iskandarīyah, there are also indications that the silting of ancient canals bringing Nile water to the Mareotic Lake substantially lowered the water level of that lake. This process apparently had begun even before the advent of the Muslims, probably fostered by political instability associated with both the military confrontations between Nicetas and Bonōsus and the Persian invasion. Certainly by the ninth century these canals had ceased to be navigable, thus impeding the transport of commodities to al-Iskandarīyah from its hinterland. When the caliph al-Mutawakkil in 870 ordered the enlargement of the port of al-Rashīd on the western distributary of the Nile, he was in fact acknowledging and at the same time exacerbating the decline of al-Iskandarīyah.[97] In any case, long before the tenth century al-Fusṭāṭ had established its right to be recognized as one of the premier Islamic capitals. By the end of that century, the city had become the nucleus of an expanding urban agglomeration that at least one topographer regarded as "the centre of the world's commerce" (p. 192 above).

Muslim and Christian authors alike writing during the first four centuries of Islam paid relatively little attention to the more southerly sectors of the Ṣaʿīd, a region that had for long been following a developmental trajectory distinct from that of Lower Egypt. In fact in 640 Uswān, unlike the cities of the Nile Delta, had been conquered not by the army of ʿAmr ibn al-ʿĀṣ but by Arab contingents that had crossed over the Red Sea from the Ḥijāz; and as late as the ninth century the governors of that district were being appointed directly from Baghdād. Uswānī cultural and economic interests at this time were directed eastward to Arabia rather than to al-Fusṭāṭ and the north. Pilgrim traffic to the Ḥaramān, trans–Red Sea trade, and gold mining in the eastern desert underpinned a web of economic activities extending in an arc from Uswān through the port of ʿAydhāb to Makkah (Mecca) and al-Madīnah in the Ḥijāz. And with economic concerns came ideologies in the form of a preference for Malīkī legal reasoning and the Pro-ʿAlid and Shīʿī sympathies prevalent in the Yaman and the Ḥijāz. Not until the mid-eleventh century was this southern nexus of relationships superseded, under Fāṭimid influence, by commercial ties running northward along the Nile to al-Fusṭāṭ. This is not to imply that Upper Egypt was at any time formally, or even conceptually, excluded from the Miṣrī *iqlīm*—which in any case would be belied by the fact that in the ninth century an Uswānī jurist was appointed chief *qāḍī* of al-Fusṭāṭ[98]—but merely that it was a distant part of the polity with its own legitimate interests that were of no great concern to the literati of Lower Egypt.[99]

It is evident that the Arabs did not change significantly the contours of the urban hierarchy of the *iqlīm* of Miṣr by adding new cities. Aside from al-Fusṭāṭ/al-Qāhirah, which was an extension of a preexisting metropolis, the highest-ranking Arab foundation in the *iqlīm* was the locationally elusive al-ʿAbbāsīyah, laid out at the behest of a daughter of Ibn Ṭūlūn, which eventually became the *qaṣabah* of the Rīf.[100] Another new, or at least refurbished, foundation of some importance was Ḥulwān, either built de novo or developed by the governor ʿAbd al-ʿAzīz ibn Marwān some thirty kilometers south of al-Fusṭāṭ as a refuge from the plague of 689–90; the city did not survive its founder. In any case such building of entirely new towns was rare. As for the agricultural settlements scattered through the black, seasonally renewed soils of both Upper and Lower Egypt, there is no evidence to show that as a group—or, more accurately, as ranks in the urban hierarchy—they grew appreciably in size. Some probably declined, although it is often difficult to ascertain whether failure to be mentioned by a topographer implied a diminution in importance or a conscious ignoring of a settlement because its population was predominantly Christian. Ṭaḥā, in Upper Egypt, affords an example of a town that was virtually destroyed during the Coptic-Qays rebellion of 829–32, but it had recovered by the tenth century, when it was well known for its woollen industry.[101] During the same period, al-Faramā had probably at least partly compensated for its reduced role in the defense of the Nile Delta by expanding its commercial facilities.[102] A group of cities that had surely grown in importance and almost certainly in size under Arab rule were the textile centers situated in the vicinity of Lake Tinnīs, although Ibn Ḥawqal reports that toward the end of the tenth century they were having a difficult time coping with the taxes imposed by the accursed Ibn Killis.[103]

Overall it must be concluded that the Arabs were reasonably capable custodians of the Miṣrī urban system rather than aggressive developers. In this essentially conservationist role the Muslims cannot but have been materially assisted by their imposition of a centralized government on what, under the Byzantine hegemony, had comprised a congeries of provinces (eparchies), each under a quasi-autonomous governor exercising both civil and military authority. Although the precise effect of the replacement of disjoined and largely unconstrained Byzantine eparchs by Muslim pagarchs answering directly to the governor in al-Fusṭāṭ can only be inferred at this time, it is a topic that would repay further investigation. In the meantime, it can be suggested that the removal or lowering of internal political barriers is likely to have facilitated virtually all modes of economic exchange between components of the urban hierarchy.[104]

Chapter Sixteen

The Urban System in al-Maghrib

> . . . the province with the most boorish, the most ill-favoured and the most deceitful people, which contains the largest number of district administrative centres *(mudun),* and which extends over the greatest area.
>
> —Al-Maqdisī, *Aḥsan al-Taqāsīm,* 33.

Al-Maghrib was the name by which al-Maqdisī, along with other early topographers, designated the Islamic lands lying to the west of Miṣr (Egypt) and comprising North Africa, al-Andalus (Islamic Spain), and Iṣqiliyah (Sicily).[1] Al-Maqdisī may have been justified in his belief that this vast tract of territory contained in aggregate a larger number of urban centers than did any of his other *aqālīm,* but it is doubtful whether the density of urban forms in this region, with the possible exception of present-day Tunisia, approached those obtaining in al-Shām (Syria), Khūzistān, or parts of Mā Wara' al-Nahr (Transoxania). Moreover, this *iqlīm* was not a functionally integrated urban region, and, like the Arabian Peninsula and al-Mashriq, it was assigned two *amṣār:* al-Qayrawān (Kairouan), which served as the metropolis of the North African urban system, and Qurṭubah (Córdoba), which played the same role in Islamic Iberia.

North Africa

Marketing and Service Centers

The metropolis of al-Maghrib in al-Maqdisī's urban system was al-Qayrawān, a city that had developed from a military encampment established by ʿUqbah ibn Nāfiʿ al-Fihrī in 670[2] as a base for operations against the Berber tribes of al-Ifrīqiyah (Tunisia and western Libya).[3] During the ensuing three centuries, the discrete tribal holdings laid out by ʿUqbah's army had been transformed into sectors of an organically functioning city in a manner broadly comparable to that described for al-Baṣrah, al-Kūfah, and al-Fusṭāṭ in chapter 2.[4] Profiting from its strategic location near the junction of three distinct ecological zones—the high *tall,* the steppe, and the coastal *sāḥil*—which meant in effect the boundary between sedentary and at least partially nomadic ways of life, by the tenth century the city had become, in al-Maqdisī's words, "the glory of Western Islam, the seat of power and one of the pillars [of the empire]."[5] The walls built by the ʿAbbāsid general Muḥammad ibn al-Ashʿath in 762–63 had been demolished in 810 by the Aghlabid Ibrāhīm I as a punishment for the city having treated with rebels, then rebuilt, and then in 824 again "razed until they were level with the ground" by Ziyādat Allāh I during his suppression of a revolt.[6] Consequently, al-Maqdisī at the end of the tenth century was able to record the unusual circumstance of a city only slightly less than three miles in diameter being unwalled.[7]

Under Aghlabid rule (800–909) al-Qayrawān became a political, economic, and cultural center of the first order.[8] Theology, jurisprudence,[9] and Maghribī poetry flourished and, indeed, continued to do so under the early Fāṭimids and the Zīrīds. Maintaining, as it did, ties of formal dependency with the Caliphate in Baghdād, the Aghlabid kingdom, and especially its capital al-Qayrawān, had become the principal cultural conduit between North Africa and the Islamic Orient, a circumstance reflected in the diversity of its population. As early as the second half of the ninth century, al-Yaʿqūbī listed among the ethnic groups crowding its streets Arabs from the tribes of Quraysh, Muḍar, Rabīʿah, and Qaḥṭān and Persian Khurāsānīs,[10] together with, as we learn from other sources, Byzantines, Afāriq (who were probably bilingual natives: compare note 72), Jews, and Christians. In connection with this last community, it is interesting to note that al-Faḍl ibn Rawḥ had authorized the building of a church in their neighborhood in 793/94.[11]

In 948 the third representative of the Fāṭimid dynasty, Ismāʿīl al-Manṣūr, transferred his residence from al-Qayrawān to the neighboring locality of Ṣabrah, on which he bestowed the honorific name of al-Manṣūrīyah. Up to this time the main *sūq* of al-Qayrawān had consisted of a roofed arcade of stalls, built in the time of the Umayyad caliph Hishām ibn ʿAbd al-Malik (r. 724–43), that stretched for more than two miles from the Rabīʿah Gate clear across the city to the Tūnis Gate; but in the third quarter of the tenth century, the Fāṭimid caliph al-Muʿizz transferred all the bazaars and crafts of al-Qayrawān to his father's palace precinct at al-Manṣūrīyah.[12]

At the level of the urban hierarchy next below the *miṣr* were five *qaṣabāt.* Farthest east was Barqah, essentially a staging post on the caravan route linking al-Ifrīqiyah to Egypt that had fully exploited both the agricultural potentialities of the middle northern slopes of the Jabal al-Akhḍār and the possibilities of maritime commerce. In addition, administrative and military responsibilities of a relatively high order had devolved on it.[13] The wall surrounding the city had been built by order of the caliph al-Mutawakkil. At the end of the ninth century the population comprised mainly Berbers, with a substantial admixture of time-expired Arab levies who had settled in the city.[14] Almost as far west of al-Qayrawān as Barqah was to the east was Ṭāhart, the regional center for the fertile Sersou plateau. At the time of the Arab conquest in the seventh century the city, under the name Tingartia, was already of considerable importance; and in 761 a group of Ibāḍī sectaries[15] under the leadership of ʿAbd al-Raḥmān ibn Rustam made it the capital of a Khārijī principality that endured until 909, when it fell to the Kutāmā Berbers of the Fāṭimid *dāʿī,* Abū ʿAbd Allāh.[16] As a result, Ṭāhart lost a good deal of its political importance. In fact al-Maqdisī's description of the city, which he refers to as "the Balkh of the Maghrib"[17] and couples in reputation with Qurṭubah and Dimashq (Damascus), would seem to relate to the Rustamid period (777–909) rather than to his own time.[18]

In the western Maghrib the two *qaṣabāt* were Fās (Fez) and Sijilmāsah. The founding and development of the former city has already been discussed in chapter 2. Suffice it here to note that, in his description of the city, al-Maqdisī seems again to be harking back to the condition of the settlement perhaps more than half a century before he was writing, certainly to a period prior to the ousting of the Fāṭimids in 972.[19] Sijilmāsah was founded (or perhaps restored) in 757 in the Tafilalt oases on the Wādī Zīz, at a point some thirteen days' march from Fās, where the steppe of what is today southern Morocco finally deteriorates into desert.[20] Al-Bakrī records two traditions regarding its origin without expressing a preference for either. According to one version, the putative ancestor of the Banū-Midrār, on his conversion to Islam, built a mosque at a spot where tribal pastoralists customarily gathered at a certain time of year for purposes of exchange. According to the other version, the earliest sedentary occupants of the site were so-called Berber *rabāḍīs* expelled from the southern suburb of Qurṭubah by al-Ḥakam I in 818.[21] Possibly two events separated by nearly a century were here run together to produce a composite myth in a manner commonly encountered among preliterate peoples, for the archetyping process that produces myth is both predominantly atemporal and anhistorical. In any case, the settlement resulting from whichever or both of these happenings was subsequently walled, according to the first of these versions by a certain Abū Manṣūr al-Yāsāʾ al-Muntaṣir. By the tenth century it had evolved into a prosperous regional center that, by virtue of its location, was able to exercise control over one of the main trans-Ṣaḥārān caravan routes.

Finally, there remains the problem of identifying and locating the *qaṣabah* of Ṭarfānah. Under this orthography the name appears twice in al-Maqdisī's *Aḥsan al-Taqāsīm,* once at the end of the schedule of *qaṣabāt* (p. 48) and again on a list of urban centers in the district of Sūs al-Aqṣā (p. 221). On no occasion does al-Maqdisī describe the settlement. Several authors have equated this toponym with the Ṭarqalah mentioned in Ibn al-Faqīh's topographical miscellany *Kitāb al-Buldān* (p. 84) and again in Yāqūt's geographical gazetteer *Muʿjam al-Buldān* (3:532).[22] Graphically, in the Arabic script *fā* for *qāf* and *nūn* for *lām* would seem not unlikely as copyist's errors, and on the evidence presented thus far the identification would seem plausible. However, Mahammad Hadj-Sadok (Muḥammad Ḥajj-Ṣadūk) has proposed an alternative solution by suggesting that Ṭarfānah should perhaps be identified with Tārūdant, the name of a settlement in the Sūs (Sous) valley.[23] As a putative copyist's mistake, this transformation is altogether less likely, and the substitution of the graphically distinctive voiceless alveolar stop *ṭā'* for the dental stop *tā'* is unacceptable unless confirmed by independent evidence. What has so far been ignored in the discussion is that al-Maqdisī's precise orthography *Ṭarfānah* also occurs in Ibn Ḥawqal's *Kitāb Ṣūrat al-Arḍ* (pp. 65 and 86), and is in fact placed on his map in close proximity to Saʿ, Jurāwah, Tilimsān, Afkān, and Yālah,[24] that is, roughly in the border zone between present-day Morocco and Algeria.

I suspect that al-Maqdisī, who was not especially well informed about the Maghrib, incorporated Ṭarfānah in his account of that province on the authority of Ibn Ḥawqal or some other topographer without having any precise idea as to its location. A close reading of the topographical literature of the ninth and tenth centuries has failed to reveal any other reference to the name, but al-Bakrī, in the second half of the eleventh century, did mention a city that he called Ṭarfalah. "This locality," he wrote, "has no equal on earth, and its inhabitants say, 'Ṭarfalah is part *(ṭarf)* of Paradise.'"[25] In fact he seems to have located the city in the vicinity of the present-day Hudnah (Hodna) Mountains. This is considerably farther eastward than Ibn Ḥawqal's map would imply, but al-Bakrī was writing nearly a century later and, being a Spaniard, may have possessed more accurate information than his predecessor. Moreover, the graphical transformation from Ṭarfānah to Ṭarfalah in a copyist's script is readily understandable. Although the matter is still very uncertain, in figure 2 (p. 74) I have—with some misgivings but as the least disagreeable of several dubious alternatives—assigned the *qaṣabah* of Ṭarfānah to east-central Algeria.

Below the rank of *qaṣabah* al-Maqdisī enumerated a stratum of four *mudun,* to which I have added one more on general functional grounds:

1. ***Qafṣah*** (Gafṣah), the classical Capsa, about which the Arab topographers had little to say beyond mentioning its heritage of Roman streets and buildings, the stones of which had frequently been incorporated in later structures.[26] The city stood on the right bank of the Oued Baiech in dry steppe country. Like Gafṣah, its present-day counterpart, it was an important node in the transportation network of al-Maghrib, where routes from all four quarters of the compass were channelled through a col cut by the Baiech River.
2. ***Al-Masīlah,*** a tenth-century foundation, having been established on the plain of Hudnah and endowed with the honorific style of al-Muḥammadīyah as recently as 925 by Abū al-Qāsim Ismāʿīl, son of ʿUbaydallāh al-Mahdī, first of the Fāṭimid caliphs.[27] Al-Maqdisī was not personally acquainted with the city, so that he could write only that "According to the description that has been given us, it is a well-known region of al-Maghrib."[28] Nevertheless, al-Masīlah clearly was the administrative seat for the whole of the Zāb District; was of substantial size, with several *sūqs* and baths; and was exploiting a powerful nodality at a point where three routes leading westward from al-Qayrawān came together before climbing up to the High Plateaux.
3. ***Tilimsān,***[29] an impressively fortified regional market center on the northern flank of the mountains forming the western sector of the High Plateaux of present-day Algeria. It had been built by a paramount chief of the Banū-Īfran during their brief political domination of northwestern Algeria in the eighth century. In the tenth century the city possessed extensive *suqs*, a congregational mosque, and several *masjids*, and enjoyed a reputation as a seat of learning.[30]
4. ***Ṭanjah*** (Tangiers), a foundation of great antiquity. In the sixth century B.C. it had been a Phoenician trading station, subsequently being occupied by Carthaginians. As Tingis it had functioned as the capital of the Roman province of Mauretania Tingitana. In 429 the settlement was captured by the Vandals, in 541 by the Byzantines, and in 621 by the Visigoths. In 682 it fell to the Arab armies under ʿUqbah ibn Nāfiʿ, and in 707 an Arab garrison was stationed there permanently. During the tenth century its control was disputed by the Umayyads of al-Andalus and the Idrīsids of Morocco. By that time the focus of settlement had already migrated from the shore of the Mediterranean Sea up the eastern slope of what is today Tangier Point, in search of protection from Idrīsid forces, which had occupied Sabtā. In any case, only small boats unloaded cargoes at the port, for the roads were too exposed to easterly winds for large vessels to venture there.[31]
5. ***Ījlī,*** "a large city on a plain," which, according to

al-Bakrī (but unconfirmed by any other topographer), was the capital of the district of al-Sūs al-Aqṣā.[32] From al-Bakrī's meager comments it is to be concluded that the city was a regional market center in the Sūs valley, which had allegedly been colonized by ʿAbd al-Raḥmān ibn Marwān, brother of that Muḥammad al-Jādī who fathered the last of the Umayyad caliphs.

The lowest rank in al-Maqdisī's urban hierarchy in the Maghrib probably had a more diverse composition than that in any other of his *iqlīms*. One of its unusually prominent components was the smaller princely foundation that owed its origin directly to Arab or Berber initiative. Muslim rule ultimately extended over an area of North Africa considerably larger than that to which the Greeks or Romans had laid claim and—as the responsibilities of Islam, including those of government, could be discharged fully only in a group setting—numerous new settlements were integrated into the existing pattern. On occasion the new foundation might be the palace enclave of a dynast, as, for example, were the fortified enceinte eventually known as al-Qaṣr al-Qadīm, founded in 800 by Ibrāhīm ibn al-Aghlab, the first of his dynasty, two miles southeast of al-Qayrawān and which he endowed with the honorific al-ʿAbbāsīyah in acclaim for the ruler in whose name he read the *khuṭbah;*[33] Raqqādah, to which Ibrāhīm II ibn al-Aghlab transferred his residence in 876, and which continued as the seat of that dynasty until Ziyādat-Allāh III fled before the Fāṭimids in 909;[34] al-Mahdīyah, the new capital inaugurated by ʿUbaydallāh al-Mahdī in 921 near the site of the old Carthaginian city of Zella;[35] and Qalʿat Banī-Ḥammād, the capital constructed by the Ḥammādid dynasty a short distance northeast of al-Masīlah early in the eleventh century.[36]

Most of these *villes créés,* however, were humbler foundations such as Ashīr, in the Ṣanhājah country of the Ṭiṭṭarī Mountains, which was transformed from a village into a fortified town by Yūsuf Buluggīn ibn Zīrī in 977/78;[37] Tanas, founded in 875 by adventurers from Ilbīrah (Elvira) and Mursiyah (Murcia) on a site overlooking the estuary of the Oued Allālah;[38] Sūq Ḥamzah, built by one Ḥamzah ibn al-Ḥasan on the site of present-day Bourdj Bouīra;[39] Wahrān (Oran), where in 902/3, as at Tanas, the stimulus toward urbanization was provided by the settlement of a band of Andalusian mariners;[40] Fakkān, constructed by the Īfranid Yaʿlā ibn Muḥammad ibn Ṣāliḥ in 949;[41] Jurāwah, founded in 872 by a certain Abū al-ʿAysh some six miles up the Kiss River;[42] Arashkūl, the port of Tilimsān, already a rendezvous of merchants when ʿĪsa ibn Muḥammad ibn Sulaymān, brother of the first Idrīsid ruler, took possession of it toward the end of the eighth century;[43] the new settlement built alongside an already existing one at Ujdah soon after 1048;[44] Nākūr, allegedly founded by Saʿīd ibn Idrīs, grandson of Ṣāliḥ ibn Manṣūr, the Ḥimyarite who conquered the territory, in the reign of the Umayyad caliph al-Walīd I (705–15);[45] Dhāt al-Ḥumām, "established by an *amīr* at the time when the Fāṭimid took possession of Egypt;[46] and al-Aqlam, founded by Yaḥyā ibn Idrīs in the tenth century.[47] It should not pass without comment, though, that all the really important cities founded by the Muslims, with the principal exception of al-Mahdīyah, were inland—a development encouraged by the existence of Roman roads running south from the Mediterranean to forts on the *limes.*

Among cities rebuilt or significantly enlarged by the Arabs were Ṭubnah, the classical Thubunae, first walled by order of al-Manṣūr, the second ʿAbbāsid caliph, and subsequently largely reconstructed by Abū Jaʿfar ʿUmar ibn Ḥafṣ al-Muhallabī, who was appointed governor of Ifrīqiyah in 768;[48] the ancient port of Malīlah (Melilla), allegedly rebuilt by a son of al-Būrī ibn Abī al-Afīyah the Miknāsian and subsequently conquered in 926 by the Spanish Umayyad ʿAbd al-Raḥmān III al-Nāṣir, who walled the whole settlement;[49] Sabtā (Ceuta), another ancient city walled by the same monarch;[50] Marsā Mūsā, a small port between Ṭanjah and Sabtā that was also rebuilt by this same ʿAbd al-Raḥmān after being destroyed by the Banū-Muḥammad and the Masmūdah in 914;[51] and Zalūl, reconstituted to the order of Ḥasan ibn Kannūn al-Ḥasanī al-Fāṭimī.[52]

The local service centers constituting the majority of the urban forms at this lower level of the urban hierarchy were spread very unevenly through the vast territory of North Africa, but corresponded closely with the availability of agricultural land. In present-day Libya they were almost confined to a narrow coastal zone that broadened somewhat in Cyrenaica to include the slopes of the Jabal al-Akhḍār. Farther westward, throughout the fifteen hundred miles of Barbary, the zone of urban settlement lapped about and between the several Atlas ranges, finally running out to the Atlantic coast of Morocco. Fairly representative of this class of service centers largely (sometimes entirely) dependent on the agricultural productivity of their local trading areas were Bājah, styled by al-Bakrī as "the granary *(al-hūrī)* of al-Ifrīqiyah;[53] Barashk, where, although cereal harvests surpassed the needs of the population, cattle constituted the principal resource of the district;[54] Māsīnah, where irrigation permitted Berber cultivators to raise abundant crops of cotton, wheat, and barley;[55] and Qasṭīliyah, "the locality whence the Ifrīqiyah acquires[56] its dates."[57] The exceptions transgressing the limits of this distribution were the service centers situated in oases on the fringe of the Ṣaḥārā: Zawīlah, a large, unwalled city in the Fazzān;[58] Nafṭah[59] and Tawzir[60] in the Jarīd (Djerīd); Biskarah,[61] Ṭawlaqā,[62] and Banṭiyūs[63] in the Zibān oases; and several settlements in the Tafilalt group of oases.[64]

Within this broad category of urban centers there were, not unexpectedly, fairly wide degrees of variation in population size and extent of city trade areas—ranging from, say, Tabassā, which, as Theveste, had once been the military headquarters of Roman Africa,[65] down to local service centers consisting of little more than a *jāmiʿ*, a *sūq*, and a sprinkling of habitations. The designation *sūq* in the names of a relatively high proportion of these settlements, particularly in the highlands, betrayed their recent past as rural, often periodic and/or tribal, markets: Sūq al-Ḥamzah, Sūq ibn Ḥablah, Sūq ibn Khalaf, Sūq ibn Mablūl, Sūq Ibrāhīm, Sūq Karā, Sūq al-Kutāmī, Sūq Fanqūr, Sūq Huwārah, and Sūq Banī-Maghrāwah, to name but a few.

Transportation Foci

Cities adapted to the institutional demands of long-distance trade tended to occur most commonly in two distinctive ecological zones of North Africa: along the Mediterranean coast and along the northern edge of the Ṣaḥārā. In the former zone ecological adaptations inevitably took the form of break-of-bulk facilities associated with port development. Such ports generally tended to be larger and more numerous in the western sectors of the coast than in the Tripolitanian or Cyrenaican sectors. Moreover, within the western sectors they were particularly numerous along the coast of the peninsula facing Gibraltar and where the coast of northeastern Tunisia thrust out toward Sicily. In fact it was not until Muslim armies had secured substantial footholds in Sicily in the second half of the ninth century that Islamic maritime commerce began to burgeon.

Several of the major Maghribī ports have been mentioned already; others of the first or second rank included the Jazā'ir Banī-Mazghannā (present-day Algiers), founded in 944 by Buluggīn ibn Zīrī, the then-Fāṭimid governor of al-Ifrīqiyah;[66] Banzart;[67] Tūnis, the main port for those travelling between al-Andalus and the holy city of al-Qayrawān and, additionally, recreator of the role of Carthage as the regional focus of what is now northern Tunisia;[68] Sūsah (al-Sūs) refortified by the Aghlabids in 827 when it served as the port of embarkation for the invasion of Sicily;[69] Munastīr, which took its name from a Christian monastery that once stood on the site of the present *qaṣabah;*[70] Asfāqus (present-day Sfax), which prospered under Aghlabid rule;[71] Qābis (Gabès), a large city on the site of the Roman colony of Tacapae;[72] Aṭrābulus (Tripoli), the ancient Oea, which was captured for Islam by ʿAmr ibn al-ʿĀṣ as early as 644 and where in the second half of the tenth century "merchant vessels fetched to anchor by day and night, bringing all sorts of merchandise and provisions from the Byzantine realm and the Maghrib";[73] and Surt, a walled town featuring a *jāmiʿ*, a *ḥammām,* and several *sūqs*, the inhabitants of which enjoyed an evil reputation for sharp trading.[74] Other significant ports were Ṭabarqah, whose location in what is now northern Tunisia attracted many Andalusian merchants doing business in the Ifrīqiyah;[75] Tanas, described by Ibn Ḥawqal as the largest port serving the Andalusian trade and the chief port of entry for travellers to other parts of the Maghrib;[76] and Wahrān, a port offering safer anchorage, according to Ibn Ḥawqal, than any other in the Berber territories except Marsā Mūsā, and the mart where Andalusians exchanged Spanish goods for Maghribī cereals.[77] At Arashkūl the same author reported the presence of numerous cisterns providing water both for shipping calling at the port and for livestock.[78]

In an age when the physical plant necessary for the handling and transshipment of goods was minimal, tertiary ports were so numerous along the three thousand or so miles of the Maghribī coastline as to almost defy listing. The only topographer to treat them reasonably systematically was al-Bakrī. Although the Atlantic seaboard of the Maghrib, al-Aqṣā, offered commodious harbors and roadsteads, it was too remote from the foci of civilization and commerce around the shores of the Mediterranean to support anything but small havens. Between Ṭanjah and the Sūs River estuary, however, al-Bakrī recorded no less than fifteen of these, disposed in three groups: seven along the coast immediately south of Ṭanjah and sharing in the general trading activity that took place in and around the Strait of Gibraltar, three on the coast between present-day Rabāṭ and Casablanca, and five between Cape Cantin and the Sūs.

The greater part of the Rīf coast of Morocco and Algeria is steep-to, and such harbors as it does provide, while offering shelter from westerly winds, usually lie open to the north. Tertiary ports were most numerous in three sectors of this coast, namely in the neighborhood of Malīlah and the estuary of the Mūlawiyah River, in the vicinity of the Jazā'ir Banī-Mazghannā, and along the coast between Jījil (Djidjelli) and Būnah (Bône, modern Annaba). Another group of such havens was strung in close proximity along the coast of northeast Tunisia (twenty-four between Banzart and Asfāqus [Sfax]). The Tripolitanian coast—known to ancient mariners as Σύρτις or "The Drag-Net" on account of its being a shoaling lee shore under the prevailing Etesian winds of summer (the sailing season in the Mediterranean)—afforded few havens, and those were mostly small. The following bald comments by al-Bakrī sufficiently convey the character of these small Maghribī harbors serving very restricted hinterlands and providing an occasional wintering for casual traders from farther afield:

- Marsā Maghīlah: "affords a summer anchorage, but it is exposed to gusty winds."[79]
- Al-Marsā al-Madfūn: "the sea is always treacherous and often engulfs vessels" (84).
- Khafānis: "ships can winter there" (84).
- Qaṣr al-Daraq: "where the sea is always calm" (85).
- Amugdūl: "a sure anchorage good to winter in" (87).
- Qūz: "ships arrive at all seasons, but they can put to sea only in the rainy season . . . when land breezes are favourable. . . . On the other hand, if the sky is cloudless and the atmosphere clear, a wind off the sea to the west raises waves sufficiently large to thrust a vessel on to the desert shore. In such a wind it is rare for a ship to escape" (153–54).
- Marsā Bāb al-Yamm: "an open roadstead" (105).
- Marsā Mūsā: "a sure anchorage, even in winter, that provides shelter from all winds except that from the southeast" (105).[80]

On the southern fringe of the Maghrib the land ports of the desert enjoyed a greater freedom of location than did the seaports of the north and were less rigorously confined to a particular boundary between contrasting environments, but institutionally they exhibited similar types of adaptations. On the whole they were best developed on the approaches to the great trans-Ṣaḥārān caravan trails. One such assembly point for caravans was Sijilmāsah, capital of the Tafīlalt oasis, whence it was two months' journey to Ghana (Ghānah) in the "Country of the Blacks."[81] Another was Aghmāt, or, rather, "the Aghmāts," for there were two urban centers bearing this name: Aghmāt Aylān, where the chief resided, and Aghmāt Warīkah, which appears to have been a ritual center of some sort, for no foreigner was allowed to enter it. Consequently it was in Aghmāt Aylān that long-distance traders congregated.[82] Farther eastward the cities of the Zibān oases functioned in similar fashion as desert-border emporia handling trade with Tūggūrt, Warqlah (Ouargla), and the settlements of the Tademait. From Tawzir and other cities of the Jarīd, caravans set out to tap the trade of the central Sūdān. In addition, Tawzir was situated in the middle of one of the chief date-producing regions of North Africa: al-Bakrī remarks that almost daily a thousand camels left the city loaded with this fruit.[83]

From Aṭrābulus another caravan trail led southward to Zawīlah in the Fazzān, from which it was a journey of forty days to the Bornu kingdom of Chad. Of Zawīlah al-Bakrī writes, "It is a city without walls, situated in the middle of the desert but as large as Ajdābiyah. It is there that the countries of the Blacks begin. The city incorporates a *jāmiʿ*, a *ḥammām* and several *sūqs*. It is an entrepôt for caravans which converge there from all directions and then separate to go their different ways."[84] In particular, Zawīlah was one of the chief slave marts of North Africa, acquiring its human merchandise from the Berber town of Kūwwar, some fifteen days' march to the south, in return for lengths of red cloth.[85] A caravan trail once linked Egypt and the kingdom of Ghana across "vast wastes of sand . . . whose incessant winds buffeted the caravans . . . not a few of which were lost . . . not to mention the depredations of desert marauders," but by the time when Ibn Ḥawqal was writing, this route had been abandoned in favor of a safer traverse by way of Sijilmāsah. From this trade enterprising merchants could reap immense profits, scarcely to be equalled in any other part of the Muslim world. Ibn Ḥawqal recalled seeing a promissory note, signed by a merchant of Awdaghust and duly witnessed, for a sum of no less than forty-two thousand *dīnārs*.[86]

Nor, despite their importance in these frontier zones, were caravan cities restricted to such regions. Many of them marked the stages along internal trade routes within the Maghrib. One such city was Tabassā, a prominent feature of which was the vaulted halls where caravans sheltered from the elements. One of these halls alone was capable of accommodating two thousand pack animals.[87] Another important node in the caravan network was the old Idrīsid capital of Fās (chapter 2 and p. 202 above), at a point where the most convenient route between the western and central Maghrib intersected that from Ṭanjah to the Tafīlalt. Two other important centers were Barqah[88] and Qābis,[89] both on the great highway from Egypt to Qayrawān, while the Fāṭimid ʿUbaydallāh (r. 909–34) once decreed that pilgrims en route to Makkah (Mecca) must pass through his new capital of al-Mahdīyah, where they were subjected to special imposts.

Industrial and Craft Centers

Specialist craft manufacture was not particularly prominent in Maghribī cities in the tenth century, although food processing and the production of implements and utensils were common to most urban centers and even villages. Carafes made in Tūnis of a pottery so thin as to be almost translucent enjoyed a high reputation throughout North Africa,[90] and at Marsā al-Kharaz (present-day La Calle) coral from an offshore reef was polished in specially equipped workshops. Rarely were there fewer than fifty vessels, each with a crew of twenty or so, engaged in collecting the coral.[91] Warships for raiding the Christian lands to the north were built at the same port and at Sūsah.[92]

The general impression of underdeveloped craft industries in the Maghrib of the tenth century probably owes a good deal to the relatively feeble development of the textile industry in the region. "Of all parts of the civilized Muslim world during the first four centuries," writes Professor Serjeant, "the Maghreb is probably the least productive of textiles of distinction."[93] Furthermore, what the industry did achieve is but poorly documented.[94] *Ṭirāz* factories existed at al-Qayrawān, Sūsah, and Fās when al-Bakrī was writing, and probably in earlier centuries,[95] while al-Idrīsī in 1154 referred to such a factory as operating at an unspecified "former time."[96] But the quality of their cloth apparently fell below that produced in Egypt and the more easterly *iqlīms*, and enjoyed no reputation outside the Maghrib. In fact manufactured textiles do not figure prominently among Maghribī exports.

The principal raw material was wool from sheep raised on the extensive steppelike pastures characteristic of so much of North Africa. Barqah,[97] Ajdābiyah,[98] Surt (Madīnat al-Sulṭān),[99] Aṭrābulus,[100] Qābis,[101] Sūsah,[102] Būnah,[103] and the whole of the Qasṭīliyah District, focused on Tawzir, exported that commodity either abroad or to other parts of the Maghrib.[104] In the neighborhood of Yarārah a breed of sheep said to have been brought from the island of Qays off the coast of Fārs produced wool of exceptionally high quality, which was used at Sijilmāsah in the manufacture of—for the Maghrib—uncharacteristically expensive cloth.[105] At Fās, too, raw wool and woollen stuffs dominated the trade of the city, which was perhaps even better known for the skill of its dyers.[106] Indigo, a dyeing agent only recently introduced into the Arab world from Persia, it should be noted, was grown widely throughout the western Maghrib and at al-Qasṭīliyah.[107]

Silk textiles were produced in only a few locations, of which Qābis was the most important, not only by reason of the volume of its manufactures[108] but also because of the high quality of its cloth.[109] The *ṭirāz* factory mentioned by al-Idrīsī had apparently specialized in the production of high-quality silks.[110] If the same author's reference to a court of silk merchants *(fundūq al-ḥarā'irīyah)* in Tūnis possibly as early as 994[111] is to be believed, the trade in that commodity, if not its manufacture, reached out well beyond the local Qābis hinterland. Cotton was certainly grown more widely, with Ṭubnah[112] and al-Masīlah (85–86) being important service centers for two of the principal producing regions; while al-Baṣrah in the far west of the Maghrib sent at least part of its crop to al-Ifrīqiyah (80), and Tūnis, actually in the Ifrīqiyah, exported its cotton harvests to the capital of al-Qayrawān at a substantial profit (74). Flax *(kattān)* was mentioned by the topographers from time to time but seems to have been of significant commercial importance only near Sabībah, in the hinterland of al-Qayrawān (84).

Fortified Settlements

One could almost say that in the tenth century the premier industry of North Africa was war. The Maghrib preserved longer than any other realm of the Islamic world, with the possible exception of the Amū Daryā frontier, its early image as Dār al-Ḥarb, territory where rewards both spiritual and material might be won fighting for the Faith. Indeed, some of the warriors of Islam may have believed the tradition—had they ever heard it—that the Prophet himself had located one of the gates of Paradise in al-Ifrīqiyah.[113] Through three centuries other traditions no less apocryphal were combined into a corpus that reflected changing expressions of a nevertheless consistent view of North Africa as "l'éternel champ des martyrs de l'Islam."[114] The material manifestations of this heroic role in the destiny of Islam were the *ribāṭāt,*[115] at once products and sustainers of *ḥadīth.* Already at the end of the ninth century, al-Yaʿqūbī was describing a chain of fortified barracks, the habitations of *al-ʿibād wa-l-murābiṭūn,* from Asfāqus to Banzart;[116] but it was the tenth and early eleventh centuries that witnessed the most intensive developments of *ribāṭāt* in the Barbary lands. The ʿAbbāsid governors were the prime movers in founding such fortified enclaves in al-Ifrīqiyah, with the *amīr*s of the Banū-Aghlab performing a comparable role in the west.

The topographers, who provide the bulk of the material relating to these foundations, were writing at too late a date to be able to provide reliable information about the origin of the institution, but the earliest implementation on present evidence would seem to have been the *ribāṭ* at Munastīr, which was established in 796 by the ʿAbbāsid governor of the Ifrīqīyah, Harthamah ibn Aʿyān.[117] Just over a quarter of a century later, in 821, the *ribāṭ* of Sūsah was founded.[118] Subsequently Aṭrābulus acquired a considerable number;[119] six *maḥāris* (sing. *maḥras*) were built in the purlieus of Asfāqus;[120] and, in the words of Georges Marçais, the city of Munastīr was one great *ribāṭ.*[121] North of Sūsah along the Tūnisian coast were the *ribāṭāt* of al-Ḥammān,[122] Qaṣr al-Ḥajjamīn (83), and Qaṣr Abī al-Sakhr (83). Between Ṭabarqah and Sabtā such fortified posts were less common,[123] but west of that point they became numerous again, among them Ishiburtāl,[124] Azīlla,[125] Salā,[126] Qūz,[127] and Māssah, on the south bank of the Wādī Sūs.[128]

These *ribāṭāt* were evidently concentrated in two zones: the coast of present-day Tūnisia and the Atlantic coast of Morocco. In the former area they served as defenses against incursions from, and as bases for raids against, the lands of Christian Europe. In the northern sector of the latter realm they constituted protection against depredations by the Normans (Majūs); in the southern sector, against raids by heretical Barghawāṭah tribesmen. More often than not such *ribāṭāt* were established in accordance with official military policy, but some were founded by pious Believers who, although themselves unable to participate in the Holy War, sought by such actions to win the mercy of Allāh. "It was the pious sentiments of the people of Aṭrābulus," writes Ibn Ḥawqal, "that led them to raise numerous *ribāṭs*";[129] al-Bakrī refers—somewhat ambiguously, it is true—to the *ribāṭ* of Azīlah as the work "of the inhabitants of the country";[130] and a tradition asserts that flanking towers had been added to the walls of Munastīr *ribāṭ* by pious devotees.[131] It was also considered meritorious to contribute to the support of an existing *ribāṭ* either in money or in kind, or perhaps most profitably, by *waqf* donations. We find Ibn Ḥawqal, for example, reporting that in the tenth century "In Ifrīqiyah there are several *waqfs* consecrated to the support of the *ribāṭs* of Munastīr and Shaqāniṣ, which also receive subventions from all the Muslim countries of the world."[132]

Finally, it may be relevant to an understanding of the urbanization process that certain *ribāṭāt* sponsored fairs on a large scale, often timed to coincide with the seasonal recruitment of new forces. Al-Bakrī's account of the *ribāṭ* of Azīlah on the Atlantic coast of al-Maghrib is especially informative on this point. There a fair, associated with the induction of recruits, was held three times a year: in the month of Ramaḍān, on the tenth of Dhū al-Ḥijjah, and on the tenth of Muḥarram.[133] Eventually the merchants' temporary tents were replaced by the houses of permanent residents, a mosque and a citadel were built, and the whole complex walled by al-Qāsim ibn Idrīs, thus reconstituting the city that had occupied the site in classical times. Similar fairs were held, but only once a year, under the auspices of *ribāṭāt* at Māssah and Munastīr.[134]

Religious Centers

Al-Maghrib had been imperfectly Christianized prior to the Islamic conquest. Its annexation phase had been prolonged until the beginning of the eighth century, and it had not been consolidated until the beginning of the ninth. Consequently the venerable sites associated with ancient pre-Islamic prophets that were so common in southwest Asia were wholly absent in the territories, and those shrines that did exist were either connected with more recent events or were holdovers from a not-so-distant pagan or Christian past. The following are reasonably representative: the tomb of Ruwayfiʿ ibn Thābit, one of the Companions, at Barqah;[135] the house, which subsequently became the mausoleum, of the great jurisconsult Ibn Abī Zayd al-Qayrawānī; the grave of the poet Daʿbil ibn ʿAlī al-Khuzāʿī in Zawīlah;[136] the shrine of a woman ascetic named Zūragh at Arkan in the Jabal Nafūsah; the tomb of ʿUqbah ibn Nāfiʿ, founder of al-Qayrawān, at Sīdī ʿUqbah, an oasis in the neighborhood of Biskarah;[137] and a stone image worshipped by Berber tribesmen three days' journey along the route from Waddān to Aṭrābulus.[138]

Commentary

Even without Spain and Sicily, al-Maqdisī's *iqlīm* of al-Maghrib was an artificially contrived urban system. Throughout the first four centuries of the Islamic era, North Africa was apportioned among several politically defined, but continually fluctuating urban hierarchies. By the ninth century these had crystallized into the following pattern of state organizations.

In the far west, Tāmasnā Province, extending along the Atlantic coast of Morocco from Salā to Safiʾ, was dominated by a confederation of Berber tribes known collectively to Arab chroniclers and topographers as Barghawāṭah. Welded into an embryonic state in the mid-eighth century by a process reminiscent of that by which the Prophet himself had forged the first Islamic polity in the Ḥijāz, and adopting a Berberized version of Sunnī Islam, the Barghawāṭah traded profitably with Fās, Aghmāt, Sūs, and Sijilmāsah over a span of several centuries. In 963 they sought to establish diplomatic relations with the Umayyad court in Qurṭubah,[139] but their heretical religious practices generally tended to isolate them politically and culturally from the Arabo-Islamic world of the Maghrib. To Ibn Ḥawqal, for instance, they were no better than infidels to be vanquished by pious *ghāzīs* from the *ribāṭāt* of Salā. The location of the paramount's capital has not been determined.

About the regions south of the Barghawāṭah, designated by the topographers vaguely as al-Sūs, even less information is available. On the north coast of the region, however, it is possible to point to two territorial enclaves asserting some autonomy during the ninth century. One focused on the port of Nākūr, which maintained its independence throughout the century and was in fact recognized by at least one Umayyad *amīr* of al-Andalus;[140] the other centered on Sabtā and, for most of the ninth century, was ruled by a Berber dynasty owing only minimal allegiance to the Idrīsids of Fās.[141] In spite of attempts to subdue the tribal groups of what is today western Morocco—notably incursions by Jaʿfar al-Andalusī, a client of the Umayyads, in 977/78; by Buluggīn ibn Zīrī in about 982/83; and by one of al-Manṣūr ibn Abī ʿĀmir's commanders in 998/99—Arab administrative control over the territory was hardly ever more than nominal.

In the most easterly sectors of the Maghrib, territories conquered by the Arabs remained administratively attached to Egypt until 705, when they were constituted as the separate *wilāyah* of Ifrīqiyah, with al-Qayrawān as its capital. Even then Cyrenaica remained under Egyptian control, leaving Tripolitania, Tunisia, and eastern Algeria as the core of the new *wilāyah*. However, Ibn Nuṣayr's conquest of northern Morocco in the years 705/6–708/9 and the ensuing occupation of the Iberian Peninsula extended the *wilāyah* briefly to include everything between the Pyrenees and the eastern boundary of Tripolitania. Not unexpectedly, this vast area proved to be beyond the control of the governors of al-Ifrīqiyah, and a Khārijī rebellion in 739/40 so weakened caliphal authority that it was unable to prevent the rise of independent dynasties in eastern Morocco and western Algeria. In the agriculturally productive Awrabah territories there crystallized a rather rudimentary, patrimonial-style kingdom under the authority of a succession of religio-political leaders owing their authority to putative descent from the Prophet through the ʿAlid line and their power to the backing of the Awrabah, one of the most powerful Berber tribes of northern Morocco. These leaders were the Idrīsids, with their capital at Fās,[142] which, as the seat of *shurafā'*[143] and the site of both the Qarawīyīn and Andalusīyīn mosques, emerged as the premier religious center of the western Maghrib.

But in the ninth century the Idrīsid kingdom began to disintegrate, a dissolution expedited when, on the death of Idrīs II in 828, it was apportioned as patrimonial-style benefices among the ruler's several sons. Even so, Islam and Arab culture continued to diffuse through the urban system, which at its maximum extent reached from the Shālif valley in present-day Algeria to Sūs in southern Morocco. But the process largely ceased at the city walls: the countryside remained predominantly Berber in custom and language, a place where heterodox, and even heretical, Islamic doctrines exercised a special appeal as symbolic rejections of the legitimacy of caliphal authority. The Idrīsid kingdom finally came to an end when a Fāṭimid army occupied Fās in 921, although branches of the dynasty survived in remoter parts of Morocco for another half century.

Whereas the Idrīsids seem to have been moderate Shī'ite Muslims, three other kingdoms that arose in the territories between the Mūlawiyah (Moulouya) valley and the Zāb District espoused the radical, egalitarian doctrine of Khārijism. Each in its own way exemplified the exploitation of Berber religious and political dissent as a means of gathering power into the hands of Arab opponents of the Caliphate. As Hichem Djaït has phrased it, with only the slightest tincture of exaggeration, "la tragédie de la conquête et l'installation de l'Islam par la violence avaient fait naître le monde berbère au sens de sa destinée historique." The least enduring of these principalities was established by a paramount chief of the Banū-Īfran in 765, with Tilimsān as the capital of a Ṣufrite imāmate.[144] Although this ruler succeeded in involving most of the tribes of the central Maghrib as far east as Ṭubnah in concerted military enterprises and was able to repulse several attacks by the 'Abbāsid army, from early in the 770s the Banū-Īfran began to cede their paramount status among the Khārijī tribes to the Rustamids. Thereafter they figured more as clients of the Rustamid rulers than as a dominant confederacy. In 786 their power was totally crushed when the Maghrāwah of Muḥammad ibn Khāzir overran Tilimsān, to be followed three years later by an Idrīsid conquest.

The fluid confederacy of Ibāḍī Berber tribes succeeding the Banū-Īfran as the paramount power in the central Maghrib was consolidated in 761, when 'Abd al-Raḥmān ibn Rustam—of Persian ancestry but raised in al-Qayrawān—was elected its *imām,* thereby establishing a dynasty that survived into the tenth century. However, the imāmate could persist as a supra-tribal embodiment of legitimate political authority only because the Ibāḍī religious scholars were prepared to make doctrinal compromises on such matters as hereditary succession to the office of *imām* and the principle of institutionalized consultation *(shūrā).* Even so, schismatic secessionist movements constituted an ever-present threat to the integrity of the kingdom.[145]

The core of the confederacy was the city of Ṭahart, planned as a military base but evolving into a religious center that became the cynosure for Khārijī throughout the Maghrib: from the Nafūsah of present-day Libya to the Ṣidrātah of Warqlah oasis, and including powerful groups in the Awrās Mountains. Almost immediately after the founding of the city, tribesmen from the Lawaṭah, Hawwārah, Zawāyhah, Maṭmāṭah, Zanātah, and Miknāsah groups settled in its environs;[146] many Persians and Christians also lived there. Ṭāhart enjoyed considerable material prosperity, underpinned by its function from the turn of the ninth century as an emporium of the trans-Ṣaḥārān caravan trade. The tribal basis of this prosperity was aptly attested by al-Shammākhī, doyen of Ibāḍī historians, when he particularized the twin pillars of the Imāmate as the Nafūsah sword and Mazātah treasure.[147] But during the ninth century a typically patrimonial looseness in the administrative structure of the Rutamid confederacy, evident from the beginning, was exacerbated as secessionist tendencies progressively subverted the unifying function of Ibāḍī doctrine. Consequently, despite the forging of an alliance with the Spanish Umayyads, the polity offered little resistance to the Fāṭimids when they occupied Ṭāhart in 909.

The third Khārijī confederation to establish itself in North Africa in the eighth century was the Ṣufrite principality of the Banū-Midrār, with its capital at Sijilmāsah in the Tafilalt oasis. Trans-Ṣaḥārān trade was clearly the basis of the city's prosperity and the attraction that brought a cosmopolitan population of veiled Ṣanhājah, black Africans, Jews, Andalusians, and Berbers and Arabs from all over the Maghrib to rub shoulders in its dusty streets. Nonetheless, its rulers did not lack territorial ambitions, which led them to extend their control over Berber gold and silver miners in the Wādī Darʿah, far to the west of Tafīlalt. Despite continual internal conflicts between Khārijī factions—the more moderate Ibāḍī of which eventually triumphed over and prepared the way for the adoption of Sunnī orthodoxy at the end of the tenth century—the confederation endured for some two centuries. It survived three Fāṭimid invasions, in 909, 922, and 960, respectively, before finally being conquered in 976/77 by a Maghrāwah ally of the Spanish Umayyads.[148]

Whereas tribalism in the guise of confederation was fundamental to political life in the western Maghrib, the *wilāyah* of al-Ifrīqiyah witnessed the rise of a territorially based state modelled on that of Baghdād and at the same time nominally subject to the ʿAbbāsids. Not that tribal concerns played no part in the government of this polity, but they were considerably subordinated to the regulatory measures of its still patrimonial-style administration. This polity came into being in 800, when the caliph Hārūn al-Rashīd granted al-Ifrīqiyah as a hereditary benefice to Ibrāhīm ibn al-Aghlab, then governor of the Zāb. For the next century the Aghlabids governed the Ifrīqiyah in the name of the ʿAbbāsids but with a de facto political autonomy that manifested itself in, among other things, the striking of coins in their own name. As far as the caliph in Baghdād was concerned, Aghlabid territory subsumed the whole of North Africa from Cyrenaica westward, but in practice the *amirs*[149] controlled only present-day Tunisia, eastern Algeria, and Tripolitania—that is, no more than the Africa of the Caesars.

Within that heartland, however, the Aghlabid *dār al-imārah* was transferred from the *wilāyah* capital at Qayrawān to a fortified enceinte some two miles distant, which was accorded the honorific al-ʿAbbāsīyah.[150] But the Aghlabids were never able to distance themselves adequately from the *jund,*[151] which, directing its loyalty to Arab immigrants who had settled permanently in the Ifrīqiyah rather than to transient representatives of the caliph, rebelled frequently throughout the life of the dynasty. In 824–27 its uprising was so successful that Aghlabid rule was preserved only through the intervention of Ibāḍī Berbers from the Nafzāwah region. An attempt by Ibrāhīm II (r. 875–902) to rid himself of the Arab aristocracy, including prominent Mālikī scholars and senior officers of the *jund,* was unnecessarily brutal and, in any case, came too late to save the dynasty.[152] As it was, it only intensified opposition to the Aghlabids at the very time when they were threatened by a rising power among the Kutāmā Berbers,[153] where a shared Ismāʿīlī faith was apparently superseding the *ʿaṣabīyah* of the tribe as the principal agent of communal solidarity. In fact, Raqqādah fell to the Ismāʿīlīs in 909, and in the following year their leader revealed himself as the Commander of the Faithful *(Amīr al-Muʾminīn),* thereby inaugurating the Fāṭimid dynasty, which in 948 moved its capital to Ṣabrah, a suburb of al-Qayrawān.[154]

The expansion of the Fāṭimid kingdom seemed to promise a substantial degree of political unity for the Maghrib as the caliph ʿUbaydallāh al-Mahdī, with the support of the Kutāmā, conquered both the Aghlabid *amīrs* of al-Ifrīqiyah and the Khārijī Rustamids of Ṭāhart and made tributaries of the Idrīsids of Fās. And under the Zīrīds, who functioned as loyal viceroys of the Fāṭimids after the latter had transferred their capital to al-Qāhirah (Cairo) in 972, the promise might have seemed to be fulfilled. From 978, when the Fāṭimids relinquished direct control of Tripolitania, the authority of the Zīrīds notionally encompassed the whole of North Africa to the west of Cyrenaica.[155] In fact, however, in northwest Algeria and Morocco their rule was continually disputed by both nomadic Zanātah tribes and the Spanish Umayyads, so that their writ ran effectively only in Tunisia and eastern Algeria.

This was the period when the unity of the Caliphate, a fundamental tenet of orthodox Islamic political theory, was shattered. The Ismāʿīlī Fāṭimid ʿUbaydallāh had proclaimed himself caliph in 910, and the Umayyad ʿAbd al-Raḥmān III had followed suit in 929. The result was that for the rest of the century the Maghrib became a battle zone where the ambitions of the two western caliphs were put to the test. The Umayyads naturally allied themselves with those groups most threatened by the Fāṭimids, especially the prevailingly nomadic Zanātah Berbers. As the Fāṭimid army comprised mainly levies of sedentary Sanhājah, some have seen reason to view the conflict as one between nomads and agriculturalists,[156] but the truth is that it was more a struggle between urbanized communities for control of the trade routes.[157] The Fāṭimids had already conquered the commercial centers of Ṭāhart and Sijilmāsah. By the 950s the Umayyads had established a de facto protectorate over most of northern Morocco, including petty chieftainships in Ṭanjah and Fās and an Idrīsid statelet in the Rīf ruled by a line of princes known as the Banū-Gannun. A decade later the Fāṭimids had recovered that territory except for Ṭanjah and Sabtā, only to lose much of it again in 973 and 974. In any case, the Umayyad caliphs were loath to involve themselves too deeply in North Africa and on the whole left Zanātah paramounts, especially those of the Maghrāwah, Banū-Īfran, and Miknāsah, to exercise dominion over Morocco in their name. It was with this deputed authority, for instance, that in the tenth century the Miknāsah established their own tribal center—apparently a cluster of large villages—at Miknāsat al-Zaytūn (modern Meknès) west of Fās.

Such was the pattern of shifting political and religious allegiances, each with its own social and economic concomitants expressing themselves in a characteristic urban hierarchy, that occupied al-Maqdisī's *iqlīm* of the Maghrib. It was not only a composite urban system but also a fluctuating, and in some periods a volatile, one. Clearly al-Maqdisī had in mind an idealized view of the Fāṭimid empire in which Ismāʿīlī authority was unquestioned from al-Qāhirah (Cairo) to Ṭanjah. Such a situation never obtained, and, even when the Fāṭimids had approached that ideal most closely by subduing the Aghlabids, Rustamids, and Idrīsids, they never succeeded in integrating all the cities under their control into anything approaching a unitary urban hierarchy. Beneath the formal political overlay former capitals survived and new ones arose as foci of persistent centroids of economic power.

Although the Fāṭimids transferred their own capital to al-Qāhirah in 972, al-Qayrawān continued to be an important city politically, economically, and above all culturally, for the rest of the century: one of the pillars of the empire, as al-Maqdisī puts it; *le centre irradiant,* in Hichem Djaït's felicitous phrase.[158] Indeed, under the early Zīrīds the city enjoyed an enviable prosperity even though the dynasts themselves resided in the old Fāṭimid enceinte of Ṣabrah al-Manṣūrīyah, immediately adjacent to al-Qayrawān. Its jurists were renowned far beyond the boundaries of the Maghrib, with the Mālikī *faqīḥ*s Ibn Abī Zayd al-Qayrawānī (died in 996) and Ibn al-Qābisī (935–1012) and the Ashʿarī al-Qālānisī (died ca. 970) being perhaps the best known.[159] Throughout the ninth and tenth centuries al-Qayrawān maintained its position at the apex of the Maghribī sacral hierarchy; the accumulated *barakah* of its shrines, tombs, scholars, and saints were challenged only distantly by that of Fās. But by the end of the tenth century the commercial underpinnings of the city had begun to collapse, a decline exacerbated by exhorbitant taxation and by an epidemic early in the eleventh century.[160]

Other capitals in the *iqlīm* almost always survived the demise of their dynasties in only slightly reduced circumstances. Tilimsān, for instance, prospered under a succession of rulers after the Banū-Īfran lost their paramountcy in the last quarter of the eighth century, and in the tenth earned an enviable reputation as a center of learning.[161] The Banū-Midrār capital at Sijilmāsah similarly maintained its prosperity through a change of rulers.[162] Fās (fig. 16), after surviving the struggle between the Spanish Umayyads and the Fāṭimids of al-Ifrīqiyah for control of northern Morocco, flourished during the last two decades of the tenth century as a protectorate of the former. Ṭāhart, by contrast, affords an example of a capital that regained neither its political nor its economic status after it was conquered by the Fāṭimids.[163]

Provincial, regional, and district capitals tended to survive such vicissitudes of fortune so long as they could rely on a strong economic base, whether agricultural, commercial, or logistical. One example must serve for all. Qābis, a port on the gulf of the same name, changed hands at least seven times between 700 and 772, when its capture by the founder of the Muhallabid dynasty brought a quarter century of peace. Under the Aghlabids it was constituted the seat of a governor, but early in the tenth century passed into the hands of the Fāṭimids, who bestowed it as a benefice on the Banū-Luqmān of the Kutāmā confederacy. In 972 a Khārijī revolt devastated the town's suburbs, after which it was administered by the Banū-ʿĀmir on behalf of the Zīrīds. This is not the end of the story, but it is as far as we need take it. The point is that, on the none-too-plentiful evidence available, through all these vicissitudes Qābis continued to be both a port and regional service center of some importance.[164] And there

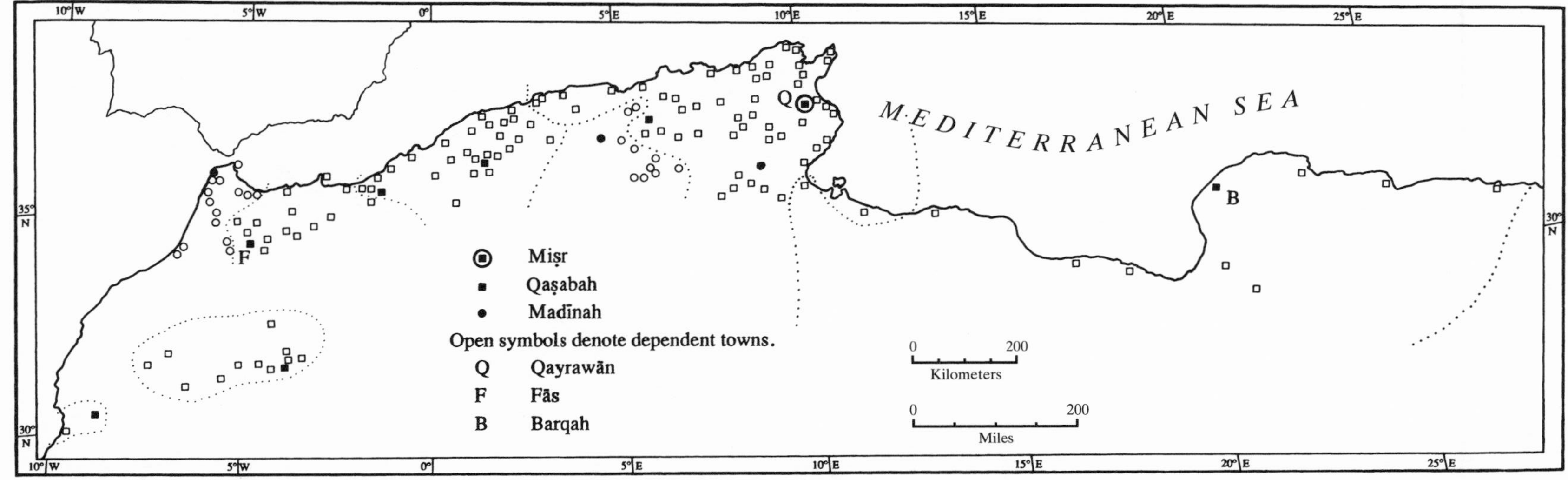

Figure 16. The middle and upper ranks of the settlement hierarchy in the Maghrib (excluding al-Andalus [Islamic Spain] and Iṣqiliyah [Sicily]) in the second half of the tenth century. Based broadly on information provided by al-Maqdisī, with that author's evident misconceptions (mistaken attributions, erroneous transcriptions, and repetitions, especially in the supposed interpolation on pages 55–56) whenever possible corrected by reference to contemporary writers. See also the comment appended to figure 15.

is no reason to suppose that numerous other medium- and small-sized towns fared any worse during the often violent fluctuations in political fortune that characterized the Maghrib between the seventh and tenth centuries.

Before the Arabs burst into North Africa, extensive tracts of the region had been colonized and governed by a succession of alien powers, including Carthaginians, Romans, Greeks, and Vandals. All had focused their attention on what is now Tunisia and eastern Algeria, that northeastward projection of the African continent that offered both agricultural potential and command of the narrow seas separating the Maghrib from Europe at the waist of the Mediterranean. In later Roman times permanent settlement in Tripolitania and Cyrenaica was still restricted to a relatively narrow coastal zone and certain oases in the interior desert.

In the Province of Africa Proconsularis, which encompassed modern Tunisia with a westward extension into the vicinity of Bône (Būnah) in Algeria,[165] Roman influence was pervasive. The *Tall* in the northern part of the province was densely settled, with the villages of the Berber population being transformed into Italian-style towns featuring wide, arcaded streets. On the olive-growing steppes in the center of the province, cultivation and settlement were only slightly diminished, although they became much less intensive southward toward the *shutts (chotts)*. The *Sāḥil* from Hadrumetum (Sousse, al-Sūs) to Taparura (Sfax) was perhaps even more densely populated than the *Tall*. Throughout settled parts of the province the small, agriculturally supported town was the characteristic settlement form, with the whole urban system being served by a network of roads, most of which had been built not directly for military purposes—as was a common occurrence in the provinces of the Roman empire—but as a response to economic development, which meant in fact linking the needs of fertile regions in the interior to ports on the north coast.

Roman influence was also strong in the provinces occupying what is now eastern and central Algeria, namely Numidia and Mauretania Sitifensis, with population densest on the coastal plains, in the broader river valleys, and on the central plains. In the eastern sector pacification and settlement reached as far south as the Awrās Mountains, which were ringed by military posts to contain dissident Berber tribesmen; but in Mauretania the frontier of Roman settlement lay much farther north, while the Kabylie massif was never effectively settled or controlled. However, within the limits specified, Roman towns, in their hierarchical grades of civic dignity as *oppida, municipia, civitates,* or *coloniae,* disseminated Italian culture, the Latin language, and the Christian religion among their inhabitants. In the countryside the prevailing language was usually one of the Berber dialects, with Punic being common in Africa Proconsularis. Originally the Roman Maghrib had ranked with Egypt as the granary of Italy, but, as Egyptian grain was increasingly funnelled to Constantinople, Rome came to rely almost exclusively on Africa and Numidia for its supplies. Farther west the provinces of Mauretania Caesariensis and Mauretania Tingitana appear to have been only thinly populated even by indigenous groups, and there were few Roman or Romanized settlements except in especially favored coastal locations.

In 430 Roman dominion west of Africa Proconsularis was ended by a Vandal chief who conquered all three Mauretanias together with Numidia, only to be overthrown in 533 by a general of the Byzantine emperor Justinian. Although Byzantine rule never encompassed the whole of Roman Africa, it did add some two centuries to the life of Roman civilization in many parts of the region. In addition, despite heavy taxation and religious schisms, the towns in Proconsular Africa, Byzacenia, and Numidia recovered some of the prosperity of which a century of Vandal domination had deprived them.[166] This was also the time when many towns were either fortified for the first time or refortified (Theveste is an entirely representative example),[167] policies testifying to a weakening of central authority, intensified exploitation of those who worked the land by those who owned it, and resulting tensions between the landed and the landless.

Nevertheless, when the Arabs took control of the Ifrīqiyah and lands to the west at the turn of the ninth century (as opposed to raiding, which had been going on since 647), they inherited a series of urban systems that were at least going concerns, even if they were not maximally efficient. With only a few exceptions, of which Sijilmāsah in the Tafīlalt and certain oases in the Libyan Desert were notable examples, the Arabs did not extend the territorial base of the system. They did, however, contribute an unusually large number of new foundations in the form of administrative centers at all levels—including al-Qayrawān, which al-Maqdisī chose as the metropolis of al-Maghrib—and *ribāṭāt* disposed along strategic sectors of the coast.[168] There is also reason to believe that urbanization increased incrementally during the eighth, ninth, and tenth centuries, resulting more from increases in the sizes of cities than from the establishment of new foundations, numerous though these were. In other words, the urban hierarchy expanded vertically (though not, as we have already noted, spatially) by a sort of inflationary process without significantly changing the structure it had inherited from the Romans and the Byzantines.

Within this framework the distinguishing feature of the Maghribī urban system was the dual nature of its economic base, in which commerce was as important overall as agriculture. It is frequently maintained that during the half millennium from the third to the eighth century A.D., the economy of the Maghrib had oscillated between stagnation and decline, subverted sequentially by the exploitative character and the inefficiency of large Roman estates, which both caused a drop-off in trade and stimulated Berber revolts; Vandal incursions, which often involved the destruction of urban defenses; heavy Byzantine taxation and religious schisms; and the Arab conquest and ensuing Khārijī wars.

This picture of debilitation is probably exaggerated and in any case would likely have held most closely only for "Roman Africa," that is, the northeast, the region having a monetary economy. Whatever view is taken of this matter, few would deny that the ninth century witnessed a signal economic recovery. Toward the close of that century al-Yaʿqūbī testified implicitly to the prosperity of the Ifrīqiyah as exemplified by the flourishing orchards in the Qafṣah District; the olive groves of the Sāḥil, "where villages lie so thick on the ground that they all but touch one another"; the date palms of the Jarīd; the grainfields of the Qarwānī plain and the Fās District with its allegedly three thousand grain mills powered by the Fās River; and the mines at Majjānat al-Maʿādin from which were extracted silver, antimony, iron, and lead.[169]

In the more westerly territories of the Aghlabid polity, the Numidia of Late Antiquity, al-Yaʿqūbī leaves the impression of predominantly Berber agriculturalists and stockmen living in villages served by relatively few towns. Here economic recovery appears to have been less complete, primarily because development in these territories, where the authority of Qarwānī, let alone Dimashqī or Baghdādī, governments was at best attenuated, had always lagged behind the Ifrīqiyah. However, still farther west, in the Rustamid kingdom focused on Ṭāhart, evidence of prosperity begins to be cited again; is equally prominent in the description of the Idrīsid kingdom of Fās, "a magnificent city, immensely wealthy and densely populated"; and only slightly less so in the account of Sijilmāsah, the territories of which were credited with near-fabulous mines of gold and silver.[170] Although written as a description of one particular locality, al-Yaʿqūbī's account of the territories of the then-independent principality of Nākūr is broadly applicable to the countrysides in much of the more truly Mediterranean zone of the Maghrib in the ninth century, encompassing as it did "numerous buildings, fortresses, villages, post-stations, cultivated fields, flocks and herds, and pasture lands."[171]

Toward the middle of the tenth century al-Iṣṭakhrī did a good deal to confirm this impression of fertility by his prodigal use of such terms as "productive," "prosperous," "fertile," and "abundant."[172] In the case of Ṭāhart, two of these epithets were run together as part of a more comprehensive characterization: "a large city set in an extensive, fertile countryside with ample water and abundant crops"; while Saṭīf was "a large, strongly defended city in a region with numerous villages almost touching one another." In his elaboration of al-Iṣṭakhrī's work in the second half of the same century, Ibn Ḥawqal documented the agricultural productivity of the Maghrib in considerable detail.[173] In Tūnis, for instance, "very large profits could be made and the return to landowners was substantial. The surrounding countryside was fertile and harvests plentiful."[174] Būnah had "handsome markets where goods found a ready *(maqṣūd)* sale yielding substantial profits. The soil of the region was fertile and prices remarkably low. Fruit was grown in orchards that stretched almost continuously *(qarīb)* across the district . . . wheat and barley were grown in almost inexhaustible quantities."[175] The Berbers living in northern Morocco "enjoyed an easy competence and an excellent diet, especially those in the neighbourhood of al-Habaṭ, who were subject to the authority of ʿAbd-Allāh ibn Idrīs ibn . . . —May the blessings of God be on him and his line!—and who were the beneficiaries of a remarkable fertility, as well as cheap, good quality and palatable victuals."[176] And so on: there is a great deal more in the same vein.

Ibn Ḥawqal's picture of an agriculturally prosperous Maghrib is echoed clearly, though more faintly, by al-Maqdisī[177] and the *Ḥudūd al-ʿĀlam.*[178] In all such instances, here drawn from the ninth and tenth centuries, the environmental context is, of course, the Mediterranean climatic regime, which is characterized by alternating seasons of mild, rainy winters and hot, drought-ridden summers; separated by short and poorly defined transitional periods in spring and autumn; and grading southward into progressively more desiccated steppe and ultimately true desert. In the purest manifestation of this regime, which occurs only in northern Cyrenaica and in a relatively narrow zone inland from the Barbary Coast, the agricultural response took the form of the cultivation of winter grain and summer fruit. This was the ecotype that Ibn Ḥawqal had primarily in mind when he wrote, "In a zone extending from al-Ifrīqiyah to the farthest bounds of the districts of Ṭanjah and from one to ten days' march wide, one encounters settlements and towns whose dependent farming districts adjoin one another, just as do their cultivated fields."[179]

It was here that in Roman times agriculture had gained ascendancy over, though by no means replaced, stock raising to generate a composite farming system sensitively responsive to the vagaries of the Mediterranean climatic regime, including those induced by aspect and altitude. And it was in this zone that were to be found nearly three out of every four Maghribī cities. To the south of this belt of diversified agriculture, as desiccation increased, stock raising became increasingly important, first in conjunction with cereal cultivation but ultimately as nomadic and seminomadic herding on the broad steppes of the Hauts Plateaux and similar environments.[180] Most of the remaining cities of the Maghrib were in the more northerly parts of this zone. Finally, south of the High Atlas and the Ṣaḥārān Atlas ranges in the western part of the *iqlīm,* and almost always within one hundred miles of the coast (sometimes much closer), in Tripolitania and Cyrenaica the steppe deteriorated into true desert having a progressively more uncertain mean annual rainfall of less than five inches and an exiguous, xerophytic vegetation. In this environment, urban forms were restricted to a few of the larger oases, notably those of the Tafīlalt, the Jarīd, and the Fazzān. In smaller oases, such as some of those in the Libyan Desert, urban development was inevitably incipient and tentative.

All this amounted to a substantial degree of agricultural prosperity in the Maghrib of the ninth and tenth centuries that would have been quite capable of supporting a reasonably elaborate urban hierarchy. However, as it so happened, this prosperity was considerably enhanced by a concomitant development of interurban trade, often under Ibāḍī auspices, particularly in the Ifrīqiyah and regions to the west. What I have in mind here is neither the exchange of goods and services between a city and its surrounding service area, which would have justified its being called a central place (chapter 3); nor the long-distance commercial transactions that took place typically in the state capitals, the northern ports, and the southern caravan cities. The exchanges to which I refer were effected between city-trade areas rather than within or across them, and could be initiated by individuals, groups, or local governments. Such trade was also largely unaffected by retailing or wholesaling going on in the same city in which it was being prosecuted, except possibly for some of its commodities being fed into the local *sūqs*. What follows is a selection of instances of such interregional trading culled mainly from Ibn Ḥawqal's account of the Maghrib.

In Barqah crowds of traders chaffered for wool, honey, wax, olive oil, pine tar held to be the best in North Africa, and all sorts of provisions; dispatched pelts to Miṣr; and imported dried dates from the oasis of Awjilah.[181] Qābis was a center of the wool and silk trade, and it exported fruit to al-Qayrawān and skins tanned with the juice of acacia leaves throughout North Africa (70). The coral-processing port of Marsā al-Kharaz was wholly dependent on food supplies sent in from neighboring regions, for it could not raise significant quantities of cereals or fruit (75). Būnah exported iron manufactures both within and outside the Maghrib (76). From Marsā al-Dajjāj, figs "large and plump" were sent to far distant parts of the land (76).[182] The Jazāʾir Banī-Mazghannā exported surplus honey, butter, and figs to al-Qayrawān and elsewhere.[183] Al-Baṣrah in the far west sent its cotton clear across the Maghrib to al-Ifrīqiyah (80). Al-Masīlah, capital of the Zāb region, supplied al-Qayrawān with quinces (85–86), at the same time as Tūnis found markets in the same city for its cotton, hemp, caraway, safflower, honey, butter, cereals, olive oil, and cattle (74). A city growing prosperous on this type of interurban and interregional trade was exemplified as well as anywhere by al-Qasṭīliyah, which Ibn Ḥawqal characterizes as "surpassing others in that part of the country [the Jarīd] in wealth, the tempo of its market transactions, and the number of travellers who provision themselves there and engage in commercial dealings. Wool and woollen fabrics are sold in all quarters of the city and its manufactures are exported far and wide (94).

These mutually supportive agricultural and commercial economies were nicely underpinned by the diversity of terrain, and consequently of ecotypes, in the Maghrib. A broad zonation of land uses deriving from latitudinally imposed climatic regimes was frequently interrupted by altitudinally induced variations that amplified the inventory of natural products available for exchange while localizing, and thereby according trade value to, individual items. And in the kingdoms of Fās (Idrīsid), Ṭāhart (Rustamid), and al-Qayrawān (Aghlabid, Fāṭimid, and Zīrīd), taxation systems were devised specifically to tap the surplus in both sectors of the economy. Of course, interregional trade can be documented in other *iqlīms* but, on the evidence available, seldom on such a scale as in the Maghrib.[184] On the other hand, it was not equally developed throughout the *iqlīm*. Among the Barghawāṭah, for instance, as among some quasi-independent groups in what is now eastern Algeria, agriculture was always more important than commerce, while, contrariwise, among those Zanātah communities that controlled the approaches to the trans-Ṣaḥārān trade routes and in the Sijilmāsah kindgom commerce outweighed agriculture as a source of revenue. But overall the dual basis of the urban economy of much of the Maghrib contributed a distinctive component to an urban system also characterized by its fragmentation; the importance of trading ports and specialized caravan cities along its northern and southern fringes; and the cordon of guard posts established along the more exposed sectors of its coasts.

Al-Andalus

It was during the second half of the tenth century that the Muslims achieved greater control of the Iberian Peninsula than at any period before or after.[185] At that time the *Sharīʿah* ran through some three-quarters of the peninsula. Constituted after the Muslim conquest in the second decade of the eighth century as a garrison state, al-Andalus had a decentralized administrative system that was faced with the task of accommodating profound cultural and social cleavages within a plural society. It was subsequently transformed into a unified state exercising centralized administrative and economic control while affording opportunities for the fusion of Arab and Neo-Muslim elements within the population.[186]

It is often said that the urban system of Islamic Spain was essentially inherited from Roman times in that most of the important cities of al-Andalus stood on the sites of former Roman settlements. Qurṭubah (Córdoba), Ishbīliyah (Hispalis, modern Seville), Qādis (Gades, modern Cadiz), Ṭulayṭulah (Toletum, modern Toledo). Saraqusṭah (Caesaraugusta, modern Zaragoza), Balansiyah (Valentia, modern Valencia), and Māridah (Emerita Augusta, modern Mérida) are archetypically representative of such cities, and there are a great many others. However, by the close of the Visigothic era many of these Hispano-Roman (or even earlier) foundations were in decline, with not a few actually ruined and some partly buried.[187] The result was that the Roman municipal institutions almost invariably failed to survive the Visigothic hegemony. When the urban physical plant persisted, subsequent expansion of the system in Islamic times more often than not submerged the Hispano-Roman ground plan. In fact the only major component of the old Roman urban hierarchy evident in the tenth century was its spatial arrangement; its vertical, or organizational, dimensions, in contrast, had been almost totally transformed. The Muslims founded few new cities, and those were almost always intended to serve strategic purposes or as coastal bases to deter Fāṭimid encroachments and Norman (Majūs) raids in the western Mediterranean. Representative of such foundations were Mursiyah, established in the ninth century as a replacement for the old town of Ello;[188] al-Marīyah, a coastal observation post *(mirʾā)* that developed into a *ribāṭ* serving as an arsenal and naval base in the tenth century;[189] Qalʿat Rabāḥ, founded by the Umayyads and peopled by refugees from Ūrīṭ when this latter city was razed;[190] Qalʿat Ayyūb, a fortress town in the Upper March named after the *tābiʿ* Ayyūb ibn Ḥabīb al-Lakhmī and rebuilt by the *amīr* Muḥammad in 862;[191] and Tuṭīlah, established by ʿAmrūs ibn Yūsuf at the order of al-Ḥakam I (r. 796–822).[192]

Wholly unrepresentative were the two great palatine-administrative complexes of Madīnat al-Zahrāʾ[193] and al-Madīnah al-Zāhirah. In the first of these ʿAbd al-Raḥmān III (r. 912–61) laid out a caliphal enclave, including a palace employing no fewer than fourteen thousand domestics and amply served by markets, baths, and caravanserais, to which he lured a supporting population with a subvention of four hundred *dirhams* to anyone "who would build a residence in the vicinity."[194] The second of these complexes, al-Madīnah al-Zāhirah, was constructed to the order of the Ḥājib al-Manṣūr ibn Abī ʿĀmir between 978 and 980. At that time the whole apparatus of government was transferred there, together with grain storage facilities and *sūqs*. In addition, high government officials seized the opportunity afforded by the generous grants of land to construct imposing palaces and pleasure pavilions in the immediate neighborhood.[195]

Marketing and Service Centers

Like virtually all topographers and historians of the period, al-Maqdisī designated Qurṭubah as the *miṣr* of al-Andalus.[196] Situated where the Guadalquivir River valley, beginning to broaden westward, is crossed by routes through the Betio Cordillera and the Sierra Morena, the city had been the capital of the Roman province of Hispania Ulterior, but little importance had accrued to it under Vandals, Byzantines, or the Germanic military aristocracy of the Visigoths. Immediately after the Muslim conquest, the capital of the newly acquired territories had been established at Ishbīliyah (in succession to the Visigothic capital of Toletum) but had been transferred to a more central location in Qurṭubah in about 717.

At first the city had been the administrative center of a province ruled by a governor appointed from Dimashq. With the founding of the Umayyad Amīrate in 756, however, it embarked on a period of commercial prosperity and cultural splendor that, under an absolute monarch styling himself Commander of the Faithful in defiance of Baghdād, would establish it as a metropolis second in the Muslim world only to Baghdād and, eventually, al-Qāhirah. Ibn Ḥawqal justly observes that in his day Qurṭubah had no equal in the Maghrib, Upper Mesopotamia (al-Jazīrah), Syria (al-Shām), or Egypt with respect to the size of its population, the area it covered, the extent of its markets, the cleanliness of its buildings, the architecture of its mosques, and the proliferation of its baths and caravanserais (he was writing prior to the flowering of al-Qāhirah). On the authority of "several travellers from the city who had visited Baghdād," the same author reports that Qurṭubah was approximately of the size of one of the quarters of the imperial capital.[197] Al-Maqdisī could do no better than characterize the city in excessively general—and, as we have noted, secondhand—terms as "an important metropolis, gracious and pleasant, where justice, wisdom, political acumen, benevolence, and religion prevail, and where there is evident prosperity."[198] And this was certainly the image that Qurṭubah projected to the rest of the world as it prospered in what the late A. J. Arberry called its "serene impregnability."[199]

In al-Andalus alone out of all the territories of the Muslim world, al-Maqdisī failed to establish an urban hierarchy. Noting apologetically that he had not had an opportunity to travel through and enumerate the Spanish territorial circumscriptions, he simply furnished a generalized overview of the urban system. The situation appears to have been further complicated by the fact that districts that would elsewhere have been called *rasātiq* (sing. *rustāq*) in al-Andalus were locally designated *aqālīm* (sing. *iqlīm*), a term used consistently by al-Maqdisī to denote the principal provinces of the Muslim world.[200] The *aqālīm* appear, in fact, to have denoted *kuwar* (sing. *kūrah*), provincial districts that as often as not corresponded to Visigothic administrative units and appear to have derived from even earlier Roman practice.

The upshot was that al-Maqdisī provided an unranked list of seventeen cities that he believed were district capitals. Subsequently another informant persuaded him to add Libīrah and Ukhshūnubah, making a total of nineteen.[201] Among these Qurṭubah was specified at the *miṣr* of al-Andalus, but there is no way of discovering for certain which among the other eighteen cities, by reason of administrative responsibility, would have qualified as *qaṣabāt*—unless, of course, all of them did. And the other tenth-century topographers, including al-Iṣṭakhrī and Ibn Ḥawqal, who might have been expected to provide some guidance in this matter, are in fact not helpful. In accordance with al-Maqdisī's practice of categorizing administrative centers of politically marginal territories as *mudun*, it might be anticipated that the headquarter cities of the Upper *(al-Aʿlā)*, Middle *(al-Awsaṭ)*, and Lower *(al-Adnā)* Marches *(Thughūr)* separating Muslim from Christian Spain—respectively Saraqusṭah, Ṭulayṭulah, and Māridah—would each have been classified as a *madīnah* in that author's schema. However, although I have not scrupled to amend al-Maqdisī's hierarchy of urban forms in individual instances, I have shirked the responsibility of foisting onto him a ranked urban system for which he has left us no warrant other than dubious analogy and the name ofthe *miṣr*.

What is beyond dispute is that the basic stratum of towns in the Andalusī urban hierarchy was supported by agriculture. The Islamic period saw a generalized shift of emphasis in the agrarian economy from the dry farming (predominantly by Hispano-Romans) and the herding (predominantly by Goths) that had prevailed in Visigothic times toward increased reliance on irrigated crops. This movement has been seen by some as a response to a climatic modulation toward warmer and drier conditions in the western Mediterranean allegedly beginning in the third century A.D. and continuing into the High Middle Ages.[202] To that end, the Arabs introduced not only technological innovations such as the water-lifting device of the noria *(nāʿūrah)*, which allowed the irrigation of entire huertas of individually owned small holdings;[203] but also institutional frameworks, not infrequently derived from Syria or even the Yaman, for the management of irrigation water.[204]

Al-Andalus was also one of the territories benefiting most from the introduction and acclimatization of the new crops, often ultimately of South Asian origin, associated with what has been aptly called the Arab agricultural revolution.[205] Among edible crops introduced into al-Andalus at this time were olives, artichokes, carob, rice, saffron, sugarcane, jujubes, eggplants, carrots, parsnips, lemons, oranges, grapefruit, and apricots. Thomas Glick describes the pattern of agricultural practice that had emerged by the tenth century as characterized by the predominance of crops dependent on irrigation, an enhanced economic significance of shepherding, and—somewhat surprisingly—an inferred diminution in the acreage of land under wheat, probably stemming from the migration of Mozarabs from al-Andalus to the Christian north and the movement of Neo-Muslims from the countryside to the cities. And sectors of this pattern exhibited strong ethnic associations, with Arabs and their Neo-Muslim[206] or Christian tenants monopolizing the fertile and irrigable lowlands; Berbers maintaining pastoral and arboricultural ecotypes in the uplands; and an indigenous population, whether Christian or Muslim, continuing to rely on cereal dry farming.[207] Adaptions of these, and very frequently of intermediate, ecotypes are presented clearly enough in the pages of al-Rāzī. A few representative examples must suffice for all.

- ***Tuṭīlah,*** in the upper Ebro valley: "Of remarkable fertility and unequalled as a producer of cereals. Excellent country for stockraising, and its orchards yield fruit of incomparable flavour."[208]
- ***Ṭulayṭulah*** (Toledo), in the heart of the Meseta: "The best possible land for grain growing. The climate is excellent and grain can be stored for a lengthy period without deteriorating; in fact it can be kept in silos for seventy years without suffering any ill effects. This is why in time of war Ṭulayṭulah does not go short of wheat. Its saffron *(al-zaʿfarān)* is the finest in al-Andalus with respect to both colour and perfume" (82).[209]
- ***Baṭalyawth,*** a strategic settlement at the confluence of the Guadiana and Rivallas Rivers and a regional service center.
- ***Extremadura:*** "A large territory which is among the most productive of cereals in all al-Andalus. There is also a large acreage of vines, and the region is as good as any for stockraising, hunting, and fishing."[210]
- ***Ukshūnubah,*** on the south shore of the Algarve in what is today southernmost Portugal: "A fertile and very flat territory with many orchards and field crops, and which also includes uplands devoted to stockraising" (91).
- ***Lablah,*** in the southwest of the peninsula: "A district lending itself to both stockraising and crops. It has numerous orchards, especially olives and vines, and produces large quantities of high-quality safflower, which can be used to make a beautiful red dye" (92).
- ***Ishbīliyah*** (Seville), in the valley of the lower Guadalqivir: "Lends itself to the cultivation of cereals, stockraising, and arboriculture.

  "There is a large tract of territory planted to olives . . . producing excellent oil that is exported to the Muslim Orient. Oil is so abundant that, if it were not exported, the inhabitants of the region would not be able to charge the least price for it. . . . There is a lot of very good honey and many excellent figs which, when dried, last a very long time without deteriorating. There is also a great deal of cotton which is exported throughout al-Andalus and North Africa" (93).[211]

- ***Shantarīn,*** a nodal city in the lower Tejo valley: "On the plain the soil is of such natural fertility that it is possible to reap two harvests [of cereals] a year. When the Tejo floods it completely covers its floodplain. When the water recedes, the peasants undertake a late sowing, and the soil retains sufficient moisture to allow them to harvest the grain even earlier than normal" (88).[212]
- ***Qulumrīyah,*** on the right bank of the Mondego River in what is now central Portugal: "It possesses a lowland particularly suited for cereal cultivation, even without irrigation. When the river overflows its banks, it completely inundates this plain. When the water recedes, the local farmers sow their grain, from which they reap a harvest sufficient to meet their needs for two years—and this in spite of the fact that the plain is only 15 miles long by 4 wide. The city of Qulumrīyah has numerous productive orchards and olive groves." (89).[213]

A factor to be borne in mind when discussing the economic functions of primarily agricultural towns in al-Andalus is that their provisions were often supplied from estates owned by members of the urban elite rather than from the holdings of a true peasantry. To that extent the transactions involved in the provisioning of the cities would have partaken of the nature of redistribution and mobilization rather than market exchange. This is not to deny, of course, that market exchange played an important part in the Andalusī economy, although Pedro Chalmeta Gendrón has suggested that the role of urban-owned estates *(munyāt)* in the provisioning of towns may have usurped the function of many rural *sūqs*.[214]

Industrial and Craft Centers

It will come as no surprise that the majority of Andalusī industries involved an artisanal processing of agricultural products that was all but ubiquitous in villages and towns alike. More restricted in its choice of locations was the considerable mining industry, which yielded a wide range of metals, including gold, silver, iron, lead, copper, and tin, as well as cinnabar, the principal ore of mercury. But there can be no doubt that the internationally most prominent industry, as well as the technologically most advanced, was that concerned with textiles of various sorts.[215] No less than six *ṭirāz* factories were in operation in al-Andalus at one time or another, specifically at Qurṭubah, al-Marīyah, Basṭah, Finyānah, Ishbīliyah, and Malaqah, but it is not certain that all had been established by the tenth century.

Ibn ʿIdhārī states explicitly that an ʿAbd al-Raḥmān introduced *ṭirāz* factories into al-Andalus and expanded the range of their manufacture.[216] The presumption that the ruler referred to was ʿAbd al-Raḥmān II al-Mutawassiṭ is confirmed by al-Suyūṭī's remark that the wearing of embroidered garments *(libs muṭarraz)* was introduced by the ʿAbd al-Raḥmān who succeeded to the Amīrate in 822.[217] Robert Serjeant has speculated that the first *ṭirāz* would have been that attached to the palace of the above-mentioned ʿAbd al-Raḥmān in Qurṭubah,[218] but, if so, there is no record of it in extant sources. However, Ibn Ḥawqal confirms that there was more than one *ṭirāz* factory in al-Andalus in the tenth century, from which cloth was regularly exported to Egypt and sometimes "to the farthest bounds of Khurāsān."[219] One of these factories was certainly in Ishbīliyah, where, according to Ibn ʿIdhārī, the rebel Ibrāhīm ibn al-Ḥajjāj ibn ʿUmayr al-Lakhmī (d. 900) had his name embroidered on the cloths, "just as the Sulṭān had been accustomed to do."[220] By the turn of the twelfth century al-Marīyah evidently had surpassed all other Andalusī cities, including Qurṭubah, as the premier textile-manufacturing center,[221] but there is no way of determining whether this preeminence can be projected back to the tenth century. There is a record, however, that in 997 the Ḥājib Ibn Abī ʿĀmir, the future al-Manṣūr, bestowed on both Muslim and Christian allies in a successful campaign 2,285 pieces of *ṭirāzī* silk *(shiqqah),* 21 lengths of sea-wool *(ṣūf al-baḥr)* fabric, 2 robes impregnated with ambergris *(ʿanbarī),* 11 pieces of *ṣiqlāṭūn,* 15 striped cloths *(murayyash),* 7 brocade carpets *(namaṭ),* 2 robes of Rūmī brocade, and 2 marten *(fanak)* furs.[222]

The fullest account of the Andalusī textile industry in the tenth century is provided by Ibn Ḥawqal:

A variety of woollen goods are manufactured, among them very expensive pieces *(qiṭaʿ*; sing. *qiṭʿah)* resembling the best Armenian carpets with their deep pile *(maḥfūr)*,[223] to say nothing of the high-quality carpets *(namaṭ)* produced there. In the matter of dyeing wool and cloth, marvellous results are obtained by the use of plants *(ḥashīsh)* peculiar to al-Andalus. It is with these that the high-quality and costly Maghribī felts *(lubūd*; sing. *libd)* are dyed, as well as whatever colours of floss-silk and raw silk are desired. Brocade is exported, and no craftsmen anywhere in the world can compete with them in the manufacture of felts. Sometimes [so-called] "thirty-felts" *(lubūd thalāthīnīyah)* are woven for the Sulṭān, a single one of which is valued at 50 to 60 *dīnār*s, even though it is only 5 to 6 spans *(shibr)* wide, for they are exquisitely coloured furnishings *(fursh)*. Also manufactured there are floss-silk and close-woven silk-stuffs *(al-khazz al-sakb)*[224] of a quality surpassing those made for the ruler of ʿIrāq. A waxed *(mushammaʿ)* variety protects the wearer from rain. . . .

In several parts of the country cheap linen for clothing is made and exported to different places, some going as far as Egypt. Robes manufactured in Bajjānak are sent to Egypt, Makkah, Yaman and elsewhere. Linen woven both for the people at large and for the Court is in no way inferior to Dabīqī of either the compact type or the fine, soft *sharb* variety, and is comparable to the best *Shaṭāwī* cloth.[225]

One thing that Ibn Ḥawqal failed to mention was that the *ṭirāz* cities were all in southern al-Andalus, reasonably close to the seat of government; Qurṭubah was the most northerly. Textile towns listed by al-Rāzī but not so far mentioned as such included Lāridah, the center of a flax-growing district in the Upper March,[226] Saraqusṭah,[227] and Laqant, a small but fairly prosperous seaport in the *kūrah* of Tudmīr.[228]

Agriculture and craft industries, together with mining and metalworking and defensive functions in the Marches and along the southeast coast, would have been quite capable of generating and maintaining a maturely developed urban hierarchy. As it so happened, however, it was commerce that provided the generative force in the expansion of the system. With the shattering of Byzantine naval power in 827 and the resulting opening of the eastern Mediterranean, al-Andalus became an important unit implanted in a larger economic network—specifically the international trade network of the Islamic Empire. And it was participation in this network that underwrote, from the second quarter of the ninth century, the rapid development not only of certain individual cities but also of the urban system as a whole. As Thomas Glick explicates the process, the international market encouraged the location and expansion of artisanal industries in towns, where a monetary economy allowed urban entrepreneurs to acquire country properties *(munyāt)* in the surrounding huertas. The agricultural surpluses generated by these symbiotically linked town-and-country complexes in turn accelerated urban growth, including the further expansion and refinement of craft industries. Although, as we have seen, al-Andalus exported products of its craft industries, including olive oil, woods, ironware, steel swords, and, particularly, textiles, its trading links with North Africa and the Eastern Caliphate were generated principally by its own role as a consumer society. Its standard of living and its purchasing power were both high in comparison with those of eastern Islam; its economy was monetarized by the end of the eighth century; and the caliphal state of the tenth century was capitalized by an influx of Sūdānese gold, tribute from the Christian kingdoms of the north, and a favorable balance of trade with the rest of the Islamic world.[229]

The diversion of natural resources into urban craft industries and the concomitant creation of new urban structures necessitated new instruments of social and political control embodied in a more responsive administrative system. This was effected when ʿAbd al-Raḥmān II (r. 822–52) undertook the administrative reorganization of the amīrate on ʿAbbāsid lines. Whereas the Umayyads in Dimashq had instituted a decentralized, tribally oriented system of administration vesting considerable authority in town governors (sing. *wālī*), ʿAbd al-Raḥmān centralized political power by concentrating it in the person of the *amīr*. Within a hierarchically ordered bureaucracy that included new court officials based ultimately on Persian models, the dominant bureau was the treasury. At the same time, political was merged with economic control in the establishment of state monopolies and governmental intervention in urban markets. At the specifically urban level, a variety of ʿAbbāsid-style officials were introduced, most notably the market master (*muḥtasib;* in this case with widened jurisdiction) and the town prefect (*ṣāḥib al-madīnah).*[230] By the tenth century, ʿAbd al-Raḥmān III al-Nāṣir (r. 912–61) was ruling through a hierarchy of slaves and Berber mercenaries brought from North Africa to assist in his military adventures on the northern frontier of al-Andalus. This process of centralization and unification from the ninth century onward was possible only because the expanding economies of the principal southern cities furnished the *amīr,* and subsequently the caliph, with the financial resources with which to implement tighter administrative and economic controls.

Commentary

It is ironic that during the centuries when the Umayyads, without recourse to justification by heretical dogma, were consolidating a state completely independent of the main Islamic polity, there should have been taking place a "Syrianization" of the Andalusī landscape in its rural and urban expressions. The settlement of Syrian contingents (*junds*) in cities such as Ishbīliyah and Balansiyah, the importation of Syrian customs by Umayyad clients who arrived in large numbers after 756, and the deliberate policy of introducing Syrian agricultural practices, Syrian irrigation techniques, Syrian architectural modes and decorative motifs, and even vegetation native to the Levant, all combined to impart a distinctively Levantine aspect to Andalusī towns and their rural environs. It is no surprise that Ishbīliyah, which had been settled by Syrian *junds*, should have been referred to by Arab writers as Ḥims al-Andalus.[231] But let Ibn Ḥawqal, for once transcending his Fāṭimid bias, have the last word:

> All the towns [in al-Andalus] I have mentioned are known for their grain crops, their articles of commerce, their vineyards, their buildings, their markets, their taverns, their baths, and their caravanserais. . . . In the whole of al-Andalus I did not find a single dilapidated mosque . . . nor a city that was not well populated, that was not surrounded by an extensive [cultivated] rural area . . . with numerous villages and prosperous farm workers owning flocks and herds, efficient implements, work animals, and fields. Their lands either receive enough rainfall to yield good harvests in spring or are irrigated by well maintained and well constructed water-distribution systems.[232]

Iṣqiliyah

Although Iṣqiliyah (Sicily) had proved a potent lure for Muslim raiders almost from the establishment of the Caliphate,[233] it was not until 827 that a sustained attempt was mounted to conquer and occupy the island. In that year the Aghlabid *amīr* Ziyādat Allāh I harnessed the energies of rebellious *jundī*s to the zeal of pious activists in a holy war against the Iṣqiliyan Christians.[234] Four years later, the Arabs seized Balarm (Palermo), the second-most important city on the island, which they made their capital; but the subjugation of Iṣqiliyah was destined to be a lengthy undertaking, hindered by rivalries between African and Andalusī contingents in the army and intermittent defensive measures undertaken by the Byzantines, as well as by interventions by Venetians and the Carolingian emperor. Although Muslim armies occupied Massīnah in 843, thereby preventing Byzantine vessels from using the strait to enter the western Mediterranean, it was not until 859, after thirty years of campaigning, that they managed to take the town of Enna. They renamed it Qaṣr Yānī,[235] and it earned the sobriquet "Belvedere of Iṣqiliyah." In 878 Saraqūsah (Syracuse) fell to the Muslims, and in 902 Ṭabarmīn, after which they controlled the whole island except for a few unimportant and scattered settlements.[236]

Marketing and Service Centers

Both al-Maqdisī and Ibn Ḥawqal, as well as every subsequent writer on Iṣqiliyan history and topography, agree that Balarm remained the seat of government, the *qaṣabah* in al-Maqdisī's classification, throughout the tenth century and beyond.[237] At first the seat of an Aghlabid governor, it subsequently became the center of the Fāṭimid government on the island, during which time the fortified enclave of al-Khāliṣah was built on the outskirts of the old city. Here resided the *amīr* with his retainers and palace guard, and here were located the various administrative bureaus of the *kūrah,* as well as an arsenal *(dār al-ṣināʿah),* a small Friday mosque, and a couple of baths. The merchants and the nobility lived in the *qaṣr* of old Balarm, while the markets of the city were dispersed through the other principal quarters, of which the Ḥarāt al-Ṣaqālibah (Slav Quarter) was the most populous. In the tenth century, Ibn Ḥawqal estimated that there were almost two hundred butchers' shops in the city.[238]

In 948 a dissident governor, al-Ḥasan ibn ʿAlī al-Kalbī,

established a local dynasty under Fāṭimid suzerainty that, during its near-century of hegemony, was to preside over the apogee of Muslim power and culture on the island. Indeed, when al-Muʿizz transferred the Fāṭimid capital to al-Qāhirah, his Zīrīd lieutenant in al-Ifrīqiyah was denied jurisdiction over Iṣqiliyah. Under Kalbite rule the population of Balarm was cosmopolitan enough to include Arabs, Berbers, Greeks, Lombards, Jews, Slavs, Persians, Turks, and blacks. What is more, according to Ibn Ḥawqal, more than three hundred mosques dotted the urban complex, including Khāliṣah and the extramural suburbs—a number he believed exceeded that in any city of twice the size known to him. And the vast majority of these mosques were well maintained.[239] All of which accords well with al-Maqdisī's comment that the two *ʿīd* festivals, on respectively the expiration of the fast of Ramaḍān and the tenth of Dhū al-Ḥijjah, the month of pilgrimage, were more revered in Iṣqiliyah than in almost any other place.[240] Of course, when speaking of Islam in Iṣqiliyah, it must be remembered that the Arab conquest had proceeded broadly from west to east. As a result, even at the end of the tenth century, while the Val di Mazara (in the west of the island) was predominantly Muslim, the Val di Noto (in the south) was considerably less so, and the Val Demone (the northeastern corner) was still prevalently Christian.[241]

As in al-Andalus, al-Maqdisī did not order Iṣqiliyan cities hierarchically, but it is certain that the vast majority at all levels were agriculturally based. Although information for the tenth century is exiguous, there is every reason to suppose that the two strongly contrastive ecosystems evident in subsequent centuries were already well developed at that time: on the one hand, intensely cultivated, often irrigated fruit and vegetable farming on a narrow, and not infrequently discontinuous, coastal strip; on the other hand, extensively farmed cereal cropping in the interior. Both systems benefited from the agricultural revolution that we have already seen transforming the landscape of al-Andalus. In the lowlands, irrigation systems already incorporating Roman siphon technology were enhanced by the introduction of Persian hydraulic techniques.[242] At the same time, the Arabs were bringing sugarcane and a knowledge of sugar refining, mulberries, silkworms, papyrus, fruit, and root and green vegetables *(baḥayrah)* to the island.[243] Māzar,[244] Lantīnī,[245] and Jirjant[246] were adequately representative of service centers in fruit- and vegetable-farming districts; Baṭarliyah[247] and Qurliyūn,[248] of those in the interior.

Capital generated by a commerce burgeoning from the island's central position in the Caliphate's vast economic commonwealth presumably found its way into the countryside occasionally as investments in the large estates of a territorial nobility and smaller, intensively farmed holdings surrounding some of the larger cities. But that did not save the olive-oil industry. Between 400 and 900 the olive tree virtually disappeared from the Iṣqiliyan landscape, probably eliminated by the depredations of warring armies; the production of olive oil was relinquished to the North African territories.

Industrial and Craft Centers

A considerable mining industry, including the extraction of gold, silver, lead, mercury, sulphur, naphtha, vitriol, antimony, and alum, was concentrated in the vicinity of Mount Etna, but seems to have exercised little influence on the Iṣqiliyan urban system. Presumably this industry gave rise to villages rather than towns. At Balharah, however, a mine in the ownership of the sovereign provided iron for the needs of the navy and the ruler's carriages.[249] There must also have been the usual array of craft industries essential to an agricultural society, although, apart from textiles, they are poorly documented. And even in the case of textiles, most of the extant information is of post-tenth-century origin.[250] The earliest reference seems to be Ibn Ḥawqal's mention of a Ṭirāz-Manufacturers' Market *(Sūq al-Ṭirāzīyīn)* in the New Quarter *(al-Ḥārah al-Jadīdah)* of Balarm, which must necessarily have been established at some time subsequent to the occupation of the city by the Muslims in 831.

In addition to listing cotton merchants *(kaṭṭānūn)* and carders of cloth *(ḥallājūn)* among the artisans of Balarm,[251] Ibn Hawqal also recorded wool and goat hair *(shaʿr)*, together with linen garments, among the products of the island. Furthermore, he did not allow his poor opinion of Sicilians generally to subvert his reporting of the claim that these particular textiles were unequalled in quality and cheapness. The tailored kind, cut into two lengths of from fifty to sixty *rubāʿī*, was of a quality superior to that of a similar type sold in Miṣr for as much as fifty or sixty *dīnārs*.[252] Al-Maqdisī's only contribution to the roster of textile manufacturers was "close-woven *(maʿṣūr)* garments," which were presumably what he had in mind when he listed among the manufactures of Āmid in the *Jazīrah* "garments of wool and linen of Iṣqiliyan type."[253] In subsequent centuries Sicilian silk stuffs earned a considerable reputation abroad, and probably in the tenth century as well, though no record of this exists from that time.

Fortified Settlements

A distinctive feature of the Iṣqiliyan landscape was the prevalence of fortresses and fortifications; more than three hundred existed in the second half of the tenth century.[254] These served two functions: fortified posts against the infidel and havens for populations of dependent territories. In the first place, Iṣqiliyah was—as Ibn Ḥawqal phrases it—a marcher country confronting the European enemy, "where the holy war had been pursued ceaselessly and the call to arms had resounded continuously ever since the Muslim conquest." The governor of the island exempted from this duty only those having an irrefutable excuse to avoid military service or who paid an exemption fee.[255] Fortified posts involved in the struggle against the infidel, for obvious reasons, occupied predominantly coastal locations, especially in the northern sectors of the island. Qalʿat al-Qawārib,[256] Ṭirmah,[257] and Qarīnash[258] are sufficiently representative of such Ṣūfī *ribāṭāt.* But, wherever they were situated, they found little favor with Ibn Ḥawqal, who depicts them as nests of duplicity and hypocrisy, filled with a shameless rabble of rogues and sanctimonious slanderers.[259] The other type of fortress settlement included towns such as Baṭarliyah[260] and Qalʿat al-Ballūt,[261] where the population of dependent territories could take refuge in all-too-frequent times of war. In fact every *iqlīm*[262] on the island supported at least one such fortified refuge, the *iqlīm* capital that, incidentally, almost invariably boasted a cathedral mosque, the salient symbol of Muslim control.

Commentary

The Iṣqiliyan urban system of Islamic times that can be elicited from contemporary sources is no more than a sketch. Nonetheless, the evidence of both pre- and post-Islamic conditions on the island does nothing to contradict what al-Maqdisī had heard about it, namely that it was one of the most highly urbanized regions of the Muslim world.[263] Certainly, commerce flourished as Iṣqiliyah benefited from its central position in the vast economic commonwealth of the Islamic world.[264] The decline in living standards that Ibn Ḥawqal claims to have witnessed in 973 was temporary and perhaps less severe than he depicts it.[265] In any case, prosperity was clearly restored by the Kalbite Jaʿfar ibn Muḥammad and his successors during the last two decades of the tenth century.

PART III

The Places where Men Pray Together

Chapter Seventeen

The Urban Fabric

Urbanism in its grossest connotation signifies no more than a particular level of sociocultural integration that becomes meaningful only when contrasted with pre-urban, nonurban, or (presumably soon-to-be) post-urban society. However, this generalization conceals the fact that each society mediates the integrative process according to its own distinctive combination of functional subsystems[1] and the values and norms of its structural subsystems. There are, in fact, two modes of integration operating in, respectively, cultural and broadly socioeconomic contexts: whereas symbolic elements are integrated logically and meaningfully into systems of beliefs, ethics, and so forth, the technosocial system is integrated causally and functionally. It follows that it is analytically profitable to discriminate two generalized types of institutional transactions taking place in the representative city: those involved in the exchange and processing of information and those involved in the exchange and processing of material goods. The former are obviously concerned with administration and ceremony, the latter principally with modes of economic exchange.

The societal node where these informational, service, and commodity transactions take place is invariably accorded material expression in a localized nexus of architectural forms that is recognized, in whatever cultural context it may occur, as a theater for the acting out of a distinctive manner of life characterized as urban. It is the forms and functions of these nexuses that constitute the subject matter of conventional urban studies, with inquiries focusing on the built form as follows:

- An arena for the interplay of creative and destructive tensions in the disposition of volume and space. Spatially it is disposed in a combination of (1) legislated and unlegislated patterns of land use reflecting a division of labor and (2) residential neighborhoods reflecting apportionment of rewards; both of these arrangements are coordinated through the agency of (3) organizational structures that generate and control a complex flow of messages, persons, and commodities through a network of ramified institutional channels.[2] By virtue of these transactions the city functions as an institution of institutions, the critical locality where the organizational output of one institution becomes the input of another.
- A locale promoting a characteristic style of life, production, and thought that, whatever its cultural and civilizational context, can be aptly rendered in English as "urban." Withal the city is a macroscopic role system within which social process and spatial form are continuously interacting to fashion a cultural recorder. On this are chronicled both the best and the worst of human achievements, and everything between.
- A component in a hierarchy of centers of societal

control in the form of a system of cities, the development of which can be viewed as an increase in societal scale involving extension of the radii of societal interdependence; intensification of the degree of that interdependence; enlargement of the range and content of the information flows that integrate societal action; and a consequent expansion of the sphere of compliance with, and control by, the metropolitan center. The extension of city influence into the surrounding countryside means that increasing numbers of people become involved in one way or another in the affairs of the city. Whether or not they live within its physical limits, they come under the influence, and more often than not the control, of its institutions. This means that an urbanized society subsumes two functionally distinct components. On the one hand there is the city dweller proper, the resident within the urban enclave; and on the other there is the urbanized countryman who lives in terms of the city but not in it, who is bound to the city in an asymmetrical structural relationship that requires him to produce in one form or another a fund of rent payable to power brokers based, if not always resident, within the urban enceinte.[3]

As the nodes in the communications networks are situated in cities, the messages they transmit originate predominantly with, and inevitably reflect the point of view of, those who reside at the hub of the network. Consequently the messages flowing outward to the rest of society are impregnated with urban norms. The city, by virtue of encompassing the organizational foci of society, contrives, prescribes, modulates, and disseminates order throughout the subsystems of that society. Its most crucial export, as Scott Greer has reminded us,[4] is control. To that extent the structure of the city can be said to epitomize the pattern of the larger society of which it is a part, which is what is meant when it is characterized as a creator of effective space,[5] when it is allegorized as the summation of society,[6] or when it is designated a living repository of culture.[7] And because of its regulation of the communications (and as often as not the transportation) networks, the city is always likely to become a focus of innovation, a generative force disseminating new concepts and novel technologies through the larger society.

Chapters 4 through 16 of this work have focused almost exclusively on the changing external relations of the cities of North Africa and the Middle East. Emphasis has been placed squarely on their roles within developing urban hierarchies—that is, on the horizontal (spatial) and vertical (organizational) components of a series of urban systems. Elements of the internal structures of these cities have been mentioned only when they have served to validate the assignment of a city to a particular rank in the hierarchy, as often happens, for example, in the case of a *masjid al-jāmiʿ*, a *dār al-imārah*, a palatine complex, or a *sūq* of particular type or size. However, the reader who has persisted this far may well have developed some curiosity as to the structure of the urban nodes, themselves systems of institutionalized transactions, that in the aggregate constitute the larger hierarchical systems. This chapter is intended partially to allay that curiosity and to direct the reader to sources where it can be more fully satisfied.

In what follows, attention will be directed to the epiphenomenal expression of selected classes of institutions located within the city proper, specifically those concerned with government and administration, religion, economic exchange, shelter, and certain specialized functions. A final section will provide sketches of the morphologies of representative cities during the first four centuries of the Islamic era, but with special emphasis on the tenth century. Nor do I apologize for the summary character of this chapter, which serves much in the manner of an epilogue to the more detailed systemic studies that precede it. Whereas the hierarchical ordering of urban centers during these centuries has hitherto received only incidental, and often allusive, mention, the internal structures of at least the larger cities have already received a good deal of scholarly attention, the details of which there is no call to recapitulate here. The following pages offer no more than an overview of certain features visually prominent in representative cities of the early Islamic world and occasionally suggest a shift in emphasis in a prevailing interpretation.

Signatures of Power in the Urban Landscape

"O Ye Who Believe, obey God, and obey the Messenger and those among you with authority."[8] It was on this Qur'ānic injunction that the Muslims based their theory of government, the primary purpose of which was to make possible the service of God (*ʿibādah*). On the death of Muḥammad the sequence of vicegerents (sing. *khalīfah*) who succeeded to the administrative functions of his office (though not to his prophethood) preserved the fundamental conception that the Caliphate constituted both the religious and the political leadership of the Muslim community. It was their responsibility to disseminate the great truths revealed by the Prophet, mediate disputes within the *Ummah*, internally maintain an appropriate level of public order, and externally extend Muslim territorial conquests for the general benefit of the community. At lower levels in the hierarchy, governors and other officials administered provinces, districts, and cities on essentially the same principles and with proportionately devolved authority.

In the earlier phases of the Muslim hegemony the material expression of the institution of government in the urban landscape was the *dār al-imārah*. Unfortunately, archaeology thus far has contributed little to our knowledge of the structure of such buildings, while the textual sources fail us in two respects: they seldom describe the architectural features of a *dār* and virtually never provide a comprehensive schedule of the governmental functions performed within its walls. Usually a canvass of textual references affords little certainty beyond the fact that government activities took place there and, more often than not, that a ruler, governor, or other high official resided there.[9] It should also be noted that, contrary to the situation in, say, al-Baṣrah or al-Kūfah, the *dār al-imārah* was not necessarily built specifically for that purpose but was a term applicable to any structure appropriated for government at the regional level and commodious enough to house a *diwān*.

It has long been a subject of comment that in the early centuries of Islamic dominance this focus of political power was almost invariably sited in the heart of the city in close proximity to the settlement's principal mosque, the center of religious authority. More recently it has been realized that the *dār al-imārah* was equally frequently—customarily is probably no exaggeration—positioned on the *qiblah* side of that mosque. The most illuminating exposition of this architectural linkage has been provided by Jere L. Bacharach, from whom I have adopted the structure of this and the following paragraph as well as a good deal of their substance.[10] The earliest recorded instance of this organic articulation between congregational mosque and *dār al-imārah*, the two most important communal institutions of the *Ummah*, occurred in al-Kūfah. In this cantonment the house of government was sited from the beginning on the *qiblah* side of the congregational mosque, although separated from it by an alley. Subsequently the two structures were combined in a single architectural feature, apparently on the advice of a *dihqān* called Rūzbih ibn Buzurgumihr, with the *dār al-imārah* still on the *qiblah* side of the *jāmiʿ*.[11] The rationale for this particular architectural composition has been lost in the mists of time, and no amount of speculation is likely to resolve the issue.

Reasonably close juxtaposition of buildings housing respectively administrative and religious institutions does not require special comment, as it has been the norm in virtually all cultures. But this does not explain the positioning of the *dār al-imārah* relative to the *qiblah* of the *jāmiʿ*. Nor do the reasons offered by the Islamic chroniclers inspire confidence: namely to protect the treasury *(bayt al-māl)*, which was housed in the *dār al-imārah*,[12] by placing the latter against the wall of the *jāmiʿ*; and to provide the commander-in-chief or governor with immediate access to his private chamber *(maqṣurah)* within the mosque. The first of these goals could have been achieved had the *dār al-imārah* been on any of three sides of the mosque. Moreover, the ruler could have entered the *jāmiʿ* from any of the three sides and still have been shielded by a barrier from the rest of the worshippers. Perhaps the linkage should be sought at a deeper level of Islamic culture than that involved in routine management. A speculative suggestion, presently devoid of confirmatory evidence, is that Saʿd ibn ʿAbī Waqqāṣ, the founder of al-Kūfah, was attempting to recreate certain aspects of the spatial ordering of the Prophet's house and prayer courtyard in al-Madīnah (Medina). However that may be, during the next two centuries the arrangement was adopted in numerous settlements under Islamic control and, intentionally or not, embodied a nicely symbolic evocation of the dual responsibilities, religious and secular, of the Muslim rulers of the time.[13] Prayer to God throughout the Muslim world was directed down the *qiblah* to Makkah (Mecca), the locus where it was most efficacious; but in the cities we are discussing it also passed through the official residence of a Muslim ruler. Did it inform his decisions, or validate them, or simply signify the role of the ruler within the *Ummah*, or none of these? In the year of the *Hijrah* 1416 the answer is still unknown.

A similar relationship of *dār al-imārah* to mosque is implicit in Donald Whitcomb's reconstruction of the city of Iṣṭakhr as it was made over by Ziyād ibn Abīhi (659–62).[14] It is also recorded that Ziyād, when he was *ʿāmil* over al-Baṣrah (665–75), moved the government *dār* to the south side of the *jāmiʿ*. Although al-Balādhurī, who has preserved this snippet of information,[15] does not state categorically that the two buildings were conjoined, Ziyād's role as governor in both Iṣṭakhr and al-Baṣrah is sufficient inducement for Bacharach to suggest that the axial architectural arrangement found in the former city may have been repeated in al-Baṣrah.[16] In Damascus it is often alleged that the Muslims at first appropriated as their place of prayer the western half of the Church of St. John, while leaving the eastern half still in the hands of Christians. This division was denied by al-Wāqidī (748–823),[17] and is incompatible with the recollection of the monk Arculf, who visited Damascus in about 670.[18]

Even if this tale is no more than a legend,[19] there is no doubt that Muʿāwiyah, when governor of al-Shām (Greater Syria), constructed for himself a residence on the *qiblah* side of an already existing *masjid al-jāmiʿ* and inaugurated a new architectural tradition by raising over it a structure known as "The Green Dome" *(al-Qubbat al-Khaḍrāʾ)*. This feature would become an integral part of the architecture of several governmental administrative buildings in the eastern half of the Caliphate during the ensuing two centuries. In 703 al-Ḥajjāj constructed a *dār al-imārah* on the *qiblah* side of the *masjid al-jāmiʿ* in his newly founded cantonment at Wāsiṭ and furnished the former with a green dome;[20] but the culmination of this practice was the famed Qubbat al-Khaḍrāʾ rising over the Golden Palace *(al-Qaṣr al-Dhahab)* in the heart of the caliph al-Manṣūr's City of Peace (Baghdād).[21] Once again the focus of administration was placed on the *qiblah* side of the mosque, even though the space available would have permitted a site on any of the other three sides. It is also worthy of comment that the fortifications of the imperial city were such as to negate the need for security as a reason for juxtaposing palace and mosque in the first place. Nor was this the only palace-mosque complex of this type built by al-Manṣūr: in 768 he began a palace on the *qiblah* side of a second principal mosque in the Baghdādi suburb of al-Ruṣāfah, which was completed in 776 in the reign of his son al-Mahdī. Bacharach believes that the presence of a virtually complete suite of formal spatial relationships probably implies the existence of a green dome over the palace.[22] Finally, it was reported that Abū Muslim, architect of the ʿAbbāsid revolution, built a domed *dār al-imārah* adjacent to a *masjid al-jāmiʿ* at Marv al-Shāhijān between 748 and 755,[23] and that in about 796 Hārūn al-Rashīd constructed a palace with a green dome in al-Rāfiqah on the Euphrates River, but no description of this latter building has survived.[24]

The precise significance of the green *qubbah* surmounting a caliphal or other official residence is uncertain. However, the dome was prominent in the architecture of both the Byzantine and the Sāsānian Empires, where it symbolized the heavens and, in the former at any rate, was often decorated with iconic representations of divine beings and Elysian furniture.[25] As such the dome signified possession of divine power, and Muʿāwiyah and al-Manṣūr, each in his time, undoubtedly perceived it as symbolizing caliphal authority. Presumably their lieutenants in Wāsiṭ and Marv were affirming the supremacy of dynasties rather than of their own governorships. In any case, the dome, by reason of its size and elevation, was an especially efficacious visual statement capable of defining the locus of power for Muslim and unbeliever alike throughout a settlement.

However that may be, after the establishment of the ʿAbbāsid government in Sāmarrā in 836, the so-called green dome atop a palace was abandoned in the former Sāsānian territories. Other discontinued design features included the axial arrangement of the *dār al-imārah* against the *qiblah* wall of the mosque and the implementation of certain ratios between their dimensions. However, in more westerly lands the spatial relationship of *dār* to mosque continued for several decades, although the dome was always lacking. In the Levant, in addition to the architectural composition at Damascus, the pattern can be discerned in Jerusalem, where, until the earthquake of 749, it is likely that a *dār al-imārah* existed on the *qiblah* side of the Aqṣā Mosque, to which it was eventually connected by a bridge;[26] probably at ʿAnjar; and possibly, with the eye of faith, at Khirbat al-Mafjar.[27] Farther west the relationship is clearer. In the cantonment known by that very name, al-ʿAskar, in 751 a *dār* was attached to the principal mosque on the *qiblah* side;[28] in 870 Ibn Ṭūlūn constructed a palace on the southern side of the famous mosque that bears his name;[29] and it appears that in al-Qayrawān (Kairouan) an analogous relationship also obtained.[30] But by the beginning of the tenth century the architectural combination of *dār al-imārah* and *masjid al-jāmiʿ* had disappeared in North Africa as completely as it had in the Eastern Caliphate. Yet the persistence of this organic relationship over two centuries and its wide dispersal through the Islamic world accord poorly with the relative triviality and seeming arbitrariness of its alleged origin.

Quite early in the history of Islam, communal interests began to diverge from those of the Caliphate. As Ira Lapidus has shown in a perceptive study, Arab rebellions fostering the crystallization of sectarian movements within the *Ummah* joined with the emergence of religious activity independent of caliphal authority and the rise of the Ḥanbalī law school to establish for most practical purposes a persistent distinction between secular and religious authority.[31] As Lapidus has phrased it, "The traditionists expected the Caliphate to uphold the truth and law, but not to define its content, because as the ultimate object of Muslim devotion, the law stood beyond the Caliph."[32] Religious and political life came to develop as distinctive spheres of endeavor with their own values, leaders, and organizations. By about the mid-ninth century effective control of the empire was passing from caliphs into the hands of governors, bureaucrats, and generals, who presided over essentially secular regimes.

A sociocultural transformation of these dimensions could not but have epiphenomenal repercussions on the nature and architectural expression of the institutions assembled in cities. In the sphere of government, the more important offices tended to be incorporated in elaborately planned administrative complexes, located outside existing cities and thereby symbolizing the growing separation of the rulers from their subjects. In addition to the ruler and his family, of whatever degree in the administrative hierarchy they might be, *dār al-imārah* and palace enclave alike housed a corps of officials and a retinue of servitors. In the case of a caliphal or palatine complex, the high officials might include the chamberlain *(ḥājib);*[33] the commander-in-chief of the army; the chief of police *(ṣāḥib al-shurṭah);* the chief *qāḍī;* the *wazīr,* often in his own palace nearby; secretaries (in the specifically Arabo-Islamic sense of *dīwān* officials);[34] and a body of eunuchs serving as confidential agents of the caliph. Other eunuchs served in less prestigious positions as domestic servants and *ḥarīm* attendants, where they mingled with a vast assortment of musicians, dancers and storytellers, physicians, astrologers, jewellers, textile workers, metal- and woodworkers, copyists and illuminators, falconers, grooms and ostlers, camel men, porters, water carriers, boatmen, slaves, and a host of other roles necessary to sustain the lifestyle proper to an important Muslim ruler.

The Sacred in the Urban Landscape

The most impressive structure in any city in the Islamic world between the seventh and tenth centuries was likely to be the *masjid al-jāmiʿ*, the congregational mosque. It was also the principal architectural expression of the unity of the Muslim community, the place where Believers joined together in ritual prayer at Friday noon and acknowledged the authority of a vicegerent of God's Prophet, while for unbelievers it was a manifest sign of Islamic hegemony.

The earliest mosque architecture derived from domestic rather than religious models and was hypostyle in form. Prior to the *Hijrah,* Muḥammad and his followers appear to have gathered for prayer in any convenient location in and around Makkah.[35] The Prophet himself is said to have occasionally performed the prayer ritual in the neighborhood of the Kaʿbah. However, when Muḥammad arrived in al-Madīnah, a simple compound *(dār)* of sun-dried brick *(labin)* was built for him and incorporated within its perimeter a space that could be used for ritual prayer. As it is portrayed in *ḥadīths,* this structure comprised lateral apartments *(ḥujarāt)* for the Prophet's wives, a roofed portico *(ẓullah),* and a smaller shelter *(ṣuffah)* for rootless Companions, who became known appropriately enough as the People of the Portico *(Ahl al-Ṣuffah),* all within or without a walled square having one-hundred-cubit (approximately sixty meters) sides. In effect, the place of prayer, which was also a meeting place for Believers, was the shared courtyard of the Prophet's compound, an architectural arrangement involving an enclosed courtyard *(ṣaḥn)* with a variable number of covered colonnades that would become standard practice in mosque construction in future centuries.[36] Al-Kūfah offers a good example: the mosque that Ziyād ibn Abīhi rebuilt in the center of that city in 670 was essentially an elaborate recreation of the Prophet's *ṣaḥn,* with a foss *(khandaq)* replacing the Madīnan wall and pillars from Jabal Ahwāz substituted for portico palm trunks. It was said, surely not without exaggeration, to be large enough to accommodate forty thousand worshippers.

The Semitic root of the word *masjid* occurred as early as the fifth century B.C. in Aramaic papyri *(msgdʾ),* subsequently in Epigraphic South Arabian *(msʾgd)* and in Nabataean inscriptions, in each form denoting a place of worship.[37] In Arabic *sajada* means "to prostrate oneself (before God)" and *masjid* the place where that is done. In the Qurʾān this latter form appears to have signified any place, architecturally defined or not, where God was worshipped, although it is debatable whether the noun was adopted directly from Aramaic or formed from a borrowed verb.[38] As to Muḥammad's establishment, there is no convincing evidence that it was planned as a sanctuary, or even treated as such, during the Prophet's lifetime. However, it was the place wherein virtually all official activities of the Muslim *Ummah* took place, including hebdomadal collective worship, revelation, dissemination of secular information, community discussion and liturgical decision making, formal profession of both the Faith and political allegiance, administration of justice, and governance of the incipient Muslim polity. And as the focus of Muslim life, the source of Islamic authority, and the very burial site of the last of the Prophets, the house gradually came to assume a distinctively Muslim sacrality in the collective memory of the *Ummah,* and ultimately to provide a basic model for *masjid* design.[39]

The Muslims who invaded the Fertile Crescent (as distinguished from Arabs already settled there) seem to have gravitated to already sacred locales as sites for their prayer places. In Jerusalem, for example, ʿUmar is said to have laid out such an enceinte in 638, which was still only a primitive structure as late as 670 or thereabouts, when the pilgrim Arculf arrived in the city. "The Saracens," he reports, "frequent a quadrangular house of prayer *(domus orationis)* rudely constructed by setting boards and great beams on some ruins surviving on the famous spot where the Temple once stood in all its splendor."[40] The same author estimated that the enceinte could accommodate three thousand men. A further example is furnished by the al-Jilāʾ mosque in Ṣanʿāʾ, which seems to have been an adaptation of a Jewish synagogue.[41] It was also fairly common for the Muslims to convert a church into a mosque, especially when the town had been acquired by conquest rather than capitulation. One tradition has the Muslims taking over no less than fifteen churches in Damascus, and in Ḥamā the largest church was converted into a mosque; while in Egypt numerous churches were transformed into mosques during al-Maʾmūn's campaign against the Copts. In al-Qāhirah (Cairo) the Rāshīdal Mosque was said to have been originally an unfinished Jacobite church. Yāqūt also reports that the chief mosque in Balarm (Palermo) had once been a church. And it comes as no surprise that what must have at first appeared as a more or less inconsequential prerogative of authority should eventually have been deemed in need of authoritative support, as when, for instance, Zayd ibn ʿAlī pronounced, "Perform thy *ṣalāt* in churches and synagogues and it will not harm thee."[42] Nor were churches alone in being adapted to this purpose. After the conquest of al-Madāʾin in 637, when the abandoned houses of the former Sāsānian capital had been apportioned among victorious Muslims, Khusraw's Īwān was converted into a mosque.[43] Between al-Ḥillah and Karbalā a temple of Shamash was adapted as a mosque; not far from Iṣṭakhr a fire temple was converted into the Masjid Sulaymān, as was another fire temple within the city; and in Maṣṣīṣah al-Manṣūr built a mosque on the site of an ancient temple.[44]

Occasionally it is claimed that Muslims actually shared a church building with Christians, but few of the relevant texts are totally convincing. We have already seen that in the case of the Church of St. John in Damascus the tradition of such a division was not incontrovertible,[45] and the same might reasonably be suspected of al-Balādhurī's assertion that after the conquest, one-fourth of the Kanīsat Yūḥannā in the city of Ḥimṣ (Emesa) was reserved as a mosque.[46] Archaeology and the Greek chronicler Theophanes are not in conflict with such a division without actually confirming it, while al-Maqdisī differs from al-Balādhurī only in assigning the Muslims a full half of the building.[47] Al-Iṣṭakhrī and his reviser Ibn Ḥawqal both wrote of the division as existing in the tenth century.[48] From all that is known of conditions in the Levant at that time, this was an unlikely conjunction of faiths. Presumably Ibn Ḥawqal had taken it on trust from al-Iṣṭakhrī, who in turn may have accepted it in good faith from al-Balkhī, within whose conceptual framework he was writing. But in even the early years of the tenth century, the period when al-Balkhī probably prepared the annotations to his maps, it would have been distinctly unusual for Islam to have shared a common building with any brand of Christianity. If the whole story is anything more than a topos incorporated in a historical narrative, the division surely pertained to the earlier centuries of Muslim occupation: perhaps during, or more likely before, the earlier decades of the eighth century, when, for instance, Khālid ibn ʿAbd Allāh al-Qaṣrī, governor of ʿIrāq, is said to have built a church for his Christian mother immediately adjoining the *qiblah* wall of the *masjid al-jāmiʿ* in al-Kūfah.[49] Furthermore, elsewhere in the *Ṣūrat al-Arḍ* (p. 342), Ibn Ḥawqal himself referred to the *masjid* at Ḥimṣ as adjoining the church, not within it. A similar juxtaposition of church and mosque was in fact recorded for the predominantly Christian city of Dabīl (Dwīn) in Armīniyah.[50] The frequently cited idea that a preexisting church at Diyārbakr was ever apportioned between Muslims (two-thirds) and Christians (one-third) has been discredited by the combined testimony of Greek historical records and archaeology.[51]

Irrespective of whether the mosque was introduced as an element in a newly founded settlement or either intruded into or adapted in a conquered city, its basic form was universally modified, the better to accommodate the requirements of religious ritual. Although Muslim prayer *(ṣalāh)* may be performed virtually anywhere, corporate prayer traditionally has been more highly esteemed and has been obligatory for the noon service on Friday *(ṣalāt al-jumʿah).* Its coming to be performed with the participants ranged in parallel rows under the guidance of a leader *(imām)* facing Makkah, which was also the direction of the devotional prostration *(sujūd),* confirmed the basic simplicity of the early prayer places as transmitted to later ages. Specifically, these places took the form of a large rectangular sanctuary *(ḥaram)* with a courtyard *(ṣaḥn)* and a covered area for prayer on the Makkah side. The orientation of the faithful during the service—which ensured that all, in countless settlements throughout the Islamic world, achieved devotional communion with those actually praying at the navel of the earth—required that the mosque have one wall directed toward Makkah (although there were sometimes unexpectedly large discrepancies between mosque alignment and true bearing).[52] In this, the *qiblah,* wall was an often richly decorated niche *(miḥrāb)* symbolically commemorating the role of the Prophet as *imām* leading his people in the Friday prayers. As an architectural feature, the *miḥrāb* seems to have been formalized under the Umayyads and generalized throughout the Muslim world by the early ʿAbbāsid period.[53] Although *maḥārib* were originally restricted to Friday mosques, they subsequently featured in all mosques everywhere. At the same time, the requirement of ablution *(wuḍūʾ* or *ghusl)* before prayer eventually necessitated the placing of a basin or fountain outside the prayer hall, but this seems not to have become customary much before the ninth century. And as it was incumbent on a Muslim ruler to preach to his community and vocalize its political allegiance to higher authority at the Friday prayer service (both acts together constituting the *khuṭbah),* so the *minbar,* which in the time of the Prophet had been a simple preaching chair, evolved into an often elaborately ornate pulpit for the pronouncement of the *khuṭbah.*[54] As such it became a symbol of legitimate authority and signified that the mosque within which it was placed was maintained by a central authority; that it was in fact a *masjid al-jāmiʿ*. Early *manābir* apparently were located variously within their respective mosques, with Syrian and Spanish Umayyads going so far as to commission readily mobile wheeled models;[55] but by the ninth century the *minbar* was invariably placed to the right of the *miḥrāb.*

Finally, there remained the problem of communicating to non-Muslims, the predominant population in the early Islamic centuries, the function of the mosque as the principal focus of Muslim confessional life. The requisite monumental expression was achieved in ʿAbbāsid times, when towers were first regularly attached to mosques: symbolic architectural features, seemingly introduced in the first half of the ninth century, that projected the presence of Islam clear across a district or even a town. Although the Umayyads had furnished the Mosque of the Prophet in al-Madīnah with four towers to signify its unique status as the house-cum-prayer place of God's Messenger, circumstantial evidence would imply that the custom of attaching one or more such structures to a mosque became established first in ʿAbbāsid Baghdād; since then the practice has become ubiquitous in the Islamic world. As Jonathan Bloom has argued most persuasively, height, which had been an exclusive feature of secular administrative, chiefly palatine, architecture, became an expected element of religious structures at the start of the ninth century. With the passage of time, and despite sporadic Shīʿah resistance, it became a diagnostic attribute of the mosque and, long after the period with which we are concerned, the very symbol of Islam.

The most lasting significance of the tower attached to a mosque was that it became utilized for, and adapted to, the call to prayer *(adhān)*, perhaps as early as the ninth century but consistently only in the eleventh. Prior to this time the *muʾadhdhin* had uttered the call to prayer from a rooftop or other raised structure. The tower became, in fact, the architectural feature known in the West as the minaret.[56] During the earlier centuries of Islam, the Syrian type of minaret, derived from the characteristically square towers of Christian churches, prevailed from the Levant westward and extended into the Eastern Caliphate. However, in ʿIrāq a helicoidal form of minaret, based on certain Sāsānian spiral towers, appeared at Sāmarrā, whence it was subsequently adopted in the Mosque of Ibn Ṭūlūn in al-Qaṭāʾiʿ. Neither cylindrical minarets of the type common in Īrān from the eleventh century nor the composite minarets that drew on a wide range of regional architectural vocabularies in later times have been identified in the period with which we are concerned.

Over the first three centuries of Islam, these and other architectural elements were combined into structures manifesting great regional and temporal diversity within a simple and remarkably constant integrating framework, namely a spacious courtyard bordered on three sides by covered colonnades *(riwāq;* pl. *arwiqah)* giving access to chambers of varying size and function. The *miḥrāb*, the *minbar*, and the *maqṣūrah* (a secluded space for the exclusive use of the caliph or governor) were the essential Islamic features within the complex, while a permanent water supply and, from early in the ninth century, monumental towers were the external identifying features. Among the many mosques constructed on this plan were some of the most impressive Muslim architectural achievements. In their geographical distribution (e.g., Dimashq [Damascus], Sāmarrā, al-Qāhirah [Cairo], al-Qayrawān [Kairouan], and Qurṭubah [Córdoba]) they represented the principal realms of the Islamic world; in their temporal order (respectively Umayyad, ʿAbbāsid, Ṭūlūnid and Fāṭimid, Aghlabid, and Spanish Umayyad), the correspondingly prestigious dynasties.

The Friday Mosque

It appears that quite early on, a simple *masjid* became formally differentiated from a *masjid al-jāmiʿ;* the mosque served the whole of a particular Muslim community as the venue for the compulsory Friday communal prayer service, and hence was often known as a Friday mosque.[57] Only the latter category of mosque, financed and supervised as it was by a central Muslim authority, was allowed to install a *minbar*, thereby designating it as an inviolable precinct wherein allegiance was sworn to a lawful representative of the Prophet. Moreover, the Ḥanafī *madhhab* insisted that the Friday service be held only in an important (signifying sizable) settlement and always in a Friday mosque. Shāfiʿites further restricted the venue for the Friday service to one mosque in each settlement. But inevitably, population densities and political interests combined to generate pressures to increase the number of *masjid al-jāmiʿ* in the larger cities. Yet as late as the beginning of the tenth century, in Baghdād the *khuṭbah* was pronounced each Friday in only two *masjids*, one situated within the Round City itself and the other on the far side of the river in al-Ruṣāfah. Not surprisingly, this arrangement eventually proved inadequate to the demand, so that on Fridays, excluded worshippers lined streets as far back as the Tigris River and followed as best they could the gesticulations of signallers imitating the gestures of the *imām*. At much the same time al-Fusṭāṭ had only two Friday mosques, which were actually located in separate cities, namely the ʿAmr Mosque in al-Fusṭāṭ proper and the Mosque of Ibn Ṭūlūn in the cantonment to its north known as al-Qaṭāʾiʿ. Al-Baṣrah, although blessed allegedly with some seven thousand places of worship in the ninth century, had only two Friday mosques, and no more than three in the tenth. Al-Iṣṭakhrī, writing in the mid-tenth century, still considered it worthy of comment that al-Ḥajjāj had built a *jāmiʿ* on the western bank of the Tigris, even though one already existed on the eastern, mainly Persian-populated, bank.[58]

From that time forward, the number of Friday mosques

throughout the Islamic world slowly began to adjust to the needs of the *Ummah*—though not without a good deal of negotiation and occasional political intrigue. Al-Maqdisī hints as much when he laments the efforts required of the inhabitants of Baykand, on the road from Bukhārā to the Amū Daryā, before they were granted permission to build a congregational mosque.[59] In this predominantly Ḥanafī territory the congregational prayer could be performed only in a metropolitan mosque, in this case Bukhārā, where the *amīr* resided. Al-Narshakhī is especially informative about other such deprivations in the Bukhārā region. The substantial settlement of Iskijkat, for example, was without a congregational mosque until the second half of the eleventh century, when a wealthy tax collector built a magnificent one for celebrating the Friday prayer service. Not unexpectedly, given the Ḥanafī predisposition of the Bukhārān *imāms*, the communal prayer with its associated *khuṭbah* was forbidden, and the mosque remained empty on Fridays until ʿUmar ibn Tughrul Khān became *amīr* of Bukhārā at the turn of the twelfth century. He razed the mosque and used its timbers to build a religious school near the stalls of the vegetable vendors in Bukhārā. The settlement of Shargh was similarly deprived of a congregational mosque until Maḥmūd ibn Sulaymān, great *oaghan* of the Qarakhanids, constructed one at his own expense at the end of the eleventh century. By contrast, the people of Farakhshā, on the western boundary of the oasis but within its outer walls, actually rejected a Friday mosque that *Amīr* Ismāʿīl Sāmanī attempted to foist on them. "A cathedral mosque," they insisted, "was unnecessary and an unreasonable imposition on their settlement"—with one recension adding "since this is not Egypt."[60] Karmīn, on the other hand, although described as "one of the dependencies of Bukhārā" and taxed accordingly, yet possessed its own congregational mosque, as did Nūr, a pilgrimage center on the road to Samarqand much frequented by the people of Bukhārā.

The mosque long retained the multipurpose functions implicit in its origins. Not until the Turkish conquests did it become principally, though still not exclusively, a place of prayer. For most of the first four centuries of Islam, the mosque was not a sanctuary in the strict sense of a building reserved for the worship of a god, but rather the center of the intellectual and social, as well as the religious, life of the *Ummah*. Open by day and by night, it served as a popular meeting place for gossiping townsmen; a forum for the dissemination of sacred knowledge and secular opinion; a venue for creative interaction among special interest groups; a retail outlet for hawkers of food and drink; and the preferred stage for a variety of entertainers and others who are best described as mountebanks, all encouraging subcultural allegiances in a minor way to be founded on social characteristics rather than on mere spatial proximity.

Most of the topographers paid special attention to the condition of the mosques in the parts of the Islamic world with which they happened to be dealing, but none more so than al-Maqdisī, whom André Miquel has aptly designated "le géographe de la mosquée."[61] It is true that every mosque worth mentioning he mentioned, and almost all meriting a description he described. This author's account of an evening visit to the congregational mosque in al-Fusṭāṭ nicely evokes the bustle and activity within the building at that hour. During the last two prayers of the day, the mosque was filled with groups of students sitting in circles *(ḥalaq)* studying jurisprudence, instructors in Qurʾānic recitation, men of letters, and philosophers. Arriving there with a party of friends from Jerusalem, al-Maqdisī found himself jammed in between two circles of study, his own conversation drowned out by voices from neighboring groups. All the mosques in al-Fusṭāṭ, he assures us, were equally crowded; in fact he counted altogether 110 such study groups.[62] At much the same time, Ibn Ḥawqal was lamenting that hawkers of bread and water carried on flourishing businesses in the mosque precincts and that their customers sometimes brought their purchases right into the prayer hall.[63] Moreover, the mosque always offered lodging to the traveller and the homeless, although some legal experts opined that this was mandatory only if no other shelter was available.[64]

Naturally, all this traffic took its toll not only on the structure of the mosque but also on its management. Although daily cleaning and maintenance of at least the larger mosques were usually the responsibility of officially appointed caretakers, not all were equally conscientious in the performance of their duties, and certainly not all the worshippers were excessively fastidious. Al-Maqdisī, observant as always of mosque behavior, notes that in al-Fusṭāṭ worshippers were apt to fidget during the prayer, hawk phlegm, blow their noses, and slip the mucus under the mats.[65] Even amid the surroundings of the al-Aqṣā Mosque in Jerusalem, worshippers (and no doubt casual visitors as well) strewed remains of meals about the floor. Nor were all mosques adequately maintained. It is by no means unusual to find one described much in the manner of the mosque at ʿAdan: dilapidated, disorderly, and filthy.[66]

Expectoration had been forbidden from early in the Islamic period, although some traditionists qualified the prohibition with "not in the direction of the *qiblah,* only to the left."[67] Shoes were also being removed on entry to some mosques certainly by the eighth century and perhaps as early as the time of the caliph ʿUmar, although even by the former date the custom was not universal. In the Umayyad Mosque in Damascus at that time, shoes were being removed only in the *maqṣūrah,* implicitly because the floor of the prayer hall was covered with mats, but in 827 bare feet formally became a condition of entry.[68] From this time onward a corpus of regulations designed to enhance the dignity of the mosque was developed; some regulations were enforced, while others were merely viewed as desirable. One's best clothes should be worn to the Friday service, for instance; public announcements about strayed animals were not to be made, as happened, it was noted, only too frequently in *badū* assemblies; and one should not call loudly across the congregation. From time to time efforts were made to curtail various forms of retailing in mosques. Even in Makkah hawkers called their wares in the mosques, and much more widely than that women sold thread and similar personal and domestic items. At least one tradition was concerned with the prohibition of wine within the mosque. Dr. Pedersen observes correctly that Ibn al-Ḥājj's schedule of activities unacceptable within the hallowed precincts leaves one "with the impression of a regular market-place,"[69] which in turn reminds us that in the cathedral mosque in Shīrāz the cries of the beggars sometimes drowned out the sermon.[70] Through the crowd moved the animals that visitors had brought inside the building instead of tethering them outside, and above the hubbub sounded the cries of water sellers and beggars. The congregational mosque in al-Ahwaz fared no better, for its precincts were the haunt of rogues, vagabonds, reprobates, and loafers.[71] Eventually, most of these adventitious activities attracted to the "place of prayer" by reason of its function as the political, religious, and social center of the community were eliminated. Even so, the dignified decorum and calm sobriety proper to the solemn invocation of God generally pertained to later centuries than those with which we are here concerned.

It was inevitable that, as the sanctity of the mosque increased, its exclusivity became an issue. Ibn al-Ḥājj would have preferred to deny access to women (citing ʿĀʾishah as his authority), but from early times they were tolerated within the mosque, usually in specially reserved sections and, according to some traditionists, unperfumed. Under the early Umayyads, Christians were still permitted to enter a mosque. Later the Ahl al-Kitāb retained that right but not polytheists; and finally the privilege became restricted to Muslims, with Ibn al-Ḥājj going so far as to recommend that Christian monks who wove mats for a mosque be prohibited from laying them.[72] By the ninth century exclusivity in access promoted pride in the physical structure of the mosque, including both architecture and interior decoration. Under this latter category were included lamps. In Islamic worship light had a special significance, borrowed in large part from the Church, over and above its practical consideration. Ibn al-Faqīh believed that al-Muʿāwiyah was the first to use oil lamps to illuminate the Kaʿbah and, writing at about the turn of the tenth century, reported that some sixteen hundred lamps were being lit every evening in Jerusalem.[73] About a century later al-Maqdisī observed that in the mosques of al-Shām (Greater Syria) oil lamps (*qanādīl;* sing. *qindīl*) were kept lit continuously and suspended on chains as at Makkah.[74] By ʿAbbāsid times such lamps had become a regular part of mosque furniture. In fact it is recorded that the caliph al-Maʾmūn (r. 813–33) decreed the placing of lamps in all mosques with the dual purpose of preventing crime and facilitating study of the Qurʾān. As for the other fittings that came to be incorporated in a well-appointed mosque, it suffices to cite part of the inventory of the al-Azhar Mosque as set out in its deed of endowment in the year 1009: Abbadān and plaited mats; Indian aloe, camphor, and musk for perfuming during Ramaḍān and other festive occasions; candles and lamps; charcoal for incense burners; 4 ropes, 6 leather water bags, and 200 brooms; oil for lamps; 2 very large silver lanterns; and 27 silver candlesticks.[75]

Location of Mosques

In the new cities that they founded, the Muslims almost invariably accorded the *masjid al-jāmiʿ* a broadly central location; in the cities that capitulated to them or that they conquered, they were often attracted to sites already sacred to Christian, Zoroastrian, or pagan beliefs. In either case, the mosque, and particularly the so-called cathedral mosque, was likely to be more or less centrally situated and to become the focus of a street pattern on any appropriate scale between citywide and quarterwide. Not infrequently a topographer would find reason to insist on the urban centrality of a *jāmiʿ*, as did al-Maqdisī when writing of Marj Juhaynah, al-Ḥasanīyah, Balad, Naṣībīn, and Āmid (Diyarbakir), all within the *Jazīrah.*[76] Within that generalized location a favorite site virtually throughout the Muslim world was actually within or on the edge of the *bāzār (sūq).* In the eastern *iqlīm* of al-Mashriq, for instance, at least thirty congregational mosques were described explicitly as being situated in *sūq*s.[77] Nor were such locations uncommon in other parts of the Islamic world, as witness the *sūq*-invested Friday mosques in the Fārsī port city of Sīrāf and at Astarābād, Ābaskūn, and Bisṭām, this last rising like a fortress in the midst of the chaffering market habitués. It is noticeable, though, that al-Maqdisī considered it worth reporting that in both Zabīd and ʿAdan the *jāmiʿ* was situated at a distance *(nāʾin)* from the *sūq*s.[78]

In any case, where an inner (and usually older) city was adjacent to or surrounded by a "suburb," the Friday mosque was likely to be in the former, close to the *dār al-imārah* and the treasury.[79] Representative examples from, say, North Africa could include Baghayah, Biskarah, Marsah al-Dajjāj, and Ṭubnah.[80] At Sijilmāsah the cathedral mosque was actually within the fortified keep,[81] as it was also in Qubā, while at Shāsh in Transoxania it was built into the wall of the *quhandiz.*[82] Another site that occasionally claimed a *masjid al-jāmiʿ* was the vicinity of a main urban gate, as at Bukhārā, where the Friday mosque abutted the Gate of the Citadel on the Rīgistān;[83] Firabr, where it stood at the Bukhārā Gate of the City;[84] Nasaf/Nakhshab, where it bordered the Ghūbadhīn Gate;[85] and Mīlah in the Zāb, where it adjoined the eastern gate of the city, the Bāb al-Ruʾūs. In Mukhā, Galāfiqah, al-Sharjah, al-Ḥirdah, and ʿAṭanah, all in southwest Arabia, the mosques were on the seashore.[86] Not infrequently, especially when extramural growth had outpaced that of an older city, the chief mosque had come to be situated in a suburb. In the case of Naysābūr it had been built by ʿAmr the Ṣaffārid facing the reviewing square (al-Muʿaskar) in the suburb;[87] in Zaranj it was also in the outer town, specifically on the Fārs road.[88] At other times cathedral mosques were found in various residential-cum-occupational quarters: at Karūkh in the Sabīdan quarter;[89] at Sinjar in the Shoemakers' Quarter;[90] at al-Rāfiqah in the Goldsmiths' Quarter (141), and at al-Raqqah in the Drapers' Quarter (141). Other locations where I have encountered congregational mosques include on the edge of the town (Ḥarrān in Aqūr and Dulāb in al-Daylam) (141, 360), inside *ribāṭāt* and similar fortified structures (Kūfan, where the fortress in question had been built by ʿAbd Allāh the Ṭāhirid in the ninth century [321],[91] and Tūnkath, where the Friday mosque also stood within a fortress);[92] and tucked away in an alley *(zuqāq)* at Asadāwadh.[93]

Despite the teachings of doctors of the law, especially those of the Ḥanāfī and Shāfiʿī persuasions, the number of Friday mosques increased steadily in response to demographic and confessional needs, so that by the tenth century it was not uncommon to find a plurality of such buildings in large cities. Marv al-Shāhijān, for instance, supported three Friday mosques, namely the Mosque of the Banū-Māhān in the citadel, the Masjid al-ʿAtīq ("Old Mosque") at the Bāb al-Madīnah (Inner City Gate) on the road to Sarakhs, and the New Mosque that had been built by Abū Muslim in the great western suburb of Mājān. Hurmuzfarrah, only a small settlement just beyond the suburban fringe of Marv, nevertheless was provided with a Friday mosque, as also were each of the even smaller neighboring settlements of Bāshān, Kharak, and al-Sūsanqān.[94] In the Būsht district of Qūhistān, a region of considerable agricultural prosperity, no less than seven settlements each had its own Friday mosque in the tenth century, in addition to the splendid mosque, allegedly rivalling that of Damascus, in the important town of Turshīz.[95] At Ṭāhart (Tiaret) in present-day Algeria, where a recently founded town on lower ground was rapidly draining the commercial vitality of Old Ṭāhart on a hill above, each sector of the city had acquired its own Friday mosque and its own *imām*.[96] Not more than a couple of leagues up the Sughd River above the populous town of Karmīniyah were the three small settlements of Khudīmankān, Madhyāmajkath, and Kharghānkath, each the proud possessor of a Friday mosque.[97] Banṭiyūs in the Zāb of North Africa offers an especially interesting division of religious responsibility. The name itself was applied to three neighboring settlements inhabited respectively by tribes of Persian origin, by persons of mixed blood, and by Berbers. Each settlement had its own Friday mosque, but only two served orthodox Sunnī Muslims, the third being reserved for Berber Ibāḍī schismatics.[98] Of course, there eventually came to be numerous neighborhood mosques dispersed through the cities of the Muslim world, sometimes in numbers that are believable only if they are held to have subsumed chapellike, private places of worship. Ibn Ḥawqal's figure of more than three hundred in Sicilian Balarm (Palermo), for example, lends itself to this interpretation.[99] In Egypt as a whole in the year 1012, a total of 830 mosques were supported entirely by pious foundations initiated by the government.[100]

Then there was a small minority of towns that for one reason or another lacked mosques of any description, a fact that was usually commented upon by one or another of the topographers. Akhsīsak, at an important crossing of the Jayḥūn (Āmū Daryā) River, was one such town, whose inhabitants had to cross the river to pray in the Friday mosque at Zamm on the Khurāsān bank.[101] Another was Barvān, *qaṣabah* of the still-undeveloped territory of Daylam.[102] At Biyār in Qūmis, the original home of al-Maqdisī's maternal grandfather, there was no congregational mosque, only a simple *masjid* within an inner fortress. Similarly, Khawst lacked a Friday mosque, even though it enjoyed considerable importance as the eastern terminus of a desert route to Kirmān.[103] Some little distance north of Samarqand the benefices of the Marzubān Ibn Turgash, one of several Sughd *dihqān*s who had been summoned to the caliph's court, were still without a Friday mosque toward the end of the tenth century.[104] In at least two instances known to me, sectarianism had prevented rather than encouraged the provision of a mosque: at Juwayn, on the Farah River in Sijistān, a Khārijite population had no need of a *minbar* (as al-Maqdisī puts it) for a Sunnī *imām* who, by their lights, had deviated from the true path, while at al-Aḥsā' Qarmaṭī rejection of the outward manifestations of orthodox Islam had allowed the Friday mosque to fall into disrepair. However, in this latter city a Persian pilgrim eventually provided a new mosque for use by orthodox travellers.[105] Turning to the Maghrib, in Sharūṣ, chief town of the Jabal Nafūsah, sectarian dissent in the mid-eleventh century was also hindering the construction of a Friday mosque, not only in the inner city but also in any of its numerous suburbs: although it was populous, its inhabitants were principally Ibāḍī. In Waddān in Jufrah oasis the city's only *jāmi*ʿ was situated midway between two quarters inhabited by opposed Arab tribal factions. In the Kutāmā settlement, the name of which al-Bakrī transcribed as Tanaguelalt, it appears simply that a tribally organized society had not yet assumed religious responsibilities commensurate with its economic prosperity, perhaps because of its propinquity to Mīlah.[106] We have already remarked on the absence of a mosque in an unexpectedly high proportion of Egyptian cities and on the apparent absence of mosques in the economically prosperous Maghribī towns of Izmāmah, Tamaghīlt, and Tamedalt.[107] However, despite lacunae such as these in the record, it can be safely asserted that by the tenth century the mosque had become the defining feature of the Islamic city in a band of territories stretching from the Atlantic Ocean to the Indus River and from the Caspian Sea to the Sūdān. And increasingly these mosques were being furnished with towers as monumental symbols of the Islamic presence, with some perhaps already being used for the call to prayer.

Instruments of Economic Exchange in the Urban Landscape

The early Islamic city—like the vast majority of cities throughout the world at any time—was potentially the site of four primary modes of exchange, each corresponding to one of the functional subsystems of society. Most fundamental of these modes of economic integration was generalized *reciprocity,* in the sense of a network of instrumental exchanges grounded in family and neighborhood morality and with the quid pro quo unspecified as to time, quality, and quantity. It needs no emphasis that this was in no way an exclusively urban activity but was of universal occurrence throughout the world. If it appeared to be more prominent within city walls, it was only because of the presence there of a greater number of persons per unit area.

Redistribution and *mobilization,* by contrast, although not operationally confined to urban milieus, were characteristically administered from such centers. The former involves the allocation of rewards and facilities in conformity with the integrative requirements of society; the latter provides mechanisms for the acquisition, control, and disposal of resources in the pursuit of collective goals. In other words, whereas redistribution operates to maintain and consolidate social stratification, mobilization channels goods and services into the hands of those pursuing primarily political aims. The preferred means for implementing both redistributive and mobilizative policies in the Islamic world were the land tax *(kharāj),* the poll tax *(jizyah),* and the tithe *(ʿushr),* supplemented by a whole repertoire of ad hoc levies, taxes, and such mobilizative instruments as corvée, eminent domain, forced contracts, and selective service.[108] In the early Islamic era the principal centers of allocation were often the main centers of decision making as well, so that there was a strong tendency toward locational isomorphism between administrative and economic hierarchies, a conjunction not infrequently inducing an otherwise unanticipated degree of stability in the urban system. However, redistribution and mobilization—which in any case are not always easily distinguishable in their institutional aspects and hardly ever in their architectural expressions—were both administrative functions of the *dār al-imārah* or other government bureaus and are best discussed under that heading.

The fourth mode of exchange, and the only one to be treated in this section, is *bāzār exchange,* the sphere of operation of specialized economic instruments that have evolved to enable the adaptive subsystem of society to achieve a variety of goals in a virtually unlimited range of contexts. Unlike redistribution and mobilization, which are concerned not with direct economic action but with economically relevant action, bazaar exchange is governed to a much greater extent by the institutionalized values of economic rationality, and its morphological expression is the *sūq.*[109] Whereas redistribution and mobilization are state-supporting modes of economic exchange, market exchange is, generally speaking, city-supporting. It is the market in this narrow sense that provides victuals for the mass of the city's population and raw materials for its domestic craftsmen. The only point at which administered exchange interacts with market transactions—and then only minimally—is when a few of the commodities brought together in the city by administrative fiat find their way serendipitously into the public markets. Of course, wealth accumulated by a state through coercive administration may be used for the beautification or defense of a city, especially when it is a national capital.

The *Sūq* and Marketing

Descriptions of markets or *bāzārs (sūq;* pl. *aswāq),* whether their precise locations, the products they handled, or their habitués *(al-sūqah),* are rare in the early centuries of Islam; the temptation is to project values and customs backward from intensively studied markets of the present day to the Middle Ages. Without doubt, certain practices are common to both eras; the question is, which? And the answer more often than not is *non liquet.* What can be assumed with some degree of confidence is that the *sūq* was simultaneously a specialized type of economic organization, a subculture within the larger entity of urbanized society, and a morphological feature of the urban landscape. With regard to the first of these characteristics, it is evident from topographical and *adab* literature alike that the *sūq* was made up predominantly of producer-retailers dealing in small-bulk, readily transportable, and easily stored commodities, with each unit being an independent enterprise producing essentially the same type of good or service as others in its particular category, and each subsuming indifferently within its range of activities production, distribution, and sales.

Furthermore, a substantial fraction of urban handicraft and service industries, whether in terms of value or volume of production or of numbers employed, was structurally integrated into the *sūq.* Mostly these activities were involved in food preparation, textile weaving and garment making, craft manufacture of small hardware items, and sometimes jewelry making. In the absence of reliable standardized weights and measures, where poor communications subverted attainment of an overall view of the market, and with no more than minimal control over quality (even when the *muḥtasib* choose to exercise his authority), value assessments had to be the responsibility of the individual buyer—hence the universal use of the sliding-price technique, in which participants in a transaction explored the zone of price uncertainty through a sequence of offers and counteroffers.

Establishments in the *sūq* were generally small in size and operated in a state of near-perfect competition (today the profit-and-loss margins among the numerous traders in a large *sūq* are so exiguous that no one of them can significantly influence the market by any policy of his own). The commodities in which they dealt (principally foodstuffs, hardware, and textiles) were those that have traditionally permitted marginal alterations in the scale of trading operations rather than requiring discontinuous investment, and that have consequently rendered it nearly impossible for the *sūq* trader to progress from hawking and stall holding to merchandising. It was presumably not fortuitous that moderate- to large-scale traders were found mainly in the textile business, as that was the most obvious enterprise having an investment curve continuous along its entire length. In this connection it is not without interest that the Prophet himself—in a tradition picked up by Shaybānī early in the ninth century—allegedly urged the Arabs to become cloth merchants.[110] The prevailingly small size of *sūq* enterprises functioning in what appears to have been a state of near-perfect competition, together with (for the *sūq* trader) inadequate means of mobilizing capital and prohibitively high interest rates, must certainly have exerted some influence on the supply-and-demand mechanism. Most probably it brought about the outcome typical of bazaar economies in many parts of the world in more recent times, that is, supply and demand are equilibrated by changes in the number of producer-retailers in business rather than by large fluctuations in price.[111]

That the *sūq* was a way of life as well as an assemblage of instruments for the prosecution of market exchange is self-evident. The ability to operate effectively under these conditions calls for certain skills and personality traits that are developed early in life. But however valuable these skills may be within the *sūq*, they do not invariably command respect among the populace at large, with the result that Arabic (and indeed Persian and Turkish) literature is replete with tales of unscrupulous traders, the memory of which lingers yet in the saying *al-tujjār fujjār* (merchants are scoundrels). It is to be inferred, though, that this unfortunate reputation did not arise—as Max Weber and others seem to have thought—from an uninhibited acquisitive impulse so much as from role asymmetry between *sūq* habitué and outsider.

It should be noted that the obloquy attaching to *sūq* trading did not extend (in its generalized form, at any rate) to enterprises undertaken by members of the governing and religious elites, for whom entrepreneurship was but one of many avenues to status and affluence. As early as the second half of the second century A.H., books were being written seeking to prove that, contrary to the teachings of mendicant ascetics, honorable commerce was not only approved by Islamic morality but was in fact a religious duty, and as such more pleasing to God than was government service. The earliest work in this vein appears to have been *Kitāb al-Kasb* by Muḥammad Shaybānī (d. 804). The book itself has long been lost, but substantial portions have survived in an abridgment prepared by the author's pupil Ibn Samāʿah (d. 847) under the title *al-Iktisāb fī al-Rizq al-Mustaṭāb* (al-Qāhirah, A.H. 1357). In support of his argument, Shaybānī adduced a number of *ḥadīth*s (which are certainly apocryphal), including one attributed to the caliph ʿUmar: "I prefer to die on my camel saddle in pursuit of trade rather than be killed in the Holy War. Has not God mentioned those seeking the bounty of Allāh before those who fight on the warpath of God?"[112] On no better authority a hero of Qādisīyah was credited with saying that he would rather earn one *dirham* by commerce than ten as military pay.[113] Shaybānī further cited relevant passages from the Qur'ān, such as *Sūrah* 2 *(al-Baqarah)*, verses 198, 275, and 282 and *Sūrah* 62 *(al-Jumuʿah)*, verse 10, as well as pointing out that Abū Bakr, the first caliph, had been a cloth merchant and ʿUthmān a successful grain importer.

There is no doubt that in the early years of Islam the first choice of most members of the new Muslim aristocracy was either appointment to a government post *(ʿamal)* or receipt of a pension *(ʿaṭā')* from the state. Some, however, continued to pursue their ancient callings while a number of others put their newly acquired wealth to work for them in commercial enterprises. In fact it eventually became the norm for a high government official to engage in commerce, and not infrequently became a subject of comment when he did not. And because his government service was likely to involve him in some way with at least one form of economically relevant action, and because his assigned territory almost inevitably included a significant node in the redistributive-mobilizative hierarchy, he was well positioned to benefit from insider's knowledge, and perhaps foreknowledge.

By the beginning of the third Islamic century the merchant class had insinuated itself into the highest social strata of the Muslim world. This almost symbiotic relationship between wealth and prestige requires further research, but Professor Goitein has collected an apparently representative sampling of names, among them Ibn ʿAmmār al-Ṭaḥḥān, a wealthy merchant from lower ʿIrāq who became al-Mu ʿtaṣim's first *wazīr;* Zayyāt, the same caliph's most famous *wazīr,* who was responsible for implementing the design of Sāmarrā;[114] Ibn Jaṣṣās, a wealthy jeweler and financier who served the Ṭūlūnid ruler of Egypt, Khumārawayh, as confidential envoy to Baghdād;[115] Ibn Killis, a Jewish merchant from ʿIrāq who reorganized the fiscal basis of the Fāṭimid Empire and ultimately converted to Islam; Abū Saʿd Tustarī, another Jewish merchant who rose to high office in the Fāṭimid state; and Abū al-Ḥasan al-Khiraqī, the cloth merchant whom al-Muttaqī raised to be chief *qāḍī* of Baghdād, not to mention the ʿIrāqī Persian family of Mādharāʾī who served as high-level administrators and revenue officers in Egypt and Syria between 879 and 946, and who have been called the leading capitalists of the third Islamic century.[116] The point I am making is that these government officials were merchants rather than *sūq* stall holders (though a family name such as Ṭaḥḥāh or Khayyāṭ occasionally hints at plebeian origins in a past generation). Their evident success in both administered trade and as entrepreneurs on their own account only affirms Karl Polanyi's glittering paradox, "Whereas he who trades for the sake of duty and honor grows rich, he who trades for filthy lucre remains poor."[117] As Adam Mez sums things up, "The wealthy tradesman had become the carrier of Muḥammadan civilization"; and he provided a good deal of material illustrative of this dictum.[118]

The greater part of the early Islamic world was encompassed within the zone of low- and middle-latitude aridity that ran discontinuously eastward as tracts of desert and steppe from the Atlantic Ocean to the Indus River. In these environments, and given the technologies of the time, it was inevitable that, apart from especially favored locales such as the supposedly idyllic earthly paradises, fertility and productivity were likely to be low. In such circumstances even today, the maximum range of a commodity (that is, under isotropic conditions the radius generating a circle within which all consumers are willing to purchase at least some of the commodity) often proves to be less than the minimum range of a firm (the radius generating the base of the demand cone just large enough to ensure the viability of the enterprise).[119] As a result, prevailingly high transportation and opportunity costs unite with elastic demand to reduce the dimensions of demand cones to the point where they are less extensive than retailers' minimum ranges, as likely as not already inflated by predominantly low income levels.

At this point the retailer faces the choice of going out of business or of repositioning himself in space by means of a series of moves that ultimately enable him to capture an aggregate market area at least equivalent to the minimum range necessary for his viability. Evidently, the optimal length of each move undertaken by an itinerant trader is roughly equal to the maximum range of the commodity he is selling. In this way he neither wastes time attempting to attract already satiated customers nor ignores potential buyers. However, the number of moves he has to undertake to attain his survival threshold for any given maximum range is a function of the minimum range of the item he is selling. Clearly, adoption of a peripatetic mode of retailing does not guarantee viability. Each move that the trader makes generates not only additional revenue but also additional costs, so that he can continue to move only until his marginal cost equals his marginal revenue. If the number of moves required for viability exceeds the number he can afford, his business will still fail. It must be remembered, though, that it will probably not be impossible for him to re-enter the *sūq* community when times improve.[120]

Periodic Markets and Fairs

That this process, or at any rate a closely similar one, was operating among small-scale traders in the early centuries of Islam is attested by not infrequent mentions of periodic markets that were held chiefly in rural areas. Presumably it was the realization that two or more peripatetic retailers plying their several wares at the same place at the same time were likely to fare better than a single trader operating in isolation that gave rise in the aggregate to periodic markets, that communicated individual behavioral patterns to community exchange institutions.

Even though the periodic market has traditionally been more common in villages than in cities, the early topographers did not fail to mention urban examples from time to time. The following are more or less representative instances called at random from the available literature. In Sughd, Vardānah and Afshīnah held markets on one unspecified day each week.[121] The Sunday *sūq* held outside the Kurdish Gate of Bardhaʿah in Arrān has been mentioned earlier. In Khūzistān, Sūq al-Thalāthāʾ owed its very name to the Tuesday market that was its *raison d'être;*[122] in al-Mawṣil (Mosul) a Wednesday market in a space or building known as the Murabbaʿah served not only for the exchange of commodities but also as an employment mart for hired hands and harvesters;[123] Iskijkat, on the outskirts of Bukhārā, had a Thursday market[124] and Ghāfiq in what is now Tunisia a Friday one;[125] around Khān Ṭawq in Khūzistān were six villages, each named after the day of the week on which its market was held;[126] and all along the Wādī Darʿah in southern Morocco Berber-speaking villages had established separate markets for each day of the week, and apparently the same rotation was common in al-Daylam.[127]

Economic forces precisely similar to those I have been describing underpin the periodicity of the exchange marts known in English as fairs: vendor and buyer alike escape the discipline of space by submitting to the discipline of time. Technically, a fair may be defined as a relatively large, regularly occurring, organized gathering of merchants coming from substantial distances.[128] Archetypically it contrasts with the market, an institution mediating local exchange, in being concerned primarily with commercial transactions over greater distances, by exhibiting a longer periodicity, by lasting for a greater length of time, and by involving larger numbers of participants. The two institutions are also generally distinguished in that at markets vendors tend to sell to consumers, whereas at fairs merchants are more likely to trade among themselves. It should be noted, though, that our sources do not discriminate consistently between periodic market/*bāzār* and fair, so that the exchange venues mentioned in medieval texts have to be assigned to one or the other category based on what can be learned about their operation. For what it is worth, fairs sensu stricto have been virtually ignored as an institution of exchange by Muslim jurists.

In Arabia of the *Jāhilīyah,* exchange gatherings appropriately designated as fairs (and almost invariably so characterized by modern authors) were to be found throughout the length and breadth of the Arabian Peninsula, from al-Ḥīrah on the border of Mesopotamia[129] to Mināʾ, Dhū al-Majāz, Majannah, and ʿUkāẓ in the Ḥijāz, of which the last became for subsequent generations the most celebrated. In most if not all instances, these fairs were associated with pilgrimage to a tribal shrine, and trading was conducted in intervals between cult observances (sacrifice, lapidation, visitation, procession, circumambulation), adjudicatory transactions (commendation, ratification, arbitration, condemnation), political accommodation (covenanting, negotiation, treaty agreement, alliance confirmation), and social and cultural diversions (athletic contest, literary tournament, lineage reunion, marriage contract). Commercial transactions entered into on such occasions doubtless owed their binding force largely to the sanctity of the site and the rites validating them. Makkah itself was the venue for just such a concourse during the annual pilgrimage to the Kaʿbah, and the incorporation of this and other local shrines into Islamic ritual to the exclusion of competing sanctuaries was partially responsible for the decline of Arabian fairs after the mid-seventh century. In any case, their cultic functions could have played only an insignificant role in an Islamic context in which cosmic and soteriological holiness combined to focus attention on the supreme sanctity of Makkah (Mecca). At the same time, the economic functions of these fairs were being subverted by a progressively stricter exclusion of infidels from the Ḥijāz and, most effectively, by the involvement of *badū* tribesmen in wars of conquest that diverted trade flows to new routes; directed into the peninsula a great influx of commodities in the form of booty; and accustomed tribesmen to accommodation and cooperation on a scale vastly greater than was attainable during the temporary truce of the fair. Meanwhile, the institutionalization of the *Ḥajj* was creating at

Makkah what was virtually an annual Islamic fair that would endure into the earlier decades of the twentieth century.[130]

Elsewhere in the Islamic realm it is often difficult to discover what happened to a particular fair after the conquest. In 635, for instance, an Arab army plundered a village close to the future site of Baghdād where the merchants of Ctesiphon (al-Madā'in) had been in the habit of sponsoring an annual fair; it is tempting to suppose that this gathering was the forerunner of the monthly fair known to have been held on the same site until the founding of the ʿAbbāsid capital. In about 670 the pilgrim Arculf mentioned an unusually large annual fair at Jerusalem that lasted for several days, beginning on the fifteenth of September. Brunschwig has plausibly suggested that this was probably a continuation into Islamic times of the Christian feast of the Exaltation of the Cross, the timing of which had been fixed by Emperor Constantine at 14 September.

In the Sughd territories a fair of very ancient origin that continued to flourish in Islamic times was held in Bukhārā. Writing in the tenth century, al-Narshakhī left an account of this fair that was subsequently abridged by a Persian editor as follows:

> In Bukhārā there was a bazaar called the bazaar of [the day of] Mākh. Twice a year for one day there was a fair, and every time there was this fair idols were sold in it. Every day more than 50,000 *dirhams* were exchanged (for the idols). Muhammad ibn Jaʿfar [that is al-Narshakhī himself] has mentioned in his book that this fair existed in his time, and he was very astonished that it should be allowed. He asked the elders and shaikhs of Bukhārā the reason for this. They said that the inhabitants of Bukhārā in olden times had been idol-worshippers. They were permitted to have this fair, and from that time they have sold idols in it. It has remained thus till today. Abu'l-Ḥasan Nīshāpūrī in his book "The Treasury of the Sciences," says that in Bukhārā in ancient times was a king who was called Mākh. He ordered this market to be built. He ordered carpenters and painters to prepare idols each year. On a certain day they appeared in the bazaar and sold the idols, and people bought them. When their idol was lost, broken, or old, the people bought another when the day of the fair came. Then the old one was thrown away. That place, which today is the grand mosque of Mākh, was a grove on the river bank. There were many trees, and the fair was held in the shade of those trees. That king came to this fair and sat on a throne in the place which is today the mosque of Mākh to encourage the people to buy idols. Everyone bought an idol for himself and brought it home. Afterwards this place became a fire-temple. On the day of the fair, when the people had gathered, all went into the fire-temple and worshipped fire. The fire-temple existed to the time of Islam when the Muslims seized power and built a mosque on that place. Today it is one of the esteemed mosques of Bukhārā.[131]

There can be little doubt that the painted wooden (and probably also terra cotta) statuettes referred to in this passage were Buddhist figurines, so that this particular fair appears not only to have survived the vicissitudes of three religious regimens but also to have preserved vestigially at least one Buddhist ritual act into Zoroastrian and Muslim times.[132]

The annual fair at Ṭawāīs, specializing in seconds and lasting for ten days, has already been described, as has another at Marsamandah in Ushrūsanah, which, though of only a single day's duration, yet managed to transact one hundred thousand *dinārs*' worth of business. In the tenth century a fair was held for ten days during the winter at Shargh, halfway between Bukhārā and Ṭawāīs; but by the second half of the twelfth century, when al-Narshakhī's work was abridged, this annual fair appears to have devolved into two weekly markets: one in Shargh on Fridays, the other across the Sāmjan River in Iskijkat on Thursdays.[133] Again in the tenth century, the small town of Dih Nūjīkat in the district of Shāsh supported a fair specializing in cheap meats that each year extended over the three months of spring,[134] while the settlement at Varaksha held a fair for fifteen days every year except when it fell at the end of a year, in which case it continued for a further five days, thereby apparently ushering in the Persian New Year.[135] At about the same time, Ibn Ḥawqal mentioned two other fairs, one at the little town of Sūq al-Aḥad in ʿIrāq serving primarily Kurdish tribesmen of the Great Zāb River valley,[136] and the other in the Adharbayjānian (Azerbaijanian) city of Ushnuh, where Kurdish herdsmen who pastured their flocks in the neighborhood during the summer provided both ready buyers and willing sellers at the appropriate seasons of the year.[137]

On the far western edge of the Islamic world, a fair connected with the induction of recruits into the service of a *ribāṭ* at Azīlah was held three times a year in the tenth century. However, by the time that al-Bakrī came to compile his topographical description of North Africa, in response to changing consumer demand within the developing city the one-time fair had been transformed into a weekly market held on Fridays.[138] Fairs were similarly associated with *ribāṭāt* at Māssah (161) and Munastīr (36). To these should probably be added an annual fair sponsored by the *ribāṭāt* of Sharshāl, although al-Bakrī does not attribute predominantly commercial interests to "the crowds that gathered there each year" (82). It is worth noting that each of these events was designated a *mawsim*, a word that in present-day Morocco still connotes all or each of a religious festival, a pilgrimage, and a fair.

*Sūq*s in al-Baṣrah

Detailed morphological descriptions of *sūq*s in the early centuries of Islam are rare, but in the case of al-Baṣrah the deficiency has been partially remedied by a meticulous analysis of relevant texts undertaken by A. J. Naji and Y. N. Ali.[139] The earliest *sūq* was incorporated in the Mirbaḍ, which seems to have developed spontaneously on the desert fringe west of the cantonment—itself a telling comment on the cultural orientation of the original settlement. However, during the ensuing twenty years, al-Baṣrah refocused its interests on the Shaṭṭ al-ʿArab, a dozen or so miles to the east, to which it was already connected by three canals: the Nahr Maʿqil, the Nahr al-Fayd, and the Nahr al-Ubullah. The first of these served vessels heading for Baghdād; the last, those doing business in the Gulf. The commercial possibilities of the great waterway combined with agricultural development of the terrain between al-Baṣrah and the Shaṭṭ to persuade the governor ʿAbd Allāh ibn ʿĀmir (646–57) of the need for establishing a new *sūq* in the eastern sector of the settlement. The site he selected, which ran beside a branch of the Fayd canal known as Umm ʿAbd Allāh, continued to dominate market exchange in the eastern part of the city until almost the end of the Umayyad period, when, jammed in as it was among residential districts, it proved incapable of accommodating the huge population increases engulfing the city. Consequently it was relocated to a site alongside the Nahr Bilāl, a canal newly constructed to link Nahr Maʿqil and Nahr Fayd.

By the middle of the second Islamic century, al-Baṣrah appears to have supported four main retailing centers. The most important, whether measured by area occupied or volume of transactions, and probably by number of traders, was the Mirbaḍ. While retaining its original function as a caravanserai and *sūq*, this tract of dusty earth also had become a meeting place for literati and others who were unwittingly but nevertheless irrevocably laying the groundwork for the Arab humanistic sciences. Poets, traditionists, lexicographers, and grammarians were especially prominent, as this was the locale where they could most readily hear undefiled *badū* speech and collect tribal traditions. Nor was it only storytellers and common versifiers who congregated in the Mirbaḍ: as Charles Pellat's researches have confirmed, "Les plus grands noms de la poésie arabe venaient se mesurer avec leurs adversaires et leurs rivaux."[140] The Mirbaḍ was actually a collection of *sūq*s rather than a unitary market (fig. 17). Among the individual exchange centers were Sūq al-Ibil, which, in spite of its name (= "The Camel Market"), was best known for its vendors of sheep, birds, fat, and camel hobbles; Sūq al-Ṭabbanīn (straw sellers); Sūq al-Wazzānīn (makers of scales); Sūq al-ʿAṭṭārīn (perfumers and druggists) adjoining Sūq al-Ṣaydallānīn (apothecaries); Sūq al-Dabbāghīn (leatherworkers); Sūq al-Dhibāb (purveyors of gazelle skins); and Sūq al-Warrāqīn (paper sellers, although this *sūq* also encompassed booksellers, bookbinders, book copiers, and ink sellers).[141]

Al-Kallā' was, as its name implies, a mooring berth for vessels on the eastern edge of the city, where a collection of *sūq*s had grown up at the break-of-bulk point, their shops and stalls stretching along the Fayd canal. The largest of the constituent *sūq*s was known alternatively as the Dār al-Rizq or Madīnat al-Rizq ("The Subsistence Market"), which included the Sūq al-Ṭaʿām, famous in Arabic literature for its array of foodstuffs. Other *sūq*s in the complex were Sūq al-ʿAllāfīn (provender suppliers), which had its own mosque built by Ziyād ibn Abīhi; Sūq al-Khallālīn (pickle vendors); Sūq al-Saqaṭ (junk sellers), which specialized in used clothing, household utensils, cheap jewelry, pepper, and chickpeas; Sūq al-Qaṣṣābīn

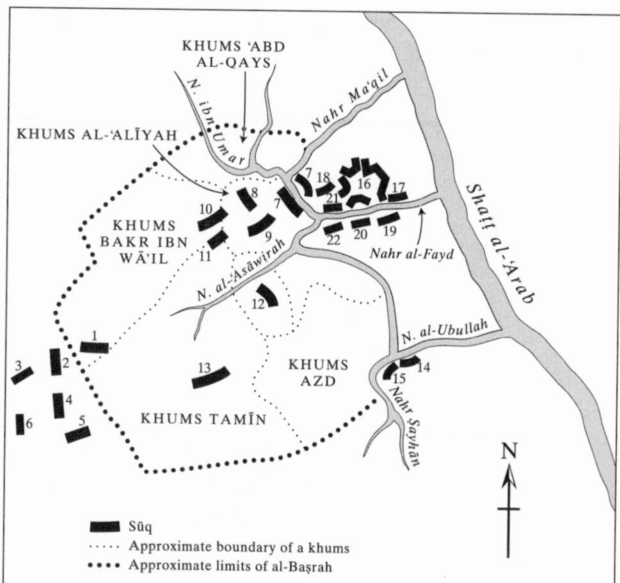

Figure 17. The principal *sūqs* of al-Baṣrah in the tenth century. *Al-Mirbad:* 1. Sūq al-Dabbāghīn; 2. S. al-Ibil; 3. S. al-Ṭabbanīn; 4. S. al-ʿAṭṭārīn; 5. S. al-Wazzanīn; 6. S. al-Dhibāb. *Sūq al-Kabīr:* 7. *Sūqs* of Nahr Bilāl; 8. S. al-Qadīm; 9. S. al-Shaʿārrīn; 10. S. Bāb ʿUthmān; 11. S. Bāb al-Masjid al-Jāmiʿ; 12. *Sūqs* of the Banū-Yashkur; 13. S. al-Ṭaḥḥānīn; 14. Al-Bārjah; 15. S. Nahr Ṣayhūn. *Al-Kallāʾ:* 16. Dār al-Rizq; 17. Sūq Aṣḥāb al-Saqaṭ; 18. S. al-Daqīq; 19. S. al-Ḥabl; 20. S. al-Qaṣṣabīn; 21. S. al- Khallālīn; 22. S. al-ʿAllāfīn. For *khums* as tribal holdings, see pp. 43–44 above.

(butchers), with Sūq al-Ghanam (sheep and goats) situated directly on the square at its center;[142] Sūq al-Qayyārīn (asphalt purveyors);[143] and Sūq al-Qaflāʿyūn (marine wreckers and repairers). From time to time, references to other Kallāʾ *sūqs* are encountered in medieval literature, but no records of their locations have survived. However, Naji and Ali have suggested, plausibly enough, that vendors of mats, dates, reeds, palm fronds, and bulrushes would have been likely to set themselves up at no great distance from Sūq al-ʿAllāfīn,[144] while the dealers in teakwood *(sāj)* would have had reason enough to associate themselves with the Qaflāʿyūn.

The third noteworthy retail center in al-Baṣrah was originally known as Sūq Bāb ʿUthmān, after ʿUthmān ibn al-ʿĀṣ al-Thaqafī, who founded it. Subsequently its location in front of the Friday mosque led to its being designated the Sūq Bāb al-Masjid al-Jāmiʿ, and its shops extended thence westward along the Sikkat al-Mirbaḍ, the axial avenue linking the eastern port district to the caravanserais on the edge of the western desert. This was the *sūq* serving principally, and located mainly within, the city proper. Its units included wine and flour vendors, butchers, money changers, booksellers, makers of slippers, retailers of textiles, and doubtless other undertakings not now recoverable. The Sūq al-Raqīq (slaves), though, was an integral part of the Kallāʾ complex.

The fourth center of retailing was al-Sūq al-Kabīr ("The Big Market"), also known as Nahr Bilāl because of its situation alongside the canal of that name. Its strategic position on the river route between Baghdād and al-Baṣrah paid off handsomely, and many of its individual enterprises are mentioned in topographical and *adab* literature: for instance, Sūq al-Ṣayyārifah (money changers); Sūq al-Qaddāḥīn (vendors of drinking cups); Sūq al-Ballūrīyīn (makers of glass and crystal, who enjoyed a great reputation during the Middle Ages); Sūq al-Ṣaffārīn (coppersmiths); Sūq al-Ḥaddādīn (ironworkers); Sūq al-Najjārīn (carpenters); Sūq al-Ṣāghah (goldsmiths); Sūq al-Qallāʾīn (vendors of fried foods); Sūq al-Rawāsīn (vendors of sheep heads); Sūq al-Rayḥān (dispensers of aromatics); and Aṣḥāb al-Fākihah (fruit sellers). Finally, and very importantly, the al-Kabīr market subsumed a whole range of *sūqs* specializing in textiles of one sort or another. Prominent among them were Sūq al-Bazzāzīn (cloth makers); Sūq al-Naddāfīn (cotton carders); Dār al-Qaṭṭān (cotton vendors); Sūq al-Ḥarīr (silk market, as well as specialists in Tūzī cloth from al-Fārs, Harawī cloth from Khurāsān, Sābūrī cloth from Bishāpūr,[145] and Dastuwānī cloth from Khūzistān);[146] and Sūq al-Ziyādī, where vendors dealt in used garments and clothes cobbled together from remnants.[147]

When al-Maqdisī came to write his description of al-Baṣrah in the second half of the tenth century, he reported only three market complexes: Sūq al-Kallāʾ, al-Sūq al-Kabīr, and Sūq Bāb al-Jāmiʿ.[148] The notable omission in his list, of course, was the Mirbaḍ, which is known from other sources to have declined in importance, especially from the second half of the tenth century.[149] Sporadic references have also been made to isolated markets spread virtually throughout the city, although seldom ascribed a precise location. It is known, for instance, that from early times there was a *sūq* for woollen goods in the *khiṭṭah* of the Banū-Bakr and one for flour in that of the Banū-Māzin; a butcher's *sūq* on the southern edge of the cemetery of the Banū-Yashkur, long a gathering place for that tribe; a pottery *sūq* near the Sayhān Canal in the southeastern sector of the city; and a large fish market called the Bārjāh nearby.[150] However, the implications of the Naji-Ali analysis are clear enough: a progressive shift occurred in the economic orientation of al-Baṣrah, from its desert to the west, eastward toward the port through which it was linked to the imperial capital and the sea route to Asia. Al-Sūq al-Kabīr exploited its riverine connections with an effectiveness that the Mirbaḍ could never match on its desert land routes, and for which its humanistic associations could not compensate. The result was that the Kabīr grew into the largest of al-Baṣrah's market complexes, with a solid base of goods for general consumption combined with specialist and high-quality craft industries and, above all, textiles. Al-Kallā' not only served the shipping needs of a port but, if we read its retail profile aright, probably provided a good deal of ships' chandlery. Sūq Bāb al-Jāmiʿ served principally the interior of the city with both items of general consumption and a suite of specialisms that had arisen in response to the proximity of the Friday mosque.

The structure of these *sūqs* is nowhere explicitly described, but Naji and Ali have collected a number of allusions from which a sketchy background can be compiled. For example, Wakiʿ asserts that a vendor could set out his wares during daylight hours anywhere in the *sūq* that he wished.[151] It is also implied by some texts that wares were often displayed on the ground, particularly in the early days of the settlement, while al-Jāḥiẓ refers to vendors who rented space in front of already established shops.[152] And, as frequently happens in markets worldwide, itinerant traders were apt to inconvenience other inhabitants of the *sūq* and thereby attract the attention of the *muḥtasib*.[153] It is noteworthy that Ziyād ibn Abīhi, governor of the city from 666 to 672, mandated the fitting of stalls with wooden or reed screens to protect against theft. But the most unexpected information comes from a time half a century or so subsequent to the period with which we are concerned. Writing in 1051, Nāṣir-i Khusraw recalled that

> [t]he procedure at the bazaar [in al-Baṣrah] is as follows: you turn over whatever you have to a moneychanger and get in return a draft; then you buy whatever you need, deducting the price from the moneychanger's draft. No matter how long one might stay in the city, one would never need anything more than a moneychanger's draft.[154]

It can only be a matter for speculation whether this surprisingly modern procedure (as employed in, say, numerous types of outdoor entertainment in the contemporary United States) was in operation in al-Baṣrah in the tenth century.

Although Naji and Ali perforce have had to leave unanswered many fundamental questions about the structure and function of the Baṣrian *sūqs*, the account that they have managed to tease out of their fragmented and often equivocal sources is fuller than that available for almost any other city during the early Islamic centuries. Usually we have to settle, even in the case of important cities, for a bare list of the categories of traders represented in the *sūqs*. Here is the schedule furnished by Ibn Ḥawqal for Balarm, the Muslim regional capital *(qaṣabah)* for Iṣqiliyah (Sicily), which incidentally is one of the fullest surviving accounts of a tenth-century retail complex:

> Most of the *sūqs* are situated between the [cathedral] Mosque of Ibn Saqlāb and the New Quarter *(al-Ḥārat al-Jadīdah)*. They include all the [olive] oil vendors,[155] flour merchants, moneychangers, apothecaries, blacksmiths, sword-cutlers, wheat merchants, embroiderers, fishmongers, grain merchants, a corporation of butchers *(al-qaṣṣābīn)*, sellers of potherbs, greengrocers, vendors of aromatic plants, sellers of jars, bakers, rope-makers, a corporation of perfumers, slaughterers *(al-jazzārīn)*, shoemakers *(al-asākifah)*, tanners, carpenters, and potters. The dealers in lumber have located outside the city. In Balarm itself there are a corporation of butchers, sellers of jars, and shoemakers. The butchers own almost two hundred shops (sing. *ḥānūt*) there for the sale of meat, and there is a smaller number in the inner city, where they congregate at the head of the main avenue. Close by are the cotton merchants, the carders, and the sandal makers *(al-haḍḍā'ūn)*.[156]

It is noteworthy that Ibn Ḥawqal further records explicitly that neither *sūqs* nor inns *(fanādiq;* sing. *funduq)* existed in the administrative enclave known as the Khaliṣah, which was reserved for the various *dīwāns*, a small cathedral mosque, the Kalbite ruler's residence and military guard, an arsenal, and two (presumably public) baths.

Sūqs in Other Cities

The siting of *sūqs* within medieval cities of the Islamic world manifested an astonishing variety of locations. From a spatial point of view, the primary dichotomy was between those within an original, or inner, city and those outside the walls (be these actual or metaphorical). Among Western historians such extramural settlements are often designated "suburban," but if that term is adopted, it holds only in its etymological sense of "below the walls," not with its modern U.S. designation of a largely autonomous residential settlement, often at some distance from the city to which it is linked by diurnal commuter flows. Within an inner city or in a small city devoid of extramural settlement, the principal *sūqs* tended to be fairly centrally located and, as often as not, clustered around the Friday mosque. That in such cases the topographers almost invariably wrote of the mosque as being in the middle, or sometimes on the edge, of the *sūq* should not be allowed to obscure the fact that the determinative locational factor was the mosque. Traders gathered in its environs not only to provide goods and services proper to worship and prayer but also to tap more diversified consumer demand at a point where every adult male Muslim in the community was expected to pass at least once a week. At Turshīz on the northwest frontier of Qūhistān, al-Maqdisī shows us the process actually working itself out: "Beside the Friday mosque," he writes, "is a *sūq* newly built, as are all the other shops around it."[157]

Within cities *sūqs* might occur in almost every possible location, although there seems to have been a preference for main streets. It was by no means unknown, for instance, for shops to border such a street from gate to opposing gate, as they did at Ṭabarīyah (Tiberias) and al-Qayrawān (Kairouan) well into the tenth century,[158] but more commonly they were grouped to serve a defined neighborhood. In cities exhibiting cardinal axiality or a roughly orthogonal plan, this sometimes gave rise to a cruciform distribution *(muṣallabah)* of retailing as shops clustered around the central intersection and extended outward along the principal streets, but the pattern could be replicated at any level in the *sūq* hierarchy. Dabīl in the Riḥāb and Arrajān in Fārs were representative examples.[159] In Harāt city there was a market on the inner side of each of four city gates, presumably benefiting from the conjoined demands of inner city and suburbs.[160]

The effects of the growth of urban population virtually throughout the Muslim world, stemming principally from rural-to-urban migration, are evident enough in the prevalence of *sūqs* in numerous so-called suburbs: Adhakhkath, Baghayah, Bāmiyān, Baykand (allegedly with about one thousand stalls),[161] Bust, Jamūkat, Kishsh, Marv al-Shāhijan, Qābis (Gabès), Shāsh (Tashkent), and Utlukh are sufficiently representative. At Thubayrah, a small town in Kirmān, the effectively independent ruler Muḥammad ibn Ilyās erected a market clear outside the town. At Bārab, on the Sayḥūn (Sīr-Daryā) River, a number of small shops *(ḥawānīt)* persisted within the old fortress *(ḥiṣn)*, probably because that was also the site of the congregational mosque.[162] Akhsīkath, Isbijāb, and Tūnkath were instances, among many, of cities having markets in both inner and outer sectors. The same development of extramural communities is evident in al-Rayy (Rey), where the whole of the interior, including the original inner city (called the Madīnah) and a former outer city (known as al-Muḥammadīyah but by the tenth century in ruins), had lost its markets to still newer suburbs.[163] Another city that saw its *sūqs* migrate to a more recent foundation was al-Qayrawān, where, as a result of discriminatory taxation, traders abandoned the metropolis in favor of the palace precinct known by the honorific al-Manṣūrīyah. It must not be assumed, however, that bazaar traders were always welcome within palatine administrative complexes, the archetypical example where they were not being Baghdād itself. After a brief experiment permitting traders to pursue their calling within the famed Round City, al-Manṣūr interdicted all commercial and industrial activities in those precincts and settled displaced traders in the southern district of al-Karkh.[164] Benefiting from its position between the Ṣarāt and ʿĪsā Canals, two of the main transportation links between the Tigris and the Euphrates, this latter district eventually became the principal market for the whole of the imperial metropolis.

Occasionally an author provides a snippet of information subverting any idea of absolute uniformity in the arrangement of *sūqs* within medieval cities. Tendencies to repetitive patterns there were, but not preordained templates. At Jannābah in Fārs, for reasons unspecified, the *sūqs* were in alleys; at Sīnīz, although it was half a *farsakh* from the sea, the *sūq* clustered around an inlet that brought boats to its very door; at Waylah (al-ʿAqabah) reconstruction after the earthquake of 749 included a new *sūq* on the beach outside the sea wall; at Hinduwān on the lower Arrajān (Ṭāb) River the main market (adjacent to the Friday mosque) was on the inland side of the town, while the fish market had, not unnaturally, gravitated to the seaward side; in Shīrāz the stalls of vendors of cooked meats were segregated from the main market; and at al-Jurjānīyah in Khwārizm a sheep market was held on a sandy expanse that al-Maqdisī likens to the Rīgistān in Bukhārā.[165]

To sum up: it can be said with a fair degree of confidence that, of the three principal classes of retailing centers occurring in cities of the present day, that of the neighborhood residential center serving a restricted locale was ubiquitous. It seems to have exemplified a hierarchical pattern ranging between a handful of stalls strung along a lane and the great markets of, say, Nīshāpūr, or indeed those of the Karkh suburb of Baghdād already described. That is, *sūqs* of this type could function, with appropriate changes in scale and accompanying increments to the range of goods offered, as neighborhood, community, quarter, or, if the city were of sufficient size, metropolitan retailing center. *Sūqs* performing specialized functions of the sort typified by religious articles and books for sale in the vicinity of a mosque, ships' chandlery sited at portside, and textile merchants more at home in the heart of the city are also readily recognizable in the tenth-century Islamic world.

The third class of retail center, the so-called ribbon development, is problematic. The idea is that its retail establishments are oriented to serving the traffic passing through the city on an arterial highway. In the tenth century, however, such functions were usually performed in caravanserais close to the main city gates, where pack and riding animals were accommodated, bought, sold, and accoutred, and where merchants could negotiate their deals. The Mirbaḍ on the western edge of al-Baṣrah was a splendid example. That shops and stalls sometimes extended along one or both sides of a main street for up to several miles is amply attested in the sources. Even so, the resulting configurations seem to have reflected a lateral merging of neighborhood *sūqs* or an opportunistic appropriation of available space rather than a primary concern to serve specifically traffic on the throughway. From time to time a source will ascribe an ethnic orientation to a *sūq*, as when the frontier town of Ūzkand was described as a place for engaging in business transactions *(matjar)* with the Turks,[166] Barzand was characterized as "the *sūq* of the Armenians,"[167] and Fakkān in the district of Ṭāhart (Tiaret) in the Maghrib was said to have begun as a market of the Zanātah Berbers. Al-Maqdisī went out of his way to record that in Biyār in Qūmis, retailing was in the hands of women, even though those same women seldom ventured abroad during daylight hours.[168]

Sūq Morphology

The architecture and material structures of these early Islamic *sūqs* are seldom mentioned in the available sources and never described in detail. Nor has archaeology contributed significantly to the picture. Ibn Ḥawqal's account of the *sūqs* of Nīshāpūr is one that has more than most to say about the organization of a market, as distinct from the commodities it handled:

> The *sūqs* are outside the *madīnah* and the *quhandiz* in the *rabaḍ*. Two of them are especially worthy of note, one called the Great Square *(al-Murabbaʿah al-Kabīrah)*, the other the Little Square *(al-Murabbaʿah al-Ṣaghīrah)*.[169] From the Square, the *sūq* extends westward as far as the Ḥusaynid cemetery *(Maqābir al-Ḥusaynīyīn)*. In the middle of these *sūqs* are *khāns* and *funduqs* within which traders store their merchandise and warehouses of goods to be bought and sold. To each *funduq* are brought the classes of merchandise in which the proprietors are known to deal. Very few of these *funduqs* fall below the size of the largest markets of their type. They are occupied by well-heeled merchants specializing in particular branches of commerce and disposing of huge quantities of goods and financial resources. *Funduqs* and *khāns* serve the needs of the artisan class *(ahl al-mihan)*.[170] The master craftsmen *(arbāb al-ṣanāʾiʿ)*[171] own shops *(dakākīn)* that drive a very good trade, with pleasant living quarters and establishments full of workmen. Such are the hatters who occupy their own

sūq, which functions something after the manner of a *funduq*, with well stocked shops and attractive domestic quarters. The same holds for the shoemakers, the pearl dealers, the rope-makers, and other specialist businesses housed in *funduqs* within the *sūq*. The *funduqs* of the cloth merchants compare favourably with those of most other regions handling these products.[172]

Al-Maqdisī's account of the markets of Rāmhurmuz in Khūzistān is briefer but does touch, however inadequately, on the nature of the physical plant:

> [Beside a fine mosque] are most imposing *sūqs* constructed by ʿAḍud al-Dawlah. I have never encountered any that surpassed them in cleanliness and elegance. They have been decorated and provided with a stone facing,[173] as well as being paved and covered. Entrance gates[174] to the market are locked at night. Here are the clothmakers, perfumers, and mat-makers *(ḥaṣṣārīn)*.[175] In the cloth market there are substantial roofed structures *(qayāṣir)*.[176]

Sūqs were by no means always roofed, even in the larger cities of the Islamic world. In fact in the imperial *metropoleis* and regional capitals it has to be presumed that vastly the larger number of neighborhood and district *sūqs* were open to the heavens, despite the opulence of their central markets. When, for instance, we read that some of the *sūqs* of al-Yahūdīyah, incorporated in the city of Iṣfahān in the last quarter of the eighth century, were roofed and some were not,[177] it is highly likely that it was only the higher-ranking retail centers that were being considered. The large numbers of small neighborhood markets that must have existed in the great cities of Islam are hardly ever noted and never described. In at least two instances, though, in the Turkish military cantonments at Baghdād and Sāmarrā, such local markets were referred to as *suwayqāt*, that is, "little *sūqs*"; and in the case of the latter city a typical establishment would have contained several shops *(ḥānūt)* for vendors such as food sellers *(fāmiyūn)*, butchers *(qaṣṣābīn)*, and dealers in other necessary goods and services.[178] Nor was roofing invariably a reflection of market size. Ṭazar was only a small town a few miles off the old Khurāsān road in al-Jibāl, but its *sūqs* were completely roofed. Possibly this architectural feature was not unconnected with the ruins of a palace of the Khusraws that in the tenth century still existed on the edge of the town.[179] It was not unknown for Sāsānian market structures to survive into Islamic times. Tall Fāfān, on the upper Tigris, and Sābāṭ in Ushrūsanah were other small towns whose main *sūqs* were roofed. Nūzvār in Khwārizm, Saghāniyān on the upper Zāmil River, and Zamm on the Jayhūn (Amū Daryā) were examples of towns whose main *sūqs* were mostly covered.[180] It is pretty certain that, if any part of a *sūq* were roofed, it would have been that of the cloth merchants. At Āmul, a *farsakh* from the Jayhun, and at Marv al-Rūdh on the Murghāb, it is reported that the *sūqs* were shaded from the sun *(taẓallal)*.[181]

Occasionally an author drops an allusive hint as to the layout of a *sūq*, as when al-Maqdisī describes the shops of the Arrajān *sūq* as being aligned in rows *(ṣufūf)*; those at Ḥamadhān in three rows; those at Marv al-Shāhijān in some sort of helicoidal arrangement around the Upper Mosque; the balconies in one of the *sūqs* at Shīrāz so low that two laden pack animals could not walk abreast in the street; and the market at Miskiyānah in the Maghrib as "spread out like a carpet *(bisāṭ)*." At Sāmarrā the slave mart was in the form of a huge quadrangle, with individual establishments comprising both upper and lower rooms, as well as the barracoons *(ḥawānīt)*.[182] However, not all *sūqs* were arranged as regularly as those we have mentioned. At Tustar in Khūzistān, for instance, they were so complicated that strangers were said—no doubt half in jest—to lose their way among the stalls.[183] But information even of this low degree of precision is rare. *Sūqs* of all types were so ubiquitous, an inescapable part of everyday life, that only the largest or otherwise most impressive were deemed worthy of mention, let alone description, by authors of the time. Yet it was these markets that supplied necessities to burgeoning urban populations in many parts of the Islamic world, thereby underpinning a prevailing process of rural-to-urban migration; and at the same time reinforced exchange links between cities and their local trading areas.

Specialist Cities

Before the large-scale exploitation of Middle Eastern oil resources in the twentieth century, agriculture had always been by any measure the preeminent industry throughout the Muslim world. The first four Islamic centuries were especially important in the development of farming practice, for they witnessed transformations of a magnitude deserving to be characterized as an agricultural revolution.[184] During these centuries an assemblage of new crops originating predominantly in the Asian humid tropics and including rice, sorghum, hard wheat, sugarcane, cotton, watermelon, eggplant, spinach, artichoke, colocasia, sour orange, lemon, lime, banana, plantain, and in restricted areas mango and coconut[185] were integrated into indigenous farming systems, thereby reconstituting numerous cropping patterns and, in particularly favorable circumstances, replacing the traditional summer fallow with a second season of productive cultivation.

This last development offered the signal advantage of permitting the hitherto unutilized practice of crop rotation, which was always likely to result in an intensification of land use. This in turn would make heavier demands on the water resources of a district, thereby encouraging both the repair and extension of ancient irrigation systems and the construction of new works, as well as the adoption of devices for the collection, channelling, and lifting of water. The resulting increase in the amount of land under cultivation and in the proportion of that land that was irrigated, together with the circumstance that it was cropped more intensively, tended to generate higher agricultural earnings. At the same time, a wider range of available crops, some of which (notably hard wheat and sorghum) could survive long periods of storage, imparted an enhanced degree of stability to those earnings. Adopted at first selectively into the lands of the Eastern Caliphate and South Arabia, the new farming systems were subsequently carried by the Arabs and their subjects throughout the length of the Islamic world, even to the farthest bounds of the Maghrib and into al-Andalus (Islamic Spain); but wherever they were established, and whether undertaken by the state, landowning nobility, peasant proprietors, or irrigation associations, they proved highly labor intensive. And this demand for farm labor seems to have encouraged the growth of rural populations, as evidenced earlier by references to zones of continuous farming and villages and small towns lying thick upon the land.[186] In many parts of the Islamic world this rural relative prosperity permitted certain strategically positioned or otherwise favored villages to develop the size and institutional structure of towns while leaving a surplus of foodstuffs to sustain swollen *metropoleis* such as Baghdād, al-Qāhirah (Cairo), and Qurṭubah (Córdoba), to say nothing of dozens of other sizable, and often growing, cities.

The processing of farm products and the manufacture of implements and utensils for local consumption were all but universal in villages and towns scattered through the countryside; large cities, including the great capitals, invariably encompassed workshops and markets for highly skilled craftsmen in wood, leather, glass, ivory, metals, or pottery. Nor was it by any means unknown for medium-sized towns to achieve regional distinction for their crafts: for example, Tūnis for its delicate pottery creations, Marsā al-Kharaz (La Calle) for its polished coral, Shāsh (Tashkent) for its swords, Marv for its brassware, Nūqān for its serpentine jars, Sābūr (Shahristān) for its perfumes, Qazwīn for its leather goods, Qāshān for its decorative tiles, Qumm for its furniture, and Sinjār for its shoes. Typically these and other craft industries were represented in the settlement hierarchy by producer-retailers living and working in urban bazaars.

Textile Cities

Valuable as the contributions of these crafts could be to the economy of a particular region, far and away the most important manufacture in the Islamic world generally was that of textiles, the only industry other than agriculture consistently (although by no means universally) to raise employment in what would today be called the basic sector of the economy to a significant proportion of the total labor force.[187] But even then it is doubtful if it generally rose above 40 percent. Where it probably did so was in the archetypical "textile towns" of the Nile Delta or Fārs-Khūzistān. But it is difficult to know precisely what al-Maqdisī had in mind when he reports, for instance, that a majority of the inhabitants of Astarābād were weavers,[188] or what al-Bakrī meant when he notes that "many workers" in Sūsah (al-Sūs) were employed in spinning and weaving.[189] It is not unlikely, though, that in villages in specialist textile-producing regions, virtually all the adult labor force, as well as a majority of the children, were engaged in cloth manufacture on a full- or part-time basis.

Figure 18 depicts the distribution of textile-manufacturing cities in the Islamic world in the tenth century insofar as that distribution can be reconstructed from more or less contemporary records. To a very considerable extent, the structure of the Muslim textile industry had been inherited from Byzantium and Sāsānian Persia, together with selected administrative practices and a good deal of material culture. However, the Muslims had not only adopted these technologies: they had improved them and greatly diversified the industry as a whole. In fact almost as soon as the Umayyad dynasty had established itself in Damascus, textile factories in Egypt and Persia had been integrated into the imperial economy, thereby initiating (perhaps more accurately continuing) a mode of production that would ultimately lead to the system known as *ṭirāz.* By the tenth century such government-controlled factories were to be found in nearly all the large cities of the Islamic world, a distribution reflected in al-Jahshiyārī's remarking that his brother, at some time during the first half of that century, had been given charge of the *ṭirāz* factories *(dūr al-ṭuruz)* "in all the provinces."[190] Here were produced garments reserved for the use of the respective courts, the most exclusive of which bore dated inscriptions in the name of the ruler, as well as costly robes of honor *(khilaʿ;* sing. *khilʿah)* bestowed on courtiers and meritorious officials. Nor was the custom of bestowing garments annually, probably wholly or in part in lieu of monetary recompense, confined to the caliph. It was reported, for instance, that al-Ṣāḥib Ismāʿīl ibn ʿAbbād, *wazīr* to Mu'ayyad al-Dawlah, distributed 820 turbans *(ʿamāʾim)* among his servants during a single winter.[191]

Side by side with the government-controlled factories, many regions were home to flourishing private enterprises that exploited a market of enormous proportions. Islam had united under a single religion, a single language of administration, a single legal system, and for a while a single rule, a congeries of diverse regions that extended for one-fifth of the way around the globe and functioned in many respects as an economic unit, a network of industry and trade that not only always constituted a potentially immense pool of consumers but also facilitated the acquisition of raw materials and expedited the diffusion of technology. It must be remembered, moreover, that textiles, in the form of curtains, wall hangings, carpets, rugs and runners, quilts, mattresses, and pillows, comprised a large share of the furnishings of a Middle Eastern or North African home, constituting what Lisa Golombek once aptly termed "a textile mentality." It is also worth nothing that textiles were often submitted by dependencies in payment of taxes, a practice followed, if not initiated, by the Umayyads when they allowed the people of Najrān to include robes in their schedule of tribute items.[192] Ibn Khaldūn has preserved an extract from *Jirāb al-Dawlah* (I am uncertain whether this is the name of a person or the title of a book) that summarizes the Baghdād treasury receipts from the different regions of the empire as formalized in the time of al-Maʾmūn, including 500 Yamanī garments *(mataʿ)* from Kirmān, 300 checkered garments *(al-muʿayyanah)* from Sijistān, 27,000 garments (sing. *thawb*) from Khurāsān, 1,000 pieces of *ibrīsm* silk from Gurgān, 300 napkins *(mandīl)* from Ṭabaristān, and 20 embroidered carpets *(busuṭ maḥfūrah)* from Armenia.[193]

Also channeled into the textile market, at least in Egypt, were the surplus products of *ṭirāz* factories. Such is implied, for example, by al-Kindī's comment on the high cost of garments from the *ṭirāz* workshops in Tinnīs and Dimyāṭ, while Ibn Ḥawqal states explicitly that those in the Fayyūm sold directly to merchants from all over the world.[194] However, that the highly priced *ṭirāz* cloths were not always available to the public is attested by Nāṣir-i Khusraw's tale (probably greatly exaggerated) of the "King of Fārs's" (presumably Aḍud al-Dawlah's) envoys petitioning unsuccessfully for two years for a single suit of Tinnīs clothing valued at twenty thousand *dinars.*[195] It is also evident that in certain cities the *ṭirāz* was farmed out to private individuals, when the weavers as likely as not were subject to some sort of corvée system. Professor Serjeant in fact has gone so far as to speculate that the workers in the *ṭirāz* factories in Baghdād may have been slaves or *ḥarīm* girls.[196]

The four principal fibers involved in the textile industry were cotton, flax, wool, and silk, with goat and camel hair playing minor roles. The industrial characteristics of the main manufacturing centers have been outlined in preceding chapters; the following is only an overview of those regional vignettes.

Cotton

Cotton became important only after the advent of Islam. The plant was probably established in isolated parts of the

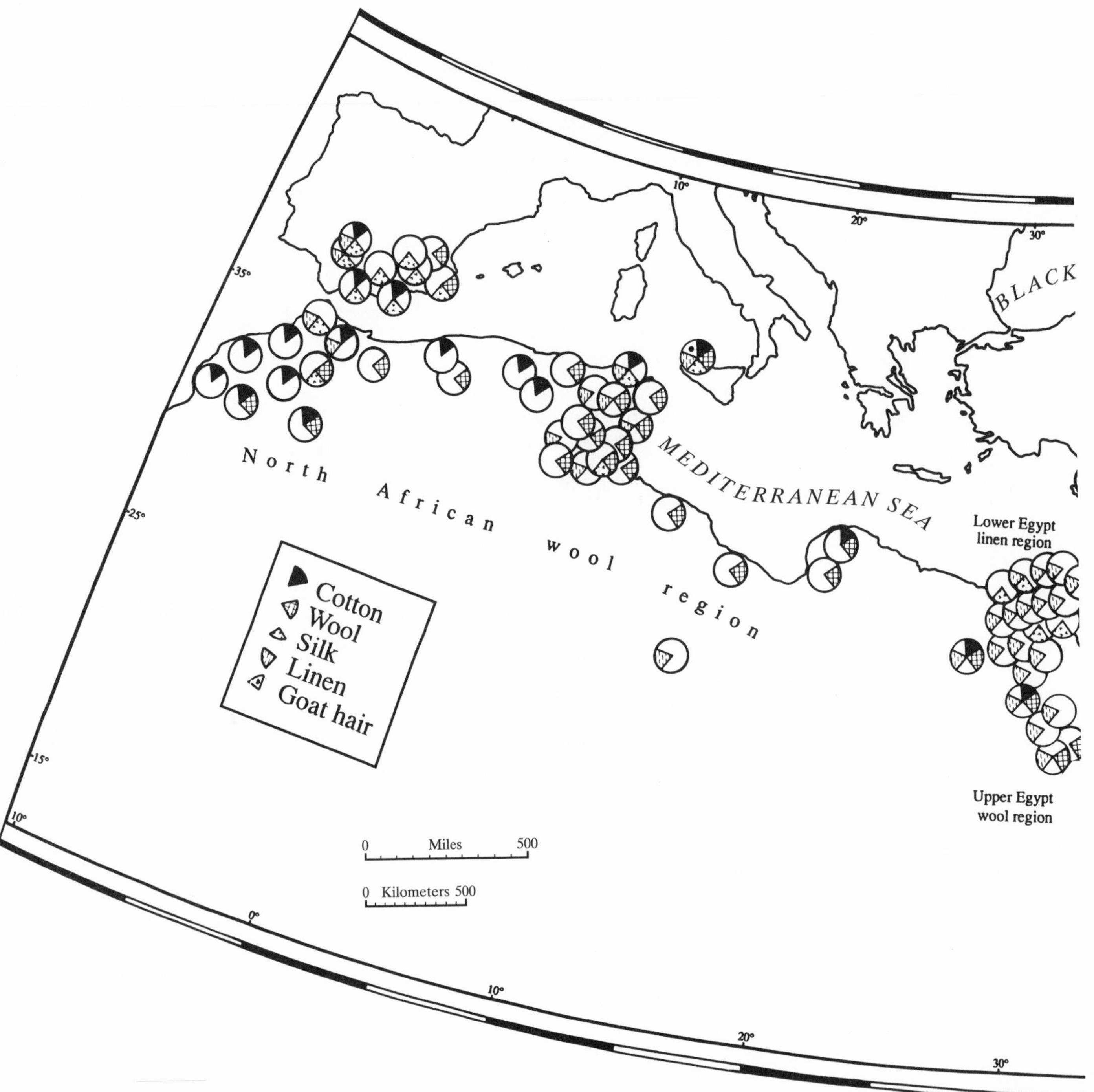

Figure 18. Textile-manufacturing regions in the Islamic world in the tenth century. For limitations inherent in these distributions, see pages 255–56.

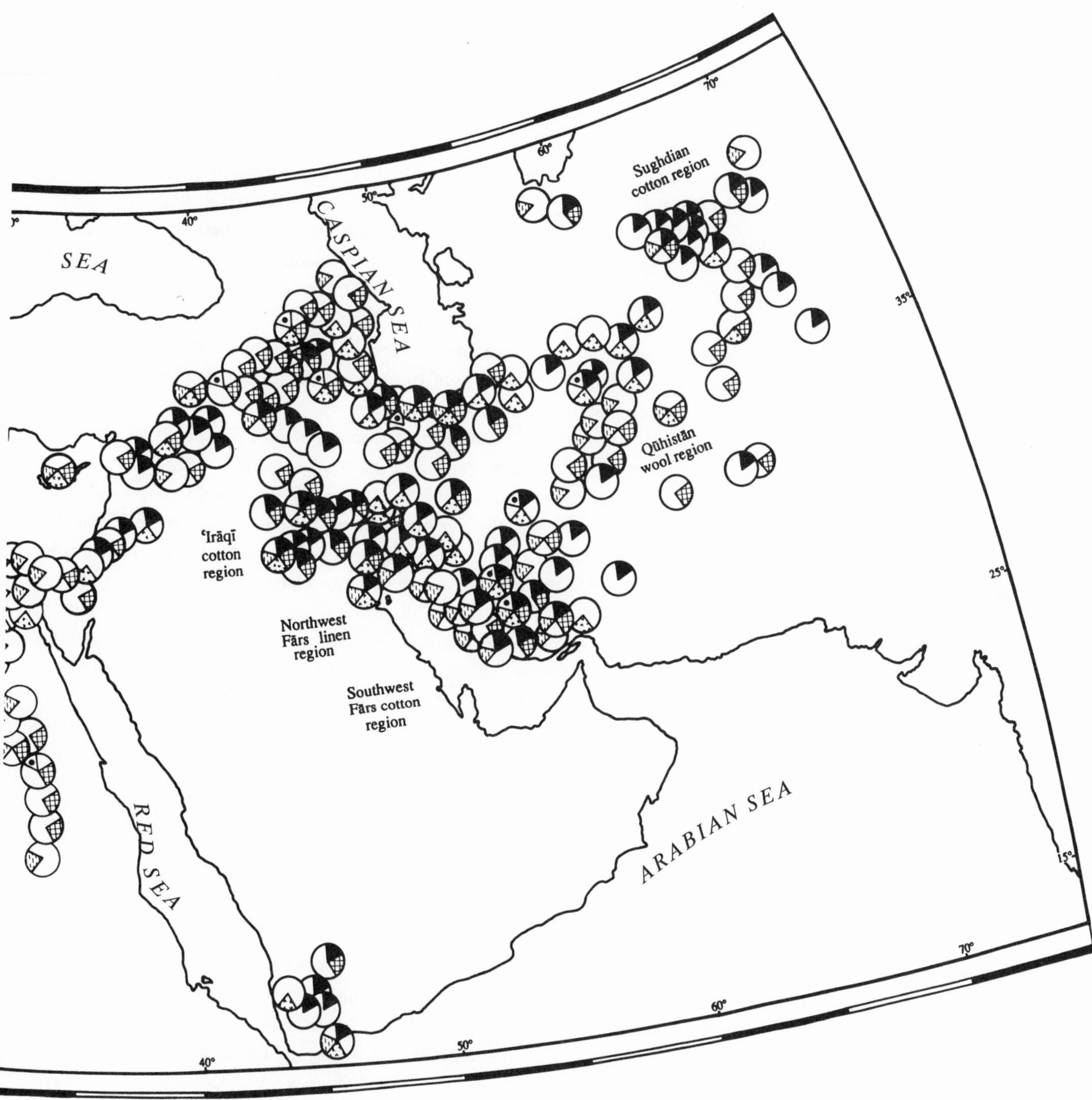
SEA
CASPIAN SEA
Sughdian cotton region
Qūhistān wool region
ʿIrāqī cotton region
Northwest Fārs linen region
Southwest Fārs cotton region
RED SEA
ARABIAN SEA
40°
50°
60°
70°
35°
25°
15°

Middle East in pre-Islamic times, notably on the shores of the Persian Gulf and in the Jordan valley, Arabia Felix, and Upper Egypt. But only with the introduction of annual varieties able to mature in shorter, cooler seasons did its cultivation diffuse virtually throughout the Islamic world, so that by the tenth century it was being grown from the Atlantic to Transoxania and south to the frontiers of Black Africa.[197] And with the crop itself went a steadily improving spinning and weaving technology. In this connection it is probably not without significance, given that this crop was adopted from the agricultural complex of monsoon Asia, that in early Islamic cloth weaving, cotton was customarily combined with one of the other fibers. Cultivation of the plant was described in detail by Ibn Waḥshīyah, probably at the beginning of the tenth century.[198]

High yields per acre, versatility in weaving, and ease of dyeing combined to ensure the spread of cotton in the manufacture of textiles from the Maghrib to the Mashriq, and much of the demand appears to have been supplied locally. However, the cotton towns par excellence were to be found mainly in the Eastern Caliphate, notably in southern Fārs, Khūzistān, al-ʿIrāq, Transoxania, northern al-Shām (Syria), and the Yaman. Among the premier producers of cotton cloth were Marv, Harāt, Nīshāpūr, and Samarqand. This is not to imply that cotton goods were the only output of textile manufacturing in those cities and regions; merely that by volume and/or value they constituted the principal products, and in some instances very distinctive features, of the industry.

Flax

Whereas by the tenth century cotton goods had become the principal product of the great textile towns of the East, flax and wool were the preferred fibers throughout most of the rest of the Islamic world. The principal center of linen manufacture was the group of towns focusing on Tinnīs and Dimyāṭ in the Nile Delta, with the latter using its more highly skilled workforce in the manufacture of pure white cloth and the former specializing in colored fabrics. The textile labor force in both cities was exclusively Coptic, even in the *ṭirāz* factories, as was also the case in the workshops of Shaṭā, which produced cloths fully capable of competing successfully with those of Tinnīs and Dimyāṭ.[199] All the stuffs produced in these factories commanded prices proportionate to their superb quality, especially the iridescent *būqalamūn* manufactured exclusively in Tinnīs. Dumayrah, Tūnah, and Dabīq (Dabquwā) also produced fine cloths, especially the last, which was renowned throughout the Islamic world for *dabīqī* pieces incorporating gold or silver threads. Eliyahu Ashtor has calculated that, if al-Thaʿālibī was correct in his reporting that taxes on Egyptian linen textiles often amounted to one hundred thousand *dinār*s a year, the total output of that industry must have accounted for almost one-fourth of the national income.[200] Ashtor's studies have also shown that the real wages of both skilled and unskilled workers were falling throughout the ninth and tenth centuries. Generally speaking, neither worked for himself but was a wage earner paid by the piece or the day.[201]

The Egyptian linen industry prospered well into the tenth century, even though its rate of expansion appears to have been levelling off at that time. In the second half of that century, however, the Fāṭimids prohibited the export of linen goods, to the great advantage of the competing industry in northwest Fārs.[202] Flax had been imported into this latter region from Egypt earlier in the century, but now it was also being grown locally, probably with the encouragement of ʿAḍud al-Dawlah, and manufactures of linen cloths on the pattern of those made in Egypt were pouring into the market. The principal manufacturing centers were Sīnīz, Jannābāʾ, Ghundijān, Tawwaj, and Kāzirūn. The circumstance that *tawwajī* (sometimes *tawwazī* or *tūzī)* became a generic term for cloth of an exceptionally delicate weave produced throughout northwest Fārs probably reflects the initial establishment of the industry in the coastal region of that part of the *iqlīm.* By the end of the tenth century, though, the center of gravity had migrated inland to the city of Kāzirūn, characterized by al-Maqdisī as the "Dimyāṭ of the Persians" because of its considerable production of *qaṣab,* a loosely woven, gauze-like material closely resembling that from the Nile Delta. It should be noted, however, that Kāzirūnī cloth retained the Egyptian name of *qaṣab* even when, as frequently happened in that district, it was made of cotton.

Wool

Almost entirely dependent on local supplies of raw materials, towns engaging in the woollen industry were inevitably located on or close to natural sheep-grazing lands, generally either steppe pastures fringing the great deserts or mountain slopes where elevation diminished tree growth. Consequently, wool was preeminent in the textile industries of Upper Egypt (e.g., Asyuṭ, Uswān [Aswan], and the towns of the Fayyūm, where it ranked coequal with flax) and North Africa more generally (e.g., Barqah, Ajdābiyah, Qābis [Gabès], Fās [Fez], and the towns of the Qasṭīliyah). Sijilmāsah actually made a name for itself by weaving relatively high-quality cloth using wool from a breed of sheep said to have been originally imported from Fārs.[203] In the Eastern Caliphate wool was the preferred fiber in many towns set amid the uplands of al-Riḥāb (notably Ardabīl, Marand, Bardhaʿah [Barda], and Baylaqān)[204] and al-Daylam (e.g., Āmul, Gurgān, and Qūmis).[205] Other regions where woollens were manufactured in significant quantities included the environs of Iṣfahān, whose carpets all but equalled the Armenian product, universally acknowledged to be the finest; certain towns of Qūhistān known for their relatively less expensive cloths; other centers in the more northerly *arbāʿ* of Khurāsān (such as Guzgān and Ṭāliqān); and sundry smaller settlements in Gharjistan (Fīrūz-kūh) specializing in carpets and felts.

Silk

Although silk, together with the basic technology for cloth production, had been transmitted from China to southwestern Asia late in the Sāsānian era, it did not become important in the Middle East until Islamic times. Eventually it gave rise to localized but flourishing industries throughout the Muslim world, but seldom, if ever, was silk the sole fiber entering into the production of a textile-manufacturing town in the way that cotton or wool sometimes monopolized an industry. The greatest concentration of looms was in Khūzistān, in cities such as Tustar (which in the early centuries of Islam had furnished the covering for the Kaʿbah), Sūs, Qurqūb, ʿAskar Mukram, and Rāmhurmuz, famous for its garments of *ibrīsm* silk. Al-Ahwāz, despite its apparent lack of a *ṭirāz* factory, manufactured "beautiful cloths *(fūṭah)* of silk for women's wear" and, as befitted the *miṣr* of the *iqlīm,* functioned as a collecting center and bourse for the whole region.[206] Other silk-based industries focused on Samarqand, Marv, groups of towns in Ṭabaristān and Gurgān (especially in the vicinity of the capital and Astarābād), Iskandarīyah (Alexandria) and al-Qāhirah (Cairo) in Lower Egypt, Qābis in the Ifrīqiyah (Tunisia and western Libya), Fās and Sabtah in the Maghrib al-Aqṣā, and ʿAdan, Sanʿāʾ, and Zabīd in the Yaman. This was a wide but fragmented distribution. In the broadest context the industry flourished only where physiographic conditions generally favored the growth of the white mulberry (*Morus alba,* Linn.), spring temperatures permitted the formation of healthy cocoons, and an appropriately committed workforce undertook the labor-intensive care of the silkworms and preparation of the thread. Within these parameters silk manufacture was found mainly in the immediate vicinity of larger cities, whose textile industries also used other fibers.

*

It is appropriate at this point to offer a caveat or two about the distribution displayed in figure 18. In the first place, the symbols on the map signify neither volume of production of all textiles in a town nor proportions of manufacture of specific types of cloth: they denote only the simple fact or facts of production in a particular town. When cloth incorporating more than one fiber is at issue (as, for example, *mulḥam* with its warp of silk and weft of some other material), all the relevant segments of the textile symbol have been activated. Second, the cities depicted on the map are only those that I have found recorded, or very occasionally inferred, as textile manufacturers in an extended reading of published medieval Middle Eastern and North African sources (but exclusive of manuscript texts), together with a much smaller number of references from Europe and Asia, including one from China.[207] The extent to which this map differs from tenth-century reality is indeterminable, but in the context of medieval Islamic history as presently understood, it appears not to be egregious. Of course, the problems of identification and location discussed in connection with figure 2 (p. 74) apply with equal force to the present distribution.

Finally, it should be noted that where, as in Egypt and Khūzistān, some form of putting-out arrangement obtained and doubtless extended into the countryside, only the urban center from which the system appears to have been organized has been plotted on figure 18. In other instances, production was recorded in villages and hamlets surrounding a city without any implication of the work being contracted out, although there can be no doubt that rural manufacture was ultimately controlled from the city, by the market mechanism if by no other means such as patron-client relationships. Representative examples of such a situation are Bukhārā, where the famed *zandanījī* cloths were woven in villages in the city hinterland;[208] and ʿAskar Mukram, where "many *ṭirāz* factories" lined the banks of the Mashruqān Canal running northward from the city.[209] In all such cases the relevant symbol has been placed over the centrally located city. In similar fashion, when, as in the case of Gīlān, the province as a whole rather than individual towns was credited with textile manufacturing, the appropriate symbol was placed in the center of the administrative region concerned. Projection forward from pre-tenth-century sources and retrojection from subsequent works have been used sparingly, and never without considerable circumstantial support. The cartographic deficiencies noted here are by no means negligible but, given the scale at which the map is reproduced, are unlikely to seriously subvert its providing a reasonably reliable visual record of the distribution of the textile industry in the tenth-century Islamic world.

Fortress Cities

In the medieval Islamic world, fortification was an almost universal attribute of settlement: rare indeed was the urban form entirely devoid of wall, fosse, citadel, or tower. Here it is proposed only to set in context the fortifications that were erected along the northern borders of the Dār al-Islam, primarily (though by no means exclusively) as defenses against Christian or subsequently Turkish incursions or as bases for the launching of Muslim raids into the Dār al-Ḥarb. No account will be taken of, for example, the fortifications at Ṭubnah, al-Masīlah, Ṭāhart (Tiaret), Sijilmāsah, or numerous other inland cities in the Maghrib; nor of the numerous castles, instruments of clan security, that diversified the Fārsī landscape; nor of fortresses such as Qaṣr Aḥnaf, Qaṣr ʿAmr Ḥiṣar-i-Zarah and numerous others in al-Mashriq; nor of the forts *(quṣūr)* constructed by al-Saffāḥ, first of the ʿAbbāsid caliphs, along the northern section of the Darb Zubaydah from al-Qādisīyah to Zubālah. In any case, many of these fortifications were covered in earlier parts of this work. The following pages, then, will treat only of the northern frontiers of the Islamic world, exclusive of al-Andalus (Islamic Spain) and Iṣqiliyah (Sicily). The several types of fortification, which were in fact never entirely discrete, will be grouped expediently under the rubrics *ribāṭāt, thughūr,* and *ʿawāṣim,* and sundry other less clearly differentiated categories.

Ribāṭāt

Ribāṭ is a term virtually incapable of unequivocal definition and consequently requires a somewhat less apodictic treatment than it was accorded in chapters 2 and 16. It must continually be set in context and, where possible, in a reasonably precise chronology.[210] At the time of the Islamic conquests the root *r.b.ṭ* was evident in a suite of derived forms, among which *ribāṭ* was to be read as a *maṣdar* (rather than a substantive) denoting the mustering of hobbled cavalry mounts prior to a *ghazū.*[211] Subsequently, either late in Umayyad times or under the early ʿAbbāsids, the term acquired the additional meaning of some type of fortified edifice, almost invariably located in a position of hazard or stress. The structure itself could vary from a simple observation tower to a small fort, a substantial fortress, or in some instances a caravanserai. As Chabbi characterizes this variability, "It seems that what is involved is the simple imposition of a noun, probably denoting the existence of danger and the need to take precautions against it, upon various pre-existing constructions, without any suggestion that there is, at the outset, such a thing as a unique type of edifice which could be called *ribāṭ.*"[212] At the same time, the term came increasingly to be associated with the ideology of *jihād* and the virtue of warfare in the way of God *(fī sabīl Allāh)* on the frontiers of Islam.[213] Eventually the *ribāṭ* on the frontier became a stereotypical idealization of the past in the works of many medieval authors. Uncertainties as to chronology then combined with ambiguities of meaning to confuse the implications of references to *ribāṭāt* in numerous parts of the Islamic world.

In figure 19, only such references to *ribāṭāt* as implied the existence of substantial fortified edifices have been plotted. Considerable effort has been made to exclude (1) references that appear to have involved no more than simple, small forts, observation towers, or caravanserais and (2) those references that seem likely to have been essentially extensions of the sense of the *maṣdar* to mean a general location involved in or conducive to the practice of *ribāṭ* as it was understood in the tenth century. At that time *ribāṭāt* were mentioned with especial frequency in two realms, respectively North Africa and Transoxania. In the former region they were found principally along the Ifrīqiyan littoral and on the Atlantic coast of Morocco (see p. 208 above). In the Ifrīqiyah the earliest authentic references point to the second half of the eighth century as a time when ʿAbbāsid coastal defenses were reinforced against raids from the Christian north. In the ninth century this policy was intensified under the Aghlabid governorate, culminating in the mounting of the first expeditions against Iṣqiliyah in 827.

It is to be noted, though, that Chabbi questions whether all the *ribāṭāt* recorded for this coast were initially established formally as *ribāṭāt* or were simply "places of *ribāṭ*" housed in whatever structures happened to be available.[214] Of the three occurrences of this term in central Tunisia reported by Ibn Ḥawqal, that relating to Munastīr—*ribaṭ yaskunu-hu ummah min al-nās*[215] (a *ribāṭ* or "a place of *ribāṭ* where a community of people reside")—could imply either an edifice or merely a place of residence. The second reference uses *ribāṭ* as a functional epithet (*qaṣr ribāṭ:* "a fort serving as a *ribāṭ*") for an establishment, known as Shaqāniṣ, situated between Munastīr and al-Mahdīyah; while the third reference involves the *maṣdar: qaṣrān ʿaẓīmān li-l-ribāṭ wa-l-ʿibādah* ("two large forts for *ribāṭ* and religious observance"). Chabbi's skepticism as to the precise function of these "*ribāṭāt*" is probably justified, but they have nonetheless been included in figure 19 on the ground that all three contexts imply a substantial degree of fortification: Munastīr, where several *ribāṭāt* were known collectively as *Quṣūr al-Munastīr;*[216] Shaqāniṣ, which was designated both *qaṣr* and *ribāṭ;* and the two coastal edifices, described specifically as forts.

Professor Chabbi is equally critical of what he perceives as an idealization of *jihād* on the eastern frontier of the empire, particularly on the Transoxanian sector.[217] In the first place he adduces persuasive reasons for discounting the idea of a generalized *jihād* based on a network of *ribāṭāt.* Instead, Ṭāhirid governors and Sāmānid *amīrs* appear to have espoused defensive strategies based on fortresses (*ḥiṣn* or Persian *quhandiz*), walled *(muḥaṣṣanah)* towns, or rampart-and-ditch defenses *(khandaq).* Moreover, Muslim forays into Turkish territory, particularly against the Qarluq, together with a conversion to Islam of many Turkish tribes along the border, seem to have established relative calm in the region. Finally, Chabbi believes that the term *ribāṭ* sometimes denoted no more than a simple hospice for travellers, and sometimes merely a halting place on an internal route. This would seem especially plausible when the "*ribāṭ*" was situated at the gate of a city, had been founded by a specifically designated individual, and was maintained by income from a *waqf.* Four *ribāṭāt* at Isbījāb, one at each gate of the city, are cited as possible examples of such hospices. Another possible example, though slightly subsequent to our period, was the "*ribāṭ* for the needy" built in the vicinity of Iskijkat by Muḥammad ibn Sulaymān, great *qaghan (arslan)* of the Western Qarakhanid kingdom.[218] Such instances have been excluded from figure 19.

Locations where Chabbi is prepared to countenance the presence of military *ribāṭāt* in the tenth century are the approaches to the mountain fortresses of the Ghūr where regular soldiers were posted *(murattabūn)* in defense of the frontier,[219] but those localities are not covered by figure 19. Where more than one *ribāṭ* is mentioned in connection with a particular location, only one symbol has been plotted on the map. In any case, some of the numbers advanced by medieval topographers are grossly inflated—probably, as Chabbi suggests, a reflection of a prevailing frontier mythology.[220] For example, both al-Maqdisī and Ibn Ḥawqal[221] credited Baykand with a thousand *ribāṭāt,* the former going so far as to discriminate between ruined *(kharāb)* structures and those in active use *(ʿāmir).* This same author[222] further attributes seventeen hundred *ribāṭāt* to Isbijāb, presumably in addition to the four mentioned above. Clearly, such figures are not only highly implausible but also raise serious questions about what these topographers understood by the term *ribāṭ.*

A third region where *ribāṭāt* were mentioned in the tenth century was that part of the Fīlastīn coast controlled from the *qaṣabah* of al-Ramlah (Ramleh). An especial component of the *ribāṭ* function there was that known as *fidāʾ*, namely the ransoming of Muslims from Christian captors.[223] Mālikī *fuqahāʾ* in the Maghrib used to recommend that such ransoms be paid in the form of pigs and wine previously offered by *dhimmīs* as part of the *jizyah.* This certainly did not happen very frequently, and apparently not at all on the Fīlasṭīn coast, where both monetary payments and direct exchanges of prisoners were practiced.

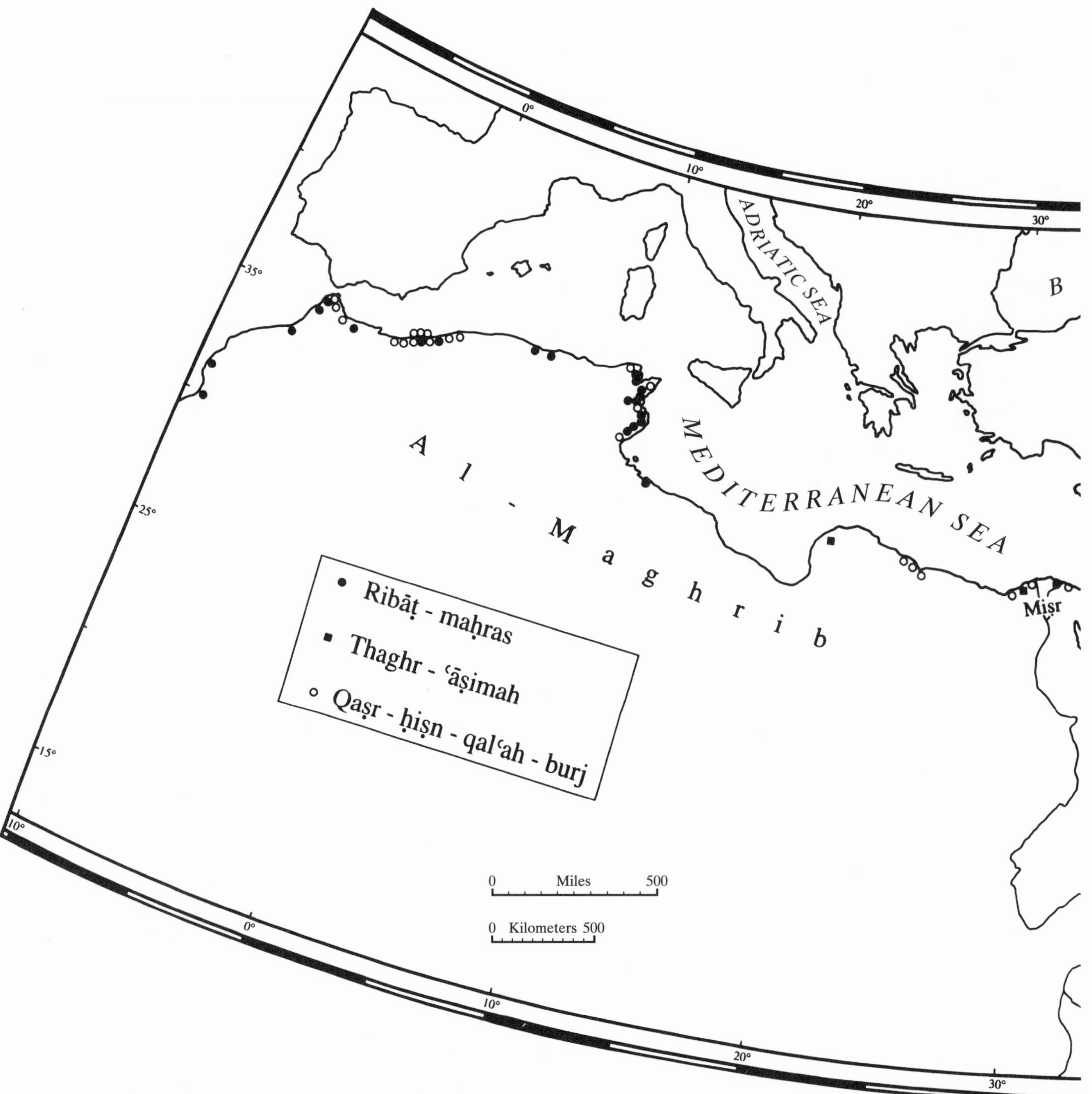

Figure 19. The principal fortified settlements along the northern frontiers of Islam about A.D. 1000, excluding al-Andalus (Islamic Spain) and Iṣqiliyah (Sicily).

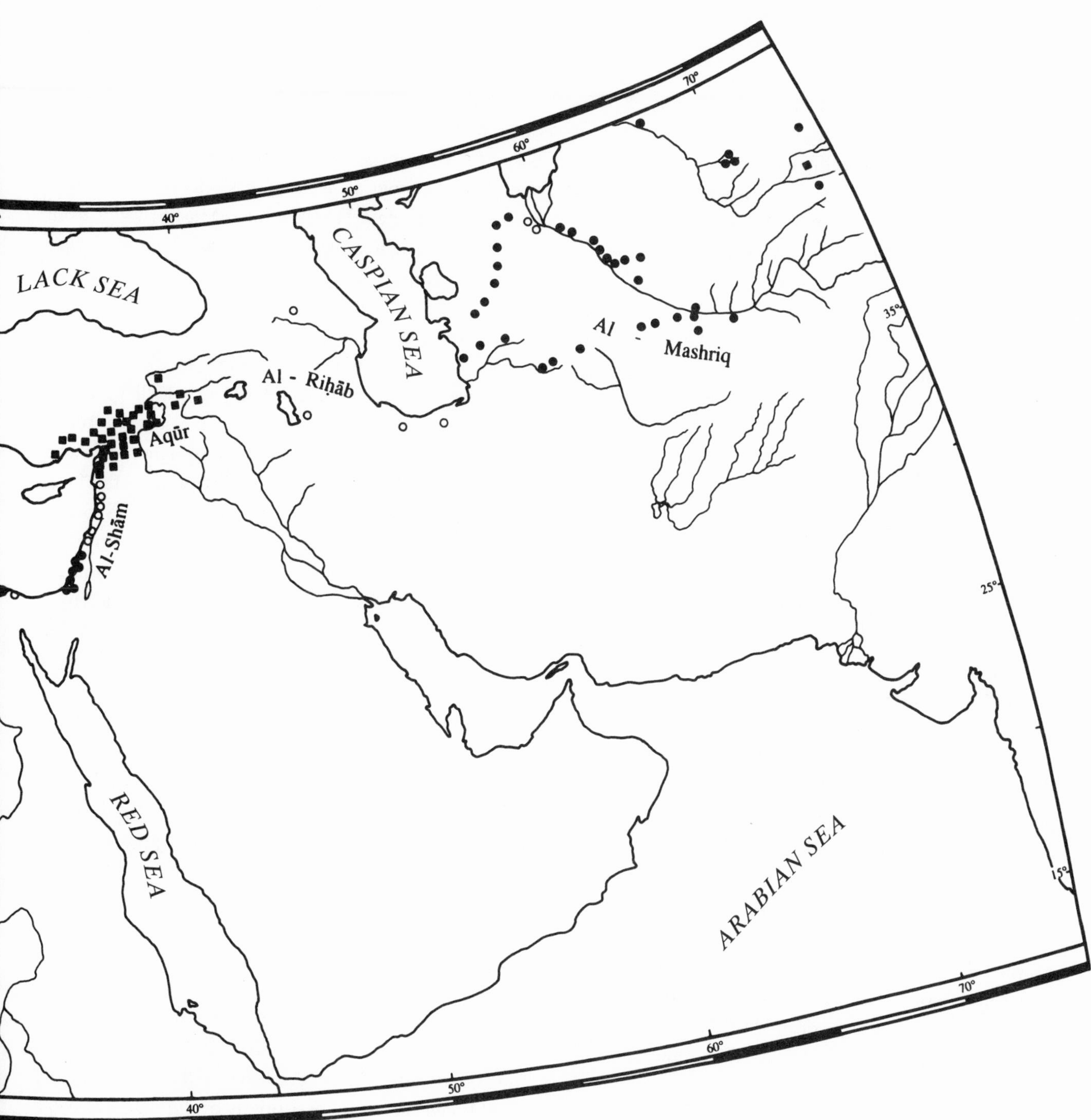
LACK SEA
CASPIAN SEA
Al - Riḥāb
Aqūr
Al-Shām
Al
Mashriq
RED SEA
ARABIAN SEA
40°
50°
60°
70°
35°
25°
15°

In figure 19 *maḥāris* (sing. *maḥras*), signifying small fortified structures with observation towers, have been subsumed within the symbol for *ribāṭ*, an expedient nicely reflective of the similarity of function of these two institutions. As in the case of *ribāṭāt*, multiple occurrences of *maḥāris* in a particular locality have been collapsed into a single symbol: for instance, the unspecified number of *maḥāris* in the neighborhood of ʿAsqalān, which was described as *kathīrat al-maḥāris;*[224] six such edifices at Asfāqus (Sfax); and five at Munastīr.[225]

Although examples of early *ribāṭāt* have not been identified with any degree of certainty in the field, Professor Chabbi is surely correct in emphasizing their great variability in size and complexity. Even later examples are extremely few, the most thoroughly studied being those at Munastīr and Sūsah (al-Sūs). The latter is the better preserved and has established itself in the relevant literature as the type-example of the fully developed *ribāṭ*, even though it is uncertain to what extent its architectural features were reproduced elsewhere. Nasser Rabbat believes that the structural characteristics of *ribāṭāt*, to the extent that they did ultimately exhibit a measure of commonality of design, developed out of nonmilitary building types such as *khān*s and caravanserais.[226] At Sūsah construction began in the last quarter of the eighth century, and the latest modifications were made to the order of the Aghlabid *amīr* Ziyādat Allāh (817–38). In its final form it comprised a fortified square enclosure having a single projecting entrance in the south wall, an attached round tower at each corner, and semiround towers in the middle of the east, west, and north sides. The southeastern tower served as a dual-purpose *manār* for observation and the call to prayer. The courtyard was surrounded by vaulted porticoes running on three sides in front of windowless cells. Similar cells were arranged around the first floor (English usage), which also housed an arcaded mosque.[227]

Thughūr and *ʿAwāṣim*

As purveyed by Arab authors of the ninth and tenth centuries, the *thughūr* and *ʿawāṣim* constituted two more or less parallel-trending zones of defensive positions established by the caliph Hārūn al-Rashīd in 786 to counter the Byzantine threat to al-Shām and al-Jazīrah. The more northerly of these systems, stretching from Ṭarsūs in Cilicia northeastward to Qālīqalā and beyond and confronting the enemy directly, was the realm of the *thughūr*, divided in Muslim topographical writing primarily into the westerly *thughūr* of al-Shām and the easterly *thughūr* of al-Jazīrah. In addition, some authors recognized a third category, *Thughūr al-Bakrīyah*, in the vicinity of Diyār Bakr. To the rear of these fortifications was a zone of strongholds known as *al-ʿAwāṣim* ("The Protectresses") because, according to al-Balādhurī, Muslim levies from the *thughūr* sought refuge in them *(yaʿtaṣimūna ilayha)* when hard pressed by the Byzantines.[228]

No doubt this was the way in which the development of these zones of fortification was perceived in the tenth century, but recently Michael Bonner has proposed an alternative reading of the evidence in which he places greater reliance on al-Ṭabarī[229] than on al-Balādhurī and adduces numismatic sources previously ignored in this context.[230] His thesis is that Hārūn's creation of the *ʿawāṣim* was an attempt to consolidate the ʿAbbāsid's northern frontier, where authority was ineffective and loyalties uncertain, into a single unified administrative unit.[231] Thereby Hārūn would curtail the power of the "viceroys" governing the region for well over a century and link this particular frontier—and the idea of *jihād* associated with it—directly with the person of the caliph.[232] It follows, on this reading, that the term *ʿawāṣim* was at that time applied to all the northern frontier strongholds. However, as the idea of the frontier as a caliphal precinct, together with the type of caliphally inspired *jihād* envisaged by Hārūn, faded from ʿAbbāsid policy, so the original meaning of *ʿawāṣim* was forgotten; al-Balādhurī in the ninth century felt it necessary to invent what amounted to a popular etymology supporting his description of the northern frontier as a dual network of fortifications that implied a probably spurious separation of the processes of conquest and settlement. As it happened, in the tenth century the ʿAbbāsids lost control of this frontier to the Ikhshīdids and Ḥamdānids, who in turn lost it to the Byzantines.

Although detailed descriptions of individual *thughūr* and *ʿawāṣim* have not survived (if they were ever written), Hugh Kennedy successfully combines a good deal of scattered evidence into a creditable, albeit generalized, account of these frontier strongholds.[233] In the plains the Muslims settled in three fairly large cities. Al-Maṣṣīṣah (Mopsuestia), the first to be colonized, had been refortified and furnished with a Friday mosque by 703. Before the end of the Umayyad period, a suburb with its own mosque had developed on the opposite bank of the Jayḥūn (Āmū Daryā) River. A third quarter was settled by order of Marwān II, last of the Umayyad caliphs, with forcibly transplanted Persians, Slavs, and Christian Nabateans, but in 756 the caliph al-Manṣūr decreed a total rebuilding of the city after it had been devastated by an earthquake. The second of the three cities, Adhanah (Adana), was apparently ignored by the Muslims until a garrison of Khurāsānīs was established there in 758–60. In 781–82 Hārūn al-Rashīd settled colonists from Dimashq (Damascus) and al-Urdunn in the city, which by the tenth century had become reasonably populous and prosperous. Ṭarsūs, although not settled by the Arabs until 779 and not formally garrisoned until 787–88, eventually became the largest city on the Cilician plain, mainly because of its command of the southern approaches to the pass across the Taurus range known as the Cilician Gates. From its fortress, summer expeditions *(ṣawā'if)* set forth annually into the Christian territories, but all this came to an end when the city capitulated to the Byzantine emperor Nicephorus Phocus in 965. Lesser centers in the Cilician basin, seemingly fortresses with garrisons and minimal numbers of service personnel, included ʿAyn Zarbah, Hārūniyah, and al-Kanīsat al-Sawdā.

Eastward, Muslim outposts were found only in valleys among the uplands, and almost invariably in the more fertile tracts of these valleys. Virtually all were isolated one from another and inevitably vulnerable to Byzantine depredations. Further west, controlling access to another pass across the mountains, was Marʿash (Marazion), rebuilt by the caliph Muʿāwiyah in the seventh century; provided with an inner keep by Marwān II, last of the Umayyad caliphs; and refortified by Hārūn. Extensive grazing on surrounding valley slopes made the town a favored base for the launching of summer raids into the Christian north. Al-Ḥadath (Adata) had been conquered by the Muslims under the caliph ʿUmar, and fortified and garrisoned under the early ʿAbbāsids. Malaṭiyah (Melitene, Modern Malatya), overlooking the valley of the Nahr Qubāqib, had a checkered history. Colonized late in Umayyad times, the city was razed by Byzantine forces, only to be rebuilt by order of the caliph al-Manṣūr in 757–58 and garrisoned with a force of four thousand. Smaller, but still substantial, fortified settlements included Ḥiṣn Manṣūr, Ḥiṣn Zibaṭrah (Sozopetra), Ḥiṣn Qalawdhiyah, and Ḥiṣn Ziyād, all of which experienced in full measure the vicissitudes of frontier conflict. Farthest east of all was Ḥiṣn Kamkh (Kamacha) in the upper Euphrates valley, with its town on the riverbank immediately below the walls of an imposing fortress.[234]

The ideal type of the *thughūr* or *ʿawāṣim* would read something as follows: It was situated on a plain (in the case of Cilicia) or more commonly in an upland valley, neither locale being seriously deficient in the resources necessary to sustain men and horses preparing for a foray. Typically it was in an isolated position and seldom able to rely on help arriving quickly from other strongholds. Al-Yaʿqūbī mirrors this situation when he describes Malaṭiyah as surrounded by mountains dominated by the Byzantines *(Rūm)*.[235] The *thaghr* or *ʿāṣimah* was almost always a preexisting Anatolian or Armenian *(au sens large)* city colonized by Arabs and perhaps fortified late in Umayyad times, and both furnished with enhanced defenses and integrated into a unitary system of provincial defense during the first fifty years of ʿAbbāsid rule. During that time it acquired a citadel, a Friday mosque, a bath, possibly a governor's residence, and a substantial Muslim community that was often still a minority but probably of a size to ensure that Christians did not sound their *nawāqīs* during the hours of Muslim prayer.

The *thaghr* city about which we are best informed is Ṭarsūs, mainly because of the preservation of extracts from al-Ṭarsūsī's *Siyar al-Thughūr* in Ibn al-ʿAdīm's biographical dictionary of Ḥalabī notables entitled *Bughyat al-Ṭalab fī Ta'rīkh Ḥalab*.[236] As this latter work, unlike the majority of such dictionaries, incorporates a good deal of topographical information, particularly in volume 1, its citations from the *Siyar* also include an unexpectedly large number of references to the urban landscape. In brief, the city was enclosed within double walls separated by a trench *(khandaq)*. Each wall was breached by five gates: those in the outer wall were fortified with iron plating *(ḥadīd mulabbas)*, while those in the inner wall were of solid iron *(ḥadīd muṣmat)*. The inner wall allegedly furnished 18,000 crenelles *(shurrāfāt)* accommodating at any one time enough men to handle 16,000 crossbows[237] and was equipped with 100 towers *(abrāj)*, nearly half of which were adapted for the use of projectile-launching engines of one sort or another. Somewhat surprisingly, these towers were owned by private individuals and served as living quarters for both a permanent population *(muta'ahhilin)* and single warriors (*'uzzāb*; lit., "bachelors") from all over the Islamic world. One of these towers, which we learn was adjacent to the *zāwiyah* of the rope makers *(al-ḥabbālīn)*, was apparently used as a paper factory *(al-waraq wa-l-kāghid)*.[238]

Within these fortifications, al-Ṭarsūsī was greatly impressed by the number of "houses" and retreats (referred to variously as [sing.] *dār, ribāṭ, zāwiyah,* and *khānqāh*) catering to *ghāzī*s motivated, as Ibn Ḥawqal phrases it, by "piety and devotion."[239] Al-Ṭarsūsī cites a count undertaken by a certain Ibn Aṭīyah in 903 that yielded a total of thirty-four thousand such establishments (an unbelievably large number even for the premier center of *jihād* on the northern frontier), dispersed through some two thousand streets and alleys *(sikak)*.[240] Apparently about two-thirds of these buildings housed *'uzzāb* while the rest, either in private ownership or endowed as *awqāf,* served as residences for the permanent population.[241] That not all were inhabited by groups or associations of *ghāzī* is evident enough if the figures just quoted have any validity at all; nevertheless, some were of considerable size. The largest *dār* in the city, according to al-Ṭarsūsī, was to be found at the end of the Street of the Carpenters. It had been founded by Shaghib (perhaps better known as Sayyidah), the slave mother of the caliph al-Muqtadir, and in the mid-tenth century housed 150 youthful slave warriors *(ghilmān)* together with blacksmiths and armorers, all supported by frontier *awqāf.* Nor was this the only *dār* sponsored by a member of a caliphal family. Qabīḥah, a slave concubine of al-Mutawakkil, had already established such a "house" in Bāb al-Ṣafṣāf Street, also for 150 *ghilmān* but this time under the command of an officer *(ra'īs)* appointed from among the *mawālī* of the caliph.

Other *dār* mentioned individually by al-Ṭarsūsī included two owned by a certain Bushrā al-Rāghibī, a small one in the Street of the Barmakīs occupied by his freedmen and freedwomen and a larger one for eunuchs and senior cavalry officers; the Dār of Ibn Qaḥṭabī in River Street (the river being the Baradān) accommodating mainly Ṣūfīs and ascetics; and a *dār* in Zuhayr ibn al-Ḥārith Street, for which al-Ṭarsūsī provides an idea of its layout. While an upper floor was given over to collective domestic arrangements, the ground floor afforded stabling for the war steeds of the leading commanders, together with storerooms and shops. *Waqf* revenues from these last supported not only the horses but also their fodder and equipment, as well as the grooms and horse doctors who cared for them.[242]

Hugh Kennedy properly emphasizes the urban character of these strongholds, and his dictum bears repeating here: "The main unit of defence was not the isolated castle but the fortified city."[243] Regular troops were stationed in virtually all these centers, about half (according to Kennedy) being brought from Khurāsān and the rest from al-Shām (Greater Syria) and al-Jazīrah. These garrisons were paid by the 'Abbāsid government at rates somewhat above those customary for the military. Their stipends were supplemented by small land grants in fee simple *(milk)*, which were subject only to the lower rate of *'ushr* (as opposed to *kharāj*) tax.[244] In addition, an unknown number of volunteers were incorporated in offensive and defensive strategies.

Finally, it should be noted that these settlements gradually shifted from a primarily military function to a developed local service economy. Prior to about 850, efforts were directed primarily toward territorial expansion, attraction of settlers, and financial exploitation of Christian *dhimmī*s. Although al-Ṭabarī refers to a "market community" *(ahl al-aswāq)* in al-Ḥadath in 785, and such almost certainly existed elsewhere, market exchange was still secondary to taxes and booty. Peter von Sivers summarizes the situation with compelling imagery when he writes, "For most thughūrians contacts with markets were probably not very different from those of a Muslim raider in 666/46 who undertook a summer campaign and after his return from enemy country spent three days in a Muslim border town to sell his booty and distribute the proceeds among his companions."[245]

During the ensuing two centuries, however, the Muslims came to realize that the rewards of military expansion were often less than the proceeds from militarily protected commerce. The frequent references to markets in the *thughūr* and *'awāṣim* imply that much of this economic activity materialized as a city-region trade on something approaching central-place principles. Even so, it seems that, from about the mid-ninth century, at least some of the frontier fortresses participated to a certain extent in long-distance trade with the Christian Mediterranean—the more especially after (1) the development of a trade route conveying spices, aromatics, and luxury goods from al-Baṣrah up the Euphrates to al-Raqqah, Ḥalab (Aleppo), and even Constantinople and (2) a fiscal reorganization of the *thughūr* in 857. However, during approximately the first half of the tenth century, the military-fiscal component in the ʿAbbāsid ruling class reasserted itself and long-distance commerce stagnated until the *thughūr* were finally lost to the Byzantines.[246]

From time to time the term *thaghr* is encountered outside the northern regions of its archetypical development as denoting a strong fortress or group of fortresses. As late as the twelfth century, for example, Geniza letters were referring to al-Iskandarīyah as al-Thaghr.

Qaṣr, ḥiṣn, burj, qalʿah are terms denoting generalized types of fortification that are encountered in medieval Islamic literature. Not infrequently, such terms were used as synonyms for *ribāṭ* and *thaghr:* for example, the *ribāṭāt* of Munastīr known collectively as Quṣūr al-Munastīr or the numerous *thughūr*/*ʿawāṣim* that incorporated *ḥiṣn* in their names (see above). In figure 19 the relevant symbol is plotted only when the edifice in question seems to have had an independent existence and, of course, formed part of the Muslim's northern defenses. Nor have Lawrence Conrad's warnings about the semantic ambiguities of the term *qaṣr,* and by implication the other terms in this rubric, been ignored.[247]

The City as an Institution of Institutions

Amṣār

It has already been sufficiently emphasized that the urban process in the Middle East and North Africa during the first four centuries of Muslim domination was principally one of adaptation and accretion rather than creation. Nevertheless, new cities were founded, and it is among the earliest and largest of these, the so-called *amṣār,* that we might expect to discern, if anywhere, traces of Ḥijāzī or more broadly Arabian urban traditions along with an incipient Islamic imprint. Unfortunately, even for the best documented of these settlements, namely al-Baṣrah, al-Kūfah, and al-Fusṭāṭ, the record is woefully inadequate. Topographers, historians, and others, writing no less than two centuries after the founding of these cities, referred incidentally to various early architectural structures such as mosques, gubernatorial residences, public treasuries, *sūqs*, and caravanserais. At the same time, they treated somewhat more fully the prevailing principles of administrative organization (e.g., *khiṭāṭ, akhmās, asbāʿ*), but were far from explicit on the spatial interrelations of these features.[248]

One of the more perspicacious evaluations of such evidence as exists bearing on early *amṣār* morphologies in general has been essayed by Jamel Akbar.[249] By analyzing the semantic implications of terms employed by Muslim writers in describing the foundations of these settlements, this author has managed to specify certain constraints that seem to have operated at that time. One commonly used suite of words derived from the root *KhṬṬ*, the form *khaṭṭ* itself meaning "line." The verb *khaṭṭa* (and, mutatis mutandis, its various derived forms) signified the claiming, with official authoritative approval, of a plot of land on which to erect a building by formally demarcating it on the ground. The noun *khiṭṭah* denoted the prospective site thus demarcated. The *maṣdar takhṭīṭ* was the laying out of such a plot; *tanzīl,* its actual occupation. For the bestowing of a specific tract of land on a specific individual by a duly constituted authority, another word altogether was used, namely *aqṭaʿah,* with the allotment itself, whether in fee simple or with rights of usufruct, being known as an *iqṭāʿ*.[250] By careful study of these and other terms, Professor Akbar shows that in these settlements locational decisions were made predominantly by the inhabitants, at most by a local rather than a central authority. As he puts it, "The town thereby became a series of adjacent properties controlled by its users, suggesting that the morphology of these towns came about as a result of the many small decisions made by the settlers themselves."[251] Furthermore, streets were determined primarily by the disposition and boundaries of quarters, while shared places such as forecourts, streets, and open spaces within a *khiṭṭah* were collectively owned and controlled. It is also implicit in early accounts that a large *khiṭṭah* could encompass a number of smaller *khiṭāṭ,* each of which in turn could enclose still smaller *khiṭāṭ.*

Al-Baṣrah

Although it has to be concluded that the Arab tribesmen were able to exercise a measure of choice in selecting the sites of their holdings, the *amṣār,* even in their early years, were not simply formless aggregations of tents, reed huts, and, in al-Baṣrah from about 670, brick dwellings spread initially over two square *farsakhs*. Al-Balādhurī, it is true, tells us that the tribesmen of al-Baṣrah "staked out their claims *(ikhtaṭṭu)* and raised their dwellings,"[252] while al-Māwardī, retailing the received information of the first half of the eleventh century, adds that certain Companions (here signifying little more than contemporaries) of the Prophet demarcated *khiṭāṭ* for their tribal peoples *(qabā'il ahlihā),* whose dwellings abutted one on another; but—significantly—none of this was undertaken until the Companions had reached agreement among themselves.[253] Although the locational principles underpinning the layout of the cantonment are not now recoverable, they almost certainly reflected fairly directly the niceties of Arabo-Islamic precedence *(sābiqah)* as worked out during the Madīnan hegemony. According to al-Ṭabarī, supervision of the myriad activities involved in establishing the cantonment was in the hands of one ʿĀṣim ibn al-Dulaf Abū al-Jarbā'.[254] What is known is that space was left in the center of the cantonment for erecting a simple mosque; a similar space *(raḥbah)* was reserved within each *khiṭṭah* for tethering horses and mustering tribesmen. What is more, a number of streets came into existence quite early in the settlement process: the main thoroughfares being sixty cubits wide, lesser streets twenty cubits, and lanes *(zuqāq)* a mere seven cubits.[255] One of the wider roads eventually became the axial thoroughfare of al-Baṣrah before continuing westward to the great market of the Mirbaḍ.[256] It is usually assumed that these streets ran more or less straight across the city, but the texts afford no firm support for that view. In this connection Nezar AlSayyad has raised the plausible possibility that the *zuqāqs* were intended less for movement than as spaces separating *khiṭāṭ*.[257] Initially the cantonment was not provided with perimeter defenses.

Al-Kūfah

Al-Kūfah was established something after the same pattern, even though the first settlers were predominantly nomadic Arab tribesmen in contrast with the more diversified contingents ensconced in al-Baṣrah. It is recorded explicitly that on this occasion the overall layout of the site was supervised by a certain Abū al-Hayyāj, a lieutenant of the army commander Saʿd ibn Abī Waqqāṣ. A space *(ṣaḥn)* allegedly some two bow shots square was reserved more or less in the center of the cantonment for a mosque and a governor's residence.[258] A council of men of sound judgment (*ahl al-ra'y:* perhaps senior tribal *shaykhs*) was empanelled to recommend to al-Hayyāj the manner in which the main streets *(manāhij)* should run. Eventually fifteen were approved: four in the direction of Makkah (indicating both the *qiblah* and a general southerly direction), five to the north, three to the east, and three to the west. These streets varied in width, allegedly on caliphal order, from 40 cubits (about 21.6 meters) to 20. Dwellings were then erected in *khiṭāṭ* fitting in between these streets and apparently separating one from another by lanes 7 cubits wide. By command of Saʿd himself, residential structures were prohibited within the *ṣaḥn,* which was delimited by a ditch *(khandaq)* "so that buildings could not encroach on it." According to Sayf ibn ʿUmar, the *ṣaḥn* was capable of holding the whole population of the *miṣr* without overcrowding.[259]

The texts clearly assert that the caliph, the army commander, his executive officer, and the advisory council of tribal representatives all had a say in the layout of the camp, but al-Ṭabarī also observes that nothing was done unless a favorable consensus was reached among the *shaykh*s of the advisory council.[260] The most reasonable interpretation of this not always consistent evidence is that the tribesmen established their *khiṭāṭ* by mutual agreement within policy parameters promulgated by the powers that were, and that al-Hayyāj functioned as a liaison officer rather than as a planner.

That *khiṭāṭ* varied in size seems to be implied by disparities in the numbers of their populations. The Nizār *khiṭṭah,* for example, was home to some eight thousand individuals, whereas that of the Ahl al-Yaman housed about twelve thousand. It is presumably to be inferred that the size of a *khiṭṭah,* despite an unspecified dimension of sixty cubits for all except the Banū Ḍabbah,[261] reflected in at least a general sense the size of its tribal muster. Furthermore, dwellers in a particular *khiṭṭah* evidently had the right to, and did, admit *rawādif* and other newcomers to their territory, a practice that could only have involved settling them on land already claimed (verb = *khaṭṭa*) but not yet physically occupied.[262] Sayf ibn ʿUmar also reports that tribal groups who could not find room in their *khiṭāṭ* for the *rawādif* desirous of joining them sometimes joined the newcomers outside the cantonment, where they presumably laid claim to larger *khiṭāṭ*. At the same time, it was not unknown for groups attracting few *rawādif* to quarter their newcomers on the vacated holdings.[263]

It would also appear that the lowest-order "streets"

were not the result of sound judgment by the advisory council but rather residual passageways left perhaps unclaimed, but surely unoccupied, when the *khiṭāṭ* were established. Al-Ṭabarī actually notes that these lanes sometimes ran parallel to and between the major streets *before merging with them,* which would appear to betoken a degree of irregularity in the shapes of bordering *khiṭāṭ;* a similar inference might be drawn from the unequal spacing of the main streets radiating from the *ṣaḥn.*[264] No perimeter defense was provided for nearly a century and a half.

Al-Fusṭāṭ

The Arab settlement at al-Fusṭāṭ has been treated at some length in chapter 2. Suffice it here to characterize that discussion as implying that the tribes each claimed their own *khiṭṭah* locations, apparently on some principle of priority of arrival, although chroniclers' accounts hint at certain effects of Islamic *sābiqah.* Al-Maqrīzī, in fact, notes that Īrānians who accompanied ʿAmr ibn al-ʿĀṣ on his Egyptian campaign "claimed and occupied the foot of the hill called Bāb al-Būn,"[265] while "the *khiṭṭah* of the Lakhm [tribesmen] began where al-Rāyah's ended and pushed up *(aṣʿadat)* toward the north." The same author further explains that the Banū-Wā'il, al-Qabbaḍ, Ahl al-Rāyah, and al-Rāshidah were able to lay claim to locationally more desirable *khiṭāṭ* simply because they had been among the first to arrive in the train of ʿAmr.[266] By contrast, the Ahl al-Ẓāhir acquired their sobriquet of "Outsider" when they arrived late in the settlement process, having been detained on military duty in Iskandarīyah (Alexandria), and found all more centrally situated sites already claimed. At any rate, that is al-Maqrīzī's interpretation of the name.[267]

At least one tribe, that of Mahrah, had done well for itself by occupying two *khiṭāṭ:* one at the foot of Yashkar Hill, where it resided, and the other on the *qiblah* side of the al-Rāyah *khiṭṭah,* close to the center of the cantonment within which it coralled its horses during the Friday prayers. Ultimately the Mahrah abandoned their holdings on the relatively distant Yashkar Hill and established themselves solely in the *khiṭṭah* adjoining that of the Ahl al-Rayah.[268] This last group, a collective body constituting an important unit in ʿAmr's army, initiated its *khiṭṭah* at the spot where it had camped during the siege of the fortress known as Bāb al-Ḥiṣn. Subsequently it extended its holding to Ḥammām al-Fār and westward to the Nile. According to al-Maqrīzī, "This *khiṭṭah* surrounded the *jāmiʿ* on all sides."[269]

The circumstance that a majority of those tribesmen privileged by lineage or service to the Faith were to be found in the centrally situated *khiṭṭah* of the Ahl al-Rāyah, where the *dār al-imārah* and the principal mosque were soon to be raised, tends to confirm our supposition that Islamic and tribal prestige played no inconsiderable role in the settlement process. That a formal claim followed by physical occupation connoted permanent right to a site is evident from al-Maqrīzī's tale of ʿAmr ibn al-ʿĀṣ's inability to prize a particular *khiṭṭah* from the hands of Qayṣabah ibn Kulthum even after it had been chosen as the site of the *jāmiʿ*.[270] Nor were strategic arguments sufficient to enable ʿAmr to compel the al-Jīzah tribesmen to transfer their *khiṭṭah* from the western to the eastern bank of the Nile.[271] The inescapable conclusion to be drawn from this evidence is that at al-Fusṭāṭ, as at al-Baṣrah and al-Kūfah, tribes competed among themselves for *khiṭṭah* sites within an overall scheme of settlement—and, of course, place of settlement—determined by authority of the army commander and his advisors. Al-Quḍāʿī says as much when he writes, "When ʿAmr returned from Iskandarīyah and abode in his pavilion, the tribes closed in on one another and competed for *[khiṭṭah]* sites."[272] The same author adds that ʿAmr thereupon charged a council of his senior lieutenants with responsibility for resolving disputes among tribes over *khiṭṭah* sites and boundaries,[273] an expedient clearly reminiscent of Saʿd's advisory council in al-Kūfah and the requirement of unanimity among the Companions at al-Baṣrah. Finally, it should be noted that not all *khiṭāṭ* were ethnically Arab. A thousand or so Jews, for example, occupied the *khiṭṭah* of the Banū-Rubil; and four hundred Byzantines who had converted to Islam, that of the Banu-al-Azraq. Rhuvon Guest accounted for a total of forty-nine *khiṭāṭ* at the foundation of al-Fusṭāṭ.[274]

Surviving evidence leaves little room for doubt that the tribes claimed and laid out their *khiṭāṭ* in at least mild competition with each other, although *sābiqah* distinctions within and between tribes almost certainly played their parts in the mediation processes of the arbitration councils.[275] Furthermore, there is no evidence that the layouts of these three *amṣār,* established during respites from fighting on their respective fronts, owed anything to a substantial and coherent tradition of urban design in either North or South Arabia. In the north, Makkah (Mecca) was essentially a shrine surrounded by a *ḥaram*, the population of which probably fluctuated from season to season; Yathrib was a collection of fortified clan settlements exploiting the possibilities of oasis agriculture; al-Ṭā'if was a walled shrine set amid palm groves and fields; Dūmat al-Jandal was a group of largely stone-built houses clustered around a shrine to the moon deity Wadd and protected by a stout fortress;[276] al-Khaybar was an agricultural settlement comprising a number of fortified towers *(ḥuṣūn)* occupied almost exclusively by Jewish and Hebraized tribal units;[277] and al-Qurā' was a staging post where southbound caravans from Syria and Egypt converged en route to the Ḥaramān,[278] and so on, while the south was heir to a tradition of religio-administrative centers supported by a developed agricultural (including irrigation) technology.[279]

None of these, nor indeed any other Arabian urban form, had been called upon to serve the precise politico-military role of the *amṣār;* consequently, none had evolved the relevant morphological features to any significant degree. Even al-Ḥīrah, the preeminent Arab city in the Fertile Crescent during the three centuries preceding the rise of Islam, and which probably began as a military encampment, cannot be invoked as a model for the foundation of the *amṣār,* although admittedly, the available evidence is meager.[280] Nor is it practicable to establish a meaningful connection between the *amṣār* and the older, more widely diffused urban tradition that predated Babylon, even though Professor Djaït appears to be somewhat sympathetic to such an idea in the case of al-Kūfah.[281]

Close juxtaposition of structures signifying, respectively, sacral authority and secular power within a centrally situated, ritually delimited enceinte enclosed within a cordon of residential dwellings that decline in status with distance from the city center—all followed ineluctably from the circumstance that ancient communications technology required the clustering in restricted locales of virtually all institutions providing leadership, reinforcement, and mediation in a polity. This was not only as true of the beginnings of urban life in ancient Sumer as of al-ʿIrāq or Egypt some three and a half millennia later but also held for the prevailing urban traditions in South and eastern Asia and the New World. When a suite of associated institutional features and their functional expressions in the landscape are distributed this widely through the world, they are clearly of very limited value in validating a case for cultural diffusion.

*

One of the more radical recent revisions of early Islamic urban history is Donald Whitcomb's suggestion that the *miṣr* was the standard unit of Arabo-Muslim settlement during the early Islamic period, both within and external to preexisting cities.[282] Integral to this interpretation is the further notion that the *miṣr* either in whole or in part was, typically, an orthogonally arranged form. In support of these conclusions Dr. Whitcomb can point to both archaeological and literary evidence indicating cantonment-like additions to a range of cities. Within the Levant, for example, was Ṭabarīyah (Tiberias), where recent archaeological investigation suggests a planned community established adjacent to the Sāsānian town in early Umayyad times;[283] and al-Ramlah (Ramleh), where the arrangement of eight city gates is held to imply an original orthogonal design with axial main streets intersecting in its center.[284] The situation in Ḥimṣ appears to have taken a different turn, for there the Arab levies were settled in *khiṭāṭ* throughout the city. As al-Balādhurī reports, "They were also settled in every place evacuated by its occupants and in every abandoned courtyard."[285] As it has been established that the pre-Islamic city was laid out on a predominantly orthogonal pattern, and as it is known to have capitulated peacefully to a Muslim army in 637, so that damage to the urban fabric would have been minimized, Islamic Ḥimṣ probably incorporated much of the original orthogonal design. Jābiyah is an especially interesting case of early Arabo-Muslim settlement because it comprised a huge Arab encampment replete with a Christian monastery, to which was attached a military cantonment at the time of the Battle of the Yarmūk.[286] It is our misfortune that the way in which these two encampments were integrated is completely unknown.

Whitcomb is also prepared to categorize as *amṣār* rectangular walled towns quartered by axial thoroughfares converging on tetrapylons, his particular examples being Waylah (al-ʿAqabah) at the head of the Gulf of ʿAqabah[287] and ʿAnjar in the Biqāʿ.[288] Furthermore, he has reinterpreted ceramic and stratigraphic data furnished by V. Tsaferis to suggest that Capernaum was in fact an Umayyad cantonment situated adjacent to a previously existing town.[289] Farther afield, Whitcomb invokes the establishment of a *miṣr* at al-Mawṣil (Mosul), which was essentially an Arab encampment adjacent to a Sāsānian settlement;[290] at Iṣṭakhr, where an apparently permanent, square settlement was laid out beside the important Sāsānian city of Stakhr;[291] and at Shīrāz, founded (probably in 684) close to a fortified Sāsānian administrative center, allegedly as a base for a Muslim army besieging Stakhr.[292] And he could, if he so wished, cite a substantial number of other *miṣr* and *miṣr*like settlements established by the Muslims, usually in reasonably close proximity to existing towns, during the course of their campaigns. Iṣfahān, al-Rayy (Rey), Qazwīn, Marv al-Shāhijān, al-Sūs, ʿAskar Mukram, and Wāsiṭ were archetypical examples in the Eastern Caliphate, as were Barqah and Qayrawān (Kairouan) in North Africa.[293]

Application of the term *miṣr* to such a wide spectrum of settlement forms in both time and space naturally prompts inquiry into the meaning of this word in early Islamic times. Reference has already been made to al-Maqdisī's four definitions pertaining to the tenth century, namely the judicial, lexicographical, popular, and technical usage that he employed in the *Aḥsan al-Taqāsīm.* It is evident from the examples appended to these definitions that professional sodalities and popular speech alike restricted the term to developed urban forms; in al-Maqdisī's work, to settlements that could justly be designated *metropoleis.* However, such a connotation could hardly have applied to the *amṣār* founded de novo close to certain Sāsānian foundations during Rāshidūn and early Umayyad times. In fact *M.S.R.* is an ancient Semitic root that in epigraphic South Arabic seems to have denoted a campaign force of some kind (perhaps "a raiding party" would be a more appropriate rendering).[294] At the same time, the word carried explicit overtones of a frontier location, a nuance apparent long before in Akkadian *miṣru* = border territory and Aramaic *miṣrā*ʾ = frontier, and retained by Ibn Manẓūr in the definition "military settlement on the frontier."[295] However, by the mid-eighth century the connotation of a fully developed urban center had become the dominant component of the cloudy halo of meanings surrounding the term *miṣr,* although—as al-Maqdisī attests—competing opinions were subsumed within the concept.[296] Ibn al-Muqaffaʿ (d. circa 756), for instance, included *amṣār* (together with *ajnād, thughūr,* and *kuwar)* among the subdivisions of the empire in a context that prevents them from being understood as any other than major cities,[297] while Ibn Durayd (d. 933) categorized "every large city such as al-Baṣrah, Baghdād, and al-Kūfah" as a *miṣr.*[298] Concurrently, al-Ṭabarī was unequivocally using the term to signify an at least regional capital: in his conceptualization, the seat from which an *ʿāmil* levied taxes.

In assessing the roles of the early *amṣār,* it must be remembered that the most detailed records of these settlements were given their present form only after a lapse of two centuries or so. To that extent they preserve early records as interpreted by literati working within an intellectual tradition that had come to associate the term *miṣr* with developed urban form. To what extent these authors were able to free themselves from ninth- and tenth-century perceptual biases is still a matter of debate. It is true that the notion of a frontier garrison post accords reasonably well with the image of the early Islamic *miṣr* that is dimly discernible through the refracting lens of Islamic tradition. Certainly, such settlements were established as holding bases for tribesmen between, and possibly at the conclusion of, campaigns, and consequently can be said to have performed garrison and security functions. And there is confirmation in the sources that the locations of these camps were chosen, as they had to be, with the logistics of food supply in mind: provisions for the tribesmen and provender and grazing for their animals. In view of this latter need, it should occasion no surprise that some of the largest *amṣār* were sited on the desert fringe. At the same time, segregating tribesmen in these cantonments facilitated control over their activities, thereby preventing spoliation of the surrounding countryside, and facilitated disbursements from the *dīwān.* Perhaps most important of all, the camps went far toward insulating newly converted Arabs and their dependents from the blandishments and temptations of Jews, Christians, and Magians, toward establishing the exclusivity of the Muslim community in the ethno-religious kaleidoscope of the Middle East.[299] In so doing they furnished the warriors of Islam with *dūr al-hijrah,* quintessentially Islamic refuges that enabled the fullest participation in the social and religious experiences of the *Ummah.*[300] Yet, if the Tradition is to retain any credence at all, it has to be acknowledged that by no means did all tribesmen take readily to life in the *amṣār,* a topic already touched upon in chapter 2.

The layouts of these settlements are often still matters of dispute involving both archaeological inference and textual interpretation. There are those, including Djaït, Al-Sayyad, and Whitcomb, who argue for an orthogonal framework,[301] and there are those, chiefly of an earlier generation, who see in the larger *amṣār* little other than labyrinths of lanes and alleys winding through makeshift camps.[302] The texts are inconclusive on this matter (in my reading at any rate), so that archaeology will have to be the arbiter in this matter—assuming, of course, that it ever overcomes the incubi of past destruction and present construction, which currently inhibit its progress in this area. Perhaps the question properly should be not, Were the *amṣār* laid out orthogonally? but rather, To what extent did some of them incorporate orthogonal elements? In this connection it should also be observed that orthogonality itself can manifest a variety of forms: that invoked in, say, the cases of Waylah and ʿAnjar, with their strongly developed axiality,[303] the form is fundamentally different from the reticulate grid postulated for classical Emesa (Ḥimṣ).[304]

Tentatively, I am interpreting the available evidence as implying only a weak rectangularity in those settlements actually designated as *amṣār*—in some instances involving even approximate right angles hardly at all. This expediential phrasing immediately raises the corollary question as to how widely the term *miṣr* should be applied. Is every Islamic settlement founded under the Rāshidūn and early Umayyads justifiably called a *miṣr*, or only certain of them? Was the early *miṣr* simply an instrument of administrative and/or fiscal convenience regularly resorted to by the Arabs in the wake of their conquests in alien lands? And what is an appropriate rendering of the triptote *miṣr* in English (as opposed to the diptote Miṣr = Egypt)? "Military camp" enjoyed considerable favor among Western scholars earlier in this century, as also did "garrison town." The military reference is unexceptionable: the *amṣār* were indeed army bases (although they may have had other functions as well) during and after the Muslim campaigns of conquest in southwestern Asia and North Africa. However, the word *camp* carries overtones of temporariness, or at least impermanence, that appear inappropriate to those scholars (like Djaït in the case of al-Kūfah and Whitcomb more generally) who believe that the *amṣār* were established from the beginning as potentially urban centers designed "intentionally to reconstitute the social organization of the conquered lands."[305] AlSayyad is even more specific when he writes that "ʿUmar tried to establish in Basrah and Kufah the ideal Islamic settlement."[306]

Of course, any settlement founded in the way described had to have begun as a camp of sorts, as a community of mechanical solidarity manifested in moral and social homogeneity and held together by superordinate power and authority. That was the limit achievable by caliphs and army commanders given the circumstances under which the *amṣār* were established: when they had laid out, or supervised the laying out, of a "camp" and furnished the authority to ensure its orderly functioning, they had accomplished all that was immediately possible. Only with the passage of time could these military camps be transmuted into diversified communities of organic solidarity integrated through the complementarity of functions that is characteristic of developed urban life.[307] The fact that this did indeed transpire in the cases of al-Fusṭāṭ, the ʿIrāqān, and certain other *amṣār* does not automatically resolve the question of intentionality. The Tradition has little to say about the long-term goals of the founders, concerning itself primarily with the immediate business of settlement. The consolidatory mechanisms of governance, social differentiation, economic exchange, and religious worship certainly combined over the centuries to generate some of the premier cities of Islam, but I doubt if we shall ever learn precisely what were the ultimate purposes of ʿUtbah ibn Ghazwān, Saʿd ibn Abī-Waqqāṣ, ʿAmr ibn al-ʿĀṣ, or ʿUqbah ibn Nāfiʿ al-Fihrī—or, indeed, if they thought in such terms—when they committed their troops to cantonments at al-Baṣrah, al-Kūfah, al-Fusṭāṭ, and al-Qayrawān, respectively. In despair at being unable to resolve these problems satisfactorily, I have come to favor *cantonment,* a term largely neutral as to both form and long-term intention, as the preferred rendering of *miṣr* insofar as it relates to Rāshidūn and early Umayyad times.

In attempting to place the *amṣār* in the cultural perspective of the seventh century, it should not go unremarked that sizable Arab tribal cantonments were by no means unknown in the Middle East of that time. Al-Ḥīrah has already been cited as a seasonal nomad settlement that had evolved into a polynuclear urban center serving as the capital of the Lakhmid dynasty and a permanent base for tribes of the Tanūkh federation. Another city that had grown from comparable origins was Boṣrah, which eventually became the Nabaṭaeans' northern capital and, from 106, the administrative seat of the Roman province of Arabia. ʿĀnat, on the Euphrates, was a third such city having *ḥērthā* origins.[308] It is unlikely that any of these urban developmental trajectories from the relatively distant past were in the minds of the Arabs who founded the three great *amṣār.* They may well have been cognizant, however, of more recent encampments of this type in Ghassān territory. There, in 542, Theodore, an Arab monk from the monastery of Pesīlota on Mount Izala, was consecrated Bishop of the Encampments *(ḥirtāt).*[309] The principal cantonment was the previously mentioned Jābiyah in the Jawlan, which featured a shrine dedicated to Mār Sarjis; but there were others at Jillīq in the Ghūṭah and at Ṣaydah, just east of Uḍruḥ. These, as well as an undetermined number of similar settlements, clearly encompassed permanent structures and fortified towers *(quṣūr),* and some also sheltered lineage tombs.[310] Encampments of apparently similar functions but known by the technical term *ḥāḍir* were to be found on the outskirts of Emesa (Ḥimṣ), Antioch (Anṭākiyah), Chalkis (Qinnasrīn), and probably elsewhere in northern Syria.[311] Of the last named, al-Balādhurī notes, "It had been inhabited by the Tanūkh since they first arrived in al-Shām and pitched their tents there. Subsequently they built houses."[312]

Finally, more or less permanent nomad encampments designated as *parembolai*[313] in the relevant sources were scattered fairly widely through the Levant. One of the first of these was established under the aegis of the anchorite Euthymius in the Wādī al-Zarāʿah toward the mid-fifth century. In its heyday it comprised a church, a bishop's residence (it was the seat of the Diocese of the Parembolai and for a time the capital of a small phylarchate), and some two hundred houses for an estimated fifteen hundred people, all surrounded by a wall some four or five feet high. The number of wells attested outside the wall has led excavators to infer that the majority of the population were seasonal residents who pitched tents outside the cantonment proper.[314] Among the other settlements that at one time or another were designated *parembolai* was Tema in the Hawrān, which figured in a Greek inscription: στρατ[ηγ]ὸς παρε[μ]βολῶν [ν]ομάδω[ν].[315] What is more, if the Book of Acts is to be believed, such an institution existed in close proximity to the temple in Jerusalem as early as the first century A.D.[316] Camps such as these were certainly known to many seventh-century Arabs, and it is tempting to speculate on the influence they may have exerted on the form and function of the *amṣār.* If such questions are ever to be answered, it will most probably be by archaeology or, less likely, by a reevaluation of texts.

In any case, evidence abounds for the evolution of *amṣār,* regardless of their founders' intention, into fully developed urban forms—among them some of the premier cities of the Islamic world. More often, however, Muslim cantonments planted near pasture and water resources adjacent to preexisting urban centers were eventually assimilated into those cities, thereby reinforcing rather than restructuring the hierarchy.

Palatine Complexes

The earlier caliphs had established their governments in or very close to existing urban centers. The first three Rāshidūn caliphs followed Muḥammad in ruling from al-Madīnah (Medina), but the fourth, ʿAlī, felt sufficiently threatened in the Ḥijāz to transfer his residence to al-Kūfah, founded nearly a score of years previously in Lower Mesopotamia. A few years later Muʿāwiyah, who had already governed Syria for twenty years, transformed Damascus from a regional capital to the imperial seat of the Umayyad dynasty; and so it continued until the ʿAbbāsid victory in 749.

Although Abū Muslim, architect of the ʿAbbāsid uprising in Khurāsān, had located his headquarters at Marv al-Shāhijān, the city near which the last Sāsānian ruler had perished; and although al-Saffāḥ, founder of the ʿAbbāsid line, had adopted first al-Kūfah and then Anbār as his capital, the ʿAbbāsids initiated a practice that would become almost standard among rulers not only in the Eastern Caliphate but also in North Africa from the eighth to the eleventh centuries: the construction of large architectural assemblages combining the principal administrative agencies of government with imposing caliphal residences. Customarily these palatine complexes were situated in relatively poorly populated locales, and almost without exception outside existing cities so as to distance their residents from turbulent urban factions. Although at its inception such a complex was far from being an organically functioning city but simply a center of imperial or regional administration, the service and craft industries attracted to its purlieus or compelled to locate there almost inevitably would eventually stimulate the socially consolidatory processes requisite for full urban status. In the case of imperial capitals, palatine complexes were the cynosures toward which were channelled the redistributive and mobilizative resources of their kingdoms, making them the primary symbols of their rulers' *dawlah* and renown as well as the ultimate standard for material prodigality and intellectual achievement alike.

Baghdād

The archetype of all such palatine complexes was that raised by the caliph al-Manṣūr on the west bank of the Tigris near the village of Baghdād.[317] Known familiarly as the Round City *(al-Mudawwarah),* its official name in documents and on coins and *ṭirāz* was Madīnat al-Salām ("City of Peace"), apparently in recognition of the Paradise invoked in *Sūrah* 6 of the Qur'ān.[318] The layout and development of the complex have been sketched in chapter 2; suffice it here to note that the presumed site of the Round City has never been formally excavated, so that the details of its plan and architectural execution have to be based exclusively on literary records.[319] Unfortunately, these are fragmentary, often ambivalent, and sometimes uncritical of their sources, to the extent that Jacob Lassner, the scholar who has contributed most to our understanding of these matters, can characterize the task of reconstructing the Round City as "highly theoretical and very speculative."[320] The sources are in agreement, though, that the foundations were laid at a precise time in 762–63 (A.H. 145) chosen by Nawbakht, one of al-Manṣūr's court astrologers. Both skilled and unskilled labor was imported from—according to al-Ṭabarī[321]—Syria, al-Mawṣil (Mosul), al-Jabal, al-Kūfah, Wāsiṭ, and al-Baṣrah, with al-Yaʿqūbī estimating the total number of workers in excess of one hundred thousand (probably an exaggeration).[322] Although the caliph seems to have taken up residence in the royal precinct in 765, construction almost certainly continued until 766–77.

Lassner distinguishes three functionally distinct architectural components in the Round City as constructed to the orders of al-Manṣūr: outer fortifications in the form of two concentric walls separated by an interval *(faṣīl)* and surrounded by a moat; an interior residential zone of symmetrically arranged streets inhabited by government functionaries, the caliph's immediate family, and palace servants;[323] and a huge inner domain *(raḥbah)* containing the caliphal residence *(Qaṣr al-Dhahab)* and mosque. In Lassner's reconstruction these features were integrated into an eponymous circular design featuring four equidistant gateways (fig. 20). The whole complex, with a diameter of about two thousand meters, was built of mud bricks and baked bricks.[324] It was protected from the depredations of hostile troops not only by its walls but more importantly by a network of interlinked waterways—including the Tigris, at some distance the Euphrates, and a series of canals—at the same time that it clearly benefited from the centripetalizing influence of these waterways and the commodities travelling over them. Al-Manṣūr's likening of his great administrative center to an island between the Tigris to the east and the Euphrates to the west (strictly the canals connecting it to the Euphrates) is almost certainly apocryphal, but as an illustrative trope is true enough.[325] However, the claim by the Khaṭīb al-Baghdādī and al-Yaʿqūbī that no other circular city was known anywhere in the world was false.[326] In fact cities having circular, or at least elliptical, plans had existed even in parts of the Middle East since Assyrian times, chiefly in an arc of territory extending from eastern Asia Minor to western Īrān.[327]

It is not immediately apparent why the Round City of al-Manṣūr should have been modelled on any one of these earlier ones. And a further point needs to be made: Madīnat al-Salām was designed as a center of imperial administration, not as an organically functioning city, and should not be compared with such. Some scholars have thought they saw in its design the lineaments of the old Asiatic *uranopoleis* that from time immemorial had been constructed as reduced models of the cosmos, thereby ensuring harmony between the planes of existence.[328] Of this I have found no evidence. It is true, of course, that ʿAbbāsid court ritual owed something to venerable Īrānian traditions, but certain vaguely realized morphological similarities between the Round City and the ideal-typical *uranopolis* in no way imply an identity of functions and institutions. Even though some components of this ancient system of cosmological relationships are

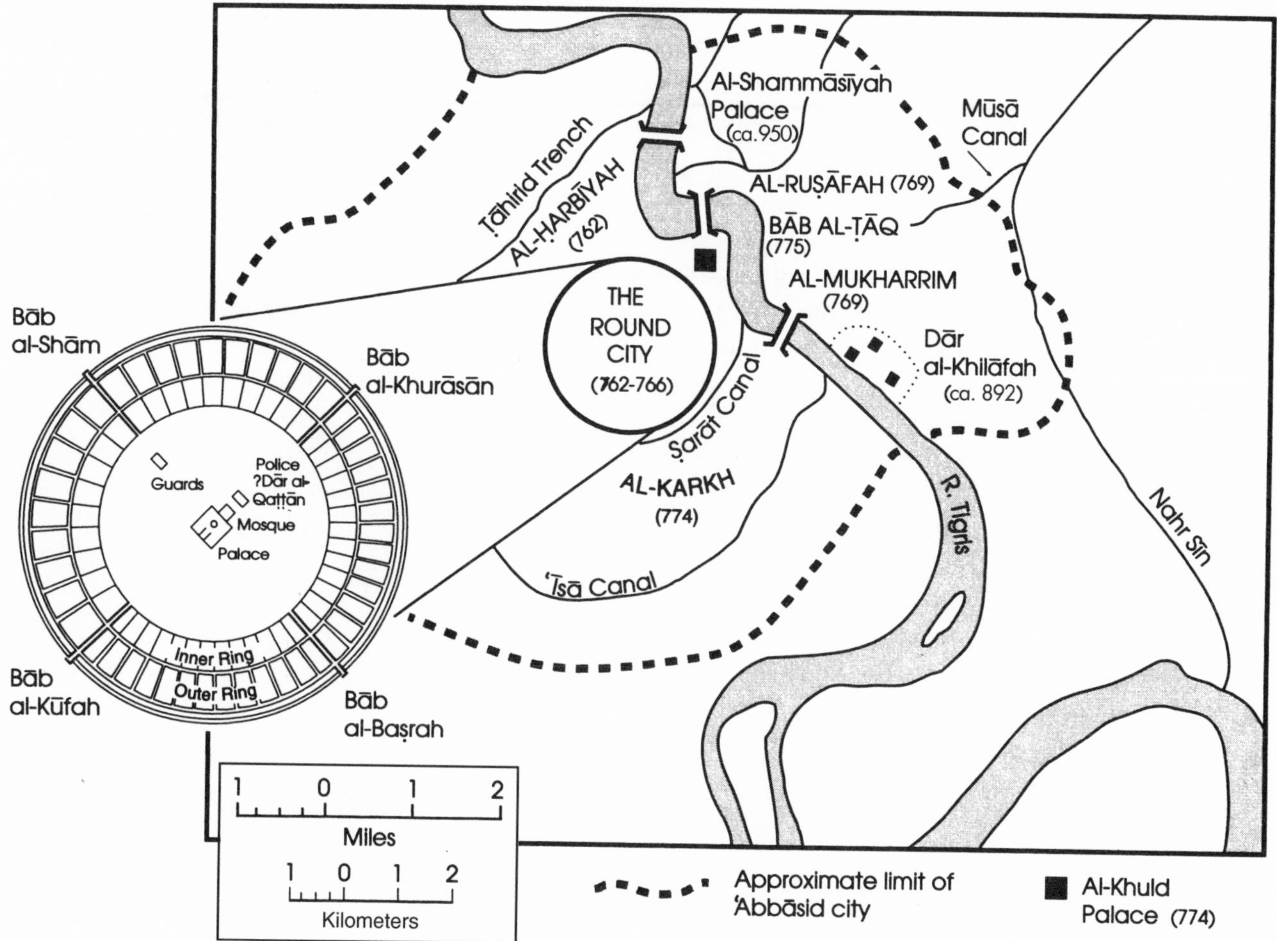

Figure 20. The chronological development of Baghdād to the end of the tenth century. Adapted from Jacob Lassner, *The Shaping of ʿAbbāsid Rule* (Princeton, N.J., 1980), 186–87.

represented in Muslim *ḥadīth* literature, none to my knowledge was ever incorporated in the actual planning of an Islamic city, and neither was the associated technical terminology apparent in either the official or other nomenclature of Madīnat al-Salām—or any other Islamic city, for that matter. I am inclined to take Muḥammad ibn Khalaf, Wakīʿ at his word when he asserts that al-Manṣur built his administrative enclave in circular form so that, ensconced in his centrally situated palace, he would be equally distant from all sectors of the complex, in the interests of efficiency.[329] Perhaps the caliph was also aware of the economies in construction costs that would be likely to accrue to a circular design. In any case, the Round City presented a dramatic expression of the centralized rule that al-Manṣūr was desperately seeking to institutionalize.

Our constant cicerone in matters concerning Madīnat al-Salām is Jacob Lassner, who is also the only modern author so bold as to castigate the planning of Baghdād, including the Round City, as a "conspicuous failure."[330] Further, he brings to light the irony that the exceptionally rapid growth of both the Round City and its surrounding cordons of settlement generated the economic forces that finally subverted the original design.[331] This is not to imply, though, that the conceptualization of the Round City contained no flaws, which, incidentally, the sources attribute to the caliph himself. To begin with, the sheer size of the enclave raised formidable problems of security.[332] The circumstance that trade and industry were excluded from the precinct altogether and only limited access permitted to the residential sectors created difficulties in the victualling and servicing of the palace complex, soon necessitating the presence of *sūqs* within the ambit of the Round City. When these came to be perceived as a possible threat to palace security, the inner plaza was forbidden to all but pedestrian traffic and the markets relocated to sectors of the large, vaulted arcades (*ṭāqāt al-kubrā;* see fig. 21) once serving as barracks for palace guards. Finally, in 774, when it had become evident that the *al-sūqah* was still too close for caliphal comfort, especially when the *muḥtasib* was implicated in a seditious conspiracy,[333] the markets were transferred clear out of the Round City to the suburb of al-Karkh. When the situation of the principal mosque adjacent to the Qaṣr al-Dhahab brought an influx of possible undesirables into the near neighborhood of the caliph for the mandatory prayer service every Friday, al-Manṣūr built a second mosque in al-Karkh, a suburb about which more will be said shortly. There are also hints in the sources that the water supply within the central enclosure was not entirely satisfactory;[334] and then there was always the likelihood that, although external forces might have difficulty breaking into the inner sancta of the Round City, the caliph might encounter equally severe hazards in escaping from what was in fact a giant cul-de-sac.

For a few years relatively minor adjustments were made in attempts to combine security with administrative and logistical efficiency,[335] but ultimately, in 775, al-Manṣūr forsook the Round City in favor of the newly constructed but magnificently appointed Palace of Eternity *(Qaṣr al-Khuld)* on the banks of the Tigris beyond the Khurāsān Gate. Here he would be almost as insulated from the populace at large as he had been in the Round City, with the added benefits of a large security force nearby and, as a last resort, ready access to the walled enclave of the Round City. At the same time, al-Manṣūr was building the splendid palace complex later known as al-Ruṣāfah[336] still farther north on the other side of the Tigris, which was crossed at this point by a pontoon bridge. In 776 the heir apparent al-Mahdī entered into residence there, and subsequent caliphs down to al-Muʿtaṣim (r. 833–42) spent at least part of their time in this palace. But the removal of the caliphs to palaces in the northeast-

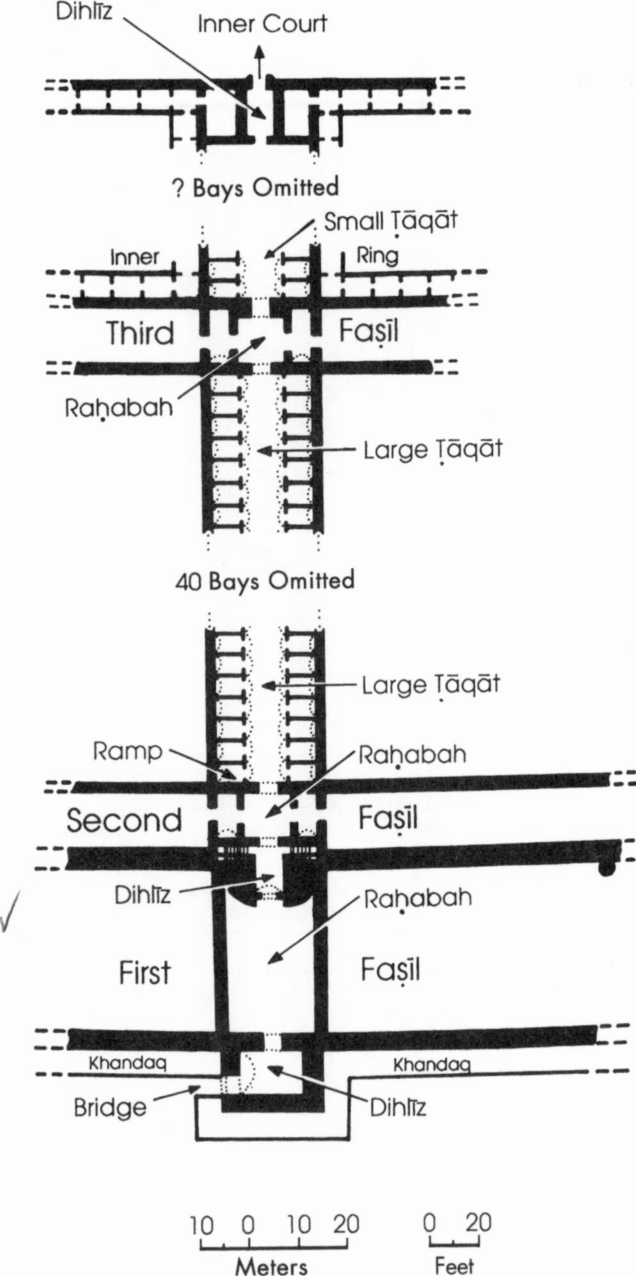

Figure 21. Large arcades *(ṭāqāt al-kubrā)* and a gate complex in the Round City. After Jacob Lassner, *The Shaping of ʿAbbāsid Rule* (Princeton, N.J., 1980), 191.

ern sector of the developing city signified more than the tightening of security and a general strengthening of defenses on the river side: it transformed the very nature of the government sector from a unitary and localized precinct to a congeries of caliphal residences and military cantonments occupying extensive sites on both sides of the Tigris. From this time onward the Round City lost its importance, and by 800 had fallen into disrepair.

The sheer size of the Round City becomes apparent not only in the morphological extent of the complex but also in its developmental sequence and the rate of growth of its peripheral settlements. Several villages already existed in the locality where al-Manṣūr was to build his governmental complex, including Baghdād and al-Karkh, the latter of which seems to have been the site of a district fair.[337] But population was sparse until al-Manṣūr assembled the massive labor force mentioned earlier. One need not accept al-Yaʿqūbī's estimate of one hundred thousand to concede that this workforce constituted the population of a very large city by the standards of the time, implying in turn that many artisans and laborers had to be housed in close proximity to the site even while the Round City was under construction. Presumably, many of them ran up quasi-permanent shelters not fundamentally different from the spontaneous settlements—shantytowns, as they are often called—that encrust the fringes of numerous present-day Middle Eastern cities. It is thought that they tended to cluster in the neighborhood of al-Karkh, which they appear to have soon transformed from a village into a sizable suburb south of the Round City between the Ṣarāt and ʿĪsā Canals. Military personnel of all ranks in the Khurāsānī army, by contrast, were quartered on a tract of land northwest of the Round City known as al-Ḥarbīyah.[338] There they were settled in territorial and tribal groups, each under the jurisdiction of a military *(qāʾid)* and a civilian *(raʾīs)* official.[339] Subsequently other army commanders were settled amid their troops *(wa bayna al-qaṭāʾiʿ manāzil al-jund)*[340] beyond the Tigris to the northeast, that is, in the vicinity of al-Ruṣāfah. Nor did these personnel exhaust the roster of what Lassner has called "a military presence of staggering variety and dimensions,"[341] involving not only regular army units but also the caliph's palace guard, police, and various auxiliary levies.

Running in an arc to the south of the Round City, Rabaḍ al-Karkh prospered as the principal market in the rapidly growing settlement, initially owing to al-Manṣūr's transference thither of the markets formerly housed in the arcades of his administrative complex. Within the new *sūq* the shops were arranged in rows *(ṣufūf)* according to the particular type of establishment.[342] As part of a program to develop the whole area between the Ṣarāt and ʿĪsā waterways in the interests of enhanced security, some sources have al-Manṣūr letting the shops rent free, a policy reversed by al-Mahdī in 783.[343] Other important markets included the Sūq al-Thalāthāʾ,[344] serving the upper-class residential communities in the southern sectors of the Mukharrim; and the Sūq al-ʿAṭash, catering to the needs of the Bāb al-Ṭāq.[345] In time this latter became the principal *sūq* on the east side of the river, worthy to be ranked with al-Karkh in the west.

By the beginning of the tenth century agglomerative tendencies generated by a concentration of power in the shape of palaces for rulers, their families, and their high ministers had spawned an extent of urban real estate vaster than had been experienced anywhere else in the Islamic world—at its maximum in the first half of the tenth century, probably as much as eight and one-half by just more than seven kilometers.[346] But this sprawling aggregation of population did not constitute a unitary city whose institutions were arranged in a prevailingly hierarchical configuration: instead it was an agglomeration of semi- and quasi-autonomous districts, localities, precincts, enclaves, and architectural complexes brought into being at different times by both authoritative intent and accidents of history. As such it conformed fairly closely to the type of polynuclear urban region that Patrick Geddes some twelve hundred years later would term a conurbation.[347]

At the very heart of the dynamism of the city were the palaces and *dīwāns* of the ruling classes. The Qaṣr al-Dhahab, Qaṣr al-Khuld, and al-Ruṣāfah have already been mentioned. To them may be added al-Mahdī's pleasure palace *(mustaqirrah)* of ʿĪsābādh;[348] the magnificent Qaṣr Ḥasanī, originally built by the Barmakid *wazīr* Jaʿfar ibn Yaḥyāʾ but which eventually became the residence of al-Maʾmūn's father-in-law and the center of a group of caliphal palaces, including two constructed by al-Maʾmūn in the district of Mukharrim and al-Muʿtaṣim's original palace;[349] the Qarār Palace, which provided a home for Hārūn al-Rashīd's widow Zubaydah; Qaṣr al-Tāj on the bank of the Tigris, begun by al-Muʿtaḍid but completed by al-Muktafī; two miles to the east the Qaṣr al-Thurayyā, one of the group mentioned above, which were built and adapted by ʿAbbāsid caliphs after the dynasty had returned to Baghdād from Sāmarrā, and which came to be known collectively as the Residence of the Caliphate *(Dār al-Khilāfah);* the Shammāsīyah Palace, to which the Buwayhid Muʿizz al-Dawlah brought seven iron doors from the old Round City; and the former residence of the chamberlain Sebuktigin in the upper Mukharrim, which Muʿizz converted into the Dār al-Imārah of the Buwayhids.

Also in the city were many other such princely residences, whose names, and sometimes sites, can be culled from the relevant sources.[350] Yet despite their numbers, it is no simple matter to delimit precisely the specifically governmental foci within the city, that is, to discriminate between sites of administrative and military functions on the one hand and those supporting civilian populations and their private activities on the other. Under al-Manṣūr and al-Mahdī the primary divide seems to have been the Ṣarāt Canal, which separated the Round City and the cantonments of the imperial army in al-Ḥarbīyah on the north from the great suburb of al-Karhk to the south. However, even in these early years government functions were being located beyond the Tigris, eventually extending from al-Ruṣāfah south to the Dār al-Khilāfah. In short, government and administration tended to take place in an arc curving around the northern edge of the Round City, with an extension northward beyond the Khandaq Ṭāhir (Ṭāhirid Trench) in the shape of al-Zubaydīyah (named for Zubaydah, who quartered her servants there) and which much later was occupied by the caliph al-Muqtadir.[351]

The remainder of the greater urban area consisted mainly of a mosaic of semiautonomous neighborhoods differentiated from one another by history, ethnicity, occupation, and location relative to caliphal political strategy.[352] A fairly strong indicator of the composite character of the city was the number of its cathedral mosques, each of which was held to signify a substantial degree of administrative autonomy. In the first half of the tenth century al-Iṣṭakhrī listed three such mosques, all associated with caliphal palaces: specifically Madīnat al-Manṣūr, al-Ruṣāfah, and the Dār al-Khilāfah.[353] Later in that century, however, at least three new cathedral mosques were added. One was at Barāthā, a district bordering the Nahr ʿĪsā in the vicinity of al-Muḥawwal, which apparently lay outside the city limits as understood by Ibn Ḥanbal and presumably therefore was entitled to claim a cathedral mosque as an autonomous settlement. Such a mosque did, in fact, exist there until the caliphate of al-Muqtadir, when it was destroyed in reprisal for Shīʿite sedition. However, it was rebuilt under al-Rāḍī (r. 934–40) and reconstituted as a principal mosque by al-Mattaqī in 941.[354] A second *masjid al-jāmiʿ* was established in the fief of Umm Jaʿfar on the ground that the holding was a *balad* in its own right;[355] a third was set up in the Ḥarbīyah. As this last district constituted part of the city proper, for a quarter of a century it was denied permission to build a cathedral mosque. Finally, in 993 the caliph al-Qādir Billāh, on the advice of his jurists, sanctioned the establishment of such a principal mosque.[356] A sizable number of lesser mosques were scattered throughout the urban area, but it was the restricted roster of principal mosques that testified most strongly to the fragmented administrative structure of what may be appropriately termed Greater Baghdād.

The rest of the urban area comprised a network of grudgingly interdependent institutions and localities bound by a compelling desire to share in the wealth of the empire. Markets were everywhere: from the acres of producer-retailers in al-Karkh and Bāb al-Ṭāq, through the *sūqs* in al-Ḥarbīyah,[357] to the neighborhood markets that sprang up wherever there seemed to be an opportunity for profit, intruding themselves into and between residential units at any level of status or occupation. Even within the princely residences, producer-retailers were to be found practicing the noble trades to serve the needs of a luxury-loving élite. Representative of these different ranks in the market hierarchy were the Sūq al-ʿAtash,[358] the principal market serving the upper east side of the city (that is, mainly al-Mukharrim) as Sūq al-Thalāthāʾ served the lower east side; Sūq al-ʿAtīqah ("The Old Market"), originally known as Sūq Baghdād; one food market known as *Sūq al-Maʾkul* on the east side[359] and another in al-Karkh known as *Sūq al-Ṭaʿām;* the Market of the Pack Animals; the Market of the Fodder Merchants *(ʿAl-lāfīn);* the Lamb Market; the Slave Market; the Butchers' Market *(Sūq al-Qaṣṣābīn);* the Clothes Merchants' Market *(Sūq al-Bazzāzīn);* the Cobblers' Market *(Sūq al-Kharrāzīn);* the Market of the Flour Merchants *(Sūq al-Sawwāqīn);* the Market of the Reed Weavers *(Aṣḥāb al-Qaṣab);* and the Market of the Soap Makers *(Aṣḥāb al-Ṣābūn).* The neighborhood markets traditionally referred to as *suwayqāt* have already been mentioned. Clearly these were, generally speaking and as their name implies, initially small and served restricted, sometimes specialized clientele. Reasonably typical of this level of retailing were the Sūqs of al-ʿAbbāsah in the Murkharrim; ʿAbd al-Wahhāb on the Ṣarāt Canal opposite the Kūfah Gate;[360] ʿAbd al-Wāḥid ibn Ibrāhīm in al-Khuwarizmīyah close to the site of the Round City; Abū al-Ward[361] and Ḥajjāj al-Waṣīf, both clients of al-Mahdī; al-Haytham ibn Shu ʿbah ibn Zuhayr, a client of al-Manṣūr; Khuḍayr, a client of the Khurāsānī Ṣāliḥ Ṣāḥib al-Muṣallā, "who sold jars there";[362] and the *wazīr,* Abū ʿUbayd Allāh ibn Yāsar al-Ashʿarī in the Mukharrim Quarter. The Dār al-Baṭṭīkh ("The Melon House") was a fruit market strategically situated at the junction of the Nahr ʿĪsā and the Nahr Tābaq.[363]

Residential construction subsuming all types of housing, from palace to villa to townhouse to hovel, was the principal occupier of urban space. A significant part of this development was initiated as early as the caliphate of al-Manṣūr. The fairgrounds of al-Karkh received a powerful boost when in 774 the markets of the Round City were transferred to that place and a second congregational mosque built in the already developing suburb. Al-Yaʿqūbī tells us that in his day the quarter comprised a maze of *sūq*s covering an area of some two by one *farsakh*s. Within each *sūq,* types of retailing were kept separate, and "no craft practised outside its designated location."[364] The Khaṭīb cites a statement by ʿUmar al-Wāqidī, who had died in 822, to the effect that the whole district was "infested with the lowest rabble," but then hastens to interpret this remark as referring to the Rāfiḍites who inhabited certain neighborhoods rather than to, say, footloose vagrants of the type known in the tenth century as Banū-Sāsān.[365]

Concurrently, originally discrete nuclei of settlement on the west side were becoming fused by the interstitial building of barracks and civilian housing. Also during this time, the siting of imperial and less-exalted palaces on the east side induced comparable developments there, particularly during the caliphates of al-Muʿtaḍid, al-Muktafī, and al-Muqtadīr (892–932). It should be noted, moreover, that al-Karkh was developed at least in part with funds provided by the caliph al-Manṣūr.[366] According to al-Yaʿqūbī, implementation of the project, which appears to have involved virtually the entire south side of the city, was entrusted to the triumvirate of al-Musayyab ibn Zuhayr, al-Manṣūr's client al-Rabīʿ, and ʿImrān ibn al-Waḍḍāḥ—that is, as Lassner aptly reminds us, a military officer ensured security, a government official supervised financial expenditures, and an appropriately qualified artificer provided technical expertise.[367]

Caliphal investment of this magnitude not only paid off handsomely in revenues—allegedly twelve million *dirham*s annually from the property tax on markets at the end of the ninth century[368]—but also encouraged other members of the establishment to follow suit. Among the numerous fiefs recorded by al-Yaʿqūbi and the Khaṭīb al-Baghdādī, it is remarkable how many were designated as *sūq*s or *suwayqah*s, presumably implying that retailing had at some time proved to be an attractive proposition on the site.[369] And in and around these suburbs, which were seamed with a network of canals, were the support services generated by a great city, notably small mosques, cemeteries, and bathhouses (sing. *ḥammām*). Of these last, al-Yaʿqūbī reports that in the time of al-Manṣūr already as many as five thousand existed on the east side and ten thousand on the west.[370] By the first half of the tenth century, a figure of twenty-seven thousand was being quoted;[371] by the middle of that century, sixty thousand.[372] All these figures were surely exaggerated, even though they apparently included small baths in private houses.[373] What is clear, though, is that the numbers declined precipitously under the Buwayhids, almost as if the count had been restricted to larger public baths. By 992, for instance, there were allegedly only fifteen hundred.

The distribution of cemeteries also changed dramatically during the first four centuries of Islam.[374] At the founding of the Round City a burial ground was placed outside each of the four gates. In subsequent centuries the oldest cemetery in all Baghdād was held to be that outside the Damascus Gate, where a group of distinguished scholars, traditionists, and jurists were buried. East of the Baṣrah Gate was the Bāb al-Dayr (Convent Gate) Cemetery, which boasted of the tomb of the venerated Maʿrūf al-Karkhī, who died in 815–16. The Syrian Gate Cemetery became the resting place of prestigious descendants of ʿAlī ibn Abī Ṭālib and of Ibn Ḥanbal (founder of the rite that bears his name) and along the way became known as the Qurashī Cemetery. Lassner has suggested that the Khaṭīb's rather confusing account of this cemetery should be understood to imply that it was in fact but one component in a complex of burial grounds extending all along the northern border of the city.[375] There were others as well, but the Khaṭīb doubtless spoke for an important segment of the population when he repeated a tale in which the graves of four Saints of God (Ibn Ḥanbal, Maʿrūf al-Karkhī, Bishr al-Ḥāfī, and Manṣūr ibn ʿAmmār), "a bulwark for the inhabitants of Baghdād against all misfortunes," were held to compensate for the wholesale corruption within the city.[376]

A possibly unanticipated feature of the urban landscape was the number of infirmaries scattered around the city. The oldest was founded by Hārūn al-Rashīd on the west side, inspired by and partly staffed from the medical school at Jundaysābūr, an institution that long antedated the coming of Islam. A second was established in the Mukharrim district during the caliphate of al-Muʿtaḍid (892–902), marking the beginning of a spate of foundations during the tenth century: by al-Muqtadir's *wazīr* ʿAlī ibn ʿĪsā in al-Ḥarbīyah in 914; a large institution by Sinān ibn Thābit in 918 on the east side, which became known as Bīmāristān al-Sayyidah, and also that year by the same benefactor, a smaller one called the Māristān al-Muqtadirī at the Damascus Gate; and in 924 yet another at Darb al-Mufaḍḍal by the *wazīr* Abū al-Ḥasan ibn al-Furāt.[377] Al-Maqdisī[378] also mentions an infirmary established by ʿAḍud al-Dawlah. These infirmaries were truly eleemosynary foundations, funded by *waqfs* established by wealthy individuals, and as such were distributed throughout the urban area where they were most needed. Among all urban institutions, the infirmaries appear to have been the ones least tied locationally to centers of power.

Independent as the aforementioned urban units might like to think they were, they were nevertheless knit together by circulation networks, not only of streets (sing. *darb*) and alleys (sing. *sikkah*)[379] but also of waterways.[380] As settlement spread to the east bank of the Tigris, pontoon bridges (sing. *jisr*) came to play an ever more important role in the life of the city, these being the structures most readily adaptable to vagaries in the flow of the river. A comparison of not always unambiguous surviving sources seems to imply there were either four or five such bridges across the Tigris until the time of al-Maʾmūn (r. 813–33), but thereafter probably only three.[381] Elsewhere in the city, masonry bridges (sing. *qanṭarah*) were by no means uncommon, as attested by the following half-dozen examples culled from a list of more than twenty surviving names: Qanṭarat Abū al-Jawn, Bāb Ḥarb, al-Bustān, al-Maʿbadī, al-Rūmīyah, and al-Ushnān. But in addition to its multifunctional waterways, the urban area was well supplied with wells, so that the entire population in normal times drank reasonably fresh water. In fact al-Yaʿqūbī reports that at the end of the ninth century,

> The inhabitants had such an abundance of water that they were able to grow palms brought from al-Baṣrah. This is the reason why palm groves are more evident in Baghdād than in al-Baṣrah, al-Kūfah, or in the Sawād. Several different types of trees are planted there which produce fruit of the highest quality. Orchards and gardens have multiplied throughout the suburbs of Baghdād as a result of the quantity and quality of its water.[382]

Lassner may have been correct in asserting that urban planning in Baghdād was a conspicuous failure,[383] but only if by Baghdād is meant essentially the governmental and administrative enclave as the Khaṭīb would have us believe Ibn Ḥanbal had defined it.[384] As we have seen, the Round City incorporated certain fundamental design flaws that prevented it ever functioning with full effectiveness and that ultimately ensured its abandonment; but that was not the case on the east bank of the Tigris, especially on the upper east side in the neighborhood of the bazaar (that is, small-business) neighborhoods of Bāb al-Ṭāq and al-Mukharrim; nor did it hold for the vast, commercially focused districts constituting the suburb of al-Karkh. Moreover, it would be futile to deny the success of Baghdād not only as a regional center for the lower Diyālah plain but also as a metropolis of empire, a reflex of political and economic power deployed on a vast scale, and seat of the ruler whose function it was to protect and nurture the very legacy of the Prophet.

That in its golden age during the late eighth and the ninth centuries the city was for Muslims the cultural and intellectual capital of the world is amply attested by contemporary authors, but nowhere is the specifically Islamic perception of Baghdād exemplified more graphically than in accounts of the reception of Byzantine ambassadors in

918 as preserved by several medieval authorities.[385] These accounts are neither wholly in agreement among themselves nor internally consistent, but the gist of their reports seems to be that the ambassadors were conducted from the Shammāsīyah Gate by way of the riverbank to the Dār al-Khilāfah, and then lodged in the palace of Ṣāʿid ibn Makhlad. According to the Khaṭīb, "The *sūqs* on the east side of the city, together with its boulevards, streets *(maslak),* and rooftops, were crowded with watching people. All the shops and balconies had been rented for exorbitant sums." On the Tigris, boats of all sorts were tastefully decorated and drawn up in order.

During a period of waiting of uncertain length determined by protocol before the envoys were granted an interview with the caliph al-Muqtadir, they were introduced to the wonders of the city, including the palace of the *wazīr* Ibn al-Furāt and the Khān al-Khayl (Cavalry Post), a peristyle court where five hundred horses with gold and silver saddles were drawn up opposite five hundred with brocade saddlecloths, each in the charge of a lavishly attired groom. These dignitaries were also shown the zoological park, which featured one hundred lions along with four elephants caparisoned in brocade and silk, and the Jawsaq al-Muḥdith (New Villa), boasting an artificial pond of white lead "more lustrous than polished silver," on the surface of which floated four boats adorned with Dabīqī brocades and covered with gold work, the whole being set amid four hundred date palms bearing exquisitely luscious fruit.

When the ambassadors were finally granted an audience with the caliph, they found no less than 160,000 troops lining the route all the way from the palace of Ṣāʿid to the Dar al-Khilāfah. In or on their way to the Tāj Palace, they visited twenty-three other palaces, including the Qaṣr al-Firdaws (where ten thousand gold breastplates were hung in the corridors); a connecting passage housing ten thousand pieces of armor in the form of shields, helmets, casques, cuirasses, coats of mail, ornamented quivers, and bows, and with two thousand white and black servants in attendance; and the Tree Room *(Dār al-Shajarah),* with an artificial tree whose gold and silver birds were set in motion by the breeze. Even more eye-catching was the hydraulically operated automaton in al-Muqtadir's throne room in which whistling silver birds perched on a silver tree emerging from within a cupola.

Special care was taken to render the caliphal palace overwhelmingly impressive in its magnificence. The chamberlains, together with their staffs, and the servants were ranged by rank along the gates, corridors, passageways, courts, and audience rooms.[386] Altogether, thirty-eight thousand curtains from Baṣinnā, Armenia, Wāsiṭ, Bahnasā, and Dabīq were displayed in al-Muqtadir's palaces, together with twenty-two thousand rugs and carpets from Jahram, Dārabjird, and Dawraq (not including "the carpets from Ṭabaristān and Dabīq in alcoves and audience halls which were to be seen but not walked upon"). Finally, and climacterically, the ambassadors were admitted to the presence of al-Muqtadir, seated on an ebony throne covered with gold-embroidered Dabīqī cloth. Suspended to the right of the throne were nine necklaces in the form of rosaries, and on the left seven providing settings for exceptionally fine jewels, "the largest of which eclipsed the daylight with its brightness." Before the caliph sat five of his sons. And there is a good deal more in this vein, all of which, our authors assure us, astonished and amazed the ambassadors. Although these accounts were written by Muslims, there are reasons to believe that they embody only pardonable hyperbole. Baghdād was certainly one of the two or three largest urban agglomerations in the world, was indisputably the equal of any in science and the arts, and was governed by one of the most powerful rulers on the face of the earth. This was the way in which Baghdādians viewed themselves not only in their heyday but also for several centuries subsequently,[387] and it was this aura of a culturally resonant and economically vibrant metropolis that eventually provided the backdrop for the tales of the *Thousand and One Nights.*[388]

This was Baghdād in its prime. In the tenth century, however, the balance of forces guaranteeing the prosperity of the city began to change. The dissolution of the empire, with serious dissidence first manifesting itself in the Mediterranean borderlands and subsequently in the eastern territories, subverted the centripetally directed redistributive and mobilizative flows supporting the imperial capital. The symbolism of a unitary community on a grand scale that the city was designed to project could not compensate for this loss of wealth, and Baghdād began to revert to being a regional capital.[389] At the same time, its regional underpinnings were being jeopardized by seemingly endless series of civil disturbances. From 896 onward, when the populace revolted against the exactions of the black eunuchs, constant uprisings demolished huge tracts of the built-up area. In 905 associations known as *ʿayyārūn*[390] were ruling the streets of al-Karkh. By the end of the tenth century they were wreaking damage throughout the city: robbing and looting, terrorizing the inhabitants, setting fires, and extorting money from merchants. The caliph no longer had the power to arbitrate disputes between urban factions, and certainly not to mediate the bitter conflicts between Sunnī and Shīʿī that were especially frequent between 925 and 940. Then in 949 Sunnī vigilantes sacked the Karkh suburb where Shīʿī sectaries were commemorating the death of the martyr al-Ḥusayn; and there were equally violent clashes in 957 and 959. There were also street battles between rival military contingents as early as 924 while Turk and Daylamī mercenaries, recruiting partisans from among the lower classes, pillaged virtually at will.[391]

This rending of the social fabric was facilitated, if not encouraged, by a prevailing disconnectedness among urban institutions. Where corporate collectivities were either wholly absent or at best only poorly developed,[392] centralization of power was achieved most effectively through the manipulation of alliances and patron-client relationships. When these were disrupted, control of the city devolved on local leaders, with whom central governments had no choice but to cooperate. This is more or less what was happening during the first half of the tenth century; but the disintegrating effects of social disorder, military incursions, and urban banditry were exacerbated by successions of natural disasters such as recurring floods of the Tigris, fires, and famines.[393] It must be emphasized, however, that the decline of the once-great metropolis, "the most beautiful possession of the Muslims," as al-Maqdisī calls it,[394] was not measured in a regular contraction of its boundaries nor in a uniform deterioration of its neighborhoods. It was as if the social fabric of the city were being rent asunder by socioeconomic forces that neither caliph nor military, religious, or local leaders could control, and which visited destruction unequally throughout the urban environment. Even when some of the quarters surrounded themselves with protective walls, it did not save them from destruction. For example, Ibn Ḥawqal, referring to a time toward the middle of the tenth century, mentions a zone some five miles long that had been abandoned and the buildings destroyed. Then he adds for good measure, "Most of the neighborhoods have fallen into decay."[395] At the same time, because of a lack of traffic and a need for expensive repairs, one of the two bridges leading across the Tigris to Bāb al-Ṭūq had been closed. Yet through all the social upheavals, the caliphal palaces, isolated within their lofty walls, survived as islands of sumptuous living, inordinate extravagance, and cultural exclusiveness, even though their taste may not always commend itself to the present age.

Beginning in 979 Aḍud al-Dawlah made a serious effort to stem the decline. He commanded that the houses and streets that arson and demolition had reduced to piles of rubble be rebuilt (with the assistance of treasury loans, if necessary), that the mosques be refurbished and their eleemosynary services re-funded, that silted feeder canals throughout the city be cleared, and that bridges be repaired, especially the main Baghdād Bridge across the Tigris, which was broadened to the width of a main road and provided with railings. But, apart from the social-service aspect of the mosques, Aḍud al-Dawlah focused almost exclusively on architectural and engineering renovations rather than on the structural disjunctions undermining the social fabric of the city. Toward the end of the tenth century al-Maqdisī's prognosis was pessimistic; by the earlier decades of the thirteenth century he had been proved right: the city was almost literally splitting apart, even while new suburbs were being added from time to time on its outer fringes. Already by the end of the eleventh century certain quarters were characterized as ruins *(kharabāt)*, and in 1225 Yāqūt noted that no less a formerly thriving inner-city district than al-Ḥarbīyah had become for all intents and purposes a separate, walled urban center, with its own *sūqs* and cathedral mosque, at some distance from the Baghdād of his day.[396]

Sāmarrā

Sāmarrā was a huge administrative complex nearly eighty miles higher up the Tigris that from 836–92 served eight caliphs as the ʿAbbāsid imperial capital. In principle the morphology of this settlement followed the pattern established in Baghdād, in which a line of caliphs successively sought to isolate themselves from their subjects and armies by retreating within the confines of ever more extravagantly furnished palaces; but, contrary to what happened in Baghdād, they do not seem to have invested at all heavily in the development of adjacent urban districts.

Unlike Baghdād, Sāmarrā has received a good deal of archaeological attention and, in fact, still persists into the modern world in the form of extensive ruins, with some (especially in the northern sectors) so well preserved as to reveal their general plan without resort to excavation.[397]

Extant historical sources unanimously attribute the migration of the ʿAbbāsid court to Sāmarrā to al-Muʿtaṣim's desire to circumvent recurrent conflicts between his Turkish regiments and the population of Baghdād. His first architectural essay, situated on the east bank of the Tigris, was the palace and governmental enclave known variously to annalists as Surra Man Raʾā, Dār al-Khilāfah, Dār al-Sulṭān, and Dār Amīr al-Muʿminīn. Within this complex al-Jawsaq al-Khāqānī was the residence of the caliphs and their families, while the Dār al-ʿĀmmah was the administrative center where the caliph sat in audience on Monday and Thursday of each week.[398] The preparatory work is reminiscent of that undertaken for al-Manṣūr's Round City in Baghdād:

> The Caliph [al-Muʿtaṣim] issued a written order to assemble workmen, masons, those with special skills, blacksmiths, carpenters, and other artisans, and to import all sorts of wood, especially teak, together with palm trunks from al-Baṣrah and its neighborhood, even from Baghdād and the Sawād, and from Anṭākiyah and all the Syrian littoral. He also recruited experts in the cutting and laying of marble[399] and opened marble workshops in Lādhiqīyah and some other cities.[400]

The principal avenue of the settlement extended southward for some three and one-half kilometers to the cathedral mosque and the main *sūq*. To the west of this axis lay the cantonment of the Turk Waṣīf; to the west that of the Maghāribah, a military unit thought to have been of Egyptian origin; and to the north of the Jawsaq that of Khāqān ʿUrtuj. Two other such cantonments were established well outside the main enclave, specifically that of the Ushrūsānīyah at Maṭīrah to the south and that of the Turkish *jund* in al-Karkh to the north—both, so al-Yaʿqūbī informs us, well removed from the *sūqs* of this last cantonment:

> When Ashnās al-Turkī and his followers were enfeoffed with a holding called al-Karkh in the far west of the built-up area . . . he was ordered not to allow strangers, whether merchants or others, to live among them nor to permit his troops to consort with non-Arab Muslims *(al-muwalladūn)*. . . . Between [the locality known as] al-Dūr (= the Houses) and other holdings, mosques and baths were built for their use, and in each locality there was established a small market *(suwayqah)* comprising shops of corn dealers *(al-fāmīyīn)*,[401] butchers *(qaṣṣābīn)*, and such like selling basic goods that could not be done without.[402]

It was actually the building of a splendid new palace designated al-Hārūnīyah by al-Muʿtaṣim's successor al-Wāthiq that encouraged the perception of the settlement as a permanent foundation rather than—as it was often called—a ʿAskar al-Muʿtaṣim, and which thereby stimulated parallel undertakings by Muslim grantees. During the first decade of al-Mutawakkil's caliphate (847–57), Surra Man Raʾā reached its greatest extent. A new congregational mosque, built between 849 and 851, and as many as twenty palaces, costing between 250 and 300 million *dirhams*, are listed among that caliph's architectural projects by various sources. Prominent among the latter were al-Iṣṭabulāt, seemingly a palace that also housed perhaps as many as thirty thousand to forty thousand men-at-arms, situated twelve and one-half kilometers south of the main caliphal enclave;[403] and Balkuwārā,[404] a palace set on the edge of the cantonment occupied by a newly formed army commanded by al-Muʿtazz, al-Mutawakkil's second son.[405] It was some six kilometers south of Surra Man Raʾā. Building densities generally were lower in Sāmarrā than in Baghdād, so that individual houses tended to be more spacious—or so al-Yaʿqūbī believed.[406]

Evidently, despite the ad hoc character of the building pattern—in which a variety of street grids each reflected the orientation of a palace or other distinguished residence, thereby imparting to the settlement plan a markedly disjunctive appearance—by about 855 Surra Man Raʾā was beginning to nurture certain consolidatory societal processes that promised to transform the mechanical integration of its original units into the organic interrelatedness of a truly urban center. As many as seven parallel avenues transected the built-up area,[407] at least two of which facilitated communication throughout the whole length of the cantonments. The one closest to the Tigris, the Shāriʿ al-Khalīj, afforded access to quays used by the riverboats providing inhabitants with luxuries and staples alike. In the northwestern sector were the caliph's stables, the slave market, the police station, the principal prison, and the main *sūq*, which had developed around the mosque of al-Muʿtaṣim. All markets incorporated the principle of segregation by profession already in operation in Baghdād. It would seem likely, though, that the *suwayqāt* established by authority in the cantonments were redistribution outlets, or at least partially redistributive in function, rather than wholly autonomous markets. In the far south of the complex was the tax registry *(Dīwān al-Kharāj al-Aʿẓam)*, to the east three horse-racing courses,[408] and "in a walled enclosure on a spacious plain" the caliph's menagerie.

It can only be a matter for speculation how far the urbanization process might ultimately have progressed, for in 859 al-Mutawakkil undertook construction of a new administrative complex that would be designated as Madīnat al-Mutawakkilīyah on its coinage and as both al-Jaʿfarīyah and al-Māḥūzah in literary sources.[409] The new foundation lay to the north of al-Karkh at the head of an inlet known as the Qāṭūl al-Kisrawī. Al-Yaʿqūbī reports that al-Mutawakkil "assigned *qaṭāʾiʿ* in the neighborhood to his heirs, his other children, his commanders and secretaries, his troops, and the populace collectively,"[410] and transferred the *dīwān*s of government there from Surra Man Raʾā.[411] His own palace, the Jaʿfarīyah, was situated some two kilometers north of the main settlement, the whole assemblage being strung along a spinal avenue of unusual width (one hundred meters). Again relying on al-Yaʿqūbī: "Buildings succeeded one another without interruption [southward] from the Jaʿfarīyah to the locality known as Dūr, then on to al-Karkh and Surra Man Raʾā, and as far as the district where the caliph's son Abū Allāh al-Muʿtazz was living [that is, the Balkuwārā]. For all that distance there were no empty spaces, vacant lots, nor places devoid of buildings. The total distance could be as much as 7 *farsakhs*." And, as al-Yaʿqūbī was led to exclaim: "It was all done in about a year."[412] Markets were established in unoccupied spaces, but they were also located at each crossroads and in each residential district. As in the Round City of Baghdād, al-Mutawakkil's palace complex evidently accommodated not only the caliph's family but also the principal instruments of his government. However, when al-Mutawakkil was assassinated in 861, the Jaʿfarī palace was abandoned and the building materials shipped to Baghdād.

The total area involved at one time or another, and often continuously, in the great Sāmarrān enterprise measured some thirty-five by five kilometers. It comprised an elongated agglomeration of large, mostly enclosed palaces, each adjacent to holdings of retainers and troops arranged as rectangular grids. Although service institutions such as markets and baths together with adjuncts of caliphal splendor such as racecourses and game parks were interspersed among the fiefs, the predominant impression conveyed by aerial photographs of the ruin field is one of an overwhelming military presence. In fact Alastair Northedge has characterized the site as "the last and best preserved of the Iraqi garrison cities."[413] Of course, when comparing Sāmarrā to Baghdād it must be remembered that the former functioned as a seat of imperial government for only little more than half a century, whereas we have followed the urbanization of Baghdād for nearly five times as long. Who is to say what organic societal interactions would have developed in Sāmarrā over an equal span of time? As it turned out, political instability and military unrest led to the withdrawal of the army from the cantonments during the 870s, while in 892 difficult communications and a prevailingly inadequate water supply finally persuaded al-Muʿtaḍid to restore the seat of government to Baghdād. In view of the enormous expenditures required to manifest adequately the glories of eight caliphs; the maintenance of harmonious relations between troops and civilian residents not being finally resolved; the extraordinary, elongated form of the settlement; and the caliphs' eventual abandonment of the site, it is difficult to dissent from J. M. Rogers's characterization of Sāmarrā as "an act of folly on a vast scale."[414] However, the site was not abandoned entirely with the departure of al-Muʾtaḍid: some of the *sūq*s continued to function, and certain of the former population nodes such as al-Karkh and al-Maṭīrah retained a considerable proportion of their inhabitants. But it is not without relevance that in 903 the Jawsaq Palace was nothing but a ruin. From the tenth century onward, Sāmarrā became best known as a pilgrimage center where the Shīʿī *imāms* ʿAlī al-Hādī (d. 868) and al-Ḥasan al-ʿAskarī (d. 874) were buried close to the soteriologically sanctified site, first accentuated architecturally by the Ḥamdānid Nāṣir al-Dawlah in 944, where the twelfth *imām* had occulted.

A final, perhaps unexpected comment: there is no

reason to suppose that the establishment of a rival capital ever seriously detracted from the prosperity of Baghdād. The wharfs bordering the Tigris in Sāmarrā accommodated vessels from—in al-Yaʿqūbī's enumeration—Baghdād, Wāsiṭ, Kaskar and the rest of the Sawād, al-Baṣrah, al-Ubullah, al-Ahwāz and adjacent regions; al-Mawṣil (Mosul), Baʿarbāyā, and Diyār Rabīʿah and its vicinity,[415] but there was an equally large number of boats, some from even greater distances, loading and unloading cargoes on the quays in Baghdād. At the hub of an empire that at its greatest extent reached one-fifth of the way around the world, there was more than enough trade to support two major ports. In any case, even under conditions of severe competition, Baghdād would have benefited enormously both from the momentum of some seventy years of prior economic growth and from its superior accessibility by river and canal. Moreover, some of its more highly specialized markets appear not to have been duplicated in Sāmarrā—or so al-Yaʿqūbī believed.[416] He further implies that the communities that were emerging virtually continuously between Baghdād and Sāmarrā for some reason benefited the former more than the latter. But the primary distinction between the two capitals was that over the two and a half centuries with which we are concerned, Baghdād developed a range of urban functions appropriate to an imperial city, whereas Sāmarrā remained to the end of its half century essentially an aggregate of military cantonments featuring only inchoate integrative institutions.[417] Modish and recherché though his sentiments might be, Abū al-Faḍl ibn al-ʿAmīd, the great prose stylist and *wazīr* to Rukn al-Dawlah, would never have propounded the literary conceit of measuring a man's intellect by his appreciation of Sāmarrā, as he did readily enough in the case of Baghdād.[418]

Al-Qāhirah

A third great palatine complex deserving placement in the first rank of such foundations not only in the Middle East of its day but in the contemporary world at large was al-Qāhirah (Cairo). When the Fāṭimid caliph al-Muʿizz ordered his general Jawhar al-Ṣiqillī to lay out an Ismāʿīlī ritual palace at the head of the Nile Delta, he was opting for a locality that could look back on a long line of politically, ritually, and commercially important settlements, of which ancient Memphis and Heliopolis (ʿAyn Shams) are probably the best known.[419] In the Islamic period the foundation of al-Fusṭāṭ has already been treated in some detail; its transmutation into an organically functioning metropolis was sketched in chapter 15. However, on the fall of the Umayyads, the ʿAbbāsid governor of the province established a new military cantonment, al-ʿAskar, a short distance northeast of al-Fusṭāṭ, perhaps partially in response to a fire that had destroyed extensive tracts of that city.[420]

The enclave initially comprised a governor's palace surrounded by barracks and residences of certain notables, and from 785 a mosque erected by the *amīr* al-Faḍl ibn ʿAlī. Its streets ran predominantly from east to west, and it ultimately came to support a range of service institutions such as infirmaries, a police force, night patrols, market inspectors, and a taxation system. Although the cantonment was interdicted to the public at large, several reasonably sized *sūqs* were established within its confines, presumably catering only or mainly to residents, but it is uncertain whether they arose spontaneously or were mandated by authority. Certainly the Qubbat al-Hawā ("Dome of the Air"), a pleasure resort on a spur of the Muqaṭṭam, was built at the initiative of an ʿAbbāsid governor circa 810. In any case, al-ʿAskar remained the seat of government in Egypt for roughly a century, isolated and for the most part remote from the uprisings and revolts of Copts and Muslim schizmatics that bedevilled Egyptian administration during that time. It is of no little significance for an understanding of the Miṣrī urban hierarchy, though, that al-Fusṭāṭ continued to expand and prosper throughout al-ʿAskar's century. It is obvious where economic, as opposed to political, power still resided.

When Ibn Ṭūlūn consolidated his rule over Egypt in 868, he sought to symbolize his regime by constructing on the site of abandoned Christian and Jewish cemeteries on the Jabal Yashkūr a new capital worthy to rank in splendor with the palace complexes he had known as a youth in Sāmarrā, where his father had held high office. In fact his new foundation, called al-Qaṭāʾiʿ ("The Wards"), was modelled on Sāmarrā, even to the name[421] and in some instances the architecture. In addition to a splendid palace far surpassing anything of the kind existing in al-Fusṭāṭ,[422] at the very beginning of the enterprise Ibn Ṭūlūn built the magnificent mosque bearing his name; its ornament was an amalgam of the three styles employed at Sāmarrā. This structure can be properly characterized as an "ʿIrāqī building planted down on the soil of Egypt,"[423] almost certainly implying the presence of ʿIrāqī craftsmen on the Jabal Yashkūr between 876 and 880.

The cantonment was originally laid out over a grid of one thousand wards within an area of one square mile. Markets were instituted at various locations within the enceinte, and a large area was reserved for military exercises, parades, horse racing, and polo. In addition, entire districts were devoted to the growth of fodder crops for the huge complex of Ṭūlūnid stables. Especially worthy of note is the first large infirmary in Islamic Egypt, which was founded in 873 and reserved exclusively for civilians. Nor were ʿIrāqī artisans the only foreigners in the settlement. Large sections of the army were composed of Turks, Byzantine mercenaries, Nubian infantry, and *badū* allies while Ibn Ṭūlūn's son and successor, Khumārawayh, instituted a special corps of black Africans. Al-Maqrīzī reports that when they marched in review in their black turbans and black tunics, they created the effect of "a swelling ocean of blackness."[424] It should not go unremarked, though, that most officials not involved in the routine of the palace continued to reside in al-Fusṭāṭ, which remained much larger and more populous in addition to being the economic capital of Egypt.

For the thirty-seven years of their dynasty, the Ṭūlūnids funnelled resources into al-Qaṭīʾiʿ, mostly acquired as loot from pharaonic tombs and as spoils from their foreign campaigns. But in 905 the ʿAbbāsids exacted their revenge by razing the palace complex. Al-Fusṭāṭ also suffered severely but recovered within a few years; its *sūqs* reclaimed whatever business they may have lost to al-Qaṭāʾiʿ. With the reinstatement of an ʿAbbāsid governor, al-ʿAskar was once again constituted as the seat of government, but the times were unpropitious. After a Berber army dispatched by the Fāṭimids of Qayrawān (Kairouan) brought chaos to the Nile Delta, dissatisfaction became rife in the army, and a contest for the governorship threatened civil war. However, in 935 another Turkish dynasty, the Ikhshīdids, ushered in more than three decades of relatively peaceful development, manifested in, among other projects, the construction of Kāfūr's Palace[425] and the replacement of the shipyard at Rawḍah by a larger one on the Nile opposite al-Fusṭāṭ.

Then in 969 the settlement cycle began all over again when the Fāṭimids, fresh from their conquest of the Delta, laid out a fortified palace enclosure, specified as twelve hundred yards square, some two miles north of al-Fusṭāṭ (fig. 22). The complex was said to have exhibited not only the basic layout but also the architectural style of the previous Fāṭimid capital of al-Manṣūrīyah, and for the first four years of its existence was known by the same honorific. Only with the arrival of al-Muʿizz in 973 was the name formally changed to al-Qāhirah ("The Victorious") in commemoration of the Fāṭimid triumph or, as some sources prefer to express it, to counteract the unpropitious aspect of the planet Mars *(Qāhir al-Aflāk)* when the first mattocks had bitten into the earth some four years previously.[426] Of the purpose of the construction Ibn Duqmāq leaves us in no doubt: Jawhar al-Ṣiqillī built the palatine complex "to ensure that al-Muʿizz, his companions and his troops were separated from the general public"[427]—a sentiment that would have applied equally to the Round City of Baghdād or Surra Man Raʾā.

The Great Eastern Palace occupied the central sector of the enclave and a smaller Western Palace for the *ḥarīm* was added subsequently. In 970 Jawhar laid the foundations to the south of the palaces of the Mosque of al-Qāhirah, which would become known throughout the Islamic world as the al-Azhar Mosque; the first Friday prayer was held there on 7 Ramadān 361/972.[428] Between the two palaces stretched a parade ground, known appropriately to our sources as Bayn al-Qaṣrayn, where ten thousand guardsmen could be deployed at one time. The perimeter wall was also aptly named al-Maḥrūsah ("The Guarded"), for entrance was by permit only and even ambassadors had to be escorted in on foot by guards. The principal street, which was also the main processional way, ran clear across the enclave from the Bāb al-Futūḥ and the Bāb al-Naṣr in the north to the Bāb Zuwaylah in the south, whence it continued as the main commercial artery of al-Fusṭāṭ. The rest of the space within the walls was taken up by precincts *(ḥārāt)* inhabited by grant holders and various ethnic divisions of the army, among them Kutāmah and Qarwānī Berbers, Kurds, Turks, Persians, and Masmūdī blacks. It is noticeable, though, that al-Muʿizz quartered his Sūdānī troops at ʿAyn Shams (Heliopolis), well to the north, presumably to minimize the likelihood of ethnic frictions. On the bank of the Nile to

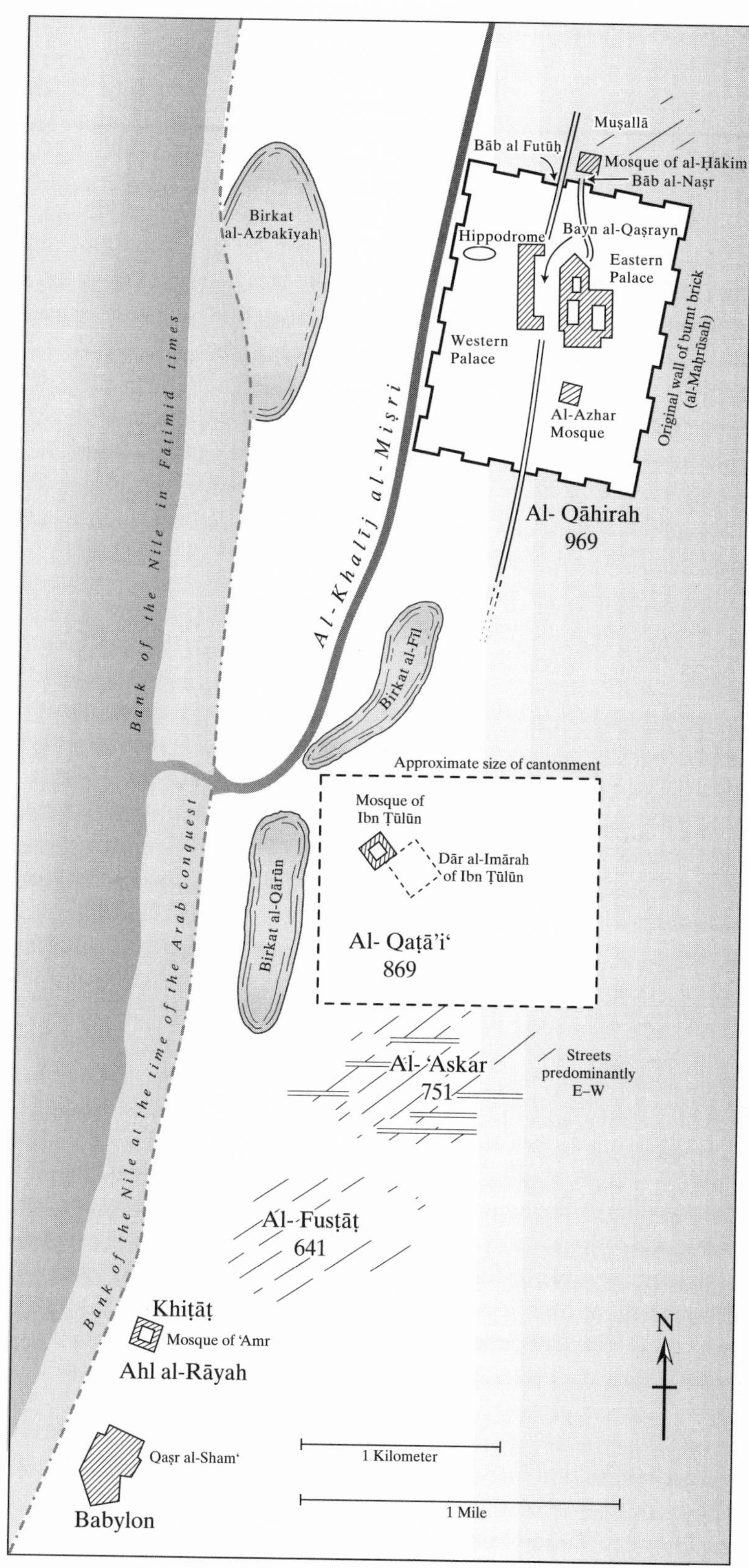

Figure 22. The chronological development of the Fusṭāṭ-al-Qāhirah (Cairo) conurbation from the seventh to the tenth century.

the west a new shipyard was constructed which in a short time had built six hundred vessels.

Curiously, no account of the early days of the settlement mentions *sūqs*. Was this an accident of historiography? Or were supplies brought in wholly from outside, which seems a priori unlikely? Or were there redistributive centers not recognized as true markets by virtue of their function or deemed unworthy of mention by reason of their size? At all events it is evident that al-Qāhirah was originally intended as a residence for the ruler with accommodations for his officers of state and his troops, not as a fully developed urban form. However, with the passage of time, the aggregative power of the palace complex attracted a large peripheral population. This was already apparent in the caliphates of al-ʿAzīz (975–96) and al-Ḥākim (996–1021), but it is equally clear that the caliph kept socioeconomic developments under tight control. As late as the mid-eleventh century Nāṣir-i Khusraw testified that

> there are no less than 20,000 shops in al-Qāhirah, all belonging to the Sulṭān. Many shops are rented for as much as 10 *dīnārs* a month, and none for less than 2. There are numerous caravanserais, bathhouses, and other public buildings—all the property of the Sulṭān, for no one owns any property other than houses and what he himself builds. I heard that in New Qāhirah and Old Qāhirah there are 8,000 buildings belonging to the Sulṭān that are on lease, with rents collected monthly. They are leased and rented on tenancy-at-will, and no sort of coercion is employed.[429]

Then Nāṣir added,

> In the midst of the houses in the city are gardens and orchards watered by wells. In the Sulṭān's *ḥarīm* are the most beautiful girls imaginable. Waterwheels have been constructed to irrigate these gardens. Trees have been planted and pleasure parks built even on the roofs. At the time I was there, a house on a lot 20 × 12 ells was being rented for 15 *dīnars* a month. The house was four storeys tall, three of which were rented out. . . . These houses are so magnificent and fine that one might suppose they were made of jewels rather than plaster, tile, and stone. All the houses in al-Qāhirah are built separate from one another, so that no one's trees or outbuildings abut on anyone else's walls. Consequently, whenever anyone needs to, he can open the walls of his house and add to it, since it inconveniences no one.[430]

Most of the institutional integration that would eventually constitute al-Qāhirah as one of the premier *metropoleis* of Islam took place after the period with which we are concerned. At the end of the tenth century it was still very much a palace complex designed to isolate and protect the caliph while yet projecting the greatness of the *Ummah* as epitomized by the ruler. There was an important respect, however, in which al-Qāhirah differed from either Baghdād or Sāmarrā: it was conceived and made to function as an Ismāʿīlī ritual enclave. As a result, the growth of the settlement was intimately related to elaboration of its ceremonial, with transformations in the signification system encoded in the cityscape initiating semantic modifications in discursive fields both ideological and political and, of course, vice versa. The intertextuality of these signifying systems for the whole of the Fāṭimid period has been explicated with great sensitivity by Paula Sanders:[431] here only a few introductory comments will be offered, bearing in mind that the major elaborations of both city fabric and ideology occurred subsequent to the period covered by this book, notably in the twelfth century, when court ceremonies had evolved a complex urban language. This is not to deny, though, that certain of the fundamentals of Fāṭimid ceremonial were manifest in al-Qāhirah from the beginning, not infrequently having been brought from North Africa.

Although ʿAbbāsid and Fāṭimid insignia and ceremonial shared a good deal in common, both asserting claims to political and religious leadership of the *Ummah* and proclaiming the relative ranks of caliphal appointees, they differed in the urban and processional character of the latter. Whereas ʿAbbāsid caliphal ceremonies tended to be static and restricted almost entirely to a palace milieu, the Fāṭimids constructed al-Qāhirah as an Ismāʿīlī ritual artifact capable of virtually endless reinterpretation as societal change might prescribe. At the root of all such protocols was the *imām*, "the terrestrial incarnation of the universal intellect, the first principle emanating from the Creator Himself."[432] Al-Muʿizz had bound his dynasty indissolubly to his new foundation by transporting the coffins of the first three Fāṭimid *imāms* across the North African desert from al-Manṣūrīyah to the Great Eastern Palace, where their joint mausoleum became known as the Tomb of al-Muʿizz *(al-Turbah al-Muʿizzīyah)* or the Saffron Tomb *(Turbat al-Zaʿfarān)*. But the palace was not only the physical setting for the luminosity of the *imāms,* both past and present: it was also the repository of the spiritual knowledge *(ʿilm)* and books *(kutub)* entrusted to them. The celebrated Fāṭimid library was, in fact, a symbol of the spiritual authority of the *imāms* and the palace a specially privileged venue for dissemination of knowledge, primarily through the medium of lectures.

It has to be emphasized, though, that the palace originally did not exercise administrative functions. Even after the founding of al-Qāhirah, government continued to be focused in the Mosque of ʿAmr[433] in al-Fusṭāṭ and the Mosque of Ibn Ṭūlūn, one of the few structures to have survived the ʿAbbāsid destruction of al-Qaṭāʾiʿ. The public treasury *(bayt al-māl),* for instance, was housed in the former building. Furthermore, the Mosque of ʿAmr continued to play a ritual and ceremonial role for all communities within the composite settlement of Fusṭāṭ-Qāhirah, including to a limited extent the Copts. In this connection it is significant that when Jawhar reached Egypt in 969 he and his troops had held their first Friday service not in the larger Mosque of Ibn Ṭūlūn, the administrative focus for al-Fusṭāṭ, but in the older, smaller, cramped Mosque of ʿAmr at the very heart of Egyptian economic and commercial life.[434] In al-Qāhirah itself, most ritual celebrations took place in the open prayer ground *(muṣallā)* reserved by Jawhar just outside the Victory Gate *(Bāb al-Naṣr)* as early as Ramaḍān 969. In fact the northern sector of al-Qāhirah became the ritual center of the evolving city, linked physically and liturgically to the palace when in 990 al-ʿAzīz rode in state between his residence and the *muṣallā* outside the north wall for the festival prayer; unbroken lines of Ismāʿīlī devotees sacralized the route by reciting the *takbīr* along its whole length.[435]

During his two decades of rule (975–96), al-ʿAzīz accomplished a good deal else to increase the density of the ritual landscape, including construction of a mosque outside the Gate of Conquest *(Bāb al-Futūḥ)* that would come to be known as the Mosque of al-Ḥākim. In so doing he established the ritual unity of al-Qāhirah in specifically Ismāʿīlī terms. Equally significant was al-Ḥākim's formal integration of al-Fusṭāṭ into the Fāṭimid ritual capital at the very beginning of the eleventh century, even though the former remained morphologically separate and distinct. By architectural trope and ceremonial protocol he succeeded in consolidating several locationally and functionally discrete settlements into a single, unitary ritual city, the stage on which Fāṭimid political and religious dramas would be enacted for nearly two centuries.[436] It is unlikely, though, that the settlements were viewed by their inhabitants as a unified city much before the time of Ṣalāḥ al-Dīn (r. 1169–93).

Mention of al-Fusṭāṭ is a reminder that that city appears not to have suffered egregiously in economic competition with the dynastic capitals instituted seriatim to the north. Virtually every commentator on it highlighted its commercial prosperity. Ibn Ḥawqal, writing in 978, praised its fine *sūqs* and its brick houses of five, six, or even seven storeys, each of which might accommodate as many as two hundred persons. The same author thought that the city was about one-third the areal extent of Baghdād.[437] Al-Masʿūdī in 956 wrote that

> [a]ll the kingdoms of the Two Seas[438] which border the country (Miṣr) bring to this emporium all the most unusual, the rarest and the finest perfumes, spices, drugs, jewels, and slaves, as well as staples of food and drink, and all kinds of cloth.

And he finished with the confident assertion that "The merchandise of the entire universe flows to this market."[439] Both al-ʿAskar and al-Qaṭāʾiʿ, by contrast, were fading from the landscape. By the end of the tenth century they served only as sources of building materials for use in al-Qāhirah or al-Fusṭāṭ.[440] Of the once impressive palace complex at al-Qaṭāʾiʿ only the cathedral mosque survived intact, around which a few descendants of Ibn Ṭūlūn's soldiery conjured but faint echoes of that glorious past.

Qurṭubah

There were numerous other palatine foundations scattered through the Islamic world, but none is as well documented as the three already discussed, and certainly none offers the archaeological rewards potentially attainable at Sāmarrā. One of these for which there is a good deal of extant information is Madīnat al-Zahrā', built some four miles to the west of Qurṭubah (Córdoba) by the Umayyad caliph Abd al-Raḥmān III and his successors over a period of twenty-five years in the mid-tenth century. Occupying about one hundred acres and at one time reportedly employing fourteen thousand servants of one sort or another, this palace complex was a visual projection of the power of the Spanish Umayyads at the same time as it affirmed their cultural preeminence. A much later author preserves a more or less contemporary estimate that ten thousand workmen and eighteen hundred pack animals were daily engaged in its construction, which cost the very large sum of three hundred thousand *dīnārs*.[441] Marble pillars were brought from as far afield as Carthage and Asfāqus (Sfax); the ceiling of the throne room was of alabaster and gold, and one of the palace roofs was of silver and gold tiles. Pools of quicksilver, automata, elaborate pictures of birds and animals, translucent alabaster windows, and jewelled doors were all reminiscent of certain of the palaces of Baghdād, as indeed is Ibn al-ʿArabī's account of the reception accorded Byzantine ambassadors to the Umayyad court.[442] And, like the caliphal palaces of Baghdād, Sāmarrā, and al-Qāhirah (Cairo), Madinat al-Zahrā' insulated the ruler from the population at large at the same time that it attracted communities of artisans and tradesmen to its periphery, encouraged—as we have seen—by subventions authorized by the caliph himself.

Where this complex differed most conspicuously from those others was in the relative preponderance of its pleasance aspects at the expense of military and administrative functions. Palaces, pavilions, mosques, baths, workshops, and barracks can all be documented, but military cantonments on the scale of those in Baghdād and Sāmarrā were not in evidence. It is noteworthy, moreover, that the central secretariat remained in the Umayyad palace in Qurṭubah until 981, when a more inclusive governmental precinct was established (see below). Of course, the architectural expression of Ismāʿīlī ritual that distinguished al-Qāhirah was entirely absent in al-Zahrā'. There was one feature, however, common to all these foundations, namely a dense and circuitous architectural plan that served to isolate and thereby emphasize the awesome power of the caliph, whose very remoteness imparted an aura of mystery to an already impressive ceremonial image. And in al-Zahrā' gardens were everywhere, both within the enclave and around its periphery. In fact it was the striking contrast of the white palaces nestled amid the dark foliage of these gardens that led an Arab poet to liken Madīnat al-Zahrā' to "a concubine in the arms of a black eunuch."[443]

But neither the splendors and extravagances nor the very real cultural achievements and amenities of al-Zahrā' could ensure its future, and in 981 the regent of Hishām II al-Mu'ayyad laid out to the east of Qurṭubah a new palatine complex, styled al-Madīnah al-Zāhirah, to which were transferred the caliphal court and, on this occasion, the central secretariat as well. Although al-Zahrā' was sacked and al-Zāhirah razed during a Berber revolt in 1013, they both figured prominently in the evocative image of Qurṭubah transmitted to succeeding generations, making the city, in one often quoted encomium, "the highest of the high, the furthest of the far, the place of the standard, the mother of towns, the abode of the good and godly, the homeland of wisdom, its beginning and its end; the heart of the land, the fount of science, the dome of Islam, the seat of the *imām;* the home of right reasoning, the garden of the fruits of ideas," and so forth.[444]

Fās and Other Maghribī Complexes

The Idrīsids certainly established two neighboring cities at ***Fās*** (Fez), but details of their intentions and of the institutional and spatial structures of the foundations are meager until the third quarter of the tenth century, when the Spanish Umayyads overthrew that dynasty. Not until the second half of the eleventh century were the twin cities brought within a single, continuous rampart. Throughout this period there were no explicit indications of luxurious pleasances isolated from the populace at large that characterized the palatine complexes already described. Available evidence leaves rather the impression of two initially administrative centers, both surrounded by residential sectors for ethnically diverse inhabitants, service institutions, and—after the founding of prestigious mosques in the two enclaves—powerful religious functions stemming from the ruling dynasts' privileged positions as descendants of the Prophet's grandsons.[445] Only in 1276 did a Marīnid *sulṭān* lay out on the periphery of Fās a walled enceinte encompassing palaces, *diwāns*, elite residences, an elegant mosque, and barracks for the palace guard, the whole complex being known at the time as the White

City *(al-Madīnah al-Bayḍah).* Market exchange was only poorly developed in the new complex, where it seems to have operated mainly through minor distributive outlets, but flourished in the old city. It is evident enough that the White City was functionally analogous to the palatine complexes discussed above, but it falls well outside the temporal limits of the present study and need not be particularized here.[446]

Other dynastic seats in the Maghrib that yet lacked the isolation and material prodigality manifested by, say, the Round City of Baghdād or al-Qāhirah included the two Aghlabid foundations of ***al-ʿAbbāsīyah,*** just outside the purlieus of al-Qayrawān (Kairouan), and ***Raqqādah,*** some five miles from the same city. Even the Fāṭimid foundation of ***al-Mahdīyah*** on a coastal site in what is now eastern Tunisia, despite its palaces and mosque, conveyed the aura of a garrison town (specifically a naval port, army post, and arsenal) rather than a princely pleasance.[447]

It was a different matter with ***al-Manṣūrīyah,*** constituted by the Fāṭimid Ismāʿīl al-Manṣūr as his capital in 948. Here, on the outskirts of al-Qayrawān, at the very spot where al-Mansūr had finally defeated the Khārijī rebel Abū Yazīd, palaces more splendid than any in the Maghrib were raised and accorded Persian honorifics. Even allowing for the nostalgia prevalent among authors writing after the calamity of the Banū-Hilal invasion, who are our principal sources for the period, it is evident that al-Manṣūrīyah, with its imposing residences remote from everyday life, its indulgent elite culture, lavish state receptions and celebrations, and annual round of festivals, came close in both form and function (though on a smaller scale) to the great palatine complexes described above.[448] It will be recalled that in due course it would become the model for General Jawhar's Egyptian capital of the same name, ultimately to be designated al-Qāhirah.

In the Eastern Caliphate, ***al-Rāfiqah*** was a barely diminished example of a caliphal retreat. Founded by the caliph al-Manṣūr adjacent to al-Raqqah in the Middle Euphrates valley in 772, it was conceived on a circular plan allegedly based on that of the Round City in Baghdād. Subsequently Hārūn al-Rashīd extended the enceinte and built three palaces outside its walls to the northeast.[449] Furthermore, it cannot be doubted that some of the so-called Umayyad castles in the Syrian desert region such, for instance, as those known today as al-Mshattā, Qaṣr al-Ḥayr al-Sharqī, and Qasṭal, should be regarded as early and relevantly modest examples of this category of settlement.

Other New Foundations

The majority of new settlements established by Muslims during the first four Islamic centuries did not qualify as palatine foundations of the type we have been describing, even though a proportion of them did incorporate palaces of rulers and high officials. Generally speaking, they were directed initially toward more purely administrative and military functions, which in turn were sometimes able to generate broad spectra of social and economic institutions. Three reasonably representative examples that were eventually designated by al-Maqdisī as *metropoleis* of all or, in one case, part of their *iqlīms* were ***al-Mawṣil*** (Mosul), Shīrāz, and Zabīd.

The first of these was originally laid out in 641 as a forward garrison of Kūfan troops who were quartered either inside or outside (or both) a fortress that had been built by the Sāsānian king Khusraw II but that had subsequently been utilized as a monastery. Tribal holdings *(khiṭāṭ)* were apportioned on the standard pattern for such army camps[450] and the cantonment provided with a congregational mosque and a *dār al-imārah.* But the settlement remained small throughout the Sufyānid period, essentially a symbol of Islamic authority in a populace of Nestorian, Melkite, and Monophysite beliefs and in a milieu where key administrative offices more often than not remained in the hands of Christian bureaucrats. Not until the Marwānids intensified the Islamization of the *Jazīrah* in the first half of the eighth century and thereby stimulated the administrative and economic potentialities inherent in the settlement's strategic location did al-Mawṣil begin to manifest the characteristic features of a developed urban form. Marwān II (r. 744–50), in particular, is remembered as a builder of roads, walls, and a pontoon bridge over the Tigris and, probably more significantly, as reconstituting the structure of city government. Practically the last Umayyad contribution to al-Mawṣil's urban development was the designation of the city as the capital of the *Jazīrah,* resulting in its acquisition of its first *diwān,* almost certainly a land-tax register establishing a revenue system comparable to those in other provinces of the Caliphate. Under the ʿAbbāsids al-Mawṣil further developed its functions as a regional center, at the same time benefiting no doubt from the concurrent migration of political power from al-Shām eastward.

In spite of sharing in the vicissitudes of fate that afflicted most cities of the Diyār Rabīʿah between the eighth and tenth centuries,[451] al-Mawṣil maintained its ranking as the chief city of the *Jazīrah* and was incorporated in al-Maqdisī's urban hierarchy as a *miṣr*.[452] The topographers, especially Ibn Ḥawqal and al-Maqdisī, tell us something about the morphology of the city but not nearly enough to enable us to reconstruct its layout in any degree of detail. It was described generally as being in the form of a *ṭaylasān,* from the circulation pattern of which al-Maqdisī chose to mention eight streets *(durūb;* sing. *darb*),[453] although he advanced no rationale for his choice. At the heart of the city, at a point where the Zubaydah canal joined the Tigris was the citadel, known locally both as al-Murabbaʿah ("The Square") and, because of the Wednesday market ensconced within its walls, as the Sūq al-Arbaʿā. The congregational mosque, which had been built by the last of the Umayyad caliphs, stood at the head of a flight of steps leading up from the Tigris. Most of the main markets were roofed, with many commodities having a plurality of *sūqs*, each comprising up to a hundred shops. The caliphal palace *(qaṣr)* was situated half a *farsakh* from the far side of the river, overlooking the ruins of ancient Nineveh (Arabic Ninawayh). Al-Maqdisī and Ibn Ḥawqal both praised the urban ambience of al-Mawṣil with its magnificent residences, fine baths, inns, and imposing vistas. With the exceptions of its low water table and unhealthy south wind, it offered an agreeable environment that, according to Ibn Ḥawqal, in the second half of the tenth century was attracting migrants from far and near.[454] Yet the topographers leave the distinct impression that even at that time the city constituted a predominantly Arab enclave in an overwhelmingly Kurdish countryside.[455]

The developmental trajectory of ***Shīrāz*** shared a good deal in common with that already sketched for al-Mawṣil. It, too, was established initially as an advanced army camp but remained small until it was constituted as the seat of the Ṣaffārid quasi-independent polity in the second half of the ninth century. This was presumably the phase in the urbanization process that al-Iṣṭakhri depicted toward the mid-tenth century:

> It was an army camp *(muʿaskar)* of the Muslims when they set about conquering Iṣṭakhr. When they had conquered Iṣṭakhr they settled in that place [that is, the camp], and the *muʿaskar* developed into [the capital of] Fārs. And [the Muslims] built a *madīnah*. . . . Here were the commissariat of the Fārsī army, the Fārsī government bureaux, and residences of the highest civil and military officials.[456]

A further century of steady but unspectacular growth received renewed impetus when the Buwayhids made it the principal seat of their government. By the second half of the tenth century Shīrāz had become a stone-built city almost a *farsakh* across, with eight gates *(durūb)* piercing the walls erected by the Buwayhid *amīr* Ṣamṣām al-Dawlah at the end of that century.[457]

Among topographers it did not enjoy a high reputation as a place to live. "Filthy and congested" is al-Maqdisī's epitomization. In particular its streets, including those serving as the main *sūqs*, were inordinately narrow, so much so that al-Maqdisī brings up the matter no less than four times in his description of the city, concluding with the comment that the low balconies of bordering buildings often prevented two pack animals from proceeding abreast. However, the mosque,[458] "incomparable in the eight [non-Arab] regions"—or so al-Maqdisī maintains[459]—stood imposingly amid the *sūqs*, with the *bāzār* of the cloth merchants right beside it. At some distance was one of the finest hospitals in the whole of Islam, supported by a generous *waqf* and furnished with skilled practitioners and the best medicaments. Elsewhere were numerous industrial establishments, most notably textile workshops, a wide range of markets, a well-equipped observatory, a palace, and at least three Zoroastrian temples, enduring material expressions of Īrānian sentiments that led to the decoration of the *sūqs* on what were to al-Maqdisī infidel festivals.[460]

In its earlier days, at any rate, the city projected a feeling of spaciousness attributed by al-Yaʿqūbī at the end of the ninth century to the large number of gardens within its residential sectors.[461] However, the most impressive part of the urban complex toward the close of the tenth century was the palace enclave, built by ʿAḍud al-Dawlah half a *farsakh* outside the city. Its gardens of native and exotic plants measured a *farsakh* across. ʿAḍud channelled through them water from some thirty miles away, crowned the buildings with domes, and excavated cisterns. This combination of architecture, vegetation, and water, in al-Maqdisī's words, evoked the delights and enchantments of Paradise. The palace allegedly contained 360 rooms *(ḥujarāt)*, some of which were set off with Chinese terra cotta, some in marble or other stone, some gilded, and some decorated with pictures. According to al-Maqdisī, who claimed to have been shown around by the head custodian, each room—one for each day of the year—was unique in its construction, furnishings, draperies, and arrangement, and "furnished with every kind of contrivance and convenience"; but the largest interior hall housed a library comprising whatever volumes ʿAḍud al-Dawlah was able to acquire in all branches of knowledge.[462] The palace complex, on which, incidentally, ʿAḍud bestowed his own family name of Kard Fanā Khusraw, is clearly in the tradition of the great palatine foundations discussed earlier. However, because it was not the primary reason for the existence of Islamic Shīrāz, it is treated here as merely a factor, albeit an important one, in the political and economic development of the city that al-Maqdisī would choose as the metropolis of his Fārsī urban hierarchy. In any case Fanā Khusraw barely survived its founder. When al-Maqdisī was writing, it had been for all intents and purposes abandoned and its market closed.

Zabīd was another Islamic foundation that, despite a checkered history, prospered; in the tenth century it was perceived as the metropolis of southwestern Arabia. Founded by a recalcitrant ʿAbbāsid governor in 820, the city capitalized on its strategic location on the principal land route between ʿAdan and Makkah (Mecca), which meant in effect the main route by which goods from the Asian Orient reached the Mediterranean. At the same time, it exploited to the full the productive potential of the irrigated tracts of its local region. The Ziyādite dynasty ruled the city from 821 until 1012, and even during its declining decades, specifically in 977, could rely on tithe revenues of half a million ʿAtharīyah *dīnār*s, supplemented by a further two hundred thousand in trade tolls.[463]

Our sources are unanimous on the growth of Zabīd—larger and more prosperous than Makkah was the way al-Maqdisī categorizes it—but have very little to say about the institutions that generated its prosperity or their material expression in the landscape. Ibn al-Mujāwir, writing in the second half of the thirteenth century but often dependent on earlier material, described a circular walled city with concentric zones ringing what he termed the Madīnah Zabīd,[464] but no tenth-century or earlier topographer advanced this claim. Al-Maqdisī reported the existence in his day of a brick-built fortress *(ḥiṣn)* with four gates, known from the settlements they led to as Bāb Ghalāfiqah, Bāb ʿAdan, Bāb Hishām (presumably for Sihām), and Bāb Shabāriq. At an early period in the history of the city an imposing palace had been built of baked brick *(ājurr)* and plaster *(jiṣṣ)* at the principal crossroads of the settlement—which was presumably where the main streets joining the four gates intersected. According to Ibn al-Mujāwir, it was surrounded by a deep and wide fosse; and the same author noted that it served as the residence of the rulers of Zabīd right down to his own time in the thirteenth century. In a rare reference to location, and then only in a relative sense, al-Maqdisī observes that the congregational mosque, clean and with a cement floor, was at some distance from the market.[465]

Other Muslim foundations that eventually sent roots deep into the sociocultural substrata of the Middle East included the following:

- ***Al-Ramlah*** (Ramleh), founded in the first or second decade of the eighth century to supersede Ludd as the capital of the *Jund* of Filasṭīn. To establish the settlement as a going concern, the whole population of Ludd was transferred there, fortifications installed, and a palace *(qaṣr)* and a congregational mosque constructed. Interestingly, the financial management of the construction of these last two buildings was in the charge of a Christian from Ludd. Another structure that was mentioned in the sources as early as the palace was "the house of the dyers" *(dār al-sabbāghīn)*, which was furnished, not unexpectedly, with a huge cistern, but the reasons for the prominence of this landmark so early in the history of the city can only be matters of speculation. By the tenth century local and regional locational advantages, initially under caliphal favor, had combined to generate a city that covered a square mile. Consequently, al-Maqdisī could not but designate it, according to his scheme, the *qaṣabah* of its province. The same author spoke highly of the congregational mosque, which had finally been completed by the caliph Hishām (r. 724–43);[466] of the *khāns*, baths, and dwellings of quarried stone and baked brick; and of the broad streets so arranged as to serve eight city gates—which, we have seen, some believe implied an orthogonal design for the original Arab encampment.[467]

- ***Askar Mukram*** was founded as a military encampment on both banks of the Masruqān Canal near the turn of the eighth century, but little is known of its development until the tenth century, when it became a mint city under the Buwayhid *amīr* Muʿizz al-Dawlah. At that time the western half of the city was the larger and encompassed both the congregational mosque and most of the *sūqs*. The waterway featured two pontoon bridges. The city ranked as a *qaṣabah* in al-Maqdisī's urban hierarchy.
- ***Sīrāf*** seems to have functioned as a minor port in Sāsānian times but did not come into its own until the eastward orientation of the ʿAbbāsids brought an almost preternatural expansion of commerce to the Gulf. In the mid-tenth century it comprised an elongated but congested settlement running for more than a mile and a half along the edge of a shallow bay. The congregational mosque was more or less centrally situated, bordering the main *sūq*, which was described by its excavator as "a maze of streets, warehouses and shops."[468] One residential quarter occupied rising ground on the landward side of the settlement, while another stretched along the waterfront westward from the congregational mosque. Beyond that was the potters' quarter and the wall marking the edge of the settlement in that direction. In the mid-tenth century al-Iṣṭakhrī judged the city to be almost as large as Shīrāz. Shortly thereafter, however, a series of earthquakes severely damaged its infrastructure at the very time when the weakening of Buwayhid power was allowing a wholesale restructuring of commercial relations on the Fārsī coast.
- ***Al-Aḥsā*** was established by a Qarmaṭī chief in 899. Little is known of its subsequent development beyond the fact that it was capable of supporting an expansionist, patrimonial-style *shaykh*dom for nearly seventy years. One surviving item of interest: Qarmaṭī religious belief allowed the disintegration of the congregational mosque, which was eventually replaced by an orthodox structure underwritten by a Persian pilgrim. Apparently a fortress known as al-Muʾminīyah was added to the settlement in 926.
- ***Al-ʿAbbāsīyah,*** *qaṣabah* of the Egyptian Rīf, may have been founded as late as 893. In the second half of the tenth century it is known to have been characterized by residences more spacious than those in Miṣr itself and to have boasted an impressive brick-built congregational mosque—yet the precise location of the city is a matter of speculation.

The information relating to the aforementioned cities is fairly typical of that available for urban forms throughout the early Islamic world: allusions to, and sometimes descriptions of, institutions, buildings, and occasionally architectural complexes abound in a variety of texts but seldom are their precise locations specified so that they can be combined into integrated urban morphologies. In only a small proportion of cases does archaeological investigation contribute significantly to an understanding of city internal structure. It will not have escaped notice that for not one of the eight cities just discussed was it practicable to specify a detailed perimeter.

Two instances where archaeology has proved to be the principal source for urban morphology are the sites of ***Waylah*** (al-ʿAqabah) at the head of the Gulf of ʿAqabah and Anjar in the Biqāʿ. The first, excavated by Donald Whitcomb between 1986 and 1995, took the form of a stone-walled, rectangular enclosure, 165 by 140 meters, divided by axial streets intersecting in a roofed structure reminiscent of the classical tetrapylon. Where the main streets pierced the outer walls they were each flanked by two towers, while the walls themselves were replete with four corner towers and a series of intervening U-shaped towers. Although the town was most probably founded in the mid-seventh century, its formal plan bore such a close resemblance in both layout and proportions to that of the typical legionary fort of the late Roman period that it would be unreasonable, despite the intervening centuries, to deny the likelihood of a causal relationship between them. However that may be, the town prospered, serving as a trade emporium *(khizānah)* for the Ḥijāz; an assembly point *(ijtimāʿ)* for pilgrims en route to Makkah from al-Shām (Greater Syria), Miṣr (Egypt), and the Maghrib;[469] and a center for legal and traditionist studies.

It is unknown when the first congregational mosque was built, but, as part of the reconstruction following the earthquake of 749, a new building was raised in the northeastern sector of the city.[470] Meanwhile, the central structure seems to have been converted into an elite residence, perhaps for a governor. Whereas the earlier houses, such as those bordering both sides of the street leading from the northwestern gate to the central structure, were originally of cut stone and brick, in Fāṭimid times internal repairs were often entirely of mud brick. There was also a substantial pottery industry, located to the north and west of the town, that provided not only wares for local domestic use but also specialized containers in the form of amphorae for the transport of agricultural products in ships' holds. The excavator of Waylah envisions grains, vegetable oils, and similar products being assembled in warehouses there, stored, and then ultimately loaded into amphorae for transshipment by sea:[471] hence the appropriateness of the designation "emporium" invoked by al-Maqdisī. By the end of the ninth century the city's commercial, pilgrimage, and intellectual functions had ensured that its inhabitants comprised a mélange of ethnic groups whose diversity attracted the attention of al-Yaʿqūbī,[472] and there is no reason to suppose that circumstances changed significantly during the tenth century.

The settlement at ***ʿAnjar*** was excavated by the *amīr* Maurice Chehab (Shihāb) in the 1950s and subsequently analyzed by his son Hafiz K. Chehab. It took the form of a stone-walled, rectangular enclosure 370 by 310 meters, with a hollow, three-quarter-round tower at each corner and intervening, solid, half-round towers. Axial colonnaded streets, analogous to, if not derived from, the Roman *cardo* and *decumanus,* intersected in a central, purely classical tetrapylon of four groups of four columns and pierced the centers of their respective walls between twin towers. The two defining avenues of the settlement were bordered by shops whose entrances corresponded broadly to the intercolumniations.[473] The only sector for which complete numeration was practicable was the west side of the north-south avenue *(cardo),* where there were 32 shops, but no less than 114 have been counted along these axes altogether. The road between the columns was 7½ meters wide and the distance between shop fronts 19 meters.

The congregational mosque, 47 by 30 meters, stood in the southeastern angle of the intersection of the axial avenues, with a door immediately west of the *miḥrāb* affording direct access from what was almost certainly a palace incorporating a *dār al-imarah.* A lesser palace-style structure was situated in the northeast angle of the intersection, with what appears to have been an enclosed *sūq* of twenty-two shops immediately behind it and another courtyard building facing it across the *cardo.* A *ḥammām* complex was situated just inside the north gate, a location suggesting to Hillenbrand public rather than exclusively elite use, and a second smaller bath just west of the same gate. The northwestern quadrant contains two rectangular but empty enclosures, aligned with the perimeter walls but of unknown function. Domestic housing seems to have been restricted virtually to the southwest quadrant.

Clearly, ʿAnjar in its general dispositions was a larger version of Waylah, and to that extent was equally likely to have incorporated a morphological, though not necessarily a close functional, generic affinity with late-Roman fortresses or coloniae. The parallels were especially close between Waylah and ʿAnjar on the one hand and the Diocletian-type legionary forts at al-Lajjūn and Uḍruḥ (both second through fifth centuries) on the other. With these latter may be classed the camps at al-Faramā and al-Aqṣūr.[474] Within the Islamic world the closest correspondences were with the Large Enclosure at Qaṣr al-Ḥayr al-Sharqī and Mshattā (both eighth century). The architectural elements of rectangular form, fortified aspect, gates in the middles of sides, U-shaped towers, central tetrapylonlike structures, and overall proportionality (though not actual dimensions) at these sites presumably stem from similarities of intention effected through an at least partially shared technology. Dr. Whitcomb introduces additional precision into this interpretation when he posits seventh-century Waylah as transitional between pre-Islamic Lajjūn and eighth-century Qaṣr al-Ḥayr.[475] The precise ekistic functions performed by the settlement at ʿAnjar are matters of dispute.

During the first four centuries of Islam, Muslims founded other new settlements throughout the Middle East and North Africa, but most were small and for hardly any are there sustained records of their subsequent development. Not a few remained undistinguished or totally failed to establish niches for themselves in the urban hierarchy. One that did succeed was ***al-Raḥbah*** in the middle Euphrates valley, often referred to as Raḥbah Mālik ibn Ṭawq, thereby perpetuating the memory of Mālik ibn Ṭawq ibn ʿAttāb al-Taghlibī. He founded the city, allegedly in the shape of a *ṭaylasān,* during the caliphate of al-Maʾmūn (813–33). Despite an appalling record of usurpation and civil war,[476] the city prospered, partly from its caravan trade but equally from the productivity of its surrounding region. In the mid-tenth century al-Iṣṭakhrī thought it was larger than Qarqīsiyah, while al-Maqdisī regarded it as the principal city in the Euphrates district (*ʿamal al-Furāt,* al-Furātīyah);[477] but nothing is known of its morphology beyond the existence of walls, a fortress, and a suburb.

Two other settlements founded in ʿAbbāsid times that became important nodes in the urban hierarchy of Aqūr were ***Jazīrat ibn ʿUmar,*** in a loop of the Tigris at the effective head of navigation on that river, and ***ʿImādīyah,*** in the upper Zāb valley. The former was said to have been established by al-Ḥasan ibn ʿUmar ibn al-Khaṭṭāb al-Taghlibī (d. 865); the latter, by ʿImād al-Dawlah in the first half of the tenth century. For neither settlement is there anything more than a passing allusion to morphology, and then, in the case of Jazīrat ibn ʿUmar, only to a wall surrounding stone-built dwellings. Altogether, though, Jazīrat was considered a comfortable place to live (except in the depths of winter, when its streets were inordinately muddy) and a profitable venue for those who would tap into Armenian trade flows.

In the Maghrib the small walled town of ***Bilizmah*** played a similar role. Founded by Arabs as a garrison post in the first half of the tenth century, its agricultural resources ensured that it developed into a pleasant enough town. According to Ibn Ḥawqal, descendants of its founders numbered among its residents—implying, I think, that they constituted an Arab island in a Berber sea.[478] One middle-sized town for which archaeological investigation has both confirmed and supplemented a meager literary account was ***al-Baṣrah*** in the far western Maghrib. Laid out as a very irregular, walled rectangle of thirty hectares by Idrīs II (r. 804–28) and named after the celebrated *miṣr* in al-ʿIrāq, the settlement developed into one of the most important towns in the peninsular territories of northern Morocco. In about 978 it was sacked by the Zīrīds, and apparently was still in ruins when al-Maqdisī[479] was collecting his information, although it was subsequently rebuilt at least in part. The enclosure covered two eminences and an intervening valley, within the last of which the majority of the population was settled. Pottery kilns were excavated in the western sector of the town.

Farther east, on the west bank of the Nākūr River, ***Madīnat al-Nākūr*** was one of the earliest Islamic settlements to be established in what is now Morocco. As the site has been greatly disturbed by modern dam construction, the prognostication for archaeological investigation must be guarded. To date, that line of inquiry has failed to confirm the existence of the wall, with its four gates, the *ribāṭ,* the mosque, baths, and *sūq*s that were attested by al-Bakrī in the eleventh century and some of which certainly figured in the tenth-century city. However, the excavations do imply that brick was favored over stone as a construction medium (al-Bakrī states explicitly that the city walls were of brick) and provide rare evidence of a group within the city espousing non-Islamic burial practices. Not surprisingly, archaeology has yet to confirm al-Bakrī's record of a Mājūs (Norman) pillaging of the city in 858.[480] Finally, mention should also be made of the other new Islamic foundations in the Maghrib listed earlier, but for none is it possible to reconstruct an urban fabric.

Adapted Cities

Vastly the larger number of cities within the medieval Islamic world were adapted settlements. They came as functioning units within conquered or surrendered territories and were utilized by Muslim authorities in whatever ways best fit the circumstances of time and place. More often than not, the process of adaptation has to be inferred from textual allusion or archaeological remains: seldom is it described, and even then, almost inevitably, only partially. The region where the manner in which Muslims adapted preexisting cities to their own use has received most attention is the Levant, al-Maqdisī's *Iqlīm al-Shām.*

The starting point was a series of publications by Jean Sauvaget in the 1930s. In them he argued that the orthogonally reticulate street pattern characteristic of Roman and Byzantine cities in the Levant tended sooner or later to be obscured by the superimposition of urban quarters, the outward expressions of internally self-governing Islamic communities, each provided with its own set of communal facilities in the form of a mosque, public bath, well, market, bakery, and so forth.[481] Sauvaget based his interpretation on analyses of changing street plans in the three cities of Dimashq (Damascus), al-Lādhiqīyah (Latakia), and Ḥalab (Aleppo), but traces of rectangular urban grids similarly overlain by discordant circulation patterns have been glimpsed in early reconstructions of sites such as, among others, Anṭākiyah, (Antiochia) Ḥimṣ, Ṭabarīyah (Tiberias), and Qayṣārīyah (Caesarea).[482] Sauvaget also emphasized that these new sociocultural configurations crystallized around already established, functionally homologous sites, a process ensuring a substantial persistence of locational values from age to age for certain urban entities—notably the enclosing walls, the principal sanctuary (compendiously exemplified by the succession Temple of Hadad, Temple of Jupiter Damascenus, Church of St. John the Baptist, and Great Mosque of Damascus), and craft specialisms. Markets, by contrast, were often reorganized. Whereas neighborhood *sūqs* continued to establish themselves in hierarchical orders throughout the urban areas, new alignments made their appearance in the form of lines of shops bordering main streets, converting intercolumnar spaces into shops, and even encroaching on the public way. The street in Damascus called Straight, the main avenue in Ladhiqīyah, and at least some parts of the axial streets at ʿAnjar afford signal instances of this development.

These transformations of morphology, and others of a closely similar nature, undeniably occurred in Levantine cities in Islamic times, but, as subsequent authors have been at pains to point out, Sauvaget may have been too ready to ascribe a causative role to Islam.[483] In the first place, it has become increasingly evident that the degradation of urban grids was already well under way before the advent of Islam, in some cities as early as the second century A.D. In the second place, it is difficult to connect the wholesale reconstitution of neighborhoods with specifically Islamic positive actions over a relatively short period of time. Rather are quarters of this type, whether Islamic or otherwise, the creations of secular agglomerative tendencies operating in conjunction with accessibility factors. They are the natural outcome of community differentiation consequent on economic and sociocultural elaboration and intensification over extended periods of time, and are never created overnight.[484] It is still impracticable to generalize about the precise contribution of an evident weakness of regulated rights in Islamic law to the mechanics of this transformative process, but it is noteworthy that some scholars have been inclined to see the origin of at least some urban quarters in Byzantine parochial divisions.[485]

When the Muslims came into possession of a city, they might seek a lodging within its confines or outside its walls, or both, depending on whether it had been acquired by force of arms or capitulation and what the immediate needs of the troops were for water, pasture, billets, and defense. Al-Balādhurī, writing a history of the Islamic conquests toward the end of the ninth century, offered the generalization: "When the Muslims conquered a city [in the Levant], whether it dominated a broad expanse of territory or was situated on the coast, they used to station within it as many Muslims as might be necessary. If the [Christian] inhabitants should revolt, Muslims would crowd into the city as reinforcements. When ʿUthmān ibn ʿAffān became Caliph, he wrote to Muʿāwiyah [Governor of al-Shām] instructing him to fortify and garrison the coastal cities and to assign fiefs to those who settled there." Then the same author added, invoking a different *isnād,* "He commanded him to furnish the garrison with holdings, apportion among them any houses that had been evacuated, to build new mosques, and enlarge those established in previous caliphates."[486] As a result, men from all parts of the Middle East migrated to these coastal cities.[487]

It was not only the coastal cities of the Levant that were physically occupied in this way. As the Muslim army approached ***Emesa*** (Ḥimṣ) it camped beside the Orontes River, where the inhabitants of the city supplied it with rations and forage before formally capitulating. At this time the army commander al-Simṭ ibn al-Aswad al-Kindī divided the city into *khiṭāṭ,* in each of which a Muslim could build a house. Furthermore, he made the tribesmen "settle in every space that had been evacuated and in every courtyard that had been deserted."[488] The implication of the relevant texts is that the agora of the classical city remained an open space until the second quarter of the eighth century. Certainly in 638 Abū ʿUbaydah ibn al-Jarrāḥ camped his forces at this spot, which he referred to as the (principal) plaza of Ḥimṣ *(fināʾ madīnat Ḥimṣ),* when he was preparing to repel a Byzantine counterattack. In the eighth century, however, this space was converted into a market known as Sūq al-Rastān.[489] We have already had occasion to comment on the common medieval assertion that the Muslims shared the Kanīsat Yūḥanna with Christians.

Another city in which Muslims settled under similar conditions was ***Damascus.*** Initially a bishop had supplied the Muslim army with rations at municipal expense (an expedient closely similar to that followed at Emesa and by no means unknown elsewhere in the Middle East), but when the city accepted the Pact of Allāh, that instrument of capitulation guaranteed that the city wall would not be demolished and that Muslims would not be billeted in private homes. Nevertheless, a substantial proportion of the inhabitants fled to Aleppo, where the Byzantine emperor Heraclius was encamped, abandoning houses that were eventually occupied by Muslims.[490] Other instances of Muslim settlement within Levantine cities, almost always after formal capitulation, included ***Tiberias,*** where lives, possessions, children, churches, and houses were spared, with the exception of those homes that were to be vacated to make room for the construction of a mosque; ***Aleppo,*** where an almost identical pact, in addition to the usual guarantees, required only a site for a mosque, although Muʿāwiyah, as governor, subsequently settled troops in the city and assigned them fiefs; ***Bālis,*** most of the inhabitants of which had fled to Byzantine territory, leaving the city to be settled by Arab levies, other Arabs long resident in al-Shām who had adopted Islam betimes, and remnants of the Qays tribe who drifted in from the desert; ***Qāṣirin,*** where wholesale evacuations occurred, but the army commander, for reasons unstated, was unable to persuade Arab settlers to remain; and ***Ḥamā,*** where a peace covenant *(ṣulḥ)* sanctioned the conversion of the city's largest Christian church into a mosque.

In ***Lādhiqīyah*** (Latakia), Christians who initially had fled were eventually permitted to return to assigned holdings (and, of course, the *kharāj*) and to retain their church at the same time that a congregational mosque was being built. After the Byzantines destroyed the city in 719, it was rebuilt by order of the caliph ʿUmar ibn ʿAbd al-ʿAzīz (or, some say, his successor) and garrisoned with Arab troops. When ʿUmar ibn al-Khaṭṭāb proposed assigning fiefs among the Muslims of ***al-Jābiyah*** in accordance with the custom when a settlement was taken by force of arms, he was opposed by a certain Muʿādh ibn Jabal on the ground that Islamic inheritance law would tend to concentrate holdings in the hands of a few men (Muʿādh actually postulated an ultimate single fief holder), so that there would be too few lots available for equally deserving tribesmen at a later date. ʿUmar took this advice, but we are not told how he implemented it. In ***Qinnasrīn*** the Arab commander Abū ʿUbaydah ibn al-Jarrāḥ found members of the Tanūkh tribe, who had originally pitched their tents in the neighborhood, already dwelling in houses. Some of them accepted Islam but not the Banū-Salīḥ ibn Ḥulwān, who held fast to their Christian faith. In ***Tripoli,*** the city of three fortresses, the population slipped away by night during the Muslim siege, leaving vacant space to which Muʿāwiyah, as governor, transferred a large contingent of Jews—an ethnic group still clustered in the harbor precincts when al-Balādhurī was writing, about 869.

For the inhabitants of ***Baʿlabakk,*** modern ʿAyn Shams (who were categorized revealingly as Greeks, Persians, and Arabs) the instrument of capitulation specified protection not only for the usual personal and community possessions but also, uncommonly, for mills. The Greeks, however, while permitted to pasture their cattle up to a distance of fifteen miles from the city, were forbidden to exploit already inhabited localities "until [the months of] Rabīʿ and Jumādah I had passed, when they could go whither they would."[491] Virtually all the Muslim topographers emphasize the impressiveness of the architecture of the city, some of it of venerable antiquity, some more recent.[492] Only al-Maqdisī notes explicitly that many of the buildings were in ruins, and he alone observes that there were noticeably extensive cultivated lands within the ramparts of the city.[493] The manner in which landholdings could sometimes remain largely intact through a succession of owners, and occasionally outlast dynasties, is nicely exemplified by al-Balādhurī's paragraph on one particular village in the Balqāʾ:

> Abū Sufyān ibn Ḥarb, who traded with al-Shām in the Jāhilīyah, possessed a village . . . called Qubbash. It [eventually] passed into the hands of Muʿāwiyah and his son but, at the installation of this [ʿAbbāsid] dynasty, suffered confiscation and became the property of certain sons of [the Caliph] al-Mahdī. . . . Thence it passed under the control of a Kūfan family of oil merchants known as the Banū-Nuʿaym.[494]

Jerusalem

Without doubt the most impressive adaptation of any preexisting city occupied by the Muslims took place in Jerusalem, known to the Arabs at the time of the conquest as Īliyā' (< Roman Aelia [Capitolina]) and subsequently as Bayt al-Maqdis,[495] but the record is sporadic and difficult to interpret. During the centuries immediately preceding the Islamic conquest, Aelia was constituted as a very imperfectly rectangular, walled city, some fifteen hundred by one thousand yards in extent, the interior of which seems to have been disposed in a series of orthogonal grids.[496] Archaeology and a mosaic map from the floor of a Byzantine church at Madaba attest that in the last quarter of the sixth century at least two of the principal thoroughfares, running longitudinally through the city to converge at the (northern) Neapolis Gate, were bordered for much of their length by colonnades, behind which it is presumed were rows of shops.[497]

From 324 to 638 Christianity was ascendant in Jerusalem, so it comes as no surprise that the population should have clustered as close as was practicable to the holy shrines of that faith, specifically around the hills of Zion and Golgotha in the western sector of the city, where the Church of the Holy Sepulchre and its associated structures served as a generative focus. However, the Christians paid relatively little attention to the Jewish shrines on Mount Moriah in the eastern sector of the city, which, for scriptural reasons, remained unexploited save for a memorial church to Saint James in the southwest corner.[498] As for the Herodian temple platform, its surface was littered with the architectural debris left by invading armies and the passage of time. To the south of the ruins of the great temple was a group of Christian hostels and monasteries, but little else. Apparently the southern wall of the city (the so-called Eudokia Wall) encompassed the whole of Zion hill and the southern spur of Mount Moriah.

In 614 the Persian general Shahr-Barz sacked Jerusalem, burned its churches,[499] and either sold into slavery or carried captive to Ctesiphon (al-Madā'in) many of the inhabitants, including the patriarch Zacharias.[500] However, the Persians did not constitute the city as their provincial capital; instead they established their headquarters at Caesarea. Fifteen years later the emperor Heraclius reestablished Byzantine control over the city, but virtually nothing is known of structural changes in the urban fabric during these troublous times.

The Muslims came into possession of Aelia by capitulation in 638[501] and almost immediately began to clear the precincts of the ruined Herodian temple. In about 680 the Christian bishop Arculf noted the existence in a part of the temple complex known as Kapitolion of a Muslim "place of prayer," a simple rectangular enclosure of wood capable of accommodating some three thousand worshippers.[502] The architecture of this mosque is unknown, but it probably partook of the hypostyle arrangement, deriving ultimately from the Prophet's compound in al-Madīnah, that would become an integral component of mosque design for centuries to come.

Further significant developments on the site of the temple complex (the platform known since Ottoman times as al-Ḥaram al-Sharīf) had to await the caliphate of ʿAbd al-Malik (685–705), who sought to sacralize that already hallowed ground by emphasizing its association with the Last Days.[503] To this end he initiated an extremely ambitious building program designed to exalt the religious, and thereby derivatively the political, status of Jerusalem. Among the resulting structures, pride of place must go to that one, unique in the annals of Islamic architecture, known as the Qubbat al-Ṣakhrah ("The Dome of the Rock"). This comprises two octagonal ambulatories around a dome-surmounted cylinder twenty and one-third meters high and set over an irregular outcrop of natural rock that forms the summit of Mount Moriah. A date equivalent to 691–92 is inscribed on the outer face of the octagonal arcade.[504]

We need not enter here into the debate as to whether this extraordinary monument was intended to rival Makkah (Mecca), a symbol of cultural superiority over Byzantines and Sāsānians, a glimpse of Paradise on earth, or the *baldaquin* (also *qubbah*) over the throne of God,[505] but the soteriological implications of its design are evident enough. Names of two gates to the dome built by ʿAbd al-Malik, Bāb Isrāfīl and Bāb al-Jannah, both referred to the Judgment Day, while Dr. Rosen-Ayalon has shown with a high degree of probability that the ornamental and architectural elements incorporated in the design were in fact representations, ideas, and symbols relating to that supreme eschatogical event.[506] It is likely that the rock enclosed by the Qubbat al-Ṣakhrah was the same "pierced stone" *(lapis pertusus),* noted by the Bordeaux Pilgrim in about 333, that was honored annually by the Jews with rites of lamentation.[507] It is also to be inferred that the site had traditionally been associated with the place where Ibrāhīm had prepared to sacrifice his son and was so regarded by the Muslims from early in their occupation. However, the currently better-known associations with the Prophet's Night Journey *(Isrā')* and Ascension *(Miʿrāj)* in their present forms seem to have been later, and probably independent, accretions to the ritual validation of the Qubbat al-Ṣakhrah.[508] As for the physical structure of the building, let one of the foremost authorities summarize prevailing opinion:

> The building is a remarkably thought-out composition whose every detail in plan and in evaluation has been most accurately measured so as to create the most impressive effect. Its conception, and almost every architectural detail in the interior arrangement (piers, columns, capitals, arches, etc.), belong to the architectural repertory of Byzantine art and more specifically to the *martyrium* tradition of Jerusalem buildings like the Holy Sepulchre or the Church of the Ascension. It is from the same tradition that derives its internal decoration of marble panelling and especially of mosaics covering almost all wall surfaces above the capitals and cornices of piers and columns.[509]

In short, it is scarcely an exaggeration to characterize the Qubbat al-Ṣakhrah as an assemblage of appropriately modified traditional lore sheltered within a structure molded to the architectural canons of Byzantine Christianity. It was not by chance that the dimensions of the building were essentially those of Byzantine imperial monuments.[510] In fact the absolute dimensions of the drum were precisely those of the Anastasis, which had been completed in about 335. The internal alternation of piers and columns was adopted from the same source, while the inner circle of the dome had the same radius as the rotunda of the Church of the Ascension on the summit of the Mount of Olives.[511] From a broader viewpoint, circular domed structures were not rare within the sphere of Roman influence, where they had become the preferred form for mausolea. Within the Levant the earliest such dome, like the Dome of the Rock a wooden structure, was that surmounting the Marneion in Gaza, which had been constructed in the second century in honor of the god Marnas.[512]

The Qubbat al-Ṣakhrah did not stand alone on the Ḥaram platform but was an integral part of a larger sacralization program undertaken by ʿAbd al-Malik. On the southern edge of the platform stood the Masjid al-Aqṣā, which may have been essentially a reconstruction of the primitive mosque noted by Arculf in the time of Muʿāwiyah. However, as the development of the area is presently understood, the building of the Aqṣā Mosque must be attributed to ʿAbd al-Malik, with fairly substantial renovations being undertaken by his son al-Walīd (r. 705–15), perhaps necessitated by a series of earthquakes in 713–14.[513] In addition, the Umayyad building program included an extension of the Ḥaram platform northward to encompass the Ṣakhrah, a shoring up of its foundations; the construction of three smaller domed structures, namely the Qubbat al-Silsilah ("Dome of the Chain"),[514] the Qubbat al-Nabī ("Dome of the Prophet"), and the Qubbat al-Miʿrāj ("Dome of the Ascension of the Prophet")[515]; the completion of the Ḥaram wall with its sacred gates; and the building of a complex of six large structures immediately outside the southern and southwestern edges of the platform, which is thought to have included a two-storeyed *dār al-imārah* with storage facilities and—significantly—a bridge leading directly from the *qiblah* side of the Aqṣā Mosque to the palace.[516]

The symbolic significance and the disposition of the architectural features on the Ḥaram in Umayyad times have been subjects of extended debate. The most inclusive interpretation at the aggregate level, as opposed to that of the individual building, has recently been advanced by Dr. Whitcomb, who views virtually the whole of east Jerusalem as an Umayyad palatine complex founded, as often happened elsewhere, alongside a preexisting city.[517] In the first place, the Christian rulers of Jerusalem had left the Temple Mount, the focus of Jewish ritual, almost totally unused, which meant in fact that a huge area overlooking most of the Christian sector became available to Muslims in a city where the institute of capitulation forbade more direct expropriation of Christian buildings. From close study of the architectural features on and adjacent to the Ḥaram, Whitcomb has reconstructed the outline of an orthogonally arranged enclave that, incidentally, he regards as the standard layout for a Muslim army cantonment. Ben-Dov had already shown that the Arab architectural presence had extended through the lower city into the Tyropoeon valley. The shared axis of the Dome of the Rock and the Aqṣā Mosque, together with its continuation to the south of the Ḥaram, are to be understood as the *cardo* of an extensive complex exhibiting a substantial degree of cardinal orientation and axiality. For Whitcomb and Rosen-Ayalon, the Dome of the Rock marked the intersection of the axial "streets," and as such functioned as an unbelievably impressive elaboration of the conventional tetrapylon or ciborium.

This construction of a monumental enclave with attached government facilities is not in conflict with Elad's contention that the Umayyads intended Jerusalem to be their capital.[518] Whether this were so or not, they did undertake a massive resacralization of the Herodian Temple enceinte—what Grabar has aptly epitomized as "a monumental and ideological Islamisation of an ancient site"—that appears sometimes to have spilled over the edges of even the extended platform; in so doing they imbued religious and architectural symbols often of great antiquity with new semantic content. Others have recognized the Ḥaram as an integrated complex devised to exalt the status of Jerusalem, but so far only Whitcomb has sought to relate its form to contemporary urban design. If he is able to substantiate his claims, he will not only have advanced our understanding of the Ḥaram, and particularly the Dome of the Rock, but will also have helped to validate his own interpretation of the urbanization process in the Levant during early Islamic times. In the meanwhile, I shall take refuge in the cautious conclusions of Amikam Elad, without, of course, pretending to his knowledge of the relevant texts: "ʿAbd al-Malik was . . . concerned with emphasizing the central place of Jerusalem, of the Ḥaram, and of the Ṣakhrah within the religious landscape of early Islam. There is no contradiction in arguing that he built the Dome of the Rock on the site of the Temple of Solomon as a symbol of the Last Days and also as a rival to Mecca, which was then in the hands of his political opponent Ibn al-Zubayr."[519]

Some scholars have seen this colossal effort to establish Muslim Jerusalem as a religious center equal, if not superior, to any other in the Middle East, including both Makkah and west Jerusalem with its Anastasis, as beginning with Muʿāwiyah ibn Abī Sufayān (r. 661–80). However that may be, it is evident that it peaked in the caliphate of ʿAbd al-Malik but lost momentum fatally under Sulaymān ibn ʿAbd al-Malik (r. 715–17), who constituted al-Ramlah as the *qaṣabah* of the *Jund* of Filasṭīn. When the ʿAbbāsids transferred their capital to Baghdād, imperial patronage became negligible, with the result that the southernmost (the so-called Eudokia) wall was abandoned in favor of the late-Roman southern trace while most of the city's other walls fell into disrepair. When al-Maqdisī came to describe his native city in about 985, however, the walls had been rebuilt, presumably by order of a Fāṭimid caliph (probably al-ʿAzīz or possibly al-Muʿizz). Other than that, the fabric of the city seems not to have changed greatly between the mid-eighth and the early tenth centuries. Al-Maqdisī lists eight iron[-covered] gates piercing the walls, the identification of which has spawned a great deal of ongoing discussion. This conundrum cannot be resolved here; suffice it to note that the primary difference of opinion is between those who fail to discern topographical order in al-Maqdisī's schedule and those who read it as a counter-clockwise sequence.[520]

One of the principal undertakings by the ʿAbbāsids on the Ḥaram was al-Mahdī's rebuilding of the Aqṣā Mosque after it had been severely damaged by an earthquake. Nor were more secular facilities neglected. By the end of the tenth century water was abundant virtually throughout the city. Channels in the streets conducted water to three reservoirs serving baths close by. Twenty underground cisterns in the vicinity of the Aqṣā Mosque supplied water to drinking fountains throughout the city. Furthermore, the cisterns in the mosque were topped up each spring by water brought in aqueducts from two reservoirs in a valley some six miles away. Bearing in mind the relative productivity of Filastīn and the soteriological sacredness of Jerusalem, it is not difficult to understand why al-Maqdisī, himself a loyal Hierosolymite, should have eulogized his birthplace as

> the most exalted of cities because it unites in itself the advantages of both This World and the Next. He who is of This World but yearns for the things of the Next, finds a well stocked market for them [here]. And he who would embrace the Next World yet cleaves to the good things of This, likewise finds them here.[521]

Jerusalem, in al-Maqdisī's view at any rate, would have been the nonpareil among cities if only its baths had been cleaner and fewer Christians and Jews were to be seen on its streets.[522] One other matter touched our author even more directly, accustomed as he apparently was to opportunistic trading on his travels. That was the total restriction of trading to hostelries *(fanādiq)*, where stiff taxes were imposed on all transactions and guards were posted at the gates to dissuade those who might be inclined to take their business elsewhere. "There is little profit to be made in such circumstances" was al-Maqdisī's dismissive rejoinder to these curbs imposed on exchange transactions.[523]

Alexandria

Similar adaptive strategies appear to have been employed in North Africa, although explicit evidence is meager in the extreme. The most revealing is probably that relating to Alexandria, which capitulated late in 641 and was occupied by a Muslim garrison, known in the texts as a *ribāṭ*, that was rotated from al-Fusṭāṭ at six-month intervals. Subsequently ʿAmr ibn al-ʿĀṣ, the conquerer of Egypt, reinforced the garrison with contingents from the Lakhm, Judham, Kindah, al-Azd, Ḥaḍrami, Juzāʿah, and al-Mazāʿinah tribes.[524] The most surprising aspect of the occupation was the almost complete absence of *khiṭāṭ* in the allocation of residential lots, the holding of Zubayr ibn ʿAwwam being the sole exception. Instead, Ibn ʿAbd al-Ḥakam used the term *akhadha,* which he defined as "to take over a house and live in it, together with one's kin *(wa banū-abīhi)*."[525] Although the dictionaries concur broadly that the term (and its derivatives) connoted, primarily if not exclusively, the occupation and management of real estate,[526] it is not at all clear precisely how an *ikhādhah* differed from a *khiṭṭah.*

That the settlement process was drawn out and not always wholly harmonious, though, is attested by al-Balādhurī when he describes how the settlers (seemingly the military contingent mentioned above) who had moved into the city after the initial capitulation were likely to find other Muslims occupying their holdings when they returned after a Byzantine revolt had been crushed and the city recaptured by force of arms. To diffuse the situation, ʿAmr decreed that a house should belong to him who thrust his lance into it. But, as more than one person might lay claim to the same property in this way, a house often came into multiple ownership. Al-Balādhurī further quotes Yazīd ibn Abi-Ḥabīb to the effect that houses such as these could "neither be sold nor bequeathed but served [only] as dwelling places for Muslims while they were on post [in the city]."[527] Finally, al-Balādhurī notes that when a garrison's tour of duty expired, its houses were (always, often, sometimes?) reoccupied by Byzantines.

Classical and Byzantine Alexandria took the form of an elongated grid of streets running roughly from east to west between the Mareotic Lake and the Mediterranean Sea. In his report to his caliph, the Muslim commander announced that he had received the capitulation of a city containing 4,000 "palaces" (meaning elite residences), 4,000 baths, 400 theaters, 12,000 vendors of green vegetables, and 40,000 taxable Jews. This is clearly an overstatement, but one that probably did not figure in ʿAmr's original letter and that almost certainly was not introduced by Ibn ʿAbd al-Ḥakam, the immediate transmitter of the information. More likely it was the result of the cumulative quantitative inflation that was endemic to the time whenever prestige was at issue.[528] The two principal avenues, running respectively east–west from the Sun Gate to the Moon Gate and north–south from the sea to the lake, were both colonnaded; where they intersected was the Soma, the mausoleum holding the body of Alexander himself. To its north, fronting on the harbor, was the Brucheion, which seems to have constituted the civic heart of Alexandria. Here stood the palaces of the Ptolemies; the Museion (which Butler aptly epitomized as "the centre of the learning of the world");[529] the Tetrapylon, where Alexander was said to have laid the bones of the prophet Jeremiah; the Church of St. Mary Dorothea, built by Eulogius; the Church of St. Mark (which at that time probably still sheltered the bones of the apostle); and the great church called the Caesarion, with twin Pharaonic obelisks of red Uswān (Aswan) granite standing in its forecourt. Originally begun in honor of Caesar, it was completed by Augustus but converted by Constantine into a Christian church.

In the southwestern part of the city known as the Egyptian Quarter, a group of buildings constituting the Serapeum, a temple dedicated to the compound god

Serapis, stood right on the ancient citadel of Rhakotis,[530] while the world-famous lighthouse dominated both Alexandrine harbors from a spot on Pharos Island.[531] By the fourth century A.D., however, the urban fabric was already deteriorating—the Brucheion had been severely damaged by civil strife, earthquakes,[532] and subsidence, and the Soma of Alexander had been reduced to a shadow of its former glory[533]—and the decline was hardly arrested under the Muslims. In fact the reorientation of trade patterns under the new dispensation further reduced Alexandria's standing relative to other Islamic *metropoleis,* although it has to be noted that commodities continued to be imported from traditional sources in small quantities until the end of the seventh century.

Information about the interaction of Greek and Arab elements in the city during the earlier Islamic centuries is meager in the literary sources and, apart from Rodziewicz's excavations at Kaum al-Dikkah, is equally so in archaeological reports, this author going so far as to categorize the eighth century as "the darkest period of Alexandria from the archaeological point of view."[534] It is known that a considerable number of Greeks abandoned the city when the Arabs took it over; the Church of St. Theonas was incorporated in the huge Mosque of a Thousand Columns; the Church of St. Athanasius also became a mosque; and the Mosque of the Prophet Daniel was raised on the Mausoleum of Alexander. The great monuments of the past, however, including the Caesarion, the Mouseion, the Pharos, and the Ptolemaic palace, fell into desuetude.

What does seem to have survived into the medieval period was the basic pattern of the urban grid, or, perhaps more accurately, sections of it. In fact as late as the fifteenth century a governor of the city likened the street net to a chessboard, and there is no doubt that many of the orthogonal components in the mesh persisted right down to the Turkish invasion in 1517.[535] To that extent, Alexandria differed from some of the Levantine cities previously discussed in the durability of its street pattern, while that very pattern also set it apart from al-Fusṭāṭ, where the streets were narrower and less regular in width and direction. A salient feature of the residential areas was that at least a proportion of the houses, dated to the eighth century, incorporated columns supporting as many as three storeys—apparently a practice deriving from Roman times. The perimeter walls of the city were remodelled *(banā)* by both al-Mutawakkil (r. 848–61) and Ibn Ṭūlūn (r. 868–84), as also at a later date by Ṣalāḥ al-Dīn and Baybars; but al-Mutawakkil's defenses enclosed only about half the area of the Hellenistic-Roman settlement. Ibn ʿAbd al-Ḥakam believed that, at the time of the Muslim conquest, Alexandria had comprised three separate walled enclaves *(mudun)* all encompassed within a containing wall.[536] Butler assumed that this was a reference to Coptic, Byzantine, and Jewish quarters, but no other historian or topographer repeated this information, the real significance of which is still obscure. The same author also listed five important mosques in Iskandarīyah in the ninth century[537] that, in spite of uncertainties as to their precise locations, appear to have been distributed fairly evenly throughout the city. By the end of the tenth century, al-Maqdisī deemed it necessary to mention only two mosques, and neither by name.[538] Probably they were the two categorized by al-Nuwayrī respectively as the eastern and western mosques.[539] In the western sector of the city was a governmental precinct, including the Dār al-Sulṭān, Dār al-ʿAdl, Dār al-Imārah,[540] Qaṣr al-Silāḥ, and Dār al-Ṭirāz. A very unusual feature of the ʿAbbāsid city was the existence of a Muslim necropolis just within the southern wall. The most prestigious cemetery, however, where places of pilgrimage *(mazārāt)* were dispersed among the colonnaded mausolea of scholars, pious devotees, and other notables, occupied ground outside the northern wall at the al-Akhḍar Gate; it was opened to the public only on Fridays.

The specifics of the transformation of Iskandarīyah's urban fabric at this stage are not recoverable, but C. E. Fraser was surely close to the truṭh when he concluded that "under the Orthodox caliphs and the Umayyads the city had been both largely militarized and arabized."[541] There can be no doubt, though, that the architectural assemblages of the city—"testimony," as Ibn Ḥawqal writes, "to [past] sovereignty and power"[542]—left a lasting impression on the Muslims. Particularly was this true of the great monuments of antiquity, "the immense columns and all sorts of marble ashlars, each requiring thousands of labourers to move it, yet raised several cubits into the air on pillars." Alexandria was clearly a type of city that the Muslims did not encounter every day, and their historians and topographers wove wondrous tales about its marvels, culminating in the archetyped assertion, repeated time after time, that the city's architectural fabric shone so brightly by night that a tailor could thread his needle by its light. The origin of this idea was prosaic enough: simply that the principal facades of the city were of marble and lesser structures painted white,[543] so that both gleamed by moon- or torchlight.

Al-Qayrawān and Other Maghribī Cities

In North Africa ***al-Qayrawān*** (Kairouan) was founded on the ruins of an ancient town named Qūniyah or Qamūniyah.[544] It was referred to variously by early authors as a *qayrawān* (presumably implying some sort of garrison cantonment) and once, by al-Malikī, as a *madīnah* (seemingly denoting a seat of governmental authority). After a period of locational instability ʿUqbah ibn Nāfiʿ, governor of al-Ifrīqiyah (Tunisia and western Libya) in the caliphate of Muʿāwiyah, designated specific sites for the congregational mosque and the *dar al-imārah* at the same time that he allocated tribal holdings *(khiṭāṭ)* within a perimeter of seven and one-half kilometers,[545] very much in the manner of the great *amṣār* of al-Fusṭāṭ and the ʿIrāqayn. But precise information is much less plentiful for al-Qayrawān than for those settlements. In fact we are dependent in the earlier years on chance allusions rather than descriptions, as when it transpires, in connection with the enlargement of the congregational mosque, that in the caliphate of Hishām (724–43) the Fihr clan of the Qurashī founder of the cantonment held title to land abutting the north side of the *masjid.*[546] In the ninth century there were incidental references to several ethnic and/or confessional identities: for instance, Ḥārat Yaḥsub,[547] Raḥbat al-Qurashīyīn,[548] Darb al-Firshāsh,[549] and Sūq al-Yahūd.[550] And there is no doubt that stone, derived principally from preexisting ruins, played a prominent role in the building of the cantonment, which yet remained unwalled until 762. The subsequent vicissitudes that befell the walls built at that time have been touched on in chapter 16.

At the beginning of the ninth century, when the burgeoning city became the capital of an independent kingdom, the ʿAbbāsīyah palace complex was built some three miles to the southeast. It encompassed not only the palace styled al-Ruṣāfah (thereby recalling similarly named institutions in Damascus and Baghdād) but also an impressive congregational mosque, baths, inns, *sūqs*, and a *ṭirāz* factory, all arranged around a large square, called al-Maydān, ideally adapted to the requirements of parades and reviews. Several gates provided access to the precinct.[551] In 877 the even more luxurious palace enclave of Raqqādah was laid out. For al-Qayrawān itself the governorship of Yazīd ibn Ḥātim al-Muhallabī (722–28) was especially beneficial: he it was who reorganized the principal *sūqs* and regulated the exchanges taking place within them. Unfortunately, the advantages of al-Muhallabī's foresight were subverted some two centuries later when the Fāṭimid caliph al-Muʿizz transferred all *sūqs* and their associated craft workshops to the palatine complex known as ***al-Manṣūrīyah.***

The additional water required by the greatly expanded urban population was provided by a series of fifteen masonry cisterns, the largest of which was built by Abū Ibrāhīm Aḥmad between 860 and 863.[552] According to al-Bakrī,[553] toward the mid-eleventh century there were forty-eight *ḥammāms* distributed through the city, while in one unspecified year no fewer than 950 oxen (yielding some two hundred tons of meat) were butchered for the feast of al-ʿAshūrā. Talbī has used these figures, in conjunction with assumed overall dimensions of four by four kilometers, to infer "a population of several hundred thousand people."[554] My estimate would be considerably fewer. Toward the end of the tenth century, al-Maqdisī described a city with fifteen main thoroughfares *(durūb),* of which he named eight: Darb al-Rabīʿ, Darb ʿAbd Allāh, Darb Tūnis, Darb Asram, Darb Aslam, Darb Sūq al-Ahad (Sunday Market), Darb Nāfiʿ, and Darb al-Hadhdhāʾīyīn (Shoemakers).[555] However, it is not known how they were disposed within the city beyond the fact that in the eleventh century the main street, known as al-Simāṭ, ran north to south along the eastern edge of the great congregational mosque for a total distance of four km.[556] As we have seen, the city was unwalled when al-Maqdisī was writing. Finally, the substantial Jewish and Christian components in the population deserve mention, especially the latter. Construction of a church had, in fact, been authorized by al-Faḍl ibn Rawḥ near the end of the eighth century,[557] and ʿIyād mentioned several heads of that confession in the ninth century.[558] Even as late as the eleventh century, Christians were using Latin in their funerary inscriptions.

Nearly one thousand miles farther west, the ancient town of ***Ṭanjah*** (Tangiers) was apportioned in *khiṭāṭ* by the conquering Muslims, probably in 682.[559] Subsequently, for defensive reasons the nucleus of the town migrated from the shore to the slopes of Tangier Point, forming what was in effect a new settlement.[560] But information about the precise relationship of conqueror and conquered in the cities of North Africa in early times is rare, and it has to be inferred that the Arabs and their allies lodged themselves either within the city or in its immediate vicinity. The number of times that classical ruins are mentioned in close proximity to, indeed often among, Muslim settlements affords considerable support for this point of view. Ibn Ḥawqal, for example, notes that the ruins of the ancient city of Nākūr were still visible in his day and that those of ancient Ashrashāl were in evidence in the port area of the town at roughly the same time;[561] but it was al-Bakrī who provided the most consistent record of this situation. The fact that he was writing in the second half of the eleventh century guarantees the existence in earlier centuries of such classical ruins as he chose to mention. The following are a selection of representative examples.[562]

- ***Ancient Carthage*** (Qarṭajannah) was, of course, the prime example, with several marble columns still rising for as much as forty cubits above the soil and numerous remains of architectural structures long since reduced to ruins. Al-Bakrī takes his leave of the locality with the comment that "The ruins of Qarṭajannah are covered with fine villages, prosperous and populous."
- ***Azūr,*** encompassing "extensive monumental remains that strike the traveller with astonishment."
- ***Jalūlah,*** incorporating ruins of ancient structures, including still-standing towers.
- ***Al-Madīnah*** (Medina), "the governmental centre," a name preserving a memory of earlier times, was a walled settlement with a congregational mosque, a bath, and a bazaar, all set amid ruins of the past.
- ***Muzyah,*** apparently a Muslim foundation beside "a large city of ancient time but now deserted." Built principally of ashlars *(jalīl),* it included a *qaṣr* known as the Tower of Thirst *(Qaṣr al-ʿAṭash)* that watched over a pool of saline water.
- ***Qafṣah*** (Gafṣah), built almost entirely of rubble on the marble foundations of pre-Islamic structures.
- ***Sūsah*** (al-Sūs), built almost entirely of ashlars. Within the city was a Roman amphitheater, "a vast edifice of ancient construction," while in its immediate neighborhood were "ruins of enormous size and great antiquity."
- ***Ṭabarqah,*** a coastal city "enclosing ancient buildings of very sound construction."
- ***Tīfāsh,*** a *madīnah* (in the broad sense of the governmental sector of a town) incorporating numerous classical ruins.
- ***Tabassā,*** where "several vaulted halls each furnishing shelter from rain and snow for as many as 2,000 pack animals" were almost certainly pre-Muslim structures.

For what al-Bakrī referred to as "the splendid town of ***al-Mughayryah,***" a little more information is available: "It contains several churches that are impressive monuments of antiquity. These edifices are so solidly built that they are still standing and are very well preserved. Looking at them, one would suppose that the craftsmen had just finished their work."[563] At Ṭubnah the vaulted chambers of a pre-Islamic fortress provided offices for those charged with local administration.[564] Unfortunately, for none of these cities is there a full accounting of the way in which the Muslims disposed themselves among the indigenous population. In fact, seldom does an author go beyond Ibn al-Ṣaghīr's bald statement that people began, among other things, to inhabit Ṭāhart, put up buildings, and cultivate gardens.[565]

Makkah and al-Madīnah

In Arabia the premier cities in Muslim eyes were the Ḥaramān, both of which manifested an absence of comprehensive planning but surely not of local and ad hoc control when the situation demanded it. The cosmologically endowed city of Makkah (Mecca) occupied a narrow corridor, just more than half a mile wide, held as in a vise between bare rock outcrops rising in places to two thousand feet. Even so, houses would have preempted virtually all sites overlooking the Kaʿbah had it not been for caliphal intervention, ʿAbd al-Malik (r. 685–705) and his son al-Walīd (r. 708–715) going so far as to define the precincts of the sacred shrine by encircling galleries (sing. *ẓullah*). The enlargement and embellishment of the *ḥaram* continued under the earlier ʿAbbāsids, particularly al-Manṣūr and Hārūn, who undertook respectively no fewer than seven and nine pilgrimages to the Holy City. Tradition has it that the old Dār al-Nadwah, which in the Prophet's time is said to have served as a Qurashī assembly hall, was pressed into service as a residence for visiting caliphs from the time when it was acquired by Muʿāwiyah until Hārūn constituted another building as an official *dār al-ʿimārah*.[566] From then on, the fabric of the Dār al-Nadwah deteriorated until it was refurbished in the time of al-Muʿtaḍid (r. 892–902) and incorporated as an annex to the Masjid al-Ḥarām.

Meanwhile, Hārūn built a palace for himself and his princes on the northern edge of the shrine, another for his wife on the western side, and a third for his mother; at the same time, officials at all levels of the government administrative hierarchy from Barmakid *wazīrs* to *ḥaram* appointees, together with well-heeled retirees anxious to reserve niches for themselves in Paradise, were appropriating prime sites for their residences along the sides of the *wādī*. By the beginning of the ninth century the *ḥaram*, delimited by a lofty wall with twenty-three gates, had almost attained the dimensions that would endure into the nineteenth century.[567] Tradition credits the caliphate of Muʿāwiyah (661–80) with having witnessed the first general use for construction purposes of baked brick (as opposed to mud brick) bonded with mortar, but by the end of the tenth century the most prominent building material was a smooth black stone set off with white trim and diversified with projecting windows of teakwood. Multistoreyed houses were common.[568] It should be noted, though, that relatively little of this development would have proved practicable without the control of run-off within the *wādī*, allegedly initiated by the caliph ʿUthman with the aid of Christian engineers, and the provision of potable water, which was a concern of caliphal households and territorial magnates at all times.

Clearly the strangulated form of this settlement deviated markedly from the prevailing compactness of contemporary Middle Eastern cities. To an inordinate degree, topography conditioned morphology. As al-Maqdisī puts it, "Its [apparently referring to Makkah, which is rubricated six lines previously, a common enough construction in Arabic texts] width is the extent of the *wādī*."[569] Almost equally anomalous, although for different reasons, was the second component of the Ḥaramān, the settlement that under the Muslims became known as al-Madīnah, "the seat of government."[570] But here dispersion rather than constriction was the distinguishing characteristic. It has already been established in chapter 1 that pre-Islamic Yathrib comprised a dispersed oasis settlement encompassing fortified subtribal compounds set amid groves of date palms, irrigated cropland, and intrusive tongues of desert. At least some of these *āṭām* were multistoreyed and thereby appropriately designated as tower houses.

It is to be presumed that the principal locus of power and authority in the settlement as a whole, if and when such existed, migrated from district to district in response to changing lineage predominance. Information as to what happened immediately following the *Hijrah* is not unduly scarce but is only too frequently ambivalent. However, it is evident that the dispersed character of the settlement persisted for a considerable period of time. Within a particular tribal subgroup the *āṭām* might be in close proximity one to another, in the case of the Banū-Zayd ibn Malik's fourteen such compounds in the Anṣārī quarter of Qubāʾ sufficiently close for their inhabitants to "borrow fire" from one another.[571] Elsewhere they were clearly somewhat farther apart, whether in the Upper or Lower *(Sāfilah)* sectors of the settlement, as Samhūdī, on the authority of Ibn Zabālah, reports for the Khaṭmah, who lived "dispersed in their fortresses."[572] Michael Lecker has also drawn attention to larger strongholds, apparently found only in the ʿĀliyah, that in time of need could serve as places of refuge for whole tribal groups.[573] Memories of four such fortresses have been preserved in the sources, two of which belonged to the Jewish tribes of Naḍīr and Qurayẓah and two to Arab subtribes allied with the same Jewish community. The tradition that ʿUthmān ibn ʿAffān demolished the *āṭām* of al-Madīnah is surely an exaggeration, perhaps an elaboration of a very limited number of instances effected in pursuit of military concerns or urban order.[574] Samhūdī preserved a curious record of the upgrading of two *qaṣrs* into *ḥiṣns* by Muʿāwiyah, and there are a few instances of fortresses being converted into mosques.[575] It is Lecker's conclusion that the eastern ʿĀliyah was "the most fortified area in Medina."[576] And clustered around and between these various types of forts were unfortified dwellings known to the record as *manāzil* (sing. *manzil*) and neighborhood *sūqs*.[577]

It will require a great deal of work of the technical caliber and interpretative subtlety manifested in Lecker's recent book to elicit with any degree of precision the manner in which competing tribal groups in al-Madīnah evolved into a unitary, patrimonial-style polity, which means in effect specifying the processes by which traditional lineage structures were adapted to accommodate incipiently class-defining, religio-political loyalties. That these transformations were not achieved easily or, in the short-term view, quickly is evident enough in the sources—although often overlooked in present-day exegesis. In fact the fundamental matter of the conversion of the inhabitants of the oasis to Islam was a rather lengthy process.[578] It is impossible at this time to document the locations of the primary power centers in the settlement. Muḥammad's compound was surely one of them; but his role was that of arbiter, from which flowed an almost certainly fluctuating degree of authority but apparently no special political power. For at least the first five years of his mediation Muḥammad's role was essentially that of a judge offering sanctified opinions to a tribal *majlis*. Only after the conquest of Makkah in 630 does he begin to appear as a military and political commander, but even then many Muslims in the Qubāʾ sector of al-Madīnah were strongly opposed to his influence, including some who hoped for the return of the formerly powerful but exiled Abū ʿĀmir.[579] Dissension was endemic in the settlement and dissident opinions were expressed even within the Muslim community, as is witnessed by the provocative invective attributed to those known to the Qurʾān and Tradition as *munāfiqūn*,[580] to say nothing of the strong Jewish presence in the oasis. The still somewhat obscure affair of the Masjid al-Ḍirār (Mosque of Dissension) in Zayd ibn Mālik territory in A.H. 9, which Lecker construes as a dispute between two mosques in Qubāʾ, may have marked a significant phase in the process of unification.[581]

In any case, by the time of Muḥammad's death in 632, his branch of the Muslim community in al-Madīnah had established a reasonably secure hegemony over the whole oasis. This achievement had almost certainly benefited from the collaborations necessary for the mounting of the more than seventy raids *(maghāzī)* that had been undertaken since the *Hijrah* and which then (if not earlier) justified the connotation of the Aramaic origin of the settlement's new Arabicized name as "seat of government." And the resulting centralization of power continued under the Rāshidūn caliphs, becoming especially evident in the time of ʿUmar (r. 634–44).[582] However, the open and seemingly dispersed character of the settlement is implicit in that even the center of the city was not walled until 974, when a Buwayhid *amīr* felt it to be threatened by the eastward advance of the Fāṭimids.

The likely origin of the town's first mosque has been discussed in the second section of this chapter. Within a decade of the *Hijrah* there were already nine tribal mosques in the Sāfilah as well as other unspecified ones elsewhere, together with the original mosque in Qubāʾ[583] and, of course, the Prophet's Mosque itself. This last had been enlarged by the caliphs ʿUmar and ʿUthmān but completely rebuilt by order of al-Walīd with the involvement of Greek and Coptic craftsmen, and again extended by al-Mahdī (r. 775–85).[584] When al-Maqdisī was writing, it boasted twenty gates. The city itself had four imposing *(hāʾil)* gates, called respectively al-Baqīʿ, al-Thanīyah, Juhaynah, and al-Khandaq,[585] and a loftily constructed keep *(ḥiṣn)*. The principal marketplaces were close to the Prophet's Mosque. The prevailing building material was clay.

Sūsa

Almost one thousand miles to the northeast, on the northern edge of the Khūzistān embayment, the old city of Sūsa, which could boast a history going back for at least two millennia, was acquired by the Arabs, apparently by capitulation, in 638 (or possibly the following year). The site was already diverse and extensive. On a tepe on the east bank of the Shāwūr River were the still imposing ruins of the palaces of Darius and Artaxerxes; on another tepe to the southeast were the remains known to present-day investigators as the Royal City, presumably what in other contexts we have designated a palatine complex. It is among these vestiges of an illustrious past that the earliest Islamic structures have been detected, either imposed on or inserted among the ruins, while the archaeological inventory testifies to the presence there not only of Muslims but also of Zoroastrians, Christians, and Jews

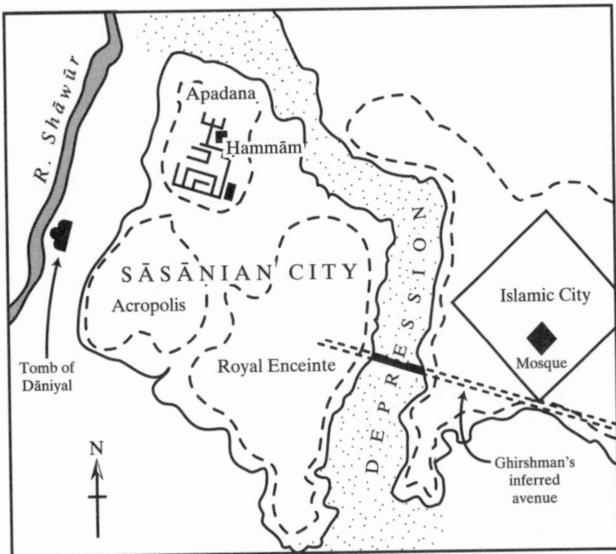

Figure 23. Skeletal layout of al-Sūs based on excavations by Kervran and Ghirshman as interpreted by Hardy-Guilbert and Whitcomb.

(fig. 23). In Arabic sources the city was rubricated as al-Sūs.[586] Then in the second half of the seventh century, on the site of an abandoned cemetery occupying the summit of a third but lower tepe eastward of a roughly longitudinal depression, the Muslims laid out a new settlement. This took the form of a square enceinte of approximately one hundred meters per side and oriented to the *qiblah* of a mosque situated to the south of its center. This mosque is believed to have been built in about 640 but enlarged and refurbished probably in the ninth century in much the same way as happened at Sīrāf at roughly the same time.[587] An ʿAbbāsid complex within the enceinte has been identified by Monique Kervran as a *khānqāh* (monastery), mainly on the basis of al-Maqdisī's remark that in the tenth century most of the inhabitants of the city belonged to the Ṣūfī sect of Ḥubbīyah.[588]

There is a certain irony in the circumstance that the archeological support frequently invoked as a potential arbiter of ambiguities in the literary record in the present instance should have given rise to opposing views of the organization of this extensive site—the other circumference of which, incidentally, appears not to have been walled. On the one hand, Claire Hardy-Guilbert has argued for the integrity of the site as a unitary urban entity, in the ninth century at least.[589] On the other hand, Donald Whitcomb has proposed the recognition of an ancient city comprising the *apadana,* fortress, and palatine complexes on the western tepes as distinct from a new, Muslim, mosque-focused foundation on the eastern tepe. He sees in the relative positions of these architectural remains a design principle analogous to that which he has elicited for Iṣṭakhr and posited for several other early Islamic foundations. The matter is further complicated by Ghirshman's reading of an air photograph as showing a possible boulevard-style artery running from northwest to southeast to link the two halves of the city. Only further archeological investigation will resolve this debate.

In any case, by the ninth century the relatively modest town that the Arabs had inherited from the Sāsānians had become a reasonably prosperous mint city, seemingly not greatly afflicted by the political troubles enveloping Khūzistān at the time. In the tenth century the whole site occupied the not inconsiderable area of four square kilometers, but archaeology testifies to a concomitant migration of population from the western sectors of the city to the Muslim settlement in the east, which must have been what al-Maqdisī had in mind when he noted that "the administrative complex *(al-madīnah)* is in ruins and the populace lives in the outer city *(al-rabaḍ).*"[590] On the far western edge of the site the alleged tomb of the prophet Dāniyāl, believed to be in the bed of the Shāwūr River with a handsome *masjid* on the west bank supposedly opposite the precise spot, was a popular attraction for pilgrims from far and near.[591] Generally speaking, al-Maqdisī approved of the quality of life in al-Sūs, rating the markets as excellent, the baths as first-rate,[592] and the congregational mosque as near-perfect. The worst failings he could impute to the inhabitants were a lack of respect for their preachers (who were Ḥanbalites, whereas he was a Ḥanafite) and a moral laxity that permitted the setting up of houses of prostitution at the very doors of the congregational mosque during the summer months.[593]

Mayyāfāriqīn

On a tributary of the Baṭmān-Ṣu, which drains into the upper Tigris, the fortified city known in Syriac texts of the time as Mīpherqēt, in Armenian as Muphargin, and to the Arabs as Mayyāfāriqīn (modern Silvan) offered the conquering Muslims, who gained control of it by capitulation in 639, an urban milieu markedly different from that of al-Sūs.[594] It had been founded probably in about

400, after which it had a checkered history until Justinian in 527 established it as a strategic military center. Procopius furnishes a detailed description of the town walls and ancillary defensive systems in the sixth century,[595] and Ibn al-Azraq provides legend-encrusted accounts of the origins and principal architectural features, including eight gates. To these may be added an impressive basilica and the Church of the Virgin, the ruins of both of which are visible today. Even after the Muslim conquest, Mayyāfāriqīn continued to be an important center of oriental Christianity. In fact Christians served as officials in the Marwānid government when there was a Melkite church in the city.[596] In the tenth century a mummified figure in the monastery of St. Thomas *(Dayr Tūmā)* a *farsakh* outside the wall was believed to have been the remains of a disciple of Jesus Christ.[597] A century later the city was the seat of a Jacobite bishop.

The precise actions of the Muslims when they came into control of the settlement are not known, but in the tenth century al-Iṣṭakhrī was impressed with the perimeter defenses,[598] which soon afterwards were repaired by the Ḥamdānid Ṣayf al-Dawlah, who from time to time held court in the citadel. Not unexpectedly, this same ruler reorganized the water supply. When Nāsir-i Khusraw passed through the city in 1046–47, it was the wall with its towers and crenellations that most attracted his attention; but when he remarked that the top of the wall "looked as though the master builder had just finished working on it,"[599] it is uncertain whether he was implying that that were indeed the case or that Ṣayf's constructions had been kept in impeccable repair. According to Nāṣir, the wall was pierced by only one gate, and it had a solid iron door. One congregational mosque was situated within the city proper and another, set amid caravanserais, *sūqs*, and baths, in the *rabaḍ*. The inference is that by the mid-eleventh century the commercial and social life of Mayyāfāriqīn had moved from the old, inner administrative focus to the outer city. But that may not have been the end of the story. Nāṣir also mentions an otherwise unknown New Town (Muḥdathah) a short (but unfortunately unspecified) distance to the north of Mayyāfāriqīn that was endowed with its own congregational mosque, bathhouses, and *sūqs*. It looks very much as if Muḥdathah were in the process of becoming a still larger *rabaḍ* on the way to appropriating the life-sustaining and life-enhancing functions of the earlier one that had drawn such activities out of the inner city.

Since the publication of the research of Wilhelm Barthold from 1928 onward, some of which was rendered into Western European languages in the 1930s and 1940s, the early Islamic cities of al-Mashriq have conventionally been assigned a ternary structure.[600] Archetypically, this took the form of a citadel (*quhandiz;* sometimes designated a *qalʿah* by Arab authors)[601] that more often than not had been the seat of a Sāsānian government official, and below the walls of which had developed an administrative center having the requisite service facilities, known to the Persians as a *shahristān* and to the Arabs as a *madīnah.*[602] This also typically had been part of the Sāsānian settlement and was itself walled. However, in the Islamic period new residential, commercial, and industrial clusters began to form outside the *shahristān;* from the tenth century onward they either usurped, or competed seriously for, the economic and social life of the *shahristān.* A peripheral settlement of this type, which in turn was often walled, was termed in Persian a *bīrūn,* in Arabic a *rabaḍ.* Not infrequently the whole settlement was referred to as a *balad.* There is no doubt that the type city of the Mashriq in one way or another subsumed these morphological components, but there has been an unfortunate tendency to construe them as arranged in roughly concentric circles or ellipses. In actuality, however, the *quhandiz* was more likely to be located eccentrically within or even outside the *shahristān,* with the *rabaḍ* initially as a discontinuous peripheral settlement that with the passage of time tended to generate its own fully urban level of social and economic integration. In other words, Barthold's formulation is an ideal type of morphology rather than a constructed type, and must be treated as such. What that means in practice will be sufficiently evident from the following brief discussions of selected Mashriqī cities.

Nīshāpūr

Tenth-century Nīshāpūr has already been described in chapter 14; the comments that follow can be regarded as supplementing that account.

Shimuzu Kosuke has set the city in a threefold hierarchical framework involving the triadically structured, built-up area of the metropolis itself, the district lying within a day's walk of it, and a dependent region up to one hundred to two hundred kilometers further out.[603] In fact this hierarchy of spaces is not very different from that espoused in the present work, namely Nīshāpūr as the built form of a *miṣr,* the city's sustaining trade area, and the *rubʿ* of which Nīshāpūr was the capital (in effect the *qaṣabah,* although in al-Maqdisī's account that function is masked by the emphasis placed on the role of *miṣr*). Indeed, Shumuzu might well have added the whole of Khurāsān—the territory that al-Maqdisī conceived as having been, or ideally ought to have been, administered from Nīshāpūr—as a fourth rank in his hierarchy.

When we turn to the internal structure of the city, the primary concern of this section, the most comprehensive attempt at reconstruction is that undertaken by Richard Bulliet by the melding together of literary sources, archaeological excavation, and such evidence as can be gleaned from air photographs.[604] The Sāsānian city appears to have conformed fairly closely to the ideal type specified above: a *quhandiz* beside a walled *shahr.* That the fosse *(khandaq)* around the *quhandiz* merged with the fosse around the *shahr*[605] reflects the fact that in this instance the citadel was outside, but close to, the wall of the *shahristān.* There is also mention of a quarter called Anbārdih ("Granary Town"), which Bulliet suggests may have persisted into Muslim times under the name Shāhanbar ("Royal Granary").[606]

It has usually been assumed that the Islamic city that followed on the conquest of Sāsānian Nīshāpūr by ʿAbd Allāh ibn ʿĀmir in 651 or 652 was built on the site of the old city. Charles Wilkinson denies such a continuity on the basis of a lack of archaeological evidence,[607] but Professor Bulliet probably makes the stronger case when he argues for a single site, the topographical and descriptive evidence in his opinion outweighing the lack of pre-Islamic materials in Wilkinson's test excavations.[608] In any case, immediately after the Muslim conquest ʿĀmir established his headquarters in Shāhanbar and built three mosques, one on the site of the city's fire temple in the *quhandiz* (also known as the Old Congregational Mosque *[al-Jāmiʿ al-ʿAtīq]*), one on Maʿqil Street, and one in the *maḥallah* of Shāhanbar.[609] At this time the city was of little importance and its development slow. In fact in 656/57 the Arabs were expelled from the city for a whole year. In 662/63 a new governor of Khurāsān took up residence in the city, but Umayyad authority was never secure until 692, when a rebellion by ʿAbd Allāh ibn Khāzim was finally suppressed. Even then Nīshāpūr was of less consequence than Marv, the Arabs' first capital in the Mashriq. Its economic and sociocultural development really began when a Ṭāhirid governor of Khurāsān constituted it as his capital, a status it was forced to surrender under the Ṣaffārids but which it regained early in the tenth century under Sāmānid rule.

By this time Nīshāpūr had become one of the premier cities in Islam—as al-Maqdisī characterizes it, "The treasure house *(khizānah)* of the two Orients, the emporium for East and West."[610] But in attaining this prosperity, the city had undergone an almost total morphological eversion: burgeoning population migrations from country to city, and from even farther afield, had shifted the focus of social, cultural, and economic life from the *shahristān* to the *rabaḍ.* Here were the principal congregational mosques, built by ʿAmr the Ṣaffārid around an earlier structure raised by Abū Muslim toward the end of the ninth century; the two main *sūqs* (described in the section on economic exchange above); and, significantly, the *dār al-imārah,* situated on Maydān al-Ḥusaynīyīn,[611] together with a prison. There were two gates to the *quhandiz,* one of them leading to the *shahristān,* the other to the *rabaḍ;* and four gates to the *shahristān,* namely the Bridge-Head Gate *(Raʾs al-Qanṭarah),*[612] the Maʿqil Street Bridge, the Fortress Gate *(Bāb al-Quhandiz),* and the Gate of the Takīn Bridge. There is no record of the *rabaḍ* having been walled, although it is credited with having numerous entrances, the most used of which seem to have been the Gate of Domes *(Bāb al-Qibāb),* through which passed travellers heading for ʿIrāq and Jurjān; the Jīq Gate, opening toward Marv, Balkh, and Transoxania; and the Aḥwaṣābād Gate, facing in the direction of Fārs and Quhistān.[613] Al-Maqdisī reports in excess of fifty streets crossing the city, in directions he failed to specify but which Bulliet is inclined to interpret as evidence of an at least partly orthogonal grid.[614] Aerial photographs strongly imply that the main artery of the city ran from northwest to northeast below the southern wall of the *shahristān.*[615]

According to al-Maqdisī, Nīshāpūr comprised 44 quarters *(maḥallāt),* although al-Naysābūrī lists 47 and a few more are known from other sources. Of the 47 names listed, more than 20 also appear in a schedule of 65 villages that al-Naysābūrī claims were incorporated in an expanding Nīshāpūr,[616] a clear enough indication of the growth of the *rabaḍ.* Bulliet has tentatively identified 25 of the *maḥallāt,*[617] among them al-Ḥīrah, a prosperous commercial quarter that had grown up around the southeastern angle of the *quhandiz.*[618] Others included the wealthy residential district of Mūlqābād and the quarter of Bāb Muʿammar best known for its cemetery, both of which were in the vicinity of al-Ḥīrah; Shāhanbar, already mentioned, not far distant from the main market area; Diz, presumably adjoining the citadel; Maydān al-Ḥusaynīyīn, where was situated the *dār al-imārah;* the neighboring Bāb ʿUrwah; Talājird, with the shrine of Muḥammad Maḥrūq; the Silk *(Qazz)* Quarter, occupying an undetermined position in the northern sector of the *rabaḍ;* Bāghak, on the city's east side; Naṣrābād, a renaming of the village formerly known as Shāpūr, presumably at the time of the Islamic conquest, where both merchants and scholars resided; Maydān Ziyād ibn ʿAbd al-Raḥmān, named for a ninth-century notable; Jīq, at the eastern end of the main avenue; Darābjird, Bāb Abī al-Aswad, and Manāshik, all located on the northern fringe of the city; al-Jūr, the site of the festival prayer ground *(ʿaidgāh),* Bidistān,[619] and Janzarūd, all in the southern sector; the Quarter of the Domes *(al-Qibāb),* where the road to al-ʿIrāq left the city; Shādyākh, in the ninth century the dynastic seat and palatine complex of the Ṭāhirids but subsequently razed by the Ṣaffārids, and visible in the present-day landscape as the remains of a circuit wall enclosing 125 hectares in the southwestern sector of the *rabaḍ;* the wealthy community of Muḥammadābād, which seems to have evolved its own ekistical personality within the larger quarter of Shādyākh; and Khūlast to its south.

Almost half the quarters known to have existed cannot now be identified at all, and it is especially unfortunate that among these should be the Weavers' Quarter (Jūlāhkān);[620] Dharwān, where the Sāsānian Lord of the Marches *(Kanārang)* had had his palace in pre-Muslim times; and two Jewish enclaves *(do dīh yahūd).* It is Bulliet's conclusion that the north and northwest sectors of the city, which encroached on the desert fringe, were populated by the poorer and less prestigious classes in contrast to the better-watered east and northeast.[621] However, this author is at pains to warn us that the sources available for this type of reconstruction "cannot possibly be relied upon for complete accuracy."[622] What can be relied on as rough approximations are al-Maqdisī's description of the city as one square *farsakh*[623] and Ibn Ḥawqal's distancing of the congregational mosque at one quarter of a *farsakh* from the *dār al-imārah.*[624]

Whatever may be the truth about the minutiae of the internal structure of Nīshāpūr, there can be no doubt but that the straggly *rabaḍ* of earlier times had become by the tenth century an urban center in its own right. When Abū ʿAli al-ʿAlawī jestingly pointed out to Abū Saʿīd al-Jūrī in effect that all his native *maḥallah* (al-Jūr) needed to become a fully developed town was a drum, a banner, and the jurisdiction of an *amīr,*[625] he was saying precisely that for what was only a very small part of the *rabaḍ.* And when al-Maqdisī asserts that Nīshāpūr (for which he uses the honorific Īrānshahr) was more extensive than al-Fusṭāṭ, more populous than Baghdād, better integrated than al-Baṣrah, more impressive than al-Qayrawān (Kairouan), cleaner than Ardabīl, and more flourishing than Hamadān,[626] his florid hyperbole was clearly inspired by life in the *rabaḍ;* even the *quhandiz* receives only incidental mention. And the same is true of al-Naysābūrī's more restrained account.

In the 1950s the Soviet scholar A. Yu. Yakubovskii sought to explain this tendency for *rabaḍ*s to preempt the destiny of Mashriqī cities in strictly Marxist terms. For him, as indeed for his numerous followers down to quite recent times, the *shahristān* was a "pre-feudal" settlement from which indigenous "aristocrats" controlled a "closed manorial economy." In the eighth century "craft industry" began to replace "cottage industry" in the newly forming *rabaḍ,* a development that in the ninth century entailed the emergence of a largely autonomous artisanate and, so Yakubovskii claimed, artisanal corporations. At this point the resulting dominance of the outer city signified the establishment of a fully "feudal" society.[627] In spite of the allegiance that this formulation commanded in the Soviet Union, it was never popular in either the Western or the Islamic world. The idiolectal jargon presents a serious problem and, even when it can be transcribed into familiar Western terminology, the resulting societal succession is not always in accord with available evidence. However, Yakubovskii was correct in his perception that the *shahristān* and the *rabaḍ* represented successive phases of urban development, as well as important sociocultural and economic transformations, and that the locus of these changes was the outer city; but Professor Bulliet put it all more clearly, and in my opinion more accurately, when he said simply, "Nishapur grew greatly as a result of becoming a major Muslim administrative center . . . and this growth occurred outside the old walled city."[628]

Balkh

Balkh, in al-Maqdisī's hierarchy the *qaṣabah* of the eastern *rub*ʿ of Khurāsān, was a city of high antiquity.[629] After the conquests of Alexander the Great it had been an important center of successively the Graeco-Bactrians, the Kushans, and the Hayṭal. In immediately pre-Islamic times Buddhism seems to have competed with Zoroastrianism, with the former represented by the famous Naw Bahār and the latter by at least five temples. The walls that had protected the city since the time of Alexander proved ineffective (if they still existed) when in 653 the Arab commander al-Aḥnaf ibn Qays imposed a tribute settlement and when a decade later the city was finally conquered by the Muslims. Even then, it was not totally subdued until early in the eighth century. Frequent revolts against Arab rule had taken such a toll on the city that al-Ṭabarī implies it was in ruins in about 705. In any case, the Arabs did not immediately occupy the city but established a garrison cantonment at Barūqān, some two *farsakh*s removed from it. Not until 727 did the governor of Khurāsān, one Asad ibn ʿAbd Allāh al-Qaṣrī, rebuild the old city of Balkh and install the garrison there—to the detriment of Barūqān, of course, which apparently faded from the landscape.[630] But it was the transference of the Khurāsānī capital from Marv to Balkh in 736 that actually initiated the revival of the city. Under the ʿAbbāsids the governors of the province treated it virtually as a personal benefice, with descendants of Khuttal princes ruling for a time in Balkh under the style Abū Dāʾūdids. In 870 Yaʿqūb ibn Layth, founder of the Ṣaffārid dynasty, overran the city, but his line was driven out thirty years later by the Sāmanids, under whom Balkh attained a level of sociocultural and economic development for which it would long be remembered.

In spite of the unpropitious beginning to Muslim rule, when the city was destroyed, bypassed, and then rebuilt and repossessed, and despite its politically ambiguous status for much of the next two centuries, Balkh prospered and grew in size. Its nodal location with respect to the Eastern Īrānian world more than compensated over time for its political vicissitudes.[631] Already by the closing years of the ninth century, al-Yaʿqūbī—who was in a position to know, having served the Ṭāhirid dynasty in Khurāsān—was lauding it as the most important city in Khurāsān. He also testified that it conformed to the archetypical morphology of Mashriqī cities, encompassing both an inner *shahristān* and an outer *rabaḍ*, which he seems to be describing as concentric.[632] According to the same author, there were four gates to the *rabaḍ*, but Barthold has provided good reason to believe that al-Yaʿqūbī is here referring to the *shahristān*, which by analogy with other Khurāsānī settlements would be expected to have had four gates. The distance between the walls of these two sectors was specified as a *farsakh*. And circling the outer boundary of the city's immediate, at least partially cultivated, environs, separating the oasis from the desert, was a feature more in keeping with Transoxanian than Khurāsānī settlements: twelve *farsakh*s of wall, in this instance pierced by twelve gates.[633] From the edge of the *shahristān* to this outer defense was a distance of five *farsakhs*. The *shahr* was one *farsakh* in diameter.[634]

By the closing decades of the tenth century, Balkh had come to rank with Marv and Harāt as a commercial emporium and cultural center, but the old triadic structure of the city was still very much in evidence. A *quhandiz*, which had not been mentioned in the earlier Islamic centuries, is now implied.[635] It is noticeable, though, that the *rabaḍ* enclosed the *shahristān* on only the east, south, and west sides, allowing quasi-rural terrain to reach right up to the city on its northern edge.[636] The walls encircling the outermost fringe of the oasis appear to have fallen out of use by this time, but the presence of the congregational mosque amid the principal *sūq*s in the *rabaḍ*[637] is sufficient testimony to the process of settlement eversion that was evident across the whole of the Mashriq as government and its derivative economic and social functions drew migrants mothlike into the expanding orbit of Islam. The four gates of the *shahristān* mentioned by al-Yaʿqūbī had become seven when al-Maqdisī was writing, specifically Bāb Naw Bahār, Bāb Raḥbah ("Gate of the Square"), Bāb al-Hadīd ("Iron [-clad] Gate"), Bāb al-Hinduwān (of the Indians), Bāb al-Yahūd (of the Jews), Bāb Shast [-band][638] (Sixty [dykes]), and Bāb Yaḥyā.[639] A structure which persisted in Muslim memory[640] long after the Arabs had destroyed it was the Buddhist temple Naw

Bahār, apparently situated in what later became the *rabaḍ*, where a *stupa* called al-Ustun rose 100 ells above 360 cells for resident and visiting monks. When the Chinese Buddhist pilgrim Hsüan Tsang arrived in the first half of the seventh century, he learned that there were as many as one hundred Buddhist monasteries and three thousand monks in Balkhī territory, while there are indications that the Naw Bahār was attracting devotees as late as the beginning of the eighth century.[641] Both houses and defensive walls were of unfired brick.

Harāt

Another city having ancient roots was Harāt, which probably capitulated to the Muslims in 652.[642] Its history during the ensuing century is obscure but was certainly not uneventful, for it was the scene of unsuccessful revolts in 661 and 702 and figured in the disorders preceding the ʿAbbāsid usurpation. It was under this dynasty that the city flourished as a regional center for the productive Harī Rūd valley; as an emporium for the southern trade with Sijistān and the south Persian provinces, including Fārs (the main east–west trade route passed from Nīshāpūr to Sarakhs to Marv al-Shahijān); and in al-Maqdisī's estimation as the *qaṣabah* of the southern *rub*ʿ of Khurāsān.

Under the Sāsānids, Harāt had been both a prosperous producer of agricultural commodities and an important military base for raids against the Hayṭal, but the morphology of the city at that time can only be a matter for speculation. By the tenth century, however, it is evident that it conformed closely to the Mashriqī type, with a *quhandiz* in the interior of a bustling *(a*ʿ*mar) shahristān/madīnah,* and a *rabaḍ* developed on the periphery. The *shahristān* was one-half of a *farsakh* long and as much wide, and it was there that the congregational mosque had been raised and attracted the principal *sūqs* to its neighborhood. The *dār al-imārah,* by contrast, was completely outside the city, at a place known as Khurāsānābād "some third of a *farsakh* along the road to Būshang."[643] The prison was close to the *masjid* in the *rabaḍ,* where a second fortress *(ḥiṣn)* had been erected. The gist of not wholly unambiguous accounts by tenth-century topographers seems to be that the city exhibited at least token cardinal orientation and axiality, with the two axial streets running clear across both *rabaḍ* and *shahristān,* and the gates into both sectors sharing the same names. As listed by al-Maqdisī,[644] these were Bāb Ziyād, facing the direction of Nīshāpūr; Bāb Fīrūz;[645] Bāb Sarāy (Palace Gate), toward Balkh; and Bāb Khushk, toward Ghūr. And close to each gate (presumably of the *rabaḍ*) there had developed a *sūq.*[646] It is evident from the tenor of the tenth-century authors that Harāt at that time was no mean city, but it is also apparent that, unlike the situation in Nīshāpūr and Balkh, the *rabaḍ* had not totally drained off the vitality of the *shahristān.* A prime reason for this is that the latter encompassed the site of the congregational mosque, described as the best attended in all Khurāsān,[647] which drew to its vicinity traders, scholars, jurists, and a host of others.

Marv al-Shāhijān

Marv al-Shāhijān was another city of ancient lineage that, initially at any rate, lost none of its prestige and prosperity under Muslim hegemony, even though its morphology was altered in no uncertain ways.[648] The settlement appears to have been founded by the Seleucid king Antiochus I Soter (r. 280–261 B.C.). It subsequently prospered as the principal seat of authority in the lower Murghāb River valley, from early times an intensively irrigated farming region,[649] and from its nodal position on the great caravan route that from Parthian times linked western Asia to China. Originally the whole oasis was surrounded by a wall which in Sāsānian times was some forty miles (fifteen hundred *stadia*) in length.[650] There are no extant records relating directly to Marv in the Sāsānian period except for mention of this wall by a seventh-century Syriac author, but a modicum of information can be inferred from the configuration of the settlement that came into possession of the Muslims in 651. The citadel *(quhandiz)* was certainly in evidence on a low eminence, and a supporting settlement had consolidated below its walls. This was the enclave that tenth-century Arabo-Persian authors came to designate the *shahristān* or *madīnah* but which in earlier times had been the capital of the *marzbān* of the northeastern frontier. Before 553 it had been the seat of a Nestorian bishop, and subsequently a metropolitanate.

When the Muslim governor of Khurāsān invested Marv, the resulting treaty of submission stipulated that the Arab garrison of four thousand men was to be quartered in the houses of the inhabitants of the *madīnah.* Exactly twenty years later, fifty thousand families from al-Baṣrah and al-Kūfah were settled in the villages dotting the oasis.[651] These infusions of population stimulated agricultural production, sometimes underwritten by government as well as private resources, and economic development, both of which encouraged the crystallization of new classes of society: notably, wealthy merchants and administrative officials who lorded it over free artisans and peasants. The *madīnah,* where these changes were probably most evident, was on the site of present-day Gavur-Qalʿah. In the tenth century it had four gates: Bāb al-Madīnah, Bāb Sanjān, Bāb Bālīn, and Bāb Dār Mashkān, which were probably, as in several other large cities of the Mashriq, situated at or close to the cardinal points of the compass.[652] Even under the Umayyads, however, a *rabaḍ* had begun to develop to the west of the *shahristān* in a neighborhood now known as Sultān Qalʿah.[653] Despite a decline in the overall prosperity of the city when the Ṭāhirids transferred the capital of Khurāsān to Nīshāpūr, this *rabaḍ* eventually developed into a virtually new city, helped not a little by Marv's role as the eastern focus for the ʿAbbāsid *daʿwā* and subsequently as the headquarters of al-Maʾmūn first when he was governor of the eastern provinces and then in the early years of his caliphate. This thriving, largely independent settlement had grown into a roughly triangular shape elongated from north to south, and boasting an extent equal to that of the *shahristān.*[654] And with commercial prosperity came administrative and religious functions, together with élite residences.

When Khurāsān and the Hayṭal territories were united under a single dynasty ruling from Nīshāpūr, however, Marv lost a good deal of its administrative and military importance; add to which disruptions caused by feuding among ambitious military commanders toward the end of Sāmānid rule. When al-Maqdisī was writing, the *quhandiz* was in ruins[655] and a third of the *rabaḍ* demolished, its houses decayed and their roofs fallen in, just as if it were all a relic of the distant past.[656] And the population had declined proportionately. The old *jāmiʿ* in the center of the *shahristān* had been demoted to a simple *masjid,* its role as a congregational mosque having been preempted by a building in the *rabaḍ* serving mainly Ḥanafites, and dating from the dawn of the ʿAbbāsid era. Close by was a domed *dār al-imārah* built by Abū Muslim, while a second *masjid* (as opposed to a *jāmiʿ*) was endowed at the beginning of the ninth century for the benefit of Shāfiʿīs. Originally the city's market had grown up around the gate leading from the *shahristān* to the *rabaḍ*—this was the small market *(suwayqah)* mentioned by al-Maqdisī[657]—but the retail center had long since been reconstituted actually within the outer city, particularly in the extensive Mājān district surrounding the *maydān.* Of this great mart Ibn Ḥawqal enthused, "It is the best maintained of markets, selling everything one might want by day or night."[658]

A salient feature of the physical infrastructure of this city, even in its decline toward the close of our period, and one that the topographers did not fail to mention, was the provision of flowing water to virtually every quarter of the complex. From a dam on the Murghāb River at the village of Zarq one *farsakh* south of Marv, four canals delivered sluice-regulated water to the numerous quarters. From west to east these conduits were the Hurmuzfarrah; the Mājān, carrying the main flow of the Murghāb; the Razīq; and the Asʿadī.[659] Even after the city had lost its privileged position in Khurāsān, its baths were rated highly.[660] The two settlements were surrounded by a wall of baked brick, and there appear to have been some interior walls separating quarters; but by the end of the tenth century the old *shahristān* and the new city to its west were morphologically, and probably functionally, distinct entities, manifesting some of the features of the twinned cities to be discussed later. And both were experiencing a decline that was reversed only with the Saljūk hegemony.

Zaranj

Zaranj, in al-Maqdisī's hierarchy, was the *qaṣabah*[661] of Sijistān. It was not unknown to Īrānian mythology, which attributed its founding to Garshāsp, a hero who was also credited with the establishment of the polity of Sijistān. In Sāsānian times, Zaranj was the seat of a *marzbān.*[662] Not least of the factors contributing to the high status of the city was the presence some three *farsakh*s down the road to Harāt, at a place called Karkūyah, of the premier fire temple of the province, which legend ascribed to no less a potentate than Kai Khusraw at the time when he was also rebuilding the citadel at Zaranj. Although the *Taʾrīkh-i Sistān* designated the city as the seat of a Mōbadh-Mōbadhān, the chief dignitary of the Zoroastrian faith, Clifford Bosworth is probably correct in his surmise that in actuality this priest may well have ranked somewhat lower in the hierarchy.[663] According to the anonymous author of the *Taʾrīkh-i Sīstān,* the *shahristān* was so strongly fortified that it acquired a sobriquet rendered by the Arabs as "The Inviolate City" *(Madīnāt al-ʿAdhrā)*.[664] Nothing else is known of the urban morphology of Zaranj under Sāsānian rule and precious little about the changes that followed on the capitulation of the city to the Muslims in 652/53. It almost immediately became a mint city for coins of Arab-Sāsānid type and a forward base for campaigns into al-Rukhkhaj and Zamīndāwar; but it can be inferred that it did not entirely escape the tribal feuds engulfing Sijistān, Khārijī unrest, and the prolonged rebellion of Ḥamzah ibn Ādharak against ʿAbbāsid authority. Nevertheless, by the closing years of the ninth century the city was surrounded by a fosse *(khandaq)*, some four *farsakh*s in circumference, crossed by five entrances *(abwāb)*.[665]

As is true of numerous Mashriqi cities, we have to wait until the second half of the tenth century for any substantial information about the layout of Zaranj; then Ibn Ḥawqal provides an unexpectedly full description.[666] A citadel stood, in typical Īrānian fashion, within a *madīnah/shahristān*,[667] with an extensive[668] and densely populated *rabaḍ* beyond, in which were to be found the residences of the Ṣaffārid princes, together with unloading facilities[669] and *funduqs*. The congregational mosque was, significantly, in the *madīnah*,[670] with the prison close by. Here too was the original *dār al-imārah*, which in the tenth century had been transferred to a palace *(qaṣr)* built by Yaʿqūb ibn al-Layth in the *rabaḍ*. Another palace built by his brother ʿAmr was also located in the same neighborhood, that is, between the Bāb al-Ṭaʿām and Bāb Minā (for which see below). Also within the *madīnah*, between the Karkūyah and Nīshak Gates (see below), was an imposing architectural complex known as *Ark* (for Persian *arg*), built by ʿAmr ibn al-Layth to serve as his treasurehouse *(khizānah)*.[671] It is to be inferred that this was the same structure that al-Maqdisī located in the *madīnah* but designated a *qalʿah*.[672] Five gates pierced the wall surrounding the *madīnah*[673] and as many as thirteen the wall and moat guarding the *rabaḍ*.[674] Although the original markets that had grown up around the congregational mosque in the *madīnah* were still driving a good trade *(aʿmar)*, they were now matched by others in the *rabaḍ* that had been founded by ʿAmr. This latter *sūq*, stretching all the way from the Fārs Gates to the Mīnā Gate, a good half *farsakh*, yielded a daily return of one thousand *dirhams* that were apportioned among the city's congregational mosque (an interesting instance of a *rabaḍ* supporting a *madīnah*), the local infirmary *(bīmaristān)*, and the Kaʿbah in Makkah (Mecca). A network of waterways and reservoirs drawing from the canalized Sanārūdh fed the outer moat, brought water to most houses, and in the northeastern sector of the city powered grain mills.[675] The preferred, indeed almost exclusive, building material was unfired brick *(ṭīn)*.

The implications of Ibn Ḥawqal's account are clear enough: Zaranj was sharing in the typical Mashriqī population movement to the *rabaḍ*. The Ṣaffārid investments in that part of the city were paying off, but, as in the case of Harāt, they had not extinguished the vitality of the *madīnah*, where both mosque and market were still very much alive and, as we have seen, in at least one respect mutually supportive. However, Ibn Ḥawqal leaves us in no doubt that the city was not exempt from the threat of environmental subversion. From May to September a low-pressure system centered over what is today West Pakistan generates northwesterly winds of great regularity and steadiness over the lower Helmand region, with wind speeds sometimes exceeding seventy miles per hour. Ibn Ḥawqal took note of the effects of these gales as they whirled loose sand and saline deposits across the open landscape, and of the windbreaks of brush and reed that farmers constructed to protect their villages and crops. More immediately to the point, he retails an involved account that he had acquired from a Sijizī travelling companion to the effect that in 970[676] sand driven by especially violent winds was engulfing the congregational mosque and threatening other sectors of the city—a disaster avoided only by recompensing a young expert in shelter-belt strategies to the tune of twenty thousand *dirhams*. Although Ibn Ḥawqal's tale is doubtless overdrawn, it surely conveys something of the reality of life in Zaranj, and by implication in certain other cities of Sijistān, during the season of the Wind of 120 Days.

The fullness of Ibn Ḥawqal's account inevitably invites an attempt to reconstruct a convincing plan of the city. In fact André Miquel has accepted just this challenge with remarkable success. The resulting dispositions, which the author modestly characterizes as "sinon le plan exact, du moins un schéma de la ville," assigns each of the features previously mentioned to an approximate location within

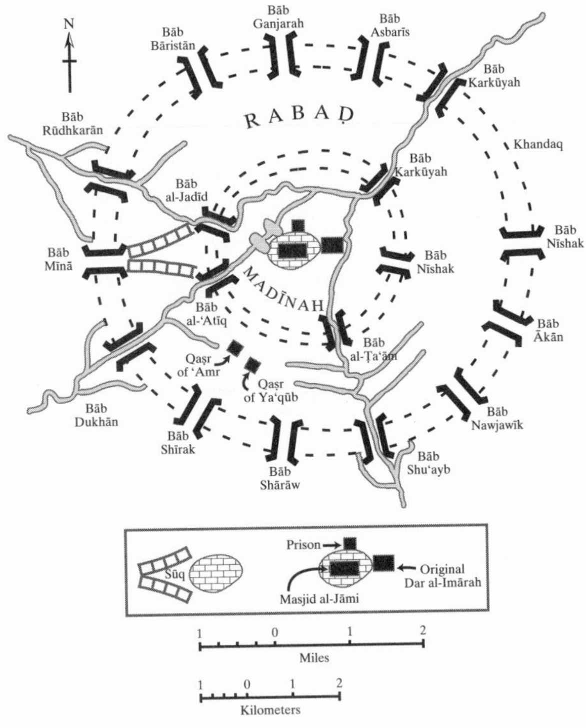

Figure 24. Approximate relative positions of some important elements in the cityscape of Zaranj in the tenth century; the precise alignments of both inner and outer walls are unknown. After Andre Miquel, *La Géographie Humaine,* 4:212.

a ternary urban framework (fig. 24).[677] The two principal discrepancies between Professor Miquel's interpretation and mine arise from slight differences in our reading of the text. First, as explained in note 667, Professor Miquel does not find a *ḥiṣn* within the *madīnah,* but rather "a fortified inner city *(madīnah),*" with no mention of a citadel. Second, there is no proof, either literary or archaeological, for the precise run of the walls enclosing the inner and outer cities. However, Professor Miquel relies on Ibn Ḥawqal's use of the word *dā'ir* in relation to the outer wall of the *rabaḍ* to infer a "ville ronde . . . ou du moins de type circulaire, parfait ou non" that had grown spontaneously by concentric increments around an initial nucleus;[678] and he adduces in support of this view the existence of other more or less circular cities in the Eastern Caliphate[679] and the alignment of three inner gates with three outer gates.[680] "L'essentiel reste," he concludes, "que le cercle est souligné, et fortement."

This is the way in which Professor Miquel has depicted the city in his reconstruction. Although these arguments are surely not without merit, I am afflicted with lingering doubts as to their validity. The force of *dā'ir,* I believe, in this context signifies no more than "circumference," "periphery," or "circuit." The supporting arguments are just that, and cannot of themselves sustain the notion of a circular city. Consequently, I have to conclude with a *non liquet,* although with some predisposition to prefer an irregular form. In short, I am uncertain not only as to what the text actually says but also as to what degree of circularity has to be involved in order for a settlement to be meaningfully characterized as a *ville ronde.*

Samarqand

Away in the northeastern corner of the Mashriq, in the intensively irrigated valley of the Nahr Ṣughd,[681] where high agricultural productivity had long coexisted with control of a virtually Asiawide commercial network, were two of Islam's premier cities, Samarqand and Bukhārā. The first of these, which al-Maqdisī designated as the *miṣr* of Mā Warā' al-Nahr, that is, Transoxania, first entered the light of history as disputed territory in the campaigns of Alexander of Macedon. The earliest mention of Muslims in the city relates to the early years of the eighth century under the Khurāsānī governorship of Qutaybah ibn Muslim, but Arab authority seems to have run only within the walls, and then only with respect to the maintenance of local order. In fact it was a Soghdian prince who ruled in Samarqand until 738, while an Arab garrison remained all but impotent in his city until the governor Naṣr ibn Sayyār finally established a Muslim hegemony over most of Soghdia. The earliest coins minted in the city date from 759 to 762. Even so, the early ʿAbbāsid years witnessed numerous disturbances in the city and its neighborhood, notably the Neo-Mazdakite revolt led by al-Muqannaʿ and the uprising of Rāfiʿ ibn al-Layth from 806 to 809. Although it was Bukhārā that became the Sāmānid capital at the close of the ninth century, Samarqand remained the chief commercial center of Transoxania, not least because of its near monopolies of the highest quality of Turkish slaves[682] and paper, the latter newly introduced from east Asia.[683]

The earliest surviving description of Islamic Samarqand, by Ibn al-Faqīh, depicts the city as surrounded by a wall twelve *farsakhs* long and pierced by twelve gates,[684] but this may have been a literary topos, and this author's further details of urban morphology are not totally free of ambivalence. Subsequent topographers were more explicit, particularly al-Maqdisī: "In the middle [of the city] is a *madīnah* with four gates: Bāb al-Sīn ("The China Gate"),[685] Bāb Naw Bahār [in the western sector], Bāb Bukhārā [in the north], and Bāb Kish [in the south]. . . . The congregational mosque is in the *madīnah*, beside the *quhandiz*."[686] The same author adds that the *madīnah* was surrounded by a wall and fosse *(khandaq)*—according to al-Tabarī, constructions ordered by Abū Muslim[687] and, according to al-Yaʿqūbī, restored by Hārūn al-Rashīd toward the end of the eighth century.[688]

Although the *dār al-imārah* and the prison *(ḥabs)* remained in the *quhandiz* as late as the tenth century, there is no doubt that the focus of economic life by that time was firmly rooted in a *rabaḍ*.[689] Here were all the principal markets of the city, together with elite palaces, *khāns*, baths, and a huge extent of residential building. Eight avenues *(durūb)*, all paved with stone flags, traversed the *rabaḍ*. However, their relationship to the institutional foci of that sector of the city is unknown beyond the fact that they converged on the Raʾs al-Tāq, a central square whence markets radiated outward along the main roads.[690] Ibn Ḥawqal is explicit in his statement that the *rabaḍ* and the principal *sūq* extended across the river from the *madīnah* northward to the locality known as Afshīnah near the Kūhak Gate, whence the perimeter ran in an arc to the Warsanīn Gate, the Fanak Gate, the Riyūdad Gate, the Qaṣr Asad Gate, and the Ghadāwad Gate, where it met the river again.[691] The river served, as it were, as the chord of the arc, a distance of two *farsakhs*. In the tenth century the Sāmānid government retaliated for an insurrection within the city by razing all the gates of the *rabaḍ*.[692]

It is evident that Samarqand—in the tenth century, at any rate—exhibited the main features anticipated of a Mashriqī city, in particular the tripartite division and the economic and sociocultural development of the *rabaḍ*. Markets had all but abandoned the *madīnah*, and the *dār al-imārah*, which al-Iṣṭakhrī had found in the *quhandiz*, was reported by Ibn Ḥawqal as in ruinous condition. However, a new complex of *dīwāns* had been constructed, interestingly enough, in the *madīnah* and, as noticed by Ibn Ḥawqal, at the instigation of the Sāmānids.[693] According to Yāqūt, in the thirteenth century the *madīnah* occupied twenty-five hundred *jarībs*; the outer town, ten thousand *jarībs*.[694] The principal shrine in the city had been promoted by the ʿAbbāsids as the tomb of Qutham ibn ʿAbbās, the Prophet's cousin, but may possibly have had a pre-Islamic origin.[695]

The topographers agreed that the city afforded an attractive environment for people from all walks of life: an elegant and comfortable metropolis, as al-Maqdisī called it, where an abundance of slaves made life as easy as possible for the rest of the population[696] and brought ample returns to those who dealt in that merchandise. A water distribution system was constructed throughout both the *madīnah* and the *rabaḍ*, with water being channelled into the city from the Sughd River through lead pipes by way of a pre-Islamic aqueduct over the moat at the Kish Gate. Where these pipes reached the Raʾs al-Tāq, they apparently took the form of open channels raised on stone supports.[697] Altogether there were two thousand points within greater Samarqand where iced water was provided free to the public, courtesy of charitable benefactors. Another result of the ready availability of water was the amount of vegetation that adorned, yet half-concealed, the city. Residential and public buildings, both usually constructed of brick and wood,[698] were apt to disappear behind clumps of greenery. When Ibn Ḥawqal climbed to the top of the citadel (as he said he did), he looked out on an intricate tapestry of natural and cultural features apparently in a state of long-standing harmony—"the most beautiful spectacle imaginable," he calls it—with verdant groves, resplendent villas *(quṣūr)*, fast-flowing streams, and productive fields. And he ends his encomium with "What a sight to capture the hearts of men!"[699] An unexpected item in this fairly lengthy tribute to the delights of Samarqand is Ibn Ḥawqal's reference to topiary in the gardens and on the streets, especially when he describes how cypress trees were trimmed *(qaṣṣaṣa)* into the shapes of elephants, camels, oxen, and savage beasts confronting each other as if preparing to attack—all of which would seem to have been an open flouting of Islamic rules of representation.

Although Qutaybah ibn Muslim had erected a congregational mosque in the *madīnah* early in the eighth century and Buddhism had almost certainly been eliminated by the middle of the same century, Islamization was evidently slow. At the beginning of the eighth century a Nestorian Christian bishopric based in the city was actually raised to a metropolitan see. In the tenth century a Christian community *(ʿumr)* from ʿIrāq had established endowed monastic cells on the inviting slopes of the Shāwdhār hill a few *farsakhs* to the south of Samarqand,[700] while a monastery of Manichaeans whose adherents called themselves *nighūshāk* (listeners) was to be found within the city itself.[701] Subsequent events imply that Christians prospered in Samarqand until the time of Ulugh Beg, but the Muslim topographers not unexpectedly preserved only a poor record of them, their shrines and monuments, and their cultural contribution to the life of the city. What is certain is that Samarqand in the tenth century was a more diverse environment than the topographers were usually prepared to admit. Nor must it be forgotten that Samarqand projected an image of earthly paradise far beyond the bounds of the Islamic world, in fact clear across Serindia to the farthest frontier of Asia. To the Chinese, who in the seventh century had claimed Soghdia as a nominally tributary kingdom, it was a source of highly prized exotica, including the famed "golden peaches" whose color fitted them for planting in the imperial orchards. On two occasions this emblematic but so far unidentified fruit was brought to the Chinese capital of Chʿang-an and with appropriate ceremony transplanted into Chinese earth, symbols of Western mystery and felicity.[702]

Bukhārā

Somewhat less than 40 *farsakhs* (about 150 miles) downstream from Samarqand, or from six to seven days' journey along the Royal Road, was the great city of Bukhārā.[703] Relatively little information exists about this city in pre-Islamic times; the earliest literary occurrence of the name dates only from Hsüan Tsang's visit in the seventh century A.D., although numismatic evidence points to its existence several centuries previously. When Qutaybah ibn Muslim, after a series of largely abortive summer raids, finally took Bukhārā for the Muslims in 709, he permitted the local dynasty of Bukhār Khudāhs to coexist side by side with an Arab governor. The city over which he had acquired dominion consisted of a walled settlement *(shahristān)* on a low eminence, with a citadel *(quhandiz)*, approximately a mile in circumference, a short distance to the west. Qutaybah quartered his garrison troops in the *shahristān* and turned his attention to pacifying the region.

As al-Narshakhī (or, more accurately, his editor) tells it, the inhabitants had earned a reputation as idolaters who embraced Islam when Arab armies arrived in the summer but apostasized when they withdrew in the winter. To combat this deviousness, in 712/13 Qutaybah built a congregational mosque on the site of a former temple in the citadel. Then he appropriated one-half of the total number of houses in the *shahristān* as residences for members of various Arab tribes, so that, as Narshakhī puts it, "the Arabs might be with them and informed of their sentiments." Furthermore, the inhabitants were required to make over to the Arabs one-half of their cultivated land, together with firewood and fodder for their horses, all over and above whatever was levied as taxes. As an incentive to approved Muslim behavior, if not yet belief, Qutaybah promised two *dirhams* to everyone who participated in the Friday prayer service—for which al-Narshakhī announces sententiously that "God the Exalted would reward the people of Bukhārā at the final judgment."[704] These new converts simply had no choice but to read the Qurʾān in Persian, and al-Narshakhī notes that they were prompted by a Persian speaker during the required bowings and prostrations. Subsequently Qutaybah's mosque was replaced by a grander structure set among pre-Islamic palaces in the space between the *shahristān* and the *quhandiz*, which eventually became known as the Rīgistān. The older building came to be used as a revenue office *(dīwān al-kharāj)*. Close by the new building was the chief weaving office.

In the interim, opportunities for profitable exchange under the improved economic environment attendant on Muslim rule were nurturing an outer city *(rabaḍ)* that, according to al-Narshakhī, was joined to the *shahristān* within a single wall in 849/50. In the tenth century enhanced economic activity under relatively benevolent Sāmānid rule required the construction of a new wall enclosing an even greater space. Long before this the city had assumed the tripartite, urban physical structure characteristic of the Mashriq, although in this case the *quhandiz* was outside the *shahristān* instead of constituting its nucleus. As reported by al-Iṣṭakhrī, the *quhandiz* had two gates: the Rīgistān Gate on the west and the Gate of the Friday Mosque on the east, which were linked by a main avenue.[705] Within this citadel in the tenth century was the palace of the Sāmānid ruler, King of the Orient, as the *Ḥudūd* calls him, which Barthold almost certainly correctly identifies with the castle *(kākh)* that al-Narshakhī claimed was built in the seventh century by the Bukhār-Khudāh Bīdūn.[706] The *shahristān* had the unusual number of seven gates.[707] In the earlier Islamic period the Arab houses had clustered in the quarter of Faghsadara, close against the gate leading to the citadel, but in the tenth century that neighborhood was already in ruins.[708] The wall of the *shahristān,* which meant in effect the limits of the pre-Sāmānid settlement, was pierced by eleven gates.[709] Curiously enough, the wall of the *rabaḍ* had the same number,[710] which would probably be interpreted as a dittography if it were not backed up by actual names.

It is evident that, although the *shahristān* was still a force to be reckoned with (*aʿmar* = "very flourishing" was al-Maqdisī's term), the *rabaḍ* was the engine of economic growth. Just how extensive the changes that supervened there in fact were is well illustrated by the same author's comments on the street pattern within the *rabaḍ*—which, incidentally, Ibn Ḥawqal characterizes as "long and wide."[711] After listing the ten principal roads in this outer city, al-Maqdisī adds, "Development has proceeded apace so that there are 10 other roads, now abandoned and often under different names, that mark previous phases of urban growth."[712] Another inescapable sign of economic growth generating population increase, almost certainly by migration into the city, was the inability of the congregational mosque in the Rīgistān to adequately serve the huge number of new believers, which led to the building in 971 of a new house of prayer *(muṣallah)* to absorb some of the overflow a half-*farsakh* along the road to the village of Samatīn. In the Rījistān, hard by the citadel, the Sāmānid *amīr* Saʿīd Naṣr ibn Aḥmad ibn Ismāʿīl (r. 913–43) had erected a palace, and adjoining it accommodation for ten bureaus of state, namely, as explicated by Barthold, *Dīwāns* of the *Wazīr (Khwājah-i Buzurg),* the Treasurer *(Mustawfī),* Archives and Documents *(ʿAmīd al-Mulk),* the Captain of the Guards *(Ṣāḥib-Shurat),* the Postmaster *(Ṣāḥib-Barīd),* the Superintendent *(Mushrif)* of [the Amīr's] Private Domains, the Chief of [Municipal] Police *(Muḥtasib),* Religious Endowments *(Awqāf),* and the Religious Judge *(Qāḍī).*

Finally, on the outer edge not of the city but of the oasis, the governor Abū al-ʿAbbās Faḍl ibn Sulaymān al-Ṭūsī (r. 783–87) had begun to construct an encompassing wall to protect the city from incursions by Turkish nomads. When it was completed in 830 it enclosed an area that al-Iṣṭakhrī estimated at twelve *farsakhs* by twelve,[713] with towers and gates at half-mile intervals. It crossed the Samarqand road at a distance of more than seven *farsakhs* and the Khurāsān road at a distance of three *farsakhs*. The upkeep of this wall placed a heavy burden on the populace, so it is not surprising that the Sāmānids were constrained to relax their demands as soon as they had pacified the region at the end of the ninth century. From that time forward the wall began to crumble into ruins, so much so that in the twelfth century it was known by the dismissive sobriquet "The Old Woman" *(Kempirak).*

Despite the circumstance that Bukhārā is better served by historians and topographers than most other Transoxanian cities, it is still not possible to reconstruct the interior layout in detail. Barthold collected virtually all the information then available for incorporation in his St. Petersburg dissertation of 1900, which became known to the West as *Turkestan Down to the Mongol Invasion,* and O. A. Sukhareva essayed a plan of the major streets in both *shahristān* and *rabaḍ* during the tenth and eleventh centuries in a work in Russian in 1958;[714] in the absence of new and informative texts, that is just about all that can be done. About the city's water-supply facilities, however, it is possible to be rather more confident, courtesy of al-Narshakhī, al-Iṣṭakhrī, Ibn Ḥawqal, and al-Maqdisī.[715] Apparently water was drawn from the Sughd River in the neighborhood of the Kallābādh Gate and, its flow modulated by sluices at a place called Fāshūn, directed into distribution channels (sing. *ariq*),[716] the principal one of which was the Rūd-i Zar (Golden River), bisecting the city. Lesser *ariqs*, which seem to all have branched off from the Zar and which sometimes furnish clues as to the locations of urban quarters, included the Fashīdīzah *ariq,* whose half-*farsakh* length[717] was bordered by two thousand "estates" (or villas, palaces: *quṣūr)* together with their accompanying grounds; Jūybar Bakār *ariq* (Reliable Canal), which provided water for one thousand "estates"; Juybār al-Qawārīrīyīn *ariq* ("Canal of the Glaziers"); Baykand *ariq,* which began near the Street of the Guide (Khutaʿ) and brought water to sectors of the *rabaḍ;* Nawkandah *ariq* ("Newly Dug Canal"), which flowed through the southwestern part of the outer city before losing itself in the steppe; Ṭaḥūnah *ariq* ("Mill Canal"), so called because it powered numerous grain mills; Kushnah *ariq,* which supported many estates, gardens, and even agricultural activities; Rabāḥ *ariq* ("Revenue Canal"), with one thousand estates along its banks; Rīgistān *ariq;* and Zughārkanda *ariq,* which flowed for a *farsakh* through the northwestern part of the city. At various internal strategic points open cisterns *(ḥiyād)* had been constructed, complete with attached cabins for ablutions.

In order to revive a faint memory of the vibrant physical texture of the tenth-century city, I shall cite a selection of representative features from the list assembled by Barthold, mainly from the schedules of al-Narshakhī:[718]

- Inside the Bazaar Gate to the left was the Street of the Drunkards *(Kū-i Rindān),* and behind it was the Mosque of the Banū-Ḥanẓalah, a conversion of an originally Christian church.
- Inside the Shahristān Gate to the right was the Street of *Wazīr* ibn Ayyūb ibn Ḥassān, named for the first Arab *amīr* of Bukhārā and home to all his successors. Close by the walls of the *shahr* were vegetable stalls and the *sūq* of the shellers of pistachio nuts.
- Inside the Banū-Ṣaʿd Gate was the mosque of the same name. Nearby, Ḥasan ibn ʿAlāʾ Sughdī had developed an estate, complete with an impressive villa, which yielded a monthly revenue of twelve hundred *dīnārs.*
- Adjacent to the Banū-Asad Gate was the residence of the *amīr* of Khurāsān.
- Near the Ḥaqq-rāh Gate, in the northwestern section of the *shahristān,* the cell of the ascetic Khwājah *imām* Abū Ḥafs had been preserved. One of the most honored teachers of Bukhārā, it was he "who was [primarily] responsible for the inhabitants of the city being educated [in the ways of their faith], for the diffusion of knowledge there, and for the *imāms* and sages being so honoured."[719] Close to this shrine was a large tumulus believed to be the tomb of the mythical Afrāsiyāb.
- Near New Gate was the Mosque of the Quraysh, founded by Muqātil ibn Sulaymān. In the southeast quarter of the city, later known by the name Gate of the Mākh Mosque, was the Mākh-rūz *bāzār* that was described earlier.
- The Fort of the Magians *(Kūshk-i Mughān),* probably in the northwest sector of the city, as would be expected, had originally been the principal locale for the temples of the fire worshippers. At the time of the conquest, however, the inhabitants, who seem to have been mainly foreign merchants called Kash-Kushans, had surrendered their houses to the Arabs and built no less than seven hundred "villas," together with housing for their clients and servants, in the *rabaḍ.* When the Sāmānids made Bukhārā their capital, officers of the guard began to buy land in Kūshk-i Mughān, raising the price first to four thousand *dīrhams* per *jift* and then, as reported by al-Narshakhī (quoting Nūh ibn Naṣr), to twelve thousand *dirhams.* When disputes arose between these obviously successful landowners and the probably less well-off Muslim population, the latter stormed the predominantly Zoroastrian district and incorporated the gates of the villas in the extension of the cathedral mosque currently taking place. An interesting footnote to this story is that the spirit protectors depicted on the gates of the residences in this district were preserved on the gates of the mosque, although with their faces erased.

Al-Narshakhī also offers a conspectus of the residences of the rulers of Bukhārā at different times.[720] The structure most admired was built in Jū-i Mūliyān district by the *amīr* Ismāʿīl (r. 907–14). Other palaces occupied sites almost the whole way from the Rīgistān Gate to the citadel. One such was built by Naṣr ibn Aḥmad, burned by rebels in 961, rebuilt by the *amīr* Manṣūr, and less than a year later again burned to its foundations. Afterward the *amīr*'s property rights were transferred to Jū-i Mūliyān, to the great detriment of the Rīgistān but the great benefit of his clients, who received houses and gardens in that district.

The second half of the tenth century witnessed an insidious decline in the prosperity of Bukhārā. The centralization of power in the Sāmānid bureaucracy inevitably weakened the *dihqān* class, the backbone of Bukhārān society, whether still working the land or as urban tradesmen and retailers. In any case, productivity seems to have fallen off throughout the oasis, land values certainly declined, and there are indications that the desert was encroaching on the western edge of cultivation as al-Ṭūsī's great wall crumbled away. Certainly, investment in land diminished as *dihqāns* either could not, or chose not to, maintain their holdings, at the same time as religious endowments *(awqāf)* and the granting of tax exemptions to *sayyid*s and governmental favorites, to say nothing of a series of palace revolts, went far toward subverting the fiscal integrity of the Sāmānid state. Out in the oasis where Ibn Ḥawqal boasted that a man could support a family and other dependents on a single *jarīb* of land, the number of villas melted away to almost none. Then in 992 a Turkish army from the East finally rang down the curtain on the glories of Bukhārā, even though the Sāmānid dynasty managed to survive into the new millennium.

One thing on which the topographers were virtually unanimous was the tribulation of actually living in Bukhārā. Although the arterial avenues, all paved with stone from quarries near the village of Warkah, two *farsakh*s along the road to Nasaf, were as wide as those in Samarqand, the housing stock was execrable: "fetid and verminous" al-Maqdisī calls it, with its houses crowded together.[721] Ibn Ḥawqal elaborates on this situation with "Buildings are consistently *(taqdīr)* crowded one against another *(ishtibāk)* following the lie of the land so that citadels *(quhandizāt)* and the very contiguity of the houses together constitute a fortification."[722] "Nowhere in Khurāsān or Mā Warā᾽ al-Nahr," writes this same author, "is there a denser population than in Bukhārā";[723] and within the wall encompassing *rabaḍ* and *shahristān* "there is no waste ground, no ruins, and no uncultivated land to be seen."[724] An inevitable concomitant of this housing density was the ever-present threat of fire to buildings constructed mostly of unbaked brick, lime, plaster, and wood, and which were sometimes several storeys high. Al-Narshakhī, for instance, alludes to two major conflagrations in respectively 929 and 937. On the latter occasion, an outbreak that destroyed the palace of the *amīr* Manṣūr ibn Nūḥ touched off a firestorm that enveloped a substantial area of the city, including several *bāzār*s, and inflicted damage estimated at one hundred thousand *dirhams*.

To the density of housing must also be attributed other disagreeable features of urban living noted by travellers, litterateurs, and even poets: dark and dank *bāzārs*, polluted waterways, and noisome lavatories—all constituting Bukhārā as "the dunghill of the region, the most depressed *(ḍayyiq)* city in the Mashriq." As Ismāʿīl ibn Aḥmad is alleged to have said, "I can only liken the contrast between the disorder and filth of the *shahristān* of Bukhārā and the healthful agreeableness of its environs to a man whose internal organs have decayed while his outward appearance has remained well enough."[725] It should be remarked, though, that at the same time as al-Maqdisī was deprecating certain of the amenities of Bukhārā, he was also praising its mosques (magnificent), markets (excellent), baths (superb), and foods (wholesome).[726]

In any case, Bukhārā survived in Muslim memory not as the foulest sewer of the Sughd valley but as "the shrine of empire," the very hearth of the New Persian Renaissance, which fused the Īrānian tradition of the past with the religion and mores of the Arabs and in so doing raised Islam to the status of a universal culture. The sheer number of humanists and scientists attracted to this center of power and authority, security and opportunity, knowledge and inquiry, intellectuality and sensibility established it among the first rank of Islamic cultural foci, "The Cupola of Islam in the Eastern Lands," as Juvaynī was to call it. Ibn Sīnā considered its book *bāzār* unequalled anywhere in the known world, and the royal library not only housed a great number of manuscripts but also underwrote ambitious copying programs, sometimes replacing parchment with the newly introduced paper. Al-Thaʿālibī is guilty of only the slightest tincture of exaggeration when he characterizes Bukhārā as "the resort of the outstanding intellects of the age," whether poets, *udabā*, philosophers, historians, topographers, geographers, medical men, astrologer-astronomers, or, not least, the distinguished doctors of Ḥanafī jurisprudence attracted to the city by the celebrated Khwājah *imām* Abū Ḥafs.

Among the more important of the numerous other cities of the Mashriq that assumed the tripartite division were the following.[727]

- ***Būnjikath,*** the *qaṣabah* of Ushrūsanah, comprised a *quhandiz* outside a *shahristān,* with an extensive *rabaḍ* beyond that. The congregational mosque was in the *shahr,* but the *sūq*s were distributed between the inner and the outer cities. According to al-Maqdisī, two gates, Madīnah Gate and the Upper Gate, gave access to the former, while the latter was served by four roads: Darb Zāmīn, Darb Marsmandah, Darb Nūjakath, and Darb Kahlabādh.[728] Ibn Ḥawqal estimated the male population (presumably potential military levies) at ten thousand.[729]
- ***Kish,*** the principal settlement on the upper reaches

of the landlocked stream now known as the Khashka Daryā, may have been founded as late as the seventh century[730] but by the beginning of the next had become the chief administrative center *(madīnah)* for the whole of Soghdia.[731] Under the earlier Sāmānids, however, the city began to decline, probably as a result of that dynasty's investments in Samarqand and Bukhārā. Of the customary three major components of a Mashriqī city, the *quhandiz* and the *shahristān* (by some authors designated *madīnat al-dākhilah* = "the inner city") were largely ruined, although the congregational mosque and the prison remained there throughout the tenth century. The *rabaḍ*, by contrast, was a hive of activity *(aʿmar),* stimulated by the principal *sūqs* of the city. The *dār al-imārah,* however, was outside both *shahristān* and *rabaḍ* at a location known as the Musallā.[732] Where Kish was unusual was in the circumstance that yet a second "suburb" was developing outside the first *rabaḍ,*[733] but it is uncertain whether that extension of the settlement was coincident with that of the Musallā district or was an entirely different enterprise. What does seem to be established is that the decay of the inner city and citadel had not only been compensated by the development of a lively *rabaḍ,* but that additional growth of the city in Sāmānid times was being accommodated by a process of ekistic superfetation on its outer fringe.[734]

- ***Akhsīkath,*** the *qaṣabah* of Farghānā situated on the north bank of the Sīr Daryā River just below the mouth of the Kasānsay, encompassed the same three components of urban form, but there is some dispute as to their relative locations. Whereas Ibn Ḥawqal located the *quhandiz* in the *shahristān,* al-Maqdisī was equally certain it was within the *rabaḍ.*[735] Possibly this apparent dissonance would be resolved if the *quhandiz* had been close against the wall of the *shahristān,* perhaps built into it, at a point where, as Ibn Ḥawqal puts it, "a *rabaḍ* adjoined it." The *dār al-imārah* and the prison were inside the *quhandiz,* the congregational mosque in the *shahristān,* and the markets throughout the city, although the heaviest concentration was in the *rabaḍ.* Nevertheless, one is left with the impression that the city was still a functional unity, that the economic burgeoning of the *rabaḍ* had not sucked all the life out of the *shahristān,* a conclusion confirmed by al-Maqdisī when he notes that "the *jāmiʿ* and [significantly] most of the buildings were in the inner city *(madīnah dākhilah).*"[736] As in Bukhārā and Samarqand, the space reserved for festival prayers lay along the riverbank. Al-Maqdisī also volunteered the information that the periphery of the city was half as long again as that of al-Ramlaḥ (Ramleh).
- ***Binkath*** (Tashkent), the administrative headquarters of Shāsh district, merits attention for the same reason as did Kish: the unusual development of its *rabaḍ.* Al-Maqdisī reports simply that there were two *rabaḍs*, each fortified, but Ibn Ḥawqal is a little more explicit: "There is a *rabaḍ* surrounded by a wall, beyond which is another walled *rabaḍ,* together with gardens and houses."[737] Presumably the reasons for this centrifugal growth were essentially those specified for Kish, but in this instance there is no evidence of catastrophic decay within the inner city. The *dār al-imārah* and the prison were within the *quhandiz,* and the *jāmiʿ* beside it; and although most of the *sūqs* were somewhere in the outer city, the *shahristān* was apparently also adequately served. The inner *rabaḍ* was traversed by eight avenues *(durūb),* the outer by seven.[738] The whole complex "from one rampart of the outer *rabaḍ* to the rampart on the opposite side of the city" was estimated at about a *farsakh.*[739] Within the walls life could be pleasant enough, especially in the *rabaḍs*, where substantial dwellings were dispersed among large cultivated holdings, where in fact there was scarcely a residence *(manzil)* without its garden, stable, and vineyard. It was, as al-Maqdisī epitomizes it, "A settlement *(balad)* where the advantages compensated for the disadvantages and excellence weighed equally with imperfection."[740] And round the whole city and its immediately dependent territory, ʿAbad Allāh ibn Ḥumayd ibn Thawr had constructed a wall as a protection against the Turkish raids that were endemic before the Sāmānids pacified those territories.[741] This wall ran from Jabal Safflagh against the Turk river all around the plain of Qilāṣ as far as the Sayḥūn (Sīr Daryā) River; and a *farsakh* beyond even that was a fosse linking the same hill to the same river.[742]

- ***Isbījāb,*** on the Arīs River, a right-bank affluent of the Sayḥūn, manifested a fairly typical Transoxanian morphology, with the usual tripartite division. However, in this case the *quhandiz* was nothing but a ruin. By contrast the walled *shahristān*[743] was a busy place, within which were the *dār al-imārah,* prison, cathedral mosque, and *bāzārs*, among which al-Maqdisī chose to mention specifically that of the cotton merchants *(Sūq al-Karābīs).* This inner city had four gates,[744] each with its own guardhouse *(ribāṭ):* Ribāṭ Nakhshabīyīn, R. al-Bukhārīyīn, R. al-Samarqandīyīn, and R. Qarātakīn. This last guardhouse had been named for a certain Qarā-tagīn, whom we also encounter as ruler of Balkh in the time of Naṣr ibn Aḥmad (r. 864–92), and close by was his tomb, as well as that of his son Manṣūr, who died in 951. In the same neighborhood there was a *sūq* whose revenues of seven thousand *dirhams* a month were devoted to charitable purposes, in particular the provision of bread and other food to the debilitated.

It is evident, though, that the prosperity of the *shahristān* was matched by that of the *rabaḍ* that had grown up beyond its walls, and which I suspect owed its development to two main factors. Isbijāb had become an advanced base for traders pushing eastward into Central Asia by way of Ṭarāz and Mīrkī, so it comes as no surprise that there were some seventeen hundred stabling facilities *(ribāṭāt)* deployed throughout the city. Second, and probably more significant, Isbijāb was an important base *(thaghr)* for *ghāzīs* assembled to defend the Faith against the depredations of Turkish tribes to the north. As al-Maqdisī puts it, this was a realm of war *(dār jihād).*[745]

The growth of the city generally, and of the *rabaḍ* in particular, probably benefited additionally from the circumstance that for much of the century Isbijāb Province enjoyed a substantial degree of autonomy. Even in the tenth century it was ruled by a Turkish dynasty that accorded it unusual privileges. Ibn Ḥawqal, for instance, was surprised to find that "Isbijāb is the only city in the whole of Khurāsān and Mā Warā al-Nahr not subject to the land tax."[746] The four *dāniqs* and a symbolic broom that the ruler of the province remitted annually to the Sāmānid government in lieu of taxes were clearly an immensely profitable investment. The city was described as one-third the extent of Binkath, although there is also a not very informative reference to a wall built by Nuḥ ibn Asad soon after 840 that enclosed "all its vineyards and other crop land"[747]—presumably after the pattern of the walls surrounding Bukhārā and Samarqand.

- ***Kāth,*** the ancient capital of Khwārizm, prior to the tenth century comprised a *quhandiz* within a *shahristān* situated on the right bank of the Jayḥūn (Āmū Daryā) River somewhat more than one hundred miles above its entry into the Aral Sea. The *quhandiz* itself, known as Fīl or Fīr and defended by triple concentric ramparts, had contained the congregational mosque, *dār al-imārah,* prison, and, most imposingly, the palace of the native ruler, the Khwārizm-*shāh,* which could be seen from ten miles away; but by early in the tenth century floodwaters of the Jayḥūn had undermined the *quhandiz,* swept away the gates of the city, and rendered the *shahristān* uninhabitable.[748] By the end of that century the *quhandiz,* together with the cathedral mosque and the prison, had completely disappeared,[749] and the population—except for a minority who moved to Jurjānīyah and other Khwārizmian towns—had migrated eastward to higher ground. The new settlement, called simply the Capital *(Shahristān),* ultimately became almost as large as Nīshāpūr: according to Ibn Ḥawqal, three *farsakhs* across, although other authors reported the distance as one-third of a *farsakh.* Here a new *dār al-imārah* was established and a new congregational mosque erected that, as so often happened, attracted an array of *bāzārs* to its vicinity. Both *shahristān* and *bāzārs* were bisected by the Jardūr canal, water from which was carried throughout the city in street channels. Commerce flourished,[750] *ghāzīs* filled the streets, and the architecture was effectively functional;[751] but the Jayḥūn floods were slowly drowning the city, forcing the inhabitants farther and farther toward the edge of the floodplain.

What was in fact happening was the abandonment of the old city in favor of a "suburb" in the twentieth-century American sense of a locationally distinct and functionally autonomous satellite settlement. But the term *rabaḍ* is not used in any text known to me, the new town always being treated as a separate foundation. Nor was it an attractive locale, not least because the inhabitants used the water runnels in their streets as public latrines and collected the waste in pits, prior to spreading it on their cropland. So filthy were the streets, bemoaned al-Maqdisī, strangers could walk about the city only in daylight. Worse still, the natives simply sloshed through it, and inevitably carried it into their neighborhoods on their feet.[752]

Al-Rayy

It was not only in the Mashriq as strictly defined that this tripartite urban structure occurred: indeed, it was common throughout the Īrānian culture realm. Among the instances on the western fringe of that realm were two of the best-known cities of Islam, al-Rayy (Rey) and Qazwīn. Al-Rayy, in northeastern Jibāl *Iqlīm,* was an instructive example of a city where a commercially strategic location and agriculturally productive environs over four centuries outweighed a politically troubled history, to the point where Ibn Ḥawqal could characterize it as "Except for Baghdād, the most flourishing city in the Orient."[753] As ancient Rhagā and Greek Rhages, it already had a long history when Muslims arrived on the scene at a variously reported time between 639 and 644. It was not an easy conquest. Despite a capitulation agreement granting "security for the inhabitants of al-Rayy and others in their households on [payment of] tribute, as much as each one can provide annually on attaining puberty,"[754] resistance by the Mihrān family, whose fief included the city, was sufficiently strong and protracted to induce the Arab commander to at least partially raze the city, which henceforth would be known as the Old Town (al-ʿAtīqah).

At the same time, a renegade Persian, al-Zīnabī Abū al-Farrukhān, who had assisted the Arabs in the storming of the city, was appointed governor *(marzaba-hu)* and authorized to build a new al-Rayy. It is noteworthy that as late as 690 a "king" from the Farrukhān family was mentioned in association with an Arab governor. Apart from a short-lived occupation by supporters of Abū Muslim in 753, the early years of the ʿAbbāsid dynasty were uneventful, but the pace of development quickened when Muhammad al-Mahdī, son of the caliph al-Manṣūr and governor of the Orient, virtually rebuilt the city and accorded it the honorific Muḥammadīyah. At the same time, those who had been forced by the rebuilding to cede property in the city were resettled in a suburblike area outside the wall that came to be known as Mahdī-ābādh.

But in 865 conflict arose in al-Rayy between the Zaydī ʿAlids of Ṭabaristān and the Ṭāhirids, a conflict in which Turkish generals in the service of the caliph played a prominent part, and which continued for two decades until in 885 Adhgü-tagīn of Qazwīn seized al-Rayy from the ʿAlids. In 894 the caliph al-Muʿtamid appointed his son to the governorship. In 912, however, the Sāmānid *amīr* Ismāʿīl ibn Aḥmad occupied the city and in 919 was formally invested with the governorship of the Orient by al-Muqtadir in the city of al-Rayy. Four years later the Sāmānid representative was driven out by the Adharbāyjānī Yūsuf ibn Abī al-Sāj, who minted his own coinage at Muḥammadīyah.[755] Subsequently the city passed successively into the hands of three Daylamī lords and in 925 under the control of Mufliḥ, a slave of Yūsuf. The Sāmānids soon re-established their authority, only to have their Daylamī general Asfār proclaim his independence and then in 930 be replaced by his Gīlāni lieutenant Mardāwij, first of the Ziyārid dynasty. After the assassination of Mardāwij in 935, al-Rayy became part of the domain territory of the Buwayhid Rukn al-Dawlah, a change of government that brought relative peace and great prosperity to the region throughout the remainder of the century. And this was the period when some of the most influential of the topographers were compiling their treatises.

Al-Rayy had twice been rebuilt, or at least once rebuilt and once extensively renovated—a circumstance engendering a certain ambivalence in our reading of the relevant texts. When al-Maqdisī remarks that the outer city *(al-madīnah al-khārijah)* was populous *(ʿamir)* but devoid of markets in contrast to the *rabaḍ,* where bazaars and important buildings *(ʿimārāt)* were concentrated, he presumably was referring to the sector of the city that had been rebuilt by al-Farrukhān and further developed by al-Mahdī; in which case the inner city *(al-madīnah al-dākhilah),* which had its own population, must have been the ʿAtīqah that had survived destruction in 643.[756] Two markets having more than local reputations were the Rūdhah, with shops and warehouses ranged along both banks of the river of the same name, and the Courtyard of the Watermelon *(Dār al-Baṭṭīkh),* a term often used to denote a city fruit market. The citadel *(qalʿah),* which was in ruins in the tenth century, had once stood on an eminence outside the so-called outer city, whence it had commanded a fine prospect over the whole settlement.[757] The congregational mosque, part of al-Mahdī's rebuilding program, stood between the citadel and al-Maqdisī's inner city.[758] The whole settlement at the end of the tenth century was upwards of a *farsakh* in extent in every direction. Its superficies were smaller than in the case of Nīshāpūr, but the density of its buildings raised its population to a comparable level, with a substantially equivalent standard of living.[759] It was "an elegant and clean city," with abundant water, excellent *khāns* and baths, and flourishing commerce.[760]

It is worth noting that, despite its having been the birthplace of Hārūn al-Rashīd, al-Rayy was not an Arab city in any meaningful sense. As late as the closing years of the ninth century, al-Yaʿqūbī noted that the Arab population was very small, with the majority of the inhabitants being different types *(akhlāt)* of Persians;[761] and there is no reason to suppose that the composition of the population changed significantly under Sāmānid rule. The fact that the Dār al-Kuttub (library), one of the finest, was housed in a *khān*[762] nicely points the twin pillars of al-Rayy's prosperity, culture and commerce, in not always seemingly propitious times.

Qazwīn

Qazwīn in al-Maqdisī's hierarchy was designated a *madīnah* overseeing territories fronting the border regions of Daylam and Ṭabaristān. Prior to its conquest in 644 by al-Barāʾb ibn ʿĀzib and Zayd ibn al-Jabal al-Ṭaʾī, it had been a frontier outpost of the Sāsānians, repelling raids from the turbulent north. As an alternative to rendering the *jizyah,* the populace is said to have converted to Islam. At the same time, garrison troops were awarded pensions and landholdings that became the foundation of a flourishing Arab community noticed by Ibn al-Faqīh some two centuries later. The first congregational mosque was built late in the seventh century by Muḥammad, son of al-Ḥajjāj, the best-known governor of Arab ʿIrāq; to subsequent generations it became known as the Bull Mosque *(Masjid al-Thawr).* The sources also seem to imply that Muḥammad either rebuilt or added to the old Sāsānian city, but the main extensions were the suburblike settlements initiated at a later date by respectively Mūsā al-Hādī and the Turkish freedman Mubārak, which Hārūn al-Rashīd eventually brought within a single encircling wall.[763]

By the second half of the tenth century Qazwīn was exhibiting the tripartite division that we have come to expect of a city in the Īrānian sphere, namely an inner town *(madīnah),* an outer town *(rabaḍ),* and, significantly, in the latter a fort *(ḥiṣn).*[764] What makes for special interest in this case is that the thirteenth-century geographer Zakarīyā ibn Muḥammad al-Qazwīnī, relying ultimately on a seventh-century source, describes the city as "two settlements, one within the other" and surrounded by an incipient von Thünen–style sequence of land uses, specifically gardens and vineyards followed by cropland and, impliedly, pasture or wasteland.[765] Indeed, he goes further and illustrates this layout by means of a diagram depicting perfectly circular concentric zones.[766] On the basis of this evidence combined with not wholly conclusive inferences from photographs and surviving earthworks in the present-day landscape, Ardavan Amirshahi has postulated a circular city in Sāsānian times, with axial avenues dividing it into four more or less equal segments.[767] As an accordant context for this arrangement he cites the ruins of Fīrūzābād, Takht-i Solaymān, and Dārābgird that are conventionally adduced as examples of Persian round cities. Then, by interpreting the second circle from the center in al-Qazwīnī's diagram as the wall begun by Hārūn, Amirshahi is able to ascribe a circular form to the ʿAbbāsid city at the beginning of the ninth century. In fact he epitomizes Qazwīn as "passant de l'enceinte circulaire shâpûrî à l'enceinte circulaire hârûnî."[768]

As far as the Sāsānian city was concerned, the circularity may have held, although the evidence is by no means conclusive. However, with the Islamic settlement the argument becomes rather less persuasive. In the first place, even minor variations in physiography would have subverted the strict circularity of al-Qazwīnī's land-use zones (as depicted in his diagram, though not in his text); these then cast doubt on the circularity of his urban interiors. Nor does such geometrical regularity jibe well with the record of sequential accretions to the original city.[769] Nor does Ḥamd Allāh Mustawfī's failure to mention a circular shape in his rather detailed account of the city during the earlier Islamic centuries afford support for the idea of a strictly circular urban plan.[770] To characterize the space enclosed by Hārūn's wall as it looped around the three nuclei, I would suggest a term such as *orbicular* or *ovoid.* In any case, al-Qazwīnī's diagram was surely an abstract schematic gloss on his text rather than a record of actual urban form. And whatever the truth of its internal structure, Qazwīn prospered as a frontier post that also attracted scholars of jurisprudence and philosophy[771] under a sequence of rulers including ʿAlids of Ṭabaristān, Ṭāhirids, Ṣaffārids, Sāmānids, and Buwayhids.

*

In the cities just described, as in most others in the Īrānian and Ṭūrānian culture realms, the ternary internal structure of *quhandiz, shahristān,* and *rabaḍ* was the organizing principle in the deployment of architectural volume and space; but, as we have seen, this was no rigid developmental template. In the first place, insofar as the sources permit an opinion, there seems to have been a near absence of geometrical symmetry in the internal structures of these cities. The nucleus appears to have been typically a Sāsānian settlement with a citadel either within or close outside its walls. When military expedients required the presence of Muslim troops in the region and subsequently Muslim administration stimulated economic development, thereby inducing a cityward flow of migrants, most of the new population occupied land outside the *shahristān.* In succeeding centuries this new settlement—or perhaps more usually, series of settlements—almost invariably expanded, not infrequently incorporating preexisting hamlets and villages in the process. In extreme cases this could result in a more or less complete eversion of the city plan, with the *rabaḍ* preempting the vital life of the city. Nor was it unknown for a second *rabaḍ* to form outside the first in a process of metaphorical societal superfetation. In a few instances a hypertrophic *rabaḍ* so dominated its city that it became in effect an independent foundation, while the *shahristān* was to all intents and purposes abandoned. When a *shahristān* maintained its vitality, it was usually through the agglomerative functions of government *dīwāns* or a prominent mosque: the principal city markets almost without exception were in the *rabaḍ,* leaving only neighborhood *sūqs* to serve the *shahristān.*

There can be no doubt that under the Sāmānids in particular (although not negligibly under the Ṭāhirids and Ṣaffārids), the agents of urban development were located overwhelmingly in the *rabaḍs*. It is unfortunate that our sources seldom permit us to specify the precise location of a *rabaḍ* in relation to its *shahristān:* whether, for example, it completely surrounded the inner city (as has commonly been assumed) or merely adjoined it in a particular district. The fate of the citadel followed a different course. Sometimes victorious Muslims would establish a *dār al-imārah* within the citadel of a conquered town, but only rarely did this arrangement persist for an extended period of time. More often the *dār al-imārah* was reconstituted as a palace, together with *dīwāns* and a prison, elsewhere in the *shahristān* or the *rabaḍ*. Equally frequently, however, the Muslims ignored the citadel altogether, leaving it to fall into disrepair, and located their headquarters initially in the *shahristān.* By the ninth century few citadels were still fully functional, and not infrequently new fortresses serving the same purpose were being erected in the *rabaḍs*. This tripartite ordering of city morphology in the Īrānian sphere was so common as to constitute the norm, but it has to be understood as an organizing principle rather than as inflexible planning practice. Any degree of internal sociopolitical reorganization or any external event could introduce variations on the theme, so that there were almost as many trajectories of morphological evolution and nuances of form within the prevailing paradigm as there were Īrānian cities.

Twin Cities

The circumstance that the Islamic empire encompassed some of the most highly urbanized regions of the Middle East and North Africa ensured that many of the new Islamic foundations were in fairly close proximity to already existing cities. Al-Kūfah, for instance, was only a few miles from the old city of al-Ḥīrah. Baghdād itself was scarcely a score of miles from the former Sāsānian administrative capital that came to be known to the Arabs as al-Madāʾin,[772] and al-Ramlah (Ramleh) was set down specifically to usurp the locational advantages of Ludd. In such cases the cities, although adjacent one to another, functioned as discrete entities. In fact one was usually in the process of displacing the other.

Not infrequently, it also happened that topographical or sociocultural cleavages were responsible for major disjunctions in the urban fabric. A classic example is afforded by the Aghlabid capital of ***Fās*** (Fez) in the ninth

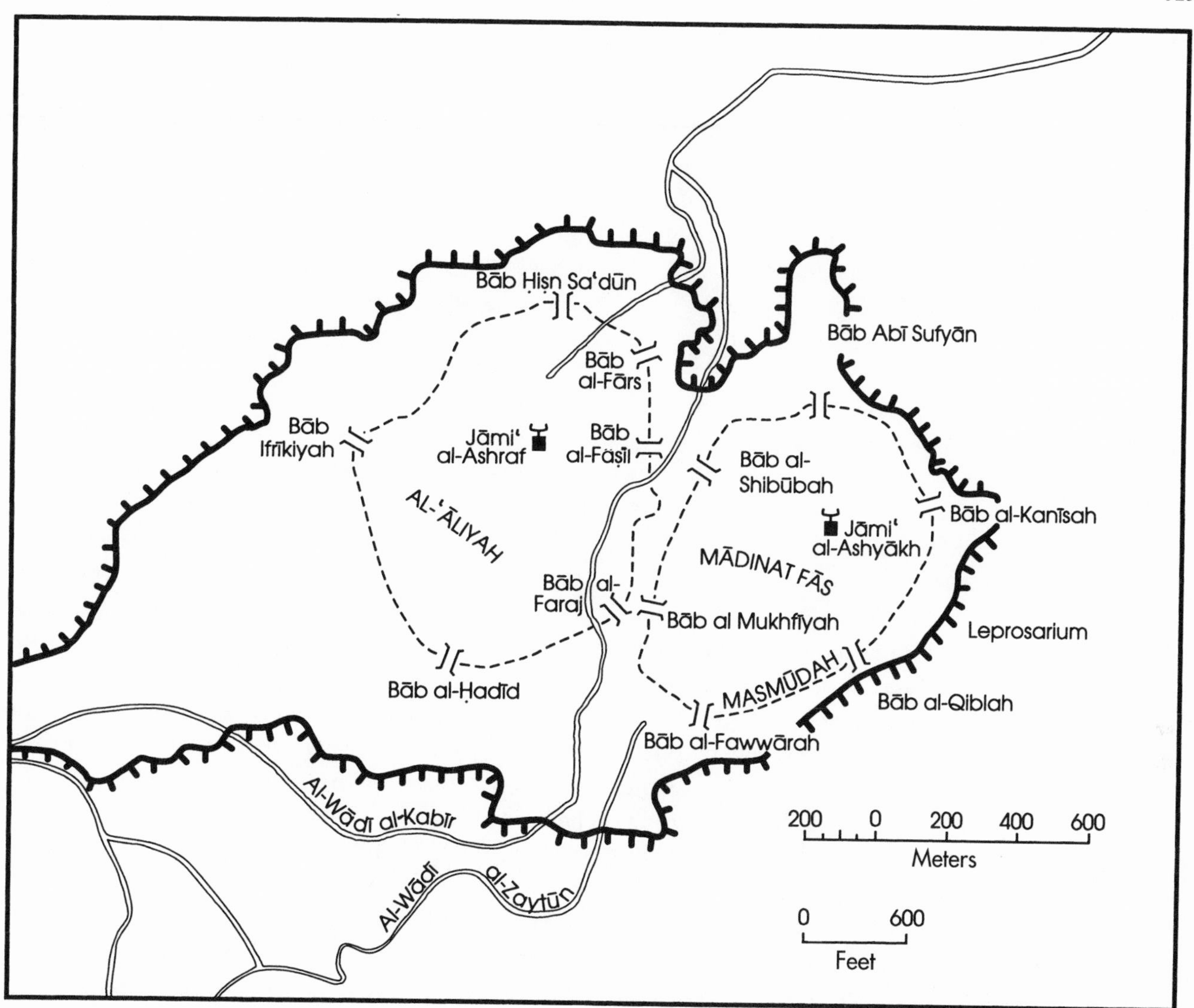

Figure 25. The layout of Fās (Fez) after the two enclaves of the Idrīsīd city had been brought within an encompassing wall in the second half of the eleventh century. The approximate configurations of the ninth- to tenth-century enclaves were still plainly evident within the unified city at that time.

century (fig. 25), where Arabs dominated the left bank of the Wādī Fās *('Adwat al-Qārawīyīn)* and Berbers, many fleeing from Umayyad Spain, the right bank *('Adwat al-Andalus).* Another instructive example was the city of ***Wāsiṭ,*** chief administrative center of the district of Kaskar. In 708 or thereabouts al-Ḥajjāj, governor of Arab 'Irāq, had established a palatine complex on the west bank of the Tigris, opposite a Sāsānian city on the east bank. In his new enclave he built a *dār al-imārah* with a green cupola *(al-Qubbat al-Khaḍrā)* that became famous throughout the Islamic world, together with a congregational mosque. By the tenth century this mosque had fallen into ruin, but another had been built in the eastern sector, and the two halves of the city linked by a pontoon bridge *(jisr),* at each end of which was a place where ships could pass through. Although the old Persian nobility still virtually monopolized the east bank as late as the end of the ninth century whereas Arab administration and residence were focused in the western sector, a rampart encircling the whole city symbolized the essential unity of the settlement.[773] ***Quṣdār,*** in the eastern Makrān, was similarly divided in two, this time by a dry *wādī* bed that was unbridged. On one (unspecified) side was the palace *(dār)* of the *sulṭān* and a fort *(qalʿah);* the other, called Būdīn, was occupied by merchants' houses and depots—which must have been numerous because caravans arrived regularly from Khurāsān, Fārs, Kirmān, and India. Although tenth-century topographers tended to accord the *sulṭān* a substantial degree of autonomy, he actually pronounced the *kuṭbah* in the name of the ʿAbbāsids, but in 977/78 was forced to transfer his allegiance to the Ghaznawids.[774]

With ***Jurjān,*** in al-Maqdisī's schedule both the metropolis of his Daylam *Iqlīm* and the *qaṣabah* of Jurjān Province, we encounter a divided city in which the two halves appear to have exercised a substantial degree of independence from each other.[775] When Yazīd ibn al-Muhallab finally conquered the valley of Andarhāz (present-day Gurgān) at the rather late date of 716/17, he occupied a small Sāsānian town on the riverbank and promptly assigned a total of forty *khiṭāṭ* to his tribal contingents for residences and the erection of mosques. Some of these were within the Sāsānian town on the eastern bank of the river and some in a *mirbaḍ* on the eastern bank.[776] Professor Bulliet has noted that twenty-one of the twenty-four mosques named were associated with specific Arab tribes, and one more was designated solely for individuals whose tribes were not well represented in the settlement *(afnaʾ al-arab)* and who consequently had to be placed under the protection of the community as a whole.[777] The other two named mosques were respectively that of the Reds *(Ḥamrāʾ),* which Bulliet suggests may have denoted "a contingent of fair-skinned Iranian troops who [had] joined the Arab army," and that of the Converts *(Mawālī).*

By the tenth century the old settlement on the east bank could be described as "a prosperous, noble town, prestigious and respected,"[778] the venerable Gurgān, half-concealed in gardens, trees, and plots of sugarcane, but known to the locals simply as Shahristān.[779] Al-Maqdisī lists nine streets within this sector of the city, which focused on a public square *(maydān)* flanked by the governor's residence *(dār al-amīr).*[780] On the opposite side of the Andarhāz River, a turbulent torrent during the winter rains although spanned by an arched bridge in the tenth century, the Arab settlement in the *mirbāḍ* had grown into a populous town *(madīnah ʿimarah)* bearing the name Bakrābād(h), famous for its silk crafts, which supplied both silkworm eggs and silk thread to the Ṭabaristān textile industry.[781] Al-Maqdisī felt constrained to mention the well-run *masjids* in Bakrābād, as well as the extensiveness of its cemeteries *(maqābir),* this last being a reflection of the unhealthiness of the region, which he characterized as a scythe mowing down the immigrant.[782] For the inhabitants, though, who were apparently immune to the disease vectors that perturbed al-Maqdisī, Jurjān appears to have been a gracious enough city in which to do business—or, rather, cities, for Bakrābad with its flourishing textile industry seems to have functioned more or less independently of the administrative center across the river. Even so, the two sectors together made up the largest city in the Caspian region.

In the case of ***Ṭūs*** in northwest Khurāsān, the functional independence of each of its twin cities is implied unambiguously when al-Maqdisī treats them under separate rubrics. According to al-Yaʿqūbī, in the ninth century Nūqān was the larger of the two towns, but by the second half of the tenth century it had been surpassed by Ṭābarān. The majority of the population in both towns was Persian; such Arabs as there were owed allegiance to the tribe of Ṭayyiʾ.[783] Nūqān's early dominance had been based on its manufacture of stone jars and its role as a bourse financing the mining of semiprecious jewels in the Kashaf Rūd, but subsequently by its sponsorship of the composite shrine in the village of Sanābād some four *farsakh*s from Ṭūs, where were buried side by side the caliph Hārūn al-Rashīd (d. 809) and the eighth *imām* ʿAlī al-Riḍā (d. 817). By the tenth century this shrine had been walled and had emerged as a popular pilgrimage sanctuary.[784] Ṭābarān, by contrast, was flourishing as a regional marketing center; the productiveness of its hinterland was evident in its bustling markets. It was also distinguished by its fort *(ḥiṣn)* and an impressive congregational mosque embellished by one Ibn ʿAbd al-Razzāq.

As representative an example of twin cities as any is provided by ***Iṣfahān.***[785] In the tenth century the topographers present us with a picture of two settlements usually said to be two miles apart on the northern flank of the Zāyindah Rūd: to the east, Jayy, known colloquially as "The Capital" *(Shahristān);* to the west, Jewish Town (al-*Yahūdīyah*), estimated at twice the size of Jayy. How this disposition arose is a complicated tale, but one that has been ably elucidated by Lisa Golombek.[786] According to al-ʿAlavī's fourteenth-century Persian translation of al-Māfarrukhī's *Taʾrīkh Iṣfahān* (ca. 1080), Jayy in the

Sāsānian period had been a walled round city enclosing some two hundred *jarībs*, including a *quhandiz* and the state archive, and with four gates facing approximately the quarter compass points.[787] As Abū Nuʿaym al-Iṣfahānī makes clear, Sāsānid Jayy was primarily an administrative complex that could also serve as a refuge for peasants from the surrounding countryside in time of need.[788] When the Arabs came into possession of the enclave in 640, 641/42, or 644, they established their congregational mosque in the dwelling of a Persian prince of the blood *(vāspuhr)* within the city and apparently assumed the administrative responsibilities of their predecessors.[789] It is to be inferred that no great changes supervened until the ʿAbbāsids established their rule over the city. Then in 767/68 an ʿAbbāsid governor built himself a palace in the village of Khushīnān, not far removed from a settlement of Jews.[790] Arabs of the Banū-Tamīm are said to have built a congregational mosque close by. The new government soon extended its jurisdiction over fifteen villages—in the manner exemplified by Nīshāpūr—and the nucleus of the al-Yahūdīyah referred to above.

Although the Buwayhid era witnessed repeated social disorders, al-Yahūdīyah prospered. Part of the enceinte was walled, probably by Rukn al-Dawlah, and an impressive citadel erected by Fakhr al-Dawlah.[791] Al-Maqdisī lists twelve gates in the wall, which apparently enclosed an ovoid space between fifteen thousand and twenty-one thousand paces round, divided into four quarters *(maḥallāt)*: an arrangement that Dr. Golombek has been able to reconstruct relying largely on the continuity of place-names and air photographs of the site.[792] Tradition (although not much else) attributes to Buwayhid al-Yahūdīyah a royal palace known as Maydān-i Mīr and a citadel; however, the latter does not appear in extant sources until Safavid times. By the mid-tenth century al-Yahūdīyah had far outdistanced Jayy in both size and wealth to become, as Ibn Ḥawqal describes it, "the destination *(furḍah)* of [commodities from] Fārs, al-Jibāl, Khurāsān, and Khūzistān," and at the same time a transportation center and a textile-manufacturing city.[793] Yet, despite the disparity in their sizes, both settlements were doing well, with congregational mosques of no mean distinction that in al-Yahūdīyah were surrounded by both covered and open *sūqs*. An ancient market at the Jūr Gate, according to al-ʿAlavī, had developed into an annual fair where "the people of Iṣfahān [district], rich and poor, high and low, men, women and children" used to gather for New Year celebrations. And there is reason to think that Ibn Ḥawqal was treating both settlements as a unitary city when he writes, "From ʿIrāq to Khurāsān only al-Rayy exceeds Iṣbahān as a commercial centre." But that he knew (and from personal experience) that the name Iṣfahān subsumed two separate settlements is attested in the following sentence: "When a traveller from Fārs arrives at Iṣbahān and climbs the hill of Sarfarāz, he sees below him the two cities *(madīnatān)* amid their surrounding districts *(rusātiq)*, at which point he savours a prospect as captivating and pleasing as can ever meet the eye."[794] But al-Maqdisī was not so easily seduced and brings us abruptly back to the realities of life in tenth-century Jibāl by reminding us that the inhabitants of Iṣfahān dare not drink their river water for fear of the sewage that they tipped into it.[795]

The two settlements, about five hundred meters apart, that al-Maqdisī rubricated as ***Waylah*** (al-ʿAqabah) and Aylah pose a problem in this context (fig. 26). In the tenth century Waylah was a densely populated and handsome city that had probably been established in the caliphate of ʿUthman (r. 644–56), whereas Aylah was in ruins. Aylah, by contrast, was a settlement of considerable antiquity. The question is, for how long did the two coexist before Aylah fell into desuetude, and were they ever functionally discrete entities? The answer to that question will probably have to wait on progress of the excavation of Aylah currently being undertaken by Thomas Parker. About the status of the two ***Āghmāts,*** which jointly constituted the chief urban center of what is today southern Morocco, there is no doubt. Āghmāt Aylān, that is, Āghmāt of the Berber tribe Aylan (Arabic Haylānah), was a ritual-administrative enclave forbidden to all foreigners; Āghmāt Wārikah (Ūrikah), some eight miles distant, was a trading center and the city's link with the outside world. Here was the residence of the chief with whom traders sought an audience before conducting their business, and here was the weekly (Sunday) market where more than one hundred head of cattle and one thousand sheep were slaughtered.[796] In the tenth century the Āghmāts were on the southwestern fringe of the Islamic world, and there is reason to suppose that Muslims were more common as traders than as residents.[797]

The same was true of another twin city on the opposite edge of the Islamic domain. This was ***Itil*** (also Atil),

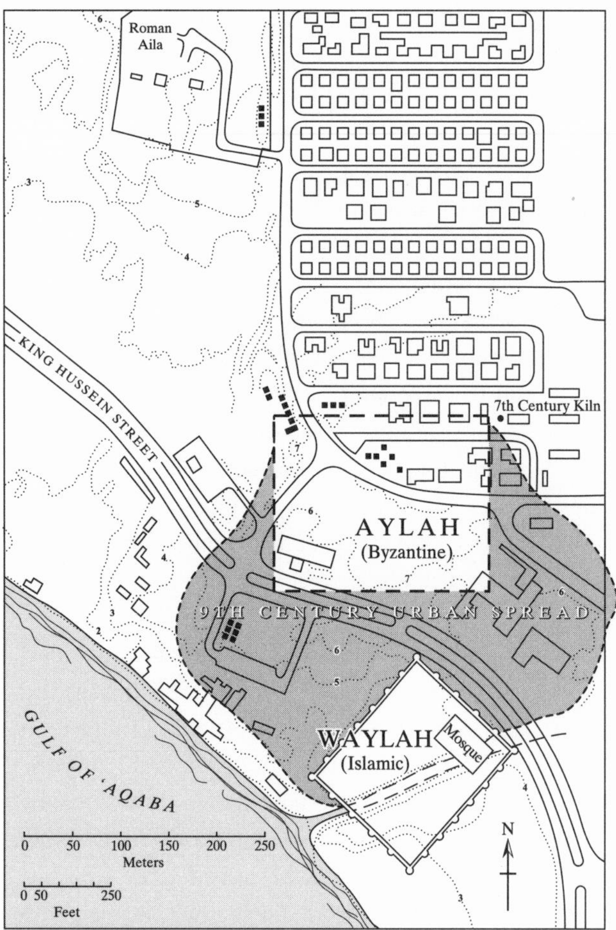

Figure 26. The spatial relation of Waylah (Islamic) to Aylah (Byzantine). Based on Donald Whitcomb, *Ayla. Art and Industry in the Islamic Port of Aqaba* (Chicago, 1994), 22 and Parker, "Preliminary report on the 1994 season of the Roman Aqaba Project," *Bulletin of the American Schools of Oriental Research* 305 (1997), fig. 4.

capital of the Khazar state, located at an undetermined point near the head of the Volga River delta.[798] Khazarān, on the west bank and the larger of the two settlements, comprised a walled enclosure extending over several miles, within which cabins of wood and felt were distributed irregularly and diversified by only a few structures of baked brick. Here, too, were the residences of the Khāqān Khazar, the Judaized ruling class, and the garrison troops. Ibn Ḥawqal reported that twelve thousand men were under arms in this sector of the city. On the east bank was Itil, a flourishing commercial center distributing furs brought down the Volga from the north to Kievan Russia in the west and Khwārizm to the east. Most of the Muslims, to the number of ten thousand by some estimates, lived in this half of the settlement, together with a sizable Christian community, pagan Ṣaqālibā, and some Rūs. In spite of the mention of *sūqs*, *ḥammāms*, and *masjids* in the city, it is evident that this was at most a frontier-style community. There is even a hint that a system of extra-territoriality was in operation whereby different ethnic groups to a considerable extent governed themselves. As the *Ḥudūd al-ʿĀlam* puts it: "This king [the Khāqān Khazar] has in this town seven governors (*ḥākim;* perhaps *headman* in this context) belonging to seven different creeds. At any hour when unusually important litigation arises (or more simply, important matters have to be decided) they ask the king for instructions or inform him of their decision."[799] Despite the relative prosperity of the two settlements, al-Maqdisī dismisses them altogether as "a wretched, barren place with a low standard of living and no fruit."[800]

And a final example from North Africa: according to al-Bakrī, who was probably relying on Ibn al-Warrāq, the town of ***Waddān*** in the date-rich Jufrah oasis comprised two sectors *(madīnatān)* inhabited by mutually antagonistic Arab tribes, specifically Sahmī and Ḥaḍramī. The sector of the former was known as Dilbāk, that of the latter as Būṣā. Appropriately enough, the town's only *jāmiʿ* was situated midway between the two sectors.

Occasionally, composite cities of more than two components are encountered: Ṭawlaqā and Bantiyūs in the Zibān oases in North Africa were archetypical examples of settlements encompassing three discrete urban units, the former based on ethnicity, the latter providing separate congregational mosques for Īrānians, Berbers, and persons of mixed blood. In the center of the Great Desert of Persia, on the route from Iṣfahān to Ṭabas, Sih Dih (as its name asserts) comprised three separate settlements, but it is more than doubtful if all three combined achieved even proto-urban status. In any case, it must be emphasized that polynucleated settlements of the type we have been discussing in no way constitute a functional category of ekistic classification: they are neither more nor less than extreme morphological expressions of forces universally at work but that happen in these instances to have been diverted by internal strains and external pressures into discrete and largely independent spatial patterns.

Epilogue

When the Muslims diffused into, conquered, or otherwise penetrated the Middle East and North Africa, they found themselves assuming dominion over some of the most highly urbanized regions of the ancient world. A possible total of twelve hundred to fifteen hundred settlements with some pretensions to urban status were already in existence at that time, although a high proportion of that number were very small by modern standards. Certainly, the larger cities preempted such essentially urban functions as regional administration (whether secular or religious), economic redistribution and mobilization, the management of long-distance trade, and certain types of manufacturing and retailing; but the lower levels of the urban hierarchy and the intervening villages (which far outnumbered all other settlements) were collectively of enormous importance in the calculus of economic productivity. Most of these cities had been founded in antiquity and barely supplemented in immediately pre-Muslim times, but they came close to exhausting the stock of spatial *locations* offering much potential for urban development under the technological and commercial restraints of the time. Potential *sites,* of course, were available in great numbers but were more likely to result in the local replacement of urban services through competition than the areal expansion or hierarchical intensification of an urban system. It was this ready availability of potential urban sites within a restricted distribution of propitious regional locations that ensured that the Muslims would establish many of their new foundations adjacent or close to preexisting settlements.

Since the publication of Adam Mez's *Die Renaissance des Islâms* in 1922, it has become customary to discriminate a number of distinctive urban traditions in the realms appropriated by Muslims and to which of necessity they had to adapt their ekistic arrangements to a greater or lesser degree. In this work these traditions have been defined as Hellenistic-Byzantine, Īrānian-Turānian (subsuming an ʿIrāqī subtradition), South Arabian, North African, and Spanish, but it must be remembered that each is a conceptual simplification of considerable cultural diversity. Insofar as the Arabian Peninsula was concerned, I have found no compelling evidence of a conscious attempt to recreate outside its borders any particular urban morphology or indeed to perpetuate the built forms of any specific urban tradition. There was no recognizable replica of Ṣanʿāʾ built in the Levant, nor of al-Madīnah (Medina) in al-ʿIrāq, nor of al-Ṭāʾif in North Africa. Institutional components of an Arabian urban form were certainly reemployed outside the peninsula, the mosque being a prime example; but never, as far as I have been able to ascertain, in a combination that could be matched to a built environment that was paradigmatically Arabian. What was transmitted from al-Madīnah was a style of government and a schedule of responsibilities. Even before the death of the Prophet, the oasis had become the focus of what some anthropologists might be tempted to call a fairly advanced confederacy, an ideological framework within which wider political alliances were believed to be possible. If the Tradition is to be believed, there had emerged at al-Madīnah an incipient theocratic polity in which an intense sanctity already legitimized the exercise of executive power by a charismatic leader; reinforced the conventions regulating the *Ummah;* minimized internal dissatisfaction by defining the requirements of society as the ultimate needs of the individual; and underpinned the nascent polity with a financial mechanism based on taxation, booty, and almsgiving. And these attributes were only confirmed and elaborated under the Rāshidūn caliphs (632–61).

The Arab Forces that first marauded northward from al-Madīnah carried no blueprint for urban design. The inchoate sociopolitical organization that they brought with them was ranked according to genealogical status. Subsequently the Muslim levies came to include representatives from all components of the Arabian ekistic hierarchy: in modern terms, *qarawīyūn, raʿīyah, shwāyah, badū;* in short, representatives of all lifestyles from *ḥaḍarī* to *aʿrāb,* from town dweller to nomad, drawn from all parts of the peninsula, and ultimately from beyond its borders. What conditioned their responses to problems of settlement and subsistence was immemorial Arab custom *(sābiqah)* as adapted to the precepts of Islam at al-Madīnah during the Prophet's lifetime and immediately thereafter. When tribesmen had to be quartered during or between campaigns, commanders and troops both responded opportunistically. For the former the primary concern must have been provisioning of men and animals. When whole armies were involved, this meant selection of a site offering pasturage, potable water (usually in the form of a river), provisions, and ready access. For the tribesmen and their followers it meant pitching camp in a prescribed location or adapting to an already established cantonment, according to the understandings of Arabo-Islamic precedence. When smaller forces had to be deployed, their commanders had the choice of laying out a cantonment outside an already existing settlement, assigning tribal holdings within its walls, or, as often happened, apportioning their troops between the two locations, their decision being contingent on the facilities offered by a city, the conditions of its capitulation or peace covenant *(ṣulḥ),* the phase of the campaign, the tribal affiliations of the troops, the resources of the neighborhood, the nature of the terrain, the season of the year, and no doubt political and administrative concerns rarely known to us at this distance of time. What all this amounted to for the inhabitants of most cities was a partial (and probably rather limited) replacement of local officials and a thin scattering of largely ignored Muslim garrisons. A sizable proportion of the populations among whom the newcomers found themselves were monotheists, no inconsiderable number were in fact Arabs, and many probably were not at all clear as to how their own ethnicity and religion differed from that of the invaders, who in any case might sometimes have been better characterized as infiltrators. In fact it was not unknown for Christian Arabs to oppose the invaders. Peter Brown got it just about right when he remarked that the occupied lands were treated less as conquered territories than as "rich neighbours of the Arabs who paid protection-money to the *Umma* . . . in return for military defence and as a sort of standing fine for not having embraced Islam."[1]

The Madīnan Arabs in the Rāshidūn armies would have recognized other confederacies both within the Arabian Peninsula and ranged around its borders (such as Ghassān and the Lakhmid polity); but the style of administration practiced in the bureaucratic empires of Byzantium and Sāsānian Persia, loosely structured though they were, would have proved largely unassimilable to the Arab concept of government founded on kinship and tribal alliance. Under the circumstances the Arabs followed the only effective course open to them by appropriating native administrations for general administrative purposes while retaining the traditional decentralized rule of the confederacy over their own community. A developed state structure they might not have, but they had brought with them a shared identity forged around adherence to the teachings of the Prophet; and it was this identity that their settlements in the conquered lands were intended to protect. This posed no problem in the great cantonments, which were overwhelmingly Arab and almost totally Muslim, but required some finesse when Muslims were constrained to take up residence within the confines of an existing city. Sometimes the previous inhabitants had fled, leaving vacant buildings that could be assigned to, or appropriated by, Muslim levies and their families; sometimes the inhabitants had to be expelled; occasionally sections of a city were razed and abandoned, or less frequently rebuilt.

In whatever type of settlement Muslims might find themselves, it was incumbent on them to create an environment maximally conducive to the service of God by endowing every aspect of life with religious significance. Fundamental to this obligation was the provision for communal worship. In the cantonments this at first amounted to little more than the setting aside of a space for communal prayer. Such an undertaking was also feasible within an inhabited city, although more often an existing church, temple, or other religious structure would be appropriated, or, less frequently, a mosque constructed on the site of a razed shrine. The stone remains of Antiquity that littered the Levant, the Īrānian world, and North Africa not only inspired some of the conquerors with superstitious awe and subsequently furnished raw materials for both Muslim moralists and Muslim builders, but also provided them with models of individual settlement features and sometimes, as in the cases of Waylah al-ʿAqabah) and ʿAnjar, of entire settlements. What is certain is that the Arabs in the early decades of their expansion adapted opportunistically to, and exploited in no uncertain terms, the ekistic situations within which they found themselves.

By the close of the Sufyānid period in 684, the old order stemming from al-Madīnah was fast consolidating into a pervasive combination of traditionalism and arbitrariness that certain later authors with little regard for the Umayyads chose to characterize as Hiraqlīyah and Kisrawīyah and that Max Weber would have had no hesitation in designating as patrimonial domain—that is, a form of traditional government in which the ruler treats political administration as an extension of his household authority, retainers hold their benefices as a form of personal service in a context of duty and respect, and questions of law and adjudication tend to be transmuted into questions of administration. As it is difficult to specify the precise point in time when Muslims first became aware of their uniqueness among a congeries of confessional groups subscribing to a range of distinct, yet mutually accordant monotheistic beliefs, so it is no easier to generalize about the times when local populations accepted the Muslims as permanent conquerors rather than transient raiders. It did not happen immediately after occupation even in the Levant, and not much before the end of the seventh century in the *Jazīrah* (al-Maqdisī's *Iqlīm* Aqūr), while even later dates are to be inferred for Sughd and other parts of Transoxania. The matter was still in doubt, for instance, in Bukhārā in the early years of the eighth century. However that may be, it is evident that by the middle of that century the Muslims had erected, on the largely crumbled foundation of the old Sāsānian settlement pattern, a vibrant urban hierarchy supporting the pyramidal political structure of the Umayyads and nurturing the cultural, religious, intellectual, and economic dimensions of their kingdom. Once again it is hazardous to attempt to assign precise dates to phases in this enhanced urbanization process, but such evidence as has been elicited in the preceding pages would seem to point generally toward the caliphate of Muʿāwiyah (661–80) initiating the transformation, with ʿAbd al-Malik (685–705) and finally Hishām (724–43) consolidating the hierarchy in the core regions of the Levant and al-ʿIrāq. The Marwānid period witnessed the first signs of a Muslim bourgeoisie in Middle Eastern cities as tribesmen and peasants alike sought fiscal relief in the seats of power, which were the places where patrons were most likely to be found, and thereby diversified urban occupational structures at the same time as they enhanced confessional conversion rates.

A problem inevitably inherent in patrimonial rule is the centrifugal tendency of the outer benefices to become detached from the central polity and to re-coalesce around largely autonomous capitals. There were stirrings in this direction under the Umayyads, but their most dire effects were postponed for half a century or so by the substitution of army generals for kinsmen and court favorites as provincial governors while new recruitment policies virtually detribalized the army. In short, whereas in the confederacy days of al-Madīnah and the Rāshidūn caliphs authority had been validated by its association with the sacred, by Marwānid times authority was beginning to effectively manipulate sanctity as a means of acquiring and retaining power. Both arrangements signified a close relationship between power and religion, but, whereas the first was metaphorically natal, the second was indisputably affinal. Nor was it without a certain irony that Dimashq (Damascus), the pivot of Roman defenses facing the desert, had become the metropolis of Arab caliphs facing the Mediterranean.

Although the Umayyads fostered a genetically diverse yet powerful urban system in the heart of the Islamic culture realm and stimulated numerous lesser systems in peripheral regions, it was under the aegis of the ʿAbbāsid Caliphate that the urbanization process registered its most rapid growth. The establishment of a bureaucratic empire on a pattern long familiar to the Middle East and wide open to oriental, especially Īrānian, influences—ruled by a prince of the blood for whom the principle of hereditary descent was only partially masked by a fictional invocation of the traditional norm of acclamation *(bayʿah),* and who exercised his (by now personalized) authority through a salaried administrative staff and his power through standing military forces, both to a great extent emancipated from the restraints of tradition—generated the foundation of new settlements, including some of the premier *metropoleis* of Islam, and an enormous influx of country dwellers into both old and new towns. Caliphal and public capital was invested in land-development schemes of every sort, the dividends from which were drawn off mainly by urban élites. Local retail trade flourished in response to the cityward migrations while an unprecedented expansion of commerce, both domestic and foreign, inspired the adoption of innovative instruments in the spheres of partnership, banking, and law.

The conjoining of a huge roster of disparate but in the aggregate complementary regions, albeit briefly and imperfectly, under a single rule within the providential framework of a shared religion, a shared though by no means exclusive language, and a shared legal system created something in the nature of an economic community of vast extent. Within this community, bureaucratically administered redistribution and mobilization collaborated with market forces to provide whatever commodities government might require or wealth and privilege desire, not excluding human merchandise. It also afforded talented individuals opportunities for social advancement, facilitated spatial mobility, and subtly encouraged the subversion of traditions that appeared inimical to creative pursuits. The result was a dramatic maturation of the urban middle class that had taken root under the later Umayyads into a cosmopolitanly inclined status group manifesting a common lifestyle defined by distance and exclusiveness in social estimation.

It was in the cities of the core regions of the Islamic world at this time, particularly in Baghdād, that there occurred the remarkable flowering of humanistic learning that has come to be known to Western scholars as the Renaissance of Islam (but which might be better viewed simply as a period of cultural exuberance within Islamic intellectualism) and which attained its apogee under the Buwayhids in the second half of the tenth century. On the outer fringes of the Caliphate older patrimonial forms of government persisted into the ʿAbbāsid period, sometimes into the tenth century: in North Africa the Idrīsids of Fās (Fez), the Sufrite Imāmate of Tilimsān, the Rustamid Imāmate based on Ṭāhart (Tiaret), and the Aghlabids in Qayrawān (Kairouan) were representative examples, all structured about impressively robust urban hierarchies culminating in *metropoleis* of no mean order. On the northern frontier, Bagratid Armenia, Vaspurakan under Ardzruni rule, and Arrān with its *qaṣabah* of Bardhāʿah (Barda), which earned the sobriquet of "The Baghdād of Arrān," were similar examples of patrimonial kingdoms. In the far west of the Maghrib and in Ṭabaristān, Jīlān, and Rūyān, certain confederacies survived even into the tenth century mainly by juggling loyalties among competing overlords or, as often as not, accepting the reality of multiple allegiances. An interpretation of the composite, hierarchical urban systems underpinning these different modes of political authority as they had evolved in the Īslamic world by the end of the tenth century comprises the substance of chapters 4 through 16. The extent to which these urban systems testified to the achievements of other than Arab Muslims is abundantly affirmed, particularly the massive contributions of resurgent Persian traditions in the eighth and ninth centuries. The salient characteristics of these structures are summarized below.

Al-ʿIrāq. Spatially, the Islamic urban system in the tenth century did not differ materially from that which had been in place under Sāsānid hegemony. Exigencies of conquest had filled some lacunae in the distribution of sites, chiefly in the upper levels of the hierarchy; but the categorical constraints of physiography decreed that settlements still be strung along rivers and other watercourses. Nor had the outer limits of the system been significantly extended. In the hierarchical dimension of the system, however, there had been important changes. Not only had the foundation of Baghdād restored a major city to the venerable centroid of political power where once Babylon and Ctesiphon (al-Madā'in) had stood, but it had also nurtured a capital of empire ranking among the two or three largest cities in the world. And because the vitality of the metropolis was a reflex of synergistic forces, both cultural and economic, operating over a vast tract of the earth's surface, it had become an example of extreme urban primacy, half again as extensive as either al-Baṣrah or al-Kūfah, the next-largest cities—and, incidentally, occupying an area some ten times that of the former Sāsānian capital of Seleucia-Ctesiphon. The primate character of the hierarchy was further accentuated by the circumstance that the four "cities" (Adams' category of settlements more than one hundred hectares in extent) in the rank immediately below the imperial capital accounted for roughly one-third of the total area of all settlements in the Diyālā River basin. This being the case, it comes as no surprise that there are occasional indications of population decline in lesser towns in the region. (See chapter 4.)

Aqūr (or al-Jazīrah). Although al-Maqdisī depicted this *iqlīm* as structured about an urban hierarchy culminating in the metropolis of al-Mawṣil (Mosul), which had succeeded to the role of ancient Nineveh, it would more accurately have been viewed as three functionally discrete systems only loosely integrated into the *iqlīm*ic hierarchy. In the middle Tigris River region, Diyār Rabīʿah supported a reasonably stable hierarchy; in the west, the hierarchy (if it can justifiably be called that) of Diyār Muḍar was rendered ekistically unstable mainly by reason of conflict between Greeks and Arabs; while to the northwest, Diyār Bakr was essentially a frontier province where settlements, apart from the *qaṣabah* of Āmid and the fortified town of Mayyāfarīqīn (Silvan), were predominantly small. The fractured network of the Jazīran *thughūr* did not constitute, or contribute to, a functional hierarchy. (See chapter 5.)

Al-Shām. Al-Shām (Greater Syria) was a highly urbanized region to which the Muslims added few new cities, but for part of the time it was divided among competing empires: Ikhshīdids and Fāṭimids in the south, Ḥamdānids in the north. The latter proved the most disruptive in that after 944 it imposed a patrimonial-style amīrate on the northern third of the *iqlīm;* but its own organizational weaknesses were exposed in 970, when it was forced to cede its westernmost territories to the Byzantines. In the frontier zone of the north the inherent instability of the urban system had degenerated into virtually total disintegration—as Ibn Ḥawqal noted poignantly enough. Although the hierarchy in the southern two-thirds of the *iqlīm,* in spite of its fluctuating political fortunes, suffered fewer and less violent disruptions, it did experience a prevailing decline in prosperity among its coastal cities and the urban centers on its desert eastern and southern fringes, to the evident advantage of the intervening tracts. A salient feature of the Shāmian urban system as a whole was the dissonance between the administrative and sacral hierarchies. (See chapter 6.)

The* Jazīrah *of the Arabs. In spite of al-Maqdisī's attempt to disguise the fact by positing two *metropoleis,* the Arabian Peninsula encompassed not one, nor two, but three essentially discrete urban systems ranged around the desert heart of the subcontinent and all cultivating centrifugally vigorous ties to the outside world: the Ḥijāz, with the western arm of the Fertile Crescent and Egypt; the Yaman, with the Horn of Africa; and ʿUmān, with the Īrānian lands. Although these subsystems were functionally discrete and generated only minimal interaction among themselves, each was a reasonably well integrated hierarchy in its own right. In the Ḥijāz the Muslims, by their development of the Ḥaramayn and al-Qurah, had generated a primate distribution of urban forms that had been completely absent in earlier periods. In the Yaman they refocused the hierarchy in a new lowland, as opposed to an upland, metropolis but did not otherwise significantly distort the ancient pattern. In ʿUmān the system remained essentially static except for an exaggerated primacy generated by Ibāḍī-controlled foreign trade in Ṣuḥar. To generalize about the peninsula as a whole, increases in the rate of urbanization stemmed not from the founding of new cities but from growth in the size of individual settlements. It should also be noted that it was in this *iqlīm* that the sacral hierarchy achieved its most comprehensive development. (See chapter 7.)

Al-Jibāl. The evolution of the urban hierarchy may

be generalized as follows: Under the Umayyads the Arabs established cordons of dispersed settlements surrounding already existing cities. Under the ʿAbbāsids these extended settlements were consolidated by a process of imperially sponsored synoecism. The resulting compact cities, which included some of the premier foci of the Islamic world, afforded fertile bases from which to disseminate ʿAbbāsid military and administrative policies, but at the end of our period what had crystallized out was a more tightly structured adaptation of a fundamentally Sāsānian urban hierarchy. Internal interactions between cities had been intensified, but the basic geometry of the system had not been changed significantly, nor its borders extended. (See chapter 8.)

Khūzistān. Khūzistān was one of the most highly urbanized regions in the Islamic world, with its relatively undifferentiated topography and abundance—sometimes overabundance—of water permitting an unusual freedom of choice of settlement sites. Without doubt it encompassed the greatest concentration of high-level administrative foci to be found in any *iqlīm,* but the urban hierarchy as it was described in the tenth century was not wholly a Muslim creation. Rather, it was a Muslim elaboration and consolidation of a preexisting Sāsānian system, particularly insofar as administration, textiles, and transport were concerned. (See chapter 9.)

Fārs. The urban hierarchy in Fārs was also largely a legacy of antiquity. Although its metropolis was an Arab foundation, it represented a substitution of site rather than of location, thereby perpetuating the Persian practice of maintaining a major administrative focus reasonably close to the geometrical center of the province. After the Arab conquest the urban system experienced relatively few significant changes until the second half of the ninth century and the first half of the tenth, and again under the Buwayhid hegemony. Even then the Muslim contribution was primarily an increase in the sizes of individual cities through investment in virtually all sectors of the economy but without an accompanying extension of the territorial base of the system. Textile-manufacturing towns and port cities were among the most dynamic components in the hierarchy during the tenth century. (See chapter 10.)

Kirmān. The position of this *iqlīm* in a transitional zone between locally productive and relatively densely populated Fārs and the virtually empty Persian desert, parts of which repelled even nomadic settlement, subverted from the beginning the development of a mature urban hierarchy. Segmented lineage loyalties within ecologically circumscribed oases were not the stuff from which a stable and resilient urban system was likely to be forged. Nor did the reputation of the province as a refuge for bandits and renegades encourage such stability. The cumulative outcome, even as late as the tenth century, was an urban hierarchy both attenuated and discontinuous. It is not without interest, however, that whereas the transference of the metropolis from al-Sirjān to Bardasīr had moved the *miṣr* somewhat nearer the geometrical center of the *iqlīm,* it had at the same time distanced the hub of the urban system from the centroid of highest population density. It was no aberration that the tenth-century topographers described a road system focused on al-Sirjān rather than Bardasīr. (See chapter 16.)

Al-Riḥāb. This frontier *iqlīm,* with its violently fractured topography, was served by a correspondingly disjunctive urban system that, except for a period of Musāfirid dominance in the tenth century, ranked among the least integrated of any in the Islamic world. Fundamentally, this system comprised three patrimonial-style kingdoms, each with its own capital, set within a shifting matrix of lesser confederacies and continually subjected to the predations of more powerful neighbors. In short, in spite of the emergence of a few relatively persistent and sometimes powerful nodes in the urban hierarchy, as a whole it amounted to hardly more than an aggregate of largely autonomous entities at varied levels of sociopolitical integration. Although this congeries of urban systems that al-Maqdisī tried unsuccessfully to meld together as an integrated hierarchy underwent no major structural changes during the first four centuries of Islam, there is abundant evidence that the level of urbanization in the province increased: in some instances (so it is to be inferred) through Arab immigration into selected cities, at other times by reason of the aggregating stimuli of textile manufacturing or strategic commercial locations. (See chapter 12.)

Al-Daylam. Al-Daylam was another frontier zone where diversified physiography and a partially unconsummated conquest subverted the development of a tightly integrated urban system, but which al-Maqdisī felt constrained to force into an artificially conceived, Ziyārid-period assemblage of ill-matched patrimonial kingdoms and confederacies. What eventually crystallized out of this matrix seems to have been a polynuclear urban system in which the effective (although not necessarily the formal) apex oscillated between center (Āmul) and periphery (Gurgān). At the close of the tenth century this composite but still unconsolidated province was as ekistically fragmented as it had been in Sāsānian times, even though the Muslim presence had stimulated the growth of certain cities specializing in transportation facilities and textile manufacture. (See chapter 13.)

Al-Mashriq. This *iqlīm* encompassed an enormous extent of rain-deficient territory where settlement was tied ineluctably to water resources. Because of its history and ethnology, Al-Maqdisī had no choice but to apportion this vast tract of country among two urban hierarchies, each culminating in a metropolis of great renown in the Islamic world. In both regions the Arabs had inherited urban systems of considerable antiquity. In Khurāsān they had adapted the old Sāsānian system to their own governmental needs and in some instances intensified the interactions among its components. This took the form of a process of selective urbanization in which the Arabs stimulated agricultural and industrial development in the environs of cities that had been chosen not for their potential productivity but for their roles in regional administration and frontier defense. In any case, it was less the attraction of life in these cities that stimulated their growth than the in-migration of peasants and some members of the *dihqān* class seeking to escape an egregiously oppressive rural taxation system. Beyond the Āmū Daryā River, in Ḥaytal territory, Muslim rule had transformed what had been at best an occasional confederacy of petty statelets into the relatively stable heart of the Sāmānid polity focused on the two great conurbations of the Zarafshān. A zone of frontier fortress cities along the northern fringe of Mā Warā al-Nahr (Transoxania) was already in decline in the second half of the tenth century as conversion of Turkic peoples to Islam obviated the need for the *ghāzīs* who had earlier flocked to the defense of the Faith. The settlement systems in Qūhistān, Sijistān, and Khwārizm that al-Maqdisī attempted to bring under the umbrella of al-Mashriq not only fit less than comfortably into his ekistic schema but were also themselves of a composite nature that subsumed virtually all levels of political integration from patrimonial kingdoms to confederacies. In sum, although Muslim dominance failed to overcome the physiographically prescribed, segmental character of urban development in the Mashriq, it did encourage, and often effected, the analytically distinct processes of consolidation, intensification, elaboration, and adaptation—but not to any significant degree areal extension. (See chapter 14.)

Miṣr. Al-Maqdisī's analogically derived reticence in discussing the urban system in the Nile valley has been touched upon in chapter 15. Moreover, as other topographers added only a minimal number of cities to al-Maqdisī's roster, it must be presumed that they too labored under the same inhibition. As best the urban hierarchy can be reconstructed, under the Umayyads it comprised a reasonably compact settlement system focused on Lower Egypt. Initially, Arab priority was the maintenance of the stability necessary to sustain the high level of agricultural and industrial productivity that had prevailed under Byzantine hegemony; al-Fusṭāṭ apart, the Muslims added few new foundations to what was already one of the most highly urbanized regions in the Middle East. Even by the tenth century they had not changed significantly the structure of the urban system. Neither the narrow corridor of agricultural land stretching along the Nile River for five hundred miles to the vicinity of Uswān (Aswan) nor the Fayyūmī oasis in the western desert was ever fully integrated into the Miṣrī urban hierarchy. It is true, though, that the Muslims restored the metropolis of the Delta to the hallowed articulation point of the two halves of the pharaonic kingdom and thereby transposed the external focus of the *iqlīm* from the Mediterranean world to southwestern Asia. Although this did not fundamentally change the configurative structure of the urban system, it did enhance the primate status of the Fusṭāṭ-Qāhirah (Cairo) conurbation beyond anything attained by earlier capitals. Islamic urban policy at the time can be generalized appropriately as primarily conservationist, although it did encourage the uninhibited growth of textile-manufacturing centers. (See chapter 15.)

Al-Maghrib. This *iqlīm* was an artificially conceived aggregation of fluid political and religious alliances, the fringes of which were treated only cursorily by Muslim topographers. But even without al-Andalus (Islamic Spain) and Iṣqiliyah (Sicily), al-Maghrib hardly ever supported anything more than a loosely composite and continually fluctuating urban system, or, perhaps better, a series of systems capable under the right conditions of varying degrees of interdigitation. Urban systems in

Cyrenaica and lands to the eastward were always linked more closely to those of Egypt than to polities in the central and western Maghrib, where a series of patrimonial-style kingdoms each extended across a latitudinal zonation of ecotypes that was clearly reflected in their north–south sequence of patterns of city distributions. With only a few significant exceptions, the Muslims did not extend the territorial base of the urban hierarchy in North Africa, but they did contribute a disproportionately large number of new foundations, mainly in the form of prevailing grandiose palatine complexes and humbler coastal defensive settlements. There is also abundant evidence that the Muslim presence had stimulated an enormous increase in both retail and interregional trade, which in turn was expressed as a general increase in city sizes at all levels of the hierarchy. In brief, between the seventh and tenth centuries the hierarchy expanded vertically by what I have likened to an inflationary process, but without doing more than minimal violence to the old Roman and Byzantine systems, and certainly without significantly reducing the fragmentation that was an enduring characteristic of the hierarchy. (See chapter 16.)

*

So much for the thirteen urban hierarchies of the early Islamic world insofar as they can be reconstructed from extant sources. When we turn to the individual cities that constituted these systems, we are confronted by a daunting diversity of forms. When Claude Cahen writes,

> La ville musulmane . . . me parait continuer sur une lancée qui prolonge, avec des transformations, mais sans rupture, la ville du Bas Empire, ou la ville sāsānide d'Iran. . . ;

or when he adds,

> Je crois tout de même que la vraie rupture n'est pas à situer à la conquête arabe, mais lors des transformations générales profondes qu'on peut en gros placer autour du XIe siècle. . . .[2]

he was evidently responding to the Weberian idea of administrative autonomy and autocephaly underpinned by vigorous, legally constituted, self-governing, corporate associations as necessary (though not sufficient) criteria of urban life. However that may have been, and whatever the degree of organic solidarity involved, it is abundantly evident that between the seventh and tenth centuries the fabric of the representative Middle Eastern city had experienced numerous and occasionally profound changes in both form and appearance; and it is these transformations that are discussed summarily enough in chapter 17 (in any case, the Weberian definition of urban status is not that adopted in this work). For one thing, the Muslims added to the kaleidoscopic array of existing urban forms a not inconsiderable number of new foundations. Among the earliest of these were the giant cantonments known to the Tradition as *amṣār.* Although Arab encampments had been common in the Middle East in earlier times (the *ḥaḍir* outside Chalkis was a prime example), anything on a scale involving whole armies and their camp followers had seldom, if ever, been recorded. An interesting aspect of the larger of these settlements was that, although they were imposed on alien communities, their evolution followed a trajectory more commonly associated with spontaneously initiated cities in realms of primary urban generation: that is, the progressive differentiation of autonomous institutional spheres and the emergence of specialized collectivities and roles as primarily a response to internal societal pressures.

Although the general direction of overall development as an Islamic settlement was in each case subject to external authority, the socially consolidatory processes of segregation and centralization required to induce the level of organic interaction connotative of an urbanized society were generated very largely internally. Relatively seldom did caliph or governor intervene at the tribal level or below; Ziyād ibn Abīhi was the prime example of one who did. Smaller cantonments on the outskirts of preexisting cities sometimes followed the same developmental patterns to a point where they absorbed or replaced original settlements, but just as frequently were themselves engulfed by expanding urban forms. A restricted number of new foundations also coalesced around shrines and fortresses, of which even fewer eventually secured places in the upper ranks of the hierarchy.

The vast majority of Middle Eastern cities, however, were pre-Muslim in origin, and as often as not of considerable antiquity. Many of the smaller of these were almost totally ignored by Muslim authority for other than taxation purposes in the decades immediately following the conquests and became fully absorbed into the Islamic polity only in the eighth century or later. In other instances the Muslims initiated programs of accommodation and adaptation that would both protect and confirm their emergent identity but which often had the additional effect of eventually stimulating a surge of urban growth unparalleled in the Middle East in previous times. In the earlier centuries of Islam it seems to have been established practice for the *dār al-imārah* to be positioned on the *qiblah* side of the congregational mosque, perhaps to suffuse administrative decisions with the power of prayer flowing down the *qiblah* to Makkah (Mecca). Although this formal architectural relationship was found at various times from Egypt to western Khurāsān, by the end of the ninth century it had apparently been discontinued. However, as religion and government began to assert substantial degrees of autonomy in their operational spheres, there developed a tendency for caliphal residences and government *dīwāns* to be incorporated in elaborately conceived extramural palatine complexes, sometimes well removed from main population foci. A number of these foundations subsequently attracted dense peripheral populations, the cultural and economic activities of which raised a few of them, including the imperial capital of Baghdād, to the first rank among Islamic cities.

By the tenth century the primary process of foundation and the evolutional process of adaptation, operating conjointly within a wide range of natural environments and culture realms, had generated a spectrum of urban morphologies the diversity of which subverts easy generalization. The circumstance that institutions of secular power and sacral authority were frequently sited in close proximity to one another should occasion no surprise: it has been a juxtaposition of virtually universal occurrence in the cities of the traditional world. Nor is it to be wondered at that the complex as often as not was situated deep within the interior of the city, somewhere in the vicinity of its functional center (the peak land-value intersection as it would be called today, which was not necessarily the same, or even particularly close to, the geometrical center). Certainly, there was nothing specifically Islamic about these arrangements. What was Islamic was the formal spatial relationship obtaining for some two centuries or so between the *dār al-imārah*, the *masjid al-jāmiʿ*, and the *qiblah* (of course, architectural features directly expressive of Islamic beliefs and values were always present: I speak here only of the prevailing structural morphology of the city). At the same time, the mosque was being transformed from a primarily spatial structure into a functionally very effective coalescence of both volume and space. Nor have I been able to distinguish specifically Islamic templates determining the manner in which instruments of economic exchange were ideally dispersed through the city. Reciprocity was integral to the daily life of all peoples, whether Muslim, *Ahl al-Kitāb*, or pagan. Redistribution and mobilization were taken care of in the *dīwān*, wherever in the city that might be. And, in spite of Eugen Wirth's claim that the integrated *sūq* developed pari passu with Islamic hegemony, I have found no compelling evidence for a specifically Islamic impress on the deployment of structures housing either retailing activities or wholesaling transactions—although Islamic values certainly informed the business conducted within their precincts, first under the watchful eye of the *ʿāmil al-sūq* but subsequently under the more general surveillance of that guardian of community morality, the *muḥtasib*. The three *sūq* distributions commonly encountered in the modern city, namely compact neighborhood, localized specialty, and extended lineal (though this last probably differed genetically from its present-day counterpart), were all evident in the Middle Eastern city of the tenth century. *Funduqs* and *khāns* were most commonly located on main thoroughfares reasonably close to the outer edges of the city. High-class residential compounds, the complexes often rubricated as *diyār* or sometimes as *quṣūr*, tended to cluster in especially favorable sectors of the city; middle- and lower-class homes were spread throughout the built-up area, often in client relationships with more powerful establishments, and with noticeable concentrations around commercial and industrial foci.

Of course, this latter housing stock was usually the spatially most extensive class of land use in a city, but it receives only incidental treatment in this work for two reasons. First, apart from generalized allusions to prevailing modes of construction, it was virtually ignored by authors of the time (presumably as being such a universal feature of everyday life as not to require description) while archaeology, except for a few notable excavations at such sites as al-Fusṭāṭ, Sīraf, Sāmarrā, Raqqah, and Sūsah (al-Sūs), has provided an inadequate basis for effective generalization. Second, this work has been concerned primarily with hierarchies and urban structures rather than with architecture. The most that can be said here is that the traditional courtyard house of the ancient Middle East continued to prevail during the first four Islamic centuries, with multistoreyed structures occurring from time to time, notably in the Yaman and certain distinctive cities such as Alexandria, Sīrāf, and Syrian Aṭrābulus (Tripoli). Nor is it at all clear how in these early centuries the distribution of other than élite housing was related to juridical and gender distinctions in the still developing legal systems of the time. Such questions will be more easily answered in studies of subsequent ages blessed with a greater abundance of information.

Although the social institution of the *ḥammām* had been a legacy of the Hellenistic and Roman worlds, the Islamic insistence on the need for ritual purity before prayer ensured a substantial increase in the number of such amenities, especially as Muslims, abandoning their initial prejudice against its foreign origin, came to espouse the public bath as furnishing facilities not only for the prescribed ablution but also for relaxation and social interaction. The larger baths functioned essentially as annexes to important congregational mosques, but others, both public and private, were distributed more or less according to the density of population. Both the close spatial relationship of congregational mosque and *ḥammām* and the substantial number of the latter scattered through even modestly sized cities, not infrequently more than one to a street, must be accounted direct effects of Islamic doctrine and practice—although not of a specific, preconceived urban design. The locational mobility of infirmaries following the distribution of poorer populations was also a direct expression of Islamic values, namely eleemosynary obligations and the institution of the *waqf.*

Defensive features were emphasized less than might have been expected. When Muslims occupied all or part of a preexisting city, they usually left its fortifications intact. Occasionally a *dār al-imārah* was established temporarily in a subjugated citadel, but more commonly such structures were ignored and allowed to fall into disrepair. Settlements founded by Muslims, including some of the most prestigious, often went unwalled until the eighth century or later, although the centers of a few early foundations, notably Waylah (al-ʿAqabah) and ʿAnjār, were walled on the pattern of some Roman and Byzantine legionary fortresses. The major compounds comprising a palatine complex, by contrast, were customarily walled at their inceptions. Within the urban enceinte, however it might be delimited and according to its size, was an agglomeration of quarters, neighborhoods, and enclaves differentiated one from another by accidents of history, ethnicity, and occupation, the whole mosaic being integrated into a functioning whole by circulatory networks of boulevards, streets, alleys, and in some instances canals. It is well known, of course, that certain activities such, for instance, as potteries, tanneries, or cemeteries were banished to the urban fringe.

Generally speaking, in the palatine sectors of these cities space was anterior to mass in the sense that the whole settlement, or at least a substantial part of it, comprised a preconceived arrangement of architectural volumes constituting nothing less than a formalized expression of dynastic ambition; whereas in those parts of the city given over to community affairs, mass can be said to have prevailed over space, which tended to become dislocated, suppressed, and sometimes dissipated altogether. But it cannot be emphasized too strongly that this aggregate of ekistic units, at whatever rank in the urban hierarchy it might occur, was hardly ever—and then only in readily explicable circumstances—a static entity. The representative city of the time was a congeries of interacting subsystems signifying both societal evolution and spatial expansion, at the same time as it substantially enhanced the content of the information flows promoting sociocultural and economic integration. This expansion is most clearly revealed in the topographic accounts of the cities of the Eastern Caliphate in ʿAbbāsid and Buwayhid times, with their repetitive emphasis on *rabaḍs* as integral components of the urbanization process; but urban intensification and expansion were all but universal during the first four Islamic centuries, beginning under the Rāshidūn caliphs, gaining momentum under the Umayyads, and eventually reaching a crescendo in response to the synergistically integrative forces of the ʿAbbāsid Empire. At that time a city without a *rabaḍ* was one that had either failed in the competition for the fruits of suzerainty or been physically destroyed by its enemies.

These brief comments summarizing the substance of chapter 17 make it clear that the specifically Islamic element in the Middle Eastern city during the Early Islamic period, especially during the first two centuries or so, resided less in the spatial deployment of its institutional foci than in the design and decoration of individual architectural components. The morphological structure of the representative city of the time was more directly reflective of familial, tribal, and ethnic concerns than of specifically Islamic values, and cultural continuity generally prevailed over developmental disjunction (Armenia being a possible exception). By the ninth or tenth century, however, depending on location and local circumstance, religion had come to contextualize virtually all perceptions and expectations of urban life, past, present, and future. A representative (governor or comparable official) of the Vicegerent of the Prophet (the caliph) ideally furnished security and stability, a *qāḍī* dispensed justice as prescribed in the *Sharīʿah,* a *ṣāḥib al-shurṭah* maintained a more or less desirable level of public order, and a *muḥtasib* arbitrated questions of transactional morality and uncontested liability. But what made the assortment of tenth-century administrations Muslim, as Ibn Taymīyah would acknowledge some three centuries subsequently, was less their intrinsic qualities than their unqualified support of the One Faith and its communities.

The somewhat more than two thousand cities lying between the Atlantic Ocean and the Indus River, the Caspian Sea and the Sūdān, in the tenth century each had their own distinctive sights, sounds, colors, and smells; but such ambient characteristics have proved all but irrecoverable from contemporary, or contemporarily relevant, texts. The imbricately structured layers of meaning, memory, and association evoked by these urban forms, in retrospect seemingly scaled harmoniously to the measure of humanity, can only be imagined. Indeed, the whole *Lebenswelt,* the "constitutive becoming" appropriate to a phenomenological understanding of cities in the first four Islamic centuries, is almost totally denied to us by the nature of our sources, and with it the cultural multicoding of urban space on which a semiotic analysis would have to be based. Instead of attempting (vainly, as I believe it would have turned out) to retroject a phenomenological, reductive specificity from more amply documented later centuries or to project it forward from an earlier period, as might have been partially practicable in a very few rare instances such as Jerusalem or Alexandria, I have settled for a reconstruction of the manner in which agglomerative and accessibility factors combined over some four centuries to recast the settlement pattern of North Africa and the Middle East into thirteen functionally discrete, politically determined, and hierarchically ordered systems. To flesh out the bones of these skeletal hierarchies, I have appended a supplementary discussion of selected representative cities as epiphenomenal expressions, concentrated and intensified, of interactions and contradictions operative throughout the wider Islamic world. Together these approaches can constitute a benchmark for future study of the urban hierarchies that in later times came to epitomize both the best and the worst of Muslim achievements—the most noble and the most ignoble deeds, in al-Fārābī's phrase—as well as a basis for further discussion of the vexed question of what may have been specifically Muslim about the so-called Islamic city.

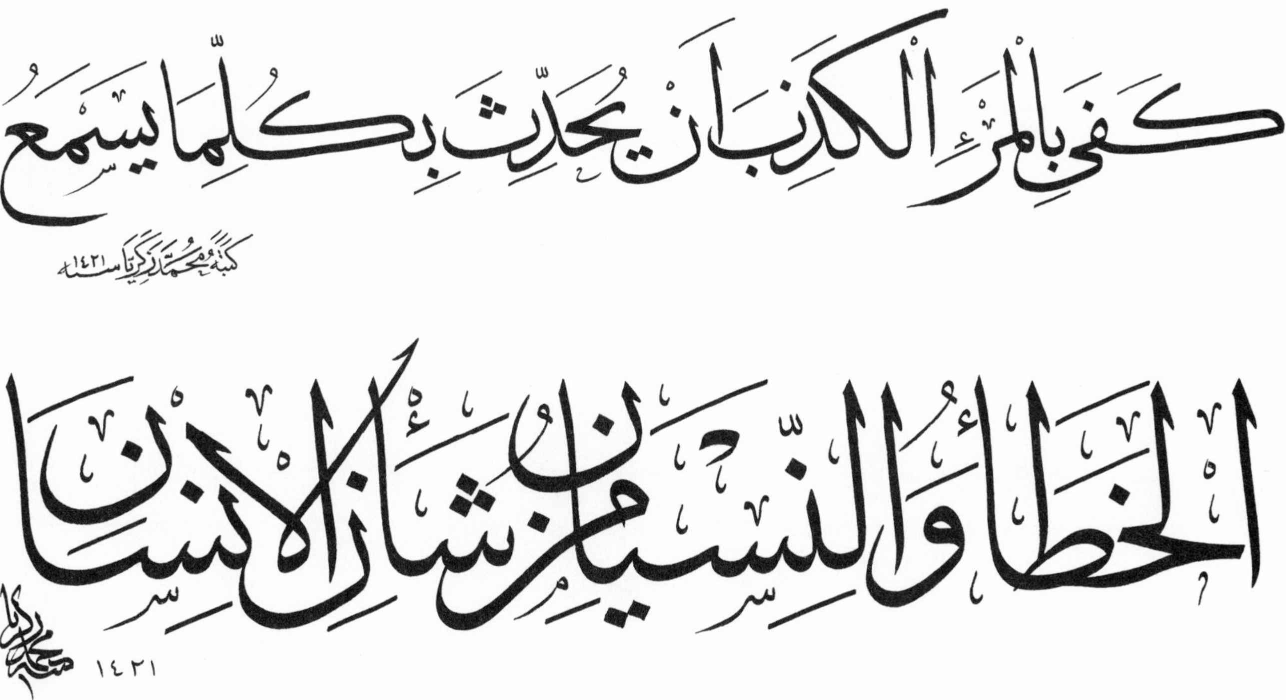

Appendix A: The Principal Islamic Dynasties, A.D. 632–circa 1000

(Hijrī dates precede their *anno domini* equivalents. Terminal dates relate to the centuries covered by the present work; several dynasties survived for substantially longer periods of time.)

I: Caliphs

Rightly Guided Caliphs *(al-Khulafāʾ al-Rāshidūn)*

11/632 Abū Bakr
13/634 ʿUmar b. al-Khaṭṭāb
23/644 ʿUthmān b. ʿAffān
35–40/656–61 ʿAlī b. Abī-Ṭālib

Umayyads

41/661 Muʿāwiyah I b. Abī-Sufyān
60/680 Yazīd I
64/683 Muʿāwiyah II
64/684 Marwān I b. al-Ḥakam
65/685 ʿAbd al-Malik
86/705 al-Walīd I
96/715 Sulaymān
99/717 ʿUmar b. ʿAbd al-ʿAzīz
101/720 Yazīd II
105/724 Hishām
125/743 al-Walīd II
126/744 Yazīd III
126/744 Ibrāhīm
127–32/744–50 Marwān II al-Ḥimār

ʿAbbāsids

132/749 al-Saffāḥ
136/754 al-Manṣūr
158/775 al-Mahdī
169/785 al-Hādī
170/786 Hārūn al-Rashīd
193/809 al-Amīn
198/813 al-Maʾmūn
201–3/817–19 Ibrāhīm b. al-Mahdī, in Baghdād
218/833 al-Muʿtaṣim
227/842 al-Wāthiq
232-847 al-Mutawakkil
247/861 al-Muntaṣir
248/862 al-Mustaʿīn
252/866 al-Muʿtazz
255/869 al-Muhtadī
256/870 al-Muʿtamid
279/892 al-Muʿtaḍid
289/902 al-Muktafī
295/908 al-Muqtadir
320/932 al-Qāhir
322/934 al-Rāḍī
329/940 al-Muttaqī
333/944 al-Mustakfī
334/946 al-Muṭīʿ
363/974 al-Ṭāʾiʿ
381/991 al-Qādir
422/1031 al-Qāʾim

II: al-Andalus

Spanish Umayyads

138/756 ʿAbd al-Raḥmān I al-Dākhil
172/788 Hishām I

180/796 al-Ḥakam I
206/822 ʿAbd al-Raḥmān II al-Mutawassiṭ
238/852 Muḥammad I
273/886 al-Mundhir
275/888 ʿAbd Allāh
300/912 ʿAbd al-Raḥmān III al-Nāṣir
350/961 al-Ḥakam II al-Mustanṣir
366/976 Hishām II al-Muʾayyad, *first reign*
399/1009 Muḥammad II al-Mahdī, *first reign*

III: North Africa

Idrīsids

172/789 Idrīs I
177/793 Idrīs II
213/828 Muḥammad al-Muntaṣir
221/836 ʿAlī I
234/849 Yaḥyā I
? Yaḥyā II
? ʿAlī II
? Yaḥyā III al-Miqdām
292/905 Yaḥyā IV
310–14/922–26 al-Ḥasan al-Hajjām

Rustamids

160/777 ʿAbd al-Raḥmān b. Rustam
168/784 ʿAbd al-Wahhāb (or ʿAbd-al-Wārith) b. ʿAbd al-Raḥmān
208/823 Abū Saʿīd Aflaḥ
258/872 Abū Bakr b. Aflaḥ
? Abū-l-Yaqẓān Muḥammad
281/894 Abū Ḥātim Yūsuf, *first reign*
284/897 Yaʿqūb b. Aflaḥ
288/901 Abū Ḥātim Yūsuf, *second reign*
294–96/907–9 Yaqẓān b. Muḥammad

Aghlabids

184/800 Ibrāhīm I b. al-Aghlab
197/812 ʿAbd Allāh I
210/817 Ziyādat Allāh I
223/838 Abū ʿIqāl al-Aghlab
226/841 Muḥammad I
242/856 Aḥmad
249/863 Ziyādat Allāh II
250/863 Abū-l-Gharānīq Muḥammad II
261-875 Ibrāhīm II
289-902 ʿAbd Allāh II
290–96/903–9 Ziyādat Allāh III

Zīrids

361/972 Yūsuf Buluggīn I b. Zīrī
373/984 al-Manṣūr b. Buluggīn
386/996 Nāṣir-al-Dawlah Bādīs
406/1016 Sharaf-al-Dawlah al-Muʿizz

IV: The Fertile Crescent

Ṭūlūnids

254/868 Aḥmad b.Ṭūlūn
270/884 Khumārawayh
282/896 Jaysh
283/896 Hārūn
292/905 Shaybān

Ikhshīdids

323/935 Muḥammad b.Ṭughj al-Ikhshīd
334/946 Ūnūjūr
349/961 ʿAlī
355/966 Kāfūr *(originally regent for ʿAlī)*
357–58/968–69 Aḥmad

Fāṭimids

297/909 ʿUbayd Allāh al-Mahdī
322/934 al-Qāʾim
334/946 al-Manṣūr
341/953 al-Muʿizz
365/975 al-ʿAzīz
386/996 al-Ḥākim
411/1021 aẓ-Ẓāhir

Ḥamdānids

Mawṣil branch

293/905 Abū-l-Hayjāʾ ʿAbd Allāh *(governor of Mawṣil for the caliph)*
317/929 Nāṣir al-Dawlah al-Ḥasan
358/969 ʿUddat al-Dawlah Abū-Taghlib
369/979 Būyid conquest
379–89/981–91 Ibrāhim, al-Ḥusayn } *restored by the Būyids as joint rulers*

Ḥalab branch

333/945 Sayf-al-Dawlah ʿAlī I
356/967 Saʿd-al-Dawlah Sharīf I
381/991 Saʿīd-al-Dawlah Saʿīd
392/1002 ʿAlī II
394/1004 Sharīf II

Mazyadids

ca. 350/ca. 961	Sanā'-al-Dawlah 'Alī I b. Mazyad
408/1018	Nūr-al-Dawlah Dubays I

Marwānids

'Uqaylids

In Jazīrat ibn 'Umar, Niṣībīn, and Balad

ca. 380/ca. 990	Muḥammad
386/996	Janāḥ-al-Dawlah 'Alī
390/1000	Sinān al-Dawlah al-Ḥasan
393/1003	Nūr al-Dawlah Muṣ'ab

In Mawṣil

ca. 382/ca. 992	Muḥammad
386/996	Ḥusām al-Dawlah al-Muqallad
391/1001	Mu'tamid al-Dawlah Qirwāsh

V: The Arabian Peninsula

Qarāmiṭah

281/894	Abū Sa'īd al-Ḥasan al-Jannābī
300/913	Abū-l-Qāsim Sa'īd
311/923	Abū Ṭāhir Sulaymān
322/944	Abū Manṣūr Aḥmad
361–66/972–77	Abū Ya'qūb Yūsuf

Zaydī Imāms of the Yaman (Rassids)

?	Tarjumān al-Dīn al-Qāsim ar-Rassī, d. 246/860
246/860	al-Ḥusayn
280/893	Yaḥyā al-Hādī-ilā-l-Ḥaqq I
298/911	Muḥammad al-Murtaḍā
301/914	Aḥmad al-Nāṣir
?	Al-Ḥusayn al-Muntakhab
324/936	al-Qāsim al-Mukhtār
?	Yūsuf al-Manṣūr al-Dā'ī
?	al-Qāsim al-Manṣūr
393/1003	al-Ḥusayn al-Mahdī

VI: The Mashriq and the Caucasus

Bāwandids

45/665	Bāw
60/680	*interregnum of Walāsh*
68/688	Surkhāb I
98/717	Mihr Mardān
138/755	Surkhāb II
155/772	Sharwīn I
181/797	Shahriyār I
210/825	Shāpūr or Ja'far
222/837	Qārin I
253/867	Rustam I
282/895	Sharwīn II
318/930	Shahriyār II
?	Rustam II
355/966	Dārā
358/969	Shahriyār III
396/1006	Rustam III

Musāfirids (Sallārids, Kangarids)

before 304/916	Muḥammad b. Musāfir *(lord of Ṭārom in Daylam)*
330/941	Marzubān I b. Muḥammad *(in Ādharbāyjān and Arrān)*
330/941	Wahsūdān b. Muḥammad *(in Ṭārom)*
346/957	Justān I b. Marzubān *(in Ādharbāyjān)*
349/960	Ibrāhīm I b. Marzubān *(in Ādharbāyjān* until d. 373/983)
355/966	Marzubān II b. Ismā'īl b. Wahsūdān *(in Ṭārom until 374/984)*
387/997	Ibrāhīm II b. Marzubān II *(re-established at Ṭārom, still alive 420/1029)*

Rawwādids

?	Muḥammad b. Ḥusayn ar-Rawwādī
ca. 340/ca. 951	Ḥusayn I b. Muḥammad
?	Abū-l-Hayjā' Mamlān I or Muḥammad
391/1000	Abū Naṣr Ḥusayn II b. Mamlān
416/1025	Wahsūdān b. Mamlān

Shaddādids

ca. 340/ca. 951	Muḥammad b. Shaddād *(in Dvīn)*
360/971	'Alī Lashkarī I b. Muḥammad *(in Ganjah)*
368/978	Marzubān b. Muḥammad
375/985	Faḍl I b. Muḥammad
422/1031	Abū-l-Fatḥ Mūsā

Ziyārids

315/927	Mardāwīj b. Ziyār
323/935	Ẓahīr al-Dawlah Vushmagīr
356/967	Ẓahīr al-Dawlah Bīsutūn
367/978	Shams al-Ma'ālī Qābūs
402/1012	Falak al-Ma'ālī Manūchihr

Buwayhids (Būyids)

In Fārs and Khūzistān

322/934	'Imād al-Dawlah 'Alī
338/949	'Aḍud al-Dawlah Fanā-Khusraw
372/983	Sharaf al-Dawlah Shīrzīl

380/990 Ṣamṣām al-Dawlah Marzubān
388/998 Bahāʾ al-Dawlah Fīrūz
403/1012 Sulṭān al-Dawlah

In Kirmān

324/936 Muʿizz al-Dawlah Aḥmad
338/949 ʿAḍud al-Dawlah Fanā-Khusraw
372/983 Ṣamṣām al-Dawlah Marzubān
388/998 Bahāʾ al-Dawlah Fīrūz
403/1012 Qiwām al-Dawlah

In Jibāl

320/932 ʿImad al-Dawlah ʿAlī
335–66/947–77 Rukn al-Dawlah Ḥasan
(a) Branch in Hamadān and Iṣfahān
366/977 Muʾayyid al-Dawlah Būya
373/983 Fakhr al-Dawlah ʿAlī
387/997 Shams al-Dawlah
412–ca. 419/1021–ca. 1028 Samāʾ al-Dawlah (under Kākūyid suzerainty)
(b) Branch in Rayy
366/977 Fakhr al-Dawlah ʿAlī
387–420/997–1029 Majd al-Dawlah Rustam

In ʿIrāq

334/945 Muʿizz al-Dawlah Aḥmad
356/967 ʿIzz al-Dawlah Bakhtiyār
367/978 ʿAḍud al-Dawlah Fanā-Khusraw
372/983 Ṣamṣʿām al-Dawlah Marzubān
376/987 Sharaf al-Dawlah Shīrzīl
379/989 Bahāʾ al-Dawlah Fīrūz
403/1012 Sulṭān al-Dawlah

Ṭāhirids

205/821 Ṭāhir I b. al-Ḥusayn, called Dhū-l-Yamīnayn
207/822 Ṭalḥah
213/828 ʿAbd Allāh
230/845 Ṭāhir II
248–59/862–73 Muḥammad

Sāmānids

204/819 Aḥmad I b. Asad b. Sāmān *(governor of Farghānah)*
250/864 Naṣr I b. Aḥmad *(originally governor of Samarqand)*
279/892 Ismāʿīl I b. Aḥmad
295/907 Aḥmad II b. Ismāʿīl
301/914 al-Amīr al-Saʿīd Naṣr II
331/943 al-Amīr al-Ḥamīd Nūḥ I
343/954 al-Amīr al-Muʾayyad ʿAbd-al-Malik I
350/961 al-Amīr al-Sadīd Manṣūr I
365/976 al-Amīr al-Riḍā Nūḥ II
387/997 Manṣūr II
389/999 ʿAbd al-Malik II
390–95/1000–1005 Ismāʿīl II al-Muntaṣir

Ṣaffārids

253/867 Yaʿqūb b. Layth al-Ṣaffār
265/879 ʿAmr b. Layth
288/901 Ṭāhir b. Muḥammad b. ʿAmr
296/908 Layth b. ʿAlī
298/910 Muḥammad b. ʿAlī
298/911 first Sāmānid occupation, and usurpations of Kuthayyir b. Aḥmad and Aḥmad b. Qudām
299/912 ʿAmr b. Yaʿqūb b. Muḥammad b. ʿAmr
300/913 Second Sāmānid occupation
310/922 Aḥmad b. Muḥammad b. Khalaf b. Layth b. ʿAlī *(originally appointed governor for the Sāmānids)*
352/963 Walī al-Dawlah Khalaf b. Aḥmad
393/1003 Ghaznavid occupation

Khwārizm-*shāhs*
Afrīghids of Kāth

?–385/?–995 Abū ʿAbd Allāh Muḥammad

Maʾmūnids of Gurgānj

ca. 382/ca. 992 Abū ʿAlī Maʾmūn I
387/997 Abū-l-Ḥasan ʿAlī
399/1009 Abū-l-ʿAbbās Maʾmūn II

Qarakhanids

? ʿAlī b. Mūsā
388/998 Aḥmad I Arslan Qara Khan or Toghan Khan
406/1015 Mansūr Arslan Khan

Ghaznavids

366/977 Nāṣir al-Dawlah Sebüktigin *(governor on behalf of the Sāmānids)*
387/997 Ismāʿīl
388/998 Yamīn al-Dawlah Maḥmūd
421/1030 Jalāl al-Dawlah Muḥammad, *first reign*

Based principally on Eduard von Zambaur, *Manuel de Généalogie et de Chronologie pour l'Histoire de l'Islam* (Hanover, 1927) and, with especial benefit, Clifford Edmund Bosworth's abridged revision of that work, *The Islamic Dynasties: a Chronological and Genealogical Handbook* (Edinburgh, 1967).

Appendix B: Modern and Variant Place-Names

Modern Name	Variant Name(s)
Ahlat	Akhlāṭ, Khlatʿ
al-Ahvāz	Hurmuz-Shah, Sūq al-Ahwāz
ʿAkkā	Accho, Ptolemasis, St. Jean d'Acre, Acre
Aleppo	Beroia, Ḥalab
Alexandria	al-Iskandarīyah
Algiers	Jazā'ir Banī-Mazghannā
ʿAmmān	Rabbah / Rabath, Philadelphia
Āmū Daryā River	Oxus, Jayḥūn River
Annaba	Bône, Būnah
Anṭakiyah	Antioch, Antiochia
Anṭarṭūs	Antaradus
al-ʿAqabah	Elath, Ælana, Aylah, Waylah
Aral Sea	Oxianus Lacus, Buḥayrah Khwarizm
Aras River	Araxes River
Arashkūl	Portus Sigensis
Ardabīl	Bādhān Fayrūz
Argandhāb River	Khardarūy River
Arīḥā	Jericho
Arwād	Arados
ʿAsqalān	Ascalon
Aswan	Uswān
ʿAyn Shams	Heliopolis, Baʿlabakk
Azerbaijan	Ādharbāyjān
Azīlah	Zilis, Julia Constantia
Baghdād	al-Mudawwarah, Madīnat al-Salām
Baku	Bākūyah
Baljuan	Munk
al-Balqā'	Moab
Bāniyās	Paneas, Caesarea Philippi
Barda	Pērōzāpāt, Bardhāʿah
Bayt Dajan	Beth Dagon, Dājūn
Bayt Jibrīn	Baetogabra, Eleutheropolis, Bayt Jibrīl
Beirut	Bayrūt
Bethlehem	Bayt Lahm
Biskarah	Vescera
Bitlis	Badlīs
Bourdj Bouīra	Sūq Ḥamzah
Bulunyās	Balanea, Valania
Cadiz	Qādis, Gades
Cairo	al-Qāhirah
Caspian Sea	Baḥr al-Khazar
Ceuta	Abyla, Julia Trajecta, Septem Fratres, Sabtā
Cherchell	Caesarea, Qaysariyah
China	al-Ṣīn
Constantine	Cirta, Qusṭanṭīnah
Córdoba, Cordova	Qurṭubah
Cyrenaica	Barqah (province)
Damascus	Dimashq
Darande	Darandah
Derbend	Bāb al-Abwāb, Darband
Diyarbakir	Āmid
Egypt	Miṣr
Enna	Enna, Qaṣr Yānī, Castrogiovanni
Erciş	Arjīsh
Erzurum	Theodosiopolis, Karin, Qālīqalā
Euphrates River	al-Furāt River

Modern Name	Variant Name(s)
Fez	Fās
Fiḥl	Bikhil, Pella
Fīrūzābād	Jūr
Fīrūz-kūh	Gharj al-Shār, Gharjistān
Gabès	Qābis
Gafṣah	Capsa, Qafṣa
Gandava	Qandābīl
Gaza	Ghazzah
Georgia	Iveria, Gurjistān
Golan Heights	Jawlan Heights
Gulf of Sidra	Khalīj Surt
Hamadān	Ekbatana
Harput	Kharput
Hebron	Habrā, Khalīl
Ḥimṣ	Emesa
Islamic Spain	al-Andalus
Jaffa	Yāfah
Jandak, Biyābānak	Jarmak
Jānkānt-Qalʿah	Yāngi-känt, al-Qarīyat al-Jadīdah, Shahrkänt
al-Jazīrah	Upper Mesopotamia
Jerusalem	Aelia, Īliyā', Bayt al-Maqdis, al-Quds, al-Balaṭ
al-Jīzah	Giza
Jordan River	Urdunn River
Jordan River valley	al-Ghawr
Kairouan	al-Qayrawān
Khalīl Rūd	Dīv Rūd
Khayrābād	al-Fāryāb
Khirbat Saylūn, Shiloh	Saylūn
Khroy	Khuy, Khawī
Khūzistān	Sūsiana
Kirmān	Bardasīr
Kūhbanān	Cobinan
Kur River	Cyrus River
Kurgan-tepeh	Halāward
Kushkah River	Nahr al-Qaṣṣārīn
La Calle	Marsā al-Kharaz
Lake Manzālah	Buḥayrat Tinnīs
Lake Sevan	Gukchah Lake
Lāmis River	Lámos River
Laqant	Lucentum
Latakia	Laodikeia ad Mare, al-Lādhiqīyah
Maʿāb	Aeropolis, Ar-Moab
al-Madā'in	Ctesiphon, Taysafūn
Madīnat al-Sulṭān	Surt
Maʿīn	Minaea
Malatya	Malaṭiyah
Marāghah	Qariyat al-Marāghah, Afrāzah Rūdh
Marrakesh	Marrākush
Mecca	Makkah
Medina	Yathrib, al-Madīnah
Meknès	Miknāsat al-Zaytūn
Melilla	Malīlah
Merida	Emerita Augusta, Māridah
Mosul	al-Mawṣil
Muʿizzīyah	Ṭabarmīn
Mutawakkilīyah	Shamkūr
Nābulus	Flavia Neapolis
Naftah	Aggarsel Nepte
Nineveh	Ninawayh
Nīshāpūr	Nīv-Shāhpuhr, Abrashar
Oran	Wahrān
Pakistani province	al-Sind
Palermo	Balarm
Panjgūr	Fannazbūr
al-Qarīnayn	Barakdiz
Qinnasrīn	Chalkis
Ramleh	al-Ramlah
al-Raqqah	Callinicum
Rey	Rhagā, Rhages, Europus, Muḥammidīyah, al-Rayy, al-ʿAtīqah
al-Rukhkhaj	Arachosia
Sabzivār	Asfuzār
al-Ṣaʿid	Upper Egypt
Sakīnah	Shechīnā
Sayrām	Isbījāb
Seville	Hispalis, Ishbīliyah
Sfax	Asfāqus, Taparura
Shabwah	Sabbatha, Sabota
Shahristān	Shāpūr, Sābūr
Sicily	Isqiliyah
Sidon	Ṣaydā
Sifwah	al-Nahrawān
Silvan	Mayyāfāriqīn, Mīpherqēt, Muphargin
Sīr-Daryā River	Jaxartes, Ṣayhun River
Sulwān	Siloam
Sūr	Tyre
Surkhāb River	Wakhshāb River
al-Sūs	Hadrumetum, Justiniapolis, Sūsah
Syracuse	Siracusa, Saraqūsah
Syria (Greater Syria)	al-Shām
Tadmur	Palmyra, Tadmor
Tangiers	Tingis, Ṭanjah

Modern Name	Variant Name(s)
Tashkent	Chăch, Shāsh, Binkath
Tawzir	Thusuros
Tblisi	Tiflīs
Tiaret	Ṭāhart
Tiberias	Tabarīyah
Tigris River	Dijlah River
Timnaʿ	Tamnaʿ
Toledo	Ṭulayṭulah, Toletum
Trabzon	Ṭarābazandah, Trebizond
Transoxania	Transoxiana, Mā Warāʾ al-Nahr
Tripoli	Oea, Aṭrābulus
Ṭubnah	Thubunae
Tūnis	Tunes
Tunisia and western Libya	al-Ifrīqiyah
al-ʿUlah	Daydān, Liḥyān
Urfa	Edessa, al-Ruhā
Valencia	Valentia, Balansiya
Viranşehir	Viran Shahr
Volga River	Nahr al-Rūs
Yavneh	Jabneh, Jamnia, Yubnā
Yazīdīyah	al-Shammākhīyah
Zaragosa, Zaragoza	Salduba, Caesaraugusta, Saraqushtah
Zohreh River	Arrajan, Ṭāb River

Notes

Chapter One

1. The term *al-Jāhilīyah* denotes the period when Arabia lacked a dispensation, a revelation, and a prophet, and is consequently explicated by Muslims as "the Age of Ignorance." Although in one sense it subsumes the whole period from the creation of Adam to the coming of Muḥammad, its connotation is customarily restricted to the period of a little more than a century immediately prior to the revelation of Islam by the Prophet. Cf. Qur'ān 3 *(Āl ʿImrān):*154; 5 *(al-Mā'idah):*50; 33 *(al-Aḥzāb):*33; 48 *(al-Fatḥ):*26; also Ignaz Goldziher, *Muhammedanische Studien* (Halle, 1889–90), 219–28.

2. Vocalization unknown. For an early discussion of this question see J. Henninger, "Das Opfer in den altsüdarabischen Hochkulturen," *Anthropos* 37–40 (1942–45): 779–810. Cf. Akkadian *karābu* = "to sacrifice"; modern South Arabic *krb* = "to set fire to." *MKRB* is interpreted as "he who makes the sacrifice," and also as "a sanctuary": cf. Ethiopian *mekuerāb.* In translating *MKRB,* authors have customarily attempted to combine the role of priest and sovereign in a single office by employing such terms as *Priesterfürst, Opferfürst* (F. Hommel, "Ethnologie und Geographie des alten Orients," in *Handbuch der Klass. Altertumswiss.* [München, 1926], vol. 3, pt. 1, sec. 1, p. 77; Nikolaus Rhodokanakis, ibid., 111; Maria Höfner, "War der sabäische Mukarrib ein 'Priesterfürst'?" *Wiener Zeitschrift für die Kunde des Morgenlandes,* 54 [1957]: 77–85), *prêtre-prince, prince-sacrificateur* (Gonzague Ryckmans, *Les Religions Arabes Préislamiques,* 2d ed. [Louvain, 1951], 25). However, more recently A. F. L. Beeston has shown conclusively that *MKRB* was "a title used purely formally by the king [*malik:* sc. paramount chief] of a dominant *šaʿb* [a grouping of two or more village communities] in a commonwealth of *šaʿb* groups [a chiefdom]": "Kingship in ancient South Arabia," *Journal of the Economic and Social History of the Orient,* 15 (1972): 265.

3. *Maʿīn* ("springwater") was a later vocalization of an original Arabic form *Maʿān;* cp. biblical *Māʿōn, Meʿūn, Meʿīn. YTL* (usually resolved as Yathīl), despite its wall, may have been a purely religious center exercising authority rather than political power—and possibly in this respect analogous to, int. al., Nippur in Sumeria, Delphi in ancient Greece, or Ile-Ifẹ in the Yoruba territories. It has been identified with present-day Barāqish in southern al-Jawf: see Glen W. Bowersock, *Roman Arabia* (Cambridge, Mass., 1983), appendix 1.

4. The relatively meager information available for the state of affairs in southern Arabia in pre-Islamic times derives from epigraphy (both indigenous and from neighboring countries), archaeological investigation, and classical authors both Western and Muslim, the last of whom preserved a considerable corpus of oral verse and tradition. See Gonzague Ryckmans, "On some problems of South Arabian epigraphy and archaeology," *Bulletin of the School of Oriental and African Studies* 14 (1952): 1–10 and Jacques Ryckmans, *L'institution Monarchique en Arabie Méridionale avant l'Islam (Maʿīn et Saba)* (Louvain, 1951). For an overview of conditions in ancient southern Arabia see Adolf Grohmann, *Arabien* (München, 1963); Carl Ratjens, "Kulturelle Einflüsse in Südwest-Arabien von den ältesten Zeiten bis zum Islam, unter besonderer Berücksichtigung des Hellenismus," *Jahrbuch für Kleinasiatische Forschung,* 1: (1950–51), 1–42; and more generally G. Levi della Vida, "Pre-Islamic Arabia," in *The Arab Heritage,* ed. N. A. Farris (Princeton, N.J., 1944); M. Guidi, *Storia e Cultura Degli Arabi Fino alla Morte di Maometto* (Florence, 1951); Régis Blachère, *Le Problème de Mahomet* (Paris, 1952); M. Gaudefroy-Demombynes, *Mahomet* (Paris, 1957); Ahmed Fakhry, *An Archaeological Journey to Yemen,* 2 vols. (Cairo, 1952); Wendell Phillips, *Qatabān and Sheba* (New York, 1955); Theodor Nöldeke, *Geschichte der Perser und Araber zur Zeit der Sasaniden* (Leyden, 1879); Ditlef Nielsen, ed., *Die altarabische Kultur,* vol. 1 of *Handbuch der alterabischen Altertumskunde*

(Copenhagen, 1927); Julius Wellhausen, *Reste arabischen Heidentums,* 2d ed. (Berlin, 1897); Henri Lammens, *Le Climat—les Bedouins,* vol. 1 of *Le Berceau de l'Islam. L'Arabie Occidentale à la Vielle de l'Hégire* (Rome, 1914); and, especially valuable for its illustrations and bibliography, Brian Doe, *Monuments of South Arabia* (Naples and Cambridge, 1983).

In these paragraphs I have followed what is known as the "short" chronology, which is based on the view that the kingdoms of Sabā' and Maʿīn were contemporary (whereas the "long" chronology assumes that the kings of Maʿīn ruled before the institution of kingship in Sabā' and dates the earliest Minaean inscriptions to the twelfth century B.C.): see F. Hommel, *Südarabische Chrestomathie* (München, 1893), 91–112; D. H. Müller, "Die Burgen und Schlösser Südarabiens nach dem Iklîl des Hamdânî," *Sitzungsberichte der Akademie der Wissenschaften in Wien,* Phil.-Hist. Kl., Bd. 94 (1879): 335–423, Bd. 97 (1881): 955–1050; J. H. Mordtmann, "Zur südarabischen Altertumskunde," *Zeitschrift der Deutschen Morgenländischen Gesellschaft* 46 (1892): 320–23, 47 (1893): 397–417; M. Hartmann, *Der Islamische Orient,* bd. 2: *Die Arabische Frage, mit einem Versuche der Archäologie Jemens* (Leipzig, 1909), 126–32; K. Mlaker, "Chronologisches," in *Zur südarabische Epigraphik und Archäologie II. Wiener Zeitschrift für die Kunde des Morgenlandes* by M. Höfner, K. Mlaker and Nikolaus Rhodokanakis 41 (Wien, 1934): 67–106; Rhodokanakis, "Die Bodenwirtschaft im alten Südarabien," *Anzeiger der Kaiserlichen Akademie der Wissenschaften in Wien,* Philologische-Historische Klasse 53 (1916): 173–204; F. V. Winnett, "The place of the Minaeans in the history of Pre-Islamic Arabia," *Bulletin of the American Schools of Oriental Research* 73 (1939): 3–9; W. F. Albright, "The chronology of ancient south Arabia in the light of the first campaign of excavation in Qataban," *Bulletin of the American Schools of Oriental Research* 119 (1950): 5–15, and "The chronology of the Minaean kings of Arabia," loc. cit., 129 (1953): 20–24; Jacqueline Pirenne, *Le royaume Sud-Arabe de Qatabān et sa Datation* (Louvain, 1961); Jacques Ryckmans, *L'Institution Monarchique,* chap. 4; G. Ryckmans, "On some problems of South Arabian epigraphy," passim; J. Ryckmans, "La Chronologie des Rois de Saba' et d̲ū-Raydān," *Nederlands Historisch-Archaeologisch Instituut in het Nabije Oosten,* vol. 16 (Istanbul, 1964); Albert Jamme, "On a drastic current reduction of South Arabian chronology," *Bulletin of the American Society for Oriental Research* 145 (1957): 28 et seq.; A. F. L. Beeston, *Epigraphic South Arabian Calendars and Datings* (London, 1956); A. G. Lundin, "Eponymat sabéen et chronologie sabéenne," in *XXVI Congrès International des Orientalistes, Conf. Pres. par la Delegation de l'USSR* (Moscow, 1963); and A. G. Loundine (Lundin) and Jacques Ryckmans, "Nouvelles données sur la chronologie des rois de Saba et D̲ū-Raydān," *Le Muséon* 77 (1964): 407–27.

For a brief discussion of early South Arabian towns from a different point of view from that adopted here, see A. F. L. Beeston, "Functional Significance of the Old South Arabian 'Town,'" in *Proceedings of the Seminar for Arabian Studies* 1 (1971): 26–31.

5. Hermann von Wissmann, "Ḥimyar, ancient history," *Le Muséon* 77 (1964): 429–99.

6. Raydān is explicated by Arab historians as the name of the royal stronghold in Ẓafār, and Jacques Ryckmans has deduced that the term *Dhū-Raydān* in the royal style was an ethnikon denoting the peoples ruled from that stronghold (*L'Institution Monarchique,* 158–62). See also Christian Robin, "Aux origines de l'état ḥimjarite *[sic]*: Ḥimyar et Dhû-Raydân," in *Arabian Studies in Honor of Mahmoud Ghul,* ed. Moawiyah M. Ibrahīm (Wiesbaden, 1989), 104–12.

7. The territory of Yamanāt may at this time have comprised more or less the whole of the South Arabian coastal district.

8. *mlk / sb' / wdhrydn / wḥḍrmwt / wymnt / w'ʿrbhmw / ṭwdm / wthmt.* These attributions occur in two inscriptions, one of Abkarib 'Asʿad and one of Maʿad-karib Yaʿfur. For the difficult reading of *Ḥa[ḍramaw]t* in the second of these inscriptions see G. Ryckmans, "On some problems of South Arabian epigraphy," 6 n. 1; he has also published both texts in *Le Muséon* 54 (1951): 97–106. See also Sidney Smith, "Events in Arabia in the 6th century A.D.," *Bulletin of the School of Oriental and African Studies* 16 (1954): 435.

9. See A. G. Lundin, "Južnaja Aravija v VI. veke," *Palestinskij Sbornik* 8 (1961): 17 et seq. For what it is worth, Ḥamzah al-Iṣfahānī (d. 961) referred to the last *tubbaʿ* as "Lord of Makkah and al-Madīnah *(Ṣāhib Makkata w l-Madīnah)*": *Ta'rīkh Sinī Mulūk al-Arḍ wa-l-Anbiyā',* ed. I. M. E. Gottwaldt (Lipsiae [Leipzig], 1844), 131. Also translated into Latin by Gottwaldt (Lipsiae, 1848).

10. This is a rendering into Weberian terms of conclusions reached by, int. al., Hermann von Wissmann, *Zur Archäologie und antiken Geographie von Südarabien. Ḥaḍramaut, Qatabān und das ʿAden-Gebiet in der Antike.* Nederlands Historisch-Archaeologisch Instituut te Istanbul, publication no. 24 (Istanbul, 1968), 79 and explicatory notes; Maria Höfner, "Die Kultur des vorislamischen Südarabien," *Zeitschrift der Deutschen Morgenländischen Gesellschaft* 99 (1945–49): 15–28; Fred McGraw Donner, *The Early Islamic Conquests* (Princeton, N.J., 1981), 37–42; and Hermann von Wissmann and Maria Höfner, *Beiträge zur historischen Geographie des Vorislamischen Südarabiens* (Mainz, 1953). There is a great deal of relevant, though often severely dated, information in Jawād ʿAlī, *Ta'rīkh al-ʿArab qabl al-Islam,* 4 vols. (Baghdād, 1951–56). See also A. G. Lundin, "Le régime citadin de l'Arabie du Sud aux IIe–IIIe siècles de notre ère," in *Proceedings of the Sixth Seminar for Arabian Studies* (London, 1973), 26–28 (first published in Russian in *Pis'mennye Pamjatniki i Problemy Istorii Kul'tury Narodov Azii* 5 [1969]: 55–57) and N. Pigulevskaja, "Les rapports sociaux à Nedjrān au début du VIe siècle de l'ère chrétienne," *Journal of the Economic and Social History of the Orient* 4 (1961): 1–14.

11. The Līsharḥ ibn Yaḥṣub of Yāqūt (1179–1229), *Kitāb Muʿjam al-Buldān,* ed. Ferdinand Wüstenfeld (Leipzig, 1866–73), 3: 811; all subsequent references are to the Wüstenfeld edition unless otherwise indicated. The ruins of Ghumdān as they existed in the tenth century A.D. were described in considerable detail by the Yamanī topographer al-Ḥasan ibn Aḥmad al-Hamdānī (d. 945): *Al-Iklīl min Akhbār al-Yaman,* 8, ed. Nabih Amin Faris (Princeton, N.J., 1940); translation by Faris under the title *The Antiquities of South Arabia* (Princeton, N.J., 1938; reprint, Westport, Conn., 1981), 8–19; see also note 120 to chapter 3 below. Cf. also Müller,

"Die Burgen und Schlösser Südarabiens," which incorporates selections from *al-Iklīl,* together with German translations.

12. In Aksūmite epigraphy of the fourth century A.D. the Abyssinian ruler claimed to be "King of Aksūm, Ḥimyar, Raydān, Ḥabashah, Salḥ, and Tihāmah." See Nielsen, *Die Altarabische Kultur,* 104. Cf. also N. V. Pigulevskaja, "Efiopiya i Khimyar v ikh Vzaimootnojeniyakh s Vostotchnorimskoy Imperiei," *Vestnik Drevnei Istorii* (Moscow, 1948), 1:87–97.

13. Procopius, *History of the Wars,* ed. and trans. H. B. Dewing, bk. 1, chap. 20 (London, 1904), pars. 9–12.

14. *Al-Qalīs* (also *al-Qulays, al-Qullays*) < Gk. *ekklēsia* = "church" (despite the efforts of traditional Arab commentators to derive the word from an Arabic root).

15. Al-Hamdānī, *Al-Iklīl* (Faris translation), 35; al-Masʿūdī (d. 956), *Murūj al-Dhahab wa-Maʿādin al-Jawhar,* ed. and trans. C. Barbier de Meynard and Pavet de Courteille under the title *Les Prairies d'Or et les Mines de Pierres Précieuses* (Paris, 1864), 3:366. (All subsequent references are to the de Meynard-de Courteille edition and translation unless otherwise indicated. For other editions of this work, consult note 125 to chapter 3); al-Iṣfahānī, *al-Arḍ wa-l-Anbiyā',* 126; and Yāqūt, *Muʿjam,* 4:383.

16. Albert Jamme, *Sabaean inscriptions from Maḥram Bilqīs (Marib),* Publications of the American Foundation for the Study of Man, vol. 3 (Baltimore, 1962). There are descriptions of the ruins of Ma'rib in Nazīh M. al-ʿAẓm, *Riḥlah fī Bilād al-ʿArab al-Saʿīdah,* pt. 2 (al-Qāhirah, n.d.), 50 et seq. and Doe, *Monuments of South Arabia,* 189–204. On irrigation in ancient South Arabia see Richard LeBaron Bowen Jr., "Irrigation in Ancient Qatabân (Beihan)," in *Archaeological Discoveries in South Arabia,* by Bowen and Frank D. Albright (Baltimore, 1958), 43–131 and Gertrude Caton-Thompson and Elinor Wight Gardner, "Climate, irrigation, and early man in the Hadramawt," *The Geographical Journal* 93 (1939): 18–38.

17. In ancient times the terms *Arabia Eudaemon* and *Arabia Felix* denoted the entire peninsula south of al-Nufūd; only in the medieval period did they come to connote specifically the Yaman. It is probable that *felix* was originally a translation of the Arabic *yumn* = "happiness," itself confused with *yaman* = "on the right hand" (southwest Arabia being so called because it was situated on the right hand, that is, to the south, of al-Ḥijāz).

18. Strabo, *Geographica,* bk. 16, ch. 4, par. 4.

19. Cf. Qur'ān 34 (Sabā'):18–19. It is alleged that Daydān, subsequently the capital of Liḥyān, originated as a Minaean colony at the northern end of this trade route.

20. For an extended discussion of the trade in aromatics during these centuries of South Arabian decline, see J. Innes Miller, *The Spice Trade of the Roman Empire, 29 B.C. to A.D. 641* (Oxford, 1969).

21. Compendious accounts of the Nabataean kingdom, with pertinent bibliographies, can be found in Philip Hammond, *The Nabataeans: Their History, Culture and Archaeology,* Studies in Mediterranean Archaeology, no. 37 (Gothenburg, 1973) and Karl Schmitt-Korte, *Die Nabatäer: Spuren einer arabischen Kultur der Antike* (Hannover, 1976), but the most up-to-date and authoritative interpretation of events in that polity is woven into the text of Bowersock, *Roman Arabia,* which is also furnished with a comprehensive bibliography. See also J. Cantineau, *Le Nabatéen,* vol. 1 (Paris, 1930) and vol. 2 (Paris, 1932), which still affords the most comprehensive treatment of the Nabataean language and script; and on relevant epigraphic materials F. V. Winnett and W. L. Reed, *Ancient Records from North Arabia* (Toronto, 1970). The origin of the Nabataean tribe is summarized compendiously by Ernst Axel Knauf, "Nabatean Origins," in Ibrahīm (ed.), *Arabian Studies in Honour of Mahmoud Ghul,* 56–61.

22. The name *Petra* is itself presumably evidence of Hellenistic influence, being a Greek translation of the Hebrew *Selaʿ* ("rock") mentioned in Isa. 16:1 and 42:11, and in 2 Kings 14:7. Summaries of available information relating to this city are to be found in M. Lindner, *Petra und das Königreich der Nabatäer,* 3d ed. (München, 1968) and Iain Browning, *Petra* (London, 1973), and there is a great deal of relevant material, shrewdly evaluated, in Bowersock, *Roman Arabia,* passim.

Apart from archaeological finds and epigraphy (for which see G. A. Cooke, *A Text-Book of North-Semitic Inscriptions* [Oxford, 1903]), the chief sources for the history of the Nabataean kingdom are Diodorus Siculus (first century B.C.), *Bibliotheca Historica,* bk. 19, and Josephus (died ca. A.D. 95), *The History of the Jewish War,* bk. 1 and *The Jewish Antiquities,* bk. 14.

23. *Dūshara* < *Dhū-Sharā'* (or *Sharāh*) = "Lord of the Sharā'," that is, the high country overlooking the Wādī al-ʿArabah in southern Jordan; rendered in Greek as *Dousares.* Cf. Dominique Sourdel, *Les Cultes du Hauran à l'Époque Romaine* (Paris, 1952), 59–68.

24. Ar. al-Ḥārith; Gk. Aretas.

25. Cf. A. Alt, "Das Territorium von Bostra," *Zeitschrift des Deutschen Palästina-Vereins* 68 (1951): 235–45. Also Sulaiman A. Mougdad, *Bosra: Historical and Archaeological Guide,* trans. by Henry Innes MacAdam (Damascus, 1978); A. Spijkerman, *The Coins of the Decapolis and Provincia Arabia,* Studii Biblici Franciscani Collectio Maior no. 25 (Jerusalem, 1978), 68–77 for epithets applied to Bostra; and especially Maurice Sartre, *Bostra, des Origines à l'Islam* (Paris, 1985) and Henry Innes MacAdam, "Bostra Gloriosa," *Berytus* 34 (1986): 169–92.

26. Ar. *Tadmur.* As "Tadmar of Amurru" it figured in an inscription of Tiglath-Pileser I (1115–1077 B.C.): see D. D. Luckenbill, *Ancient Records of Assyria and Babylonia,* vol. 1 (Chicago, 1927), pars. 287 and 308. There is a plan of the city as it was in Roman times in Alfons Gabriel, "Recherches archéologiques à Palmyre," *Syrie,* vol. 7 (1926), plate 12. See also D. Schlumberger, *La Palmyrène du Nord-Ouest* (Paris, 1951); J. G. Février, *Essai sur l'Histoire Politique et Économique de Palmyre* (Paris, 1931); Iain Browning, *Palmyra* (Park Ridge, N.J., 1979); and Bowersock, *Roman Arabia,* chap. 9.

27. Lat. Odenathus; Ar. Udhaynah.

28. Palmyrene *bt zby;* Ar. al-Zabbā', Zaynab.

29. Probably a Greek rendering of Wahb-Allāth (Ar. Wahballāt) = "Gift of al-Lāt" < al-Ilāhah = "The Goddess," one of the three daughters of Allāh.

30. See Abū al-Fidā' (1273–1332), *Mukhtaṣar Ta'rīkh al-Bashar* (Istanbul, 1869), 1:76–77; al-Iṣfahānī, *al-Arḍ Wa-l-Anbiyā'*, 115–22; al-Masʿūdī (d. 956), *Murūj* 3:217–21; and Ibn Qutaybah (d. 889), *Kitāb al-Maʿārif*, ed. Ferdinand Wüstenfeld (Göttingen, 1850), 314–16. According to another work of al-Masʿūdī, *Kitāb al-Tanbīh wa-l-Ishrāf* (ed. M. J. de Goeje [Leyden, 1893], 202), the Ghassānids chose the year of the breaking of the Ma'rib dam to inaugurate their dynastic era. It is still worthwhile consulting Theodor Nöldeke, *Die Ghassânischen Fürsten aus dem Hause Gafna's. Abhandlungen der Königlichen Akademie der Wissenschaften zu Berlin* (Berlin, 1887; Arabic translation by Pendali Jousé and Costi Zurayk under the title *Umarāʿ Banī Ghassān* [Bayrūt, 1933]) on general matters relating to the Ghassānid confederation, but see also Irfan Kawar (Irfan Shahīd), "The Arabs in the peace treaty of A.D. 561," *Arabica* 3 (1957): 181–213, and "Ghassān and Byzantium: a new terminus *a quo*," *Der Islam* 33 (1958): 145–58; Ismāʿīl R. Khālidi, "The Arab kingdom of Ghassān: its origins, rise, and fall," *Moslem World* 46 (1956): 193–206; P. Goubert, "Le problème Ghassanid à la veille d'Islam," in *Congrès des Etudes Byzantines* 1 (1950): 103–18; and Donner, *The Early Islamic Conquests*, 43–45.

31. Irfan Kawar, "The last days of Salīḥ," *Arabica* 5 (1958): 145–58.

32. Gk. Aretas. By Arab chroniclers al-Ḥārith was given the *laqab* (nickname) of al-Aʿraj = "The Lame." For Greek accounts of his reign see Procopius, *History of the Wars*, bk. 1, chap. 17, par. 47–48 and Joannes Malalas, *Chronographia*, ed. L. Dindorf (Bonn, 1831), 435 and 461ff. Cf. Irfan Kawar, "Arethas, son of Jabalah," *Journal of the American Oriental Society* 75 (1955): 205–16 and "Procopius on the Ghassānids," loc. cit., 77 (1957): 79–87.

33. This was the next-highest rank to that of the emperor, and in Arabic was rendered as *malik* = "king." On this and related topics see Rudi Paret, "Note sur un passage de Malalas concernant les phylarques arabes," *Arabica* 5 (1958): 251–62.

34. Cf. Leone Caetani, *Annali dell'Islam* (Milano, 1910), 3:928. For a fervid but apocryphal description of the Ghassān court, at one time ascribed to the Madīnese poet Ḥassān ibn Thābit, see Abū al-Faraj al-Iṣfahānī, *Kitāb al-Aghānī* (Būlāq, A.H. 1285/A.D. 1868; reprint, Bayrūt, A.H. 1421/A.D. 1970), 16:15. Although the *Aghānī* is a prime source for Arab material culture from the *Jāhilīyah* through the ninth century and will be cited as such from time to time in the following pages, it has to be admitted that its reliability *for this purpose* is not infrequently in question—a caveat raised forcefully by Régis Blachère, *Histoire de la Littérature Arabe des Origines à la Fin du XVe siècle de J.C.* (Paris, 1952), 1:133–38.

35. Abū Jaʿfar Muḥammad ibn Jarīr al-Ṭabarī (838–923) (*Ta'rīkh al-Rusul wa-l-Mulūk*, ed. M. J. de Goeje et al. [Leiden, 1879–1901] 2:612; all subsequent references are to the de Goeje edition unless otherwise indicated) categorizes the Tanūkh as *ʿArab al-Ḍāḥīyah*, signifying dwellers in the borderlands. More recently Glen Bowersock (*Roman Arabia*, 132) has characterized the confederacy as "the consolidated enemies of Palmyra." For a recent evaluation of the epigraphic evidence relating to the Tanūkh see this same work, 132–35.

36. Alamundarus in Byzantine chronicles. To the Arabs, al-Mundhir III was known as Ibn Mā' al-Samā' = "Son of the Water of Heaven," a sobriquet of his mother Mārīyah or Māwīyah.

37. Meir J. Kister, "Mecca and Tamim (aspects of their relations)," *Journal of the Economic and Social History of the Orient* 8 (1965): 115. See also note 280 to chapter 17.

38. Ibn Rustah, *Kitāb al-Aʿlāq al-Nafīsah*, in *Bibliotheca Geographorum Arabicorum*, ed. M. J. de Goeje (Lugduni Batavorum, 1892), 7:192, 217; all subsequent references are to the de Goeje edition unless otherwise indicated. Cf. also Ibn Qutaybah, *al-Maʿārif*, 273–74. Louis Massignon characterized al-Ḥīrah as "un 'port du désert', une *caravan-city*, lieu d'échanges intermittents entre officiers iranisés et grands bédouins chameliers, lieu de symbiose aussi entre citadins (ou ruraux) araméens fortement christianisés et humbles tribus arabes moutonnières, bergers refoulés et domestiqués": "Explication du plan de Kûfa (Irak)," in *Mélanges Maspéro* (Le Caire, 1935–40), 3:338.

The most comprehensive account of the Lakhmid confederacy is still that compiled at the end of the nineteenth century by Gustav Rothstein, *Die Dynastie der Laḥmiden in al-Ḥîra. Ein Versuch zur arabisch-persischen Geschichte zur Zeit der Sasaniden* (Berlin, 1899). It has been considerably updated by Meir J. Kister, "Al-Ḥīra: some notes on its relations with Arabia," *Arabica* 15 (1968): 143–69, and summarized by Donner, *The Early Islamic Conquests*, 45–47. See also Bowersock, *Roman Arabia*, chap. 9, especially pp. 132 et seq. The main references to the Lakhmids in al-Ṭabarī's *Ta'rīkh* are vol. 1, pp. 821ff., 858, 2016ff., and 2038ff.; vol. 3, pp. 645–46.

39. The ethnikon *Thamūd* was rendered as *Tamudaei* by Pliny (*Historia Naturalis*, bk. 6, chap. 32). For cuneiform references see Luckenbill, *Ancient Records*, vol. 2, pars. 17, 18. Thamūdic inscriptions, apparently ranging in date from the fifth century B.C. to the fourth century A.D., are discussed in F. V. Winnett, *A Study of the Lihyanite and Thamudic Inscriptions* (Toronto, 1937). On Thamūd generally see E. Littmann, *Thamūd und Ṣafā* (Leipzig, 1940); Albertus van den Branden, *Histoire de Thamoud*, Publications de l'Université Libanaise, Section des Etudes Historiques, no. 6 (Beyrouth, 1960); and Joëlle Beaucamp, "Rawwafa et les Thamoudéens," *Supplément au Dictionnaire de la Bible*, no. 9 (1979), 1467–75. For interesting comments on the contribution of the Thamūd to "The bedouinization of Arabia," see Werner Caskel's paper with that title in *Studies in Islamic Cultural History*, ed. G. E. von Grünebaum; memoir no. 76 of The American Anthropological Association (Menasha, Wis., 1954), 36–46.

40. René Dussaud, *Les Arabes en Syrie avant l'Islam* (Paris, 1907), 57–73.

41. The Lechieni of Pliny, bk. 6, chap. 32. For comprehensive discussions of Liḥyān see Werner Caskel, *Das altarabische Königreich Lihjan* (Krefeld, 1950) and *Liyhan und Lihyanisch* (Köln and Opladen, 1954).

42. The Dedan of Isa. 21:13, Jer. 25:23, and Ezek. 25:13. The ruins at al-ʿUlah are described in Eduard Glaser, *Skizze der Geschichte und Geographie Arabiens* (Berlin, 1890), 2:98–127 and

A. Jaussen and R. Savignac, *Mission Archéologique en Arabie* (Paris, 1909), 250–91.

43. Al-Iṣfahānī, *al-Arḍ wa-l-Anbiyā'*, 140; Ibn Qutaybah, *al-Maʿārif*, 308; and Gunnar Olinder, *The Kings of Kinda of the Family of Ākil al-Murār,* Lunds Universitets Årsskrift, Ny Fôljd, Fôrsta Avdelningen, vol. 23, no. 6 (Lund, 1927), 38–39. For the results of recent excavations at Qaryat al-Faw, the site of one capital of the Kindah confederacy, strategically situated where the Wādī Dawāsir breaks through the Tuwayq range, see A. R. al-Ansary, *Qaryat al-Fau: a Portrait of Pre-Islamic Civilisation in Saudi Arabia* (Riyādh, 1982).

44. The rivalry between the Kindah and the Lakhmids is recorded in the verse, bitter as gall, of Imru' al-Qays (died ca. 540), a descendant of the Kindah ruling family and author of one of the most venerated odes in the *Muʿallaqāt.* An earlier, and seemingly more transitory, confederacy whose memory has been preserved in tradition was that of Tanūkh, which came into being when a number of tribes pasturing in Baḥrayn formed a network of offensive and defensive alliances (*ʿAlā-l-tawāzur wa-l-tanāṣur:* al-Ṭabarī, *Ta'rīkh,* 1:746; cf. also Nöldeke, *Geschichte der Perser und Araber,* 23 n. 2; Aloys Sprenger, *Die alte Geographie Arabiens als Grundlage der Entwicklungsgeschichte des Semitismus* [n.p., 1875]; E. Tyon, *The Encyclopaedia of Islam,* 2d ed., s.v. "*ḥilf*"). Of the semilegendary Farasān confederacy mentioned by Ibn Durayd, hardly anything is known other than its name (*Kitāb al-Ishtiqāq,* ed. Ferdinand Wüstenfeld [Göttingen, 1854], 8).

45. *Ḥaḍarī* (also *ḥadharī*) are sometimes referred to as *ahl ṭīn* (= "dwellers in mud [houses]").

46. Ferdinand Wüstenfeld, "Die Wohnsitze und Wanderungen der arabischen Stämme . . . " (being a partial translation of Abū ʿUbayd ʿAbd Allāh al-Bakrī, *Muʿjam Mā Istaʿjama al-Bakrī*), in *Abhandlungen der Gesellschaft der Wissenschaften zu Göttingen* (1868–69), 14:93–172.

47. On the *badū* way of life in general see, int. al., Max A. S. von Oppenheim, *Die Beduinen,* vols. 1 and 2 (Leipzig, 1939 and 1943; vols. 3 and 4 ed. Werner Caskel [Wiesbaden, 1952 and 1968]); Werner Caskel, *Die Bedeutung der Beduinen in der Geschichte der Araber* (Köln and Opladen, 1953); ʿAbd al-Jalīl al-Ṭāhir, *Al-Badū w-al-ʿAshā'ir fi-l-Bilād al-ʿArabīyah* (al-Qāhirah, 1954); Makkī al-Jamīl, *Al-Badāwah wa-l-Badū fi-l-Bilād al-ʿArabīyah* (al-Qāhirah, 1962); and Jibrail S. Jabbur, *The Bedouins and the Desert. Aspects of Nomadic Life in the Arab East* (Albany, N.Y., 1995). On nomadism more generally see Robert Montagne, *La Civilisation du Désert. Nomades d'Orient et d'Afrique* (Paris, 1947); Douglas L. Johnson, *The Nature of Nomadism: a Comparative Study of Pastoral Migrations in Southwestern Asia and Northern Africa,* University of Chicago, Department of Geography Research Paper no. 118 (Chicago, 1969), chaps. 1 and 2; Cynthia Nelson, ed., *The Desert and the Sown: Nomads in the Wider Society,* University of California, Institute of International Studies Research Series no. 21 (Berkeley, 1973); Brian Spooner, *The Cultural Ecology of Pastoral Nomads* (Reading, Mass., 1975); and Elizabeth E. Bacon, "Types of pastoral nomadism in Central and Southwest Asia," *Southwestern Journal of Anthropology* 10 (1954): 44–68. Specifically Arabian examples are discussed in P. G. N. Peppelenbosch, "Nomadism on the Arabian Peninsula—a general appraisal," *Tijdschrift voor Economische en Sociale Geografie,* 59 (1968): 335–46; H. S. Helaisi, "Bedouins and tribal life in Saudi Arabia," *International Social Science Journal* 11, no. 4 (1959): 532–38; Saad E. Ibrahim and Donald P. Cole, "Saudi Arabian Bedouin," in *Cairo Papers in Social Science,* vol. 1 (Cairo, 1978); Donald P. Cole, *Nomads of the Nomads. The Āl Murrah Bedouin of the Empty Quarter* (Chicago, 1975); Alois Musil, *The Manners and Customs of the Rwala Bedouin* (New York, 1928) and *The Northern Ḥeǧâz* (New York, 1926); Carl Raswan, *Black Tents of Arabia* (New York, 1935; reprint, New York, 1971) and "Tribal areas and migration lines of the North-Arabian bedouins," *Geographical Review* 20 (1930): 494–502; Wilfred Thesiger, "The badu of southern Arabia," *Journal of the Royal Central Asian Society* 37 (1950): 53–61; Louise E. Sweet, "Camel Pastoralism in North Arabia and the Minimal Camping Unit," in *Man, Culture, and Animals. The Role of Animals in Human Ecological Adjustment,* ed. Anthony Leeds and Andrew P. Vayda (Washington, 1965), 129–52; and Joseph Chelhod, *Le Droit dans la Société Bédouine* (Paris, 1971). The cycle of nomadic migration is evoked with a rare immanence in a Nabaṭī-style poem by ʿAbd Allāh al-Ḥmūd ibn Sbayyil, who knew the life at first hand. The poem is included in the *Dīwān* of Ibn Sbayyil as published by Kh. M. al-Faraj: *Dīwān al-Nabaʿt,* 2 vols. (Dimashq, A.H. 1371); trans. Saad Abdullah Sowayan under the title *Nabaṭi Poetry* (Berkeley and Los Angeles, 1985), 26–27.

Reconstructions of tribal organization during the *Jāhilīyah* and early Islamic times are to be found in Werner Caskel, "Der arabische Stamm vor dem Islam und seine gesellschaftliche und juristische Organisation," in *Atti del Convegno Internazionale sul Tema: Dalla Tribu allo Stato (Roma, 13–16 aprile 1961)* (Roma, 1962), 139–49; ʿUmar Riḍā Kaḥḥālah, *Muʿjam Qabā'il al-ʿArab,* 3 vols. (Bayrūt, 1968); C. A. Nallino, "Sulla costituzione delle tribù arabe prima dell-islamismo," in *Raccolta di Scritti Editi e Inediti* no. 3, *Istituto per l'Oriente* (Roma, 1941), 64–86 (reprint of a paper written in 1893); Lammens, *Le Climat—les Bédouins;* Georg Jacob, *Altarabisches Beduinenleben* (Berlin, 1897; reprint, Hildesheim, 1967); Maria Höfner, "Die Beduinen in den vorislamischen arabischen Inschriften," in *L'Antica Società Beduina,* ed. Francesco Gabrieli (Roma, 1959); W. Montgomery Watt, *Muhammad at Medina* (Oxford, 1956), chap. 4; Erich Bräunlich, *Bisṭām ibn Qais. Ein vorislamischer Beduinenfürst und Held* (Leipzig, 1923); and Robert F. Spencer, "The Arabian matriarchate: an old controversy," *Southwestern Journal of Anthropology* (1952): 478–502. Superseded expositions of Arabian kinship systems which nevertheless repay the reading are William Robertson Smith, *Kinship and Marriage in Early Arabia* (London, 1903; reprint, Boston, n.d.) and Otto Procksch, *Über die Blutrache bei den vorislamischen Arabern und Mohammeds Stellung zu Ihr* (Leipzig, 1899), while Eldon Rutter has some sound things to say in "The habitability of the Arabian desert," *The Geographical Journal* 76 (1930): 512–15.

48. Musil, *Manners and Customs of the Rwala Bedouin,* 48. *Ahl* also has two alternative connotations: a group of distinct tribes

united in pursuit of a common purpose, as in the phrases *ahl al-jabal* sometimes applied to hill tribes, or *ahl al-dīrah* denoting sedentary Arabs; and a social group united by shared values, aims, and sentiments, as in the phrase *ahl al-dīn,* "god-fearing men."

We are evidently dealing here with lineages of the type commonly, but somewhat inaccurately, designated by anthropologists as "conical clans"; see Paul Kirchhoff, "The principles of clanship in human society," *Davidson Journal of Anthropology* 1 (1955): 1–10; cf. also Marshall D. Sahlins's comments in *Tribesmen* (Englewood Cliffs, N.J., 1968), 52 n. 5. Such lineages form the framework within which Arabian tribal society is customarily analyzed by academic intruders from the Western world. However, William Lancaster, one of the few anthropologists to have actually participated in the harsh life of the *badū* (in his case the Ruwalah tribe of the ʿAnāzah confederacy), reports that at the present time these tribesmen perceive genealogical linkages in spatial rather than temporal terms. He writes, "When a man says 'I am A son of B son of C of the Zuwaiyid Nseir of the Murath tribal section of the Rwala Aneze', he is not thinking in terms of time, of dead individuals, but in terms of spatial, ever-expanding inclusive groups of living people. . . . Thus, despite the fact that a man or a woman is identified genealogically . . . and despite the fact that inter-group relationships are conceived in genealogical terms, the genealogy is so fluid as to be relatively unimportant. It is simply the accepted way of explaining pragmatically determined groups, a structural framework to account for present reality" (Lancaster, *The Rwala Bedouin Today* [Cambridge, 1981], 152–54).

Furthermore, Lancaster discerns a conceptual break in the perceived structure of the tribal genealogy immediately below the level of the tribal section. Upward from this point genealogical terminology is figurative only. The persons and cascading father-son successions that constitute the patrilineal genealogy are not regarded as realities but simply as connoting generalized relationships within an inclusive group. Manipulation of these higher-level relationships is always a weighty political act. Below the level of the tribal section, the suppression of genealogical links with more inclusive, higher-level entities deprives named groups of anything more than figurative associations with tribal sections. They become simply small groups ("minimal sections," in Lancaster's terminology) making up a larger group. In the absence of genealogical links with higher levels of the tribal hierarchy, there is no basis for claims of supremacy over other groups. In other words, there is an uncharacteristic jural equality of groups below the level of the tribal section, which means that genealogies can easily be adjusted to fit political or economic reality without threatening the structure of the whole Ruwalah system of social relations (Lancaster, *The Rwala,* chap. 1).

On the political content of Arabian genealogies more generally see Erich Bräunlich, "Beiträge zur Gesellschaftsordnung der arabischen Beduinenstämme," *Islamica* 6 (1934): 68–111, 182–229.

49. See, for example, Walter M. Patton, "Blood revenge in Arabia and Israel," *American Journal of Theology* 5 (1901): 703–31; Michael J. L. Hardy, *Blood Feuds and the Payment of Blood Money in the Middle East* (Leiden, 1963); and for informative case studies Joseph Ginat, *Blood Disputes among Bedouin Rural Arabs in Israel: Revenge, Meditation, Outcasting, and Family Honor* (Pittsburgh, 1987).

50. Both inscriptions and texts attest the use of the term *kabīr* to denote a tribal chief in ancient times. For instance, Abū Sufyān, on whom the *ashrāf* of Quraysh relied to avenge their defeat at Badr, was characterized as the *shaykh Quraysh wa-kabīr-ha.* Cited by R. B. Serjeant, *The Saiyids of Ḥaḍramawt. An Inaugural Lecture Delivered on 5 June 1956* (School of Oriental and African Studies, University of London, 1957), 5 n. 4.

51. Philip Hitti, *History of the Arabs: From the Earliest Times to the Present,* 6th ed. (New York, 1956), 28. Numerous extant pre-Islamic genealogies evidently were molded in the interests of rivalries between tribal groups during the early Islamic centuries. The conflict between "northerners" (ʿAdnān or Maʿadd) and "southerners" (Qaḥṭān or al-Yaman) was especially important in this connection (see Goldziher, *Muhammedanische Studien,* 1:89–98), but it was during late Umayyad and early ʿAbbāsid times that the science of comprehensive genealogy developed— and with it the formalization of the great body of genealogical literature as we now know it—as a response to the disintegration of the original Arab tribal organization: cf. Werner Caskel, *Ǧamharat an-Nasab: das genealogische Werk des Hišām ibn Muḥammad al-Kalbī,* 2 vols. (Leiden, 1966). However, if genealogies were formulated in ancient times in the same way as they presently are among the Ruwalah, many of them were probably to a greater or lesser degree fictionalized even before the time of Muḥammad. Cf. note 48 above and William Lancaster's further conclusion: "For them [the Ruwalah] the main point of a genealogy is to provide a framework for legitimising present political relationships between groups. This does not mean that they seek to ratify a relationship by reference to the genealogy, but rather that an existing or proposed relationship is an inevitable result of a mutually agreed genealogy. It is not *the* genealogy leading to *a* relationship, but rather *the* relationship leading to *a* genealogy" (*The Rwala,* 151).

In light of this analysis, it may not be unduly skeptical to assume that the traditionists of the eighth and later centuries were manipulating genealogies that had already undergone substantial adaptation by tribesmen responding to social and political pressures in Makkah and al-Madīnah during the seventh century. Al-Balādhurī (d. 892) furnishes a nicely apposite instance of the tribe of Thaqīf manipulating its genealogy to accord with political realities in the seventh century A.D. (*Ansāb al-Ashrāf,* vol. 1, ed. Muḥammad Ḥamīdullāh [al-Qāhirah, A.H. 1379/A.D. 1959], 25); and Charles-André Julien draws attention to "numerous examples of tribes [in the Maghrib] supposedly descended from a single ancestor but in reality made up of unrelated elements united by a single way of life" (*History of North Africa* [London, 1970], 16).

52. Sahlins, *Tribesmen,* 24.

53. Ibid., 15.

54. Ibid., 84.

55. The following discussion of the sectoral organization of the reciprocatively integrated *badū* economy is adapted from Marshall Sahlins's generalized analysis in "On the Sociology of Primitive Exchange," in Michael Banton, ed., *The Relevance of Models for Social Anthropology,* Monographs of the Association of Social Anthropologists, no. 1 (London and New York, 1965), 139–236.

56. Ibn Qutaybah, al-Shiʿr wa-l-Shuʿarāʾ, ed. M. J. de Goeje (Leyden, 1904), 124. For a more recent example see T. E. Lawrence's comments on the magnificent hospitality offered to guests by ʿAwda Abū Ṭayyiʾ, chief of the Ṭayyiʾ *qawm* of the eastern Ḥuwayṭāt, in *Seven Pillars of Wisdom* (London and Toronto, 1926), 222.

57. The term *negative reciprocity* was coined by Alvin W. Gouldner: "The norm of reciprocity: a preliminary statement," *American Sociological Review,* 25 (1960): 161–78.

58. Cf. Louise E. Sweet, "Camel raiding of North Arabian bedouin: a mechanism of ecological adaptation," *American Anthropologist* 67 (1965): 1132–50; Lothar Stein, "Zum Problem der Raubzüge (ġazū) bei den Šammar-Ğerba," *Annals of the Naprstek Museum,* 2 (1963): 51–68; and more generally William Irons, "Livestock raiding among pastoralists: an adaptive interpretation," *Papers of the Michigan Academy of Science, Arts, and Letters* 50 (1965): 393–414.

59. Werner Caskel, "Aijām al-ʿArab. Studien zur altarabischen Epik," *Islamica* 3 (1930): 1–99.

60. Al-Iṣfahānī, *al-Aghānī,* 2:162.

61. Muḥammad ibn Isḥaq (d. 768), *Sīrat Sayyidinā Muḥammad Rasūliʾllāh,* in *Das Leben Muhammeds nach Muhammed ibn Ishâk, Bearbeitet von ʿAbd al-Malik ibn Hischâm,* ed. Ferdinand Wüstenfeld (Göttingen, 1858–60), 1:117–19 (all subsequent references are to the Wüstenfeld edition unless otherwise indicated); English translation by Alfred Guillaume under the title *The Life of Mohammad* (Oxford, 1955), 82 and Yāqūt (1179–1229), *Muʿjam,* 3:579.

62. Al-Iṣfahānī, *al-Aghānī,* 4:140–52; Ḥabīb ibn Aws Abū Tammām (died ca. A.D. 845), *Dīwān al-Ḥamāsah,* ed. as *Hamasae Carmina cum Tebrisii Scholiis, Ashʿār al-Ḥamāsah* by G. Freytag (Bonn, 1828), 420–23; and Ibn ʿAbd-Rabbih (860–940), *al-ʿIqd al-Farīd,* vol. 3 (al-Qāhirah, A.H. 1302), 95.

63. Al-Iṣfahānī, *al-Aghānī,* 9:150 and 7:150.

64. Preserved by Abū Tammām in his anthology *Ashʿār al-Ḥamāsah,* in *Hamasae Carmina,* ed. G. Freytag (Bonn, 1828), 171.

65. Abū Dāʾūd Sulaymān ibn al-Ashʿath (d. 888), *Kitāb al-Sunan* (Al-Qāhirah, A.H. 1280), 1:89, quoted in Hitti, *History of the Arabs,* 24. This same fierce independence and pride in self and ancestry is clearly evident in the boast attributed to Abū Rabīʿ of the Ghanī tribe in the second half of the first Islamic century: "The best of all people are the Arabs, and among those the Muḍar tribes; among those Qays; among those the clan of Yaʿṣur; among those the family of Ghanī; and of the Ghanī I am the best man. Hence I am the best of all men" (Al-Mubarrad, *al-Kāmil,* ed. William Wright [Leipzig, 1864] 352, quoted in Goldziher, *Muslim Studies,* 15).

66. Rudi Paret, "Les Villes de Syrie du Sud et les routes commerciales d'Arabie à la fin du VI siècle," in *Akten des XI. Internationalen Byzantinisten-Kongresses,* München 1958 (München, 1960), 438–44. It can hardly be fortuitous that the resurgence of these trade routes followed closely on the replacement of wheeled vehicles by pack animals, chiefly camels, throughout the Middle East: see Richard W. Bulliet, *The Camel and the Wheel* (Cambridge, Mass., 1975), passim.

67. The only oasis in the tract of corrugated and fissured lava country *(al-ḥarrah)* lying between Yathrib (Medina) and Makkah (Mecca): cf. al-Iṣfahānī, *al-Aghānī,* 2:179. There is a study of all the *ḥarrah* terrain of Arabia as described in numerous entries in Yāqūt's *Muʿjam al-Buldān* in Otto Loth, "Die Vulkanregionen (Ḥarra's) von Arabien nach Jaḳut," *Zeitschrift der Deutschen Morgenländischen Gesellschaft* 22 (1868): 365–82.

68. Now al-Ḥāʾiṭ.

69. See Lammens, *Le Berceau de l'Islam,* passim.

70. Qurʾān 6 *(al-Anʿām):*92 and 42 *(al-Shūrā):*7. In its original revelation, this phrase most probably referred to al-Madīnah, but in subsequent Islamic writings it has invariably been taken, as it is here, to denote Makkah: for example, Ibn Ḥawqal, *Kitāb Ṣūrat al-Arḍ* (ca. 988), ed. J. H. Kramers, *Opus Geographicum Auctore Ibn Haukal,* vol. 2 of *Bibliotheca Geographorum Arabicorum* (Lugduni Batavorum, 1938), 2:18 (all subsequent references are to the Kramers edition unless otherwise indicated); French translation by J. H. Kramers and G. Wiet under the title *Configuration de la Terre,* vol. 1 (Paris, 1964), 1:18.

Since this chapter was first drafted, Patricia Crone has published a thoroughly revisionist study of Makkah, and, by implication, Arabia, during the concluding phases of the *Jāhilīyah: Meccan Trade and the Rise of Islam* (Princeton, N.J., 1987). In this study she argues that the commerce and sanctity of pre-Islamic Makkah are fabrifications perpetrated by early Muslim traditionists. Dr. Crone's interpretation has proved highly controversial, provoking some rather intemperate responses, particularly that by Robert B. Serjeant: "Meccan trade and the rise of Islam: misconceptions and flawed polemics," *Journal of the American Oriental Society* 110, no. 3 (1990): 472–86. For Crone's rejoinder see "Serjeant and Meccan trade," *Arabica,* 39, fasc. 2 (1992): 216–40. A work written a decade before Crone's book but strongly opposed to her style of interpretation (and incidentally equally strongly supportive of Serjeant's views) is Mardsen Jones, "Al-Sīra al-Nabawiyya as a Source for the Economic History of Western Arabia at the Time of the Rise of Islam," in *Proceedings of the First International Symposium on the History of Arabia, 23rd–28th April, 1977* (1977), 15–23.

For my part, I am sympathetic to Dr. Crone's skepticism of the value of early historical sources for understanding the rise of Islam. I accept in principle, though with some reservations, her characterization of the Islamic exegetical tradition as "tendentious, its aim being the celebration of an Arabian *Heilsgeschichte,*" together with the corollary that "this tendentiousness has shaped the facts as we have them, not merely added some partisan statements that we can deduct" (230). And I believe that there is a good deal of truth to her contention that, during the first century and a half of the Islamic era, spurious information tended to drive genuine information out of circulation so that the Muslim "recollection of the past was reduced to a common stock of stories, themes and motifs that could be combined and recombined in a profusion of apparently factual accounts" (225).

It is possible, though, that Dr. Crone has occasionally placed too great a reliance on negative evidence in explicating certain sources that are both fragmentary and selective in the first place. Perhaps she has also failed to discriminate adequately between truth and authenticity in medieval Arabic texts. It is evident, for example, that *akhbārīyūn* such as al-Wāqidī customarily wove together an array of disparate traditions (which were authentic enough by any standard) in order to shape a discursive field that became something much more than a record of truthfully remembered events: a new code of signification, in fact (for pertinent comments on this aspect of al-Wāqidī's work see Rizwi S. Faizer, "The issue of authenticity regarding the traditions of al-Wāqidī," *Journal of Near Eastern Studies* 58, no. 2 [1999]: 97–106). Even so, while the dates, places, and sequences of events are only too often irrecoverable, it is often still practicable to elicit developmental patterns as manifested in types of actions and forms of interrelationships—in short, to arrive at some notion of generalized institutional evolution. The question then arises, of course, as to the date to which this paradigmatic view of the past relates: in this case, is it to the early seventh century or to the eighth or later? Or, as is perhaps more likely, is it compounded of successive additions and elaborations? In what follows I have tried to chart a course between, on the one hand, the almost total acceptance of the tradition in the manner of Henri Lammens and Montgomery Watt and, on the other hand, the extreme skepticism of Dr. Crone. My emphasis has been on patterns of institutional development; where I have strayed beyond that, I have done so with trepidation.

Dr. Crone has elaborated her views on the nature of the Islamic tradition in further works that collectively constitute one of the few contemporary examples of cumulative research in early Islamic studies. Of direct relevance here are *Hagarism: The Making of the Islamic World,* authored jointly with Michael Cook (Cambridge, 1977) and *Slaves on Horses: The Evolution of the Islamic Polity* (Cambridge, 1980). It is in the latter work (p. 6) that she presents her most arresting description of the early Islamic tradition: "For over a century the landscape of the Muslim past was thus exposed to a weathering so violent that its shapes were reduced to dust and rubble and deposited in secondary patterns, mixed with foreign debris and shifting with the wind. Only in the latter half of the Umayyad period, when the doctrinal structures of Islam began to acquire viability, did the whirlwind gradually subside." However, it is not impossible that the sedimentary deposits to which Dr. Crone refers may sometimes envelop durable fragments of information from earlier disintegrated strata that can be salvaged and, with appropriate caution, used in the partial reconstruction of an earlier age. In fact Lawrence I. Conrad has already provided some idea of one way in which such a salvage operation might be essayed in a paper entitled "Abraha and Muḥammad: some observations apropos of chronology and literary *topoi* in the early Arabic historical tradition," *Bulletin of the School of Oriental and African Studies,* 50, pt. 2 (1987): 225–40. Conrad approaches the structure of the *sīrah* tradition not only as a problem of historiography but more exigently as a question of social perceptions, as commonly exemplified in "the use of literary topoi to advance subtle arguments in the form of symbolic messages and images" (226–27). He concludes that "the historiographical problems are serious and complex, but do not seem to warrant the conclusion that nothing about *sīra* can be extracted from the Islamic sources, or indeed, from any sources" (239).

For a splendid exposition modelling the process by which Umayyad storytellers indeed integrated fragmentary and undifferentiated materials into an unhistorical narrative laced with topoi, schemata, and other stereotypical motifs, see Lawrence I. Conrad, "The Conquest of Arwād: A Source-Critical Study in the Historiography of the Early Medieval Near East," in *Problems in the Literary Source Material,* vol. 1 of *The Byzantine and Early Islamic Near East,* ed. Averil Cameron and Lawrence I. Conrad (Princeton, N.J., 1992), 317–401. The substantial degree of instability pervading the Arab-Islamic tradition as late as the second half of the ninth century has recently been demonstrated with exemplary clarity by Stefan Leder, *Das Korpus al-Haiṯam ibn ʿAdī (st. 207/822). Herkunft Überlieferung, Gestalt früher Texte der Aḫbār Literatur* (Frankfurt, 1991), passim and "Authorship and transmission in unauthored literature: the *Axbār* attributed to al-Haiṯam ibn ʿAdī," *Oriens* 31 (1988). More than two decades ago Albrecht Noth drew attention to the transfer of material between traditions ("Iṣfahān-Nihāwand. Eine quellenkritische Studie zur frühislamischen Historiographie," *Zeitschrift der Deutschen Morgenländischen Gesellschaft* 118 [1968]: 274–96). Noth took full account of the instability of the *futūḥ* tradition in his *Quellenkritische Studien zu Themen, Formen und Tendenzen frühislamischer Geschichtsüberlieferung:* 1, *Themen und Formen* (Bonn, 1973), especially pp. 174–92, where he elicits the manner in which comparatively unimportant events were elaborated with the aid of stock narrative motifs and schematic tropes into happenings of much greater significance. There are some thought-provoking reflections on the revisionist history of early Islam in Christian Decobert, *Le Mendiant et le Combattant* (Paris, 1991).

71. R. B. Serjeant, "Professor A. Guillaume's translation of the Sīrah," *Bulletin of the School of Oriental and African Studies,* 21 (1958): 7. Cf. also Serjeant's reading of a difficult line of verse in the *Sīrah:* "One who makes a votive offering to a benefactor, makes a votive offering at it [Zamzam]": loc. cit., 8. For implications of the contradiction between the alleged antiquity of Zamzam and traditions about its later digging see G. R. Hawting, "The disappearance and re-discovery of Zamzam and the 'well of the Kaʿba,'" *Bulletin of the School of Oriental and African Studies* 43 (1980): 44–54. The well of Zamzam still flows in the courtyard of the Kaʿbah.

72. "Tangled scrub in a wādī bed" *(muʿtalij al-baṭḥāʾ)* in Ibn Hishām's phrase: *Sīrah,* 1:65. Cf. Serjeant, "Meccan trade," 485–86. Cf. also the need for food to be imported into Makkah in Qurʾān 2 *(al-Baqarah):* 126, 16 *(al-Naḥl):* 112, and 28 *(al-Qaṣaṣ):* 57.

73. Al-Maqdisī, *Aḥsan al-Taqāsīm fī Maʿrifat al-Aqālīm* (985/6), in *Descriptio Imperii Moslemici Auctore al-Moqaddassi,* vol. 3 of *Bibliotheca Geographorum Arabicorum,* ed. M. J. de Goeje (Lugduni Batavorum, 1877), 95. All subsequent references are to the de Goeje edition unless otherwise indicated.

74. Henri Lammens, "La Mecque à la veille de l'Hégire," in *Mélanges de l'Université Saint-Joseph, Beyrouth (Syrie)* 9 (1924): 180[84]–181[85].

75. Claudius Ptolemaeus, *Geographia,* bk. 6, chap. 7, par. 32.

76. Ethiopic *mekwerāb.* Cf. Ar. *maqrab* = the place of *qurbān* = "sacrifice," "oblation," or sometimes "theophany." It is only fair to note that, although this identification has been widely accepted, it has been vigorously opposed by Patricia Crone (*Meccan Trade and the Rise of Islam,* 134–36).

77. E.g., Ibn Isḥāq, *Sīrah,* 1:73–80; Guillaume's translation, 48–56. For insightful comments on the credibility of the canonized genealogy of Muḥammad, see Daniel Martin Varisco, "Metaphors and sacred history: the genealogy of Muhammad and the Arab 'tribe,'" *Anthropological Quarterly* 68, no. 3 (1995): 139–65.

78. Robert B. Serjeant, "Ḥaram and Ḥawṭah, the Sacred Enclave in Arabia," in *Mélanges Ṭāhā Ḥusain: Offerts par ses Amis et ses Disciples à l'Occasion de son 70ième Anniversaire* (Le Caire, 1962), 53. In the Ḥaḍramawt, the guardian of a *ḥaram* (there called a *ḥawṭah*) holds the title of *manṣab* or *manṣūb.*

79. Aḥmad al-Nuwayrī, *Nihāyat al-Arab fī Funūn al-Adab* (al-Qāhirah, 1955), 16:30 et seq. The vignette is not implausible, because it continued to represent the situation near Makkah for centuries subsequent to the advent of Islam. Indeed, the lower part of Makkah, including the Masjid al-Ḥaram, is still subject to flash flooding, with a particularly severe instance occurring in 1950.

80. Henri Lammens, "Les sanctuaires préislamites dans l'Arabie occidentale," *Mélanges de l'Université Saint-Joseph* 2 (1926): 39–173, and "Le culte des bétyles," *Bulletin de l'Institut Français d'Archéologie Orientale,* vol. 17 (Cairo, 1919).

81. Information about pre-Islamic religions in Arabia is not abundant. Such as it is, it derives from allusions in the verse of the *Jāhilīyah;* from traditions preserved in later Islamic literature and collected by Hishām ibn al-Kalbī (d. 819) in his *Kitāb al-Aṣnām,* ed. Aḥmad Zakī Pasha (al-Qāhirah, A.H. 1330) (all subsequent references are to the Pasha edition unless otherwise indicated); from relics of early paganism incorporated in Islamic lore; and from a handful of inscriptions. See Julius Wellhausen, *Reste arabischen Heidentums* (Berlin, 1887); 2d ed., with additions and corrections (Berlin, 1897; reprint, Berlin, 1927 and 1961); Goldziher, *Muhammedanische Studien* (Halle, 1889–90), English translation under the title *Muslim Studies* (London, 1966; Chicago, 1967), chap. 1; Ryckmans, *Les Religions Arabes Préislamiques;* Joseph Henninger, "La religion bédouine préislamique," in *L'Antica Società Beduina,* ed. Francesco Gabrieli (Roma, 1959), 115–40; Werner Caskel, "Die alten semitischen Gottheiten in Arabien," in *Le Antiche Divinità Semitiche,* ed. Sabatino Moscati (Roma, 1958), 95–117; Joseph Chelbod, *Les Structures du Sacré chez les Arabes* (Paris, 1964); Toufic Fahd, *Le Panthéon de l'Arabie Centrale à la Veille de l'Hégire* (Paris, 1968); Henri Charles, *Le Christianisme des Arabes Nomades sur le Limes et dans le Désert Syro-Mésopotamien aux Alentours de l'Hégire* (Paris, 1936); Arent Jan Wensinck, *Mohammed en de Joden te Medina* (Leiden, 1908), English translation under the title *Mohammad and the Jews of Medina* (Freiburg, 1975); and Meir J. Kister, "Labbayka, Allāhumma, labbayka . . . : on a monotheistic aspect of a Jāhiliyya practice," *Jerusalem Studies in Arabic and Islam* 8 (1986): 47–48. A paper nicely illustrative of the manner in which information about pre-Islamic religion can sometimes be recovered from beneath an overlay of subsequent Muslim exegesis is A. F. L. Beeston's "The so-called harlots of Ḥaḍramaut," *Oriens* 5 (1952): 16–22. Professor Beeston shows that the unfortunate ladies in question, who are mentioned in both al-Baghdādī's *al-Muḥabbar* and al-Ṭabarī's *Taʾrīkh,* were in fact priestesses of the old pagan religion of South Arabia, and in at least some cases of high social class (three of those named were of the *ashrāf* class and four belonged to the royal tribe of Kindah). Cf. also K. Mlaker, *Die Hierodulenlisten von Maʿin* (Leipzig, 1943).

Certainly, the description of pre-Islamic religions presented here is no more than a gross cartoon of the complex religious system of which the Makkan sanctuary was one, although perhaps not the most important, expression. It should be noted, moreover, that certain revisionist historians, impressed by an apparent lack of archaeological confirmation of the literary sources, have suggested that accounts of Jāhilī religion may be "back-projections of a paganism actually known from later and elsewhere." See J. Koren and Y. D. Nevo, "Methodological approaches to Islamic studies," *Der Islam* 68 (1991): 102.

82. Ibn Isḥāq, *Sīrah,* 1:71; Guillaume's translation, 45.

83. Yāqūt, *Muʿjam,* 1:434; al-Qazwīnī (d. 1283), *ʿAjāʾib al-Makhlūqāt wa-Gharāʾib al-Mawjūdāt,* ed. Ferdinand Wüstenfeld (Göttingen, 1849), 200.

84. Al-Kalbī, *al-Aṣnām,* 18, 20; Yāqūt, *Muʿjam,* 3:772–73.

85. Ibn Isḥāq, *Sīrah,* 1:22; Guillaume's translation, 14–16. Al-Ṭabarī, *Taʾrīkh,* 1:922.

86. Ibn Isḥāq, *Sīrah,* 1:844; Guillaume's translation, 568–69.

87. For example, Nasr (= "vulture": Qurʾān 71 *(Nūḥ):*23) and ʿAwf (a large bird). See Henri Lammens, *Les Chrétiens à la Mecque à la Veille de l'Hégire: l'Arabie Occidentale avant l'Hégire* (Beyrouth, 1928), 145.

88. Bernard Lewis, *The Arabs in History* (New York, 1960), 30.

89. Cf. E. E. Evans-Pritchard's remarks on Nuer religion: "Mighty and celestial phenomena and great and terrible happenings, such as plagues and famines, and the moral order which concern all men are attributed to God *[Kwoth],* while processes and events which do not have so general a range of impact tend to be attributed to whichever particular refraction or type of refraction

the situation and context evoke" (*Nuer Religion* [Oxford, 1956], 211).

90. Sahlins, *Tribesmen,* 103.

91. This phrase would not necessarily have implied celestial family relationships comparable to those obtaining in the Greek pantheon, for in the Semitic culture realm the terms *son* and *daughter* were often used to denote the abstract notion of subordinancy: cf. W. Montgomery Watt, *Islam and the Integration of Society* (London, 1961), 188.

92. Al-Kalbī, *al-Aṣnām,* 18–19.

93. Nielsen, *Handbuch,* 1:236.

94. Mentioned by Herodotus under the orthography *Alilat* (bk. 3, chap. 8). For a comprehensive, although sometimes controversial, discussion of this goddess see Susanne Krone, *Die arabische Gottheit al-Lāt,* Heidelberger Orientalistiche Studien 23 (Heidelberg, 1992).

95. Cf. Ar. *manīyah* = "fate"; Heb. *Mĕni* in Isa. 65:11.

96. Al-Kalbī, *al-Aṣnām,* 13.

97. Cooke, *Text-Book,* 217, 219. Even Muḥammad at first recognized the power of these goddesses, but subsequently retracted his advocacy and reconstituted *Sūrah* 53 *(al-Najm):* 19–20 to read as at present:

> Have ye given thought to al-Lāt and al-ʿUzzā,
> And Manāt, the third, the other [goddess]?

According to tradition, when first revealed these verses were followed by two others that were subsequently expunged:

> These are the birds [literally, cranes] exalted,
> Whose intercession is to be hoped for.

Cf. al-Bayḍāwī, *Anwār al-Tanzīl wa-Asrār al-Taʾwil,* ed. H. O. Fleischer (Leipzig, 1846–48), 1:636–37 and Abū Jaʿfar Muḥammad ibn Jarīr al-Ṭabarī (838–923), *Jāmiʿ al-Bayān fī Tafsīr al-Qurʿān* (Būlāq, 1905–11), 17:131 and 27:34ff.

98. Al-Isfahānī, *al-Aghānī,* 7:149–50; Ibn Qutaybah, *Kitāb al-Maʿārif,* 130; Theodor Nöldeke, in *Encyclopedia of Religion and Ethics,* Hastings ed., s.v. "Arabs"; and Albert Jamme, "Le panthéon sud-arabe préislamique d'après les sources épigraphiques," *Le Muséon* 60 (1947): 55–147. Hubal < Aramaic for "vital breath."

99. Winnett, *A Study of the Lihyanite and Thamudic Inscriptions,* 30.

100. A loanword from Aramaic through Nabataean: see F. Buhl, *The Encyclopaedia of Islam,* 1st ed., s.v. "Ḥanīf"; Caetani, *Annali,* 1:181–92; Richard Bell, "Who were the Ḥanīfs?" *Moslem World,* 20 (1930): 120–24; N. A. Faris and H. W. Glidden, "The development of the meaning of the Koranic Ḥanīf," *Journal of the Palestine Oriental Society* 19 (1939): 1–13; Arthur Jeffery, *The Foreign Vocabulary of the Qurʾān,* Gaekwad Oriental Series, no. 74 (Baroda, 1938), 112–15; and M. J. Kister, "A bag of meat," *Bulletin of the School of Oriental and African Studies* 33 (1970): 267–75.

101. Cf. Robert B. Serjeant, "Hūd and other pre-Islamic prophets of Ḥaḍramawt," *Le Muséon* 67 (1954): 121–78.

102. V. V. Barthol'd, "Musaylima," *Bulletin de l'Académie des Sciences de Russie* 19 (1925); W. Montgomery Watt, *Muhammad at Medina* (Oxford, 1956), 134–37; and Dale F. Eickelman, "Musaylima: an approach to the social anthropology of seventh century Arabia," *Journal of the Economic and Social History of the Orient* 10 (1967): 17–52. Musaylimah was a diminutive of this prophet's real name, Maslamah, as Ṭulayḥah was a derisive diminutive of Ṭalḥah.

103. Al-Azraqī, *Kitāb Akhbār Makkah,* in *Die Chroniken der Stadt Mekka,* ed. Ferdinand Wüstenfeld (Leipzig, 1857–61), 104–107 and Uri Rubin, "The Kaʿba. Aspects of its ritual, functions and position in pre-Islamic and early Islamic times," *Jerusalem Studies in Arabic and Islam* 8 (1986): 97–131. *Kaʿbahs* also existed elsewhere on the Arabian Peninsula, notably at Najrān and Ṣanʿāʾ, while there were similar shrines at Petra and al-Ṭāʾif.

104. The tradition related by Ibn Isḥāq (*Sīrah,* 1:50 *et seq.;* Guillaume's translation, 35 et seq.) that this idol had been brought by a certain ʿAmr ibn Luḥayy from either Moab or Mesopotamia may have preserved a kernel of truth, for the name Hubal was derived from an Aramaic word meaning "vapor," "spirit," or "vital breath."

105. Qurʾān 2 *(al-Baqarah):* 125, 127.

106. Cf. Biblical Hebrew *ḥērem.* See Serjeant, "Ḥaram and Ḥawṭah," 41–58. *Ḥawṭah* is contemporary South Arabian usage for *ḥaram.*

107. This is the customary reading of Muslim scholars, who tend to follow the Qurʾān 9 *(al-Tawbah):* 36, the months in question being Dhū al-Qaʿdah (eleventh), Dhū al-Ḥijjah (twelfth), al-Muḥarram (first), and Rajab (seventh); but elsewhere the Qurʾān refers to "the" sacred month (2 *[al-Baqarah]:*194, 217; 5 *[al-Māʾidah]:* 2, 97). Some scholars, W. Montgomery Watt among them (*Muhammad at Medina,* 8), have viewed this discrepancy as representing a compromise between varying practices in different localities.

108. See Serjeant, "Ḥaram and Ḥawṭah," 52. There are also references in al-Isfahānī, *al-Aghānī* (12:121, 21:63), to a *ḥaram* of the Ghaṭafān, which was destroyed by Zuhayr ibn Janāb.

109. A good deal of popular etymological speculation has accumulated around the ethnikon *Quraysh,* most of it tracing the name to a root meaning "to collect together." None of it is soundly based but usually adjusted to the image of the tribe as it appeared to other, and often later, Arabs. One interpretation derives the name from the fact that the Quraysh "collected together" all their migratory kinship units around the Kaʿbah; another from their having "collected together commodities from all sides for sale" (Ferdinand Wüstenfeld, *Geschichte der Stadt Mekka nach den arabischen Chroniken,* vol. 4 [Leipzig, 1864], 25, 28). Still another etymology, no better based than the former but reflecting even more explicitly the Arabian view of the Quraysh, derives their name from a word meaning "to profit from trade" (Ferdinand Wüstenfeld, *Das Leben Mohammeds nach Muhammed Ibn Ishāk,* vol. 1 [Göttingen, 1858], 46). In fact the ethnikon seems to mean "shark" and probably originated as an ancient tribal totem (Maxime Rodinson, *Mahomet* [Paris, 1961]; English trans. New York, 1971, 39).

110. Ibn Isḥāq, *Sīrah,* 1:83; Guillaume's translation, 55–56.

111. *Fol.* 177r, cited by Kister; see reference in note 116 below.

112. Cf. Al-Balādhurī, *al-Ashrāf,* 1:68 (where ʿAbd al-Muṭṭalib's companion is given as ʿAmr ibn ʿĀʾidh al-Makhzūmī); al-Faḍl ibn al-Ḥasan al-Ṭabarsī/al-Tabrisī, *Majmaʿ al-Bayān fī Tafsīr al-Qurʾān,* 10 vols. (Bayrut, A.H. 1380/A.D. 1961), 3:234–37; and Muḥammad Bāqir ibn Muḥammad Taqī Majlisī, *Biḥār al-Anwār,* 110 vols. (Tehrān, 1379), 15:134–37 (as cited by Kister). Ibn Isḥāq gives a quite different account of Quraysh involvement with Abrahah: *Sīrah,* Guillaume's translation, 21–28.

113. Caetani, *Annali,* 1:148.

114. Cited in and adapted from Wüstenfeld, *Das Leben Muhammeds,* 1:85.

115. Al-Mufaḍḍal al-Ḍabbī (died ca. 785), *al-Mufaḍḍalīyāt,* trans. and annotated by C. J. Lyall, 2 vols. (Oxford, 1918), 2:254; Arabic text in vol. 1 (1921), 621. The poet in question was the picaresque al-Ḥarith ibn Dhālim, whom Lyall correctly characterizes as a "man of blood and violence."

116. Quoted in M. J. Kister, "Some reports concerning Mecca from Jāhiliyya to Islam," *Journal of the Economic and Social History of the Orient,* 15 (1972): 62. On the *Nihāyah* see Edward G. Browne, "Some account of the Arabic work entitled 'Niháyatu'l-irab fi akhbāri'l-Furs wa'l-'Arab' . . . ," *Journal of the Royal Asiatic Society* (1900): 195–204, and note 79 above. The remainder of Kister's long paper deals with the substance of the *Nihāyah.*

117. Julius Wellhausen, *Skizzen und Vorarbeiten,* vol. 3 (Berlin, 1887), 88. These fairs, together with the one at Ḥabashah, were those annual gatherings of *badū, shwāyah, ḥaḍarī,* and merchants of which accounts have been preserved, but there were certainly others, including one at Makkah. In Muslim tradition they were believed to have occurred at specified times and in a given rotation, beginning with ʿUkāẓ on the first of Dhū al-Qaʿdah, and ending with Dhū al-Majāz and Mināʾ, which were held between the ninth and the final days of the Great Pilgrimage. Ḥabashah probably denoted a locality in the Ḥaḍramawt (cf. note 12 above: although Azraqī [*Kitāb Akhbār Makkah,* 131] prefers al-Yaman and others, such as al-Bakrī, have assumed a site close to Makkah); of the other fairs, only ʿUkāẓ can be assigned a regional location with certainty, namely between Nakhlah and al-Ṭāʾif. For a discussion of these matters see Lammens, "La Mecque," 153 [57]–154 [58] and F. Krenkow, "The annual fairs of the pagan Arabs," *Islamic Culture* 21 (1947): 111–13. There is a passage describing these pre-Islamic fairs in Muḥammad ibn Ḥabīb (d. A.D. 850), *Kitāb al-Muḥabbar,* ed. Ilse Lichtenstädter (Ḥaydarābād, 1942), 263ff., and an expanded version of the same material is provided by the later author al-Marzūqī, *Kitāb al-Azminah wa-l-Amkinah,* 2 vols. (Ḥaydarābād, 1913), 2:161–70. Both accounts derive from a now-lost work by al-Kalbī (d. 819). A different list of Arabian fairs is included in the Yamanī topographer Abū Muḥammad al-Ḥasan ibn Aḥmad al-Hamdanī (d. 945), *Ṣifat Jazīrat al-ʿArab,* 2 vols., ed. D. H. Müller (Leiden, 1884–91), 1:179 ff. (cf. note 119, chapter 3 below). The most comprehensive modern discussion of these fairs is in Saʿīd al-Afghānī, *Aswāq al-ʿArab fī-l-Jāhilīyah wa-l-Islam* (Dimashq, 1960), passim.

118. The conventional view of this trade was summarized by Aloys Sprenger, *Das Leben und die Lehre des Moḥammed,* 3 vols. (Berlin, 1869), 3:94–95 and by Henri Lammens, *Les Chrétiens à la Mecque à la Veille de l'Hégire: l'Arabie Occidentale avant l'Hégire* (Beyrouth, 1928), 22–23. Cf. also Wellhausen, *Skizzen und Vorarbeiten,* 3:183:

> In dem tumultuarischen Wirrwar, der die Wüste füllt, bilden die Feste, zu Anfang jedes Semesters, den einzigen erfreulichen Ruhepunkt. Ein nicht kurz bemessener Gottesfriede unterbricht dann die ewige Fehde. Die verschiedensten Stämme, die sonst einander nicht über den Weg trauen, wallfahren unbesorgt, durch Freundes oder Feindes Land, gemeinschaftlich zu der selben heiligen Stätte. Der Handel wagt sich heraus, und es entsteht ein lebhafter, allgemeiner Verkehr. Man atmet auf und fühlt sich eine Zeit lang frei von den Schranken, die sonst jeden Stamm einschliessen und von den anderen trennen; man lernt sich kennen: alle hervorragenden Männer, auch wenn sie durch weiteste Entfernungen getrennt wohnen, wissen von einander und haben sich in der Regel auch gesehen. Die Feststätten werden zu Messen und Märkten; in Ukâtz [ʿUkāẓ] gibt sich ganz Arabien ein jährliches Rendezvous. Dem Austausch der Waren folgt der geistige Austausch; er erstreckt sich auch auf die Poesie und die Tradition. Eine Gemeinschaft geistiger Interessen entsteht, die ganz Arabien umfasst; eine allerdings illiterate Literatur, eine über den Dialekten stehende Sprache, eine gewisse allgemeine Bildung und Anschauungsweiese.

To illustrate the extent of the trade activities in which one particular family was involved, that of Hishām ibn al-Mughīrah, Kister ("Some reports concerning Mecca," 92) cites the following verses from the *Dīwān* of al-Ḥuṭayʾah, ed. Nuʿmān Amīn Ṭāhā (Qāhirah, A.H. 1378/A.D. 1958), 320 (commentary, 322):

> fa-hallā amartī bnay hishāmin fa-yamkuthā:
> ʿalā mā aṣābā min miʾīnah wa min alfī
> min al-rūmī wa-l-uḥbūshī ḥattā tanāwalā:
> bi-bayʿihimā māla al-marāzibatī al-ghulfī
> wa-mā kāna mimmā aṣbaḥā yajmaʿānihī:
> min al-mālī illā bi-l-taḥarrufī wa-l-ṣarfī.

119. Sprenger, *Das Leben,* 96. Based on the Byzantine *solidus,* the *mithqāl* was a unit of weight used more particularly for precious metals. The remembrance of the Makkan caravan trade in the Prophet's day, partly mythologized though it was, became a prominent theme in the Tradition. Cf., for example, al-Wāḥidī's story about the seven caravans belonging to Jews of al-Madīnah that arrived in Makkah from Bostra and Adhruʿāt in a single day bearing cloth, perfumes, jewels, and "products of the sea" *(amtiʿat al baḥr): Asbāb al-Nuzūl* (al-Qāhirah, A.H. 1388/A.D. 1968), 187. Cf. also al-Qurṭubī, *al-Jāmiʿ li-Aḥkām al-Quaʾān,* 10 vols. (al-Qāhirah, A.H. 1387/A.D. 1967), 10:56 (both quoted by Kister, "Some reports concerning Mecca," 77 n. 1). Dr. Crone rightly castigates this episode as "a crude piece of exegetical invention": *Meccan Trade,* 96 n. 37. Cf. also 140 n. 36, 216 n. 60.

120. Muḥammad ibn ʿUmar al-Wāqidī (747–823), *Kitāb al-Maghāzī,* ed. Alfred von Kremer (Calcutta, 1855–56); abridged trans. by Julius Wellhausen under the title *Muhammed in Medina; das ist Vakidis Kitab al-Maghazi in verkürzter deutscher Wiedergabe* (Berlin, 1882), 34, 39.

121. Lammens, "La Mecque," 233 [137]. See also the same author's "La république marchande de la Mecque vers l'an 600 de notre ère," *Bulletin de l'Institut Egyptien,* 5th ser., 4 (1910): 23–54. Cf. Charles C. Torrey (*The Commercial-Theological Terms in the Koran* [Leyden, 1892]), who drew attention to the manner in which the Qurʾān often uses commercial terms to express fundamental points of doctrine. Qurʾānic passages cast in the idiom of mercantile exchange include 39 *(al-Ḥāqqah):* 19, 25; in 84 *(al-Inshiqāq):* 7, 10, men's deeds are entered in a book (signifying ledger); 69 *(al-Ḥāqqah):* 20, 26, and 84 *(al-Inshiqāq):* 8: the Day of Judgment as an accounting or reckoning; 21 *(al-Anbiyā):* 47 and 101 *(al-Qāriʿah):* 6: men's deeds are weighed in the balance; 52 *(al-Ṭūr):* 21 and 74 *(al-Muddaththir):* 38: man's soul held as a pledge; 2 *(al-Baqarah):* 13, 16; 57 *(al-Ḥadīd):* 18, 28; 84 *(al-Inshiqāq):* 25; and 95 *(al-Tīn):* 6: man is rewarded for his services; 2 *(al-Baqarah):* 245; 57 *(al-Ḥadīd):* 11, 18; 64 *(al-Taghābun):* 17; and 73 *(al-Muzammil):* 20: supporting the Prophet's cause is likened to making a loan to Allāh.

122. Al-Wāqidī, *al-Maghāzī,* 39. The information in this passage is expanded and annotated by Lammens, "La Mecque," 282 [186]–285 [189].

123. Aḥmad ibn Yaḥyā al-Balādhurī (d. 892), *Kitāb Futūḥ al-Buldān,* ed. M. J. de Goeje under the title *Liber Expagnationis Regionum . . .* (Lugduni Batavorum, 1906); trans. under the title *The Origins of the Islamic State* by Philip K. Hitti, pt. 1 and F. C. Murgotten, pt. 2, Columbia University Studies in History, Economics and Public Law, vol. 68 (New York, 1916, 1924), passim. All subsequent references are to the de Goeje edition unless otherwise indicated.

124. This alleged evidence of a monetary economy in Makkah at the time of the Prophet was collected by Eric R. Wolf from the works of such authors as al-Balādhurī, Ibn Hishām, al-Wāqidī, Muḥammad ibn Ismāʿīl al-Bukhārī (810–70) (*al-Jāmiʿ al-Ṣaḥīḥ* [Būlāq, 1878]), and from the *Mufaḍḍalīyāt.* See "The social organization of Mecca and the origins of Islam," *Southwestern Journal of Anthropology* 7, no. 4 (1951): 334.

125. Wüstenfeld, *Geschichte der Stadt Mekka,* 36.

126. Al-Mufaḍḍal al-Ḍabbī, *al-Mufaḍḍalīyāt,* Lyall's translation, 2:308; Arabic text, 1:721. *Qad thāba* in the text may be rendered colloquially as "is up again": cf. Lyall, "has risen in the market." The original meaning of *thāba* is "it returned," and the word was often used in connection with the recovery of a well that had been drained. The poet in question was Ḥājib ibn Ḥabīb of the tribe of Asad.

127. Al-Wāqidī, *al-Maghāzī,* ed. Marsden Jones, 3 vols. (Oxford, 1966), 340; all subsequent references are to the Jones edition unless otherwise indicated.

128. Caetani, *Annali,* 1:73 *et seq.*

129. Francesco Gabrieli, Geschichte der Araber (Stuttgart, 1963), 20.

130. A. J. Wensinck, *The Encyclopaedia of Islam,* 1st ed., 514 et seq.

131. Lammens, "La Mecque," 148 [52].

132. Harris Birkeland, *The Lord Guideth. Studies on Primitive Islam* (Oslo, 1956), 123.

133. Kister, "Mecca and Tamīm," 121.

134. W. Montgomery Watt, *Muhammad at Mecca* (Oxford, 1953), 13. An approach broadly similar to that of Watt characterizes the works of F. E. Peters, "The Commerce of Mecca before Islam," in *A Way Prepared. Essays on Islamic Culture in Honor of Richard Bayly Winder,* ed. Farhad Kazemi and R. D. McChesney (New York, 1988), 3–26 and Mahmood Ibrahim, *Merchant Capital and Islam* (Austin, Tex., 1990), chaps. 1–4.

135. Eric R. Wolf, "The social organization of Mecca," 329–56.

136. Entirely representative of such interpretations are Aḥmad Shalabī, *al-Taʾrīkh al-Islamī wa-l-Ḥaḍārah al-Islāmīyah* (al-Qāhirah, A.H. 1378/A.D. 1959), 54 and ʿAlī Ibrāhīm Ḥasan, al-Taʾrīkh al-Islāmī al-ʿāmm (al-Qāhirah, A.H. 1383/A.D. 1963), 101.

137. Probably the most authentic record of these commercial arrangements is that provided by Muḥammad ibn Saʿd (d. 845), *Kitāb al-Ṭabaqāt al-Kabīr,* 9 vols., Eduard Sachau et al. (Leyden and Berlin, 1904–40), vol. 1, pt. 1, p. 45. The tradition is reported on the authority of ʿAbd Allāh ibn Nawfal ibn al-Ḥārith. Cf. also al-Qālī (d. 967), *Dhayl al-Amālī, wa-l-Nawadir,* 3 vols. (Bayrūt, A.H. 1384/A.D. 1964), 3:199 et seq. Other references are cited in Kister, "Mecca and Tamīm," passim. Ibn Saʿd denotes the treaties with the alleged rulers of neighboring powers by the term *ḥilf,* al-Qālī by *ʿahd* or *amām,* al-Balādhurī by *ʿiṣmah,* and al-Ṭabarī by *ʿiṣmah* and *ḥabl.*

138. For example, int. al., al-Yaʿqūbī, *Taʾrīkh,* in *Historiae,* ed. M. Th. Houtsma, 2 vols. (Leiden, 1883), 1:280–82; al-Ṭabarī, *Taʾrīkh,* 3:1089; Ibn Ḥabīb, *al-Muḥabbar,* 162, *Kitāb al-Munammaq,* cited from an unpublished Lucknow manuscript by Muḥammad Ḥamīdullāh, and "Al-īlāf ou les rapports économico-diplomatiques de la Mecque préislamique," in *Mélanges Louis Massignon* (Damas, 1957), 299–300, 309–10 (see below); Ibn Saʿd, *al-Ṭabaqāt,* vol. 1, pt. 1, 43–46; al-Balādhurī, *Al-ashrāf,* 1:59, section Hāshim; al-Masʿūdī, *Murūj,* 3:121–22; and al-Zamakhsharī, *al-Fāʾiq,* ed. Muḥammad Abū al-Faḍl Ibrahīm-Bijāwī, 1:40. Summarized in Kister, "Mecca and Tamīm," passim but especially 116–21. See also (though with caution because it accepts as fact much legendary material) Muḥammad Ḥamīdullāh, "Al-īlāf," 2:292–311.

139. The most incisive analysis of sources bearing on the institutional character of the *īlāf* is Robert Simon's "Ḥums et īlāf, ou commerce sans guerre (sur la genèse et le caractère du commerce de La Mecque)," *Acta Orientalia Academiae Scientiarum Hungaricae* 23 (1970): 205–32, but there is much useful material in Kister, "Mecca and Tamīm," especially pp. 116–21. Cf. also Birkeland's examination of lexical explications of the word *īlāf* in *The Lord Guideth,* 106–7, and note 161 below.

How closely *ʾilf/ilāf/īlāf* was associated with the Quraysh is attested by some verses of Musāwir ibn Hind ibn Qays that were incorporated in Abu Tammām's *Dīwān al-Ḥamāsah* (al-Qāhirah, A.H. 1325), 178: "You [the Banū-Asad] consider yourselves to be the equals of the Quraysh; [but you are not] for they have *ʾilf* and you have not an *ʾilāf.*" Although the quantity of the first syllable in each of these two words is metrically attested, it is difficult to see why both forms should occur in the same poem. However, that they denoted the same covenant granting security to Quraysh traders is not in doubt.

It is only fair to note that at least one contemporary scholar is more than half inclined to regard the traditions purporting to define the *īlāf* as "no more than the blossoming of one particular line of speculation to which an obscure Koranic verse has given rise" (Michael Cook, *Muhammad* [Oxford, 1983], 72). Cf. Crone, *Meccan Trade,* passim but especially chap. 5.

140. This point was first made by Lammens, "La république marchande," 26 et seq.

141. Simon, "Ḥums et īlāf," 220–29. The best overview of political relations in the Middle East during the centuries immediately preceding the rise of Islam is N. V. Pigulevskaja, *Araby u granic Vizantii i Irana v IV–VI vv* (Moscow and Leningrad, 1964). There is also a great deal of useful material in Smith, "Events in Arabia," 425–68.

142. Al-Balādhurī, *Ansāb al-Ashrāf,* vol. 11 ed. W. Ahlwardt (Greifswald, 1883); vol. 5 by S. D. F. Goitein (Jerusalem, 1936), vol. 1 by Muḥammad Ḥamīdullāh (al-Qāhirah, 1959), and vol. 4A by Max Schloessinger and M. J. Kister (Jerusalem, 1971). The relevant passage is here quoted by Kister from MS. fol. 811a in "The campaign of Ḥulubān: a new light on the expedition of Abraha," *Le Muséon* 78 (1965): 429–32. Cf. Ḥamīdullāh, "Al-īlāf," 302 (although Kister points out [p. 432] that this author misinterprets an important phrase in the text).

143. Simon, "Ḥums et īlāf," 223.

144. Ibid. and 229–30. Al-Ḥilf al-Fuḍūl is usually rendered into English as "The Confederation of the Virtuous," but this would appear to be a rationalization by later traditionists. Several versions exist of the *raison d'être* of this institution, but most involve a refusal by a Makkan (usually a Sahmī) to honor a debt to a Yamanī merchant: for example, al-Isfahānī, *al-Aghānī* 17:210; al-Masʿūdī, *Murūj,* 4:123; and Maḥmud Alūsī-Zada, *Bulūgh al-ʿArab fī Maʿrifat Aḥwāl al-ʿArab,* 2 vols. (al-Qāhirah, A.H. 1341/A.D.1923–24), 1:275. Ibn Isḥāq (*Sīrah,* 2:85–86; Guillaume's translation, 57) and al-Yaʿqūbī (*Taʾrīkh,* 2:16) were among those who offered different accounts of the origins of the Fuḍūl. Among modern scholars, Caetani considered, unrealistically enough by Jāhilī standards, the Ḥilf al-Fuḍūl to be a league against injustice (*Annali,* 1: 164–66). Watt is nearer the truth by characterizing it as an alliance formed by the less prosperous clans in Makkah for the purpose of claiming a share in the Yaman trade (*Muhammad at Mecca,* 15). But whatever the precise circumstances of its formation may have been, Simon is probably correct when he writes that "l'événement en question [the formation of the Ḥilf al-Fuḍūl] constitua pour ainsi dire le dernier acte d'un processus plus long, au cours duquel les Quraiš éliminèrent définitivement les marchands du Yemen du commerce de la route de l'encens" ("Ḥums et īlāf," 222). Participants in the alliance included the clans of Hāshim, al-Muṭṭalib, Asad, Zuhrah, Taym, and probably al-Ḥārith ibn Fihr (Ibn Isḥāq, *Sīrah,* 2:86; Guillaume's translation, 57–58), and Watt may be correct in viewing it as a development of an earlier faction within the Quraysh al-Baṭāʾih, known as al-Muṭayyabūn, "The Perfumed Ones." For the origin of this name see Ibn Isḥāq, *Sīrah,* 2:85; Guillaume's translation, 56–57.

145. Simon "Ḥums et īlāf," 224–25. The story of al-Ḥuwayrith is related by, int. al., al-Musʿab al-Zubayrī, *Nasab Quraysh,* ed. E. Lévy-Provençal (al-Qāhirah, 1953), 209 and al-Fāsī in *Die Chroniken der Stadt Mekka,* ed. Ferdinand Wüstenfeld (Leipzig, 1859), 2:143. The events in question are summarized by Lammens, "La Mecque," 367[271]–375[279] and Watt, *Muhammad at Mecca,* 15–16. Cf. also Maxime Rodinson, *Mahomet,* 2d ed. (Paris, 1968); English translation by Anne Carter (New York, 1971), 108.

146. *Ḥarb* (or *Ayyām*) *al-Fijār,* "War (or Days) of Transgression," so called because they fell within the sacred months when raiding was prohibited for tribes within the Makkan confederacy. Simon ("Ḥums et īlāf," 227 n. 75) draws attention to the fact that even as late as the last decade of the sixth century Lakhmid caravans from al-Ḥīrah came regularly to the fairs at ʿUkāz: cf. al-Yaʿqūbī, *Taʾrīkh,* 2:14; Ibn Saʿd, *al-Ṭahaqāt,* vol. 1, pt. 1, p. 80; and al-Iṣfahānī, *al-Aghānī,* 22:64. An additional advantage accruing to the Quraysh as a result of the Ḥarb al-Fijār was assumption of authority over the fair at ʿUkāẓ, which had previously been a prerogative of the Hawāzin—at least according to al-Azraqī (*Akhbār Makkah,* 1:124), an authority followed in recent times by Simon ("Ḥums et īlāf," 215). However, al-Marzūqī (*al-Azminah wa-l-Amkinah,* 2: 167) assigned control of the fair to the Banū-Tamīm. Kister apparently assumes that the Tamīm were accorded that privilege at Qurashī discretion, for he writes, "Tamīm was invested with the *ifāḍah* [the so-called dispersing to Muzdalifah during the *Ḥajj*] in Mecca itself and with the control of the fair at ʿUkāẓ" ("Mecca and Tamīm," 146).

147. Al-Iṣfahānī, *al-Aghānī,* 13:207. In 17:283 it is implied that the Lakhmid ruler al-Nuʿman Abū-Qābūs had granted control over the caravan route to al-Ḥīrah, and therefore its profits, to the *shaykh*s of the Banū-Ṭayyiʾ.

148. See, for example, George F. Hourani, *Arab Seafaring in the Indian Ocean in Ancient and Early Medieval Times,* Princeton Oriental Studies no. 13 (Princeton, N.J., 1951), 5; Smith, "Events in Arabia in the 6th century A.D.," 429; and Simon, "Ḥums et īlāf," 223–24.

149. Simon, "Ḥums et īlāf," 228–29. For the elaboration of certain details in this interpretation see Simon, "L'inscription Ry 506 et la préhistoire de La Mecque," *Acta Orientalia Academiae Scientiarum Hungaricae* 20 (1967): 325–37.

150. All the relevant sources imply the close association of pilgrimages and fairs, so it is not altogether surprising that Qurʾān 2 *(al-Baqarah):*198 should have allowed Muslims to "seek bounty from your Lord" (i.e., to trade) during the pilgrimage. This is only

one of the many occasions on which Allāh conferred His imprimatur on a custom of pre-Muslim Arabia. Cf. also al-Azraqī, *Akhbār Makkah,* 1:121.

151. Al-Qālī (*al-Amālī,* 3:199), who, though referring to the time of Hāshim, Muḥammad's great-grandfather, was probably drawing his information from a much later stratum of evidence.

152. Abū Manṣūr ʿAbd al-Malik ibn Muḥammad al-Thaʿālibī, *Thimār al-Qulūb fī al-Muḍāf wa-l-Mansūb* (al-Qāhirah, A.H. 1326/A.D. 1908), 89, quoted in Kister, "Mecca and Tamīm," 118 and Simon, "Ḥums et īlāf," 216.

153. Al-Azraqī, *Akhbār Makkah,* 474; al-Fākihī, *Taʾrīkh Makkah,* MS Leiden, Or. 463, fol. 461v, both quoted in Kister, "Some reports concerning Mecca," 77.

154. Simon, "Ḥums et īlāf," 215, citing al-Marzūqī, *al-Azminah wa-l-Amkinah,* 2:166; Kister, "Mecca and Tamīm," 156, relying on the same source.

I have resorted to the term *fair* in discussing these types of transactions even though the word used in the texts, *al-sūq,* is customarily translated as "market." Not only is *fair* widely sanctioned in the relevant European literature, but it also denotes with reasonable accuracy the type of exchanges that occurred at these annual assemblies. In European writings on modes of exchange the term *fair* is customarily reserved for relatively large, organized gatherings, at more or less regularly spaced intervals of time, of merchants coming from some distance, whereas *market* denotes local retailers (in the broadest sense) selling to local folk either daily or at specified, short intervals. At a fair, merchants sell to merchants (which is what seems to have been happening a good deal of the time at ʿUkāẓ et al.); in a market, retailers sell to consumers. See *La Foire,* vol. 5 of *Recueils de la Société Jean Bodin* (Bruxelles, 1957), passim.

For a Talmudic parallel to the literary treatment of the Abrahah story that goes a long way toward confirming the archetyped character of its framework, see Gordon D. Newby, "Abraha and Sennacherib: a Talmudic parallel to the *tafsīr* on *Sūrat al-Fīl,*" *Journal of the American Oriental Society* 94, no. 4 (1974): 431–37.

155. Ibn Isḥāq, *Sīrah,* 1:33–34; Guillaume's translation, 25; al-Ṭabarī, *Taʾrīkh,* 1:98; and al-Masʿūdī, *Murūj,* 3:260. The whole tale of ʿAbd al-Muṭṭalib sitting on a carpet beside Abrahah and stubbornly demanding the return of his camels is reminiscent of Wilfred Thesiger's vignette of an audience before *Shaykh* Zayīd ibn Sulṭān at Muwayqih, one of the small settlements making up the Buraymī oasis, in 1949:

> Perhaps an Arab would get up from the circle, sit down immediately in front of Zayīd, hit the ground a wallop with his stick and attract attention, and interrupting us as we spoke together, would say: "Now Zayīd, what about those camels which were taken from me?" Zayīd, who might be in the middle of a sentence, would stop and listen to the man's complaint. Most of the complaints were about camels" (*Arabian Sands* [London, 1959; Penguin edition, Harmondsworth, Middlesex, England, 1964], 270).

156. Cf. the numerous accounts of raiding and retribution in this century among the tribes of the Ḥaḍramawt and ʿUmān that are related in Thesiger's *Arabian Sands.* Elsewhere, writing of the *badawī*'s concern for his camels, Thesiger recalls: "Some years ago, when we arrived in the Hadhramaut out of the desert, I remember the enormous meals which were provided for us, such as my always hungry companions cannot even have dreamed of; yet next day they were frantic to get back to the desert where there would be proper grazing for their animals" ("The badu of southern Arabia," 57).

157. Dated by Simon, "L'inscription RY 506," 334.

158. Lammens, "La Mecque," passim but especially 12–32. In his *Taʾrīkh Makkah* (MS Leiden, Or. 463, fol. 458a), al-Fākihī notes that Abyssinians dwelt in the Dar al-ʿUlūj in the quarter of the Banū-Makhzūm (quoted in Kister, "Some reports concerning Mecca," 73).

159. W. Montgomery Watt, *Islamic Political Thought. The Basic Concepts* (Edinburgh, 1968), 3.

160. Qurʾān 16 *(al-Naḥl):* 112.

161. This *sūrah,* although short, presents several difficult lexical and exegetical problems, not the least of which is the opening phrase *li-ʾīlāfi Qurayshin ʾīlāfihim.* There is a discussion of this passage in Lane's *Arabic-English Lexicon,* p. 79, cols. b and c, but the most thorough lexical investigation is that by Birkeland, *The Lord Guideth,* 102–30. This author has established that the precanonical reading *li-yaʾlafa (li-yālafa) Qurayshun ʾilfahum* was abandoned by about 800 at latest in favor of the version cited above, which became the *textus receptus* followed by all of the canonical Seven Readings except that of the Damascene Ibn ʿĀmir. It is now the reading of the official Cairene edition of the Qurʾān (See note 176 below), which preserves the supposed ʿUthmānic text with the Kūfan reading of Ḥafṣ *an* ʿĀṣim. Birkeland has also demonstrated that early lexicographers construed the term *īlāf* (together with the variant readings *ʾilāf* and *ʾilf,* which have been adopted by some exegetes) in its Qurʾānic association with the Quraysh as signifying "protection" or the like, as opposed to the more usual rendering of "a uniting" or "a bringing together" (*The Lord Guideth,* 106–8), even though that meaning is not advanced by either al-Ṭabarī or later commentators (with the exception of al-Ālūsī and Abū Ḥayyān, this last being added to Birkeland's analysis by Kister, "Mecca and Tamīm," 120).

In Birkeland's view, the revealed reading was rejected by commentators at an early date because the recitation of a *sūrah* associating protection of Qurashī caravans with the Lord of the Kaʿbah would have been egregiously inappropriate in al-Madīnah at a time when Muḥammad's followers were raiding those very caravans (108). The last two lines of the *Sūrah* are customarily held to have referred respectively to the special functions of commerce in the arid neighborhood of Makkah where agriculture was impracticable and to the beneficial effect of the prohibition of hostilities within the *ḥaram.* That the "journeys" referred to in *Sūrah* 106 were those of caravans to the south and north respectively is the conventionally accepted view, but there has been occasional dissent. Fakhraddīn al-Rāzī, for instance, suggested as an alternative (though less likely) interpretation that the *riḥlas* might be referring to the Greater and Lesser Pilgrimages to Makkah, which were occasions of intensified trading activity; on the other hand, a Persian tradition represented by Saʿīd ibn Jubayr ibn ʿAbbās asserts that the passage is alluding to the Qurashī oligarchs' supposed practice of wintering in Makkah and summering in al-Ṭāʾif. For a total rejection of the idea of Qurashī winter and summer caravans see Crone, *Meccan Trade,* 204–13.

162. Wüstenfeld, *Geschichte der Stadt Mekka,* passim but especially 58–75. The Quraysh al-Baṭāʾiḥ (al-Biṭaḥ) were held to have comprised essentially all the descendants of Quṣayy's great-grandfather Kaʿb, sometimes with the addition of al-Ḥārith ibn Fihr and ʿĀmir.

163. Specifically by commingling of blood and by an oath sworn in the Kaʿbah: Smith, *Kinship and Marriage in Early Arabia,* 50–51. In *al-Mufaḍḍalīyat,* a Jāhilī poet by the name of al-Ḥusayn ibn al-Ḥumām refers to a client bound to a tribe by a ritual kinship arrangement as a "cousin knit to us by oath": Lyall edition, Arabic text in 1:101; English translation, 2:35. Cf. Goldziher, *Muhammedanische Studien,* 1:105: "cousins by oath" contrasted with "cousins by birth." It has often been asserted that many of Muḥammad's earliest converts came from among the clients and slaves of Makkah: e.g., Caetani, *Annali,* 1:240; Procksch, *Über die Blutrache,* 81–82; and Hitti, *History of the Arabs,* 113. But note W. Montgomery Watt's insistence that these earlier converts often being "cousins by oath" does not imply that they necessarily, or even probably, came from humble social strata. See *Muhammad at Mecca,* 86–99; *Muhammad, Prophet and Statesman* (Oxford, 1961), 37; and *Islam and the Integration of Society,* 12–13.

164. Wolf, "The social organization of Mecca," 335.

165. Joseph Hell, *Neue Huḍailiten-Diwane* (Leipzig, 1933), 1:10.

166. Cited by Lammens, *Les Chrétiens à la Mecque,* 145.

167. Wellhausen, *Skizzen und Vorarbeiten,* 3:190.

168. See Wolf, "The social organization of Mecca," 340–44.

169. Olinder, *The Kings of Kinda,* 81.

170. Gustav Rothstein, *Die Dynastie der Laḫmiden in al-Ḥîra,* 136–37. Not generally accepted is Lammens's belief that this guard, supposedly used primarily for the protection of caravans, was composed of foreign mercenaries under the command of Kinānah cadres, tribesmen who were genealogical (though not necessarily biological) kinsmen of the Makkan oligarchs (Lammens, *Les Chrétiens à La Mecque,* 244–83).

171. Cf. G. E. von Grünebaum, *Islam. Essays in the Nature and Growth of a Cultural Tradition,* 2d ed. (London, 1961), 31, 142–43.

172. Qurʾān 96 *(al-ʿAlaq):*1–5.

173. Qurʾān 51 *(al-Dhāriyāt):*50–51, 67 *(al-Mulk):*26, and 74 *(al-Mudaththir):*1–7. The literature dealing with the life of Muḥammad is enormous, but all attempts to construct a biography of the Prophet must base themselves ultimately on allusions in the Qurʾān; on narrative accounts in the Traditions *(aḥādīth,* sing. *ḥadīth)* as preserved by al-Ṭabarī (d. 922), al-Wāqidī (d. 822), Ibn Saʿd (d. 845), al-Bukhārī (810–70), Muslim ibn al-Ḥajjāj (d. 875), and others; and on information in the *sīrahs,* that is, the biographies compiled by Islamic historians from the eighth century onward. Especially important is the earliest extant biography, the *Sīrat Sayyidinā Muḥammad Rasūlīʾllah* by Muḥammad ibn Isḥāq (d. 768). Despite severe criticisms of the trustworthiness of many of the traditions and poems included in this book, in the recension of the traditionist ʿAbd al-Malik ibn Hishām (died ca. 833) it became and has remained the principal authority for the life of Muḥammad. It has been edited by Ferdinand Wüstenfeld, *Das Leben Muhammeds nach Muhammed ibn Ishâk, bearbeitet von ʿAbd al-Malik ibn Hischâm,* 2 vols. (Göttingen, 1858–60) and by Muṣṭafā al-Saqqā, Ibrāhīm al-Abyarī, and ʿAbd al-Ḥafīẓ Shalabī (Qāhirah, A.H. 1355/A.D. 1937). This latter edition has been translated into English by Alfred Guillaume under the title *The Life of Mohammad* (Oxford, 1955). On Ibn Isḥāq see J. Fück, *Muḥammad ibn Isḥāq* (Frankfurt-am-Main, 1925). There is a succinct evaluation of the *Sīrah* literature, of which Ibn Isḥāq's biography is a selective summary, in M. J. Kister, "The Sīrah Literature," in *Arabic Literature to the End of the Umayyad Period,* ed. A. F. L. Beeston et al. (Cambridge, 1983), 352–67.

Muḥammad Maher Ḥamadeh, in an unpublished doctoral dissertation submitted to the University of Michigan, has listed more than fifteen hundred works dealing explicitly with the life of the Prophet ("Muhammad the Prophet: a Selected Bibliography" [Ann Arbor, 1965]), and the number of those in which the topic is treated incidentally must be at least three or four times as large. Among those produced by Western writers, James E. Royster has distinguished two dominant methodologies, which he terms the normative and the descriptive ("A study of Muḥammad: a survey of approaches from the perspective of the history and phenomenology of religion," *The Muslim World* 82 (1972): 49–70). The former, which evaluates Muḥammad's conduct in terms of a norm external to the available data, found its most extreme representations in the nineteenth and early twentieth centuries, archetypically in Washington Irving's *Mahomet and His Successors* (New York, 1849), a wholly representative paragraph of which ends with the sentiment that Muḥammad "died in the delusive belief of his mission as a prophet" (197). Another example in the same vein is Sprenger's *Das Leben und die Lehre des Mohammed.*

The descriptive (or empirical) methodology, insofar as it focuses on observable features of Muḥammad's life while eschewing the invocation of norms external to the Islamic tradition, represents the penetration of a positivistic point of view into the field of biography. It can involve one or more of the following approaches:

- ***the historicist,*** to portray Muḥammad "as he really was": R. V. C. Bodley, *The Messenger: The Life of Mohammed* (Garden City, N.Y., 1946), 8; also Emile Dermenghem, *Mohamet,* 2d ed. (Paris, 1950) which, while yielding a good deal of certitude, denies significance to all that cannot be "proved" (in terms of supposedly reputable traditions) to have happened;

- ***the reductionist,*** whether naturalistic, which seeks to explain, or explain away, religious phenomena such as miracles in terms of natural happenings; psychological, which casts religious manifestations in psychic categories; cultural, or functionalist, which attempts to elicit Muḥammad's significance in the context of his time; or exordial, which is primarily concerned with uncovering origins, sources, and influences; and
- ***the phenomenological,*** which endeavors to depict Muḥammad as understood by Muslims. Biographies by Westerners meeting this last criterion are rare. Perhaps the closest approach, although one occasionally lapsing into a normative ideology, is the portrait that emerges from Watt's cumulative researches: *Muhammad at Mecca; Muhammad at Medina,* but note R. B. Serjeant's critical comments on these works in "Professor A. Guillaume's translation of the Sīrah," *Bulletin of the School of Oriental and African Studies,* 21 (1958): 187–88; and *Muhammad, Prophet and Statesman.*

Other accounts of the Prophet's life that incorporate varying combinations of the above approaches include D. S. Margoliouth, *Mohammed* (London, 1939); Frants (P. W.) Buhl, *Muhammeds Livs* (n.p., 1903), German translation by Hans Heinrich Schaeder under the title *Das Leben Muhammeds* (Leipzig, 1930); Tor Andrae, *Mohammed, sein Leben und sein Glaube* (Göttingen, 1932); Blachère, *Le problème de Mahomet;* Muḥammad Ḥamīdullāh, *Le Prophète de l'Islam: sa Vie, son Oeuvre,* 2 vols. (Paris, 1959); Sir William Muir, *The Life of Mohamet; with Introductory Chapters on the Original Sources . . . ,* 4 vols. (London, 1858–61; rev. abridged ed., Edinburgh, 1923); Gaudefroy-Demombynes, *Mahomet;* Rodinson, *Mahomet,* 2d ed. (Paris, 1968); Rudi Paret, *Mohammed und der Koran: Geschichte und Verkündigung des arabischen Propheten,* 2d ed. (Stuttgart, 1966); and Antoine Wessels, *A Modern Arabic Biography of Muḥammad: A Critical Study of Muḥammad Ḥusayn Haykal's 'Ḥayāt Muḥammad'* (Leiden, 1972)—Haykal's book was first published in 1935; 10th ed., 1969. The most recent, as well as the most unorthodox (though by no means unsympathetic), interpretation of Muḥammad's achievement is contained in Cook's *Muhammad.*

174. This is how D. Z. H. Baneth interprets the signification of the term *islām* at the time of Muḥammad ("What did Muḥammad mean when he called his religion 'Islam'? The original meaning of aslama and its derivatives," *Israel Oriental Studies* 1 [1971]: 183–90). Basing his interpretation on Helmer Ringgren's analysis of the occurrence of the Arabic root *SLM* in the Qur'ān, in the *Ḥadīth,* and in the poetry of the *Jāhilīyah* (*Islam, Aslama and Muslim,* Horae Soederblomianae no. 2 [Uppsala, 1949]), Baneth has shown that its semantic emphasis inhered in the idea of "belonging to one only," of "being the exclusive property of one [in this case Allāh]." The more usual rendering (as espoused by, int. al., Andrae, Ahrens, Gibb, Goldziher, Grimme, von Grünebaum, Horovitz, Jeffery, Lewis, Nöldeke, Pautz, Torrey, and Watt) of "submission [or 'surrender' or 'resignation'] to the will [of Allāh]," which is apparently adopted from certain medieval Arabic dictionaries and Qur'ānic commentaries (e.g., al-Ghazzālī, *Iḥyā'; *al-Bayḍāwī, *Anwār*), was substituted for the earlier reading at a later date when polytheism was no longer a threat to the Islamic faith. For critiques of earlier, and now mostly unacceptable, explanations of the term by Margoliouth, Lidzbarski, Künstlinger, and Bravmann, see Ringgren, *Islam,* passim; and for a recent explication of the term as a "Samaritan calque," Crone and Cook, *Hagarism,* 19–20.

175. For the Qur'ānic emphasis on the need for rescue rather than salvation see von Grünebaum, *Islam. Essays in the Nature and Growth of a Cultural Tradition,* 2–3.

176. Muslim knowledge of the Islamic past was transmitted orally for about a century and a half (notwithstanding Fuat Sezgin's argument that the Tradition was cast in written form from the time of Muḥammad (*Geschichte des arabischen Schrifttums,* vol. 1 [Leiden, 1967], 53ff. and 237ff.). Few Western scholars now accept the Tradition according to which a comprehensive collection of Muḥammad's revelations was assembled from "pieces of papyrus, flat stones, palm-fronds, animal scapulae and ribs, fragments of leather and wooden boards, as well as from the hearts of men" during the caliphate of Abū Bakr (632–34); see, int. al., al-Khaṭīb al-Tibrīzī, *Mishkāt al-Maṣābīh,* 10 vols. (St. Petersburg, 1898), 1:343, but there is less reason to dissent from the received belief that whatever had been preserved of the Prophet's utterances was consolidated into a standard lectionary *(al-Qur'ān)* at the instigation of the caliph 'Uthmān (644–56). It should be noted, though, that there is no confirmatory evidence for the existence of any version of the Qur'ān prior to the last decade of the seventh century, while the Tradition relating these matters is not attested before the mid-eighth century.

Copies of the new recension allegedly were dispatched to the main centers of the faith and previous partial collections ordered to be destroyed, with the result that the text has remained inviolate from that day to this. It takes the form of 114 sections called *suwar* (sing. *sūrah*) arranged, apart from an initial brief prayer, roughly in order of decreasing length, but there is a large measure of agreement among both Muslim and secular scholars as to the chronological sequence of their revelation. The *sūrah*s are divided into verses termed *āyāt* (sing. *āyah*), which have not been imposed on the text (as the verse divisions of the Christian Bible often have) but are integral to the original form of the revelations.

For Muslims this text is the word of God revealed to His Messenger Muḥammad through the intermediacy of the angel Jibrīl. Except in the opening prayer and in a few other passages put into the mouth of Muḥammad or of the angel, the speaker throughout is God. Consequently, for Muslims there can be no question of a changing literary style or of a developing doctrine. Such matters are, and can be, a concern only of secular research. Among Western scholars the most widely used edition of the Arabic text has been that prepared by Gustav Flügel (*Corani Textus Arabicus* [Leipzig, 1834, with numerous subsequent editions]), even though it is based on an inferior text and the verse numbers differ from those of the standard Egyptian edition, *Al-Muṣḥaf al-Sharīf* or *Al-Qur'ān al-Karīm,* which was authorized by King Fu'ād I of Egypt in A.H. 1344/A.D. 1924.

As the Qur'ān was directly dictated by God into His chosen language, Arabic, no translation can officially be anything more than a commentary prepared for teaching purposes. However, an authorized translation into Turkish has been permitted, and a number of unauthorized interlinear, free translations into foreign languages exist. And, of course, European scholars have prepared their own translations from the twelfth century when Peter the Veneragle, ninth abbot of Cluny, sponsored a Latin version by Robert of Ketton (Robertus Ketenensis) which circulated in manuscript for some four centuries before being published at Basel in 1543 under the editorship of Thomas Bibliander (Buchmann). In 1647 André du Ryer, "Sieur de la Garde Malezair," published a French translation that two years later was rendered into English by Alexander Ross under the title *The Alcoran of Mahomet . . . newly* Englished, *for the satisfaction of all that desire to look into the* Turkish *vanities . . .* (In an edition of 1688 the title was extended to include *with a needful caveat or admonition, for them who desire to know what use may be made of, or if there be danger in reading the* ALCORAN) (Randal Taylor, London). The early English translation that has best withstood the test of time is George Sale's *The Korân* (London, 1734). Based on the readings of Muslim commentators, especially al-Bayḍāwī, it remained the standard English translation for a century and a half and was justifiably incorporated in the *Wisdom of the East* series. Not the least of its virtues was that it explicated the Qur'ānic text according to traditional Sunnī interpretations while yet discriminating carefully between text and exegesis.

By common consent, the most successful translation of the Qur'ān into a European language—if success be defined as an accurate rendering of the text as understood by a seventh-century Ḥijāzī—is that by Rudi Paret: *Der Koran: Übersetzung von Rudi Paret,* 2 vols. (Stuttgart, 1962), which is intended to be used with the same author's *Der Koran: Kommentär und Konkordanz* (Stuttgart, 1971), a truly indispensable aid to Qur'ānic study. Second only to Paret's translation in my estimation is Richard Bell's *The Qur'ân Translated,* 2 vols. (Edinburgh, 1937, 1939), which incorporates an attempt to reconstruct the history of the text. Cf. also Bell's *Introduction to the Qur'ân* as revised and enlarged by W. Montgomery Watt (Edinburgh, 1970). A. J. Arberry's *The Koran interpreted,* 2 vols. (London, 1955) is a *tour de force* in its imitations of "the rhetorical and rhythmical patterns which are the glory and the sublimity of the Koran." Mohammed Marmaduke Pickthall's *The Meaning of the Glorious Koran: An Explanatory Translation* (London, 1930; Arabic and English edition, New York, 1970) most of the time is a knowledgeable rendering of a traditional Muslim interpretation rather than a literal translation. Its author was an Englishman who converted to Islam. N. J. Dawood's *The Koran* (Harmondsworth, Middlesex, 1956; 4th rev. ed., 1978) is a readable but overly free translation by an 'Irāqī. The standard French version of the *Qur'ān* is Régis Blachère, *Le Coran: Traduction selon un Essai de Reclassement des Sourates,* 3 vols. (Paris, 1947–51; 2d ed., 1966; reprint, 1973), and the standard French introduction is the same author's *Introduction au Coran,* 2d ed. (Paris, 1959). Together these volumes provide an accurate and judicious presentation of the sacred text. 'Abdullāh Yūsuf 'Alī's *The Holy Qur'ân: an Interpretation in English, with the Original Arabic Text in Parallel Columns . . .* (Lahore, 1934) is reliable but occasionally allows later theological views to influence the translation. Muhammad Zafrulla Khān's *The Quran. The Eternal Revelation Vouchsafed to Muhammad, the Seal of the Prophets,* 2d rev. ed. (London and New York, 1975) tends to paraphrase rather than translate, and follows an Indian-Pakistani system of verse numbering in which the introductory *bismillāh* is counted as the first verse. Pīr Ṣalāḥud-Dīn's *The Wonderful Koran: A New English Translation* (Eminabad, n.d.) employs the same numbering system but incorporates valuable extracts from classical commentaries whenever the text is ambiguous or unclear. Hashim Amir-Ali's *The Message of the Qur'an* (Rutland, Vt., and Tokyo, 1974), is also predominantly paraphrastic, what the author calls "a perspective presentation." There is a comprehensive bibliography of translations of the Qur'ān into European languages by J. D. Pearson in Beeston et al., eds., *Arabic Literature,* 502–20.

No discussion of the Qur'ānic text can omit to mention the foundation of all modern studies of it, namely Theodor Nöldeke's *Geschichte des Qorāns,* an enlarged version of a prizewinning work first published at Göttingen in 1860. The preparation of a second edition, which involved three new authors, Friedrich Schwally, Gotthelf Bergsträsser, and Otto Pretzl, took forty years, being first suggested in 1898 (3 vols., Leipzig, 1909–38). Gustav Flügel's *Corcordantiae Corani Arabicae* (Leipzig, 1842) was intended as a concordance to his edition of the Qur'ān and is now rather badly dated. Ignaz Goldziher's *Die Richtungen der islamischen Koranauslegung* (Leiden, 1920, 1952) is a classic of its kind but now needs to be supplemented with more contemporary works such as J. M. S. Baljon, *Modern Muslim Interpretation (1880–1960)* (Leiden, 1961) and J. J. G. Jansen, *The Interpretation of the Koran in Modern Egypt* (Leiden, 1974). Josef Horowitz's *Koranische Untersuchungen* (Berlin and Leipzig, 1926) is still a basic resource for any study of the technical terms and fundamental concepts of the Qur'ān. See also Birkeland, *The Lord Guideth* and Jacques Jomier, *Le Commentaire Coranique du Manâr: Tendances Modernes de l'Exégèse Coranique en Egypte* (Paris, 1954).

A recent sophisticated attempt to reconstruct the correct *(richtig)* or original *(ursprüngliche)* verse divisions of the Qur'ān is Angelika Neuwirth, *Studien zur Komposition der mekkanischen Suren,* Studien zur Sprache, Geschichte, und Kultur des islamischen Orients, n.s., vol. 10 (Berlin, 1981). Some of Dr. Neuwirth's conclusions are controversial, especially her claim that the Makkan *sūrahs* comprise groups of verses arranged in numerical patterns, often in balanced proportions. In fact critical opinion on the chronology, composition, and history of the Qur'ān is still very much divided. Representative of a skeptical approach to the historicity of the

Qur'ān and the Islamic tradition that has gained ground in recent years is John Wansbrough, *Quranic Studies: Sources and Methods of Scriptural Interpretation* (Oxford, 1977) and *The Sectarian Milieu: Content and Composition of Islamic Salvation History* (London, 1978). There is implicit in Dr. Wansbrough's exegeses the conclusion that the Qur'ān is a relatively late and imperfect redaction of materials drawn from a plurality of traditions.

177. Those passages which are (1) regarded as early by both Nöldeke (note 176 above) and Bell *(The Qur'ân)* and (2) in which opposition to Muḥammad is not mentioned or implied, have been analyzed by Watt in *Muhammad at Mecca,* chap. 3, and *Muhammad, Prophet and Statesman,* chap. 2.

178. This despite the so-called satanic verses, mentioned in note 97 above, which were subsequently abrogated according to the principle of *nāsikh* and *mansūkh.*

The utterances of the *kāhin,* the *ṭāghūt* (arbiter), and the *shāʿir* (bard) were, of course, the only models available to Muḥammad when first he strove to communicate in language the sensory manifestations of his revelations, even though the *Sīrah* has the Prophet declaring his dislike of such persons in no uncertain terms (1:153; Guillaume's translation, 106; al-Ṭabarī, *Taʾrīkh,* 2:1150). In this connection, there can be little doubt that al-Zuhrī's (d. 742) account of Muḥammad "entering Khadījah's chamber and saying 'Cover me *(zammilūnī),* cover me'," once after a revelation and once after a vision, (al-Ṭabarī, *Taʾrīkh,* 2:1147, 1155) refers to the mantle in which the *kāhin* wrapped himself when prophesying—an interpretation already suggested by Maxime Rodinson, *Muhammad* (New York, 1980), 81.

179. Montgomery Watt writes that the thought underlying the term translated as "presumption" seems to be "of a man who presses on regardless of obstacles, regardless of moral and religious considerations, and full of confidence in his own powers." The word translated as "pride of wealth" in the religious context of the Qur'ān came to mean "not only the actual possession of wealth, but also the spiritual attitude which the possession of wealth fostered among the Meccan merchants" (*Muhammad, Prophet and Statesman,* 29; cf. also *Muhammad at Mecca,* 66–67).

180. Watt, *Muhammad at Mecca,* 133–36; *Muhammad, Prophet and Statesman,* 57–59; and "Economic and social aspects of the origin of Islam," *The Islamic Quarterly* 1–2 (1954–55): 90–103.

181. Watt, *Muhammad at Mecca,* passim; *Muhammad at Medina,* passim; and *Islam and the Integration of Society,* chap. 3. Note especially *Muhammad, Prophet and Statesman,* 48–49: "The essential situation out of which Islam emerged was the contrast and conflict between the Meccans' nomadic outlook and attitudes and the new material (or economic) environment in which they found themselves." For some reason, G. H. Bousquet has characterized Watt's style of argument as Marxist: "Observations sociologiques sur les origines de l'Islam," *Studia Islamica* 11 (1954): 61–87. Cf. also the same author's "Observations sur la nature et les causes de la conquête arabe," *Studia Islamica* 6 (1956): 37–52 and "Quelques remarques critiques et sociologiques sur la conquête arabe et les théories émises à ce sujet," in *Studi Orientalistici in Onore de Giorgio Levi della Vida,* vol. 1 (Roma, 1956), 52–60. Maxime Rodinson has presented some restrained criticisms of Watt's interpretation in "The life of Muhammad and the sociological problem of the beginnings of Islam," *Diogenes,* no. 20 (1957): 28–51. Cf. also the same author's "Comment est né l'Islam," *Le Courrier Rationaliste* (Paris, 23 September 1956), 136–41. For subsequent slight modifications in Watt's views see his "Ideal factors in the origin of Islam," *Islamic Quarterly* 2 (1955): 160–74.

182. Robert B. Serjeant, review of *Muhammad at Medina,* by W. Montgomery Watt. *Bulletin of the School of Oriental and African Studies* 21 (1958): 187.

183. This is Robert B. Serjeant's phrasing: "Ḥaram and Ḥawṭah," 42. Cf. his "'Constitution of Medina,'" *The Islamic Quarterly* 8 (1964): 8. For documented instances in which (contra Schacht, Watt, Wolf, and virtually all Muslim writers) Muḥammad "kept to the existing body of *sunnahs* that formed the law, adapting some ancient *sunnahs* and adding a few new ones, justified on occasion by Quranic revelation," see Serjeant, "Early Arabic Prose," in *Arabic Literature,* ed. Beeston et al., 132–33. It is to be inferred from the so-called satanic verses in the Qur'ān (note 97 above) that the new sect at one time even honored the traditional Jāhilī divinities and respected their shrines as lesser elements in a sort of henotheistic hierarchy. Cf. also al-Ṭabarī, *Taʾrīkh,* 2:1192. Not unnaturally, the continuity of Muḥammad's belief and actions with the values and institutions of the Arabian past has been depreciated in Muslim tradition in order to enhance the uniqueness of his teaching.

184. Leone Caetani, *Studi di Storia Orientale,* vol. 1 (Milano, 1911), passim. but especially 21 et seq. and 366–68.

185. Carl Heinrich Becker, *Vom Werden und Wesen der islamischen Welt, Islamstudien* (Leipzig, 1924), 1:1–23.

186. E. A. Belyaev, *Araby, Islam i Arabskii Khalifat v Rannee Srednevekovʾe,* 2d ed. Moscow, 1966.

187. Hubert Grimme, *Mohammed,* vol. 1: *Das Leben* (Münster i. W., 1892). Grimme makes his view of Muḥammad as a sort of nineteenth-century German Social Democrat patently clear:

> Doch hat der Islam in seiner frühesten Form es auch gar nicht nötig, auf eine vorher bestehende Religion zurückgeführt und durch sie in seinen Lehrmeinungen erklärt zu werden; denn näher betrachtet ist er keineswegs als ein Religionssystem ins Leben getreten, sondern als ein Versuch sozialistischer Art, gewissen überhandnehmenden irdischen Missständen entgegenzutreten.
>
> Die Bedingungen, unter welchen in der Geschichte sozialistische Bewegungen aufzutreten pflegen, waren zu Mohammeds Zeit in Mekka vorhanden. (14)

188. Bendelī Jawzī, *Min Taʾrīkh al-Ḥarakāt al-Fikrīyah fī-l-Islām,* vol. 1: *Min Taʾrīkh al-Ḥarakāt al-Ijtimāʿīyah* (Jerusalem, n.d. but preface dated A.H. 1347/A.D. 1928). I have not seen this work, which is quoted in Rodinson, "The life of Muhammad," 35–36. Jawzī was a member of the Tatar community of Kazan who, when he wrote this paper, occupied a chair at the University of Baku.

189. Barbara C. Aswad, "Social and Ecological Aspects in the Formation of Islam," in *Peoples and Cultures of the Middle East*, vol. 1, ed. Louise Sweet (Garden City, N.Y., 1970), 53–73. This paper is a revision of "Social and ecological aspects in the origin of the Islamic state," *Papers of the Michigan Academy of Sciences, Arts, and Letters* 48 (1963): 419–42.

190. Wolf, "The social organization of Mecca," 329–56.

191. An egregiously uncritical example of this genre of writing is afforded by ʿAbbās Muḥmūd al-Aqqād, *ʾAbqarīyat Muḥammad* (al-Qāhirah, n.d.). Dermenghem's *Mohamet* (Paris, 1958), although discriminating between allegedly strong and weak traditions, also explicates the rise of the Islamic state in exclusively religious terms.

192. François-Marie Arouet de Voltaire, *Le Fanatisme ou Mahomet le Prophète*, passim but especially act 2, scene 5; in *Oeuvres Complètes, Théatre*, vol. 3 (Paris, 1877), 124–28.

193. For discussions of various aspects of the nature of the Muslim *Ḥadīth* (pl. *aḥādīth*) and the mode of its transmission, consult Ignaz Goldziher, "Über die Entwicklung des Hadith," in *Muhammedanische Studien*, vol. 2 (Halle, 1890), and more briefly in *Vorlesungen über den Islam* (Heidelberg, 1910; 2d ed., 1925); Alfred Guillaume, *The Traditions of Islam. An Introduction to the Study of the Hadith Literature* (Oxford, 1924); Joseph Schacht, *Origins of Muhammadan Jurisprudence*, 4th ed. (Oxford, 1967), passim; L. Bercher, *Etudes sur le Hadīth* (Alger, 1952); Josef Horovitz, "Alter und Ursprung des Isnad," *Der Islam* 8 (1918), and "The earliest biographies of the Prophet and their authors," *Islamic Culture* 1 (1927): 535–59; J. Fück, *Muḥammad ibn Isḥaq;* and Watt, *Muhammad at Mecca*, xi–xvi and *Muhammad at Medina*, excursus A. An example of a conservative reaction to the highly skeptical approach of Goldziher and his successors to *ḥadīth* studies (to say nothing of the work of Patricia Crone, Michael Cook, and John Wansbrough), and a defense of the authenticity of the Tradition is Fazlur Rahman's *Islam*, 2d ed. (Chicago, 1979), chap. 3. For recent Egyptian discussions of this topic see G. H. A. Juynboll, *The Authenticity of the Tradition Literature: Discussions in Modern Egypt* (Leiden, 1969). Recent summaries of various aspects of the *ḥadīth* literature are provided by Beeston et al., eds., *Arabic Literature*, chaps. 10–14 inclusive.

194. For an interpretation of the Tradition evidence relating opponents of Muḥammad's teaching to the dispute between the Confederacy of the Fuḍūl (see p. 16 above and note 144) and another group known as the Aḥlāf or Confederates, see Watt, *Islam and the Integration of Society*, 8–10. In Watt's view the Aḥlāf (sing. *ḥilf*, "mutual alliance") were committed to the exclusion of Yamanī merchants from the Makkan market, whereas the membership of the Fuḍūl probably comprised predominantly those clans unable to organize independent caravans to al-Yaman, and therefore unable to participate in the profitable southern trade but for the visits to Makkah of Yamanī merchants.

195. Qurʾān 2 *(al-Baqarah):*125, 127; 3 *(Āl ʿImrān):*96–97; and 14 *(Ibrāhīm):*35, 37.

196. Cf. Arent J. Wensinck, "The ideas of the Western Semites concerning the navel of the earth," *Verhandelingen der Koninklijke Akademie van Wetenschappen te Amsterdam*, Afdeeling Letterkunde, n.s., 17, no. 1 (1916), passim. For broad conspectuses of this cosmo-magical symbolism, not necessarily relating to the Middle East, see Mircea Eliade, *Le Mythe de l'Eternel Retour: Archétypes et Répétition* (Paris, 1949), chap. 1 and Paul Wheatley, "La pelle sospesa. Riflessioni su un modello abbandonato di struttura spaziale," chap. 1 in *La Città come Simbolo* (Brescià, 1981).

197. For the making of the Ptolemaic *Geographia* see Leo Bagrow, "The origin of Ptolemy's Geographia," *Geografiska Annaler*, 27, pts. 3–4 (1945), 318–87. Bagrow's views are summarized in the same author's *History of Cartography*, revised and enlarged by R. A. Skelton (London, 1964), 34–37. Additionally O. A. W. Dilke, "The Culmination of Greek Cartography in Ptolemy," in *The History of Cartography*, ed. J. B. Harley and David Woodward, vol. 1 (Chicago, 1987), chap. 11.

198. For example, Ibn Isḥāq, *Sīrah*, 1:80; Guillaume's translation, 52–53; al-Bakrī in *Das geographische Wörterbuch des al-Bekrī*, ed. Ferdinand Wüstenfeld (Göttingen and Paris, 1876–77), 58; and Aḥmad al-Nuwayrī, *Nihāyat al-ʿArab*, vol. 16 (al-Qāhirah, 1955), 30 et seq. See also al-Alūsī, *Bulūgh al-ʿArab*, 1:235.

199. P. 12 above and note 71. It is said that ʿAbd al-Muṭṭalib sprinkled raisins in the well of Zamzam to improve the taste of the water and furnished pilgrims to the Kaʿbah with milk and honey (al-Azraqī, *Akhbār Makkah*, 1:70). Other traditions credit Suwayd ibn Harmī with being the first to provide the pilgrims with milk (al-Muṣʿab ibn ʿAbd Allāh al-Zubayrī, *Nasab Quraysh*, 342; al-Zubayr ibn Bakkār, *Jamharat Nasab Quraysh wa-Akhbārihā:* not seen but quoted in Kister, "Mecca and Tamīm," 127 from MS. Bodley. Marsh. 384, fol. 153r), and Abū Umayyah ibn al-Mughīrah al-Makhzūmī, together with Abū Wadāʿah al-Sahmī, the first to offer honey (Muḥammad ibn Ḥabīb, *al-Muḥabbar*, 177). Even today camel's milk is the first thing offered to a stranger arriving at a *badū* encampment, if possible the sweet froth of new-drawn milk: see, for example, Charles M. Doughty, *Travels in Arabia Deserta* (first published in 1888; Dover reprint of the third edition, New York, 1979), passim, but typically 2:257–58; and Thesiger, *Arabian Sands*, passim.

200. Ibn Durayd, *al-Ishtiqāq*, 94.

201. Lammens, "Le culte des bétyles," 106–7.

202. Serjeant, *The Saiyids of Ḥaḍramawt*, 3–4. At any rate, that is what Ibn Isḥāq apparently believed had happened during the time of Quṣayy when the *rifādah* (provisioning of pilgrims) could properly be described as a levy paid by the Quraysh to the lord of the Kaʿbah during the annual pilgrimage (note 110 above). And it is also what happened until very recently in the *ḥawṭahs* of Ḥaḍramawt when a *manṣab* offered pilgrims food from his *maṭbakh* ("kitchen") (Serjeant, *The Saiyids of Ḥaḍramawt*, 4; "Ḥaram and Ḥawṭah," 53; and "Hūd and other pre-Islamic prophets of Ḥaḍramawt," 138).

203. Cf. the line from a *qaṣīdah* by Abū Qays that is quoted by Ibn Isḥāq, *Sīrah*, 1:179; Guillaume's translation, 128: "And the sin

of breaking the taboo on travel-worn gazelles." As recently as the late 1940s when Wilfred Thesiger visited the *ḥawṭah* at Mughshin, on the southern edge of the Rabʿ al-Khālī, hares were protected within the sacred enclave (*Arabian Sands,* 111).

204. Ibn Saʿd, *al-Ṭabaqāt,* vol. 1; al-Balādhurī, *al-Ashrāf,* 1: 58; al-Yaʿqūbī, *Taʾrīkh,* vol. 1; and al-Ḥalabī, *Insān al-ʿUyūn,* (al-Qāhirah, 1932), 1:14. The fact that this all sounds very much like a traditionist's elaboration does not necessarily invalidate its essential verisimilitude: if the prohibition was a common feature in the eighth century A.D. and later, it may well have been true of the Makkan *ḥaram* in still earlier times. The felling of trees was also taboo in the *ḥawṭah* at Mughshin and in several others visited by Thesiger: cf. note 203 above.

205. It should be remembered, though, that it is the Qurashī version of these events (or, as some would have it, nonevents) that predominates in the Tradition.

206. Al-Jāḥiẓ, *Rasāʾil,* ed. H. al-Sandūbī (al-Qāhirah, 1933), 70.

207. Ibn Isḥāq, *Sīrah,* 1:630; Guillaume's translation, 419.

208. Robert B. Serjeant, "Two tribal law cases (documents): (Wāḥidī Sultanate, South-West Arabia)," *Journal of the Royal Asiatic Society* (1951): 167–68.

209. *Ḥums* (pl.); *aḥmas* (sing.). Cf. Ibn Isḥāq, *Sīrah,* 1:126–29; Guillaume's translation, 87–89; Ibn Saʿd, *al-Ṭabaqāt,* 1:41; al-Azraqī, *Akhbār Makkah,* 1:113–15; and Ibn Durayd, *Kitāb al-Ishtiqāq* (al-Qāhirah, 1958), 250. The most succinct modern elucidations of the significance of this term are Kister, "Mecca and Tamīm," 132–41, and particularly Simon, "Ḥums et īlāf," passim. The connection of the *Ḥums* with the Kaʿbah is evident from the fact that the latter was occasionally referred to as al-Ḥamsāʾ (Kister, "Mecca and Tamīm," 139).

210. For example, Ibn Isḥāq, Ibn Saʿd, Ibn Qutaybah, al-Jāḥiẓ, al-Anbārī, al-Marzūqī, al-Qurṭubī, Abū Ḥayyān, Ibn Ḥabīb. The discrepancies in these lists are summarized by Kister, "Mecca and Tamīm," 132–33.

211. Whereas Ibn Isḥāq (*Sīrah,* 1:126; Guillaume's translation, 87) was uncertain whether it was before or after Abrahah's invasion that the Quraysh developed the institution of the *Ḥums,* al-Azraqī (*Akhbār Makkah,* 1:113) had no doubt that it occurred after the campaign. For a summary of available evidence bearing on the date, see Simon, "Ḥums et īlāf," 217–18.

212. Ibn Ḥabīb, *al-Muḥabbar,* 180; Yāqūt, *Muʿjam,* s.v. "Makkah"; and Ibn al-ʿArabī, *Muḥāḍarat al-Abrār wa Musāmarāt al-Akhyār,* vol. 1 (al-Qāhirah, A.H. 1324/A.D. 1906), 150, 162. Summarized by Kister, "Mecca and Tamīm," 138. Variant traditions are preserved, however, in al-Ṭabarī, *Tafsīr,* ed. Maḥmūd and Muḥammad Shākir (al-Qāhirah, A.H. 1374/A.D. 1954), *Sūrah* 2, p. 189 and in al-Suyūṭī, *al-Durr al-Manthūr,* vol. 1 (Tehran, A.H. 1377/A.D. 1957), 204 et seq. The religious rites of the *Ḥums* are summarized in C. Snouck Hurgronje, *Oeuvres Choisies* (Leyden, 1957), 181 and Caetani, *Annali,* 1:148 et seq.

213. Al-Jāḥiẓ, *Mukhtārāt Fuṣūl,* quoted in Kister, "Mecca and Tamīm," 136–37 from MS British Museum Or. 3183.

214. Ibn al-Faqīh al-Hamadhānī, *Kitāb al-Buldān,* in *Compendium Libri Kitâb al-Boldân,* vol. 5 of *Bibliotheca Geographorum Arabicorum,* ed. M. J. de Goeje (Lugduni Batavorum, 1885), 18. According to al-Zubayr ibn Bakkār, *Nasab Quraysh* (cited after Kister, "Mecca and Tamīm," 136 n. 1: cf. note 199 above), the Quraysh used to donate special clothes to pilgrims for the circumambulation of the Kaʿbah, upon which the *badū* would discard their own desert garments. Ibn Bakkār also noted that a *qawm* hosting *badū* pilgrims was entitled to a share of the meat of the camels slaughtered for the guests' sustenance.

215. According to Ibn Ḥabīb (*al-Muḥabbar,* 179), the Ḥillah comprised all the Tamīm (with the exceptions of Yarbūʿ, Māzin, Ḍabbah, Ḥumays, Ẓāʿinah, and al-Ghawth ibn Murr); all the Qays ʿAylān (except Thaqīf, ʿAdwān, and *Āmir* ibn Ṣaʿṣaʿah); all Rabīʿah ibn Nizār; all Quḍāʿah (except ʿIlāf and Janāb); the Anṣār; Khathʿam; Bajīlah; Bakr ibn ʿAbd Manāt ibn Kinānah; Hudhayl; Asad; Ṭayyiʾ; and Bāriq. Ibn Ḥabīb (ibid.) mentions a third group, the *Ṭuls,* who, like the Ḥillah, followed a different ritual when performing the *Ḥajj.* The Ṭuls were made of up tribes from al-Yaman and Ḥaḍramawt, together with the ʿAkk, Ujayb, and Īyād. A fourth group, the *Basl,* consisting of the *ʿāmir* ibn Luʾayy (also known as ʿAwt ibn Luʾayy and Murrah ibn ʿAwf ibn Luʾayy), were believed to have recognized no less than eight sacred months (al-Kalāʾī, *Kitāb al-Iktifāʾ fī Maghāzī al-Mustafā wa-l-Thalātha,* in *Bibliotheca Arabica* no. 6, vol. 1, ed. H. Massé [Alger, 1931], 78; Ibn Kathīr, *al-Bidayah wa-l-Nihāyah,* vol. 2 [al-Qāhirah, A.H. 1351/A.D. 1932], 204; and Abū Dharr, *Sharḥ al-Sīrah,* ed. Brönnle [al-Qāhirah, 1911], 235).

All these groups—Ḥums, Ḥillah, Ṭuls, and Basl alike—recognized the sanctity of the Makkan *ḥaram.* However, there was yet another categorization in which some traditionists discriminated between the tribes, including the Ḥums and those tribes of the Ḥillah who undertook the pilgrimage and acknowledged the sanctity of Makkah *(Muḥrimūn)* on the one hand and those who totally rejected the sanctity of the *ḥaram* and did not respect the sacred months *(Muḥillūn)* on the other (al-Jāḥiẓ, *Kitāb al-Ḥayawān,* ed. ʿAbd al-Salām Hārūn [al-Qāhirah, 1960], 7:216 et seq; al-Yaʿqūbī, *Taʾrīkh,* 1:221; and al-Marzūqī, *al-Amkinah,* 2:166. Cf. also al-Najīramī, *Aymān al-ʿArab fī al-Jāhilīyah,* ed. Muḥibb al-Dīn al-Khaṭīb [al-Qāhirah, A.H. 1346/A.D. 1928], 12 and Ibn Ḥabīb, *al-Muḥabbar,* 319). It was against these latter that the famous imprecation was uttered: "I [an intercalator] make it lawful to shed the blood of the Muḥillūn, Ṭayyiʾ and Khathʿam. Slay them wherever you encounter them if they harass you" (al-Balādhurī, *al-Ashrāf,* fol. 900v: quoted [slightly modified] in Kister, "Mecca and Tamīm," 142). Al-Jāḥiẓ numbers among the Muḥillūn all the Ṭayyiʾ and Khathʿam, together with many *qawms* of Quḍāʿah, Yashkur, and al-Ḥārith ibn Kaʿb, but the lists offered by other authors differ considerably both from that of al-Jāḥiẓ and from one another.

216. Cf. preceding note.

217. Kister, "Mecca and Tamīm," 142–43.

218. Al-Yaʿqūbī, *Taʾrīkh,* 1:221.

219. For highly suggestive statements on ritual as a social regulatory mechanism see Roy A. Rappaport, "The sacred in human evolution," *Annual Review of Ecology and Systematics* 2 (1971): 23–44 and "The obvious aspects of ritual" and "Sanctity and lies in evolution," both in the same author's *Ecology, Meaning, and Religion* (Richmond, Calif., 1979), 173–221, 223–46.

220. See al-Marzūqī, *al-Amkinah,* 2:161.

221. Ibn Ḥabīb, *al-Muḥabbar,* 181.

222. Quoted in al-Ḥalabī, *Insān al-ʿUyūn,* 1:242.

223. It is instructive to compare the following two passages written at an interval of a millennium:

> If Qurashī merchants took the route from Makkah [to Dūmat al-Jandal] by way of al-Ḥazn, they did not require the protection of any of the tribes until they returned because the Muḍar did not raid Muḍarī caravans, nor were [the merchants] raided by an ally of Muḍar. That was the accepted custom between them. And when they departed from al-Ḥazn or journeyed thither, they passed by the wells of Kalb. Kalb were in alliance with Tamīm and consequently did not attack them. When they passed through the lowland, they encountered the Asad and reached the Ṭayyiʾ. The Ṭayyiʾ did not raid them because of their alliance with the Asad. Muḍar used to say "The Quraysh performed for us the religious obligations that we inherited from Ismāʿīl" (al-Marzūqī, *al-Amkinah,* 2:162. A substantially similar account is included in Ibn Ḥabīb's *al-Muḥabbar,* 264–65).

> To travel safely among the Duru we needed a *rabia (rabīʾah)* or companion, who could frank us through their territory. He could be either from the Duru or from some other tribe entitled by tribal custom to give his travelling companions protection among the Duru while they were in his company. A *rabia* took an oath: "You are my companions and your safety, both of your blood and your possessions, is in my face." Members of the same party were responsible for each other's safety, and were expected to fight if necessary in each other's defence, even against their own tribes or families. If one of the party was killed, all the party were involved in the ensuing blood-feud. No tribe would be likely to attack a party which was accompanied by a tribesman from a powerful tribe to which they were allied, but a *rabia* could belong to a small and insignificant tribe and still give protection. The question of how and where each tribe could give protection was complicated. It often amused my companions to argue hypothetical cases as we rode along, and their arguments sometimes became so involved that I was reminded of lawyers disputing (Thesiger, *Arabian Sands* [Penguin ed., Harmondsworth, Middlesex, England, 1964], 171).

The parallelisms exhibited by these two passages are typical of the apparent institutional similarities between Arabia of the *Jāhilīyah* and of the very recent past that are becoming increasingly evident as we compare current ethnographic reports with ancient texts.

Of course, the implications of parallels such as those noted above must not be pressed too far: there is always the chance that morphologically similar institutions may have functioned quite differently within the sociocultural framework of pre-Islamic Arabia from the way their apparent analogues operate in the twentieth century (for a summary of the possibilities and limitations of ethnographic analogy see Bryony Orme, "Twentieth-century prehistorians and the idea of ethnographic parallels," *Man,* n.s., 9 (1974): 199–212). Even so, the cumulative implications of the sets of ancient and modern parallelisms that, for example, Robert Serjeant has elicited cannot be ignored by anyone trying to reconstruct conditions in Arabia of the seventh century. The following, from Serjeant's paper "Ḥaram and Ḥawṭah," is nicely illustrative of the way in which fieldwork can illuminate the possibilities of an ancient text:

> As an extension of the influence of the ḥaram or of the ḥawṭah, we may consider the celebrated caravan of Quraish and its summer and winter journey. Turning once more to present-day Southern Arabia, we find that if a Manṣab wishes a tribesman to visit the shrine, or should the tribesman himself desire to do so, the Manṣab will send him a thread or some other emblem of security. Al-Marzūqī reports what appears to be the same custom from the pre-Islamic period, and I believe this was the usage amonst the Ashrāf of Mecca in medieval if not even later times. The tribesman may then walk to the sanctuary protected by it from his foes. Arising from the basic principle that wherever a Manṣab or a member of his family goes, he will not only be secure, but able also to extend that security to others, we find that he can accompany caravans to protect them. The medieval writer, al-Sharjī, refers in several places to a caravan from Yemen to Mecca known as Qāfilat Ibn ʿUjail accompanied first by the celebrated Yemenī saint, Ibn ʿUjail, then later by his descendants which had complete inviolability *(ḥurmah wāfirah)* from attack. No one of the Bedouin of these districts, says al-Sharjī, will molest them—nay, if there be a small boy of them in the caravan or one of their slaves, nobody will molest them. They have an effective control (ḥukm nāfidh) over them, and their command is obeyed through the barakah of the shaikh. (54–55)

224. Ibn Isḥāq, *Sīrah,* 1:80; Guillaume's translation, 53.

225. Translation by Kister, "Mecca and Tamīm," slightly modified. The passage is abstracted from al-Balādhurī, *Ansāb,* MS fol. 869r.

226. For the term *kabīr* as signifying "tribal chief" in ancient inscriptions and texts, see note 50 above.

227. Ibn Isḥāq, *Sīrah,* 2:238; Guillaume's translation, 164. The passage is also translated by Robert Serjeant, *The Saiyids of Ḥaḍramawt,* 5.

228. Al-Ṭabarī, *Taʾrīkh,* 1:1278.

229. Qurʾān 2 *(al-Baqarah):*217. There is a commentary on the ambush of the caravan near Nakhlah, sympathetic to Muḥammad but showing no great understanding of the nature of *badū*

raiding—the whole episode is treated as if it were a planned platoon foray in World War II—in Watt, *Muhammad at Medina,* 5–9.

230. Ibn Isḥāq, *Sīrah,* 1:445; Guillaume's translation, 301.

231. Ibid., 1:230–32; Guillaume's translation, 159–61. Serjeant ("Early Arabic prose," 151) suggests that the Qurashī boycott shows certain procedural similarities to the Sabaean penal law declaring a man an outlaw and thereby depriving him of civil protection. As the Qurashī proscription was said to have been hung up inside the Kaʿbah, so the Sabaean interdiction also was proclaimed in a sanctuary *(maḥram).* Cf. A. F. L. Beeston, "A Sabaean penal law," *Le Muséon* 64 (1951): 306.

232. This view of the ekistic character of Makkah in the seventh century is essentially that implied by Uri Rubin, "The Kaʿba," cited in note 103 above. In fact the settlement at Makkah that Muḥammad knew probably did not appear greatly dissimilar to, although probably somewhat larger than, that at Qabr Hūd described by Robert Serjeant in the early 1950s ("Hūd and other pre-Islamic Prophets of the Ḥaḍramawt," 150 et seq.). Plate 2 (between pp. 148 and 149; comments on p. 178) shows the *sūq* in what appears to be a small town, with the shrine of the saint at the far end, an assortment of residences bordering the *sūq,* and at the end distant from the shrine the booths and shelters of merchants and *badū.*

For an argument that the architectural details of the supposed Jāhilī shrine at Makkah were in fact appropriated from the pagan shrines familiar to eighth-century traditionists—whence the conflict between archeological and literary evidence, as well as the lack of agreement among traditionists—see Yehuda D. Nevo and Judith Koren, "The origins of the Muslim descriptions of the Jāhilī Meccan sanctuary," *Journal of Near Eastern Studies* 49, no. 1 (1990): 23–44.

At this point I should mention a particularly radical interpretation proposed by Goto Akira. This author starts from much the same conceptual foundation as that proposed—perhaps assumed would be a more accurate term—by Lammens, Watt, and others, namely Makkah in the Prophet's time as a merchant republic. Whereas Watt sees this commercial environment as inducing a societal malaise inhibiting adaptation to a changing world, Goto views Makkah as a "free city" entirely lacking "an official system of headmen, councils, or public institutions." On this view the basic unit of Makkan society was the "free person" entering entirely independently into contracts and agreements with other equally "free" individuals. Although Goto was almost certainly correct in imputing degrees of flexibility to both the prevailing lineage system and the kinship exclusiveness of the *īlāf,* his insistence on a "total absence of institutionalization [of social and administrative practices]" runs directly counter to the primary import of the evidence adduced in this chapter. Nor does the author explain how such an atomistic society could have maintained its integrity as a functioning entity. Moreover, the grain of truth at the core of his argument seems to me to relate to the eighth rather than the early seventh century. A representative selection of Goto's writings on these topics includes "Isuramu bokkoki no Arabu shakai no kozo," *Isuramu Sekai* 7 (1970) and 11 (1977); "Jiyu toshi Mekka" in *Nairikuajia Nishiajia no Shakai to Bunka,* ed. Mori Masao (Tokyo, 1983); "Jiyu toshi Mekka no hitobito," *Isuramusekai no Hitobito* 5 (Tokyo, 1984); and "7 Seiki no Mekka to Medina," *Shicho,* n.s., 26 (1989).

233. P. 18 above and note 160.

234. Kister, "Mecca and Tamīm," 140–41. The passages from the *Ansab* as transcribed by Kister are as follows:

Fakharnā wa-l-umūru lahā qarārūn
bi-Makkatinā wa-bi-l-baladi ʾl-ḥarāmi.
Wa-annā lā yurāmu lanā harīmūn
wa-annā lā nurawwaʿu fī ʾl-manāmi.
Wa-annā lā tusāqu lanā kiʿābūn
khilala ʾl-naqʿi bādiyatu l-khidāmi.
Maʿādha ʾllāhi min hādhā wa-hādhā
fa-inna ʾllāha laysa lahū musāmī.

Tufākhirunī maʿāshiru min Qurayshin
bi-Kaʿbatihim wa-bi-l-bayti ʾl-ḥarāmi.
Fa-akrim bi-ʾlladhī fākharū wa-lākin
maghāzī ʾl-khayli dāmiyatu ʾl-kilāmi.
Wa-ṭaʿnun fī ʾl-ʿajājati kulla yawmin
nuḥūra ʾl-khayli bi ʾl-asali l-dawāmi.
Aḥabbu ilayya min ʿayshin rakhiyyin
maʿa ʾl-Qurashiyyi Ḥarbin aw Hishāmi.
Wa-mā ʿayshu ʾbni Judʿānin bi-ʿayshin
yajurru ʾl-kazza fī ʾl-baladi ʾl-tihāmī.

235. Al-Yaʿqūbī (*Taʾrīkh,* 2:49) provides a list, probably apocryphal, of the tribes from whom these Jews were supposedly descended. Cf. also Julius Wellhausen, *Medina vor dem Islam* (Berlin, 1889). For a useful footnote to the situation of the Jews in Yathrib see Robert B. Serjeant, "The *Sunnah Jāmiʿah,* pacts with the Yathrib Jews, and the *taḥrīm* of Yathrib: an analysis and translation of the documents comprised in the so-called 'Constitution of Medina,'" *Bulletin of the School of Oriental and African Studies* 41, pt. 1 (1978): 2–3 and note 9.

236. Aram. *Medīntā* = "juridical circumscription" (< *dīn* = "judgment"), with a subsequent extension of meaning to denote "province": cf. F. Buhl, *The Encyclopaedia of Islam,* 1st ed., s.v. "al-Madīna." The gloss of al-Madīnah as "The City [of the Prophet]" appears relatively late in the Tradition. It follows that in the earliest Islamic literature there is always the likelihood that al-Madīnah should be understood as "the seat of authority" rather than as the proper name of the settlement.

237. Ibn Isḥāq, *Sīrah,* 1:286 et seq.; Guillaume's translation, 197 et seq.

238. Serjeant, "Two tribal law cases (documents)," 33–45, 156–69; "Ḥaram and Ḥawṭah," passim; and *The Saiyids of Ḥaḍramawt,* passim. An appendix to the first of these papers (166–68) recounts the election of a *manṣab* of the Mashāyikh in the late 1940s. For an account of the manner in which a powerful Qurashī *shaykh* arbitrated in a dispute about blood money, see Ibn Isḥāq, *Sīrah,* 1:273–75; Guillaume's translation, 187–89.

239. Ibn Isḥāq, *Sīrah,* 1:281–85; Guillaume's translation,

194–97. It is possible that the Banū-Ḥanīfah rejected Muḥammad's overtures because they had already declared their allegiance to a monotheistic prophet, the so-called Musaylimah (p. 13 above and note 102).

240. Ibn Isḥāq, *Sīrah,* 1:279–81; Guillaume's translation, 192–94.

241. Ibid., 1:288–90, 293–97; Guillaume's translation, 198–99, 201–4. This is the standard version of events, but ʿUrwah ibn al-Zubayr has preserved a somewhat different account, which is thought to have been influenced by clan loyalties: cf. Watt, *Muhammad at Medina,* 145–46; al-Ṭabarī, *Taʾrīkh,* 2:1224–25. According to Ibn Isḥāq (ibid.), the Pledge of Women was so called because "we pledged ourselves to the Prophet after the manner of women," presumably implying that no fighting was involved.

242. In pre-Islamic usage the term *ummah* apparently denoted a religious community, as employed, for example, by the Christian poet al-Nābighah (*Diwān al-Nābighah al-Dhubyānī,* ed. Shukrī Fayṣal [Bayrūt, A.H. 1388/A.D. 1968], 51; quoted in Denny, "The meaning of *ummah,*" 37). In the Qurʾān the term first figures in *sūrah*s that are usually assigned to the end of the Makkan period, when it had come to denote those groups (not exclusively Muslim) to whom a messenger *(al-rasūl)* or a warner *(al-nadhīr)* had been sent and who had accepted his teaching. Not until the Madīnan period do we encounter instances of *Ummah* denoting a totally Islamic community. See Frederick Mathewson Denny, "The meaning of *ummah* in the Qurʾān," *History of Religions* 15 (1975): 34–69 and "*Ummah* in the Constitution of Medina," *Journal of Near Eastern Studies* 36 (1977): 39–47. For earlier studies consult Rudi Paret, *The Shorter Encyclopedia of Islam,* ed. H. A. R. Gibb and J. H. Kramers (Leiden, 1954), s.v. "*ummah*" and Louis Massignon, "L'Umma et ses synonymes: notion de 'communauté sociale' en Islam," *Revue des Etudes Islamiques* 15, pt. 1 (1941–46, but published in 1947), 151–57.

Most modern scholarship derives the term *Ummah* from the Hebrew *ummā* or Aramaic *umetha,* both ultimately from Akkadian *ummatu:* cf. Jeffery, *The Foreign Vocabulary of the Qurʾān,* 69 and Josef Horovitz, *Koranische Untersuchungen,* 52. Earlier attempts to derive the term from a Semitic root signifying "mother" are not now acceptable: for example, William Robertson Smith, *Kinship and Marriage in Early Arabia,* 32; Massignon, "L'Umma," 152; Louis Gardet, *La Cité Musulmane: Vie Sociale et Politique,* 3d ed. (Paris, 1969), 61–63; Julius Wellhausen, *The Arab Kingdom and Its Fall,* trans. Margaret Graham Weir (London, 1927; reprint, Beirut, 1963), 11 (this is an English translation of *Das arabische Reich und sein Sturz* [Berlin, 1902]).

There are more general discussions of the institutional significance of the term *Ummah* in W. Montgomery Watt, *Islam and the Integration of Society,* 57–59, 147–48 and C. A. O. van Nieuwenhuijze, "The *ummah*—an analytic approach," *Studia Islamica,* vol. 70 (1959), pp. 5–22.

243. Qurʾān 49 *(al-Ḥujurāt):*13.

244. Al-Wāqidī, *al-Maghāzī,* ed. Alfred von Kremer (Calcutta, 1956), 338. A graphic, if inevitably archetyped, example of the sundering of lineage ties by converts to the new faith is afforded by the tale of the two Thaqīf tribesmen Abū Mulayḥ ibn ʿUrwah and Qārib ibn al-Aswad, who forswore all dealings with Thaqīf, even their maternal uncle Abū Sufyān ibn Ḥarb (celebrated as the Qurashī commander of the Makkan caravan attacked by Muḥammad's forces at Badr), when they elected to "choose God and His apostle": Ibn Isḥāq, *Sīrah,* 1:918; Guillaume's translation, 617.

245. Ibn Isḥāq, *Sīrah,* 1:341–46; Guillaume's translation, 231–35.

246. Abū ʿUbayd al-Qāsim ibn Sallām, *Kitāb al-Amwāl,* ed. M. K. Harās (al-Qāhirah, 1968), 290 et seq. There is also a late copy of the document made by Ismāʿīl ibn Muḥammad ibn Kathīr, *al-Bidāyah wa-l-Nihāyah,* vol. 3 (al-Qāhirah, A.H. 1351/A.D. 1932), 224 et seq.

247. Patricia Crone, *Slaves on Horses,* 7.

248. Al-Zuhrī's tradition was allegedly based on the authority of Anas ibn Mālik (died ca. 709), in whose house at least two of the treaties may have been contracted: Serjeant, "The 'Constitution of Medina,'" 6–7. On al-Zuhrī see A. A. Durī, "Al-Zuhrī: a study on the beginnings of history writing in Islam," *Bulletin of the School of Oriental and African Studies* 19 (1957): 1–12.

249. R. B. Serjeant, "The *Sunnah Jāmiʿah,*" 7.

250. For example, Julius Wellhausen, "Muhammads Gemeindeordnung von Medina," in his *Skizzen und Vorarbeiten,* vol. 4 (Berlin, 1889), 75ff; Hubert Grimme, *Mohammed,* vol. 1 (Münster, 1892), 76; Tor Andrae, *Mohammed,* 135ff; Frants P. W. Buhl, *Das Leben Muhammeds* (Leipzig, 1930), 211; Watt, *Muhammed at Medina,* 221–28; Muḥammad Hamīdullāh, *Le Prophète de l'Islam,* 1: 128ff; Serjeant, "The 'Constitution of Medina,'" passim; "The *Sunnah Jāmiʿah,*" passim; and "Early Arabic Prose," 134–39; and Moshe Gil, "The Constitution of Medina: a reconsideration," *Israel Oriental Studies* 4 (1974): 44–66. What most distinguishes the works of Serjeant and Gil from those of previous authors is that they both interpret the so-called Constitution in terms of pre-Islamic tribal custom.

251. Crone and Cook, *Hagarism,* 7.

252. Gil, "The Constitution of Medina," 48; al-Diyārbakrī, *Taʾrīkh al-Khamīs fī Aḥwāl Anfas Nafīs* (al-Qāhirah, A.H. 1302/A.D. 1884), 1:398.

253. Serjeant, "The *Sunnah Jāmiʿah,*" passim.

254. Serjeant (ibid., 14–15) adds significant semantic overtones to this received definition: "On the basis of my work in the Yemen I have come to regard the *Muhājir* as a person seeking protection in a place and with a people not his own—like Yemeni *sayyids* seeking *hijrah* with the Zaydī tribes. Documents A and B may then be regarded as basically an agreement between members of the Bayt of Quraysh, that is to say the Holy House, seeking security and a secure dwelling-place which they are accorded by the two arms-bearing tribes, Aws and Khazraj, settled at Yathrib." Protection for the Prophet himself was, of course, guaranteed by the two ʿAqabah treaties (p. 25 above).

It is to be noted that, according to tradition, the Muhājirūn did not monopolize a special quarter in al-Madīnah but were dispersed among the Anṣār (Wellhausen, *Skizzen und Vorarbeiten,* vol. 4 [Berlin, 1884–99], 68).

255. On the signification of *Mu'minūn* see M. M. Bravmann, *The Spiritual Background of Early Islam: Studies in Ancient Arab Concepts* (Leiden, 1972), 26 and Serjeant, "The *Sunnah Jāmi'ah,*" 12–15.

256. This rendering of *min dūni-l-nāsi* follows a suggestion by Gil, "The Constitution of Medina," 49–50. Serjeant's version is "set apart from the people" ("The *Sunnah Jāmi'ah,*" 18 and "Early Arabic Prose," 135); Watt's reading is "distinct from (other) people" (*Muhammad at Medina,* 221).

257. Qur'ān 21 *(al-Anbiyā'):*92 appears to be a direct reference to the *Ummah* of Document A: "This confederacy *(ummah)* of yours is a single confederacy *(ummatun wāḥidatun),* and I am your Lord, so worship Me." And the final clause in Document B is close to Qur'ān 42 *(al-Shūrā):*10: "And in whatsoever you differ, the verdict is the prerogative of Allāh," and even more so to 4 *(al-Nisā'):* 59: "If you are in dispute about any matter, refer it to Allāh and the Messenger, if you [truly] believe in Allāh and the Last Day."

258. Ibn Isḥāq, *Sīrah,* 1:553–54; Guillaume's translation, 369.

259. Al-Wāqidī is evidently referring, if not to this very treaty, at least to its substance, in *al-Maghāzī,* 1:176. Cf. also al-Ṭabarī, *Ta'rīkh,* 2:1395.

260. On this term see Serjeant, "The 'Constitution of Medina,'" 13–14 and "The *Sunnah Jāmi'ah,*" 27. The same author derives *Munāfiqūn* (those who paid the *nafaqah* only reluctantly) from the same root, its more familiar Qur'ānic sense of "hypocrites" being a later development. Rodinson regards the term as a borrowing from the ritual language of the Christian church of Abyssinia, where it connoted "men of two minds, people of little faith" (*Muhammad,* 184, 339). Serjeant ("The *Sunnah Jāmi'ah,*" 11) compares the *nafaqah* to the *ghurm* that the Zaydī tribes until recently imposed upon themselves in emergencies.

261. The Jawf (= depression; a geomorphological basin) of Yathrib is the relatively level area lying between the mountainous terrain to the north and west of the settlement and the upland lava tracts (the *lābatayn* or *ḥarratayn*) to the east and south. Several traditions allege that the boundaries of the *ḥaram* were specified in the proclamation *(taḥrīm)* document, but that is not true of the text as transmitted to us. Probably the boundaries incorporated in the traditions are later elaborations. Cf., for example, al-Bukhārī, *al-Jāmi' al-Ṣaḥīḥ, bāb* "Ḥaram al-Madīnah" and Ibn al-Athīr, *al-Jāmi' al-Uṣūl* (al-Qāhirah, A.H. 1369/A.D. 1949), 10:190, 193.

262. This is the first time in the treaties that Muḥammad has been referred to in this way, a circumstance presumably indicative of an enhancement of his authority, if not also of the power at his disposal, during his six or seven years at al-Madīnah. Note, though, that the term does occur in Ibn Isḥāq's introduction (p. 26 of the present text).

263. The Banū-Qurayẓah were clients of the Arab tribe of Aws, specifically the *ḥulafā'* and *mawālī* of the *naqīb* Sa'd ibn Mu'ādh. For the term *naqīb* see Serjeant, "The *Sunnah Jāmi'ah,*" 10–11.

264. *Khandaq* is a Persian word, and the Tradition has it that the expedient of defending the northern flank of the settlement with a ditch was suggested by a Persian freedman named Salmān. Although such fortifications were entirely alien to the *badū* style of raiding, they were employed in al-Yaman and apparently were not unknown in al-Ṭā'if.

265. Al-Wāqidī, *al-Maghāzī,* 2:455–56.

266. Ibn Kathīr, *al-Bidāyah wa-l-Nihāyah,* vol. 4 (al-Qāhirah, 1932), 103.

267. Al-Wāqidī (*al-Maghāzī,* 2:485, quoting a Companion, Abū Shurayḥ) and Yāqūt (*Mu'jam,* 4:619) both cite rules of the *ḥaram* at Makkah closely similar to those stipulated in this article.

268. Serjeant, "Ḥaram and Ḥawṭah," 45. In reproducing this passage, I have italicized technical terms in accordance with the practice in the rest of this volume.

Serjeant goes on (45–46) to show how such an agreement between *manṣab* and tribes worked out in practice, specifically in the case of the engagement entered into in 1922 by the Ahl Shamlān with the *Manṣab* of the Thibī *ḥawṭah,* near Tarīm. The document concludes with articles (summarized by Serjeant) again remarkably reminiscent of those preserved by Ibn Isḥāq:

> An old or a recent resident in the *ḥawṭah* is a protected person, neither entitled to commit an offence, nor may an offence be committed against him; but should any trouble arise between him and a tribe he must leave the *ḥawṭah,* and any warlike actions must be carried on outside it. The *Manṣab* is not to show preference for any particular group or person, and the Āl Shamlān on their part undertake to do all that will "adorn the Lord of the place, and preserve the *ḥawṭah* and its inviolability." The agreement concludes with an oath taken by the tribes—the oath by God, his Book, and their *shaikh,* the 'Aidarūs Saiyid (i.e. the *Manṣab*), to observe the afore-going stipulations.

It is of no little interest that this author indicates a Sayyid of the Mawlā al-Dawīlah family referred to the tribes supporting this saint's *ḥawṭah* as *anṣār*—the term used in the Qur'ān, the *Sīrah,* and the Tradition generally to denote Muḥammad's Madīnan supporters (cf. p. 26 above).

269. Qur'ān 8 *(al-Anfāl):*72. Although traditionally regarded as having been revealed shortly after the battle at Badr, this *sūrah* exhibits all the indications of a cumulative text. Bell suggests that some verses, such as 29, were revealed before the battle but that others were at least as late as the Day of the Trench (i.e., 627). Cf. also p. 25 and note 244 above.

270. Qur'ān 2 *(al-Baqarah):*111–12.

271. And perhaps the Qur'ān also: cf. Richard Bell's comment on *Sūrah* 2:85 (79 in Bell's translation, which follows the Flügel numbering): *The Qur'ān Translated,* vol. 1 (Edinburgh, 1937), 12 n. 2.

272. Cf. 1 Kings 8:29–30, Dan. 6:10. The Hierosylite *qiblah,* according to the Tradition, had been among the Jewish practices adopted by Muḥammad after the *Hijrah*—perhaps out of genuine respect for the customs of Arabia's premier monotheists, perhaps to secure the support of the Madīnan Jews.

273. Qur'ān 2 *(al-Baqarah):*144. Verses 142–52 also deal with the change of *qiblah* but not entirely consistently, which led Bell to suggest that they were revealed at different times. There is a tradition that, on the occasion of (one of) the revelation(s), the Prophet was worshipping at the prayer place in the quarter of the Banū-Salimah. This event is interesting inasmuch as the Banū-Salimah was the tribe of al-Barā' ibn Ma'rūr, a participant in the Pledge of War at al-'Aqabah (prior to the *Hijrah,* be it noted) who even then had insisted on praying toward the Ka'bah (Ibn Isḥāq, *Sīrah,* 1: 294–95; Guillaume's translation, 202: cf. also p. 427, trans. p. 289, though for an incompatible date see p. 381, trans. p. 258). See also, int. al., al-Diyārbakrī, *Ta'rīkh al-Khamīs,* 1:414 and al-Bukhārī, *al-Jāmi' al-Ṣaḥīḥ, Ṣalāt* (8), *bāb* 32.

When reproached with rejecting the *qiblah* that "he used to face when claiming to follow the religion of Ibrāhīm," Muḥammad was vouchsafed the revelation that, "We [Allāh] appointed the *qiblah* which thou has been observing only that we might know those who would follow the Messenger from those who would turn on their heels," that is, as a test of devotion to the word of Allāh (Qur'ān 2 *[al-Baqarah]:*143; cf. Ibn Isḥāq, *Sīrah,* 1:381; Guillaume's translation, 259). In instances such as this it is difficult to disagree with Frants Buhl's delicately nuanced comment on the way in which "die späteren Offenbarungen mitunter seinen allerniedrigsten Neigungen zu Hilfe kommen" (*Das Leben Muhammeds* [Leipzig, 1930], 141).

For an interpretation that envisages the choice of Makkah for the site of the premier Muslim sanctuary as "a sort of compromise between a preexisting pagan sanctuary and sanctuary ideas which had developed first in a Jewish milieu"—and that only "at a relatively late date in the Islamic period, not at its beginning as has been generally accepted"—see G. R. Hawting, "The Origins of the Muslim Sanctuary at Mecca," in *Studies on the First Century of Islamic Society,* ed. G. H. A. Juynboll (Carbondale, Ill., 1982), pp. 23–47.

274. 'Āshūrā = Arabized Aramaic for "the tenth."

275. Ibn Isḥāq, *Sīrah,* 1:545–47; Guillaume's translation, 363–64; al-Wāqidī, *al-Maghāzī* (von Kremer edition), 92–94; and al-Ṭabarī, *Ta'rīkh,* 3:1360–362.

276. Ibn Isḥāq, *Sīrah,* 1:652–56; Guillaume's translation, 437–439; al-Wāqidī, *al-Maghāzī,* 2:353–62; and al-Ṭabarī, *Ta'rīkh,* 3: 1448–53.

277. Ibn Isḥāq, *Sīrah,* 1:684–99; Guillaume's translation, 461–69; al-Ṭabarī, *Ta'rīkh,* 3:1485–98.

278. This point has already been made by Serjeant, "Ḥaram and Ḥawṭah," 52.

279. Ibn Isḥāq, *Sīrah,* 1:546; Guillaume's translation, 363–64. Cf. Qur'ān 5 *(al-Mā'idah):* 51 (which was supposedly revealed at this time): "O ye who believe! take not Jews and Christians as clients: they are clients to one another. Whoever takes them as clients belongs with them. Of a truth, Allāh doth not guide wrongdoers." 'Ubādah is reputed to have told 'Abd Allāh ibn Ubayy, "The disposition of [men's] hearts has changed and Islam has abrogated [our] treaties" (al-Wāqidī, *al-Maghāzī,* 2:499).

280. Ibn Isḥāq, *Sīrah,* 1:688–90; Guillaume's translation, 463–64.

281. For example, Ibn Isḥāq, *Sīrah,* 1:415ff; Guillaume's translation, 281ff; al-Wāqidī, *al-Maghāzī,* passim. A list of the raids carried out at Muḥammad's instigation between the *Hijrah* and his death are in Watt, *Muhammad at Medina,* excursus B, 339–43. The first complete chronology of these raids is that compiled by al-Wāqidī (above), most recently edited by Marsden Jones, 3 vols. (Oxford, 1966).

282. The most celebrated of all such raids in the Tradition was that which took place at Badr in March 624, when some three hundred Muslims were supposed to have waylaid a caravan of a thousand camels and subsequently defeated a relief force dispatched from Makkah (p. 15 above). The first of the recorded raids specifically on Qurashī caravans resulted in the affair at Nakhlah mentioned on p. 23.

283. In this connection it may be noted that the Makkan *qiblah* was established while Muḥammad was residing in al-Madīnah. The conventionally accepted date was the fifteenth of Sha'bān, A.H. 2 (11 February A.D. 624).

284. I am using *power* in the sense of "ability to produce intended effects, specifically the capacity of an individual or group of individuals to modify the conduct of other individuals or groups in a manner that they desire." It is the threat of sanctions that differentiates power from influence in general. *Authority* is "the right accorded by an individual or group to another individual or group to exercise power." To say that a person has authority is to say that the political formula assigns him power, and that those who adhere to the formula regard his exercise of that power as just and proper. Authority alone is power of low weight. For a classic discussion of this distinction see Harold D. Lasswell and Abraham Kaplan, *Power and Society. A Framework for Political Inquiry* (New Haven, 1950), passim.

285. Robert Serjeant has pointed out that the process by which the *Ummat Allāh* came into being paralleled that obtaining among the pre-Islamic kingdoms of South Arabia as reconstructed by Jacques Ryckmans: "La tribu sud-arabe réunissait, sous la direction d'un clan privilégié, divers groupes ethniques ou économico-sociaux en vue de l'exploitation du territoire au profit du dieu national ou du patron tribal, par l'intermédiaire du temple . . . Dans le royaume sabéen, la notion de l'Etat était exprimée par la formule: 'Almaqah (le dieu national), Karibi'l (le souverain), et Saba'" ("Early Arabic Prose," 133–34).

For a different interpretation of events in the Ḥijāz during the decade or so prior to 622, see Fred M. Donner, "Muḥammad's political consolidation in Arabia up to the conquest of Mecca: a reassessment," *The Muslim World* 69 (1979): 229–47.

286. See, int. al., Ibn Isḥāq, *Sīrah,* 1:802–32; Guillaume's translation, 540–61; al-Balādhurī, *Futūḥ al-Buldān,* 40; Hitti's translation, 66. Cf. also Qur'ān 17 *(al-Isrā'):* 81. It is surely not without significance that one tradition has Muḥammad wearing a black turban as he entered Makkah, presumably in acknowledgement of the fact that he was violating the *ḥaram.* At any rate, this interpretation would be in accordance with the words that Ibn Isḥāq put into the mouth of the Prophet on the day following his entry into the sacred precinct: "God made Makkah holy on the day He created heaven and earth, and it is the holy of holies until the resurrection day. It is not lawful for anyone who believes in God and the last day to shed blood therein, nor to cut down trees therein. It was not lawful to anyone before me and it will not be lawful to anyone after me. *Indeed, it is not lawful for me except at this time because of God's anger against the inhabitants.* Now it has regained its former holiness" (Ibn Isḥāq, *Sīrah,* 1:823–24; Guillaume's translation, 555; my italics).

Fred M. Donner has suggested that the Muslim conquest of Makkah was helped to at least some degree by a famine in the settlement, which was probably exacerbated when Madīnan raids on Makkan caravans not only disrupted Qurashī commerce but also, intentionally or incidentally, effected a blockade of their food supplies ("Mecca's food supplies and Muhammad's boycott," *Journal of the Economic and Social History of the Orient* 20, pt. 2 (1977): 249–66). His argument relies in places on textual sources susceptible of alternative interpretation, and in any case the effectiveness of such a blockade would have depended greatly on the type of settlement that Makkah was. Whereas Professor Donner clearly regards it as a maturely developed urban form, I envisage it as having been "a town more in name than substance" (cf. p. 24 above and note 232). Whatever may be the truth of the matter, al-Madīnah provided Muḥammad with a strategically positioned base from which to intercept caravans from Syria, which may well have been bringing cereals, oil, and dried fruit from the country that Arabians of the time regarded as flowing with milk and honey.

Representative of current revisionist trends in Islamic historiography is G. R. Hawting's claim that the accounts of the conquest of Makkah as they have come down to us have been elaborated from early materials in which the sanctuary role of the settlement was only poorly developed: "Al-Hudaybiyya and the conquest of Mecca: a reconsideration of the tradition about the Muslim takeover of the sanctuary," *Jerusalem Studies in Arabic and Islam* 8 (1986): 1–23.

287. Ibn Isḥāq, *Sīrah,* 1:821; Guillaume's translation, 552.

288. Procksch, *Über die Blutrache,* vol. 5, pt. 4, p. 66.

289. Cf., for example, al-Mufaḍḍal al-Ḍabbi, *al-Mufaḍḍalīyāt,* vol. 1 (Lyall edition), 599; vol. 2 (Lyall's translation), 237.

290. In a revelation immediately after the encounter at Badr, Allāh justified Muḥammad's share of a fifth of the booty by charging him with responsibility for the care of orphans, the poor, and travellers (*Qur'ān* 8 *[al-Anfāl]:*41):

> And know that whatever ye take as booty, verily a fifth of it belongs to Allāh, and to the Messenger and the kinsmen, orphans, the indigent, and the travellers, if ye believe in Allāh and that which We revealed to Our servant of the Day of Discrimination *(Furqān)* [of the just from the unjust], the day when the two armies met. Allāh hath power over everything.

Muḥammad is reported to have appointed Maḥmīyah ibn Jaz' al-Zubaydī, a brother-in-law of his uncle al-ʿAbbās, as his agent to superintend the collection and distribution of the "fifth": Ibn Isḥāq, *Sīrah,* 1:783; Guillaume's translation, 527; al-Wāqidī, *al-Maghāzī,* Wellhausen's translation, 177, 221; and Ibn Saʿd, *Ṭabaqāt,* 4:146. There is a list of the *ʿummāl* dispatched to various tribal groups newly converted to Islam in Watt, *Muhammad at Medina,* 366–68.

291. Rodinson, *Mahomet,* 258.

292. This correspondence has been collected into a single volume by Muḥammad Ḥamīdullāh, *Majmūʿāt al-Wathā'iq al-Siyāsīyah* (Bayrūt, 1969). It is summarized by Serjeant ("Early Arabic Prose," 139–40), who accepts some of the documents as genuine (cf. the same author's "The 'Constitution of Medina,'" 3). I am not convinced of this, although they probably preserve something of the spirit and form of treaties and guarantees concluded during Muḥammad's lifetime.

293. Al-Maqdisī (*Aḥsan* [985–86], 112) noted that two routes between Makkah and al-Ṭā'if were in use in his day, one being easier but somewhat longer than the other. Cf. John Lewis [Johann Ludwig] Burckhardt, *Travels in Arabia, Comprehending an Account of those Territories in Hedjaz which the Mohammedans Regard as Sacred,* (London, 1829), 1:108–28. A brief survey of historical references to these routes in Arabic literature is incorporated in Henri Lammens, "La cité arabe de Ṭāif à la veille de l'hégire," *Mélanges de l'Université Saint-Joseph, Beyrouth (Syrie)* 8, fasc. 4 (1922): 132[20]–134[22].

294. The comparison with Syria was often made in early times: for example, al-Maqdisī, *Aḥsan,* 79. Cf. al-Hamadhānī, *al-Buldān* (903), 22: "What a man was that Qasī [the founding ancestor of the Banū-Thaqīf]! What a wonderful nest he discovered in which to shelter his brood." For more recent characterizations see, int. al., Burckhardt, *Travels in Arabia,* 1:122 and Maurice Tamisier, *Voyage en Arabie* (Paris, 1840), 1:260, 298, 299.

295. Al-Iṣfahānī, *al-Aghānī,* 4:75.

296. The tribe of the Banū-Thaqīf consisted of two sections known respectively as the Banū-Mālik, politically the more influential group, and the Aḥlāf ("Confederates"). The former were associated with the Hawāzin confederacy, while the Aḥlāf appear to have had ties with the group at Makkah who went under the same name.

297. There are several references to this wall in the *Sīrah* of Ibn Isḥāq (1:870–73; Guillaume's translation, 587–89). During the as-

sault on al-Ṭā'if in 630, the Muslims eventually breached the wall under cover of a testudo. Cf. also al-Balādhurī, *Futūḥ al-Buldān,* 56.

298. Serjeant, "Early Arabic Prose," 139.

299. Ibn Isḥāq, *Sīrah,* 1:918; Guillaume's translation, 617. Subsequently other tribal groups were rewarded with the establishment of *ḥimā*'s at Jurash, al-Muẓallalah, al-Naqī', Rabadhah, and Sharāf, at least one at the instigation of Muḥammad himself: cf. Fred M. Donner, *The Early Islamic Conquests,* 72, 298 n. 83. Defense of tribal *ḥimā*'s against raids by neighboring communities became a staple ingredient of *mufākharah* verse.

300. Cf. Watt, *Muhammad at Medina,* p. 104.

301. Hitti quotes a figure of 17 percent for the proportion of urban dwellers to total population in al-Ḥijāz in the later decades of the *Jāhilīyah* (*History of the Arabs,* 98) but neither cites his source or method of computation nor specifies what institutional assemblage he would regard as constituting an urban settlement.

The morphological development of the Ḥaramān is further discussed in chapter 17.

Chapter Two

1. It is unlikely that Abū Bakr himself used this title: later traditionists probably bestowed it on him. It has been claimed that 'Umar, second of the Rāshidūn caliphs, first assumed the title of *Khalīfah* with the implication of *Khalīfat Khalīfat Rasūl Allāh* (the Deputy of the Vicegerent [i.e., Abū Bakr] of God's Messenger), a style subsequently abbreviated, according to Ibn Sa'd on account of its length, but perhaps more probably through ignorance of the original form. See Ibn Sa'd (d. 845), *al-Ṭabaqāt,* vol. 3, pt. 1, p. 202. It has been plausibly argued, however, that from the time of 'Uthmān to the end of the Umayyad dynasty the style *khalīfat Allāh* was in common use, only to be largely replaced by *Kalīfat Rasūl Allāh* under the 'Abbāsids: see Patricia Crone and Martin Hinds, *God's Caliph. Religious Authority in the First Centuries of Islam* (Cambridge, 1986).

2. Elias Shoufani, in a recent study of the Ḥurūb al-Riddah, deduces that the term *riddah* was originally applied only to certain tribal groups in Najd and Eastern Arabia who withheld their taxes from the government in al-Madīnah (Medina), and who were consequently known as *Ahl al-Riddah.* These appear to have included the more powerful clans of the Ghaṭafān, Tayyi', and Tamīm (*Al-Riddah and the Muslim Conquest of Arabia* [Toronto, 1973], chap. 3). Subsequently the term was broadened to subsume all the conflicts that took place in Arabia immediately following the Prophet's death, and was finally given its conventional sense of apostasy by later jurists and historians.

3. Hugo Winckler, "Arabisch-Semitisch-Orientalisch," *Mitteilungen der Vorderasiatischen Gesellschaft* no. 4 (1901), 85–90.

4. Caetani, *Studi di Storia Orientale,* 1:133–35, 136 et seq.

5. Karl W. Butzer, "Der Umweltfaktor in der grossen arabischen Expansion," *Saeculum* 8 (1957): 359–71.

6. Sir William Muir, *The Caliphate: Its Rise, Decline and Fall* (London, 1898; reprint, Beirut, 1963), 45.

7. Lammens, *Le Climat—les Bédouins,* 177. It is noteworthy that all the protagonists of this style of argument have ignored the very significant differences between an intertribal *ghazū* undertaken for the prosecution of a blood feud or the seizure of livestock and an organized military campaign in a distant country against culturally and socially alien peoples.

8. Carl H. Becker, "Die Ausbreitung der Araber" in the same author's *Islamstudien,* vol. 1 (Leipzig, 1924; reprint, 1967), 66–145. An English translation of this paper, under the title "The Expansion of the Saracens," appears as chaps. 11 and 12 of *The Cambridge Medieval History,* vol. 2, ed. H. M. Gwatkin et al. (Cambridge, 1913; reprint, 1967). The fundamental question raised by Becker was whether the whole phenomenon of conquest and migration would be conceivable without Islam, and he seemed inclined to answer yes.

9. Marius Canard, "L'expansion arabe: le problème militaire" in *L'Occidente e l'Islam nell'Alto Medioevo,* vol. 1 of *Settimane di Studio del Centro Italiano di Studi sull'Alto Medioevo,* XII, 2–8, aprile 1964 (Spoleto, 1965), 37–63.

10. Muhammad Abdulhayy Shaban, *Islamic History,* A.D. *600–750 (*A.H. *132). A New Interpretation* (Cambridge, 1971), 24–25.

11. Al-Balādhurī, *Futūḥ al-Buldān,* 107, Hitti's translation, 165.

12. Ibid., 256–57; Hitti's translation, 411–12.

13. Abū Tammām, *Dīwān al-Ḥamāsah,* 795; supplementary commentary in 2 vols. (Bonn, 1847, 1851). Translation of the quotation by Hitti, *History of the Arabs,* 144.

14. Bousquet, "Observations sur la nature," 37–52.

15. Rodinson, "The life of Muhammad," 28–51, but especially p. 29: "At the base of the Arab conquest is the preaching of the prophet Muhammad." Cf. also the same author's "Comment est né l'Islam?" 136–41.

16. John J. Saunders, "The nomad as empire builder: a comparison of the Arab and Mongol conquests," *Diogenes,* no. 52 (1965), 79–103.

17. Francesco Gabrieli, *Muhammad and the Conquests of Islam* (New York and Toronto, 1968), chap. 6.

18. Laura Veccia Vaglieri, "The Patriarchal and Umayyad Caliphates," in *The Cambridge History of Islam,* ed. P. M. Holt, Ann K. S. Lambton, and Bernard Lewis (Cambridge, 1970), 1:60.

19. Claude Cahen, *Vom Ursprung bis zu den Anfängen des Osmanenreiches,* vol. 1 of *Der Islam* (Frankfurt-am-Main, 1968), 22–23.

20. Gustave E. von Grünebaum, *Classical Islam: a History, 600* A.D.*–1258* A.D. (Chicago, 1970), 53.

21. Crone and Cook, *Hagarism,* 9. Cf. also chap. 4, especially pp. 24–25, and Cook, *Muhammad,* 76.

22. Donner, *The Early Islamic Conquests,* 271.

23. Ibid., 269.

24. Ibid., 267.

25. Ibid., chap. 3 for a comprehensive critical summary of the

conquest of the territories now known as Syria. There is also some useful material in Philip Mayerson, "The First Muslim Attacks on Southern Palestine (A.D. 633–634)," in *Transactions and Proceedings of the American Philological Association* 95 (1964): 155–99.

26. For a critical summary of the conquest of the plains of the lower Tigris-Euphrates valley (i.e., al-ʿIrāq) see Donner, *The Early Islamic Conquests,* chap. 4. In this detailed reconstruction of the campaign Donner emphasizes both the relatively small number of tribesmen involved (between six thousand and twelve thousand at the Battle of al-Qādisīyah and some two thousand to four thousand active in southern al-ʿIrāq, as compared with perhaps twenty thousand to forty thousand at the Battle of Yarmūk in Syria) and the strong, centralized direction of the conquests from al-Madīnah.

27. Of the Arab campaign in Egypt, Alfred J. Butler's *The Arab Conquest of Egypt and the Last Thirty Years of the Roman Dominion* (Oxford, 1902) is still, after more than three quarters of a century, the standard account, although it needs revision in numerous details. It was reissued in 1978 with additional documentation and a critical bibliography by P. M. Fraser. There is a concise summary of the conquest, incorporating some alternative intepretations by Leone Caetani, in Gabrieli, *Muhammad and the Conquests of Islam,* chap. 9.

28. Cf. M. Caudel, *Les Premières Invasions Arabes dans l'Afrique du Nord et l'Orient au Moyen Âge* (Paris, 1900); Becker, "Die Ausbreitung der Araber" (see note 8 above); William Marçais, "Comment l'Afrique du nord a été arabisée," *Annales de l'Institut d'Etudes Orientales de l'Université d'Alger,* 17 (1938): 1–22, and "Les siècles obscurs du Maghreb," *Revue Critique d'Histoire et de Littérature* (1929), 255–70; reprinted in the same author's *Articles et Conférences: Publications de l'Institut d'Etudes Orientales, Faculté des Lettres d'Alger* 21 (Paris, 1961): Évariste Lévi-Provençal, "Un nouveau récit de la conquête de l'Afrique du nord par les Arabes," *Arabica* 1 (1954): 17–43; Charles-André Julien, *Histoire de l'Afrique du Nord,* rev. 2d ed. by Roger Le Tourneau (Paris, 1952), chap. 1; and Michael Brett, "The Arab Conquest and the Rise of Islam in North Africa," in *Cambridge History of Africa,* vol. 2, ed. J. D. Fage and Roland Olivier (Cambridge, 1978), 490–544. Several bold theoretical constructions by Émile Félix Gautier have failed to stand the test of time, although they have sparked valuable reappraisals of the evidence: *L'Islamisation de l'Afrique du Nord. Les Siècles Obscurs du Maghreb* (Paris, 1927); 2d ed. published under the title *Le Passé de l'Afrique du Nord. Les Siècles Obscurs* (Paris, 1952). See also Jamil M. Abun-Nasr, *A History of the Maghrib in the Islamic Period* (Cambridge, 1987), chap. 2.

29. Originally the term *Ahl al-Dhimmah* was applied only to scripturaries *(Ahl al-Kitāb),* chiefly Jews, Christians, and Ṣābians, but subsequently was extended by readily comprehensible analogy to include Zoroastrians *(Majūs),* Hindus, certain heathen communities in Ḥarrān, and pagan Berbers.

30. Al-Balādhurī, *Futūḥ al-Buldān,* 121; translation after Hitti and Murgotten, *The Origins of the Islamic State,* pt. 1, p. 187, modified. A later treaty on the same pattern was that which ʿAbd Allāh ibn ʿĀmir concluded with the *ʿaṭhīm* of Harāt: ibid., 405; Hitti and Murgotten, pt. 2, p. 163. For the changing meaning of the term *jizyah* see note 35 below.

31. Cf., for example, Aḥmad ibn Abī Yaʾqūb al-Yaʿqūbī, *Kitāb al-Buldān,* ed. M. J. de Goeje under the title *Kitâb al-Boldân Auctore . . . ,* in *Bibliotheca Geographorum Arabicorum,* ed. de Goeje (Lugduni Batavorum, 1892), 7:257 (all subsequent references are to the de Goeje edition unless otherwise indicated) and Ibn Khaldūn, *Muqaddimah,* Franz Rosenthal's translation (New York, 1958), 1:421 et seq. The one Umayyad ruler who was granted the title of *Khalīfah* by traditional Muslim historians was the pious ʿUmar II (r. 717–20).

32. Bernard Lewis, noting that the Byzantine chronicler Theophanes described Muʿāwiyah, first of the Umayyad rulers, not as king or emperor but as *Protosymboulos* or first councillor, adds, "This is not an inept description of the nature of the authority which he exercised" (*The Arabs in History,* 65).

33. Ibid., 66.

34. Such leases were modelled on the Byzantine *emphyteusis.*

35. Under the early caliphs, *jizyah* already technically denoted a poll tax, but *kharāj* (< Gk. *chorēgia,* possibly through Aram. *kᵉrāgā*) was used generically for any kind of tax, with a developing implication of the gross tribute levied by the Arabs from a region. By the beginning of the eighth century, *jizyah* had acquired the specific meaning of a poll tax payable by non-Muslims, and *kharāj* had come to denote the land tax.

36. See Wellhausen, *Das Arabische Reich,* chap. 8; H. A. R. Gibb, *The Arab Conquests in Central Asia* (London, 1923); and Francesco Gabrieli, "Muhammad ibn al-Qasim e la prima penetrazione araba nel Sind," in *Rendiconti Lincei* (Roma, 1965), 345–62.

37. The standard account of the Muslim conquest of the Iberian Peninsula was established by Reinhardt Dozy in his *Histoire des Musulmans d'Espagne,* 711–1110, first published at Leiden in 1861 and translated into English under the title *Spanish Islam* (London, 1913). Évariste Lévi-Provençal published an updated edition in three volumes (Leiden, 1932), and subsequently commenced a new work of his own, of which only three volumes appeared before his death: *Histoire de l'Espagne Musulmane* (Paris, 1944–53). This whole Dozy/Lévi-Provençal tradition is conveniently summarized in W. Montgomery Watt, *A History of Islamic Spain* (Edinburgh, 1965), chap. 1. Cf. also note 197 to chapter 16.

38. *Akhbār Majmūʿah fī Fatḥ al-Andalus,* ed. Lafuente y Alcántara (Madrid, 1867), 25 and Shihāb al-Dīn ibn Muḥammad al-Maqqarī, *Nafḥ al-Ṭīb* (originally published in Dimashq, A.H. 1038–40/A.D. 1628–30), ed. Iḥsān ʿAbbās (Bayrūt, A.H. 1388), vol. 1, p. 146, line 3 (all subsequent references are to the ʿAbbās edition unless otherwise indicated).

39. See, for example, Clifford E. Bosworth, *The Ghaznavids: Their Empire in Afghanistan and Eastern Iran* (Edinburgh, 1963), chap. 1.

40. Ramesh Chandra Majumdar, ed., *The Struggle for Empire,* vol. 5 of *Bharatiya Vidya Bhavan's History and Culture of the Indian*

People (Bombay, 1957), chap. 4 and Majumdar et al., eds., *The Delhi Sultanate,* vol. 6 of *BVB's History and Culture of the Indian People* (Bombay, 1960).

41. Sayyid Qadratullah Fatimi, *Islam Comes to Malaysia* (Singapore, 1963). For an exposition of the role of Ṣūfīs in the propagation of Islam in Southeast Asia see A. H. Johns, "Sufism as a category in Indonesian literature and history," *Journal of Southeast Asian History* 2 (1961): 10–23.

42. Kuwabara Jitsuzō, "On Pʿu Shou-keng, a man of the western regions . . . ," *Memoir of the Research Department of the Tōyō Bunkō* 2 (1928): 1–79 and 7 (1935): 1–104 (this is an English translation of an article that was originally published in *Shigaku Zasshi,* 26–29 [1915–18]) and Paul Wheatley, "Geographical notes on some commodities involved in Sung maritime trade," *Journal of the Malayan Branch of the Royal Asiatic Society* 32 (1959): 1–140.

43. J. Spencer Trimingham, *A History of Islam in West Africa* (Oxford, 1970).

44. Von Grünebaum, *Islam: Essays in the Nature and Growth of a Cultural Tradition,* 4.

45. For the *ḥisbah* see pp. 231–38 below.

46. For those, like Sir William Muir, Father Henri Lammens, and Professors Eric Wolf and Montgomery Watt, who regarded Makkah (Mecca) and al-Madīnah as developed urban centers, it seemed natural enough to see Islamic urban ideology as reflective of Muḥammad's personal experience of life in those settlements. The late Francisco Benet put this view succinctly enough when he wrote of Islam as "a predominantly urban religion . . . arising first in the minds of town merchants" ("The Ideology of Islamic Urbanization," in *Urbanism and Urbanization,* ed. Nels Anderson [Leiden, 1964], 114). But what if, as I contend (p. 24 above), Makkah in the time of the Prophet was "a town more in name than substance"? The evidence, as I read it, is unequivocal in its implication that the settlement was shot through with the norms of desert and steppe rather than pervaded by a characteristically urban style of life, production, and thought. As for al-Madīnah, it appears to have been even less of an urban focus than was Makkah (chapter 1, pp. 24–25).

It is, of course, undeniable that the original corpus of Islamic doctrine was subsequently formalized, codified, interpreted, and sometimes elaborated by men living in highly urbanized settings who doubtless impregnated their glosses and commentaries with norms of urban conduct. The point to be emphasized is that, in the interpretation being proposed here, Islamic urban ideology was in no way a direct legacy of Ḥijāzī town life in the seventh century but rather was induced in subsequent centuries by the sociocultural demands of the developing Muslim *Ummah* seeking to create an environment maximally conducive to the service of the One God. The resulting urban forms actually manifested only the most distant similarities to the Jāhilī settlements of al-Ḥijāz, as will be shown in later chapters.

47. In that section of his work dealing with cities known by more than one name, al-Maqdisī listed two additional designations for Jerusalem: *Iliyah* (< [Colonia] Ælia [Capitolina]) and al-Balāṭ (*Aḥsan,* 3:30). This topic is addressed further in chapters 6 and 17.

48. Adam Mez discriminated the urban traditions in the core region of Islamic culture on slightly different principles, viz., die hellenistische Mittelmeerstadt, die (süd)arabische Stadt wie Sanʿâ —auch Mekkah und Fostât gehören zu diesem Typus—, die babylonische und die östliche Stadt (*Die Renaissance des Islâms* [Heidelberg, 1922], 389).

49. *Tamṣīr* probably originally denoted the transformation of the separate sections of a military encampment into the quarters of a developed city (cf. Massignon, "Explication du plan de Kûfa [Irak]," 339), but has often been used subsequently by Muslim historians to mean the establishment of the camps in the first instance, particularly those in al-ʿIrāq. In the title to the present section I have used the term in an even broader sense to subsume the urban creation and transformation that accompanied the diffusion of Islam throughout southwest Asia and North Africa. For the implications of the term *miṣr* (pl. *amṣār*) see note 55 below.

50. For example, Georges Marçais, "La conception des villes dans l'Islâm," *Revue d'Alger* 2, no. 10 (1945): 517–33 (This author appears to have derived the notion of this particular dichotomy from certain remarks made by Pierre Lavedan in his *Géographie des Villes* [Paris, 1936], 11); Edmond Pauty, "Villes spontanées et villes créées en Islam," *Annales de l'Institut d'Etudes Orientales* 9 (1951): 52–75; and Xavier de Planhol, *Le monde Islamique: Essai de Géographie Religieuse* (Paris, 1957); English translation under the title *The World of Islam* (Ithaca, N.Y., 1959), 2–5. Cf. also G. E. von Grünebaum, "Die islamische Stadt," *Saeculum* 6 (1955): 138–53.

51. Marçais, "La conception des villes," 517.

52. Massignon, "Explication du plan de Kūfa," 338.

53. In the mid-twentieth century the populations of these once great capitals were al-Qayrawān (Kairouan), twenty-three thousand; al-Mahdīyah, eighty-five hundred. In the case of al-Qayrawān, the length of the original perimeter laid out in the ninth century had been reduced by more than half.

54. Benet, "The Ideology of Islamic Urbanization," 112–13.

55. The term *miṣr* (pl. *amṣār*) has borne a variety of connotations at different periods in history and, indeed, for different authors. For Arab historians of the Rāshidūn and Umayyad periods it seems to have meant "military cantonment." In the tenth century al-Maqdisī (*Aḥsan,* 47) offered four not wholly congruent definitions: (1) According to Muslim jurists, it signified "a city with a large population, courts of justice and a resident governor, which meets public charges from its own revenue, and is the focus of authority for surrounding territory." The examples offered by al-Maqdisī within this category were ʿAththar, Nābulus, and Zūzan. (2) Lexicographers allegedly restricted in term to "a settlement located at the boundary between two regions," as in the cases of al-Baṣrah, al-Raqqah, and Arrajān. (3) The common people, by contrast, supposedly understood the term to apply to any large and important settlement *(balad)* such as al-Rayy (Rey), al-Mawṣil (Mosul), or al-Ramlah (Ramleh). (4) Al-Maqdisī himself used the

word with the specific connotation that today attaches to the term *metropolis*, that is, "the locale *(balad)* where the supreme ruler of a territory resides, where the departments of state concerned with fiscal administration *(aʿmāl)* are located, and which exerts a dominant influence over all other urban centres in an *iqlīm*." We shall return to this particular use of the term *miṣr* in the next and subsequent chapters.

For a discussion of the way in which Muslim urban foundations were named, see Giovanna Calasso, "I nomi delle prime città di fondazione Islamica nel *Buldān* di Yāqūt: etimologie e racconti di origine," in *Studi in Onore di Francesco Gabrieli nel suo Ottantesimo Compleanno*, ed. R. Traini (Roma, 1984), 1:147–61.

56. Qayrawān (< Pers. *kārwān*) signified "garrison camp." For the founding of this city see M. Talbi, *The Encyclopaedia of Islam*, new ed., 4:825–27; also see chapter 16.

57. A Berber word signifying "camp." Strictly speaking, Tagrart was originally a siege position established during an investment of the older city of Agadir.

58. Aloys Sprenger's phrase: "Versuch einer Kritik von Hamdânis Beschreibung der arabischen Halbinsel," *Zeitschrift der Deutschen Morgenländischen Gesellschaft*, 45 (1891): 361. Cf. Aḥmad ibn Ḥanbal's phrase "men of the dug and udder": *al-Musnad*, ed. Aḥmad Muḥammad Shākir (al-Qāhirah, A.H. 1368–), 3:163.

59. Ibn Saʿd, *al-Ṭabaqāt*, vol. 3, pt. 1 (1904), 246.

60. Procksch, *Über die Blutrache*, vol. 5, pt. 4, 58.

61. Ibn Ḥanbal, *Musnad*, 3:161; Muḥammad ibn Ismāʿīl al-Bukhārī (810–70), *al-Jāmiʿ al-Ṣaḥīḥ*, *kitāb* 1, *bāb* 64; *kitāb* 7, *bāb* 13, 20, 33. According to al-Jāḥiẓ (*al-Ḥayawān*, vol. 4 [al-Qāhirah, 1938–45], 46), disease in the *amṣār* took a greater toll on *badū* life than did wounds on the battlefield.

62. Ibn Ḥanbal, *Musnad*, 2:176 and Ignaz Goldziher, *Abhandlungen zur Arabischen Philologie* (Leiden, 1896), 1:111 n. 1. Cf. also the following tradition preserved by al-Bukhārī (810–70), by universal consent the greatest of all collectors of *ḥadīths*. Converts from the tribes of ʿUkl and ʿUraynah, after having dwelt in al-Madīnah for some time, announced to the Prophet,

> "We are people accustomed to the udders of our camels; we are not people of the soil and al-Madīnah is uncomfortable for us. Life there does not become us." The Prophet then gave them a herd, placed a herdsman at their disposal, and permitted them to leave al-Madīnah to return contentedly to their accustomed way of life. Hardly had they reached the Ḥarrah when they reverted to their old beliefs, slew the herdsman, and appropriated the animals (Al-Bukhārī, *al-Jāmiʿ al-Ṣaḥiḥ*, quoted in Goldziher, *Muslim Studies*, 16).

63. Ibn Saʿd, *al-Ṭabaqāt*, vol. 4, pt. 2, par. 66, sec. 3 and Ibn Ḥanbal, *Musnad*, 2:160. On the *badū* distaste for life in the *amṣār* generally see Henri Lammens, "La 'bādia' et le 'ḥīra' sous les Omayyades: le problème de Mśattā," *Mélanges de la Faculté Orientale [de Beyrouth]* 4 (1910). Reprinted in Lammens, *Etudes sur le Siècle des Omayyades* (Beyrouth, 1930), 325–50.

64. Ibn Ḥanbal, Musnad, 3:370.

65. Benet's term for "backsliding into Bedouinism": "The ideology of Islamic urbanization," 116. Perhaps it would be strictly more accurate to speak of the magnitude of the *badū* anachorein *as perceived by traditionists of the eighth century and later.*

66. For succinct expositions of this theme see A. Leo Oppenheim, *Ancient Mesopotamia. Portrait of a Dead Civilization* (Chicago, 1964), 109–42 and "Mesopotamia—Land of Many Cities," in *Middle Eastern Cities. A Symposium on Ancient, Islamic, and Contemporary Middle Eastern Urbanism*, ed. Ira M. Lapidus (Berkeley and Los Angeles, 1969), 5–18; and M. B. Rowton, "Urban autonomy in a nomadic environment," *Journal of Near Eastern Studies* 32 (1973): 201–15.

67. Ziyād's *khuṭbah* is summarized in Lammens, "Ziad ibn Abihi, vice-roi de l'Iraq," in *Etudes sur le Siècle des Omayyades*, 27–163; pp. 61–62 include comments on the authenticity of Ziyād's homily. Cf. also Lammens, "La cité arabe de Ṭāif," 308 [196]; Wellhausen, *The Arab Kingdom and Its Fall* (Beirut, 1963), 122–23; and Gustave E. von Grünebaum, *Classical Islam: A History, 600 A.D.–1258 A.D.* (Chicago, 1970), 70–71.

68. Cf., int. al., the lines of a contemporary poet which have been preserved by al-Ṭabarī (838–923) (*Taʾrīkh*, 2:78) as rendered by Lammens in "La cité arabe de Ṭāif," 309:

> Esprit libéral, tu apparus, au milieu d'un siècle inique,
> où le mal s'affichait publiquement;
> Où, les hommes divisés par leurs passions, les coeurs ne
> prenaient plus la peine de dissimuler leurs haines.
> Le sédentaire tremblait; les alarmes enveloppaient le
> nomade en marche ou au campement.
> A ce moment paru l'épée d'Allah, Ziad . . .

It must be remembered, of course, that in the struggle after ʿUthmān's death, al-ʿIrāq generally had supported ʿAlī, so that a Sufyānī-appointed governor probably would have been biased against one of the province's premier Arab settlements in any case.

69. The chief primary sources for the settlement of the tribes in al-Baṣrah are al-Balādhurī, *Futūḥ al-Buldān* (892); *Ḥudūd al-ʿālam* (982), translated from the Persian by V. Minorsky (London, 1937), 138–39 (all subsequent references are to Minorsky's translation unless otherwise indicated); al-Maqdisī, *Aḥsan;* and Yāqūt, *Muʿjam*. The information in these works has been interpreted by Guy Le Strange, *The Lands of the Eastern Caliphate* (Cambridge, 1905); Else Reitemeyer, *Die Städtegründungen der Araber im Islam nach dem Arabischen Historikern und Geographen* (München, 1912); Massignon, "Explication du plan de Kûfa," appendix 1 and "Explication du plan de Baṣra (Irak)," in *Westöstliche Abhandlungen: Rudolf Tschudi zum Siebzigsten Geburtstag überreicht von Freunden und Schülern*, ed. Fritz Meier (Wiesbaden, 1954), 154–74 (neither work being wholly reliable); Charles Pellat, *Le Milieu Baṣrien et la Formation de Ǧāḥiẓ* (Paris, 1953), 2–4 (Arabic translation by I. Keilani, Dimashq, 1961); and Ṣāliḥ Aḥmad al-ʿAlī, "Khiṭaṭ al-Baṣrah," *Sumer* 8 (1952): 72–83, 281–302 and *al-Tanẓīmāt al-Ijtimāʿīyah*

wa-l-Iqtiṣādīyah fī-l-Baṣrah fī-l-Qarn al-ʾAwwal al-Hijrī (Baghdād, 1953). There is an interpretive summary of Arab settlement in the cantonments of both al-Baṣrah and al-Kūfah in Richard W. Bulliet, "Sedentarization of Nomads in the Seventh Century: The Arabs in Basra and Kufa," in *When Nomads Settle,* ed. Philip C. Salzman (Brooklyn, N.Y., 1980), 35–47, and pertinent analytical comments in Donner, *The Early Islamic Conquests,* chap. 5. For the *amṣār* (and Arab settlement generally) as instruments of economic progress see Ira M. Lapidus, "Arab Settlement and Economic Development of Iraq and Iran in the Age of the Umayyad and Early Abbasid Caliphs," in *The Islamic Middle East, 700–1900: Studies in Economic and Social History,* ed. A. L. Udovitch (Princeton, N.J., 1981), 177–208.

70. Al-Balādhurī, *Futūḥ al-Buldān,* 346; Murgotten's translation, 60, modified.

71. Al-Balādhurī's text reads *qaṣabah,* but should perhaps be amended to read *qaḍabah* (nutritious plants). Cf. Murgotten's translation, 60 n. 3.

72. Al-Balādhurī, *Futūḥ al-Buldān,* 341; Murgotten's translation, 52.

73. The several strands in these two traditions have been analyzed and explicated by Caetani, *Annali,* 3:292–309, 769–84.

74. Al-Masʿūdī, *al-Tanbīh wa-l-Ishrāf,* 357–58.

75. Caetani finally came to favor this latter year: *Annali,* 3:769.

76. Pellat, *Le Milieu Baṣrien,* 2–3.

77. Ibn al-Faqīh al-Hamadhānī, *al-Buldān* (903), 187 and Abū Isḥāq al-Iṣṭakhrī, *al-Masālik wa-l-Mamālik* (c. 950), in *Viae Regnorum Descriptio Ditionis Moslemicae,* vol. 1 of *Bibliotheca Geographorum Arabicorum,* ed. M. J. de Goeje (Lugduni Batavorum, 1870), 80.

One *parasang* (a customary European rendering of the Perso-Arabic *farsakh*) is equal to three Arab miles. The term was used mainly in the provinces of the Caliphate lying to the east of the Euphrates.

78. It would seem that the name al-Baṣrah was in some way related to the nature of the local terrain, although the derivations proposed by early Muslim authors have all the appearance of folk etymology conjured up to explain an unfamiliar word. Al-Balādhurī (*Futūḥ al-Buldān,* 341) and Abū Ḥanīfah Aḥmad ibn Dāwūd al-Dīnawarī (d. 895) (al-Akhbār al-Ṭiwāl, ed. V. Guirgass [Leiden, 1888], with variants and index by I. J. Kračkovskij [al-Qāhirah, A.H. 1330/A.D. 1912], 117), for example, took it as denoting "black pebbles," as did subsequently also al-Maqdisī (*Aḥsan,* 118) and Yāqūt (*Muʿjam,* 1:637). Others took it to imply a white stone or a white dust, and in one case proposed a spurious Persian derivation from *bas rāh,* "many ways" (Ḥamzah al-Iṣfahānī [died ca. 961], *al-Arḍ wa-l-Anbiyāʾ;* see Goldziher, *Muhammedanische Studien,* 1 [1890]: 211). On the significance of the name in general see Caetani, *Annali,* 3:297 n. 2 and Pellat, *Le Milieu Baṣrien,* 4 n. 1.

79. Al-Iṣṭakhrī, *al-Masālik wa-l-Mamālik,* 81; Ibn Ḥawqal, *Ṣūrat al-Arḍ* (977), 120; Badīʿ al-Zamān al-Hamadhānī (d. 1007), *Maqāmāt,* ed. Muḥammad ʿAbduh (Bayrūt, 1889), 69; Abū ʿUthmān ʿAmr ibn Baḥr al-Jāḥiẓ (d. 868/9), *Kitāb al-Bukhalāʾ,* ed. Ḥājirī (al-Qāhirah, A.H. 1368/A.D. 1948), 24, 259–60.

80. Al-Balādhurī, *Futūḥ al-Buldān,* 347; Murgotten's translation, 61.

81. Al-Maqdisī, *Aḥsan,* 117. The *ṭaylasān* was a pointed black hood or stole thrown over the head and shoulders (sometimes including the turban): see Yedida K. Stillman, *Dictionary of the Middle Ages,* vol. 11, 507–9. At first peculiar to *faqīhs,* it eventually came to be worn by men of distinction in sundry other walks of life. The simile of the *ṭaylasān* was a favorite one with al-Maqdisī, who uses it again in his descriptions of al-Mawṣil (138) and al-Raḥbah (142). *Ṭaylasān* was a loanword in Arabic from Middle or New Persian *tālashān:* cf. Aramaic *ṭalshanā.*

82. Al-Yaʿqūbī, *al-Buldān* (891–92), 323.

83. Al-Ṭabarī, *Taʾrīkh,* 2:1379.

84. Ibid., 3:373–74; ʿIzz al-Dīn ibn al-Athīr (1160–1234), *al-Kāmil fī al-Taʾrīkh,* ed. C. J. Tornberg under the title *Ibn al-Athiri Chronicon quod Perfectissimum Inscribitur . . .* (Leyden, 1867–76), 6:2; and Reitemeyer, *Städtegründungen,* 25.

85. *Mirbaḍ* originally denoted the floor on which dates were dried (see Yāqūt, *Muʿjam,* 4:484 and al-Sayyid Murtaḍā al-Zabīdī, *Tāj al-ʿArūs* [al-Qāhirah, A.H. 1307/A.D. 1889], s.v. "*RBḌ*"), but at some unspecified time acquired the additional meaning of stabling for camels or pens for migrant flocks: cf. Pellat, *Le Milieu Baṣrien,* 11.

86. Yāqūt, writing in the early years of the thirteenth century (*Muʿjam,* 4:484), notes that by his time the street leading to the Mirbaḍ was in disrepair and its bordering buildings in ruins, so that the former suburb appeared as an oasis in the desert. Al-Maqdisī, in the tenth century (*Aḥsan,* 118), also observes that "the desert side of al-Baṣrah has now fallen into ruins."

87. Al-Balādhurī, *Futūḥ al-Buldān,* 346. "Freestanding" because Saʿd ibn Abī Waqqaṣ had previously set up a *minbar* in the Sāsānian audience hall (the Īwān Kisrā) at al-Madāʾin after the Muslim conquest of that city in 637 (al-Ṭabarī, *Taʾrīkh,* 4:2442–44).

88. Al-Balādhurī, *Futūḥ al-Buldān,* 347; Yāqūt, *Muʿjam,* 1:642.

89. Al-Balādhurī, *Futūḥ al-Buldān,* 347; Yāqūt, *Muʿjam,* 1:642; and Ibn Rustah (d. 903), *al-Aʿlāq,* 192.

90. Al-Ṭabarī, *Taʾrīkh,* 1:3455.

91. Ibid., 2:726 and al-Balādhurī, *al-Ashrāf,* 4B:112. Cf. Julius Wellhausen, *Das Arabische Reich,* 164. The three most comprehensive, though not wholly accordant, explications of the somewhat ambiguous evidence are those undertaken by Pellat, *Le Milieu Baṣrien,* 22–34; Massignon, "Explication du plan de Baṣra," 154–74; and al-ʿAlī, "Khiṭaṭ" and *al-Tanẓīmāt* (cf. note 69 above).

92. In a recent paper Fred M. Donner ("Tribal Settlement in Basra during the First Century A.H.," in *Land Tenure and Social Transformation in the Middle East,* ed. Tarif Khalidi [Beirut, 1984], 97–120) questions the extent to which we can rely (as here) on Arabic narrative sources to reconstruct the *tamṣīr* process, and essays a quantitative analysis of the tribal affiliations of individuals mentioned in the relevant biographical dictionaries. However, his

tentative findings appear not to be in fundamental disagreement with the reconstruction proposed here.

93. Cf. Meir J. Kister, "Tamīm in the Period of the Jahiliyya: A Study in Tribal Tradition" (Ph.D. diss., Hebrew University, Jerusalem, 1964). The Tamīm who settled in al-Baṣrah were divided among the clans of the Banū-Saʿd, Banū-ʿAmr, and Banū-Ḥanẓalah.

94. Yāqūt and Masʿūdī were exceptional in that the former refers to the indigenous folk of the Sawād as Persians (*Muʿjam,* 3:31) and the latter writes of the Chaldaeans of the Baṭāʾiḥ (*al-Tanbīh,* 161. Note: *Baṭāʾiḥ* and its plural *Baṭīḥah* are used interchangeably to denote the Great Swamp north of al-Baṣrah). The best account of the Aramaic speakers in al-ʿIrāq at the time of the Muslim conquest is provided by Michael G. Morony, *Iraq after the Muslim Conquest* (Princeton, N.J., 1984), chap. 4. On p. 170 Morony observes that the term *Anbāṭ* seems to have connoted a sedentary way of life rather than a language group.

95. Al-Balādhurī, *al-Ashraf,* 4B:109 and al-Ṭabarī, *Taʾrīkh,* 2:458, 995. Cf. also A. Christensen, *L'Iran sous les Sassanides,* 2d ed. (Copenhagen, 1944), 113. This piece of information crops up in a not wholly reliable context but itself appears to bear an imprint of considerable verisimilitude.

96. Al-Masʿūdī, *Murūj,* 2:241. Cf. also Christensen, *L'Iran sous les Sassanides,* 508–9 and Morony, *Iraq after the Muslim Conquest,* chap. 5.

97. Al-Balādhurī, *Futūḥ al-Buldān,* 410; al-Ṭabarī, *Taʾrīkh,* 2:170; and Yāqūt, *Muʿjam,* 1:520, 522. Cf. also Narshakhī's account of Bukhārā in Richard N. Frye's translation, *The History of Bukhara* (Cambridge, Mass., 1954), 38.

98. Al-Balādhurī, *Futūḥ al-Buldān,* 366, 373. The Zuṭṭ are discussed by Gabriel Ferrand in *The Encyclopaedia of Islam,* 1st ed., 4:1305–6. On the Zuṭṭ in the vicinity of al-Baṣrah see M. J. de Goeje, *Mémoire sur les Migrations des Tsiganes à travers l'Asie* (Leyde, 1903).

99. Al-Balādhurī, *Futūḥ al-Buldān,* 375. Kaskar was the district, east of al-Kūfah, within which the city of Wāsiṭ was later established.

100. Ibid., 321, 373. The Sindian provenance of the Asāwirah has been established by de Goeje (*Mémoire sur les Migrations des Tsiganes,* 17).

101. Gabriel Ferrand, *The Encyclopaedia of Islam,* 1st ed., s.v. "Sayābidja": Sayābiga, sing. Saibagī, Sābagī, Sābag = Zābag < Jāvaka = Indonesians. Cf. also de Goeje, *Mémoire sur les Migrations des Tsiganes,* 86 et seq. For *Sayābijah,* see al-Iṣfahānī, *al-Aghānī,* 14:46, which reads *Satāyijah;* and al-Athīr, *al-Kāmil,* 2:281, which reads *Sabābijah.* Cf. al-Ṭabarī, *Taʾrīkh,* 1:1961.

102. Al-Balādhurī, *Futūḥ al-Buldān,* 373–75.

103. Ibid., 376. Other early authors speak of only forty Sayābijah in the service of the treasury.

104. See Louis Massignon, *The Encyclopaedia of Islam,* 1st ed., s.v. "Zanğ."

105. Al-Jāḥiẓ, *Kitāb al-Bayān wa-l-Tabyīn,* ed. ʿAbdal-Salām Muḥammad Hārūn (al-Qahirah, A.H. 1367), 3:36.

106. Al-Ṭabarī, *Taʾrīkh,* 1:2378, 2385: between three hundred and five hundred men; al-Balādhurī, *Futūḥ al-Buldān,* 35 and Yāqūt, *Muʿjam,* 1:641: eight hundred men; Ibn Rustah, *al-Aʿlāq,* 195: about three hundred.

107. Pellat, *Le Milieu Baṣrien,* 5. Al-Ṭabarī (*Taʾrīkh,* 1:3156, 3224) claims that five thousand Baṣrians were killed at the Battle of the Camel in 657, but Pellat indicates (loc. cit., note 5) that this number is grossly exaggerated and incompatible with the figures advanced by the same author when he discusses the apportionment of the booty (loc. cit., 1:3227).

108. Al-Balādhurī, *Futūḥ al-Buldān,* 350 and Yāqūt, *Muʿjam,* 1:644.

109. Al-Ṭabarī, *Taʾrīkh,* 2:1290–91.

110. Pellat, *Le Milieu Baṣrien,* 6.

111. Some five and a half centuries after the event, Yāqūt incorporated highly valuable information about the founding of al-Kūfah in his geographical dictionary *Muʿjam al-Buldān.* There is also a limited amount of material preserved in al-Ṭabarī's *Taʾrīkh.* Several early works devoted to al-Kūfah are now known only by their titles and by quotations in later authors' works. Among these are four essays by Haytham ibn ʿAdī (d. 822): *Kitāb Khiṭaṭ al-Kūfah,* on which al-Yaʿqūbī probably based his account of al-Kūfah; *Kitāb Wilat al-Kūfah,* exploited by al-Ṭabarī; *Kitāb Quḍāt al-Kūfah wa-l-Baṣrah,* on which Ibn Saʿd drew for his *al-Ṭabaqāt;* and *Kitāb Fakhr Ahl al-Kūfah ʿalāʾ al-Baṣrah,* which considerably influenced the writing of Ibn al-Faqīh. For citations from these works see Massignon, "Explication du plan de Baṣra," 357 n. 5 and Kāẓim al-Janābī, *Takhṭīṭ Madīnat al-Kūfah ʿan al-Maṣādir al-Tārīkhīyah wa-l-Athārīyah* (Baghdād, 1967). There are useful comments on both the texts and the settlement process in M. H. Zubaydī, *Al-Ḥayāt al-Ijtimāʿīyah wa-l-Iqtiṣādīyah fī al-Kūfah fī al-Qarn al-Awwal al-Hijrī* (Baghdād, A.H. 1379; al-Qāhirah, A.H. 1390); Martin Hinds, "Kûfan political alignments and their backgrounds in the mid-seventh century A.D.," *International Journal of Middle East Studies,* 2 (1971): 346–67; and Donner, *The Early Islamic Conquests,* chap. 5. Something can also be gleaned from Muḥammad ʿAlī Muṣṭafā, "Preliminary report on the excavations in Kūfa during the Third Season," *Sumer* 19 (1963): 36–64. But after half a century the most comprehensive reconstruction of the disposition of the tribes in al-Kūfah is still Louis Massignon's "Explication du plan de Kûfa" (Cf. note 69 above). In his extremely thorough discussion of the city, Hichem Djaït (*Al-Kūfa: Naissance de la Ville Islamique* [Paris, 1986]) apparently accepts many of the conclusions advanced in Massignon's paper, which he praises as *un texte capital* (p. 83) while yet revising others in light of a closer reading of Sayf ibn ʿUmar (in al-Ṭabarī's *Taʾrīkh*).

112. Al-Yaʿqūbī, *al-Buldān,* 310.

113. Al-Ṭabarī, *Taʾrīkh,* 1:2360.

114. See Louis Massignon, *Mission en Mésopotamie (1907–*

1908), vol. 1 (Le Caire, 1910), 31–51, especially p. 49 and Morony, *Iraq after the Muslim Conquest,* chaps. 4, 6.

115. Yāqūt, *Muʿjam,* 4:323–24 and Ibn Saʿd, *al-Ṭabaqāt,* 6:10.

116. Al-Ṭabarī, *Taʾrīkh,* 1:2487–88 and al-Janābī, *Takhṭīṭ,* 75–78.

117. For administrative purposes, principally the payment of stipends, these migrants were known collectively as *al-rawādif* ("those who come after"). For a definition of *rawādif* see Ibn Manẓūr, *Lisān al-ʿArab,* ed. Y. Khayyat and N. Marʿashlī (Bayrūt, n.d.), 1:1152.

118. Cf. Hinds, "Kûfan political alignments," passim. For *al-rawādif* see preceding note.

119. Massignon, "Explication du plan de Kûfa," 341–42, based on al-Ṭabarī, *Taʾrīkh,* 1:2495; but for certain reservations as to Massignon's placing of the *khiṭāṭ* see Djaït, *Al-Kūfa,* chap. 8. Contra Massignon, this author believes that mapping the tribes in the *khiṭāṭ* "se heurte à des difficultés quasi insurmontables" (121). Al-Janābī (*Takhṭīṭ,* 77) envisages the camp as laid out on an orthogonal plan, while Saleh al-Hathloul believes that tribes were assigned a *khiṭṭah* by a central authority ("Tradition, Continuity, and Change in the Physical Environment" [Ph.D. diss., Massachusetts Institute of Technology, 1981], 35). Both readings of the situation are opposed by Jamel Akbar ("Khaṭṭa and the territorial structure of early Muslim towns," *Muqarnas. An Annual of Islamic Art and Architecture* 6 [1989]: 22–32) and the present author. This topic will be discussed in chapter 17.

120. On this lineage see, int. al., Ibn Rustah, *al-Aʿlāq,* 205, 229; al-Ṭabarī, *Taʾrīkh,* 2:728, 1044, 1132; Ibn al-Faqīh, *al-Buldān,* 172; al-Iṣfahānī, *al-Aghānī,* 5:145, 18:35, 42; and Ibn Saʿd, *al-Ṭabaqāt,* 6:290. For the role of so-called Yamanī tribes, preeminently Madhḥij, Hamdān, Ḥimyar, and Ḥaḍramī, in the early years of the *miṣr* see Hichem Djaït, "Les Yamanites à Kūfa au Ier siècle de l'Hégire," *Journal of the Economic and Social History of the Orient* 19 (1976): 148–81.

121. The Tamīm were generally known by the name of their putative ancestor Muḍar.

122. For *al-ḥamrāʾ* as Persian knights see Julius Wellhausen, "Die religiös-politischen Oppositionspartei im alten Islam," *Abhandlungen der Königlichen Gesellschaft der Wissenschaften zu Göttingen,* Phil.-Hist. Klasse, n.s. 5, no. 2 (1901): 58 n. 1, but Donner (*The Early Islamic Conquests,* 347 n. 77) suggests "it is conceivable that the references at times are to tribesmen of Azd or Lakhm."

123. The Bakr ibn Wāʾil were generally known by the name of their putative ancestor Rabīʿah.

124. Balādhurī, *al-Ashrāf,* cited in Caetani, *Annali,* 9:129; al-Dīnawarī, *al-Akhbār al-Ṭiwāl,* 148. Al-Ṭabarī (*Taʾrīkh,* 1:3174) omits the first and fourth groups in the list as reproduced here. See also Massignon, "Explication du plan de Kûfah," 342.

125. Ibn al-Faqīh, *al-Buldān,* 183.

126. Massignon, "Explication du plan de Kûfah," 342–43.

127. Ibn al-Faqīh, *al-Buldān,* 190. The lineages in question were those of Ahl Zurārah of the Dārim clan (Tamīm), Ahl Zayd of the Fazārah clan (Qays), Ahl Dhī al-Jaddayn of the Shaybān clan (mainly Bakr), and Ahl Qays of the Zubayd clan (Madhḥij). It is noteworthy, however, that al-Faqīh did attempt to maintain a degree of symmetry in his narrative by observing that there were also four important (though presumably less so) lineages among the tribes of al-Baṣrah: al-Muhallab (Azd), Ibn ʿAmr al-Bāhilī (Qays), Mismaʿ (Bakr), and al-Jarūd (ʿAbd al-Qays). Djaït (*Al-Kūfa,* 87–89), relying on information provided by Sayf ibn ʿUmar, accorded the settlement an extremely rapid development—*une urbanisation concertée, rationnelle, et d'une étonnante rapidité*—but he seems to have been influenced more by layout and building materials than by societal change.

128. Whereas Massignon attached considerable significance to the function of al-Baṣrah as a "port fluvial où les colis, avant de partir du *mirbad* à dos de chameau, étaient déchargés des navires" ("Explication du plan de Baṣra," 340), Pellat minimizes the importance of trading activities (*Le Milieu Baṣrien,* 12).

129. On this theme see Pellat, *Le Milieu Baṣrien,* 42 et seq. Both Pellat (loc. cit.) and Massignon (loc. cit.) ascribe considerable influence on Baṣrian development to the Īrānicized elements within the settlement.

130. Ziyād was governor of all al-ʿIrāq and the East from about 669 to 673.

131. Al-Ṭabarī, *Taʾrīkh,* 2:131, 255, 644, 701, 857, 1702.

132. This office was a good deal older than Ziyād's reconstitution of the tribes. From the early days of the settlement the *ʿarīf* had been the head of an *ʿirāfah,* or stipend (*ʿaṭāʾ*), unit. In the time of Muḥammad the *ʿirāfah* seems to have comprised either ten or fifteen tribesmen, but by the middle of the seventh century it had developed into a stipendiary institution of varying size. According to al-Ṭabarī (*Taʾrīkh,* 1:2496), the *ʿirāfahs* were first introduced into al-Kūfah after the Battle of Qādisīyah in 637. The same author (1:2496) also notes that, prior to Ziyād's reorganization, the Dīwān disbursed its payments first to the *shaykhs* in charge of the "sevenths" and to the tribal standard-bearers (*aṣḥāb al-rāyāt*), who then distributed them to the heads of the *ʿirāfahs,* the *naqībs* and the *amīns,* who in turn conveyed them to individuals. After an examination of the scanty evidence available, Professor Donner has concluded that the commanders of the "sevenths" were responsible for the disbursement of civilian stipends; the standard-bearers, for the military payroll (*The Early Islamic Conquests,* 238).

133. Lammens, "Ziad ibn Abihi vice-roi de l'Iraq," *Rivista degli Studi Orientali* 4 (1911–12): 127–32.

134. Al-Ṭabarī, *Taʾrīkh,* 1:2488–90.

135. Massignon, "Explication du plan de Kûfa," 348.

136. Al-Yaʿqūbī, *al-Buldān,* 310.

137. Al-Balādhurī, *Futūḥ al-Buldān,* 275–76. Cf. also al-Ṭabarī, *Taʾrīkh,* 1:2481. On the internal layout of al-Kūfah see Djaït, *al-Kūfa,* chap. 7 and chapter 17 of the present text.

138. Al-Ṭabarī, *Taʾrīkh,* 1:2494.

139. Ibid., 1:2492; Ibn Jubayr, *Riḥlah,* ed. M. J. de Goeje, vol. 5 of the Gibb Memorial Series (Leyden, 1907), 211 (all subsequent references are to the de Goeje edition unless otherwise indicated); and K. A. C. Creswell, *A Short Account of Early Muslim Architecture* (Harmondsworth, Middlesex, England, 1958), 13.

140. Al-Balādhurī, *Futūḥ al-Buldān,* 289.

141. Massignon, "Explication du plan de Kûfa," 347.

142. Ibid., 351–52.

143. Paul Pelliot, "Des artisans chinois à la capitale Abasside en 751–762," *T'oung Pao* 26 (1928): 110–12, citing *T'ung Tien* (A.D. 766–801), chap. 191.

144. Al-Ṭabarī, *Ta'rīkh,* 2:268, 735; Ibn Sa'd, *al-Ṭabaqāt,* 6: 280; and Massignon, "Explication du plan de Kûfa," 354–55.

145. Al-Balādhurī, *Futūḥ al-Buldān,* 289. Djaït (*Al-Kūfa,* 287) believes that the incorporation of *jabbānāt* in the cantonment was a practice introduced by Yamanī settlers.

146. Ibn al-Faqih, *al-Buldān,* 172.

147. Al-Balādhurī, *Futūḥ al-Buldān,* 350. Cf. Yāqūt, *Mu'jam,* 1: 644 and Reitemeyer, *Städtegründungen,* 25.

148. Al-Jahshiyārī (d. 942), *Kitāb al-Wuzarā' wa-l-Kuttāb,* published by Hans von Mžik (Leipzig, 1926) and edited by Mustafā al-Saqqā' et al. (al-Qāhirah, A.H. 1357/A.D. 1938), 52b. All subsequent references are to the von Mžik edition unless otherwise indicated.

149. Massignon, "Explication du plan de Kûfa," 345.

150. This name probably arose as a Greek corruption of the ancient Egyptian *Pi-Hapi n-On* (the temple of Apis of Heliopolis) and was apparently transmitted to the Crusaders, and so to western Europe, by the Copts who inhabited the region. See Paul Casanova, *Essai de Reconstitution Topographique de la Ville d'al-Foustât ou Miṣr,* 3 vols. together constituting vol. 35 of *Mémoires Publiés par les Membres de l'Institut Français d'Archéologie Orientale du Caire* (Le Caire, 1913–19). The reference is to vol. 1, fasc. 3, p. xxv. Cf. also Casanova, "Les noms coptes du Caire," *Bulletin de l'Institut Français d'Archéologie Orientale du Caire* 1 (1901): 197.

151. This is the common interpretation of medieval Muslim authors, but more probably the name was derived from the Byzantine Greek *φοσσᾶτον* = "encampment," although the variety of orthographies employed by early Muslim authors would seem to imply some uncertainty as to the true origin of the word.

152. There is doubt about the precise significance of the term *maḥras* in this conext. A. Rhuvon Guest translates it as "guard-house" or "watchtower" ("The foundation of Fustat and the khittahs of that town," *The Journal of the Royal Asiatic Society of Great Britain and Ireland* [1907]: 79–80), Gaston Wiet as "caravanserai" (*Ya'ḳūbī. Le Pays* [Le Caire, 1937], 184).

153. See note 132 above.

154. Al-Ya'qūbī, *al-Buldān,* 330–31. Other sources that incorporate materials relating to the founding of al-Fusṭāṭ, and in much greater abundance to its subsequent history, include Ibn 'Abd al-Ḥakam (ca. 805–71, and therefore closest of extant authors to the founding of the settlement, as well as scion of a notable Fusṭāṭ family), *Kitāb Futūḥ Miṣr wa-l-Ifrīqiya,* ed. Charles C. Torrey (New Haven, Conn., 1922) (all subsequent references are to the Torrey edition unless otherwise indicated); al-Maqdisī, *Aḥsan* (cf. note 47 above); Yāqūt, *Mu'jam* (cf. note 38 above); Ṣārim al-Dīn Ibn Duqmāq, *Kitāb al-Intiṣār li-Wāsiṭat 'Iqd al-Amṣār,* 2 vols. (Būlāq, A.H. 1308/A.D. 1890–91); Taqī al-Dīn Aḥmad al-Maqrīzī (1364–1442), *al-Mawā'iẓ wa-l-I'tibār fī Dhikr al-Khiṭaṭ wa-l-Āthār,* 2 vols. (Būlāq, A.H. 1270/A.D. 1853. Edited by Gaston Wiet [Le Caire, 1911] [all subsequent references are to the Wiet edition unless otherwise indicated]; and Jalāl al-Dīn al-Suyūṭī (1445–1505), *Ḥuṣn al-Muḥāḍarah fī Akhbār Miṣr wa-l-Qāhirah,* 2 vols. (al-Qāhirah, A.H. 1321/A.D. 1903). These and other works relating to al-Fusṭāṭ are evaluated by Guest, "The foundation of Fustat," 49–83; Casanova, *Essai de Reconstitution,* which includes detailed plans of virtually every sector of the city; and, most comprehensively, Wladyslaw B. Kubiak, *Al-Fustat: Its Foundation and Early Urban Development* (Cairo, 1987), chap. 1. This last author, in addition to being a competent Arabist, is a practicing field archaeologist who worked with the Fusṭāṭ Expedition mounted by the American Research Center in Egypt as recently as the 1960s. Consequently he has been able in certain instances to revise Casanova's conclusions. In particular his Plans 1 and 4 must be held to supersede the parallel reconstructions in the *Essai de Reconstitution.* Whatever remains of value in the work of Aly Bahgat Bey and Albert Gabriel (*Fouilles d'al-Foustât* [Paris, 1921]) and G. Salmon ("Études sur la topographie du Caire," *Mémoires Publiés par les Membres de l'Institut Français d'Archéologie Orientale du Caire* 7 [1902]) has been expertly subsumed by Kubiak's inclusive study and even more recently by Roland-Pierre Gayraud, "Fostat: Evolution d'une capitale arabe du VIIe au XIIe siècle d'après les fouilles d'Istabl 'Antar," in Gayraud (ed.), *Colloque International d'Archéologie Islamique,* 435–60.

155. In the early years of al-Fusṭāṭ's existence, Sharaf al-Raṣad was sometimes called al-Sanad = "The Cliff" (e.g., al-Maqrīzī, *al-Mawā'iẓ,* 1:125). Jabal Yashkur was apparently so known in early times, but the third hillock seems to have lacked a distinctive name.

156. Al-Maqrīzī, *al-Mawa'iẓ,* 2:177. The name al-Rawḍah was actually applied to this island only in the eleventh century; before then it was known simply as al-Jazīrah or Jazīrat Miṣr.

157. Cf. al-Maqrīzī, *al-Mawā'iẓ,* 1:286. On Qaṣr al-Sham' see Ugo Monneret de Villard, "Ricerche sulla topografia di Qasr eš-Šam'," *Bulletin de la Société Géographique d'Égypte* 12 (1923–24): 205–32 and 13 (1924–25): 73–94.

158. Cf. Balādhurī, *Futūḥ al-Buldān,* 213–20 and al-Ḥāzimī, cited by al-Maqrīzī, *al-Mawā'iẓ,* 1:287. The most detailed recreation of the Roman and Byzantine setting that would become the site of al-Fusṭāṭ is provided by Kubiak (*Al-Fustat,* chaps. 2 and 3), who joins Caetani (*Annali,* 4:551) in opposing the existence of any town outside the walls of Babylon (56). In any case, the district became a focus of hostility to Byzantine rule to which many Copts gravitated when the Council of Chalcedon in A.D. 451 declared Monophysitism heretical.

159. Cf., for example, al-Suyūṭī, *Ḥuṣn al-Muḥāḍarah,* 1:77, 79; al-Maqrīzī, *al-Mawā'iẓ,* 1:296; and Ibn Duqmāq, *al-Intiṣār,* 2:3, 64.

160. Al-Maqrīzī, *al-Mawāʿiẓ,* 1:296; Ibn Duqmāq, al-Intiṣār, 2:2; Guest, "The foundation of Fustat," map following p. 83; Casanova, *Essai de Reconstitution,* vol. 1, fasc. 3, plate III; and Kubiak, *Al-Fustat,* Plan 4, p. 176. Guest was of the opinion that al-Maqrīzī and Ibn Duqmāq, both of whom appear to have drawn their information from a common source, may have omitted some of the tribal *khiṭāṭ:* see "The foundation of Fustat," p. 60 and list on p. 83.

161. As illustrated, for example, by the story of Qayṣabah ibn Kulthūm, the original occupant of the site of the mosque of ʿAmr: al-Maqrīzī, *al-Mawāʿiẓ,* 2:246. See also the expanded discussion in chapter 17 of the present text.

162. The wall built subsequently at an unknown date enclosed only a portion of the site occupied by the original encampment.

163. Al-Maqrīzī, *al-Mawāʿiẓ,* 1:297–98.

164. There are detailed descriptions of the mosque in the time of ʿAmr in Ibn Duqmāq, *al-Intiṣār,* 2:59 and al-Maqrīzī, *al-Mawāʿiẓ,* 2:246. The many modifications, often amounting to rebuilding, that it underwent are retailed by Yāqūt, *Muʿjam,* 3:899–900. It should be remarked that, for reasons stated in note 52 to chapter 17, remarkably few mosques at any period have been precisely oriented.

165. Al-Maqrīzī, *al-Mawāʿiẓ,* 2:246. Ibn Duqmāq describes numerous *masjids* as *khiṭṭī,* that is, as laid out from the inception of the camp.

166. Muḥammad ibn Yūsuf al-Kindī (d. 961), *Kitāb al-Umarā (al-Wulāt) wa-Kitāb al-Quḍāt,* ed. R. Guest (Leyden, 1908–12). It is noteworthy, though, that Ibn Duqmāq also refers to the Dār al-Raml as being used by some governors of al-Fusṭāṭ.

167. Guest, "The foundation of Fustat," 77–78.

168. Ibid., 82. The evolution of predominantly single-tribe *khiṭāṭ* into urban quarters with more diversified populations has been traced, so far as literary texts and archaeological evidence permit, by Kubiak, *Al-Fustat,* chap. 6.

169. F. R. Wingate, *Ten Years' Captivity in the Mahdi's Camp 1882–1892, from the Original Manuscripts of Father Joseph Ohrwalder,* 2d ed. (London, 1892), chaps. 12, 16, and 19.

170. Harry St. J. B. (subsequently ʿAbdullāh) Philby, *Arabia* (London, 1930), 224–27. Cf. also K. S. Twitchell, *Saudi Arabia* (Princeton, 1947), 121 et seq.

171. Cited in Philby, *Arabia,* 227.

172. *Western Arabia and the Red Sea.* Geographical Handbook Series, Naval Intelligence Division (1946), 286. Philby was probably the author of this section of the book. Rihānī had estimated the population of the colonies to be as high as one hundred thousand in 1927, but this was almost certainly an exaggerated figure.

173. Benet, "The Ideology of Islamic Urbanization," 113 n. 1.

174. The term used in the Arabic texts was *ʿashīrah.*

175. As an illustration of the persistence of tribal loyalties into the second quarter of the eighth century, Richard Bulliet has aptly cited the history of Khālid al-Qasrī, governor of al-ʿIrāq, conveniently summarized by Wellhausen in *The Arab Kingdom and Its Fall,* 326–36 and 358–62 ("Sedentarization of Nomads in the Seventh Century," 47 n. 10).

176. Donner lists these as the Banū-Aslam, Banū-Ghifār, Banū-Muzaynah, Banū-Ashjaʿ, Banū-Juhaynah, Banū-Kaʿb ibn ʿAmr, and sections of the Banū-Sulaym, Banū-Ṭayyiʾ, Banū-Tamīm, Banū-Asad, Banū-Ghaṭafān, Banū-Bajīlah, and certain Yamanī tribes (*The Early Islamic Conquests,* 88). See also Shoufani, *Al-Riddah and the Muslim Conquest of Arabia,* chap. 4.

177. The Arabic plural is *ribāṭāt.* The distinction in principle between the functionally convergent institutions of the *ribāṭ,* military and Arab, and the *khānqah,* mystical and Persian, has been examined by Max van Berchem in *Matériaux pour un Corpus Inscriptionum Arabicarum: Égypte* (Paris, 1894), 163 n. 3 and 408 n. 4. See also chapter 17.

178. Much material relating to the *ribāṭāṭ* of North Africa is summarized in Georges Marçais, "Note sur les ribâṭs en Berbérie," in *Mélanges René Basset,* 2 (Paris, 1925): 395–430; but for certain reservations see chapter 17 of the present text.

179. These and other *ribāṭāṭ* are mentioned, together with references to original sources, in W. Barthold, *Mussulman Culture.* Translated from the Russian by Shahid Suhrawardy (Calcutta, 1934); *Turkestan down to the Mongol Invasion,* 3d ed. (London, 1968), passim; and *An Historical Geography of Iran,* trans. Svat Soucek (Princeton, N.J., 1984), passim; see also *Ḥudūd al-ʿālam,* Minovsky's translation, 2d ed. (London, 1970).

180. Yāqūt, *Muʿjam,* 4:687 and al-Iṣfahānī, *al-Aghānī,* 14:115. For a pioneering discussion of these desert "palaces" see Jean Sauvaget, "Châteaux umayyades de Syrie. Contribution à l'étude de la colonisation arabe aux Ier et IIe siècles de l'Hégire," *Revue des Etudes Islamiques* 35 (1967): 1–49.

181. Yāqūt, *Muʿjam,* 4:95. *Qasṭal* < Lat. *castellum* = "fortress." For relevant bibliography see Pauline Carlier, "Qastal: Château Ommeyade?" 2 vols., Ph.D. diss., University Aix-Marseilles, 1984 and Denise Homès-Fredericq and J. Basil Hennessy, eds., *Archaeology of Jordan,* vol. 2, part 2 (Leuven, 1989), 458–65.

182. Al-Ṭabarī, *Taʾrīkh,* 2:1743.

183. R. E. Brünnow and A. von Domaszewski, *Die Provincia Arabia,* vol. 2 (Strassburg, 1905), 105–76; B. Schulz and J. Strzygowski, "Mschatta," *Jahrbuch der Königlich-Preussischen Kunstsammlungen* 25 (1904): 205–373; Henri Lammens, "La 'bādia' et la 'ḥīra' sous les Omayyades," 325–50, esp. 338ff; Ernst Kühnel, "Mschatta," in *Bilderhefte der Islamischen Kunstabteilung,* pt. 2 (Berlin, 1933); Oleg Grabar, "Al-Mushatta, Baghdād, and Wāsiṭ," in J. Kritzeck and R. Bayly Winder, eds., *The World of Islam: Studies in Honour of Philip K. Hitti* (London, 1959), 99–108; and K. A. C. Creswell, *The Umayyads,* vol. 1 of *Early Muslim Architecture,* 2d ed. (Oxford, 1969), 578–606, 614–41, and bibliography 604–6.

184. There is a splendid report on excavations undertaken at Qaṣr al-Ḥayr East by Oleg Grabar, Renata Holod, James Knustad, and William Trousdale: *City in the Desert,* 2 vols., Harvard Middle Eastern Monographs 23/24 (Cambridge, Mass., 1978). For Quṣayr ʿAmrah see Alois Musil, "Ḳuṣejr ʿAmra und andere Schlösser östlich

von Moab," *Sitzungs-Berichte der Philos.-Hist. Klasse der K. Akad. der Wissenschaften* 144, pt. 7 (Wien, 1902): 5ff. and *Ḳuṣejr ʿAmra: I, Textband* (Wien, 1907); A. Jaussen and Savignac, *Les Châteaux Arabes de Qeseir ʿAmra, Harāneh et Tūba,* 2 vols. (Paris, 1922); and M. Almagro et al., *Qusayr ʿAmra. Residencia y Baños Omeyas en el Desierto de Jordania* (Madrid, 1975). Musil thought that the palace was constructed by al-Walīd II. Quṣayr ("little palace") ʿAmrah is the present-day name of the site, whose eighth-century appellation is unknown. For al-Mafjar see R. W. Hamilton, *Khīrbat al-Mafjar. An Arabian Palace in the Jordan Valley* (Oxford, 1959) and, for recent modifications in the dating of the site, Donald Whitcomb, "Khirbet al-Mafjar reconsidered: The ceramic evidence," *Bulletin of the American Schools of Oriental Research* 271 (1988): 51–67.

185. Ibn al-Athīr, *al-Kāmil,* 5:220; *Kitāb al-ʿUyūn wa-l-Ḥaqāʾiq,* ed. M. J. de Goeje and P. de Jong (Leyden, 1869), 150.

186. Al-Yaʿqūbī, *al-Buldān,* 237. After leaving al-Kūfah, al-Saffāḥ established his court at Qaṣr Ibn Hubayrah, a city already founded by the last Umayyad governor of al-ʿIrāq, Yazīd ibn ʿUmar ibn Hubayrah. When the populace persisted in referring to the city by the name of its founder, al-Saffāḥ built a new city opposite Qaṣr ibn Hubayrah, but in 752 again moved, this time to a site near al-Anbār, where he died before completing the construction of yet another royal capital. The story of these early ʿAbbāsid capitals is admirably told by Jacob Lassner in *The Shaping of ʿAbbāsid Rule* (Princeton, N.J., 1980), chap. 6. See also p. 100 below.

187. For the meaning of this name see note 317 to chapter 17.

188. Al-Yaʿqūbī, *al-Buldān,* 237–38. Cf. also al-Ṭabarī, *Taʾrīkh,* 3:272. For the political context in which al-Manṣūr settled in Baghdād see Lassner, *The Shaping of ʿAbbāsid Rule,* 158–62.

189. Al-Balādhurī, *Futūḥ al-Buldān,* 295; Ibn Qutaybah (properly Muḥammad ibn Muslim al-Dīnawarī), *al-Maʿārif,* 192; al-Ṭabarī, *Taʾrīkh,* 3:277; al-Masʿūdī, *al-Tanbīh,* 360; al-Maqdisī, *Aḥsan,* 121; al-Khaṭīb al-Baghdādī (d. 1071), *Taʾrīkh Baghdād:* edition of G. Salmon under the title *L'Introduction Topographique à l'Histoire de Baghdadh . . .* (Paris, 1904), 79 (all subsequent references are to the Salmon edition unless otherwise indicated); and Yāqūt, *Muʿjam,* 4:680, 682. The definitive modern exposition of the layout of early Baghdād has been provided by Jacob Lassner in *The Topography of Baghdad in the Early Middle Ages. Text and Studies* (Detroit, 1970), and summarized, with some modifications, by the same author in *The Shaping of ʿAbbāsid Rule,* chaps. 7 and 8. Cf. also Saleh Ahmad el-Ali (Ṣāliḥ Aḥmad al-ʿAlī), "The Foundation of Baghdād," in *The Islamic City: A Colloquium,* ed. Albert Hourani and S. M. Stern (Oxford, 1970), 87–101.

190. Al-Khaṭīb, *Taʾrīkh,* 1:66–70; al-Ṭabarī, *Taʾrīkh,* 3:276, 326; al-Yaʿqūbī, *al-Buldān,* 238; and Yāqūt, *Muʿjam,* 4:683. Al-Maqdisī states the cost as 4,833,000 *dirhams.*

191. Al-Khaṭīb, *Taʾrīkh,* 1:79–80.

192. Al-Ṭabarī, *Taʾrīkh,* 3:1179–81; al-Masʿūdī, *Murūj,* 7:118 et seq.; and Yāqūt, *Muʿjam,* 3:16–17.

193. Despite several attempts to relate Ernst Herzfeld's archaeological discoveries to available literary evidence, the layout of this composite city is still not elucidated in all its details; see, int. al., Maximilian Streck, *Die Alte Landschaft Babylonien nach den Arabischen Geographen,* 2 vols. (Leiden, 1900–1901); Reitemeyer, *Städtegründungen;* E. Herzfeld, *Samarra, Aufnahmen und Untersuchungen zur Islamischen Archäologie* (Berlin, 1907); "Mitteilungen über die Arbeiten der Zweiten Kampagne von Samarra," *Der Islam* 5 (1914): 196–204; *Der Wandschmuck der Bauten von Samarra* (Berlin, 1923); "Geschichte der Stadt Samarra," *Ausgrabungen von Samarra,* vol. 6 (1948); H. Viollet, "Description du Palais d'al-Moutasim . . . à Samarra . . . ," *Mémoires de l'Académie des Inscriptions et Belles-Lettres* 12, pt. 2 (Paris, 1909): 577–94; ʿIrāq Government Department of Antiquities, *Excavations at Samarra 1936–1939* (Baghdād, 1940); J. M. Rogers, "Sāmarra. A Study in Medieval Town Planning," in *The Islamic City,* ed. A. H. Hourani and S. M. Stern (Oxford, 1970), 119–55. There is an evaluation of the significance of recent archaeological excavations at Sāmarra in Alastair Northedge, "Archaeology and New Urban Settlement in Early Islamic Syria and Iraq," in *The Byzantine and Early Islamic Near East,* ed. G. R. D. King and Averil Cameron (Princeton, N.J., 1994), 231–65 and figs. 42–57. See also the same author's *Samarra: Residenz der ʿAbbasidenkalifen 836–892 v. Chr. (221–279 Higri)* (Tübingen, 1990).

194. Al-Yaʿqūbī, *al-Buldān,* 267.

195. Ibn Abī Zarʿ al-Fāsī, *Rawḍ al-Qirṭas fī Akhbār Mulūk al-Maghrib wa-Taʾrīkh Madīnat Fās* (ca. 1320), ed. J. H. Tornberg (Uppsala, 1843), Arabic text, 15 (all subsequent references are to the Tornberg edition unless otherwise indicated). Latin translation by Tornberg under the title *Annales Regum Mauritaniae* (Uppsala, 1845), 21 et seq.; French translation by Beaumier under the title *Histoire des Souverains du Maghreb et Annales de la Ville de Fès* (Paris, 1860). For the bibliography of this work see Évariste Lévi-Provençal, "La fondation de Fès," *Annales de l'Institut d'Études Orientales de l'Université d'Alger* 4 (1938): 23–53; reprinted in Lévi-Provençal, *Islam d'Occident* (Paris, 1948), 1–41; and Abū al-Ḥasan ʿAlī al-Jaznaʾī, *Zahrat al-Ās* (first half of the fourteenth century), ed. and trans. A. Bel under the title *Zahrat al-Ās (La Fleur du Myrte) Traitant de la Fondation de la Ville de Fès* (Alger, 1923). These authors have transmitted what may be termed the received version of the origin of Fez, namely that Idrīs II established a capital on the right bank of the Oued Fès (Wādī Fās) in 808, and in the following year founded another city on the left bank. (Meager references in the works of Ibn Ḥawqal [fl. 943–77] and al-Bakrī [d. 1094] apparently support this tradition: see Ibn Ḥawqal, *Ṣūrat al-Arḍ,* 2:90 and Régis Blanchère, "Fès chez les géographes arabes du moyen âge," *Hespéris* 18 [1934]: 41–48.) However, a less well-known, but earlier, version of the event was recorded by Aḥmad ibn Muḥammad ibn Mūsā al-Rāzī in the tenth century. This particular work of al-Rāzī has long been lost, but fortunately the section relating to Fez was incorporated in the writings of several later historians, notably Ibn al-Athīr's *al-Kāmil* (Cf. also Claudio Sanchez-Albornoz, "Rasis fuente de Aben Alatir," *Bulletin Hispanique* 41 [1939]: 5–59); Abū ʿAbd Allāh Muḥammad ibn al-Abbār (1199–1260), *Kitāb al-Ḥullah*

al-Siyarā', ed. in part by R. Dozy under the title *Notices sur Quelques Manuscrits Arabes* (Leyden, 1847–51); Ibn Sa'īd al-Maghribī (d. 1274), whose disquisition on the Maghrib has been only fragmentarily preserved in the works of al-'Umarī (see the translation of the section relating to Fez in M. Gaudefroy-Demombynes, *L'Afrique Moins l'Égypte* [Paris, 1927], 159); and Abū al-'Abbās Aḥmad al-Qalqashandī (d. 1418), *Kitāb Subḥ al-A'shā fī Ṣinā'at al-Inshā'*, 14 vols. (al-Qāhirah, A.H. 1331–40). According to this earlier tradition, it was Idrīs I who, in 789, founded the city on the right bank of the Oued Fès but possessed insufficient resources to develop it. Twenty years later Idrīs II chose to establish a new capital to inaugurate his reign rather than resuscitate the moribund foundation of his father. After an exhaustive examination of the evidence, Évariste Lévi-Provençal concludes that this earlier tradition approximates more closely to the truth than the better known version (*Islam d'Occident* [Paris, 1948], 1–41).

196. Now known as Córdoba la Vieja.

197. Ḥājib (chamberlain), an office much the same as that of the vizier *(wazīr)* in the Eastern Caliphate.

198. Building had commenced in 978. See Ibn 'Idhārī al-Marrākushī, *al-Bayān al-Maghrib fī (Ikhtisar) Akhbār Mulūk al-Andalus wa-l-Maghrib*, ed. G. S. Colin and E. Lévi-Provençal under the title *Histoire de l'Afrique du Nord et de l'Espagne Musulmane, Intitulé kitab al-Bayan al-Maghrib* (Leiden, 1948–51), 2:267–69; Abd al-Rahmān ibn Khaldūn, *Kitāb al-'Ibar wa Dīwān al-Mubtada'* . . . , ed. Naṣral-Hūrīnī, vol. 4 (Būlāq, A.H. 1284/A.D. 1867), 147–48 (all subsequent references are to the al-Hūrīnī edition unless otherwise indicated); Ibn al-Athīr, *al-Kāmil* 9:124–25; and Lisān al-Dīn ibn al-Khaṭīb (1313–74), *al-Iḥāṭah fī Akhbār Gharnāṭah*, abbreviated ed., vol. 2 (al-Qāhirah, A.H. 1319/A.D. 1901), 67–69.

199. Ibn Abī Zar', *Rawḍ al-Qirṭas*, 1:88–89.

200. Yāqūt, *Mu'jam*, 4:694–96; al-Mas'ūdī, *al-Tanbīh*, 334; and Abū 'Abd Allāh Ibn Ḥammād, *Akhbār Mulūk Bani-'Ubayd*, ed. and trans. M. Vonderheyden under the title *Histoire des Rois Obaïdites* (Alger, 1927), 9–10.

201. S. D. Goitein, "Cairo: An Islamic City in the Light of the Genzia Documents," in *Middle Eastern Cities*, ed. Lapidus, 84.

202. Abū 'Abdallāh Ibn al-Ḥājj al-Fāsī (d. 1336), *Mudkhal al-Shar'al-Sharīf*, vol. 3 (al-Qāhirah, A.D. 1929/A.H. 1348), 139–40: trans. G. E. von Grünebaum, "The Sacred Character of Islamic Cities," *Mélanges Ṭāhā Ḥusain: Offerts par ses Amis et ses Disciples a l'Occasion de son 70ième Anniversaire* (Le Caire, 1962), 27–28, modified.

203. One Shī'ite tradition relates that 'Alī's burial site was chosen, in accordance with his dying wish, by the wanderings of an unreined camel bearing his corpse. Another tradition asserts that he was buried within the Great Mosque of al-Kūfah (e.g., al-Maqdisī, *Aḥsan*, 46). The earliest detailed description of the shrine at al-Najaf was provided by Ibn Ḥawqal, *al-Masālik wa-l-Mamālik*, ed. Johannes Henrik Kramers (Lugduni Batavorum, 1938–39), 240.

204. Cf. Lammens, "La 'bādia' et la 'ḥīra' sous les Omayyades," 325 and Donner, *Early Islamic Conquests*, chap. 3, especially 148–55.

205. These culturally modified urban forms will be discussed further in chapter 17.

206. Robert Brunschvig, "Urbanisme médiéval et droit musulman," *Revue des Études Islamiques* 15 (1947): 155.

207. Von Grünebaum, *Islam. Essays in the Nature and Growth of a Cultural Tradition*, 149. These paragraphs should not be held to imply that Islamic ideals alone were responsible for the transformation of Middle Eastern cities, a point that will be taken up in chapter 17.

208. Nikita Elisséeff, "Damas a la lumière des théories de Jean Sauvaget," in *The Islamic City*, ed. Houvani and Stern, 167–68.

209. Ibid., 174.

210. E. Ashtor-Strauss, "L'administration urbaine en Syrie médiévale," *Rivista degli Studi Orientali* 31 (1956): 81–82.

211. As exemplified, for instance, in Damascus, where the Temple of Jupiter was succeeded on the same site by the Church of St. John the Baptist, and that in turn by the congregational mosque of the Umayyads. On "la loi de la permanence topique du sanctuaire" see Jean Sauvaget, "Esquisse d'une histoire de la ville de Damas," *Revue des Etudes Islamiques*, vol. 8 (1934), 421–80; and for further comments on the permanence of site values during the Roman, Byzantine, and Islamic periods, the same author's *Alep*, Bibliothèque Archéologique et Historique, vol. 36 (Paris, 1941), passim.

212. This Persian term does not figure in histories and topographies by Arab authors.

213. Etymologically *bāzār*, apparently originally neither an Īrānian nor a Semitic word, signified "business at the gate": Barthold, *Mussulman Culture*, 32.

214. Ibid., 31–32 and *Turkestan down to the Mongol Invasion*, 78. For a general discussion of these cities see N. Pigulevskaja, *Les Villes de l'État Iranien aux Époques Parthe et Sassanide: Contribution a l'Histoire de la Passe Antiquité* (Paris and La Haye, 1963). In Arabic texts *shahristān* is rendered as *madīnah*, and *bīrūn* as *rabaḍ*. Several Persian cities were described by Arab authors in terms of a *madīnah dākhilah*, or inner city, and a *madīnah khārijah*, or outer city; for example, Bukhārā, Samarqand, Marw (Marv), and Naysābūr.

Chapter Three

1. This manner of conceptualizing a settlement pattern was first stated formally by Chauncy D. Harris and Edward L. Ullman in "The nature of cities," *The Annals of the American Academy of Political and Social Science* 242 (1945): 7–17. Because of its functional basis, simplicity, and comprehensiveness, it has proved remarkably durable in the flux of competing formulations proposed during the ensuing forty years and, moreover, is easily rendered operational in terms of the data available for the Islamic world of the tenth century.

2. Walter Christaller, *Die zentralen Orte in Süddeutschland: eine ökonomisch-geographische Untersuchung über die Gesetzmässigkeit*

der Verbreitung und Entwicklung der Siedlungen mit städtischen Funktionen (Jena, 1933). The idea of a more or less regular distribution of retailing and service centers in rural areas had been advanced in embryonic form as early as 1841 by J. Reynaud (cf. M. C. Robic, "Cent ans avant Christaller. Une théorie des lieux centraux," *L'Espace Géographique* 11 [1982]: 5–12), adumbrated again independently by Léon Lalanne in 1863 ("Essai d'une théorie des réseaux de chemin de fer, fondée sur l'observation des faits et sur les lois primordiales qui président au groupement des populations," *Comptes Rendus Hebdomadaires des Séances de l'Académie des Sciences* 42:206–10), and subsequently restated in more detail by C. J. Galpin (*The Social Anatomy of an Agricultural Community*, Research Bulletin no. 34, Agricultural Experiment Station of the University of Wisconsin [Madison, 1915]), but it was Christaller who first formally elaborated the concept. The first use of the term *central place* in English in this technical sense was probably in a paper by Mark Jefferson, who wrote, "Cities do not grow up of themselves, countrysides set them up to do tasks that must be performed in central places" ("Distribution of the world's city folks," *The Geographical Review* 21 [1931]: 454), but it is a moot point whether Christaller had this paper in mind when he entitled his monograph *Die zentralen Orte.*

3. In other words, assuming a uniform distribution of population and purchasing power, uniform terrain and resource distribution, and transportation facilities equally deployed in all directions; all of which imply that travel and transportation costs are a function solely of distance travelled. These environmental assumptions were explicit in *Die zentralen Orte,* but others were also implicit in Christaller's argument, namely the economy of the isotropic surface (presumably a featureless plain) is static, and changes in agricultural location do not affect the siting of towns. In addition, it is possible to elicit from Christaller's formulation a number of interrelated behavioral assumptions, most notably that both producers and consumers are economically rational individuals in the sense that they seek to minimize purely economic costs and to maximize their purely economic profits. This behavior implies that producers minimize the number of production sites (or, put differently, maximize the degree to which they agglomerate), while consumers travel only to the nearest central place offering the goods and services they require. On this topic see particularly P. Saey, "Three fallacies in the literature on central place theory," *Tijdschrift vóór Economische en Sociale Geografie* 64 (1973): 181–94.

4. Because of the competitive economic basis to this solution in which it is assumed that all areas can be served from a minimum of central places, Christaller characterized the system as organized according to a "marketing principle." The progressive increase in numbers of market areas at successively higher levels of the hierarchy by a rule of threes led subsequent investigators to refer to the hierarchy developed on this principle as a K-3 network. *K* in hierarchies based on the marketing principle = the bifurcation ratio *k* for central places + 1; that is, it refers to the number of settlements at a given level in the hierarchy served by a central place at the next-higher level.

A statement of the simplest model of a hierarchy of cities in mathematical form has been provided by M. J. Beckmann ("City hierarchies and the distribution of city size," *Economic Development and Cultural Change* 6 [1958]: 243–48); and M.-A. Prost has compared the model with the results obtained empirically by Christaller in Germany: *Hierarchie des Villes* (Paris, 1965), 70–74. As early as 1931 W. J. Reilly advanced a Law of Retail Gravitation, which included a formula providing a ready approximation of the extent of market areas: *The Law of Retail Gravitation* (New York).

Christaller himself postulated two alternative hierarchies arranged according to (1) a "transportation priciple," which permits maximization of the number of central places located on major transportation routes and which results in a nesting of complementary regions according to a rule of fours (K-4); and (2) an "administrative principle" requiring the sociopolitical separation of complementary regions, which is achieved when each central place controls six lower-order places. Nesting is accordingly by rule of sevens (K-7). Recently J. B. Parr, in the course of examining possible forms of structural change that may occur in a central-place hierarchy, has demonstrated that a general model in which the value of *K* is allowed to vary from level to level within the hierarchy yields predictions for southern Germany closer to the observed frequencies of central places than those obtained by Christaller's use of fixed K-values ("Frequency distributions of central places in southern Germany: a further analysis," *Economic Geography* 56 [1980]: 141–54).

During the last fifty years Christaller's exposition of Central-Place Theory has undergone considerable modification and elaboration. August Lösch, in particular, has greatly strengthened its theoretical foundation (*Die räumliche Ordnung der Wirtschaft* [Jena, 1944]. Cf. also S. Valavanis, "Lösch on location," *American Economist* 45 [1955]: 637–44; H. O. Nourse, *Regional Economics* [New York, 1968]; Alton C. Thompson, "Some comments on Lösch," *Geographical Analysis* 2 [1970]: 397–400; and Michael J. Webber, "Empirical verifiability of classical Central Place Theory," *Geographical Analysis* 3 [1971]: 15–28). Whereas Christaller had assumed that, once generated by regional development, K-values would remain constant, Lösch incorporated in his theoretical statement all possible hexagonal solutions, with the fixed-K assumptions of the marketing, transportation, and administrative principles represented only as special limiting cases. By rotating the nest of possible hexagonal patterns all centered on one point—which he designated the metropolis, the highest order of central place in his system—Lösch effected maximum coincidence in the locations of cities, the minimization of the aggregate distance between all settlements, the maximization of effective local demand, and consequently minimization of the number of shipments and total length of transport lines.

The pattern that emerges from this manipulation of hexagonal market areas comprises twelve sectors of alternating many and few central places, each of which exhibits considerable variation in incidence of urban forms with distance from the metropolis. Such alternating sectors have, in fact, been discerned around large metropolitan centers in the United States (see D. J. Bogue, *The Structure of the Metropolitan Community: a Study of Dominance and Subdominance* [Ann Arbor, Mich., 1949]). This hierarchy is less rigid than that developed by Christaller, and comprises a relatively continuous sequence of central places in contrast to the distinct tiers of settlements postulated in the earlier model. It follows, moreover, that cities of the same size do not inevitably perform the same functions, and that the functions of larger central places do not necessarily subsume all those of smaller central places.

It appears that Christaller's formulation is likely to throw more light on the distribution of retail and service businesses, while Löschian analysis is probably more relevant to an understanding of the spatial distribution of market-oriented manufacturing (Edwin von Boventer, "Towards a unified theory of spatial economic structure," *Papers of the Regional Science Association* 10 [1962]: 163–87. However, J. Tinbergen's model of market-oriented location, developed on an isotropic plain and minimizing total costs of production and transportation, apparently generates a tiered hierarchy not dissimilar to that of Christaller: "The spatial dispersion of production: an hypothesis," *Schweizerische Zeitschrift für Volkwirtschaft und Statistik* 97 [1961]: 412–19 and "Sur un modèle de la dispersion géographique de l'activité économique," *Revue d'Economie Politique* 74 [1964]: 30–44). It is also possible that Christaller's model is better adapted to studying systems of cities developed in areas of sparse settlement, whereas that of Lösch may provide a more satisfactory framework for analyzing settlement patterns in regions of dense, long-established settlement.

A conspectus of Central-Place Theory, including its antecedents, and a summary of the types of investigation to which it has given rise are provided by Leslie J. King in a compact volume entitled *Central Place Theory* (Beverly Hills, Calif., 1984). The geometry of central-place structures is examined and some of their mathematical properties established in a collaborative work by Nurudeen Alao et al., *Christaller Central Place Structures: An Introductory Statement,* Northwestern University Studies in Geography, no. 22 (Evanston, Ill., 1977). Keith S. O. Beavon's *Central Place Theory: A Reinterpretation* (London, 1977) is an attempt to provide a theoretical basis for a continuum of central places at the intrametropolitan scale. Each of these books incorporates a bibliography relevant to its theme. See also Gerard Rushton, "Postulates of Central-Place Theory and the properties of central-place systems," *Geographical Analysis* 3 (1971): 140–56.

5. Karl Polanyi, "The economy as instituted process," in Polanyi, Conrad M. Arensberg, and Harry W. Pearson, eds., *Trade and Market in the Early Empires* (Glencoe, Ill., 1957), 255.

6. This broadly "cultural" component in the nexus of factors controlling the location and size of market centers has been only one impediment in the search for empirical evidence with which to test the validity of Central-Place Theory. Another is the circumstance that the formulation is derived from a theory of demand that itself is inherently unverifiable by reference to empirical evidence (cf. G. P. E. Clarkson, *The Theory of Consumer Demand: a Critical Appraisal* [Englewood Cliffs, N.J., 1963], passim).

Faced with the difficulty of matching in the so-called real world the isotropic surface postulated by Christaller, experimental investigators have tended either to view the inevitable discrepancies—such as irregularities in the distribution of population and purchasing power, diversified terrain, unequal incidence of resources and transport facilities—simply as operational reasons for the incongruence of actual spatial patterns with those predicted by theory, or to incorporate negative evidence in the formulation as morphological variants.

More than forty years ago Brian J. L. Berry and William L. Garrison somewhat simplified the problem when, using only the concepts of range and threshold, they were able to restate the theory in a manner that no longer required the assumptions of a uniform distribution of population and a hexagonal shape for market areas, thus permitting its application to intra-urban and highway ribbon development ("Recent developments of Central Place Theory," *Papers and Proceedings of the Regional Science Association* 4 [1958]: 107–20. The operational use of the restated theory was subsequently demonstrated by Berry in "Ribbon developments in the urban business pattern," *Annals of the Association of American Geographers* 49 [1959]: 145–55).

Subsequently various probabilistic interpretations have been introduced into the theory. E. N. Thomas, for example, by using a normal curve of error to determine whether cities were of *significantly* similar populations and at *significantly* similar distances apart, established the relative stability of their population-size and distance relationships ("Towards an expanded central place model," *Geographical Review* 51 [1961]: 400–11; "The Stability of Distance-Population-Size Relationships for Iowa Towns from 1900–1950," in *Human Geography,* vol. 24 in Lund Studies in Geography, Series B [1962], 13–30 and "The Spatial Behavior of a Dispersed Non-Farm Population," in *Papers and Proceedings of the Regional Science Association* 8 [1962]: 107–33).

More recently Michael Dacey has conceived Central-Place Theory in terms of an equilibrium solution for a spatial arrangement of settlements subject to the influence of external forces, but with inconclusive results ("A probability model for central place location," *Annals of the Association of American Geographers* 56 [1966]: 550–68). In fact, the error-term incorporated in the data from Dacey's study area (presumably induced by noneconomic forces) is so large that it is unlikely ever to be susceptible to treatment by the classical theory of errors. Dacey also pointed out that the theory as explicated by Christaller and Lösch was algebraic, and hence deterministic rather than probabilistic; that because it did not allow for deviations from precisely stated relations and locations, there was no chance of accumulating evidence verifying the theory.

7. J. H. Kolb and E. de S. Brunner, *A Study of Human Society,* 2d ed. (Boston, 1940). Kolb had in fact been working on this problem since 1923, when he had published *Service Relations of Town and Country,* Research Bulletin no. 58, Agricultural Experiment Station of the University of Wisconsin (Madison). To this extent he was a forerunner of Christaller, and even in his 1940 book was uninfluenced by the German scholar.

8. W. J. Reilly, *The Law of Retail Gravitation* (New York, 1931).

9. Cf. O. Tuominen, "Das Einflussgebiet der Stadt Turku im System der Einflussgebiete S.W. Finnlands," *Fennia* 71 (1949): 114–21.

10. See, for example, John E. Brush, "The hierarchy of central places in southwestern Wisconsin," *Geographical Review* 43 (1953): 380–402; M. F. Dacey, "Analysis of Central Place and Point Patterns by a Nearest Neighbor Method," in *Human Geography,* vol. 24 in Lund Studies in Geography, Series B (1962), 55–75; B. J. L. Berry, H. G. Barnum, and R. J. Tennant, "Retail Location and Consumer Behavior," in *Papers and Proceedings of the Regional Science Association* 9 (1962): 65–106; S. Godlund, "Bus Service in Sweden," in *Human Geography,* vol. 17 of Lund Studies in Geography, Series B (1956); J. E. Brush and H. E. Bracey, "Rural service centers in southwestern Wisconsin and southern England," *The Geographical Review* 45 (1955): 559–69; and G. Olsson and A. Persson, "The Spacing of Central Places in Sweden," in *Papers and Proceedings of the Regional Science Association* 12 (1964), 87–93.

11. Leslie J. King, "A multivariate analysis of the spacing of urban settlements in the United States," *Annals of the Association of American Geographers* 51 (1961): 222–23 and "A quantitative expression of the pattern of urban settlements in selected areas of the United States," *Tijdschrift vóór Economische en Sociale Geografie* 53 (1962): 1–7.

12. Preliminary analyses of selected data from the great geographical dictionary *Muʿjam al-Buldān,* completed in 1228 (some three centuries later than the period with which we are concerned here) by Yāqūt ibn ʿAbd Allāh al-Ḥamawī and which includes a great deal of material not available for the tenth century, especially as concerns the lower levels of the settlement hierarchy, appear to favor the cluster model. This inquiry will be the subject of a future work. Recent work by Ian W. J. Hopkins on the urban hierarchy in Roman Palestine seems to point to a similar conclusion ("The city region in Roman Palestine," *Palestine Exploration Quarterly* 112 [1980]: 19–32): e.g., p. 30, "a tendency for minor towns to flourish at some distance from the local city, usually on the periphery of that city's region." Cf. p. 22 and figures 4 and 6 in the same article.

A Network System of urban distributions recently proposed by Paul M. Hohenberg and Lynn Hollen Lees (*The Making of Urban Europe 1000–1950* [Cambridge, Mass., 1985], chap. 2) as an alternative to Central-Place Theory appears to be based on the locational imperatives of wholesale exchanges and long-distance trade rather than on the retailing and servicing of city trade areas that lie at the heart of the Christaller model.

The reference for al-Azharī is Abū Manṣūr Muḥammad ibn Aḥmad al-Azharī, *Tahdhīb al-Lughah* (Beirut, 1967), quoted by A. N. Wohaibi, *The Encyclopaedia of Islam,* 2d ed., vol. 4 (1978), 680.

13. G. K. Zipf, *Human Behavior and the Principle of Least Effort* (New York, 1949). The Rank-Size Rule can be expressed algebraically as

$$P = K(R)^{-q},$$

where q (which approximates unity) and K are constants for a given group of cities, and P is the population of a particular city of rank R in the descending array of settlements. For computational purposes, this equation can be cast in logarithmic form as

$$\log P = \log K - q(\log R).$$

Although the Rank-Size Rule is customarily associated with the name of Zipf, who certainly did much to popularize it, the principle had been enunciated nearly forty years earlier by F. Auerbach ("Das Gesetz der Bevölkerungskonzentration," *Petermanns Geographische Mitteilungen* 59 [1913]: 74–76) and further developed by A. J. Lotka ("The law of urban concentration," *Science* 94 [1941]: 13).

14. Beckman, "City hierarchies," 243–48.

15. H. A. Simon, "On a class of skew distribution functions," *Biometrica* 42 (1955): 425–40.

16. B. J. L. Berry and W. Garrison, "Alternate *[sic]* explanations of urban rank-size relationships," *Annals of the Association of American Geographers* 48 (1958): 83–91.

17. It should be noted, though, that just under a quarter of the thirty-eight countries studied yielded intermediate distributions, and the ascription of several to one or the other of the two main groups can be justified only by invoking the operation of an array of cultural and historical factors: see B. J. L. Berry, "City size distributions and economic development," *Economic Development and Cultural Change* 9 (1961): 573–88. Cf. also Auerbach, "Das Gesetz der Bevölkerungskonzentration," 74–76; G. R. Allen, "The 'Courbes des Populations': a further analysis," *Bulletin of the Oxford University Institute of Statistics* 16 (1954): 179–89; R. Vining, "A description of certain spatial aspects of an economic system," *Economic Development and Cultural Change* 3 (1955): 147–95; C. T. Stewart, "The size and spacing of cities," *Geographical Review* 48 (1958): 222–45; and B. J. L. Berry, "Cities as Systems within Systems of Cities," in *Papers and Proceedings of the Regional Science Association* 13 (1964): 147–63.

For a critical review of the value of the rank-size distribution as an explanatory tool, see Jan de Vries, *European Urbanization 1500–1800* (Cambridge, Mass., 1984), chap. 6. In the same work De Vries also demonstrates beyond a doubt that the Law of Proportionate Effect never operated in any phase of European urbanization (p. 103).

The concept of metropolitan primacy was first enunciated by Mark Jefferson ("The law of the primate city," *Geographical Review* 29, no. 2 [1939]: 226–32). See also Arnold S. Linsky, "Some generalizations concerning primate cities," *Annals of the Association of American Geographers* 55, no. 3 (1965): 506–13 and Surinder K. Mehta, "Some demographic and economic correlates of primate cities: a case for revaluation," *Demography* 1, no. 2 (1964): 136–47.

18. Mez, *Die Renaissance des Islâms.*

19. The *nisbah* of this author was first made familiar in Europe by Aloysius Sprenger (*Die Post- und Reiserouten des Orients. Abhandlungen für die Kunde des Morgenländes,* vol. 3, pt. 3 [Leipzig, 1864], xviii) as al-Muqaddasī, an orthography still retained by some

present-day Arabists (notably Charles Pellat, *Description de l'Occident Musulman au IVe–Xe Siècle.* Bibliothèque Arabe-Française no. 9 [Alger, 1950] and André Miquel, *Aḥsan al-Taqāsīm fī Maʿrifat al-Aqālīm* [Damas, 1963] and *La Géographie Humaine du Monde Musulman jusqu'au Milieu du IIe Siècle* [Paris and La Haye, 1967], 313–30. See also A. Fischer, "Al-Maqdisi und al-Muqaddasi," *Zeitschrift der Deutschen Morgenländischen Gesellschaft,* vol. 60 [1906]: 404–10). However, al-Maqdisī, denoting (as does al-Muqaddasī) a Hierosolymite birth, seems to be the preferable transcription. While admitting as much, Pellat yet retains the reading al-Muqaddasī on the strength of custom (*Description,* 7 n. 1). Miquel (*Aḥsan,* xv n. 5) justifies this practice on the ground that it has "le mérite de distinguer l'auteur d'autres personnages, pour lesquels la forme Maqdisī a prévalu, entre autres l'auteur du *Kitāb al-badʾ al-ḫalq wa t-taʾrīḫ*" (i.e., al-Muṭahhar ibn Ṭāhir al-Maqdisī). This apologia is repeated in the same author's *La Géographie Humaine,* 212 n. 2. Al-Maqdisī's full name, as inscribed on the first page of the Berlin recension of his work, was Shams al-Dīn Abū ʿAbd Allāh Muḥammad ibn Aḥmad ibn Abī Bakr al-Bannāʾ al-Shāʾmī al-Maqdisī al-maʿrūf bi-l-Bashshārī. In Yāqūt's *Muʿjam al-Buldān* he is invariably cited as al-Bashshārī.

20. This is the title of the older of two Berlin manuscripts, but a Constantinople manuscript bears the rubric *Kitāb al-Masāfāt wa-l-Wilāyāt,* while in one of the surviving fragments of his history of Jerusalem Mujīr al-Dīn (end of the fifteenth century) refers to Maqdisī's work as *al-Badīʿ fī Tafḍīl Mamlakat al-Islām* (text published at Būlāq in A.H. 1283/A.D. 1866; trans. H. Sauvaire under the title *Histoire de Jérusalem et d'Hébron* [Paris, 1876], where the reference is to p. 11). For the Berlin and Constantinople manuscripts, see below.

21. Cf. p. 152 of the de Goeje edition of the *Aḥsan;* see next note.

22. M. J. de Goeje, *Bibliotheca Geographorum Arabicorum, Pars Tertia: Descriptio Imperii Moslemici auctore al-Moqaddassi,* 1st ed. (Lugduni Batavorum, 1877); rev. ed., 1906; all subsequent references are to the revised edition unless otherwise indicated. De Goeje also discusses al-Maqdisī and his work in the *Praefatio* to *BGA,* vol. 4 (1879), vi–viii (in Latin). Despite the passage of time, de Goeje's edition remains remarkably reliable, requiring unexpectedly few emendations.

Until recently, there has been no complete translation of the *Aḥsan* into any European language—or, as far as I am aware, into any other language at all—although partial translations have not been uncommon. One of the most ambitious of these latter is an abundantly annotated English rendering of the first 202 pages (about two-fifths of the territorial coverage of the entire work) of de Goeje's text by G. S. A. Ranking and R. F. Azoo, *Aḥsanu-t-Taqâsîm fî Maʿrifati-l-Aqâlîm,* Bibliotheca Indica, Asiatic Society of Bengal, vol. 1, fascs. 1–4 (no more published: Calcutta, 1897–1910). Prior to this J. Gildemeister had published a rather unsatisfactory German translation of the greater part of the chapter on al-Shām (i.e., "Greater Syria, including Palestine": 151–255 of de Goeje's text): "Beiträge zur Palästinakunde aus arabischen Quellen," *Zeitschrift des Deutschen Palästinavereins* 7 (1884), 143–72, 215–30. This same chapter was subsequently translated in its entirety by Guy Le Strange ("Description of Syria, including Palestine. By Mukaddasi [circa 985 A.D.]," *Palestine Pilgrims' Text Society* 3 (1886): i–xvi, 1–116: reprint, New York, 1971) and again by Miquel (*Aḥsan* [see note 19]). Another sustained translation of a sizable section of the work is Pellat's highly competent French version of those parts dealing with the Maghrib, for which he also furnishes the Arabic text: *Description* (see note 19). Miquel has also rendered the chapter on Miṣr (Egypt) into French: "L'Egypte vue par un géographe arabe du IVe/Xe siècle: al-Muqaddasī," *Annales Islamologiques* 11 (1972): 109–39. Other parts of the *Aḥsan* have been translated into French by G. Baldacchino in a Thèse de 3e Cycle, Université de Paris-III, 2 vols. (1978), but this work has not been available to me. Jean Sauvaget translated short passages of the text in his *Historiens Arabes* (Paris, 1946), 65 et seq., and Basil A. Collins did the same in *Al-Muqaddasi: The Man and His Work,* Michigan Geographical Publication No. 10 (Ann Arbor, 1974). Five Russian partial translations prepared between 1908 and 1994 have not been accessible to me. Le Strange, Miquel, and Collins incorporate substantial background discussions of al-Maqdisī and the *Aḥsan* with their translations. A.-S. Marmardji also included French translations of al-Maqdisī's descriptions of Palestinian towns in his *Textes Géographiques Arabes sur la Palestine, Recueillis, Mis en Ordre Alphabétique et Traduits en Français* (Paris, 1951). Only very recently has Basil Collins published a complete, but unannotated, English translation of the *Aḥsan: Al-Muqaddasī. The Best Divisions for Knowledge of the Regions* (Reading, Pa., 1994).

23. De Goeje, *Bibliotheca Geographorum Arabicorum,* rev. ed., 4:vi. The version that has survived bears an Islamic date equivalent to A.D. 1259/60.

24. Miquel, *Aḥsan,* xxvii–xxviii.

25. Konrad Miller, *Mappae Arabicae,* vol. 1, pt. 1 (Stuttgart, 1926), Tafel 4. Maqdisī's maps are reproduced *in toto* in Collins, *Al-Muqaddasi,* together with English-Language keys.

26. This and subsequent references are to al-Maqdisī, *Aḥsan,* de Goeje edition.

27. An echo of Qurʾān 3 *(āl ʿImrān)*:104, which was subsequently developed into the *ḥisbah* obligation.

28. Maqdisī, *Aḥsan,* 2.

29. Twenty-fourth caliph of the ʿAbbāsid dynasty (974–91). The author's phrase that I have rendered as "maturity" was "my fortieth year." However, in the ancient and medieval Middle East, "forty" was a common topos connoting perfection, completion, or culmination. By associating the *Aḥsan* with the age of forty, al-Maqdisī was asserting that he had written it at the height of his intellectual powers (note that medieval Islam came to assign the birth of Muḥammad to a date forty years before the beginning of his mission). For a discussion of such topoi in Middle Eastern literature, see Conrad, "Abraha and Muhammad" and "Seven and the *tasbīʿ*: on the implications of numerical symbolism for the

study of medieval Islamic history," *Journal of the Economic and Social History of the Orient* 31 (1988): 42–73.

30. Fifth of the ʿUbaydī caliphs (Fāṭimids), and the second to rule in Egypt (975–96).

31. In place of the latter half of this sentence the Constantinople manuscript reads, "and in the days of his Excellency al-Amīr Abū al-Qāsim Nūḥ ibn Manṣūr [seventh of the Sāmānid amīrs], the vassal of the Commander of the Faithful." It is curious that Yāqūt (*Muʿjam,* 1:653), possibly using an amended version of al-Maqdisī's original text, ascribes its completion to A.H. 378 (A.D. 988).

32. For a discussion of the works of the two schools of Islamic geography that are conveniently designated the Balkhī and the ʿIrāqī, see S. Maqbul Ahmad, *The Encyclopaedia of Islam,* 2d ed., s.v. "Djughrāfiyā," 579–82 and especially Miquel, *La Géographie Humaine,* vol. 1, chaps. 3 and 8.

33. M. J. de Goeje, "Die Iṣṭaḫrî-Balḫî Frage," *Zeitschrift der Deutschen Morgenländischen Gesellschaft* 25 (1871): 42–58; Johannes Henrik Kramers, "La question Balḫî-Iṣṭaḫrî-Ibn Ḥauqal et l'atlas de l'Islam," *Acta Orientalia* 10 (1932): 9–30; V. Minorsky, "A false Jayhānī," *Bulletin of the School of Oriental and African Studies* 13 (1949): 89–96; and, most authoritatively, Gerald R. Tibbetts, "The Balkhī School of Geographers" in *The History of Cartography,* ed. J. B. Harley and David Woodward, vol. 2, bk. 1 (Chicago, 1992), 108–36.

34. Ahmad, *The Encyclopaedia of Islam,* 2d ed., s.v. "*Djughrāfiyā,*" 581.

35. The most enlightening evaluation of al-Maqdisī's place in the development of Islamic geography is provided by Miquel, *La Géographie Humaine,* 313–30.

36. Ibid., 295.

37. ʿAbd al-Raḥmān ibn Khaldūn's formal discussion of the nature and evolution of urban institutions occurs in the *Muqaddimah* (prologue) to his history of the Islamic world, *Kitāb al-ʿIbar,* al-Hurīnī edition. The text of the *Muqaddimah,* corresponding to vol. 1 of the *ʿIbar,* was published by E. M. Quatremère under the title *Prolégomènes d'Ebn-Khaldoun,* as vols. 16–18 of *Notices et Extraits des Manuscrits de la Bibliothèque du Roi . . . publiés par l'Institut Impérial de France* (Paris, 1858) and has been translated into English by Franz Rosenthal under the title *The Muqaddimah, an Introduction to History,* 3 vols. (New York, 1958).

38. Maqdisī, *Aḥsan,* 43.

39. *Harīsah* (pl. *harāʾis*) = pottage compounded of bruised wheat boiled to a consistency, to which is added meat, butter, cinnamon, and aromatic herbs: gloss in de Goeje, *Bibliotheca Geographorum Arabicorum,* 3: 369–70; references ibid., 203, 311, 326, 430. Cf. Maxime Rodinson, "Recherches sur les documents arabes relatifs à la cuisine," *Revue des Etudes Islamiques* (1949), 103, 139, 150 and Ranking and Azoo, *Aḥsanu,* 111 n. 8.

40. *Tharīdah* (pl. *tharāʾid*) = dumplings of crumbled bread containing small pieces of meat, and the whole soaked in broth: gloss in de Goeje, *Bibliotheca Geographorum Arabicorum,* 4:200. Cf. Ranking and Azoo, *Aḥsanu,* 74 n. 2 and Rodinson, "Recherches," 133, 148.

41. *ʿAṣīdah* = a sort of pudding concocted either by heating wheat flour moistened with clarified butter or by pouring boiling water over flour, clarified butter, and sometimes honey: see Ranking and Azoo, *Aḥsanu,* 74 n. 3.

42. In the tenth century, and even down to recent times, Mount Lebanon enjoyed a reputation as the home of exceptionally holy men, where indeed dwelt the forty *abdāl* (sing. *badal*), who constituted one of the degrees in the Ṣūfī hierarchical order of sainthood (*The Encyclopaedia of Islam,* 2d ed., 1:94–95).

43. *Nawāqīs* (sing. *nāqūs:* a loanword in Arabic from Syriac *nāqūshā*) = thin pieces of wood or metal struck with rods to summon a Christian congregation to divine service. Such a flagrant violation of Islamic law relating to the tolerated religions was possible only where Muslims were few in number; hence al-Maqdisī implies that he had travelled on the very fringes of the Dār al-Islām.

44. The word rendered as "songs" is not at all clear in the printed text but Ranking and Azoo (*Aḥsanu,* 75 n. 2) are surely correct in their view that al-Maqdisī is here alluding to an anecdote related in al-Iṣfahānī's *al-Aghānī,* 1:23, about an *amīr* of al-Ḥijāz who, on arriving at a tent in the desert, was given water only when he began to sing.

45. *Kanīsah;* pl. *kanāʾis.*

46. The *samūm* is a powerful flow of hot, dry air drawn in from the south before the passage of a depression. It is almost invariably accompanied by driving sand and dust. In Egypt the same phenomenon is known as the *khamsīn,* in Libya as *ghiblī,* and in the Levant as *shilūq.*

47. In the *adab* literature, weavers were portrayed as proverbially lacking in intelligence: one author asserts that the intelligences of one hundred weavers would only equal that of a single eunuch, while another more charitably fixes the number at forty.

48. *Sawīq* = a syrup of barley and honey drunk ritually by pilgrims to Makkah: see M. Gaudefroy-Demombynes, *Le Pèlerinage à la Mekke* (Paris, 1923), 80–101. Cf. also Charles Schéfer's translation of Nāṣir-i Khusraw's *Safar Nāmah* under the title *Sefer Nameh. Relation du Voyage de Nassiri Khosrau en Syrie, en Palestine, en Egypte, en Arabie et en Perse* (Paris, 1881), 207; also W. M. Thackston Jr. (trans.), *Nāṣer-e Khosraw's Book of Travels (Safarnāma)* (New York, 1986), 78.

49. The text is not entirely clear, but the term *sīq* (cf. Syriac *shūqā* = market street; Gk. σηκός = sacred enclosure) seems to refer to a Syrian monastery of the Melchite rite. Cf. M. J. de Goeje, "*Sīq,*" *Zeitschrift der Deutschen Morgenländischen Gesellschaft* 54 (1900): 336–38 and Miquel, *Aḥsan,* 112 n. 14.

50. See note 114 to chapter 6. *Khalīl* (= "friend") was a standard epithet applied to Ibrāhīm. It derived immediately from Qurʾān 4 *(al-Nisāʾ):* 125: "Allāh took Ibrāhīm as a friend," but ultimately from the Bible, specifically 2 Chron. 20:7, Isa. 41:8, and James 2:23.

51. Sing. = *al-waqf.*

52. *Bidʿah* = "innovation" in the sense of that which is contrary to the *sunnah* or has no foundation in it.

53. Without a doubt allusions to, respectively, ʿAmīd al-Dawlah Fāʾiq, *amīr* of Khurāsān when al-Maqdisī was compiling the *Aḥsan;* and to the *qāḍī* Abū al-Ḥasan ʿAlī ibn al-Ḥasan, to whom he dedicated his work (66), and who served as a *wazīr* to the aforementioned amīr.

54. The *ʿayyārūn* (sing. *ʿayyār*) were military-style fraternities, often no more than urban gangs, bound in varying degrees by the code of medieval chivalry *(futūwwah).* See Fr. Taeschner, *The Encyclopaedia of Islam,* 2d ed., 1:794. There are also some useful comments in Roy P. Mottahedeh, *Loyalty and Leadership in an Early Islamic Society* (Princeton, N.J., 1980), 157–58.

55. The baths of Ṭabarīyah (Tiberias) were built over hot springs in the neighborhood of the town: cf. Maqdisī, *Aḥsan,* 161; al-Harawī, *Kitāb al-Ishārāt ila Maʿrifat al-Ziyārāt,* ed. and trans. J. Sourdel-Thomine under the title *Guide des Lieux de Pèlerinage,* 2 vols. (Damascus, 1953, 1957), 20–21 of the Arabic text; Yaʿqūbī, *Kitāb al-Buldān* (see notes 134 and 135 below), 179.

56. Al-Maqdisī was here almost certainly referring to the ruins of Persepolis, the ritual capital of the Achaemenid dynasty: Erich F. Schmidt, *Persepolis,* Publications of the Oriental Institute, vols. 68 and 69 (Chicago, 1953, 1957) and Arthur U. Pope, "Persepolis as a ritual city," *Archaeology* 10 (1957): 123–30.

57. As far as I have been able to ascertain, no record of this festival has survived.

58. The (Christian) Feast of Saint Barbara was celebrated on 4 December. On p. 182 of the *Aḥsan,* al-Maqdisī records the Syrian saying, "When the Feast of Saint Barbarah comes round, the bricklayer takes up his flute, meaning that he may stay at home [because the rainy season has begun]."

59. Biʾr Buḍāʿah was (and is) situated outside the Bāb al-Shāmī (the Syrian or northwestern gate) of al-Madīnah (Medina) on the road to Uḥud. Tradition has it that when the Prophet spat into the well its water was transformed from saline to sweet.

60. Yāqūt (*Muʿjam,* 3:220) inclines to the belief that Yaʿqūb's home was at Saylūn (the Shiloh of the Old Testament), although he takes note of other interpretations.

61. The Mihrajān, the Sadhah, and the Nawrūz are Persian festivals celebrated respectively at the autumnal equinox, the tenth of Bahman-Māh, and the vernal equinox. According to Muḥammad ibn Abdūs al-Jahshīyārī (*Kitāb al-Wuzarāʾ,* ed. M. al-Saqqāʾ et al. [al-Qāhirah, A.H. 1357/A.D. 1938], 21), the Persian custom of offering gifts to the monarch at Mihrajān and Nawrūz was revived by ʿAbd Allāh ibn Darrāj, who thereby added ten million *dirhams* in gifts to the yield of taxes. Mār Sarjah = Saint Sergius, whose feast day falls on 7 October in the churches of both Eastern and Western Christendom.

62. *Aḥsan,* 45. Al-Maqdisī tells us that, in collecting the information on which his book is based, he had acquired no less than thirty-six *nisbahs* and *laqabs* (43): *Maqdisī* (Hierosolymite: cf. note 19 above), *Filasṭīnī* (Palestinian), *Miṣri* (Egyptian), *Maghribī* (North African), *Khurāsānī* (Khurasanian), *Salamī* (from Salamīyah, a town in Syria), *Muqrī* (Teacher of Qurʾānic Reading), *Faqīh* (Canon Lawyer), *Ṣūfī* (Mystic), *Walī* (Holy Man: lit., "Friend [of God]"), *ʿĀbid* (Devotee), *Zāhid* (Ascetic), *Sayyāḥ* (Pilgrim), *Warrāq* (Copyist of Manuscripts), *Mujallid* (Book Binder), *Tājir* (Merchant), *Mudhakkir* (Reciter), *Imām* (Leader in Communal Prayer), *Muʾadhdhin* (Muezzin), *Khaṭīb* (Preacher), *Gharīb* (Foreigner), *ʿIrāqī* (from al-ʿIrāq), *Baghdādī* (from Baghdād), *Shāmī* (Syrian), *Ḥanīfī* (Devotee of Abū Ḥanīfah: see note 63 below), *Mutaʾaddib* (Neophyte Scholar), *Karī* (Lodger [in the precincts of an endowment: Ranking and Azoo, *Aḥsanu,* 74]), *Mutafaqqih* (Jurisconsult), *Mutaʿallim* (Savant), *Farāʾiḍī* (= pl. of *farīḍah:* Specialist in Inheritance Law), *Ustādh* (Teacher), *Dānishūmand* (< Pers. *dānishmand* = possessor of knowledge: Sage), *Shaykh* (Elder), *Nishāstah* (Man of Learning), *Rākib* (Courier), and *Rasūl* (Envoy). Al-Maqdisī may have merited most or all of these sobriquets, but the number, thirty-six, of those that he chose to list is a manifestation of Islamic numerical symbolism (3 × 3 × 4), of which there eventually developed thirteen different systems: cf. Ibn Sīnā, *Kunūz al-Muʿaẓẓimīn,* ed. Jalāl al-Dīn Homāʾī (Tehran, A.H. 1331/A.D. 1912), 40. There is a highly informative discussion of the numerological values and symbolism of the letters of the Arabic alphabet, based on the *Jafr Jāmiʿ* of al-Nasībī and the *Shaṭaḥīyat* of al-Baqlī, in Louis Massignon, *Essai sur les Origines du Lexique Technique de la Mystique Musulmane* (Paris, 1954), 90–101.

63. There are at least twenty-two references to Abū Ḥanīfah on, sequentially, pp. 37, 38, 39, 40, 41, 75, 113, 116, 121, 128, 130, 180, 182, 282, 311, 323, 327, 357, 359, 415, 439, and 481. On p. 43 al-Maqdisī tells us that one of his many *nisbahs* (cf. note 62 above) was Ḥanīfī = devotee of Abū Ḥanīfah (as distinct from *Ḥanafī* = a follower of Abū Ḥanīfah's teaching). See also p. 39 of the *Aḥsan.*

For al-Maqdisī's view of *istiḥsan* see *Aḥsan,* 156: "In our branch of knowledge, *istiḥsan* not infrequently takes precedence over *qiyās* (reasoning by analogy) [which might be put more bluntly as "reasoned argument is often sacrificed to expediency"], as is indeed the case in questions affecting registration [of covenanted slaves] *(fī masāʾilī al-makātib).* It is well known that deferment of payments over the Nayrūz (New Year's Day in the Persian calendar) or the Mihrajān (a Persian feast day celebrated at the autumn equinox) is deemed legally irregular, yet is admissible in the case of [contracts of] *kitābat* by reason of *istiḥsan.*"

64. This author was in error in transcribing *ʿilmun* for *ʿilmin.* Al-Maqdisī's question on p. 156 of the same edition is wholly representative of his use of this type of reasoning: "Why not apply the same analogical reasoning *(qiyās)* [as has just been applied to Ḥalab and Anṭākīyah] to Shīrāz by reckoning Iṣṭakhr and its towns as dependencies of that city?"

65. For example, "Muḥammad [ibn al-Ḥasan al-Shaybānī] uses [the name al-Shām] for the sake of simplicity and in accordance with the conventional usage *(mutaʿāraf)* of the people of ʿIrāq, just as it is customary to designate Khurāsān as al-Mashriq

(= "The East") even though the East [properly speaking] lies beyond this."

66. For example, "It is worthy of note that there are villages in this province (al-Shām) more important and larger than most of the chief towns in the Arabian Peninsula. . . . But because they have the characteristics of villages, they are [here] reckoned as such. This practice, as we have said, is based on common usage *(ta'āruf)*" (155). See also p. 32, and cf. Miquel's assessment: "[*Al-ta'āruf* in the *Aḥsan*] est avant tout un principe méthodologique, armature de raisonnements et de discussions où se révèle, beacoup plus qu'un vulgarisateur, un juriste ferré à glace" (*La Géographie Humaine,* 349).

67. Maqdisī, *Aḥsan,* 43.

68. By the expression *ṭarīq al-āḥād,* al-Maqdisī denoted a tradition based on the authority of a single Companion of the Prophet or on that of one of the Successors *(al-tābi'ūn),* that is, persons who were separated from the Prophet by no more than one transmitter.

69. This point has already been made by Miquel (*Aḥsan,* xxix).

70. The context leaves no doubt that *akhbār* here connotes Prophetic traditions, that is, *aḥādīth.*

71. These verses read:

He has made the two seas flow together;
[But] between them is a barrier they cannot transgress
[i.e., the Isthmus of Suez].

72. 'Abd Allāh ibn 'Amr ibn al-'Āṣ enjoyed a reputation as one of the most learned among the Companions of the Prophet. He died in A.H. 65/A.D. 683.

73. The five seas is an idea that goes back to Ptolemy: cf. also al-Mas'ūdī, *Murūj,* 1:183–84. The bodies of water that al-Maqdisī designated the two seas were, respectively, that stretching from the East African coast to China, together with its several extensions; and the Mediterranean, together with its Atlantic approaches and peripheral embayments.

74. Maqdisī, *Aḥsan,* 17.

75. There can be little doubt that by *mashāyikh* (sing. *shaykh*) al-Maqdisī denoted the *mu'allimūn,* or master navigators, who piloted vessels through the Arabian Sea and the Indian Ocean: cf. Gabriel Ferrand, *Introduction à l'Astronomie Nautique Arabe,* vol. 3 of *Instructions Nautiques et Routiers Arabes et Portugais* (Paris, 1928), 177 et seq.

76. *Ashātimah;* sing. *ishtiyām.* Cf. de Goeje's gloss *oneris in nave impositi curator* (*Bibliotheca Geographorum Arabicorum,* 4:271).

77. The precise significance of *riyāḍī* must remain obscure in the absence of an attached qualifying term, but it presumably related to some form of calculation. Although it is just possible that it denoted those practicing some type of religious exercise, it does not seem likely that such persons would have been mentioned among captains, supercargoes, agents, and merchants.

78. *Wukalā';* sing. *wakīl.*

79. Maqdisī, *Aḥsan,* 10.

80. *Al-khazā'in* (sing. *khizānah*). For a description of medieval Islamic archives and libraries see F. Krenkow and W. Heffening, *The Encyclopaedia of Islam,* 1st ed., 2:1105–8; Johannes Pedersen, *Den Arabiske Bog,* English translation by Geoffrey French under the title *The Arabic Book* (Princeton, N.J., 1984), chap. 9; O. Pinto, "The libraries of the Arabs during the time of the Abbasids," *Islamic Culture* 3 (1929): 525–37.

81. The Constantinople manuscript (p. 4) includes a statement by al-Maqdisī (missing in the Berlin recension) to the effect that he had seen this work, in seven volumes but without an author's name affixed, in the library of 'Aḍud al-Dawlah (949–83), most illustrious of the Buwayhid line. We know that Sābūr, minister of 'Aḍud al-Dawlah, founded a Shī'ite library in Baghdād in A.H. 381/A.D. 991 (Cf. H. Laoust, La Vie et la Philosophie d'Abū al-'Alā' al-Ma'arrī, *Bulletin d'Etudes Orientales d'Institut Français des Etudes Arabes de Damas,* 10:127), but this would appear to have happened too late for the library to have been the one referred to by al-Maqdisī. This author provides a fairly detailed description of the particular library of 'Aḍud al-Dawlah, which he consulted on p. 449 of the *Aḥsan.* He also notes that some of the local scholars ascribed the authorship of the work in question to Ibn Khurradādhbih. However, in Nīshāpūr (Nīsābūr) he had actually seen two small volumes, authored respectively by al-Jayhānī and Ibn Khurradādhbih, the contents of which were very similar; and the confusion may have arisen from this circumstance. For additional comments on al-Jayhānī, see p. 69.

82. Cf. p. 64. In the Constantinople manuscript, p. 5, al-Maqdisī recalls having seen copies of al-Balkhī's treatise in the library of the Buwayhid *wazīr* al-Ṣāḥib ibn 'Abbād, where its authorship was disputed. He had also seen other copies of the same work in Nīsābūr and Bukhārā.

83. Cf. pp. 71–72. In the Constantinople manuscript, p. 5, al-Maqdisī notes that the version of Ibn al-Faqīh's work he had consulted comprised five volumes.

84. Cf. pp. 70–71.

85. Probably the most frequently quoted writer of *belles-lettres* in the whole of Arabic literature. He died in 868.

86. In the Constantinople manuscript, p. 4, al-Maqdisī tells us that the one of Jāḥiẓ's many works he had in mind was the *Kitāb al-Amṣār wa 'Ajā'ib al-Buldān,* for which see Carl Brockelmann, *Geschichte der Arabischen Literatur, Supplement,* vol. 1 (Leiden, 1937): 246.

87. A representative example of such a chain of authorities is as follows: "I have it from Abū Bakr Aḥmad ibn 'Abdān al-Ahwāzī, who heard it from Muḥammad ibn Mu'āwīyah al-Anṣārī, after Ismā'īl ibn Ṣabīḥ, Sufyān al-Ḥarīrī, 'Abd al-Mu'min, Zakarīyā' Abū Yaḥyā, and al-Aṣbagh ibn Nabātah, who heard 'Alī—May God be gracious to him—say that" (Maqdisī, *Aḥsan,* 42–43).

88. See, for example, chapter 16.

89. See p. 65 above.

90. See C. E. Bosworth, *The Encyclopaedia of Islam,* 2d ed., 4:667–69. For textual references attesting al-Maqdisī's familiarity with Karrāmite doctrine and ritual, consult Miquel, *Aḥsan,* xx n. 1.

It may not be without significance that Ibn Karrām, the founder of the sect, was buried in Jerusalem, al-Maqdisī's birthplace.

91. A puritanical movement rising to prominence in Marwānid times on the basis of a scholastic-style theology *(kalām)* that emphasized the free responsibility of man and divine justice (as opposed to the divine power and mercy of the orthodox schools). Muʿtazilite influence was preeminent at the caliphal court during the first quarter of the third century A.H. For citations of passages in which al-Maqdisī evinces Muʿtazilite sympathies, see Miquel, *Aḥsan*, xx n. 3, 88 n. 16, and 94 n. 32.

92. For citations from the *Aḥsan* supporting this statement see Miquel, *Aḥsan*, xx nn. 4, 5. Note also al-Maqdisī's frequent reliance on Shīʿite traditionists.

93. Plural = *duʿāt*. Cf. Marius Canard, "L'impérialisme des Fatimides et leur propagande," *Annales des Etudes Orientales* 4 (1942–47): 156 n. 2.

94. Miquel, *Aḥsan*, xx and *La Géographie Humaine*, 316, 319, 237.

95. Miquel, *Aḥsan*, 126.

96. The degree to which the principle of *taqīyah* (dissimulation of religious belief under duress) played a part in al-Maqdisī's apparent eclecticism is uncertain. André Miquel, who has studied the evidence of the *Aḥsan* bearing on this question, does not entirely exclude the possibility but accords more importance to al-Maqdisī's commitment to objectivity, which "entraîne l'auteur à essayer de voir lucidement, dans chaque école, le pour et le contre, cette lucidité ne pouvant aboutir, on s'en doute, qu'à un scepticisme foncier quant à la lettre des doctrines" (*Aḥsan*, xx–xxi). This is a generous interpretation by the modern scholar who knows al-Maqdisī most intimately, but it should also be remembered that, whereas *taqīyah* has been accepted as a legitimate ethical principle by other Muslims (on the authority of *Qur'ān* 3 *[Āl ʿImrān]*:29), particularly some Khārijite groups, by the Shīʿīs it was raised to the level of a fundamental tenet designed to protect not only the individual but also his coreligionists. As a *dāʿī*, al-Maqdisī was clearly at risk, and as a Shīʿah sympathizer he probably harbored few scruples about resorting to *taqīyah*. However, while I am more suspicious than is Dr. Miquel, I too can only conclude with a *non liquet*.

97. Whereas Yāqūt and Western scholarship invariably refer to this author as al-Iṣṭakhrī, Ibn Ḥawqal used the *nisbah* al-Fārisī. Al-Maqdisī employed both al-Fārisī and al-Karkhī, the latter *nisbah* presumably referring to a well-known quarter of Baghdād.

98. The *Surat al-Ma'mūnīyah* was a world map prepared by the collective efforts of the topographers working in Baghdād during the reign of the caliph al-Ma'mūn (813–33). Masʿūdī (*al-Tanbih*, 33) regarded it as superior to the maps of both Ptolemy and Marinos of Tyre.

99. M. J. de Goeje, *Viae Regnorum. Descriptio Ditionis Moslemicae Auctore Abu Ibn Ishák al-Fārisí al-Istakhrí*, Editio Secunda, photomechanice iterata (Lugduni Batavorum, 1927). M. Jābir ʿAbd al-ʿĀl al-Ḥīnī's edition of this work was published at Qāhirah (Cairo) in A.H. 1381/A.D. 1961. Although in what follows I have relied principally on de Goeje's edition, I have consulted al-Ḥīnī's redaction in all cases of dubious readings. The most informed exposition of al-Iṣṭakhrī's contribution to the development of Islamic geography is incorporated in Miquel, *La Géographie Humaine*, 292–99.

100. Cf. p. 67 above. For a discussion of Ibn Ḥawqal's Shīʿite sympathies see Miquel, *La Géographie Humaine*, 300–302. Note especially this author's remark: "Il [Ibn Ḥawqal] a sans doute glissé du muʿtazilisme au šīʿisme." For Ibn Ḥawqal in the role of a Fāṭimid *dāʿī* see Reinhardt Dozy, *Histoire des Musulmans d'Espagne, 711–1110* (Leiden, 1861), 3:17. Prince P. H. Mamour's argument to the contrary, in *Polemics on the Origin of the Fatimi Caliphs* (London, 1934), 158, has not prevailed.

101. This redaction was dedicated to the Ḥamdānid Sayf al-Dawlah, who died in 967.

102. M. J. de Goeje, *Bibliotheca Geographorum Arabicorum* (Lugduni Batavorum, 1873). This edition was based on manuscripts in Leiden and Oxford, supplemented by Arabic MS no. 2214 in the Bibliothèque Nationale at Paris (which de Goeje designated as *Epitome Parisiensis*).

103. Johannes Hendrik Kramers, *Opus Geographicum Auctore Ibn Ḥauḳal (Abū'l-Ḳāsim ibn Ḥauḳal al-Naṣībī) secundum textum et imagines codicis Constantinopolitani conservati in Bibliotheca Antiqui Palatii no. 3346 cui titulus est "Liber Imaginis Terrae,"* 2d ed. (Lugduni Batavorum, 1938–39). This edition is essentially the text of a single manuscript (Arabic MS. no. 3346 in the Old Seray Library, Istanbul), which was copied in A.H. 479/A.D. 1086 and differs significantly from those utilized by de Goeje. The *Epitome Parisiensis* (note 102) turns out to be an abridgment of this text, which also incorporates annotations relating to the period of the redactor, specifically A.H. 534–80/A.D. 1139–84.

Kramers distinguished the twelfth-century additions by brackets in his edition of the text and by italic type in his translation. A revision of a translation of this text prepared by Kramers, and reproducing Ibn Ḥawqal's maps, has been published posthumously by Gaston Wiet: Kramers and Wiet, *Ibn Hauqal. Configuration de la Terre*, 2 vols. (Beyrouth and Paris, 1964). Cf. also Brockelmann, *Geschichte*, vol. 1 (Leiden, 1945), 263 and *Supplementband 1* (Leiden, 1937), 408; R. Blachère and H. Darmaun, *Extraits des Principaux Géographes Arabes du Moyen Age* (Paris, 1957), 134–36; I. Yu Kračkoviskiy, *Arabskaya Geografičeskaya Literatura* (Moscow-Leningrad, 1957), 198–205; and Miquel, *La Géographie Humaine*, 299–309 and *The Encyclopaedia of Islam*, 2d ed., vol. 3 (Leiden and London, 1968), 786–88.

104. *Khudūd al-ʿĀlem. Rukopis' Tumanskayo. S vvedeniem i ukazatelem V. Bartol'da. Edition of the Academy of Sciences of the U.S.S.R. (Leningrad, 1930).*

105. Tehran University Publication no. 727 (A.H. 1340/A.D. 1962). Cf. also article by Manūchir Sutūdah in *Farhang-i Īrān-zamīn*, vol. 7, pts. 1–3 (1959), 334–46.

106. Pages 1–114, with Barthold's *Index* reproduced on 115–49.

107. V. Minorsky, trans., *Ḥudūd al-ʿĀlam*. E. J. W. Gibb Memorial Series, n.s., 11 (London, 1937); 2d ed. by C. E. Bosworth

(London, 1970). Subsequently Minorsky has suggested that the author of the *Ḥudūd* may have been a certain Ibn Farīghūn, who compiled an encyclopedia of the sciences entitled *Jawāmiʿ al-ʿUlūm* ("Ibn Farīghūn and the Ḥudud al-ʿĀlam," in *A Locust's Leg. Studies in Honour of S. H. Taqizadeh* [London, 1962], 189–96).

108. This and subsequent references are to the *Ḥudūd*, Minorsky's translation, Bosworth edition, unless otherwise indicated.

109. Minorsky, *Ḥudūd*, xliii (citing a letter from Gulpāyagānī to Tumansky dated 2 Rabīʿ II, 1310 = 25 October 1892) and xlix–l.

110. Minorsky (*Ḥudūd*, xlix) has advanced the argument that the peculiar order of enumeration of places in some regions is the result of the author of the *Ḥudūd* having read his text off a map.

111. Cf. p. 64 above. In his preface to the Russian edition of the text in 1930 (translated in loc. cit., 18), Barthold suggests that Abū Zayd al-Balkhī's (d. 934) lost topographical treatise may have been in the nature of an exposition of al-Khāzin's maps. For an evaluation of al-Khāzin's contribution to the development of the discipline of geography, see J. Samsó, *The Encyclopaedia of Islam*, 2d ed., 4:1182–83.

112. Maqdisī, *Aḥsan*, 3–4.

113. Minorsky, *Ḥudūd*, passim.

114. André Miquel, *La Géographie Humaine*, xxvii.

For the life of al-Hamdānī see, int. al., Yāqūt, *Muʿjam al-Udabāʾ*, ed. by D. S. Margoliouth (Leyden, 1907–26), 3:9; ʿAlī ibn Yūsuf al-Qifṭī, *Ikhbār al-ʿUlamāʾ bi Akhbār al-Ḥukamāʾ*, ed. Julius Lippert (Leipzig, 1903), 163; Jalāl al-Dīn al-Suyūṭī, *Bughyat al-Wuʿāh* (al-Qāhirah, A.H. 1326/A.D. 1908). *Ṣifat Jazīrat al-ʿArab*, or the *Ṣifah*, has been edited by D. H. Müller under the title *Ṣifa: al-Hamdânî's Geographie der arab. Halbinsel*, 2 vols. (Leyden, 1884–91; reprint, Leiden, 1968; all subsequent references are to the Müller edition unless otherwise indicated. 2d ed. by Muḥammad ibn ʿAlī al-Akwaʿ [Riyāḍ, A.H. 1394/A.D. 1974]). There is a partial translation by L. Forrer, *Südarabien nach al-Hamdānī's "Beschreibung der arab. Halbinsel". Abhandlungen für die Kunde des Morgenlandes*, vol. 27, pt. 3 (Leipzig, 1942).

115. Only four of the original ten books of the *Iklīl* have survived. A facsimile edition of volumes 1 and 2, detailing the genealogy of Mālik ibn Ḥimyar, was published in Berlin in 1943. Book 1 was edited by (1) O. Löfgren in *Bibliotheca Ekmaniana*, vol. 58 (Uppsala, 1954, 1965) and (2) Muḥammad ibn ʿAlī al-Akwaʿ al-Ḥiwālī (al-Qāhirah, A.H. 1383/A.D. 1963). The final section of book 2 has been edited by Löfgren, *Südarabisches Muštabih.* in *Bibl. Ekmaniana*, vol. 57 (Uppsala, 1954). A poorly collated edition of book 8, which is mainly a description of the antiquities of the Yaman interspersed with a good deal of verse, was published by Anastās Mārī al-Karmalī under the title *al-Iklīl, al-Juzʾ al-Thāmin* (Baghdād, 1931). Subsequently Nabih Amin Faris issued an improved version (Princeton, N.J., 1940) and translated the text under the title *The Antiquities of South Arabia* (Princeton, N.J., 1938; reprint, Westport, Conn., 1981). Cf. also Müller, "Die Burgen und Schlösser Südarabiens," which includes selections from *al-Iklīl*, together with German translations. Book 10, which specifies the genealogies of the Hamdānid tribes Ḥāshid and Bakīl, has been edited by Muḥibb al-Dīn al-Khaṭīb (al-Qāhirah, A.H. 1368/A.D. 1948).

116. Ar. *haft iqlīm*. In this system the world was divided into seven equal circles (each constituting a *kishwar*), disposed in such a manner that the fourth circle, which included Īrānshahr, was centrally located with respect to the other six: see Ahmad, *The Encyclopaedia of Islam*, 2d ed., vol. 2 (1965), s.v. "Djugrāfiyā," 577.

117. Cf. note 32 above.

118. See Charles Pellat, *Mélanges Ṭahā Ḥusain: offerts par ses amis et ses disciples à l'occasion de son 70ième anniversaire* (Le Caire, 1962), 37 and Miquel, *La Géographie Humaine*, 205–8.

119. Miquel, *La Géographie Humaine*, 205–8. Aḥmad Shboul has rejected this suggestion on the ground that there is no evidence that al-Masʿūdī left ʿIrāq when the Buwayhids came to power. For reference see note 120.

120. Masʿūdī, *Murūj al-Dhahab wa-Maʿādin al-Jawhar*, ed. and trans. C. Barbier de Meynard and Pavet de Courteille under the title *Les Prairies d'Or et les Mines de Pierres Précieuses*, 9 vols. (Paris, 1861–77). Subsequent references are to this edition as revised and corrected in 5 vols. by Charles Pellat, Publications de l'Université Libanaise, Section des Etudes Historiques, vol. 11 (Beirut, 1966–74). Pellat has also published two supplementary volumes in Arabic devoted exclusively to indices, which contain a wealth of biographical and historical information. Also edited by Yūsuf Asʿad Dāghir in 4 vols. (Bayrūt, 1965–66).

A challenge to the customary translation of *murūj* as "meadows" advanced by J. Gildemeister ("Über den Titel des Masudischen Werkes *Murūj al-Dhahab*," *Zeitschrift für die Kunde* 9: 202–4), and adopted by Carl Brockelmann in the first edition of his *Geschichte der Arabischen Literatur*, vol. 1 (Leipzig, 1901), 110—these authors prefer "[gold] washings"—has been successfully refuted by Tarif Khalidi (*Islamic Historiography: The Histories of Masʿūdī* [Albany, N.Y., 1975], 2 n. 2). This last work is also the best available general introduction to the *oeuvre* of Masʿūdī, although there are shrewd comments and a great deal of useful information in Ahmad M. H. Shboul, *Al-Masʿūdī and His World: A Muslim Humanist and His Interest in Non-Muslims* (London, 1979).

121. Edited by M. J. de Goeje, *Bibliotheca Géographorum Arabicorum*, vol. 8 (Leiden, 1893–94; reprint, Beirut, 1965); translated by Baron Carra de Vaux under the title *Le Livre de l'Avertissement et de la Revision* (Paris, 1897).

122. Cf. Ibn al-Nadīm, *Kitāb al-Fihrist*, ed. Gustav Flügel (Leipzig, 1871–72), 1:154; Tāj al-Dīn al-Subki, *Ṭabaqāt al-Shāfiʿīyah*, ed. Maḥmūd Muḥammad al-Ṭanāḥī and Muḥammad ʿAbd al-Fattaḥ al-Ḥilw 2:307; [E.] Quatremère, "Sur la vie et les ouvrages de Masoudi," *Journal Asiatique*, ser. 3, vol. 7, pp. 1–31; and Brockelmann, *Geschichte*, vol. 1 (Leiden, 1945), 141–43.

123. The unique manuscript of this work (Add. MS. 23,379, The British Museum, London) has been edited by H. von Mžik (*Bibliothek Arabischer Historiker und Geographen*, no. 5 [Leipzig, 1930]). It has been dated between 902 and 945 by Guy Le Strange on the basis of its description of Baghdād architecture ("Descrip-

tion of Mesopotamia and Baghdād, written about the year 900 A.D. by Ibn Serapion . . .," *Journal of the Royal Asiatic Society* [1895], 2). As Ibn Sarābiyūn refers to himself in his introduction as Suhrāb, it is usually inferred that he was of Persian origin. However, André Miquel interprets Suhrāb as the pseudonym of an otherwise unknown redactor who prepared a new version of the *Kitāb Ṣūrat al-Arḍ* of al-Khwārizmī, which he then attributed to an equally unknown (today at any rate) Ibn Sarābiyūn (Ibn Serapion) (*La Géographie Humaine,* xxviii, 79–80).

124. Muḥammad ibn Mūsā al-Khwārizmī (780–ca. 850), *Kitāb Ṣūrat al-Arḍ,* ed. H. von Mžik (Wien, 1926); Miquel, *La Géographie Humaine,* 80.

125. See Brockelmann, *Geschichte,* 1:261 and *Supplement* (Leiden, 1937–42), 1:406; Kračkoviskiy, *Arabskaya* (Moscow, 1959), 97–99; *The Encyclopaedia of Islam,* 2d ed., 3:929–30; and Miquel, *La Géographie Humaine,* 79–80.

126. Cf. Brockelmann, *Geschichte,* 1:156–157 and *Supplement,* 1:231; Kračkoviskiy, *Arabskaya,* 165–66; and Évariste Lévi-Provençal, "La 'Description de l'Espagne' d'Aḥmad ar-Rāzī," *Andalus* 18 (1953): 51–108. See also note 186 to chapter 16.

127. His grandfather's Īrānian name was transliterated *Kh.r.dā.dh.b.h* and apparently vocalized as either Khurdādhbih (= "Excellent Gift of the Sun") or, more probably, Khurradādhbih (= "Created by the Excellent Sun"): see M. Hadj-Sadok, *The Encyclopaedia of Islam,* 2d ed., vol. 3 (1968), 839.

128. Maqdisī, *Aḥsan,* 392.

129. See Brockelmann, *Geschichte,* 1:225–26; Masʿūdī, *Murūj,* 1:72, 8:80; Ibn al-Nadīm, *al-Fihrist,* 149; C. Barbier de Meynard, "Le livre des routes et des provinces par Ibn-Khordadbeh," *Journal Asiatique* 5 (1865): 5–127, 227–96; M. J. de Goeje, *Bibliotheca Geographorum Arabicorum,* Pars Sexta: *Kitāb al-Masālik wa'l-Mamālik (Liber viarum et regnorum) auctore Abu'l-Kâsim Obaidallah ibn Abdallah ibn Khordâdhbeh et excerpta e Kitâb al-Kharâdj auctore Kodâma ibn Djaʿfar quae cum versione Gallica edidit, indicibus et glossario instruxit* (Lugduni Batavorum, 1889), preface; J. Marquart, *Osteuropäische und ostasiatische Streifzüge* (Leipzig, 1903), 390; Carra de Vaux, *Les Penseurs de l'Islam,* vol. 2 (Paris, 1921), 7; Blachère and Darmaun, *Extraits,* 21; I. Yu Kračkoviskiy, *Izbrannïe sočineniya,* vol. 4 (Moscow-Leningrad, 1957), 147 et seq.; M. Hadj-Sadok, *The Encyclopaedia of Islam,* 2d ed., vol. 3 (1968), 839–40; and Miquel, *La Géographie Humaine,* 87–92.

Ibn Khurradādhbih's reputation varied considerably among litterateurs in the century following his death. Whereas al-Iṣfahānī (d. 967), author of the *Kitāb al-Aghānī,* castigated him for reporting as fact "mere conjectures unsupported by authority" (1:19, 5:3), al-Masʿūdī considered the *Kitāb al-Masalik wa-l-Mamalik* to be "a valuable book, an inexhaustible mine of information that can always be worked with profit," while yet deprecating its emphasis on routes and distances to the virtual exclusion of discussions of states and governments (*Murūj,* 1:13, 2:70). Ibn Ḥawqal kept a copy of the work by him at all times (*al-Masālik wa-l-Mamālik,* 329), and in the Constantinople recension of the *Aḥsan* (6) al-Maqdisī implies that al-Jayhānī (probably first half of the tenth century, although there is more than a little doubt about this author's identity: see Charles Pellat, *The Encyclopaedia of Islam,* new ed., *Supplement,* fascs. 5–6 [1982], 265–66) had used it as the basis of his own book of the same title. Al-Maqdisī himself (*Aḥsan,* 4–5) dismissed it as too concise to be of much use. Nevertheless, he, like al-Masʿūdī and Ibn al-Faqīh, did not hesitate to borrow information from the father of the roadbook genre.

130. His full name was Aḥmad ibn Abī Yaʿqūb ibn Jaʿfar ibn Wahb ibn Wāḍiḥ al-Kātib al-ʿAbbāsī al-Yaʿqūbī.

131. Al-Yaʿqūbī's style is simple and unencumbered with the fabulous ornament that plays such a large part in the works of many other medieval Arab topographers. For substantiation of al-Yaʿqūbī's Shīʿite sympathies as revealed in his *Mushākalat al-Nās li-Zamānihim wa-mā Yaghlibu ʿalayhim fī kulli ʿaṣrin,* see William G. Millward, "The adaptation of men to their time: an historical essay by al-Yaʿqūbī," *Journal of the American Oriental Society* 84 (1964): 329–44.

132. T. G. J. Juynboll (1861), cited in *Bibliotheca Geographorum Arabicorum,* vol. 7: see next note.

133. M. J. de Goeje, *Kitāb al-Boldân Auctore Ahmed ibn Abî Jaʿkûb ibn Wâdhih al-Kâtib al-Jaʿkûbî, Bibliotheca Geographorum Arabicorum,* vol. 7 (Lugduni Batavorum, 1892).

134. Gaston Wiet, trans. and annot., *Yaʿḳūbī. Les Pays* (Le Caire, 1937). For a compendious evaluation of al-Yaʿqūbī's role in the development of Islamic geography, see Miquel, *La Géographie Humaine,* 102–4, 285–92.

135. Edited by M. J. de Goeje, *Bibliotheca Geographorum Arabicorum,* vol. 7 (Lugduni Batavorum, 1892), and translated by Gaston Wiet under the title *Les Atours Précieux* (Le Caire, 1955). Cf. Brockelmann, *Geschichte,* 1:227; Clément Imbault Huart, *Littérature Arabe* (Paris, 1923), 297; and Blachère and Darmaun, *Extraits,* 32–53.

136. Ibn Rustah, *Al-Aʿlaq,* 151.

137. Miquel, *La Géographie Humaine,* 202.

138. Extensive extracts from the *Kitāb al-Kharāj* have been edited by M. J. de Goeje, *Bibliotheca Geographorum Arabicorum,* vol. 6, Arabic text, 184–296; French translation, 144–208. Edition completed by A. Makkī under the title *Qudāma b. Ǧaʿfar et Son Oeuvre* (Paris, 1955), mimeo. Book 7 has been translated and edited by A. Ben Shemesh, *Taxation in Islam,* 2d rev. ed., vol. 2 (Leiden and London, 1965). Cf. Brockelmann, *Geschichte,* 1:228; Huart, *Littérature,* 297; Blachère and Darmaun, *Extraits,* 53–69; and Miquel, *La Géographie Humaine,* 95–101.

139. Miquel (*La Géographie Humaine,* 99) believes that Qudāmah was the earliest extant author to use the term "empire of Islam" *(mamlakat al-Islam):* de Goeje's Arabic text, 234; translation, 177.

140. Blachère and Darmaun, *Extraits,* 70. Cf. also Brockelmann, *Geschichte,* 1:227 and Huart, *Littérature,* 296. The *Kitāb al-Buldān* has been edited by M. J. de Goeje, *Compendium Libri Kitâb al-Boldân auctore Ibn al-Faḳîh al-Hamadhânî quod edidit, indicibus*

et glossario instruxit: Bibliotheca Geographorum Arabicorum, vol. 5 (Lugduni Batavorum, 1885). It was in the introduction to this work that de Goeje deduced the author and date of the abridged version. Cf. also A. Z. Validov (= A. Z. Validi Toğan), "Meshkhedskaya Rukopis Ibnu-l-Fakikha," *Izvestiya Russkoy Akad. Nauk,* no. 1 (1924): 237–48.

141. Maqdisī, *Aḥsan.* An exception was Hamadān, Ibn al-Faqīh's native city, for which he provided many details (219ff.).

142. Cf. Miquel's characterization of the *Kitāb al-Buldān* as a work: "où ne serait consigné que ce qui échappe au spectacle quotidien, et systématiquement noté que ce qui n'est pas systématique" (*La Géographie Humaine,* 162).

143. Miquel's phrase: ibid., 162.

144. Ibid., 188. This author's chapter on Ibn al-Faqīh (153–89) is the most discerning evaluation of this topographer to date. Cf. also H. Massé, *The Encyclopaedia of Islam,* new ed., 3:761–62.

145. That part of the text of al-Bakrī's *Kitāb al-Masālik wa-l-Mamālik* dealing with North Africa has been edited and translated by Baron Mac Guckin de Slane under the title *Description de l'Afrique Septentrionale par Abou-Obeïd-el-Bekri* (Alger, 1857–58; 2d ed., Alger, 1911–13; reprint, Paris, 1965). Cf. also Brockelmann, *Geschichte,* 1:476 and Huart, *Littérature,* 300. For further items of bibliography see *The Encyclopaedia of Islam,* new ed., 1:157.

146. Cf. Pons Boigues, *Ensayo Bio-Bibliográfico sobre los Historiadores y Geógrafos Arábigo-Españoles* (Madrid, 1898), 80 n. 1; Brockelmann, *Geschichte: Supplement,* 1:233; Kračkoviskiy, *Izbrannîe,* 165; Robert Brunschvig, "Un aspect de la littérature historico-géographique de l'Islam," in *Mélanges Gaudefroy-Demombynes,* Series of the Institut Français d'Archéologie Orientale du Caire (Le Caire, 1935–45), 147–58; and Miquel, *La Géographie Humaine,* xxxi–xxxii, 259–62.

147. The *Niẓām al-Marjān* has been edited by ʿAbd al-ʿAzīz al-Ahwānī (Madrid, 1965). Cf. also Évariste Lévi-Provençal, *La Péninsule Ibérique au Moyen Age d'après le "Kitab ar-Rawd al-Miʿṭār* (Leyden, 1938), xxiii–xxiv and Miquel, *La Géographie Humaine,* 269 n. 1. For his information on Christian Spain (which will be of only passing concern in the following pages), al-Bakrī's principal source was a now-lost work of the Jew Ibrāhīm ibn Yaʿqūb al-Isrāʾīlī al-Ṭurṭūshī, who lived at the beginning of the tenth century.

148. The *Safar Nāmah* of Nāṣir-i Khusraw (began his pilgrimage in 1045; died between 1072 and 1077), first published, together with an annotated French translation by Charles Schéfer in the series of the Ecole des Langues Orientales Vivantes (*Sefer Nameh. Relation du Voyage de Nassiri Khosrau* . . . [Paris, 1881]), has been edited more recently by Muḥammad Dabīr-Siyāqī (Tehrān, A.H. 1335/A.D. 1956) and translated into English by W. M. Thackston Jr. under the title *Nāṣer-e Khosraw's Book of Travels (Safarnāma)* (New York, 1986). All subsequent references are to Thackston's translation unless otherwise indicated.

149. Guy Le Strange and Reynold A. Nicholson, eds., *The Fárs-Náma of Ibnu'l Balkhī,* Gibb Memorial Series, n.s., 1 (London, 1921); English translation by Le Strange under the title "Description of the Province of Fars, in Persia, at the beginning of the twelfth century A.D., translated from the MS. of Ibn-al-Balkhī in the British Museum," *Journal of the Royal Asiatic Society* (1912): 1–30, 311–39, 865–89. The name of the author of this work is unknown, but Ibn al-Balkhī is the conventionally accepted and convenient manner of referring to one who states in his preface that an ancestor was a native of Balkh.

150. Al-Idrīsī, scion of a noble Maghribī family, travelled widely in Europe, Africa, and the Levant before settling at the court of Roger II in Sicily. The *Nuzhat* is prefaced by a brief description of the earth as a globe, after which follows a lengthy account of the regions of the world derived from an artificial subdivision of the seven main Ptolemaic *klimata.* Sicily at this time was the rendezvous of navigators from the whole of the Mediterranean, as well as from the Atlantic shores of Europe, so that al-Idrīsī was, generally speaking, better informed about current events in the western realms of Islam than were those of his contemporaries who were writing in Asia. Unfortunately for our present purpose, he was not overly interested in the past of those regions.

A synopsis of the text of the *Nuzhat,* together with its seventy-one maps, was printed at Rome as early as 1592. It was translated into Latin in 1619 by two Maronite scholars, Jibrāʾīl al-Ṣahyūnī (Gabriel Sionita) and Yūḥannah al-Ḥaṣrūnī (Joannes Hesronita). Partial editions of the text have since appeared at different times in Leiden, Madrid, Rome, and Bonn, but the only translation currently available, and not an especially reliable one at that, is A. Jaubert's *Géographie d'Edrisi,* 2 vols. (Paris, 1836–40). Cf. also Brockelmann, *Geschichte,* 1:477; Huart, *Littérature,* 300; and Blachère and Darmaun, *Extraits,* 190–200.

151. The *Riḥlah* of Ibn Jubayr was edited and published by William Wright (Leiden, 1852), and subsequently re-edited by M. J. de Goeje as vol. 5 of the Gibb Memorial Series (Leyden and London, 1907) and by Ḥ. Naṣṣar (al-Qāhirah, A.H. 1374/A.D. 1955). There are translations into Italian by C. Schiaparelli (Roma, 1906); English by R. J. C. Broadhurst (1952); and French by M. Gaudefroy-Demombynes in *Documents Relatifs à l'Histoire des Croisades,* 3 fascs. (Paris, 1949–56). Cf. also Brockelmann, *Geschichte,* 1:478 and *Supplement,* 1:879; Huart, *Littérature,* 301; Blachère and Darmaun, *Extraits,* 318–48; and Charles Pellat, *The Encyclopaedia of Islam,* 2d ed., 3:755.

152. Yāqūt al-Rūmī (or, according to a genealogy that he subsequently assumed, Shīhāb al-Dīn Abū ʿAbd Allāh Yaʿqūb ibn ʿAbd Allāh al-Ḥamawī) spent his life as a merchant, copyist, and bookseller in various parts of the Islamic world ranging from Alexandria to Balkh, so that he was not unfitted by training and experience to undertake the compilation of a geographical dictionary. Yet his *Muʿjam al-Buldān* contains very little original information, being in effect a collection of borrowings from earlier writers. In the present context this has not proved totally a defect, for Yāqūt quoted freely from virtually all his predecessors in the field of Islamic topography, including some from the tenth century.

The *Muʿjam* has been published by Ferdinand Wüstenfeld

under the title *Jacut's geographisches Wörterbuch,* 6 vols. (Leipzig, 1866–73); by Amīn al-Khānojī, 10 vols. with a supplement (al-Qāhirah, A.H. 1324/A.D. 1906–1907); and again in an uncritical edition of 5 vols. at Bayrūt, A.H. 1374–76/A.D. 1955–57. Cf. also Brockelmann, *Geschichte,* 1:479–81; Huart, *Littérature,* 301; and Blachère, *Extraits,* 264–75. *Al-Marāṣid al-Iṭṭilā' 'alā Asmā' al-Amkinah wa-l-Biqā',* an abridged version of the *Mu'jam* by 'Abd al-Mu'min ibn 'Abd al-Ḥaqq, which appeared within three-quarters of a century of Yāqūt's original work, has been edited by T. G. J. Juynboll, *Lexicon Geographicum cui Titulus est Marāṣid al-Iṭṭilā 'ala Asmā al-Amkina wa-l-Biqā,* 6 vols. (Leyden, 1851–64). In the second half of the fifteenth century Jalāl al-Dīn al-Suyūṭī also prepared an abridged version entitled *Mukhtaṣar Mu'jam al-Buldān.* Yāqūt himself seems to have realized that the great size of the *Mu'jam* was likely to daunt many readers, for he himself executed a shorter version entitled *al-Mushtarik Waḍ'an wa-l-Mukhtalif Ṣaq'an,* which was edited by Wüstenfeld (Göttingen, 1846). In any case, the usefulness of the full work has been enhanced by the publication of an index to Wüstenfeld's edition: Oskar Rescher, *Sachindex zu Wüstenfeld's Ausgabe von Jacut's "Mu'ğam al-Buldān"* (Stuttgart, 1928). The articles in the *Mu'jam* relating to Persia have been translated into French by C. Barbier de Meynard in *Dictionnaire Géographique, Historique et Littéraire de la Perse et des Contrées Adjacentes. Extrait du Modjem el-Bouldan de Yaqout* (Paris, 1861), and Wadie Jwaideh has provided an English translation of chapters 1–5: *The Introductory Chapters of Yāqūt's Mu'jam al-Buldān* (Leiden, 1959).

The *Mu'jam* has proved a rich quarry for topographers in later periods, including the present, and particularly for those seeking to reconstruct the journey of Abū Dulaf Mis'ar (ibn Muhalhil al-Khazrajī al-Yanbū'ī: the *nisbah* is invariably written in this way even though the accepted orthography of the name of the port from which it derives is Yanbu') through northern and western Persia and al-Riḥāb in about the mid-tenth century. However, since the publication of an authentic (although not the original) copy of the manuscript of the so-called Second *Risālah* of Abū Dulaf, resort to Yāqūt's text in this respect has been rendered unnecessary. See V. Minorsky, "La deuxième risala d'Abu-Dulaf," *Oriens* 5 (1952): 23–27 and *Abū Dulaf Mis'ar ibn al-Muhalhil's Travels in Iran (circa A.D. 950)* (Cairo, 1955), which reproduces the Mashhad text (discovered in 1923) of the second *risālah,* together with an English translation and a detailed commentary; Miquel, *La Géographie Humaine,* 139–45; and *The Encyclopaedia of Islam,* 2d ed., 1:116.

A topographer who is still known only through 55 quotations in Yāqūt's *Mu'jam* and at least 135 in the *Mukhtaṣar Ta'rīkh al-Bashar* of Abū al-Fidā' (1273–1332) is al-Ḥasan ibn Aḥmad al-Miṣrī al-Muhallabī (d. A.H. 380/A.D. 990), the author of a *Kitāb al-Masālik wa-l-Mamālik* dedicated to the Fāṭimid caliph al-'Azīz, and known familiarly as *al-Kitāb al-'Azīzī.* Judging from the extant quotations from what was clearly a large work, al-Muhallabī was familiar at firsthand with Egypt, Syria, and 'Irāq, but was otherwise dependent on secondhand accounts. However, descriptions of urban forms figure prominently in the surviving fragments of his work, together with their histories, traditions, monuments, holy places, peoples, and products. For a succinct summary of what can be inferred about al-Muhallabī's role in the development of Islamic geography see Miquel, *La Géographie Humaine,* 309–12.

153. The text of Ḥamd-Allāh Mustawfī's *Nuzhat al-Qulūb* was lithographed at Bombay in A.H. 1311/A.D. 1894, under the editorship of Mīrzā Muḥammad Shīrāzī. In 1915 Guy Le Strange published a variorum edition of the third, or geographical, part of this work (E. J. W. Gibb Memorial Series, vol. 23 [Leyden and London]), followed by an English translation (vol. 23, 2) in 1919. Like Yāqūt, Mustawfī incorporated in his narrative a good deal of material relevant to earlier centuries.

154. For a general discussion of these local histories see Franz Rosenthal, *A History of Muslim Historiography* (Leiden, 1952), 130–49.

155. Published in 14 vols. at al-Qāhirah in A.H. 1349/A.D. 1931. Of the *Ta'rīkh,* Ibn Khallikān remarked (*Wafayāt al-A'yān wa-Anba Abnā' al-Zamān,* de Slane translation, 1:27), "Had the Khaṭīb al-Baghdādī written nothing but this, it would have been sufficient to ensure his reputation." Al-Khaṭīb's introductory chapter on the topography of Baghdād (*Ta'rīkh,* 1:4–101ff.) has been published and translated by G. Salmon under the title *L'Introduction Topographique à l'Histoire de Bagdâdh . . .* (Paris, 1904). Cf. also J.-P. Pascual, *Index Schématique du Ta'rīḫ Baġdād* (Paris, 1971). A new translation of the *Ta'rīkh* has recently been used to good effect by Jacob Lassner to reconstruct the topography of Baghdād: *The Topography of Baghdād* with revisions in chaps. 7 and 8 of Lassner, *The Shaping of 'Abbāsid Rule.*

156. Al-Narshakhī's full name was Abū Bakr Muḥammad ibn Ja'far ibn Zakarīyā ibn Khaṭṭāb ibn Sharīk al-Narshakhī. The *nisbah* implies that he was from a village near the city about which he was writing. The original Persian translation of al-Narshakhī's text, *Ta'rīkh Bukhārā,* was the work of Abū Naṣr Aḥmad al-Qubāvī in 1128, who also brought the history down to 975. Half a century later this translation was abridged by a certain Muḥammad ibn Zufar ibn 'Umar. There are several editions of this abridgment, including most recently that of Mudarris Razavī [Riḍawī] (Tehrān, n.d. but probably in about 1939) and an earlier publication by Charles Schéfer under the title *Description Topograpique [sic] et Historique de Boukhara . . . par Mohammed Nerchaky, 943 (332 H.)* (Paris, 1892: reimpression, Amsterdam, 1975). For the variant versions of Narshakhī's text, a bibliography, and a translation, see Richard N. Frye, *The History of Bukhara* (Cambridge, Mass., 1954).

157. Of this work the Turkish bibliographer Ḥājjī Khalīfah (d. 1658), who was apparently able to consult the original version, writes:

> My eyes have never seen a more excellent chronicle; I place it first among books referring to individual provinces. The majority of the persons mentioned in it are his [i.e., Ibn al-Bayyi'] shaykhs [i.e., teachers] or the shaykhs of his shaykhs. He mentions also the Companions and Followers who came to Khurāsān and settled there, and gives a brief

account of their origin and their history. Next [he enumerates] the second generation of Followers, then the third and fourth generations. He divides them all into six categories; the men of each generation are enumerated in alphabetical order, and the sixth and last category includes those persons who transmitted *ḥadīths* between the years [A.H.] 320 and 380. (*Kitāb Kashf al-Ẓunūn ʿan Asāmi al-Kutub wa-l-Funūn,* ed. Gustav Flügel [Leipzig, 1835–58], vol. 2, pp. 155–56: cited in W. Barthold, *Turkestan down to the Mongol Invasion,* 3d ed. [London, 1968], 16, modified).

A condensed Arabic version of the text of al-Bayyiʿ, *Taʾrikh Naysābūr,* now exists only in excerpts in a Persian translation of the original book. A second Arabic book based on the work of al-Bayyiʿ, titled *Kitāb al-Siyāq li-Taʾrīkh Nīsābūr,* was written by ʿAbd al-Ghāfir ibn Ismāʿīl al-Fārisī, who died in 1134. Today only the second part of this book survives. However, the entire work was epitomized by a certain Ibrāhīm ibn Muḥammad al-Sarīfīnī, who died in 1243. The so-called Persian recension, the second part of al-Fārisī's version, and al-Sarīfīnī's epitome have been reproduced in facsimile by Richard N. Frye, *The Histories of Nīshāpūr* (The Hague, 1965), while an index of the personal and place-names contained in al-Fārisī's text has been compiled by Habib Jaouiche: *The Histories of Nīshāpūr* (Wiesbaden, 1984). The epitome has also been edited by B. Karīmī (Tehrān, A.H. 1339/A.D. 1960). The value of the materials contained in these histories for a reconstruction of the social history of Nīshāpūr has been splendidly demonstrated by Richard W. Bulliet in *The Patricians of Nishapur. A Study in Medieval Islamic Social History* (Cambridge, Mass., 1972).

158. *Taʾrīkh Wāsiṭ,* compiled by Aslam ibn Sahl Baḥshāl; published at Baghdād in A.H. 1387/A.D. 1967. See Brockelmann, *Geschichte: Supplement,* 1:210.

159. *Kitāb Dhikr Akhbār Iṣbahān,* ed. S. Dedering, 2 vols. (Leiden, 1931). This work is essentially a collection of biographies of scholars and other prominent persons associated with Iṣbahān. For a later (A.H. 729/A.D. 1329) Persian history of the same city see ʿAbbās Iqbāl, ed., *Tarjuma-yī Maḥāsin-i Iṣfahān* (Ṭihrān, A.H. 1328) and Edward G. Browne, "Account of a rare manuscript History of Iṣfahán," *Journal of the Royal Asiatic Society* (1901), 411–46 and 661–704. This last manuscript, by Ḥusayn ibn Muḥammad al-ʿAlawī, was translated from an Arabic original, *Kitāb Maḥāsin Iṣfahān,* composed in 1030 by al-Mufaḍḍal ibn Saʿd ibn al-Ḥusayn al-Māfarrūkhī, and consequently incorporates some material from the tenth century or earlier. It has been edited by Sayyid Jalāl al-Dīn Ṭihrānī (Ṭihrān, A.H. 1312). There are some relevant secondary materials in Shaykh Ḥasan Jābirī Anṣārī, *Taʾrīkh-i Iṣfahān va-Rayy* (Tihrān, A.H. 1321/A.D. 1944).

160. Published and edited by Sayyid Jalāl al-Dīn Ṭihrānī (Ṭihrān, A.H. 1353/A.D. 1934). Cf. also A. Houtum-Schindler, *Eastern Persian Irak* (London, 1896), 60–76 and Ann K. S. Lambton, "An account of the *Tārīkhi Qumm,*" *Bulletin of the School of Oriental and African Studies* 12 (1948): 585–96. The surviving five chapters include fairly detailed descriptions of Qumm and its dependent villages, as well as their revenue assessments and the settlement of Ashʿarī Arabs in the region.

161. Ibn Zarkūb Shīrāzī, *Shīrāz-Nāmah,* ed. Bahman Karīmī (Tehrān, A.H. 1310/A.D. 1931). Pertinent information is also summarized in a nineteenth-century history by Muḥammad Jaʿfar al-Ḥusaynī Khurmūjī, *Taʾrīkh-i Shīrāz* [or *Āthār-i Jaʿfarī*] (Tehrān, A.H. 1276/A.D. 1860).

162. Abū Zakarīyāʾ Yazīd ibn Muḥammad ibn Iyās ibn al-Qāsim al-Azdī, *Taʾrīkh al-Mawṣil,* ed. ʿAlī Ḥabībah (al-Qāhirah, A.H. 1387/A.D. 1967) from a manuscript copied in A.H. 624/A.D. 1256 by Ibrāhīm ibn Muḥammad ibn Jamāʿah ibn ʿAlī. For an excellent example of how the information in this history can throw light on the functioning of the urban hierarchy in one sector of the *iqlīm* of al-Jazīrah, consult Paul G. Forand, "The governors of Mosul according to al-Azdī's *Taʾrīkh* al-Mawṣil," *Journal of the American Oriental Society* 89 (1969): 88–105.

163. There is apparently a Russian translation of the Persian version by W. Vyatkin that I have not seen. For the reference see W. Barthold, *Turkestan down to the Mongol Invasion.* E. J. W. Gibb Memorial Series, n.s., 5 (London, 1968), 15 n. 8.

164. Al-Bayhaqī, *Tarīkh-i Bayhaq,* ed. A. Bahmanyār (Ṭihrān, A.H. 1317/A.D. 1968). Bayhaq is present-day Sabzavār in Khurāsān.

165. The *Taʾrīkh Madīnat Ṣanʿāʾ* has been edited by Ḥusayn ibn ʿAbd Allāh al-ʿAmrī and ʿAbd al-Jabbār Zakkār (Dimashq, A.H. 1395/A.D. 1975).

166. Ibn ʿAsākir (full name: Al-Ḥāfiẓ Thiqat al-Dīn Abū al-Qāsim ʿAlī ibn Abī Muḥammad al-Ḥasan ibn Hibat Allāh ibn ʿAbd Allāh ibn al-Ḥusayn al-Dimashqī al-Shāfiʿī), *Taʾrīkh Madīnat Dimashq,* ed. Ṣalāḥ al-Dīn al-Munajjid, 2 vols. (Dimashq, 1951–54); vol. 2 of this edition has been translated by Nikita Elisséeff under the title *La Description de Damas d'Ibn ʿAsākir* (Damas, 1959). Ibn ʿAsākir's sources for the ninth and tenth centuries are summarized diagrammatically opposite p. 48 of the translation.

Among the early "histories" of cities which have not survived were three works dealing with Marw, two with Harāt, and one with Balkh, all alluded to in the *Tarīkh-i Bayhaq,* as well as several histories of Hamadhān mentioned by Ḥājjī Khalīfah (*Kitāb Kashf al-Ẓunūn,* 1:310); but many others are cited in Arabic, Persian, and Turkish literature from virtually all historical periods. It is especially unfortunate that a history of al-Baṣrah by ʿUmar ibn Shabbah (d. 876), which circulated widely in the tenth century, has not survived: see Ibn Ḥawqal, *al-Masālik wa-l-Mamālik,* 238 and al-Nadīm, *al-Fihrist,* Bayard Dodge's translation, 1:246–47.

167. Al-Khushanī, *Ṭabaqāt ʿUlamāʾ Ifrīqiyah,* ed. and trans. into Spanish by Ribera y Tarragó (Madrid, 1914).

168. Maqdisī, *Aḥsan,* 9.

169. For a discussion of Chinese notices of Meroë see V. Velgus, "The countries of Mo-lin and Po-sa-lo (Lao-po-sa) in Chinese medieval reports on Africa," *Africana,* n.s., 90 (1966): 104–21 and Wheatley, "Analecta Sino-Africana Recensa," in *East Africa and the Orient: Cultural Syntheses in Pre-Colonial Times,* ed. H. Neville Chittick and Robert I. Rotberg (New York, 1975), 76–114.

170. For early Arab accounts of the East African littoral see J. Spencer Trimingham, "The Arab Geographers and the East African Coast," in Chittick and Rotberg, *East Africa and the Orient,* 115–46. Al-Maqdisī (*Aḥsan,* 97–98) relates that he himself was prevented from mounting a trading expedition to East Africa *(Bilād al-Zanj)* only by the death of his business partner—an eventuality that probably deprived the world of what would have turned out to be the only topographical description of, as opposed to simple references to, the Azanian region prior to Ibn Baṭṭūṭah in the fourteenth century and the Chinese accounts of the early fifteenth century: see note 169. For the opening of the trade route from the Middle East to East Africa at the very time when al-Maqdisī was collecting information for his book, see Mark Horton, "The Swahili corridor," *Scientific American* 257 (1987): 86–93.

171. Written Ātil in Minorsky, *Ḥudud,* 75, 80, 161, 452; Ibn Ḥawqal, *al-Masālik wa-l-Mamālik,* 389–393; and some other works; Ithil in Iṣṭakhrī, *al-Masālik wa-l-Mamālik,* 222.

172. Maqdisī, *Aḥsan,* 48.

173. Cf. Lassner, *The Topography of Baghdād,* 180, citing *Kitāb al-Fiqh ʿalā al-Madhāhib al-Arbaʿah, Qism al-ʿIbādat,* 2d ed. (Qāhirah, A.H. 1345/A.D. 1931), 346–48. The term *masjid al-jāmiʿ*, here translated as "congregational mosque," signified the Great Mosque, where Friday prayers were said weekly and the *khuṭbah* preached. In European writings it is often called the cathedral mosque, a custom that E. Diez believes was originally inspired by the resemblance of early mosques to the Nestorian churches of Īrān (*Glaube und Welt des Islam* [Stuttgart, 1941], 165–68). In later times the term *masjid al-jāmiʿ* was replaced by *masjid al-jumʿah* = the Friday mosque, a rendering frequently applied in European writings to the congregational mosque of the classical period.

174. Maqdisī, *Aḥsan,* 273.

175. A comparable situation could have been observed in Nasaf District in Transoxania, where sizable settlements were ignored by early topographers because they lacked mosques (see p. 183 below).

176. In the Ifrīqiyah (Tunisia and western Libya), by contrast, this author accepted as cities settlements which, "although smaller than many villages in other provinces, are customarily recognized as urban" (228). For settlements of up to ten thousand men in al-Jibāl Province which yet lacked mosques, see p. 138 below. For *taʿāruf* see p. 65 above.

177. For a compendious exposition of Arab perceptions of the illustrious past of Babylon, see Caroline Janssen, *Bābil, the City of Witchcraft and Wine* (Ghent, 1995), passim.

178. Bakrī, *al-Masālik wa-l-Mamālik,* 76. This and the following toponyms are apparently Baron Mac Guckin de Slane's restorations of Berber vocalizations.

179. Maqdisī, *Aḥsan,* 93–94, 356, 360. See also note 24 to chapter 7.

180. See also note 55 to chapter 2.

181. In constructing figure 5 I have added to the *mudun* enumerated by al-Maqdisī a handful of other cities that appear to have fallen appropriately into this category.

Al-Maqdisī employed two plural forms of the noun *madīnah,* namely *mudun* and *madāʾin.* The former he appears to have reserved generally as a technical term for district capitals in his urban hierarchies while using *madāʾin* to denote cities or towns in a more general sense.

182. Iṣṭakhrī, *al-Masālik wa-l-Mamālik,* 270; cf. also Yaʿqūbī, *al-Buldān,* 287; Ibn Ḥawqal, *al-Masālik wa-l-Mamālik,* 321–22; and Minorsky, *Ḥudūd,* 107.

183. Iṣṭakhrī, *al-Masālik wa-l-Mamālik,* 181; Ibn Ḥawqal, *al-Masālik wa-l-Mamālik,* 239; Maqdisī, *Aḥsan,* 377; Yaʿqūbī, *al-Buldān,* 271; Minorsky, *Ḥudūd,* 143; and Ibn Rustah, *al-Aʿlāq,* 106.

184. It should be noted in passing that identification of a city is not necessarily the same thing as the location of its site. Toponymic identification presented some difficulties, but they were nothing so severe as those arising from site identification.

185. An additional difficulty in this instance: whereas al-Maqdisī (*Aḥsan,* 355) stated that the name of the provincial capital was Barvān (Barwān: cf. Yaʿqūbī, *al-Buldān,* 288), other authors seem to have referred to it as Rūdhbār (lit., "river": Iṣṭakhrī, *al-Masālik wa-l-Mamālik,* 204–5 and Yāqūt, *Muʿjam,* 2:831).

186. Al-Maqdisī is especially helpful to the present-day student seeking to locate the urban centers mentioned in his text, for he presented his itineraries in terms of a set of conventions to which, as far as I have been able to ascertain, he adhered rigorously (*Aḥsan,* 106):

> With regard to distances, it is to be noted that the word "and" *(waw)* is copulative, that the word "then" *(thumma)* expresses sequence, and that the word "or" *(aw)* denotes an alternative. For example, when we say ". . . to such and such a place and such and such a place" it is implied that the two places are in the same locality, as are Khulays *AND* Amaj, Mazīnān *AND* Bahmanabādh. When we use the word "then," it is to be read in conjunction with the word [immediately] preceding it, as for example: ". . . to Baṭn Marr, *THEN* to ʿUsfān," ". . . to Ghazzah, *THEN* Rafaḥ." And when we write "or" we advert back to the word before the last, as when we say "from al-Ramlah to Īliyah *OR* to ʿAsqalān," "from Shīrāz to Juwaym *OR* to Ṣāhah." We have assumed a *marḥalah* (stage) of 6 or 7 *farsakhs.* If it happens [in a particular instance] to exceed this distance, we place two dots over the *-hā* [the last letter of the word *marḥalah*]; if it exceeds 10 *farsakhs,* we place two dots below the *lām* [the penultimate letter of the word *marḥalah*]; if it is fewer than 6 *farsakhs* we place one dot above the *-hā.* [The punctuation and stylistic emphases incorporated in this passage are not reproduced in de Goeje's transcription of the text.]

187. Yaʿqūbī, *al-Buldān,* 290.

188. Ibn Ḥawqal, *al-Masālik wa-l-Mamālik,* 304; Minorsky, *Ḥudūd,* 110.

189. Maqdisī, *Aḥsan,* 140. The Persian myth of the scorpions of Naṣībīn (the Nisibis of classical authors) is recounted in Yāqūt, *Muʿjam,* 4:787.

190. Maqdisī, *Aḥsan,* 76.

191. This mosque was so called from its location on a *khayf,* a mountain shoulder immediately above the edge of a valley, in this instance the Wādī Makkah.

192. According to Muslim tradition this mosque was founded by Lubābah, daughter of ʿAlī ibn ʿAbd Allāh ibn al-ʿAbbās, on a rock at the foot of the hill of Thabīr, where Ibrāhīm is said to have sacrificed a ram in place of his son: hence *al-Kabsh.* See Azraqī (died ca. 858), *Akhbār Makkah,* 401.

193. This is the ʿAqabah where Muḥammad had concluded an agreement with the Anṣār of al-Madīnah prior to the *Hijrah* (cf. chapter 1, p. 25).

194. Abū al-Ḥasan ʿUbaydullāh ibn al-Ḥasan al-Karkhī (d. 951) was a celebrated doctor of the Ḥanafite school. The Karkh to which his *nisbah* refers was a quarter of Sāmarrā, not the better known sector of Baghdād.

195. Abū Ḥanīfah al-Nuʿmān ibn Thābit (d. 767), founder of the earliest, largest, and most tolerant school of Islamic law. Cf. p. 65 above.

196. Baghūlan was a village in the district of Naysābūr. Abū Ḥāmid ibn Ibrāhīm ibn Muḥammad (d. 993) was the leading Ḥanafite doctor of his age. He taught jurisprudence at Naysābūr for more than sixty years.

197. Qurʾān 22 *(al-Ḥajj):*33.

198. Qurʾān 5 *(al-Māʾidah):*95.

199. Maqdisī, *Aḥsan,* 76. It is evident that, in reporting the verdicts of these distinguished jurists, al-Maqdisī adopts the definition of *miṣr* that he elsewhere claims was common among the mass of the population, namely "a large and important settlement," while ignoring the definition that he had previously attributed to jurisconsults in general (p. 47: cf. note 55 to chapter 2 of the present work). In citing the opinions of others he would naturally not be expected to impose his own conception of the *miṣr* (discussed on p. 77 above). The rendering of *miṣr* as "metropolis" would have been incompatible with the context of this passage.

200. Maqdisī, *Aḥsan,* 115. Al-Bandanījayn in Yāqūt, *Muʿjam,* 1:745, who records the original Persian name of the settlement as Wandanīgān, although Mustawfī (*Nuzhat al-Qulūb,* 137; all subsequent references are to the Le Strange translation unless otherwise indicated) cites a form Bandanīgān. Cf. also Ibn Khurradādhbih, *Kitāb al-Masālik wa-l-Mamālik,* 6; Iṣṭakhrī, *Masālik al-Mamālik,* 94; Ibn Ḥawqal, *al-Masālik wa-l-Mamālik,* 176; and Abū Dulaf, *Risālah,* Arabic text, 13; English translation, 44. A somewhat similar problem of settlement classification in contemporary times was described by the authors of the volume on *Western Arabia and the Red Sea* ([British] Naval Intelligence Division, Oxford, 1946), p. 541 in the following words: "Rābigh 'town' is a group of hamlets in a scattered but extensive oasis of palm-groves . . . to the east of the Wādī Rābigh. It is the headquarters of the Zobeid [Zubayd] section of the Ḥarb tribe, and contains a shrine which attracts Moslem pilgrims."

201. Iṣṭakhrī, *al-Masālik wa-l-Mamālik,* 202, 228–231; Ibn Ḥawqal, *al-Masālik wa-l-Mamālik,* 288–91; Maqdisī, *Aḥsan,* 390; and Abū Dulaf, *Risālah,* Arabic text, 19; English translation, 51.

202. Bakrī, *al-Masālik wa-l-Mamālik,* 4; Maqdisī, *Aḥsan,* 245; Qudāmah, *al-Kharāj,* Arabic text, 221, French translation, 168; and Ibn Khurradādhbih, *al-Masālik wa-l-Mamālik,* 84.

203. Maqdisī, *Aḥsan,* 462.

204. Bakrī, *al-Masālik wa-l-Mamālik,* 75.

205. Ibn Ḥawqal, *al-Masālik wa-l-Mamālik,* 301.

206. Maqdisī, *Aḥsan,* 321. Cf. note 109 to chapter 14.

207. Iṣṭakhrī, *al-Masālik wa-l-Mamālik,* 266; Ibn Ḥawqal, *al-Masālik wa-l-Mamālik,* 318; and Maqdisī, *Aḥsan,* 330.

208. Bakrī, *al-Masālik wa-l-Mamālik,* 7.

209. Ibid., 114.

210. Ibid., 141.

211. Iṣṭakhrī, *al-Masālik wa-l-Mamālik,* 104.

212. Bakrī, *al-Masālik wa-l-Mamālik,* 142.

213. Ibn Ḥawqal, *al-Masālik wa-l-Mamālik,* 322.

214. Maqdisī, *Aḥsan,* 317–18.

215. Iṣṭakhrī, *al-Masālik wa-l-Mamālik,* 244; Ibn Ḥawqal, *al-Masālik wa-l-Mamālik,* 301; and Maqdisī, *Aḥsan,* 297.

216. Ibn Ḥawqal's categorization (*al-Masālik wa-l-Mamālik,* 363) of the villages near Iṣbahān (Iṣfahān) as being "as numerous as the days of the year" is obviously to be understood in the general sense of "thick on the ground." In the thirteenth century Yāqūt recorded dependent villages for the Islamic cultural realm rather more consistently than the tenth-century topographers had done, and Mustawfī frequently provided such information in his fourteenth-century description of al-ʿIrāq and Persia under the Mongols.

217. Bakrī, *al-Masālik wa-l-Mamālik,* 6.

218. Ibid., 4.

219. Maqdisī, *Aḥsan,* 67–95.

220. On another page (ibid., 84), al-Maqdisī writes that Zabīd was "on the whole more thriving and busier and possessed of greater natural resources than Makkah," but it is clear from other remarks that he ranked Zabīd below Makkah (Mecca) in general importance, and almost certainly in size and population.

221. Unfortunately, the location of Jabalah and Mahāyiʿ, the latter "situated on the edge of the valleys known by the name of Sāyah," cannot be identified.

222. Other tenth-century authors do little either to confirm or elaborate the skeletal urban hierarchy that can be elicited from al-Maqdisī's account. The *Ḥudūd* (145–51), drawing eclectically on earlier topographies and travel books, furnishes only brief descriptions of Arabian cities and their best-known products, with no attention to relative size. Makkah, for instance, is (following Ibn Khurradādhbih) "a large town, prosperous *(ābādhān),* populous." Ṣanʿāʾ is also "a flourishing and prosperous town." Only for Zabīd does the formula vary: it was the second-largest town in al-Yaman after Ṣanʿāʾ. Ibn Rustah and al-Iṣṭakhrī add nothing of significance about the relative sizes of Arabian cities, nor does al-Ḥamdānī. Although this last author devoted a whole book to South Arabia, the surviving sections deal only with genealogies and antiquities (cf. note 115 above). Ibn Ḥawqal (*al-Masālik wa-l-Mamālik,* 30) confirms that al-Madīnah was less than half the extent of Makkah, but

he notes that it was larger than otherwise unknown Khiḍrimah (31). He adds that Juddah was larger than Jār, the port of al-Madīnah (31); Juḥfah was roughly the same size as Fayd (33); and al-Ṭā'if was about equal to Qurḥ (32). As Qurḥ was the second-largest city of the Ḥijāz and al-Ṭā'if was rated as small, it is to be inferred that in the tenth century Ḥijāzī urbanism was still only poorly developed.

223. Iṣṭakhrī, *al-Masālik wa-l-Mamālik,* 325–47; Ibn Ḥawqal, *al-Masālik wa-l-Mamālik,* 379–405; Maqdisī, *Aḥsan,* 325–47; and Minorsky, *Ḥudūd,* 112–19, 351–58.

224. Pers. Chāch. The city was often also known by the Tūrānian name of Binkath (e.g., Maqdisī; Bīkath in *Hudud al-ʿĀlam* [and, incidentally, in Yāqūt two and a half centuries later] through an error in pointing). The modern name Tashkent (Tāshkand) is most probably derived from *Chāch* + Turk. *kand* = village; *chāch* > *tash* through a dissimulation on the pattern of *čaθr-* > Middle Pers. *tas-; Shūshtar* > Ar. *Tustar.* See Minorsky, *Ḥudūd,* 357.

225. Pers. = Fanākant. After being razed by Chinggis Khan in the thirteenth century, the city was rebuilt in 1415 by order of *Shāh* Rukh, son of Tīmūr, and received the honorific of Shāhrukhīyah.

226. Sometimes written Tūkath owing to an error in pointing.

227. *Ispēchāb. Present-day Sayrām: cf. Minorsky, *Ḥudūd,* 357–58, citing Maḥmud al-Kāshgharī, *Dīwān Lughāt al-Turk,* ed. Kilisli Muʿallim Rifʿat Bey (Istanbul, A.H. 1333–35/A.D. 1917), 1:78.

228. Probably for Panjikath; also written Banjakath and Bunūjkath by medieval authorities, and erroneously as Navīnjkath in *Ḥudūd,* 115. The city was also known, after the province of which it was the capital, as Madīnat Ushrūsanah. Its site is presently evidenced by the ruins at Shahrastān, some sixteen miles southwest of Ura-tepeh: Barthold, *Turkestan down to the Mongol Invasion,* 166.

229. Chimkant, Chimīkant in Sharaf al-Dīn ʿAlī Yazdī, *Ẓafar-Nāmah* (Calcutta, A.H. 828/A.D. 1425), 1:166, 2:633, 636. Published in Calcutta, 1887–88 by Maulawi Muhammad Ilahdad and translated into French by Pétis de la Croix under the title *Histoire de Timur-Bec,* but here quoted from Le Strange, *The Lands of the Eastern Caliphate,* 484. *Jamūkat* is the orthography used by al-Maqdisī (*Aḥsan,* 263, 272, 275).

230. Also Fārāb. To Arab topographers the suburb of the city was known as Kadar. In the *Ḥudūd* Pārāb is described as "a pleasant district of which the chief place is called Kadir" (118). In later centuries the city was known as Utrār or Uṭrār. This Bārāb on the Sayḥūn is not to be confused with the Bārāb (also Fāryāb) in Jūzjān.

231. Also Arsubānīkath.

232. Apparently the same place as that known to ʿAlī of Yazd as Yassī (*Ẓafar-Namah,* 1:466, 557; 2:9, 636, 642).

233. Also Ṣabrān. Ṣahrān in *Ḥudūd,* 119.

234. Also Khāsh, Khās, and Khāṣ.

235. Maqdisī, *Aḥsan,* 262, 273.

Chapter Four

Author's note: al-Maqdisī, who has furnished the framework for our discussion of urban systems, followed the practice of the Balkhī school of geographers in according Arabia the place of honor at the head of his exposition. I have found it more convenient, however, to begin with the metropolitan province of the ʿAbbāsid Empire, although its power had been greatly reduced by the tenth century.

1. The earlier Arab geographers tended to delimit the northern edge of the province as coinciding with a line running from present-day Ramadī to Takrīt: cf. Le Strange, *The Lands of the Eastern Caliphate,* 24–25. The usage adopted here does not conflict with a recent warning by Moshe Gil and Shaul Shaked that *sawād* "did not mean 'lower Iraq' but rather 'province' and was used in a non-specifying manner": review of *Iraq after the Muslim Conquest,* by M. J. Morony, *Journal of the American Oriental Society* 106 (1986): 820. A list of works useful for reconstructing the urban hierarchy in early Islamic ʿIrāq and Aqūr is incorporated in a bibliography of modern Arabic writings relating to the historical geography of Mesopotamia: G. ʿAwaḍ, "Mā ṭubiʿah ʿan buldān al-ʿIrāq bi al-lughat al-ʿArabīyah," *Sumer* 10 (1954): 40–72.

2. The formation of the Great Swamps *(al-Baṭā'iḥ;* sing. *al-Baṭīḥah)* late in Sāsānian times is described by Balādhurī (*Futūḥ al-Buldān,* 292).

3. Diminutive of Dijlah = Tigris. The name Dujayl had originally denoted a channel running from the Euphrates to the Tigris some distance to the north of the Nahr ʿĪsā. When its western sectors had become choked with silt by the beginning of the tenth century, the name was transferred to the new channel referred to here, which in fact led into the easternmost sector of the old Dujayl.

4. The canal network of al-Sawād was described by Iṣṭakhrī, *al-Masālik wa-l-Mamālik,* 84–85; Ibn Ḥawqal, *al-Masālik wa-l-Mamālik,* 165–66; and Maqdisī, *Aḥsan,* 124; and has been explicated in modern times by Guy Le Strange, "Description of Mesopotamia and Baghdad," 1–76, 255–315; and "On the mediaeval castle and sanctuary of Abrīḳ, the modern Arabkir; with some further notes on Mesopotamia as described by Ibn Serapion," idem, 739–49. See also a summary statement in the same author's *The Lands of the Eastern Caliphate,* 25–30, and generally in chaps. 2–5; and M. Streck, *Die alte Landschaft Babylonien.*

5. ʿAbdasī (< Pers. Afdāsahī) in Yāqūt, *Muʿjam,* 4:468, and some other authors.

6. Often designated specifically as Sīb of the Banū-Kūmā. Although only a small town, it enjoyed some renown in Islamic annals as the site of the battle where in 862 the troops of the caliph al-Muʿtamid had routed the forces of Yaʿqūb the Ṣaffārid.

7. Al-Maqdisī (*Aḥsan,* 123) notes that in his time al-Anbār was greatly diminished from the days when al-Saffāḥ, the first ʿAbbāsid caliph (749–54), had resided there. See also note 22 below.

8. Ibid., 122. ʿAbertā had been a large city in Sāsānian times and continued to be so throughout the Early Islamic and Sāmarrān periods. During the tenth century, however, agricultural productivity generally deteriorated in the surrounding countryside, occasioned partly by breaching of the banks of the what is today called Nahrawān Canal upstream of the city.

9. Also called Jisr Nahrawān (= Nahrawān Pontoon). The ancient city was on the site of present-day Sifwah.

10. Al-Jāmiʿān, "The Two Mosques." In the tenth century the

city was situated mainly on the east bank of the Euphrates a few miles below the ruins of Babylon. In about the seventh decade of that century the city and its surrounding territory came under the control of the Banū-Mazyad, who eventually founded al-Ḥillah, "The Encampment," on the opposite bank. This latter city, which controlled the bridge of boats where the pilgrim road from Baghdād to al-Kūfah crossed the Euphrates, soon eclipsed the older settlement of al-Jāmiʿan. See George Makdisī, "Notes on Ḥilla and the Mazyadids in mediaeval Islam," *Journal of the American Oriental Society* 74 (1954): 249–62 and ʿAbd al-Jabbār Nājī, *al-Imārah al-Mazyadīyah, Dirāsah fī Waḍʿihā al-Siyāsī wa-l-Iqtiṣādī wa-l-Ijtimāʿī 387–558 h.* (al-Baṣrah, n.d. [1971?]), 59 et seq.

11. Maqdisī, *Aḥsan,* 122. Nevertheless, Maqdisī ranked Sāmarrā as a *qaṣabah* in his urban hierarchy.

12. Preserved in Yāqūt, *Muʿjam,* 3:176; an abbreviated version is given in Abū al-Fidāʾ, *Mukhtaṣar Taʾrīkh al-Bashar,* 2:75.

13. In pre-Sāmarrān times called Karkh Fayrūz, and said also to have been known as Karkh Bājaddā: Yāqūt, *Muʿjam,* 4:256.

14. Quoted by al-Thaʿālibī (d. 1038), *al-Laṭāʾif al-Maʿārif,* ed. Ibrāhīm al-Abyārī and Ḥasan Kāmil al-Ṣayrafī (al-Qahīrah, A.H. 1380/A.D. 1960), 167. English translation and commentary by C. E. Bosworth under the title *The Book of Curious and Entertaining Information. The Laṭāʾif al-Maʿārif of Thaʿālibī* (Edinburgh, 1968), 123. All subsequent references are to the al-Abyārī/al-Ṣayrafī edition and the Bosworth translation unless otherwise indicated.

15. Quoted by Thaʿālibī, *al-Laṭāʾif al-Maʿārif,* 167; Bosworth's translation, 123. It should be remembered that from 657 to 661 al-Kūfah had been the capital of that part of the Islamic world recognizing ʿAlī ibn Abī-Ṭālib as caliph—although the evidence is all against ʿAlī having intended to make it his permanent capital: see Hinds, "Kûfan political alignments," 361.

16. Iṣṭakhrī, *al-Masālik wa-l-Mamālik,* 82.

17. Maqdisī, *Aḥsan,* 116–17.

18. Cf. note 53 to chapter 2.

19. Maqdisī, *Aḥsan,* 117–18: "This city is, in my view, superior to Baghdād by reason of the amplitude of its resources and the great number of godly people living there. I was once present in a company comprising most of the doctors of Baghdād and its learned men when the conversation turned to Baghdād and al-Baṣrah. The final consensus was that, if the inhabited parts of Baghdād were [notionally] compacted and the ruined sectors disregarded, the city would be no larger than al-Baṣrah."

20. *The Encyclopaedia of Islam,* 2d ed., 5:350.

21. Wāsiṭ (= "The Middle [City]") was probably so called because it was roughly equidistant from the *amṣār* al-Kūfah and al-Baṣrah, although al-Maqdisī (*Aḥsan,* 135) went further and declared that it owed its name to its being fifty *farsakh*s distant from each of Baghdād, al-Kūfah, al-Baṣrah, Hulwān, and al-Ahwāz. Yaʿqūbī (*al-Buldān,* 322) stated that a city had existed in the vicinity of Wāsiṭ on the east bank of the Tigris in pre-Islamic times and that the population was still predominantly Persian in the ninth century. In 703 al-Ḥajjāj had disbanded the ʿIrāqī *muqātilah* and built a new settlement for the Syrian garrison on the west bank, surrounding a palace (al-Qubbat al-Khaḍrāʾ) and congregational mosque. As a result, he created a dual city, the two halves of which were connected by a pontoon bridge *(jisr).* Wāsiṭ was one of the relatively few cities with two congregational mosques, in this case one for each half of the city. Cf. al-Jāmiʿān (note 10 above), where a similar situation had also resulted in the building of two congregational mosques.

Baḥshal al-Wāsiṭī's *Taʾrīkh Wāsiṭ,* surviving only in an incomplete Cairene manuscript, is the oldest extant history designed as an aid for *ḥadīth* scholars. It has relatively little to say about the material fabric of the city or its environs. It has been published by Kurkīs ʿAwwād (Baghdād, A.H. 1387). For reconstructions of the city in early Islamic times, see ʿAbd al-Qādir Sulaymān al-Maʿāḍīdī, *Wāsiṭ fī al-ʿAṣr al-Umawī* (Baghdād, A.H. 1396) and *Wāsiṭ fī al-ʿAṣr al-ʿAbbāsī* (Baghdād, A.H. 1403).

22. Al-Anbār = "The Granaries," so called, it is said, because the Persian kings had stored rations *(al-rizq)* for their troops in the city. According to Yāqūt (*Muʿjam,* 1:367), its Persian name was Fīrūz Sābūr (cf. Gk. Perisabor) in honor of its founder, the Sāsānian monarch King Shāpūr I (A.D. 241–72). Cf. al-Dīnawarī, *Kitāb al-Akhbār al-Ṭiwāl,* ed. V. Guirgass (Leiden, 1888), 131, 372.

23. Named after Ītākh the Turk, a captain of the guard under the caliph al-Muʿtaṣim. The city stood at the point where the Qanṭarah Kisrawīyah ("Bridge of the Khusraws") crossed the Nahrawān Canal.

24. Known to Ibn al-Athīr (1160–1234) as al-Baṭīḥah: *al-Kāmil,* ed. C. J. Tornberg, 13 vols. (Leyden, 1867–74), 9:22, 35.

25. Ibn al-Athīr (loc. cit.) also testified to the good government of the independent rulers of al-Ṣalīq.

26. Maqdisī, *Aḥsan,* 119.

27. On strict central-place principles, it would be expected that the marketing and administrative hierarchies, by no means inevitably spatially coincident, would have articulated differently. Whereas the city administrative areas must, by definition, have been discrete at all levels, with each lower-level unit appertaining to only a single unit at the next higher level, the marketing systems would have been discrete only at the lowest level, with each lower-order area being shared typically between two or three systems at the level above. This principle implies that, unlike the administrative systems, the marketing systems would have been integrated into interlocking networks; or that, in central-place jargon, although a degree of marketing efficiency was maintained, each lower-order central place would have been located wholly within the city trade area of the next-largest center. But the evidence available for al-ʿIrāq is insufficient to justify the assumption of a central-place hierarchy in the strict sense, and an urban system of the type postulated by Kolb and Brunner remains a possibility.

28. The fullest account of the post roads traversing al-ʿIrāq relates to the ninth century and is to be found scattered through various sections of al-Yaʿqūbī's *Kitāb al-Buldān,* chiefly in the second half of that work; but there are good reasons for believing that the road system was not significantly different in the tenth century.

There is also a good deal of relevant information in other roadbooks of the ninth century, notably those by Ibn Khurradādhbih, Qudāmah, and Ibn Rustah. In addition, the systematic topographers of the tenth century also furnish updated accounts: e.g., al-Iṣṭakhrī and Ibn Ḥawqal (incidentally) and al-Maqdisī (stage by stage; *Aḥsan,* 134).

29. Yaʿqūbī, *Kitāb al-Buldān,* 234. *Redistribution* is the mode of exchange that allocates rewards and facilities in accordance with the integrative requirements of society; *mobilization,* that which provides mechanisms for the acquisition, control, and disposal of resources in the pursuit of collective goals. Cf. Talcott Parsons and Neil J. Smelser, *Economy and Society. A study in the integration of economic and social theory* (London, 1956); summarized in Smelser, "A comparative view of exchange systems," *Economic Development and Cultural Change* 7 (1959): 173–82.

30. The Arab mile was probably something in excess of two thousand yards.

31. In Ibn Khurradādhbih *(al-Masālik wa-l-Mamālik)* and Qudāmah *(al-Kharāj)* the reading appears to be Dayr Bāzamā; in Ibn Rustah *(al-Aʿlaq),* Dayr Tīrmā.

32. Maqdisī, *Aḥsan,* 135.

33. Ḥulwān was celebrated both for its pomegranates, which were supposedly unequalled in the medieval world, and for the excellence of its figs (cf. p. 92). The city is said to have been founded by the Sāsānian Qubād, who reigned at the end of the fifth and beginning of the sixth century A.D.

34. According to Yāqūt (*Muʿjam,* 4:210), the term *quhandiz* (Pers. *kuhan* = old and *diz* = citadel) was applied to a fortress situated within the enceinte of a reasonably sized city, more particularly a city in Khurāsān or Transoxania.

35. Maqdisī, *Aḥsan,* 123.

36. Daskarat al-Malik is apparently to be identified with Dastagird, a palace city of Khusraw Parwīz that was razed by the Byzantine emperor Heraclius in A.D. 628. Ibn Rustah (*al-Aʿlāq,* 164) notes that at the end of the ninth century it still possessed a citadel that had been erected in Sāsānian times.

37. Al-Maqdisī (*Aḥsan,* 121) notes that pilgrims en route to Makkah (Mecca) would put up for the night in the eastern quarter of the city before continuing their journey across the bridge of boats spanning the canal.

38. Ibn Rustah (*al-Aʿlāq,* 164) reports that the ruins of the Sāsānian palace still existed in the ninth century A.D.

39. Qur'an 3 *(al-ʿImrān)*:96–97.

40. This was the Qādisīyah where, in 635, the Muslim armies had won their first major battle against the Persians, thus opening the way for the subjugation of al-ʿIrāq. It was often called al-Qādisīyah of Kūfah to distinguish it from the city of the same name on the Tigris below Sāmarrā. Cf. also Minorsky, *Ḥudūd,* 140.

41. Maqdisī, *Aḥsan,* 117. For the first half century of ʿAbbāsid rule, it was not unknown for pilgrims from all over the Eastern Empire to assemble at a predetermined time in Baghdād and make the crossing of the Arabian Desert in the train of a caliph, the whole ensemble appearing much like an army on the march. The last ʿAbbāsid caliph to undertake the pilgrimage to Makkah was Hārūn al-Rashīd (r. 786–809), after which the duty was delegated to an *amīr al-ḥajj.*

42. *Farj* (= an opening) *al-Hind* in Ṭabarī, *Taʾrīkh,* 1:2223. The city was also categorized as *Furḍat al-Baḥrayn wa-ʿUmān wa-l-Hind wa-l-Ṣīn* (the harbor [whence ships set sail] for Baḥrayn, ʿUmān, India, and China) by ʿUtbah ibn Ghazwān in his report of its conquest to the caliph ʿUmar in 635–36 or 637–38 (the date is contested): Balādhurī, *Futūḥ al-Buldān,* 341; Murgotten's translation, 53. The name al-Ubullah is the Arabic rendering of the Greek Ἀπόλογος.

43. The site of this city is now well inland as a result of progradation of the shore at an average rate of one and one-half miles per century.

44. Nothing is recorded about this port other than that it "was a benefice belonging to ʿUbayd ibn Qusayṭ, Commander of the Patrol in the time of al-Ḥajjāj. In it lived an ascetic named Sulaymān ibn Jābir, after whom it was named"; Balādhurī, *Futūḥ al-Buldān,* 364. Yāqūt (*Muʿjam,* 1:645) explains the forms Sulaymānān and ʿAbbādān as resulting from the Baṣrians' habit of converting personal into place-names by adding the termination *-an.* Hence Sulaymānān < Sulaymān and ʿAbbādān < an otherwise unknown ʿAbbād.

45. Yaʿqūbī, *al-Buldān,* 241, 244; Ibn Sarābiyūn, *ʿAjāʾib al-Aqālīm al-Sabʿah,* Le Strange's translation, 71; Ibn Ḥawqal, *al-Masālik wa-l-Mamālik,* 242 (for the need to transship commodities between the ʿĪsā and Ṣarāt Canals); and Yāqūt, *Muʿjam,* 4:432.

46. Yaʿqūbī, *al-Buldān,* 251. ʿAttābī cloth took its name from ʿAttābīyah, a particular sector of the city where it was manufactured. Although Baghdād was celebrated for its textiles, the early topographers largely ignored its *ṭirāz* factories, which must have been extensive. Ultimately the Buwayhid *amīr*s appropriated the *ṭirāz* for their own use, for which time Abū Naṣr Muḥammad ibn ʿAbd al-Jabbār al-ʿUtbī provided a certain amount of apparently reliable information about that institution: *al-Taʾrīkh al-Yamīnī* (al-Qāhirah, A.H. 1286/A.D. 1869). Al-ʿUtbī died in 1036 or 1039–40.

47. Minorsky, *Ḥudūd,* 138. "Crystals turned on a lathe" is Minorsky's rendering of *ābgīna-yi makhrūṭ,* "glazed ware," of *ālāt-hā-yi mad-hūn;* and "electuaries," of *maʿjūn.* ʿAttābī cloth was a silky fabric striped like the coat of a zebra (cf. R. B. Serjeant, *Islamic Textiles. Material for a History up to the Mongol Conquest* [Beirut, 1972], 28).

48. Maqdisī, *Aḥsan,* 128 and Ibn Rustah, *al-Aʿlāq,* 186.

49. Ibn Rustah, *al-Aʿlāq,* 186–87.

50. Maqdisī, *Aḥsan,* 130 note *p:* cf. also p. 128. On p. 113 the same author remarks nostalgically that Baṣrian dates are unforgettable.

51. Ibid., 130: after Ranking and Azoo, *Aḥsanu,* 208–10, modified. Ibn Ḥawqal (*al-Masālik wa-l-Mamālik,* 235) provides a shorter list of venerated sites in al-Baṣrah but includes in it the tomb of Muḥammad ibn Sīrīn, a celebrated traditionist who died in 728.

52. Cf. Qur'ān 21 *(al-Anbiyā')*:69.

53. Cf. Qur'ān 11 *(Hūd)*:40.

54. But see p. 57 above. Cf. Ibn Ḥawqal, *al-Masālik wa-l-Mamālik,* 240 and Minorsky, *Ḥudūd,* 140. As al-Maqdisī espoused the tradition that ʿAlī was buried in al-Kūfah, there was no cause for him to mention the Mashhad ʿAlī at Najaf, some two *farsakhs* outside the city, which a competing tradition still maintains is ʿAlī's burial place. When Ibn Ḥawqal visited the spot "close to the corner of the cathedral mosque" in Kūfah where some believed ʿAlī to have been secretly buried, he found it occupied by a fodder merchant's shop.

55. Cf. pp. 56–57 above.

56. Ṭalḥah ibn ʿUbaydallāh, one of the ten foremost Companions who, on the field of Uḥud, had saved the life of the Prophet. He was killed at the Battle of the Camel in 656, and buried some distance outside al-Baṣrah. Only subsequently was his corpse reinterred within the city, where his tomb became a popular visitation site.

57. Al-Zubayr ibn al-ʿAwwām, husband of the Prophet's aunt. One of the chief among the Companions, he was killed on the day of the Battle of the Camel in the Wādī al-Sibāʿ, outside al-Baṣrah, where he was buried.

58. ʿAbd Allāh ibn al-Ḥārith ibn ʿAbd al-ʿUzzā al-Saʿdī, the foster brother of Muḥammad.

59. One of the most eminent of the Tābiʿūn. He was born at al-Madīnah (Medina) in 642 and died at al-Baṣrah in 728. For his life see Ibn Khallikān (1211–82), *Wafayāt,* 1:228.

60. The domestic servant of Muḥammad while he was in al-Madīnah. On the death of the Prophet he moved to al-Baṣrah, where he became one of its most revered *imāms* in Tradition. He died allegedly at a very advanced age in 712, and was buried at a spot a *farsakh* and a half outside the city, which subsequently became known as Qaṣr Anas.

61. ʿImrān ibn al-Ḥusayn al-Khuzāʿī, one of the Companions, who embraced Islam in 628 and died at al-Baṣrah in 672.

62. A native of al-Kūfah, who migrated to al-Baṣrah in 772 and died there six years later.

63. One of the Tābiʿūn and a native of al-Baṣrah, who became one of the city's leading exponents of Tradition. He died in 741.

64. See Ibn Baṭṭūṭah, *Tuḥfat al-Nuẓẓār fī Gharā'ib al-Amṣār wa-ʿAjā'ib al-Asfār,* ed. C. Defrémery and B. R. Sanguinetti (third impression, Paris, 1879–93), 2:15; trans. H. A. R. Gibb under the title *The Travels of Ibn Baṭṭūṭa* A.D. *1325–1354,* vol. 2: Hakluyt Society, 2d ser., no. 117 (Cambridge, 1962): 279. Gibb, citing Abū Nuʿaym al-Iṣfahānī, *Ḥilyat al-Awliyā',* vol. 6 (al-Qāhirah, A.H. 1355), 226–38, notes that ʿUtbah ibn Abān, called al-Ghulām ("The Deacon") because of his assiduity in religious exercises, was killed in battle against the Greeks at Miṣṣīṣah.

65. Muḥammad ibn Wāsiʿ ibn Jābir al-Azdī, one of the Tabiʿūn who died according to most traditions in 739, but according to Ibn al-Athīr (*al-Kāmil,* 5:259) in 745.

66. A traditionist who died in 788.

67. Ayyūb ibn Abī-Tamīmah, who died of plague at al-Baṣrah in 749.

68. Abū Muḥammad Sahl ibn ʿAbd Allāh ibn Yūnus al-Tustarī, a celebrated saint and thaumaturge, who was born at Tustar in 816 and died at al-Baṣrah in 896.

69. A Baṣrian woman revered for the saintliness of her life. (Incidentally, in stating that her tomb was on the outskirts of Jerusalem, Ibn Khallikān [*Wafāyāt,* 1:515] was confusing her with Rābiʿah al-Badawīyah, another woman greatly revered for her holiness.)

70. Founder of the heretical sect of al-Sālimīyah, which is discussed by al-Maqdisī on p. 126 of his treatise.

71. Cf. note 63 of chapter 3.

72. A contemporary of al-Maqdisī and a scholar of high repute, whose house served as a salon for the learned of Baghdād.

73. A well-known disciple of Abū Ḥanīfah. He was born in Baghdād in 731 and died there in 798.

74. Aḥmad ibn Ḥanbal (d. 855), a student of al-Shāfiʿī and founder of the Ḥanbalite rite, which enjoins a rigorous adherence to the very letter of the *ḥadīth.* In Baghdād, Ibn Ḥanbal's fundamentalist respect for the Tradition was the main bulwark against Muʿtazilite innovation.

75. One of the preeminent saints of his age. He died in Baghdād in 815–16.

76. A saint who was born in Marw in 767 and died in Baghdād in 842.

77. Salmān al-Fārisī ("The Persian"), who, according to tradition, advised Muḥammad to defend Madīnah with a trench and was the first Persian to adopt Islam: see Louis Massignon, "Salmân Pâk et les prémices spirituelles de l'Islam iranien," *Publications de la Société des Etudes Iraniennes,* no. 7 (1934).

78. Al-Madā'in (= "The Cities") was the Arab name for five settlements that in the tenth century existed amid the ruins of the former twin capitals of Persia, Ctesiphon (Ar. = Ṭaysafūn) and Seleucia. Ctesiphon was a site of ancient occupation on the east bank of the Tigris, not improbably the Casiphia mentioned in Ezra 8:17. Seleucia, on the west bank, was also an ancient foundation, which had taken its name from Seleucus I Nicator (301–280 B.C.). In more recent times Anūshirwān the Just, conqueror of Seleucia on the Orontes, had transported the inhabitants of that city to his capital at Ctesiphon, where he had settled them in a new quarter on the east bank of the Tigris, opposite the old Seleucia. When the Arab armies conquered al-ʿIrāq, this suburb was known as al-Rūmīyah, "The Greek Settlement."

Although early Arab authors mentioned no less than seven separate settlements as comprising the city of al-Madā'in, only five appear to have been inhabited when al-Yaʿqūbī (*al-Buldān,* 321) was writing in the ninth century. These were al-Madīnah al-ʿAtīqah (= "The Old City" = Ctesiphon) on the east bank, furnished with an elegant congregational mosque dating from the time of the Muslim conquest; Asbānbur, one mile to the south; al-Rūmīyah nearby; and on the opposite bank of the Tigris, Bahurasīr (< Pers. Bih-Ardashīr), with Sābāṭ (Persian Balāsābād) one league downstream.

In the tenth century al-Maqdisī referred to al-Madā'in as "a flourishing city built of brick, with its mosque in the market-place" (*Aḥsan,* 122).

The ancient site is described by J. M. Fiey, "Topography of al-Mada'in," *Sumer* 23 (1967): 3–38 and by Sāliḥ Aḥmad al-ʿAlī, "Al-Madā'in fī al-Maṣādir al-ʿArabīyah," loc. cit., 47–65; there is still a good deal of relevance in older works by M. Streck, *Die Alte Landschaft Babylonien,* vol. 2 (Leiden, 1901), 246–79 and "Seleucia und Ktesiphon," *Der Alte Orient* 16 (1917). A compendious summary of available knowledge by Streck (revised by Michael G. Morony) is included in *The Encyclopaedia of Islam,* 2d ed., vol. 5 (1984), 945–46.

79. G. E. von Grünebaum, "The Sacred Character of Islamic Cities," in *Mélanges Ṭāhā Ḥusain: Offerts par ses Amis et ses Disciples à l'Occasion de son 70ième Anniversaire* (Le Caire, 1962), 25–37.

80. Ibid., 27.

81. Ibid., 27. This author's note *a* (p. 35) reads as follows:

> Avicenna (d. 1037), *Traités mystiques,* ed. A. F. von Mehren (Leiden, 1889–99), III, 46–47 (transl, pp. 26–27), argues from the oneness of the chain of being for the transmissibility of spiritual force. The souls of the saints visited effectively act on the devout. Avicenna [Ibn Sīnā] also seems to have realized that when gathered in large numbers at holy places the pilgrims will be more receptive to the influence emanating from their superiors in the creaturely order. The concept that the souls of the purified saints may have a direct effect on bodies not their own is set forth by Avicenna with a view to explaining their miracles; cf. his treatise *Fi Bayân al-Muʿjizât wa'l-Karâmât, Ms. Pertev Pasha 617,* ff. 268v–269v, ed. by G. N. Atiyeh, *Avicenna's Conception of Miracles,* Ph.D. Diss, Chicago, 1954 (typescript).

For the *ḥadīth* cited in the quotation, see p. 118 of chapter 6.

82. Al-Tadmurī (d. 1429). Ed. C. D. Matthews, "The Muṭir al-Gharām of Abū-l-Fidā' of Hebron," *Journal of the Palestine Oriental Society* 17 (1937): 108–37, 149–208; translation by Matthews under the title *Palestine—Mohammedan Holy Land* (New Haven, Conn., 1949), 43–137. Cf. also G. E. von Grünebaum, review of *Palestine,* in *Journal of Near Eastern Studies* 11 (1952): 230–32 and pp. 66–67 and 117–18 in the present text.

83. Qur'ān 4 *(al-Nisā'):*125.

84. Published by J. Sourdel-Thomine under the title *Guide des Lieux de Pèlerinage,* 2 vols. (Damascus, 1953, 1957).

85. Yāqūt, *Muʿjam,* 4:554–55.

86. Von Grünebaum, "The Sacred Character of Islamic Cities," 27, 31.

87. Cf. pp. 56–57 above. Although Shīʿite tradition ranked the congregational mosque at al-Kūfah as fourth in prestige after those of Makkah, al-Madīnah, and Jerusalem, the consensus of the Muslim community never accorded it a level of soteriological sanctity approaching that of these other cities. For details of the Shīʿite tradition see M. J. Kister, "'You shall only set out for three mosques,'" *Le Muséon* (1969): 188–91.

88. René Berthelot, *La Pensée de l'Asie et l'Astrobiologie* (Paris, 1949), passim. There are a number of comments relative to this theme in Charles Wendell, "Baghdād: *imago mundi,* and other foundation-lore," *International Journal of Middle East Studies* 2 (1971): 99–128.

89. Berthelot, *La Pensée de l'Asie,* chap. 2: "Les antécédents de l'astrobiologie et son role dans la formation de la science," especially pp. 54–55:

> Dans cette phase "bio-astrale," puis "bio-solaire," les hommes transportent aus objects célestes, au astres, et, tout d'abord, à la lune comme au soleil, la vie et dans quelque mesure la conscience qu'ils attribuent aux êtres qui les entourent sur la terre. Ils s'en tiennent à la périodicité, conçue sans précision rigoureuse et numérique, que l'observation courante révèle, surtout en pays plus ou moins tempéré, dans la vie des plantes et les mouvements du soleil: naissance, croissance, floraison, fructification, mort et renaissance des plantes annuelles, cultivées par eux; rhythme quotidien selon lequel le soleil chaque jour se lève, monte à l'horizon, se couche et par lequel la nuit succède au jour, puis de nouveau le jour à la nuit; rhythme annuel, enfin, suivant lequel les saisons se succèdent conformément à la position du soleil dans le ciel.

According to Berthelot, the bio-astral worldview differed from the astrobiological chiefly in that the numerical regularities deduced from the motions of heavenly bodies had not yet been adapted to the biological cycles of earth. Cf. p. 62:

> A cette époque apparaît l'astrobiologie proprement dite: les hommes (c'est-à-dire d'abord les observateurs et calculateurs professionels) transportent aux événements terrestres l'idée des relations numériques précises et invariables, des lois mathématiques, qu'ils ont établies pour les mouvements célestes (astrologie et calendrier de plus en plus perfectionné) tout en conservant aux êtres célestes le caractère vivant et animé que leur prêtait l'époque antérieure et en attribuant éventuellement ce caractère au Ciel dans son ensemble ou même à l'univers entier, Ciel et Terre à la fois.

90. Walter F. Otto, *The Homeric Gods: The Spiritual Significance of Greek Religion* (New York, 1954), 287. This is a translation by Moses Hadas of *Die Götter Griechenlands: Das Bild des Göttlichen in Spiegel des Griechischen Geistes,* 2 vols. (Frankfurt-am-Main, 1947).

91. Premodern modes of thought have been analyzed by, int. al., Ernst Cassirer, *Philosophie der Symbolischen Formen, II: Das Mythische Denken* (Berlin, 1925); Lucien Lévy-Bruhl, *L'Âme Primitive* (Paris, 1927) and *Le Surnaturel et la Nature dans la Mentalité Primitive* (Paris, 1931); Rudolf Otto, *Das Heilige,* new ed. (München, 1947); and Henri and H. A. Frankfort, John Wilson, and Thorkild Jacobsen, *The Intellectual Adventure of Ancient Man* (Chicago, 1946), reprinted under the title *Before Philosophy* (Harmondsworth, 1949).

The basic modes of cosmomagical symbolism have been systematized by Mircea Eliade in *Traité d'Histoire des Religions* (Paris, 1948), chap. 10, English translation under the title *Patterns in Comparative Religion* (New York, 1958); *Le Mythe de l'Éternel Retour,* chap. 1, English translation under the titles *The Myth of the Eternal Return* (New York, 1954) and *Cosmos and History* (New York, 1959); *Das Heilige und das Profane* (Hamburg, 1957), chap. 1, translated from the original French, and subsequently rendered into English under the title *The Sacred and the Profane* (New York, 1959); and "Centre du monde, temple, maison," in *Le Symbolisme Cosmique des Monuments Religieux,* Serie Orientale Roma XIV (Roma, 1957), 57–82.

For the expression of this symbolism specifically in urban design, see Eliade, *Comentarii la Legenda Meşterului Manole* (Bucharest, 1943); Werner Müller, *Die Heilige Stadt* (Stuttgart, 1961); and Wheatley, *City as Symbol,* inaugural lecture delivered at University College, London, 20 November 1967 (London, 1969) and *The Pivot of the Four Quarters. A Preliminary Enquiry into the Origins and Character of the Ancient Chinese City* (Edinburgh and Chicago, 1971), chap. 5. Cf. also Ernst Topitsche, *Vom Ursprung und Ende der Metaphysik: Eine Studie zur Weltanschauungskritik* (Wien, 1958) and Th. H. Gaster, "Myth and story," *Numen* 1 (1954): 184–212, especially p. 191, where the author, after referring to "earthly cities, temples or religious institutions [which] have their duplicates in some transcendental sphere, often identified with the heavens," observes that "the intrinsic *identity* of real with transcendental cities (or temples) tends to be conveyed in terms of an artificial *identification* of an earthly with a heavenly structure."

92. See W. H. Roscher, "Neue Omphalosstudien," *Abhandlungen der Königlich Sächsischen Gesellschaft der Wissenschaft, Phil.-Hist. Klasse,* vol. 31, pt. 1 (1915) and Wensinck, "The ideas of the Western Semites."

93. Cf. 1 Kings 8:29–30 and Dan. 6:10.

94. J. L. Austin, *How to Do Things with Words* (Oxford, 1962), passim.

95. Robert McC. Adams, *Land Behind Baghdad. A History of Settlement on the Diyala Plains* (Chicago and London, 1965). The fundamental principles of topographic archaeology, in the context of conditions on the Mesopotamian plain, were propounded by Thorkild Jacobsen during the course of a reconnaissance survey in the Diyālā region in the field season 1936–37: (1) since ancient sites necessarily lay close to the watercourses upon which they were dependent, the approximate courses of now-vanished streams and canals could be plotted from the positions of ruins adjoining them; and (2) of primary importance in the present discussion, the periods of occupation of the ancient sites—and thus also of the watercourses connecting them—could be determined from an examination of their surface remains. Cf. Adams, *Land Behind Baghdad,* appendix A.

96. Jacob Lassner, *The Topography of Baghdad,* 164–68.

97. Ibid., 166.

98. Ibid., 168.

99. For the concept of urban primacy see chapter 3. For the contention that, at the present time, primate distributions are characteristic of small territories recently urbanized and possessing relatively simple political and economic institutions, see Berry, "City size distributions and economic development," 573–88.

100. Maqdisī, *Aḥsan,* 36. It must be remembered, though, that al-Maqdisī had his personal reasons for denigrating the ʿAbbāsid capital: cf. chapter 3.

101. [The Ṣāḥib] Abū al-Qāsim ibn ʿAbbād, cited by Thaʿālibī, *al-Laṭāʾif al-Maʿārif,* 171; Boswell's translation, 125.

102. Sāmarrā (100 ha.?), ʿUkbarā (130 ha.), Buṣrā (5 ha.), Dayr al-ʿAqūl (20 ha.), al-Madāʾin (20 ha.?), Humānīyah (20 ha.), Jarjarāyā (20 ha.), Nahrawān (25 ha.), al-Daskarah (20 ha.?), Shahrābān (20 ha.?), Barāz al-Rūz (20 ha.?), Hārūnīyah (20 ha.), Baʿqūbah (30 ha.?), Bājisrā (10 ha.?), ʿAbertā (4 ha.), and Uskāf Banī-Junayd (20 ha.?).

103. Tall Mukherij (16 ha.), Tall Daymat al-ʿUdah (12 ha.), Tall Jubayl (10 ha.), Tall Mirhij (21 ha.), Tall Abū Khansīrah (16 ha.), Tall Maʿbūd (12 ha.), Mayyah al-Sharqī (19 ha.), and Tulūl al-Shuʿaylah (10 ha.).

104. Adams, *Land Behind Baghdad,* 104.

105. Ibid., ix.

106. For a general discussion of the urban system under the Sāsānian imperium, see Pigulevskaja, *Les Villes de l'État Iranien,* pt. 2, and a few pertinent comments in Heinz Gaube, *Iranian Cities* (New York, 1979), 21–30.

107. Ira M. Lapidus has provided substance for this conclusion in "Arab Settlement and Economic Development in Iraq and Iran," 177–207. There is a very full account of al-ʿIrāq under the Umayyads in Morony, *Iraq after the Muslim Conquest,* passim.

108. Balādhurī, *Futūḥ al-Buldān,* 333; Yāqūt, *Muʿjam al-Buldān,* 1:341; and Ibn Sarābiyūn, *ʿAjāʾib al-Aqālīm al-Sabʿah,* Le Strange translation, 52–53.

109. Ṭabarī, *Taʾrīkh,* 1:2482, 2:504.

110. Balādhurī, *Futūḥ al-Buldān,* 290.

111. Yaʿqūbī, *al-Buldān,* 322.

112. Ṭabarī, *Taʾrīkh,* 1:2473–74.

113. Ibid., 2:773.

114. Lapidus, "Arab Settlement and Economic Development of Iraq and Iran," 178.

115. Yāqūt, *Muʿjam,* 2:258.

116. For a discussion of possible factors entering into that decision, see Lassner, *The Shaping of ʿAbbāsid Rule,* 139–43.

117. Ibid., 143–51, sets forth Lassner's persuasive arguments in favor of this location.

118. Ṭabarī, *Taʾrīkh,* 3:20–21, 34, 37; ʿA. ʿA. Dūrī (ed.), *Akhbār al-Dawlah al-ʿAbbāsīyah* (Bayrūt, 1971), 374–75, 388. Although al-Ḥīrah had been displaced as a regional center of government after the Arab conquest of al-ʿIrāq, it enjoyed a moderate resurgence of influence late in the Umayyad period, when the provincial governor Yūsuf ibn ʿUmar al-Thaqafī reconstituted it as the seat of local rule and stationed contingents of the Syrian army there (summa-

rized by Lassner, *The Shaping of ʿAbbāsid Rule,* 147–150, on the basis of information provided in al-Ṭabarī's *Taʾrīkh* and al-Yaʿqūbī's *Taʾrīkh*). Subsequently two Umayyad governors of al-ʿIrāq established their official residences in the revivified city.

119. At any rate, this is the sequence elicited by Lassner (*The Shaping of ʿAbbāsid Rule,* 151–62) from a *mélange* of ambiguous and sometimes contradictory texts. See also the same author's article on "Ḳaṣr ibn Hubayra" in *The Encyclopaedia of Islam,* 2d ed., 4:728–29.

120. Gerlof van Vloten, *De Opkomst der Abbasiden in Chorasan* (Leiden, 1890) and *Recherches sur la Domination Arabe, le Chiitisme et les Croyances Messianiques sous le Khalifat des Omayades* (Amsterdam, 1894); Bernard Lewis, "Hās͟himiyya," *The Encyclopaedia of Islam,* 2d ed., 3:265.

121. See pp. 53–54 above.

122. See pp. 54–55 above. Gaston Wiet has made the interesting point that the founding of Sāmarrā had no appreciable effect on the prosperity of Baghdād, which had already established itself as a supraregional market: *Baghdad, Metropolis of the Abbasid Caliphate* (Norman, Okla., 1971), 41, citing Yaʿqūbī, *al-Buldān.*

123. Yaʿqūbī, *al-Buldān,* 266–67.

124. Cf. p. 37 above.

125. These agricultural developments in al-ʿIrāq have been summarized succinctly by Lapidus in "Arab Settlement and Economic Development of Iraq and Iran," 178–91, from which the preceding comments have been abstracted.

126. This is Lapidus's conclusion: ibid., 190. An official lawyer's interpretation of treasury responsibilities by Abū ʿAbd Allāh Muʿāwiyah ibn ʿUbayd Allāh (reported by Qudāmah, *al-Kharāj,* 99–100; Ben Shemesh translation, 62) runs as follows:

> all the expenses of digging, including [provision of] supporting stakes, the construction of culverts and bridges, the clearing of rivers, and the maintenance of post-stations and dams on the great rivers, are to be borne by the Treasury. [The author] based his interpretation on the circumstance that the banks of the great rivers are not in the possession of private individuals, who might [nevertheless] suffer if the banks were not repaired and who consequently would have to undertake the work. Therefore, the cost should be borne by the Treasury, which would suffer loss and damage if the matter were not rectified.

127. In this connection Lapidus points to a passage in al-Balādhurī's *Futūḥ al-Buldān* (143–44; Hitti's translation, 221):

> After the time of Sulaymān ibn ʿAbd al-Malik [governor of the province of Palestine], the costs of [maintaining] the wells and canal of al-Ramlah (a town in Palestine) were underwritten by the Banū-Umayyah; and when the Banū-al-ʿAbbās assumed the caliphate, they [also] paid the [necessary] expenses. The authorization for these expenses was issued yearly by each of the caliphs, but when al-Muʿtaṣim succeeded to that office, he promulgated a permanent decree concerning these expenses, thereby obviating the need for the caliph to issue an order on each occasion. Thereafter, such [maintenance] was treated as a current expense which the *ʿāmils* disbursed and accounted for.

128. Lapidus, "Arab Settlement and Economic Development of Iraq and Iran," 181.

129. Mean annual precipitation in the Sawād is about five and one-half inches, falling on an average of twenty-eight separate days in winter and spring. Summers are entirely without rainfall.

Chapter Five

1. For changing views as to the southern limits of this province, see note 2 to chapter 4. A more usual Arab term for this province was al-Jazīrah—"The Island" or "The Peninsula," that is, the lands encompassed by the upper courses of the Tigris and Euphrates Rivers. In ancient times these territories had constituted the heartland of the Assyrian Empire. The origin and significance of al-Maqdisī's name *Iqlīm* Aqūr is not known, but see Yāqūt, *Muʿjam al-Buldān,* 1:119, 340 and 2:72. Whereas the Rabīʿah and Bakr tribal groups were predominantly *qarawīyūn* or *rāʿīyah* (see chapter 1), the Muḍar were more purely nomadic, characteristics reflected in the types of terrain on which the groups settled.

2. The only full-scale published treatment of the Ḥamdānid dynasty with its twin amīrates based respectively in al-Mawṣil (Mosul) and Ḥalab (Aleppo) is Marius Canard's *Histoire de la Dynastie des H'amdanides de Jazîra et de Syrie,* Publications de la Faculté des Lettres d'Alger, 2d ser., 21 (Paris, 1953), although G. W. F. Freytag, "Geschichte der Dynastien der Hamdaniden in Mosul und Aleppo," *Zeitschrift der Deutschen Morgenländischen Gesellschaft* 10 (1856) and 11 (1857) can still be consulted with profit, but also with the caution appropriate to a work of that vintage. The substance of Canard's volume is summarized by the same author in *The Encyclopaedia of Islam,* 2d ed., 3:126–31, and a very brief history of the Mawṣil Amīrate is incorporated in ibid., 2:523–24. See also Ramzi Jibran Bihazi, "*The Ḥamdānid Dynasty of Mesopotamia and North Syria*" (Ph.D. diss., University of Michigan, 1981) and especially Karin Bartl and Stefan R. Hauser, eds., *Continuity and Change in Northern Mesopotamia from the Hellenistic to the Early Islamic Period,* Berliner Beiträge zum Vorderen Orient 17 (Berlin, 1996), passim.

3. Maqdisī, *Aḥsan,* 146. In the thirteenth century Yāqūt (*Muʿjam,* 1:446) noted that the stream flowing through Baʿashīqā powered numerous mills and irrigated olive, date, and orange groves. There was a substantial *qayṣarīyah,* excellent bathhouses, and, despite the fact that the population was still predominantly Christian, a fine congregational mosque with an elegant minaret.

4. Or Mār Juhaynah: Maqdisī, *Aḥsan,* 139.

5. Ibn Rustah, *al-Aʿlāq,* 106; Ibn Ḥawqal, *al-Masālik wa-l-Mamālik,* 219–20; Minorsky, *Ḥudūd,* 140; and Maqdisī, *Aḥsan,* 139–40.

6. Cf. Iṣṭakhrī, *al-Masālik wa-l-Mamālik,* 73; Ibn Ḥawqal, *al-Masālik wa-l-Mamālik,* 214; Maqdisī, *Aḥsan,* 140; and Ibn Rustah, *al-Aʿlāq,* 97, 106.

7. Rās al-ʿAyn = spring head. Numerous springs made the locality a veritable garden stretching, according to Ibn Ḥawqal (*al-Masālik wa-l-Mamālik,* 143), for twenty leagues beyond the city. Cf. also Maqdisī, *Aḥsan,* 140 and Minorsky, *Ḥudūd,* 141.

8. Syriac Mīpherqēṭ; Arm. Nphkert, subsequently Muphargin. As Martyropolis (transcribed by Yāqūt as Madūrṣālā: *Muʿjam,* 4: 702), the city had been the capital of Roman Armenia. Al-Maqdisī (*Aḥsan,* 141) described Mayyāfarīqīn (Silvan) as the latrine of the province on account of its filthy streets. Cf. also Minorsky, *Ḥudūd,* 143. There is a twelfth-century account of the founding and early Islamic history of Mayyāfarīqīn in Ibn al-Azraq al-Fāriqī, *Taʾrīkh Mayyāfāriqīn wa-Āmid,* known only from *MS Or. 5803* in the British Library, London (which I have not seen), although the Marwānid sections, 983–1085, have been edited by B. A. L. ʿAwaḍ (al-Qāhirah, A.H. 1379/A.D. 1959). Half a century after Ibn al-Azraq was writing, Yāqūt (*Muʿjam,* 4:703) gave a condensed account of the founding of the city.

9. Early Arab authors relied on folk etymology to explain the name Mawṣil, deriving it either from the city's alleged function of connecting *(waṣala)* Mesopotamia with Syria or from its location where a series of anastomotic river courses coalesced to form the main channel of the Tigris River. In fact the word was probably an Arabic rendering of Mespila, the name of an ancient Assyrian city. In Sāsānian times it, or another city close by, had been known as Būdh Ardashīr (cf. Yāqūt, *Muʿjam,* 4:682–84: *Bawardashīr*), although al-Maqdisī (*Aḥsan,* 138) claims it was originally called Khawlān. In the time of this latter author, the mounds marking the ruins of Nineveh, across the river from al-Mawṣil, were known as Tall al-Tawbah ("The Hill of Repentance"), allegedly the spot where the prophet Yūnus (Jonah) had attempted to convert the inhabitants of Nineveh to monotheism.

10. Balādhurī, *Futūḥ al-Buldān,* 331–32 and Ibn al-Faqīh, *al-Buldān,* 128–29.

11. Azdī, *Taʾrīkh al-Mawṣil,* 169–70. The early Islamic history of al-Mawṣil is summarized by Saʿīd al-Daywajī al-Dewuchī/al-Dīwuhjī, "Khiṭaṭ al-Mawṣil," *Sumer* 17, no. 1 (1951), 88–98 and explicated at greater length in the same author's *Taʾrīkh al-Mawṣil,* vol. 1 (Baghdād, A.H. 1402), which deals with the location and structure of prominent buildings, literary luminaries, handicrafts, agriculture, commerce, the army, social life, and sectarian matters from pre-Islamic times to the collapse of the Zangid dynasty in the thirteenth century. See also ʿAbd al-Mājūd Aḥmad al-Sulaymān, *al-Mawṣil fī al-ʿAhdayn al-Rāshidī wa-l-Umawī* (al-Mawṣil, A.H. 1405).

12. Lapidus, "Arab Settlement and Economic Development of Iraq and Iran," 180.

13. These conclusions were formulated by Forand on the basis of information contained in the *Taʾrīkh al-Mawṣil:* "The governors of Mosul," 88–105. The *Taʾrīkh* covers only the period 719–838 (i.e., from the last year of the caliphate of ʿUmar II through the sixth year of the caliphate of al-Muʿtaṣim), and the administrative status of the city under the later ʿAbbāsids is usually uncertain. Page 105 of Forand's article contains a map of al-Mawṣil's administrative district under the governorship of al-Ḥurr ibn Yūsuf (724/25–731/32). There is also a good deal of relevant information in L. Dillemann, *Haute Mésopotamie Orientale et Pays Adjacents* (Paris, 1962).

14. Ibn Ḥawqal, *al-Masālik wa-l-Mamālik,* 143–45.

15. Maqdisī, *Aḥsan,* 138. See also Yaʿqūbī, *al-Buldān,* 237, 263, 265; Ibn Rustah, *al-Aʿlāq,* 106; and Minorsky, *Ḥudūd,* 140.

16. Maqdisī, *Aḥsan,* 140. In later times the city became known, as at the present time, by the name of the district of which it was the *qaṣabah,* Diyār Bakr. The settlements and countryside along the upper Tigris River are discussed at some length in J. Markwart, *Süd-armenien und die Tigrisquellen Nach Griechischen und Arabischen Geographen* (Wien, 1930).

17. Ibn Ḥawqal, *al-Masālik wa-l-Mamālik,* 153. Al-Raqqah occupied a site close to that of the ancient Hellenistic city of Nikephorion, which had been founded by Seleucus I Nikator (301–281 B.C.) but which subsequently became known as Callinicum after a Sophist named Callinicus who died there. In Byzantine times it was redesignated by the style Leontopolis. The Arabic term *al-Raqqah* is merely a descriptive appellation denoting a riverine floodplain.

18. Maqdisī, *Aḥsan,* 141. For the founding of al-Rāfiqah see Balādhurī, *Futūḥ al-Buldān,* 179; Hamadhānī, Ibn al-Faqīh, *al-Buldān,* 132; and Yāqūt, *Muʿjam,* 4:208. Cf. Minorsky, *Ḥudūd,* 141: "Two large and flourishing towns joined to one another." See also J.-Chr. Heusch and M. Meinecke, *Die Residenz des Harun al-Raschid in Raqqa* (Damaskus, 1989). Cf. also p. 287 and note 449 of chapter 17.

19. At any rate, this is the version of events preserved by Mustawfī (*Nuzhat al-Qulūb,* 165), but other authorities ascribe the founding of ʿImādīyah to ʿImād al-Dīn, founder of the Zangid line in northern Mesopotamia and Syria. In any case, there is no doubt that this latter ʿImād carried out extensive restorations in the city even if he did not found it.

20. Maqdisī, *Aḥsan,* 142.

21. Le Strange, *The Lands of the Eastern Caliphate,* 106. Once having established his court at Ruṣāfah, Hishām very seldom left the city during the remainder of his reign: Francesco Gabrieli, *Il Califfato di Hisham. Studi di Storia Omayyade* (Alexandria, 1935), 134.

22. Al-Ḥadīthah, "The New City," had been similarly named in Persian times: Nawkird. Cf. Ibn Rustah, *al-ʿAlāq,* 106; Ibn Ḥawqal, *al-Masālik wa-l-Mamālik,* 219; Maqdisī, *Aḥsan,* 139; and Minorsky, *Ḥudūd,* 141.

23. Ibn Ḥawqal, *al-Masālik wa-l-Mamālik,* 224; Maqdisī, *Aḥsan,* 139; and Yāqūt, *Muʿjam,* 2:79. The site has been identified with that of the Roman (and earlier) fortress of Bāzabdā.

24. Maqdisī, *Aḥsan,* 136.

25. An apposite example is afforded by Marj Juhaynah (= "Juhaynah Meadow"), on the Tigris River one stage south of al-Mawṣil, where cattle, as well as sheep and goats, were raised (Ibn Ḥawqal, *al-Masālik wa-l-Mamālik,* 217).

26. Maqdisī, *Aḥsan,* 138.

27. Ibn Ḥawqal, *al-Masālik wa-l-Mamālik,* 220, 227; Maqdisī, *Aḥsan,* 145.

28. Maqdisī, *Aḥsan,* 140.

29. Cotton was listed among the more important products of Ḥarrān, Arābān, and Mākisīn (also transcribed as Maykasān) and was attributed more generally to the valleys named. Mustawfī (*Nuzhat al-Qulūb,* Le Strange's translation, 102–105) listed Irbīl, Bāṣabdah, Arzān, Ra'ṣ al-ʿAyn, Barṭallā, and Mardīn specifically as centers of cotton-growing districts.

30. Ibn Ḥawqal, *al-Masālik wa-l-Mamālik,* 225.

31. Maqdisī, *Aḥsan,* 145 and Ibn Ḥawqal, *al-Masālik wa-l-Mamālik,* 181. The *manah* was a weight of approximately two pounds.

32. Ibn Ḥawqal, *al-Masālik wa-l-Mamālik,* 217.

33. Ibid., 217. Al-Maqdisī (*Aḥsan,* 146–47) notes the presence of a plant in the neighborhood of Bāʿashīqā (a small town some three or four *farsakh*s north of al-Mawṣil) blessed with the property of curing both scrofula and hemorrhoids "in those who tear it up by the roots."

34. Maqdisī, *Aḥsan,* 145.

35. Ibn Ḥawqal, *al-Masālik wa-l-Mamālik,* 214: the *Ḥudūd,* 393 renders *jawāhir al-zajāj* by *sang-i ābgīna.* Yāqūt (*Muʿjam al-Buldān,* 2:188) remarks on an iron mine in the vicinity of Ḥānī, a town on a minor tributary of the Tigris north of Āmid (Diyarbakir) but no earlier topographer had referred to it. Cf. also Mustawfī (*Nuzhat al-Qulūb,* 165), who mentions Ḥānī but not the mine.

36. These post routes are described by Ibn Khurradādhbih, *al-Masālik wa-l-Mamālik,* 93; Qudāmah, *al-Kharāj,* 214; Maqdisī, *Aḥsan,* 135, 148, 149; and in the fourteenth century by Mustawfī, *Nuzhat al-Qulūb,* 195. The precise locations of the post stations on the caravan road between al-Mawṣil and Naṣībīn, which appear ambiguous in the topographical accounts, have been clarified by J. M. Fiey, "The Iraqi section of the Abbassid road Mosul—Nisibin," *Iraq* 26 (1964): 107–17.

37. Ibn Ḥawqal, *al-Masālik wa-l-Mamālik,* 215. Al-Maqdisī (*Aḥsan,* 138) confirms this claim when he observes that "all the caravans of al-Riḥāb converge on the city" (al-Riḥāb is the term by which al-Maqdisī denotes the upland province encompassing Adharbāyjan [Azerbaijan], Armīniyah, and Arran).

38. Ibn Ḥawqal, *al-Masālik wa-l-Mamālik,* 225.

39. Iṣṭakhrī, *al-Masālik wa-l-Mamālik,* 73; Ibn Ḥawqal, *al-Masālik wa-l-Mamālik,* 221. Whereas in the ninth century Barqaʿīd had supported about two hundred shops, by the thirteenth century it had sunk to the level of a village that caravans went out of their way to avoid.

40. Ibn Ḥawqal, *al-Masālik wa-l-Mamālik,* 219. For *urūb* see Aly Mazahéri, *La Vie Quotidienne des Musulmans au Moyen Âge Xe au XIIIe siècle* (Paris, 1951), 277.

41. Probably Ḥānī, which Ibn al-Athīr mentions under the orthography Ḥānā.

42. Maqdisī, *Aḥsan,* 141.

43. Balādhurī, *Futūḥ al-Buldān,* 185; Yaʿqūbī, *al-Buldān,* 238, 362; Ibn Rustah, *al-Aʿlāq,* 107; Minorsky, *Ḥudūd,* 149 (where it is listed among Syrian towns and categorized as "the largest frontier post *[thaghr]* on this side of Mount Lukkām [= Amanus range]; and Maqdisī, *Aḥsan,* 139. For extended remarks on the frontier strongholds abutting the Byzantine territories, see chapter 6, p. 117. Malaṭiyah < Gk. Melitene.

44. Yāqūt, *Muʿjam,* 4:26. Malaṭiyah (Malatya) was described as a substantial urban center by al-Iṣṭakhrī (*al-Masālik wa-l-Mamālik,* 62) in the tenth century.

45. Present-day Harput.

46. Called Perrhe by the Byzantines; presently Adiamān. The city was named after Manṣūr of the Qays tribe, who was its commander under the Umayyad caliph Marwān II. It was refortified by Hārūn al-Rashīd during the caliphate of his father, al-Mahdī (775–85). Ibn Ḥawqal (*al-Masālik wa-l-Mamālik,* 120) notes that the city suffered greatly from the ravages of border skirmishes, and changed hands frequently.

47. Ḥiṣn Maslamah, nine leagues south of Ḥarrān, was named after Maslamah, a son of the Umayyad caliph ʿAbd al-Malik (685–705). It is one of the fortress cities for which a certain amount of information is available. Standing about one and one-half miles from the Balīkh River, the fortress occupied one-third of an acre (one *jarīb*), and its walls were fifty ells high. Water was brought from the river by a canal and stored in a cistern two hundred ells square and twenty deep. The canal also served to irrigate fields and gardens (Yāqūt, *Muʿjam,* 1:453–54, 734).

48. Gk. Taranta; present-day Darande, situated on the Qubāqib River three marches above Malatya. As early as 702 a Muslim garrison was stationed there, but the post was abandoned in 719. In the ninth century the city became one of the strongest fortress cities of the Paulicians (Ar. al-Baylaqānī): cf. note 63 below.

49. Gk. Sozopetra or Zapetra. The ruins of this city are probably to be identified with those of Vīrān Shahr (Vivanşehir), to the south of Malaṭiyah. Captured by the Byzantines on several occasions, it was rebuilt by both al-Manṣūr and al-Ma'mūn: see Balādhurī, *Futūḥ al-Buldān,* 191 and Iṣṭakhrī, *al-Masālik wa-l-Mamālik,* 63.

50. Another fortress which was for many years alternately in Greek and Arab hands. It was rebuilt by the caliph al-Mahdī in 779 and restored by Hārūn al-Rashīd (786–809). In 954 it was finally prized out of Greek hands and again rebuilt by the Ḥamdānid Sayf al-Dawlah.

51. The incursions of the Banū-Ḥabīb into Diyār Muḍar are recounted by Ibn Ḥawqal, *al-Masālik wa-l-Mamālik,* 211–13 and summarized by Canard, *Histoire de la Dynastie des H'amdanides,* 139–40, 303, 737–39. This latter author complements Ibn Ḥawqal's version with materials from Ibn Ẓāfir Jamāl al-Dīn's *Kitāb Akhbār al-Zamān fi Ta'rīkh Banī-al-ʿAbbās* (MS Br. Mus., Or. 3685), which I have not consulted.

52. Qālīqalā (Erzurum) was also known to the Arab topographers as Arḍ (or Arzan) al-Rūm, to Armenians as Karin, and to the Greeks as Theodosiopolis. Ibn Serapion knew the Western Euphrates as the Nahr al-Furāt (Le Strange, *The Lands of the Eastern Caliphate* 117).

53. Also transcribed as Mināzjird, Manzikart, and Milāsgird.

54. Maqdisī, *Aḥsan,* 376.

55. Ibn Ḥawqal, *al-Masālik wa-l-Mamālik,* 211, 225.

56. Maqdisī, *Aḥsan,* 146.

57. Ibid., 146.

58. Ibid., 139, citing Wahb ibn Munabbih. The authorities for the tradition were Abū Saʿīd ibn Ḥamdān; Abū Ḥāmid al-Julūdī; Abū Hani' and his father; ʿAbd al-Munʿim ibn Idrīs and his father; and the above-mentioned Wahb ibn Munabbih. Cf. Qur'ān 11 *(Hūd):* 48.

59. Edessa: Ar. al-Ruhā < Aram. Orhāy (cf. Arm. *Urhay*) < Gk. Kallirrhoe. The modern name Urfa is presumably derived from Ruhā by way of a form Rufā, according to a common principle in Turkish of mutation of *h* to *f*: see J. Deny, *Principes de Grammaire Turque ('Türk' de Turquie)* (Paris, 1955), 109.

60. Iṣṭakhrī, *al-Masālik wa-l-Mamālik,* 79 and Ibn Ḥawqal, *al-Masālik wa-l-Mamālik,* 226. On the "napkin of ʿĪsā, son of Maryam," see also Masʿūdī, *Murūj,* 2:331 and Ibn al-Athīr, *al-Kāmil,* 8:302. This relic was accorded especial reverence by the Melkites, one of the three main sects of Aqūr Christianity (the others being the Nestorian Dyophysites and the Monophysites). The story of the sacred napkin bearing an imprint of the features of Jesus is summarized by J. B. Segal, *Edessa, "The Blessed City"* (Oxford, 1970), 214–16.

61. Maqdisī, *Aḥsan,* 141, 147. More than a century earlier Ibn Khurradādhbih (*al-Masālik wa-l-Mamālik,* 161) had reported that "The Romans pretend that no building constructed of stone surpasses in beauty the cathedral at Ruhā." Presumably both authors were referring to the Melkite cathedral built by Bishop Amazonius soon after 525.

62. Ibid., 146.

63. Qudāmah, *al-Kharāj,* 254 and Masʿūdī, *Murūj,* 8:74. Abrīq < Gk. Tephrike or Aphrike: also al-Abrūq in ʿAlī Yazdī, cited by Yāqūt, *Muʿjam,* 1:87. The Paulicians (*παυλικιανοί* [< Arm. *Payli keank*] = adherents of a minor Paul), a heretical sect of allegedly Manichaean (although actually Adoptionist Christian) persuasion which seems to have been inspired by the teachings of Paul of Samosata, patriarch of Antioch from 260 to 272, occupied Tephrike with the tacit consent of the caliphs. For some years they served as a buffer between Christians and Muslims.

64. Cited by Segal, *Edessa,* 206. Cf. also the same author's "The Planet Cult of Ancient Harran," in *Vanished Civilizations,* ed. E. Bacon (New York, 1963), 211–20. Ḥarrān had long been a stronghold of the Qays tribe, and for a brief period in the eighth century had been constituted the imperial capital by Marwān II, last of the Umayyad caliphs.

65. Morony, *Iraq after the Muslim Conquest,* 132. Morony aptly suggests that this spatial division of responsibilities was adopted in the interests of "greater efficiency, discipline, and control."

66. See ibid., 214–35 for an excellent, succinct summary of Arab settlement in Sāsānian ʿIrāq and Aqūr in pre-Islamic times.

67. Balādhurī, *Futūḥ al-Buldān,* 178.

68. This region had been known to the Greeks as Osrhoene. The vicissitudes of Ruhā under Muslim rule are compendiously set forth in Segal, *Edessa,* chap. 5, from which the following remarks are abstracted.

69. Balādhurī, *Futūḥ al-Buldān,* 178; but note Lapidus's query as to the implications of this statement ("Arab Settlement and Economic Development of Iraq and Iran," 204 n. 8): "Did they [ʿUthmān and Muʿāwiyah] actually prescribe territories for the various groups or merely ratify established Arab settlements?"

70. It may well have been in Diyār Muḍar, even in al-Ruhā, that al-Maqdisī had heard, as he puts it, "the sound of *nawāqīs* in the night" (cf. p. 65 above).

71. Cited by Segal, *Edessa,* 200 from J. B. Chabot, *Anonymi Auctoris Chronicon ad Annum Christi 1234 Pertinens (CSCO 81-2, Ser. syri 36-7)* (1953).

72. Maqdisī, *Aḥsan,* 137.

73. Ibn Ḥawqal, p. 221.

74. For example, in March 740: cf. Segal, *Edessa,* 204.

75. For example, locusts in March 842: cf. ibid.

76. For example, in 952–53: cf. ibid., 216.

77. Cited by ibid., 205 from J. B. Chabot, *Incerti Auctoris Chronicon Pseudo-Dionysianum Vulgo Dictum (CSCO 91, 104, Ser. syri 43, 53)* (1952–53).

78. For examples of such exactions in al-Ruhā see Segal, *Edessa,* 197–200.

79. Ibn Ḥawqal, *al-Masālik wa-l-Mamālik,* 216.

80. The author of the *Ḥudūd* in 982–83 still regarded Naṣībīn as "the most prosperous town in al-Jazīrah" (140).

Chapter Six

Author's note: The toponymy and topography of the territories comprising present-day Syria and Lebanon in medieval times are reconstructed in detail by R. Dussaud in *Topographie Historique de la Syrie Antique et Médiévale* (Paris, 1927), and for what was formerly Palestine by Guy Le Strange in *Palestine under the Moslems* (London, 1890). There is a vast amount of general information relevant to this chapter in Moshe Gil, *A History of Palestine, 634–1099* (Cambridge, 1992; originally published in Hebrew by Tel Aviv University, 1983). For a thorough discussion of the changing administrative structure of the southern sectors of the *iqlīm,* see A. Walmsley, "The Administrative Structure and Urban Geography of the Jund of Filastin and the Jund of al-Urdunn," Ph.D. diss., University of Sydney, 1987. Virtually all Arabic descriptions of Palestine from the ninth to the eighteenth century have been assembled in gazetteer form and translated into French by Marmardji in *Textes Géographiques Arabes sur la Palestine.*

1. P. 35 above.

2. P. 105 above.

3. For this city in the tenth century see p. 114 below.

4. A settlement on the road from Damascus to Palmyra. On early Arab settlement in the Levant more generally see Hugh Kennedy, "The Towns of Bilād al-Shām and the Arab Conquest," in *Proceedings of the Symposium on Bilād al-Shām during the Byzan-*

tine Period . . . , ed. M. A. Bakhit and M. Asfour (Amman, 1986), 2:88–99.

5. See chapter 3.

6. Miquel, *La Géographie Humaine,* 2d ed. (Paris and La Haye, 1973), 280 n. 3.

7. Cf. p. 103 above.

8. For an analysis of the transformation of this city in Umayyad times see Sauvaget, "Esquisse d'une histoire de la ville de Damas," 444–49.

9. Among numerous examples: Ibn Jubayr, *Riḥlah,* 234–35: "If Paradise be on earth, Dimashq must be it; if it be in Heaven, Dimashq can match and equal it"; also al-Maqdisī (*Aḥsan,* 151): "Dimashq, the garden of the world." Cf. further al-Khwārizmī as quoted by al-Thaʿālibī in *al-Laṭāʾif al-Maʿārif,* 157–58; and Yāqūt, *Muʿjam,* 2:589. Ibn Baṭṭūṭah, writing in the fourteenth century, incorporated a representative selection of eulogistic verses about Dimashq (Damascus) in his *Tuḥfat al-Nuẓẓār,* vol. 1 (Paris, 1853), 187–97.

10. Maqdisī, *Aḥsan,* 155. For Ḥalab (Aleppo) under the Umayyads, ʿAbbāsids, and Ḥamdānids see Sauvaget, *Alep,* chaps. 6, 7. Cf. also Ibn Ḥawqal, *al-Masālik wa-l-Mamālik,* 177 and Minorsky, *Ḥudūd,* 150.

11. Maqdisī, *Aḥsan,* 156. Cf. also Yaʿqūbī, *al-Buldān,* 324–25; Ibn Khurradādhbih, *al-Masālik wa-l-Mamālik,* 75–76; Masʿūdī, *Murūj,* 1:125, 312; Ibn Rustah, *al-Aʿlaq,* 83, 97, and 107; Iṣṭakhrī, *al-Masālik wa-l-Mamālik,* 61; Minorsky, *Ḥudūd,* 150; and Ibn Ḥawqal, *al-Masālik wa-l-Mamālik,* 176. Even as late as the tenth century, the districts into which al-Maqdisī partitioned al-Shām (Syria) reflected in their extents the Roman and Byzantine administrative units that the Arabs seem to have adopted as military districts (sing. *jund*) at the time of the conquest. These comprised Dimashq, Ḥimṣ, al-Urdunn, and Filasṭīn, to which the caliph Yazīd I (680–83) added Qinnasrīn in the far north. However, with the establishment of Ḥalab as the Ḥamdānid capital, the old "provincial" capital of Qinnasrīn (ancient Chalkis) sank into insignificance. For pertinent comments on the *junds* of al-Shām see Irfan Shahīd, "The Jund System in Bilād al-Shām: Its Origin," in *Proceedings of the Symposium on Bilād al-Shām during the Byzantine Period (1983),* ed. Bakhit and Asfour, 2:45–52.

That Ḥimṣ should have experienced developmental difficulties in the ninth century is not unexpected given that the city rebelled on no less than seven occasions between 855 and 882, first against ʿAbbāsid governors but subsequently against Ṭūlūnid authority. Some of these uprisings were suppressed with extreme severity (Tabarī, *Taʾrīkh,* al-Faḍl Ibrāhīm edition, 9:197, 199–200, 259, 276, 510, 551).

12. Yaʿqūbī, *al-Buldān,* 327; Iṣṭakhrī, *al-Masālik wa-l-Mamālik,* 58; Ibn Ḥawqal, *al-Masālik wa-l-Mamālik,* 173; and Maqdisī, *Aḥsan,* 161. For the initial Islamic occupation of this site see Timothy P. Harrison, "The early Umayyad settlement at Ṭabariyah: a case of yet another *miṣr?*" *Journal of Near Eastern Studies* 51 (1992): 51–59.

13. Balādhurī, *Futūḥ al-Buldān,* 143; al-Qalqashandī, *Subḥ al-Aʿshā,* 4:99–100; Ibn Ḥawqal, *al-Masālik wa-l-Mamālik,* 171; and Maqdisī, *Aḥsan,* 164–65. It has been suggested that ʿAbd al-Malik's decision to establish al-Ramlah (Ramleh) was influenced by the circumstance that its site lay in the territory of the Yamanī tribes on whom he relied for support against the Qaysī faction within the Umayyads: see Kennedy, "The Towns of Bilād al-Shām and the Arab Conquest," 97. Yaʿqūbī (*al-Buldān,* 328) notes that the inhabitants of Ludd were transferred to the new city, so that the old provincial capital decayed. The mosque referred to, known as al-Abyaḍ ("The White Mosque"), was built by Hishām, tenth caliph of the House of Umayyah. Al-Maqdisī (*Aḥsan,* 165) adds, "In all Islam there is not a larger *miḥrab* than the one in this mosque, and its pulpit is the most exquisite that is to be seen after that at Bayt al-Maqdis (Jerusalem)." Cf. M. Rosen-Ayalon and A. Eitan, *Ramla Excavations: Finds from the VIIIth century* C.E. (Jerusalem, 1969); Dominique Sourdel, "La fondation umayyade d'al-Ramla," in *Studien zur Geschichte und Kultur des Vorderen Orients: Festschrift für Bertold Spuler,* ed. H. R. Roemer and A. Noth (Leiden, 1981) and Walmsley, "Administrative Structure and Urban Geography," 62–64. See also pp. 228–29 below.

14. Also Zughar and Sukar. It is a moot point whether Ṣughar was the Zoar of Gen. 19:22, 23, and 30, although Ibn Ḥawqal (*al-Masālik wa-l-Mamālik,* 185) and al-Maqdisī (*Aḥsan,* 178) clearly made that identification. In this connection it may be noted that the form *Ṣughar* is close to the Hebrew Ṣoʿar (= "small thing") used in that work. Furthermore, al-Iṣṭakhrī (*al-Masālik wa-l-Mamālik,* 56) and Ibn Ḥawqal located the city in the neighborhood of "the dwellings of Lot's people" (*diyār-i qawm Lūṭ: jāy-i qawm-i Lūṭ* in Minorsky, *Ḥudūd,* 151), while al-Maqdisī explicitly characterized Ṣughar as "a vestige of the cities of Lūṭ" (*Aḥsan,* 178).

15. Cf. Maqdisī, *Aḥsan,* 178: "He who finds that the Angel of Death delays for him should come here, for in all Islam I know of no place with such an evil climate." This author also related that "The people of the two neighboring districts call the town Ṣaqar (= Hell), and a native of Jerusalem, writing thence to his friends, once addressed his letter, 'From the lower Ṣaqar to the upper Paradise.'"

16. The phrase is al-Maqdisī's, ibid. Cf. also Ibn Ḥawqal, *al-Masālik wa-l-Mamālik,* 184–85. For a discussion of Ṣughar as "an Islamic regional center," see Donald Whitcomb, "Southern Ghors and Northeast ʿArabah Archaeological Survey," in *Archaeological Survey of the Southern Ghors and Northeast ʿArabah,* ed. B. MacDonald (forthcoming). Walmsley suggests that Ṣughar was constituted as the capital of al-Sharāʾ by the early Fāṭimids, probably mainly al-ʿAzīz (975–96), as a means of consolidating their control over the revitalized Red Sea and Ḥijāzī trade routes ("Administrative Structure and Urban Geography," 181).

17. Maqdisī, *Aḥsan,* 160. In spite of its relatively small size, Nawā was the principal town in the Ḥawrān.

18. Present-day Bethshean: Maqdisī, *Aḥsan,* 162. Interestingly, some two and a half centuries later Yāqūt (*Muʿjam,* 1:788) could see only two solitary palms in the vicinity of the settlement.

19. Maqdisī, *Aḥsan,* 162.

20. Ibid.

21. Bāniyās < Paneas, the Greek name of the city more commonly called Caesarea Philippi. The population of the city had been greatly increased by an influx of Muslim refugees from the northern frontier districts after the conquest of Ṭarsūs by the Greeks in 965.

22. The Heliopolis of the Greeks. See Yaʿqūbī, *al-Buldān,* 325; al-Faqiḥ, *al-Buldān,* 118; Masʿūdī, *Marūj,* 4:87; Iṣṭakhrī, *al-Masālik wa-l-Mamālik,* 61; Ibn Ḥawqal, *al-Masālik wa-l-Mamālik,* 175; Minorsky, *Ḥudūd,* 150; and Maqdisī, *Aḥsan,* 160. For a general description of Baʿlabakk in ancient times see Friedrich Ragette, *Baalbek* (Park Ridge, N.J., 1980). The Muslim city is discussed on pp. 71–79.

23. For a reading of this phrase, which has the Sea of Rūm facilitating exports from al-Shām, see Miquel, *Aḥsan,* 153. The *Ḥudūd* (148), however, would seem to confirm my interpretation: "Whatever is produced in the Maghrib, Egypt, Byzantium, and Andalus is brought [to al-Shām]." For the road system of southern al-Shām during the ʿAbbāsid and early Fāṭimid periods see Walmsley, "Administrative Structure and Urban Geography," chap. 5.

24. Ibn Ḥawqal, *al-Masālik wa-l-Mamālik,* 182.

25. Maqdisī, *Aḥsan,* 174. See also Yaʿqūbī, *al-Buldān,* 329. Also transcribed as Yāfā.

26. The early topographers did not have much to say about al-Suwaydīyah, although it was mentioned (but no more) by both Ibn Ḥawqal (*al-Masālik wa-l-Mamālik,* 165) and al-Maqdisī (*Aḥsan,* 154). Some two and a half centuries after these two authors were writing, Yāqūt (*Muʿjam,* 1:385) characterized al-Suwaydīyah as "a little town . . . where the ships of the Franks cast anchor, and whence their goods are carried on horses and mules to Anṭākiyah."

27. The classical Laodikeia ad Mare, founded by Seleucus I Nicator early in the third century B.C. and peopled mainly by Macedonians (see Jones et al., *The Cities of the Eastern Roman Provinces,* 243). Cf. Yaʿqūbī, *al-Buldān,* 325–26, where it is stated that toward the end of the ninth century, the population of the town included a large contingent of Yamanī tribesmen; and Maqdisī, *Aḥsan,* 154. The city was captured by Nicephorus Phocas in 968.

28. Ibn Ḥawqal, *al-Masālik wa-l-Mamālik,* 178 and Maqdisī, *Aḥsan,* 154. The city had been captured by Nicephorus Phocas in 968 when, according to Ibn Ḥawqal (ibid.), some thirty-five thousand men, women, and children had been taken into captivity—which sounds like an exaggeration if it was intended that they all came from Jabalah town.

29. Gk. Balanea; the Valania of the Crusaders. Cf. Ibn Ḥawqal, *al-Masālik wa-l-Mamālik,* 165 and Maqdisī, *Aḥsan,* 154, 160.

30. The ancient Antaradus. Cf. Ibn Ḥawqal, *al-Masālik wa-l-Mamālik,* 176–77 and Maqdisī, *Aḥsan,* 154.

31. Maqdisī, *Aḥsan,* 154; also mentioned by Ibn Khurradādhbih, *al-Masālik wa-l-Mamālik,* 76. At a later date categorized as "Rafanīyah of Tadmur" by Yāqūt, *Muʿjam,* 2:796.

32. Iṣṭakhrī, *al-Masālik wa-l-Mamālik,* 61 and Ibn Ḥawqal, *al-Masālik wa-l-Mamālik,* 175: meaning, presumably, the main port for Dimashq District rather than for the city itself. When Sufyān ibn Mūjib al-Azdī besieged Aṭrābulus (Tripoli) in 644, the inhabitants fled by sea to Byzantine territories, which allowed Muʿāwīyah, then governor of Syria, to replace them with a colony of Jews (Baladhuri, *Futūḥ al-Buldān,* 127). Al-Yaʿqūbī (*al-Buldān,* 327), while asserting that the colonists were Persians, adds that the harbor could shelter as many as a thousand vessels.

33. Classical Berytus, perhaps the Berothai of the Hebrew Scriptures. Yaʿqūbī (*al-Buldān,* 327) notes that in his day Bayrūt (Beirut) "was populated by Persians settled there by the Caliph Muʿāwīyah." See also Iṣṭakhrī, *al-Masālik wa-l-Mamālik,* 65; Ibn Ḥawqal, *al-Masālik wa-l-Mamālik,* 176 ("It is a centre for maritime imports and exports"); al-Maqdisī, *Aḥsan,* 154; and more generally Ṣāliḥ ibn Yaḥyā, *Taʾrīkh Bayrūt,* ed. Francis Hours, S.J. and Kamal Salibi (Beirut, A.H. 1389/A.D. 1969).

34. Yaʿqūbī, *al-Buldān,* 327; Ibn Ḥawqal, *al-Masālik wa-l-Mamālik,* 165, 187; and Maqdisī, *Aḥsan,* 160.

35. Maqdisī, *Aḥsan,* 163–64; also Iṣṭakhrī, *al-Masālik wa-l-Mamālik,* 59 and Ibn Ḥawqal, *al-Masālik wa-l-Mamālik,* 174.

36. Accho of the Old Testament; classical Ptolemais; St. Jean d'Acre of the Crusaders. See Maqdisī, *Aḥsan,* 162–63. Cf. Walmsley, "Administrative Structure and Urban Geography," 96–97.

37. Maqdisī, *Aḥsan,* 174; Iṣṭakhrī, *al-Masālik wa-l-Mamālik,* 66; and Ibn Ḥawqal, *al-Masālik wa-l-Mamālik,* 165, 186. After the Muslim conquest of Caesarea (Cherchell) in 640 or 641, the city appears to have been abandoned by the majority of its population; its port, denied access to the maritime commerce of the Mediterranean, became moribund. Not until Muʿāwiyah, when governor of the Levant, restored its fortifications, constituted it as a *ribāṭ,* garrisoned it with volunteers from the Īrānian world, and built its first mosque, did the city begin to recover. Despite being occupied by Byzantine forces from 685 to 690 and again briefly by the army of John I Tzimisces in 975, and despite the relative neglect that the ʿAbbāsids visited upon the Levant as compared with their eastern provinces, Qayṣārīyah prospered as the focus of a productive agricultural region, but its port never recovered the commercial pre-eminence it had enjoyed in pre-Islamic times. For a summary of archaeological investigation of the city, see Kenneth G. Holum and Robert L. Hohlfelder, eds., *King Herod's Dream: Caesarea on the Sea* (New York, 1988), especially chap. 6. Note also Walter E. Kaegi, "Some seventh-century sources on Caesarea," *Israel Exploration Journal* 28 (1978): 177–81. Cf. Walmsley, "Administrative Structure and Urban Geography," 65–67 and C. J. Lenzen, "The Byzantine/Islamic Occupation at Caesarea Maritima as Evidenced through the Pottery" (Ph.D. diss., Drew University, 1983). The specifically Islamic aspects of the city are discussed in considerable detail in Avner Raban, ed., *The Richness of Islamic Caesarea* (Haifa, 1999).

38. Maqdisī (*Aḥsan,* 174) notes that, although the city was "spacious, wealthy, healthy, and strongly defended," its harbor was treacherous.

39. Ibid.

40. Ibid., 178. A century earlier, al-Yaʿqūbī (*al-Buldān,* 340) had noted that the city was a meeting place for pilgrims from Syria, Egypt, and the Maghrib en route to Makkah (Mecca), a fact already observed by the Piacenza Pilgrim in Byzantine times: Antoninus Placentinus, *Itinerarium,* no. 39; cited by John Wilkinson, *Jerusalem Pilgrims before the Crusades* (Warminster, England, 1977), 87–88. Waylah (also Aylah) = the Elath of the Old Testament and the Ælana of classical authors. Nelson Glueck has concluded, on the basis of archaeological excavations, that Elath and the Ezion-geber of the biblical narrative were one and the same place (*The Other Side of the Jordan* [New Haven, Conn., 1940], 89, 105, 107–8, and 112–13). For an earlier discussion of Waylah see Ph. Schertl, "Ela-ʿAḳaba," *Orientalia Christiana Periodica* 2 (1936): 33–77, and for recent excavations at the site Donald Whitcomb, "Excavations in Aqaba: First preliminary report," *Annual of the Department of Archaeology of Jordan* 31 (1987): 247–66; "Evidence of the Umayyad Period from the Aqaba Excavations," in *The Fourth International Conference on the History of Bilād al-Shām during the Umayyad Period,* ed. M. Bakhit and R. Schick, English section, 2:164–84; *Aqaba—Port of Palestine on the China Sea* (Amman, 1988); *Ayla: Art and Industry in the Islamic Port of Aqaba* (Chicago, 1994); and "Out of Arabia: Early Islamic Aqabah and Its Regional Context," in *Colloque International d'Archéologie Islamique,* ed. Gayraud, 403–18. There is a summary of the information available up to 1960 in *The Encyclopaedia of Islam,* 2d ed., 1:783–84. Paul M. Cobb has provided a discriminating footnote to Early Islamic historiography with implications extending far beyond Waylah in "A note on ʿUmar's visit to Ayla in 17/638," *Der Islam* 71, pt. 2 (1994): 283–88.

It may or may not be significant that al-Maqdisī reserved the name Waylah for the contemporary town, while asserting that Aylah was the name of a ruined settlement in the same neighborhood. However, he notes that popular custom persisted in applying the latter name to the new settlement. Al-Maqdisī also repeated the popularly held belief that old Aylah was the place referred to in Qur'ān 7 *(al-Aʿrāf)*:163: "Ask them about the town by the sea [where certain Jews were punished for fishing on the Sabbath]." Cf. Yāqūt, *Muʿjam,* 1:422; Abū ʿUbayd al-Bakrī, *Muʿjam mā Istaʿjama,* 1:135; and al-Qazwīnī, *Āthār al-Bilād wa Akhbaār al-ʿIbād,* ed. F. Wüstenfeld (Göttingen, 1848), p. 103. Whitcomb has given reasons for inferring that Waylah was founded in about A.D. 650: "The Miṣr of Aylah: Settlement at al-ʿAqaba in the Early Islamic Period," in *The Byzantine and Early Islamic Near East,* ed. King and Cameron, 2:157–58 and *Ayla,* 25.

Al-Maqdisī's characterization of Waylah as "the port of Filasṭīn" should be understood to mean "the port of Filasṭīn [on the Sea of China]" as Yāfah (above) was "the emporium of Filasṭīn [on the Sea of Rūm]." By "the emporium of the Ḥijāz," al-Maqdisī obviously meant "the [Filasṭīn] emporium for trade with the Ḥijāz." The pilgrim cited earlier in this note added to his comments there recorded that Indian shipping brought a variety of spices to the port of Aylah. The date at which he was writing was circa 570 (Wilkinson, *Jerusalem Pilgrims before the Crusades*). In any case Dr. Whitcomb's discovery of amphorae (used as specialized containers for grains, oils, and produce to be packed in ships' holds) and the nearby kilns where they were fired afford independent testimony to the commercial and industrial importance of the town.

41. Yūsuf Ghawanmah, *Aylah (al-ʿAqabah) wa-l-Baḥr al-Aḥmar* (Irbid, Jordan, A.H. 1406/A.D. 1984), where names and sources are cited in full. On the history of the settlement more generally see Ṣalāḥ Daradkah, "Lamaḥāt min ta'rīkh Aylat al-ʿAqabah," *Dirāsāt Ta'rīkhīyah,* vols. 15–16 (1984), 67–110.

42. Maqdisī, *Aḥsan,* 154; also Ibn Jubayr, *Riḥlah,* 251 and Yāqūt, *Muʿjam al-Buldān,* 1:437, 603, 664 and 2:200.

43. Ibn Ḥawqal (*al-Masālik wa-l-Mamālik,* 179) notes that in his day (or at least when he was composing the later editions of his work) Khunāsirah was prospering as a provisioning center for travellers who chose to follow the interior route rather than risk Byzantine incursions or Ḥamdānid exactions along the conventional caravan trails through the heart of the province.

44. Cf. pp. 5 and 7 above.

45. Cf. p. 5 above.

46. Originally the chief settlement of the Ammonites, when it was known as Rabbah or Rabbath, that is, "the capital," this city was restored by Ptolemy Philadelphus (285–246 B.C.) and renamed Philadelphia. Cf. Maqdisī, *Aḥsan,* 175. See also A. Almagro, *El Palacio Omeya de Amman I: La Arquitectura* (Madrid, 1983) and Alastair Northedge, "Qalʿat ʿAmman in the Early Islamic Period" (Ph.D. diss., London University, 1984).

47. Ar-Moab, one of the capitals of the Moabites; classical Areopolis. Cf. Maqdisī, *Aḥsan,* 178; also mentioned by Yaʿqūbī, *al-Buldān,* 326.

48. Maʿāb and Udhruḥ (also Adhruḥ) were the two principal urban centers of the Jabal al-Sharā': see Abū al-Fidā' (1273–1332), *Taqwīn al-Buldān,* 2:24. Cf. Maqdisī, *Aḥsan,* 178. For recent excavations at the site of Uḍhruḥ see A. C. Killick, "Udruh: the frontier of an empire," *Levant* 15 (1983): 110–31 and (ed.) *Udhruh: Caravan City and Desert Oasis* (Romsey, England, 1987).

49. Iṣṭakhrī, *al-Masālik wa-l-Mamālik,* 65 and Ibn Ḥawqal, *al-Masālik wa-l-Mamālik,* 185. Al-Dimashqī, writing in about 1300, records that Maʿān had originally been built as a desert retreat by the Umayyads, some of whose descendants still inhabited the town in Ibn Ḥawqal's time (see al-Dimashqī, *Nukhbāt al-Dahr fī ʿAjā'ib al-Barr wa-l-Baḥr,* ed. A. F. Mehren under the title *Cosmographie de Chems-ed-Din . . .* [St. Petersburg, 1866], 213).

50. Maqdisī, *Aḥsan,* 176.

51. Ibid., 177.

52. Ibid., 176.

53. Iṣṭakhrī, *al-Masālik wa-l-Mamālik,* 58; Ibn Ḥawqal, *al-Masālik wa-l-Mamālik,* 172, 186; Minorsky, *Ḥudūd,* 150; and Maqdisī, *Aḥsan,* 174. Ghazzah (Gaza) was a settlement of great antiquity; for its pre-Islamic status see M. A. Meyer, *A History of the City of Gaza* (New York, 1907) and, more specifically, Glanville Downey, *Gaza in the Early Sixth Century* (Norman, Okla., 1963).

54. Maqdisī, *Aḥsan,* 172–73; also Iṣṭakhrī, *al-Masālik wa-l-Mamālik,* 57 and Ibn Ḥawqal, *al-Masālik wa-l-Mamālik,* 172 (where the town is referred to as Masjid Ibrāhīm, as it is in Minorsky, *Ḥudūd,* 150). Al-Maqdisī adds that the hospitality offered at the shrine was funded by a *waqf* established by Tamīm (ibn Aws) al-Dārī, a Companion of the Prophet who embraced Islam in the year A.H. 7. He died in Filasṭīn in A.H. 40 and was buried in Bayt Jibrīl (Bayt Jibrīn).

The Constantinople recension adds: "The Amīr of Khurāsān [Nūḥ ibn Manṣūr, 977–97]—May God confirm his dominion—has donated to this foundation a thousand *dirhams* yearly; and, in addition, the ruler (al-Shār [of Gharjistān]) al-ʿĀdil has made large bequests to this house. In all Islam, I know of no charity or almsgiving *(ṣadaqah)* as well regulated as this one. Hungry travellers may here partake of wholesome food, thereby continuing the custom of Ibrāhīm."

55. Minorsky, *Ḥudūd,* 150, which is only a slight elaboration of information provided by Iṣṭakhrī, *al-Masālik wa-l-Mamālik,* 65 and Ibn Ḥawqal, *al-Masālik wa-l-Mamālik,* 184.

56. Cf. Ibn Ḥawqal, *al-Masālik wa-l-Mamālik,* 177.

57. Ancient Barbalissus; an important river port where caravan routes converged: cf. Iṣṭakhrī, *al-Masālik wa-l-Mamālik,* 62; Ibn Ḥawqal, *al-Masālik wa-l-Mamālik,* 180; Minorsky, *Ḥudūd,* 149; and Maqdisī, *Aḥsan,* 155.

58. The nodal position of Dimashq in earlier times was imaginatively illustrated by James Elroy Flecker in his poem entitled "Gates of Damascus."

Itineraries for the principal roads and trails in al-Shām are provided with varying degrees of completeness by Ibn Khurradādhbih, *al-Masālik wa-l-Mamālik,* 98–100 and Yaʿqūbī, *al-Buldān,* 324–30 (for the second half of the ninth century); Qudāmah, *al-Kharāj,* 219 and the abridged al-Faqīh, *al-Buldān,* index (for the first half of the tenth century); Ibn Ḥawqal, *al-Masālik wa-l-Mamālik,* 185–88; and Maqdisī, *Aḥsan,* 190–92 (for the second half of the tenth century).

59. Iṣṭakhrī, *al-Masālik wa-l-Mamālik,* 61 and Ibn Ḥawqal, *al-Masālik wa-l-Mamālik,* 176. Cf. also Minorsky, *Ḥudūd,* 150.

60. Iṣṭakhrī, *al-Masālik wa-l-Mamālik,* 62 and Ibn Ḥawqal, *al-Masālik wa-l-Mamālik,* 179–180. Cf. also Masʿūdī, *Murūj,* 2:406, 407 and 4:55, 91.

61. Maqdisī, *Aḥsan,* 164.

62. Ibn Ḥawqal, *al-Masālik wa-l-Mamālik,* 171.

63. P. 112 above.

64. For example, al-Ramlah (Maqdisī, *Aḥsan,* 164), Aṭrābulus (Ibn Ḥawqal, *al-Masālik wa-l-Mamālik,* 175), and Iskandarūnah (Iṣṭakhrī, *al-Masālik wa-l-Mamālik,* 63; and Ibn Ḥawqal, *al-Masālik wa-l-Mamālik,* 182).

65. For example, Ḥimṣ (Ibn Ḥawqal, *al-Masālik wa-l-Mamālik,* 176), Ḥamāh (*ibid.,* 177), Baʿlabbak (Maqdisī, *Aḥsan,* 160), and Anṭākiyah (Ibn Ḥawqal, *al-Masālik wa-l-Mamālik,* 179–80).

66. Maqdisī, *Aḥsan,* 175: quoted by Yāqūt, *Muʿjam,* 3:760. For archaeologically based comments on farming practices in this region, see Henry I. MacAdam, "Settlements and Settlement Patterns in Northern and Central Transjordania: ca. 550–ca. 750," in *The Byzantine and Early Islamic Near East,* ed. G. R. D. King and Averil Cameron; vol. 2: *The Byzantine and Early Islamic Near East* (Princeton, N.J., 1994).

67. Maqdisī, *Aḥsan,* 161, 163 (Constantinople recension only). In view of the general productivity of the Ghūṭah, this statement must have referred primarily to cereals. Cf. ibid., where Maqdisī describes the town of Bāniyās, on the western edge of the Jawlan, as "the granary of Dimashq."

68. Maqdisī, *Aḥsan,* 164.

69. Ibid., 7, 165.

70. For example, Maʿarrat al-Nuʿmān (Ibn Ḥawqal, *al-Masālik wa-l-Mamālik,* 178), al-Farāḍiyah (Maqdisī, *Aḥsan,* 162), and Baʿlabbak (Maqdisī, *Aḥsan,* 160). The best-quality raisins were known as ʿAynūnī and Dūrī after the villages of Bayt ʿAynūn and Dūrah, near Ḥabrā (Hebron) (Maqdisī, *Aḥsan,* 180).

71. Ibn Ḥawqal, *al-Masālik wa-l-Mamālik,* 178.

72. Maqdisī, *Aḥsan,* 164.

73. Ibid., 176. Yubnā was the Jabneh of 1 Macc. 4:15 and the Jamnia of classical authors. A variety of small fig, growing wild, known as *quṭṭayn* (< Gk. *κόττανον* was a product of Filasṭīn (Maqdisī, *Aḥsan,* 180).

74. Maqdisī (ibid., 174) made special mention of Nābulus, where "olive trees abound." This city, near the biblical Shechem, the chief sanctuary of the Samaritans, had been founded as Flavia Neapolis in A.D. 71–72; see Jones et al., *The Cities of the Eastern Roman Provinces,* 276.

75. Maqdisī, *Aḥsan,* 172: cf. Iṣṭakhrī, *al-Masālik wa-l-Mamālik,* 57 and Ibn Ḥawqal, *al-Masālik wa-l-Mamālik,* 172.

76. Maqdisī, *Aḥsan,* 172.

77. Ibid., 162.

78. Ibn Ḥawqal, *al-Masālik wa-l-Mamālik,* 176; Maqdisī, *Aḥsan,* 161. Sugarcane probably had been introduced into the Middle East from South Asia during the last century of Sāsānian rule, but it did not spread at all widely until the Islamic period. There is no record of its cultivation in the Levant before the references cited here. For the diffusion of the cane through the Islamic world from the seventh to the tenth century, see Andrew M. Watson, *Agricultural Innovation in the Early Islamic World. The Diffusion of Crops and Farming Techniques, 700–1100* (Cambridge, 1983), 24–30 and S. Hamarnah, "Zirāʿat qaṣab al-sukkar wa-ṣināʿatuhu ʿinda al-ʿArab al-Muslimīn," *Annual of the Department of Antiquities [of Jordan]* 22 (1977–78):12–19. The archaeological remains of a series of sugar mills *(tawāḥin al-sukkar)* in southern Ghawr are discussed by Whitcomb, "Southern Ghors and Northeast ʿArabah," 3–5, 9.

79. Maqdisī, *Aḥsan,* 160.

80. Ibid., p. 179. For the diffusion of this crop in early Islamic times, see Watson, *Agricultural Innovations,* chap. 8.

81. For example, Ṣughar (Ibn Ḥawqal, *al-Masālik wa-l-Mamā-*

lik, 184–85). One particular saffron-colored variety of date from this city, known as *al-inqilā,* was held to surpass any "found in al-ʿIrāq or elsewhere" (ibid.).

82. *Indigofera tinctoria,* Linn., the source of indigo dye, had been introduced into the Arab world from India through the intermediacy of Persia, probably in the sixth century A.D. (cf. Berthold Laufer, *Sino-Iranica. Chinese Contributions to the History of Civilization in Ancient Iran,* Field Museum of Natural History Publication 201: Anthropological Series vol. 15, no. 3 [Chicago, 1919], 370). Al-Maqdisī (*Aḥsan,* 175, 180) reports that indigo was grown in the neighborhoods of Jericho (Arīḥā) and Baysān, and Ibn Ḥawqal (*al-Masālik wa-l-Mamālik,* 184–85) noted that it was grown commercially in the vicinity of Ṣughar.

83. Maqdisī, *Aḥsan,* 175: also p. 180, where lambs are listed among the products of ʿAmmān. More than two centuries later Yāqūt (*Muʿjam,* 3:760) would note that ʿAmmān, the district capital, was a refuge for *badū* of the Syrian Desert.

84. Although the indigo was of high quality (at least that from Jericho: Maqdisī, *Aḥsan,* 180), for dyeing purposes it was apparently less than the best (Ibn Ḥawqal, *al-Masālik wa-l-Mamālik,* 184–85).

85. A sweetmeat of fig paste pressed into the form of small bricks: cf. Rodinson, "Recherches," 140 n. 4.

86. *Munayyar* was a silken cloth of double warp or weft, and consequently of great durability. *Baʿlīsī* has not been identified, although Serjeant has suggested that possibly *Baʿlabakkī* should be read for *baʿlīsī* (*Islamic Textiles,* 117 n. 23).

87. For the terminology that al-Maqdisī employed to express degrees of excellence, see *Aḥsan,* 6–7. *Maʿṣūr* for *maqṣūr* = closely woven: see Serjeant, *Islamic Textiles,* 253.

88. Maqdisī, *Aḥsan,* 174. It is ironic that, for an *iqlīm* as industrially developed as al-Shām, textile manufacturing is less fully documented than for almost anywhere else in the Islamic world.

89. Cf. ibid., 128.

90. Maqdisī, *Aḥsan,* 174; also 152. Bayt Jabrīl today is popularly known as Bayt Jibrīn (= "The House of Giants"), probably because it is close to Gath, the supposed home of Goliath's (Jālūt) family. The city had been founded by Septimus Severus in A.D. 199 as Eleutheropolis on the site of the village of Baetogabra (Jones, *The Cities of the Eastern Roman Provinces,* 278).

91. Ibn Ḥawqal, *al-Masālik wa-l-Mamālik,* 184. Bitumen occurs in the country rock surrounding the Dead Sea and is often found floating in the water, especially after earthquakes.

92. These are the *ʿawāṣim* listed by al-Balādhurī (*Futūḥ al-Buldān,* 132) and repeated by Yāqūt (*Muʿjam al-Buldān,* 3:742), but other authors furnished different schedules: for example, Ibn Khurradādhbih (*al-Masālik wa-l-Mamālik,* 75) added al-Jūmah, Būqā, Bālis, and Ruṣāfah Hishām; Ibn Ḥawqal (*al-Masālik wa-l-Mamālik,* 176, 187) also included Bālis, Sanjah, and Sumaysāṭ; Ibn Shaddād (*al-Aʿlāq al-Khaṭīrah,* ed. Ch. Ledit in *al-Mashriq* 30 (1935): 179–223; all subsequent references are to this edition) provided still another variant, adding Baghrās, Darbasāq, Artāḥ, Kaysum, and Tall Qabbāsīn.

93. Ibn Ḥawqal, 179, 187. It should be noted, though, that this same author (p. 187) observed that there was no recognized administrative center for the frontier, where "each town is independent." Cf. p. 120 below.

94. Minorsky, *Ḥudūd,* 148–49.

95. Maqdisī, *Aḥsan,* 152.

96. Iṣṭakhrī, *al-Masālik wa-l-Mamālik,* 55–68.

97. Ibn Ḥawqal, *al-Masālik wa-l-Mamālik,* 182. For additional information on the *ʿawāṣim* and *thughūr* see Balādhurī, *Futūḥ al-Buldān,* 159–63; Ibn al-Faqīh, *al-Buldān,* 3:120; Yāqūt, *Muʿjam,* 1:927; and Abū al-Fidā', *Mukhtaṣar Ta'rīkh al-Bashar,* 233. See also Le Strange, *Palestine under the Moslems,* 25–27, 36–38, 45–47; Marius Canard, *Histoire de la Dynastie des H'amdanides,* 1:226–35; and *The Encyclopaedia of Islam,* 2d ed., 1:761–62.

98. Maqdisī, *Aḥsan,* 156; also Dussaud, *Topographie Historique de la Syrie,* 117 et seq.

99. Ibn Ḥawqal, *al-Masālik wa-l-Mamālik,* 176–77 (where the name is transcribed as Ṭurṭusah).

100. Maqdisī, *Aḥsan,* 160.

101. Ibid., 174.

102. Ibid., 163–64. Cf. also Ibn Ḥawqal, *al-Masālik wa-l-Mamālik,* 174. Late in the ninth century, Yaʿqūbī (*al-Buldān,* 327), had noted the existence of shipyards (*dār al-ṣināʿah* at Ṣūr, where were constructed vessels used in expeditions against the Greeks.

103. Al-Maqdisī's account of the construction of the harbor defenses is as follows:

> My grandfather said, "It is a simple matter: let large and strong beams of sycamore lumber be brought." He then floated these beams on the surface of the water as a projection seaward of the land fortifications and bound them to one another, while leaving on the western side an opening for a wide entrance. Upon these beams he raised a structure of stones and cement, reinforcing it with great columns after every five courses. As the beams came to bear increasingly heavy loads, they began little by little to sink. When my grandfather judged that they rested firmly on sand, he left them for a whole year so that they might become firmly embedded; after which he resumed construction where he had left off. At each point where the new construction [now no longer sinking] abutted the old [city walls] he joined them together, riveting the new work to the old. Then he built a bridge across the [western] entrance; and every night, when the [authorized] vessels have entered the harbour, a chain is drawn across the entrance, just as at Ṣūr. (163)

The construction technique described by al-Maqdisī appears to have been of a type in common use in the ancient world, and to have been of the same order of undertaking as that described by Vitruvius, *De Architectura,* bk. 5, chap. 12. A chain as a harbor defense was also recorded by al-Dimashqī (*Nukhbāt,* 209) at Lādhiqīyah (Latakia).

104. Maqdisī, *Aḥsan,* 177. Māḥūz (Aram.) = port, haven.

105. *Shalandīyāt* < Gk. *χελάνδιον.*

106. Maqdisī, *Aḥsan,* 177. For contemporary, analogous prisoner exchanges across the Lāmis (Gk. Lámos) River, the then-frontier between the Caliphate and the East Roman Empire, see Arnold Toynbee, *Constantine Porphyrogenitus and His World* (London, 1973), 388.

107. Maqdisī, *Aḥsan,* 151. *Al-Abdāl,* or Substitutes (sing. *Badal*), according to some so called as the surrogates of the prophets and sustainers of cosmic order. The identities of these righteous persons, "who know God and His attributes in so far as is possible," are divulged only to God, but their number is maintained constant (some say seventy, others as few as seven or as many as three hundred): when one dies, another is substituted in his place. One tradition locates all the Abdāl in Syria: for example, Thaʿālibī, *al-Laṭāʾif al-Maʿārif,* 156; Bosworth's translation, 118. Cf. also Lane's *Arabic-English Lexikon,* s.v. "*Abdāl*" and "*ʿAṣāʾib*"; Ignaz Goldziher in *The Encyclopaedia of Islam,* 1st ed., and H. J. Kissling, 2d ed., s.v.; and S. D. Goitein, "The Sanctity of Jerusalem and Palestine in Early Islam," in that author's *Studies in Islamic History and Institutions* (Leiden, 1966), 135–48.

108. Muḥammad prayed toward the Temple of Jerusalem for sixteen months after his arrival in al-Madīnah (Medina), but then changed the *qiblah* to the Kaʿbah in Makkah (Mecca): cf. chapter 1, p. 28.

109. In some traditions (e.g., one reported by al-Maqdisī, *Aḥsan,* 172) the Resurrection and the Last Judgment are assigned to a locality near the Church of the Ascension on the Mount of Olives, which is known by reference to Qurʾān 79 *(al-Nāziʿāt):* 14 as al-Sāhirah. Another tradition, which is both biblical and Muslim, places the Resurrection in the Wādī al-Jahannam ("The Valley of the Kidron").

110. The Temple of Jerusalem, whither Muḥammad was transported by night from Makkah, and whence he was carried through the seven heavens to the presence of God. Cf. Qurʾān 17 *(al-Isrāʾ):*1.

111. In one tradition, al-Shām as a whole is referred to as the *muhājar* of Ibrāhīm, that is, "the country to which he migrated." For localities in al-Shām preserving the memory of Ibrāhīm, see Harawī, *al-Ishārāt,* Sourdel-Thomine translation, passim, but especially pp. 12, 24, 30–31, 85, and 92 of the Arabic text.

112. Ibrāhīm was allegedly buried on a low hill three miles outside Hebron: see Harawī, *al-Ishārāt,* Arabic text, 3–31; Le Strange, *Palestine under the Moslems,* 309–27; L. H. Vincent, E. J. H. Mackay, and F. M. Abel, *Hébron, le Haram al-Khalil, Sépulture des Patriarches* (Paris, 1923), chaps. 3 and 7. The patriarch is said to have kept an open house for guests (which is not surprising, as it was in any case the custom of the *badū*), whence he is often called "The Father of Guests" *(Abū al-Dhīfān).* In the time of al-Maqdisī a free table was still kept in Hebron for the needy.

113. According to al-Masʿūdī (*Murūj,* 1:91), Ayyūb roamed the steppes of Ḥawrān and al-Bathanīyah between Dimashq and al-Jābiyah. His tomb was venerated in a village near Nawā. Whereas the spring that God opened for him (Qurʾān 38 *[Sād]:*42) was in this same village, his well (Biʾr Ayyūb) was to be found on the outskirts of Jerusalem. Al-Maqdisī may have been confusing the two.

114. For the *Miḥrāb* of Dāwūd see Qurʾān 38 *(Ṣād):* 21 and Masʿūdī, *Murūj,* 1:109. His gate was one of those giving access to the Masjid al-Aqṣā in Jerusalem.

115. Yāqūt (*Muʿjam al-Buldān,* 4:593) offers a selection of the wonders associated with Sulaymān in Bayt al-Maqdis (Jerusalem). Among cities associated with Sulaymān, al-Maqdisī (*Aḥsan,* 186) includes Baʿlabakk (ʿAyn Shams) and Tadmur, and might well have added Ghazzah (where Sulaymān was supposedly born) and Hebron (within which he raised the first structure). See also Ibrāhīm ibn Waṣīf Shah, *Mukhtaṣar al-ʿAjāʾib:* trans. Carra de Vaux under the title *L'Abrégé des Merveilles* (Paris, 1898), 122; al-Masʿūdī, *Murūj,* 1:106–12, and Harawī, *al-Ishārāt,* 21, 25, 27, and 32 of the Arabic text.

116. Just outside Hebron, in the same cave (that of Machpelah) as that within which Ibrāhīm was buried.

117. At Bayt Laḥm (Bethlehem): cf. Yāqūt, *Muʿjam,* 1:779, but Ibn Baṭṭūṭah (*Tuḥfat al-Nuẓẓār,* 1:124) mistakenly assigned the cradle to Jerusalem (Gibb's translation, vol. 1, 2d ser., no. 110, p. 80).

118. Ṭālūt's native village was Gibeah, between Jerusalem and Rāmah. Curiously enough, Yāqūt (*Muʿjam,* 3:341) records a minority belief that Ṭālūt hailed from Duzdān in the district of Shahrazūr. Ṭālūt's river was presumably that used by him to test the endurance of his followers (Qurʾān 2 *[al-Baqarah]:*249), and said to be the Urdunn (Jordan). It would seem that this anecdote was confused with a similar one related of Gideon in Judg. 7:4–7.

119. The fight between Dāwūd and Jālūt is said to have taken place in the valley of Elah, in the territory of the tribe of Judah (Masʿūdī [*Murūj,* 1:108] was wrong in locating it near Baysān, which was actually where Ṭālūt was supposedly killed). The so-called Castle (*ḥiṣn, qaṣr*) of Jālūt was perched on a hill overlooking the city of Rabbath-Ammon (= ʿAmmān: cf. note 46 above). Cf. Maqdisī, *Aḥsan,* 175 and Yāqūt, *Muʿjam,* 3:760.

120. Cf. Jer. 38:6.

121. The reference is to Uriah the Hittite, who was killed under the walls of Rabbath-Ammon, where indeed al-Maqdisī (*Aḥsan,* 175) locates his tomb. It must be presumed that the house of Uriah was in Jerusalem, but it should be noted that the word has all the appearance of a tautologous insertion intended to complete a binary phrase of a type not uncommon in the *Aḥsan.* Cf. 2 Sam. 11:3ff.

122. The Dome of the Prophet *(Qubbat al-Nabī)* is one of the four domes on the platform in the center of the court of the Masjid al-Aqṣā. The Gate of Muḥammad is one of the entrances to this mosque.

123. The rock near which Mūsā met with al-Khiḍr (Qurʾān 18 *[al-Kahf]:*63), located by some on the coast near Anṭākiyah, by others near Shirwān.

124. Cf. Qur'ān 23 *(al-Mu'minūn)*:50. According to some authors this hill, "furnished with security and a flowing spring," was Mount Qāsiyūn, near Dimashq: cf., for instance, Ibn Baṭṭūṭah, *Tuḥfat al-Nuẓẓār,* 1:233–34 (Gibb's translation, 1:46) and, for an elaboration of the legend, Ibn ʿAsākir, *Taʾrīkh Madīnat Dimashq,* 1:96–98; Elisseéf's translation, 177–80. Others, however, have refuted this identification (e.g., Harawāi, *al-Ishārāt,* Arabic text, 11; Sourdel-Thomine's translation, 25–26), some believing that "The Blessed Hill" *(al-Rabwah)* represents Jerusalem, while still others—al-Maqdisī among them—believed that it signified a location in Egypt.

125. Within the Masjid al-Aqṣā. Cf. Qur'ān 19 *(Maryam)*: 11.

126. Presumably a reference to the story of the blood of John the Baptist fermenting on the ground until seventy thousand men were slain thereby; cf. Ibn al-Athīr, *al-Kāmil,* 1:216. For the interpretation "battle-ground" see Ranking and Azoo, *Aḥsanu,* 245 n. 4. Miquel (*Aḥsan,* 148 n. 18) has proposed an alternative reading not without merit except that it involves emending the text: *maʿrak* (battleground) to read *mugharraq* = "place of immersion." In spite of the attractive appositeness of this reading, I prefer the first alternative as not requiring emendation of the text.

127. Three localities in al-Shām are associated with Ayyūb in Islamic lore: his native settlement of al-Bathanīyah, in Ḥawrān between Dimashq and Aḍriʿāt; Nawā, where his main encampment was situated; and Dayr Ayyūb ("Job's Monastery"), where he suffered his tribulations and was finally buried (cf. Maqdisī, *Aḥsan,* 160, and note 113 above.)

128. Yaʿqūb is usually said to have dwelt in the village of Saylūn (Shiloh) in Nābulus District (cf. Yāqūt, *Muʿjam,* 4:311), but al-Iṣṭakhrī (*al-Masālik wa-l-Mamālik,* 59) and Ibn Ḥawqal (*al-Masālik wa-l-Mamālik,* 174) prefer a locality in the Jordan valley.

129. The Great Mosque at Jerusalem, built on the site of the Temple of Solomon. It was designated "The Farthest Mosque" *(Masjid al-Aqṣā),* that is, the most remote of the venerated mosques of Islam, in Qur'ān 17 *(al-Isrā')*:1. Cf. p. 118 below.

130. The site of the ascension of al-Nabī ʿĪsā.

131. Jabal Ṣiddīqā, in the Shephelah between Ṣūr and Bāniyās, which al-Maqdisī (*Aḥsan,* 188) lists among the sacred hills of al-Shām. Ṣiddīq was the son of the prophet Ṣāliḥ. Al-Maqdisī goes on to mention a mosque

> in honour of which a festival is held on the middle day of the month of Shaʿbān, when a great concourse of people from the cities [of Ṣūr, Qadas, Bāniyās, and Ṣaydah] make a pilgrimage to the tomb [of Ṣiddīq], and a representative of the Sulṭān is also present. It so happened that once when I was sojourning in this part of the country, the middle of Shaʿbān fell on a Friday and, at the invitation of the Qāḍī Abū al-Qāsim ibn al-ʿAbbās, I preached before the congregation. In my address I urged them to restore this mosque, which they did, and they also constructed a pulpit for it. One story I have heard told is that when a dog pursues a wild animal to the boundaries of this sanctuary, it [thereupon] stops short. And there are other tales of a similar kind told [about this shrine].

132. Cf. Deut. 34:6: "And he buried him in a valley in the land of Moab, over against Beth-peor [the present-day district of al-Balqā']: but no man knoweth of his sepulchre unto this day." Nevertheless, Yāqūt (*Muʿjam,* 3:210) located the grave on a mountain near Sayḥān, a village just outside Maʿāb. Still other traditions place the tomb in the vicinity of Jericho: cf. Miquel, *Aḥsan,* 149 n. 22.

133. The cave of Machpelah, near Hebron, where Ibrāhīm is said to have slept after seeing the cities of Lūṭ in midair: cf. Maqdisī, *Aḥsan,* 173 and note 111 above.

134. In ʿAsqalān was the sanctuary where the head of al-Ḥusayn, the younger son of the caliph ʿAlī and the Prophet's daughter Fāṭimah, was interred before it was transferred to Cairo by the Fāṭimid caliph in 1153: cf. Ibn Baṭṭūṭah, *Tuḥfat al-Nuẓẓar,* 1:126; Gibb's translation, 1:81.

135. Cf. John 9:7. Yāqūt (*Muʿjam,* 3:125) reports that in his time the spring was accounted miraculous, and its water used for curative purposes. Cf. also Harawī, *al-Ishārāt,* Arabic text p. 27.

136. Cf. Qur'ān 31 *(Luqmān)*: 12. According to Yāqūt (*Muʿjam,* 3:512), Luqmān's grave was east of the Sea of Ṭabarīyah (Galilee). See also Harawī, *al-Ishārāt,* 19.

137. As al-Maqdisī (*Aḥsan,* 161) subsequently refers to Ṭabarīyah as the principal city in the Wādī of Kanʿān, it would appear that the Wādī denoted the Ghawr (or Jordan valley).

138. Lūṭ is mentioned in no less than fourteen Qur'ānic *sūrahs.* Cf. also Gen. 14:1–12 and 19:1–28.

139. This expression refers to the tradition that on the Day of the Gathering, Paradise will be established in Jerusalem (cf. Yaʿqūbī, *al-Buldān,* 94), an event the anticipation of which endowed the Holy City with an increment of proleptic sanctity.

140. As it was the policy of ʿUmar, second of the Rāshidūn caliphs, to erect a mosque wherever a Christian church already existed (Yāqūt, *Muʿjam,* 1:779), numerous Syrian mosques came to bear his name. Prominent among them were mosques at Baysān and Dimashq and on the Mount of Olives.

141. This was an extensive garden near the village of Siloam (Sulwān) that had been bequeathed as a *waqf* to the poor of Jerusalem by ʿUthmān ibn ʿAffān, third of the Rāshidūn caliphs (cf. Maqdisī, *Aḥsan,* 171). Some have considered the site to be the royal garden referred to by Neh. 3:15: "the wall of the pool of Siloah by the King's garden, and unto the stairs that go down from the city of David."

142. Cf. Qur'ān 5 *(al-Mā'idah)*:27. Although the gate referred to has traditionally been identified with one of those of Arīḥā (Jericho: see, for example, Blachère, *Le Coran,* 3:1120), André Miquel (*Aḥsan,* 150 n. 30) has suggested that it just as probably may have been the Desert Gate *(Bāb al-Tih)* of Jerusalem for—here referring to the Qur'ānic *sūrah*—"Ce désert [était] celui où le peuple d'Israël fut condamné à erreur à la suite de son refus d'obéissance."

143. Cf. Qur'ān 38 *(Ṣād)*:21. Cf. also Ibn Ḥawqal, *al-Masālik wa-l-Mamālik,* 171.

144. Cf. Qur'ān 57 *(al-Ḥadīd)*:14. The reference is to the "wall with a door in it," which will separate Believers from unbelievers on the Day of the Gathering.

145. The sacred rock in the Temple of Jerusalem from which "the herald [the archangel Isrāfīl] will make proclamation from a place near at hand": Qur'ān 50 *(Qāf)*:41.

146. This shrine was connected in some way with the tradition of al-Jassāsah, the beast that will bring news to the Antichrist (*al-Masīḥ al-Dajjāl* < Aram. *Meshīḥa Daggāla:* see Matt. 24:24, Rev. 13:1–18, and Dan. 11:36. See also Ranking and Azoo, *Aḥsanu,* 247 n. 2.

147. The Gate of Forgiveness. Cf. Qur'ān 2 *(al-Baqarah)*:58: "When We said, 'Enter this town, and eat easefully from it wherever ye please; enter in at the gate with obeisance, and say Ḥiṭṭah [? Heb. *ḥēṭ'* = sin], and We shall forgive you your transgressions and increase those who do good.'" The gate is in the southwestern wall of the Ḥarām at Jerusalem.

148. One of the gates under the Dome of the Rock in Jerusalem, now known as "The Gate of Paradise" *(Bāb al-Jannah).*

149. Cf. Maqdisī, *Aḥsan:*

> At the distance of a *farsakh* from Ḥabrā is a low hill, overlooking the Lake of Ṣughar (Dead Sea) and the sites of the cities of Lūṭ, on which stands a mosque built by Abū Bakr al-Ṣabāḥī and called Masjid al-Yaqīn. In this mosque is to be seen the resting-place of Ibrāhīm, sunk about a cubit into the stony ground. It is related that when Ibrāhīm first saw from here the cities of Lūṭ in the air, he lay down on the ground, saying "Verily, I now bear witness that the word of the Lord is the Truth *(al-Yaqīn).*"

Cf. also Harawī, *al-Ishārāt,* Arabic text, 29–30; Sourdel-Thomine's translation, 71.

150. The tomb of the Virgin Mary is reputedly in a church close to the Garden of Gethsemane, outside the wall of Jerusalem, in the valley of Jehoshaphat. Rachel's grave is a short distance from the village of Bayt Laḥm: cf. Gen. 35:19.

151. Qur'ān 18 *(al-Kahf)*:60. The "two seas" have been glossed by most commentators as the Mediterranean and the Persian Gulf, but al-Maqdisī himself (*Aḥsan,* 19) contends that "God has actually called the Sea of al-Rūm by the name of 'the two seas.'"

152. Qur'ān 57 *(al-Ḥadīd)*:14.

153. Qur'ān 2 *(al-Baqarah)*:248. Sakīnah < Heb. Shechīnā. The precise implications of the term in this context are obscure. In the Qur'ān the word generally has the sense of "assurance," but it is doubtful if it bears that connotation on this occasion (cf. Richard Bell, *The Qur'ān* [Edinburgh, 1937], 1:36 n. 2). Other commentators have chosen to translate it as "glory" or "divine presence."

154. A small cupola standing in the shadow of the Qubbat al-Ṣakhrā within the Ḥarām al-Sharīf, and said by some (e.g., Mujīr al-Dīn, *al-Uns al-Jalīl fī-Ta'rīkh al-Quds wa-l-Khalīl* [Cairo, A.H. 1283/A.D. 1866], 241; all subsequent references are to this edition) to have served as a model at a reduced scale for the Qubbat al-Ṣakhrā. The chain referred to was the so-called Chain of David, allegedly used to discriminate truth from falsehood: the innocent could reach it, the guilty could not (but note that al-Maqdisī himself, on p. 46 of the *Aḥsan,* admits that this chain was equally likely to have been in al-Jashsh).

155. A reference to the tradition that shortly before the Day of the Gathering the Ka'bah will be removed from Makkah to Jerusalem.

156. I am particularly indebted to Ranking and Azoo, *Aḥṣanu,* 242–47, for identification and explication of several of the allusions in this passage from al-Maqdisī.

157. For the extension of the term *holy* from Jerusalem to Filasṭīn to the whole of al-Shām, see Goitein, "The Sanctity of Jerusalem and Palestine in Early Islam," 146. Typical of the vast range of works, both general and special, in which the sanctity of Filasṭīn was transmitted and discussed were Ibn al-Faqīh, *al-Buldān,* 93–97 and Nuwayrī, *Nihāyat al-Arab,* 1:325–39. For expositions of the consecrated status of Jerusalem and the surrounding territory in Islamic tradition, see al-Musharraf (d. 1099), *Kitāb Faḍā'il Bayt al-Maqdis wa-l-Shām* (cf. Brockelmann, *Geschichte, Supplement,* 1: 576, 876) and Ibn 'Asākir (d. 1203), *Kitāb al-Jāmi' al-Mustaqṣā fī Faḍā'il al-Masjid al-Aqṣā* (cf. Brockelmann, *Geschichte, Supplement,* 1:567 et seq.).

In early Islamic literature the full name of Jerusalem was Īliyā' (< Rom. Aelia) Madīnat Bayt al-Maqdis = "Aelia, the City of the Temple," (Ṭabarī, *Ta'rīkh,* 1:2360), but most commonly either Īliyā' or Bayt al-Maqdis was used alone. The latter term is the Arabicization of Aramaic Bēth Maqde'shā = "The Sacrosanct House," or "The Temple." Al-Quds (< Aram. Qudsha = "sanctuary"), which ultimately became the commonest Arabic name for Jerusalem, seems to have come into use only in the tenth century. It has not been found in any ninth-century works and occurs only once in Muṭahhar's *al-Bad',* written in 966 (vol. 6, p. 91: see next note), but is used fairly frequently by al-Maqdisī (ca. 985). Various Arabic renderings of Hebrew Shālēm and Aramaic Urishlem (Arabicized as Urshalīm) also occur from time to time, together with (in poetry only) al-Balāṭ = "royal residence" < Lat. *palatium* or "paved area" < Gk. *πλατεῖα.* See S. D. Goitein, *The Encyclopaedia of Islam,* 2d ed., 5:322–39 and note 520 to chapter 17 of the present text.

158. Muṭahhar ibn Ṭāhir al-Maqdisī, *Kitāb al-Bad' wa-l-Ta'rīkh* (966). See Cl. Huart, *Journal Asiatique* 18 (1901): 16–21. Throughout most of the Eastern Caliphate, this work was known simply as *Ta'rīkh-i-Maqdisī.*

159. Ibn Kathīr, *al-Bidāyah wa-l-Nihāyah,* 8:280.

160. Ibn Taymīyah, *Qā'idah fī Ziyārat Bayt al-Maqdis,* ed. Ch. D. Mathews, "A Muslim iconoclast (Ibn Taymiyyah on the 'merits' of Jerusalem and Palestine)," *Journal of the American Oriental Society* 56 (1936): 1–21.

161. Goitein, "The Sanctity of Jerusalem and Palestine in Early Islam," 141–42.

162. Ibid., 142.

163. It will be recalled from chapter 3 that al-Maqdisī was in no way ill disposed toward Ṣūfīs, actually having accepted the hospitality of followers of Sufyān al-Thawrī in their monastery on the Jawlān (Golan) Heights (*Aḥsan,* 188).

164. Cf. ibid., 184: "The greater proportion of holy places are to be found in the vicinity of Bayt al-Maqdis, although they occur in smaller numbers throughout Filasṭīn and, even more rarely, in Urdunn province."

165. Ibn Ḥanbal, *Musnad,* 12:177, no. 7191 and 241, no. 7248. Literally, the passage reads: "The [girths of the] camel saddles shall not be cinched except for [pilgrimages to] three mosques: the Masjid al-Ḥarām, my mosque, and the Aqṣā Mosque" *(lā tushaddu al-riḥālu illā ilā thalāthati masājida: ilā al-masjidi al-ḥarāmi wa-masjidī hādhā wa-l-masjidi al-aqṣā).* For a discussion of the implications of this particular *ḥadīth* and an exhaustive bibliography of similar versions, see Kister, "'You shall only set out for three mosques,'" 173–96. From time to time attempts, only partly reflected in the canonical collections of *ḥadīths*, were made to minimize the importance of Jerusalem vis-à-vis Makkah and al-Madīnah, to add to the list (e.g., al-Ṭūr), or to substitute another mosque for the one in Jerusalem (e.g., al-Kūfah by certain Shīʿites), but ultimately the claims of Jerusalem prevailed.

Al-Maqdisī and the other early topographers touched only the surface of the eschatological significance of Jerusalem. For a conspectus of Muslim traditions relating to the city, see J. W. Hirschberg, "The sources of Moslem traditions concerning Jerusalem," *Rocznik Orientalistyczny* 17 (1951–52): 314–50; also H. Lazarus-Yafeh, "The sanctity of Jerusalem in Islamic tradition," *Molad* 21 (1971): 219–27 (in Hebrew and not accessible to me).

166. In the earliest Islamic exegesis the Masjid al-Aqṣā was explicated as a heavenly sanctuary, possibly (as *The Encyclopaedia of Islam,* 1st ed., s.v. "Miʿradj" suggests) the highest of the seven heavens in which angels sing the praises of Allāh. Only subsequently (but long before the tenth century) was it accorded a terrestrial locus in Jerusalem.

167. The description is included in *Itinera et Descriptions Terrae Sanctae Lingua Latina, Saec. IV–XI. Exarata, Sumptibus Societatis Illustrandis Orientis Latini Monumentis,* ed. T. Tobler (Genève, 1877), 1:145, and translated from Latin into English in James Rose MacPherson, "Pilgrimage of Arculfus in the Holy Land (about the year A.D. 670)," *Palestine Pilgrims' Text Society* (London, 1889), 4–5. Cf. also P. Geyer, ed., *Itinera Hierosolymitana* (Prague, 1898), 226–27 and Adamnanus, *De Locis Sanctis,* ed. L. Bieler in *Itineraria et Alia Geographica,* 2 vols.: Corpus Christianorum, Series Latina, vols. 175 and 176 (Turnhout, Belgium, 1965), 1:186.

168. The Ṣakhrā is mentioned in the Talmud and Targums, but its legendary associations received their greatest elaboration in Muslim traditions: see, for example, *The Encyclopaedia of Islam,* 1st ed., s.v. "Ḳubbat al-Ṣakhrā."

169. Mujīr al-Dīn, *al-Uns al-Jalīl,* 1:240–43.

170. The late Professor Goitein argued strongly against what he called the "Shīʿite fable" propounded by al-Yaʿqūbī (*Taʾrīkh,* 2:11) and subsequent historians and topographers who copied from him—as well as by virtually all modern writers prior to the publication of Goitein's paper—that ʿAbd al-Malik built the Qubbat al-Ṣakhrā with the intention of diverting the *Ḥajj* from Makkah to Jerusalem. See "The Sanctity of Jerusalem and Palestine in Early Islam," 135–40, 147. Interestingly, among early writers, al-Maqdisī (*Aḥsan,* 159) was the one who, quoting his uncle, viewed the building of the Qubbat al-Ṣakhrā as a response to the cultural needs of the second generation of Muslims, as an irrefutable statement of the greatness and preeminence of Islam: "Is it not evident that ʿAbd al-Malik, observing the grandeur and magnificence of the Dome of the Dunghill (*al-Qumāmah:* a deliberate distortion of *al-Qiyāmah* = "The Resurrection," the name by which Christian Arabs knew the Church of the Anastasis, which had been erected over the supposed Holy Sepulchre in the time of Constantine) and fearing that it would seduce the hearts of Muslims, was moved to erect above the Ṣakhrā the dome which is now to be seen there?" For a recent critique of Goitein's views see Amikam Elad, "Why Did ʿAbd al-Malik Build the Dome of the Rock? A Re-Examination of the Muslim Sources," in *Bayt al-Maqdis: ʿAbd al-Malik's Jerusalem,* pt. 1, ed. Julian Raby and Jeremy Johns (Oxford, 1992), 33–58.

171. This date has been established, in spite of conflicting testimony among Arab authors, by K. A. C. Creswell (*A Short Account of Early Muslim Architecture,* 43) by means of information contained in contemporary papyri from Aphrodito in Upper Egypt: see H. I. Bell, *Greek Papyri in the British Museum,* vol. 4: *The Aphrodito Papyri,* 75–76.

172. The *Wuqūf,* "the standing [before God]" at ʿArafāt, constitutes the most essential part of the *Ḥajj;* in the succinct phrasing of the Tradition, "the Wuqūf is the Ḥajj." The ritual procedure as carried out in the provincial capitals was known as *ʿarraf (taʿrīf)* after Mount ʿArafāt, where the original ceremony took place: see Ibrāhīm Rifʿat, *Mirʾāt al-Ḥarāmyn* (al-Qāhirah, A.H. 1345/A.D. 1925), 1:141. Other cities known to have observed the custom of the *taʿrīf* included al-Baṣrah and al-Fusṭāṭ.

173. Nāṣir-i Khusraw, *Safar Nāmah,* trans. Guy Le Strange, *Palestine under the Moslems,* 88; Schéfer's translation, 66; Thackston's translation, 21.

174. Note that Nāṣir reports twenty thousand as the total population of both Jerusalem (*Safar Namāh,* Thackston's translation, 88) and Aṭrābulus (Thackston's translation, 349).

175. Qurʾān 21 *(al-Anbiyāʾ):* 71; cited by Maqdisī, *Aḥsan,* 173.

176. Maqdisī, *Aḥsan,* 157; cf. Ibn Ḥawqal, *al-Masālik wa-l-Mamālik,* 174: "a congregational mosque which surpasses in the elegance of its architecture all others in the lands of Islam."

177. Maqdisī, *Aḥsan,* 174.

178. Ibid., 178. The mantle had been given by Muḥammad to Yuḥannah ibn Rūbah, the so-called king of Waylah, who had negotiated with the Prophet in Tabūk during the Muslim expedition against the Greeks in the ninth year of the *Hijrah.* The text of the treaty is preserved in Ibn Hishām's recension of Ibn Isḥāq's *Sīrat*

Rasūl Allāh, Muṣṭafā al-Saqqā et al. edition, 902, where it is also noted that (in the eighth century) the people of Udhruḥ still retained a copy of the document. Although Udhruḥ was seemingly of small importance when al-Maqdisī and Ibn Ḥawqal were writing, a century earlier al-Yaʿqūbī (*al-Buldān,* 326) had designated it as the capital of al-Sharā' province.

179. Ibn Ḥawqal, *al-Masālik wa-l-Mamālik,* 182, 176–77. Other holy relics and sacred sites are mentioned by later authors, such as Yāqūt and al-Harawī, with the implication that they existed in the tenth century. Unless the implication is so strong as to amount to certainty, such sites are omitted from figure 12.

180. Yāqūt, *Muʿjam,* 3:761.

181. Ibn Ḥawqal, *al-Masālik wa-l-Mamālik,* 181–82; Yāqūt, *Muʿjam,* 2:218.

182. Ibn Ḥawqal, *al-Masālik wa-l-Mamālik,* 187.

183. And, incidentally, by *badū* who came out of the Syrian steppe to scavenge what the Greeks had left: ibid., 176.

184. Ṭarsūs had been reestablished by the ʿAbbāsid caliph al-Ma'mūn at the foot of the Taurus range, which, in Ibn Ḥawqal's words, "formed a barrier between the two worlds [of Islam and Christianity]."

185. Al-Ṭarsūsī (see chapter 17) purports to purvey the substance (he can hardly be quoting the actual words) of a peroration delivered by Abū ʿAbd Allāh al-Ḥusayn ibn Muḥammad al-Khawwās during the last Friday worship in the city's great mosque on 10 Shaʿbān 354/10 August 965:

> Hear me, O men of Ṭarsūs, as I speak to you.
> Here it was that the exalted Book of God used to be recited.
> Here it was that forays were launched into Byzantine territories.
> Here it was that all the affairs of the *thughūr* took their origin.

A curious feature of this last Muslim worship in Ṭarsūs was that al-Khawwās addressed the *Khuṭbah* to al-Muʿtaḍid (r. 892–902) as if he were still reigning, presumably implying that there had been no caliph worthy of the name since that time. See Marius Canard, "Quelques observations sur l'introduction géographique de la Bughyat at'-T'alab de Kamâl ad-Dîn ibn al-ʿAdîm d'Alep," *Annales d'Etudes Orientales d'Alger* 15 (1957): 41–53.

Al-Maqdisī (*Aḥsan,* 160) reports that, when Ṭarsūs fell to the Greeks, most of the inhabitants of the district *(ahl al-thughūr)* migrated to Bāniyās on the western slopes of the Syrian Jawlān. For further comments on Ṭarsūs see chapter 17.

186. Ibn Ḥawqal, *al-Masālik wa-l-Mamālik,* 177–78.

187. There is a useful statistical comparison of the urban systems of the *Junds* of Filasṭīn and al-Urdunn in late-Byzantine and ʿAbbāsid times in Walmsley, "Administrative Structure and Urban Geography," passim.

188. See H. Bietenhard, "Die Dekapolis von Pompeius bis Traian: ein Kapitel aus der neutestamentlichen Zeitgeschichte," *Zeitschrift des Deutschen Palästina-Vereins* 79 (1963): 24–58 and, in expanded form, *Die Dekapolis von Pompeius bis Trajan* (Frankfurt, 1963); S. T. Parker, "The Decapolis reviewed," *Journal of Biblical Literature* 94 (1975): 437–41. There is also a good deal of information about individual cities in Spijkerman, *The Coins of the Dekapolis and Provincia Arabia,* as well as in E. Schürer, *The History of the Jewish People in the Age of Jesus Christ* (Edinburgh, 1979), 2:130–55.

189. The cities cited here are those listed by Pliny the Elder, *Naturalis Historia* (A.D. 77), vol. 5, par. 74. Ptolemy, *Geographia* (ca. A.D. 150), bk. 5, chap. 7, offered a schedule of eighteen names from which, curiously, Raphana was missing.

190. Ibn Khurradādhbih, *al-Masālik wa-l-Mamālik,* Arabic text, 77–78; English text, 56–57. Cf. a shorter list in al-Faqīh (c. 903), *al-Buldān,* 116. Skythopolis, Pella, Gadara, Hippos, Gerasa, Dion, Abila, and Philadelphia had all been listed by both Hierocles *(Synecdemus)* and Georgius ("Description") probably late in the sixth century: see E. Honigman, *Le Synekdémos d'Hiéroklès et l'Opuscule Géographique de Georges de Chypre* (Bruxelles, 1939); also Jones, *The Cities of the Eastern Roman Provinces,* table 40.

191. See, for example, the papers presented to the Workshop on Late Antiquity and Early Islam held at the School of Oriental and African Studies, University of London, 25–27 April 1991 and subsequently published as *The Byzantine and Early Islamic Near East,* ed. King and Cameron.

192. This earthquake has customarily been dated to 747/48 (e.g., K. W. Russell, "The earthquake chronology of Palestine and Northwest Arabia from the 2nd through the mid 8th century A.D.," *Bulletin of the American Schools of Oriental Research* 260 [1985]: 47–49), but Yoram Tsafrir and Gideon Foerster have recently proposed a date of 749 based on a correlation of numismatic evidence with other available sources: "The dating of the earthquake of the sabbatical year 749 C.E.," *Tarbiz* 58 (1989): 357–62 (in Hebrew; revised English version in press).

193. Michael Avi-Yonah, "Scythopolis," *Israel Exploration Journal* 12 (1962): 123–34; Baruch Lifschitz, "Scythopolis: l'histoire, les institutions et les cultes de la ville à l'époque hellénistique et impériale," *Aufstieg und Niedergang der Römischen Welt* 2 (1978): 262–92; Gideon Fuks, *Greece in the Land of Israel—Beth Shean (Scythopolis) in the Graeco-Roman Period* (Jerusalem, 1983) (in Hebrew—not seen); and Yoram Tsafrir, "From Scythopolis to Baysan—Changing Concepts of Urbanism" (paper presented at the Workshop on Late Antiquity and Early Islam, School of Oriental and African Studies, University of London, 25–27 April 1991): cf. note 66 above.

It is curious that no Muslim topographer mentioned the linen manufacture for which Skythopolis had once been renowned. Its products had been praised in the Talmud and the fourth-century *Expositio Totius Mundi et Gentium,* while an edict of Diocletian at the end of the third century had permitted the highest prices to be charged for its cloths. See Tsafrir, "From Scythopolis to Baysan," 9–10. I am inclined to think that the industry had failed to reestablish itself after the earthquake of 749—although such speculation is hazardous in view of the meager attention that Muslim topographers paid to the textile industry of al-Shām (cf. note 88 above).

194. As early as the fourteenth century B.C., the city had figured in the Amarna correspondence as Bikhil (< Sem. *p.ḥ.l*). Macedonian colonists who settled there late in the fourth century B.C. honored it with the similarly sounding name of the Macedonian city of Pella. To that extent Yāqūt was only half correct when he characterized Fiḥl as "a foreign name without meaning in the Arabic tongue" (*Muʿjam,* 3:853 and *Marāṣid,* 2:365).

195. Yaʿqūbī, *al-Buldān,* 327.

196. On the history of Pella (Fiḥl) generally see Robert Houston Smith, *Pella of the Decapolis,* vol. 1 (Wooster, Ohio, 1973), and vol. 2 (1989). The Byzantine and early Islamic periods are treated in 1:57–76; Smith, "Pella of the Decapolis," *Arts and the Islamic World* (Spring 1984): 58–60; Alan Walmsley, "Ceramics and the social history of early Islamic Jordan: the example of Pella (Tabaqat Fahl)," *al-ʿUṣūr al-Wusṭā* 9, no. 1 (1997): 1–3, 12; A. W. McNicoll and A. Walmsley, "Pella/Fahl in Jordan during the Early Islamic Period," in *Studies in the History and Archaeology of Jordan,* no. 1, ed. Adnan Hadidi (Amman, 1982), 339–45; Rami G. Khouri, *The Antiquities of the Jordan Rift Valley* (Amman, 1988), 21–27; and Robert Houston Smith, "Trade in the Life of Pella of the Decapolis," in *Studies in the History and Archaeology of Jordan,* no. 3, ed. Hadidi (1987), 53–58. See also MacAdam, "Settlements and Settlement Patterns," 30–31.

197. C. H. Kraeling, ed., *Gerasa, City of the Decapolis* (New Haven, 1938); Iain Browning, *Jerash and the Decapolis* (London, 1982); Rami G. Khouri, *Jerash: A Frontier City of the Roman East* (London, 1986); and MacAdam, "Settlements and Settlement Patterns," 70–71, 76–77, which includes a bibliography of recent archaeological excavations.

198. MacAdam, "Settlements and Settlement Patterns," 85. This economic and social decline was typical of a general impoverishment of urban life in the Byzantine East in the century immediately preceding the Islamic conquest: see Hugh Kennedy, "The last century of Byzantine Syria: a reinterpretation," *Byzantinisches Forschungen* 10 (1985): 141–83. There is a discussion of the incidence of plague in al-Shām in Lawrence Conrad, "The Plague in Bilād al-Shām in Pre-Islamic Times," in *Bilād al-Shām* 1986, 2:143–63. For earthquake chronology in the region see note 192 above.

199. Henry I. MacAdam, "The History of Philadelphia in the Classical Period," in *Studies on the Citadel of Amman,* ed. Alastair Northedge (forthcoming) and Rami G. Khouri, *Amman: A Brief Guide to the Antiquities* (Amman, 1988).

200. Thomas Weber and Rami G. Khouri, *Umm Qais: Gadara of the Decapolis* (Amman, 1989) and Birgit Mershen and Ernst Axel Knauf, "From Gadar to Umm Qais," *Zeitschrift des Deutschen Palästina-Vereins* 104 (1988): 128–45.

201. W. Harold Mare, "Quwailiba: Abila of the Decapolis," *Archiv für Orientforschung* 33 (1986): 206–209; Michael Jeffrey Fuller, "Abila of the Decapolis: A Roman-Byzantine City in Transjordan," (Ph.D. diss., Washington University, 1987); Fuller, ed., *Abila Reports* (St. Louis Community College, Florissant Valley, 1986); and MacAdam, "Settlements and Settlement Patterns," 71–72.

202. Alison McQuitty, "Bait Ras," *Archiv für Orientforschung* 33 (1986): 153–55; C. J. Lenzen and E. A. Knauf, "Beit Ras/Capitolias: a preliminary evaluation of the archaeological and textual evidence," *Syria* 64 (1987): 21–46; and Lenzen, "Beit Ras excavations: 1988 and 1989," *Syria* 67 (1990): 474–76.

203. MacAdam, "Settlements and Settlement Patterns," 72.

204. Bert de Vries, "Umm al-Jimal in the Third Century," in *The Defence of the Roman and Byzantine East,* by P. W. M. Freeman and D. L. Kennedy (Oxford, 1986), 227–52; de Vries, "Urbanization in the Basalt Region of North Jordan in Late Antiquity: The Case of Umm el-Jimal," in *Studies in the History and Archaeology of Jordan,* ed. Adnan Hadidi, vol. 2 (London, 1985), 249–61; de Vries, "The Umm el-Jamil project, 1972–77," *Bulletin of the American Schools of Oriental Research* 244 (1981): 53–72 (figure 5, p. 102, is a plan of the city); Ernst Axel Knauf, "Umm el-Jimāl: an Arab town in late Antiquity," *Revue Biblique* 91 (1984): 578–86 (a summary of suggested identifications of this site with ancient names is presented on pp. 580–81); and Maurice Sartre, "Le peuplement et le développement du Hauran antique à la lumière des inscriptions grecques et latines," in *Hauran I: Recherches Archéologiques sur la Syrie du Sud à l'Époque Hellénistique et Romaine,* ed. J.-M. Dentzer, pt. 1 (Paris, 1985), passim but especially pp. 201–2.

205. Jean-Baptiste Humbert and Alain Desreumaux, "Huit campagnes de fouilles au Khirbet es-Samra (1981–1989)," *Revue Biblique* 97 (1990): 252–69 and MacAdam, "Settlements and Settlement Patterns," 73–74.

206. MacAdam, "Settlements and Settlement Patterns," 75–76.

207. Most such sites are listed and described in *Archaeology of Jordan,* ed. Dénise Homès-Fredericq and J. Basil Hennessy, 2 vols. (Leuven, 1986–89, continuing).

The so-called desert retreats of the Umayyads ought perhaps to be treated separately, as they were specialized, and in the long term transient, elements that for the most part were never fully integrated into the settlement hierarchy of al-Shām. In addition to those sites known respectively as Quṣayr ʿAmrah, Muwaqqar, Qasṭal, al-Azraq, al-Mshattā, al-Mafjar, al-Minyah, ʿAnjar, and the separate sites both called Qaṣr al-Ḥayr (listed in chapter 2 above), mention should also be made of Qaṣr Mushāsh, Qaṣr Kharānah, Dayr Kahf, Qaṣr Burquʿ, and Qaṣr Hallābāt. It must also be acknowledged that there is far from complete agreement on the functions of certain of these settlements. Some, such as Muwaqqar and Qasṭal, are documented in literary sources specifically as caliphal retreats, but in other instances the precise function is debatable or multiple purposes are suspected. Certainly there is no marked uniformity in the design of their structures. An interesting but not totally verified hypothesis as to the function of Qaṣr Kharānah has been advanced by Heinz Gaube ("Die syrischen Wüstenschlösser: einige wirtschaftliche und politische Gesichtspunkte zu ihrer Enstehung," *Zeitschrift des Deutschen Palästina-Vereins* 95 (1979): 182–209), and followed by Stephen Urice (*Qasr Kharana in the Trans-*

jordan [Durham, N.C., 1987], 88), namely that the settlement was established to serve as a meeting place for Umayyad and tribal leaders in the latter's territory. Cf. also Gaube, "Khirbat al-Bayda: A Reconsideration" (paper presented to the Workshop on Late Antiquity and Early Islam, University of London, 25–27 April 1991). Much the same interpretation has been advanced for Qaṣr Hallābāt by Ghazi Bisheh, "Qasr al-Hallabat: An Umayyad Desert Retreat or Farm-Land?" in *Studies in the History and Archeology of Jordan,* ed. Hadidi, 2:263–65; while others have seen in some of these constructions primarily a caravanserai function. Moreover, both Sauvaget ("Châteaux umayyades de Syrie," 1–49) and Grabar et al. (*City in the Desert,* chap. 8) have noted the probable role of local agriculture in the provisioning of these settlements. Nor would it be wholly unrealistic to suggest that some of the less grandiose of these establishments might have been desert estates of the type held by ʿAbd Allāh ibn ʿAmr al-ʿĀṣ (the scholar son of the conqueror of Palestine and Egypt) in the second half of the seventh century. See Michael Lecker, "The estates of ʿAmr b. al-ʿAṣ in Palestine: notes on a new Negev Arabic inscription," *Bulletin of the School of Oriental and African Studies* 52 (1989): 24–37. For similar estates in the Ḥijāz in the first Islamic century see Saleh A. El-Ali, "Muslim estates in Hidjaz in the first century A.H.," *Journal of the Social and Economic History of the Orient,* 2 (1959): 247–61. For an informative discussion of the range of possible functions that researchers have attributed to these desert complexes see R. Hillenbrand, "*La dolce vita* in early Islamic Syria: the evidence of later Umayyad palaces," *Art History* 5 (1982): 1–35.

Uncertainty often surrounds the dates and functions of these desert complexes, as does doubt regarding their patrons. The following ascriptions are probably reasonably close to prevailing scholarly opinion. It is likely that Khirbat al-Minyah, Usays, and ʿAnjar were built during the reign of al-Walīd I (705–15), with the first two being almost certainly intended as royal residences; Hishām (r. 724–43) constructed palaces at a place called Zaytūnah (identified by Grabar et al., *City in the Desert,* 13 as Qaṣr al-Ḥayr al-Sharqī) and at Quṭayyifah (Yaʿqūbī, *al-Buldān,* 325); Yazīd II (r. 720–24) spent a good deal of time at al-Muwaqqar and Bayt Ra's (Yāqūt, *Muʿjam,* 4:686; al-Iṣfahānī, *al-Aghānī,* 13:165); and al-Walīd II (r. 743–44) remodelled a Roman fort called al-Bakhrā, which was probably situated some twenty-five kilometers to the south of Palmyra (Tadmur) (D. Derenk, *Leben und Dichtung des Omaiyadenkalifen al-Walīd ibn Yazīd. Ein Quellenkritischer Beitrag* [Freiburg im Bresgau, 1974], 46 and Hillenbrand, "*La dolce vita,*" 22 n. 9), and lived at various times at Qasṭal (al-Iṣfahānī, *al-Aghānī,* 6:113), Zīzah, Ubāyir (possibly present-day Qaṣr Bāyir), and most frequently at al-Azraq. Al-Mshattā was probably the palace that he is known to have commissioned when he succeeded to the throne (Hillenbrand, "*La dolce vita,*" 22). According to R. W. Hamilton (cf. note 181 to chapter 2), Khirbat al-Mafjar was built by Walīd ibn Yazīd while he was heir apparent to Hishām, but Whitcomb is inclined to favor a later date.

208. Three Byzantine sites in the southern Ḥawrān that on present evidence failed to survive the conquest were southern Dayr Qīnn, Sabaʿ Asir, and Bāyir, but it is not impossible that their abandonment was unconnected with the Arab hegemony.

209. This conclusion is being voiced with increasing frequency and confidence by archaeologists concerned with the transitional period from late Byzantine to early Umayyad times. Not at all atypical is a paper by A. H. Zeyadeh, "Settlement Pattern: An Archaeological Assessment. Case Studies from Northern Palestine and Jordan" (presented to the Workshop on Late Antiquity and Early Islam, University of London, 25–27 April 1991). The same theme is reported to be the burden of the author's "An Archeological Assessment of Six Cities in al-Urdun [sic]: From the Fourth Century to the Mid-Eighth Century A.D.," in *The Fifth International Conference on the History of Bilād al-Shām during the ʿAbbāsid Period,* ed. Muḥammad ʿAdnān Bakhit and Muḥammad Yūnus al-ʿAbbadī, Arabic section (Ammān, 1992), 3–31.

210. The vexed question of the sequence of events involved in the Muslim siege of Arados/Arwād and its implications for the use of topoi and other stereotypical motifs in early Islamic tradition are discussed by Conrad, "The Conquest of Arwād," 317–401.

211. Peter Brown, *The World of Late Antiquity* (London, 1971), 202. It is not without interest that Seleucia-in-Pieria, the former outport of Antiocheia, was never integrated into this system of coastal defense.

212. This term has in fact been applied to the situation on the Ḥawrān by Kennedy, "The Towns of Bilād al-Shām and the Arab Conquest," 93.

213. Ibid., 95.

214. Yaʿqūbī, *al-Buldān,* 327.

215. I have found very little evidence that could be construed as supporting Walmsley's claim that "the towns of the eastern Wādī ʿArabah experienced a relative economic boom during the later 3rd/9th and 4th/10th centuries" ("Administrative Structure and Urban Geography," 278)—with the exception, of course, of Ṣughar.

The combination of forces responsible for urban decline on the desert borders is not at all clear but may well have involved the interaction of environmental as well as human factors. This is in fact the conclusion of Benjamin Z. Kedar, whose analyses of the incidence of arboreal pollen from boreholes in several parts of the Levant have led him to suggest that "the regional climate may have deteriorated in the seventh century" ("The Arab conquests and agriculture: a seventh-century apocalypse, satellite imagery, and palynology," *Asian and African Studies* 19 [1985]: 15). Although the curve of pollen content peaks in the mid-seventh century (or even at the end of the second century if the olive is included in the count), it continues to decline until late in the ninth century, implying thereby that the environment in at least parts of al-Shām, and those most likely the more arid areas, was turning at least mildly maladaptive throughout most of the period with which we are concerned. It is also worth noting that in this same paper Kedar has some interesting things to say about the implications for the Shāmī ecosystem of comments in the *Pirqe de-Rabbi Eliezer* (early ninth century), the *Nisterot Rabbi Shim'on ben Yokhay* (mid-eighth century), and the *Apocalypse of Pseudo-Methodius* (second half of the seventh century).

216. A. H. M. Jones et al., *The Cities of the Eastern Roman Provinces,* 2d ed. (Oxford, 1971).

Chapter Seven

Author's note: Jazīrah connotes essentially an island, but by extension a peninsula (as here) and even land lying between rivers (cf. chapter 5) or separated from centers of civilization by an expanse of desert. For al-Hamdānī the term *Jazīrat al-ʿArab* included not only the Arabian Peninsula proper but also al-ʿIrāq west of the Euphrates River and Greater Syria up to the frontier with Asia Minor (*Ṣifat Jazīrat al-ʿArab,* Müller's edition, 1:47–51). This author justified the use of the term *jazīrah* on the ground that the territory was surrounded by seas and rivers, including the Euphrates. Ibn Ḥawqal's name for the same area was *Diyār al-ʿArab* (*al-Masālik wa-l-Mamālik,* 18–41). Al-Maqdisī delimited his *Iqlīm Jazīrat al-ʿArab* as depicted in figure 3, thereby exluding all of al-Shām and a good deal of territory lying to the west of the Euphrates.

1. A reference to the circumstance that in Arabia, the heartland of Arab culture, there were originally no *dhimmīs* to pay either land tax *(kharāj)* or poll tax *(jizyah),* but only Arabs paying a personal religious tithe.

2. For details and illustrative texts see Ferdinand Wüstenfeld, *Die Chroniken der Stadt Mekka,* 4 vols. (Leipzig, 1858–61; reissued at Hildesheim, 1981), vols. 1 and 2. One such pretender in al-Madīnah, Muḥammad al-Nafs al-Zakīyah, had his claim to the caliphate certified by no less a scholar than Mālik ibn Anas (ca. 715–95), author of the first written compendium of Islamic law.

3. The Qarāmiṭah, usually classed as an aspect of the Ismaʿīlī movement, drew their inspiration from the Messianic ideals of radical Shīʿism. Their relationship to the Fāṭimids of North Africa has not yet been fully explained. See M. J. de Goeje, *Mémoire sur les Carmathes du Bahraïn et les Fatimides* (Leyden, 1886); W. Ivanow, "Ismailis and Qarmations," *Journal of the Bombay Branch of the Royal Asiatic Society* 16 (1940): 43–85; W. Madelung, "Fatimiden und Baḥrainqarmaṭen," *Der Islam* 34 (1959): 34–88; and *The Encyclopaedia of Islam,* 2d ed., vol. 4 (1978), 660–65.

4. Wüstenfeld, *Die Chroniken,* 2:205 ff.

5. Maqdisī, *Aḥsan,* 104.

6. The best account of the Yuʿfirids is still Charles L. Geddes, "The Yuʿfirid Dynasty of Ṣanʿāʾ" (Ph.D. diss., University of London, 1959). For the Zaydī Imāmate cf. C. van Arendonk, *Les Débuts de l'Imāmat Zaidite au Yemen* (Leyden, 1960), passim (this is a French translation of a doctoral thesis, "De Opkomst van het Zaidietische Imamaat in Yemen" University of Leiden, 1919).

For the symbolism inherent in the name Yaman see Suliman Bashear, "Yemen in early Islam: an examination of non-tribal traditions," *Arabica* 36 (1989): 327–61.

7. The Ziyādids claimed to be descended from Ziyād, the reputed son of Abū Sufyān of the Quraysh clan, but al-Maqdisī (*Aḥsan,* 104) accorded them a descent from the Hamdān, a powerful Ḥimyarite tribe. No other author made this claim, but it is true that the founder of the dynasty was already a dweller in al-Yaman when he was appointed to the governorship of the country by the caliph al-Maʾmūn. For a history of this dynasty through the nearly two centuries of its existence see Henry Cassells Kay, *Yaman, Its Early Mediaeval History* (London, 1892; reprint, Farnborough, Hampshire, 1968). The immediately relevant part of this volume is the text and annotated translation of a history of the Yaman written in the twelfth century by Najm al-Dīn ʿUmārah al-Ḥakamī at the behest of the Qāḍī al-Fāḍil, confident of Ṣalāḥ al-Dīn and one-time chief secretary in the Fāṭimid bureaucracy (see Ibn Khallikān, *Wafāyāt,* 2:367). Clearly, ʿUmārah's account of events that had transpired more than three centuries before his time is not wholly reliable in its details, although its general framework seems to be sound enough. In any case, it is the best available. ʿUmārah apparently derived some of his material from a now lost (except for fragmentary quotations) *Kitāb al-Mufīd fī Akhbār Zabīd* by Abū al-Ṭāmī Jayyāsh, a king of the Banū-Najāḥ dynasty.

An abridged history of Zabīd compiled in the fifteenth century by ʿAbd al-Raḥmān ibn ʿAlī ibn al-Daybaʿ al-Shaybānī al-Zabīdī, which survives in manuscript form in Cambridge and Paris, has been edited by Muḥammad al-Akwaʿ under the title *Qurrat al-ʿUyūn fī Akhbār al-Yaman al-Maymūn* (al-Qāhirah, A.H. 1397/A.D. 1977). A Latin abstract by C. T. Johannsen was published at Bonn as long ago as 1828. There is also much relevant information in the *Tārīkh al-Mustabṣir* attributed to the traveller Yaʿqūb ibn al-Mujāwir (ed. O. Löfgren under the title *Descriptio Arabiae Meridionalis, Taʾrīḫ al-Mustabṣir,* 2 vols. [Leiden, 1951–54]), who, although he was writing about 1260, often incorporated in his text material deriving ultimately from earlier periods.

It should be noted that, although Zabīd developed into a prestigious city under the aegis of the Banū-Ziyād, a less important settlement called Ḥuṣayb had existed on the site long before the beginning of the ninth century: see Hamdānī, *Ṣīfat Jazīrat al-ʿArab,* Akwaʿ edition, 73. For a detailed discussion of the city in early Islamic times see J. Chelhod, "Introduction à l'histoire sociale et urbaine de Zabīd," *Arabica* 25, pt. 1 (1978): 48–88.

8. Maqdisī, *Aḥsan,* 84–85. For a preliminary report on an archaeological survey undertaken by the Zabīd Project of the Royal Ontario Museum in 1982, see Edward J. Keall, "The dynamics of Zabid and its hinterland: the survey of a town on the Tihamah plain of North Yemen," *World Archaeology* 14, no. 3 (1983): 378–92. A collection of papers resulting from the Zabīd Project has been assembled by the Royal Ontario Museum under the title *Zabid: A Composite* (Toronto, n.d., although one paper is dated as recently as 1993).

9. Maqdisī, *Aḥsan,* 84.

10. Ibid., 77, 83. The Banū-Jaʿfar were the descendants of Jaʿfar ibn Abī Ṭālib, the caliph ʿAlī's brother who was killed at Muʾtah in 629 during the first Muslim campaign against the Greeks. He had three sons by his wife Asmāʾ, but of these only one, ʿAbd Allāh, had

issue. Al-Hamdānī (*Ṣifah,* al-Akwaʾ edition, 1:48) and al-Maqdisī (*Aḥsan,* 77) both noted that al-Juḥfah marked the point *(mīqāt)* at which Syrian pilgrims undertaking the *Ḥajj* should begin observing the canonically prescribed ritual requirements.

It is only fair to note that some revisionist historians and archaeologists doubt that Arabs played any significant role in the Ḥijāz before the reign of Muʿāwiyah, in which case the lack of growth of the settlement hierarchy would hardly be surprising: Koren and Nevo, "Methodological approaches to Islamic studies," 87–107, especially 100–3 and 104–6.

11. Maqdisī, *Aḥsan,* 80.

12. Ibid., 83. Ibn Ḥawqal (*al-Masālik wa-l-Mamālik,* 33) noted that the Ḥasanid family was still managing *waqfs* in Yanbuʿ that had been endowed by ʿAlī some three centuries previously. See also ʿArrām ibn al-Aṣbagh, *Kitāb Asmāʾ Jibal al-Tihāmah wa Makāniha* (ca. 845), ed. ʿAbd al-Salām Hārūn in Nawādir al-Makhṭūṭāt, vol. 2 (al-Qāhirah, A.H. 1374/A.D. 1954), 397–98; Hamdānī, *Ṣifah,* 1:171, 181, 219.

13. Maqdisī, *Aḥsan,* 79–80.

14. Ibid., 83. This author uses the orthography *Qurḥ.* For an archaeological survey of a site thought to be that of al-Qurāʾ, see A. A. Nasif, "The identification of the Wâdi ʾl-Qurâ and the ancient Islamic site of al-Mibyât," *Arabian Studies* 5 (1979): 1–19.

There is a good deal of useful ekistic information relating to al-Ḥijāz (and to elsewhere in Arabia) in the Early Islamic period in ʿArrām ibn al-Aṣbagh, *Asmāʾ Jibāl al-Tihāmah wa Makāniha,* 388–421; and Abdullah al-Wohaibi has made good use of this source in his *The Northern Hijaz in the Writings of the Arab Geographers 800–1150* (Beirut, 1973).

15. It is in this sense that I read Maqdisī, *Aḥsan,* 83.

16. Also known as Abū al-ʿAbbās (died ca. 688). He was a cousin of Muḥammad and ancestor of the ʿAbbāsid dynasts. So extensive was his knowledge of sacred and profane tradition, so sound his Qurʾānic exegesis, and so great his skill in jurisprudence, he became known by the title Sage of the *Ummah (Ḥibr al-Ummah).*

17. Died between 709 and 711.

18. Died in 693.

19. Cf. for example, al-Iṣfahānī, *al-Aghānī,* 14:164–72 and 17: 94, 97, 101–2; Ibn Khallikān, *Wafāyāt,* 1:377; Ibn Saʿd, *al-Ṭabaqāt,* 8:349; and Ibn Qutaybah, *al-Maʿārif,* 101, 109–110, 113, 122, 289–90. Persian and Byzantine slave singing-girls *(qiyān)* were numerous in al-Madīnah as early as Umayyad times, and the *Aghānī* (21: 197) contains references to houses of assignation patronized by no less a poet than al-Farazdaq (ca. 640–732). For an elaboration of this theme see Gaston Wiet, "La vie de plaisir, à la Mecque et à Médine au premier siècle de l'Islam," *Académie des Inscriptions et Belles-Lettres* (Paris, 1960), 417–25.

20. Cf., for example, Iṣfahānī, *al-Aghānī,* 3:103, 10:60.

21. Al-Maqdisī (*Aḥsan,* 86) is not entirely consistent on this point, but the general tenor of his remarks seems to imply that Ṣanʿāʾ was a larger city than Zabīd. See also Ibn Ḥawqal, *al-Masālik wa-l-Mamālik,* 36–37 and Minorsky, *Ḥudūd,* 146–47. The governor of Ṣanʿāʾ from 963/64 to 997 was the *amīr* ʿAbd Allāh ibn Qaḥṭān, grandnephew of Asʿad ibn Yuʿfur, last of the Yuʿfurid line to maintain his independence: see Kay, *Yaman,* note 8 on pp. 223–31. For a fairly full account of medieval Ṣanʿāʾ that is nearly a century earlier than al-Maqdisī's, see Ibn Rustah, *al-Alāq,* 109–13. Although this author did not visit the Yaman, he is known to have been in the Ḥijāz in 903 and seems, as far as his descriptions can be checked, to have consulted reliable informants. Al-Hamdānī's *Ṣifah* and *Iklīl,* from the first half of the tenth century, also contain much useful information, as does al-Rāzī's *Taʾrīkh Madīnat Ṣanʿāʾ* from the first half of the eleventh century.

22. Maqdisī, *Aḥsan,* 86. The early Islamic history of Ṣanʿāʾ is discussed with authority in Robert B. Serjeant and Ronald Lewcock, eds., *Ṣanʿāʾ. An Arabian Islamic City* (London, 1983), chaps. 5–7 and 10, and more briefly in Ronald Lewcock, *The Old Walled City of Ṣanʿāʾ* (Paris, 1986), 26ff. The argument that Ṣanʿāʾ was a sacred enclave in pre-Islamic times is advanced by Serjeant in chap. 5, "Ṣanʿāʾ the 'Protected' *Hijrah*" in the former of these two volumes.

23. The progenitor of this particular branch of the descendants of ʿAlī was Abū Muḥammad al-Qāsim of the Banū al-Rassī who died in 860. His grandson Yaḥyā ibn al-Ḥusayn was acknowledged as *imām* of Ṣaʿdah in 909–10. See the summary account of the history of the ʿAlawīyah dynasty provided by Najm al-Dīn ʿUmārah al-Ḥakamī as published by Kay, *Yaman,* 135–38 of the Arabic transcription, 184–90 of the English translation, and note 127 on pp. 314–16.

24. Ibn Ṭarf, who owed allegiance to Abū al-Jaysh Isḥāq ibn Ibrāhīm of the Ziyādite dynasty until the latter died in 981/82, ruled over territories extending along the Tihāmah from Ḥaly to al-Sharjah. By Ḥaḍramawt, al-Maqdisī was presumably referring to the ancient town of Shibām, which as early as the seventh century an agent of the Prophet is said to have constituted as the seat of Islamic government for the western sector of the Wādī. Al-Hamdānī records that by the beginning of the tenth century it was prospering as the principal commercial center of the Wādī, with no fewer than thirty mosques. Even after being pillaged by Kindah tribes, it seems to have recovered, for in 1055 it successfully resisted an incursion by Yamanī Ṣulayḥids. For ʿAdan see below.

25. Maqdisī, *Aḥsan,* 94–95; Ibn Ḥawqal, *al-Masālik wa-l-Mamālik,* 25; and Nāṣir-i Khusraw, *Safar Nāmah,* Schéfer's translation, 225–33; Thackston's translation, 86–90. Archaeological research in al-Ḥasaʾ district is summarized in Donald S. Whitcomb, "The archaeology of al-Hasaʾ oasis in the Islamic period," *Atlal: The Journal of Saudi Arabian Archaeology* 2 (1978): 95–113.

26. Maqdisī, *Aḥsan,* 94. For a brief summary of the little that is known about the coastal tracts between al-Baḥrayn and the Bāṭinah in the early Islamic period, see J. C. Wilkinson, "A sketch of the historical geography of the Trucial Oman down to the beginning of the sixteenth century," *The Geographical Journal* 130 (1964): 337–47.

27. See George Percy Badger, *History of the Imams and Seyyids of 'Omân, by Salîl-ibn-Razîk, from* A.D. 661–1856. Hakluyt Society, 1st ser., no. 44 (London, 1871), xv n. 1. Certainly, this nineteenth-century compilation is not an especially reliable source for events of the tenth century. For archaeological discoveries relating to northern ʿUmān in Islamic times, see Donald S. Whitcomb, "The archaeology of Oman: a preliminary discussion of the Islamic periods," *The Journal of Oman Studies* 1 (1975): 123–157: "Early Islamic" (A.D. 630–1055/A.H. 9–447) on pp. 125–26. The early Islamic history of the whole region is sketched briefly but insightfully by J. C. Wilkinson in "The Origins of the Omani State," in *The Arabian Peninsula: Society and Politics,* ed. Derek Hopwood (London, 1972), 67–88. This author shows that from Nazwah the *imām* was able to directly control virtually all the important tribal groupings in the early ʿUmānī state, which were in fact represented by important clans in the villages of the Jawf. But Wilkinson also cautions that the terms *seat of government* or *capital* should be used with discretion. "The whole structure of imamate government," he writes, "deriving in large measure from the structure of bedu society, militate[d] against a sophisticated government machinery or any court society. Whilst the imam's residence represent[ed] the focal point in the Ibadi community physical power remain[ed] vested in the hands of the leaders of the community" (78).

28. Ibn al-Athīr, *al-Kāmil,* 8:419.

29. Maqdisī, *Aḥsan,* 92. See also Ibn Ḥawqal, *al-Masālik wa-l-Mamālik,* 38–39. There is a good deal of useful information on this city and its hinterland in J. C. Wilkinson's "Ṣuḥār (Sohar) in the Early Islamic Period: The Written Evidence," in *South Asian Archaeology,* ed. M. Taddei, vol. 2 (Naples, 1979), 887–907, and an excellent discussion of the environmental setting of Ṣuḥār in the early Islamic period by P. M. Costa and T. J. Wilkinson, "The hinterland of Sohar. Archaeological surveys and excavations within the region of an Omani seafaring city," *The Journal of Oman Studies* 9 (1987): whole issue, especially chap. 5, "The Early Islamic Cultivation Systems of Sohar."

30. Ibn Ḥawqal, *al-Masālik wa-l-Mamālik,* 33.

31. Ibid., 34. The bifurcating caravan route from ʿAdan to Makkah by way of either Zabīd or Ṣanʿāʾ is clearly depicted on al-Maqdisī's map of Arabia (most conveniently reproduced in Konrad Miller, *Mappae Arabicae,* extracts and index arr. Heinz Gaube under the title *Beihefte zum Tübinger Atlas des vorderen Orients,* Reihe B. Geisteswissenschaften no. 65, 2 vols. [Wiesbaden, 1986], Tafelband, 26, 27; see also Tibbetts, "The Balkhī school of geographers," 124 and Collins, *al-Muqaddasī,* 71, with place names transcribed on p. 442). On another map from the Balkhī school, attributed specifically to al-Iṣṭakhrī and dating from up to half a century earlier, however, only the eastern route through Ṣanʿāʾ is depicted, while the nodal position of al-Madīnah (Medina) is emphasized even though Makkah (Mecca) is represented as the undisputed sacral center. Routes from Maʿān, al-Raqqah, al-Kūfah, al-Baṣrah, al-Baḥrayn, Ḥajar, and Makkah are all shown converging on al-Madīnah (Miller, *Mappae Arabicae,* Tafelband, 24, 25). I am indebted to Dr. Donald Whitcomb for bringing this latter map to my attention.

32. Al-Maqdisī underestimated the distance from Ṣuḥār to Biʾr al-Silāḥ, assigning a total of only eighty-four miles to what was in fact rather more than twelve degrees of longitude.

33. Maqdisī, *Aḥsan,* 110–11. This author's map of the Arabian Desert is reproduced in Tibbetts, "The Balkhī school of geographers," 124 and Collins, *al-Muqaddasī,* 224.

34. Aḥmad ibn Abī Yaʿqūb al-Yaʿqūbī, *Mushākalat al-Nās li-Zamānihim wa-mā Yaghlibu ʿalayhim fī Kulli ʿAṣrin,* trans. William G. Millward under the title "The adaptation of men to their time: an historical essay by al-Yaʿqūbī," *Journal of the American Oriental Society* 84 (1964): 339–40. It was al-Fākihī, an historian of Makkah writing in 885, who furnished *Kitāb Akhbār Makkah,* the fullest account of Zubaydah's benefactions (*Kitāb Akhbār Makkah,* ed. Ferdinand Wüstenfeld under the title *Die Chroniken der Stadt Mekka,* vol. 2 [Leipzig, 1861], 33, 35). So numerous were they along the pilgrim road from al-Kūfah to Makkah that it was known popularly as the Darb Zubaydah and became the stuff of which legends were made, as when the former queen assured an interrogator from beyond the grave that Allāh had forgiven her transgressions with the first stroke of the mattock on the Makkah road: Al-Khaṭīb al-Baghdādī, *Taʾrīkh,* 14:433–34. In fact at least three of the post stages on that route bore the name Zubaydīyah. See also Saʿd A. al-Rāshid, *Darb Zubaydah. The Pilgrim Road from Kufa to Mecca* (al-Riyāḍ, 1980).

35. For Ibn Salāmah see Ronald Lewcock, *Wādī Ḥaḍramawt and the Walled City of Shibām* (Paris, 1986), 32. Ibn Āmir is quoted in M. J. Kister, "Some reports concerning Mecca," 91, citing Balādhurī, *Ansāb al-Ashrāf,* MS. fol. 799b. The pilgrim routes through the northern Ḥijāz are analyzed with exemplary thoroughness by Wohaibi, *The Northern Hijaz in the Writings of the Arab Geographers,* pt. 2, 315–95.

36. The "Sea of China" was the name used by al-Maqdisī (*Aḥsan,* 12–13) to denote the Indian Ocean in general. Al-Ṣīn (< MPers. *Čin* < Anc. Chin. **Dzʿi̯ĕn* = the style of the dynasty that unified most of China in 221 B.C.: cf. Paul Pelliot, *Notes on Marco Polo,* vol. 1 [Paris, 1959], p. 270) in the Middle Ages referred to all the lands lying beyond present-day Singapore or thereabouts on the sea route to the East, but al-Maqdisī used the term *Sea of China* in the sense of "the sea stretching as far as China," a phrase that he did in fact employ on p. 97. The sea of the Franks, also called the sea of al-Shām (Greater Syria), was the Mediterranean.

37. Maqdisī, *Aḥsan,* 34, 86, 92.

38. Ibid., 92. See also Ibn Ḥawqal, *al-Masālik wa-l-Mamālik,* 38–39 and more generally A. Williamson, *Sohar and Omani Seafaring in the Indian Ocean* (Muscat, 1973); also the same author's "Persian Gulf commerce in the Sasanian period and the first two centuries of Islam," *Bastanshenasi va Honar-i Iran,* vols. 9–10 (1972).

39. Maqdisī, *Aḥsan,* 93. Testimony to the role of al-Masqaṭ in Eastern commerce is provided by Ibn al-Faqīh (*al-Buldān,* 11–12),

who, late in the ninth century, designated it as the port of departure for vessels sailing to Kūlam Malaya = Kollam (Quilon) in the Malaya country, that is, Malabar. Cf. also the anonymous *Akhbār al-Ṣīn wa-l-Hind,* compiled in 851: ed. Jean Sauvaget (Paris, 1948), 7–8.

40. Ibn Ḥawqal, *al-Masālik wa-l-Mamālik,* 37 (who, contradicting al-Maqdisī, notes that ʿAdan was only a small city: "there are larger cities in al-Yaman which are not so well known"); Maqdisī, *Aḥsan,* 85; and Minorsky, *Ḥudūd,* 147.

41. On this point see R. Simon, "Ḥums et īlāf," 23:223 n. 61, citing Azraqī, *Akhbār Makkah,* in *Die Chroniken der Stadt Mekka,* ed. Ferdinand Wüstenfeld, vol. 1 (Leipzig, 1858), 99. Cf. also Frants Buhl, *Das Leben Muhammeds* (Leipzig, 1930), 106 n. 24. For discussion of the possibility of Juddah having existed in pre-Muslim times (as was claimed by Ibn al-Mujāwir, *Tārīkh al-Mustabṣir* (1: 42), see G. R. Hawting, "The origin of Jedda and the problem al-Shuʿaybah," *Arabica* 31 (1984): 318–26. Ḥamad al-Jāsir's attempt to locate al-Shuʿaybah (*Fī Shamāl Gharb al-Jazīrah* [Riyāḍ, A.H. 1390], 173–74), which several Islamic traditions designate as the port of Makkah in Jāhilī times, does not carry conviction.

42. Maqdisī, *Aḥsan,* 79; but contrast Ibn Ḥawqal (*al-Masālik wa-l-Mamālik,* 31–32), who reported a decline in the prosperity of the port consequent on the flight of many of its patrician class when the Makkan Sharifate was established. Was al-Maqdisī's information outdated or had the trade of the port revived by the last decades of the century, in which case Ibn Ḥawqal would have been at fault? The Persian connection was emphasized by Ibn al-Mujāwir (*Tarīlch al-Mustabṣir,* 1:42) and is attributed by Hawting ("The Origin of Jedda," 321) to the decline of the Gulf port of Sīrāf.

43. Maqdisī, *Aḥsan,* 83.

44. Ibid., 83, and 97, where al-Jār is bracketed with Juddah as one of the two principal ports of entry for Egyptian grain destined for Makkah. Ibn Khurradādhbih (*al-Masālik wa-l-Mamālik,* 153) notes that in his day, both Juddah and al-Jār were frequented by Muslim traders coming alike from the east and the west. See also Yaʿqūbī, *al-Buldān,* 341; Ibn Rustah, *al-Aʿlaq,* 99; and Iṣṭakhrī, *al-Masālik wa-l-Mamālik,* 23.

45. Maqdisī, *Aḥsan,* 83.

46. Ibid., 86.

47. A resin exuded from the bark of *Callitris quadrivalvis* and used as incense and in the making of a pale-colored varnish; also known as juniper resin.

48. Probably the plural of *sharb:* See Serjeant, *Islamic Textiles,* s.v. in the very full index.

49. Maqdisī, *Aḥsan,* 97.

50. Abū Zayd al-Sīrāfī, supplement to *Akhbār al-Ṣīn wa-l-Hind,* cited from J. T. Reinaud's edition of the text in *Relations des Voyages Faits par les Arabes et les Persans dans l'Inde et à la Chine dans le IXe Siècle de l'Ère Chrétienne,* vol. 1 (Paris, 1845), 92; also Gabriel Ferrand, *Voyage du Marchand Arabe Sulaymān . . . Suivi de Remarques par Abū Zayd Ḥasan* (Paris, 1922).

51. Masʿūdī, *Murūj,* 307.

52. The vexed question of the location of Kalah is discussed in the light of Arabo-Persian texts in G. R. Tibbetts, *A Study of the Arabic Texts Containing Material on South-East Asia.* Oriental Translation Fund, n.s., 44 (Leiden, 1979), s.v. in the index; and from the perspective of East Asian sources in Paul Wheatley, *Nāgara and Commandery. Origins of the Southeast Asian Urban Traditions,* University of Chicago, Department of Geography Research Papers no. 207–8 (Chicago, 1983), 234–36 and 254 n. 28. For additional bibliographical materials consult note 24 to chapter 10.

53. Cf. Minorsky, *Ḥudūd,* 148. Frankincense, a gum resin produced by several members of the genus *Boswellia,* in Arabia grows only in Dhufar between longitudes 53° and 55° east and from the central zone of the coastal plain to the lower slopes of the Qarah Mountains, a distribution almost certainly related to the belt of summer rain induced by a seasonal monsoonal indraft. Myrrh is a fragrant gum resin yielded by the genus *Commiphora,* which appears at all times to have been restricted to the southwest corner of Arabia—in which case Shiḥr must have been an entrepôt handling long-distance trade to the east. Mining at unspecified localities in ʿUmān is mentioned by al-Masʿūdī, *Murūj,* 1:242. Production in the ninth and tenth centuries is summarized by Whitcomb, "The archaeology of Oman," 126 and 131 n. 12 and documented archaeologically by G. Weisgerber, "Archaeological evidence of copper exploitation at ʿArja," in Costa and Wilkinson, "The hinterland of Sohar," chap. 8. For archaeological excavations in the Wādī al-Jizzī in general and at ʿArjah in particular see ibid., chaps. 6 and 7. Al-Hamdānī's report in the *Iklīl* that ʿUmān manufactured a thousand hauberks (sing. *dirʿ;* pl. *durū, adruʿ*) annually is evaluated by David Nicolle in "Arms manufacture and the arms trade in South-Eastern Arabia in the Early Muslim period," *The Journal of Oman Studies* 6 (1983): 231–38.

54. Following a textual emendation to p. 98 of al-Maqdisī's text by Ranking and Azoo (*Aḥsanu,* 149).

55. Considerable esteem attached to the cotton stuff from Suḥūlā in the Yaman because Tradition asserted that the corpse of the Prophet had been shrouded in three pieces of this *suḥūlīyah;* cf., for example, O. Houdas and W. Marçais, trans., *El-Bokhâri: Les Traditions Islamiques,* vol. 1 (Paris, 1905), 409 (*bāb* 19) and Al-Zamakhsharī, *Kitāb al-Amkinah wa-l-Jibāl wa-l-Miyāh,* ed. S. de Grave (Leyden, 1856), 85.

56. Abstracted mainly from Maqdisī, *Aḥsan,* 98, supplemented by incidental comments in Ibn Ḥawqal, *al-Masālik wa-l-Mamālik,* and the *Ḥudūd.*

57. Hamdānī, *Ṣifah,* 1:202.

58. Cf. the works of Wensinck and von Grünebaum cited in notes 80 and 91 to chapter 4.

59. Azraqī (died ca. 858), *Akhbār Makkah,* Wüstenfeld edition, 1:1. Kʿab al-Aḥbār, a converted Jew, was a contemporary of the Prophet. He died in 652 or 654.

60. Qurʾān 79 *(al-Nāziʿāt):* 30.

61. Wüstenfeld, *Die Chroniken der Stadt Mekka,* 3:442, citing Ibn Sabʿīn (Quṭb al-Dīn, ca. 1217–69), *al-Ajwibah ʿan al-Asʾilah al-Ṣiqilliyah* (unpublished).

62. ʿAlī ibn Burhān al-Dīn al-Ḥalabī (d. 1634), *al-Sīrat al-*

Ḥalabīyah, vol. 1 (al-Qāhirah, A.H. 1329/A.D. 1911), 196. ʿAbd Allāh ibn ʿAbbās died probably in 687–88.

63. Wensinck, "The ideas of the Western Semites," 15, citing al-Kisāʾī, *ʿAjāʾib al-Malakūt* (Leiden MS. Wanner 538), fol. 15r.

64. Ferdinand Wüstenfeld, *Zakarija ben Muhammed ben Mahmud el-Cazwinis Kosmographie,* vol. 1: *Kitāb ʿAdjīʾib al-Makhlūqāt* (Göttingen, 1848). For a discussion of *pars pro toto* as a figure of cosmological thought see Wheatley, *The Pivot of the Four Quarters,* 428–36.

Dr. Whitcomb has pointed out that the Balkhī-style map of Arabia designated Iṣṭakhrī II and dated to the mid-tenth century discriminates very clearly between the nodal position of al-Madīnah as the focus of routes from all parts of the *iqlīm* and the relative isolation of Makkah. In fact the seasonally utilized pilgrimage routes are almost totally ignored (Whitcomb, "Urbanism in Arabia," 50 n. 12), although Makkah is depicted unmistakably as a preeminent religious center. It should not go unnoticed, however, that this distinction is not apparent on al-Maqdisī's map of Arabia (Collins, al-Muqaddasī, 71).

65. Thaʿālibī, *al-Laṭāʾif al-Maʿārif,* 155; Bosworth's translation, 117–18. Al-Thaʿālibī also repeats a story that he had picked up from the works of al-Jāḥiẓ (*al-Ḥayawān,* 3:142–43) and Ibn Rustah (*al-Aʿlaq,* 59):

> Al-Madīnah has acquired the alternative name of Ṭaybah on account of its fragrance counteracting the unpleasantness of its situation. This fragrance diffuses itself through the currents of the earth, into the odour of its soil, and into the breezes of its atmosphere. The delectable scent characteristic of its streets and gardens is an indication that when the city was constituted a *ḥaram,* it also became a miraculous symbol. Perfumes, incense, and aromatic substances are several degrees more fragrant at al-Madīnah than in other lands, even though these latter may be more costly and more highly esteemed. Whereas in many places, such as the capital city al-Ahwāz and Anṭākiyah, perfume undergoes a transformation and its fragrance evaporates, in al-Madīnah a pinch of salt placed, together with a small piece of aromatic substance (which, because it is so common there, is of low value) on the head of a young black slave-girl acquires a sweet odour and fragrance unequalled even by the bridal chamber of a woman of high rank. Even soaked date stones, which are considered by the people of al-ʿIrāq to have an excessively unpleasant smell when immersed in water for a long time, would be extremely sweet-smelling at al-Madīnah.

66. According to Yaʿqūt (*Muʿjam,* 1:423), Muḥammad had given this particular mantle to Yuḥannah ibn Ruʾbah, the *shaykh* of Waylah, who had visited him at Tabūk during his expedition against the Greeks in 630.

67. Hūd was the prophet sent to, but rejected by, the tribe of ʿĀd in the Ḥaḍramawt: see Qurʾān 46 *(al-Aḥqāf)*:21.

It is a moot point whether the tomb of Eve—first mentioned by al-Idrīsī and Ibn al-Jubayr in the twelfth century and surviving until its destruction by Wahhābīs in 1926—was in existence in Juddah in the tenth century: see Hawting, "The Origin of Jedda," 319. On this tomb more generally consult Nallino, *Raccolta di Scritti Editi e Inediti,* vol. 1 (Roma, 1939), 155 and A. Pesce, *Jiddah: Portrait of an Arabian City* (London, 1974), 126–30.

68. Maqdisī, *Aḥsan,* 80.

69. Ibid.

70. Saleh A. el-Ali, "Muslim estates in Hidjaz in the first century A.H.," *Journal of the Social and Economic History of the Orient* 2 (1959): 251, 254.

71. Tabari, *Taʾrīkh,* 2:1910.

72. Al-Maqdisī's phrase: *Aḥsan,* 87.

73. *Julandā* was originally the title of an Arab chieftain who exercised local control over the settled tracts of ʿUmān under Sāsānian hegemony. When, a few years after the Islamic conquest, the caliphate relinquished direct administration of the region, the Julandā resumed authority over a fragmented tribal system that Wilkinson characterizes as differing little from that of the desert *badū* ("The Origins of the Omani State," 74). See also J. C. Wilkinson, "The Julanda of Oman," *The Journal of Oman Studies* 1 (1975): 97–108.

74. Nazwah succeeded Rustāq as chief town in the interior of ʿUmān, a position it had held since Sāsānian times.

75. Al-Maqdisī's phrase: *Aḥsan,* 93.

Chapter Eight

Several valuable tools in the form of secondary analytical works are available for reconstructing the urban systems of the tenth-century Īrānian culture realm. Among these, pride of place must go to Barthold's (Bartol'd) *Istoriko-Geograficheskii obzor Irana.* A contemporary of Barthold was Josef Markwart (Marquart), whose *Ērānšahr nach der Geographie des Ps. Moses Xorenacʿi. Mit Historisch-Kritischen Kommentar und Historischen und Topographischen Excursen* (Abhandlungen der Königlichen Gesellschaft der Wissenschaften zu Göttingen, Phil.-Hist. Kl., n.s., vol. 3 [Berlin, 1901]) is nominally a translation of an inconsequential Armenian topography, but on which the translator lavished a massively erudite commentary that a century later still throws light on the topography and toponymy of the Persian-speaking territories in medieval times. Third, there is Paul Schwarz's utterly comprehensive *Iran im Mittelalter nach der Arabischen Geographen,* 9 vols. (Leipzig, Zwickau, Stuttgart, Berlin, 1896–1936; reissued Hildesheim, 1969). It must be understood, though, that each of these storehouses of immensely valuable information is still only a descriptive work concerned with the mechanics of historical reconstruction. Indeed, al-Maqdisī, with his concern for urban hierarchies and functional urban systems, offers a more sophisticated conceptualization; but as textual exegetes making the substance of difficult texts available to an unspecialized readership, Barthold, Markwart, and Schwarz were probably unsurpassed in any textual tradition.

In the English-speaking world, Le Strange's *The Lands of the Eastern Caliphate* still affords a valuable reconstruction of the Īrānian settlement pattern to the end of the ʿAbbāsid period; while *The*

Cambridge History of Iran, vol. 4, *The Period from the Arab Invasion to the Saljuqs,* ed. Richard N. Frye (Cambridge, 1975) provides a comprehensive overview of the period with which we are concerned. The continuing *Encyclopedia Iranica,* edited by Ehsan Yarshater (3 volumes published to date), is a mine of information and bibliographical reference for the topics that have been covered thus far. For German-speaking scholars Bertold Spuler has made available a vast amount of information on the Īrānian cultural realm in his *Iran in Früh-Islamischer Zeit: Politik, Kultur, Verwaltung und Öffentliches Leben Zwischen der Arabischen und der Seldschukischen Eroberung 633 bis 1055* (Wiesbaden, 1952). I must also note the existence of a huge secondary literature in Russian relevant to this and the following six chapters, the substance of which has been accessible to me only through the medium of Svat Soucek's translation of Barthold's *Historical Geography* and by title and brief description in Masashi Haneda and Toru Miura, *Islamic Urban Studies: Historical Review and Perspectives* (London and New York, 1994), 83–184, 235–328.

1. During the twelfth century, under the later Saljuks, al-Jibāl Province came to be known as Persian ʿIrāq (ʿIrāq ʿAjamī, *ʿajamī* being a word originally used to denote any foreigner but subsequently becoming restricted to the Persian foreigner); cf. Yāqūt, *Muʿjam,* 2:15 and Le Strange, *The Lands of the Eastern Caliphate,* 185–86.

2. The most comprehensive exposition of the physiography of Īrān, including al-Jibāl, is to be found in *The Cambridge History of Iran,* vol. 1, *The Land of Iran,* ed. W. B. Fisher (Cambridge, 1968), chaps. 1–8.

3. The name of this city was usually written Hamadhān by Arab topographers; Gk. Ekbatana probably < *hangmata* = "[place of] gathering"; Ahmatan and Hamatan in Armenian sources; Aḥmetā in Ezra 6:2. In Parthian and Sāsānian times the city had been a royal resort during the summer months. It is greatly to be regretted that neither Abū Shujāʿ Shīrawayh ibn Shahvdār's early twelfth-century history of Hamadān nor any of the other histories of the city listed by Ḥājjī Khalīfah (*Kashf al-Ẓunūn,* 1:310) have survived.

4. Maqdisī, *Aḥsan,* 392.

5. Ibn Ḥawqal, *al-Masālik wa-l-Mamālik,* 256, 260.

6. Ibn al-Faqīh, *al-Buldān,* 219. The *sāruq* (< Pers. *srk/srwk* = fortress) is believed by A. S. Shahbazī here to have denoted the state treasury ("From Parsa to Taxt-e Jamšid," *Archäologische Mitteilungen aus Iran* 10 [1977]: 197–207). For the broader implications of this identification see Donald S. Whitcomb, *Before the Roses and Nightingales: Excavations at Qasr-i Abu Nasr, Old Shiraz* (New York, 1985), 229–50.

7. Maqdisī, *Aḥsan,* 392.

8. Masʿūdī, *Murūj,* 2:396.

9. Ibn al-Athīr, *al-Kāmil,* 8:404. On this city generally see Schwarz, *Iran,* 5:513–34.

10. Also Qirmāsīn, Qirmāshīn, Qarmāsīn, etc.; Pahlavi Kirmānshāhān. The site of the city in Islamic times was on elevated ground to the northwest of present-day Kirmānshāh. See Laurence Lockhart, *Persian Cities* (London, 1960), 101–3; Schwarz, *Iran,* 445ff.; and A. K. S. Lambton, *The Encyclopaedia of Islam,* 2d ed., 5:167–71.

11. Cf. especially Maqdisī, *Aḥsan,* 257 ff., although this author's dating of the foundation to the end of the fifth or first third of the sixth century is not supported by all early topographers: see, for example, Barthold, *Historical Geography,* 197.

12. Ibn Ḥawqal, *al-Masālik wa-l-Mamālik,* 256, 265.

13. Maqdisī, *Aḥsan,* 393.

14. Al-Rayy < Raga; Gk. Rhages.

15. Maqdisī, *Aḥsan,* 391.

16. Iṣṭakhrī, *al-Masālik wa-l-Mamālik,* 207.

17. This is what the texts appear to imply, although their import is by no means unambiguous: cf. Yaʿqūbī, *al-Buldān,* 275; Ibn Rustah, al-Aʿlaq, 168; Ibn Ḥawqal, *al-Masālik wa-l-Mamālik,* 265, 269–70; Maqdisī, *Aḥsan,* 390–91; and Yāqūt, *Muʿjam,* 2:153 and 894–95, 3:855, and 4:431. Comparison of the descriptions of the several tenth-century authors with an old topographical account preserved by Yāqūt would seem to indicate that the Madīnah, originally developed under the walls of a hilltop citadel, had become the focus of activity during the earlier years of the Islamic period. However, when the future caliph al-Mahdī reconstructed the old citadel precinct under the name of Muḥammadīyah, the center of gravity of the city reverted to its original site.

18. Ibn Ḥawqal, *al-Masālik wa-l-Mamālik,* 265. For a brief conspectus of the turbulent political and sectarian history of al-Rayy (Rey) during the tenth century, particularly insofar as it was influenced by the Ismāʿīlīs, see S. M. Stern, "The early Ismāʿīlī missionaries in north-west Persia and in Khurāsān and Transoxania," *Bulletin of the School of Oriental and African Studies* 23 (1960): 62–63.

19. Maqdisī, *Aḥsan,* 386. For the history of the Jewish community in Iṣfahān see W. J. Fischel, "Isfahan. The Story of a Jewish Community in Persia," in *Joshua Starr Memorial Volume* (New York, 1953), 111–28.

20. Rendered in Arabic as *al-Madīnah* by Maqdisī, *Aḥsan,* 386–89. Ibn Rustah (*al-Aʿlaq,* 160–62), at the turn of the tenth century, estimated the diameter of the city as half a *farsakh* and its area as two thousand *jarībs* (approximately six hundred acres). It is not surprising that this author should have bequeathed us the most detailed description of Jayy in the early Islamic period, as he was a native of that city. For the etymology of Jay (> Ar. *Jayy,* Old Iranian **Gaba-,* Mid. Pers. *Gay*) see W. B. Henning, "Gabae," *Asia Major,* n.s., 2 (1952), 144.

21. Nāṣir-i Khusraw, *Safar Nāmah,* Schéfer's translation, 93; Thackston's translation, 98–99. For general comments on the city see Shaykh Ḥasan Jābirī Anṣārī, *Taʾrīkh-i Iṣfahān va Rayy* and ʿAlī Jawāhir Kalām, *Zanda-rūd yā Jughrāfiyā-i Tāʾrīkhī-yi Iṣfahān va Julfā* (Tehrān, A.H. 1390–91/A.D. 1970–71); and for Pre-Ṣafavid Iṣfahān, Lisa Golombek, "Urban Patterns in Pre-Safavid Iran" in Renata Holod, ed., "Studies on Isfahan," *Iranian Studies* 7 (1974): 18–44, including a reconstruction of the settlement pattern in the vicinity of the two cities circa 768 on p. 42. Note that the relative

sizes of al-Yahūdīyah and Shahristānah in 768 were the reverse of those that would be posited by al-Maqdisī more than two centuries later. See "Comments" by Renata Holod, 45–48.

22. Known to the Persians as Nīmrāh (= "Halfway House"), on account of its situation midway between Ctesiphon (al-Madā'in) and Shīz, sites of the two premier fire temples of Sāsānian times: Ibn Muhalhal (tenth century), cited by Yāqūt, *Muʿjam*, 3:216, 340, and 4:988. The ruins of the old city are today known as Yasīn Tappah. See Spuler, *Iran in Früh-Islamischer Zeit*, index s.v., especially pp. 126ff.

23. *Māh* < Old Iranian *mada-* = "Media": annotation by V. A. Livshits in Barthold, *Historical Geography*, 208 n. 4.

24. In the tenth century Ibn Ḥawqal (*al-Masālik wa-l-Mamālik*, 260) estimated Dīnawar to be two-thirds the size of Hamadān. Cf. also Iṣṭakhrī, *al-Masālik wa-l-Mamālik*, 198; Maqdisī, *Aḥsan*, 394; and Minorsky, *Ḥudūd*, 132. After the Muslim conquest the city acquired the sobriquet "Māh al-Kūfah" in recognition of its revenues being used to fund the state pensions of the inhabitants of the ʿIrāqī city. Cf. note 23 above.

25. Ibn Ḥawqal, *al-Masālik wa-l-Mamālik*, 258, 262; Maqdisī, *Aḥsan*, 394; Minorsky, *Ḥudūd*, 132, 201; and Ibn Khurradādhbih, *al-Masālik wa-l-Mamālik*, 241. When the Dulafid line came to an end in 897, the city reverted to dependence on the central government. Less than a decade later Ibn al-Faqīh found the city unprepossessing and poverty-ridden (*al-Buldān*, 237, 239, 261).

26. Ibn Ḥawqal, *al-Masālik wa-l-Mamālik*, 258, 262 and Yāqūt, *Muʿjam*, 1:596, 2:737.

27. Ibn Ḥawqal, *al-Masālik wa-l-Mamālik*, 259, 263, 271 and Maqdisī, *Aḥsan*, 391. The inner fortress had been built by Mubārak, a Turkish freedman, whence it was called the Mubārakīyah (or Madīnah Mubārak), while the locality within which it stood became known as Mubārakābād. The outer suburb was known as Madīnah Mūsā, after its builder, Mūsā, subsequently the caliph Hādī. Writing toward the mid-fourteenth century, Mustawfī (*Nuzhat al-Qulūb*, 145–46) recalled that it was the caliph Hārūn al-Rashīd who had enclosed both the Mubārakīyah and Madīnah Mūsa, together with an earlier Persian settlement called Shād-i Shāpūr, within a single wall.

There is a great deal of useful information on Qazwīn in the tenth century in Roy P. Mottahedeh, "Administration in Būyid Qazwīn," in *Islamic Civilisation 950–1150*, ed. D. S. Richards (Oxford, 1973), 33–45. More general accounts are incorporated in Husayn Qūlī Sutūda, "Tārīkh Qazwīn," in *Barrasīhā-i Tārīkhī*, vol. 4 (1969–70), 97–132, 156–210; and Ardavan Amirshahi, "Le développement de la ville de Qazwīn jusqu'au milieu du VIIIe/XIVe siècle," *Revue des Études Islamiques* 49 (1990): 1–20. See also *The Encyclopaedia of Islam*, 2d ed., 4:857–63.

28. Ibn Rustah, *al-Aʿlaq*, 165–69; Ibn Khurradādhbih, *al-Masālik wa-l-Mamālik*, 19–22; Qudāmah, *al-Kharāj*, 198–200; Ibn Ḥawqal, *al-Masālik wa-l-Mamālik*, 256–58; and Maqdisī, *Aḥsan*, 400–402.

29. Sābūrkhwāst < Pers. Shāpūrkhwāst. In the tenth century this city came under the rule of the local Kurdish Ḥasanūyah lineage. Cf. Iṣṭakhrī, *al-Masālik wa-l-Mamālik*, 197; Maqdisī, *Aḥsan*, 401; Ibn Ḥawqal, *al-Masālik wa-l-Mamālik*, 259, 264; and Minorsky, *Ḥudūd*, 383; also Spuler, *Iran in Früh-Islamischer Zeit*, 116, 304 (s.v. Šāpūrḫvāst).

30. It is traditionally reported, though without much supporting evidence (e.g., in the *Tāʾrīkh-i Qumm*), that Qumm was founded in 720 on the site of an older Persian settlement by a colony of Shīʿite Ashʿarī Arabs seeking refuge from Umayyad persecution; but cf. p. 139 below.

31. Ibn Ḥawqal, *al-Masālik wa-l-Mamālik*, 359–60.

32. Ibid., 258; Maqdisī, *Aḥsan*, 395–96; and Minorsky, *Ḥudūd*, 132. *Munayyar* denotes a silk fabric woven with a double thread in either warp or weft.

33. Ibn Rustah, *al-Aʿlaq*, 153; Iṣṭakhrī, *al-Masālik wa-l-Mamālik*, 199; Minorsky, *Ḥudūd*, 131, 382; Ibn Ḥawqal, *al-Masālik wa-l-Mamālik*, 363; Ibn al-Faqīh, *al-Buldān*, 50, 254; and al-Jāḥiẓ (attrib.), "Al-Tabbaṣṣur bi-l-Tijārah," ed. Hasan H. ʿAbd al-Wahhāb, *Revue de l'Académie de Damas*, 12 (1932): 337, 345 (For the authorship of this work see Charles Pellat, "Ǧāḥiẓiana, I: *Le Kitāb al-Tabaṣṣur bi-l-Tiǧāra* attribué à Ǧāḥiẓ," *Arabica* 1 [1954]: 153–65.). Ibn Ḥawqal (ibid.) ranks Iṣfahān *ʿattābī* above all others in quality. *Washī* was a figured cloth; *siqlāṭūn*, a heavy, figured silk stuff. Ibn al-Faqīh's quip (*al-Buldān*, 267) that there were more Jews, weavers, and adulterers in Iṣfahān than anywhere else need not be taken too seriously, but the fact that he places weaving in this context testifies to the prominence of textile manufacture in the urban economy of the time. For a succinct summary of textile manufacture in Jibāl Province, see Serjeant, *Islamic Textiles*, chap. 8.

34. *Ghaḍāra* in Minorsky, *Ḥudūd*, 132.

35. This is a summary of information provided by al-Maqdisī, *Aḥsan*, 395–96. Al-Thaʿālibī (*al-Laṭāʾif al-Maʿārif*, 184) notes that the mantles of al-Rayy were called *ʿAdanīyāt*, in allusion to those manufactured at ʿAdan in al-Yaman. Serjeant (*Islamic Textiles*, 82–83) speculates that the original design may have been transmitted from ʿAdan to Persia during the Sāsānian domination of South Arabia. Cf. also Minorsky, *Ḥudūd*, 132, 384.

36. Minorsky, *Ḥudūd*, 133.

37. Ibn Ḥawqal, *al-Masālik wa-l-Mamālik*, 363, 368.

38. Mustawfī, *Nuzhat al-Qulūb*, 75, 148–49.

39. Yāqūt, *Muʿjam*, 2:901. For Shīʿism in al-Jibāl more generally, see Schwarz, *Iran*, 853–54 and S. M. Stern, "The early Ismāʿīlī missionaries," 56–90.

40. Ibn Ḥawqal, *al-Masālik wa-l-Mamālik*, 363, 379. Among the large functionally urban dependencies of al-Rayy lacking mosques, Ibn Ḥawqal lists Sudd, Warāmīn, Āranbūyah, Warzanīn, Dizak, and Qūsīn. See also Schwarz, *Iran*, 781, 794–95.

41. Yāqūt, *Muʿjam*, 3:216.

42. Maqdisī, *Aḥsan*, 394 and Lambton, "An account of the *Taʾrīkh-i Qumm*." The *Taʾrīkh-i Qumm*, composed in Arabic by Ḥasan ibn Muḥammad ibn Ḥasan Qummī in A.H. 378/A.D. 988, is no longer extant; but a Persian translation was made by Ḥasan ibn

ʿAlī ibn Ḥasan ibn ʿAbd al-Malik Qummī for Ibrāhīm ibn Maḥmūd ibn Muḥammad ibn ʿAlī al-Ṣafī in A.H. 805/A.D. 1403, of which only the first five chapters have survived. Among the items of information that they contain are a reasonably detailed description of the towns, villages, and lands controlled from Qumm and of its irrigation system; a summary of its revenue assessments; and an account of Arab settlement in the city. The Persian translation has been edited by Sayyid Jalāl al-Dīn Tehrānī (Tehrān, A.H. 1313/A.D. 1895).

43. Guy Le Strange, trans., *The Geographical Part of the Nuzhat-al-Qulub Composed by Ḥamd-Allāh Mustawfī* (Leyden and London, 1919), 68.

44. I am indebted to Lapidus for an explanation of this distinction ("Arab Settlement and Economic Development of Iraq and Iran," 191–97).

45. Yaʿqūbī, *al-Buldān*, 274; Wiet's translation, 76–77.

46. Baladhurī, *Futūḥ al-Buldān*, 314; Hitti's translation, 488.

47. Or possibly Jūzdān-Maribīn: the sources are inconclusive on this point.

48. Ibn Rustah, *al-Aʿlaq*, 200; Wiet's translation, 234 (Abū Nuʿaym gives an earlier date for this event, namely 656–61). The early (and partly legendary) history of Iṣfahān is recounted by al-ʿAlawī in his translation of al-Māfarrukhī's *Taʾrīkh Iṣfahān:* cf. Browne's synopsis, "Acccount of a rare manuscript History of Iṣfahán," *Journal of the Royal Asiatic Society* (1901); and biographies of the city's notables are incorporated in Abū Nyʿaym's *Dhikr Akhbār Iṣbahān.* See also Schwarz, *Iran,* 5:582–670.

49. Baladhurī, *Futūḥ al-Buldān,* 321; Murgotten's translation, 10.

50. Lapidus, "Arab Settlement and Economic Development of Iraq and Iran," 193.

51. For the pre-Muslim history of Qazwīn, see Mustawfī's *Nuzhat al-Qulūb* as abstracted by C. Barbier de Meynard, "Description historique de la ville de Kazvin," *Journal Asiatique,* ser. 5, vol. 10 (1857): 257–308. See also Schwarz, *Iran,* 6:705–39.

52. This is Yāqūt's version of events (*Muʿjam,* 7:159–61), but the *Tārīkh-i Qumm* claims that the Kūfan refugees were welcomed by the Persian population: Lambton, "An account of the *Tārīkh-i Qumm,*" 596.

53. Lambton, "An account of the *Tārīkh-i Qumm,*" 588ff. For background information on Qumm in Umayyad times see A. Houtum Schindler, *Eastern Persian Iraq* (London, 1896), 60–76 and Schwarz, *Iran,* 5:560–61.

54. Balādhurī, *Futūḥ al-Buldān,* 316–20; Murgotten's translation, 521–25; Yaʿqūbī, *al-Buldān,* 275–76; Wiet's translation, 79–80; and Ibn al-Faqīh, *al-Buldān,* 269, 282.

55. This and the following paragraphs are based on the sources cited in notes 45–54 to this chapter, and more generally in note 1.

56. Cf. note 27 above.

57. Minorsky, *Ḥudūd,* 133.

58. Lapidus, "Arab Settlement and Economic Development of Iraq and Iran," 197.

59. Ibn Ḥawqal, *al-Masālik wa-l-Mamālik,* 260.

60. Ṭabarī, *Taʾrīkh,* 2:994.

Chapter Nine

Author's note: For secondary works bearing on the urban system of Khūzistān in the tenth century, see the author's note to chapter 8, especially Schwarz, *Iran,* 289–455 and Le Strange, *The Land of the Eastern Caliphate,* chap. 16. For more general statements on the history of the province, consult Muḥammad ʿAlī Imām Shushtarī, *Tārīkh wa Jughrafiyā-yi Khūzistān* (Tehran, A.H. 1331/A.D. 1952) and Dānishjū, *Khūzistān va Khūzistāniyān* (Tehran, A.H. 1326/A.D. 1947).

1. In early Islamic times the Kārūn was known to the Arabs as the Dujayl (= "Little Dijlah [Tigris]) of al-Ahwāz," but by the fourteenth century al-Mustawfī was referring to it as the Dijlah of Tustar, at that time the most important city on its banks (*Nuzhat al-Qulūb,* 207). Although the Kārūn now flows into the Shaṭṭ al-ʿArab, there are indications that even within historical times it entered the Persian Gulf through its own estuary, the Shaṭṭ al-Aʿmā, and Le Strange does so depict it (*The Lands of the Eastern Caliphate,* map 2, p. 25). It is said that the present-day course of the Kārūn was initiated by the digging of a canal joining that river to the Shaṭṭ al-ʿArab in the time of the Buwayhid *amīr* ʿAḍud al-Dawlah (r. 949–983): cf. V. Minorsky, *Abū-Dulaf Misʿar ibn al-Muhalhil's Travels in Iran (circa A.D. 950)* (Cairo, 1955), 109 n. 1.

2. Maqdisī, *Aḥsan,* 419.

3. Ibid., 405. Baṣunnay in Minorsky, *Ḥudūd,* 131.

4. Maqdisī, *Aḥsan,* 408.

5. Al-Maqdisī designates Īdhaj as one of the finest towns of Khūzistān. Great Lur (Lur-i Buzurg) was the name that al-Mustawfī (*Nuzhat al-Qulūb,* 73–74) ascribed to the territory within (i.e., on the south side of) the great bend of the Kārūn River.

6. Maqdisī, *Aḥsan,* 413 and Ibn Ḥawqal, *al-Masālik wa-l-Mamālik,* 257.

7. Ibn Ḥawqal, *al-Masālik wa-l-Mamālik,* 253–54 and Mustawfī, *Nuzhat al-Qulūb,* 107–8.

8. Iṣṭakhrī, *al-Masālik wa-l-Mamālik,* 88–90; Ibn Ḥawqal, *al-Masālik wa-l-Mamālik,* 258–59; and Maqdisī, *Aḥsan,* 402–6, 414–20; also Spuler, *Iran in Früh-Islamischer Zeit,* index s.v. In Sāsānian times this city had been known as Hurmuz-Shahr (variously as Hurmuz Awshīr and Hurmuzd-Ardashīr). It was renamed by the Arab conquerers Sūq al-Ahwāz = "The Bazaar of the Hūzī [or Ḥūzī or Khūzī]" people, that is, the people of Khūzistān, whence the abbreviated form al-Ahwāz. Al-Balādhurī (*Futūḥ al-Buldān,* 383; Murgotten's translation, 121–22), citing al-Thawrī, maintained that al-Ahwāz was in fact a popular corruption of al-Akhwāz. Al-Thawrī had supported his argument by a quotation from verses by al-Aʿrābī:

Do not send me back again to al-Akhwāz
And Qaʿqaʿān beside the market.

9. Ibn Khurradādhbih, *al-Masālik wa-l-Mamālik,* 170; Iṣṭakhrī, *al-Masālik wa-l-Mamālik,* 88; Ibn Ḥawqal, *al-Masālik wa-l-Mamālik,* 171; Maqdisī, *Aḥsan,* 406, 410; and Abū Dulaf, *Risālah,* par. 65: pp. 61–62 of the English text, p. 28 of the Arabic text.

10. Minorsky, *Ḥudūd,* 130.

11. Maqdisī, *Aḥsan,* 407; 414–19. See also Spuler, *Iran in Früh-Islamischer Zeit,* index s.v.

12. V.ndū-shāvūr (< * *Gundē-Shāpūr*) in Minorsky, *Ḥudūd,* 131. Al-Tabarī (*Ta'rīkh,* 1:826) derived the name of this city, which was founded by the Sāsānian monarch Shāpūr I in the mid-third century A.D., from a form *Bih az Andaw-i Shāpūr* (an interpretation probably adopted from Ibn Muqaffaʿ). J. Marquart interpreted the name as "better [is] the [new] Antiochia of Shāhpūr." Note that Shāhpūr I (r. 241–72) had extended the city for the purpose of housing the many prisoners he had captured at the conquest of Antioch in al-Shām (*A Catalogue of the Principal Capitals of Ērānšahr,* ed. G. Messina [Rome, 1931], 98; amending an earlier interpretation in *Ērānšahr nach der Geographie des Ps. Moses Xorenacʿi*). In Marquart's Middle Persian list of towns in the *Catalogue,* Gundē-Sābūr appears as *V.ndwy* (or *V.ndwg*)*-Shahpuhr,* which the editor emends to *Van<iy>og-Shahpuhr.* In his commentary on the *Ḥudūd,* Minorsky writes, "the fact is that *V.ndwy/g* exactly corresponds to the first part of the Byzantine βενδοσαβόων and to our *V.ndū-shāvūr,* which all agree in showing that the people simplified the name into a compound Vindōy-Shāpūr" (382). For the name *Vindōy* see Ferdinand Justi, *Iranisches Namenbuch* (Marburg, 1895), 370. H. Hübschmann explains the Armenian orthography *Vndoy* (borrowed from Middle Persian) as a familiar form of some Old Persian name such as *Vindafarnah,* "he who achieves glory" (*Armenische Grammatik* [Leipzig, 1897], 85). The site of the medieval city is now evidenced by the ruins called Shāhābādh: see Robert McC. Adams and Donald P. Hansen, "Archaeological reconnaissance and soundings in Jundī Shāhpūr"; appendix by Nabia Abbott, "Jundī Shāhpūr: a preliminary historical sketch," *Ars Orientalis* 7 (1968): 53–73. Cf. also Barthold, *Historical Geography,* 187–88. Virtually all commentators have rejected the *Volksetymologie* involving Jund-i Shāpūr = "army" or "camp of Shāpūr."

13. Maqdisī, *Aḥsan,* 405.

14. Pers. = Shushtar. Cf. ibid., 405. See more generally Raḍī al-Dīn Sayyid ʿAbd Allāh Jazāʾirī, "Faqīr," *Tārīkh-i Shushtar* (Calcutta, A.H. 1342/A.D. 1924) and Spuler, *Iran in Früh-Islamischer Zeit,* index s.v. "Šūštar."

15. According to Ibn Serapion (p. 32) and Ibn Ḥawqal (*al-Masālik wa-l-Mamālik,* 172–75), in the tenth century the Masruqān channel did not rejoin the main stream of the Kārūn (Dujayl) at ʿAskar Mukram but continued on a course more or less parallel to that river down to the tidal estuary. For an exposition of the drainage pattern of Khūzistān at that time see Le Strange, *The Lands of the Eastern Caliphate,* 235–38, with a few additional pertinent remarks in Minorsky, *Ḥudūd,* 214 n. 39.

16. Arabicized as Rustaqubādh. The version of events outlined here, which is the received record, has been preserved by Balādhurī (*Futūḥ al-Buldān,* 382–83), but the same author also advances an alternative account in which the city was named after a certain Mukram ibn Muṭarrif during the ʿIrāqī governorship of Muṣʿab ibn al-Zubayr. According to Mustawfī (*Nuzhat al-Qulūb,* 112; Le Strange's translation, 110), the old Persian city of Rustam Qawādh had been renamed Burj Shāpūr after Shāpūr I had greatly enlarged it. The same author adds that even as late as the fourteenth century ʿAskar Mukram was popularly called "The Camp" (Pers. = Lashkar). The site of the medieval city is now betrayed only by the ruins known as Band-i Qīr (= "The Bitumen Dyke").

17. Iṣṭakhrī, *al-Masālik wa-l-Mamālik,* 95 and Maqdisī, *Aḥsan,* 412.

18. Iṣṭakhrī, *al-Masālik wa-l-Mamālik,* 92–93; Ibn Ḥawqal, *al-Masālik wa-l-Mamālik,* 175–76; and Maqdisī, *Aḥsan,* 407, 413. Ibn Sawwār is otherwise unknown. The city had been named after King Hurmuz, grandson of Ardashīr Bābgān.

19. Also Lurdagān and Lurkān.

20. It has been suggested that the Kārūn in the tenth century flowed directly into the Persian Gulf at or near Sulaymānān (p. 91 and note 1 to this chapter), but the channel (or another like it) was considered dangerous to shipping. It appears that most vessels preferred to thread their way through the channels leading from Bāsiyān to Dawraq and so into the Nahr al-Sidrah (Lotus River): see Le Strange, *The Lands of the Eastern Caliphate* and Barthold, *Historical Geography,* 191–92. Later geographers (e.g., Yāqūt and Qazwīnī) mentioned a port of Dawraqistān, not far from Bāsiyān, where ships from India made their landfall; but there is no reference to this port in the tenth or earlier centuries.

21. Maqdisī, *Aḥsan,* 411.

22. Maqdisī appears to have been the only topographer using this name in the tenth century or earlier, and even he sometimes refers to the city simply as "The Bridge" (al-Qanṭarah). Ibn Rustah (*al-Aʿlaq,* 90) knew it as Qanṭarah al-Rūdh ("The River Bridge"); Ibn Serapion (p. 32), as Qanṭarah al-Rūm, "The Greek Bridge," in recognition of its construction supposedly having been supervised by captive Roman engineers in the time of Shāpūr I (L. Lockhart, *The Encyclopaedia of Islam,* new ed., 2:350). Iṣṭakhrī (*al-Masālik wa-l-Mamālik,* 93) preserved the old Persian name of Andāmishk under the Arabic form Andāmish. Another name in use in the tenth century was Qaṣr al-Rūnāsh.

23. Yāqūt, *Muʿjam,* 1:416. The bridge was known as the Qanṭarah Khurrah Zād, after the mother of King Ardashir. It was repaired in the tenth century by a *wazīr* of Rukn al-Dawlah.

24. Cited by Laufer, *Sino-Iranica,* 377. E. O. von Lippmann (*Geschichte des Zuckers* [Leipzig, 1890], 93) propounded the theory that sugar refining from the *Saccharum* cane was developed by Christians in the city of Gundē-Shāpūr (Junday Sābūr). Previously, Carl Ritter (*Geschichte der Erdkunde* . . . herausgegeben von H. A. Daniel [Berlin, 1861]) had postulated Sīrāf as the port through which the cane entered Persia, a point of view subsequently

opposed by Paul Schwarz ("Die Zuckerpressen von Ahwāz," *Der Islam* 6 [1916]: 269–79), who preferred Hurmuz as the point of entry. A more recent study (E. Wiedemann, "Beiträge zur Geschichte der Naturwissenschaften: LII, Über den Zucker bei den Muslimen," in *Aufsätze zur Arabischen Wissenschaftsgeschichte*, ed. W. Fischer [Hildesheim, 1970], 2:304–13) concludes that the cane was introduced into Ahwāz at about the time of the Arab conquest, a date obviously at variance with the testimony of Moses of Khorene.

25. Maqdisī, *Aḥsan*, 416. Cf. Minorsky, *Ḥudūd*, 130: "All the red and white sugar *(shakar)* and refined sugar *(qand)* of the world come from ʿAskar Mukram."

26. Thaʿālibī, *al-Laṭāʾif al-Maʿārif*, 174; Bosworth's translation, 126. This author also noted that fifty thousand *riṭls* of ʿAskar Mukram sugar had at one time been demanded by the central government annually in addition to the land tax.

27. The receipt of a robe of honor by a courtier or official was a signal mark of distinction. *Ṭirāz*, an Arabicized version of a Persian word, is described in the first edition of *The Encyclopaedia of Islam*, 4:785–93, as follows: "The word originally means 'embroidery'; it then comes to mean a robe adorned with elaborate embroidery, especially one ornamented with embroidered bands with writing on them, worn by a ruler or person of high rank; finally, it means the workshop in which such materials or robes are made." Cf. also J. von Karabaček, *Zur Orientalischen Altertumskunde, I. Die Arabischen Papyrusprotokolle: Sitzungsb. Phil.-Hist. Kl., Akademie, Wien*, vol. 161 (1909) and Ernst Kühnel, "Tirāzstoffe der Abbassiden," *Der Islam* 14 (1925): 82–88. The available information relating to the *ṭirāz* cities of Khūzistān has been assembled by Serjeant in *Islamic Textiles*, chap. 4, which has afforded a basis for this paragraph (although I have furnished references to my own editions of the sources). See also more generally Pigulevskaja, *Les Villes de l'Etat Iranien*, 161–69.

28. For example, al-Thaʿālibī, *Histoire des Rois des Perses*, ed. and trans. H. Zotenberg (Paris, 1900), 530; Yāqūt, *Muʿjam*, 2:496; Masʿūdī, *Murūj*, 2:185–86; and F. Wüstenfeld, ed., *El-Cazwini's Kosmographie* (Göttingen, 1846–48), 2:114—all cited by Serjeant in *Islamic Textiles*, 41.

29. Ibn Taghrībirdī, *al-Nujūm al-Zāhirah fī Mulūk Miṣr wa-l-Qāhirah*, ed. F. G. Juynboll and B. F. Matthes under the title *Abūʾl-Mahasin ibn Tagri Bardii Annales* (Leyden, 1855–61), 2:192.

30. Thaʿālibī, *al-Laṭāʾif al-Maʿārif*, 174: Bosworth's translation, 126. The *Ḥudūd* (131) claims that the brocaded covering for the Kaʿbah *(parda-i Makka)* was made in Tustar, but Ibn Ḥawqal (*al-Masālik wa-l-Mamālik*, 175) states explicitly that in the tenth century this was no longer so. For an interpretation of the confused rubrication of this section of the *Ḥudūd*, see Minorsky, *Ḥudūd*, 130 and 381 n. 14.

31. Iṣṭakhrī, *al-Masālik wa-l-Mamālik*, 92.

32. Ibn Ḥawqal, *al-Masālik wa-l-Mamālik*, 175.

33. Maqdisī, *Aḥsan*, 409.

34. Thaʿālibī, *al-Laṭāʾif al-Maʿārif*, 174; Bosworth's translation, 126; Iṣṭakhrī, *al-Masālik wa-l-Mamālik*, 93; Ibn Ḥawqal, *al-Masālik wa-l-Mamālik*, 175; Maqdisī, *Aḥsan*, 416–17; and Minorsky, *Ḥudūd*, 131.

35. Maqdisī, *Aḥsan*, 408.

36. Iṣṭakhrī (*al-Masālik wa-l-Mamālik*, 93) notes that some of the curtains that were exported "to all regions" with *ʿamal Baṣinnā* ("made in Baṣinnā") woven into them were in fact the products of other, though neighboring, towns. Cf. also Ibn Ḥawqal, *al-Masālik wa-l-Mamālik*, 171; Minorsky, *Ḥudūd*, 131; and Maqdisī, *Aḥsan*, 416, who comments on the frequency with which other than Baṣinnā curtains were sold as the genuine article, even as far afield as Wāsiṭ. Despite the high quality of Baṣinnā cloth, there is no record of a *ṭirāz* factory ever having operated in the city.

37. Cf. J. von Karabaček, *Die Persische Nadelmalerei Susandschird* (Leipzig, 1881); Schwarz, *Iran*, 2:97; and Serjeant, *Islamic Textiles*, 45. The name denotes a textile that was a product of both weaving and embroidery: cf. German *Nadelmalerei, Webstickerei*. In Fasā the process was practiced on a woolen base; in Qurqūb, on a less suitable silk base. In the *Ḥudūd* (131) the word is rendered *sūzan-kard*, in two words, thereby emphasizing the etymological implication of "needle-work"; but in popular speech *sūzan* (= needle) was replaced by *sūsan* (= lily), and the final *-kard* became *-*gird* (*-jird* in Arabic transcription), in compliance with a phonetic change attested in other contemporary place-names—for example, Dārābkart (= "Built by Dārāb") > Dārābgird (Ar. = *Dārābjird). See Manuchihr Sutudah in Minorsky, *Ḥudūd*, xvi–xvii.

38. Maqdisī, *Aḥsan*, 412. Because carpets *(busuṭ)* and runners *(ankhākh)* from Dawraq figured among fineries put on display for a Byzantine ambassador, Serjeant (*Islamic Textiles*, 47) has suggested that the city may have had a *ṭirāz* factory, even though such an enterprise is not mentioned in any extant text.

39. "The best variety is pure and lovely coloured in kind, free of all variations [in colour or texture] and stains which confuse some of its threads. The threads should be of one shape and not some coarse and some fine, nor bulging." Quoted by Serjeant, *Islamic Textiles*, 201 from Jaʿfar ibn ʿAlī al-Dimashqī, *al-Ishārah ilā Maḥāsin al-Tijārah* (al-Qāhirah, A.H. 1318/A.D. 1900), 25.

40. Iṣṭakhrī, *al-Masālik wa-l-Mamālik*, 93.

41. Ibn Ḥawqal, *al-Masālik wa-l-Mamālik*, 176.

42. Maqdisī, *Aḥsan*, 405.

43. Iṣṭakhrī, *al-Masālik wa-l-Mamālik*, 92; Minorsky, *Ḥudūd*, 131; and Mustawfī, *Nuzhat al-Qulūb*, 269.

44. It is also true that the *Ḥudūd*, which might have been expected to provide a modicum of independent testimony, relies almost exclusively on al-Iṣṭakhrī's *Masālik wa-l-Mamālik*, 88–96 for its information on Khūzistān.

45. For a compendious statement on the nature and effects of this agricultural revolution see Andrew M. Watson, *Agricultural Innovations* and more briefly in "The Arab agricultural revolution and its diffusion, 700–1100," *The Journal of Economic History* 34, no. 1 (1974): 8–35. Because a high proportion of the new crops had origi-

nated in the tropical regions of South and Southeast Asia, the well-watered plains of Khūzistān—with their intensely hot and oppressive summers, in which mean temperatures exceed 90°F for four consecutive months under extremely humid conditions—proved to be fertile ground for agricultural innovation, and the province became a center of diffusion of new crops and farming practices.

46. Minorsky, *Ḥudūd,* 129.

47. Serjeant, *Islamic Textiles,* 9. This author is inclined to associate the establishment of these state functions in Sāsānian Persia with the administrative policy of soliciting products for which particular provinces were especially noted as part of their tax schedules. The conventional date of A.D. 484–88 for the institution of this practice probably signified only its standardization, for there are indications that it had already had a long history in the Persian culture realm. It is only fair, though, to acknowledge that others, including von Karabaček (*Die Arabischen Papyrusprotokolle,* note 27 above), have sought the origin of the *ṭirāz* system in the Coptic textile factories of pre-Muslim Egypt.

48. Maqdisī, *Aḥsan,* 413.

49. Thaʿālibī, *al-Laṭāʾif al-Maʿārif,* 174; Bosworth's translation, 126. Cf. Minorsky, *Ḥudūd,* 130: "Anyone who settles in Ahwāz loses his mind."

50. Maqdisī, *Aḥsan,* 410.

51. Quoted by Thaʿālibī, *al-Laṭāʾif al-Maʿārif,* 176–77; Bosworth's translation, 127.

Chapter Ten

Author's note: For commentary and exegesis bearing on the urban system of Fārs, see author's note to chapter 8, especially Schwarz, *Iran,* 1–211 and Le Strange, *The Lands of the Eastern Caliphate,* chaps. 17–20. There is also a great deal of pertinent material in Spuler, *Iran in Früh-Islamischer Zeit.* A valuable primary Persian source specific to this *iqlīm* but dating from a few years subsequent to the period with which we are primarily concerned is the *Fārs-Nāmah,* ed. Guy Le Strange and R. A. Nicholson in the E. J. W. Gibb Memorial Series, n.s., 1 (London, 1921); English translation by Le Strange under the title *Description of the Province of Fars, in Persia, at the Beginning of the Twelfth Century* A.D. . . . (Asiatic Society Monographs, vol. 14 [London, 1912]). Originally published in *Journal of the Royal Asiatic Society* (1912): 1–30, 311–39, 865–89. Cf. also Ḥasan Fasāʾī, *Fārs-Nāma-yi Nāṣirī* (Tehran, A.H. 1314/A.D. 1896). A map illustrative of this work, which was published separately, is very rare. I have not seen it, but a copy was in the possession of Professor Minorsky when he was preparing his translation of the *Ḥudūd al-ʿĀlam* (see p. 376). See also more generally Bahman Karīmī, *Jughrāfiyā-yi Tāʾrīkhī-yi Mufaṣṣal-i Gharb-i Īrān* (Tehran, A.H. 1317/A.D. 1938). The contributions of archaeology to our understanding of trade and urbanization in Fārs Province in the earlier Islamic periods are evaluated by Donald S. Whitcomb in "Trade and Tradition in Medieval Southern Iran" (Ph.D. diss., University of Chicago, 1979).

1. Iṣṭakhrī, *al-Masālik wa-l-Mamālik,* 120 and Mustawfī, *Nuzhat al-Qulūb,* 119; Le Strange's translation, 117.

2. Iṣṭakhrī, *al-Masālik wa-l-Mamālik,* 110 and Minorsky, *Ḥudūd,* 128. The name of this city is also transcribed as Nawbanjān and Nūbandagān.

3. Minorsky, *Ḥudūd,* 129. It should be noted that the section on Fārs in the *Ḥudūd* is essentially an abridgment, often mutilated, of Iṣṭakhrī's *al-Masālik* or perhaps, as Minorsky suggests (p. 376), of a Persian translation of that work.

4. Medieval authors were not wholly in agreement as to the significance of the old Sāsānian settlement for the subsequent development of Shīrāz. Some merely noted, as did the author of the *Ḥudūd al-ʿĀlam,* that "This city was built in the Islamic period *(īn shahr-rā ba rūzgār-i Islām karda-and)*" [126]; cf. Ibn Ḥawqal, *al-Masālik wa-l-Mamālik,* 279), but others, including Mustawfī (*Nuzhat al-Qulūb,* 114; Le Strange's translation, 112–13), accorded it an ancient, although not continuous, history. Incidentally, Mustawfī observed that it had fallen into ruin before the Muslim conquest. Possibly the most reliable account is that of the historian of Shīrāz, Ibn Zarkūb, who in his *Shīrāz-Nāmah,* written in about 1342 (edited by Bahman Karīmī [Tehran, A.H. 1310/A.D. 1931]), attributed either the founding or the restoration of the city to a brother of al-Ḥajjāj (cited in Arthur J. Arberry, *Shiraz. Persian City of Saints and Poets* [Norman, Okla., 1960]). The early Islamic history of Shīrāz is examined with exemplary thoroughness by Donald S. Whitcomb in *Before the Roses and Nightingales,* 221–33. This volume also contains a great deal of information on the Shīrāz region in pre-Islamic times. See also Muḥammad Jaʿfar Ḥusayni Khurmūjī, *Tārīkh-i Shīrāz* (Tehran, A.H. 1276/A.D. 1860) and Muʿīn al-Dīn Junayd Shīrāzī, *Shadd al-Izār fī Khaṭṭ al-Awzār ʿan Zuwwār al-Mazār* (Tehran, A.H. 1338/A.D. 1940).

5. The first substantial walls around Shīrāz were built by either Ṣamṣām al-Dawlah or Sulṭān al-Dawlah, respectively son and grandson of ʿAḍud.

6. Maqdisī, *Aḥsan,* 429–30, 456.

7. Ibid., 449.

8. For a possible derivation of this word through Syriac from Greek *χώρα* see Th. Nöldeke, *Geschichte der Perser und Araber,* 3.

9. Ar. Sābūr < Pers. Shāpūr < Bih-Shāpūr < Wih-Shāpūr = "the excellence of Shāpūr"; cf. Le Strange, *The Lands of the Eastern Caliphate,* 262 and Minorsky, *Ḥudūd,* 379 n. 19. For a different, and certainly erroneous, etymology, see Mustawfī, *Nuzhat al-Qulūb,* 126; Le Strange's translation, 125–26. Cf. also Iṣṭakhrī, *al-Masālik wa-l-Mamālik,* 118, 150 and Minorsky, *Ḥudūd,* 128. Excavations undertaken at the site of the ancient city by French archaeologists in 1935–41 are summarized by R. Ghirshman (*Bichapour* [Paris, 1971]), whose conclusions are, however, criticized severely by Whitcomb ("Trade and Tradition," 67–70).

10. Ibn Ḥawqal, *al-Masālik wa-l-Mamālik,* 278.

11. Maqdisī, *Aḥsan,* 424, 432, 444. By the beginning of the twelfth century, Shāpūr (Shahristān) had been abandoned (*Fārs-*

Nāmah, ff. 74b, 75a; Le Strange's translation, 331), and by the middle of the fourteenth its very name had been transferred to the Kāzirūn District (Mustawfī, *Nuzhat al-Qulūb*, 125–26; Le Strange's translation, 125). For the rise of Kāzirūn as a textile-manufacturing center see p. 149.

12. *Araghān* (a colloquial vocalization) in the *Ḥudūd* (Minorsky, 127, 378–79); cf. also Mustawfī, *Nuzhat al-Qulūb*, 129–30; Le Strange's translation, 129.

13. Ibn Ḥawqal, *al-Masālik wa-l-Mamālik*, 282; and for further comments, 269. Cf. also Iṣṭakhrī, *al-Masālik wa-l-Mamālik*, 128, 134, 152 and Maqdisī, *Aḥsan*, 425. For more recent impressions of the city, consult C. A. de Bode, *Travels in Luristan*, vol. 1 (London, 1845), 295, 297. There is a comprehensive discussion of the historical geography of the Arrajān region from the seventh to the eighteenth century A.D. in Heinz Gaube, *Die Südpersische Provinz Arrağān/Kūh-Gīlūyeh von der Arabischen Eroberung bis zur Safawidenzeit* (Wien, 1973). Like Shāpūr, by the fourteenth century Arrajān city had been abandoned by its inhabitants, and its function as a regional center usurped by the city of Behbehān (Mustawfī, *Nuzhat al-Qulūb*, 129; Le Strange's translation, 129).

14. Iṣṭakhrī, *al-Masālik wa-l-Mamālik*, 123.

15. Ibn Ḥawqal, *al-Masālik wa-l-Mamālik*, 277. Cf. also Maqdisī, *Aḥsan*, 435. For an interpretative study of the archaeological evidence from Iṣṭakhr and its vicinity, see Donald S. Whitcomb, "The City of Istakhr and the Marvdasht Plain," *Akten des VII. Internationalen Kongresses für Iranische Kunst und Archäologie, München 7.–10. September 1976* (Berlin, 1979), 363–70; and for the sequence of settlement patterns in much the same area derived by the techniques of topographic archaeology pioneered by Robert McC. Adams (chapter 4, pp. 95–97), see W. M. Sumner, "Cultural Development in the Kur River Basin, Iran: an Archaeological Analysis of Settlement Patterns" (Ph.D. diss., University of Pennsylvania, 1972).

16. Maqdisī, *Aḥsan*, 428. Cf. also Iṣṭakhrī, *al-Masālik wa-l-Mamālik*, 123, 155. See also Whitcomb, "Trade and Tradition," 43–46.

17. For general discussions of Sīrāf see J. Aubin, "La ruine de Sīrāf et les routes du Golfe Persique aux XIe et XIIe siècles," *Cahiers de Civilisation Médiévale* 2 (1959): 295–301; A. Lamb, "A visit to Siraf, an ancient port on the Persian Gulf," *Journal of the Malayan Branch of the Royal Asiatic Society* 37, pt. 1 (1964): 1–19; and S. M. Stern, "Rāmisht of Sīrāf, a merchant millionaire of the twelfth century," *Journal of the Royal Asiatic Society* (1967): 10–14.

18. David Whitehouse, "Excavations at Sīrāf. First interim report," *Iran* 6 (1968): 10–22; "Second interim report," loc. cit., 7 (1969): 39–62; "Third interim report," loc. cit., 8 (1970): 1–18; "Fourth interim report," loc. cit., 9 (1971): 1–17; "Fifth interim report," loc. cit., 10 (1972): 63–87; "Sixth interim report," loc. cit., 12 (1974): 1–30; "Sīrāf: a medieval port on the Persian Gulf," *World Archaeology* 2, no. 2 (1970): 141–58; and "The houses of Siraf, Iran," *Archaeology* 24 (1971): 255–62.

19. Iṣṭakhrī, *al-Masālik wa-l-Mamālik*, 34, 106, 116, 127, 141, 154. Cf. also Maqdisī, *Aḥsan*, 422, 426–27.

20. Whitehouse, "Sīrāf," 150–152 and figs. 5, 7; and "The houses of Siraf," passim.

21. Iṣṭakhrī, *al-Masālik wa-l-Mamālik*, 154.

22. Maqdisī, *Aḥsan*, 426.

23. Tadeusz Lewicki, "Les premiers commerçants arabes en Chine," *Rocznik Orjentalistyczny* 11 (1935): 176–81.

24. For the location of Kalah see G. R. Tibbetts, "The Malay Peninsula as known to the Arab geographers," *The Malayan Journal of Tropical Geography* 7 (1955): 24–33 and *A Study of the Arabic Texts Containing Material on South-East Asia*, 9–10, 37–42, 112–14, 118–28, 132–37; Paul Wheatley, *The Golden Khersonese* (Kuala Lumpur, 1961), 216–224 and "Desultory Remarks on the Ancient History of the Malay Peninsula," in *Malayan and Indonesian Studies. Essays Presented to Sir Richard Winstedt on His Eighty-fifth Birthday*, ed. John Bastin and R. Roolvink (Oxford, 1964), 68–70; Sayyid Qadratullah Fatimi, "In quest of Kalah," *Journal [of] Southeast Asian History* 1, no. 2 (1960): 62–101; and most recently Wheatley, *Nāgara and Commandery*, 234–36, 254. For general comments on Arab and earlier trade with the East, see G. F. Hourani, *Arab Seafaring in the Indian Ocean in Ancient and Early Islamic Times;* Sauvaget, *ʿAḫbar aṣ-Ṣīn wa l-Hind;* D. Whitehouse and A. Williamson, "Sasanian maritime trade," *Iran* 11 (1973): 29–49; and Moira Tampoe, *Maritime Trade between China and the West: An Archaeological Study of the Ceramics from Siraf (Persian Gulf), 8th to 15th Centuries A.D.*, British Archaeological Reports, International Series, 555 (Oxford, 1989).

25. Fīrūzābād = "The Abode of Fortune," so styled when ʿAḍud al-Dawlah began to use the city as a summer residence for hunting and other leisure pursuits, as the original name of Jūr (= grave) was considered inauspicious (Maqdisī, *Aḥsan*, 432).

26. Iṣṭakhrī (cf. note 18) listed the South and East Asian imports that eventually found their way to Shīrāz as aloeswood, amber, camphor, gemstones, bamboo, ivory, ebony, paper, sandalwood, Indian perfumes, drugs, and condiments.

27. Nāṣir-i Khusraw, *Safar Namāh*, Schéfer's translation, 247; Thackston's translation, 97. Cf. also Minorsky, *Ḥudūd*, 127.

28. Iṣṭakhrī, *al-Masālik wa-l-Mamālik*, 34, 128; Maqdisī, *Aḥsan*, 426; and Minorsky, *Ḥudūd*, 127. According to Yāqūt (*Muʿjam*, 1: 502, 3:221), large sectors of Sīnīz were devastated by Qarmaṭians in 933, but the port seems to have recovered rapidly: less than twenty years later al-Iṣṭakhrī described it as larger than Mahrubān. Neither Maqdisī nor the author of the *Fārs-Nāmah* mentioned the Qarmaṭian attack.

29. Iṣṭakhrī, *al-Masālik wa-l-Mamālik*, 32, 34, 119, 128 and Maqdisī, *Aḥsan*, 426. It is uncertain which present-day river corresponds to the Shādhkān. Jannābāʾ was also the birthplace of Abū Ṭāhir Sulaymān, the Qarmaṭian who seized Makkah in 930 and carried off the Black Stone from the Kaʿbah.

30. Maqdisī, *Aḥsan*, 422 and Minorsky, *Ḥudūd*, 127.

31. Mustawfī, *Nuzhat al-Qulūb,* 119–20; Le Strange's translation, 118.

32. For the history of the Banū-Qayṣar, who ruled the island for the three centuries preceding its conquest by the Atābek Abū Bakr, see ʿAbd Allāh Sharaf ibn Faḍl Allāh Shīrāzī Waṣṣāf, *Taʾrīkh-i Waṣṣāf,* vol. 1 (Bombay, A.H. 1269/A.D. 1853), 170ff.

33. Mustawfī, *Nuzhat al-Qulūb,* 120; Le Strange's translation, 118.

34. Also known as Dīkbāyah and Ḥiṣn ibn ʿUmārah. See also note 77 below.

35. Also transcribed as Shahrū, and, anomalously, as Tūsar by Mustawfī (*Nuzhat al-Qulūb,* 187).

36. *Fārs-Nāmah,* ff. 73b–74a; Le Strange's translation, 222–23.

37. Qazwīnī, *ʿAjāʾib al-Makhlūqāt,* 2:161.

38. These caravan routes were described in considerable detail by Ibn Khurradādhbih and Qudāmah in the ninth century; by Iṣṭakhrī, Ibn Ḥawqal, and Maqdisī in the tenth; in the *Fārs-Nāmah* at the beginning of the twelfth; and by Mustawfī in the fourteenth.

39. Iṣṭakhrī, *al-Masālik wa-l-Mamālik,* 120; Ibn Ḥawqal, *al-Masālik wa-l-Mamālik,* 282; and Minorsky, *Ḥudūd,* 127.

40. Maqdisī, *Aḥsan,* 435.

41. Mustawfī, *Nuzhat al-Qulūb,* 128; Le Strange's translation, 127. There is a detailed examination of the nature and structure of trade in medieval Fārs in Whitcomb, "Trade and Tradition," chap. 3.

42. Iṣṭakhrī, *al-Masālik wa-l-Mamālik,* 113–15 and Ibn Ḥawqal, *al-Masālik wa-l-Mamālik,* 265, 269–71.

43. Legal alms; strictly almsgiving not of a prescribed amount (in contrast to *zakāt*).

44. Ibn Ḥawqal, *al-Masālik wa-l-Mamālik,* 302–3. It should be noted, though, that Iṣṭakhrī (*al-Masālik wa-l-Mamālik,* 158) gave a somewhat different account, according to which taxes in the tribal territories were assessed as proportions of crops (or, presumably, livestock) specified in charters (*ʿuhūd*) granted mainly by the early caliphs.

45. Ibn Ḥawqal, *al-Masālik wa-l-Mamālik,* 271.

46. Al-Sarī ibn Aḥmad al-Kindī al-Raffāʾ (a poet at the court of Sayf Al-Dawlah who died in 976/77), quoted by Thaʿālibī, Laṭāʾif al-Maʿārif, 178; Bosworth's translation, 127.

47. Iṣṭakhrī, *al-Masālik wa-l-Mamālik,* 155.

48. There are, for example, no less than fifty words and phrases with this implication in the relevant chapter of the *Ḥudūd* alone (126–29), not including the prefatory statement (126) that "[Fārs] is a prosperous and wealthy *(tuvangar)* province with manifold resources *(niʿmat-hā-yi gūnāgūn).*"

49. For the *ṭirāz* system see note 27 to chapter 9. As in chapter 9, I draw heavily on Robert B. Serjeant's *Islamic Textiles,* chap. 5, for information on the textile industry in early Islamic Fārs. Both Iṣṭakhrī (*al-Masālik wa-l-Mamālik,* 152) and Ibn Ḥawqal (*al-Masālik wa-l-Mamālik,* 212) describe the products of the individual *ṭirāz* factories in Fārs Province.

50. Maqdisī, *Aḥsan,* 442. At a considerably later date (1107) the author of the *Fārs-Nāmah* (p. 63) described the Sīnīzī cloths as "very thick and soft," although not wearing well. Under the Sāsānians and the Umayyads they had been used as tent cloth; al-Manṣūr, second of the ʿAbbāsid caliphs, was the first to replace them with the coarser cloth known as *khaysh* (Serjeant, *Islamic Textiles,* 49 n. 5). Cf. also Ibn al-Faqīh, *al-Buldān,* 254; Masʿūdī, *Murūj,* 1:238; Ibn Ḥawqal, *al-Masālik wa-l-Mamālik,* 126; and Minorsky, *Ḥudūd,* 127.

51. Ibn al-Faqīh, *al-Buldān,* 254 (emending *jubbāʾiyah* to read *jannābī,* as suggested by Serjeant, *Islamic Textiles,* 53 n. 27); Masʿūdī, *Murūj,* 1:238; and Ibn Ḥawqal, *al-Masālik wa-l-Mamālik,* 185.

52. Maqdisī, *Aḥsan,* 435; Minorsky, *Ḥudūd,* 127; and Thaʿālibī, *al-Laṭāʾif al-Maʿārif,* 235; Bosworth's translation, 145. To Yāqūt, writing in the thirteenth century, *tawwajī* was "a fine cloth of light and delicate weave *(muhalhal al-nasaj),* rather like a fine sieve-cloth *(munkhal).* Its colours are lovely and it has golden *ṭirāz* borders" (Serjeant's translation, *Islamic Textiles,* 53). The essay "Al-Tabaṣṣur bi-l-Tijārah," formerly attributed to al-Jāḥiẓ, refers to "Sābirī linen garments of Tawwaj" (12:337), which Serjeant (53) suggests may imply that Sāsānian-style fabrics were being manufactured under the *tawwajī* name.

53. Maqdisī, *Aḥsan,* 433–34. Cf. Yāqūt, who repeats this information in the *Muʿjam* (4:225). Interestingly, al-Iṣṭakhrī *(al-Masālik wa-l-Mamālik,* 136) claimed that in his day Kāzirūn did not have a *ṭirāz.*

54. Maqdisī, *Aḥsan,* 435. Clearly, the author of the *Ḥudūd* (127) was in error when he stated that "All the *tavazī* textiles come from Tavaz (Tawwaj)." The *Fārs-Nāmah* (55–57) provides a detailed account of the manufacture of *tūzī (tawwazī, tawwajī)* cloth as it was organized in Kāzirūn at the beginning of the twelfth century. A part of this account, which may refer to the later years of the tenth century, runs as follows:

> In times past it was all after this wise. The brokers would make up the bales of Kāzirūnī cloth; the foreign merchants would come and buy the bales as they stood thus made up, for they placed reliance on the brokers; and in any city to which they were carried the certificate of the Kāzirūnī broker was merely requested and the bales would then be sold at a profit without being opened [for examination]. Thus it would often happen that a load of Kāzirūnī bales would pass from hand to hand ten times over without being opened. But now, in these latter days, fraud has become rife, and with the people becoming dishonest, all confidence is gone, for the goods with the treasury stamp are often found deficient, so that foreign traders have come to avoid the merchandise of Kāzirūn.

The same source reports that after the flax fiber had been spun, the thread was washed in the waters of the Rāhbān canal, to which was attributed its whiteness. At the time when the *Fārs-Nāmah* was written, the Rāhbān waterway was the property of the royal treasury, with the profits from the linen industry accruing to the *amīr*. The weavers performing the several processes worked for the treasury in a putting-out system. The prices of the various cloths were set by brokers, who sealed the bales under the watchful eye of a treasury inspector.

55. Iṣṭakhrī, *al-Masālik wa-l-Mamālik,* 152 and Ibn Ḥawqal, *al-Masālik wa-l-Mamālik,* 212.

56. Iṣṭakhrī, *al-Masālik wa-l-Mamālik,* 152; Ibn Ḥawqal, *al-Masālik wa-l-Mamālik,* 184; Minorsky, *Ḥudūd,* 129; and Maqdisī, *Aḥsan,* 442.

57. Iṣṭakhrī, *al-Masālik wa-l-Mamālik,* 152. For *susanjird* see note 37 to chapter 9.

58. Maqdisī, *Aḥsan,* 442–43.

59. Al-Jaḥiẓ, "Al-Tabaṣṣur," 336–37. *Qirmiz* dye was extracted from the insect *Kermococcus vermilis,* Planchon, which feeds on the oak *Quercus coccifera:* see R. A. Donkin, "The insect dyes of western and west-central Asia," *Anthropos* 72 (1977): 849–53, 859–63 and, more briefly, "Spanish red: an ethnogeographical study of cochineal and the opuntia cactus," *Transactions of the American Philosophical Society* 67, pt. 5 (1977): 9–10. *Qirmiz* is, of course, the origin of the English *crimson* by way of Low Latin *carmesinus* and Old French *cramoisi(n).*

60. A stuff having either a double woof or a double weft.

61. Cf. note 33 to chapter 8.

62. A type of linen cloth. The list of manufactures was compiled from the works of Ibn al-Faqīh, *al-Buldān,* 254; Iṣṭakhrī, *al-Masālik wa-l-Mamālik,* 152; Ibn Ḥawqal, *al-Masālik wa-l-Mamālik,* 212; and Maqdisī, *Aḥsan,* 442.

63. Maqdisī, *Aḥsan,* 442.

64. Iṣṭakhrī, *al-Masālik wa-l-Mamālik,* 152; Ibn Ḥawqal, *al-Masālik wa-l-Mamālik,* 212. No tenth-century (or earlier) author, as far as I am aware, discussed either the silk industry of Yazd—based on the prevalence of the mulberry tree, which the author of the *Fārs-Nāmah* (p. 20) would mention at the beginning of the twelfth century—or the manufacture of fine brocades, which, he said, owed their excellence to the circumstance that the Yazdīs "reared no sheep, but only goats, the hair of which is very strong." It is uncertain whether these manufactures developed after the tenth century or were, for reasons unknown, ignored by the tenth-century topographers. The former is the more likely, I think.

65. Maqdisī, *Aḥsan,* 442–43.

66. Ibid., 433.

67. Iṣṭakhrī, *al-Masālik wa-l-Mamālik,* 155.

68. Ibid., 154; Ibn Ḥawqal, *al-Masālik wa-l-Mamālik,* 214; and Maqdisī, *Aḥsan,* 442–43.

69. Maqdisī, *Aḥsan,* 442.

70. Ibid., 443.

71. Iṣṭakhrī, *al-Masālik wa-l-Mamālik,* 155 and Maqdisī, *Aḥsan,* 430.

72. Serjeant, *Islamic Textiles,* 57.

73. Maqdisī, *Aḥsan,* 431.

74. Ibn Ḥawqal, *al-Masālik wa-l-Mamālik,* 184. This point was first made by Serjeant, *Islamic Textiles,* 54.

75. Cf. chapter 9, pp. 142–43 above.

76. Ibn Ḥawqal, *al-Masālik wa-l-Mamālik,* 272. Cf. also Iṣṭakhrī, *al-Masālik wa-l-Mamālik,* 116. In the B recension of the *Aḥsan,* Maqdisī repeats Iṣṭakhrī's figure (p. 447, citing that author as al-Fārisī), but in the C recension the number is quoted as five hundred (ibid.).

77. Mustawfī, *Nuzhat al-Qulūb,* 130; Le Strange's translation, 129.

78. Ibn Ḥawqal, *al-Masālik wa-l-Mamālik,* 272. Cf. also Iṣṭakhrī, *al-Masālik wa-l-Mamālik,* 140. The *ḥiṣn* of Dīkbāyah, also known as Qalʿah al-Dīkdān and Ḥiṣn Ibn ʿUmārah, could provide safe anchorage for as many as a score of vessels.

79. Maqdisī, p. 435.

80. Ibid. For the significance of the term *Kurd,* see p. 148 above.

81. Al-Baṣrī (d. 728) was highly esteemed as a transmitter of *ḥadīths,* since he was believed to have known personally no less than seventy of the participants in the Battle of Badr. Numerous religious movements within Islam derived their doctrines ultimately from his works: see Ibn Khallikān, *Wafāyāt,* 1:228.

82. Also transcribed as Abarqūyah and Barqūh.

83. Mustawfī, *Nuzhat al-Qulūb,* 122; Le Strange's translation, 120.

84. Ibn Ḥawqal, *al-Masālik wa-l-Mamālik,* 273. Cf. also Iṣṭakhrī, *al-Masālik wa-l-Mamālik,* 118 and B. M. Tirmidhi, "Zoroastrians and their fire temples in Iran and adjoining countries from the 9th to the 14th centuries *[sic]* as gleaned from the Arabic geographical works," *Islamic Culture* 24 (1950): 271–84.

85. Maqdisī, *Aḥsan,* 439.

86. Barthold, *An Historical Geography,* 149. Iṣṭakhrī (*al-Masālik wa-l-Mamālik,* 123) notes that the Persians identified Sulaymān with their mythical king Jamshīd.

87. This idea was formalized by, among others, al-Maqdisī (*Aḥsan,* 421) in his statement that the city lay sixty leagues from the frontiers of Fārs in the cardinal compass directions and eighty leagues from each of the four corners of the province. For the extent to which Persian administrative and imperial traditions survived the Arab invasion, see Heribert Busse, *Chalif und Grosskönig. Die Buyiden in Iraq (945–1055)* (Beirut, 1969), with the discussion continued in "The Revival of Persian Kingship under the Būyids," in *Islamic Civilisation, 950–1150,* ed. D. S. Richards (Oxford, 1973), 47–69.

88. Maqdisī, *Aḥsan,* 429, 441. See also Spuler, *Iran in Früh-Islamischer Zeit,* 191–92 and Barthold, *An Historical Geography,* 155.

89. Busse, "The Revival of Persian Kingship," 59. Iṣṭakhrī (*al-Masālik wa-l-Mamālik,* 150) and al-Maqdisī (*Aḥsan,* 445) both described the rock carvings of Bīshāpūr. There is a bibliography of Sāsānian monuments in the vicinity of this city in L. Vanden

Berghe, *Archéologie de l'Iran Ancien* (Leiden, 1959), 54–57, 158–59, 242.

90. Maqdisī, *Aḥsan,* 444. The dam was also known as the Band-i Amīr, and one section of the complex as the Sikr (Weir) of Fanā Khusraw Kūrah.

91. P. 148 above.

92. *Fārs-Nāmah,* 34: "A great deal of cotton is grown [in the vicinity of Jahram], which [significantly] is also exported"; also Mustawfī, *Nuzhat al-Qulūb,* 125; Le Strange's translation, 124. In the Mandistān desert region, lying along the lower course of the Sakkān River, Mustawfī notes that plentiful winter rains could nurture a spring crop of cotton a thousandfold larger than the quantity of seed planted (120; Le Strange's translation, 118).

93. Iṣṭakhrī, *al-Masālik wa-l-Mamālik,* 136.

Chapter Eleven

Author's note: For commentary and exegesis bearing on the urban system of Kirmān in the tenth century, see author's note to chapter 8. There is a survey of the tribal groups as they were constituted at the time in J. A. Markwart (Marquart), *A Catalogue of the Provincial Capitals of Ērānshahr,* 74–81. For references to the name Kirmān in antiquity see Barthold, *Historical Geography,* 133. For a good deal of general information about the province in early times, see Afḍal al-Dīn Aḥmad ibn Ḥāmid Kirmānī (died before 1218; by Bāstānī Pārīzī accorded the sobriquet "The Bayhaqī of Kirmān"), *ʿIqd al-ʿUlā li-l-Mawqif al-Aʿlā,* ed. ʿAlī Muḥammad ʿĀmirī Nāʾinī (Tehran, A.H. 1311). Cf. Th. Houtsma, *Recueil de Textes Relatifs à l'Histoire des Seldjoukides,* vol. 1 (Leyden, 1886). The nineteenth-century historian of Kirmān, Aḥmad ʿAlī Khān Vazīrī, relied on the *ʿIqd al-ʿUlā* for much of the information in his *Tārikh-i Kirmān (Tārikh-i Sālārīyah),* to which Muḥammad Ibrāhīm Bāstānī Pārīzī added further citations in his annotated edition of the text. Publications of the Farmān-Farmāyān Memorial Library, no. 1 (Tehran, A.H. 1340/A.D. 1961). Cf. C. E. Bosworth, "The Banū Ilyās of Kirmān (320–57/932–68)," in *Iran and Islam: In Memory of the Late Vladimir Minorsky,* ed. C. E. Bosworth (Edinburgh, 1971), 108–9. This author relies for his information principally on Miskawayh's (d. 1030) *Tajārib al-Umam wa Taʿāqib al-Humam,* ed. with English trans. by H. F. Amedroz and D. S. Margoliouth under the title *The Eclipse of the Abbassid Caliphate;* 3 vols. of text, 3 of trans., plus an index (Oxford and London, 1921).

1. Iṣṭakhrī, *al-Masālik wa-l-Mamālik,* 158, 163–65.

2. *Jurūm:* lit., "hot lands"; cf. present-day *garmsīr,* for which see W. B. Fisher, ed., *The Land of Iran,* vol. 1 of *The Cambridge History of Iran* (Cambridge, 1991), 284.

3. George C. Miles, "Some New Light on the History of Kirmān in the First Century of the Hijrah," in *The World of Islam: Studies in Honour of Philip K. Hitti,* ed. James Kritzeck and R. Bayly Winder (London, 1959), 89.

4. Ibn Ḥawqal, *al-Masālik wa-l-Mamālik,* 315. Bosworth has suggested that this impost was in fact tribute paid to the Sāmānids by the Ilyāsids ("The Banū Ilyās," 122 n. 30).

5. Also transcribed as al-Shīrajān and al-Sīrajān.

6. Cf. p. 112 above.

7. Ibn Khurradādhbih, *al-Masālik wa-l-Mamālik,* 49; Ibn Rustah, *al-Aʿlaq,* 286; Iṣṭakhrī, *al-Masālik wa-l-Mamālik,* 167; and Ibn Ḥawqal, *al-Masālik wa-l-Mamālik,* 312. The ruins of medieval al-Sīrjān, which are presently known as Qalʿah-i Sang or Qalʿah-i Bayḍā, are located five miles east of Saʿīdābād on the road to Baft: cf. Sir Percy Sykes, *Ten Thousand Miles in Persia* (London, 1902), 431; Guy Le Strange, "The cities of Kirmān in the time of Ḥamd Allāh . . . Mustawfī and Marco Polo," *Journal of the Royal Asiatic Society* (1901): 289; and Jean Aubin, "La question de Sīrǧān au XIIIe siècle," *Studia Iranica,* 6 (1977): 285–90.

8. Yaʿqūbī, *al-Buldān,* 286.

9. Iṣṭakhrī, *al-Masālik wa-l-Mamālik,* 166.

10. On this point see Bāstānī Pārīzī, *Tārīkh-i Kirmān,* 62 n. 2 and Bosworth, "The Banū Ilyās," 122 n. 23.

11. Maqdisī, *Aḥsan,* 464, 470. Cf. Minorsky, *Ḥudūd,* 124, where Sīrjān (here Sīrgān) is still designated the capital of Kirmān, presumably because the author of this work was basing himself almost entirely on al-Iṣṭakhrī.

12. Yāqūt, *Muʿjam,* 4:106, 265.

13. Bardasīr < Pers. *Bih-Ardashīr (whence the alternative form of the name: Guwāshīr). Cf. Ḥamzah al-Iṣfahānī, *al-Arḍ wa-l-Anbiyāʾ,* 46; Maqdisī, *Aḥsan,* 460–61; and Yāqūt, *Muʿjam,* 1:555, 2:927, 4:265.

14. Cf. Minorsky, *Ḥudūd,* 125, which comments on the sparseness of the population in the area.

15. The ruins of Jīruft, near the village of Karīmābād, are now known as the Shahr-i Daqiyānūs = "The City of Decius," the proverbial tyrant during whose reign the Seven Sleepers of Ephesus entered their cave: Qurʾān 18 *(al-Kahf):*9–14.

16. Iṣṭakhrī, *al-Masālik wa-l-Mamālik,* 166; Ibn Ḥawqal, *al-Masālik wa-l-Mamālik,* 311; Maqdisī, *Aḥsan,* 466, 470; and Minorsky, *Ḥudūd,* 124.

17. Ibn Ḥawqal, *al-Masālik wa-l-Mamālik,* 223–24; Maqdisī, *Aḥsan,* 465–66; and Minorsky, *Ḥudūd,* 125.

18. Maqdisī, *Aḥsan,* 463–64; and Minorsky, *Ḥudūd,* 125. The ruins of Narmāsīr are still visible at the place now called Chugukābād: Le Strange, *The Lands of the Eastern Caliphate,* 313.

19. Iṣṭakhri, *al-Masālik wa-l-Mamālik,* 234; Maqdisī, *Aḥsan,* 462–63; and Minorsky, *Ḥudūd,* 125.

20. Iṣṭakhrī, *al-Masālik wa-l-Mamālik,* 227–28.

21. Also Rīqān and Rīghān: ibid., 162; Maqdisī, *Aḥsan,* 463; Ibn Ḥawqal, *al-Masālik wa-l-Mamālik,* 307; and Minorsky, *Ḥudūd,* 125.

22. Maqdisī, *Aḥsan,* 463.

23. Ibid. and Minorsky, *Ḥudūd,* 125 (Bahra < *Pahra).

24. Maqdisī, *Aḥsan,* 469.

25. Gently sloping underground channels driven into water-bearing strata. *Kārīz* is the term used in the eastern sectors of the Īrānian world; elsewhere *qanāt* is the usual name for such a tunnel.

26. Minorsky, *Ḥudūd,* 125.

27. Note 16 above. For the introduction of indigo into the

Middle East see chapter 6, note 82. This crop was grown fairly widely in the southern half of the *iqlīm;* for example, Minorsky, *Ḥudūd,* 124 (Maghūn); Maqdisī, *Aḥsan,* 466–67 (Darahqān and Hurmuz); Ibn Ḥawqal, *al-Masālik wa-l-Mamālik,* 312 ("From the territories of Maghūn and Walashjird to the district of Hurmuz").

28. Ibn Ḥawqal, *al-Masālik wa-l-Mamālik,* 310.

29. Maqdisī, *Aḥsan,* 462–63.

30. These routes were described in earlier times by Ibn Khurradādhbih, *al-Masālik wa-l-Mamālik,* 48–54; Qudāmah, *al-Kharāj,* 195–96; Iṣṭakhrī, *al-Masālik wa-l-Mamālik,* 131, 168–69; Ibn Ḥawqal, *al-Masālik wa-l-Mamālik,* 313–15; Maqdisī, *Aḥsan,* 455, 473; and in the fourteenth century by Mustawfī, *Nuzhat al-Qulūb,* 201. The nodal position of Sīrjān in the route network of Kirmān is clearly evident in the Balkhī (al-Iṣṭakhrī II) map in the Bologna MS. *Cod. 3521,* fol. 47: reproduced in Miller, *Mappae Arabicae,* Gaube reprint, 48–49.

31. Maqdisī, *Aḥsan,* 463.

32. Iṣṭakhrī, *al-Masālik wa-l-Mamālik,* 169; Ibn Ḥawqal, *al-Masālik wa-l-Mamālik,* 311; and Maqdisī, *Aḥsan,* 486. Bāstānī-i Pārīzī's work (author's note above) includes numerous references to a suburb of Jīruft known as Qamādīn, "where foreign merchants from Rūm and Hind had their warehouses, and where travellers by sea and land could store their goods." In the *sūqs* of this suburb, he notes, it was possible to buy and sell goods from China, Transoxania, Hindūstān, Khurāsān, the Zanj countries, Abyssinia, Egypt, the Greek lands, Armenia, Mesopotamia, and Ādharbayjān (Azerbaijan). However, no tenth-century or earlier writer mentioned this great market, and when Marco Polo passed through Qamādīn (which he subsequently dictated as *Camadi*) toward the end of the thirteenth century, it was "of little consequence, for the Tartars in their incursions have several times ravaged it" (A. C. Moule and Paul Pelliot, *Marco Polo: The Description of the World,* vol. 2 [London, 1938], xii).

33. Maqdisī, *Aḥsan,* 466. Cf. also Minorsky, *Ḥudūd,* 124.

34. Minorsky, *Ḥudūd,* 124; Iṣṭakhrī, *al-Masālik wa-l-Mamālik,* 166; and Abū al-Fidā', *Mukhtaṣar Ta'rikh al-Bashar,* 2:103.

35. Iṣṭakhrī, *al-Masālik wa-l-Mamālik,* 166–67 and Ibn Ḥawqal, *al-Masālik wa-l-Mamālik,* 311.

36. Maqdisī, *Aḥsan,* 470, where the name of the district is written as Valashgird.

37. In addition to these references see al-Jaḥiẓ (attrib.), "Al-Tabaṣṣur," 345.

38. Maqdisī, *Aḥsan,* 459, 470. The manufacture of tutty *(tutia)* in Kūhbanān *(Cobinan)* was described by Marco Polo: Moule and Pelliot, *Marco Polo,* 1:127. For commentary see Sir Henry Yule, *The Book of Ser Marco Polo the Venetian Concerning the Kingdoms and Marvels of the East,* vol. 1 (London, 1903): 126–27. Cf. also Pedro Teixeira, *Relacion de Persia* (Amberes, 1610), 121. For the history of tutty in medieval Asia see Berthold Laufer, *Sino-Iranica,* 511–14. Ibn al-Faqīh provides a readily accessible account of the zinc mines on the slopes of Mount Dunbāvand in Ṭabaristān, for which see Schwarz, *Iran,* 252.

39. Ibn al-Faqīh, *al-Buldān,* 206; Maqdisī, *Aḥsan,* 470; and Minorsky, *Ḥudūd,* 65. In the fourteenth century Mustawfī (*Nuzhat al-Qulūb,* 204, 206; Le Strange's translation, 196, 197) mentioned turquoise and lapis-lazuli mines in the province, but there is no account of these in earlier times.

40. Ibn Ḥawqal, *al-Masālik wa-l-Mamālik,* 312; cf. also Minorsky, *Ḥudūd,* 125. The phrase *ṭayālisah muqawwarah* has not been adequately explained, and the rendering "embroidered ———" is derived from Serjeant's "possibly with some kind of raised pile or embroidery which gave the appearance of hollows": *Islamic Textiles,* 107.

41. Maqdisī, *Aḥsan,* 465, 466, 470.

42. Iṣṭakhrī, *al-Masālik wa-l-Mamālik,* 167; cf. Abū al-Fidā', *Mukhtaṣar Ta'rīkh al-Bashar,* 337 and Ibn Ḥawqal, *al-Masālik wa-l-Mamālik,* 313.

43. Ibn Ḥawqal, *al-Masālik wa-l-Mamālik,* 312.

44. Maqdisī, *Aḥsan,* 461.

45. Ibid., 462.

46. The shrine of the Ṣūfī saint Niʿmat-Allāh at Māhān, which is today revered throughout Īrān, was established only in the fifteenth century.

47. There is a brief summary of Arab settlement in Kirmān by Ann K. S. Lambton in *The Encyclopaedia of Islam,* 2d ed., 5: 153–54.

48. There is a summary of Ilyāsid building in Kirmān Province, based on information furnished by the topographers and Afḍal al-Dīn Kirmānī, in Bosworth, "The Banū Ilyās," 113–14.

49. Ibn Ḥawqal, *al-Masālik wa-l-Mamālik,* 309–10. Cf. also Maqdisī, *Aḥsan,* 471. On the Qufṣ generally see C. E. Bosworth, "The Kūfichīs or Qufṣ in Persian history," *Iran, Journal of the British Institute of Persian Studies* 14 (1976): 9–17.

50. Minorsky, *Ḥudūd,* 65.

51. Miskawayh, *Tajārib al-Umam,* 2:368.

52. Ibid., 2:299–301 and Spuler, *Iran in Früh-Islamischer Zeit,* 100–101.

53. Iṣṭakhrī, *al-Masālik wa-l-Mamālik,* 164.

54. Miskawayh, *Tajārib al-Umam,* 2:249–50.

55. Ibn Ḥawqal, *al-Masālik wa-l-Mamālik,* 309–10. For comments on the wealth of Muḥammad ibn Ilyās derived from al-ʿAwfī's *Lubāb al-Albāb* (thirteenth century), see Bosworth, "The Banū Ilyās," 119–20.

56. Maqdisī, *Aḥsan,* 489.

57. Ibn Ḥawqal, *al-Masālik wa-l-Mamālik,* 315.

Chapter Twelve

Author's note: For commentary and exegesis bearing on the urban system of al-Riḥāb in the tenth century, see author's note to chapter 8. Cf. also K. Hübschmann, "Die altarmenischen Ortsnamen," *Indo-Germanen Forschungen,* 16 (1904): 197–479; Sayyid Aḥmad Kasravī, *Pādshāhān-i Gumnām-i Īrān,* fascs. 1–3 (Tehran, A.H. 1347–49); A. Z. Validi, "Azerbaycanîn tarihî cografyasî," *Azerbaycan Yurt Bilgisi* (1932), no. 1, 35–48; no. 2, 1–15; no. 3, 123–

32; no. 4, 145–56 and "Azerbaycan etnografisine dair," loc. cit. (1953), no. 14, 49–56. It should be noted that Ibn Ḥawqal (*al-Masālik wa-l-Mamālik,* 331–35) provides an unexpectedly rich infusion of local color in his description of this *iqlīm* on the fringe of the Islamic world; and that there is a certain amount of supplementary information in the so-called Second *Risālah* of Abū Dulaf, who travelled through al-Riḥāb in the mid-tenth century: cf. note 152 to chapter 3. The most useful short commentary on the information furnished by the early topographers generally is that incorporated in Minorsky's translation of the *Ḥudūd al-ʿĀlam,* 393–411; the most comprehensive, as usual, is provided by Schwarz, *Iran,* 959–1600. There is a useful summary of the complicated history of the region by Wilferd Madelung in Frye, ed., *The Period from the Arab Invasion to the Saljuqs,* 226–49. A Russian translation of and commentary on al-Maqdisī's chapter on al-Riḥāb by Nikolai Serikoff has not been accessible to me.

1. Respectively the Cyrus and Araxes Rivers of the classical world. The Arab topographers without exception cast the name of the provine in pseudo-Arabic form as al-Rān: cf. note 8 below.

2. Pers. = Ādharbādhagān; Arm. Atrpatakan < Gk. Atropatene; cf. Barthold, *Historical Geography,* 214.

3. To Masʿūdī (*Murūj,* 1:97) and Ibn Ḥawqal (*al-Masālik wa-l-Mamālik,* 345), Lake Urmīyah was known as the Buḥayrah Kabūdhān, meaning "the Blue Lake" (from the Arabic *Buḥayrah* and the Persian *Kabūd*). It was also sometimes referred to as the Lake of Schismatics, from the prevalence of heterodox beliefs among the inhabitants of the region.

4. For the rulers of this dynasty see Justi, *Iranisches Namenbuch,* 441; Eduard von Zambaur, *Manuel de Généalogie et de Chronologie pour l'Histoire de l'Islam* (Hanover, 1927), 180; and more compendiously, Clifford E. Bosworth, *The Islamic Dynasties: A Chronological and Genealogical Handbook* (Edinburgh, 1967), 86–87. The Musāfirids were known alternatively as Sallārids, and probably also as Kangarids.

It is not without interest that Maqdisī's *iqlīm* also approximated fairly closely to the Sāsānian administrative unit of Kʿust-i Kapkoh, which had subsumed Armenia, Iberia, Albania, Ādharbāyjān (Azerbaijan), and certain small Caspian districts.

5. In spite of their often Kurdicized names (e.g., Mamlān < Muḥammad, Aḥmadīl < Aḥmad), the Rawwādids were originally Arabs of the Yamanī tribe of Azd. Under the earlier ʿAbbāsids the family had provided governors of Tabrīz.

6. For native Armenian sources, both ancient and modern—to which I have no access—consult the bibliography in *The Encyclopaedia of Islam,* 2d ed., 1:645–50. See also H. Manadean, "Les invasions arabes en Arménie," *Byzantion* 18 (1946–48): 163–92 (This is a French translation of a paper first published in Yerevan in 1932); B. Khalateantz, *Textes Arabes Relatifs à l'Arménie* (Vienne, 1919); J. Laurent, *L'Arménie entre Byzance et l'Islam depuis la Conquête Arabe jusq'en 886* (Paris, 1919); J. Muyldermans, *La Domination Arabe en Arménie: Extrait de l'Histoire Universelle de Vardan . . .* (Louvain and Paris, 1927); René Grousset, *Histoire de l'Arménie des Origines à 1071* (Paris, 1947), chaps. 9–11; and R. Vasmer, *Chronologie der Arabischen Statthalter von Armenien . . . (750–887)* (Wien, 1931). For the Bagratid period in particular see Aram Ter-Ghewondyan, *The Arab Emirates in Bagratid Armenia* (Lisbon, 1976).

7. See *Histoire des Ardzrounis,* a French translation of the work of Thomas Ardzruni (ninth to tenth century) in M. Brosset, *Collection d'Historiens Arméniens,* vol. 1 (St. Pétersbourg, 1874).

8. For the early Islamic history of Arrān see Laurent, *L'Arménie entre Byzance et l'Islam* (cf. note 6). In Greek and Latin the combined floodplains of the Kur (Cyrus) and Aras (Araxes) Rivers, lying between Iveria (Georgia) and the Caspian Sea, constituted the territory of Albania, the Armenian equivalent of which was Alvan-kʿ or Ran; in Syriac, Aran: hence the al-Rān of Islamic topographers. Marquart (*Ērānšahr nach der Geographie des Ps. Moses Xorenacʿi,* 117) characterized the province at the close of the Sāsānian era as *eminent unarisches Land,* while Moses of Khorēn castigated the Albanian language as "gutteral, rude, barbaric, and generally uncouth" (quoted by Minorsky, *A History of Sharvān and Darband in the 10th and 11th Centuries* [Cambridge, 1953], 12, from Movsēs Xorenacʿi, *Patmutʿiwn Hayocʿ,* vol. 3, chap. 54).

9. This was the Marwān who subsequently became the last of the Umayyad caliphs.

10. Ibn al-Athīr, *al-Kāmil,* 8:308–10; Masʿūdī, *Murūj,* 2:21; and Miskawayh, *Tajārib al-Umam,* 2:62–67. Cf. also D. S. Margoliouth, "The Russian seizure of Bardhaʿah in 943 A.D.," *Bulletin of the School of Oriental and African Studies* (1918): 82–95.

11. Ardavīl in Minorsky, *Ḥudūd,* 142; in Armenian, Artavet. In Sāsānian times the city had been known as Bādhān Fayrūz, but its pre-Islamic history is totally obscure. Cf. also Abū Dulaf, *Risālah,* Arabic text, 6; Minorsky's translation, 35.

12. Cf. V. Minorsky, *La Domination des Dailamites,* Publications de la Société des Etudes Iraniennes, no. 3 (Paris, 1932), passim.

13. Ibn Ḥawqal, *al-Masālik wa-l-Mamālik,* 334; Minorsky, *Ḥudūd,* 142; Abū al-Fidāʾ, *Mukhtaṣar Tāʾrīkh al-Bashar,* 2:152.

14. Ibn Ḥawqal, *al-Masālik wa-l-Mamālik,* 334.

15. Ibid., 337. Cf. also Iṣṭakhrī, *al-Masālik wa-l-Mamālik,* 182–84 and Minorsky, *Ḥudūd,* 143. The city had originally been built by the Albanian Vachʿē during the reign of the Sāsānian king Pēroz (457–84), hence its Persian name Pērōzāpāt, whence Armenian Partaw.

16. Ibn Ḥawqal, *al-Masālik wa-l-Mamālik,* 338. Eventually the wheel came full circle and the day of the week that had given its Greek name to the market became known popularly as Kurkī Day.

17. Maqdisī, *Aḥsan,* 375.

18. Also Duwīn, Dwīn, and Tovin.

19. Iṣṭakhrī, *al-Masālik wa-l-Mamālik,* 191; Ibn Ḥawqal, *al-Masālik wa-l-Mamālik,* 342; Maqdisī, *Aḥsan,* 379; and Minorsky, *Ḥudūd,* 142–43; cf. also V. Minorsky, "Transcaucasica," *Journal Asiatique* (1930): 41–56.

20. For a fairly detailed account of the history of Dabīl (Dwīn)

see Josef Marquart (Markwart), *Südarmenien und die Tigrisquellen,* 562 *et seq.*, with a great deal of additional information in V. Minorsky, *Studies in Caucasian History* (London, 1952), especially 116 et seq.; but the most compendious discussions are those by M. Canard in *The Encyclopaedia of Islam,* 2d ed., 2:678–81 and Ter Ghewondyan, *The Arab Emirates in Bagratid Armenia,* passim. There is an authoritative chronology of the city of Dabīl/Dwīn from 330 to 1236 in this latter work: appendix 1, 179–80.

21. Cf. p. 78 above.

22. See Ṭabarī, *Taʾrīkh,* 3:645 and Balādhurī, *Futūḥ al-Buldān,* 210; also Josef Marquart, *Osteuropäische und ostasiatische Streifzüge* (Leipzig, 1903), 455 and particularly Minorsky, *Ḥudūd,* 404.

23. Minorsky (*Ḥudūd,* 404) believes that, contra Yāqūt (*Muʿjam,* 4:147), who identified Yazīdīyah precisely with Shammākhīyah, the former settlement was the **lashkar-gāh* (army camp) where the *Ḥudūd* tells us the Sharvān *shāh* resided and which was a *farsakh* distant from Shammākhīyah proper. See also V. Minorsky, *A History of Sharvān and Darband,* 75. The same author has also elicited a considerable quantity of information relevant to Sharvān in the tenth and eleventh centuries from a *Taʾrīkh Bāb al-Abwāb* that now survives only in copious quotations in Aḥmad ibn Luṭf Allāh Münejjim-Bashī's *Jamīʿ al-Duwal (A History of Sharvān and Darband)* 3 vols. (Istanbul, A.H. 1285), especially 56–69, 75–85, and 116–22. A *Darband-Nāmah,* which now exists in at least eight somewhat divergent manuscripts in Azarbayjān Turkish (5) and Persian (3), is unlikely in any of its versions to be older than a Persian redaction known to have been in existence toward the end of the seventeenth century. It does deal, however, with the early days of the Muslim conquest. This text was translated into English as early as 1851 by Mirza A. Kazem-Beg: *Derbend-nâmeh, or the History of Derbend: Translated from a Select Turkish Version* (St. Petersburg).

24. Also transcribed as Mughkān and Mūqān.

25. Maqdisī, *Aḥsan,* 51, 376 and Mustawfī, *Nuzhat al-Qulūb,* 159–60.

26. Maqdisī, *Aḥsan,* 378. The commonly adduced tradition that Tabrīz had been founded by Zubaydah, wife of Hārūn al-Rashīd, although espoused by Barthold (*Historical Geography,* 217), receives no support from the early topographers, and, indeed, goes against such other evidence as is available. A similar tale is told of Warthān in Mūghān, but there is no reason to think that the lady in question ever visited the Province of al-Riḥāb. The Rawwādid dynasty ruled in Tabrīz intermittently from the mid-ninth century until Saljūk times.

27. Minorsky, *Ḥudūd,* 142.

28. Also transcribed as Khilāṭ; Armenian Khlatʿ, modern Turkish Ahlat. For the nearly four centuries being here reviewed, Akhlāṭ was ruled successively by Arab governors, Armenian princelings, and Arab local *amīrs* of the Qays tribe. In about 983 it was incorporated in the territories controlled by Bādh, founder of the Kurdish Marwānid dynasty: for which see von Zambaur, *Manuel,* 136; Bosworth, *Islamic Dynasties,* 53–54; and with profit, despite the period when it was written, H. F. Amedroz, "The Marwānid dynasty at Mayyāfāriqīn in the tenth and eleventh centuries A.D.," *Journal of the Royal Asiatic Society* (1903): 123–54. For a comprehensive bibliography of Akhlāṭ see A. Gabriel, *Voyages Archéologiques dans la Turquie Orientale,* vol. 1 (Paris, 1940), 241–51.

29. Arm. Archēsh; in the *Ḥudūd,* 143, Arjīj—perhaps influenced by the popular etymology *arčīč* > *arzīz:* see Minorsky, *Ḥudūd,* 395 n. 12. Although the city had been occupied by Arabs in the time of the caliph ʿUthmān, it remained under the authority of one or another Armenian principality until 772, when it was incorporated into the Qaysite Amīrate of Akhlāṭ (cf. note 28).

30. Also transcribed as Bahargīrī: see Iṣṭakhrī, *al-Masālik wa-l-Mamālik,* 188, 194; Ibn Ḥawqal, *al-Masālik wa-l-Mamālik,* 344, 346, 353; Ibn al-Faqīh, *al-Buldān,* 285; and Maqdisī, *Aḥsan,* 374, 383.

31. Ibn Ḥawqal, *al-Masālik wa-l-Mamālik,* 343.

32. Iṣṭakhrī, *al-Masālik wa-l-Mamālik,* 188, 194; Ibn Ḥawqal, *al-Masālik wa-l-Mamālik,* 333; Maqdisī, *Aḥsan,* 374–413; and Yāqūt, *Muʿjam,* 1:526.

33. Ibn Ḥawqal, *al-Masālik wa-l-Mamālik,* 333 and Maqdisī, *Aḥsan,* 383 (Tall Wān).

34. Also transcribed as Ṭasūj.

35. Pers. = Dih Khuwārqān.

36. Also written as Naylān.

37. Qudāmah, *al-Kharāj,* 213; Ibn Ḥawqal, *al-Masālik wa-l-Mamālik,* 336; Maqdisī, *Aḥsan,* 374–83; and Minorsky, *Ḥudūd,* 143.

38. Iṣṭakhrī, *al-Masālik wa-l-Mamālik,* 182, 194; Ibn Ḥawqal, *al-Masālik wa-l-Mamālik,* 336; Maqdisī, *Aḥsan,* 374–86; and Minorsky, *Ḥudūd,* 143.

39. The Arabic name of this city was originally Qariyat al-Marāghah = "The Village of the Pastures." In Sāsānian times it had been known as Afrāzah Rūdh. See Iṣṭakhrī, *al-Masālik wa-l-Mamālik,* 181, 190; Ibn Ḥawqal, *al-Masālik wa-l-Mamālik,* 333, 336; Qudāmah, *al-Kharāj,* 226–27; Maqdisī, *Aḥsan,* 374–84; Minorsky, Ḥudūd, 142; and al-Faqīh, *al-Buldān,* 284.

40. Ibn Ḥawqal, *al-Masālik wa-l-Mamālik,* 336–37.

41. Also Ushnūyah: Minorsky, *Ḥudūd,* 142–45 and Ibn Ḥawqal, *al-Masālik wa-l-Mamālik,* 336.

42. Ibn Ḥawqal, *al-Masālik wa-l-Mamālik,* 344.

43. Gurjistān (Georgia) became Muslim only after the campaign of Tīmūr at the end of the fourteenth century, but Tiflīs (Tblisi), its capital, figured in the writings of tenth-century topographers such as Iṣṭakhrī (*al-Masālik wa-l-Mamālik,* 185), Ibn Ḥawqal, (*al-Masālik wa-l-Mamālik,* 340), Maqdisī (*Aḥsan,* 375–79), and the author of the *Ḥudūd* (144 [derived almost entirely from Iṣṭakhrī]).

44. Nahr al-Samūr, but known to al-Maqdisī as Nahr al-Malik, "The King's River." Bāb al-Abwāb was the name by which the Arabs designated the city of Darband: Arm. *Chʿor* (**Chūr* > Ar. *Ṣul);* Mongol *Qahalgha.* Cf. Iṣṭakhrī, *al-Masālik wa-l-Mamālik,*

184; Ibn Ḥawqal, *al-Masālik wa-l-Mamālik,* 386–89; Maqdisī, *Aḥsan,* 376–81; and Minorsky, *Ḥudūd,* 145. For the early twelfth-century *Ta'rīkh Bāb al-Abwāb* and Minorsky's history based on it, see note 23 above.

45. Minorsky, *Ḥudūd,* 145. Also Iṣṭakhrī, *al-Masālik wa-l-Mamālik,* 184; Ibn Ḥawqal, *al-Masālik wa-l-Mamālik,* 339–40; and Minorsky, *A History of Sharvān and Darband,* 127.

46. As Ibn Ḥawqal remarks (*al-Masālik wa-l-Mamālik,* 339), this closing of the harbor entrance was reminiscent of the situations at Ṣūr, Bayrūt (I have not found confirmation of this particular statement), and, we may add, at ʿAkkā.

47. Also Bākū, Bākuh', Bākūh. Iṣṭakhrī, *al-Masālik wa-l-Mamālik,* 190; Ibn Ḥawqal, *al-Masālik wa-l-Mamālik,* 339–40; Abū Dulaf, *Risālah,* par. 13 (Arabic text, 5; Minorsky's translation, 35); Masʿūdī, *Murūj,* 2:21, 25 and *al-Tanbīh* (completed at the end of the author's life), 60; Minorsky, *Ḥudūd,* 145; and Maqdisī, *Aḥsan,* 376.

48. Ar. Surmāhī < Pers. *shūr-māhī* = "salt fish." It was exported to places as far distant as al-ʿIrāq (Ibn Ḥawqal, *al-Masālik wa-l-Mamālik,* 338).

49. Ibn Ḥawqal, *al-Masālik wa-l-Mamālik,* 346. Some three centuries later, Yāqūt (*Muʿjam,* 1:526) recalled that he had purchased some of this salted *ṭirrīkh* as far away as Balkh. Ar. *tirrīkh* < Arm. *tareχ*.

50. Minorsky, *Ḥudūd,* 145.

51. Abū Dulaf, *Risālah,* par. 13 (cf. note 47 above).

52. Serjeant suggests that possibly certain manufactures of Khūzistān were here intended (*Islamic Textiles,* 33).

53. High-quality cloth from Maysān in southeastern ʿIrāq.

54. A kind of brocade.

55. Al-Jāḥiẓ (attrib.), "Al-Tabaṣṣur," 12:336–37.

56. Ibid., 348. For the reputation and value of Armenian trouserbands see Serjeant, *Islamic Textiles,* 61–62. Al-Thaʿālibī includes them in a schedule of luxury fabrics relating to the second half of the tenth century (*al-Laṭā'if al-Maʿārif,* 236; Bosworth's translation), while Ibn Ḥawqal praises those made in the town of Salmās as "unequalled in the world" (*al-Masālik wa-l-Mamālik,* 344).

57. Iṣṭakhrī, *al-Masālik wa-l-Mamālik,* 152, 183, 188; Ibn Ḥawqal, *al-Masālik wa-l-Mamālik,* 344-45; Maqdisī, *Aḥsan,* 374, 380; and Minorsky, *Ḥudūd,* 142–45.

58. Iṣṭakhrī, *al-Masālik wa-l-Mamālik,* 184; cf. also Ibn Ḥawqal, *al-Masālik wa-l-Mamālik,* 339.

59. Iṣṭakhrī, *al-Masālik wa-l-Mamālik,* 183; Ibn Ḥawqal, *al-Masālik wa-l-Mamālik,* 338; Minorsky, *Ḥudūd,* 143; and Maqdisī, *Aḥsan,* 380.

60. See chapter 10.

61. Jaḥiẓ, "Tabaṣṣur," 339; Iṣṭakhrī, *al-Masālik wa-l-Mamālik,* 188; Ibn Ḥawqal, *al-Masālik wa-l-Mamālik,* 342; Minorsky, *Ḥudūd,* 142; and Ibn al-Faqīh, *al-Buldān,* 247.

62. Balādhurī, *Futūḥ al-Buldān,* 200. I owe this reference to Serjeant, *Islamic Textiles,* 65. Azdisāṭ < Arm. Artašat.

63. Minorsky, *Ḥudūd,* 143; Iṣṭakhrī, *al-Masālik wa-l-Mamālik,* 190; and Ibn Ḥawqal, *al-Masālik wa-l-Mamālik,* 347. The Arabic term for madder was *fuwwah,* the Persian *rūnās.*

64. Ibn Ḥawqal, *al-Masālik wa-l-Mamālik,* 347.

65. Minorsky, *Ḥudūd,* 144. The fortress in question was Qalʿah ibn K.nd.mān, twelve *farsakhs* east of Tiflis: cf. Iṣṭakhrī, *al-Masālik wa-l-Mamālik,* 193.

66. Mustawfī, *Nuzhat al-Qulūb,* Arabic text, 90; Le Strange's translation, 91. Other sources placed the Fountain of Life at the Confluence of the Two Seas (beyond the Pillars of Hercules = the Strait of Gibraltar).

67. Qur'ān 18 *(al-Kahf):*63. Other sources locate the Rock of Mūsā at the Confluence of the Two Seas (cf. note 66) or, for reasons that are hard to fathom, at Anṭākiyah (Antioch) in al-Shām (Syria).

68. Marquart, *Südarmenien und die Tigrisquellen,* 115.

69. Ibn Ḥawqal, *al-Masālik wa-l-Mamālik,* 347.

70. Ibid., 335.

71. Ibid., 337, 339.

Chapter Thirteen

Author's note: For secondary works bearing on the urban system of al-Daylam in the tenth century, see author's note to chapter 8, especially Le Strange, *The Lands of the Eastern Caliphate,* chapters 12 and 26 and Minorsky's commentary on the *Ḥudūd al-ʿĀlam,* 384–91. There is also a good deal of useful information relevant to this topic in Spuler, *Iran in Früh-Islamischer Zeit,* index; R. Vasmer, "Die Eroberung Ṭabaristāns durch die Araber zur Zeit des Chalifen al-Manṣūr," *Islamica* 3 (1927): 86–150; and, incidentally to an itinerary-style narrative, in H. L. Rabino (di Borgomale), *Mázandarán and Astarábád,* E. J. W. Gibb Memorial Publications, n.s., no. 7 (London, 1928); also "L'histoire du Māzandarān," *Journal Asiatique* 234 (1943–45): 211–43.

The Caspian provinces generally were not well reported by the early historians and topographers. Ibn Khurradādhbih and Qudāmah totally ignored them. Al-Balādhurī and al-Ṭabarī provided only fragmentary accounts, and al-Yaʿqūbī (*al-Buldān,* 276–77) and Ibn Rustah (*al-Aʿlaq,* 149–51) somewhat abbreviated ones. Ibn al-Faqīh, although furnishing a rather longer description (*al-Buldān,* 101–14), offered relatively little of relevance to the present inquiry. However, Iṣṭakhrī (*al-Masālik wa-l-Mamālik,* 204–17), Ibn Ḥawqal (*al-Masālik wa-l-Mamālik,* 375–85), and al-Maqdisī (*Aḥsan,* 353–73) presented reasonably systematic accounts of the region which together constitute the basis of the urban hierarchy described in this chapter. Moreover, two additional texts have provided certain information not recorded elsewhere: namely the anonymous *Ḥudūd al-ʿĀlam* (133–37), which appears to preserve personal recollections of the province of Gīlān (cf. pp. 68–69 above); and the so-called Second *Risālah* of Abū Dulaf, who travelled through Gīlān and Gurgān probably in the 940s (cf. note 152 to chapter 3). Some use has also been made of Muḥammad ibn Ḥasan Ibn Isfandiyār, *Tārīkh-i Ṭabaristān,* ed. ʿAbbās Iqbāl, 2 vols.

(Tehran, A.H. 1320/A.D. 1941); abridged English trans. by E. G. Browne (Leyden and London, 1905). The author, who was writing early in the thirteenth century, was able to consult both Arabic and Persian works that are no longer extant. (A Russian translation of and commentary on al-Maqdisī's chapter on al-Daylam by Nikolai Serikoff has not been accessible to me.)

1. Maqdisī, *Aḥsan,* 353–73. Cf. *Ḥudūd,* 133–37 and 384–91, where al-Daylamān includes Gurgān, Ṭabaristān, Qūmis (Kūmish), Daylam proper *(Daylam-i khāṣṣa),* and Gīlān.

2. Ar. = Jīlān, or perhaps more commonly in the plural form Jīlānāt, when the name was presumably intended to embrace two contrasting ecotypes, namely the lower course of the Safīd Rūd and the mountain slopes behind it; the former being the habitat of the ethnic group known to antiquity as Γέλοι (Ar. *al-Jil*), the latter that of "the pure-blooded Daylamī" *(al-Daylam al-maḥḍ).*

3. Ar. = Jurjān.

4. According to Ibn Ḥawqal (*al-Masālik wa-l-Mamālik,* 382), Gurgān was nearly as large as al-Rayy (Rey) (p. 136 above).

5. This is the orthography used by Ibn Ḥawqal (ibid.) and the *Ḥudūd* (133); Maqdisī (*Aḥsan,* 357–58) wrote Bakrābād.

6. Minorsky, *Ḥudūd,* 133.

7. The political history of al-Daylam is often obscure and inevitably complicated both by the composite character of the *iqlīm* and by its situation on the northern fringes of the Islamic world. Gīlān, for instance, was never conquered by the Arabs, and Ṭabaristān finally submitted only in the third quarter of the eighth century. In fact coins bearing Pahlavī inscriptions continued to be struck for some years even after Muslim governors were established in Āmul. Gurgān had been captured from the Chöl (Ar. Ṣūl) Turks in 716/17. For the rest of the period with which we are here concerned, several petty dynasties managed to maintain themselves in remoter areas of the *iqlīm* (ʿAlids in Ṭabaristān and Gīlān, Ziyārids in Ṭabaristān and Gurgān, Bāwandid, *Iṣpahbads* and *Ustandārs* in Rūyān, Kāwūsīyah Bāwandids in the Qārin Mountains, Justānids and Sallārids in Ṭārum, to name only some of the more important), submitting expediently to ʿAbbāsids, Buwayhids, Ṭāhirids, and Sāmānids as frontier power struggles dictated.

The most compendious account of these minor dynasties is that by Wilferd Madelung, "The Minor Dynasties of Northern Iran," in *The Cambridge History of Iran,* vol. 4: *The Period from the Arab Invasion to the Saljuqs,* ed. R. N. Frye (Cambridge, 1975), 198–249. See also the same author's *Der Imam al-Qāsim b. Ibrāhīm und die Glaubenslehre der Zaiditen* (Berlin, 1966) and "The ʿAlid Rulers of Ṭabaristān, Daylamān and Gīlān," in *Atti del III Congresso di Studi Arabi e Islamici* (Napoli, 1967); Minorsky, *La Domination des Dailamites;* H. L. Rabino (di Borgomale), "Les dynasties du Māzandarān de l'an 50 avant l'hégire à l'an 1066 de l'hégire (572 à 1597–98) après les chroniques locales," *Journal Asiatique* 228 (1936): 397–474 and "Les dynasties alaouides du Mazandéran," *Journal Asiatique* 210 (1927): 253–77; and M. Rekaya, "La place des provinces sud-caspiennes dans l'histoire de l'Iran de la conquête arabe à l'avènement des Zaydites (16–250 H./637–864 J.C.): particularisme régional ou rôle 'national'?" *Revista degli Studi Orientali* 48 (1974): 117–52. For the Ziyārids see Charles Huart, "Les Ziyārides," *Mémoires de l'Institut National de France,* Académie des Inscriptions et Belles-Lettres 42 (1922). The dynastic successions within these states are presented most fully in von Zambaur, *Manuel,* 187–89, 210–11 and more briefly in Bosworth, *Islamic Dynasties,* 83–93.

8. Thaʿālibī, *al-Laṭāʾif al-Maʿārif,* 188; Bosworth's translation, 130.

9. Cited by Thaʿālibī, ibid.; Bosworth's translation, 130–31.

10. Whence al-Dāmghān was often referred to by topographical writers as Qūmis, signifying Madīnah Qūmis = Qūmis City. However, after visiting Bisṭām in 1046, Nāṣir-i Khusraw (*Safar Nāmah,* Schéfer's translation, 7; Thackston's translation, 2) apparently regarded that city as the capital, for he referred to it as Qūmis City.

11. Yaʿqūbī, *al-Buldān,* 276.

12. Ibn Khurradādhbih, *al-Masālik wa-l-Mamālik,* 23; Qudāmah, *al-Kharāj,* 201; Ibn Ḥawqal, *al-Masālik wa-l-Mamālik,* 380, Maqdisī, *Aḥsan,* 355–56; Abū Dulaf, *Risālah,* Minorsky's translation, 57; and Minorsky, *Ḥudūd,* 135, 387, where Minorsky suggests that Dāmghān should probably be identified with the settlement of Parthian times known to the Greeks as Ἑκατόμπυλος βασίλειον. More recently J. Hansman has established conclusively that Hekatompylos occupied the site of present-day Shahr-i Qūmis, to the southwest of Dāmghān: "The problem of Qūmis," *Journal of the Royal Asiatic Society* (1968): 111–39. For the classical sources relating to Hekatompylos, the more-than-a-century-old paper by A. D. Mordtmann, "Hekatompylos. Ein Beitrag zur vergleichenden Geographie Persiens," *Sitzungsberichte der Königlichen Akademie der Wissenschaften zu München, Phil.-Hist. Kl.* 1 (1869): 497–536 is still the most useful.

In addition to the references listed in the author's note above, see Iqbāl Yaghmāʾī, *Jughrāfiyā-yi Tāʾrīkhi-yi Dāmghān* (Tehran, A.H. 1377/A.D. 1957) and Chahryār Adle, "Contribution à la géographie historique du Damghan," *Le Monde Iranien et l'Islam* 1 (1971): 69–104. It is noteworthy that the structure known as the Tarī Khāna, situated one kilometer south of the present-day town, may be the earliest remains of a mosque in Īrān—dating, it is believed, from the ninth century.

13. Iṣṭakhrī, *al-Masālik wa-l-Mamālik,* 204; Maqdisī, *Aḥsan,* 360. For difficulties in identifying the site of Barvān see p. 79 and note 185 in chapter 3.

14. After the Arab conquest, while caliphal governors resided in Āmul, the *iṣpahbads* continued to control most of Ṭabaristān from their capital of Ispahbadān, a mile or so north of Sārīyah and only two miles from the Caspian shore. Cf. Barthold, *Historical Geography,* 238.

15. Minorsky, *Ḥudūd,* 134.

16. Ibn Ḥawqal, *al-Masālik wa-l-Mamālik,* 381. The other information in this paragraph is derived from al-Maqdisī, *Aḥsan,* 360.

17. Maqdisī, *Aḥsan,* 355, 360. The precise site of Dūlāb was not specified by any early topographer, but the circumstance that it was five days' journey from Mūghān and eleven from Shālūs in western Ṭabaristān (ibid., 373) would imply a location in the western part of Gīlān.

18. Ibn Ḥawqal, *al-Masālik wa-l-Mamālik,* 381; Maqdisī, *Aḥsan,* 359; and Minorsky, *Ḥudūd,* 134.

19. Ibn Ḥawqal, *al-Masālik wa-l-Mamālik,* 378 and Minorsky, *Ḥudūd,* 135.

20. Ibn Ḥawqal, *al-Masālik wa-l-Mamālik,* 378.

21. Ibid., 376, 384; Minorsky, *Ḥudūd,* 134.

22. Ibn Ḥawqal, *al-Masālik wa-l-Mamālik,* 378 and Minorsky, *Ḥudūd,* 134. Although Mamāṭīr existed as a small settlement in pre-Islamic times, its development into a reasonably prosperous town appears to date only from the Muslim annexation of Ṭabaristān.

23. Iṣṭakhrī, *al-Masālik wa-l-Mamālik,* 213–14; Ibn Ḥawqal, *al-Masālik wa-l-Mamālik,* 378, 384; Maqdisī, *Aḥsan,* 358; and Minorsky, *Ḥudūd,* 134.

24. Ibn Ḥawqal, *al-Masālik wa-l-Mamālik,* 380.

25. Maqdisī, *Aḥsan,* 356; also Iṣṭakhrī, *al-Masālik wa-l-Mamālik,* 211 and Minorsky, *Ḥudūd,* 135. The city is said to have been founded in the sixth century A.D. by Bisṭām, a rebellious governor of Ṭabaristān, Khurāsān, and certain adjacent territories. See Marquart, *Ērānšahr, nach der Geographie des Ps. Moses Xorenacʿi,* 71 and E. Herzfeld, "Khorasan. Denkmalsgeographische Studien zur Kulturgeschichte des Islam in Iran," *Der Islam* 11 (1921): 168–69.

26. Transcribed as al-Khuwār by Arab authors. Ibn Ḥawqal, *al-Masālik wa-l-Mamālik,* 379 and Minorsky, *Ḥudūd,* 132 (in which the city—actually the westernmost substantial settlement in Qūmis—is treated as part of Jibāl *iqlīm*).

27. Ibn Ḥawqal, *al-Masālik wa-l-Mamālik,* 380 and Minorsky, *Ḥudūd,* 135.

28. But note the statement in the *Ḥudūd* (p. 136) that "They [the inhabitants of Daylam proper] have no urban centres with *minbars,*" which gives some substance to a remark by Abū al-Fidā' that the settlement at Baylamān had all the characteristics of a farmstead (*Mukhtaṣar Ta'rīkh al-Bashar,* 429; where, incidentally, the name appears as Bīmān).

29. Iṣṭakhrī, *al-Masālik wa-l-Mamālik,* 214–17; Ibn Ḥawqal, *al-Masālik wa-l-Mamālik,* 383–84; and Maqdisī, *Aḥsan,* 372–73. For information relating to these routes in the ninth century see Ibn Khurradādhbih, *al-Masālik wa-l-Mamālik,* 22–23, 124–25; Qudāmah, *al-Kharāj,* 200–201; and Ibn Rustah, *al-Aʿlaq,* 169–70.

30. Iṣṭakhrī, *al-Masālik wa-l-Mamālik,* 213 and Ibn Ḥawqal, *al-Masālik wa-l-Mamālik,* 382–83, 385. Minorsky equates Ābaskūn (or Ābaskun, as it appears in his text) with the Ptolemaic *Σωκανάα* (*Geographia* VI, *cap.* 9).

31. Maqdisī, *Aḥsan,* 358. Cf. Minorsky, *Ḥudūd,* 134: "a haunt of merchants from all the territories trading on the Khazar Sea" (i.e., the Caspian).

32. Yāqūt, *Muʿjam,* 1:242.

33. Mustawfī, *Nuzhat al-Qulūb,* 239; Le Strange's translation, 231. The volume of textile trade passing through ports at the southern end of the Caspian Sea is evidenced by Ibn Ḥawqal's remark that "The Khazars produce no clothing *(malbūs)* but import it from Gurgān, Ṭabaristān, Ādharbāyjān, Rūm, and neighbouring lands" (*al-Masālik wa-l-Mamālik,* 394–95).

34. Alhum in Minorsky, *Ḥudūd,* 135; Ahlum in Yāqūt, *Muʿjam,* 1:409.

35. Mustawfī, *Nuzhat al-Qulūb,* 160; Le Strange's translation, 157.

36. Certain Daylamī fruit enjoyed more than a local reputation in their unprocessed form. Samnān, for instance, was credited with producing better fruit than anywhere else in the *iqlīm* (Minorsky, *Ḥudūd,* 135; cf. Abū Dulaf, *Risālah,* 193b; Minorsky's translation, 56), and Ṭabaristān, generally with equally superlative oranges (*utrujj:* ibid., 193a; Minorsky's translation, 55); while Bisṭāmī apples were exported as far afield as al-ʿIrāq (Ibn Ḥawqal, *al-Masālik wa-l-Mamālik,* 380). Ṭabaristān produced a good deal of sugarcane, principally in the lowlands bordering the Caspian Sea, where Mīlah merited special mention (Minorsky, *Ḥudūd,* 134); but Abū Dulaf at least considered the quality inferior to that of Khūzistān (*Risālah,* 193a).

37. *Mā [sic] zaʿfarān* = saffron water; *mā ṣandal* = sandalwood water; *mā khalūq* = perfumed water: Minorsky, *Ḥudūd,* 134. *Khalanj,* a Persian name Arabicized, was a fine-grained hardwood from the forests of Ṭabaristān much favored for the making of bowls: Lane, *Arabic-English Lexicon,* 1:803. A. Z. Validi Togan identifies the wood as a maple (*Acer* spp): *Ibn Faḍlans Reisebericht,* in *Abhandlungen für die Kunde des Morgenlandes,* vol. 24 (Leipzig, 1939), 211–15.

38. Ibn Isfandiyār, *Tārīkh-i Ṭabaristān,* Browne's translation, 118. Lafūrajī cloth was manufactured in the town of Lapūr, a few miles south of Mamāṭīr (p. 167 above).

39. Serjeant, *Islamic Textiles,* 74.

40. Al-Ṭabarī, *Ta'rīkh,* 1:536.

41. Cf. p. 155 above.

42. Jāḥiẓ (attrib.), "Al-Tabaṣṣur," 338.

43. Serjeant, *Islamic Textiles,* 78, citing Browne's translation of Ibn Isfandiyār, *Tārīkh-i Ṭabaristān,* 33. Ibn Isfandiyār was here drawing on the work of al-Yazdādī, who was writing between 976 and 1012.

44. P. 92 above.

45. See chapter 10.

46. This rendering of *qālī-hā-yi-maḥfūrī* is based on Serjeant's translation "carpets in relief." This author is inclined to derive the term *qālī* from the Armenian city of Qālīqalā (Erzurum), supporting his argument with Yāqúts statement (*Muʿjam,* 4:20) that "In Qālīqalā are manufactured those carpets *(busuṭ)* known as *qālī,* the *nisbah* of which has been abbreviated in speech" (*Islamic Textiles,* 66).

47. Collected and discussed by Serjeant (ibid., 74–80).

48. Maqdisī, *Aḥsan,* 367.

49. Minorsky, *Ḥudūd,* 134–35.

50. Yaʿqūbī, *al-Buldān,* 276; Ibn Rustah, *al-Aʿlaq,* 170, Iṣṭakhrī, *al-Masālik wa-l-Mamālik,* 211; and Ibn Ḥawqal, *al-Masālik wa-l-Mamālik,* 380.

51. Maqdisī, *Aḥsan,* 367.

52. Minorsky, *Ḥudūd,* 135.

53. Jaḥiẓ (attrib.), "Al-Tabaṣṣur," 345.

54. Minorsky, *Ḥudūd,* 133 and Maqdisī, *Aḥsan,* 367, who lists the veils under the term maqāniʿ qazzīyāt. Abū Dulaf notes that Gurgān silk did not deteriorate during the dyeing process (*Risālah,* 194a; Minorsky's translation, 58).

55. Maqdisī, *Aḥsan,* 367. Silkworm culture was introduced into Gurgān from Marv during early Islamic times, whence it spread to Ṭabaristān.

56. Minorsky, *Ḥudūd,* 134 and Maqdisī, *Aḥsan,* 358. Cf. also Iṣṭakhrī, *al-Masālik wa-l-Mamālik,* 213 and Abū Dulaf on the expensive black silk veils made in Samnān (*Risālah,* 193b; Minorsky's translation, 57).

57. Minorsky, *Ḥudūd,* 133. Also Maqdisī, *Aḥsan,* 358–59; and Iṣṭakhrī, *al-Masālik wa-l-Mamālik,* 219 and Ibn Ḥawqal, *al-Masālik wa-l-Mamālik,* 388, although both these authors underreported the size and importance of Dihistān and, through confusion with Dihistānān-Sūr, situated it on the coast. Cf. Barthold, *Historical Geography,* 117 n. 34.

58. Maqdisī, *Aḥsan,* 358–59.

59. *Farāv* in Minorsky, *Ḥudūd,* 133; *Afrāvah* in Maqdisī, *Aḥsan,* 320.

60. Yāqūt, *Muʿjam,* 3:866. The site has been identified as present-day Qīzīl Arvat = "The Red Ribāṭ": cf. Barthold, *Historical Geography,* 89. See also Iṣṭakhrī, *al-Masālik wa-l-Mamālik,* 273 and Ibn Ḥawqal, *al-Masālik wa-l-Mamālik,* 445.

61. Minorsky, *Ḥudūd,* 135–36.

62. Qazwīnī, *ʿAjāʾib al-Makhlūqāt,* 2:238.

63. Nāṣir-i Khusraw, *Safar Nāmah,* Schéfer's translation, 7; Thackston's translation, 2. Note that Nāṣir regarded Bisṭām as the capital of Qūmis and referred to it as Qumis City (cf. note 10 above). Bāyazīd was one of the most famous ecstatic mystics of Islam. Ibn Baṭṭūṭah visited his tomb and lodged in the attached hospice, probably in 1333 (cf. H. A. R. Gibb, *The Travels of Ibn Baṭṭūṭa* A.D. 1325–1354, vol. 3. Hakluyt Society, 2d ser., no. 141 [Cambridge, 1971], 585). See also Abū Dulaf's "Second *Risālah,*" Minorsky's translation, 57 and Louis Massignon, *Lexique Technique de la Mystique Musulmane* (Paris, 1922), 243–56.

64. Minorsky, *Ḥudūd,* 133.

65. Masʿūdī, *Murūj,* 1:275.

66. Ruyanj in Ibn Ḥawqal, *al-Masālik wa-l-Mamālik,* 377. For the history of this region see Awliyāʾ Allāh Muḥammad ibn Ḥasan Āmulī, *Tāʾrīkh-i Rūyān* (Tehran, A.H. 1313).

67. Yāqūt, *Muʿjam,* 3:504.

68. Ibn Ḥawqal, *al-Masālik wa-l-Mamālik,* 377; Sāmār in Minorsky, *Ḥudūd,* 136.

69. Pers. Pirrīm. Cf. M. Rekaya, "Ḳārinids," *The Encyclopaedia of Islam,* 2d ed., 4:644–67; P. Casanova, "Les Ispehbeds de Firīm," in *ʿAjabnáma, a Volume of Oriental Studies Presented to Edward G. Browne,* ed. T. W. Arnold and R. A. Nicholson (Cambridge, 1922), 117–21; C. E. Bosworth, "Firrīm," *The Encyclopaedia of Islam,* 2d ed., suppl. fascs. 5–6 (1982), 309. Māzyār, the last representative of the Qārinid dynasty, was executed in 840, when power apparently passed to the Kāwūsīyah lineage of the Bāwandids, who continued to exercise authority in the area into the tenth century (see M. Rekaya, "Māzyār, résistance ou intégration d'une province iranienne au monde musulman au milieu du IXe siècle après J.C.," *Studia Iranica* 2 (1973): 143–92 and, for the history of the Bāwandids, R. N. Frye, *The Encyclopaedia of Islam,* 2d ed., s.v. 1:1110).

70. Minorsky, *Ḥudūd,* 135–36, which is also the principal source for information about Firrīm in the tenth century; but see also Ibn Ḥawqal, *al-Masālik wa-l-Mamālik,* 377; Yāqūt, *Muʿjam,* 3:890; and Mustawfī, *Nuzhat al-Qulūb,* 162; Le Strange's translation, 158.

71. Minorsky, *Ḥudūd,* 135.

72. Ibn Isfandiyār, *Tārīkh-i Ṭabaristān,* Browne's translation, 122–23.

73. Ibn al-Faqīh, *al-Buldān,* 306.

74. Minorsky, *Ḥudūd,* 136.

75. Ibn Ḥawqal, *al-Masālik wa-l-Mamālik,* 377.

76. Madelung, "Minor Dynasties," 200.

77. Ibid., 202.

78. Ibn al-Faqīh, *al-Buldān,* 305.

79. P. 165 above.

80. Richard W. Bulliet, *Islam: The View from the Edge* (New York, 1994), 102–3.

81. Ibn al-Faqīh, *al-Buldān,* 303–4. Also Ibn Ḥawqal, *al-Masālik wa-l-Mamālik,* 381. Ṭabaristān was one of the relatively few regions within the Islamic world where rice was the staple crop at lower elevations, although supplemented even there by wheat and barley, which in turn became dominant at higher altitudes.

82. Abū Dulaf, *Risālah,* 193a; Minorsky's translation, 56.

83. Ibid., Minorsky's translation, 103.

Chapter Fourteen

1. Maqdisī, *Aḥsan,* 7. He might have added to his sentence the phrase "at their greatest extent." Cf. also Ibn Ḥawqal, *al-Masālik wa-l-Mamālik,* 43 and Minorsky, *Ḥudūd,* 102. There is a compendious and authoritative account of the Sāmānid dynasty by Frye in *The Period from the Arab Invasion to the Saljuqs,* 136–61.

2. For commentary and exegesis bearing on the urban system of Khurāsān in the tenth century, see the author's note to chapter 8. Additionally there is a large amount of relevant information scattered through Spuler's *Iran in Früh-Islamischer Zeit,* while Elton L. Daniel (*The Political and Social History of Khurasan under Abbasid*

Rule 747–820 [Minneapolis and Chicago, 1979]) provides a reliable political and social framework for most of the first century of the ʿAbbāsid hegemony, as well as a useful bibliography. E. Herzfeld's "Khorasan," 107–74 is still of value despite the date at which it was written.

3. Ar. Naysābūr < Pers. Nīv-Shāhpuhr, so called after the city was rebuilt in the fourth century A.D. by Shāpūr II. On the coinage of the Umayyads and the early ʿAbbāsids, Nīshāpūr appeared as a mint city under the Persian name Abrashahr = "Cloud City." For the collections of patrician biographies that can be conveniently cited as *The Histories of Nīshāpūr,* see note 157 to chapter 3. Half a century after Charles K. Wilkinson, Walter Hauser, and Joseph M. Upton carried out a series of archaeological excavations in the city (1935–40, 1947), the final site reports are still in course of publication. The most relevant items for present purposes published so far are Wilkinson, "Life in early Nishapur," *Bulletin of the Metropolitan Museum of Art,* n.s., vol. 9, no. 2 (1950): 6–72 and *Nishapur: Some Early Islamic Buildings and Their Decoration* (New York, 1986).

4. Bosworth, basing himself on comparative estimates of urban populations by Nāṣir-i Khusraw (e.g., the population of Old Cairo [Miṣr] was at least five times that of Nīshāpūr), suggested a total of thirty thousand to forty thousand persons early in the eleventh century (*The Ghaznavids,* 162), and he might well have added that the population of the city was unlikely to have changed greatly during the preceding half century. Bulliet, by contrast, invokes logistical considerations and the population carrying capacity of the region in support of his higher estimate of the order of one hundred thousand persons, which seems to me to be on the high side (*The Patricians of Nishapur,* 10; also "Medieval Nishapur: a topographic and demographic reconstruction," *Studia Iranica* 5 [1976]: 87–89).

5. Maqdisī, *Aḥsan,* 314–16. Cf. also Ibn Rustah, *al-Aʿlaq,* 171; Iṣṭakhrī, *al-Aghānī,* 254–55; Ibn Ḥawqal, *al-Masālik wa-l-Mamālik,* 431–33; and Minorsky, *Ḥudūd,* 102.

6. This Persian term is not actually met with in the writings of the early topographers, who invariably employed the Arabic *rabaḍ* to denote an outer city.

7. Maqdisī, *Aḥsan,* 33.

8. Ar. Al-Shāhijān, < Pers. Shāhgān = royal.

9. Yaʿqūbī, *al-Buldān,* 278–80; Iṣṭakhrī, *al-Masālik wa-l-Mamālik,* 258–63; Ibn Ḥawqal, *al-Masālik wa-l-Mamālik,* 434–36; Maqdisī, *Aḥsan,* 310–12; and Minorsky, *Ḥudūd,* 105.

10. V. A. Livshits, in Barthold, *Historical Geography,* 42 n. 45, cites a paper by P. G. Bulgakov purporting to establish that the citadel had been razed as early as the second half of the eighth century, and apparently had not been rebuilt. Barthold himself and C. E. Bosworth, his editor, provide references to Russian works dealing with the early history of Marv, of which V. A. Zhukovskii's *Razvaliny Starogo Merva (The Ruins of Old Marv),* although published as long ago as 1894, is still extremely useful. Cf. also Bosworth, *The Encyclopaedia of Islam,* 2d ed., 6:618–21.

11. For discussions of medieval Balkh see, in addition to the titles listed in note 2 above, Paul Schwarz, "Bemerkungen zu den Arabischen Nachrichten über Balkh," in *Oriental Studies in Honour of Cursetji Erachji Pavry* (London, 1933), 434–443; A. Z. Toğan, "The topography of Balkh down to the middle of the seventeenth century," *Central Asiatic Journal* 14 (1970): 277–88. The text of a Persian history of the city, *Faḍāʾil-i Balkh,* with historical annotations, is included in Ch. Schéfer's *Chrestomathie Persane,* vol. 1 (Paris, 1883), 56–94, 65–103.

12. Or, according to some accounts, during the caliphate of al-Muʿāwiyah: cf. Balādhurī, *Futūḥ al-Buldān,* 408–9; Murgotten's translation, 168. Although the destruction extended to the great temple of New Bahār (< Skt. *nava vihāra*), that site remained sacred for Buddhists for a long time to come. Al-Ṭabarī (*Taʾrīkh,* 2: 1205), for instance, reports that the Ṭukhārian princes who revolted against Qutaybah ibn Muslim, the governor of Khurāsān, early in the eighth century, performed their ritual prayers there. The New Bahār was described by Ibn al-Faqīh in *al-Buldān,* 322–24; see also Yāqūt, *Muʿjam,* 4:817–20, citing ʿUmar ibn al-Azraq of Kirmān, and Qazwīnī, *ʿAjāʾib al-Makhlūqāt,* 2:221.

13. Interestingly, the reconstruction of the old city was entrusted to a member of the Barmakid family, which, in Sāsānian times, had provided the hereditary high priests of the Zoroastrian faith.

14. Sometimes also known as the Bānījūrids after an eponymous putative ancestor Bānījūr: see Marquart, *Ērānšahr nach der Geographie des Ps. Moses Xorenacʿi,* 300–302; R. Vasmer, "Beiträge zur muhammedanischen Münzkunde: I. Die Münzen der Abū Daʾudiden," *Numismatische Zeitschrift,* n.s., 18 (1925): 49–62; and C. E. Bosworth, *The Encyclopaedia of Islam,* 2d ed., Supplement, fascs. 1–2 (1980), p. 125.

15. Minorsky, *Ḥudūd,* 108.

16. For instance, according to Yaʿqūbī the *rabaḍ* of Balkh had four gates, whereas the topographers of the tenth century assigned it seven. Barthold (*Turkestan down to the Mongol Invasion,* 78) is probably correct in suggesting that Yaʿqūbī's statement referred to the *shahristān* rather than to the *rabaḍ,* for numerous other Khurāsānian *shahristāns* were furnished with four gates. Again, whereas Yaʿqūbī at the end of the ninth century estimated the diameter of the *shahristān* as one *farsakh,* according to Iṣṭakhrī it was only half a *farsakh.* See Yaʿqūbī, *al-Buldān,* 287–88; Iṣṭakhrī, *al-Masālik wa-l-Mamālik,* 275, 278, 280; Ibn Ḥawqal, *al-Masālik wa-l-Mamālik,* 447–48; and Maqdisī, *Aḥsan,* 301–2.

17. Harāt existed in Avestan times, but received its classical form when it was constituted as Alexandria-in-Aria by Alexander the Great. On the pre-Islamic city see Markwart (Marquart), *A Catalogue of the Provincial Capitals of Ērānshahr,* 11, 46.

18. Iṣṭakhrī, *al-Masālik wa-l-Mamālik,* 264–66; Ibn Ḥawqal, *al-Masālik wa-l-Mamālik,* 437–38; Maqdisī, *Aḥsan,* 306–7; and Minorsky, *Ḥudūd,* 103–4. For more general histories of Harāt see Sayf al-Harawī, *Taʾrīkh Nāma-i Harát,* ed. M. aṣ-Ṣiddíqí (Calcutta,

1944) and Muʿin al-Dīn al-Zamchī al-Iṣfizārī, *Rawḍat al-Jannāt fī Awṣāf Madīnat Harāt,* ed. Sayyid Muḥammad Kāẓim Imām (Tehran, 1959).

19. Also al-Yahūdān and, in Yāqūt (*Muʿjam,* 2:168 only) Jahūdān al-Kubrā = "The Great Jewry." This city occupied the site of present-day Maymanah (according to Marquart, *Ērānšahr nach der Geographie des Ps. Moses Xorenacʿi,* 78 < an ancient **Nisāk-i miyānak*), a name found in reference to the tenth century only in al-Birūnī's *al-Qānūn al-Masʿūdī* (Livshits's annotation to Barthold's *Historical Geography,* 33 n. 108). See also Spuler, *Iran in Früh-Islamischer Zeit,* 216. For the eponymous Jewish community in the city, consult Walter J. Fischel, "The Jews of Central Asia (Khorasan) in medieval Hebrew and Islamic literature," *Historia Judaica* 7 (1945): 29–50. This settlement is not to be confused, as apparently happens in Yāqūt, with the Maymand (for Maywand) in Zābulistān.

20. Yaʿqūbī, *al-Buldān,* 287; Iṣṭakhrī, *al-Masālik wa-l-Mamālik,* 270–71; Ibn Ḥawqal, *al-Masālik wa-l-Mamālik,* 442; and Maqdisī, *Aḥsan,* 198.

21. Minorsky, *Ḥudūd,* 107.

22. Maqdisī, *Aḥsan,* 321. Cf. Ibn Ḥawqal, *al-Masālik wa-l-Mamālik,* 446; Minorsky, *Ḥudūd,* 103 (Qa'īn); and Nāṣir-i Khusraw, *Safar Nāmah,* Thackston's translation, 102. For the central location of Qāyin in relation to other important settlement foci in Qūhistān, see Mustawfī, *Nuzhat al-Qulūb,* 146; Le Strange's translation, 144; and Spuler, *Iran in Früh-Islamischer Zeit,* 309, 402.

23. *Sijistān* is the early Arabic form, *sīstān* the usual Persian orthography: < MPer. Sakastān = "Land of the Śakas." The principal primary sources for Sijistān from the ninth to the thirteenth century are (1) the anonymous *Tārīkh-i Sīstān* (ca. A.D. 1062, continued to 1325 by a second author), ed. Malik al-Shuʿarā [an honorific title] Muḥammad Taqī (Tehran, A.D. 1935); English trans. by Milton Gold, under the title *The Tārikh-e Sistān,* Persian Heritage Series, no. 20 (Roma, 1976); and (2) the *Iḥyāʾ al-Mulūk* by Shāh Ḥusayn ibn Malik Ghiyāth al-Dīn (ca. A.D. 1618), ed. Manūchihr Sutūdah (Tehran, A.H. 1344/A.D. 1966). The province's medieval topography and toponymy were discussed with considerable acumen by G. P. Tate (*Seistan, a Memoir on the History, Topography, Ruins, and People of the Country,* Parts 1–4 [Calcutta, 1910–12]), and there is some useful material in Marquart's *Ērānšahr nach der Geographie des Ps. Moses Xorenacʿi,* 35–39. The definitive study of Sīstān in the first two centuries or so of Islam is Clifford Edmund Bosworth, *Sīstān under the Arabs, from the Islamic Conquest to the Rise of the Ṣaffārids (30–250/651–864)* (Rome, 1968). Cf. also the same author's *The History of the Saffarids of Sistan and the Maliks of Nimruz (247/861 to 949/1542–3)* (Costa Mesa, Calif., 1994).

24. Yaʿqūbī, *al-Buldān,* 281.

25. Maqdisī, *Aḥsan,* 305.

26. Iṣṭakhrī, *al-Masālik wa-l-Mamālik,* 239–42 and Ibn Ḥawqal, *al-Masālik wa-l-Mamālik,* 415.

27. Eastern Sijistān included the extensive tracts of territory now constituting southeastern Afghānistān but that in the tenth century were known as the regions of al-Rukhkhaj and Zamīndāwar (= "Land of the Gates or Passes": Ar. = Arḍ al-Dāwar or Balad al-Dāwar). As early as 653 a governor of Sijistān had led a military expedition into these territories, but not until the beginning of the tenth century, when they were incorporated in the Sāmānid Empire, were they brought securely under Muslim control. Even then their remoteness from Bukhārā practically ensured that local rulers retained a considerable degree of autonomy, possibly after receiving some sort of formal investiture from the Sāmānid *amīrs* (cf. Bosworth, *The Ghaznavids,* 35).

28. Cf. Minorsky, *Ḥudūd,* 110: "It is the gate of Hindūstān and a resort of merchants."

29. Iṣṭakhrī, *al-Masālik wa-l-Mamālik,* 244–45; Ibn Ḥawqal, *al-Masālik wa-l-Mamālik,* 419; and Maqdisī, *Aḥsan,* 304.

30. The form *Ghaznin* used by al-Maqdisī (*Aḥsan,* 337) and the *Ḥudūd* (111), and which Yāqūt (*Muʿjam,* 2:904–5, 3:798) asserted was the correct scholarly orthography, is thought to have derived from *Ghaznīk* or *Ghaznēn,* ultimately, by way of a metathesis of *-nz-/-nj-* to *-zn-* in eastern Īrānian, from **Ganzak* < *ganja* = treasury. This etymology has been taken to imply that the city had been the capital of Zābulistān in pre-Islamic times. Cf. C. E. Bosworth, *The Encyclopaedia of Islam,* 2d ed., 2:1048–50 and E. Benveniste, "Le nom de la ville de Ghazna," *Journal Asiatique* 221 (1935): 141–43. Also J. Marquart and J. J. M. de Groot, "Das Reich Zābul und der Gott Žūn vom 6–9 Jahrhundert," in *Festschrift Eduard Sachau* (Berlin, 1915), 248–92.

31. Ibn Ḥawqal, *al-Masālik wa-l-Mamālik,* 450.

32. Also Bannajbūr (the readings *Qannazbūr* and *Qannajbūr* of several manuscripts are the result of careless pointing) and Banjbūr (Minorsky, *Ḥudūd,* 123).

33. The site of ancient Fannazbūr is now known as Panj-gūr, and lies a day's march west of Qalʿah Nāghah: see Le Strange, *The Lands of the Eastern Caliphate,* 329 n. 2. Brian Spooner's paper "Notes on the Toponymy of the Persian Makran" in *Iran and Islam. In Memory of the Late Vladimir Minorsky,* ed. C. E. Bosworth (Edinburgh, 1971), is not without relevance to matters raised in this and some following paragraphs.

34. Maqdisī, *Aḥsan,* 478. Cf. also Iṣṭakhrī, *al-Masālik wa-l-Mamālik,* 170–71; and Ibn Ḥawqal, *al-Masālik wa-l-Mamālik,* 325.

35. Iṣṭakhrī, *al-Masālik wa-l-Mamālik,* 171, 176; Ibn Ḥawqal, *al-Masālik wa-l-Mamālik,* 226, 232; and Maqdisī, *Aḥsan,* 476–78. The name of the settlement is transcribed as Qusdhān in Minorsky, *Ḥudūd,* 123.

36. Iṣṭakhrī, *al-Masālik wa-l-Mamālik,* 273; Ibn Ḥawqal, *al-Masālik wa-l-Mamālik,* 445; Maqdisī, *Aḥsan,* 320; and Minorsky, *Ḥudūd,* 103, 326. The site of medieval Nasā is to be found near the village of Bāgīr, to the west of the town of Ashkhābād: Minorsky in commentary on the *Ḥudūd,* 326.

37. Cf. Barthold, *Turkestan down to the Mongol Invasion,* 261 and *Historical Geography,* 90.

38. Maqdisī (*Aḥsan,* 318–19) reports that its markets were larger and busier than those in Nisā. See also Spuler, *Iran in Früh-Islamischer Zeit,* 110, 165, 405–7.

39. Yaʿqūbī, *al-Buldān,* 277–78.

40. Ibn Ḥawqal, *al-Masālik wa-l-Mamālik,* 434; Maqdisī, *Aḥsan,* 319, 333, 352; and Minorsky, *Ḥudūd,* 103, 326.

41. Also transcribed as Fūshanj. This city apparently occupied the site of present-day Ghūriyān: W. Tomaschek, *Zur Historischen Topographie von Kleinasien im Mittelalter,* vol. 1 (Wien, 1891), 78.

42. Ibn Ḥawqal, *al-Masālik wa-l-Mamālik,* 440. Cf. also Iṣṭakhrī, *al-Masālik wa-l-Mamālik,* 267–68; Maqdisī, *Aḥsan,* 307; and Minorsky, *Ḥudūd,* 104.

43. Asbuzār (< *Aspuzār) in Minorsky, *Ḥudūd,* 104. Cf. also Iṣṭakhrī, *al-Masālik wa-l-Mamālik,* 267 and Ibn Ḥawqal, *al-Masālik wa-l-Mamālik,* 439–40. The city is now known as Sabzivār of Harāt (to distinguish it from the Sabzivār to the west of Nīshāpūr).

44. Le Strange, *The Lands of the Eastern Caliphate,* 412. On this interpretation the reading Jāshān (for Khāstān) that occurs in some texts is erroneous. Since the publication of the text of the *Ḥudūd al-ʿĀlam* it has become evident that the Persian original of the name was Kavāzhān (Minorsky, *Ḥudūd,* 104), which would very likely have yielded the Arabic transcription Kuwāshān.

45. Also Babnah; Baun (presumably for Bavan) in Minorsky, *Ḥudūd,* 104.

46. Iṣṭakhrī, *al-Masālik wa-l-Mamālik,* 269; Ibn Ḥawqal, *al-Masālik wa-l-Mamālik,* 441; and Minorsky, *Ḥudūd,* p. 104.

47. Qudāmah, *al-Kharāj,* 210; Iṣṭakhrī, *al-Masālik wa-l-Mamālik,* 269; Ibn Ḥawqal, *al-Masālik wa-l-Mamālik,* 441; and Minorsky, *Ḥudūd,* 105 (Marūd). This city, which should not be confused with Marv al-Shāhijān discussed above, was almost certainly sited at present-day Bālā Murghāb, as demonstrated by W. Barthold on the strength of certain remarks by Qudāmah (209) ("Merverrūd," *Zapiski Vostochnogo Otdeleniya Imperatorskago Russkogo Arkheologicheskogo Obshchestva* 14 (1901: 028–032). Cf. also Mir Hussein, "Merve Rud," *Afghanistan* 9, no. 3 (1954): 8–17 and no. 4 (1955): 19–25. The ruins at modern Maruchak, which have sometimes been proposed as the site of Marv al-Rūd, are in fact the remains of Qaṣr-i Aḥnaf, one of its dependent settlements (Bosworth, *The Encyclopaedia of Islam,* 2d ed., 6:617).

48. Transcribed variously as Bashīn (Iṣṭakhrī, *al-Masālik wa-l-Mamālik,* 271–72; Ibn Ḥawqal, *al-Masālik wa-l-Mamālik,* 443 and elsewhere; and Minorsky, *Ḥudūd,* 106), Afshīn (Maqdisī, *Aḥsan,* 50 and Minhāj al-Dīn ibn Sirāj Jūzjānī, *Ṭabaqāt-i Nāṣirī,* ed. W. Nassau Lees [Calcutta, 1863] and ʿAbd al-Ḥayy Ḥabībī, 2 vols. [Kābul, A.H. 1342–43]), and Abzhin (*The Armenian Geography:* cf. R. H. Hewsen, "Introduction to the Study of Armenian Historical Geography," [Ph.D. diss., Georgetown University, 1967]).

49. Al-Maqdisī (*Aḥsan,* 309) was essentially correct in his assertion that *Shār [Shēr]* = the style of the ruling prince (< an Old Īrānian word for *king*) and *Gharj* (< Avestan *garay-*) = "mountain" in the local dialect. There were, in fact, Shārs ruling in Bāmiyān at this time: cf. Minorsky, *Ḥudūd,* 105, 109. During the later Middle Ages the region around the headwaters of the Murghāb River was more commonly known as Gharjistān (Gharchistān) and its inhabitants as Gharchah. It corresponded fairly closely with the region now known as Fīrūz-kūh. See Bogdan Składanek, "Settlements in Gharchistān during the early Islamic period (up to the 11th century A.D.)," *Rocznik Orientalistyczny* 34 (1971): pp. 57–71; also Iṣṭakhrī, *al-Masālik wa-l-Mamālik,* 271–72 and Ibn Ḥawqal, *al-Masālik wa-l-Mamālik,* 323.

50. For sources relating to Ghūr in the ninth and tenth centuries, see A. A. Naimi, "Un regard sur Ghor. Préambule: la gégographie, l'histoire et les sites historiques," *Afghanistan* 4 (1949): 1–23 and, more generally, C. E. Bosworth, "The early Islamic history of Ghūr," *Central Asiatic Journal* 6 (1961): 116–33. There is also a brief statement in V. M. Masson and V. A. Romodin, *Istoriia Afganistana,* vol. 1 (Moscow, 1964), 255–57.

51. Iṣṭakhrī, *al-Masālik wa-l-Mamālik,* 277, 280; Ibn Ḥawqal, *al-Masālik wa-l-Mamālik,* 451; Maqdisī, *Aḥsan,* 296, 303; and Minorsky, *Ḥudūd,* 109. Al-Maqdisī seems to have described the city under the name al-Lahūm, but the reading is uncertain and the text probably corrupt at this point. According to al-Yaʿqūbī the Shārs of Bāmiyān converted to Islam early in the ʿAbbāsid period, although this author equivocated as to the precise date (*al-Buldān,* 289; in the reign of al-Manṣūr, 754–75; *Ta'rīkh,* 2:479; in the reign of al-Mahdī, 2:775–85).

52. Banjway < Īrānian Panjwāy = "Five Streams"; Rukhkhaj < Arachosia, the Hellenistic name of the region. Cf. Iṣṭakhrī, *al-Masālik wa-l-Mamālik,* 250; Ibn Ḥawqal, *al-Masālik wa-l-Mamālik,* 418; Maqdisī, *Aḥsan,* 305; and Minorsky, *Ḥudūd,* 111 (rendered as Fījuvānī). The precise location of this city has not been determined, but, from a collation of several itineraries, it is evident that it was not too far distant from present-day al-Qunduhār: namely four marches from Bust to a point where the road bifurcated, with one branch leading north in twelve days' march to Ghaznah, the other east in six days' march to Sībī. See Mir Husain Shah, "Panjwayee-Fanjuwai," *Afghanistan* 17 (1962): 23–27.

53. Iṣṭakhrī, *al-Masālik wa-l-Mamālik,* 244; Ibn Ḥawqal, *al-Masālik wa-l-Mamālik,* 418; Minorsky, *Ḥudūd,* 111; and Maqdisī, *Aḥsan,* 297 (Wālishtān), 486. Cf. also J. Markwart, *Wehrot und Arang. Untersuchungen zur Mythischen und Geschichtlichen Landeskunde von Ostiran,* ed. H. H. Schaeder (Leiden, 1938), 124.

54. Iṣṭakhrī, *al-Masālik wa-l-Mamālik,* 176; Ibn Ḥawqal, *al-Masālik wa-l-Mamālik,* 326; Maqdisī, *Aḥsan,* 478; and Minorsky, *Ḥudūd,* 123, 373.

55. Iṣṭakhrī, *al-Masālik wa-l-Mamālik,* 257, 284 (Khān Ravān: perhaps, as Minorsky suggests, for Rāvin [*Ḥudūd,* 326]; Ibn Ḥawqal, *al-Masālik wa-l-Mamālik,* 433; and Maqdisī, *Aḥsan,* 300.

56. Maqdisī, *Aḥsan,* 300.

57. Minorsky, *Ḥudūd,* 102. Cf. also Ibn Ḥawqal, *al-Masālik wa-l-Mamālik,* 433. In medieval times, the city was often called by the name of the district of which it was the capital, namely Bayhaq.

Even in the ninth century it was an important center of Shīʿism (Yaʿqūbī, *Taʾrīkh,* 2:397). For much general information see Ẓahīr al-Dīn Abū al-Ḥasan al-Bayhaqī, *Taʾrīkh-ī Bayhaq.* In spite of its focus on a later period, J. Aubin's "L'aristocratie urbaine dans l'Iran seldjukide: l'exemple de Sabzavār" (in *Mélanges Offerts à René Crozet,* ed. P. Gallais and Y. J. Rion [Poitiers, 1966], 323–32) is not totally irrelevant to the tenth century. In the thirteenth century Yāqūt (*Muʿjam,* 1:804) reported that the district of Sabzivar contained no less than 321 villages.

58. Farhādhjird in Yāqūt, *Muʿjam,* 1:280.

59. Also transcribed as Sabanj and subsequently by Mustawfī (*Nuzhat al-Qulūb,* 174; Le Strange's translation, 169) as (Rubāṭ) Savanj.

60. Maqdisī, *Aḥsan,* 318. Sabarāyin in Minorsky, *Ḥudūd,* 102 (for Siparāyin, perhaps influenced by a popular etymological derivation from *ispar-āyīn* = shieldlike: C. E. Bosworth, *The Encyclopaedia of Islam,* 2d ed., 4:107). Cf. also Ibn Ḥawqal, *al-Masālik wa-l-Mamālik,* 428.

61. Minorsky, *Ḥudūd,* 102.

62. Ibn Ḥawqal, *al-Masālik wa-l-Mamālik,* 403 and Minorsky, *Ḥudūd,* 105.

63. Note 47 above.

64. Named after al-Aḥnaf ibn Qays, the general who had first led the armies of Islam on to the plains of Turkmenistān. The settlement, which Ibn Ḥawqal (*al-Masālik wa-l-Mamālik,* 441–42) categorized as large and set amid vineyards and fine gardens, is usually located on the site of present-day Marūchāq (see note 47 above).

65. Actually five settlements (as the name indicates) strung along the Murghāb valley. Cf. Nāṣir-i Khusraw, *Safar Nāmah,* 1.

66. Described by al-Maqdisī (*Aḥsan,* 314) as a populous settlement equal in size to Qaṣr Aḥnaf.

67. According to Minorsky (*Ḥudūd,* 328), citing V. A. Zhukovskii, the original name of this settlement was Barakdiz, which is probably the form that erroneous pointing has rendered as *P.r.kdar* in the *Ḥudūd,* 105. Cf. also Ibn Ḥawqal, *al-Masālik wa-l-Mamālik,* 435–36.

68. Ibn Ḥawqal, *al-Masālik wa-l-Mamālik,* 436.

69. Ibn Ḥawqal, *al-Masālik wa-l-Mamālik,* 429, 436, 456. *Kiranj* in Maqdisī, *Aḥsan,* 310.

70. Ibn Ḥawqal, *al-Masālik wa-l-Mamālik,* 428, 436, 456.

71. Iṣṭakhrī, *al-Masālik wa-l-Mamālik,* 263; Ibn Ḥawqal, *al-Masālik wa-l-Mamālik,* 429, 437, 457; Minorsky, *Ḥudūd,* 105; Shavashkān in Yāqūt, *Muʿjam,* 3:245.

72. Ibn Ḥawqal, *al-Masālik wa-l-Mamālik,* 435–36.

73. This city, although physiographically within the Murghāb River basin, was considered to belong to Gūzgān, the westernmost district of the Balkh *rubʿ.* In the ninth century al-Yaʿqūbī (*al-Buldān,* 287) had attributed its substantial size, which was capable of supporting two Friday mosques, to its manufacture of woollen fabrics, but tenth-century authors tended to emphasize the agricultural productivity of its environs with, as Ibn Ḥawqal puts it (*al-Masālik wa-l-Mamālik,* 442), "numerous flourishing settlements." Cf. also Iṣṭakhrī, *al-Masālik wa-l-Mamālik,* 270; Maqdisī, *Aḥsan,* 299; and Minorsky, *Ḥudūd,* 107, 335. The city was razed by Chingiz Khān after a siege of half a year, but Barthold (*Historical Geography,* 37) has identified its site on the southern edge of the Qalʿah Walī valley (contra Le Strange [*The Lands of the Eastern Caliphate,* 423], who prefers a site at Chachaktu).

74. Pers. = Gurzuvān or Gurzubān. Cf. Ibn Ḥawqal, *al-Masālik wa-l-Mamālik,* 443 and Minorsky, *Ḥudūd,* 107, 335.

75. Also transcribed as Kandadram: Iṣṭakhrī, *al-Masālik wa-l-Mamālik,* 270; Ibn Ḥawqal, *al-Masālik wa-l-Mamālik,* 429, 443 (Kandarm); and Minorsky, Ḥudūd, 107 *(K.nd.rm).* In the ninth century al-Yaʿqūbī (*al-Buldān,* 287) had designated this city as a former seat of the ruler of Gūzgān, but in the tenth century the official (winter) residence of the Farīghūnids was at Anbār (Iṣṭakhrī, *al-Masālik wa-l-Mamālik,* 270; Ibn Ḥawqal, *al-Masālik wa-l-Mamālik,* 443; and Minorsky, *Ḥudūd,* 107) or, as al-Maqdisī believed (*Aḥsan,* 347), al-Yahūdīyah.

76. P. 173 above.

77. For Pers. Pāryāb. Ibn Ḥawqal, *al-Masālik wa-l-Mamālik,* 442 and Minorsky, *Ḥudūd,* 107, 335. The city was destroyed by the Mongols, but its site has been identified as that of the ruins now known as Khayrābād, near modern Dawlatābād: Le Strange, *The Lands of the Eastern Caliphate,* 425; Minorsky, *Ḥudūd,* 335; and Barthold, *Historical Geography,* 33.

78. Ushburqān in Ibn Ḥawqal, *al-Masālik wa-l-Mamālik,* 443 and Minorsky, *Ḥudūd,* 107.

79. Probably located on the site of present-day Sar-i Pul on the upper Shubūrqān River: see Minorsky, *Ḥudūd,* 335 and R. Ghirshman, *Les Chionites-Hephthalites* (Cairo, 1948), 26. Cf. also Ibn Ḥawqal, *al-Masālik wa-l-Mamālik,* 443.

80. Ibn Ḥawqal, *al-Masālik wa-l-Mamālik,* 448 (Siyāhkird).

81. Ibid., 447; Maqdisī, *Aḥsan,* 303; and Minorsky, *Ḥudūd,* 108.

82. Maqdisī, *Aḥsan,* 303 and Minorsky, *Ḥudūd,* 108–9. The city has been identified with the ruins at Haybak, set in the widest and most fertile sector of the Khulm valley: Minorsky, *Ḥudūd,* 338 and Barthold, *Historical Geography,* 22.

83. Or Ruʾb (Minorsky, *Ḥudūd,* 338). The settlement occupied the site of present-day Rūy, upstream from Khulm in the valley of the same name.

84. Ibn Ḥawqal, *al-Masālik wa-l-Mamālik,* 443; also Minorsky, *Ḥudūd,* 107. Variously Andakhud, Addakhūd, al-Nakhud, Antkhudh. According to Iṣṭakhrī (*al-Masālik wa-l-Mamālik,* 270), Andkhuy was the name of a district of which Ushturj was the chief town. It appears that in many instances Ibn Ḥawqal used the ethnikon *Kurd* as a generic term for nomads.

85. In the medieval topographies this name was also transcribed as Khwash and Khuwash. Ibn Ḥawqal (*al-Masālik wa-l-Mamālik,* 422) referred to this river as the Nahr Nīshak, owing to

its flowing through the populous region of that name to the east of Zaranj.

86. Maqdisī, *Aḥsan,* 306.

87. Ibn Ḥawqal, *al-Masālik wa-l-Mamālik,* 420: "the chief town in a rural district encompassing 60 villages and set amidst palm groves, orchards, and fields of cereals."

88. Ibid.

89. Ibid., 419; Maqdisī, *Aḥsan,* 306; and Minorsky, *Ḥudūd,* 110 (Qarnī).

90. For this district see Marquart and de Groot, "Das Reich Zābul," 248–92.

91. Ibn Ḥawqal, p. 418.

92. Ibid., 420–21 and Minorsky, *Ḥudūd,* 110.

93. Ibn Khurradādhbih, *al-Masālik wa-l-Mamālik,* 56; Yaʿqūbī, *al-Buldān,* 281; Ibn Rustah, *al Aʿlaq,* 97; and Maqdisī, *Aḥsan,* 305.

94. Ibn Ḥawqal, *al-Masālik wa-l-Mamālik,* 422.

95. Le Strange, *The Lands of the Eastern Caliphate,* 330.

96. See note 84 above.

97. Ṭuraythīth and Ṭurthīth in the earlier Arab topographers; subsequently Turshīsh, Turshīz, and Turshīs. Cf. Ibn Ḥawqal, *al-Masālik wa-l-Mamālik,* 433, 440; Maqdisī, *Aḥsan,* 317–18; and Minorsky, *Ḥudūd,* 103.

98. Maqdisī, *Aḥsan,* 317–18.

99. Ibn Ḥawqal, *al-Masālik wa-l-Mamālik,* 433 and Maqdisī, *Aḥsan,* 318.

100. Al-Dandānqān was a small but prosperous city on the southwestern edge of the Marv oasis. It exploited both its position as the service center for a productive agricultural district and its strategic situation at a place where caravans from Sarakhs and points west entered the oasis.

101. In modern terms this wilderness encompassed what Western cartographers customarily represent as the Dasht-i Lūṭ ("Lot's Desert") and the Dasht-i Kavīr (Great Desert). However, strictly speaking, neither designation is accurate. *Dasht* denotes an arid expanse having a surface of gravel or gravelly silt that remains firm even when moist. *Kavīr,* on the other hand, signifies a tract of salt slime and mud that develops a hard salt crust when dry. Both the northern and southern stretches of the desert exhibit both types of surface (cf. *Persia.* Geographical Handbook Series, Naval Intelligence Division [Oxford, 1945], 86–98 and W. B. Fisher, ed., *The Cambridge History of Iran,* vol. 1, *The Land of Iran* [Cambridge, 1968], 90–101).

102. Ibn Ḥawqal, *al-Masālik wa-l-Mamālik,* 399–410.

103. Maqdisī, *Aḥsan,* 488–89.

104. The Balūṣ, travelling mostly on foot and reserving their few camels for raiding while living largely off the nut of the *nabq* tree, enjoyed a reputation for remarkable endurance. It is to be noted that, at the time when al-Maqdisī crossed the desert, the Balūṣ were living predominantly in the eastern part of Kirmān Province. Not until the eleventh and twelfth centuries did they migrate eastward into present-day Persian and Pakistani Balūchistān as a response to the Saljūk invasion of Kirmān: see Richard N. Frye, "Remarks on Baluchi history," *Central Asiatic Journal* 5–6 (1959–61): 44–50.

105. Minorsky, *Ḥudūd,* 105 (see also note 100 above); Ibn Ḥawqal, *al-Masālik wa-l-Mamālik,* 436.

106. Ibn Ḥawqal, *al-Masālik wa-l-Mamālik,* 414–16.

107. Ibn Ḥawqal, *al-Masālik wa-l-Mamālik,* 454–55.

108. Ibid., 402–3, who, incidentally, not unreasonably counted Sanīj as part of Kirmān rather than of Sijistān. For the range of transcriptions of this place-name see Schwarz, *Iran,* 3:250ff.

109. Ṭabas al-Tamr ("Ṭabas of the Date Palm") so called to distinguish it from Ṭabas al-ʿUnnāb ("Ṭabas of the Jujube": called Ṭabas Masīnān by the Persians), also in Qūhistān, was almost archetypically a caravan city where desert trails converged before striking out eastward for Qāyin and Harāt. Well might al-Balādhurī designate it "The Gate of Khurāsān"—in the widest usage of that term, of course (*Futūḥ al-Buldān,* 403). Characteristic of the settlement's function as a desert "port" was its massive tank for the storage of water brought from the hills by *kārīz,* its excellent hot baths, and its imposing mosque (Maqdisī, *Aḥsan,* 321–22). See also note 110.

110. In fact Ibn Ḥawqal (*al-Masālik wa-l-Mamālik,* 405) refers to the whole settlement as Sih Dih = "Three Villages." The oasis now goes under the names of Jandak and Biyābānak. When Nāṣir-i Khusraw crossed the desert by this northern route in 1052, he found that the *amīr* Gīlakī of Ṭabas had established such firm control over the whole area that the Qufṣ and other robbers no longer preyed on travellers (*Safar Nāmah,* Thackston's translation, 99). So powerful an impression did this governor make on the inhabitants of the area that in the later Middle Ages Ṭabas al-Tamr (note 109) became known as Ṭabas Gīlakī. Nāṣir-i Khusraw remarks particularly on the moving sands *(rīg-ravān)* and salt swamps *(shūristān)* that beset the traveller on this northern crossing. On these oases in general see Richard N. Frye, "Biyābānak: the oases of Central Iran," *Central Asiatic Journal* 5–6 (1959–61): 182–97.

111. Ibn Ḥawqal, *al-Masālik wa-l-Mamālik,* 406.

112. Maqdisī, *Aḥsan,* 478. The same author noted that, despite the mosque in the marketplace, the inhabitants were only nominally Muslims. Balūṣī featured prominently among them. See also Iṣṭakhrī, *al-Masālik wa-l-Mamālik,* 170–71 and Ibn Ḥawqal, *al-Masālik wa-l-Mamālik,* 325. The site of the city is presently known as Panjgūr = "Five Tombs," specifically those of the five martyred warriors of the first Arab conquest.

113. Maqdisī, *Aḥsan,* 478.

114. For a compendious account of textile manufacture in Khurāsān and Sijistān, see Serjeant, *Islamic Textiles,* 87–96 and 110–111, from which most of the following remarks are derived.

115. Iṣfahānī, *al-Aghānī,* 6:240. For the *ṭirāz* see note 30 to chapter 9.

116. See chapter 15.

117. Ibn al-Faqīh, *al-Buldān,* 254. *Mulḥam* was a cloth with a

warp of silk and a woof of other fiber. At least some of that manufactured in Marv had a double warp.

118. Iṣṭakhrī, *al-Masālik wa-l-Mamālik,* 263; Maqdisī, *Aḥsan,* 324; and Minorsky, *Ḥudūd,* 105.

119. Al-Bakrī, *al-Masālik wa-l-Mamālik,* Arabic text, 93; de Slane's translation, 187.

120. Ibn ʿAbd-Rabbihī, *al-ʿIqd al-Farīd,* vol. 4 (al-Qāhirah, A.H. 1303/A.D. 1913), 267–68.

121. Al-Thaʿālibī, *al-Laṭāʾif al-Maʿārif,* 119; Bosworth's translation, 98. Bosworth has shown that the al-Mustakfī of the text should be amended to read al-Muktafī.

122. Miskawayh, *Tajārib al-Umam,* 1:44; Margoliouth's translation, 41. For *shāhijān* see note 8 above.

123. Al-Thaʿālibī, *al-Laṭāʾif al-Maʿārif,* 201; Bosworth's translation, 135. For other texts incorporating references to Marvian cloths see Serjeant, *Islamic Textiles,* 87–90, especially 90 n. 27.

124. Ibn al-Faqīh, *al-Buldān,* 254. Although Ṭāhirī cloth would appear likely to have been a fabric made up for the Ṭāhirid governors stationed in Nīshāpūr, the style of which persisted after the demise of that dynasty, Serjeant (*Islamic Textiles,* 91 n. 28) has suggested the alternative possibility that it may have taken its name from the town of Ṭāhirīyah in Khwārizm, but the circumstance that that town received no special mention as a textile center does not strengthen the argument. *Tākhtanj* and *rākhtanj* apparently denoted sorts of twisted material (ibid., 91).

125. Ibn Ḥawqal, *al-Masālik wa-l-Mamālik,* 432–33. See also Iṣṭakhrī, *al-Masālik wa-l-Mamālik,* 255 and Minorsky, *Ḥudūd,* 102.

126. A kind of cloth made with a special instrument known as a *ḥaff.*

127. It has been suggested that the term *baybāf* derived from Persian *pai-bāf* = "weaver": Serjeant, *Islamic Textiles,* 92 n. 36.

128. An unidentified fabric which, according to al-Bakrī, was manufactured at Ṣanʿāʾ in the Yaman: see M. J. de Goeje, *Bibliotheca Geographorum Arabicorum,* vol. 4, *Indices, Glossarium et Addenda et Emendanda ad Part I–III* (Lugdani Batavorum, 1967), 260 and E. W. Lane, *Arabic-English Lexicon,* vol. 1 (London and Edinburgh, 1863), 1362.

129. Also unidentified.

130. *Mushṭ* was apparently a type of weavers' card the name of which, for unexplained reasons, became attached to textiles manufactured in Nīshāpūr.

131. Maqdisī, *Aḥsan,* 325.

132. De Goeje (*BGA, Indices,* 194) suggests that this word may be derived from Persian *panba* = "cotton" ("Pannus in urbe Chorasanica Nasâ fabricatus . . . De derivatione nominis incertus sum, videtur autem inesse Persicum panba—gossypium").

133. Iṣṭakhrī, *al-Masālik wa-l-Mamālik,* 94; Maqdisī, *Aḥsan,* 319, 324, 325; and Minorsky, *Ḥudūd,* 103.

134. For example, Yāqūt, *Muʿjam,* 3:72, 343; Abū al-Fidāʾ, *Mukhtaṣar Taʾrīkh al-Bashar,* 459; and Qazwīnī, *ʿAjāʾib al-Makhlūqāt,* 2:266.

135. H. Sauvaire, *Histoire de Jérusalem et d'Hebron . . . par Moudjir ed-Dyn* (Paris, 1876), 52–53.

136. Serjeant, *Islamic Textiles,* 94.

137. Maqdisī, *Aḥsan,* 324.

138. Minorsky, *Ḥudūd,* 106.

139. Jāḥiẓ, "Al-Tabaṣṣur," 343.

140. Iṣṭakhrī, *al-Masālik wa-l-Mamālik,* 275.

141. For literary references to this cloth, consult Serjeant, *Islamic Textiles,* 95.

142. *Jāma-hā-yi farsh* (?): alternatively, "covers for carpets" (Minorsky, *Ḥudūd,* 110 n. 1).

143. Ibid., 110.

144. Kurd de Schloezer, *Abu Dolaf Misaris ben Mohalhal de Itinere Suo Asiatico* (Berlin, 1845), 28.

145. Also Ṣālaqān in Iṣṭakhrī, *al-Masālik wa-l-Mamālik,* 248; Jahalakan (*jah* = *c* ?) in Maqdisī, *Aḥsan,* 297; and *Chālkān in Minorsky, *Ḥudūd,* 110, 344.

146. Iṣṭakhrī, *al-Masālik wa-l-Mamālik,* 248. Ibn Ḥawqal (*al-Masālik wa-l-Mamālik,* 421) and Yāqūt (*Muʿjam,* 3:363) repeat this information.

147. Ibn Ḥawqal, *al-Masālik wa-l-Mamālik,* 450.

148. This information is from al-Yaʿqūbī (*al-Buldān,* 291: end of the ninth century) only; tenth-century topographers do not mention it. "The big myrobalan called Kābulī" ("chebulic" in the traditional English rendering) is the dried, astringent fruit of *Terminalia chebula,* Retz. In the Middle Ages it was used both medicinally and in the tanning process. The Arabic name was *al-ahlīlaj* or *al-halīlaj.*

149. Information on the industries touched upon in this paragraph has been abstracted principally from Iṣṭakhrī, *al-Masālik wa-l-Mamālik,* 281; Ibn Ḥawqal, *al-Masālik wa-l-Mamālik,* 411–58; Maqdisī, *Aḥsan,* 321–26; and Minorsky, *Ḥudūd,* 102–12. For the cofusion method of the manufacture (producing steel in a crucible by the cofusion of high- and low-carbon iron), see Georgina Hermann et al., "The International Merv Project. Preliminary report on the fifth season," *Iran* 35 (1997): 1–35.

150. Minorsky, *Ḥudūd,* 111. Marquart ("Das Reich Zābul," 271) locates these two settlements near Daravāt, east of Baghnī, and on the right bank of the Helmand River.

151. Tall in Iṣṭakhrī, *al-Masālik wa-l-Mamālik,* 244. On the basis of extant itineraries, this city would appear to be identical with that which al-Maqdisī (*Aḥsan,* 305) describes under the name Dāwar.

152. Maqdisī, *Aḥsan,* 321, 333; cf. also Ibn Ḥawqal, *al-Masālik wa-l-Mamālik,* 430 and Minorsky, *Ḥudūd,* p. 103.

153. Ibn Ḥawqal, *al-Masālik wa-l-Mamālik,* 434. Cf. also Minorsky, *Ḥudūd,* 103.

154. Maqdisī, *Aḥsan,* 319. Note: the great shrine of Mazār-i Sharīf, popularly supposed to shelter the remains of the caliph ʿAlī, did not feature in the sacral hierarchy of the tenth century, for the supposed grave was not discovered until A.D. 1480.

155. See note 12 above. There is a succinct description of this shrine, abstracted from the writings of early topographers, in Le Strange, *The Lands of the Eastern Caliphate,* 421–22.

156. The fullest account of this shrine is furnished by al-Qazwīnī, (*ʿAjā'ib al-Makhlūqāt,* 2:163), writing at the close of the thirteenth century, and there is no reason to suppose that it then differed significantly from the tenth-century version.

157. In the fifth century A.D. the Hayṭal (Hephthalites or so-called White Huns) had harassed the Sāsānian forces along the Jayḥun frontier to such effect that their name had come to signify for the Arabs all Transoxanian peoples. The Hephthalite kingdom had been destroyed by the Sāsānids in alliance with Turkish *khāns* between 563 and 567, with the Turks appropriating the territories to the north of the Jayḥūn and the Persians those to the south. Reconstructions of the topography and toponymy of medieval Transoxania are to be found in Wilhelm Tomaschek, "Soghdiana," *Sitzungsberichte der Wiener Akademie der Wissenschaften* 87 (1887): 67–120; W. Barthold, "Otchot o poyezdke v Sredn'uyu Aziyu, 1893–4," *Mémoires de l'Académie des Sciences de St. Pétersbourg,* VIIIe série, vol. 1, no. 4 (1897), passim and *Turkestan down to the Mongol Invasation,* E. J. W. Gibb Memorial Series, n.s., no. 5 (3d ed., London, 1968), 64–179; Marquart, *Ērānšahr nach der Geographie des Ps. Moses Xorenacʿi,* 226–37 and *Wehrot und Arang,* passim; and Le Strange, *The Lands of the Eastern Caliphate,* 433–89. Pre-Islamic times are discussed by Kurakichi Shiratori, "A Study on Su-tʿe, or Sogdiana," *Memoirs of the Research Department of the Tōyō Bunkō,* vol. 2 (Tōkyō, 1928), 81–145, with critical comments by Paul Pelliot in "Des artisans chinois à la capitale Abbasside en 751–762," *T'oung Pao* 26 (1929): 365. Cf. also O. Maenchen, "Huns and Hsiung-nu," *Byzantion* 17 (1945): 225–31.

After comparing the principal transcriptions of the ethnikon *Hephthalite* in Chinese, Arabic, Syriac, Persian, Greek, and Armenian, Franz Altheim concludes that it was an Old Turkish name that had originally designated not the people but the royal lineage: *Aus Spätantike und Christentum* (Tübingen, 1951), 109–13 (as had been proposed by Marquart [*Wehrot und Arang,* 45]). Barthold (*Historical Geography,* 19–20) follows W. Tomaschek ("Über die ältesten Nachrichten über den Skythischen Norden," *Sitzungsberichte der Kaiserlichen Akademie der Wissenschaften zu Wien,* Phil.-Hist. Kl., vol. 116 [1888], p. 751) in suggesting that *Hayṭal* was a mislection, resulting from defective pointing, of *Habṭal.* For Chinese accounts of this kingdom *(Ya-ta Kuo)* see Roy Andrew Miller, *Accounts of Western Nations in the History of the Northern Chou Dynasty,* Chinese Dynastic Histories Translations no. 6 (Berkeley, 1959), 11–12, 70–71.

Studies focusing exclusively on the Hephthalites include Albert Herrmann, "Die Hephthaliten und ihre Beziehungen zu China," *Asia Major* 2 (1925): 564–80 (now somewhat dated); A. J. van Windekens, "Huns blancs et ārçi. Essai sur les appelations du 'tokharien,'" *Le Muséon* 54 (1941): 181–86; Kazuo Enoki, "On the Nationality of the Ephthalites," in *Memoirs of the Research Department of the Toyo Bunko* vol. 18 (Tōkyō, 1959): 1–58; and especially R. Ghirshman, with the collaboration of T. Ghirshman, *Les Chionites-Hephthalites* (Le Caire, 1948), passim.

158. The Rās al-Ṭāq was called Darwāza-i Kish by Tāj al-Dīn Abū Saʿīd al-Samʿānī (112–66), *Kitāb al-Ansāb,* facsimile edition by D. S. Margoliouth in the E. J. W. Gibb Memorial Series, vol. 20 (London, 1913).

159. Ṭabarī, *Ta'rīkh,* 3:80.

160. Yaʿqūbī, *al-Buldān,* 293.

161. Barthold, *Turkestan down to the Mongol Invasion,* 88. The Chinese in question was the Taoist adept Chʿang Chʿun, whose disciple recorded the master's journey to the Western Regions in a work conventionally known as *Hsi-yü Chi.*

The earliest description of Samarqand after the Arab conquest was provided by Ibn al-Faqīh (*al-Buldān,* 325–26) after which it was treated by Iṣṭakhrī, (*al-Masālik wa-l-Mamālik,* 316–18); Ibn Ḥawqal, (*al-Masālik wa-l-Mamālik,* 492–94); Maqdisī (*Aḥsan,* 278–79); and the *Ḥudūd,* 113 (Minorsky's translation).

162. ʿAla al-Dīn ʿAṭā Malik Juwaynī, *Tarīkh-i Jahān Gushā,* ed. Mirzā Muḥammad Qazvīnī, E. J. W. Gibb Memorial Series, no. 16, 3 vols. (London, 1912, 1916, 1937).

163. Cf. note 165.

164. According to Tomaschek ("Soghdiana," 103), it was in the Hephthalite tongue that *vihāra* was vocalized as *bukhār,* but it must be noted that Richard N. Frye has raised the possibility that *buχu̯ār/buχar* was involved as the name of a people or tribe ("Notes on the history of Transoxiana," *Harvard Journal of Asiatic Studies,* vol. 19 [1956]: 106–19).

165. Richard N. Frye, *Bukhara, the Medieval Achievement* (Norman, Okla., 1965), 7–8. The name Bukhārā occurs only relatively late. The earliest dated source referring to it is the *Ta-T'ang Hsi-yü Chi* of the Buddhist pilgrim Hsüan Tsang (who travelled from China to India and back between A.D. 629 and 645), where **·ân [-si̯ək]* (Modern Standard Chinese = *An[-hsi])* is identified with **Bʿuo-χât* (MSC = *Pu-ho)* = Bukhārā (S. Beal, *Si-yu-ki, Buddhist Records of the Western World,* vol. 1 [London, 1906], 34. The *Sui Shu, chüan* 83, *fol.* 9r confirms that **·ân* [as written by Hsüan Tsang] is an apocapated form of **·ân-si̯ək).* On the name Bukhārā see Altheim, *Aus Spätantike und Christentum,* 110–12 and Frye, "Notes on the history of Transoxiana," *Harvard Journal of Asiatic Studies* 19 (1956): 106–19. The Chinese transcription **Bʿuo-χât* is discussed by W. B. Henning in "Argi and the 'Tokharians,'" *Bulletin of the School of Oriental and African Studies* 9 (1938): 549 (in the Sogdian *Nāfnāmak* "schedule of nations," it appears as no. 4: *pwγ'r*).

The *Būmijkath* of Juwaynī appears in Iṣṭakhrī (*al-Masālik wa-l-Mamālik,* 305, 313) and Ibn Ḥawqal (*al-Masālik wa-l-Mamālik,* 482) as *Nūmijkath,* in Maqdisī (*Aḥsan,* 48, 267) as *Numūjkath,* and in Narshakhī (Frye's translation, 21) as *Numijkat* and *Būmiskat.* For a detailed discussion of this name see Markwart, *Wehrot und Arang,* 161–64.

166. Iṣṭakhrī, *al-Masālik wa-l-Mamālik,* 305. Translation after Bosworth, *The Ghaznavids,* 30.

167. Narshakhī, *Ta'rīkh Bukhārā,* 31–32; Frye's translation, 25–27; Abū ʿAbd Allāh Muḥammad al-Khwārizmī, *Mafātīḥ al-ʿUlūm,* ed. G. van Vloten (Leiden, 1895), 53–79; Spuler, *Iran in Früh-Islamischer Zeit,* 337–38; and Barthold, *Turkestan down to the Mongol Invasion,* 229.

168. The most detailed account of tenth-century Bukhārā is incorporated in Narshakhī's history of that city. Of the general topographies devoting sections to the city, the most valuable is al-Maqdisī's (*Aḥsan,* 266–68), though there is also a good deal of information in Iṣṭakhrī (*al-Masālik wa-l-Mamālik,* 305–9) and Ibn Ḥawqal (*al-Masālik wa-l-Mamālik,* 482–89). Cf. also Minorsky, *Ḥudūd,* 112.

169. Iṣṭakhrī, *al-Masālik wa-l-Mamālik,* 326–27; Ibn Ḥawqal, *al-Masālik wa-l-Mamālik,* 503–4; Maqdisī, *Aḥsan,* 277; and Minorsky, *Ḥudūd,* 115. Also Banjakath, Bunūjkath, and, in error in the *Ḥudūd,* Navīnjkath. *Ushrūsanah* is the orthography adopted by Iṣṭakhrī, Ibn Ḥawqal, and Maqdisī, but Ibn Khurradādhbih (*al-Masālik wa-l-Mamālik,* 29) and Yaʿqūbī (*al-Buldān,* 293) wrote *Usrūshanah* and the *Ḥudūd, Surūshana* (or perhaps **Surūshna*). The city has been identified both with the actual site of present-day Ura-tepeh by Le Strange (*The Lands of the Eastern Caliphate,* 474) and, more plausibly, with the ruins known as "The Shahristān," which are situated some sixteen miles southwest of that city (Barthold, *Turkestan down to the Mongol Invasion,* 166).

170. Ibn Ḥawqal, *al-Masālik wa-l-Mamālik,* 503.

171. Iṣṭakhrī, *al-Masālik wa-l-Mamālik,* 325; Ibn Ḥawqal, *al-Masālik wa-l-Mamālik,* 502–3; Maqdisī, *Aḥsan,* 282; and Minorsky, *Ḥudūd,* 114. The city is identified with the site of present-day Qarshī: cf. L. Zimin in *ʿIqd al-Jumān* (Festschrift for V. Barthold) (Tashkent, 1927), 196–214.

172. Yaʿqūbī, *al-Buldān,* 299.

173. Iṣṭakhrī, *al-Masālik wa-l-Mamālik,* 324; Ibn Ḥawqal, *al-Masālik wa-l-Mamālik,* 501; Maqdisī, *Aḥsan,* 282; and Minorsky, *Ḥudūd,* 113. A more accurate orthography than that employed by the tenth-century topographers would have been *Kishsh.* The medieval city is to be identified with present-day Shahr-i Sabz (= "Green City"), a name dating from the period when Tīmūr, who was born near the city, adopted it as his favorite place of residence. See J. Marquart, *Die Chronologie der alttürkischen Inschriften* (Leipzig, 1898), 57. In *Ērānšahr nach der Geographie des Ps. Moses Xorenacʿi,* 304, Marquart adduces evidence from Chinese sources to show that Kish was not built until the seventh century A.D.

174. Iṣṭakhrī, *al-Masālik wa-l-Mamālik,* 337.

175. Maqdisī, *Aḥsan,* 283–84.

176. Ṣaghāniyān (Pers. Chaghāniyān) was probably on the site of present-day Denaw (properly Dīh-i Naw = "New Village") (see Barthold, *Turkestan down to the Mongol Invasion,* 72), although Le Strange (*The Lands of the Eastern Caliphate,* 440) identifies it with Sar-i Asyā on the upper reaches of the Ṣaghāniyān River.

177. Maqdisī, *Aḥsan,* 283–84.

178. Tomaschek ("Soghdiana," 36, 46) identifies Hulbik with the Ptolemaic *χολβισῖνα/χόλβυσσα* (*Geographia* 6, cap. 12). Cf. also Barthold, *Turkestan, down to the Mongol Invasion,* 68–70.

179. On the site of modern Baljuan: Barthold, *Turkestan down to the Mongol Invasion,* 69.

180. On the site of present-day Kurgan-tepeh: Marquart, *Ērānšahr nach der Geographie des Ps. Moses Xorenacʿi,* 233 and Barthold, *Turkestan down to the Mongol Invasion,* 69.

181. Iṣṭakhrī, *al-Masālik wa-l-Mamālik,* 278; Ibn Ḥawqal, *al-Masālik wa-l-Mamālik,* 447; Maqdisī, *Aḥsan,* 303; and Minorsky, *Ḥudūd,* 112.

182. Pers. *Chāch* (spelled *Jāj* in Minorsky, *Ḥudūd,* 118). The city was also often known by its Tūrānian name of Binkath (Bīkath in ibid. and Yāqūt, *Muʿjam,* 1:746, probably owing to an error in pointing in the Arabic script). The medieval city was on the site presently known as Old Tāshkand. Cf. Qudāmah, *al-Kharāj,* 27; Ibn Ḥawqal, *al-Masālik wa-l-Mamālik,* 508–9; and Maqdisī, *Aḥsan,* 276–77.

183. Pers. = Khashart.

184. Iṣṭakhrī, *al-Masālik wa-l-Mamālik,* 332, 345; Ibn Ḥawqal, *al-Masālik wa-l-Mamālik,* 509; Maqdisī, *Aḥsan,* 277; and Minorsky, *Ḥudūd,* 117 (using the orthography *Nūkath,* doubtless owing to an error in pointing).

185. Ibn Khurradādhbih, *al-Masālik wa-l-Mamālik,* 30.

186. Ibn Ḥawqal, *al-Masālik wa-l-Mamālik,* 512 and Maqdisī, *Aḥsan,* 27. Cf. also Iṣṭakhrī, *al-Masālik wa-l-Mamālik,* 333 and Minorsky, *Ḥudūd,* 116.

187. Cf. Barthold, *Turkestan down to the Mongol Invasion,* 161–62. Akhsīkath subsequently suffered severely in the wars of Muḥammad Khwārizm-Shāh at the beginning of the thirteenth century, and was virtually destroyed by the Mongols, after which the capital of Farghānah was transferred to Andījān.

188. Also transcribed as Isfījāb and Asbījāb.

189. Iṣṭakhrī, *al-Masālik wa-l-Mamālik,* 333; Ibn Ḥawqal, *al-Masālik wa-l-Mamālik,* 510; Maqdisī, *Aḥsan,* 272–73; and Minorsky, *Ḥudūd,* 118–19.

190. Masʿūdī, *Murūj,* 1:212 and Ibn Ḥawqal, *al-Masālik wa-l-Mamālik,* 512. Cf. also Iṣṭakhrī, *al-Masālik wa-l-Mamālik,* 310; Maqdisī, *Aḥsan,* 287–88; and Minorsky, *Ḥudūd,* 121. Yäng-i-känt = "The New Town," a meaning carried over into both the Arabic (*al-Qarīyat al-Jadīdah* or *al-Qarīyat al-Ḥadīthah*) and Persian (*Dih-i Naw*) renderings of this name. In literature the honorific style *Shahrkänt* is also met with. The settlement, which was the winter residence of the Ghuzz paramount, was on the site of present-day Jānkänt-Qalʿah. Cf. Bosworth, *The Ghaznavids,* 212–13; S. P. Tolstov, *Auf den Spuren der Altchoresmischen Kultur* (Berlin, 1953), 60–69, 228–30, 264–66 and the same author's "Goroda Guzov," *Sovetskaya Etnografiya* 3 (1947): 55–102; J. Marquart, *Osteuropäische und Ostasiatische Streifzüge,* 339; and W. Barthold, *Histoire des Turcs d'Asie Centrale* (Paris, 1945), 49.

191. The site of Jand is evidenced by the ruins of Khisht-Qalʿah in the district of Tumarutkul, and rather less than a score of miles from Perowsk: V. Kallaur, cited in Barthold, *Turkestan down to the Mongol Invasion,* 178. Cf. Ibn Ḥawqal, *al-Masālik wa-l-Mamālik,* 512 and Minorsky, *Ḥudūd,* 122. By medieval topographers the Aral Sea was often designated the Sea of Jand.

192. Also transcribed as *Juwārah* owning to an error in pointing.

193. On the Turkish world map of Maḥmūd al-Kāshgharī (A.D. 1074 or 1076–77), the lower and middle Sayḥūn (Sīr-Daryā) River bears the legend "Land of the Oghuz towns." See Miller, *Mappae Arabicae,* 5:142–48 and Albert Herrmann, "Die alteste turkische Weltkarte," *Imago Mundi* 1 (1935): 21–28.

194. Eduard Sachau, "Zur Geschichte und Chronologie von Khwārazm," *Sitzungsberichte der Wiener Akademie der Wissenschaften,* Phil.-Hist. Klasse, 73 (1873): 491(20)–495(24).

195. This is the reading of the Constantinople manuscript; the Berlin text reads ". . . is larger than Bukhārā."

196. Maqdisī, *Aḥsan,* 287–88; also Iṣṭakhrī, *al-Masālik wa-l-Mamālik,* 300–301; Ibn Ḥawqal, *al-Masālik wa-l-Mamālik,* 478; and Minorsky, *Ḥudūd,* 121 (using the orthography *Kāzh*). The ruins of the original Kāth are now known as Shāh ʿAbbās Walī, and are situated some distance southeast of the modern city: Barthold, *Turkestan down to the Mongol Invasion,* 145–46.

For comments on the topography and toponymy of medieval Khwārizm see Barthold, *Turkestan down to the Mongol Invasion,* 142–55 and *Nachrichten über den Aral-See und den Unteren Lauf des Amu-Darja* (Leipzig, 1910; Russian original, 1902).

197. Pers. = Gurganj. In later times Mongols and Turks knew the city as Urgenj. It is said that Jurjānīyah had replaced the city of al-Manṣūrah, which was overwhelmed by floodwater from the Jayḥūn. "Al-Manṣūrah" was the honorific bestowed by the Arabs on the chief city of Khwārizm, then known as al-Fīl, when they conquered it in 712 (Balādhurī, *Futūḥ al-Buldān,* 420–21; Murgotten's translation, 705–7).

198. According to M. J. de Goeje, the line of the Wadhāk Canal is traced by the present bed of the Kunya Daryā: *Das alte Bett des Oxus,* cited by Barthold, *Turkestan down to the Mongol Invasion,* 146.

199. Maqdisī, *Aḥsan,* 288–89. See also Iṣṭakhrī, *al-Masālik wa-l-Mamālik,* 299–300; Ibn Ḥawqal, *al-Masālik wa-l-Mamālik,* 350–51; and Minorsky, *Ḥudūd,* 122.

200. Ibn Ḥawqal, *al-Masālik wa-l-Mamālik,* 507 (this translation takes account of an amendment to the text proposed by de Goeje in *Bibliotheca Geographorum Arabicorum,* 4:298). Iṣṭakhrī (*al-Masālik wa-l-Mamālik,* 328–32) enumerates 27 urban centers in Shāsh and 14 in Īlāq, and al-Maqdisī (*Aḥsan,* 264–65) 34 and 17, by no means all of which can now be both identified and located. For an impressionistic representation of the relative size and spacing of urban centers in the Sayḥūn (Sīr Daryā) provinces in the tenth century, see figure 7.

201. Ibn Ḥawqal, *al-Masālik wa-l-Mamālik,* 473.

202. Maqdisī, *Aḥsan,* 288 and Ibn Ḥawqal, *al-Masālik wa-l-Mamālik,* 480.

203. Maqdisī, *Aḥsan,* 263.

204. Ibn Ḥawqal, *al-Masālik wa-l-Mamālik,* 461–62.

205. For the probable location of this town see Barthold, *Turkestan down to the Mongol Invasion,* 151–52.

206. Also transcribed as Banākit: Pers. = Fanākant. Cf. Minorsky, *Ḥudūd,* 118.

207. Maqdisī, *Aḥsan,* 288–89.

208. Ibn Ḥawqal, *al-Masālik wa-l-Mamālik,* 491.

209. Maqdisī, *Aḥsan,* 289. In the tenth century the town was still small (though it did have a cathedral mosque) and exhibiting no obvious intimations of the fame it would achieve under Uzbeg chiefs in subsequent centuries.

210. Ibid., 288.

211. Ibn Ḥawqal, *al-Masālik wa-l-Mamālik,* 514; Maqdisī, *Aḥsan,* 272.

212. Yaʿqūbī (*al-Buldān,* 290) mentions an urban center near this defile under the name Madīnat Bāb al-Ḥadīd, at the same time that he notes the Persian name Dār-i Āhanīn. The pass now goes under the name Buzgala.

213. Cf. especially Ibn Ḥawqal, *al-Masālik wa-l-Mamālik,* 492 and Minorsky, *Ḥudūd,* 113.

214. In the *Ḥudūd* (114) Tirmidh is referred to as "the emporium *(bārgah)* of Khuttalān and Chaghāniyān [Ṣaghāniyān]."

An island in the Jayḥūn that facilitated the construction of a bridge of boats combined with a location on the approach to the Balkh to make Tirmidh the most important crossing of the Jayhūn after Āmul (see pp. 176 and 177).

215. Maqdisī, *Aḥsan,* 291; also Ibn Ḥawqal, *al-Masālik wa-l-Mamālik,* 489 and Minorsky, *Ḥudūd,* 113.

216. Minorsky, *Ḥudūd,* 118. See also Iṣṭakhrī, *al-Masālik wa-l-Mamālik,* 333–34 and Ibn Ḥawqal, *al-Masālik wa-l-Mamālik,* 510.

217. Minorsky, *Ḥudūd,* 115–16.

218. Also Ṣabrān. Cf. Maqdisī, *Aḥsan,* 273–74.

219. Ibn Ḥawqal, *al-Masālik wa-l-Mamālik,* 511 and Minorsky, *Ḥudūd,* 119 (transcribed through an error in pointing as T•rār).

220. Ibn Ḥawqal, *al-Masālik wa-l-Mamālik,* 511 (where the mispointed reading is *Bīskand*): see Barthold, *Turkestan down to the Mongol Invasion,* 177 n. 3. The settlement in question was situated in the vicinity of the Qara-kul Lake.

221. Ibn Ḥawqal, *al-Masālik wa-l-Mamālik,* 513.

222. Maqdisī, *Aḥsan,* 325; Ibn Ḥawqal, *al-Masālik wa-l-Mamālik,* 477 and Minorsky, *Ḥudūd,* 97, 122, where Jurjānīyah is characterized as the Gate of Turkestān.

223. Iṣṭakhrī, *al-Masālik wa-l-Mamālik,* 305.

224. Maqdisī, *Aḥsan,* 340. A specialty of Khwārizm was the strain of melon known as *bāranj* (according to the *Taj al-ʿArūs* = coconut [?-shaped or -sized] but more probably < Pers. *bā rang* = colored), which, packed in snow inside leaden containers, was

brought down the Khurāsān road to the court of the caliph al-Ma'mūn, and subsequently to that of al-Wāthiq, in Baghdād: Thaʿālibī, *al-Laṭā'if al-Maʿārif,* 226; Bosworth's translation, 142.

225. Iṣṭakhrī, *al-Masālik wa-l-Mamālik,* 304–5. In the city of Nasā, Khwārizmian merchants had come to control, if not own outright, virtually all landed property (Maqdisī, *Aḥsan,* 320).

226. Ibn Ḥawqal, *al-Masālik wa-l-Mamālik,* 518.

227. Ibid., 490; Narshakhī, *Ta'rīkh-i Bukhārā,* Frye's translation, 20–21.

228. Ibn Ḥawqal, *al-Masālik wa-l-Mamālik,* 489 and Narshakhī, *Ta'rīkh-i Bukhārā,* Frye's translation, 20–21. The commercial importance of the Bukhārā region was affirmed when al-Narshakhī reported that all the inhabitants of Iskijkat were merchants (13)—even though he may have been guilty of some exaggeration. *Bāzār* is here rendered as "fair" rather than "market" on the authority of Frye's translation under the title *The History of Bukhara,* 13, 113 n. 57.

229. Minorsky, *Ḥudūd,* 115. Ibn Ḥawqal, *al-Masālik wa-l-Mamālik,* 506–7) states that the fair was held on the first of every month. Cf. also Maqdisī, *Aḥsan,* 278.

230. Ibn Ḥawqal, *al-Masālik wa-l-Mamālik,* 511. According to Ibn Baṭṭūṭah, in the fourteenth century the journey downstream from Tirmidh to Kāth on the Jayḥūn took ten days (H. A. R. Gibb, *The Travels of Ibn Baṭṭūṭa,* vol. 3 [Hakluyt Society, 2d ser., no. 141 (Cambridge, 1971)], 542).

231. Information derived from Le Strange's summary: *The Lands of the Eastern Caliphate,* 452–53, 467–68.

232. Ibn Ḥawqal, *al-Masālik wa-l-Mamālik,* 481. Yāqūt, who found himself on the Sayḥūn in December 1219 (*Muʿjam,* 1:191), provides a graphic account of the dangers involved in attempting to navigate the river late in the season.

233. For discussions of the road network of Transoxania in medieval times see Ibn Khurradādhbih, *al-Masālik wa-l-Mamālik,* 25–30; Qudāmah, *al-Kharāj,* 203–9; Iṣṭakhrī, *al-Masālik wa-l-Mamālik,* 334–37; and Ibn Ḥawqal, *al-Masālik wa-l-Mamālik,* 515–24, 341–44.

234. Also rendered as Khāsh, Khās, and Khaṣ: Iṣṭakhrī, *al-Masālik wa-l-Mamālik,* 332; Ibn Ḥawqal, *al-Masālik wa-l-Mamālik,* 509–10; and Maqdisī, *Aḥsan,* 278.

235. Lit., "Silver Mountain": Minorsky, *Ḥudūd,* 117. Sīm (possibly the orthography *-saym* implies a vocalization **sēm*) < [*αργύριον*] *ἄσημον* = "unminted" [silver]; cf. Syriac *sēmā:* H. H. Schaeder, "Fu-Lin," *Iranica,* no. 10 (1934): 35 and Minorsky, *Ḥudūd,* 356 n. 65. Cf. also Iṣṭakhrī, *al-Masālik wa-l-Mamālik,* 332, 345 and Minorsky, *Ḥudūd,* 117.

236. Maqdisī, *Aḥsan,* 288.

237. Iṣṭakhrī, *al-Masālik wa-l-Mamālik,* 314; Ibn Ḥawqal, *al-Masālik wa-l-Mamālik,* 490; Maqdisī, *Aḥsan,* 324; and Minorsky, *Ḥudūd,* 112. *-jī* < Sogdian suffix of origin *-čyk* or New Persian *-čī/zī:* see Frye, *Bukhara,* 115 n. 74) and Dorothy G. Shepard and W. B. Henning, "Zandanījī Identified?" in *Aus der Welt der islamischen Kunst: Festschrift für Ernest Kühnel zum 75 Geburtstag* (Berlin, 1959), 15–40.

238. Narshakhī, *Ta'rīkh Bukhārā,* Frye's translation, 20. Serjeant has suggested that the most likely time for the establishment of the *ṭirāz* workshop in Bukhārā would have been early in the ninth century, when al-Ma'mūn had resided at Marv before setting out to wrest the caliphate from his brother (*Islamic Textiles,* 97).

239. Serjeant, *Islamic Textiles,* 99.

240. For the transmission of Narshakhī's text see note 160 to chapter 3.

241. Textiles from the town of Wadhār, settled by Arabs in the Samarqand oasis. According to al-Idrīsī (*Nuzhat,* Jaubert's translation, 2:201), Wadhārī cloth was "woven of cotton on cotton . . . [Such cloths] are of a colour like to yellow saffron, soft and light to the touch, yet very thick, excellent in their wearing qualities, and durable." Their profitability for the manufacturers in Samarqand in the twelfth century was attested by al-Idrīsī's further remark that "There is not a prince, minister, or *qāḍī* in the whole of Khurāsān who does not wear a Wadhārī garment over his clothes in winter."

242. Minorsky, *Ḥudūd,* 113. Paper had been brought from China into what is now Russian Turkestan at some time between the fourth and sixth centuries. Cf. Laufer, *Sino-Iranica,* 557–59. The art of its manufacture was transmitted to the Arabs by Chinese paper makers taken captive at the Battle of the Ṭalās (Ṭarāz) River in 751. Al-Thaʿālibī writes of this event as follows:

> Its [Samarqand's] specialities include paper, which has driven out of use the Egyptian papyrus and the parchment which previous generations employed; this is because it looks better, is more supple, is more easily handled and is more convenient for writing on. It is only made in Samarqand and China. The author of the *Kitab al-Masalik wa-l-Mamalik* [presumably the roadbook of the Sāmānid vizier al-Jayhānī: see p. 69 above] relates that amongst the Chinese prisoners-of-war captured by Ziyād b. Ṣāliḥ and brought to Samarqand were some artisans who manufactured paper in Samarqand; then it was manufactured on a wide scale and passed into general use, until it became an important export commodity for the people of Samarqand. Its value was universally recognized and people everywhere used it. (*al-Laṭā'if al-Maʿārif,* Bosworth's translation, 140)

In 793/94 Hārūn al-Rashīd brought Chinese workmen to start the first paper factory in Baghdād. On the transmission of paper manufacture to the Occident generally, see Thomas Francis Carter, *The Invention of Printing in China and Its Spread Westward,* 2d ed. rev. by L. Carrington Goodrich (New York, 1955), chap. 13.

243. Ar. = *mandīl:* Maqdisī, *Aḥsan,* 324.

244. See p. 195 below.

245. Iṣṭakhrī, *al-Masālik wa-l-Mamālik,* 304–5; Ibn Ḥawqal, *al-Masālik wa-l-Mamālik,* 481; Maqdisī, *Aḥsan,* 324–25; and Minorsky, *Ḥudūd,* 112–22.

246. Barthold, *Turkestan down to the Mongol Invasion,* 176.

247. Ibn al-Athīr, *al-Kāmil,* 8:157, 370.

248. Also Kaylif.

249. Maqdisī, *Aḥsan,* 291. The *epitheton ornans* Dhū al-Qarnayn (= *bicornus*) bestowed on Alexander the Great apparently derived ultimately from the fable of King Midas's asses' ears: see Ovid, *Metamorphoses,* bk. 11, ll. 146–93; H. Ritter, "Das Proömium des Matnawī-i Maulawī," *Zeitschrift der Deutschen Morgenländischen Gesellschaft,* 93 (1939): 180–81; and John R. Krueger, "A note on Alexander's Arabic epithet," *Journal of the American Oriental Society* 81, no. 4 (1961): 426–27.

250. Maqdisī, *Aḥsan,* 291. The *Ḥudūd* (113) adds that the *Mīr-i Rūdh* (overseer of irrigation) lived in this city.

251. *Sh.lāt* in Minorsky, *Ḥudūd,* 117; *S.lāt* in Iṣṭakhrī, *al-Masālik wa-l-Mamālik,* 346.

252. Minorsky, *Ḥudūd,* 116. Cf. also Iṣṭakhrī, *al-Masālik wa-l-Mamālik,* 333 and Ibn Ḥawqal, *al-Masālik wa-l-Mamālik,* 513.

253. Cf. note 218 above.

254. Also transcribed as Mīrkī: Maqdisī, *Aḥsan,* 275; also Ibn Khurradādhbih, *al-Masālik wa-l-Mamālik,* 28 and Minorsky, *Ḥudūd,* 97, 119.

255. Minorsky, *Ḥudūd,* 115. For Vayshagirt < *Vēsh[a]gird* (the legendary city of Vaēsa) see Marquart, *Ērānšahr nach der Geographie des Ps. Moses Xorenacʿi,* 227. Minorsky (*Ḥudūd,* 353–54 n. 35) identifies it with Fayḍābād on the Īlāq River. For Shaqīq Balkhī, a hermit *(zāhid)* killed during a Muslim raid *(ghazāh)* against Kulān in the Turk country, consult Farid al-Dīn ʿAṭṭār, *Tadhkirat al-Awliyā,* ed. R. A. Nicholson, vol. 1 (London and Leiden, 1905–7), 196–202; also Ibn al-Athīr, *al-Kāmil, sub* A.H. 194 (A.D. 809).

256. Maqdisī, *Aḥsan,* 46.

257. Barthold, *Turkestan down to the Mongol Invasion,* 160, citing Jamāl Qarshī (Abū al-Faḍl ibn Muḥammad), *Mulḥaqāt al-Ṣurāḥ,* written in Kāshghar at the beginning of the fourteenth century. For Nūr see Narshakhī, *Taʾrīkh Bukhārā,* Frye's translation, 12–13; Samʿānī, *Kitāb al-Ansāb,* 570b; and Yāqūt, *Muʿjam,* 4:822.

258. Barthold, *Turkestan down to the Mongol Invasion,* 160, citing Jamāl Qarshī.

259. Narshakhī, *Taʾrīkh Bukhārā,* Frye's translation, 58.

260. Gibb, *The Arab Conquests in Central Asia,* 14 n. 6. In more recent times the course of the Arab conquest of Īrān has been summarized by ʿAbd al-Ḥusayn Zarrīnkūb in Frye, ed., *The Period from the Arab Invasion to the Saljuqs,* 1–56, and, with considerable insight, by M. A. Shaban: "Khurāsān at the Time of the Arab Conquest," in Bosworth, ed., *Iran and Islam,* 479–90: substantially reproduced as chap. 1 in Shaban, *The ʿAbbāsid Revolution* (Cambridge, 1970).

261. For example, Maqdisī on Khulm in Ṭukhāristān (*Aḥsan,* 296): "a small town surrounded by many large villages."

262. Ibid., 318.

263. Minorsky, *Ḥudūd,* 104.

264. Maqdisī, *Aḥsan,* 319.

265. Markwart, *A Catalogue of the Provincial Capitals of Ērānšahr,* 8–13.

266. The process of Arab settlement in Khurāsān has been sketched by Lapidus, "Arab Settlement and Economic Development of Iraq and Iran," 199–201.

267. At the frequently employed conversion rate of three dependents—women, children, and others—to each warrior, fifty thousand troops would have translated into a total of some two hundred thousand persons.

268. According to al-Narshakhī (*Taʾrīkh Bukhārā,* Frye's translation, 48), Qutaybah ibn Muslim expropriated half the houses in the *shahristān* of Bukhārā as quarters for his troops; while al-Ṭabarī (*Taʾrīkh,* 2:1250) reports that all the inhabitants of Samarqand were dispossessed to make room for the Arab garrison. Note, though, that other sources ascribe this evacuation to 713, after the second conquest of Sughd.

269. Shaban, "Khurāsān at the Time of the Arab Conquest," 486.

270. A member of the lesser nobility in the Sāsānian Empire. Under the early Arab Caliphate, the *dihqān*s retained many of their social and economic privileges.

271. The government went so far as to tax even the transit trade in slaves to Baghdād. Young Turkish slaves were enrolled in schools sponsored by the Sāmānid *amīr*s who trained them for military or administrative service.

272. The other principal regions bordering Khurāsān where Islam had failed to establish a foothold were large parts of Bactria (including Chaghāniyān, Tajikistān, and northern Afghānistān), the valleys of the Hindu Kush, and most of southern Afghānistān.

273. Cited by Frye in *The Period from the Arab Invasion to the Saljuqs,* 155.

274. Lapidus, "Arab Settlement and Economic Development of Iraq and Iran," 202.

275. Representative examples are Abīvard, an island of cultivation on the edge of the Marv desert; Asfuzār, in a similar situation in the Hārūd valley; Marv al-Rud at the upstream end of a zone of riverine cultivation and settlement stretching as far north as Marv al-Shāhijān; and Kāth and al-Jurjānīyah, respectively capitals of the territories on the Turkish and Persian sides of the Āmū Daryā, and both deriving their sustenance from irrigated agriculture combined with developed trade networks.

Chapter Fifteen

1. The single most valuable tool for reconstructing the settlement pattern of medieval Egypt, despite its being more than eighty years old and certainly in need of some amendments, is Jean Maspero and Gaston Wiet's *Matériaux pour Servir à la Géographie de l'Égypte,* vol. 36 of *Mémoires Publiés par les Membres de l'Institut Français de l'Archéologie Orientale du Caire* (Le Caire, 1919). Although this work ostensibly furnishes a list of the provinces, towns,

and villages cited by Taqī al-Dīn Aḥmad al-Maqrīzī (1364–1442) in his *al-Mawāʿiẓ* (for full reference see note 36 below), the annotations take account of conditions in both pre-Muslim and early Muslim Egypt—a procedure actually encouraged by al-Maqrīzī's preoccupation with antiquities. Moreover, the authors compiled, in addition to their very full commentary, schedules of the administrative divisions of Egypt as reported by the principal historians and topographers up to the time of al-Maqrīzī, sometimes with counts of the number of villages in each (pp. 173–92).

A work that serves as a partial updating of the *Matériaux* is Adolph Grohmann's *Studien zur Historischen Geographie und Verwaltung des Frühmittelalterlichen Ägypten,* vol. 77 of *Österreichische Akademie der Wissenschaften* (Wien, 1959). The maps in this volume are especially valuable, despite being poorly drafted. Less detailed but still useful are Rhuvon Guest's maps in his edition of Muḥammad ibn Yūsuf al-Kindī's *Kitāb al-Umarāʾ (al-Wulāt)* and *Kitāb al-Quḍāt,* published together under the title *The Governors and Judges of Egypt . . . ,* E. J. W. Gibb Memorial Series, vol. 19 (Leyden and London, 1908–1912); re-edition of *K. al-Wulāt* by Ḥusayn Naṣṣār (Bayrūt, A.H. 1379/A.D. 1959). Especially helpful in recovering the river and canal systems of the Delta and in tracing the itineraries, real or notional, of topographers through that region, is the same author's "The Delta in the Middle Ages. A note on the branches of the Nile and the kurahs of Lower Egypt . . . ," *The Journal of the Royal Asiatic Society of Great Britain and Ireland* (1912): 941–80. See also Prinz Omar Toussoun, *La Géographie de l'Époque Arabe I–III,* vol. 8 of *Mémoires de la Société Royale de Géographie d'Égypte* (Le Caire, 1926, 1928, 1936) and Dieter Müller-Wodarg, "Die Landwirtschaft Ägyptens in der frühen ʿAbbāsidenzeit: 750–969 n. Chr. (132–358 d.H.)," *Der Islam* 31 (1954): 174–227.

The standard account of the Muslim conquest of Egypt for nearly a century has been Butler's *Arab Conquest of Egypt.* A more recent interpretation is J. Jarry, "L'Égypte et l'invasion musulmane," *Annales Islamologiques* 6 (1966): 1–29. A succinct appraisal of the province in Umayyad and early ʿAbbāsid times is provided by Hugh Kennedy ("Egypt as a Province in the Islamic Caliphate, 641–868," in *The Cambridge History of Egypt,* vol. 1, *Islamic Egypt, 640–1517,* ed. Carl F. Petry [Cambridge, 1998], 62–85). The most detailed discussion of any period of ʿAbbāsid administration in Egypt and of the Islamization of the province is provided by Michael Collins Dunn in "The Struggle for ʿAbbāsid Egypt," (Ph.D. diss., Georgetown University, 1975), which deals with the period from the establishment of the ʿAbbāsid dynasty (750) to the appointment of Aḥmad ibn Ṭūlūn as deputy of the provincial governor (868). Sayyidah Ismāʿīl Kāshif's *Miṣr fī ʿAṣr al-Wulāt* (al-Qāhirah, n.d.), which also focuses on Pre-Ṭūlūnid Egypt, is largely derivative from earlier Western studies.

2. Whereas most medieval Arab topographers who cited the name Maqadūniyah applied it to the district around the capital, Ibn al-Faqīh used it to denote all of Egypt in ancient times. In any case the significance of the designation is not entirely clear (nor was it to Yāqūt, who admitted that he was unable to explain the relationship between this name and the Byzantine district of Macedonia), but it would seem that at least part of the Nile Delta was so called after the Alexandrian conquest of the country. Cf. Maspero and Wiet, *Matériaux,* 195–96. Note: The ingenious suggestion by Casanova ("Les noms coptes du Caire," 193–97) that Maqadūniyah might have been an Arabic transcription of *Ma-kha-to-ui* = "The Balance of the Two Kingdoms," an honorific name of the old capital in Memphis, has not found favor with later scholars.

3. Yaʿqūbī, *al-Buldān,* 330–31; Ibn Rustah, *al-Aʿlaq,* 115–16; Wiet's translation, 130–31; and Masʿūdī, *Murūj,* 2:412.

4. See Thierry Bianquis, "La prise du pouvoir par les Fatimides en Egypte (357–363/968–974)," *Annales Islamologiques* 11 (1972): 49–108.

5. Ibn Ḥawqal, *al-Masālik wa-l-Mamālik,* 143, 145–46. The approximate dates of this author's visits to al-Fusṭāṭ have been established by Régis Blachère ("L'agglomération du Caire vue par quatre voyageurs arabes du moyen âge," *Annales Islamologiques* 8 [1969]: 2–4).

Evidently Ibn Ḥawqal, since his first visit to Egypt, for reasons that are unclear and likely to remain so, had become disillusioned with the governance of the Fāṭimids, whose dynastic style he never once mentions, referring to them as "Maghribians." Al-Qāhirah, the honorific name of their capital, he mentions only once, and Al-Azhar, the name of their magnificent congregational mosque, not at all.

6. Maqdisī, *Aḥsan,* 197.

7. Ibid., 193, 197. Cf. further on p. 197, where the city is characterized as "the glory of Islam."

8. Minorsky, *Ḥudūd,* 151.

9. Maqdisī, *Aḥsan,* 197. For the layout of al-Fusṭāṭ in its early years, see chapter 2.

10. The Sin of the Hebrew Scriptures, and the Pelusium of classical authors. Ar. al-Faramā < Egypt. Peremoun = "The City of the Ooze." The ruins of the medieval city are still visible at Tīnah, close to Port Saʿīd. For recent archaeological investigations at the site see Mohammad Abd el-Maqsoud, "Excavations at Tell el-Farama (Pelusium)," *Annales de la Service des Antiquités de l'Egypte* 70 (1984–85), 3–8.

11. So called from the cisterns (sing. *al-jifrah*) that delineated its caravan trails. The district was also sometimes called Rimāl Miṣr = "The Sands of Egypt."

12. This statement is based on the Constantinople recension of al-Maqdisī's *Aḥsan,* 194. In subsequent centuries, the term came to denote the whole of Lower Egypt, and indeed the countryside generally. For comments on the implications of *al-rīf* see the discussion at the end of Goitein's paper (p. 96) cited in note 18 below. There is a long and still useful note on this term attached to an old translation by E. Quatremère: *Histoire des Sultans Mamlouks de l'Égypte,* vol. 2 (Paris, 1845), 205–10. It should be noted that al-Iṣṭakhrī (*al-*

Masālik wa-l-Mamālik, 54) ascribed al-ʿAbbāsīyah to the *kūrah* of al-Ḥawf.

13. M. J. de Goeje, *Descriptio Imperii Moslemici,* vol. 3 of *Bibliotheca Geographorum Arabicorum* (Lugdani Batavorum, 1906), 194 n. *c.* The Yāqūt reference is to *Muʿjam,* 3:600. Cf. also Grohmann, *Studien zur Historischen Geographie,* 29 and Georgette Cornu et al., *Atlas du Monde Arabo-Islamique à l'Époque Classique, IXe–Xe Siècles* (Leiden, 1985), p. 96 and Carte 10.

14. Maqdisī, *Aḥsan,* 196. Cf. also Maspero and Wiet, *Matériaux,* 187. It is certainly possible that Yāqūt and Abū al-Fidā' meant to imply that the city was reconstituted in 893 rather than actually founded.

15. Bilbays < Egypt. Phelbis. Also Bilbaythes.

16. Al-Ḥawf (= edge, fringe) probably denoted most of the country from slightly north of the latitude of ʿAyn Shams and east of the Dimyāt branch of the Nile. According to Ibn Ḥawqal (*al-Masālik wa-l-Mamālik,* 145, followed some two centuries later by Yāqūt, *Muʿjam,* 2:365), it comprised an Eastern Ḥawf, which was presumably largely steppe terrain, and a Western Ḥawf of mostly cultivated land between the steppe and the river. Georgette Cornu has interpreted Ibn Ḥawqal's testimony as implying an Eastern Ḥawf *(al-Ḥawf al-Sharqī)* constituting a transition zone between the eastern edge of the Nile Delta and the desert, and a Western Ḥawf *(al-Ḥawf al-Gharbī)* performing an analogous function on the western edge of the Delta (Cornu, et al., *Atlas du Monde Arabo-Islamique,* 101). This reading of the text does not accord well with the schedule of towns in the *kūrah* as cited by, among others, al-Maqdisī, *Aḥsan,* 193–94; but neither is the interpretation adopted here wholly satisfactory. For what it is worth, Maspero and Wiet believed that the distinction between Eastern and Western Ḥawf came into being only after Ḥawf had come to denote the eastern edge of the Delta, and was ultimately extended to the western edge in response to a felt need for symmetry elicited by a corruption of Ibn Ḥawqal's text (*Matériaux,* 75–77). Cf. also Guest, "The Delta in the Middle Ages," 945–46.

17. For example, Maqdisī, *Aḥsan,* 195: "It is large and flourishing, and has numerous villages and cultivated fields." Cf. also Ibn Ḥawqal, *al-Masālik wa-l-Mamālik,* 144.

18. Goitein, "Cairo: An Islamic City in the Light of the Geniza Documents," 82. See also *A Mediterranean Society: The Jewish Communities of the Arab World as Portrayed in the Documents of the Cairo Geniza,* vol. 4 (Berkeley, 1983), 10–12. The Cairo Geniza documents date mostly from the tenth to the end of the thirteenth century. The nature of these archives is explained in a compendious manner by Goitein in *Economic Foundations,* vol. 1 of *A Mediterranean Society,* 1–28. Published documents from the archives are listed in S. Shaked's *Tentative Bibliography of the Geniza Documents* (Paris and The Hague, 1964). Cf. also Ibn Ḥawqal, *al-Masālik wa-l-Mamālik,* 150–51; Maqdisī, *Aḥsan,* 196–97; and, for the end of the ninth century, Yaʿqūbī, *al-Buldān,* 338–39. For general discussions of medieval Alexandria see Paul Kahle, "Zur Geschichte des mittelalterlichen Alexandria," *Der Islam* 12 (1921): 29–84; Mieczyslaw Rodziewicz, "Graeco-Islamic elements at Kom el Dikka in the light of the new discoveries: remarks on early medieval Alexandria," *Graeco-Arabica* 1 (1982): 35–49; and al-ʿAbbādī, "Ibn ʿAbd al-Ḥakam ʿind al-fatḥ al-ʿArabī," in *Dirāsāt ʿan Ibn ʿAbd al-Ḥakam* (al-Qāhirah, A.H. 1395/A.D. 1975).

19. Maqdisī, *Aḥsan,* 201 and Ibn Ḥawqal, *al-Masālik wa-l-Mamālik,* 147–48.

20. Maqdisī, *Aḥsan,* 201; Ibn Ḥawqal, *al-Masālik wa-l-Mamālik,* 159–60; and Minorsky, *Ḥudūd,* 152.

21. Maqdisī, *Aḥsan,* 195.

22. Ibid., 200. The city was the Heliopolis of the Greeks.

23. Ibn Ḥawqal, *al-Masālik wa-l-Mamālik,* 140. In other texts this town is recorded under the severely apocopated form Būmīnah (e.g., Ibn Khurradādhbih, *al-Masālik wa-l-Mamālik,* 83; Yaʿqūbī, *al-Buldān,* 342; Maqdisī, *Aḥsan,* 214). Shubrū (Shabruwā) was a common element in Egyptian place-names; Yāqūt incorporated no fewer than fifty-three examples in his *al-Mushtarik.*

24. Maqdisī, *Aḥsan,* 201.

25. See p. 75 above.

26. Ibn Ḥawqal, *al-Masālik wa-l-Mamālik,* 144 and Maqdisī, *Aḥsan,* 195.

27. Maqdisī, *Aḥsan,* 200.

28. Ibid., 195.

29. At least it served these functions at a slightly later period: see Goitein, "Cairo: An Islamic City in the Light of the Geniza Documents," 82. Cf. also Ibn Ḥawqal, *al-Masālik wa-l-Mamālik,* 150–51 and Maqdisī, *Aḥsan,* 196–97.

30. Maqdisī, *Aḥsan,* 201. This author's enthusiasm led him to characterize the city as "a little Baghdād," a comparison that had already been advanced by Yaʿqūbī (*al-Buldān,* 338) about a century earlier. The memory of the city persists to this day in Tall Tanīs in Lake Manzālah.

31. The text reads ḍarʿ = "udder."

32. Maqdisī, *Aḥsan,* 195–96. To illustrate the scarcity of fuel in al-Qulzum, al-Maqdisī relates that on one occasion when he bought a *dirham*'s worth of gourds, he had been constrained to spend another *dirham* on fuel with which to cook them.

33. Ibid., 199. For *maʿāyish* = "shops" in the passage quoted see R. Dozy, *Supplément aux Dictionnaires Arabes,* 2d ed. (Paris, 1927), 2:195; M. J. de Goeje, *Bibliotheca Geographorum Arabicorum, Indices, Glossarium et Addenda et Emendanda ad Part I–III* (Lugdunum Batavorum, 1879), 307 *(taberna mercatoria);* and Miquel, "L'Égypte vue par un géographe arabe du IVe/Xe siècle: al-Muqqaddasī," 116 n. 47.

34. Al-Azraqī, *Akhbār Makkah,* 1:176. Ar. *Qibṭ* (Copt) < Gk. *Aigyptos* < Anc. Egypt. *Ha-Ka-Ptah* = Temple of the God Ptah = Memphis.

35. Serjeant, *Islamic Textiles,* 11, 136. Chap. 16 in this volume provides detailed information on the Egyptian textile industries and is the basis of the present account.

36. Cf. note 30 to chapter 9 above. For Dimyāt see Yaʿqūbī, *al-Buldān,* 338; Iṣṭakhrī, *al-Masālik wa-l-Mamālik,* 52; Ibn Ḥawqal, *al-Masālik wa-l-Mamālik,* 156; Maqdisī, *Aḥsan,* 201–2; and al-Maqrīzī, *al-Mawāʿiẓ,* 4:37–80. The city's textile industry continued to flourish despite repeated naval raids by the Byzantines. For Tinnīs see Yaʿqūbī, *al-Buldān,* 337, 338; Qudāmah, *al-Kharāj,* 247; Ibn Ḥawqal, *al-Masālik wa-l-Mamālik,* 156; and Maqdisī, *Aḥsan,* 201–2.

37. On an island in Lake Manzālah: cf. Ibn Ḥawqal, *al-Masālik wa-l-Mamālik,* 152 and Maqdisī, *Aḥsan,* 195 (C recension only), 202.

38. Also Dabqū. Cf. Ibn Ḥawqal, *al-Masālik wa-l-Mamālik,* 156 and Maqdisī, *Aḥsan,* 193. The precise location of this important textile-manufacturing town is unknown, but Gaston Wiet, relying on a comment by al-Maqrīzī (*al-Mawāʿiẓ,* 1:226), has described it as "a locality in the outer suburbs of Damietta" (*The Encyclopaedia of Islam,* 2d ed., 2:72). See also Wiet's edition of *al-Mawāʿiẓ* (*El-mawāʿiz waʾl-iʿtibān fī dhikr el-khitat waʾl-āthār* [Cairo, 1911–27]), 1:[ix]–xvi, for an exhaustive bibliography.

39. Situated on an island in Lake Manzālah. Cf. Ibn Khurradādhbih, *al-Masālik wa-l-Mamālik,* 83; Ibn Ḥawqal, *al-Masālik wa-l-Mamālik,* 156; and Maqdisī, *Aḥsan,* 194.

40. Also Damīrah: cf. Ibn Ḥawqal, *al-Masālik wa-l-Mamālik,* 156 and Maqdisī, *Aḥsan,* 194, 196.

41. Maqrīzī, *al-Mawāʿiẓ,* 1:176.

42. Ibid., 1:226 and Ibn ʿAbd Rabbihī, *al-ʿIqd al-Farīd.*

43. Reported by al-Thaʿālibī, *al-Laṭāʾif al-Maʿārif,* de Jong edition, 160; Bosworth's translation, 120. Cf. Ibn Ḥawqal, *al-Masālik wa-l-Mamālik,* 152: "Everything manufactured [in Tinnīs and Dimyāṭ] is of linen," and Nāṣir-i Khusraw, *Safar Nāmah,* Schéfer's translation, 110; Thackston's translation, 39. Of the three thousand textile fragments recovered by the Fusṭāṭ Expedition, 70 percent were undyed linens; 12 percent linens dyed medium blue; 8 percent heavy fabrics that might be woven with undyed linen, hemp, or reeds and that were probably used as floor coverings; and 10 percent patterned dyed fabrics. Although blue-and-white striped linens in plain weave constituted the largest component in this group, it also comprised about 150 distinctive fabrics in linen, wool, silk, cotton, hemp, and reeds. See Władysław Kubiak and George T. Scanlon, *Fusṭāṭ Expedition Final Report,* vol. 2 (Winona Lake, Ind., 1989), chap. 7.

44. Maqdisī, *Aḥsan,* 202, 203 (where the contrast with Dimyāṭ is drawn only in the Constantinople recension). Cf. Ibn Zawlāq (writing before 997) as cited by Yāqūt, *Muʿjam,* 3:288.

45. Preserved in Yāqūt, *Muʿjam,* 2:602; translation modified by Serjeant (*Islamic Textiles,* 145).

46. Cited by Serjeant (*Islamic Textiles,* 138) from J. B. Chabot's French translation of *Chronique de Michel le Syrien . . .* (Paris, 1899), vol. 3, p. 63.

47. For the phrase *ʿuqidat alayhim* in this passage, see de Goeje, *Indices, Glossarium et Addenda,* 302.

48. Cf. ibid., 246–47.

49. Maqdisī, *Aḥsan,* 213.

50. Ibn Ḥawqal, *al-Masālik wa-l-Mamālik,* 152.

51. Al-Kindī, *Faḍāʾil Miṣr,* cited in Serjeant, *Islamic Textiles,* 141. This brief treatise was written by ʿUmar, an otherwise unknown son of Abū ʿUmar Muḥammad al-Kindī, the historian of Egypt. It has been edited and translated into Danish by J. Østrup in *Oversigt over det Kongelige Danske Videnskabernes Selskab Forhandlinger* (Kobenhavn, 1896), 173–245.

52. Al-Jāḥiẓ (attrib.), "Al-Tabaṣṣur," 12:337. In rendering this somewhat obscure passage I have followed the sense (although not the precise wording) of Serjeant's translation in *Islamic Textiles,* 143. Cf. also Charles Pellat, "Ǧāḥiẓiana, I: Le Kitāb al-Tabaṣṣur bi-l-Tiǧāra attribué à Ǧāḥiẓ," *Arabica,* 1 (1954): 158. Yāqūt's assertion (*Muʿjam,* 4:166) that the Egyptian manufacture of *būqalamūn* had been introduced from the Greek world was probably correct, for the name appears to have been derived from *ὑποκάλαμον* (cf. Dozy, *Supplément aux Dictionnaires Arabes* [Leyden, 1881], 1:6–7), although the epithet *khusrawāni* seems to imply some connection with the Sāsānian monarchy.

53. Nāṣir-i Khusraw, *Safar Nāmah,* Schéfer's translation, 113; Thackston's translation, 40.

54. Cf. note 38 above.

55. Iṣfahānī, *al-Aghānī,* 5:424, 345.

56. Serjeant, *Islamic Textiles,* 138–41. Cf. the multicolored Dabīqī awnings *(sutūr Dabīqī mulawwanah)* raised on Nile riverboats for the ceremony of perfuming the Nilometre in 1124 (see Paula Sanders, *Ritual, Politics, and the City in Fatimid Cairo* [Albany, N.Y., 1994], 113).

57. Ibn Ḥawqal, *al-Masālik wa-l-Mamālik,* 152–53. It is usually conceded that Ibn Killīs's administration was a major factor in stimulating the economic prosperity of the Nile valley under the early Fāṭimids. Maqrīzī (*al-Mawāʿiẓ,* 2:6), for instance, recorded under this *wazīr* the revenue of the cities Tinnīs, Dimyāṭ and Ashmunayn (all textile centers) amounted to as much as 220,000 *dīnārs* a day. "This was unheard of in any other country," he added, "and continued until Muḥarram A.H. 365 (A.D. 975)." It was also almost certainly an exaggeration but nevertheless a not altogether unrealistic reflection of the reputation of this industrial complex. See Yaacov Lev, "The Fāṭimid vizier Yaʿqub ibn Killis and the beginning of the Fāṭimid administration in Egypt," *Der Islam* 58 (1981): 237–49.

58. Aḥmad al-Qalqashandī (d. 1418), *Ṣubḥ al-Aʿshā,* 4:7.

59. These references have been collected by Serjeant (*Islamic Textiles,* 147). The continuing silk trade is described by O. von Falke in *Decorative Silks,* 3d ed. (London, 1936), 7.

60. Al-Washshā, *Kitāb al-Muwashshā,* ed. R. E. Brünnow (Leyden, 1886), 124.

61. The *ṭirāz* factories of Bahnasā are mentioned by both al-Masʿūdī (*al-Tanbīh,* 22) and al-Kindī (*Fadāʾil Misr,* cited in Serjeant, *Islamic Textiles,* 154).

62. Cf. Gaston Wiet, "Tapis égyptiens," *Arabica* 6 (1959): 13.

63. Ibn Ḥawqal, *al-Masālik wa-l-Mamālik,* 159.

64. Yaʿqūbī, *al-Buldān,* 331; cf. also Maqrīzī, *al-Mawāʿiẓ,* 734.

65. Maqdisī, *Aḥsan,* 203. This name is transcribed as Būṣīr-Qūrīdis by Wiet (*The Encyclopaedia of Islam,* 2d ed., 1:1343). Note that Maqdisī here contradicts, at least in part, his statement two folios previously that the linen of the Fayyūm was of only middling quality: cf. p. 193 above.

66. Maqdisī, *Aḥsan,* 202 and Ibn Ḥawqal, *al-Masālik wa-l-Mamālik,* 159.

67. Or possibly "divided" carpets. I have followed de Goeje (*Bibliotheca Geographorum Arabicorum,* 7:332) in reading *quṭūʿ* in Yaʿqūbī's text, which Serjeant (*Islamic Textiles,* 156 n. 171) tentatively suggests should be amended to *maqṭūʿ*. Wiet (ed. and trans. of Yaʿqūbī, *Les Pays* [Le Caire, 1937], 187) reads *nuṭūʿ*, as the manuscript apparently permits, and consequently renders the phrase as *des tapis de cuir.* The *ṭirāz* factories in Akhmīm are mentioned by al-Masʿūdī (*al-Tanbīh,* 36). In Byzantine times there had been a factory in the city under Coptic control: cf. von Falke, *Decorative Silks,* 7.

68. Masʿūdī, *al-Tanbīh,* 22.

69. Nāṣir-i Khusraw, *Safar Nāmah,* Thackston's translation, 63. This author renders *dastār* as "turbans." Nāṣir-i Khusraw was, of course, writing in the mid-eleventh century. Cf. Schéfer's translation, 173.

70. Ibn Ḥawqal, *al-Masālik wa-l-Mamālik,* 158, 159; cf. also Iṣṭakhrī, *al-Masālik wa-l-Mamālik,* 53. It should also be noted that Egypt was able to acquire from its own territories three substances of great importance in the preparation and dyeing of cloth, specifically alum *(shabb)* from the desert of Upper Egypt, natron *(naṭrūn)* from the Wādī Naṭrūn, and indigo *(nīlah),* which was grown fairly widely in the *iqlīm.* Most of the relevant information is provided by Ibn Mammātī (d. 1209; *Qawānīn al-Dawānīn,* ed. A. S. Aṭiyah [al-Qāhirah, A.H. 1318/A.D. 1900–01]), whence it was copied by a number of subsequent writers, including al-Maqrīzī. Because of their uses in textile manufacturing, these natural resources were involved in a vigorous network of domestic and foreign trading, much of which was subject to government regulation. The available information, which can be retrojected to the tenth century only with caution, has been summarized by Serjeant (*Islamic Textiles,* 162–64).

71. Balādhurī, *al-Buldān,* 223; Hitti's translation, 350; Ḥakam, *Futūḥ Miṣr,* 130; and Goitein, "Cairo: An Islamic City in the Light of the Geniza Documents," 82. Of course, this is not to deny that there was probably an element of historical conventionality in this usage.

72. Maqdisī, *Aḥsan,* 202.

73. Minorsky, *Ḥudūd,* 152. Note that the third redaction of Ibn Ḥawqal's book was almost contemporary with the completion of the *Ḥudūd,* which in this instance was almost certainly purveying out-of-date information.

74. Ibn Ḥawqal, *al-Masālik wa-l-Mamālik,* 152.

75. Iṣṭakhrī, *al-Masālik wa-l-Mamālik,* 51; Ibn Ḥawqal, *al-Masālik wa-l-Mamālik,* 150; Maqdisī, *Aḥsan,* 209; and Minorsky, *Ḥudūd,* 151. Al-Shāfiʿī was interred between two of his most famous disciples, al-Muzanī and Abū Isḥāq al-Marwazī. For the site at the end of the twelfth century see al-Harawī, *al-Ishārāt,* Arabic text, 41; French translation, 83. Cf. also Gaston Wiet, "Les inscriptions du mausolée de Shāfiʿī," *Bulletin de l'Institut d'Égypte* 15 (1933): 167–85.

76. Iṣṭakhrī, *al-Masālik wa-l-Mamālik,* 53.

77. Maqdisī, *Aḥsan,* 201. Abū al-Fayḍ Thawbān ibn Ibrāhīm al-Miṣrī Dhū al-Nūn (ca. 796–861), called "The Head of the Ṣūfīs," is held to have been the first to teach the true nature of gnosis *(maʿrifah):* cf. M. Smith, *The Encyclopaedia of Islam,* new ed., 2:242.

78. Maqdisī, *Aḥsan,* 209–10.

79. Amn was no doubt derived from, or perhaps assimilated connotatively to, the Elim of Exod. 15:27 and 16:1, with its twelve water holes; a connection made most explicitly by al-Maqdisī (*Aḥsan,* 209) when he referred to twelve springs of tolerably sweet water at al-Amn.

80. Qurʾān 24 *(al-Nūr):*35.

81. Maqdisī, *Aḥsan,* 209.

82. Qurʾān 12 *(Yūsuf):*20.

83. Qurʾān 23 *(al-Muʾminīn):*50.

84. For overviews of this topic, including estimates of the progress of conversion at different times, see Dunn, "The Struggle for ʿAbbāsid Egypt," 177–89; Ira M. Lapidus, "The conversion of Egypt to Islam," *Israel Oriental Studies,* 2 (1972): 248–62; and for an attempt at quantitative interpretation, Richard W. Bulliet, *Conversion to Islam in the Medieval Period: An Essay in Quantitative History* (Cambridge, Mass., 1979), 8.

The current standard account of Coptic Egypt under Arab rule is S. Tomin, *Das christliche-koptische Ägypten im arabischen Zeit* (Wiesbaden, 1984). There is a succinct conspectus of the Roman period in A. F. Shore, "Christian and Coptic Egypt," in *The Legacy of Egypt,* ed. J. R. Harris (Oxford, 1971), 390–443 and a fuller discussion in lively, documented detail in Naphtali Lewis, *Life in Egypt under Roman Rule* (Oxford, 1983). Egypt under Byzantine rule is discussed authoritatively by Walter E. Kaegi: "Egypt on the Eve of the Muslim Conquest," in *Islamic Egypt, 640–1517,* ed. Petry 1:34–61. As would be expected, there is a great deal of relevant information in A. S. Atiya, ed., *The Coptic Encyclopedia,* 8 vols. (New York, 1991).

85. According to revenue information provided by al-Yaʿqūbī (*al-Buldān,* 339), more than half the Christian population of Egypt would have been converted to Islam during the caliphates of ʿUthmān and ʿAlī (644–61), with a consequent massive reduction in the poll tax; and there would have been substantial further conversions in later Umayyad and early ʿAbbāsid times. But D. C. Dennett has demonstrated with a high degree of probability that al-Yaʿqūbī in his calculations failed to discriminate between the poll tax and total revenues (*Conversion and the Poll Tax in Early Islam* [Cambridge,

1950], 82–88). As a matter of fact, a census of Egypt's more than ten thousand villages during the caliphate of Hishām (724–43) found most of them to be Christian (cited by Lapidus, "The conversion of Egypt to Islam," 251).

86. Lapidus, "The conversion of Egypt to Islam," 254; also Dunn, "The Struggle for ʿAbbāsid Egypt," 146–48; L. Caetani, *Annali,* 4:590–91, 597; and B. T. Evetts, ed., *The Churches and Monasteries of Egypt,* usually attributed to Abū Ṣālilḥ al-Armanī but in fact probably written by Jirjīs ibn al-Makīn (Oxford, 1894–95), 101–4, 108–10.

87. Maqrīzī, *al-Mawāʿiẓ,* 2:494.

88. Lapidus, "The conversion of Egypt to Islam," 260; cf. Dunn, "The Struggle for ʿAbbāsid Egypt," passim.

89. Maqrīzī, *al-Mawāʿiẓ,* 1:80–82.

90. Lapidus, "The conversion of Egypt to Islam," 256, 258–59. Cf. also Dominique Sourdel, "Nouvelles recherches sur la deuxième partie du *Livre des Viziers* d'al-Ǧahšiyari," *Mélanges Louis Massignon* 3 (1957): 287–89. On the whole, Dunn ("The Struggle for ʿAbbāsid Egypt," passim but especially 190–203) attaches greater importance to the Arab tribes settled in the Nile Delta as prime movers in the conversion process than does Lapidus.

91. Lapidus, "The conversion of Egypt to Islam," 260–62.

92. Ibn Ḥawqal, *al-Masālik wa-l-Mamālik,* 55.

93. Ibid., 154.

94. Maqdisī, *Aḥsan,* 57, 217, 220.

95. P. 192 above.

96. See, for example, Alan K. Bowman, *Egypt after the Pharaohs, 332* B.C.–A.D. 642 (Berkeley and Los Angeles, 1989), chap. 7.

97. Mieczyslaw Rodziewicz, "Alexandria and district of Mareotis," *Graeco-Arabica* 2 (1983): 199–216.

98. Al-Kindī, *Kitāb al-Quḍāt,* supplement by Ibn Hajar al-ʿAsqalānī, Guest edition, 532.

99. For a discussion of the role of al-Ṣaʿīd vis-à-vis the Nile Delta in Egyptian history, see J.-C. Garcin, "Pour un recours à l'histoire de l'espace vécu dans l'étude de l'Égypte arabe," *Annales—Économies, Sociétés, Civilisations* 35 (1980): 436–51.

100. P. 192 above. The only full-scale study of the Ṭūlūnid dynasty, written well over half a century ago, is Zaky Mohamed Hassan, *Les Tulunides. Étude de l'Égypte Musulmane à la Fin du IXe Siècle 868–905* (Paris, 1933).

101. P. 196 above. Ṭaḥā was the ancient Theodosiopolis. It was also the birthplace of the Ḥanafite jurist Imām Abū Jaʿfar al-Azdī, also known by the *nisbah* al-Ṭaḥāwī (844–933): cf. Maqdisī, *Aḥsan,* 202; Ibn Ḥawqal, *al-Masālik wa-l-Mamālik,* 159; Ibn Khallikān, *Wafāyāt,* al-Dīn edition (al-Qāhirah, A.H. 1367/A.D. 1948), 1:53–55.

102. Cf. p. 193 above.

103. Pp. 195–96 above.

104. As introductions to this theme, consult H. I. Bell, "The administration of Egypt under the Umayyads," *Byzantinische Zeitschrift* 28 (1928): 278–86 and Kōsei Morimoto, *The Fiscal Administration of Egypt in the Early Islamic Period* (Kyōtō, 1981).

Chapter Sixteen

1. In the eleventh century, al-Bakrī used the term *al-Maghrib* in the more restricted sense of the North African lands lying west of the Khalīj Surt (Gulf of Sidra). In subsequent centuries, writers (Ibn Khaldūn among them) customarily placed the eastern boundary of al-Maghrib in the neighborhood of present-day Bougie, and denoted modern Tunisia and western Libya by the term *al-Ifrīqiyah.*

Al-Maqdisī's treatment of the Maghrib was noticeably less detailed, as well as considerably less reliable, than were most of his descriptions of the Eastern Caliphate. He recorded a smaller proportion of the total number of cities than he did for any other *iqlīm* (he himself admits to mentioning only the more important: *Aḥsan,* 228), and seems not to have visited all those he did mention. At least the *ʿiyān* that informs so many pages of the *Aḥsan al-Taqāsīm* (p. 64 above) is largely missing from the section dealing with the Maghrib, where it is sometimes replaced with a perfunctory style of reporting—as when al-Qusṭanṭīnnīyah (*Aḥsan,* 228) is dismissed as "a Pre-Islamic town two days' journey from the capital (al-Miṣr, i.e., al-Qayrawān)." This is clearly an error: the time involved was more of the order of eight days; compare with ten stages from al-Qayrawān (Kairouan) to Saṭīf (ibid., 246). Another example of this reportorial style occurs when the commercial dealings of the whole Maghrib are summarized in less than four lines of the transcribed text (ibid., 238). It is evident, moreover, that he simply appropriated the itinerary from Barqah to Iskandarīyah (Alexandria) from Ibn Khurradādhbih's roadbook. Fortunately, these deficiencies are compensated for by the existence of two considerably more detailed topographies, namely Ibn Ḥawqal's *Ṣūrat al-Arḍ* (p. 68 above) and al-Bakrī's *Kitāb al-Masālik wa-l-Mamālik* (p. 72). Ibn Ḥawqal's chapter on the Maghrib is perhaps the finest achievement in his book. He describes his method of inquiry as follows:

> I used continually to be interrogating and cross-examining travellers who had traversed the world, as well as brokers from the markets, and I used to read works dealing with these topics. When I happened to meet a man whom I believed to be truthful and well informed on subjects that interested me, I would have him tell me about a certain occurrence on which I placed some reliance with the intention of testing his veracity. Then I would ask him to retell the same story and to listen to accounts of it that I had obtained elsewhere, thereby confronting him with another witness's version of the events he was describing. Finally I would compare these two versions with yet a third in a totally unprejudiced manner. (329)

This description may have been an idealization of the manner in which Ibn Ḥawqal collected his data, but the Maghribī section of his book (pp. 60–107) surely testifies to the extreme scrupulosity of his search for accuracy and comprehensiveness. In fact, he himself claims (p. 83) that, from Barqah to the Atlantic Ocean, he described only those cities "that he had visited and seen with his own eyes or about which he had heard from persons who had lived there."

Although the other principal topography used in the writing of this chapter, al-Bakrī's book of the routes-and-kingdoms genre, was not written until the second half of the eleventh century, it nevertheless incorporates much information relating to the tenth century and proved of prime importance in reconstructing the urban hierarchy of the Maghrib at that time. It is our good fortune that the Maghribī section is among the surviving fragments of that work.

Other authors whose works have been drawn upon from time to time include the following:

- ʿAbd al-Raḥmān ibn ʿAbd Allāh ibn ʿAbd al-Ḥakam (d. 870 in al-Fusṭāṭ), *Kitāb Futūḥ Miṣr wa-l-Ifrīqiyah.* Although for this author history was more an instrument for the establishment of points of law than a disinterested record of past events, he does furnish valuable (but uncritically evaluated) information on conditions in North Africa during the earlier Islamic centuries. The Arabic text and a French translation of those sections dealing with North Africa and Spain have been published by Albert Gateau under the title *Conquête de L'Afrique du Nord et de l'Espagne (Futūḥ' Ifrīqiya wa'l-Andalus)* (2d ed., Alger, 1947). The text reproduced by Gateau is essentially that established by Charles C. Torrey under the title *The History of the Conquest of Egypt, North Africa and Spain Known as the Futūḥ Miṣr* (New Haven, Conn., 1922). The historical sections of this text (but not those dealing with judges and traditionists) as they appear in a twelfth-century manuscript unknown to Torrey was published by ʿAbd al-Munʿim ʿĀmir in about 1961: *Futūḥ Miṣr wa-l-Maghrib li-Ibn ʿAbd al-Ḥakam* (al-Qāhirah, n.d.). For earlier publications of this text see Julien, *History of North Africa: Tunisia, Algeria, Morocco,* rev. 2d ed. (New York and Washington, 1970), 383. Originally published as *Histoire de l'Afrique du Nord* (Paris, 1952). There are also useful comments on this text in Robert Brunschvig, "Ibn ʿAbdalhʾakam et la conquête de l'Afrique du Nord par les Arabes," *Annales de l'Institut des Etudes Orientales* 6 (1942–47): 108–55. For evaluations of various aspects of Ibn ʿAbd al-Ḥakam's work given by a group of Egyptian historians, see *Dirāsāt ʿan Ibn ʿAbd al-Ḥakam* (al-Qāhirah, A.H. 1395/A.D. 1975), sponsored by Wizārah al-Thaqāfah.
- Ibn al-Ṣaghīr, who lived at Ṭāhart (Tiaret) and composed an anecdotal chronicle of the times of the Rustamid *imāms,* probably in about 903: edited with a French translation by A. de C. Motylinski under the title "Chronique d'Ibn Ṣaghīr sur les imams rostémides de Tahert," *Actes du XIVe Congrès International des Orientalistes* (Alger, 1905; third part, Paris, 1908), 3–132. Motylinski aptly characterizes this work as "la monographie de la Tāhert abādhite dans sa vie intime." Cf. also Tadeusz Lewicki, "Les historiens, biographes et traditionistes ibāḍities-wahbites de l'Afrique du Nord du VIIIe au XVIe siècle," *Folia Orientalia* 3 (1961–62): 105–6.
- Abū Zakarīyā al-Warjalānī, a Khārijī scholar who studied in the Wādī Righ under the Ibāḍī shaykh Abū al-Rabīʿ Sulaymān ibn Ikhlaf al-Mazātī. In the second half of the eleventh century he wrote *Al-Sīrah wa-Akhbār al-Aʾimmah,* the earliest record of the Ibāḍīs in the Maghrib prepared by a member of the sect. It has been edited and translated into French by Roger Le Tourneau under the title "'La Chronique' d'Abū Zakariyyā al-Wargalānī (m. 471 H = 1078 J.-C.)," *Revue Africaine* 105 (1961): 117–76. There is an early French translation under the title *Chronique d'Abou Zakaria* by Emile Masqueray (Alger, 1878).
- Ibn ʿIdhārī al-Marrākushī, a one-time *qāʾid* of Fās who lived in the second half of the thirteenth century and the early decades of the fourteenth. His extant chronicle entitled *al-Bayān al-Maghrib fī (Ikhtiṣār) Akhbār Mulūk al-Andalus wa-l-Maghrib* comprises three sections, of which the first is a condensed analytical history of al-Ifrīqiyah from the conquest of Egypt in 640/41 to the Almohad capture of al-Mahdīyah in 1205/6 (the second and third sections, which deal respectively with the Iberian Peninsula and with the Almoravid and Almohad dynasties, do not concern us at this juncture). J. Bosch-Vilá has characterized this work as "a compilation of chronicles many of which have been lost, a basic source containing sound and detailed information, indispensable to the historian of the Maghrib and of al-Andalus" (*The Encyclopaedia of Islam,* 2d ed., 3:805–6). Volumes 1 and 2 have been edited by G. S. Colin and E. Lévi-Provençal under the title *Histoire de l'Afrique du Nord et de l'Espagne Musulmane, Intitulé Kitab al-Bayan al-Mughrib* (Leiden, 1948–51). Vol. 3 had already been edited by Lévi-Provençal (Paris, 1930). There is a French translation of an edition of parts 1 and 2 prepared by R. Dozy in 1848–51 that was made by E. Fagnan as long ago as 1901–4: *Histoire de l'Afrique et de l'Espagne Intitulée Al-Bayanoʾl-Mogrib,* 2 vols. (Alger).
- Ibn Abī Zarʿ al-Fāsī, an *imām* of Fās (Fez) who died between 1310 and 1320. He composed a hagiographical and prevailingly uncritical history of Morocco entitled *al-Anīs al-Muṭrib bi-Rawḍ al-Qirṭās fī Akhbār Mulūk al-Maghrib wa-Taʾrīkh Madīnat Fās.* There have been several editions and translations of this text, beginning with Dombay's *Geschichte de mauritanischen Könige* (Agram, 1794–97) and including Moura's *Historia dos Soberanos Mahometanos* (Lisboã, 1824); C. J. Tornberg's edition and Latin translation, *Annales Regum Mauritaniae* (Uppsala, 1843–46); A. Beaumier's French translation, *Histoire des Souverains du Maghreb (Espagne et Maroc) et Annales de la Ville de Fès . . .* (Paris, 1860); and a Spanish rendering by Ambrosio Huici Miranda, *Rawd al-Qirtas,* 2d ed. (Valencia, 1964).

The relevant *ṭabaqāt* literature, represented by such authors as Abū al-ʿArab (d. 944), al-Khushanī (d. probably in 981), and al-Mālikī (fl. 967) and referring mainly to the Aghlabid and early Fāṭimid periods, proved unrewarding for present purposes except for occasional anecdotal material relating to urban life. The *ṭabaqāt* of both Abū al-ʿArab and al-Khushanī have been published and translated by Mohammed Ben Cheneb under the title *Classes des Savants de l'Ifrīqiyah (Ṭabaqāt ʿUlamāʾ Ifrīqiyah),* Publication de la Faculté des Lettres d'Alger, vols. 51–52 (Alger, 1915, 1920); and that of al-Mālikī edited by H. Muʾnis in 2 vols.: *Kitāb Riyāḍ al-Nufūs fī Ṭabaqāt ʿUlamāʾ al-Qayrawān wa-Ifrīqiyah* (al-Qāhirah, A.H. 1370/A.D. 1949).

The modern classic history of North Africa (excluding Egypt) is Julien's *Histoire de l'Afrique du Nord: Tunisie, Algérie, Maroc* (Paris, 1931; 2d ed., 2 vols., 1951–52; rev. 2d ed., 1966); English translation, see above. This work has provided the received framework for the historiography of North Africa for more than half a century despite the success of Gautier's earlier *Le Passé de l'Afrique du Nord. Les Siècles Obscurs.* More recent are Jamil M. Abun-Nasr's *A History of the Maghrib* (Cambridge, 1971) and *A History of the Maghrib in the Islamic Period* (Cambridge, 1987), and Abdallah Laroui's revisionist *L'Histoire du Maghreb: un Essai de Synthèse* (Paris, 1970; English translation, Princeton, N.J., 1977). For the eighth century there are two especially useful papers by Hicham (Hichem) Djaït: "Le Wilāya d'Ifrīqiya au IIe/VIIIe siècle: étude institutionelle," *Studia Islamica* 27 (1967): 77–121 and 28 (1968): 79–107, and, somewhat more broadly conceived, "L'Afrique arabe au VIIIe siècle (86–184 H./705–800)," *Annales: Économies, Sociétés, Civilisations* (1973): 601–21.

2. This is the traditionally received date for the founding of al-Qayrawān, but Lévi-Provençal has drawn attention to the existence of at least one other early (and seemingly more authentic) Arab tradition, according to which the military camp was established as early as 663 or 664 ("Un nouveau récit de la conquête de l'Afrique du Nord par les Arabes"). This uncertainty is entirely characteristic of the ambivalences in our knowledge of al-Maghrib in the early years of the Arab conquest, for which the chroniclers provide only meager information. Not only were they writing relatively late in time (the earliest among them dating from the second half of the ninth century A.D.), but they were almost exclusively from the eastern provinces of the Caliphate and neither well informed about, nor particularly interested in, the problems of North Africa.

It is reported that ʿUqbah intended his foundation to "perpetuate the glory of Islam to the end of time" (Abū al-ʿArab, *Ṭabaqāt,* 8 and Ibn ʿIdhārī, *Bayān,* 1:19).

3. Al-Ḥakam, *Futūḥ Miṣr,* 64–66; al-Mālikī, *Riyāḍ,* 1:6–7, 19; and Ibn ʿIdhārī, *Bayān,* 1:19–20. *Berber* is the term commonly used to designate the congeries of peoples between the Egyptian frontier and the Atlantic Ocean and reaching as far south as the great bend of the Niger River who, before their Arabicization, spoke local forms of a language of Hamitic stock. Originally the name probably had abusive or contemptuous connotations, and Berbers themselves use the ethnikon *Imazighen* (sing. Amazigh) to denote members of their linguistic subfamily in general. However, lacking a developed sense of more than regional community, they almost invariably refer to themselves by their tribal affiliations or, in recent times, accede to foreign designations such as Chaouia (Shawīyah) or Kabyle (probably from Ar. pl. *qabāʾil;* sing. *qabīlah* = tribe). The ethnographic literature on the Berbers is diffuse and fragmented, but includes a brief, somewhat popular, general account by G.-H. Bousquet, *Les Berbères (Histoire et Institutions)* (Paris, 1957) and a more detailed exposition by Robert Montagne, *The Berbers: Their Social and Political Organization,* English translation by David Seddon (London, 1973).

4. Owing to the paucity of data referred to in note 2, it is not possible to analyze the process of urbanization in al-Qayrawān in the way that was attempted for al-Baṣrah, al-Kūfah, and al-Fusṭāṭ, but there is a compendious summary of available evidence by M. Talbi in *The Encyclopaedia of Islam,* 2d ed., 4:827–30.

5. Maqdisī, *Aḥsan,* 225. This author added that the city was "more attractive than Naysābūr, larger than Dimashq, and more important than Iṣfahān." The strategic situation of al-Qayrawān in relation to the ecological zones of al-Ifrīqiyah was emphasized by al-Bakrī (*al-Masālik wa-l-Mamālik,* 24; de Slane's translation, 56) and has been explicated in considerable detail by scholars in this century, among them Jean Despois ("Kairouan: origine et évolution d'une ancienne capitale musulmane," *Annales de Géographie* 39 [1930]: 159–77 and "L'emplacement et les origines de Kairouan," *Revue Tunisienne,* vol. 33 [1927]). Cf. also Jean. Poncet, "L'évolution des genres de vie en Tunisie (autour d'une phrase d'Ibn Khaldoun)," *Les Cahiers de Tunisie,* nos. 7–8 (1954): 315–23. It must be remembered, though, that in the seventh century the immediate environs of the city were not as steppelike as they subsequently became. Ibn ʿIdhārī (*Bayān,* 1:20), for example, preserved a command of ʿUqbah to clear the forest in the area *(an yaqṭāʿū al-shajar),* while al-Bakrī (*al-Masālik wa-l-Mamālik,* 26; de Slane's translation, 61) notes that the demands of the city for wood were in no way depleting the olive groves on the surrounding plain—where, incidentally, there is today none at all. An excellent monograph in the high tradition of French regional geography that elicits many ecosystemic constants in the history of eastern Tunisia is by Jean Despois: *La Tunisie Orientale. Sahel et Basse Steppe* (Paris, 1955).

6. Ibn ʿIdhārī, *Bayān,* 1:100.

7. Maqdisī, *Aḥsan,* 225. The walls of al-Qayrawān were again rebuilt by the Zīrīd ruler al-Muʿizz in A.D. 1052: cf. Bakrī, *al-Masālik wa-l-Mamālik,* 25.

8. Compare, for example, M. Vonderheyden, *La Berbérie Orientale sous la Dynastie des Benoûʾl-Arlab (800–909)* (Paris, 1927), 61–64; Georges Marçais, *La Berbérie Musulmane et L'Orient au Moyen Âge* (Paris, 1946), chap. 2; Laroui, *The History of the Maghrib,* 119–21; and *The Encyclopaedia of Islam,* 2d ed., 4:829–30.

9. It was in al-Qayrawān that jurists such as Saḥnūn evolved the Maghribī system of jurisprudence based on the Mālikī *madhhab,* the formalism of which some have seen as particularly attractive to the Berber cast of mind: e.g., Roger Le Tourneau, "North Africa to the Sixteenth Century," in *The Cambridge History of Islam,* vol. 2, ed. P. M. Holt, Ann K. S. Lambton, and Bernard Lewis (Cambridge, 1970), 217.

10. Yaʿqūbī, *al-Buldān,* 348; Wiet's translation, 210.

11. Pseudo-Ibn al-Raqīq, *Taʾrīkh,* ed. M. al-Kaābī (Tūnis,

1968), 185: cited by M. Talbī, *The Encyclopaedia of Islam,* 2d ed., 4:829.

12. Bakri, *al-Masālik wa-l-Mamālik,* 25. As a footnote to this transfer: al-Maqdisī (*Aḥsan,* 227) notes that in his day, traders used to commute between al-Qayrawān and Ṣabrah al-Manṣūrīyah mounted on Egyptian donkeys—a mode of transportation also favored by the most successful cloth merchants in the Shāmī city of al-Ramlah, modern Ramleh (ibid., 183).

13. Iṣṭakhrī, *al-Masālik wa-l-Mamālik,* 37–38; Maqdisī, *Aḥsan,* 223; Ibn Ḥawqal, *al-Masālik wa-l-Mamālik,* 66; Bakrī, *al-Masālik wa-l-Mamālik,* 5; and A. Abdussaid, "Barqa, modern El-Merj," *Libya Antiqua* 8 (1971): 121–28, summarized in G. R. D. King, "Islamic archaeology in Libya, 1969–1989," *Libyan Studies* 20 (1989): 193–207.

14. Yaʿqūbī, *al-Buldān,* 343; Wiet's translation, 202.

15. According to Ibāḍī tradition, but erroneously, so called after a certain ʿAbd Allāh ibn Ibāḍ, who lived during the second half of the first Islamic century (cf. ʿAbd al-Karīm al-Shahrastānī, *Kitāb al-Milal wa-l-Nihal,* ed. W. Cureton [London, 1842–46], 100 [A subsequent edition of this work by Aḥmad Fahmī Maḥmūd in 3 vols. (al-Qāhirah, 1948–49) was not consulted]; al-Baghdādī, *Kitāb al-Farq bayn al-Firāq,* ed. by M. Badr (al-Qāhirah, 1328) and transl. by Philip K. Hitti under the title *al-Baghdādī's Characteristics of Muslim Sects* [Cairo, 1924], 87–88; al-Ījī, *Sharḥ ʿalā Mukhtaṣar al-Muntahā li-Ibn al-Ḥājib* [Constantinople, 1889], 356; and T. Lewicki, *The Encyclopaedia of Islam,* 2d ed., 3:648–60, esp. 653–55). This subsect of the Khārijites acquired its first North African converts among the Zanātah Berbers of the Jabal Nafūsah. Already by the mid-tenth century al-Iṣṭakhrī (*al-Masālik wa-l-Mamālik,* 39) had commented on the presence of Ibāḍites in Ṭāhart, "of which they were the masters."

16. Al-Bakrī, *al-Masālik wa-l-Mamālik,* 66–69. See also al-Ḥabīb al-Junḥānī, "Ṭahart: ʿĀsimah al-Dawlah al-Rustamīyah," *Revue Tunisienne de Sciences Sociales* 40–43 (1975); and for a conspectus of specifically Ibāḍī sources, Elizabeth Savage, *A Gateway to Hell, a Gateway to Paradise* . . . (Princeton, N.J., 1997), 7–14.

17. Cf. Yaʿqūbī, p. 353; ʿIrāq of the Maghrib."

18. Maqdisī, *Aḥsan,* 228–29. Ibn Ḥawqal (*al-Masālik wa-l-Mamālik,* 86) notes that commerce flourished more in that sector of the city which had grown up beside the old nucleus dating back to Roman times. See also p. 210 below.

19. Maqdisī, *Aḥsan,* 229. Cf. also Iṣṭakhrī, *al-Masālik wa-l-Mamālik,* 39 and Ibn Ḥawqal, *al-Masālik wa-l-Mamālik,* 90–91.

20. Cf. Maqdisī, *Aḥsan,* 231: "Sijilmāsah is in the midst of the sands." Cf. also Iṣṭakhrī, *al-Masālik wa-l-Mamālik,* 39: "It can be reached only by crossing sandy, uninhabited *(qifār)* deserts," and Ibn Ḥawqal (who visited the city in 951), *al-Masālik wa-l-Mamālik,* 99–100. The history of Sijilmāsah is summarized by Mohamed el Mellouki: "Contribution à l'Étude de l'Histoire des Villes Médiévales du Maroc: Sigilmassa des Origines à 668 (H.) 1269 (J.C.)," (doctoral thesis, University of Aix en Provence, 1985), and preliminary archaeological investigations are reported in Ronald A. Messier and Neil D. MacKenzie's *Archaeological Survey of Sijilmasa 1988* (Murfreesboro: Middle Tennessee State University, 1989). For a comprehensive overview of site and settlement, consult Dale R. Lightfoot and James A. Miller's "Sijilmassa: the rise and fall of a walled oasis in medieval Morocco," *Annals of the Association of American Geographers* 86, no. 1 (1996): 78–101.

21. Bakrī, *al-Masālik wa-l-Mamālik,* 149. Cf. note 452 to chapter 17.

22. Among others M. J. de Goeje (*Descriptio Imperii Moslemici* [Lugduni Batavorum, 1906], 221 n. *d*), who added the terse comment "Nomen urbis forte corruptum est," and Pellat, *Description,* 9, 112.

23. M. Hadj-Sadok (Muḥammad Ḥajj-Ṣadūk), *Description du Maghreb et de l'Europe du IIIe au IXe Siècle.* Bibliothèque Arabe-Française, vol. 6 (Alger, 1949), 109 n. 35 and *The Encyclopaedia of Islam,* 1st ed., 4:715. Cf. also Cornu et al., *Atlas du Monde Arabo-Islamique,* 118–19.

24. Ibn Ḥawqal's map is reproduced in J. H. Kramers and G. Wiet's *Configuration de la Terre,* vol. 1 (Paris, 1964), between pp. 60 and 61.

25. Al-Bakrī, *al-Masālik wa-l-Mamālik,* 60. The implied connection of *ṭarf* and *Ṭarfalah* is, of course, nothing more than folk etymology.

26. For example, al-Ḥakam, *Futūḥ Miṣr,* 61; Yaʿqūbī, *al-Buldān,* 349; Ibn Ḥawqal, *al-Masālik wa-l-Mamālik,* 64, 94; Maqdisī, *Aḥsan,* 55, 217, 246 (curiously enough, although al-Maqdisī lists Qafṣah, he does not describe it); and al-Bakrī, *al-Masālik wa-l-Mamālik,* 47. The ancient city of Capsa had been destroyed by the Roman general Marius in 106 B.C. in the course of the Jugurthine War, but was subsequently restored and constituted a colony by Trajan. One of Justinian's generals enclosed the city with a wall in A.D. 540, when it was renamed Justiniana. The *qaṣabah* that survives today was not built until 1494, early in the reign of the Ḥafṣid Abū ʿAbd Allāh Muḥammad V.

27. The official charged with the actual laying out of the city was ʿAlī ibn Ḥamdūn, better known as Ibn al-Andalusī, a longtime retainer of the Fāṭimid ʿUbaydallāh: cf. Bakrī, *al-Masālik wa-l-Mamālik,* 59 and Ibn Ḥawqal, *al-Masālik wa-l-Mamālik,* 85.

28. Maqdisī, *Aḥsan,* 231.

29. This is the orthography (< Berber *tilmisān,* one form of the plural of *talmas* = spring) used by Ibn Ḥawqal (*al-Masālik wa-l-Mamālik,* 89), al-Maqdisī (*Aḥsan,* 247), al-Ḥakam (*Futūḥ Miṣr,* 87, 121), Yaʿqūbī (*al-Buldān,* 356), and al-Bakrī (*al-Masālik wa-l-Mamālik,* 76, 77). Ibn Khurradādhbih (*al-Masālik wa-l-Mamālik,* 78) and Ibn al-Faqīh (*al-Buldān,* 78) used the more accurate transcription of the plural form: *Tilmasīn.* Cf. Hadj-Sadok, *Description du Maghreb,* 96 n. 109.

30. Tilimsān was not included by al-Maqdisī in his list of Maghribī *mudun* (although it was mentioned by him on p. 247 of the *Aḥsan*), but it is so scheduled here because it clearly performed the requisite functions. After the collapse of the Idrīsids early in the tenth century, the city became a regional capital of Maghrāwah

amīrs, the Banū-Khazar, and subsequently of the Banū-Yaʿlā, vassals of the Umayyads of Qurṭubah. Although modern Tilimsān was not founded until 1080, al-Bakrī refers explicitly to the prosperity of the older settlement on a site to the east of the present city.

31. Yaʿqūbī, *al-Buldān*, 357; Iṣṭakhrī, *al-Masālik wa-l-Mamālik*, 36, 39, 45, 68; Ibn Ḥawqal, *al-Masālik wa-l-Mamālik*, 79; Maqdisī, *Aḥsan*, 231, 244; and Bakrī, *al-Masālik wa-l-Mamālik*, 104–9.

32. Bakrī, *al-Masālik wa-l-Mamālik*, 161–62.

33. Ibn ʿIdhārī, *Bayān*, 1:84 and Bakrī, *al-Masālik wa-l-Mamālik*, 28. Although, as the seat of the Aghlabids, al-ʿAbbāsīyah had its own congregational mosque and quickly attracted to its vicinity numerous *sūqs*, caravanserais, and baths, it declined equally rapidly when the capital was removed to Raqqādah in 876. By the tenth century it was hardly more than an undistinguished suburb of al-Qayrawān. The settlement was also known at the time as Qaṣr al-Aghālibah.

34. Yaʿqūbī, *al-Buldān*, 348; Ibn Ḥawqal, *al-Masālik wa-l-Mamālik*, 96; and Bakrī, *al-Masālik wa-l-Mamālik*, 28. ʿUbaydallāh, the first of the Fāṭimid line, resided in Raqqādah until 921. After that time the city began to decline, with its inhabitants departing and its houses falling into ruin. Finally the Fāṭimid caliph al-Muʿizz (r. 953–75) razed the remaining buildings and drove the plow over the site, sparing only the gardens for which the city had formerly been famous.

35. The new capital, the building of which had begun in 912, was built on a mile-long but narrow peninsula projecting eastward from the Tūnisian coast, a circumstance leading al-Maqdisī (*Aḥsan*, 226) to compare it with Constantinople: "Anyone wishing to know Constantinople [al-Qusṭanṭīnnīyah written in error], instead of taking the trouble to visit that city, need only take himself to al-Mahdīyah. Like that [Greek] city, al-Mahdīyah is built on a peninsula" accessible only by a road "as narrow as a shoelace." Although initially established as a royal precinct, during the tenth century the city developed as the port through which al-Qayrawān conducted its trade with Iṣqiliyah (Sicily) and Miṣr (Egypt). Cf. Ibn ʿIdhārī, *Bayān*, 1:169, 184 and al-Qāḍī al-Nuʿmān, *Iftitāḥ*, ed. F. Dachraoui (Tūnis, 1975), 372–78. More generally see Slimane Mostfa Zbiss, "Mahdia et Ṣabra-Manṣoûriya," *Journal Asiatique* 244 (1956): 79–93; A. Lézine, *Mahdia* (Paris, 1965); and A. Masmoudi, "Les Fonctions Urbaines de Mahdia" (doctoral thesis, University of Paris, published at Tūnis, 1985).

36. See William MacGuckin, Baron de Slane, *Ibn Khaldoun: Histoire des Berbères et des Dynasties Musulmanes de l'Afrique Septentrionale. Traduite de l'Arabe*, 4 vols. (Alger, 1852–56), 2:530. De Slane had already published the Arabic text of this part of Ibn Khaldūn's comprehensive history in 2 vols. (Alger, 1847–51). See also Hady Roger Idris, *La Berbérie Orientale sous les Zirides, Xe–XIIe Siecles*, 2 vols. (Paris, 1962).

37. Buluqqīn in Modern Standard Arabic. Cf. al-Bakrī, *al-Masālik wa-l-Mamālik*, 71; Ibn Ḥawqal, *al-Masālik wa-l-Mamālik*, 90; Maqdisī, *Aḥsan*, 221, 247; and Ibn Khaldūn, *al-ʿIbar*, de Slane's translation, 2:6 et seq. and 489 et seq. It is probable that Ashīr is today represented by ruins at Benia, slightly more than sixty miles south-southwest of Algiers. Interestingly, in 934/35 Buluggīn's father, Zīrī ibn Manād, had sought permission from the Fāṭimid caliph to found a town in the same part of the Ṭiṭṭarī, thereby establishing himself as paramount chief of the principal tribe of the Ṣanhājah and acquiring a base from which to dominate the high plains to the southward. For this reconstruction of events see G. Marçais, "Achir (Recherches d'Archéologie Musulmane)," *Revue Africaine* (1922): 21–38 and *The Encyclopaedia of Islam*, 2d ed., 1: 699–700. Buluggīn's city was peopled by groups forcibly resettled from Ṭubnah, Masīlah, Sūq Ḥamzah (Bourdj Bouīra), and Tilimsān. The same ruler also founded, or perhaps more likely repopulated, the three towns of Milyānah, al-Madīyah, and Jazāʾir Banī-Mazghannā as gubernatorial benefices for his sons.

38. According to al-Bakrī (*al-Masālik wa-l-Mamālik*, 61–62), the Andalusians, who habitually wintered at Tanas, were invited by Berber tribesmen to occupy a local fort and establish a *sūq* on the shore. It would seem more than likely that the Andalusians had previously engaged in regular trading with the Berbers during their winter sojourns. In any case, the site already had a history of settlement from Phoenician times, and the fortress to which al-Bakrī refers was almost certainly a relic of the Roman colony of Cartenna, where Augustus had settled a substantial contingent of veterans. Subsequently some four hundred nomadic families from the district of Sūq Ibrāhīm adopted a sedentary mode of life on the borders of the new settlement. The harbour of Tanas offered a sure anchorage on an otherwise inhospitable coastline stretching for nearly two hundred miles between present-day Arzeu and Algiers (on this aspect of the settlement see al-Bakrī, *al-Masālik wa-l-Mamālik*, 82). See also Ibn Ḥawqal, *al-Masālik wa-l-Mamālik*, 77 and Maqdisī, *Aḥsan*, 229.

39. Maqdisī, *Aḥsan*, 217, 227–28 and al-Bakrī, *al-Masālik wa-l-Mamālik*, 65.

40. According to al-Bakrī (*al-Masālik wa-l-Mamālik*, 70–71), the Andalusians, who were under the command of Muḥammad ibn Abī ʿAwn and Muḥammad ibn ʿAbdūn (two adventurers who claimed to have served under the Spanish Umayyad general ʿAbd al-Malik ibn Umayyah), settled among the Berbers of the Nafzah and Mazghannā tribes. In 910 the city was sacked during the course of a tribal blood feud, but the governor of Ṭāhart (Tiaret) allowed the inhabitants to return in the following year. The settlement then flourished until 954, when it was occupied by Yaʿlā ibn Muḥammad ibn Ṣāliḥ, and the inhabitants transported to a city recently founded at Fakkān (see note 41), after which it remained desolate for several years. Only gradually did a minor degree of prosperity return to the city. Cf. also Maqdisī, *Aḥsan*, 219, 229; Ibn Ḥawqal, *al-Masālik wa-l-Mamālik*, 77–78; and Ibn Khaldūn, *al-ʿIbar*, de Slane's translation, 1:283.

41. Maqdisī, *Aḥsan*, 219, 229, 247; Bakrī, *al-Masālik wa-l-Mamālik*, 79; and Ibn Ḥawqal, *al-Masālik wa-l-Mamālik*, 89 (Afkān). Prior to the establishment of the city, Fakkān had been the site of a periodic market instituted by the Zanātah Berbers. The new

foundation rapidly increased its population, chiefly through the immigration into its purlieus of a group of Ṭāhartians from al-Muʿaskar on the southern slopes of the Monts des Beni-Chougran, together with others from Hilhel, Wahrān (Oran), and Qaṣr al-Fulūs, and elements from the Banū-Watīl. Before the close of the tenth century the settlement had come to constitute a fully urban center furnished with a congregational mosque, a *hammām*, *sūqs*, and several caravanserais. See Ibn Khaldūn, *al-ʿIbar*, de Slane's translation, 3:213.

42. Maqdisī, *Aḥsan*, 247 and Bakrī, *al-Masālik wa-l-Mamālik*, 77, 142–43.

43. Bakrī, *al-Masālik wa-l-Mamālik*, 77–78. In the second half of the tenth century the city was rebuilt by an *amīr* of the Miknāsah Berbers who owed vassalage to the Umayyad caliph at Qurṭubah, modern Córdoba (Ibn Ḥawqal, *al-Masālik wa-l-Mamālik*, 65 [Arashkūl], 78 [Arajkūl]). Under Muslim rule it had assumed the functions, and probably inherited the site, of the former Portus Sigensis. Today the old name survives in that of Rachgoun Island.

44. Bakrī, *al-Masālik wa-l-Mamālik*, 87–88.

45. Also Nukūr. Iṣṭakhrī, *al-Masālik wa-l-Mamālik*, 38; Maqdisī, *Aḥsan*, 220, 247; Ibn Ḥawqal, *al-Masālik wa-l-Mamālik*, 78; and Bakrī, *al-Masālik wa-l-Mamālik*, 90–99. Yaʿqūbī (*al-Buldān*, 357) citing local opinion, denied that Ṣāliḥ ibn Manṣūr was a Ḥimyarite, asserting instead that he was a Berber of the Nafzāwah tribe.

46. Maqdisī, *Aḥsan*, 224 and Ibn Ḥawqal, *al-Masālik wa-l-Mamālik*, 63. The Fāṭimid in question was al-Muʿizz li-Dīn Allāh, who arrived in Egypt in 973, four years after his armies had captured al-Fusṭāṭ.

47. Ibn Ḥawqal, *al-Masālik wa-l-Mamālik*, 80. Cf. Yāqūt, *Muʿjam*, 1:338.

48. Ibn Khurradādhbih (*al-Masālik wa-l-Mamālik*, 87): referring to Ṭubnah as "the city [signifying capital] of Zāb"; Maqdisī, *Aḥsan*, 217, 221, 247; Ibn Ḥawqal, *al-Masālik wa-l-Mamālik*, 85; Bakrī, *al-Masālik wa-l-Mamālik*, 50–51; and Ibn Khaldūn, *al-ʿIbar*, de Slane's translation 1:379. Ṭubnah was a city of impressive size, as is testified by al-Bakrī: "From al-Qayrawān to Sijilmāsah there is no city larger than Ṭubnah." Basically it comprised a citadel, "an enormous edifice of antique construction in stone" (Muḥammad ibn Yūsuf, cited by al-Bakrī, ibid., 50), within which were the congregational mosque, lodgings and offices for officials administering the district, and a huge reservoir providing water for spacious gardens. Outside the citadel were extensive suburbs. Today the ruins of Ṭubnah survive only as mounds of debris.

49. Bakrī, *al-Masālik wa-l-Mamālik*, 88–89; Maqdisī, *Aḥsan*, 220 (where the reading is *Amlīl*, perhaps for *Amellil*); and Ibn Ḥawqal, *al-Masālik wa-l-Mamālik*, 78.

50. Sabtā (Ceuta) had already had a long history prior to the Muslim conquest. It was the Abyla of the Phoenicians, the Julia Trajecta of the Romans, and late in the sixth century A.D. became the Byzantine provincial capital of Septem Fratres. In 682 it was occupied by an Arab garrison, which shortly afterward was expelled by a Berber force from Ṭanjah. The city then remained derelict until reoccupied by Muslim Berbers and, at a subsequent date, refugees from al-Andalus (Islamic Spain). From 828 to 931 it was incorporated in the Idrīsid kingdom, and from 941 to 1016 was a colony of the Spanish Umayyads. In fact when Ibn Ḥawqal was writing, it was the only foothold of the Umayyads on the Maghribī coast. In the tenth century the population comprised both Sidf Arabs of Ḥaḍramawt origin and Berbers from the districts of Azīlah and al-Baṣrah (in al-Maghrib, not the city in lower ʿIrāq). At this as at other times, Sabtā enjoyed a high reputation as a center of learning, particularly with regard to theological studies. See Ḥakam, *Futūḥ Miṣr*, 157; Ibn Khurradādhbih, *al-Masālik wa-l-Mamālik*, 89; Iṣṭakhrī, *al-Masālik wa-l-Mamālik*, 38; Ibn Ḥawqal, *al-Masālik wa-l-Mamālik*, 78–79; Maqdisī, *Aḥsan*, 219, 229; and Bakrī, *al-Masālik wa-l-Mamālik*, 102–4.

51. Bakrī, *al-Masālik wa-l-Mamālik*, 105 and Ibn Ḥawqal, *al-Masālik wa-l-Mamālik*, 79. For the history of the local Idrīsid dynasty of the Banū-Muḥammad, see Ibn Khaldūn, *al-ʿIbar*, de Slane's translation, 2:145 et seq.

52. Maqdisī, *Aḥsan*, 219 and Ibn Ḥawqal, *al-Masālik wa-l-Mamālik*, 79.

53. Bakrī, *al-Masālik wa-l-Mamālik*, 56–57. Cf. Ibn Ḥawqal (*al-Masālik wa-l-Mamālik*, 74): ". . . yields [of cereals] which I believe to be unequalled for quantity, quality, and freedom from impurities in the whole of the Maghrib."

54. Ibn Ḥawqal, *al-Masālik wa-l-Mamālik*, 77.

55. Ibid., 81.

56. *Maghūtha;* cf. de Goeje, *Bibliotheca Geographorum Arabicorum*, 4:312: "[Maghūthatun] saepe est locus unde suppetiae veniunt."

57. Ibn Ḥawqal, *al-Masālik wa-l-Mamālik*, 94; also Maqdisī, *Aḥsan*, 230, who noted that a whole camel load of dates could be bought for a few *dirhams*. The chief city of the Qasṭīliyah was Tawzir (see note 60 below and Yaʿqūbī, *al-Buldān*, 350).

58. Maqdisī, *Aḥsan*, 246; al-Bakrī, *al-Masālik wa-l-Mamālik*, 10; and Minorsky, *Ḥudūd*, 153, 416; also p. 206 below.

59. Islamic Naftah was on the site of Roman Aggarsel Nepte, almost at the western end of the Chott Djerīd. Its substantial population was totally Shīʿah, so that it was known popularly as Little Kūfah. In the tenth century the city contained several mosques and "a large number of baths": Bakrī, *al-Masālik wa-l-Mamālik*, 74–75. Al-Maqdisī mentions the settlement on three occasions (*Aḥsan*, 218, 243, 246), but found little to say about it other than to record that dog meat was offered for sale on butchers' stalls (as also happened in Qasṭīliyah [Maqdisī, ibid., 244] and Sijilmāsah [al-Bakrī, ibid., 148]).

60. Islamic Tawzir was on the site of the ancient settlement of Thusuros. Al-Bakrī (*al-Masālik wa-l-Mamālik*, 48) describes it as "A large city surrounded by a wall of stone and brick, possessing a solidly built *jāmiʿ* and several *sūqs*. All around it stretched extensive suburbs housing a multitude of people. . . ." Cf. Yāqūt, *Muʿjam*, 1:892–983.

61. Islamic Biskarah occupied the site of Roman Vescera. It was

the principal settlement of the Zibān (sing. Zāb) group of oases and, from its chief product, was often known as Biskarah of the Date-Palms *(Biskarat al-Nakhīl):* Maqdisī, *Aḥsan,* 220, 230 and Bakrī, *al-Masālik wa-l-Mamālik,* 51–53.

62. Ṭawlaqā was a composite city made up of three separate walled settlements, inhabited respectively by Arabs of Yamanī origin, Arabs of the Qays tribe, and by persons of mixed blood: Maqdisī, *Aḥsan,* 221 and Bakrī, *al-Masālik wa-l-Mamālik,* 72.

63. Banṭiyūs was another composite city made up of three separate walled settlements, each with its own congregational mosque. Two of these *jāmi*ʿ*s* were supported by orthodox Muslims, the third by Ibāḍī schismatics. The three settlements were inhabited respectively by Īrānians known as the Banū-Jurj, Berber tribesmen, and persons of mixed blood: Maqdisī, *Aḥsan,* 218, 221 and al-Bakrī, *al-Masālik wa-l-Mamālik,* 72.

64. E.g., Amarghād, Yarārah, Tāmajjāthat, Tiḥammāmīn (interestingly enough, an Arabic name Berberized, in which form it signified "hot springs"): al-Bakrī, *al-Masālik wa-l-Mamālik,* respectively pp. 107, 147, 107, and 102.

65. Theveste had been established as a Roman civil municipality in about A.D. 75. Subsequently it had been constituted as a colony by Trajan, and during the third century had profited from its nodal position at the eastern end of the Tabassā Mountains to become a road center of primary importance and one of the richest cities in North Africa (cf. S. Gsell, *Histoire Ancienne de l'Afrique du Nord,* vol. 1 [Paris, 1913]). In the fifth century it had been destroyed by the Vandals, but was subsequently rebuilt by Solomon, one of Justinian's generals. After its conquest by the Arabs in 682 the city lost much of its strategic importance, but in the tenth century was still a prosperous, if placid, local service center: Maqdisī, *Aḥsan,* 227 (under the orthography *Tabassā*), 247 *(Tabassah)* and Bakrī, *al-Masālik wa-l-Mamālik,* 141–42. See also Yāqūt, *Mu*ʿ*jam,* 1:823.

66. Jazā'ir Bani-Mazghannā = "The Islands of the Mazghannā Tribe": Maqdisī (*Aḥsan,* 217, 228, 246) erroneously reads Jazā'ir Bani-Zaghannāyah; al-Bakrī (*al-Masālik wa-l-Mamālik,* 66, 82) once refers to the port as Marsā al-Jazā'ir = "The Port of the Isles." Also Ibn Ḥawqal, *al-Masālik wa-l-Mamālik,* 76. The city stood on the site of the small Roman town of Icosium, which, in the years prior to the Arab conquest, had fallen into ruin, its dilapidated buildings providing shelter for bands of Berbers of the aforementioned Banū-Mazghannā. Al-Bakrī remarks (ibid., 66) that solidly constructed stone buildings, arches, and a theater (lit., "a house of entertainment," *dār al-mal*ʿ*ab*) as late as the eleventh century "bore testimony that in a distant period of time the city had been the capital of an empire." But in this supposition al-Bakrī was in error, for Icosium was never anything more than a relatively small urban center, the capital of Roman North Africa being Caesarea (Cherchel).

67. Maqdisī, *Aḥsan,* 217, 226; Ibn Ḥawqal, *al-Masālik wa-l-Mamālik,* 74; and al-Bakrī, *al-Masālik wa-l-Mamālik,* 58, 84. Banzart occupied the site of Hippo Diarrytus, a Phoenician colony of the fourth century B.C. and subsequently a Roman colony. The port provided excellent harborage, but poor access to the interior of the Maghrib.

68. Islamic Tūnis was on the site of ancient Tunes, a town of no special distinction in its day but which, after its conquest for Islam by Ḥassān ibn al-Nuʿmān, assumed an enhanced importance. Under the Aghlabids (A.D. 800–909) it was reputedly (though improbably) larger than al-Fusṭāṭ, but during the tenth century it suffered severely in the series of conflicts preceding the establishment of Fāṭimid supremacy. The port not only served a commercial purpose but was also a naval base from which Islamic fleets sallied forth to harry the coasts of Rūm. Both Yaʿqūbī and al-Bakrī note that it possessed an arsenal. At the same time, the city was furnished with numerous *sūqs* and caravanserais, and was famed throughout the Islamic world as a center of jurisprudence. Cf. Ḥakam, *Futūḥ Miṣr,* passim; Iṣṭakhrī, *al-Masālik wa-l-Mamālik,* 38, 46; Ibn Ḥawqal, *al-Masālik wa-l-Mamālik,* 63, 73–74; Maqdisī, *Aḥsan,* 55, 216, 240, 246; and Bakrī, *al-Masālik wa-l-Mamālik,* 37–42. There can be no truth to al-Bakrī's assertion that Tūnis was the site of biblical Tharsis, which, if it were anywhere in the western Mediterranean, should most likely be associated with Tartessus in the southeastern Iberian Peninsula.

69. Sūsah (al-Sūs) was already ancient when it was captured by the Arab armies in 689. As Hadrumetum it had been a Phoenician foundation older even than Carthage. Under Trajan it had been constituted as a Roman colony, but was razed by the Vandals in A.D. 430. Justinian rebuilt it and named it Justinianopolis. In the tenth century the city was extremely prosperous, with extensive *sūqs* displaying "an extraordinary abundance of merchandise and fruit" (al-Bakrī). A poet of the city once referred to it as "the boulevard of al-Maghrib" (cited by al-Bakrī). Cf. Ibn Ḥawqal, *al-Masālik wa-l-Mamālik,* 72–73; Maqdisī, *Aḥsan,* 217, 226, 247; and Bakrī, *al-Masālik wa-l-Mamālik,* 35–36.

70. Although not itself on the site of a classical city, Munastīr was situated in the vicinity of three such settlements, namely Leptis Minor six miles to the south-southeast, Ruspina three miles to the west, and Thapsus ten miles to the southeast. The monastery was converted into a *ribāṭ* during the ninth century: Ibn Ḥawqal, *al-Masālik wa-l-Mamālik,* 73; Maqdisī, *Aḥsan,* 217; and Bakrī, *al-Masālik wa-l-Mamālik,* 36.

71. Asfāqus (Sfax), the natural nodal point for the north-central Tunisian *sāḥil,* was originally a Carthaginian settlement and subsequently the Roman city of Taparura. In the tenth century it was a strongly fortified city featuring numerous *sūqs,* baths, and caravanserais, and was surrounded by an extensive suburb. Its port was one of the busiest along the whole of the North African littoral, and through it were exported to Miṣr, al-Maghrib (in the restricted sense of Barbary), Iṣqiliyah (Sicily), and Europe the large quantities of olive oil manufactured in the city. Even so, the physical (as opposed to the institutional) appurtenances of the port were minimal:

vessels were run up on the beach at high tide prior to being unloaded when the tide receded. Cf. Ibn Ḥawqal, *al-Masālik wa-l-Mamālik,* 70–71; Maqdisī, *Aḥsan,* 216, 226; and Bakrī, *al-Masālik wa-l-Mamālik,* 19–20.

72. Qābis (modern Gabès) stood in an oasis close to the shore of the gulf of the same name. In the tenth century it was a flourishing city built in the form of suburbs grouped on the eastern and southern flanks of a strong citadel, and incorporating numerous *sūqs* and caravanserais, a large number of baths, and a magnificent *jāmiʿ*. "The harbour," wrote al-Bakrī half a century later, "receives vessels from all parts of the world." The population comprised both Arabs and groups known to the topographers as al-Afāriqah (pl. of *al-Afrīqī* < *Afri,* the name by which the natives of Africa Proconsularis were known in antiquity), which apparently signified indigenous peoples other than those Berbers who had adopted at least some features of Greco-Latin civilization. Certainly they appear to have spoken an Africanized Latin vernacular (*al-lisān al-latīnī al-ifrīqī* is Idrīsī's phrase). In the tenth century they were to be found in Cyrenaica, Tripolitania, throughout what is today Tunisia, and in the Zāb. Cf. Ḥakam, *Futūḥ Miṣr,* 143 n. 3, 148 n. 166, 154 n. 111; Yaʿqūbī, *al-Buldān,* 249, 347, 350; Qudāmah, *al-Kharāj,* 225; Ibn Ḥawqal, *al-Masālik wa-l-Mamālik,* 70, Maqdisī, *Aḥsan,* 216, 224, 230, 244, 246; Bakrī, *al-Masālik wa-l-Mamālik,* 17–18; Georges Marçais, "La Berbérie au IXe siècle d'après el-Yaʿqoûbî," *Revue Africaine* (1941): 44–52 and *La Berbérie Musulmane et l'Orient au Moyen Âge,* 70 et seq.; Vonderheyden, *La Berbérie Orientale,* 65–67; and Tadeusz Lewicki, "Une langue romane oubliée de l'Afrique du Nord," *Rocznik Orientalistyczny* 17 (1951–52): 417–19. Ibn Abī Dīnār al-Qayrawānī, in his *al-Muʾnis fī Akhbār Ifrīqiyah wa-Tūnis* (Tūnis, A.H. 1286/A.D. 1869), which he carried down to 1685, apparently considered the Afāriqah to be descendants of the Carthaginians (vol. 18, p. 1), an interpretation to which J. F. P. Hopkins has not been unsympathetic in more recent times: cf. *Medieval Muslim Government in Barbary until the Sixth Century of the Hijra* (London, 1958), 63–65.

73. Also Ṭarābulus, Ṭarbulīṭah (citing a Greek original), and Madīnat al-Ānās, presumably for the al-Āyās of one manuscript < Gk. Ἑῴας (genitive of Ἑῴα), possibly influenced by certain Latin uses of oblique cases. Cf. Ḥakam, *Futūḥ Miṣr,* passim; Yaʿqūbī, *al-Buldān,* 346–47; Qudāmah, *al-Kharāj,* 224; Iṣṭakhrī, *al-Masālik wa-l-Mamālik,* 37–38, 46; Ibn Ḥawqal, *al-Masālik wa-l-Mamālik,* 68–69; Maqdisī, *Aḥsan,* 216, 223, 246; and Bakrī, *al-Masālik wa-l-Mamālik,* 6–7. It should be noted that, despite the volume of shipping frequenting the port, the anchorage was not considered safe under northerly winds, and visiting vessels often needed the assistance of local mariners to enter the port (Ibn Ḥawqal, *al-Masālik wa-l-Mamālik,* 69–70).

74. Ḥakam, *Futūḥ Miṣr,* 57, 139, 141; Yaʿqūbī, *al-Buldān,* 344–46; Qudāmah, *al-Kharāj,* 223; Ibn Ḥawqal, *al-Masālik wa-l-Mamālik,* 68; Maqdisī, *Aḥsan,* 224, 225; and Bakrī, *al-Masālik wa-l-Mamālik,* 17. According to Baron MacGuckin de Slane, who has been followed by virtually all subsequent authors, the ancient port of Surt was on the site of present-day Madīnat al-Sulṭān (*Description de l'Afrique Septentrionale par Abou-Obeïd-el-Bekri* [2d ed., Alger, 1911–13; reprint, Paris, 1965], 17 n. 3). For archaeological excavations at Madīnat al-Sulṭān by A. Abdussaid, M. Fehervari, R. G. Goodchild, M. Mostafa, M. Shagluf, and others, see King, "Islamic archaeology in Libya," 200–204.

75. Ibn Ḥawqal, *al-Masālik wa-l-Mamālik,* 74–75: "In spite of its small size and modest development, Ṭabarqah has become well-known for the large number of vessels that anchor there, bringing Andalusian merchants to transact business in the port"; on which, Ibn Ḥawqal adds, "They used to pay the tithe." When al-Maqdisī (*Aḥsan,* 226) was writing, the citadel was in ruins and the population had moved into a suburb. Also see Iṣṭakhrī, *al-Masālik wa-l-Mamālik,* 38.

76. Ibn Ḥawqal, *al-Masālik wa-l-Mamālik,* 77; Iṣṭakhrī, *al-Masālik wa-l-Mamālik,* 37, 38, 46; Maqdisī, *Aḥsan,* 229; and Bakrī, *al-Masālik wa-l-Mamālik,* 61–62.

77. Ibn Ḥawqal, *al-Masālik wa-l-Mamālik,* 77–78. Al-Maqdisī (*Aḥsan,* 229) notes that al-Andalus was only a day and a night's sail distant. For *ghallatun* signifying (cereal) harvest, see de Goeje, *Bibliotheca Geographorum Arabicorum,* 4:310, relying on a gloss by Idrīsī.

78. Ibn Ḥawqal, *al-Masālik wa-l-Mamālik,* 78. Cf. also note 43 above.

79. Bakrī, *al-Masālik wa-l-Mamālik,* 82.

80. Baron de Slane has already pointed out that al-Bakrī must have been in error, for Marsā Mūsā is almost completely sheltered from southeasterly winds (*Description de l'Afrique Septentrionale,* 207 n. 1).

81. Ghānah was the earliest (as well as the most stable) of the empires of the western Sūdān about which we are reasonably well informed. The name itself seems originally to have been a title borne by Soninke rulers who assumed control of the state in the eighth century A.D. During the tenth century, from a capital probably represented today by the ruins of Kumbi Ṣāliḥ, some two hundred miles north of Bamako, these Soninke controlled an empire stretching from the borders of the Tekrur in the west to the great bend of the Niger in the east, and from the Bawle and upper Senegal Rivers in the south to the southernmost Berber tribes in the north. It should be noted, though, that at no time did the medieval kingdom of Ghāna include the territory occupied by the modern state of the same name. See al-Bakrī, *al-Masālik wa-l-Mamālik,* 173–76 and, for modern accounts of the kingdoms of the western Sūdān, including ancient Ghāna, Bolanle Awe, "Empires of the Western Sudan," in J. F. Ade and Ajayi and Ian Espie, eds., *A Thousand Years of West African History* (Ibadan, 1965), 55–71; Nehemia Levtzion, *Ancient Ghana and Mali* (London, 1973); and R. Cornevin, *The Encyclopaedia of Islam,* 2d ed., 1001–3, which includes a substantial, although rather dated, bibliography. For Sijilmāsah see p. 202 above.

82. Maqdisī, *Aḥsan,* 221 (reading [Aghmāt] Waylā for Aylā[n]) and Bakrī, *al-Masālik wa-l-Mamālik,* 153. From Ibn Ḥawqal's map (de Goeje, *Bibliotheca Geographorum Arabicorum,* 2d ed., facing 66) it would appear that the Aghmāts were located in the upper valley of the Tensift River.

83. Bakrī, *al-Masālik wa-l-Mamālik,* 48. See also Yaʿqūbī, *al-Buldān,* 350; Abū al-Fidā', *Mukhtaṣar Ta'rīkh al-Bashar,* 2:200; and p. 205 above.

84. Bakrī, *al-Masālik wa-l-Mamālik,* 10–11. Cf. also Iṣṭakhrī, *al-Masālik wa-l-Mamālik,* 40, 44, 46; Maqdisī, *Aḥsan,* 246; and in recent times H. Ziegert and A. Abdussalam, "The White Mosque of Old Zuila," *Libya Antiqua* 9 and 10 (1973): 221–22. Cf. also note 58 above. Al-Yaʿqūbī (*al-Buldān,* 345) notes the presence of Ibāḍīs in the city as early as the second half of the ninth century. The Ajdābiyah referred to in this quotation was a flourishing city close to the eastern shore of the Gulf of Surt, yet hemmed in by the Libyan Desert. The inhabitants were mostly Copts. See Ḥakam, *Futūḥ Miṣr,* 73; Yaʿqūbī, *al-Buldān,* 344–45; Qudāmah, *al-Kharāj,* 222, 224; Ibn Ḥawqal, *al-Masālik wa-l-Mamālik,* 67; Maqdisī, *Aḥsan,* 55, 212, 224; and Bakrī, *al-Masālik wa-l-Mamālik,* 5–6.

85. Bakrī, *al-Masālik wa-l-Mamālik,* 11; also Yaʿqūbī, *al-Buldān,* 345. See also Elizabeth Savage, "Berbers and Blacks, Ibadi slave traffic in eighth-century North Africa," *Journal of African History* 33 (1992): 351–68.

86. Ibn Ḥawqal, *al-Masālik wa-l-Mamālik,* 61. For the likelihood that Ibn Ḥawqal met the holder of the note in Sijilmāsah rather than, as is often assumed, in Awdaghust, see Nehemiah Levtzion, "Ibn Ḥawqal, the cheque, and Awdaghost," *Journal of African History* 9 (1968): 223–33. Ibn Ḥawqal also notes the presence in Sijilmāsah of merchants from al-Baṣrah, al-Kūfah, and Baghdād—an observation reminiscent of a comment by Ibn al-Faqīh (*al-Buldān,* 11) at the beginning of the tenth century to the effect that "The people of al-Baṣrah and the Ḥimyarites are the greatest money-grubbers. A traveller in the remotest part of Farghānah or the far west of the Maghrib will surely find a man from al-Baṣrah or a Ḥimyarite there." In this connection we do well to recall the hoard of gold *dīnars* minted in Sijilmāsah near the turn of the eleventh century that came to light in the excavation of Waylah (present-day ʿAqabah): Whitcomb, *Ayla,* 18.

87. Bakrī, *al-Masālik wa-l-Mamālik,* 145–46. Cf. also note 65 above.

88. P. 202 above.

89. Ibn Ḥawqal, *al-Masālik wa-l-Mamālik,* 70.

90. Bakrī, *al-Masālik wa-l-Mamālik,* 40. Ibn Ḥawqal (*al-Masālik wa-l-Mamālik,* 73) writes of "handsome polychrome vessels and pottery as beautiful as that imported from al-ʿIrāq."

91. The method of gathering and polishing the coral is described by al-Maqdisī (*Aḥsan,* 229) and the organizational aspects of the industry by Ibn Ḥawqal (*al-Masālik wa-l-Mamālik,* 75). Government agents supervised the harvesting of the coral and exacted the relevant dues. Merchants from far and near gathered in the port to treat with dealers expert in the coral trade. Al-Bakrī (*al-Masālik wa-l-Mamālik,* 55) notes that in his day Marsā al-Kharaz had become a haven for corsairs preying on ships taking a short route to Sardinia. Cf. also C. Féraud, *Histoire des Villes de la Province de Constantine: La Calle* (Alger, 1877).

92. Yaʿqūbī, *al-Buldān,* 348 and al-Bakrī, *al-Masālik wa-l-Mamālik,* 34.

93. Serjeant, *Islamic Textiles,* 177. There is a convenient summary of industrial development in North Africa during the later phase of our period in Claudette Vanacker's "Géographie économique de l'Afrique du Nord selon les auteurs arabes (IXe–XIIe siècle)," *Annales: Économies, Sociétés, Civilisations* (1973): 659–80.

94. A further difficulty arises from the circumstance that the adjective *Maghribī* often denoted both Spain and North Africa, so that it is not always possible to discriminate between cloths from these two regions. Such is the case, for instance, when (a Pseudo-) al-Jāḥiẓ rates Maghribī felts along with the Chinese (Ṣīnī) as the best in the world ("Al-Tabaṣṣur," 12:338).

95. Bakrī, *al-Masālik wa-l-Mamālik,* 25, 36 and Serjeant, *Islamic Textiles,* 187. The latter author speculates that the *ṭirāz* factories in Fās (Fez) may not have been under direct palace control but instead may have produced fabrics on commission for palace officials.

96. R. P. A. Dozy and M. J. de Goeje, eds., *Description de l'Afrique et de l'Espagne* (Leyden, 1866), 106.

97. Ibn Ḥawqal, *al-Masālik wa-l-Mamālik,* 67: "markets where great numbers of buyers come to purchase wool." Cf. Maqdisī, *Aḥsan,* 239 and Bakrī, *al-Masālik wa-l-Mamālik,* 5.

98. Ibn Ḥawqal, *al-Masālik wa-l-Mamālik,* 67: the principal exports are medium-quality robes and lengths *(shiqqah)* of fairly good-quality woollen cloth shipped abroad on trading vessels in exchange for provisions. For a summary of, together with a bibliography relating to, archaeological work at Ajdābiyah, see King, "Islamic archaeology in Libya," 196–99, 206–7.

99. Ibn Ḥawqal, *al-Masālik wa-l-Mamālik,* 68: visiting trading vessels carry away wool.

100. Ibid., 69: "considerable export of wool."

101. Ibid., 70: "important trade in wool."

102. Bakrī, *al-Masālik wa-l-Mamālik,* 36: "Many workers are employed . . . in weaving and spinning thread, one *mithqal* of which is worth two gold *mithqals.*"

103. Ibn Ḥawqal, *al-Masālik wa-l-Mamālik,* 76: "trades in wool."

104. Ibid., 94: "wool for sale in all the quarters . . . and all that is manufactured there is exported to distant parts."

105. Bakrī, *al-Masālik wa-l-Mamālik,* 147.

106. It is probable that the prominence of the city as a center of cloth dyeing was the result of its large Jewish population (Bakrī, *al-Masālik wa-l-Mamālik,* 115). Cf. I. Epstein, *The Response of Rabbi Simon ben Ẓemaḥ* (London, 1930), translation p. 47; quoted by Serjeant, *Islamic Textiles,* 187.

107. Serjeant, *Islamic Textiles,* 181. Cf. also note 82 to chapter 6.

108. Ibn Ḥawqal, *al-Masālik wa-l-Mamālik,* 70.

109. Bakrī, *al-Masālik wa-l-Mamālik,* 17.

110. P. 207 above.

111. P. 205 above.

112. Ibn Ḥawqal, *al-Masālik wa-l-Mamālik,* 85.

113. Abū al-ʿArab, *Ṭabaqāt,* Ben Cheneb's translation, 5, 7.

114. Georges Marçais, "Note sur les ribāṭs en Berbérie," in *Mélanges René Basset,* vol. 2 (Paris, 1925), 396. Marçais draws attention to other *hadīths* (usually attributed to Muḥammad) reflecting the same point of view both in this paper (395–97) and in *La Berbérie Musulmane et l'Orient au Moyen Âge,* 19–26: for example, among others, "The holy war will have ceased in all countries excepting a locality in the West that is called al-Ifrīqiyah" (citing Abū al-ʿArab, *Ṭabaqāt,* text, 4; translation, 13; Ibn Nājī, *Maʿalim al-Īmān* [Tūnis 1320], vol. 1, p. 4; also Bakrī, *al-Masālik wa-l-Mamālik,* 22); and "He who takes post in the *ribāṭ* of Munastīr for three days has earned the right to Paradise" (citing Abū al-ʿArab, ibid., text, 3; translation, 9; al-Tijānī, *Riḥlah,* Ms. Bibl. Universitaire d'Alger no. 2014, p. 14v, trans. Alphonse Rousseau, "Voyage du Scheikh et-Tidjani dans la Régence de Tunis, pendant les années 706, 707 et 708 de l'Hégire [1306–1309]," *Journal Asiatique,* 4th ser., vol. 20 [1852]: 112). Cf. Bakrī, ibid., 8: "He whose sins are numerous had better put Libya behind him [i.e., suffer martyrdom for the Faith in the Ifrīqiyah]."

115. I am including with *ribāṭāt* the guard posts known as *maḥras* (sing.), apparently functionally and morphologically similar to *ribāṭāt* but generally smaller and less elaborately furnished: see de Goeje, *Indices, Glossarium et Addenda et Emendanda, Bibliotheca Geographorum Arabicorum,* 4:214: "habet significationem notam praesidii sensu castelli."

116. Yaʿqūbī, *al-Buldān,* 350; Wiet's translation, 213.

117. Bakrī, *al-Masālik wa-l-Mamālik,* 36; Ibn al-Athīr, *al-Kāmil,* 5:331, 6:92–96. Cf. also Yāqūt, *Muʿjam,* 5:374. Ibn Ḥawqal (*al-Masālik wa-l-Mamālik,* 73) describes how appropriately motivated Ifrīqiyans would volunteer to serve in this *ribāṭ* for specified periods each year, bringing their own provisions with them.

118. Ibn Ḥawqal, *al-Masālik wa-l-Mamālik,* 72–73 and Bakrī, *al-Masālik wa-l-Mamālik,* 35.

119. Ibn Ḥawqal, *al-Masālik wa-l-Mamālik,* 168; Bakrī, *al-Masālik wa-l-Mamālik,* 7.

120. Bakrī, *al-Masālik wa-l-Mamālik,* 20; Ibn Ḥawqal, *al-Masālik wa-l-Mamālik,* 70.

121. Marçais, "Note sur les ribāṭs en Berbérie," 400.

122. Bakrī, *al-Masālik wa-l-Mamālik,* 84.

123. I have found only four references to *ribāṭāt* along this stretch of coast: at Jījil (ibid., 82), Marsā Maghīlah (ibid., 81), Arzāw (ibid., 70), and Nākūr (Naqūr: ibid., 91).

124. Ibid., 113.

125. Ibid., 112.

126. Ibid., 87 and Ibn Ḥawqal, *al-Masālik wa-l-Mamālik,* 81–82, who estimated that at any one time, according to circumstance, one hundred thousand or so *ghāzīs* were assembled in the *ribāṭāt* ringing the city, drawn there by the need to hold the frontier against Barghawāṭah encroachments.

127. Bakrī, *al-Masālik wa-l-Mamālik,* 86, 153.

128. Ibid., 161. At the end of the ninth century, Yaʿqūbī (*al-Buldān,* 360) had characterized Māssah as an important trading port where there anchored "the sewn vessels, constructed at al-Ubullah, which voyaged as far as China."

129. Ibn Ḥawqal, *al-Masālik wa-l-Mamālik,* 168.

130. Bakrī, *al-Masālik wa-l-Mamālik,* 112 and Ibn Ḥawqal, *al-Masālik wa-l-Mamālik,* 79. Also Arzīlah. Al-Bakrī was not strictly accurate in stating that the city was no older than its *ribāṭ.* It was actually a Phoenician foundation (Zilis) that had been renamed Julia Constantia by the Romans, seized by the Goths, and captured by the Arabs in 713. Although the city had been burned by the Vikings in 843, the site had not been totally abandoned. Azīlah = the Berber rendering of ancient Zilis.

131. Cited by Marçais, "Notes sur les ribāṭs en Berbérie," 417.

132. Ibn Ḥawqal, *al-Masālik wa-l-Mamālik,* 73, to which al-Bakrī (*al-Masālik wa-l-Mamālik,* 36) adds that "The inhabitants of Qayrawān remit [to Munastir] a great deal of money and abundant alms." Cf. also a late twelfth-century text cited by Marçais that asserts substantially the same thing: "Note sur les ribāṭs de la Berbérie," 418.

133. Bakrī, *al-Masālik wa-l-Mamālik,* 112.

134. Ibid., 161, 36.

135. Ibid., 5. Ruwayfah had been appointed governor of Aṭrābulus in A.D. 666.

136. So said al-Bakrī (ibid., 10), but Ibn Khallikān (*Wayfāyāt,* de Slane's translation, 1:510) records that al-Khuzāʿi died at al-Tīb, a city rather more than fifty miles southeast of Baghdād.

137. Al-Shammākhī, *Kitāb al-Siyar* (al-Qāhirah, A.H. 1301), 240–41 and Bakrī, *al-Masālik wa-l-Mamālik,* 73.

138. Bakrī, *al-Masālik wa-l-Mamālik,* 12.

139. For information about the Barghawāṭah in pre-Almoravid times, we are dependent almost entirely on Ibn Ḥawqal (*al-Masālik wa-l-Mamālik,* 82–83) and al-Bakrī (*al-Masālik wa-l-Mamālik,* 134–41). It was probably toward the mid-ninth century that a paramount chief of this confederacy formally proclaimed himself a prophet, composed in Berber a holy book on the model of the Qur'ān, and instituted prayers, fasting, dietary laws, punishments, and so forth that appear to have incorporated Shīʿī influence and that were certainly enforced with Khārijitelike rigor. See also Ibn ʿIdhārī, *Bayān,* 1:324–31; Ibn Abī Zarʿ, *al-Anīs al-Muṭrib,* Tornberg edition, 82–84; translation, 112–14; Marçais, *La Berbérie Musulmane,* 126–28; Mohamed Talbi, "Hérésie, acculturation et nationalisme des Berbères Bargawata," in *Proceedings of the First Congress of Mediterranean Studies of Arab-Berber Influence,* ed. Micheline Galley and David R. Marshall (Algiers, 1973), 221–26; and *The Encyclopaedia of Islam,* 2d ed., 1:1043–45.

140. See note 45 above.

141. See note 50 above.

142. See p. 202 and chapter 2 above. In assessing the level of

integration of the Idrīsid polity, I incline to Laroui's revisionist views (*The History of the Maghrib,* 109–12) rather than to traditional interpretations, which have owed a good deal to Ibn Khaldūn's systemization of the history of the Idrīsids. In turn, his account relied on fourteenth-century Fāsī chroniclers who often projected onto the ninth century the glories of the city existing in their time.

143. Vocalized as *shorfā'* in Moroccan Arabic. Sing. = *sharīf* = putative descendant of the Prophet. For an interpretation emphasizing the role of the Idrīsids as religious leaders, see Laroui, *The History of the Maghrib,* 112.

144. The Ṣufrīyah, taking its name from ʿAbd Allāh ibn al-Ṣaffār, constituted a moderate branch of the Khārijī movement that had broken away from the more extreme Azāriqah. For comments on Tilimsān, see p. 203 above. Djaït's dictum is from his "L'Afrique arabe," 601.

145. See Tadeusz Lewicki, "Les subdivisions de l'Ibadiyya," *Studia Islamica* 9 (1958): 78 and "La répartition géographique des groupements ibāḍites dans l'Afrique du Nord au moyen-âge," *Rocznik Orientalistyezny* 21 (1957): 301–43; also Abū Zakariyā, *al-Sīrah,* Masqueray's translation, 128–43; Chaikh Békhri, "Le Kharijisme berbère: quelques aspects du royaume rustumide," *Annales de l'Institut d'Etudes Orientales de l'Université d'Alger* 15 (1957): 55–108; and J. C. Wilkinson, "Ibādī Theological Literature," in *Religion, Learning and Science in the ʿAbbāsid Period,* ed. M. J. L. Young, J. D. Latham, and R. B. Serjeant (Cambridge, 1990), 33–39.

146. Bakrī, *al-Masālik wa-l-Mamālik,* 67. It is worth noting that even within the territories nominally subject to the Rustamids, several chieftainships asserted their independence at one time or another during the ninth century, notably the Banū-Masālah in the Aurès, a confederation in the Hudnah-Zāb region, and other groups in the Waddān and the Wādī al-Raml.

147. Cited by Savage, *A Gateway to Hell,* 115. Cf. Marçais, *La Berbérie Musulmane,* note 111; D. al-Habib al-Janḥānī, *al-Maghrib al-Islamī: al-Ḥayāt al-Iqtiṣādīyah wa-l-Ijtimāʿīyah* (Tūnis, A.H. 1398); and Abun-Nasr, *The History of the Maghrib in the Islamic Period,* 45; but for reminders that there is no firm confirmation of this conclusion, see Tadeusz Lewicki, "L'état nord-africain de Tāhert et ses relations avec le Soudan occidental à la fin du VIIIe et au IXe siècle," *Cahiers d'Etudes Africaines* 2 (1962): 513–35 and Laroui, *The History of the Maghrib,* 115. For additional comments on Ṭāhart see Chaikh Békhri, "Le Kharijisme berbère," 55–108 and p. 202 above.

148. See also p. 202 above.

149. *Amīr,* the official style by which the Aghlabid rulers chose to be known, did not—in contradistinction to the title *wālī*—imply subservience to the ʿAbbāsid government.

150. Cf. chapter 2 and p. 204 above.

151. The regular troops of the *wilāyah.* In 876 Ibrāhīm II began to build another fortified palace at Rāqqadah, five miles southwest of Qayrawān (p. 204 above).

152. On these events see Mohamed Talbi, *L'Emirat Aghlabide, Histoire Politique* (Paris, 1966) 281–82.

153. The Kutāmā were a group of sedentary tribes within the Sanhājah branch of the Berbers.

154. P. 202 above.

155. Zīrīd control of Tripolitania was short-lived: between 1001 and 1147 it was ruled by the quasi-independent dynasty of the Banū-Khazrūn, who read the *khuṭbah* first in the name of the Fāṭimids but from the 1030s in the name of the ʿAbbāsids. See Idris, *La Berbérie Orientale sous les Zirides;* Lucien Golvin, *Le Maghrib Central à l'Epoque des Zirides: Recherches d'Archéologie et d'Histoire* (Paris, 1957).

At the beginning of the eleventh century the Zīrīd kingdom was partitioned between the main branch of the ruling lineage, which retained al-Qayrawān as its capital, and the Ḥammādid branch, which established a new capital at Qalʿat Banī-Ḥammād.

156. For example, Henri Terrasse, *Histoire de Maroc des Origines à l'Établissement du Protectorat Français,* vol. 1 (Casablanca, 1949), 175–79 and Julien, *Histoire de l'Afrique du Nord,* 2d ed., 2:58.

157. For an exposition of this point of view, see Laroui, *The History of the Maghrib,* chap. 6.

158. P. 201 above and Djaït, "L'Afrique arabe," 620. For the cultural life of al-Qayrawān at this period, see Hady Roger Idris, "Contribution à l'histoire de l'Ifriqiya. Tableau de la vie intellectuelle et administrative à Kairouan sous les Aglabites et les Fatimites . . . d'après le Riyād En Nufūs de Abū Bakr el-Mālakī," *Revue des Etudes Islamiques* 9 (1935): 105–78, 273–305; 10 (1936): 45–104.

159. Ibn Nājī, *Maʿālim al-Īmān,* vol. 3 (Tūnis, A.H. 1320/A.D. 1902/3), 135–52, and 168–80; ʿIyāḍ, *Tartīb al-Madārik,* ed. M. Talbi, vol. 3 (Bayrūt, 1965), 616–21; Ahwānī, *al-Taʿlīm fī Ra'y al-Qābisī* (al-Qāhirah, A.H. 1364/A.D. 1945); and Hady Roger Idris, "Deux juristes kairouanais de l'époque zīrīde: Ibn Abī Zayd et al-Qābisī," *Annales de l'Institut d'Etudes Orientales de l'Université d'Alger* 12 (1954): 121–98. Ibn Abī Zayd was by no means undeserving of the sobriquet "Mālik the Younger," by which he was sometimes known. Al-Qābisī was a traditionist of high repute who made known in the Maghrib the *Ṣaḥīḥ* of al-Bukhārī.

160. Ibn ʿIdhārī (*Bayān,* 1:230) noted that many Qarwānī citizens were ruined when in 976–77 six hundred of them were forced to provide the vice-regent ʿAbd Allāh al-Kātib with no less than four hundred thousand *dīnārs;* some individuals were held severally responsible for as much as ten thousand *dīnārs.*

161. Cf. p. 203 above.

162. P. 202 above.

163. P. 202 above.

164. For additional details about these events and supporting bibliography, see M. Talbi in *The Encyclopaedia of Islam,* 2d ed., 4: 335–40.

165. Under Diocletian (r. 284–305), Byzacenia, the southern part of Africa Proconsularis, was constituted as a separate province.

166. It was not only the pillage and slaughter associated with the Vandal conquest—which evidence indicates may have been exaggerated—that proved so damaging to the North African provinces: more destructive in the long run were the lack of systematic government, the deterioration in public order, and the redistribution of agricultural estates among time-expired legionaries not sufficiently familiar with North African farming practice. On the Vandal occupation generally see Christian Courtois, *Les Vandales et l'Afrique* (Paris, 1955) and, more briefly, Abun-Nasr, *A History of the Maghrib,* 45–53.

167. Cf. note 65 above.

168. There were at least thirty to forty substantial new foundations (depending on how the relevant texts are interpreted) in the *iqlīm* of al-Maghrib out of a total of between 350 and 400 recorded urban forms (again depending on the way in which the texts are read). In other words, roughly one in every ten Maghribī towns existing in the tenth century had been established during the Islamic period—easily the highest proportion in any part of the Muslim world.

169. Yaʿqūbī, *al-Buldān,* 342–60 (except 353–55, which are devoted to a description of al-Andalus). The mills are mentioned on p. 358. Laroui (*The History of the Maghrib,* 123) asserts that the metals extracted from the mines at Majjānat al-Maʿādīn were used in the shipyards of Sūsah, but I have not found direct evidence for that statement in the tenth or earlier centuries. For those who do not have access to the Arabic text, there is a convenient summary of al-Yaʿqūbī's views in Marçais, "La Berbérie au IXe siècle d'après el-Yaʿqoûbî," 40–61.

170. Yaʿqūbī (*al-Buldān,* 359) refers to "gold and silver lying like herbage on the ground" in the Wādī Darʿah—the sort of rumor that has emanated from goldfields in all parts of the world, from the Klondike to Kalgoorlie, and at all times. Yaʿqūbī probably did not visit any part of present-day Morocco, and Laroui (*The History of the Maghrib,* 124) suggests that he may have acquired his information about the Idrīsids in Tilimsān.

171. Yaʿqūbī, *al-Buldān,* 357.

172. Iṣṭakhrī, *al-Masālik wa-l-Mamālik,* 36–48.

173. Ibn Ḥawqal, *al-Masālik wa-l-Mamālik,* 60–107.

174. Ibid., 73. In this and the following quotations I have transposed the tenses to the past in order to maintain the flow of the narrative.

175. Ibid., 75–76.

176. Ibid., 103–4. I have been able neither to identify nor to locate al-Habaṭ beyond placing it in the same part of the Maghrib as Ṭanjah, Azīlah, Fās, and Tāmadīt. Ibn Ḥawqal (ibid.) adds that formerly these people had been even better off, and there had been a falling off of the prosperity that he had observed in A.H. 330/A.D. 942—presumably owing to continuing conflict between Spanish Umayyads and Fāṭimids.

177. Maqdisī, *Aḥsan,* 215–48.

178. Minorsky, *Ḥudūd,* 153–54. Although eight of eighteen entries incorporate epithets such as "prosperous," "flourishing," or "wealthy," it is not certain what importance ought to be attached to them, for this chapter seems to be little more than a summary of al-Iṣṭakhrī's account (cf. note 172 above). Furthermore, V. Minorsky, the translator of the *Ḥudūd,* thinks that the epithets are "personal additions to the names of cities by our author" (416). In any case, not all necessarily indicated agricultural, as opposed to industrial or commercial, wealth.

179. Ibn Ḥawqal, *al-Masālik wa-l-Mamālik,* 83.

180. It is Laroui's belief that the prevalence of nomadism in these regions from the third century onward represented a "renomadization" of peoples who had traditionally shifted between agriculture and stock raising. Driven south of the *limes* by the Roman legions, these groups elaborated the pastoral aspects of their economies into fully developed camel nomadism on the fringes of the Ṣaḥārā. The principal effect of the Arab conquest then would have been to drive the nomads even farther south, thereby effecting the economic integration of the Ṣaḥārā with the northern Maghrib (*The History of the Maghrib,* 70–72, 125–26). But few, if any, completely severed their ties with sedentary agriculturists or even with cities. Ibn Ḥawqal (*al-Masālik wa-l-Mamālik,* 68), for instance, tells how Berber tribesmen who raised crops in the interior would come to camp on the outskirts of the city of Surt when (autumn) rains revivified the pastures there. At the same time, the population of Namazdūwan (p. 87; Barādawan in Idrisī, *Nuzhat,* 140), a day's journey from Tījis in the Ifrīqiyah (Tunisia and western Libya), was about evenly divided between sedentary and nomadic (presumably strictly *raʿīyah:* see chapter 1) families. Equally often, however, the relationship between nomads and settled communities was one of hostility. For Ibn Ḥawqal (*al-Masālik wa-l-Mamālik,* 70), the nomads traversing the territory of Qābis were villainous rogues given to attacking travellers and on one occasion setting fire to a suburb of that city.

For information not inimical to, if not explicitly supportive of, Laroui's interpretation, see Emilienne Demougeot, "Le chameau et l'Afrique du nord romaine," *Annales: Economies, Sociétés, Civilisations* 15 (1960): 209–47 and Bulliet, *The Camel and the Wheel,* chap. 5.

181. Ibn Ḥawqal, *al-Masālik wa-l-Mamālik,* 66–67.

182. Ibn Ḥawqal also records that the prices of fruit, eatables generally, wheat, barley, milk products, and cattle were so reasonable that inhabitants of neighboring regions came to obtain provisions from the town.

183. Ibn Ḥawqal, *al-Masālik wa-l-Mamālik,* 76.

184. I believe this to be true even though Ibn Ḥawqal's chapter on the Maghrib is unusually detailed and always inclines to provide more information relevant to this theme than do any of the other topographers.

This is an appropriate point at which to refer to a model of North African urban (and state) development elicited by Charles Redman and his associates from a series of archaeological investigations in northern Morocco. Their formulation is essentially as follows (although not in their terminology):

- The Idrīsid urban hierarchy was an agrarian-based, redistributive and mobilizative, multitiered, patrimonial administrative system.
- The Almoravid, Almohad, and Marīnid urban hierarchies, by contrast, were called into being to manage long-distance trade, specifically the transport of gold between Subsaharan Africa and the countries of the Mediterranean littoral. These functions tended to promote a primate pattern of urban size distributions while fostering concurrently the emergence of the dichotomized interests of inland capitals on the one hand and coastal entrepôts on the other.
- Local service functions of the sort broadly subsumed under the central-place rubric developed to a significant degree only in the later phase of urban development.

Redman is certainly correct in his characterization of the Idrīsid polity, although relatively little is known of its settlement pattern beyond the excavations undertaken by the Moroccan-American Archaeological Project, directed by Professor Redman himself, at al-Baṣrah, Madīnat al-Nākūr, Badīs, and Tamdoult. And what he has to say about the Idrīsids is equally applicable to the Rustamids, the Banū-Īfran, the Banū-Midrar, and the Aghlabids.

The Almoravids and subsequent dynasties fall outside the scope of this work and need not concern us here. What is debatable, however, is the provision or not of services and goods for city-trade areas under the Idrīsids. It is difficult to conceive of any towns, even those serving primarily as centers of economic redistribution and mobilization, as totally lacking markets for local produce. Certainly, markets have customarily coexisted with redistributive economic regimes throughout the traditional world. It must be remembered, moreover, that even sophisticated excavation techniques are usually incapable of recovering evidence of the daily movement of fruit and vegetables from the countryside to an urban market. See Charles L. Redman, "Comparative urbanism in the Islamic Far West," *World Archaeology* 14 (1982–83): 355–77; James L. Boone and Redman, "Alternate pathways to urbanism in the medieval Maghrib," *Comparative Urban Research* 9 (1982): 28–38; Boone, J. Emlen Myers, and Redman, "Archaeological and historical approaches to complex societies: the Islamic states of medieval Morocco," *American Anthropologist* 92, no. 3 (1990): 630–46. For an earlier archaeological reconnaissance of the Baṣrian district, see Daniel Eustache, "El-Baṣra, capitale idrissite, et son port," *Hesperis* 42 (1955): 217–38.

185. *Al-Andalus* was the term customarily employed by medieval Arabic speakers to denote those territories of the Iberian Peninsula that were under Islamic control. As such, its spatial referents varied with time, predominantly waxing in the eighth century, remaining fairly stable through the tenth, but contracting from the eleventh century onward (Toledo was recaptured by Christian forces in 1085). The designation is generally thought to have derived from the ethnikon *Vandal,* although it is not immediately evident why the Arabs should have appropriated for their Iberian province the name of a people who had traversed the peninsula en route to North Africa some two centuries before the Muslim invasion. One suggestion is that North African Berbers referred to the peninsula by some such term as a hypothetical **Zamurz Wandalus* (= "Land of the Vandals"), and, as a prefixed *w-* denotes a genitive in many Berber nouns, the Arabs could perhaps have rendered the Berber name into Arabic as *Bilad al-Andalus,* signifying "Land of the [supposed] Andals." Competing theories have been advanced, but none carries any greater conviction. In any case, the name al-Andalus occurs as a translation of *Spania* on bilingual coins as early as 716: see Werner Wycichl, "Al-Andalus (Sobre la Historia de un Nombre)," *Al-Andalus* 17 (1952): 449–50; Joaquín Vallvé, "Sobre algunos problemas de la invasión musulmana," *Anuario de Estudios Medievales* 4 (1967): 361–63; and, in summary, Thomas F. Glick, *Islamic and Christian Spain in the Early Middle Ages* (Princeton, N.J., 1979), 14. For the Vandals generally, consult Courtois, *Les Vandales et l'Afrique.*

186. The first two centuries of Islamic rule are described in such meager fashion by the early topographers (e.g., Ibn Khurradādhbih, *al-Masālik wa-l-Mamālik,* 89–90; translation, 64–65; Yaʿqūbī, *al-Buldān,* 353–55; Wiet's translation, 217–21; Ibn Rustah, *al-Aʿlaq,* incidental mentions on 78, 79, 85, 98, and 129: index to Wiet's translation) that it can only be inferred that al-Andalus was then accounted of little importance by authors in the Eastern Caliphate. With the restoration of the Marwānid Caliphate at al-Qurṭubah in the tenth century, however, information becomes both somewhat fuller and better systemized.

Al-Iṣṭakhrī's account (*al-Masālik wa-l-Mamālik,* 41–44) was concerned primarily with agriculture and commerce, while enumerating fourteen itineraries into the interior of the peninsula. The author of the *Ḥudūd al-ʿĀlam* (154–56) did no more than reproduce these materials in skeletal form. This is not altogether surprising in view of the vast distance that separated this author's homeland in Gūzgānān from al-Andalus on the far western fringe of the known world; what is less expected is the meagerness of al-Maqdisī's description of the peninsula. He admitted that he had never set foot there but had acquired such information as he had from persons encountered in Makkah (Mecca) after he had already prepared a fair copy of the *Aḥsan al-Taqāsīm.* Consequently, he could provide only a brief overview of Andalusī cities, the sole exception being a somewhat more detailed account of Qurṭubah made possible by the number of informants willing to talk to him about it (57, 222, 235–36). Both more detailed and more coherent was the description compiled by Ibn Ḥawqal (*al-Masālik wa-l-Mamālik,* 108–17), who had the great advantage of having travelled in al-Andalus in 948. Évariste Lévi-Provençal has justly characterized this work, biased in favor of the Fāṭimids though it is, as "the first rational description . . . of the Cordovan Kingdom, which has come down to us" (*The Encyclopaedia of Islam,* 2d ed., 1:488).

Among native Andalusī topographers and historians of the tenth century, pride of place must be accorded Aḥmad ibn Muḥammad ibn Mūsā al-Rāzī (d. probably in 955), who prefaced his now-lost history of Islamic Spain with a description of al-Andalus. This description survives only in (1) a Castilian version, published in 1852 by Pascual de Gayangos (*Memoria sobre la Autenticidad de la Crónica Denominada del Moro Rasis. Memorias de la Real Academia de la Historia,* vol. 8 [Madrid]), which was in turn a rendering by Gil Peres of a lost Portuguese translation commanded at about the turn of the fourteenth century by King Denis of Portugal (r. 1279–1325); and (2) a second Portuguese version derived from Gil Peres's translation and published in *Crónica Geral de Espanha de 1344,* ed. L. E. Lindley Cintra (Lisboã, 1952). However, Lévi-Provençal has prepared a French translation of the Castilian version and, with the help of the extant Portuguese text, attempted to reconstruct the original Arabic: "La 'Description de l'Espagne' d'Aḥmad al-Rāzī," *Andalus* 18 (1953): 51–108. Al-Rāzī's text served as a model for most subsequent descriptions of the Iberian Peninsula, including that which Abū ʿUbayad al-Bakrī incorporated in his *al-Masālik wa-l-Mamālik* (see chapter 3). Although this section of the *Masālik* is no longer extant, it can be partially reconstructed from quotations in *al-Rawḍ al-Miʿṭār,* compiled in the fourteenth century by Ibn ʿAbd al-Munʿim al-Ḥimyarī (ed. and trans. Évariste Lévi-Provençal under the title *La Péninsule Ibérique au Moyen Âge d'après le Kitāb al-Rawḍ al-Miʿṭār fī Ḫabar al-Akṭār* (Leiden, 1938).

A late source that nonetheless preserves a good deal of otherwise unknown information culled from early works is Shihāb al-Dīn al-Maqqarī's (1591–1632) voluminous introduction to his biography of Ibn al-Khaṭīb, vizier of Gharnāṭah, entitled *Nafḥ al-Ṭīb min Ghuṣn al-Andalus al-Raṭīb.* The introduction, containing a fund of curious and valuable information, has been edited by Muḥyi al-dīn (al-Qāhirah, A.H. 1368: not seen by me), and was translated into French by R. Dozy, G. Dugat, L. Krehl, and W. Wright under the title *Analectes sur l'Histoire et la Littérature des Arabes d'Espagne,* 2 vols. (Leyden, 1855–61). There is also an old English translation by Pascual de Gayangos, *The History of the Mohammedan Dynasties in Spain,* 2 vols. (London, 1840–43), which I have not seen. It is greatly to be regretted that histories of such towns as Badajos (Aʿlam al-Baṭalyawsī, d. 1248), Malaga (Ibn ʿAskar, d. 1238), Almeria (Ibn al-Ḥajj, d. 1372), and Seville (Ibn al-Shāt, d. 1323)—*ṭabaqāt* though they probably were—should have been lost.

Until recently the prevailing historiographical tradition concerning the period prior to the fall of the Spanish Caliphate was that established sequentially by Reinhart Dozy and Évariste Lévi-Provençal. Dozy's *Histoire des Musulmanes d'Espagne . . . 711–1110* was first published at Leiden in 1861 and translated into English under the title *Spanish Islam* (London, 1913). A revised edition was edited by Lévi-Provençal (Leyden, 1932), who then began preparing an entirely new work on the same theme, only three volumes of which were published before the author's death: *Histoire de l'Espagne Musulmane* (Paris, 1944–53). Vol. 2, *Le Califat umaiyade de Cordoue (912–1031),* was translated into Spanish by E. García Gómez under the title *España Musulmana hasta la Caída del Califato de Córdoba* (2d ed., Madrid, 1957; vol. 4 of *Historia de España,* directed by Ramón Menéndez Pidal). All these works take the form of narrative political history with some attention to literature and philosophy, and even Lévi-Provençal's final synthesis is severely dated. Shorter overviews essentially in the same tradition include Henri Terrasse's *Islam d'Espagne: une Renontre de l'Orient et de l'Occident* (Paris, 1958); Juan Vernet's *Los Musulmanes Españoles* (Barcelona, 1961); Watt's *A History of Islamic Spain;* and S. M. Imamuddin's (Imām al-Dīn), *Muslim Spain 711–1492 A.D.: A Sociological Study* (Leiden, 1981). An interpretation that tends to emphasize continuity in early Spanish history, especially between the Roman and Islamic periods, is H. V. Livermore's *Origins of Spain and Portugal* (London, 1971); but the work that I have found conceptually most useful in developing this section is Glick's *Islamic and Christian Spain in the Early Middle Ages,* which combines familiarity with sociocultural theory, taking an explicitly comparative stance. Claudio Sánchez-Albornoz's *La España Musulmana,* 3d ed. (Madrid, 1973) is a useful collection of principally Islamic medieval texts. There is a great deal of material relevant to this section in Salma Khadra Jayyusi, ed., *The Legacy of Muslim Spain* (Leiden, 1992), and the relevant archaeology is summarized by Juan Zozaya in "The Islamic Consolidation in al-Andalus (8th–10th Centuries): An Archaeological Perspective," in Gayraud, ed., *Colloque International,* 245–58.

187. As attested by archaeological evidence. Cited by Glick, *Islamic and Christian Spain,* 30, 321.

188. According to al-Ḥimyarī (al-Rawḍ al-Miʿṭār, 181–82; Lévi-Provençal's translation, 218–19), Ello was destroyed "by order of ʿAbd al-Raḥmān II [r. 822–52] as an extreme means of suppressing chronic conflict between Muḍarī and Yamanī Arabs, both of whom laid claim to it." Cf. also Ibn ʿIdhārī, *Bayān,* 2:84; translation, 134; Yāqūt, *Muʿjam,* 4:497; and Díaz Cassou, "Ordenanzas y costumbres de la huerta de Murcia," in *Historia de Murcia Musulmana* by M. Caspar Remiro (Zaragoza, 1905), 48. On Ello see Reinhardt Dozy, *Corrections sur les Textes du Bayáno 'l-Mogrib* (Leiden, 1883), 40; with reference to *Bayān,* 2:85, l. 2.

189. Al-Ḥimyarī, *al-Rawḍ al-Miʿṭār,* 183–84; Lévi-Provençal's translation, 221. Cf. al-Rāzī, Lévi-Provençal's translation, 67: "Fine galleys are built there." There are also bare, uninformative mentions of al-Marīyah in Iṣṭakhrī, *al-Masālik wa-l-Mamālik,* 42; Ibn Ḥawqal, *al-Masālik wa-l-Mamālik,* 65, 110, 116; and Maqdisī, *Aḥsan,* 223–24. For a reconstruction of al-Marīyah as it was in the tenth century, see Lévi-Provençal, *Histoire de l'Espagne Musulmane,* 3:345.

190. Ḥimyarī, *al-Rawḍ al-Miʿṭār,* 163; Lévi-Provençal's translation, 196 and Ibn Ḥawqal, *al-Masālik wa-l-Mamālik,* 66, 116. Despite the authoritative approval of Lévi-Provençal (*La Pénninsule Ibérique au Moyen-Âge,* 196 n. 2), the prevalent belief that the eponymous founder of the city was the *tābiʿ* ʿAlī ibn Rabāḥ seems to have been no more than folk etymology.

191. Rāzī, Lévi-Provençal's translation, 77–78; Ḥimyarī, *al-Rawḍ al-Miʿṭār,* 163, 195–96; and al-ʿUdhrī, *al Masālik ilā Jamīʿ al-Mamālik,* ed. ʿAbd al-ʿAzīz al-Ahwānī (Madrid, 1965), index.

192. Rāzī, Lévi-Provençal's translation, 76.

193. Several of the texts available to me, as well as al-Maqqarī (*Nafḥ al-Ṭīb*, Dozy, et al.'s translation), actually use the form *al-Madīnah al-Zahrā'* instead of the expected *Madīnat al-Zahrā'*.

194. Ibn Ḥawqal, *al-Masālik wa-l-Mamālik,* 111–12 and Ḥimyarī, *al-Rawḍ al-Mi'ṭār,* 95; Lévi-Provençal's translation, 117.

195. Ḥimyarī, *al-Rawḍ al-Mi'ṭār,* 80–82; Lévi-Provençal's translation, 100–3.

196. Maqdisī, *Aḥsan,* 47–48, and 244.

197. Ibn Ḥawqal, *al-Masālik wa-l-Mamālik,* 111; cf. also Rāzī, Lévi-Provençal's translation, 64–65.

198. Maqdisī, *Aḥsan,* 233. This author's statement that he had heard an 'Uthmānī claim that Qurṭubah was more impressive than Baghdād carries no weight. 'Uthmāniyah in this context makes little sense, and Pellat is probably correct in suggesting that it may have been a mislection: *Description,* 80 n. 68.

199. A. J. Arberry, "Muslim Cordoba," in *Cities of Destiny,* ed. Arnold Toynbee (London, 1967), 171. On Qurṭubah generally, see also Évariste Lévi-Provençal, "Cordoue, capitale du Califat Umaiyade d'Occident," chap. 6 in *L'Espagne Musulmane au Xème Siècle* (Paris, 1932), 195–236 and, revised and elaborated, "Le développement urbain. Cordoue au Xe siècle," chap. 3 in *Histoire de l'Espagne Musulmane,* vol. 3: *Le Siècle du Califat de Cordoue* (Paris, 1953), 325–95. Also Robert Hillenbrand, "'The Ornament of the World': Medieval Córdoba as a Cultural Centre," in *The Legacy of Muslim Spain,* ed. Jayyusi, 112–35.

200. Maqdisī, *Aḥsan,* 222, 235–36. The seventeen cities listed by al-Maqdisī were Bajjānah, Malaqah, Balansiyah (Valencia), Tudmīr, Saraqūsah *(sic),* Yābisah, Wādī al-Ḥijārah, Tuṭīlah, Washqah, Madīnat Sālim, Ṭulayṭulah (Toledo), Ishbīliyah (Seville), Baṭalyawth, Bājah, Qurṭubah, Sadhunah, and al-Jazīrah al-Khaḍrā'. As a matter of fact, al-Maqdisī promises—on the authority of an unnamed Andalusī scholar *(shaykh)*—eighteen cities but enumerates only seventeen, perhaps (as Pellat supposes: *Description,* 80 n. 77) because he read al-Jazīrah al-Khaḍrā' as two names. He also notes that Ibn Khurradādhbih had mentioned forty cities in al-Andalus (p. 57), but in the extant version of the *Kitāb al-Masālik wa-l-Mamālik* that author cites only five by name (de Goeje transcription, 89).

201. Maqdisī, *Aḥsan,* 236. In the prefatorial digest of his book, al-Maqdisī names a total of twenty-seven notable *(madhkūrāt)* urban centers (57), not all of which could have been large.

202. Ignacio Olangüe, *La Revolución Islámica en Occidente* (Barcelona, 1974), 73–112, 224–82. What little is known of the Visigothic economy is summarized in Jaime Vincens Vives' *Economic History of Spain* (Princeton, N.J., 1969), 83–92.

203. Thorkild Schiøler, *Roman and Islamic Water-Lifting Wheels* (Copenhagen, 1973), 79–83; also more generally Julio Caro Baroja, "Sobre la historia de la noria de tiro," *Revista de Dialectología y Tradiciones Populares* 11 (1955): 15–79. The Arabs also extended the use of *qānāt*s (chain wells), ultimately of Persian origin but already employed by the Romans (for an example near Mursiyah, see Ḥimyarī, *al-Rawḍ al-Mi'ṭār,* 183; Lévi-Provençal's translation, 220). Instances of Arab hydraulic construction were to be found at Garbalyān (probably for agricultural purposes) and at Qurṭubah and Majrīt (providing urban water supplies): Glick, *Islamic and Christian Spain,* 226.

204. Not all irrigation techniques were Arab innovations. For example, there is conclusive evidence for the continuity of certain practices from Roman through Muslim times in specific localities such as the Balansiyah huerta: see Thomas F. Glick, *Irrigation and Society in Medieval Valencia* (Cambridge, Mass., 1970), 189–90.

205. Watson, "The Arab agricultural revolution," 8–35; and in more elaborate form in *Agricultural Innovations.*

206. The term customarily used among the Arabs to denote Spanish Muslims (Glick's Neo-Muslims) was *muwalladūn.*

207. Glick, *Islamic and Christian Spain,* 66. For the term *ecotype* as denoting a system of energy transfers involved in a process of ecological adaptation, see Eric R. Wolf's *Peasants* (Englewood Cliffs, N.J., 1966), chap. 2. For the Arab introduction of hard wheat into al-Andalus, cf. Glick, op. cit., 80–83.

208. Al-Rāzī, Lévi-Provençal's translation, 76. This and the following paragraphs are translated from the French of Lévi-Provençal (note 186 above); I have not had access to the original text.

209. On the conduciveness of the dry Meseta air to cereal storage, see Yāqūt, *Mu'jam,* 3:545–46 (Ṭulayṭulah wheat could be stored in silos for up to a century); Glick, *Islamic and Christian Spain,* 80–83; and Watson, "The Arab agricultural revolution," 15–16.

210. Rāzī, Lévi-Provençal's translation, 87.

211. On Ishbīliyah generally see L. Torres Balbás, "Notas sobre Sevilla en la época musulmana," *al-Andalus* 10 (1945): 177–96 and Lévi-Provençal, "Le développement urbain," 335–38, including an outline reconstruction of the city as it was in the tenth century (p. 337).

212. The extant Portuguese text adds the information that the grain could be harvested as soon as seven weeks after sowing (ibid.). A similar account is incorporated in Al-Ḥimyarī's *al-Rawḍ al-Mi'ṭār,* 113; Lévi-Provençal's translation, 139, where the Tejo inundation is compared, in principle, if not in magnitude, to that of the Nile.

213. Although Ibn al-Qūṭīyah used the form *Qulunbiriyah, Qulumriyah* is the usual rendering of this name (*Ta'rīkh Iftitāḥ al-Andalus,* trans. J. Ribera [Madrid, 1926], 200). I have not seen a more recent edition of this text prepared by 'Abd Allāh Anīs al-Ṭabbā' (Bayrūt, ?1957).

214. Pedro Chalmeta Gendrón, *El Señor del Zoco es España* (Madrid, 1973), 101–2. This author is probably correct in invoking the Andalusī monetary economy as an additional factor militating against the persistence of rural markets.

215. See Serjeant, *Islamic Textiles,* chap. 17.

216. Ibn 'Idhārī, *Bayān,* Dozy edition, 2:93.

217. Jalāl al-Dīn al-Suyūṭī (1445–1505), *Ta'rīkh al-Khulafā',* ed. by S. Lee and Mawlawī 'Abdalḥaqq (Calcutta, 1857), 539; trans. H. S. Jarret (Calcutta, 1881), 547.

218. Serjeant, *Islamic Textiles,* 169.

219. Ibn Ḥawqal, *al-Masālik wa-l-Mamālik,* 110.

220. Ibn ʿIdhārī, *Bayān,* Dozy edition, 2:130. It is uncertain whether al-Ḥajjāj had founded the *ṭirāz* in Ishbīliyah or whether he had simply appropriated a factory already established by ʿAbd al-Raḥmān. I incline to the latter view.

221. Maqqarī, *Nafḥ al-Ṭīb,* Dozy et al.'s translation, 2:148 and Yāqūt, *Muʿjam,* 4:517.

222. Maqqarī, *Nafḥal-Ṭīb,* 1:271. For *namaṭ* see Gaston Wiet, "Tapis égyptiens," *Arabica* 6 (1959): 9–10. *Namaṭ* can also mean "saddlecloth," but the context here would seem to favor a particular type of small carpet. For the still not fully understood manufacture of "sea wool" from the fine silky hairs of the byssus of the large mollusk *Pinna nobilis,* Linn., see Serjeant, *Islamic Textiles,* chap. 21.

223. So Serjeant, *Islamic Textiles,* 173, 252; but see also Wiet, "Tapis égyptiens," 13 and J. H. Kramers and Gaston Wiet, *Configuration de la Terre,* vol. 1 (Paris, 1964), 113.

224. A thin silk material manufactured in al-Kūfah: Maqdisī, *Aḥsan,* 416–17.

225. Ibn Ḥawqal, *al-Masālik wa-l-Mamālik,* 114.

226. Rāzī, Lévi-Provençal's translation, 74. Lāridah was a district (*ʿamal*) center situated at a strategically important node in the defensive system of the Upper March. For the vicissitudes of the city's history from the eighth through the tenth century as it became the prize of the Frankish and Cis-Pyrenean armies and on numerous occasions asserted its independence from the *amīr*s in Qurṭubah, see J. Bosch Vilá, *The Encyclopaedia of Islam,* 2d ed., 5:682–83. The city was reconstructed and fortified by Ismāʿīl ibn Mūsā ibn Mūsā ibn Qasī in 883/84 (the Banū-Qasī being one of the groups who dominated the history of Lāridah during the ninth and tenth centuries; the others were the Banū-Mūsā, the Banū-ʿAmrūs, the Banū-Shabrīt, and the Banū al-Muhājir). The textile manufacture to which al-Rāzī refers was actually located in a small castle town in Lāridah territory.

227. Al-Rāzī, Lévi-Provençal's translation, 78.

228. Ibid., 70–71. Another town called Laqant, situated in the neighborhood of present-day Fuente de Cantos and close to the road connecting Māridah with Ishbīliyah, existed in the tenth century but has now disappeared. The Laqant mentioned by al-Rāzī was the port known in classical times as Lucentum.

229. Glick, *Islamic and Christian Spain,* chap. 3, especially pp. 111, 125, and 129–34.

230. For the background to this administrative reorganization see ibid., 6, 39–40, 201–202.

231. Ibid., 55–56. This author also quotes a remark of the thirteenth-century writer Ibn Saʿīd to the effect that, of all eastern cities, only Dimashq (Damascus) and Ḥamāh reminded him of his home in Gharnātah. There was also some validity to al-Maqdisī's comparison (*Aḥsan,* 221, 233, 235) of al-Andalus with the lands beyond the Jayḥūn, which he refers to as the territories of the Hayṭal (= Hephthalites: the Mā Warāʾ al-Nahr [Transoxania] mentioned earlier). In al-Maqdisī's schema, each region constituted a substantial part of a larger province (al-Maghrib in the case of al-Andalus, al-Mashriq in the case of Mā Warāʾ al-Nahr), from which it was separated by a body of water (respectively the Strait of Gibraltar and the Jayḥūn River). Furthermore, both were "the homes of warriors either actually fighting the infidel or standing to arms prepared to do so, and were seats of profound learning, with a powerful ruler, specialized products, intense commercial activity, and notable resources."

232. Ibn Ḥawqal, *al-Masālik wa-l-Mamālik,* 116. Of course, the two types of farming systems referred to were not alternative uses of the same land but rather distinct ecosystems devised for contrasting environments, specifically rain-fed, winter, cereal cultivation versus summer or year-round huerta cropping, as often as not practiced by different ethnic groups. Cf. p. 219 above.

233. The earliest Arab raid against Iṣqiliyah was dispatched by Muʿāwiyah ibn Abī Sufyān in 652 while he was still governor of Syria; the second, by the same Muʿāwiyah in 667 after he had established himself as caliph.

234. For the Aghlabids in North Africa see p. 211 above.

235. > Castrogiovanni, the name by which the town was known until 1927, when the classical name Enna was revived.

236. After suppression of a revolt in 962, the name Ṭabarmīn was changed to Muʿizzīyah in honor of the Fāṭimid *imām* al-Muʿizz.

Information about the island of Iṣqiliyah in the centuries leading up to and immediately following the Muslim conquest is exiguous. The conquest itself is, of course, treated in the standard histories; but descriptions of the countryside and, except for Balarm, of the cities are meager and perfunctory. Al-Maqdisī (*Aḥsan,* 231–32) mentions thirty settlements (p. 221), not all of which can be identified, and provided sketchy comments on eighteen, but then asserts that no part of the Muslim world was more highly urbanized (p. 232)—something that would never be inferred from his own casually organized account. Ibn Ḥawqal (*al-Masālik wa-l-Mamālik,* 118–31) furnished a valuable and detailed account of Balarm (Palermo) based on a visit he had made there in 973 (p. 128) but chose to devote most of the remainder of his chapter to denigration of the Sicilians. For the rest we are dependent on later authors such as Yāqūt (e.g., *Muʿjam,* 1:309, 719–20; 2:601; 3:81, 509; 4:67, 391, 1001).

The textual basis for the history of Muslim Sicily, nearly all of which is owed to other than Sicilian authors, was assembled as long ago as 1857 by Michele Amari (*Biblioteca Arabo-Sicula,* 2 vols. [Arabic text, Lipsia; Italian trans., Torino/Roma, 1881–82]). It was Amari who also formulated the received historical interpretative framework in his *Storia dei Musulmani di Scilicia,* ed. C. A. Nallino, 2d ed., 3 vols. (Catania, 1933–39). For events prior to A.D. 1000 he had to depend heavily on retrojection of the implications of later Islamic sources; contemporary Christian chronicles were either ignorant of or failed to mention them. More recently, summaries of current knowledge have been prepared by Iḥsān ʿAbbās (*al-ʿArab fī Ṣiqillīyah* [al-Qāhirah, A.H. 1379]) and ʿAzīz Aḥmad (*A History of*

Islamic Sicily [Edinburgh, 1975]), while Denis Mack Smith's *History of Sicily: Medieval Sicily 800–1713* (London, 1968) begins with an introductory perspective on the Islamic period. See also Francesco Gabrieli, ed., "Histoire et culture de la Sicile arabe," *Revue de la Méditerranée* (Paris-Alger, mai-juin 1957), 241–59.

237. Maqdisī, *Aḥsan,* 231.

238. Ibn Ḥawqal, *al-Masālik wa-l-Mamālik,* 119–20. For a general appraisal of Ibn Ḥawqal's account of Sicily (Ṣiqiliyah), see F. Gabrieli, "Ibn Hawqal e gli Arabi di Sicilia," *Revista degli Studi Orientali* 37 (19??): 245–53.

239. Ibn Ḥawqal, *al-Masālik wa-l-Mamālik,* 120. This author asserts that a common accord prevailed among Sicilians regarding the number of mosques in Balarm, a quantity apparently inflated by the prevalence of private family mosques.

240. Maqdisī, *Aḥsan,* 183.

241. Amari, *Storia,* 2:248, 252. For an analogous scale of acculturation some two centuries later, see Jeremy Johns, "The Greek Church and the conversion of Muslims in Norman Sicily," *Byzantinische Forschungen* 21 (1995): 133–57.

242. Mack Smith, *History of Sicily,* 7.

243. Amari, *Storia,* 2:506–12. The memory of Arab horticultural expertise is preserved to this day in a stratum of loanwords in the Sicilian dialect. For *baḥayrah,* see de Goeje, *Bibliotheca Geographorum Arabicorum,* 4:185, where it is explicated as *horti olitorii.* Ibn Ḥawqal (*al-Masālik wa-l-Mamālik,* 122–23) notes that Sicilian papyrus was the only sort in the whole world that could compare with the product of the Egyptian plant. Most of the production was plaited into anchor cables, with only a small portion being reserved for government use in the manufacture of scrolls for official records.

244. Maqdisī, *Aḥsan,* 55, 221, 232.

245. Ibid., 55, 221, 232. Cf. also Amari, *Storia,* 2:303, 362 and 3:793, 797.

246. Maqdisī, *Aḥsan,* 55, 221, 232.

247. Ibid., 55, 222, 232. Cf. also Amari, *Storia,* 2:362, 457.

248. Maqdisī, *Aḥsan,* 55, 222; also Yāqūt, *Muʿjam,* 4:67 *(Qurullūn).*

249. Ibn Ḥawqal, *al-Masālik wa-l-Mamālik,* 123: *Qarrusaṭiyāt* (here rendered as "carriages") is a speculative reading suggested by Henri Massé. Cf. Kramers and Wiet, *Configuration de la Terre,* 122 n. 612a. Ibn Ḥawqal also notes that when the Aghlabids had owned the iron mine, it had been made to yield a high revenue.

250. Cf. Serjeant, *Islamic Textiles,* 191–92.

251. Ibn Ḥawqal, *al-Masālik wa-l-Mamālik,* 119–20.

252. Ibid., 131. My understanding of the relevant passage has been influenced by Serjeant, *Islamic Textiles,* 191. For a somewhat different emphasis in the interpretation, consult Kramers and Wiet, *Configuration de la Terre,* 130. *Rubāʿī* was probably a measure of cloth.

253. Maqdisī, *Aḥsan,* 239, 145.

254. Amari, *Biblioteca Arabo-Sicula,* Italian translation, 1: 199–200.

255. Ibn Ḥawqal, *al-Masālik wa-l-Mamālik,* 126. Cf. Maqdisī, *Aḥsan,* 215: "The inhabitants [of Iṣqiliyah] are continually at war with the infidel."

256. Maqdisī, *Aḥsan,* 55, 221; cf. also Amari, *Storia,* 3:794, 833.

257. Maqdisī, *Aḥsan,* 55, 222; cf. also Amari, *Storia,* 3:315 n. 3.

258. Maqdisī, *Aḥsan,* 55, 222; cf. also Amari, *Storia,* 2:495.

259. Ibn Ḥawqal, *al-Masālik wa-l-Mamālik,* 121.

260. Maqdisī, *Aḥsan,* 55, 222, 232; cf. also Amari, *Storia,* 2: 362, 457.

261. Maqdisī, *Aḥsan,* 55, 221, 232 and Yāqūt, *Muʿjam,* 1:733. Cf. also Amari, *Storia,* 1:443, 471 and vol. 2:50 n. 1.

262. The Iṣqiliyan *iqlīm,* like that of al-Andalus, has to be understood as a *kūrah:* see p. 218 above.

263. Maqdisī, *Aḥsan,* 233.

264. The phrase is Mack Smith's: *A History of Sicily,* 6.

265. Ibn Ḥawqal, *al-Masālik wa-l-Mamālik,* 130–31.

Chapter Seventeen

1. In Parsonian sociology the functional subsystems of society are specified as those concerned with pattern maintenance and tension management, adaptation (economy), goal attainment (polity), and integration: Tallcot Parsons and Neil J. Smelser, *Economy and Society. A Study in the Integration of Economic and Social Theory* (London, 1956), chap. 2.

2. This is essentially the analytical approach to urban form pursued by Professor Nezar AlSayyad in his *Cities and Caliphs. On the Genesis of Arab Muslim Urbanism* (New York, 1991), 9 and passim. It is a felicitous combination of the Lynch-Rodwin analytical system (Kevin Lynch and Lloyd Rodwin, "The Form of the City," in *Cities and City Planning,* ed. Rodwin [New York, 1981]) and the linkage and place theories of Trancik (Roger Trancik, *Finding Lost Space* [New York, 1986]). Despite the excellence of Professor Al-Sayyad's cartographic presentations, I regret that I am unable to follow him in all his analyses of textual and archaeological evidence.

3. For a synthesis of an extensive literature on this and related topics, see Wolf, *Peasants,* passim.

4. Scott Greer, *The Emerging City: Myth and Reality* (New York, 1962), 34.

5. John Friedmann, "Cities in social transformation," *Comparative Studies in Society and History* 4, no. 1 (1961): 92.

6. As was implicit, for example, in the works of Tönnies, Durkheim, Spengler, and Ortega y Gasset, among others.

7. Richard L. Meier, "The Organization of Technological Innovation in Urban Environments." In *The History and the City,* ed. Oscar Handlin and John Burchard (Cambridge, Mass., 1963), 75.

8. Qur'ān IV *(al-Nisā'):*59.

9. It should be noted that a specifically built *dār al-imārah* was not required for the administration of a city at any level of the urban hierarchy. Any building large enough to accommodate a government bureau *(dīwān)* could be pressed into service and would thereafter be referred to as the *dār al-imārah.*

10. Jere L. Bacharach, "Administrative Complexes, Palaces, and Citadels. Changes in the Loci of Medieval Muslim Rule," in *The Ottoman City and Its Parts. Urban Structure and Social Order,* ed. Irene A. Bierman, Rifa'at A. Abou-el-Haj, and Donald Preziosi (New Rochelle, N.Y., 1991): 111–28 and "The Court-Citadel: An Islamic Urban Symbol of Power," in *Urbanism in Islam,* vol. 3, ed. Yukawa Takeshi (Tokyo, 1989).

11. Ṭabarī, *Ta'rīkh,* 1:2487–95. Originally the government house had been referred to as "a house *(dār)* for Saʿd [ibn ʿAbī Waqqāṣ, the conqueror of Ctesiphon and Qādisīyah]." Only under the ʿĪraqi governorship of Ziyād ibn Abīhi in the 660s do we find the building being designated the *dār al-imārah.* The circumstance that the building was initially associated personally with Saʿd would seem to imply that he had not at that time clearly formulated a policy of permanent urban foundation. The most thorough analysis of the spatial relationship of *jāmiʿ* and *dār al-imārah* in early al-Kūfah is provided by Djaït, *Al-Kūfa,* chap. 7.

There is a short account of Rūzbih, a Hamadhānī, in Ṭabarī, 1:2494–95.

12. It is noteworthy that when al-Maqdisī was writing the *Aḥsan* in 985, the treasury in every provincial capital *(qaṣabah)* in al-Shām (Greater Syria) was housed in the cathedral mosque (182), while al-Iṣṭakhrī in 951 reported similar circumstances from Adharbayjān (Azerbaijan), where the state treasure was kept in a *bayt māl* covered by a lead roof, behind an iron door, and supported on nine columns (174).

13. This is not to deny, of course, that the symbolism *may* be more apparent to us today than it was ever to a seventh- or eighth-century Muslim.

14. Donald Whitcomb, "The city of Istakhr and the Marvdasht plain," 364, 367 and *Ayla. Art and Industry in the Islamic Port of Aqba,* 22.

15. Balādhurī, *Futūḥ al-Buldān,* 347. The precise location of the *dār al-imārah* before this time is uncertain, although K. A. C. Creswell favored a site on the northeastern side of the mosque (*Early Muslim Architecture,* 1:22).

16. Bacharach, "Administrative Complexes," 115.

17. In Balādhurī, *Futūḥ al-Buldān,* 123.

18. T. Tobler and A. Molinier, *Itinera Hierosolymitana,* vol. 1 (London, 1889), 186.

19. See Creswell, *A Short Account of Early Muslim Architecture,* rev. ed., 62–65. All subsequent references are to this edition unless otherwise indicated.

20. Creswell, *A Short Account of Early Muslim Architecture,* 40–41. Bacharach ("Administrative Complexes," 115–16) claims that this architectural complex also incorporated an axial pattern and dimensional ratios employed elsewhere in the eastern sectors of the Caliphate.

21. Lassner, *The Shaping of ʿAbbāsid Rule,* chaps. 7, 8 and Oleg Grabar, *The Formation of Islamic Art,* rev. ed. (New Haven, Conn., 1987), chap. 6.

22. Bacharach, "Administrative Complexes," 116–17.

23. Abū Muslim's *dār* in Marv is described in Iṣṭakhrī, *al-Masālik wa-l-Mamālik,* 259.

24. Bacharach, "Administrative Complexes," 117.

25. For Sāsānian domed palaces see Arthur Upham Pope, *Persian Architecture* (New York, 1965), 47–60; for the dome in Byzantine architecture, Karl Lehmann, "The Dome of Heaven," *Art Bulletin* 14, no. 1 (1945): 26ff. and E. Baldwin Smith, *The Dome* (Princeton, N.J., 1950), passim.

It has also been queried whether "green dome" is an acceptable translation of *al-quabbat al-khaḍrā',* which in Classical Arabic usage can be rendered quite satisfactorily as "the dome of heaven" (Charles Wendell, "Baghdād: *imago mundi,* and other foundation lore," *International Journal of Middle East Studies* 2 [1971]: 119–120). Moreover, *akhḍar* may have been a generic term subsuming shades of both blue and green: *al-khaḍrā'* is fairly commonly employed to denote "sky" (cf. Albert Morabia, "Recherches sur quelques noms de couleur en arabe classique," *Studia Islamica* 21 [1964], 70). The materials of which these domes were constructed are not recorded.

26. Bacharach, "Administrative Complexes," 117–18, basing his interpretation on information provided by Benjamin Mazar (*The Mountain of the Lord* [Garden City, N.Y., 1975]).

27. Bacharach, "Administrative Complexes," 118.

28. Maqrīzī, *al-Mawāʿiẓ,* 1:304.

29. Ibid., 2:269.

30. Bacharach, "Administrative Complexes," 118–19.

31. Ira M. Lapidus, "The separation of state and religion in the development of early Islamic society," *International Journal of Middle East Studies* 6 (1975): 363–85. The manner in which "Ḥanbalism fused the tradition of autonomous religious activity with the heritage of political activism and rebellion borne by the *ahl-Khurāsān*—a fusion with explosive implications for the religious authority of the Caliphate and for the regulations between state and religion" is admirably elucidated by Lapidus in the second half of this paper, pp. 370ff.

32. Ibid., 382–83.

33. For the changing function of this office in both al-Andalus (Islamic Spain) and the Eastern Caliphate, see Dominique and Janine Sourdel, *La Civilisation de l'Islam Classique* (Paris, 1968), 365–66.

34. C. E. Bosworth, "Abū ʿAbdallāh al-Khwārazmī on the technical terms of the secretary's art," *Journal of the Economic and Social History of the Orient* 12 (1969): 113–64.

35. This flexibility was subsequently rationalized in a tradition that had Muḥammad claiming that, whereas his predecessors had been constrained to pray in churches and synagogues, he had been given the whole world as a *masjid* (Wāqidī, *al-Maghāzī,* Wellhausen's translation, 403 and Muḥammad ibn Ismā'īl al-Jāmiʿ al-saḥīḥ, *Ṣalat,* in *Concordance et indices de la Tradition musulmane,* ed. A. J. Wensinck [Leiden, 1936–64], *bāb* 56). Cf. also Muslim ibn al-Ḥajjāj al-Qushayrī al-Jāmiʿ al-saḥīh, in *Concordance et indices de la Tradition musulmane,* ed. A. J. Wensinck (Leiden, 1936–64), tr. 1:

"Wherever the hour of prayer overtakes thee, thou shalt perform the *ṣalāt* and that is a *masjid*."

36. Doğan Kuban, *Muslim Religious Architecture,* part 1 of *The Mosque and Its Early Development* (Leiden, 1974); Creswell, *A Short Account of Early Muslim Architecture,* 4–17; and J. Pedersen, "Masdjid," *The Encyclopaedia of Islam,* 2d ed., 6:644–77.

37. *The Encyclopaedia of Islam,* 2d ed., 6:644.

38. Jeffery, *The Foreign Vocabulary of the Qur'ān,* 263–64. It seems that Qur'ānic *masjid* conveyed an Islamic connotation only when it was in grammatical construct with certain nouns, most commonly in reference to the Masjid al-Harām at Makkah (Mecca). Cf. Qur'ān 24 *(al-Nūr):* 36: "[Mosques are] houses of which God has allowed the construction and the pronouncement of His name therein."

39. This is essentially the process of sacralization proposed by Grabar (*The Formation of Islamic Art,* chap. 5). In explicating this approach to the origin of the Mosque, this author writes that "in the Muslim view of Islam and of its growth, there was no preconceived, theoretical notion of a holy place but an accretion of unique and at times trivial events that became accepted. It is as though the culture were psychologically reluctant to interpret abstractly the physical reality of its Muslim life."

40. Arculfus, *Relatio de Locis Sanctis,* ed. T. Tobler under the title *Itinera et Descriptiones,* vol. 1 (Genève, 1877), 195. No early Arab historian records the laying out of a place of prayer in Jerusalem at the time of its capitulation to ʿUmar in 637, and the testimony of the several Christian authors who do mention it is encumbered with evident legendary accretions. See, for example, Creswell's and Pedersen's comments as cited in note 36 above. It is usually assumed that the ruins mentioned by Arculf were those of the Royal Stoa built by Herod but destroyed by Titus in A.D. 70.

41. Serjeant and Lewcock (eds.), *Ṣanʿāʾ. An Arabian Islamic City,* 353.

42. Pedersen, "Masdjid," 649, citing *Corpus Iuris di Zaid b. ʿAlī,* ed. Griffini, no. 364. It is not inappropriate in this connection to cite Creswell's conclusion (*A Short Account of Early Muslim Architecture,* 17) that "there is no reason for believing that any mosque was built as such in Syria until the time of al-Walīd (705–15) or possibly ʿAbd al-Malik (685–705)."

43. Tabarī, *Taʾrīkh,* 1:2443.

44. For these and other examples see Pedersen, "Masdjid," 650; and for the suppression of fire temples in the eastern territories Michael G. Morony, "Conquerors and Conquered: Iran" in *Studies on the First Century of Islamic Society,* ed. G. H. A. Juynboll (Carbondale, Ill., 1982), 81 et seq.

45. What is firmly established is that the church was originally a pagan temple adapted to Christian purposes by order of the Byzantine emperor Theodosius in the last quarter of the fourth century.

46. Balādhurī, *Futūḥ al-Buldān,* 131.

47. Maqdisī, *Aḥsan,* 156.

48. Iṣṭakhrī, *al-Masālik wa-l-Mamālik,* 61 and Ibn Ḥawqal, *Ṣūrat al-Arḍ,* 176.

49. Jonathan Bloom, *Minaret, Symbol of Islam* (Oxford, 1989), 38, citing *The Kāmil of el-Mubarrad,* ed. William Wright (Leipzig, 1864), 481.

50. Iṣṭakhrī, *al-Masālik wa-l-Mamālik,* 188; Ibn Ḥawqal, Ṣūrat al-Arḍ, 342; and Maqdisī, *Aḥsan,* 377.

51. Wāqidī, *al-Maghāzī,* Niebuhr-Mordtmann's translation, 108: see Max van Berchem, *Amida* (Heidelberg, 1910), 51. See also Creswell, *A Short Account of Early Muslim Architecture,* 63.

52. Medieval Muslim mathematicians were quite capable of determining *qiblah* directions from anywhere in the Islamic world with virtually any desired degree of accuracy if the requisite data were available: see, int. al., David A. King, "Ḳibla: Astronomical Aspects," *The Encyclopaedia of Islam,* 2d ed., 5:83–88; "The earliest Islamic mathematical methods and tables for finding the direction of Mecca," *Zeitschrift für Geschichte der Arabisch-Islamischen Wissenschaften* 3 (1986), 82–149; "The orientation of medieval Islamic architecture and cities," *Journal for the History of Astronomy,* 26 (1995): 253–74; and with Richard P. Lorch, "Qibla Charts, Qibla Maps, and Related Instruments," in *The History of Cartography,* vol. 2, bk. 1, ed. J. B. Harley and David Woodward (Chicago, 1992), 189–205. However, the accuracy of an actual calculation of a particular *qiblah* direction depended on the quality of the data available at that locale, especially latitudes and longitudes, the latter of which were seldom exact; while not infrequently, *qiblahs* were not computed from terrestrial data but adopted from tradition. Consequently, mosques were often incorrectly aligned. On a site as relatively close to Makka as Aylah (al-ʿAqabah), the *qiblah* wall faced approximately southwest, while the true direction was slightly east of south, and the common *qiblah* in what are now southern Syria and Jordan was due south (Donald Whitcomb, "Water and recent excavations at Aqaba," *The Oriental Institute News and Notes,* no. 141 [1994]: 4–5). The Friday mosque at Wāsiṭ diverged from the true *qiblah* by as much as 35°. In an unpublished map, Dr. Whitcomb has depicted the main regional *qiblah* variations as far as present evidence permits: North Africa, including Egypt, approximately southeast (112°–157°); Greater Syria, south (157°–202°); Central Arabia and the Eastern Caliphate, southwest (202°–247°); Yaman, north (337°–22°).

53. The etymology of the word *miḥrāb* (pl. *maḥārīb*) is obscure, but it seems that in pre-Islamic times it denoted a revered, perhaps sacred, space within an architectural structure (G. Fehérvári, "Miḥrāb," *The Encyclopaedia of Islam,* 7:7–15). The common explanation that the *miḥrāb* was introduced initially and simply as an indication of the direction toward which one turned in prayer is no longer viable: see H. Stern, "Les origins de l'architecture de la mosquée omeyyade," *Syria* 28 (1951): 269–279; Grabar, *The Formation of Islamic Art,* 114–16; and Nuha N. N. Khoury, "The mihrab: from text to form," *International Journal of Middle East Studies* 30 (1998), passim. In this last paper the author establishes that in pre- and early Islamic times *miḥrāb* was a protean metaphor that, like a semiotic excipient, conferred notions of elevation and superiority on a range of substantive concepts, and that became attached to the *qiblah* orientation as the focus of the prayer area.

54. *Minbar* could be derived from the Arabic root *N.B.R.* = "high" but is at least as likely to have been a loanword from Ethiopic (J. Pedersen, "Minbar," *The Encyclopaedia of Islam,* 7:73–76). The *khuṭbah* is thought to have been instituted in the Umayyad period.

55. Kuban, *Muslim Religious Architecture,* 5 and F. H. Jimenez, "El almimbar movil del siglo X de la mezquita de Cordoba," *al-Andalus* 24 (1959): 381–99.

56. *Minaret* via Turkish from *manār/manārah,* which in pre-Islamic Arabia denoted an elevated site for the sending of fire or smoke signals. However, with the passage of time the word shed its association with *nār* = "fire" and came to designate boundary markers and watchtowers, and subsequently minarets in the presently accepted sense.

The interpretation presented here is based on the research of Bloom (*Minaret, Symbol of Islam,* passim), although my brief summary does much less than justice to the intricacies of that author's argument. See also Robert Hillenbrand, "Manāra, Manār," *The Encyclopaedia of Islam,* 6 (1987): 361–68 and Grabar, *The Formation of Islamic Art,* 113–14. In reading architectural height as a symbol of political power, the early Muslims were merely following contemporary practice in the region. The shift in the semiotics of Islamic architecture is summarized by Bloom on pp. 19 and 73.

57. Often rendered into English as "cathedral mosque."

58. Iṣṭakhrī, *al-Masālik wa-l-Mamālik,* 82–83; cf. Yaʿqūbī, *al-Buldān,* 322. For extended comments on the increase in the number of Friday mosques see Pedersen, "Masdjid," 655–57.

59. Maqdisī, *Aḥsan,* 282.

60. Narshakhī, Frye's translation, 12–15, 17. For other apparently urban centers lacking congregational mosques, see p. 76.

61. Miquel, *La Géographie Humaine,* 4:242.

62. Maqdisī, *Aḥsan,* 205. Cf. the same author's account of groups assembled in the congregational mosque in Shīrāz in the forenoon for study of jurisprudence *(fiqh),* glorification of God *(dhikr),* and reading of the Qurʾān (p. 441, Constantinople recension only).

63. Ibn Ḥawqal, *al-Masālik wa-l-Mamālik,* 143.

64. Cf., for instance, Ibn al-Ḥājj, *Mudkhal,* 2:43.

65. Maqdisī, *Aḥsan,* 205.

66. Ibn al-Ḥājj, *Mudkhal,* 2:53 and Maqdisī, *Aḥsan,* 85.

67. Bukhārī, *Ṣalāt, bāb* 33–34.

68. See Pedersen, "Masdjid," 654–55.

69. Pedersen, "Masdjid," 655. See also Ibn al-Ḥājj, *Mudkhal,* 2:54 and Bukhārī, *Ṣalāt, bāb* 70–71, 73.

70. Maqdisī, *Aḥsan,* 429. It must be noted, though, that this same mosque was well attended for worship while serving as a venue for scholarly discussion, Qurʾān reading, and community meetings (Maqdisī, C recension, 430).

71. Ibn al-Ḥājj, *Mudkhal,* 2:53 and Maqdisī, *Aḥsan,* 7.

72. Ibn al-Ḥājj, 2:57. For further information on this tendency to exclusivity, see Pedersen, "Masdjid," 654–55.

73. Ibn al-Faqīh, *al-Buldān,* 20, 100.

74. Maqdisī, *Aḥsan,* 182.

75. Maqrīzī, *al-Mawāʿiẓ,* 2:274; cited by Mez, *The Renaissance of Islam* 334–35.

76. Maqdisī, *Aḥsan,* 139–40.

77. The total number must remain unspecific, as I cannot claim to have exhausted all the relevant material in tenth-century historiographical, topographic, and *adab* literature throughout the extensive *iqlīm* of the Mashriq. Suffice it to say that the number has been culled from a sustained, although inevitably imperfect, attempt at comprehensive coverage.

78. David Whitehouse, *Siraf III. The Congregational Mosque and Other Mosques from the Ninth to the Twelfth Centuries* (London, 1980), 1 and Maqdisī, *Aḥsan,* 356–58, 84–85.

79. I am using the term *suburb* in its original sense of a part of a town outside, but immediately adjacent to, the wall—in no way to be equated with modern U.S. usage implying an outlying residential district.

80. Bakrī, *al-Masālik wa-l-Mamālik,* 123, 126, 154, 322 and Ibn Ḥawqal, *al-Masālik wa-l-Mamālik,* 85.

81. Maqdisī, *Aḥsan,* 231.

82. Iṣṭakhrī, *al-Masālik wa-l-Mamālik,* 333; Ibn Ḥawqal, *al-Masālik wa-l-Mamālik,* 508–9; and Maqdisī, *Aḥsan,* 276.

83. Ibn Ḥawqal, *al-Masālik wa-l-Mamālik,* 483.

84. Maqdisī, *Aḥsan,* 291.

85. Ibn Ḥawqal, *al-Masālik wa-l-Mamālik,* 502–3.

86. Bakrī, *al-Masālik wa-l-Mamālik,* 153. To these examples may be added Qādisīyah, where the congregational mosque stood adjacent to the Desert Gate (p. 91 above). Also see Maqdisī, *Aḥsan,* 86.

87. Ibn Ḥawqal, p. 431.

88. Ibid., 414–15.

89. Ibid., 439.

90. Maqdisī, *Aḥsan,* 140.

91. Constantinople recension only.

92. Ibn Ḥawqal, *al-Masālik wa-l-Mamālik,* 509.

93. Maqdisī, *Aḥsan,* 393.

94. Summarized by Le Strange, *The Lands of the Eastern Caliphate,* 398–400.

95. Ibn Ḥawqal, *al-Masālik wa-l-Mamālik,* 409 and Maqdisī, *Aḥsan,* 317–18 (Turthīth).

96. Ibn Ḥawqal, *al-Masālik wa-l-Mamālik,* 86; Bakrī, *al-Masālik wa-l-Mamālik,* 159–60. Maqdisī (*Aḥsan,* 229) included the interesting information that the two Friday mosques occupied two-thirds of the settlement *(balad).*

97. Ibn Ḥawqal, *al-Masālik wa-l-Mamālik,* 489.

98. Bakrī, *al-Masālik wa-l-Mamālik,* 169–70.

99. Ibn Ḥawqal, *al-Masālik wa-l-Mamālik,* 120.

100. Mazahéri, *La Vie Quotidienne des Musulmans,* 16.

101. Ibn Ḥawqal, *al-Masālik wa-l-Mamālik,* 477.

102. Maqdisī, *Aḥsan,* 360.

103. Ibid., 356–57 and Le Strange, *The Lands of the Eastern Caliphate,* 361–62. Biyār = "The Wells," an apposite name for a settlement on the edge of the Dasht-i Kavīr (Great Desert).

104. Ibn Ḥawqal, *al-Masālik wa-l-Mamālik,* 499–500 and Maqdisī, *Aḥsan,* 279.

105. Maqdisī, *Aḥsan,* 306 *(Kuwayn* for Pers. *Guvayn).*

106. Bakrī, *al-Masālik wa-l-Mamālik,* 25–26, 178–79.

107. For Ibn Ḥawqal's reference to a city of some ten thousand men in al-Jibāl which yet lacked a mosque, see chapter 8.

108. No fewer than twenty-one works bearing the title *Kitāb al-Kharāj* (or *Kitāb Risālah fī al-Kharāj*) are known by name, the earliest of which was written by Muʿāwiyah ibn ʿUbayd Allāh ibn Yasār al-Ashʿarī (d. 786). The three volumes that are presently extant were compiled respectively by Abū Yūsuf in the second half of the eighth century; by Yaḥyā ibn Ādam at the end of the same century; and by Qudāmah ibn Jaʿfar ibn Qudāmah early in the tenth century. This last treatise has been edited, translated, and annotated by A. Ben Shemesh under the title *Taxation in Islam,* rev. ed., vol. 2 (Leiden and London, 1965).

109. See Parsons and Smelser, *Economy and Society,* passim and Smelser, "A Comparative view of exchange systems," *Economic Development and Cultural Change* 7 (1959): 173–182. The distinction between "economic action" and "economically relevant action" was first advanced by Max Weber (*Economy and Society. An Outline of Interpretive Sociology,* vol. 1, ed. Guenther Roth and Claus Wittich [New York, 1968], 63–54 et seq.).

110. The ostensible rationale for this advice was that the Arabs would be following in the footsteps of their progenitor Ibrāhīm, but, quite apart from the lack of any source casting Ibrāhīm as a cloth merchant, this highly suspect tradition almost certainly owed its origin to the great importance of the textile industry in early ʿAbbāsid times rather than to any historical remembrance. Cf. also Jalāl al-Dīn Suyūṭī's comment in the fifteenth century that nine-tenths of all profit in this world is made in the textile trade (*Kanz al-ʿUmmāl* [Haydarābād, 1894–95]; cited from H. Ritter, "Ein Arabisches Handbuch der Handelswissenschaft," *Islam* [1916]: 20 by S. D. Goitein, *Studies in Islamic History and Institutions* [Leiden, 1968], 222).

111. The rationale for this belief is as follows. If demand increases, each establishment in the *sūq* will be able to expand its sales up to the point at which they are equal to the maximum number of articles that the shop family can produce in a given unit of time. Beyond that point the only way in which the supply of articles can be augmented is by enlarging the number of shops in the *sūq.* Contrariwise, if demand falls off, sales will decline, and as no single trader enjoys any substantial competitive advantage over another, they will decline at a rate more or less constant throughout the *sūq.* As each trader hopes for an improvement in demand, he may well for a short time continue to manufacture the same number of articles as before, so that his inevitably slender capital resources daily become more irredeemably locked up in currently unsalable goods (whence the common observation by nineteenth- and early twentieth-century travellers that much of the capital of *sūq* traders appeared to be immobilized in stocks of unsold goods). Ultimately there comes a time when, for virtually all establishments dealing in this particular commodity, the price will have fallen to a level equal to, or less than, the cost of production. At the same time, as a result of low turnover, income will eventually decline to a point at which it is insufficient to meet the cost of purchasing raw materials for continued production. At this stage the proprietor has no choice but to cease trading. In theory all traders handling this particular item should go out of business simultaneously, but, because subtle differences in trading practices and various extraneous circumstances combine to render some establishments relatively more vulnerable than others, the number of vendors still economically viable will decrease only to the point at which supply does not significantly exceed the low level of demand, and equilibrium is thus reestablished. Since businesses are small, moreover, even those traders who have gone out of business require only modest amounts of capital to gain reentry to the trading community at a level competitive with those who have survived the period of depressed demand. It follows that an intensifying of demand is likely to bring back a substantial proportion of those establishments that failed in hard times, with the result that, for certain marginal members of the *sūq,* trading is something undertaken only in times of high prices.

This is the sort of interpretation that is proposed as a means for understanding *sūqs* of the present day, which can be visually inspected and their traders interrogated. As this section is demonstrating, only the sketchiest information is available for the *sūqs* of the tenth century and earlier; yet it is difficult to believe that producer-retailers in the circumstances specified would have acted very differently from those of more recent times—or, indeed, some of those of the present.

112. The reference is to Qurʾān 73 *(al-Muzammil):*20.

113. Ibn Saʿd, *al-Ṭabaqāt,* 6:68. Cited by Goitein, *Studies in Islamic History,* 223. This particular chapter, entitled "The Rise of the Middle-Eastern Bourgeoisie in Early Islamic Times," 217–41 (first published in *Journal of World History* 3 [1957]: 583–604), offers a great deal of information relating to early Muslim attitudes toward commerce, including a summary of Shaybānī's work and mentions of prominent leaders of the Muslim community who were also successful entrepreneurs.

114. Although the family name Zayyāt signifies "oil merchant," the family seems to have made its fortune a generation earlier in purveying tents, parasols, and suchlike to the ʿAbbāsid court.

115. Ibn Jaṣṣāṣ (= "plasterer") as a family name lay buried in the past.

116. Goitein, *Studies in Islamic History,* 236–38. Jewish merchants in this period have been thoroughly researched by W. J. Fischel (*Jews in the Economic and Political Life of Medieval Islam* [London, 1937]) and the Mādharāʾī by H. Gottschalk (*Die Mādarāijjūn* [Berlin and Leipzig, 1931]). The quotation is from Becker, *Islamstudien,* 1:216.

117. Polanyi, Arensberg, and Pearson, *Trade and Markets in the Early Empires,* 259.

118. Mez, *The Renaissance of Islam,* 470ff.

119. The minimum range is often, and appositely, known as

the threshold of the firm. This type of analysis of peripatetic trading is demonstrated compendiously by James H. Stine, "Temporary Aspects of Tertiary Production Elements in Korea," in *Urban Systems and Economic Development,* ed. Forrest R. Pitts (Eugene, Ore., 1962), 68–88.

Although the two "ranges" are both related to demand characteristics, they are controlled by very different factors. The maximum range of a commodity is a function of demand elasticity and transportation costs: the higher the elasticity of demand, the shorter the maximum range (because consumers are easily induced to forgo the purchase or acquire a substitute), and the higher the cost of transportation, the shorter the maximum range. Minimum range, on the other hand, is generated by demand density per unit area and by the level of profit acceptable to a particular firm. Demand density itself is a function of population density and levels of disposable income. Generally speaking, the smaller the demand generated per unit area, the larger the minimum range. The profit level regarded as acceptable is to a great extent culturally determined, and within that context is strongly influenced by socioeconomic status: the meager pickings of a fishmonger in the *sūq* of al-Ubullah would be quite unacceptable to a cloth merchant in the *qayṣarīyah* of, say, Ḥalab.

120. Cf. note 111 above.

121. Narshakhī, *Taʾrīkh Bukhārā,* Frye's translation, 16.

122. Maqdisī, *Aḥsan,* 406.

123. Ibid., 138.

124. Narshakhī, *Taʾrīkh Bukhārā,* 11.

125. Maqdisī, *Aḥsan,* 224.

126. Ibid., 406–7.

127. Bakrī, *al-Masālik wa-l-Mamālik,* 102; Maqdisī, *Aḥsan,* 369.

128. John Gilissen, "La notion de la foire à la lumière de la méthode comparative," in *La Foire. Recueils de la Société Jean Bodin,* vol. 5, ed. Gilissen (Bruxelles, 1953), 323–32. The only attempt at a territorially comprehensive assessment of the role of fairs in the traditional economies of Islam is still Robert Brunschvig, "Coup d'oeil sur l'histoire des foires à travers l'Islam," in *La Foire,* 43–75.

129. Iṣfahānī, *al-Aghānī,* 16:95. Brunschvig ("Coup d'oeil," 43 n. 2) has drawn attention to a passage in Procopius's *De Bello Persico* (Loeb edition, 402–3) that seems to go some distance toward confirming the *Aghānī* reference to a fair at al-Ḥīrah in pre-Islamic times: "for it was the season of the vernal equinox, when the *Sharqīyīn* always dedicated some two months to their god, and during this time never undertook any incursions into the territories of other peoples." A period of cultic celebration when raiding was prohibited was precisely the type of situation in which fairs are known to have developed in the Islamic world in later times. For the implications of the term *Sharqīyīn* see Irfan Shahīd, *Rome and the Arabs: A Prolegomenon to the Study of Byzantium and the Arabs* (Washington, D.C., 1984), chap. 9.

130. For elaboration of these and related topics, see Brunschvig, "Coup d'oeil," passim. Traditional exegesis has interpreted Qurʾān 2 *(al-Baqarah):*194 as sanctioning, if not encouraging, pursuit of trade during the *Ḥajj.* In any case, without such adventitious income, countless of the faithful would have had to forgo the pilgrimage to Makkah (Mecca). In later times the notion of remunerative exchange both along the route and at Makkah became firmly entrenched in the minds of Believers, as is attested by the threefold supplication of pilgrims recorded by C. Snouck Hurgronje late in the nineteenth century: a pilgrimage acceptable to God, a transgression forgiven, and no interference with trade (*Ḥajj mabrūr wa-dhanb maghfūr wa-tijārat lan tabūr* [*Mekka in the Latter Part of the Nineteenth Century* (Leiden and London, 1931), 3]).

131. Narshakhī, *Taʾrīkh Bukhārā,* Frye's translation, 20–21.

132. In this context it is worth recalling al-Ṭabarī's report (*Taʾrīkh,* 3:1841) that in 871 Yaʿqūbī ibn al-Layth dispatched to Sāmarrā "idols" he had seized in Kābul.

133. Narshakhī, *Taʾrīkh Bukhārā,* 13, 15. The circumstance that, whereas participants in the economic exchanges at Shargh in the tenth century "came from far districts to trade and bargain," those at the same site in the twelfth century "came from the city [Bukhārā] and surrounding districts" is wholly in accord with the distinction we have made between market/*bāzār* and fair.

Shargh, also Jargh in Yāqūt (*Muʿjam,* 3:276) < Chargh.

134. Maqdisī, *Aḥsan,* 274. In the *Ḥudūd al-ʿĀlam,* 118, Nūjīkat (here Nūjakath) is described as the settlement "from which come the boatmen *(kashtībānān)* working on the rivers Parak (= Chirchik) and Khashart (for Yaksart, that is, the Syr Darya)."

135. Narshakhī, *Taʾrīkh Bukhārā,* 18. Frye's comments on this passage are on p. 118, note 90. The five days mentioned in the text appear to have been connected in some way with the epagomenae of the Persian and/or Magian calendars.

136. Ibn Ḥawqal, *al-Masālik wa-l-Mamālik,* 217.

137. Ibid., 336.

138. Bakrī, *al-Masālik wa-l-Mamālik,* 111–13.

139. A. J. Naji and Y. N. Ali, "the suqs of Basrah: commercial organization and activity in a medieval Islamic city," *Journal of the Economic and Social History of the Orient* 24:298–09.

140. Pellat, *Le Milieu Baṣrien,* 12.

141. The approximate locations of these and other *sūqs* in al-Baṣrah are mapped in Naji and Ali, "The suqs of Basrah," 303, 305, 307.

142. Sūq al-Ghanam had been moved to this location from the ʿUthmān Gate about 730.

143. Asphalt was used for coating the insides of boats and the outsides of reservoirs.

144. Naji and Ali, "The suqs of Basrah," 306.

145. This is the identification of this cloth proposed by Serjeant, *Islamic Textiles,* 56–57, although the matter is not completely settled.

146. Dastuwānī garments are mentioned by Ibn ʿAbd Rabbihi, *al-ʿIqd al-Farīd,* 4:267 and Yāqūt, *Muʿjam,* 2:574. Al-Suyūṭī (*Lubb al-Albāb,* ed. P. J. Veth under the title *Specimen e Litteris Orientalibus . . .* [Leyden, 1840–51], 105) identified Dastuwā as a cloth-

exporting settlement near Ahwāz, but it is not otherwise known.

147. *Kitāb al-Uyāun wa-l-Ḥadā'iq fi akhbar al-haga'iq*, ed. 'Umar Sa'idi (Dimashq, 1972), 3:15.

148. Maqdisī, *Aḥsan*, 117. Nāṣir-i Khusraw, in the mid-eleventh century, also recorded three market complexes in al-Baṣrah but listed them under different names, specifically Sūq Shuzā'ah (Bazar of the Khuzā'ah tribe), Sūq 'Uthmān (see above), and Sūq al-Qaddāḥīn (*Safar Nāmah*, Thackston's translation, 90–91). Although this last market still bore the name signifying vendors of drinking cups, the implication of Nāṣir's information is that by his time it had become important enough to give its name to the whole of the old Sūq al-Kabīr, of which it was formerly only a part.

149. Al-Maqdisī's omission of the Mirbaḍ from his list of Baṣrian market complexes may have been influenced by its never having been brought within the city wall and thereby projecting an aura of autonomy. Nevertheless, its decline is attested independently, and al-Maqdisī himself observed that the desert side of the city had fallen into ruin (chapter 2, note 86).

150. The references for these statements are furnished by Naji and Ali, "The suqs of Basrah," 309.

151. Waki', *Akhbār al-Quḍāt* (al-Qāhirah, A.H. 1366–69), vol. 1, p. 339: cited by Naji and Ali, "The sūqs," 339. In this connection it can be noted that al-Ṭabarī (*Ta'rīkh*, 13:71) reported that market sites were assigned on a first-come basis in the central sector of al-Kūfah.

152. Naji and Ali, "The suqs of Basrah," 300, citing al-Jāḥiẓ, *Kitāb al-Bukhalā'*, 120.

153. Cf. al-Māwardī, *Kitāb al-Aḥkām al-Sulṭānīyah* (al-Qāhirah, A.H. 1380), 258. In this connection it is not without interest to invoke al-Ṭabarī's account, citing Sayf ibn 'Umār (*Ta'rīkh*, 2493–94), of the disruption ensuing when noise from *sūqs* adjacent to the governor of Kūfah's living quarters was so deafening as to prevent Sa'd ibn Abī Waqqāṣ from conversing normally. When Sa'd was alleged to have remonstrated with the stall holders in 638, the gate to the citadel was burned by order of the caliph 'Umār.

154. Nāṣir-i Khusraw, *Safar Nāmah*, Thackston's translation, 91.

155. It will be recalled that only miniscule quantities of olive oil were being produced on the island in the tenth century, so that the merchants in Balarm (Palermo) no doubt manipulated the North African supply to their advantage.

156. Ibn Ḥawqal, *al-Masālik wa-l-Mamālik*, 119–20. The use of specialized terms for footwear would seem to imply that the manufacture and retailing of such items were somewhat diversified in Balarm in the tenth century, a situation to be inferred for similar reasons in Baghdād at much the same time (Lassner, *The Topography of Baghdād*, 249 n. 10).

157. Maqdisī, *Aḥsan*, 318: here, *Turthīth*. As long ago as 1928 William Marçais noticed that "le bazar marche d'accord avec la mosquée" and, further, cited an opinion of Mālik ibn Anas (ca. 715–95) that would have restricted the holding of Friday services to cathedral mosques in cities that also supported markets: "L'Islamisme et la vie urbaine," in *Comptes Rendus des Séances de l'Année 1928* (Académie des Inscriptions et Belles-Lettres, Paris, 1929), 86–100: reprinted in Marçais, *Articles et Conférences*, 59–67, where the reference is to p. 65. That not all *sūqs*, even the more important, were inevitably sited in the vicinity of a mosque is abundantly attested: Zabīd and 'Adan are representative instances of cities where the two institutions were specifically said to be a considerable distance apart (Maqdisī, *Aḥsan*, 84–85).

158. Maqdisī, *Aḥsan*, 161. It seems that his was probably the case at 'Anjar, although only thirty-two such shops have so far been excavated, all on the western side of the southern sector of the north-south axial street (Creswell, *A Short Account of Early Muslim Architecture*, 122).

159. Maqdisī, *Aḥsan*, 377, 425. It is likely that the principal *sūqs* in Nīshāpūr also manifested a cruciform plan.

160. Ibn Ḥawqal, *al-Masālik wa-l-Mamālik*, 437.

161. Maqdisī, *Aḥsan*, 281–82.

162. Ibid., 273, 462–63.

163. Ibid., 391.

164. Lassner, *The Shaping of 'Abbāsid Rule*, 185, 195.

165. Maqdisī, *Aḥsan*, 426, 440, 288–89; Whitcomb, *Ayla*, 9.

166. Ibn Ḥawqal, *al-Masālik wa-l-Mamālik*, 513 and Minorsky, *Ḥudūd*, 116.

167. Maqdisī, *Aḥsan*, 378.

168. Bakrī, *al-Masālik wa-l-Mamālik*, 79 and Maqdisī, *Aḥsan*, 356–57. It should not go unnoticed that Eugen Wirth has cast the *sūq* as developing its archetypical form only after the rise of Islam. In some places he seems to be writing about all urban markets but in others to have in mind only ribbon developments along main streets (e.g., "Strukturwandlungen und Entwicklungstendenzen der orientalischen Stadt," *Erdkunde* 22 [1968]; "Zum Problem des Bazars [sūq, çarşi]," *Der Islam*, 51 [1974]: 203–60 and 52 [1975]: 6–46; "Villes islamiques, villes arabes, villes orientales? Une problématique face au changement," in *La Ville Arabe dans l'Islam*, ed. A. Bouhdiba and D. Chevallier [Tunis and Paris, 1982]). The first alternative is demonstrably incorrect (H. Solṭanzāde has cited examples of *bāzārs*, in Sāsānian cities: *Moqaddameyī bar Tārīḫ-e šahr o šahrnešīnī dar Irān* [Tehran, A.H. 1365]) and the second, if true (and I hold it doubtful), was not, as Wirth deduces, the defining characteristic of something called "the Islamic city" but, more prosaically, an outcome of the way in which some large Middle Eastern cities came progressively to be organized between the first and tenth centuries, aided in some instances by opportunistic appropriations of spaces bordering colonnaded streets abandoned by previous traders.

169. J. H. Kramers and G. Wiet translate *murabba'ah* as "carrefour," which preserves the etymological implication of four features, in this case streets (*Configuration de la Terre*, 418). Schéfer had in fact suggested this reading in his translation of Nāṣir-i Khusraw's itinerary (*Safar Nāmah*, 1881), and Bulliet ("Medieval Nishapur," 73 n. 20) has recently approved it.

170. Translation suggested by de Goeje, *Bibliotheca Geographorum Arabicorum,* 4:357. Note this author's preference for a reading *fabricatores* rather than *opifices.*

171. Kramers and Wiet (*Configuration de la Terre,* 418) render this phase as *les petits fabricants,* basing themselves on de Goeje, *Bibliotheca Geographorum Arabicorum,* 4:282–83.

172. Ibn Ḥawqal, *al-Masālik wa-l-Mamālik,* 432–33.

173. For the verb *barbaqa* see de Goeje's note in *Bibliotheca Geographorum Arabicorum,* 4:186–87, especially his quotation from Von Kremer: "das Wort *barbaqa* bedeutet die flache Terrasse eines Hauses oder die Seiten desselben mit einer Steinmasse bestreichen, um sie gegen den Regen zu sichern."

174. For this use of *durūb* see Lane, *An Arabic-English Lexicon,* 1:866–67.

175. Cf. de Goeje, *Bibliotheca Geographorum Arabicorum,* 4: 215 and Reinhart Dozy, *Supplément aux Dictionnaires Arabes,* vol. 1 (Leyde, 1881), 295.

176. Maqdisī, *Aḥsan,* 413.

177. Ibid., 388.

178. Lassner, *The Shaping of ʿAbbāsid Rule,* 229.

179. Maqdisī, *Aḥsan,* 393. Yāqūt (*Muʿjam,* 3:537) salvaged from somewhere the information that the palace in question had been built by Khusrūjird, son of Shahān.

180. Maqdisī, *Aḥsan,* 141, 277, 283, 291.

181. Ibid., 292–93, 314.

182. Ibid., 310, 392, 425, 429; Ibn Ḥawqal, *al-Masālik wa-l-Mamālik,* 84; and Yaʿqūbī, *al-Buldān,* 260.

183. Maqdisī, *Aḥsan,* 409.

184. Watson, *Agricultural Innovation,* and more briefly "The Arab agricultural revolution." It is only fair to acknowledge that the very occurrence of such a green revolution has been challenged most vigorously by Bulliet (*Islam: The View from the Edge,* 68–71).

185. This list does not take account of the numerous plants exploited for fodder, condiments, drugs, cosmetics, perfumes, dyes, or garden and ornamental features. Watson ("The Arab agricultural revolution," 9) asserts that "a complete list of even only the useful plants" would number well into the hundreds.

186. For a selection of such instances see chapter 3.

187. In contemporary urban studies, *basic goods and services* are those produced for sale outside the immediate urban area, while those produced for sale within the local community are designated *nonbasic.*

188. P. 169 above. Al-Iṣṭakhrī, Ibn Ḥawqal, and Yāqūt said the same thing about Zāliqān (also Jāliqān) in Sijistān (note 146 of chapter 14).

189. See note 102 of chapter 16.

190. Al-Jahshiyārī, *Kitāb al-Wuzarāʾ,* 249. I have not consulted the Muṣṭafā al-Saqqāʾ et al. edition of this work.

191. Cited by Serjeant, *Islamic Textiles,* 22.

192. Balādhurī, *Futūḥ al-Buldān,* 47; Ibn Saʿd, *al-Ṭabaqāt,* E. Mittwoch edition (Leyden, 1905), 1:85 and 2:36; and al-Thaʿālibī, *Thimār al-Qulūb,* 484. For addition instances of the inclusion of textiles in tax schedules, consult Serjeant, *Islamic Textiles,* 10–11; for the *kharāj* at Bukhārā paid in textile fabrics, see p. 185 above. The Lisa Golombek quotation is from "The Draped Universe of Islam," in *Content and Context of Visual Arts,* ed. Priscilla Soucek (University Park., Pa., and London, 1988), 30.

193. Franz Rosenthal, *Ibn Khaldūn. The Muqaddimah,* vol. 1 (New York, 1958), 361–65. On p. 361 Rosenthal has an informative note (120) on Jirāb al-Dawlah.

194. Ibn Ḥawqal, *al-Masālik wa-l-Mamālik,* 159. I have been unable to discern the tense differences in accounts by al-Iṣṭakhrī (*al-Masālik wa-l-Mamālik,* 153) and Ibn Ḥawqal (299) that induced Eliyahu Ashtor (*A Social and Economic History of the Near East in the Middle Ages* [Berkeley, Calif., 1976], 151) to conclude that during the tenth century Fārsī *ṭirāz* workshops were being farmed out or sold to private entrepreneurs.

195. Nāṣir-i Khusraw, *Safar Nāmah,* Schéfer's translation, 111; Thackston's translation, 39. A wish-fulfilling myth current at the time had the emperor of Byzantium so anxious to control the production of *qaṣab* and *būqalamūn* that he was prepared to exchange a hundred of his cities for Tinnīs alone (ibid.).

196. Serjeant, *Islamic Textiles,* 21.

197. The diffusion of the "Old World cottons," *Gossypium arboreum,* Linn. and *G. herbaceum,* Linn., throughout the Islamic realm has been elicited by Watson, *Agricultural Innovation,* chap. 6.

198. Abū Bakr Aḥmad ibn ʿAli al-Ṣūfī al-Qussaynī/Kasdānī, better known as Ibn Waḥshīyah (the name varies considerably from manucript to manuscript), Al-Filāḥat al-Nabaṭīyah, Agr. Ms. 490 Dār al-Kutub, al-Qāhirah. The authorship and date of this work have provoked extended controversy, but Andrew Watson's close studies of the manuscript cited above have persuaded him that "a substantial part of the work was composed at the beginning of the 10th century": *Agricultural Innovation,* 219 n. 1. I have not been able to thoroughly digest Toufic Fahd's recent two-volume edition of this text, but see the bibliography for the full citation.

199. Maqrīzī, *al-Mawāʿiẓ,* 1:163.

200. Thaʿālibī, *al-Laṭāʾif al-Maʿārif,* 161 and Ashtor, *Social and Economic History,* p. 152.

201. Ashtor, *A Social and Economic History,* 153–54 and more generally the same author's *Histoire des Prix et des Salaires dans l'Orient Médiéval* (Paris, 1969), passim but especially pp. 90–94 and 261–65.

202. See pp. 148–49 and 151 above.

203. There is some useful information about the familial organization and business practices of the Fayyūmī textile trade in Yūsuf Rāġib, *Marchands d'Étoffes du Fayyoum au IIIe/IXe Siècle d'après leurs Archives (Actes et Lettres). Supplément aux Annales Islamologiques:* vol. 1, *Les Actes des Banū ʿAbd al-Muʾmin* (Le Caire, 1982); vol. 2, *La Correspondance Administrative et Privée des Banū ʿAbd al-Muʾmin* (Le Caire, 1985).

204. See also p. 162 above.

205. See also p. 168 above.

206. Maqdisī, *Aḥsan,* 411.

207. In his *Ta-T'ang Ta-Tz'ŭ-En Ssŭ San-tsang Fa-shih,* written in 817 (Tai-Shō edition), the Chinese monk Hui Lin was already referring to the production of cotton stuffs in Marv. For inscriptions recording the manufacture of linen cloth in the same city in 891 and 906, see Gaston Wiet, *L'Épigraphie Arabe de l'Exposition d'Art Persan du Caire. Mémoires Présentés à l'Institut d'Égypte* (Le Caire, 1935), 3.

208. Narshakhī, *Ta'rīkh Bukhārā,* 35; Frye's translation, 15–16.

209. Maqdisī, *Aḥsan,* 410. The Mashruqān canal branched off from the Dujayl River at the Great Weir at Tustar and rejoined the same river at ʿAskar Mukram. In addition to its role in the textile industry, it was the chief source of irrigation water for the premier sugarcane-growing district in Khūzistān. Cf. the Narsī fabrics *(thiyāb)* woven along the banks of the Nars canal in southern ʿIrāq: al-Masʿūdī, *Murūj,* 2:115.

210. This is the burden of J. Chabbi's perceptive paper on "Ribāṭ," in *The Encyclopaedia of Islam,* 2d ed., 8:493–506.

211. In medieval Arabic dictionaries *ribāṭ* is treated as the plural of the singular *rabīṭ* (used in a passive sense), signifying either "a group of horses (almost always mares) assembled for a *ghazū*" or "the place where these mares were kept hobbled and where they were fed." However, *ribāṭ* could also be read as a *maṣdar* (verbal noun) of the Form 3 verb *rābaṭa,* when it denoted *the act of* "assembling horses in readiness for a *ghazū*" (see Chabbi, "*Ribāṭ,*" 494). Herein lies the source of the misunderstandings described in the text.

212. Ibid.

213. An association somewhat overemphasized by Georges Marçais in an otherwise useful paper: "Note sur les *ribâṭs* en Berbérie," 395–430.

214. Chabbi, "Ribāṭ," 502.

215. Ibn Ḥawqal, *al-Masālik wa-l-Mamālik,* 73.

216. Maqdisī, *Aḥsan,* 4–5. More than two centuries later Yāqūt (*Muʿjam,* 4:661) would record five *quṣūr* enclosed within a defensive wall.

217. Chabbi, "Ribāṭ," 499–501.

218. Ibid., 500, citing Maqdisī, *Aḥsan,* 306; Narshakhī, *Ta'rīkh Bukhārā,* 15.

219. Maqdisī, *Aḥsan,* 272–73.

220. Chabbi, "Ribāṭ," 500.

221. Maqdisī, *Aḥsan,* 282 and Ibn Ḥawqal, *al-Masālik wa-l-Mamālik,* 489.

222. Maqdisī, *Aḥsan,* 273.

223. For *fidā'* see *The Encyclopaedia of Islam,* 2d ed., Supplement: 306–8.

224. Maqdisī, *Aḥsan,* 174.

225. Bakrī, *al-Masālik wa-l-Mamālik,* 36.

226. Nasser Rabbat, "Ribāṭ 2: Architecture," *The Encyclopaedia of Islam,* 2d ed., 8:506.

227. For discussions and plans of the *ribāṭ* at Sūsah (al-Sūs), see Creswell, *A Short Account of Early Muslim Architecture,* 286–88 and Alexandre Lézine, *Deux Villes d'Ifriqiya, Sousse, Tunis* (Paris, 1971), 82–88.

228. Balādhurī, *Futūḥ al-Buldān,* 132.

229. Ṭabarī, *Ta'rīkh,* 3:545.

230. Michael Bonner, "The name of the frontier: ʿawāṣim, thughūr, and the Arab geographers," *Bulletin of the School of Oriental and African Studies* 57 (1994): 17–24. Bonner has subsequently elaborated these ideas in a volume entitled *Aristocratic Violence and Holy War: Studies in the Jihad and the Arab-Byzantine Frontier* (New Haven, Conn., 1996).

231. This reading necessitates the rendering of *ʿawāṣim* as "inviolable ones" rather than "protectoresses."

232. During the first half of the eighth century the provinces of al-Jazīrah, Mawṣil, Armīniyah, Arran, Adhārbayjān (Azerbaijan), and sometimes Junjistān formed an inchoate and unstable conglomeration of administrative units, not infrequently assuming a quasi-independent status, which has been conveniently characterized by present-day scholars on numismatic grounds as "the Umayyad North." See M. Bates, "The dirham mint of the northern provinces of the Umayyad Caliphate," *Armenian Numismatic Journal* 15 (1989): 89–111 and D. A. Spellberg, "The Umayyad North: numismatic evidence for frontier administration," *Armenian Numismatic Society Museum Notes* 33 (1988): 119–27. This was the hitherto unmanageable aggregation of fiefdoms that Hārūn al-Rashīd was attempting to reorganize.

233. Hugh Kennedy in J. F. Haldon and Kennedy, "The Arab-Byzantine frontier in the eighth and ninth centuries: military organisation and society in the borderlands," *Recueil des Travaux de l'Institut d'Etudes Byzatines* (Belgrade) 19 (1980): 79–116. This paper deals with both Byzantine and Muslim frontier districts; Kennedy's contribution to the latter runs from p. 106 to p. 116.

234. For example, Ibn Serapion, in Le Strange, "Description of Mesopotamia and Baghdād," 48. *Kamḥ* in Yāqūt, *Muʿjam,* 4:304.

235. Yaʿqūbī, *al-Buldān,* 362; Wiet's translation, 230.

236. Abū ʿAmr al-Ṭarsūsī's tenth-century discussion of the *Thughūr (Siyar al-Thughūr)* has long been lost but is quoted extensively by Ibn al-ʿAdīm (1192–1262) in his *Bughyat al-Ṭalab fī Ta'rīkh Ḥalab.* Many of the citations from al-Ṭarsūsī have been extracted by Iḥsan ʿAbbās in *Shadharāt min Kutub Mufqūdah fī Ta'rīkh* (Bayrūt, A.H. 1408), to which the reader is here referred. See also C. Edmund Bosworth, "The city of Tarsus and the Arab-Byzantine frontiers in Early and Middle ʿAbbāsid times," *Oriens* 33 (1992): 268–86 and "Abū ʿAmr ʿUthmān al-Ṭarsūsī's *Siyar al-Thughūr* and the last years of Arab rule in Tarsus (Fourth/Tenth century)," *Graeco-Arabica* 5 (1993): 183–95. A good deal of al-Ṭarsūsī's information is confirmed in al-Muhallabī's *Kitāb al-Masālik wa-l-Mamālik* (usually known as *al-ʿAzīzī*), a work now lost except for fourteen folios mainly on Jerusalem and Damascus but preserved fragmentarily in writings by Yāqūt, Abū al-Fidā', and al-Qalqashandī.

237. *Qisiyy al-rijl.* For *shurrāfah* see de Goeje, *Bibliotheca Geographorum Arabicorum,* Indices, 4:273–74. Presumably the implied distinction between bows and bowmen means that at least some archers were responsible for more than one bow. It will be recalled that in medieval European warfare an archer shooting

from a platform or embrasure was usually accompanied by a varlet whose job it was to load a second bow while the first was being discharged.

238. Ṭarsūsī in Iḥsan ʿAbbās, *Shadharāt,* 446–49.

239. P. 120 above.

240. Ṭarsūsī (in Iḥsan ʿAbbās, *Shadharāt,* 452) notes that he himself had acquired this information not directly from Ibn Aṭīyah but from one Abū Naṣr Muḥammad ibn Aḥmad ibn al-Miḥāl.

241. Ibid., 452.

242. Ibid., 451–53. The Bushrā al-Rāghibī mentioned in the text was a *mawlā* of al-Muwaffaq, virtual ruler of the Caliphate during the time of al-Muʿtamid. The Qaḥṭabī family had descended from al-Ḥasan ibn Qaḥṭabah al-Ṭāʾī, who had quartered troops from Khurāsān, Khwarizm, and Transoxania in Ṭarsūs during the caliphate of al-Mahdī (r. 775–85). For additional information on al-Ṭarsūsī and his city, especially the disposition of the tithe revenues *(aʿshār)* from the farmlands surrounding Ṭarsūs, see Bosworth, "Abū ʿAmr ʿUthmān al-Tarsūsī's *Siyar al-Thughūr,*" 188–95.

243. Kennedy and Haldon, "The Arab-Byzantine frontier," 109.

244. Ibid., 112.

245. Peter von Sivers, "Taxation and trade in the ʿAbbāsid thughūr, 750–962/133–351," *Journal of the Economic and Social History of the Orient* 25, pt. 1 (1982): 81.

246. For the dire consequences arising from the fundamental incompatibility between fiscal and commercial interests in the ʿAbbāsid ruling class, see von Sivers, "Taxation and trade in the ʿAbbāsid thughūr," passim but especially pp. 89–99.

247. Lawrence I. Conrad, "The *quṣūr* of medieval Islam. Some implications for the social history of the Near East," *Al-Abhāth* 29 (1981): 7–23. Conrad's arguments closely parallel those advanced by Chabbi with respect to the variable forms and functions of *ribāṭs.* It may be noted in passing that the term *ḥiṣn* in the perspective of the whole Islamic world may sometimes invite a more varied definition than that espoused by de Goeje in *Bibliotheca Geographorum Arabicorum,* Indices, 4:216: "murus qui circumdat urbem."

248. The formation and development of the *amṣār* are summarized in chapter 2. This usage of the term is to be clearly differentiated from the same word's occurrence in al-Maqdisī's technical vocabulary.

249. Akbar, "Khaṭṭa," 22–32. See also the same author's *Crisis in the Built Environment: The Case of the Muslim City* (Singapore, 1988), chap. 4.

250. The concepts deriving from the root *KhṬṬ* are neatly summarized by Ibn Manẓūr (d. 1312) in his *Lisān al-ʿArab,* 1:858. Fee simple was denoted by Arabic *iqṭāʿ tamlīk,* usufruct by *iqṭāʿ istighlāl.*

251. Akbar, "Khaṭṭa," 29.

252. Balādhurī, *Futūḥ al-Buldān,* 342.

253. Literally, "They did not do that until they had arrived at an agreed opinion" *(wa-lam yafʿalū dhālika illa ʿan raʾyin attafaqū ʿalayhi):* al-Māwardī, *al-Aḥhām al-Sulṭānīyah,* 179–80.

254. Al-Ṭabarī, *Taʾrīkh,* 1:2488.

255. One cubit in this context = a little more than fifty centimeters.

256. Jamel Akbar, citing al-Māwardī, *al-Aḥkām al-Sulṭānīyah,* notes that the main thoroughfares functioned as *mirbaḍs,* which he defines as horse stalls (presumably in addition to their roles as corridors of movement): "Khaṭṭa," 26 and *Crisis in the Built Environment,* 86. It is true that Ibn Manẓūr (*Lisān al-ʿArab,* 1:1105) defined *mirbaḍ* in this way, but he was invoking a meaning that had become attached to the term relatively recently. In texts relating to the founding of the *amṣār,* I think it is best to retain the earlier meaning of *mirbaḍ* as "a floor for the drying of dates." Cf. chapter 2, note 85. A late source (Yāqūt, *Muʿjam,* 2:635) reports that the open space in the center of the settlement was called al-Dahnāʾ.

257. Nezar AlSayyad, *Cities and Caliphs,* 51.

258. Ṭabarī (*Taʾrīkh,* 1:2487) relates the almost certainly archetyped tale that the dimensions of the *ṣaḥn* were determined by an archer standing on the site designated for the mosque and shooting arrows in four directions. The whole tone of the account of the founding of al-Kūfah is strongly ritualistic, even to the extent of being furnished with an ex post facto prophecy that "A town shall be built on the site, whose people shall bring about the destruction of the Persians" (Ibn al-Faqīh, *al-Buldān,* 162). Charles Wendell is inclined to suspect Persian influence in the method of determining the dimensions of the central square of the cantonment ("Baghdād," 109). Certainly, al-Kūfah was close to Sāsānian foundations such as al-Hīrah, Sadīr, and al-Khawarnaq, and the columns of the colonnade *(ẓullah)* of the cathedral mosque were actually appropriated from nearby buildings (*wa kānat ẓullatuhā miʾatay dhirāʿin ʿalā asātīni rukhāmin kānat li-l-Akāsirati:* Ṭabarī, *Taʾrīkh,* 1:2489). Furthermore, it cannot be without relevance in this context that, after the Battles of Qādisīyah, al-Madāʾin, and Jalūlāʾ, all in 637, no less than four thousand Daylamite converts to Islam had settled in al-Kūfah (Balādhurī, *Futūḥ al-Buldān,* 280). Cf. also Djaït, *Al-Kūfa,* 92.

In Ibn Maẓūr's *Lisān al-ʿArab* a bowshot *(ghilwah)* is specified as one twenty-fifth of a *farsakh* (15:132–33), that is, 240 meters.

It should not go unremarked that al-Kūfah, like al-Baṣrah, was founded before a centralized Islamic administration had been put in place in al-ʿIrāq.

259. Ṭabarī, *Taʾrīkh,* 1:2489.

260. *Ḥattā idhā aqāmū ʿalā shayʾ:* lit, "when they agreed upon something" (Tabarī, *Taʾrīkh,* 1:2488).

261. Balādhurī, *Futūḥ al-Buldān,* 276–77; Ṭabarī, *Taʾrīkh,* 1: 2488. The reason for this exception is nowhere explained.

262. In later times special *khiṭāṭ* reserved for members of small tribes incapable of sustaining *khiṭāṭ* of their own were known as *afnīyah,* sing. *fināʾ* (a term that had originally denoted the open space adjacent to a *badawī*'s tent where outsiders under the owner's protection would pitch their own tents). A representative example comes from Gurgān, where a mosque was named for such a tribally diverse community. See Bulliet, *Islam,* 74.

263. Ṭabarī, *Taʾrīkh,* 1:2490–91.

264. Sayf in ibid., 1:2490. In my reading of the sources, they do not support al-Janābī's reconstruction of al-Kūfah as a rigor-

ously orthogonal cantonment (*Takhṭīṭ,* 77), an interpretation subsequently adopted by Nezar AlSayyad (*Cities and Caliphs,* 55–69). Hichem Djaït (*Al-Kūfa,* 118) seems to favor this interpretation in principle, although he concedes that "Le symétrie . . . n'est pas parfaite dans le schéma de Sayf [ibn ʿUmar]" and that "Nous ne pouvons que procéder par touches, impressions, nous fonder sur le probable, jamais sur le certain." It is also to be noted that Sayf continues, "The *khiṭaṭ* were situated in the space beyond and between the roads."

265. The Arabic sentence is *fa ikhtaṭṭū biha wa-akhadhū safḥ al-jabal:* Maqrīzī, *al-Mawāʿiẓ,* 1:298.

266. Literally, "They settled before other people and [therefore] possessed these places" *(fa-nazalū fī muqaddimati al-nās wa-hādhihi al-mawāḍiʿ):* ibid.

267. Ibid., 1:297. See also Caetani, *Annali,* 4:589 et seq. The Ahl al-Ẓāhir in Jāhilī times appear to have been tribal outcasts who banded together as brigands. Captured and then freed by Muḥammad, in early Islamic times they became known as al-ʿAtaqa' (= "Freedmen").

268. Maqrīzī, *al-Mawāʿiẓ,* 1:297.

269. Ibid. The Ahl al-Rāyah (= "People of the Banner") comprised members from several tribes, among which the most prestigious were Quraysh and Anṣār (this latter group being Madīnan agriculturalists of the Banū-Aws and Khazraj tribes). Other groups who mustered under this banner (allegedly bestowed on them by ʿAmr) were Ghifār, Jarīsh, Kinānah, Thaqīf, ʿAbs, and Tamīm, together with individuals from so-called South Arabian tribes and the ʿAtaqa' (cf. note 267 above): see ʿAbd al-Ḥakam, *Futūḥ Miṣr,* 116; Ibn Duqmāq, *al-Intiṣār,* 4:3; Maqrīzī, *al-Mawāʿiẓ,* 1:296; and al-Qalqashandī, *Ṣubḥ al-Aʿshā,* 3:327; also Caetani, *Annali,* 4:584, 588. Kubiak (*Al-Fustat,* 62) estimates that the Ahl al-Rāyah never exceeded four hundred, or at most five hundred, men.

270. Maqrīzī, *al-Mawāʿiẓ,* 1:246. This account seems to have derived ultimately from al-Kindī's lost work on the Masjid Ahl al-Rāyah, but less detailed versions probably traceable to al-Quḍāʿi (d. 1062) were preserved by both Yāqūt (*Muʿjam,* 3:898) and Ibn Duqmāq (*al-Intiṣār,* 62).

271. Maqrīzī, *al-Mawāʿiẓ,* 1:297.

272. Cited by ibid. and Ibn Duqmāq, *al-Intiṣār,* 4:3.

273. The members of the council were Muʿāwiyah ibn Ḥudayj of the Tujīb, Sharīk ibn Sumayy of the Ghuṭayfah branch of the Murād, ʿAmr ibn Qaḥzam of the Khawlān, and Ḥayawīl ibn Nāshirah of the Maʿāfir. This list is preserved in several late works, but only al-Maqdisī ascribes it to al-Quḍāʿi.

274. Guest, "The foundation of Fustat," 83.

275. It behooves me to acknowledge that Saleh al-Hathloul has strongly contested this view, asserting instead that the tribes arranged themselves wholly in accordance with a preplanned, centrally organized system of *khiṭaṭ:* "Tradition, Continuity, and Change in the Physical Environment," 39–40.

That the type of settlement process envisaged here is not totally alien to present-day *badū* pasturing in the Levant and North Arabia is attested by Jabbur in *The Bedouins and the Desert:*

> When they *(badū)* reach the land where they are going to camp, they wait until the shaykh selects a place to pitch his tent. Then the tribe spreads out around him and the master of every household selects a place to pitch his own tent. (291)
>
> When they make camp their tents are usually arranged in lines, each line about 60 meters from the next, so that there will be space for the tent ropes and for the passage of camels between them. A single camp may sometimes be as large as 300 tents, if the available water supplies can support such a number and if the tribe is this large. (289–90)

Certainly, citations of current ethnographic practice have no probative value for the tenth century, but they cannot on that account be denied a certain limited suggestiveness.

276. Khaleel Ibrahim al-Muaikel, *Study of the Archaeology of the Jawf Region, Saudi Arabia* (Riyadh, A.D. 1994/A.H. 1414). On Wadd in Dūmat al-Jandal see Yāqūt, *Muʿjam,* 5:366–67.

277. Abdullah al-Wohaibi, *The Northern Hijaz in the Writings of the Arab Geographers,* 113–19 and Laura Veccia Vaglieri, *The Encyclopaedia of Islam,* 2d ed., 4:1137–43. Al-Wāqidī repeatedly characterizes the people of Khaybar as living in fortresses and on one occasion has al-Tābūt refer to their "impregnable lofty towers" (*al-Maghāzī,* Jones edition, 176). Half a millennium later Yāqūt (*Muʿjam,* 2:503–5) lists seven *ḥuṣūn* within the environs of Khaybar.

278. Wohaibi, *The Northern Hijaz in the Writings of the Arab Geographers,* 293–300. Other Arabian settlements that have been investigated in recent years, most effectively by archaeologists, include the following:

- ***Al-Maʿbīyāt,*** believed to be the site of al-Qurah/Qurā'/Qurḥ, where residential structures from the tenth and eleventh centuries appear to have been grouped so as collectively to form an irregular defensive perimeter (cf. note 14 to chapter 7 and M. Gilmore, M. Ibrahim, G. Mursi, and Dh. Al-Talhi, "A preliminary report on the first season of excavations at al-Mabiyat, an early Islamic site in the northern Hijaz," *ATLAL* 9 [1985]: 109–25).
- ***Najrān,*** in northern Yaman, had already a long history before the Islamic conquest. It was, in fact, the principal center of Christianity in South Arabia, with Monophysitism prevailing over various other denominations. The apogee of the city's prestige extended over the half century from 525, when, under Byzantine protection, it functioned as one of the premier pilgrimage centers on the peninsula and a martyropolis of renown (*τὴν πόλιν τῶν μαρτύρων* in the *Martyrium Arethae,* ed. E. Carpenter, *Acta Sanctorum,* vol. 10 [1861], 721–59), responsibilities that were expressed architecturally in the building of churches and monasteries and in the pilgrim-attracting martyrion known as Kaʿbat Najrān, under the custodianship of the Banū al-Ḥārith ibn Kaʿb, the chief Arab tribe in Najrān (Hishām ibn Muḥammad ibn al-Kalbī [d. 819 or 820], *al-Aṣnām,* Faris translation, 38–39). The core of the settlement at this time appears to have been a stone citadel known today as al-Ukhdūd, within which the excavator of the site has tentatively identified the Kaʿbah

mentioned above. The walls give the impression of having been composite constructions, much in the manner of al-Maʿbīyāt, rather than unitary architectural enterprises (J. Zarins et al., "Preliminary report on the Najrān/Ukhdūd survey and excavations 1982/1402 A.H.," *ATLAL* 7 (1983): 22–40). During the Byzantine and early Islamic periods there was a movement of population to a mud *(libn)*-built settlement stretching northeastward from the citadel. Even if this migration was initiated in pre-Muslim times, it was accelerated when the caliph ʿUmar (r. 634–44) ordered the almost exclusively Christian inhabitants of Najrān to evacuate their city. Nevertheless, Christian bishops were recorded in the city in the ninth and tenth centuries, and al-Bakrī mentions the existence of a fine, mosaic-decorated church at an undetermined date (al-Bakrī, *Muʿjam mā Istaʿjama,* Wüstenfeld edition, 1:367). In any case, a considerable number of the Banū al-Ḥārith eventually converted to Islam and helped form a small town that, in the tenth century, was well known for its leather crafts. No traces of town walls or gateways have come to light in this *extra muros* settlement, which presumably comprised Islamic Najrān.

It is not possible to connect the architectural form of al-Ukhdūd (pre-Islamic Najrān) directly with that of any early Muslim foundation in the Levant. Although it shared a square perimeter with, say, ʿAnjar or Waylah (al-ʿAqabah), the international dispositions of the two cities were fundamentally different, and the composite construction of the walls of al-Ukhdūd contrasted not only with the Levantine cities named but also with other South Arabian sites such as Maʾrib, al-Asdahil, or al-Baydāʾ. It is, however, a technique not unknown in the ʿAsīr highlands today and in the uplands south of Sanaʿāʾ. See G. R. D. King, "Settlement in Western and Central Arabia and the Gulf in the Sixth–Eighth Centuries A.D.," in King and Cameron, *Land Use and Settlement Patterns,* 202. For societal differentiation in pre-Islamic Najrān see Pigulevskaja, "Les rapports sociaux à Nedjrān,"

- ***Al-Rabaḍah*** is best known as a relatively important station on the Darb Zubaydah, with a floruit in the later eighth and the ninth centuries. However, Ibn Rustah's assertion that the settlement had existed in the *Jāhilīyah (al-Aʿlāq,* [ca. 903], 179; Wiet's translation, 207) has been amply confirmed by recent archaeological excavations (Saʿd A. al-Rashīd, *Al-Rabadhah. A Portrait of Early Islamic Civilisation in Saudi Arabia* [al-Riyāḍ, 1986]). The sequence of occupancy seems to have been something as follows. In pre-Islamic times the settlement had functioned as the center of tracts of reserved grazing land *(ḥimā)* under the control of a nomadic *shaykh,* probably in the name of a tribal deity. Under the Islamic dispensation, which put an end to many pagan practices, *ḥimā* conveyed only a secular connotation, namely government-controlled pasturage for the camels of the Muslim armies (Māwardī, *al-Aḥkām al-Sulṭānīyah,* 322–25; Fagnan's translation, 397–401, with special reference to al-Rabadhah on p. 398). Both pre-Islamic and Islamic usage of these pastures accords well with Ibn Rustah's remark that "there is plenty of water from tanks and wells." Apparently, the Muslim *ḥimā* was constituted by the second caliph, ʿUmar ibn al-Khaṭṭāb (r. 634–44). Under the ʿAbbāsids the settlement comprised a series of fortified structures, which Rāshid has interpreted as grain stores and possibly disbursement centers, interspersed among clusters of residences. It is not unreasonable to suppose that the pre-Islamic settlement had grown up around fortified lineage strongholds, perhaps of the type *(aṭām)* recorded for Yathrib at much the same time. It is to be inferred that Umayyad influence became strong in the settlement at about the turn of the eighth century (King, "Settlement in Western and Central Arabia," 200), but its greatest expansion certainly took place under the ninth- and tenth-century ʿAbbāsids, who incorporated it in their encompassing development of the Darb Zubaydah. From this period date the congregational mosque reported by Ibn Rustah, an immense circular reservoir of the type common along the Darb, and the manufacture of metal, glass, and soapstone objects. Although these industries were small in scale, their products appear to have exceeded the requirements of the settlement, which raises the likelihood that they were in fact curios and talismans for sale to pilgrims. At the same time, the tomb of Abū Dharr al-Ghifārī was being mentioned as a noteworthy feature of the settlement. Al-Ghifārī was an ascetic Companion of the Prophet who died in al-Rabaḍa in 652–53, and it is tempting to speculate that he had gone, or been sent, there in connection with Rāshidūn administration of the *ḥimā.* In any case, Qarāmiṭah insurrections in the tenth century, together with changes in ʿAbbāsid priorities and abandonment of the great caliphal pilgrimage, resulted in a decline in the upkeep of facilities along the road; and toward the end of the tenth century al-Maqdisī noted briefly that al-Rabadhah was in ruins and its water bitter (*Aḥsan,* 108).
- ***Qanāʾ*** was well attested in pre-Islamic times as an entrepôt on the South Arabian coast for the collection and transshipment of frankincense (e.g., G. W. B. Huntingford, ed. and trans., *The Periplus of the Erythraean Sea,* The Hakluyt Society, 2d ser., 151 [London, 1980], 35, 102). During the sixth century there seems to have been a shift in the focus of the settlement from the shore to the fortress of Māwiyal on the hill known as Ḥusn al-Ghurāb. However, the lower city continued at least into Umayyad times, and Dr. Whitcomb has interpreted the remains—two rectangular enclosures of roughly the same size—respectively as Waylah (170 meters by 150 meters) and Ukhdūd (250 by 230 meters): see Whitcomb, "Urbanism in Arabia," 48–49; cf. also Piotrovsky, "Late ancient and early medieval Yemen," 219. Five seasons of Soviet excavation at this site have been summarized by A. V. Sedov: "New archeological and epigraphic material from Qana (South Arabia)," *Arabian Archaeology and Epigraphy* 3 (1982): 110–37.

Other pre-Islamic Arabian settlements are known from both texts and archaeological surveys of varying degrees of intensity—Taymāʾ, al-Qaṣīm, al-Yamāmah, Shabwah, al-Aflaj, al-Baḥrayn, Faylakah, and Sīr Banī-Yās, to cite only a few of the more promising—but none has thus far yielded a firm basis for comparative study (This material is summarized by King, "Settlement in Western and Central Arabia," 192–94, 205–12. There is a compendious overview of Sāsānian and Early Islamic al-Baḥrayn in Curtis E. Larsen's *Life and Land Use on the Bahrain Islands* [Chicago, 1983], 84–87. See also V. Bernard and J.-F. Salles, "Discovery of a Christian church at al-Qusur, Failaka [Kuwait]," *Proceedings of the Seminar for Arabian Studies* 21 [1991]: 7–21). Qaryat al-Fāw, in the early centuries A.D. the capital of the Kindah confederacy, is the best documented to date. A palace, royal tombs, domestic structures of various types, and a market complex have been unearthed, but the organization of the settlement, which inscriptions placed under the control of the nomadic tribes of Kindah, Qaḥṭan, and Madhhij, is still far from clear (A. R. al-Ansary, *Qaryat al-Fau. A Portrait of Pre-Islamic Civilisation in Saudi Arabia* [al-Riyādh, 1982]).

279. In this connection it is not without interest that Ibn ʿAbd Rabbihi (*al-ʿIqd al-Farīd,* 3:97) cites Ibn al-Kalbī as listing six *ummahāt al-qurā al-ʿarabīyah,* namely Yathrib, al-Ṭā'if, Khaybar, Wādī al-Qurā, Dūmat al-Jandal, and al-Yamāmā.

280. The archaeological evidence underpinning our perceptions of al-Ḥīrah is summarized by D. Talbot Rice, "The Oxford excavations at Ḥīra," *Ars Islamica* 1 (1934): 51–73 and more generally by Beeston and Shahīd in *The Encyclopaedia of Islam,* 2d ed., 3:462–63. The city's cantonment origin is implied both by etymology and by several legends recounted by Yāqūt (*Muʿjam,* 2: 375–79).

281. Djaït, *Al-Kūfa,* 94–95.

282. Whitcomb, "The *Miṣr* of Ayla," 155–70 and "Islam and the Socio-Cultural Transition of Palestine—Early Islamic Period (638–1099 CE)," in *The Archaeology of Society in the Holy Land,* ed. T. E. Levy (London, 1995), 488–501.

283. See Harrison, "The early Umayyad settlement at Ṭabariyah," 51–59.

284. Donald Whitcomb, "Amṣār in Syria? Syrian cities after the conquest," *ARAM* 6 (1994): 18–19 and "Islam and the Socio-Cultural Transition of Palestine," 492. The eight city gates *(durūb)* of al-Ramlah (Ramleh) as enumerated by al-Maqdisī (*Aḥsan,* 165) in the following order were those of, literally, the Soldier's Well (Bi'ir al-ʿAskar, but al-Maqdisī [*Aḥsan,* 27] notes that al-ʿAskar was the name of a particular quarter *[maḥallah]* of al-Ramlah, so the name should probably be understood as Gate of the Well of the ʿAskar Quarter); the ʿAnnabah Mosque (ʿAnnabah being a village to the west of al-Ramlah); Bayt al-Maqdis (Jerusalem); of Baylaʿah (presumably the village of Bāliʿah that Yāqūt [*Muʿjam,* 1:479] assigned to the Balqā'; identified by Ranking and Azoo [*Aḥsanu,* 271 n. 3] with ancient Kirjath-Baal, present-day Kuryet el-Enāb); Ludd; Yāfā; Miṣr (Egypt); and Dājūn (ancient Beth Dagon, now Bayt Dajan, a short distance to the east of Yāfā [Jaffa]). Whitcomb reads these gates as beginning with Bi'r al-ʿAskar in the south and proceeding in a counterclockwise direction.

285. Balādhurī, *Futūḥ al-Buldān,* 131.

286. *The Encyclopaedia of Islam,* 2d ed., 2:360.

287. See note 40 to chapter 6 and Whitcomb, "Amsār in Syria?" 25–26. Also see "Out of Arabia" and especially "Diocletian's *miṣr* at Aqaba," *Zeitschrift des Deutschen Palästinavereins* 106 (1990): 156–61.

288. Whitcomb, "Amṣār in Syria?" 19. For a summary of the excavations undertaken at the site of ʿAnjar in the 1950s, see Maurice Chehab, "The Umayyad palace at ʿAnjar," *Ars Orientalis* 5 (1963): 17–27.

289. Whitcomb, "Amṣār in Syria?" 24–25. V. Tsaferis's excavations are reported in *Excavations at Capernaum,* vol. 1: *1978–1982* (Winona Lake, Ind., 1989).

290. Balādhurī, *Futūḥ al-Buldān,* 332.

291. Whitcomb, "The city of Istakhr and the Marvdasht plain," 363–70.

292. Whitcomb, *Before the Roses and Nightingales,* especially chap. 4.

293. Al-Qayrawān (Kairouan) appears to have been established some twelve kilometers southeast of al-Qarn, where the Arab commander Muʿāwiyah ibn Ḥudayj had already planted a garrison camp *(qayrawān)* as early as 654/55. Al-Malikī (*Riyāḍ,* 1:17–18) refers to Ibn Ḥudayj as "having laid out a *madīnah* in the neighborhood of al-Qarn" *(ikhtaṭṭa madīnatan ʿind al-Qarn).*

294. A. F. L. Beeston et al., *Sabaic Dictionary (English-French-Arabic)* (Beirut, 1982), s.v. "S.R.W." and J. C. Biella, *Dictionary of Old South Arabic. Sabaean Dialect* (Chico, Calif., 1982), 431.

295. Ibn Manẓūr, *Lisān al-ʿArab,* 5:175. For pertinent comments on the etymology of *miṣr* see C. Fontinoy, "Les noms de l'Égypte en hébreu et leur étymologie," *Chronique d'Égypte* 64 (1989): 90–97. The precise relationship between the triptote *miṣr,* with its plural *amṣār,* and the diptote *Miṣr* = Egypt has not been satisfactorily explicated, despite the shared etymological origin of these words.

296. This semantic evolution of the term *miṣr* has been summarized compendiously by Paul M. Cobb: "Al-Amṣār: Civic and Semantic Development in the Early Islamic Period" (typescript, University of Chicago, 1991). Lexicographers, from the nature of their trade, tend to be conservative, so it comes as no surprise that they should have preserved longer than most the idea of *miṣr* as a border territory. Al-Azharī (quoting Aḥmad ibn Yaḥyā Thaʿlab, who died in 904), for example, defines *miṣr* as a barrier *(ḥājiz)* between two territories (*arḍān* [cited by Cobb, "Al-Amṣār," 5]).

297. Cited by Cobb, "Al-Amṣār," 3.

298. Abū Bakr Muḥammad ibn al-Ḥasan ibn Durayd, *Al-Jamharat al-Lughah* (Baghdād, A.H. 1392), 2:359.

299. For a study of this exclusivity as reflected in *ḥadīth* collections, see M. J. Kister, "'Do not assimilate yourselves . . . ,': *lā tashabbahū,*" *Jerusalem Studies in Arabic and Islam* 12 (1989): 321–71.

300. Balādhurī, in reporting the instructions of the caliph ʿUmar regarding the foundation of al-Kūfah (*Futūḥ al-Buldān,* 275), actually used the term *dār al-hijrah* and further characterized the proposed settlement as a *qayrawān,* usually rendered into English by a phrase such as "garrison camp" or "military base."

301. Djaït, *Al-Kūfa,* passim but especially p. 302 (it should be noted that this author's remarks apply only to al-Kūfah); AlSayyad, *Cities and Caliphs,* passim; and Whitcomb, "Amṣār in Syria?" 14, 18. Nor has speculation on this topic been confined to recent authors: early in the twentieth century, Jūrjī Zaydān attempted an

idealized reconstruction of a Muslim army camp that also incorporated a strong orthogonal component (*Taʾrīkh al-Tamaddun al-Islamīyah,* vol. 3 [Al-Qāhirah, A.H. 1322]). The cultural antecedents of these orthogonal grids are usually designated as Hellenistic cities and more immediately as late-Roman camps.

302. Representative evocations of supposedly chaotic tribal encampments can be found in several of the *amṣār*-related references cited in chapter 2, particularly in works by Lammens, Guest, and Massignon, together with Creswell, *Early Muslim Architecture,* not previously cited.

303. Whitcomb ("Amṣār in Syria? 25) refers to Waylah as "morphologically transitional between late Roman legionary camps and the *quṣūr,*" a statement that would presumably hold for ʿAnjar, even though it was roughly twice the size of Waylah. Then he adds, "The cultural antecedent for these patterns was the orthogonal grid derived from the Classical cities and, more immediately, from late Roman camps such as al-Lajjūn and Udhruḥ."

304. Paul M. Cobb, "The Missing *Amṣār* of Syria: Alternative Urbanization at Ḥimṣ" (typescript, University of Chicago, 1993), fig. 2.

305. Whitcomb, "Amṣār in Syria?" 28.

306. AlSayyad, *Cities and Caliphs,* 72.

307. The terminology is, of course, that of Émile Durkheim, *De la Division du Travail Social: Étude sur l'Organisation des Sociétés Supérieures* (Paris, 1893), chaps. 2, 3.

308. It will be recalled that *Ḥīrah* is an Arabicization of Aramaic *Ḥērthā.*

309. More than a century earlier, in 427, the Arab *shaykh* known most commonly as Aspebet (actually a Persian title) had been consecrated "Bishop of the Encampments" in the Judaean desert by Juvenal, bishop of Jerusalem.

310. Th. Nöldeke identified many of these features as long ago as 1875 ("Zur Topographie und Geschichte des Damascenischen Gebietes und der Haurângegend," *Zeitschrift der Deutschen Morgenländischen Gesellschaft* 29 [1875]: 419–44). It is not without interest that Markabta, the site of a Synod convened by Dādīshōʿ, Catholicos of Soleucia, in 424 was itself a *ḥērthā,* "the seat of the Ṭāyyāye (Arab. Ṭayy) confederation" (J. B. Chabot, ed., *Synodicon Orientale. Notices et Extraits des Manuscrits,* vol. 37 [Paris, 1902], 285, 676). The location of this settlement has not been identified.

311. Walter E. Kaegi, *Byzantium and the Early Islamic Conquests* (Cambridge, 1992), 55.

312. Al-Balādhurī, *Futūḥ al-Buldān,* 144–45. In addition to Tanūkh, by about 600 other Christian tribes resident within the vicinity included Taghlib and Bahrāʾ (Yaʿqūbī, *al-Buldān,* 324; Yāqūt, *Muʿjam,* 5:158).

313. There is an eminently sensible discussion of the term *parembolē* (pl. *parembolai*) by Irfan Shahīd in his *Byzantium and the Arabs in the Fifth Century* (Washington, D.C., 1989), 212–13. The fact that *pará* = "beside" and *parabállo* = "place beside" would seem to imply a distinctively subordinate settlement as well as one probably less permanent than a regular *castra.* It is extremely likely that the Greek word was rendered into Arabic as *ḥīrah.*

314. P. Féderlin in R. Génier, *Vie de Saint Euthyme le Grand* (Paris, 1909), 104–11. The exact site of this parembolē was close to Bīʾr al-Zarāʿah.

315. J. Spencer Trimingham, *Christianity among the Arabs in Pre-Islamic Times* (London and Beirut, 1979), 119, citing R. Dussaud and F. Macler, *Voyage Archéologique au Ṣafâ et dans le Djebel el-Drûz* (Paris, 1901), no. 7 and *Publications of the Princeton University Archaeological Expeditions to Syria:* (a) 1899–1900, (b) 1904–5, section A, pt. 3 (Princeton, N.J., 1908), no. 752.

316. Acts 21:34–35. In view of the fairly substantial buildings that have been brought to light at Bīʾr al-Zarāʿah, it need occasion no surprise that this *parembolē* was approached by way of a flight of steps (up which the apostle Paul was hustled). Cf. also Heb. 13:11, 13.

317. Although the name Baghdād was attested as early as 1800 B.C., modern authors have tended to regard it as transmitted through either Persian or Aramaic, the former suggesting meanings such as "gift of God," the latter "sheep enclosure" (for which see Y. Ghanīmah and A. Karmalī in *Lughat al-ʿArab,* 4:27, 6:748). There is a useful summary of this debate by A. A. Duri in *The Encyclopaedia of Islam,* 2d ed., 1:894.

318. Qurʾān 6 *(al-Anʿām)*:127: "For them is the abode of peace with their Lord"; cf. 10 *(Yūnus)*:25. Other appellations encountered in medieval sources include Madīnat Abī Jaʿfar, Madīnat al-Manṣūr, Madīnat al-Khulafāʾ, and al-Zawrāʾ. The last term (= "the crooked") probably derived from the offset entrances incorporated in the outer gateways of the surrounding wall; for a discussion of the name see Lassner, *The Shaping of ʿAbbāsid Rule,* 164–68.

319. To the references in note 189 to chapter 2, add Creswell (revised by Allan), *A Short Account of Early Muslim Architecture,* chap. 10. The interpretation of the Round City espoused here is essentially that proposed by Jacob Lassner in the two works listed under his name in note 189.

320. Lassner, *The Topography of Baghdad,* 142.

321. Tabarī, *Taʾrīkh,* 3:276.

322. Yaʿqūbī, *al-Buldān,* 238.

323. Ibid., 240–41 preserves the names of all the principal streets.

324. For comments on the dimensions of the bricks used in the building of the Round City see Creswell, *A Short Account of Early Muslim Architecture,* 230–31. Mud bricks were used in construction of the walls, burnt bricks for tunnel vaults and domes. The size of the Round City is given variously by medieval authors. The figure adopted here, on the advice of Lassner (*The Shaping of ʿAbbāsid Rule,* 291 n. 17), is a conversion to contemporary measure of the *mil* that the Khatīb al-Baghdādī (*Taʾrīkh,* 71; Lassner, *The Topography of Baghdad,* 51) attributed to Rabāḥ, the architect who built the wall of the complex.

325. Yaʿqūbī, *al-Buldān,* 237; Wiet's translation, 10.

326. Khaṭīb, *Taʾrīkh,* 67; Lassner's translation (*Khutat Baghdad fi al-ʾuhud al-Abbasiyah al-ulʾa* [Baghdad, 1984]), 46; Yaʿqūbī, *al-Buldān,* 238.

327. For a list of such cities see Creswell, *A Short Account of Early Muslim Architecture,* 236. Not unexpected, the closest parallels with the Round City (Hatra, Dārābjird, Gūr [subsequently Fīrūzābād], and Ctesiphon) date from Parthian and/or Sāsānian times.

328. Notable proponents of this cosmological interpretation of the plan of Madīnat al-Salām are H. P. L'Orange (*Studies in the Iconography of Cosmic Kingship in the Ancient World* [Cambridge, 1953], 12–14), who characterizes the caliphal precinct (which he designates Baghdād) as the "unsurpassable incarnation" of this tradition of urban design; and Wendell ("Baghdād," 99–128), for whom the Round City was "a schematic representation of the world—essentially that of the Sassanian monarchs—in purely formal aniconic terms . . . and may represent a shadowy survival of the moving camp and court of the ancient Indo-Iranian conquerors who would 'recreate' the world at each stage of their progress across Asia." Both of these authors worked in a tradition of inquiry that was known to Sir Thomas Browne in the seventeenth century; flowered in the continental European *Omphalosstudien* of the early decades of the twentieth century; was given formal coherence by Müller in his *Die Heilige Stadt;* and has recently been given new life by James S. Duncan in *The City as Text: The Politics of Landscape Interpretation in the Kandyan Kingdom* (Cambridge, 1990). For a brief overview of the urban morphologies to which this system of beliefs gave rise, see Paul Wheatley, "City as Symbol" (inaugural lecture delivered at University College London, 20 November 1967 [London, 1969]).

329. Wakīʿ in Khaṭīb, *Taʾrīkh,* 72; Lassner's translation, 52.

330. Lassner, *The Shaping of ʿAbbāsid Rule,* 229.

331. Ibid., 230.

332. According to Lassner (ibid., 194), the Round City, even without its suburban developments, was larger than "any known urban center in upper Iraq since the beginning of recorded history."

333. Khaṭīb, *Taʾrīkh,* 79–80; Lassner's translation, 60–61; and Ṭabarī, *Taʾrīkh,* 3:325.

334. The sources underpinning this inference are evaluated by Lassner, *The Shaping of ʿAbbāsid Rule,* 198–99.

335. Including widening of certain roads, razing of dwellings that interfered with this project, bringing additional water from outside the precinct, and permitting only a single greengrocer *(baqqāl)* to set up shop in each of the four quadrants, where he was allowed to sell only vegetables and vinegar (Khaṭīb, *Taʾrīkh,* 78–80 and Ṭabarī, *Taʾrīkh,* 3:322–25). These adjustments soon attracted a cocoon of validatory myths, which have been evaluated by Lassner in the works previously cited.

336. Al-Ruṣāfah = "The Causeway," but the rationale for this name is not immediately apparent. Possibly it derived from a causeway spanning swampy ground bordering the river (Lassner, *The Topography of Baghdād,* 250 n. 1). The site had originally been known as ʿAskar al-Mahdī, probably because the heir apparent had commanded a detachment of troops quartered there (ibid., although other [and altogether less convincing] reasons are advanced by a range of authorities).

337. Duri, *The Encyclopaedia of Islam,* 2d ed., 1:895.

338. Named after Ḥarb ibn ʿAbd Allāh, commander of al-Manṣūr's guard. The most systematic and detailed account of the districts within Greater Baghdād down to the time of al-Mahdī (r. 775–785) is furnished by al-Yaʿqūbī (*al-Buldān,* 237–54). This time span has been established by Lassner (*The Shaping of ʿAbbāsid Rule,* 212) on the basis of princely palaces of known date that were actually mentioned by Yaʿqūbī.

339. Yaʿqūbī, *al-Buldān,* 246.

340. Ibid., 253.

341. Lassner, *The Shaping of ʿAbbāsid Rule,* 208.

342. Khaṭīb, *Taʾrīkh,* 80.

343. Ibid., 81; Lassner's translation, 62. Among the sources reporting that rents were in fact charged in the caliphate of al-Manṣūr, al-Ṭabarī (*Taʾrīkh,* 3:323) notes that a tax *(kharāj)* was levied according to the size of the establishment; Yaʿqūbī (*Muʿjam,* 4:254), that it was assessed *ʿalā qadri-l-ṣināʿah,* perhaps signifying "according to the nature of the enterprise." Ṭabarī (ibid.) also reported that traders in government-built *sūqs* were taxed at a lower rate than those who provided their own premises. Cf. also Balādhurī, *Futūḥ al-Buldān,* 295.

344. Named for the Tuesday market held on the site in pre-Islamic times.

345. For exhaustive discussions of the locations of east-bank districts see Lassner, *The Topography of Baghdād,* 155–77.

346. Lassner's conservative estimate for the area of the city was of the order of seven thousand hectares (ibid., 158). For the widely disparate population estimates that have been advanced by various authors, see ibid., p. 160. Lassner himself seems prepared to accept a figure between about three hundred thousand and five hundred thousand: cf. his "The *ḥabl* of Baghdād and the dimensions of the city: a metrological note," *Journal of the Economic and Social History of the Orient* 6 (1963): 228–29. Most authors, however, opt for a higher figure, usually one million or more.

347. Patrick Geddes, *Cities in Evolution* (London, 1949), 14–15; Reprint of the 1915 edition, with deletions from and additions to the original. Of course, the term *conurbation* today is customarily applied to urban aggregations a good deal larger than tenth-century Baghdād.

348. Originally bestowed on al-Mahdī's son ʿIsā (Yāqūt, *Muʿjam,* 3:752–53). Subsequently al-Mahdī built a palace there known formally as Qaṣr al-Salām, and took up residence in 782. There is reason to believe that much of the imperial administration was then transferred to ʿĪsābādh.

349. For comments on the precise locations of these palaces see Lassner, *The Shaping of ʿAbbāsid Rule,* 298 n. 92.

350. Among the other palaces mentioned in the relevant literature are those of ʿAbdawayh al-Azdī, Ḥumayd ibn ʿAbd al-Ḥamīd, the Princes Sulaymān and Ṣāliḥ (sons of al-Manṣūr). ʿUmārah ibn Ḥamzah, ʿAbd Allāh ibn Ṭāhir (this residence usually known as the Ḥarīm al-Ṭāhirī), Ḥafṣ ibn ʿUthmān, Ibn Abī ʿAwn, Saʿīd al-Khaṭīb, Hāniʾ, Waḍḍāḥ al-Sharawī, Khuzaymah ibn Khāzim (a chief of police), Prince ʿUbayd Allāh, Princess Asmā, Ibn Muqlah, Ibn al-

Furāt, Ibn al-Khaṣīb, and Bānūqah, daughter of the caliph al-Mahdī. Their approximate locations can be ascertained from maps 4 and 5 in G. Le Strange, *Baghdād during the ʿAbbāsid Caliphate* (London, 1900). It is not without interest in this connection that, when the Saljūk Toghrïl Beg entered Baghdād in 1055, there were no fewer than 170 "palaces" lining the banks of the Tigris (Ibn al-Jawzī, *al-Muntaẓam fī-l-Taʾrīkh al-Mulūk wa-l-Umam*, ed. F. Krenkow, vol. 8 [Haydarābād, 1939], 232), a reference first cited by Lassner, *The Topography of Baghdād*, 295 n. 54.

351. This fief *(qaṭīʿah)*, al-Zubaydīyah, must not be confused with the district of the same name in the Nahr al-Qallaʾīn quarter of al-Karkh (Khaṭīb, *Taʾrīkh*, 110; Lassner's translation, 98). For a perceptive discussion of difficulties involved in the delimitation of the government sector of early Baghdād, see Lassner, *The Shaping of ʿAbbāsid Rule*, 223–29.

There are grounds, too, for interpreting a somewhat sibylline comment by the Khaṭīb (*Taʾrīkh*, 71) as implying that, by the ninth century, the government sector could legalistically be understood as the heart of Baghdād, and perhaps the only part truly deserving of that name. The great jurist Aḥmad ibn Ḥanbal (d. 855) was held to have opined that "Baghdād includes everything from the Ṣarāt Canal to Bāb al-Tibn (the Straw Gate: a neighbourhood *[maḥallah]* running along the north bank of the Ṭāhirid Trench opposite the fief of Zubaydah)." The Khaṭīb glossed this opinion as follows: "Aḥmad [ibn Ḥanbal], in that statement, is referring to the Madīnat al-Manṣūr and adjacent districts, since the upper (i.e., northern) part of the urban area *(aʿlā al-balad)* is the fief of Umm Jaʿfar (= Zubaydīyah). Below (i.e., south of) this fief is the *Khandaq [Ṭāhir]* that separates it from the built-over area of the actual city. In similar fashion the lower (i.e., southern) part of the urban area, comprising al-Karkh and adjacent districts, is separated from the actual city by the Ṣarāt Canal, which determines the width of the city (including its incorporated districts). Lengthwise it reaches from the bank of the Tigris to a place called al-Kabsh wa-l-Asad (the Ram and the Lion: two fairly extensive districts *[shāriʿ]* not far from the Ṭāhirid Trench in the vicinity of al-Naṣrīyah)." If the Khaṭīb's explication of Ibn Ḥanbal's statement was valid, it would have implied that in the ninth century Baghdād denoted, perhaps specifically in a legal and/or administrative sense, al-Manṣūr's Round City (much of which still survived in Ibn Ḥanbal's lifetime), together with the adjacent military cantonments of al-Ḥarbīyah. Apparently the fief of Umm Jaʿfar (and possibly other holdings north and west of the Ṭāhirid Trench), the southern suburb of al-Karkh and perhaps settlements to its west, and the palaces and quarters on the east bank of the Tigris were not subsumed, administratively at any rate, under the rubric Baghdād but were controlled by a variety of local bodies exercising substantial degrees of autonomy. Some confirmation of part of this reading is to be derived from the circumstance (adorned with miraculous trimmings) that in 991 the fief of Umm Jaʿfar was granted permission to establish its mosque as a *masjid al-jāmiʿ* on the ground that "a *khandaq* separated it from the urban area *(balad)*, thereby rendering the district in which the mosque was situated a *balad* in its own right." The relevant passage from the Khaṭīb's *Taʾrīkh* (110) is translated in full by Lassner, *The Topography of Baghdād*, 98–99.

Interestingly, the Khaṭīb observed in his day (mid-tenth century) that houses in the Kabsh wa-l-Asad "gave the appearance of a village inhabited by farmers and woodcutters." When he returned at a still later date he "saw no trace of a dwelling" (*Taʾrīkh*, 71).

352. Lassner (*The Shaping of ʿAbbāsid Rule*, 181 and elsewhere) characterizes these distinctive urban neighborhoods as "municipal entities." I am not sure that the decentralized organization of ʿAbbāsid Baghdād is wholly consonant with the idea of incorporated government inherent in the current concept of municipality, but the fact of varying degrees of administrative autonomy is indisputable.

353. Iṣṭakhrī, *al-Masālik wa-l-Mamālik*, 84.

354. Khaṭīb, *Taʾrīkh*, 109; Lassner's translation, 97–98.

355. See note 351 above.

356. Khaṭīb, *Taʾrīkh*, 110; Lassner's translation, 99.

357. Some have viewed these *sūqs* as beginning primarily as distribution centers serving the military cantonments of the area—presumably something like early versions of the PX.

358. Built by Saʿīd al-Ḥarrashī for al-Mahdī, and named the Market of Plenty *(Sūq al-Riyy)*. Only later did it become known as the Market of Thirst *(Sūq al-ʿAtash)*.

359. Lassner, *The Topography of Baghdād*, 278, citing al-Jawzī, *Manāqib Baghdād*, ed. M. M. Atharī (Baghdād, A.H. 1341), 26.

360. Eventually the whole of ʿAbd al-Wahhāb's estate *(rabaḍ)* came to be known by the name of its *sūq*.

361. The identity of Abū al-Ward is uncertain: see Lassner, *The Topography of Baghdād*, 256 n. 43.

362. Khaṭīb, *Taʾrīkh*, 93. Yaʿqūbī (*al-Buldān*, 253) reports that merchants in this *suwayqah* specialized in selling Chinese bric-a-brac *(ṭarāʾif)*.

363. Lassner, *The Topography of Baghdād*, 249 n. 10.

364. Yaʿqūbī, *al-Buldān*, 246.

365. Khaṭīb, *Taʾrīkh*, 81. *Rāfiḍī* originally denoted sectarians who rejected *(rāfaḍa)* the legitimacy of the caliphs Abū Bakr and ʿUmar, but in the tenth century signified little more than Shīʿī, particularly of The Twelver persuasion (*The Encyclopaedia of Islam*, new ed., 8:386–89). In any case, al-Wāqidī was surely employing the term in a pejorative sense, although the Imāmīs were even then embracing it as a title of respect.

366. This caliphal investment in the development of the southern suburb is stated explicitly by the Khaṭīb (*Taʾrīkh*, 79).

367. Yaʿqūbī, *al-Buldān*, 241. Cf. Lassner, *The Topography of Baghdād*, 247 n. 3.

368. Yaʿqūbī, *al-Buldān*, 254.

369. For a compendious summary of economic development in the suburbs of Baghdād, see Lassner, *The Topography of Baghdād*, appendix B.

370. Yaʿqūbī, *al-Buldān*, 254.

371. Lassner, *The Topography of Baghdād*, 283 n. 6, citing Hilāl al-Ṣābiʾ, *Rusūm Dār al-Khilāfah*, ed. M. ʿAwād (al-Qāhirah, A.H. 1383), 20ff.

372. Khaṭīb, *Ta'rīkh,* 117, citing Muḥammad ibn Yaḥyā al-Ṣūlī (d. 946 or 947). Al-Ṣūlī further noted at least five assistants (a bath attendant, a steward, a sweeper, a stoker, and a water carrier) in each *ḥammām,* which would have implied a total labor force of some three hundred thousand males.

373. In this connection it is pertinent to note that Hilāl recorded fifteen baths attached to some thirty residences in the Bāb al-Marātib district (Lassner, *The Topography of Baghdād,* 284 n. 6).

374. The Khaṭīb devotes a whole section of his work (*Ta'rīkh,* 120–27) to the cemeteries of Baghdād and incorporates numerous ad hoc references in the rest of his text.

375. Lassner, *The Topography of Baghdād,* 285–86 n. 1. Other units within the complex included the Bāb al-Tibn, Shūnīzī, the two Kāẓims (Shīʿite *imāms*), and Khayzurān Cemeteries. This last was the burial place of Muḥammad ibn Isḥāq ibn Yāsar (d. circa 767), author of a biography of the Prophet, and of the great jurist Abū Ḥanīfah.

376. Khaṭīb, *Ta'rīkh,* 121; Lassner's translation, 112.

377. The Arabic word here rendered as "infirmary" is *bīmāristān* < Pers. *bīmār* = sick + *-īstān* = place. There are summary statements about Baghdādī infirmaries by D. M. Dunlop in *The Encyclopaedia of Islam,* 2d ed., 1:1222–224 and by Lassner, *The Topography of Baghdād,* 278 n. 9, both deriving their information from Ibn Abī Uṣaybiʿah, *ʿUyūn al-Anbā' fī Ṭabaqāt al-Aṭibbā',* ed. A. Müller (al-Qāhirah and Königsberg, 1882–84), 1:174–75, 221–22, 224; ʿAlī ibn Yūsuf, *Ta'rīkh al-Ḥukamā',* ed. J. Lippert (Leipzig, 1903), 383–84; and Ibn al-Jawzī, *al-Muntaẓam,* 6:142, 174. It is worth noting that in the first half of the thirteenth century Uṣaybiʿah counted 860 licensed physicians in the city (pp. 221, 224, 310).

378. Maqdisī, *Aḥsan,* 120.

379. Khaṭīb, *Ta'rīkh,* 83–98; Lassner's translation, 66–84. Yaʿqūbī (*al-Buldān,* 250) asserts that at the end of the ninth century there were six thousand streets and alleys, an impossibly high number.

380. Khaṭīb, *Ta'rīkh,* 111–15; Lassner's translation, 100–104.

381. Ibid., 115–17; Lassner's translation, 105–6.

382. Yaʿqūbī, *al-Buldān,* 251.

383. P. 271 above.

384. Cf. note 351 above.

385. Accounts of this embassy and its reception in the Muslim capital are to be found in Miskawayh, *Tajārib al-Umam,* 1:53–55; Ibn al-Jawzī, *al-Muntaẓam,* 6:143–44; Ibn al-Athīr, *al-Kāmil,* 8:79; al-Ṣābi', *Rusūm,* 11 *et seq.;* Ibn al-Zubayr, *al-Dhakhā'ir wa al-Tuḥaf,* ed. Salāḥ al-Dīn al-Munajjid (Bayrūt, A.H. 1379), 131–39; and the Khaṭīb, *Ta'rīkh,* 100–105. This last account has been translated and annotated by Guy LeStrange: "A Greek embassy to Baghdād in 917 A.D.," *Journal of the Royal Asiatic Society* (1897): 35–45 and by Lassner, *The Topography of Baghdād,* 86–91.

386. The Khaṭīb (*Ta'rīkh,* 101) placed the number of chamberlains in caliphal service at 700, eunuchs at 7,000 (4,000 of whom were white, 3,000 black), and black pages (other than eunuchs) at 4,000.

387. Cf. the comments of Ibn Jubayr, a Spanish pilgrim who visited Baghdād in 1184 (quoted by Wiet, Baghdad, 142): "Each [inhabitant] conceives . . . that the whole world is but trivial in comparison with his land, and over the face of the world they find no noble place of living save their own. It is as if they are persuaded that God has no lands or people save theirs."

388. Nonetheless, the *Nights* received its final form in Mamlūk Qāhirah rather than Baghdād; the ruler whose exploits are archetyped in these tales was probably al-Nāṣir (r. 1180–1225) rather than Hārūn al-Rashīd.

389. Cf. Maqdisī, *Aḥsan,* 120: "As the authority of the caliphs declined, the city deteriorated, and the population dwindled."

390. Persian pl. *ʿayyārān.* This term varied in meaning according to time and place. In Baghdād from the tenth to the twelfth century it seems to have implied little more than an urban brotherhood or faction, almost always opposed to the government. See *The Encyclopaedia of Islam,* 2d ed., 1:794.

391. For comments on social unrest in Baghdād under the declining ʿAbbāsid dynasty, see Simha Sabari, *Mouvements Populaires à Bagdad à l'Époque ʿAbbāside IXe–XIe Siècles* (Paris, 1981), and for a more general view, Claude Cahen, "Mouvements populaires et autonomisme urbain dans l'Asie musulmane du moyen âge," *Arabica* 5 (1958): 225–50 and 6 (1959): 25–56, 233–65.

392. On the weak development of corporations in the Islamic world in general see S. M. Stern, "The Constitution of the Islamic City," in *The Islamic City,* ed. Hourani and Stern, 25–50, especially 47–50. Generally speaking, Islamic law knew only three categories of "legal persons": the estate of a deceased, a pious endowment *(waqf),* and the public treasury. It should not go unremarked, however, that a paucity of corporate institutions was the norm among the cities of the traditional world.

393. The Tigris River flooded at least a dozen times between 883 and 945, this last causing rents to rise throughout much of the residential area. Further devastating inundations occurred in 978, 980, and 983. Fires were especially common between 850 and 950, and were often accompanied by looting, especially in al-Karkh. Notable famines occurred in 946, 981, 983, 993, and 1002.

394. Maqdisī, *Aḥsan,* 120.

395. Ibn Ḥawqal, *al-Masālik wa-l-Mamālik,* 241–42.

396. Yāqūt, *Muʿjam,* 2:234.

397. For bibliographical references to archaeological excavations at Sāmarrā, see note 193 to chapter 2, especially the works there cited by Rogers (1970) and Northedge (1994); and ʿAbd al-Latif Janin Kettana, "A Case Study in the History of Islamic Towns: Spatial Patterns of Historic Samarra' in the Period of Abbasid Residence at Samarra' 221–279 AH/835–892 AD" (Ph.D. diss., University of Manchester, 1979).

398. The honorific title of the city was Surra Man Ra'ā ("Pleased be he who gazes upon it"); but whereas Maqdisī (*Aḥsan,* 122) and Yāqūt (*Muʿjam,* s.v.) thought Sāmarrā was simply popular usage of the honorific, it is more likely that it was an Arabic rendering of a pre-Islamic toponym and that the unusual Surra Man Ra'ā was actually a verbal conceit concocted at the caliphal court (cf. *The En-*

cyclopaedia of Islam, 2d ed., 8:1039). It is not without interest to note that exactly forty years earlier, Hārūn al-Rashīd had started to build an octagonal palace called al-Mubārak at al-Qādisīyah to the south of Sāmarrā, but it was abandoned before it could be completed. For a detailed discussion of the layout of this palace complex, see Alastair Northedge, "Analyse du plan du palais du Caliphe al-Muʿtaṣim à Sāmarrā," in *Colloque International,* ed. Gayraud, 149–79.

399. For the Levantine practice (specifically at al-Ramlah [Ramleh]) of cutting marble with toothless saws and Makkan sand as reported in the eleventh century, see Nāṣir-i Khusraw's *Safar Nāmah,* Thackston's translation, 20.

400. Yaʿqūbī, *al-Buldān,* 258.

401. For comments on the root underlying this term, defined by Paul Casanova (translation of Maqrīzī, *al-Mawāʿiẓ,* 211) as "généralement tous les grains dont on peut faire le pain," see Wiet, *Yaʿkūbī. Les Pays,* 50–51 n. 3.

402. Yaʿqūbī, *al-Buldān,* 259.

403. Alastair Northedge, "The palace at Iṣṭabulāt, Sāmarrā," *Archéologie Islamique* 3 (1992): 61–86.

404. This is the orthography adopted by al-Yaʿqūbī (*al-Buldān,* 265), but variants such as Barkuwārā, Barkuwāzā, Baruwānā, and Bazkuwārā also occur in other texts.

405. Yaʿqūbī's account of these events runs as follows:

> After the death of al-Wāthiq in the year [A.H.] 232, his successor Jaʿfar al-Mutawakkil ibn al-Muʿtaṣim took up residence in the Hārūnīyah. . . . He settled his son Muḥammad al-Muntaṣir in the palace of al-Muʿtaṣim known as the Jawsaq, another son Ibrahīm al-Muʾayyad in al-Maṭīrah, and another son Muʿtazz in a locality called Balkuwārā, beyond al-Maṭīrah to the east. Construction continued uninterruptedly from Balkuwārā to the neighbourhood of Dūr—about 4 *farsakhs* in all. (ibid., 265)

406. Ibid., 263.

407. According to Yaʿqūbī (ibid., 260–63), the principal avenue in the complex was Shāriʿ al-Sarījah, and the others were Shāriʿ Abī Aḥmad ibn Rashīd, Shāriʿ al-Ḥayr al-Awwal, Shāriʿ Barghamish al-Turkī, Shāriʿ al-Askar (or Shāriʿ Ṣāliḥ al-ʿAbbāsī), Shāriʿ al-Ḥayr al-Jadīd, and the Shāriʿ al-Khalīj mentioned above.

408. Alastair Northedge, "The racecourses at Samarra," *Bulletin of the School of Oriental and African Studies* 53 (1990): 31–56.

409. Al-Jaʿfarīyah (Yaʿqūbī, *al-Buldān,* 266) after the *ism* of al-Mutawakkil; Māḥūzah was the pre-Islamic name of the site (Ṭabarī, *Taʾrīkh,* 3:1438).

410. Yaʿqūbī, *al-Buldān,* 266.

411. Yaʿqūbī (ibid., 266–67) lists the *dīwāns* involved in the move as Dīwān al-Kharāj, Dīwān al-Ḍiyāʿ, Dīwān al-Zimām (for Zimām al-Nafaqāt: *zimām* figured in the titles of other high-ranking officials), Dīwān al-Jund wa-l-Shākirīyah, Dīwān al-Mawṣilālī wa-l-Ghilmān, and Dīwān al-Barīd.

412. Ibid., 267.

413. Northedge, "Early Islamic Syria and Iraq," 260.

414. Rogers, "Sāmarrā," 127. There are, too, hints that the planning sometimes failed to match the needs of individual units of settlement, whether palace or *qaṭīʿah,* let alone the whole aggregation of grids and enclosures. It is known, for example, that the million-dīnār canal by which al-Mutawakkil hoped to supply the Jaʿfarīyah with water functioned only imperfectly owing to miscalculations of its levels (Yaʿqūbī, *al-Buldān,* 267). Concerning the other extreme, a superfluity of water: Rogers (*"Sāmarrā,"* 145 n. 76) quotes al-Iṣfahānī (*al-Aghānī,* 20:42) to the effect that heavy thunderstorms rendered Sāmarrā streets impassible.

It is also worth noting that, unlike most of Baghdād, where the water supply was reasonably palatable (Yaʿqūbī, *al-Buldān,* 251–52), wells in Sāmarrā were unusually deep and consequently disagreeably brackish. As a result, Tigris water had to be distributed throughout the settlement in goat skins slung on the backs of mules and camels (ibid., 263).

415. Ibid.

416. Ibid., 254.

417. As a Parsonian sociologist might say, among the functional subsystems of society, goal attainment almost totally eclipsed adaptation, integration, and pattern maintenance: Parsons and Smelser, *Economy and Society.*

418. Al-Thaʿālibī, *al-Laṭāʾif al-Maʿārif,* 170–71; Bosworth's translation, 124–25.

419. To the references cited in note 154 to chapter 2, add Susan Jane Staffa, *Conquest and Fusion. The Social Evolution of Cairo* A.D. 642–1850 (Leiden, 1977), chaps. 1–3 and Sanders, *Ritual, Politics, and the City,* chaps. 1–3. To the primary sources there listed, add Abū Muḥammad ʿAbd Allāh al-Balawī, *Kitāb Sīrat Āl Ṭūlūn,* ed. Kurd ʿAlī (Dimashq, A.H. 1358). Al-Balawī's main sources are thought to have been documents preserved in the chancery office *(Dīwān al-Inshāʾ)* established by Ibn Ṭūlūn.

420. Sāwirus ibn al-Muqaffaʿ (Severus of Ushmunayn), *Historia Patriarchorum Alexandrinorum;* translation by B. Evetts under the title *History of the Patriarchs of the Coptic Church of Alexandria,* in *Patrologia Orientalis,* vols. 5:1–215; 10:357–551 (Paris, 1904–15), 5:168.

421. Land grants in Sāmarrā were usually categorized as *qaṭāʾiʿ.*

422. In its heyday, the palace was furnished with a garden of gold and silver trees, a menagerie, and a hippodrome.

423. Creswell, *A Short Account of Early Muslim Architecture,* 406.

424. Maqrīzī, *al-mawāʿiẓ,* 1:318.

425. Kāfūr was an Ethiopian eunuch who acted as regent for the sons of Muḥammad ibn Tughj, founder of the Ikhshīdid dynasty, on the death of the latter in 946, and who retained the power originally conferred by that office for twenty-two years. He also built another palace close to the Mosque of Ibn Ṭūlūn, but it was rendered uninhabitable by noxious miasmas from stagnant waters in the neighborhood.

426. This may not have been the mere literary topos that its context is often thought to imply, for astrology was held in high esteem by the Qarmaṭians and their offshoot the Fāṭimids, who fre-

quently adduced it in their propaganda. In the archetyped version of the tale it was al-Muʿizz himself who devised the corrective strategy that would ensure the settlement a propitious future.

427. Ibn Duqmāq, al-Intiṣār, 4:127.

428. Maqrīzī, *al-Mawāʿiẓ*, 2:273.

429. Nāṣir-i Khusraw, *Safar Namah*, Thackston's translation, 45 (modified).

430. Ibid., 47 (modified).

431. Sanders, *Ritual, Politics, and the City*, passim. The remarks that follow are derived from that work, especially chap. 3, "The Ritual City." However, in addition to explicating the ritualized framework first of al-Qāhirah (Cairo), and subsequently of the whole composite city, Sanders shows (1) how the New Year procession was organized to reflect twelfth-century changes in the structure of the Fāṭimid army and administration; and (2) how, in the procession to Cut the Canal and Perfume the Nilometre, the Nile was integrated into the ritual panoply of the capital, and thereby of the kingdom.

432. Ibid., 41, citing Muḥammad ibn Ḥānī', *Dīwān*, ed. Zāhid ʿAlī (al-Qāhirah, A.H. 1352), no. 1, 31: "The cause of the world which was created by Him." Cf. Canard, "L'impérialisme des Fāṭimides et leur propagande," 156–93.

Imām originally denoted a Muslim prayer leader. As a title of the caliphs it was extended to describe the leader of the *Ummah*. For Shīʿī, and more particularly Ismāʿīlī, it was used for their pretenders to the Caliphate, who were viewed as "divinely inspired religious pontiffs" (Bernard Lewis's phrase: *The Arabs in History*, 106).

433. Also known as the Old (Congregational) Mosque *(al-Jāmiʿ al-ʿAtīq)*.

434. Maqrīzī, *Ittiʿāẓ al-Ḥunafā bi-akhbar al-aʾimmah al-Fatimiyin al-khulafa*, ed. Jamal al-Din-Shayyal (al-Qāhirah, 1967), 1:114–15. Although the Mosque of ʿAmr, originally constructed at the time of the Muslim conquest, had been largely demolished and then rebuilt by Ibn Ṭāhir (as governor) in 827, it was still much smaller than the huge edifice of Ibn Ṭūlūn.

435. Maqrīzī, *al-Mawāʿiẓ*, 2:277.

436. This is as far as our present purpose requires us to go. The rest of the story, in which a succession of Fāṭimid caliphs elaborated the ritual and protocol of a changing city and reinterpreted it in response to the demands of a fluctuating political environment, is told with grace and skill in Sander's *Ritual, Politics, and the City*, passim. A splendid work that extends the study of signification systems in al-Qāhirah to written signs, but that regrettably impinges only marginally on the present discussion, is Irene A. Bierman's *Writing Signs: The Fatimid Public Text* (Berkeley, Calif., 1998).

437. Ibn Ḥawqal, *al-Masālik wa-l-Mamālik*, 146.

438. See note 73 to chapter 3.

439. Masʿūdī, *al-Tanbīh*, 20.

440. Maqrīzī, *al-Mawāʿiẓ*, 1:305.

441. Shihāb al-Dīn ibn Muḥammad al-Maqqarī (1577–1631), *Azhār al-Riyāḍ fī Akhbār al-ʿIyāḍ*, vol. 2 (al-Qāhirah, A.H. 1359), 269; *Nafḥ al-Ṭīb*, Gayangos's translation, 233.

442. Cited by Hillenbrand, "'The Ornament of the World,'" 126: "The Caliph had mats unrolled from the gates of Córdoba to the entrance of Madīnat al-Zahrā', a distance of three miles, and stationed a double rank of soldiers along the route, their naked swords, both broad and long, meeting at the tips like the rafters of a roof. . . . The fear that this inspired was indescribable. . . . From here to the palace where they were to be received, the Caliph had the ground covered with brocades. At regular intervals he placed dignitaries whom they took for kings, for they were seated on splendid couches and arrayed in brocades and silk." And so forth: there is more in the same vein.

443. Ibid.

It should be noted that Madīnat al-Zahrā' was not the first caliphal retreat erected in the vicinity of Qurṭubah: a century and a half previously, ʿAbd al-Raḥmān I, the first Umayyad ruler of al-Andalus, had built a villa that he styled Munyat al-Ruṣāfah after his grandfather's favorite Syrian retreat; he stocked its gardens with Syrian plants (Maqqarī, *Nafḥ al-Ṭīb*, Iḥsān ʿAbbās edition, 1: 466–67).

444. Anonymous author of *al-Dhakhīrah al-Sanīyah*, translated by Hillenbrand, "'The Ornament of the World,'" 112.

The main city of Qurṭubah (Cordoba), unlike Baghdād, Sāmarrā, and al-Qāhirah, was not a new foundation but rather a Muslim adaptation of a preexisting settlement—and one of considerable importance at that. Even under the Muslims the heart of Qurṭubah was the roughly rectangular, walled *madīnah* (in the sense of a fortified enclosure, not in al-Maqdisī's technical usage), whose defenses still betrayed their Roman origins. The advantage of the location commanding the broad lands bordering the middle reaches of the Wādī al-Kabīr from a site on the north bank of the river, which was then navigable up to that point, proved as powerful a stimulus under the Muslims as it had during previous centuries. From 786 ʿAbd al-Raḥmān I extended the city's ramparts, which eventually came to incorporate 13 gates and 132 towers; enlarged the old Roman bridge over the Wādī al-Kabīr; renovated the city's aqueduct; replaced the Visigothic administrative center with his own *dār al-imārah* (probably thereby invoking continuity of site as symbolizing, if not guaranteeing, legitimacy of secular authority); and raised a magnificent cathedral mosque on the site of the Christian church of St. Vincent (there are good reasons to be skeptical of al-Rāzī's claim that Muslims and Christians once shared the church, a situation suspiciously analogous to events in early Muslim Damascus that are themselves of dubious authenticity).

Outside the *madīnah* with its palaces, mansions, *dīwāns, sūqs*, and barracks (for five thousand horse and one thousand foot soldiers under al-Ḥakam I [r. 796–822], according to al-Maqqarī), there developed a lateral sequence of suburbs (sing. *rabaḍ*) stretching from Madīnat al-Zahrā' in the west to al-Madīnah al-Zāhirah in the east. The ancient Secunda (Ar. Shaqundah), to the south of the river, was demolished in 818 after a Muwalladūn revolt (the so-called Battle of the Suburbs); its inhabitants were deported to North Africa, Egypt, and Crete, and the whole district was left to be used as a huge necropolis. By the mid-tenth century there were twenty-one distinct extramural quarters, known collectively as "The Suburb" *(al-Rabaḍ),* nine being to the west, seven to the east, three to the north, and two beyond the river to the south.

The caliphal palace and cathedral mosque both fronted on the river, and the most splendid mansions were strung along the road to Madīnat al-Zahrā', some with belvederes affording panoramic views of Qurṭubah. A good proportion of the streets were paved and some lighted by lamps attached to outer doors and corners of houses. To the east of the principal mosque were the main *sūqs* and the *qayṣarīyah.* The circumstance that a merchant wishing to do business in the *sūq* was required to pay an entrance fee of four hundred *dirhams* attests to the opportunities afforded by various forms of retailing. The city is recorded as home to thirteen thousand weavers and its textiles were known throughout the Islamic world, as also were its leather work, jewelry, carved ivory, and crystal manufactures. The seventy libraries within the city sufficiently testify to its role as an intellectual center. According to Ibn Sa'īd (d. 1286), "Qurṭubah held more books than any other city in al-Andalus, and its inhabitants were the most solicitious in caring for their libraries. Such collections were regarded as symbols of status and social leadership"—though Ibn Sa'īd goes on to note that a proportion of those who acquired such libraries did so purely for reasons of social advancement with no pretensions to learning (Hillenbrand, "'The Ornament of the World,'" 120).

It is not necessary to accept one Arab author's conclusion that the conurbation as a whole in the tenth century encompassed 471 mosques, 213,077 houses of the working classes, 60,300 villas and mansions of officials and aristocrats, and 80,455 shops, which would probably imply a population of about 1 million (Arberry, "Muslim Cordoba," 171) in order to acknowledge that Qurṭubah was one of the principal cities of the Islamic world, disputing with Baghdād the intellectual leadership of the *Ummah.* Modern scholars tend to assign it a population of from 100,000 to 500,000.

Reconstructions of Qurṭubah and its environs as they were in the tenth century are included in Lévi-Provençal's *Histoire de l'Espagne Musulmane,* 3:361, 365.

445. Ar. = sing. *Sharīf,* pl. *Shurafā'* (Moroccan Ar. *Shorfā'*).

446. On the Marīnid state and its capitals see Maya Shatzmiller, *The Encyclopaedia of Islam,* 2d ed., 6:571–574 and M. Kably, *Société, Pouvoir et Religion au Maroc à la fin du Moyen Âge* (Paris, 1986).

447. A reading of the situation in no way in conflict with the well-known hagiographical rationale for the founding and location of al-Mahdīyah, including a typical *post eventum* prophecy regarding its future.

448. The context of the founding of al-Manṣūrīyah is covered in chapter 16.

449. For the circumstances surrounding the foundation of al-Rāfiqah, the sources available, and persisting uncertainties as to the relationship and nomenclature of the twin cities, see and notes 17 and 18 to chapter 5. Excavations by several groups of archaeologists are summarized by Creswell, *A Short Account of Early Muslim Architecture,* chaps. 11 and 12 and mapped in *The Encyclopaedia of Islam,* 2d ed., vol. 8, opp. p. 16, where the reconstructions are based on excavations undertaken by the German Archaeological Institute of Damascus.

As has been noted, al-Raqqah was maintained as a fortified garrison post on the main route to the Byzantine Empire from the time of its conquest in 639 or 640, when the old city of Kallinikos/Callinicum was accorded what was presumably a sobriquet denoting a riverine tract (note 17 to chapter 5). Quite early on, the governor Sa'īd ibn 'Āmir ibn Hidhyam built a congregational mosque, more or less in the center of the old city, that was subsequently enlarged to monumental proportions. Outside the city but within its sphere of influence, two members of the Umayyad family established residential estates at respectively Wāsiṭ al-Raqqah and Ḥiṣn Maslamah, the products of whose irrigated fields were often to be found in the *sūqs* of al-Raqqah itself (C.-P. Haase, "Bilād al-Shām during the 'Abbāsid Period," in *Proceedings of the Fifth International Conference on the History of Bilād al-Shām,* ed. Muḥammad 'Adnān al-Bakhīt and R. Schick [Ammān, 1991], 206–213). Then in 771 the 'Abbāsid caliph al-Manṣūr initiated construction of an entirely new foundation, which came to be known as al-Rāfiqah (= "The Companion [City]"). Situated a mere two hundred meters to the west of al-Raqqah, the new palatine complex was enclosed within a wall nearly five thousand meters long and further fortified with 132 round towers, an advance wall, and a moat (Murhaf al-Khalaf, "Die 'abbāsidische Stadtmauer von al-Ragga/ar-Rāfiqa," *Damaszener Mitteilungen* 2 [1985]: 123–31). It was said to have been modelled on the Round City at Baghdād, although such a design is not now immediately apparent in the excavated sectors of the complex, which are better described as a parallelogram bordering a semicircle—although this layout might have originated as a parallelogram tangential to a circle, with later walls masking the relationship. Close to the generating point of the semicircle, another monumentally impressive congregational mosque was raised to serve primarily the Khurāsānian garrison.

However, it was the magnificent palaces constructed within the enclave that gave al-Rāfiqah its palatine character, which was greatly enhanced when Hārūn al-Rashīd transferred his capital thither from 796 to 808. During this time a whole palatial quarter was laid out on ten square kilometers to the north of the twin cities. Altogether some twenty large complexes have been identified, including Hārūn's principal palace and, presumably, the residences of his family, court officials, and servitors: in short, here for twelve years was the administrative center of the 'Abbāsid Empire, together with its military command. By the tenth century al-Raqqah and al-Rāfiqah together comprised one of the largest urban aggregations in the Middle East, probably surpassed in size only by Baghdād. M. Meinecke estimates that al-Rāfiqah alone almost matched Damascus in areal extent (*The Encyclopaedia of Islam,* 2d ed., 8:411; also J.-Chr. Heusch and M. Meinecke, "Grabungen im 'Abbāsidischen Palastareal von ar-Raqqa/ar-Rāfiqa 1982–1983," *Damaszener Mitteilungen* 2 [1985]: 85–105).

About eight kilometers to the west of al-Rāfiqah, Hārūn built the Hiraqlah, a victory monument celebrating his conquest of the Byzantine city of Herakleia in 806. This structure comprised a massive, square building constructed of stones appropriated from frontier churches dismantled by an order of 806–7, the whole being set within a circular wall five hundred meters long (Muḥammad ibn Shaddād, *al-Aʿlāq al-Khaṭīrah,* ed. A. M. Eddé, *Bulletin d'Études Orientales de l'Institut Français de Damas,* 32–33 [1980–81]; K. Toueir, "Heraqlah: a unique victory monument of Hārūn al-Rashīd," *World Archaeology* 14, no. 3 [1983]: 296–304). It is sufficiently evident that Hārūn's departure for Khurāsān in 808, followed shortly afterward by his death, prevented the completion of this monument. Indeed, the restoration of capital functions to Baghdād at this time reduced al-Raqqah-al-Rāfiqah to the seat of a regional governor, in al-Maqdisī's hierarchy a *qaṣabah.*

In 813 an Amīn-inspired revolt resulted in the fiery destruction of the market quarter situated between the two cities, while in 944 a whole sector of al-Raqqah was razed by a similar conflagration, presumably Raqqah the Burnt (al-Raqqah al-Muḥtariqah), which al-Maqdisī (*Aḥsan,* 141) later notes was a desolate ruin. The markets (presumably he meant the main markets) in his day were roofed. However, as early as the beginning of the ninth century the great palace quarter outside the city walls was falling into disrepair, to be revived only briefly in 838 in connection with the last military foray into Byzantine territories to be conducted from al-Raqqah. Excavation has also revealed pottery and glass industries apparently from the ʿAbbāsid period, the most impressive being a glass-manufacturing workshop whose kilns were inserted into the western wall of al-Raqqah-Leontopolis (Julian Henderson, lecture to the Middle East Urbanism Seminar, The Oriental Institute, University of Chicago, 22 May 1996).

For the cultural reputation of the city see Muḥammad ibn Saʿīd al-Kushayrī (d. 945), *Taʾrīkh al-Raqqah,* ed. Ṭāhir al-Naʿsānī (Ḥamā, A.H. 1378). Al-Maqdisī sums up the situation with "It is a pleasant, restful place that was platted a long time ago *(qadīmat al-khiṭṭah),*" a phrase that surely harks back to the initial settlement of Arabs in Nikephorion-Leontopolis rather than to the subsequent establishment of the palatine complex. An ethnographic feature of the city worthy of comment was the prominent of Peoples of the Book. A Christian bishropric was seated there right through to the twelfth century and there were at least four monasteries, one of which, the Dayr Zakkā, has been excavated on Tall al-Bīʿah, one thousand meters or so to the north of al-Raqqah (M. Krebernik, "Schriftfunde aus Tall Biʿa 1990," *Mitteilungen der Deutschen Orient-Gesellschaft* 123 [1991]: 41–57). There was also a substantial synagogue serving a large and long-established Jewish community, which survived at least into the second half of the twelfth century (Marcus Nathan Adler, *The Itinerary of Benjamin of Tudela* [London, 1907], 32).

450. It should be noted that the sources relating to the foundation of al-Mawṣil (Mosul) are often ambiguous and sometimes mutually contradictory, so that the version advanced here can be no more than provisional.

References in this section that duplicate the relevant citations in chapters 4–16 will not be repeated here; however, additional references not previously adduced will be cited in full.

451. A few highlights from which: in 861 the governor of the city was deposed by the Taghlibī Ayyūb ibn Aḥmad, who installed his son in that office; in 868 ʿAzdī Allāh ibn Sulaymān lost the governorship to the Khārijīs; in 873 al-Muʿtamid appointed the Turkish general Asātigīn to the post, but the latter's son was driven out by the populace while deputizing for his father; the city was retaken by Asātigīn, who was soon again driven out; when the nominee of a son of an ʿAbbāsid-approved governor was repudiated by the townsmen, he enlisted the help of the Banū-Shaybān, who stormed the city; and shortly thereafter the victor was deposed by the Kurd ʿAlī ibn Dāwūd; in 895 Ḥamdān (the grandfather of Sayf al-Dawlah) rebelled in al-Mawṣil but was defeated by caliphal forces; in 896 the Khārijī Hārūn, whose followers were engaged in a running conflict with caliphal tribute collectors, was captured; and in 907 the Ḥamdānid Abū al-Hayjāʾ ʿAbd Allāh subdued the Kurds, who were causing trouble in and around the city; from this time forward it was the Ḥamdānid writ that ran in al-Mawṣil, first as the will of ʿAbbāsid governors but from 929 as the commands of sovereign rulers. From 996 to 1096 the city was ruled by the independent ʿUqaylid dynasty. On the history of early Muslim al-Mawṣil see al-Sulaymān, *Al-Mawṣil.*

452. In other words, a regional metropolis. At this point it is probably otiose to remind the reader that this term does not refer to the ekistic feature discussed in the *Amṣār* section of this chapter.

453. Literally, "Among its streets were . . ." The eight streets were named by al-Maqdisī (*Aḥsan,* 138) as Dayr al-Aʿlā Bāṣlūt (< Syriac Beth Ṣlothā = "Prayer House"), al-Jaṣṣāṣīn ("Vendors of Gypsum"), Banī-Maydah, al-Jassāsah ("The Gypsum Quarry"), the Amīr al-Muʾminīn's Millstone, al-Dabbāghīn ("The Tanners"), and Jamīl. These street names have been discussed by E. Herzfeld in *Archäologische Reise im Euphrat- und Tigrisgebiet,* vol. 2 (Berlin, 1920), 209.

454. Ibn Ḥawqal, *al-Masālik wa-l-Mamālik,* 215.

455. See especially ibid., 215–16 and, for a general discussion of Arabs and Kurds in the vicinity of al-Mawṣil, Canard, *Histoire de la Dynastie des H'amdanides,* 132–34.

456. Iṣṭakhrī, *al-Masālik wa-l-Mamālik,* 124–25. It was the Ṣaffārid ʿAmr ibn al-Layth who in 894 founded the first congregational mosque in Shīrāz, which in later ages would come to be known as the Masjid-i ʿAtīq ("The Old Mosque"). No other congregational mosque would be sanctioned until the Masjid Sunqur was built by the first Atabeg of the Salghurids (1148–61), to be followed by the so-called New Mosque built by the Salghurid ruler Saʿd ibn Zangī (1203–31).

457. Maqdisī (*Aḥsan,* 430) lists these gates as Bāb Iṣṭakhr, Darb Tustar, Darb Bandāstānah, Darb Ghassān, Darb Silm, Darb Kuwār, Darb Mandar, and Darb Mahandar (seemingly for Fāhandar). A parallel passage in the Constantinople recension of the *Aḥsan* substitutes Darb Sabaq for Darb Tustar and Darb Kuwān for Darb Kuwār in the above list. Although not all the names can be identified, it appears that the gates predominantly took the names of settlements to which their roads led. It is noticeable that a list of nine gate names preserved by Mustawfī (*Nuzhat al-Qulūb,* Le Strange

edition, 113) in the first half of the fourteenth century retains only two of al-Maqdisī's tenth-century appellations.

It is unusual for a topographer to use *darb* to denote a gate. In fact, in an interlinear insertion in a different hand, the plural *durūb* in the phrase translated as "eight gates" is emended to *abwāb* = "gates" (de Goeje, *Bibliotheca Geographorum Arabicorum,* 3:430, note). However, Lane does cite several examples of *darb* being used to mean "entrance" (*Lexikon,* 866–67). Is it conceivable that, despite the reasonableness of the emendation of a subsequent reader, al-Maqdisī had actually resorted to the term *darb* (with its implication of "a place of entrance between two mountains," and a derived meaning of "gate of a side street *[sikkah]*") in response to the absence of a wall around the city and consequently the existence of "entrances" rather than formal gateways?

458. Maqdisī, *Aḥsan,* 429. The other references to the narrowness of the streets are "They bump their heads against bay windows [because of the said narrowness]"; "There is not a single wide street *(shāriʿ fasīḥ)*"; "The narrowness of the *sūq* makes for congestion there." It is probable that al-Maqdisī's later mention of "the narrowness and closeness of the houses" (430) also really reflected the narrowness of the streets.

459. Cf. note 456 above.

460. Al-Maqdisī was inclined to attribute a good many other defects in the city to the Zoroastrian presence, particularly the reluctance of *dhimmīs* to wear the prescribed emblem *(ghiyār);* the prevailing lack of respect accorded the Muslim religious classes *(aṣḥāb al-ṭaylasān);* and the debased morality that, among other things, permitted the open practice of prostitution. Cf. also Spuler, *Iran in Früh-Islamischer Zeit,* 191–92.

461. Yaʿqūbī, *al-Buldān,* 362: "Each residence has a garden attached, where all sorts of fruits, flowers, and vegetables are grown."

462. The palace and library of ʿAḍud al-Dawlah are described by al-Maqdisī (*Aḥsan,* 449–50; slightly varying versions in the two recensions). Contrary to what appears to have been the case elsewhere, books in this library were stored on shelves *(wa-l-dafātir munaḍḍadah ʿalā rufūf)* instead of in boxes (see Barthold, *Historical Geography,* 155), and were both shelved and catalogued by subject. Admittance was restricted, though, to privileged members of the élite. Al-Maqdisī himself sometimes acknowledged his indebtedness to manuscripts in this library.

463. Ibn Ḥawqal, *al-Masālik wa-l-Mamālik,* 23. A century and a half subsequently, ʿUmārah (*Taʾrīkh al-Yaman,* English translation by Henry Cassells Kay under the title *Yaman, Its Early Medieval History* [London, 1892; reprint, Fairborough, Hampshire, 1968], 8 and 234 n. 12) slightly inflated these revenue figures for his own purpose, while specifying additional imposts such as those on Indian cargoes; musk; camphor; ambergris from Bāb al-Māndab, ʿAdan, Abyan, and al-Shiḥr; and pearl fisheries, and tribute from at least one dependency.

The ʿAththarīyah *dīnār* took its name from ʿAththar (also ʿAthr), a town on the Yaman coast that prospered as the principal port for Ṣanʿāʾ before coming effectively independent in 960. The coin was equal to two-thirds of a *mithqāl.* For recent discoveries at ʿAththar see J. Zarins and A. Zahrani, "Recent archaeological investigations in the southern Tihama Plain (The sites of Athar, and Sihi, 1404/1984)," *ATLAL* 9 (1985): 65–107.

464. Ibn al-Mujāwir, *Taʾrīkh al-Mustabṣir,* 1:78. See also Chelhod, "Introduction à l'histoire sociale et urbaine de Zabīd," 58.

465. Maqdisī, *Aḥsan,* 84.

466. "More magnificent and more elegant than the congregational mosque of Damascus" was al-Maqdisī's assessment (ibid., 165).

467. See note 284 in this chapter. An essay in urban reconstruction by Nimrod Luz that is based on an analogical interpretation of literary and meager archaeological evidence, and which posits "a classic orthogonal plan" closely similar to that of ʿAnjar, remains to be verified archaeologically ("The construction of an Islamic city in Palestine. The case of Umayyad al-Ramlah," *Journal of the Royal Asiatic Society,* ser. 3, vol. 7 [1997]: 27–54).

468. Whitehouse, "The houses of Siraf," 257.

469. Yaʿqūbī, *al-Buldān,* 340.

470. It should not go unnoticed that Waylah (al-ʿAqabah) was one of the minority of cities for which al-Maqdisī failed to record either the existence or the nonexistence of a mosque—possibly because the building in question was a relatively simple structure for such a flourishing settlement and deemed unworthy of mention. Or perhaps it simply slipped his mind.

471. See Whitcomb, *Ayla,* 23–25. For accounts of the excavations consult note 40 to chapter 6.

472. Yaʿqūbī, *al-Buldān,* 341.

473. This has been a common enough arrangement of *sūqs* down to modern times, as we have seen.

474. Mohammad el-Saghir, *Le camp romain de Louqsour* (Le Caire, 1986), passim.

475. Whitcomb, "The *Miṣr* of Ayla," fig. 27, which depicts the perimeters of all seven foundations on a uniform scale. Cf. also pp. 235–44 of the same article.

476. Selections from which include that the son and successor of the founder was driven out in 883 by Muḥammad ibn Abī al-Sāj, ruler of al-Anbār; in 928 the Qarmaṭī Abū Ṭāhir al-Jannābī seized the city, initiating some thirteen years of civil war; in 941 a governor despatched from Baghdād reclaimed the city; in the reign of the Ḥamdānid Nāṣir al-Dawlah, the rebel Taghlibī Jamān established the city as his base of operations and was expelled only with difficulty; after the death of Nāṣir in 969 his sons disputed possession of the city, the eventual victor rebuilding its walls but ceding control to the Buwayhid ʿAḍud al-Dawlah in 978; in 1008 the governor was killed by the ʿUqaylid ʿĪsā ibn Khalāt; and a few years later Luʾluʾ of Damascus imposed Egyptian control over al-Rahbah.

477. Iṣṭakhrī, *al-Masālik wa-l-Mamālik,* 77; Ibn Ḥawqal, *al-Masālik wa-l-Mamālik,* 227, and Maqdisī, *Aḥsan,* 142. The "Euphrates district" denoted the irrigated plain extending from Dayr al-Zawr to Abū Kamāl and including the towns, in addition to al-Raḥbah, of Dāliyah, ʿĀnah, and al-Ḥadīthah.

478. Ibn Ḥawqal, *al-Masālik wa-l-Mamālik,* 93.

479. Maqdisī, *Aḥsan,* 230.

480. See al-Bakrī, *al-Masālik wa-l-Mamālik,* 90–92 and the references in note 45 to chapter 16. The excavations referred to are summarized in the papers by Charles Redman and his associates cited in note 184 to the same chapter. Al-Bakrī lists the four gates of Nākūr as Bāb Sulaymān to the south, Bāb Beni-Waryāghal in a general easterly direction, Bāb al-Muṣalla to the west, and Bāb al-Yahūd ("The Jews' Gate") to the north. It should be emphasized that the rarity of the record does not inevitably imply rarity of practice.

481. Sauvaget's three most important contributions for present purposes are "Esquisse d'une histoire de la ville de Damas"; "Le plan de Laodicée-sur-Mer," *Bulletin d'Études Orientales* 4 (1934): 81–114; and *Alep.*

482. Timothy P. Harrison, "The early Umayyad settlement at Ṭabarīyah" and Holum and Hohlfelder, eds., *King Herod's Dream,* chap. 6.

483. See, for example, Nikita Elisséeff, "Damas," 157–77. R. S. Humphreys advances much the same type of argument in "Urban Topography and Urban Society: Damascus under the Ayyubids and Mamluks" in the same author's *Islamic History: A Framework for Inquiry* (Princeton, N.J., 1991). See also Toru Miura in Masashi Haneda and Miura, eds., *Islamic Urban Studies,* 111–12.

484. This is, of course, the case only with communities of relatively homogeneous sociocultural composition; it clearly does not apply to disparate ethnic groups settled by dictate of centralized authority, each in its own quarter and not infrequently enjoying a limited degree of autonomy.

485. Most notably Elisséeff, "Damas," 174.

486. Balādhurī, *Futūḥ al-Buldān,* 128.

487. Ibid., citing al-Waḍin.

488. Ṭabarī, *Ta'rīkh,* 1:2499. The peace covenant concluded at Emesa (Ḥimṣ) is said to have spared the lives of the inhabitants, their properties, the city wall, their churches, and their grain mills in return for a levy of 170,000 *dīnār*s and the use of a quarter of the principal church as a mosque.

489. Wilferd Madelung, "Apocalyptic prophecies in Ḥimṣ in the Umayyad age," *Journal of Semitic Studies* 31 (1986): 141–85. Rastān was the Arabicized form of Arethusa, an ancient town on the Orontes to the north of Emesa; and the *sūq* was so called because it abutted the city gate facing in that direction.

490. Balādhurī, *Futūḥ al-Buldān,* 121–23, citing Abū ʿAbd Allāh al-Wāqidī: other authorities differ to a greater or lesser degree in their accounts of the way in which control of the city passed to the Muslims.

491. An analogous, although less explicitly described, reservation of surrounding countryside for Muslims apparently figured in the instrument of capitulation for Jerusalem: ibid., 139.

492. For example, Yaʿqūbī, *al-Buldān,* 112, 114; al-Faqīh, *al-Buldān,* 118; Masʿūdī, *Murūj al-Dhahab,* 4:87; Iṣṭakhrī, *al-Masālik wa-l-Mamālik,* 61; and Ibn Ḥawqal, *al-Masālik wa-l-Mamālik,* 116.

493. Maqdisī, *Aḥsan,* 160, 179, 181.

494. Balādhurī, *Futūḥ al-Buldān,* 129. This author's references for other citations in this paragraph are pp. 116, 127, 130, 131, 133, 144–45, 150, and 151–52.

495. From Aramaic *Beth Maqd*ᵉ*ʿshā:* cf. Hebrew *Bēt ha-Miqdāsh* = sanctuary, temple. The common name al-Quds came into use only in the tenth century.

496. See John Wilkinson, "The streets of Jerusalem," *Levant,* (1975): 118–36 and "Jerusalem under Rome and Byzantium 63 BC–637 AD," in *Jerusalem in History,* ed. K. J. Asali (New York, 1990), 75–104.

497. M. Avi-Yonah, *The Madaba Mosaic Map* (Jerusalem, 1954) and J. T. Milik, "La topographie de Jérusalem vers la fin de l'époque byzantine," *Mélanges de l'Université Saint-Joseph* 37 (1960): 125–89. The map was devised in about 575. The western thoroughfare followed the ridge of the upper city, while the other passed through the Tyropoeon valley and the lower city.

498. For qualifications of the absolute reliability of this statement see Cyril Mango, "The Temple Mount AD 614–638" in *Bayt al-Maqdis,* ed. Raby and Johns, 1–16.

499. Sebēos, *Sébéos. Histoire d'Héraclius,* trans. F. Macler (Paris, 1904), 64–70.

500. Wilkinson, "Jerusalem under Rome and Byzantium," 100–102, citing Strategius, *Capture of Jerusalem,* Garitte's translation (*La Prise de Jérusalem par les Perses en 614* [Louvain, 1960]), 16.

501. The details of the instrument of capitulation are variously reported by early authors, successive generations of whom embellished their accounts with layers of validatory myth acceptable to their times. The earliest, and probably the most reliable, tradition depicts a common form of capitulation by which the city would be spared so long as the inhabitants paid the specified tribute (Balādhurī, *Futūḥ al-Buldān,* 138).

502. See note 165 to chapter 6. Arculf's description was as follows (Paul Geyer, *Itinera Hierosolymitana* [Vindobonae, 1898], 226–27): "In illo famoso loco, ubi qondam templum magnifice constructum fuerat . . . nunc Saraceni quadrangulam orationis domum, quam subrectis tabulis et magnis trabibus super quasdam ruinarum reliquias construentes vili fabricati sunt opere, ipsi frequentant quae utique domus tria hominum milia simul, ut fertur, capere potest."

A mosque capable of accommodating three thousand *homines* (= persons) would presumably imply an anticipated Muslim population of roughly that size, not all of whom need have been settlers after the conquest. At that time people known respectively as *ʿArab* (Arabic-speaking) and *Aʿrāb* (nomadic) were settled throughout the Levant and Mesopotamia, where they were adherents of some form (more often than not Christian) of monotheism, and as such probably not inherently hostile to Islam. It is also worth noting that about twenty years before Arculf's visit, Anastasius of Sinai complained that he was awakened betimes by the sound of Egyptian workmen clearing the Temple Mount: cited by Robert Hoyland, *Seeing Islam as Others Saw It. A Survey and Evaluation of Christian,*

Jewish and Zoroastrian Writings on Early Islam (Princeton, N.J., 1997), 101, 595.

503. The architectural and ritual features of the platform now known as the Ḥaram al-Sharīf (a name that did not enter into general use until Ottoman times) are discussed by, int. al., Max van Berchem, *Jérusalem Ḥaram,* pt. 2, vol. 2 of *Matériaux pour un Corpus Inscriptionum Arabicarum* (Cairo, 1925–27), *Planches,* vol. 3 (Cairo, 1920); Miriam Rosen-Ayalon, *The Early Islamic Monuments of al-Ḥaram al-Sharīf: An Iconographic Study,* Monographs of the Institute of Archaeology (Jerusalem, 1989); S. D. Goitein, O. Grabar, "al-Ḳuds," *The Encyclopaedia of Islam,* new ed., 5:322–44; Raby and Johns, eds., *Bayt al-Maqdis;* and Elad, *Medieval Jerusalem and Islamic Worship* (Leiden, 1995); and are depicted cartographically by Dan Bahat in the relevant sheets of *Carta's Historical Atlas of Jerusalem* (Jerusalem, 1983). The fortifications of the city are discussed by G. J. Wightman (*The Walls of Jerusalem from the Canaanites to the Mamluks* [Sydney, 1993], chaps. 9, 10).

504. This has almost universally been taken as a completion date, but Sheila S. Blair has made a strong case for reassessing it as a terminus a quo ("What Is the Date of the Dome of the Rock?" in *Bayt al-Maqdis,* ed. Raby and Johns, 59–87). More than a century later the name of ʿAbd al-Malik, the instigator of the dome, was replaced by that of the caliph al-Maʾmūn (r. 813–33) during an ʿAbbāsid restoration of the building, but the date remained unchanged.

505. This last interpretation has been proposed by Josef van Ess ("ʿAbd al-Malik and the Dome of the Rock. Analysis of Some Texts," in ibid., 89–103).

506. Rosen-Ayalon, *The Early Islamic Monuments,* chap. 7. This interpretation has also been espoused by Amikam Elad ("Why Did ʿAbd al-Malik Build the Dome of the Rock? A Re-examination of the Muslim Sources," in *Bayt al-Maqdis,* ed. Raby and Johns, 51–52), basing his argument on comments by ibn Kathīr *(al-Bidāyah wa-l-Nihayah).*

507. English translation by F. E. Peters, *Jerusalem* (Princeton, N.J., 1985), 143; also Geyer, *Itinera Hierosolymitana,* 21–22.

508. A particularly radical revisionist contribution to the debate concerning the purpose of the Dome of the Rock has recently been proposed by van Ess. Basing his arguments on texts by Ibn Ḥibbān, al-Wāsiṭī, Rabīʿ ibn Ḥabīb, Ibn Khuzaymah, and others, he suggests that the imprint on the rock under the dome was originally conceived as the footprint not of Muḥammad but of God. As van Ess writes, "The Syrian Muslims wanted to surpass the dome [of the Anastasis] which covered the spot from which Christ had ascended to Heaven [after the creation], by constructing a new one which covered the rock from which *God* had ascended to Heaven. The Christians proved the divinity of Christ with a footprint in the floor of the Church of the Ascension, and the Muslims were happy to produce similar evidence on the Rock" ("ʿAbd al-Malik and the Dome of the Rock," 101). In another place this author concedes, revealingly, that "ʿAbd al-Malik seems to have thought of the Rock more in connection with God than with the Prophet" (100). This reading of the evidence simply cannot prove acceptable to Muslim scholars, although van Ess does go some way toward discounting the charge of anthropomorphism implicit in the protests of those Ḥijāzī scholars who opposed the (to them) inordinate sacralization of the Ḥaram (97–99).

509. Goitein and Grabar, "al-Ḳuds," 5:340.

510. See, for example, M. Écochard, "À propos du Dôme du Rocher et d'un article de M. Oleg Grabar," *Bulletin d'Études Orientales* 25 (1972): 37–45, who has demonstrated dimensional correspondences between the Dome of the Rock and the basilica of St. Simeon Stylites at Qalʿat Simʿān (probably completed between 459, when the saint died, and the end of the century), or farther afield with San Vitale in Ravenna.

511. But the rotunda lacked an outer octagon until the time of the Crusades.

512. Mark the Deacon, *Vie de Porphyre, Évêque de Gaza,* ed. and trans. H. Grégoire and M.-A. Kugener (Paris, 1930), 52–60.

513. The sequence of events under the Umayyads has been elicited with care and acumen by Elad (*Medieval Jerusalem and Islamic Worship,* chap. 1). That al-Walīd was indeed responsible for some construction work on the Aqṣā Mosque is attested by the Aphrodito Papyri, which preserve official correspondence between a governor of Egypt (709–14) and one of his officials, including explicit statements that skilled craftsmen were sent from Egypt to work on "the mosque in Jerusalem" for periods of six months to a year (H. I. Bell, "Translation of the Greek Aphrodito Papyri in the British Museum," *Der Islam* 2 [1911]: 269–83, 372–84; 3 [1912]: 132–40, 369–73; 4 [1913]: 87–96).

514. The Dome of the Chain, in common with certain other monuments built by ʿAbd al-Malik in Jerusalem, was sanctified by both Jewish and Muslim traditions: the site was the place where King David had used a miraculous chain of light as a test of truthfulness among the Children of Israel, and was also the spot where the Prophet had met the *ḥūr al-ʿayn* on the night of the *Isrāʾ.* See Elad, *Medieval Jerusalem and Islamic Worship,* 47–48.

515. Al-Muhallabī (eleventh century) mentions two additional domes on the Ḥaram during the caliphate of al-Walād: Qubbat al-Mīzān ("Dome of the Scales") and Qubbat al-Maḥshar ("Dome of the Gathering"), but they are cited in a context that casts a measure of doubt on that author's reliability. See ibid., 48 n. 115. In any case, the precise locations of these two domes are unknown.

516. B. Mazar, *The Excavations in the Old City of Jerusalem near the Temple Mount. Preliminary Report on the Second and Third Seasons 1969–1970* (Jerusalem, 1971) and M. Ben-Dov, *The Omayyad Structures near the Temple Mount* (Jerusalem, 1971); these papers comprise a single volume.

517. Donald Whitcomb, "Meaning of the Dome of the Rock," window in Whitcomb, "Islam and the Socio-Cultural Transition of Palestine," 499. The interpretation adopted here is not in fundamental disagreement with that explicated by Oleg Grabar in his splendid volume entitled *The Shape of the Holy: Early Islamic Jerusalem* (Princeton, N.J., 1996), which unfortunately appeared too recently to be integrated into this study.

518. Cf.: "we may note that, although there survives no explicit

written testimony that the Umayyads considered Jerusalem to be their capital, their extraordinary investment of material and human resources in the city leaves no doubt that this was so" (Elad, "Why did ʿAbd al-Malik build the Dome of the Rock?" 48). Note also Hoyland's endorsement of this point of view in *Seeing Islam as Others Saw It,* 223: "Evidently Jerusalem was not only a cultic centre, but initially the capital of Muslim Palestine."

519. Elad, *Medieval Jerusalem and Islamic Worship,* 163.

520. Maqdisī, *Aḥsan,* 167. The names of the gates as preserved by this author are Bāb Ṣihyūn (Zion Gate), Bāb al-Tīh (Wilderness), Bāb al-Balāṭ (here probably = a paved area: < Gk. πλατεῖα through Aramaic; Sourdel, *The Encyclopaedia of Islam,* 1:987), Bāb Jubb Irmiyā (Jeremiah's Well), Bāb Silwān (Siloam), Bāb Arīḥā (Jericho), Bāb al-ʿAmūd (the Column), and Bāb Miḥrāb Dāwūd (David's Oratory). Other lists of gates differing in varying degrees from that of al-Maqdisī were provided by Ibn al-Faqīh (903), Ibn ʿAbd Rabbihi (ca. 913), Nāṣir-i Khusraw (1047), Ibn Fadl Allāh al-ʿUmarī (ca. 1345), and, of course, Muʿjīr al-Dīn al-ʿUlaymī (1496). See the comparative tables in Michael Hamilton Burgoyne, "The Gates of the Ḥaram al-Sharīf," in *Bayt al-Maqdis,* ed. Raby and Johns, 120–21.

The principal attempts to identify and locate these gates are as follows:

- Le Strange, *Palestine under the Moslems,* 211–17.
- L. H. Vincent and M. Abel, *Jérusalem—Recherches de Topographie, d'Archéologie et d'Histoire: II, Jérusalem Nouvelle,* 4 vols. (Paris, 1914–26).
- A. Miquel, "Jérusalem arabe: note de topographie historique," *Revue des Etudes Orientales* 16 (1958–60): 7–13.
- Yoram Tsafrir, "Muqaddasi's gates of Jerusalem—a new identification based on Byzantine sources," *Israel Exploration Journal* 27 (1977): 152–161.
- D. Bahat, "Les portes de Jérusalem selon Mukaddasi: nouvelle identification," *Revue Biblique* 93 (1986): 429–36.

The positions of these gates have been plotted on a map of ʿAbbāsid Jerusalem by Wightman (*The Walls of Jerusalem,* 239 fig. 75). In addition, an interpretation proposed by Donald Whitcomb is too recent to be included in the Wightman summary ("Islam and the Socio-Cultural Transition of Palestine," 499 window 1). In any case, there is currently no scholarly consensus as to the locations of these gates. Most of the specified authors tended to conclude that the gates were not listed in topographical order or to avoid the question altogether, whereas Tsafrir and Whitcomb agree on a counterclockwise sequence beginning in the southwestern corner of the city (an interpretive strategy already employed by Whitcomb in the case of al-Ramlah [Ramleh] and Shīrāz).

521. Maqdisī, *Aḥsan,* 166.

522. Ibid., 167. It followed from the relatively small number of Muslims in Jerusalem that its congregational mosque attracted only small congregations and assemblies while instruction in its schools had practically ceased.

523. Ibid.

524. Muḥammad ibn al-Qāsim al-Iskandarānī al-Nuwayrī, *Kitāb al-Ilmām,* ed. A. S. Aṭīyah, 6 vols. (Hyderabad, A.D. 1968–76/A.H. 1388–93), vol. 2, p. 135. On al-Nuwayrī more generally see Aṭīyah, *A Fourteenth-Century Encyclopedist from Alexandria* (Salt Lake City, 1977).

525. Ibn ʿAbd al-Ḥakam, *Futūḥ Miṣr,* 130.

526. For example, Ibn Manẓur, *Lisān al-ʿArab,* 1:474 and Lane, *Lexicon,* 28–31, especially p. 30. Several of the references cited by Lane imply that *ikhādhah* should be wasteland or at least unclaimed land; but it must also be remembered that these citations are all later than the *Futūḥ Miṣr.*

527. Balādhurī, *Futūḥ al-Buldān,* 222. This author's account of the conquest of Miṣr (Egypt) is not free of ambiguities, but I believe that my report accurately reflects al-Balādhurī's intentions. I have assumed that the lances were thrust into walls of houses, but it is not impossible that they were stood upright in the earth before the houses that they designated. It is also possible that the Muslims who found their dwellings occupied by other Muslims were being rotated from al-Fusṭāṭ, although that interpretation fits the context as reported by al-Balādhurī less well.

528. Butler made this point very forcefully in his *The Arab Conquest of Egypt,* 2d ed., 368. He also suggested that 400 palaces and baths, 40 theatres, 1,200 vendors of green vegetables, and 4,000 (tax-paying) Jews would have accorded fairly well with what is known about other contemporary *metropoleis;* and he quotes Zachariah of Mitylene as listing 1,797 magnates' residences and 926 baths in Rome at much the same time. For comments on a similar inflation in the numbers supplied by al-Ṭabarī and a proposed coefficient of correction, see Gautier H. A. Juynboll, trans., *The History of al-Ṭabarī,* vol. 13 (Albany, N.Y., 1989), xiii–xvi. Note that in the twelfth century Benjamin of Tudela, who had reason to ascertain as accurately as possible the number of Jews in the cities he visited, reported 3,000 in Alexandria (*Safer ha-Masaot,* trans. Marcus Nathan Adler [New York, 1983], 134). For an authoritative overview of the city in late antiquity see C. Haas, *Alexandria in Late Antiquity: Topography and Social Conflict* (Baltimore, 1997).

529. Butler, *The Arab Conquest of Egypt,* 371.

530. For pre-Islamic Alexandria see Heinz Heinen, "Alexandria in Late Antiquity," *The Coptic Encyclopedia,* 1:95; P. M. Fraser, "Alexandria, Christian and Medieval," *The Coptic Encyclopedia,* 1:88–92; Kahle, "Zur Geschichte des mittelalterlichen Alexandria," 29–84; and notes 18 and 97 to chapter 15.

531. The low profile of the alluvial coastline of the delta and the need to avoid offshore reefs were powerful inducements to the provision of a navigational aid on Pharos Island.

532. Fraser, *The Coptic Encyclopedia,* 1:90.

533. Cf. John Chrysostom searching in vain for this mausoleum, in Mieczyslaw Rodziewicz, "Graeco-Islamic elements at Kom el Dikka," 35.

534. Ibid., 44. See also the same author's more recent "Transformation of Ancient Alexandria into a Medieval City," in *Colloque International,* ed. Gayraud, 369–86.

535. Rodziewicz, "Graeco-Islamic elements at Kom el Dikka," 513. In fact isolated elements of the old orthogonal grid persisted into modern times, notably the Via Canopica, part of which endured as the Rue Rosette.

536. Ibn ʿAbd al-Ḥakam, *Futūḥ Miṣr,* 42, who gave the names

of the *madīnāt* as Mannah (in the vicinity of the lighthouse); Alexandria (proper), which in the ninth century became known as the Qaṣabat al-Iskandarīyah; and the not satisfactorily explicable Naqitah.

537. Ibid., 41–42, but there are not wholly accordant competing traditions, additional mosques appear to be mentioned from time to time, and a number of mosques are known to have been established in abandoned or preempted Melkite churches (Fraser, *The Coptic Encyclopedia,* 1:91 and Aziz S. Attiya, "Historic churches in Alexandria," *The Coptic Encyclopedia,* 1:92–95).

538. Maqdisī, *Aḥsan,* 197: *jāmi'ān,* but jāmi'ātān in the Constantinople recension. See *Bibliotheca Geographorum Arabicorum,* 3:197, text and note f.

539. Nuwaryī, *al-Ilmām,* 1:102.

540. The *dār al-imārah* had originally been established in 664 in "the old fortress" *(al-ḥiṣn al-qadīm),* perhaps in response to an intensification of settlement following Mu'āwiyah's assumption of the caliphate in 661.

541. Fraser, *The Coptic Encyclopedia,* 1:89.

542. Ibn Ḥawqal, *al-Masālik wa-l-Mamālik,* 150.

543. Yāqūt (*Mu'jam,* 1:256–65) alone refuted this story, asserting that by night al-Iskandarīyah (Alexandria) was no less dark than any other city he was aware of.

544. Ibn 'Abd al-Ḥakam, *Futūḥ Miṣr,* 58, 74; al-Malikī, *Riyāḍ,* 1:12, 18, 19, 21; al-Bakrī, *al-Masālik wa-l-Mamālik,* 75; and Yāqūt, *Mu'jam,* 4:399, 415. For additional comments on the development of this city see chapter 16 and note 293 above.

545. Balādhurī, *Futūḥ al-Buldān,* 228 and Ibn 'Idhārī, *Bayān,* 1:21.

546. Bakrī, *al-Masālik wa-l-Mamālik,* 23.

547. 'Iyāḍ, *Tartīb al-Madārik,* ed. M. Talbī (Bayrūt, 1965), 71. This and the following three references have been collected by Talbi in *The Encyclopaedia of Islam,* 2d ed., 4:829.

548. 'Iyāḍ, *Madārik,* 369.

549. Ibid., 359.

550. Ibid.

551. The surviving list of gates at al-'Abbāsīyah is probably not complete, but the most important were probably as follows: Bāb al-Raḥmah (Mercy), Bāb al-Ḥadīd (Iron), Bāb Ghalbūn (attributed to Aghlab ibn 'Abd Allāh ibn al-Aghlab, a minister of Ziyādat Allāh I: H. H. Abdul-Wahab, *The Encyclopaedia of Islam,* 2d ed., 1:24), and Bāb al-Rīḥ (Wind), all in the east, and Bāb al-Sa'ādah (Happiness) in the west.

552. Bakrī, *al-Masālik wa-l-Mamālik,* 26 and Ibn 'Idhārī, *Bayān,* 1:106. The Qarwānī cisterns are discussed by Creswell, (*A Short Account of Early Muslim Architecture,* 381–82).

553. Bakrī, *al-Masālik wa-l-Mamālik,* 26.

554. Talbī, *The Encyclopaedia of Islam,* 4:829.

555. Maqdisī, *Aḥsan,* 225–26.

556. Bakrī, *al-Masālik wa-l-Mamālik,* 25–26.

557. Talbī, *The Encyclopaedia of Islam,* 4:829, citing (Pseudo-) Ibn al-Raqīq, *Ta'rīkh* (Tūnis, A.H. 1388), 185.

558. 'Iyāḍ, *Madārik,* 132.

559. Balādhurī, *Futūḥ al-Buldān,* 230.

560. For references see note 31 to chapter 16. Ibn Ḥawqal reports that the ruins of the classical city were still visible along the shore in the second half of the tenth century (*al-Masālik wa-l-Mamālik,* 79).

561. Ibid., 77–78.

562. Bakrī, *al-Masālik wa-l-Mamālik,* 34, 45, 47, 53, 57, 70, 144, 146, 202.

563. Ibid., 57.

564. Ibid., 50. Note, though, that in the previous century al-Maqdisī had not incorporated Ṭubnah in his administrative hierarchy.

Of course, remains of classical structures were not restricted to urban areas but were to be found in various stages of decay scattered through the countrysides. Particularly noteworthy in al-Bakrī's narrative is the fortress *(ḥiṣn)* of Labdah, a stronghold midway between Sharūs and Tripoli occupied by one thousand Arab horsemen engaged in more or less continuous warfare against Berber tribesmen. The *ḥiṣn* itself was of pre-Muslim construction and surrounded by impressive monuments from antiquity, as well as numerous ruins (9). In the vicinity of al-Masīlah, too, there was an ancient, stone-built city whose inhabitants had long since departed (143–44), while the circumstance that Roman reservoirs in Constantine (Quṣtanṭīnah) were in use as late as the present century makes it more than likely that they were also pressed into service by the Muslims after their conquest of the Ifrīqiyah. In the eleventh century, and probably for some centuries previously, this last city was controlled by Kutāmā tribes (63; de Slane's translation, 131–32).

565. Ibn al-Ṣaghīr, Motylinski edition, 68.

566. Ibn Sa'd, *al-Ṭabaqāt,* 1:39ff; Azraqī in Wüstenfeld, *Die Chroniken der Stadt Mekka,* 1:65–67. Serjeant ("Ḥaram and Ḥawṭah," 54) has interpreted Mu'āwiyah's purchase of the Dār al-Nadwah from the 'Abd al-Dār for one million *dirhams* as "a piece of politico-religious strategy" that entitled him to preside at arbitrations and mediation of disputates. There is a summary of what is known and inferred about this institution by Rudi Paret in *The Encyclopaedia of Islam,* 2d ed., 2:128; see also chapter 7. The principal sources for the early Islamic development of Makkah (Mecca) have been brought together by Wüstenfeld in *Die Chroniken der Stadt Mekka* and *Geschichte der Stadt Mekka nach den Arabischen Chroniken bearbeitet* (Leipzig, 1861; reprint, Hildeshim, 1981).

567. See the reconstruction of the lineaments of the city in Wüstenfeld, *Die Chroniken der Stadt* (Mekka, reprint edition), vols. 3 and 4, map facing p. 344; and, for the nineteenth century, in Hurgronje, *Mekka in the Latter Part of the Nineteenth Century,* map at end of volume. It is noticeable, too, that through all the changes taking place in the city, the Ka'bah remained inviolable in its *ḥaram* so that even today it projects essentially the building that 'Abd al-Malik had in mind when he restored its fabric at the end of the seventh century.

568. Maqdisī, *Aḥsan,* 71.

569. Ibid. It is possible, though, that the reference may have been to either al-Masfalah (the lower [sector of the settlement]) or al-Ma'alāt (the upper sector), both of which are mentioned imme-

diately preceding the sentence in question and in the same line. Maqdisī cites three other cities as occupying analogous situations: ʿAmmān in al-Shām (Greater Syria), Iṣṭakhr in Fārs, and Qaryat al-Ḥamrāʾ (simply al-Ḥamrāʾ in Ibn Khurradādhbih, *al-Masālik wa-l-Mamālik,* 24) in Khurāsān.

570. A signal resource for the study of early Islamic al-Madīnah (Medina) is Michael Lecker's *Muslims, Jews and Pagans. Studies on Early Islamic Madina* (Leiden, 1995). This volume not only elicits a great deal of information about the ʿĀliyah (Upper Madīnah) but also establishes a methodological framework for further work on the city as a whole as an essential contribution to the writing of a comprehensive biography of the Prophet Muḥammad. Another valuable guide to available materials is ʿUmar ibn Shabbah, *Taʾrīkh al-Madīnah al-Munawwarah,* ed. Fahīm Muḥammad Shaltūt (Makkah, A.H. 1399); for comments on this work see Lecker, *Muslims,* 10 n. 5. Lecker's exposition relies heavily (although certainly not exclusively) on ʿAlī ibn Aḥmad al-Samhūdī's *Wafāʾal-Wafāh bi-Akhbār Dār al-Muṣṭafā,* ed. Muḥammad Muḥyī al-Dīn ʿAbd al-Ḥamīd (al-Qāhirah, A.H. 1374), who quoted extensively from the late seventh-century author Muḥammad ibn al-Ḥasan, known as Ibn Zabālah, whose book entitled *Akhbār al-Madīnah* survives only as extracts in later authors.

571. Lecker, *Muslims,* 103–4.

572. Samhūdi, *Wafāʾ al-Wafāh,* 1:198 and Lecker, *Muslims,* 17.

573. Lecker, *Muslims,* 14–18. Similar observations had been advanced by ʿAbd al-Quaddūs al-Anṣārī, *Āthār al-Madīnah al-Munawwarah* (Dimashq, A.H. 1353), 42 and ʿUbayd al-Madanī, "Uṭūm al-Madīnah al-Munawwarah," *Journal of the College of Arts at the King Saud University* 3 (1973–74): 214.

574. Lecker, *Muslims,* 13. It was Masʿūdī (*al-Tambīh,* 206) who reported the impliedly total destruction of the Madīnan *āṭām,* an event that Lecker finds improbable. Masʿūdī further observes that vestiges of their structures were still visible in the landscape of his own day.

575. Lecker, *Muslims,* 11, 16.

576. Ibid., 18. The terms *ḥiṣn* and *uṭum* appear to have been employed interchangeably for much of the time, although there are texts in which they seem to have been differentiated (ibid., 10). Later sources referred to the Jewish fortresses mentioned above by the word *qalʿah,* at least once expanded to *qahʿah ḥaṣīnah* (ibid., 15).

577. M. Lecker, "On the markets of Madina (Yathrib) in pre-Islamic and early Islamic times," *Jerusalem Studies in Arabic and Islam* 8 (1986): 133–47.

578. This is Lecker's careful assessment in *Muslims,* 19. The delayed conversion of the large subtribe of Aws Allāh, domiciled in the ʿĀliyah, is the theme of chap. 2 of Lecker's book.

579. Ibid., 145.

580. Usually rendered in English as "hypocrites" but perhaps better as "subversives."

581. Lecker, *Muslims,* 95. Chap. 4 of this work is a compendious evaluation of the several independent versions of the Ḍirār matter that furnish conflicting accounts of the manner in which certain named individuals built a mosque that was at first sanctioned by the Prophet but subsequently disapproved and razed on his order. If—as at least one commentary implies and many modern scholars believe—the conflict was between the Ḍirār Mosque and the Prophet's Mosque in Safilah, the implication of disunity in the oasis is to that extent more plausible.

582. For this and other comments on Yathrib/al-Madīnah see chapters 1 and 7.

583. Lecker, *Muslims,* 100, citing Balādhurī, *al-Ashrāf,* 1:273 and Muṭahhar ibn Ṭāhir al-Maqdisī, *al-Badʾ wa-l Taʾrīkh,* ed. C. Huart, vol. 4 (Paris, 1899), 85.

584. Jean Sauvaget, *La Mosquée Omeyyade de Médine* (Paris, 1947); Creswell, *A Short Account of Early Muslim Architecture,* 43–46; Ghazi Izzeddin Bisheh, "The Mosque of the Prophet at Madīnah throughout the First-Century A.H. with Special Emphasis on the Umayyad Mosque" (Ph.D. diss., University of Michigan, 1979); and Hillenbrand, *Islamic Architecture: Form, Function and Meaning* (New York, 1994), 73.

585. Maqdisī, *Aḥsan,* 82.

586. It is noteworthy that Susa/al-Sūs is one of the relatively few cities under discussion where interpretation of urban morphology depends more on archaeological evidence than on literary sources. The archaeological record is summarized compendiously in Donald Whitcomb's "Islamic archaeology at Susa," *Paléorient* 11, no. 2 (1985): 85–90 and Monique Kervran's "Transformations de la ville de Suse et de son économie de l'époque sasanide à l'époque abbaside," *Paléorient* 11, no. 2 (1985): 91–100. For general comments on the economic resources of the city see Rémy Boucharlat, "Suse, marché agricole ou relais du grand commerce. Suse et la Susiane à l'époque des grands empires," *Paléorient* 11, no. 2 (1985): 71–81.

587. R. Ghirshman, "Une mosquée de Suse au début de l'Hégire," *Bulletin des Études Orientales* 12 (1947–48): 77–91.

588. Maqdisī, *Aḥsan,* 407; Monique Kervran, "Le batiment oriental," in "Recherche sur les niveaux islamiques de la Ville des Artisans," by Kervran and Axelle Rougelle, *Cahiers de la Délégation Archéologique Française en Iran* (Paris, 1984), 40–52. *Khānqāh* (var. *khāniqāh;* Lane, *Lexicon,* 2:818, *khānaqāh;* < Pers. *khānagāh*) first appeared in tenth-century authors to denote the center of combined worship, teaching, and evangelism of certain Ṣūfī sects, particularly in Khurāsān and Transoxania. "Monastery," although the commonly used term, conveys only an imperfect idea of the range of functions of this institution. Furthermore, it is by no means certain that, even if the archeological remains are those of a religious structure, *khānqāh* is the appropriate term. And there is still the not totally negligible possibility that the structure in question may have been something in the manner of a *khān* or *fundūq,* or perhaps none of these.

589. Claire Hardy-Guilbert, "Contribution à l'analyse du tissu urbain de Suse à partir du XIe siècle," *Paléorient* 11, no. 2 (1985): 101–13.

590. Maqdisī, *Aḥsan,* 407.

591. Al-Maqdisī (ibid., 407–8) wisely rejected the multifaceted

myths that had grown up around this tomb with the curt statement that "The only things known about the grave is that it is in the river and there is a tale told about it."

592. A bath excavated in the *apadana* complex was similar to one found at Sīrāf (Whitcomb, "Islamic archaeology at Susa," 87, citing Monique Kervran and S. Renimel, "Suse islamique: remarques préliminaires et perspectives," *Studia Iranica* 3 [1974]: 253–66).

593. There is no confirmation in either the archaeological record or pre-eleventh-century literary sources of the claim advanced by both Yāqūt (*Muʿjam,* 1:848, citing Ḥamzah al-Iṣfahānī) and Ḥamd Allāh Mustawfī (*Taʾrīkh-i Guzīdeh,* ed. Edward G. Browne under the title *The Taʾrīkh-i-guzída; or, "select history" of Hamdaʾlláh Mustawfí-i-Qazwíní [Leiden, 1910],* 105) that al-Sūs was rebuilt by an early Sāsānian ruler in the shape of a falcon; nor, for that matter, of the same authors' assertion that the other Khūzistānī cities of Tustar and Junday-Sābūr at about the same time were given the spatial frameworks of respectively a horse and a chessboard *(ruqʿat al-shaṭranj).* The originating circumstances for these three specifically Khūzistānī tales are not immediately evident.

594. See the sources given in note 8 to chapter 5, to which should be added Carole Hillenbrand, "*The History of the Jazīra 1100–1150: the Contribution of Ibn al-Azraq al-Fāriqi*" (Ph.D. diss., University of Edinburgh, 1979).

595. Procopius, *De Aedificiis,* vol. 3 of *Procopii Caesariensis Opera Omnia,* ed. J. Haury (Leipzig, 1905–13); rev. ed. by G. Wirth (Leipzig, 1962–64). It must be borne in mind, though, that *The Buildings* (to give the title an English translation) was conceived as a panegyric in praise of not only Emperor Justinian's public works but also his imperial policy.

596. Ibn al-Azraq, *Taʾrīkh,* 149, 164.

597. Maqdisī, *Aḥsan,* 146.

598. Iṣṭakhrī, *al-Masālik wa-l-Mamālik,* 76.

599. Nāṣir-i Khusraw, *Safar Nāmah,* Thackston's translation, 7.

600. For instance, Barthold, *Mussulman Culture,* 31–32 and *Turkestan down to the Mongol Invasion,* 78.

601. *Quhandiz;* sometimes *dīz* < *kuhna dīz* = old citadel.

602. *Shahristān* = place of power; *madīnah* = administrative center, an accurate enough translation. Note: This is not al-Maqdisī's technical usage of the term *madīnaḥ.*

603. Shimuzu Kosuke, "Iranshi no naka no toshizo: 10–11 seiki no Nishapuru," *Shicho,* n.s., vol. 28 (1990).

604. Bulliet, "Medieval Nishapur," 67–89.

605. Al-Naysābūrī in Richard Frye, *The Histories of Nishapur* (Cambridge, Mass., 1965), ff. 57a–58a. This fact is confirmed by al-Iṣṭakhrī (*al-Masālik wa-l-Mamālik,* 254), Ibn Ḥawqal (*al-Masālik wa-l-Mamālik,* 432) and al-Maqdisī (*Aḥsan,* 316).

606. Shāh Hanbar in Yāqūt, *Muʿjam,* 3:246. Bulliet ("Medieval Nishapur," 71) identifies the *quhandiz* and *shahr* on the ground as represented by respectively higher and lower mounds separated by a narrow depression, presumably a vestige of the merged *khandaqs.*

607. Charles K. Wilkinson, *Nishapur: Pottery of the Early Islamic Period* (New York, 1975), xxvii.

608. Bulliet, "Medieval Nishapur," 71–72.

609. Naysābūriaī in Frye, *The Histories of Nishapur,* ff. 66b, 8b; 61b; 21b. Maʿqil Street was in the Bāghak ("Little Garden") quarter (f. 59b).

610. Maqdisī, *Aḥsan,* 315.

611. Named for the son of al-Ḥusayn ibn Muʿādh ibn Muslim, governor from 777 to 780: E. von Zambaur, *Manuel de Généalogie et de Chronologie pour l'Histoire de l'Islam* (Hanover, 1927), 48. The *dār al-imārah* had been built by ʿAmr ibn al-Layth.

612. Presumably this bridge carried "the only road" that Iṣṭakhrī describes as crossing the *khandaq* between the *quhandiz* and the *shahristān* (*al-Masālik wa-l-Mamālik,* 254).

613. Ibn Ḥawqal, *al-Masālik wa-l-Mamālik,* 432.

614. Bulliet, "Medieval Nishapur," 74: "[The ruins] suggest a general alignment of streets parallel and perpendicular to this line." Maqdisī (*Aḥsan,* 316) lists the most widely known streets as Darb al-Jīq, Darb Khushnān, Darb Bard, Darb Manīshak, Darb al-Qibāb, Darb Fārs, Darb al-Khurūj, and Darb Aswār Kārīz.

615. Bulliet's reconstruction of the layout of the medieval city is reproduced as Planche I in "Medieval Nishapur."

616. Naysābūrī in Frye, *The Histories of Nishapur,* ff. 58b–59b.

617. Bulliet, "Medieval Nishapur," 77–87.

618. According to Yāqūt (*Muʿjam,* 2:380), this settlement had originally been named after the city in ʿIrāq, although I think it at least as likely that its name reflected its origin as a tribal encampment.

619. Named for the abundance of willows *(bīd)* growing there.

620. *Jūlāh* = "weaver."

621. Bulliet, "Medieval Nishapur," 83. This conclusion is based on the number of references in the *The Histories of Nishapur,* the number of biographies preserved, and the prevalence of the lower-class Karrāmīyah sect in Manāshik, for which see C. E. Bosworth, "The rise of the Karāmiyyah in Khurasan," *Muslim World* 50 (1960): 5–14.

622. Bulliet, "Medieval Nishapur," 69.

623. Iṣṭakhrī, *al-Masālik wa-l-Mamālik,* 254.

624. In this connection it is not without relevance to note that Maqdisī (*Aḥsan,* 315), responding to a question at a gathering in Shīrāz, rated the *mahallāt* of al-Ḥīrah, al-Jūr, and Manīshak as each being about half the size of the Fārsī capital.

625. Reported by Maqdisī, ibid., 315.

626. Ibid.

627. Summarized by Hisao Komatsu in *Islamic Urban Studies,* ed. Haneda and Miura, 285–86.

628. Bulliet, "Medieval Nishapur," 72–73.

629. For references see notes 11–16 to chapter 14.

630. Ṭabarī, *Taʾrīkh,* 2:1490.

631. Al-Yaʿqūbī (*Kitāb al-Buldān,* 287) overshot the mark egregiously when he placed Balkh at thirty days' march from each of Farghānah, Rayy (Rey) Sijistān, Kābul, Qandahār, Kirmān, Qashmīr, Khwārizm, and Multān, but the point of powerful nodality that he was making was valid enough.

632. Literally, "with parallel perimeters" (Yaʿqūbī, *al-Buldān,* 287).

633. There may be grounds for reading these dimensions as standardized topoi rather than potentially verifiable lengths, for they are also attached to at least two other settlements, Bukhārā and Samarqand.

634. Iṣṭakhrī's figure of half a *farsakh* (*al-Masālik wa-l-Mamālik,* 254) is certainly an error, as it is not in accord with other statements of his.

635. Yāqūt, *Muʿjam,* s.v.

636. Ibn Ḥawqal, *al-Masālik wa-l-Mamālik,* 448.

637. Maqdisī, *Aḥsan,* 302, Constantinople recension only.

638. The *-band* is inserted on the authority of Iṣṭakhrī.

639. Ibn Ḥawqal (*al-Masālik wa-l-Mamālik,* 447–48) mentions "several gates" and, like al-Maqdisī, specifies seven: al-Naw Bahār, Wākhtah (which I read as a mislection for al-Raḥbah), Hadīd, al-Hinduwān, al-Yahūd, al-Shastaman (for Shastband = possibly an aural misunderstanding), and Bakhtī (presumably poor pointing for Yaḥyā).

640. Descriptions, not entirely devoid of fantasy, by Ibn al-Faqīh, al-Masʿūdī, Qazwīnī, Yāqūt (citing ʿUmar ibn al-Azraq al-Kirmānī), and the Chinese Buddhist monk Hsüan Tsang (cf. note 165 to chapter 14).

641. See note 12 to chapter 14. See also Minorsky, *Ḥudūd,* 108.

642. For references see notes 17 and 18 to chapter 14. Harāt (with Arabic feminine ending) Pahlavi *h'y.* Harī in Minorsky, *Ḥudūd,* 103.

643. Ibn Ḥawqal, *al-Masālik wa-l-Mamālik,* 437.

644. Maqdisī, *Aḥsan,* 307.

645. Ibn Ḥawqal (*al-Masālik wa-l-Mamālik,* 437) reads, "Fīrūzābādh, the gate which faces toward Sijistān and the south."

646. Ibid.

647. Minorsky, *Ḥudūd,* 103–5, 327 n. 20. Iṣṭakhrī (*al-Masālik wa-l-Mamālik,* 265), followed by Ibn Ḥawqal (*al-Masālik wa-l-Mamālik,* 438), said much the same thing; Maqdisī (*Aḥsan,* 307), simply that the *jāmiʿ* was well attended *(aʿmar).*

648. For references see notes 8–10 to chapter 14.

649. E. Wiedemann, *Aufsätze zur arabischen Wissenschaftsgeschichte,* vol. 1 (Hildesheim, 1970), 272–78.

650. Richard N. Frye, "The Sasanian System of Walls for Defense," in *Studies in Memory of Gaston Wiet,* ed. Myriam Rosen-Ayalon (Jerusalem, 1977), 14.

651. Balādhurī, *Futūḥ al-Buldān,* 410.

652. If the enceinte were turned so that its gates faced the intermediate cardinal directions, they would have opened on respectively Sarakhs (southwest), the Banī-Māhān district and the Asʿadī canal, the road to the Āmū Daryā, and the northwest: a suggestion made by Le Strange (*The Lands of the Eastern Caliphate,* 399).

653. It is largely owing to the excavations of V. A. Zhukovskii at the end of the nineteenth century and M. E. Masson in the 1960s that the broad outlines of Marvian morphology have been established. Both are summarized by Barthold in *An Historical Geography,* chap. 2 and A. Yu. Yakubovskii and C. E. Bosworth in *The Encyclopaedia of Islam,* 2d ed., 6:618–21.

654. Yakubovskii and Bosworth, *The Encyclopaedia of Islam,* 6:619.

655. Livshits in Barthold, *An Historical Geography,* 42 n. 45 suggests that the *quhandiz* had been razed in the second half of the eighth century.

656. Maqdisī, *Aḥsan,* 311.

657. Ibid.

658. Ibn Ḥawqal, *al-Masālik wa-l-Mamālik,* 435.

659. Ibid., Maqdisī, *Aḥsan,* 312; and retrojecting information provided by Yāqūt, *Muʿjam,* 2:777 and Mustawfī, *Nuzhat al-Qulūb,* 214.

660. Maqdisī, *Aḥsan,* 299, 311.

661. *Al-madīnah al-ʿuẓmā* in Ibn Ḥawqal, *al-Masālik wa-l-Mamālik,* 414. For references for this section see notes 23–26 to chapter 14.

662. *Ta'rīkh-i Sīstān,* Gold's translation of the Bahār edition, 1–4, 23.

663. Possibly an Āhūramazd-Mōbadh, the priest in charge of a province or city: Bosworth, *Sistan under the Arabs,* 5.

664. *Ta'rīkh-i Sīstān,* 3, 10–11. I am in no position to judge the significance of al-Maqdisī's statement that half the city had been built by the Persian monarch Ardashīr and half by Khusraw (*Aḥsan,* 305–6).

665. Yaʿqūbī, *al-Buldān,* 281.

666. Ibn Ḥawqal, *al-Masālik wa-l-Mamālik,* 414–15.

667. Ibn Ḥawqal used the term *ḥiṣn* instead of the expected *quhandiz* to denote the citadel. It is also possible to read the relevant sentence as referring to "a fortified town/enceinte," as do in fact Kramers and Wiet (*Configuration de la Terre,* 402) and Miquel (*La Géographie Humaine,* vol. 4: *Les Travaux et les Jours* [Paris, 1988], 213). I have opted for the reading offered here under the influence of al-Maqdisī, who says directly enough, "There is a *madīnah* with a *ḥiṣn* . . ." (*Aḥsan,* 305).

668. Or "with spacious buildings." The Arabic reads *wāsʿ al-abniyah.*

669. For this rendering, as opposed to the "entrepôts" of Kramers and Wiet (*Configuration de la Terre,* 402) and Miquel (*La Geographie Humaine,* 4:213), see Lane, *Lexicon,* 619 col. 2.

670. Both Ibn Ḥawqal and Maqdisī use the term *madīnah* for the inner city; neither uses *shahristān* in this description.

671. Yāqūt (*Muʿjam,* 1:210) saw fit to add the comment "Then it became the seat of the government and a fortress."

672. Maqdisī, *Aḥsan,* 305.

673. These were Bāb al-Jadīd ("New Gate") and Bāb al-ʿAtīq ("Old Gate"), a short distance apart on the west side of the city, where they faced toward Fārs (in fact later in the same passage they appear to be referred to jointly as the Fārs Gates); Bāb Karkūyah ("Karkūyah Gate"), opening onto the Khurāsān road, and Bāb Nīshak ("Nīshak Gate"), looking toward Bust, both named after towns toward which they gave access; and in the southeast sector of the city, Bāb al-Ṭaʿām ("Provisions Gate"), leading to neighboring

rural districts *(rasātīq)*. It was this last entrance that had the most traffic *(aʿmar)*, and not surprisingly so, for a city with at least one dimension of ten kilometers, even if that were not all built over, would have drawn a huge volume of supplies from its surrounding trade area. All five gates were "of iron," which probably means faced with that metal.

674. These were Bāb Mīnā, looking toward Fārs, then in anticlockwise order, Bāb Dukhān, Bāb Shīrak, Bāb Shārāw, Bāb Shuʿayb, Bāb Nawjawīk, Bāb Ākān, Bāb Nīshak, Bāb Karkūyah, Bāb Asbarīs, Bāb Ghanjarah, Bāb Bāristān, and Bāb Rūdhkarān.

675. Ibn Ḥawqal (*al-Masālik wa-l-Mamālik,* 415) compares the domestic water supply in Zaranj to that operating in Arrajān in Fārs.

676. Literally, "the previous year": Ibn Ḥawqal's encounter with the traveller occurred in 971.

677. Miquel, *La Géographie Humane,* 4:211–15; the significance of Ibn Ḥawqal's account was also noticed by Blachère and Darmaun (*Extraits,* 137–39).

678. Miquel, *La Géographie Humaine,* 4:214.

679. Ibid.: "[Zaranj] reproduit l'un des schémas favoris de la cité d'Orient, don't le modèle . . . s'incarna en Bagdad." It has to be noted, though, that the other cities of this type—and they were not numerous—were the results of integrated, preconceived plans, not of spontaneous incremental growth.

680. Which, in any case, not infrequently happened in orthogonal cities throughout the world.

681. Since the eighteenth century known as the Zarafshān.

682. Cf. Ibn Ḥawqal, *al-Masālik wa-l-Mamālik,* 494: "The best slaves in all Mā Warāʾ al-Nahr are those trained in Samarqand."

683. Iṣṭakhrī, *al-Masālik wa-l-Mamālik,* 288, whence it was (almost certainly) copied into the *Ḥudūd,* 113. The historical framework for this discussion of Samarqand is much dependent on Barthold, *Turkestan down to the Mongol Invasion,* 83–92; H. H. Schnaeder and C. E. Bosworth, *The Encyclopaedia of Islam,* 2d ed., 8:1031–34; and Frantz Grenet and Claude Rapin, "De la Samarkand antique à la Samarkand islamique: continuités et ruptures," in *Colloque International,* ed. Gayraud, 387–402, with additional references to topographers where appropriate.

684. Consult note 633 above.

685. Ibn Ḥawqal (*al-Masālik wa-l-Mamālik,* 492) adds that this gate gave onto the Jird bridge over the Sughd River.

686. Maqdisī, p. 278. Cf. Minorsky, *Ḥudūd,* 113.

687. Ṭabarī, *Taʾrīkh,* 3:80. Some authors have assumed that the wall in question surrounded a *rabaḍ* rather than the *madīnah;* in response to which I can only say that I understand the context to lean slightly toward the latter interpretation. Barthold (*Turkestan, down to the Mongol Invasion,* 83) believed that the wall of the *shahristān (madīnah)* had been constructed in pre-Muslim times.

688. Yaʿqūbī, *al-Buldān,* 293.

689. Ibn Ḥawqal, *al-Masālik wa-l-Mamālik,* 493.

690. Maqdisī, *Aḥsan,* 278–79; Iṣṭakhrī, *al-Masālik wa-l-Mamālik,* 278; and Ibn Ḥawqal, *al-Masālik wa-l-Mamālik,* 493. Al-Maqdisī lists the *durūb* as Darb Ghadāwad, Darb Isbask, Darb Sūkhashīn, Darb Afshīnah, Darb Kūhak (Little Mount), Darb Warsanīn, Darb Riyūdad, and Darb Farrukhshīd.

691. As al-Maqdisī's schedule of streets does not take account of a Bāb Fanak, it is to be inferred that it was an alternative designation for either a Bāb Isbask or a Bāb Sūkhashīn. Fanak was a village about half a *farsakh* from the city (Yāqūt, *Muʿjam,* 3:920); Ghadāwad was a *farsakh* outside the city (ibid., 3:776); Isbask lay at a distance of two *farsakhs* (Isbaskath in 1:238); Warsanīn was a *maḥallah* within the *rabaḍ;* and Riyūdad was a village a *farsakh* south of the city.

692. Ibn Ḥawqal, *al-Masālik wa-l-Mamālik,* 494. These gates were subsequently restored by the governor of the city, Abū al-Muẓaffar Aḥmad ibn Asad.

693. Ibid., 493.

694. Yāqūt, *Muʿjam,* 3:134. The *jarīb* varied with time and place, but 2,500 *jarībs* can be taken roughly as 750 acres (Le Strange, *The Lands of the Eastern Caliphate,* 464). For a summary of regional variations in this measure see Walther Hinz, *Islamische Masse und Gewichte* (Leiden and Köln, 1970), 38.

695. Schaeder and Bosworth, *The Encyclopaedia of Islam,* 2d ed., 8:1032.

696. Maqdisī, *Aḥsan,* 278.

697. The system of water distribution within Samarqand is conveniently summarized in Barthold, *Turkestan down to the Mongol Invasion,* 88–89.

698. The wood was rafted down to Samarqand from upstream forests around the headwaters of the Sughd River: Ibn Ḥawqal, *al-Masālik wa-l-Mamālik,* 497.

699. Ibid., 492.

700. Ibid., 498.

701. Minorsky, *Ḥudūd,* 113. Schnaeder and Bosworth (*The Encyclopaedia of Islam,* 8:1032) identify these Manichaean monks as ʿIrāqī refugees from persecutions in the time of al-Muqtadir.

702. *Tsʿe-fu Yüan-kuei,* 1642 edition, fol. 11b; *Tʿang Hui-yao,* 1774 edition, fol. 99.

703. For references see note 165 to chapter 14.

704. Narshakhī, *Taʾrīkh Bukhārā,* Frye's translation, 48, 53. According to Narshakhī (53), Rabīʿah and Muḍar tribesmen were assigned houses between the Gate of the Spice Merchants and the Nūn/Naw/Nūr Gate, while the rest of the appropriated area was given to Yamanīs.

705. Iṣṭakhrī, *al-Masālik wa-l-Mamālik,* 305–6. Narshakhī (*Taʾrīkh Bukhārā,* 23–24) calls the Mosque Gate the Ghūriyān Gate, and Maqdisī refers to the Rīgistān Gate as the Gate of the Plain *(Sahlah)*.

706. Barthold, *Turkestan down to the Mongol Invasion,* 100 and Minorsky, *Ḥudūd,* 112. "King of the Orient" was the *Ḥudūd's* rendering of Iṣṭakhrī "Wālī of Khurāsān of the House of Sāmān" (*al-Masālik wa-l-Mamālik,* 306).

707. Iṣṭakhrī, *al-Masālik wa-l-Mamālik,* 306 and Narshakhī, *Taʾrīkh Bukhārā,* 52–56. These gates were, in the latter author's schedule, Bazaar Gate (so called to differentiate it from the other six gates, which originally did not attract markets, but designated

by Iṣṭakhrī as the Iron Gate); Shahristān Gate (not unexpectedly called Madīnah Gate by Iṣṭakhrī); Banū-Ṣaʿd Gate; Banū Asad Gate; Quhandiz Gate (considered the strongest); Ḥaqq-rāh Gate (Way to Truth, named for the shrine of the celebrated sage Abū Ḥafs, who is said to have died in 832); and the last to be built, New Gate. Maqdisī (*Aḥsan,* 280) specifies only seven gates, all plated with iron: Bāb Nūr, Bāb Hufrah, Bāb al-Hadīd, Bāb al-Quhandiz, Bāb Banī Saʿd, Bāb Banī Asad, and Bāb al-Madīnah. Also Ibn Ḥawqal, *al-Masālik wa-l-Mamālik,* 483.

708. Narshakhī, *Taʾrīkh Bukhārā,* 55.

709. Enumerated by Iṣṭakhrī (*al-Masālik wa-l-Mamālik,* 307), proceeding counterclockwise from the northeastern quarter, as Iron Gate; Gate of Ḥassān Bridge; Gates near the Makh mosque; Rukhna Gate; Gate of the Castle of Abū Hishām al-Kinānī; Gate near the Bridge of the Little Bazaar *(suwayqah);* Farjak Gate; Darwāzjah Gate; Gate of the Street of the Magians; and Samarqand Gate.

710. Enumerated by Iṣṭakhrī (ibid., 306), proceeding counter-clockwise from the southwest corner, as Maydān Gate (leading to the much-travelled Khurāsān road); Ibrāhīm Gate; Riw Gate; Mardkushān Gate; Kallābādh Gate; Naw Bahār Gate; Samarqand Gate; Faghāskūn Gate (also known as the Maʿbid Gate); Rāmīthan Gate; Ḥadshirūn Gate; and Ghushaj Gate.

711. Ibn Ḥawqal, *al-Masālik wa-l-Mamālik,* 483.

712. The streets listed by al-Maqdisī (*Aḥsan,* 280–81) are, as would be expected, associated with the gates of the *rabḍ:* Darb al-Maydān, Darb Ibrāhīm, Darb Mardkushān, Darb Kilābādh, Darb Naw Bahār, Darb Samarqand, Darb Faghāskūn, Darb al-Rāmīthanīyah, Darb Hadsharūn, and Darb Ghushaj.

713. Iṣṭakhrī, *al-Masālik wa-l-Mamālik,* 305; but see note 633 above. It is not without interest that Masʿūdī believed that Faḍl ibn Sulaymān had in fact only restored a mural system originally built by some Soghdian prince (Barthold, *Turkestan down to the Mongol Invasion,* 112).

714. Which became the basis of an outline plan in Frye, *Bukhara,* 67.

715. Narshakhī, *Taʾrīkh Bukhārā,* 31–32; Iṣṭakhrī, *al-Masālik wa-l-Mamālik,* 307; Ibn Ḥawqal, *al-Masālik wa-l-Mamālik,* 484; and Maqdisī, *Aḥsan,* 331–32.

716. *Ariq* in Turkestān usually denotes an irrigation channel.

717. A whole *farsakh* in Ibn Ḥawqal, *al-Masālik wa-l-Mamālik,* 484.

718. Barthold, *Turkestan down to the Mongol Invasion,* 106–16.

719. Narshakhī, *Taʾrīkh Bukhārā,* 56.

720. Ibid., 110.

721. Maqdisī, *Aḥsan,* 281.

722. Ibn Ḥawqal, *al-Masālik wa-l-Mamālik,* 487. This composite type of derived fortification would seem to have had a good deal in common with those encountered at, int. al., al-Maʿbiyat and Najrān in Arabia (note 278 above).

723. Ibid., 483: lit., "more populated in relation to its extent."

724. Ibid., 482.

725. Quoted by al-Thaʿālibī in *al-Laṭāʾif al-Maʿārif,* al-Abyārī and al-Sayrafī edition, 216.

726. Maqdisī, *Aḥsan,* 281. In a subsequent summary account of conditions in the Mashriq, al-Maqdisī again takes up the matter of pollution of Bukhārā's water supply, primarily by reason of the excrement that the inhabitants threw into it: which affords him the opportunity to repeat a ditty that he had picked up from a local man of letters *(adīb):*

The *bāʾ* of Bukhārā is [merely] an augmenting *bāʾ*,
And the *alif* in the middle is of no avail,
So that nothing prevails but *kharā* (= excrement).

In the *Laṭāʾif al-Maʿārif,* p. 216, al-Thaʿālibī attributes a different version to Abū al-Ṭayyib al-Ṭāhirī (with a *nisbah* like that, clearly no devotee of the Sāmīnids):

Know that the *bāʾ* and the first *alif* of Bukhārā are superfluous.
It is unadulterated excrement *(kharā)* and its inhabitants are like birds for ever captive in its cage.

It was this spurious association of *kharā* with [Bu]khārā that seems to have fueled the evidently widespread delight of contemporary authors in denigrating the inner city of Bukhārā. Here, for example, is a pleasantry of Abū Aḥmad ibn Abī Bakr (known to his contemporaries as al-ʿAṭawānī), a litterateur and wit in the early years of the Sāmānids, as preserved by al-Thaʿālibī (ibid., 216; Bosworth's translation, modified, 140):

Bukhārā is the arsehole of the world, into which we have rushed unheeding.
Would that it fart us forth this instant for we have delayed too long.

727. The basic references will be found at appropriate points in chapter 12.

728. Maqdisī, *Aḥsan,* 277.

729. Ibn Ḥawqal, *al-Masālik wa-l-Mamālik,* 501.

730. Such was the view of Marquart (*Ērānšahr nach des Geographie des Ps. Moses Xorenacʿi,* 304), citing Chinese sources, including Hsüan Tsang.

731. Yaʿqūbī, *al-Buldān,* 299.

732. Glossed by Barthold (*Turkestan down to the Mongol Invasion,* 135) as "the place where the festival prayers were held."

733. Here I am following what seems to me to be the most compelling reading of Ibn Ḥawqal's account (*al-Masālik wa-l-Mamālik,* 501), although others, including C. E. Bosworth (*The Encyclopaedia of Islam,* 2d ed., 5:181), have thought otherwise. My interpretation seems to be supported by al-Maqdisī's bald statement that "another [development] is contiguous with the *rabaḍ*" (*Aḥsan,* 282). In fact his text is here so close to that of Ibn Ḥawqal that it is difficult not to postulate a direct borrowing, or perhaps that both authors borrowed from the same third source, presumably Iṣṭakhrī or possibly one of his predecessors.

734. This urban growth sequence has already been encountered at Mayyāfāriqīn (Silvan). The inner city of Kish had four

gates: Bāb al-Ḥadīd ("Iron[-clad] Gate"), Bāb ʿUbayd Allāh, Bāb al-Qaṣṣābīn (Butchers), Bāb al-Madīnah al-Dākhilah ("Gate of the Inner City"); and the outer city but two: Bāb al-Madīnah al-Khārijah and Bāb Biraknān.

735. Ibn Ḥawqal, *al-Masālik wa-l-Mamālik,* 513 and Maqdisī, *Aḥsan,* 271.

736. Maqdisī, *Aḥsan,* 271. Apparently there were five gates into the *shahristān,* although medieval authors differ as to their names. The city as a whole probably extended along the riverbank for a third of a *farsakh,* depending on how a sentence of Ibn Ḥawqal's (*al-Masālik wa-l-Mamālik,* 512) is constructed.

737. Maqdisī, *Aḥsan,* 276 and Ibn Ḥawqal, *al-Masālik wa-l-Mamālik,* 508.

738. Al-Maqdisī (*Aḥsan,* 276) enumerates the avenues in the inner *rabaḍ* as Darb Ribāṭ Aḥmad, D. al-Ḥadīd, D. al-Amīr, D. Farrukhān, D. Sūrkadah, D. Karmābaj, D. Sikkat Khāqān, and D. Qaṣr al-Dihqān; those in the outer *rabaḍ* as D. Farghakad, D. Khāsakath, D. Sandījā, D. Ḥadīd, D. Barkardajā, D. Sakrak, and D. Dar Thaghrabādh. The same author notes that two gates afforded access to the *quhandiz:* one from the *shahristān* (referred to as the *madīnah* by both al-Maqdisī and Ibn Ḥawqal [*al-Masālik wa-l-Mamālik,* 508]), the other from the *rabaḍ.* The *shahristān* was entered, in al-Maqdisī's schedule, through three gates: Bāb Abī al-ʿAbbās, B. Kish (B. Kuthayr in Ibn Ḥawqal's version), and B. al-Janbad (following an emendation in de Goeje, *Bibliotheca Geographorum Arabicorum,* 3:276 n. *k;* al-Janbadh in Ibn Ḥawqal, p. 508). Ibn Ḥawqal (508–9) names the following ten entrances into the inner *rabaḍ:* Bāb Ribāṭ Ḥamdīn, B. al-Hadīd al-Dākhilah, B. al-Amīr, B. Farrukhān, B. Sūrkadah, B. al-Karmānij, B. Sikkat Sahl, B. Rāshidīhāq, B. Sikkat Khāqān, and B. Qaṣr al-Dihqān; and the following seven entrances into the outer *rabaḍ:* B. Farghadh, B. Khāshkath, B. Sakandīhāq, B. al-Ḥadīd, B. Bakridīhāq, B. Sakrak, and B. Darbifaryād.

739. Ibn Ḥawqal, *al-Masālik wa-l-Mamālik,* 509.

740. Maqdisī, *Aḥsan,* 276.

741. Barthold (*Turkestan down to the Mongol Invasion,* 172) suggests that the builder of the wall may have been ʿAbd Allāh ibn Ḥumayd ibn Qaḥṭabah, whom we encounter as the governor of Khurāsān for a few months in 776.

742. Ibn Ḥawqal, *al-Masālik wa-l-Mamālik,* 509.

743. *Madīnah* in Maqdisī, *al-madīnah al-dākhilah* in Ibn Ḥawqal, *al-Masālik wa-l-Mamālik,* 510.

744. Ibn Ḥawqal, *al-Masālik wa-l-Mamālik,* 510. Al-Maqdisī's statement of this point (*Aḥsan,* 272–73) is ambiguous but more comprehensive. He lists the gates as Bāb Nūjakath, Bāb Farrukhān, Bāb Shākrānah (adopting an emendation in *Bibliotheca Geographorum Arabicorum,* 3:273 n. *a*), and Bāb Bukhārā.

745. Maqdisī, *Aḥsan,* 273.

746. Ibn Ḥawqal, *al-Masālik wa-l-Mamālik,* 510; cf. Maqdisī, *Aḥsan,* 273.

747. Barthold, *Turkestan down to the Mongol Invasion,* 211.

748. Iṣṭakhrī, *al-Masālik wa-l-Mamālik,* 301.

749. Ibn Ḥawqal, *al-Masālik wa-l-Mamālik,* 478. Al-Bīrūnī provides the more specific information that the last traces of the *quhandiz* disappeared in 994 (Barthold, *Turkestan down to the Mongol Invasion,* 145).

750. Minorsky, *Ḥudūd,* 121: "It is a resort of merchants."

751. Maqdisī, *Aḥsan,* 287: "The builders are skilful."

752. Ibid., 288.

753. Ibn Ḥawqal, *al-Masālik wa-l-Mamālik,* 371.

754. Tabarī, *Ta'rīkh,* 1:2655.

755. G. C. Miles, *The Numismatic History of Rayy* (New York, 1938), 140–42.

756. Maqdisī, *Aḥsan,* 391.

757. Ibn Rustah, *al-Aʿlaq,* 169. This was probably the *qalʿah* that Abū Dulat (*Risālah,* Minorsky's translation, 51) reports as having been built by Rāfiʿ ibn Harthamah in Ṭāhirid times.

758. Maqdisī's (*Aḥsan,* 391) phrase is "on the edge of the inner city"; but Iṣṭakhrī (*al-Masālik wa-l-Mamālik,* 208) says the mosque was in the *shahristān,* and Ibn Rustah (*al-Aʿlaq,* 168) reports that it was "behind the *jāmiʿ.*" My reconstruction of these morphological lineaments of al-Rayy (Rey) in the tenth century has not been uninfluenced by Yāqūt's account (*Muʿjam,* 2:153, 894–95), which he claims was drawn from earlier sources. A summary of a six-volume report on archaeological investigations at al-Rayy is conveniently available in Chahryar Adle and Y. Kossari, "Notes sur les première et seconde campagnes archéologiques à Rey. Automne-hiver 1354–55/1976–7," in *Contributión à l'histoire de l'Iran: Mélanges offerts Jean Perrot,* ed. F. Vallat (Paris, 1990), 295–307. See also Sylvia A. Matheson, *Persia: An Archaeological Guide* (London, 1976), 40ff.

759. Ibn Ḥawqal, *al-Masālik wa-l-Mamālik,* 371.

760. Maqdisī, *Aḥsan,* 390.

761. Yaʿqūbī, *al-Buldān,* 276.

762. Maqdisī, *Aḥsan,* 391.

763. Cf. note 27 to chapter 8. Actually, Hārūn's death brought work on the wall to a halt, and it was not finished until 868 under the caliphate of al-Muʿtazz.

764. Maqdisī, *Aḥsan,* 392.

765. J. H. von Thünen, *Der Isolierte Staat in Beziehung auf Landwirtschaft und Nationalökonomie,* 3d ed. (Berlin, 1875).

766. Qazwīnī, *Āthār al-Bilād wa-Akhbār al-ʿIbād,* 290–91. Al-Qazwīnī was an inveterate plagiarist, no less than 360 of the 600 articles in the *Āthār* having been adapted wholly or in part from Yāqūt's *Muʿjam al-Buldān* (M. Kowalska, "The sources of al-Qazwīnī's Āthār al-Bilād," *Folia Orientalia* 8 [1966]: 41–88), but the graphic representation of the city and its environs is not found elsewhere.

767. Amirshahi, "Le développement de la ville de Qazwîn," 1–20 plus illustrations. In this same paper Amirshahi (p. 4) shows that the skein of transmission of information about early Muslim Qazwīn utilized by thirteenth- or fourteenth-century authors such as al-Qazwīnī, Mustawfī, and ʿAbd al-Karīm Rāfiʿī derived ultimately, by way of al-Balādhurī and Ibn al-Faqīh, from Bakr ibn Haytham, who claimed to have heard it from a *shaykh* of al-Rayy (Balādhurī, *Futūḥ al-Buldān,* 321).

768. Amirshahi, "Le développement de la ville de Qazwîn," 10. The Shāpūr referred to was either Shāpūr Ardashir, who was be-

lieved to have founded a city on the site later occupied by Qazwīn, or Shāpūr II, who rebuilt it at the same location.

769. This record is alluded to in note 26 to chapter 8.

770. Mustawfī, *Nuzhat al-Qulūb,* Le Strange's translation, 62–64.

771. Maqdisī, *Aḥsan,* 392.

772. Better known, under what was presumably a Hellenized version of its Persian name, as Ctesiphon (> Ar. Ṭaysafūn), this capital was actually a group of five towns, one of which, called Veh Ardashir, was probably founded by the first Sāsānian ruler, and another of which, Veh Antiok Khusrau, had been settled by Khusrau I with prisoners of war from Antioch (Anṭakiyah). The names of the other three towns are not known, nor is the collective honorific for the whole group.

773. Mostly from Ya'qūbī, *al-Buldān,* 322.

774. Ibn Ḥawqal, *al-Masālik wa-l-Mamālik,* 324; Maqdisī, *Aḥsan,* 478; and Minorsky, *Ḥudūd,* 123, 373.

775. For general comments on this city in early Islamic times, see A. von Dietrich, "Die Moscheen von Gurgan zur Omaijadenzeit," *Der Islam* 40 (1964): 1–17; Muhammad Yousef Kiani, "Urbanization and Urban Planning in Iran during Islamic Period. An Introduction to the City of Jurjan," in *The Proceedings of the International Conference on Urbanism in Islam, Oct. 22–28, 1989,* vol. 2, ed. Yukawa Takeshi (Tokyo, 1989), 75–111.

776. Ḥamzah al-Sahmī, *Ta'rīkh Jurjān aw Kitāb Ma'rifat 'Ulamā' Ahl Jurjān* (Ḥaydarābād, A.H. 1387), 10. This information occurs in a preface on the Arab conquest of Jurjān in what is otherwise a *rijāl* work recounting lives and achievements of the city's scholars.

777. Bulliet, *Islam,* 73–75. Bulliet has amended *afna'* to real *finā'* (or plural *afniyah*): see 215 n. 10.

778. Maqdisī, *Aḥsan,* 357.

779. Ibn Ḥawqal, *al-Masālik wa-l-Mamālik,* 382.

780. Maqdisī, *Aḥsan,* 358. The streets were recorded as Darb Sulaymān, Darb al-Qūnisīyīn, Darb al-Shāri' Hayyān, Darb Kandah, Darb al-Bādinjān, Darb Bārikāh, and Darb Khurāsān.

781. Ibn Ḥawqal, *al-Masālik wa-l-Mamālik,* 382, following Iṣṭakhrī, *al-Masālik wa-l-Mamālik,* 213. It is not unlikely that Bakrābād preserved the name of the Arab Bakr tribe, even though there is no confirmatory evidence of that tribe having participated in the original Muslim settlement.

782. Maqdisī, *Aḥsan,* 358.

783. Ya'qūbī, *al-Buldān,* 277 and Maqdisī, *Aḥsan,* 319.

784. Ibn Ḥawqal, *al-Masālik wa-l-Mamālik,* 434. This shrine was, of course, the nucleus of what by the fourteenth century had become the holy city of Mashhad.

785. For references see notes 19–21 to chapter 8; also R. D. McChesney, "Four sources on the building of Isfahan," *Muqarnas* 5 (1988): 103–35.

786. Golombek, "Urban patterns in Pre-Safavid Isfahan," 18–44.

787. 'Alawī, *Maḥāsin-i Iṣfahān,* ed. by 'Abbās Iqbāl (Ṭihrān, A.H. 1312); Browne abstract and commentary ("Account of a rare manuscript History of Iṣfahán"), 417–18. Also Ibn Rustah, *al-A'laq,* 160. The gates were reported at the end of the ninth century as Bāb Khūr, Bāb Isfīj, Bāb Ṭīrah, and Bāb Yahūdīyah. The precise spacing of the gates had been determined by the directions of the rising and setting of the sun at the summer and winter solstices. According to the *Tarjuma* (Browne, "Account of a rare manuscript History of Iṣfahán," 417), the archive had been located in Jayy because of its dry soil and pure air.

788. Abū Nu'aym Aḥmad al-Iṣfahānī (d. 1038), *Kitāb Dhikr Akhbār Iṣbahān (Geschichte Isbahans),* ed. S. Dedering (Leiden, 1931), 1:15–16.

789. Historians of the Kūfan and Baṣran schools provide both conflicting dates for the capture of Jayy and irreconcilable accounts of the manner of its surrender.

790. Abū Nu'aym, *Dhikr Akhbar Isbahān,* 1:16 and Luṭf Allāh Hunarfar, *Ganjinah-i Athār-i Ta'rīkh-i Iṣfahān* (Iṣfahān, A.H. 1344), 18.

791. Shaykh Ḥasan Jābiri Anṣārī, *Ta'rīkh-i Iḍfahān va Rayy* (Tehrān, A.H. 1321), 18.

792. Golombek, "Urban patterns in Pre-Safavid Isfahan," 25–27.

793. Ibn Ḥawqal, *al-Masālik wa-l-Mamālik,* 362. *Furḍah:* cf. Lane, *Lexicon,* s.v.: "The place where ships unload," "where ships are stationed near the bank of a river."

794. 'Alawī (Browne, "Account of a rare manuscript History of Iṣfahán," 418); Ibn Ḥawqal, *al-Masālik wa-l-Mamālik,* 363.

795. Maqdisī, *Aḥsan,* 389. The Constantinople recension alone adds that the populace acquired its potable water from sweet wells.

796. Al-Bakrī, *al-Masālik wa-l-Mamālik,* 340.

797. This was not always so. In the earlier decades of the eleventh century, when Āghmāt was the seat of a Berber paramountcy ruled by a Maghrāwah chief, numerous scholars and jurists from Qurṭubah (Córdoba) and Qayrawān (Kairouan) sought refuge in the city from the disturbances when afflicting the Ifrīqīyah, modern Tunisia and western Libya (E. Lévi-Provençal, *The Encyclopaedia of Islam,* 2d ed., 1:250–51).

798. Iṣṭakhrī, *al-Masālik wa-l-Mamālik,* 220–25; Ibn Ḥawqal, *al-Masālik wa-l-Mamālik,* 389–93; Minorsky, *Ḥudūd,* 161–62, with a thorough examination of the difficulties inseparable from the study of sources for Khazar history on pp. 450–60; and Maqdisī, *Aḥsan,* 360–61.

799. Minorsky, *Ḥudūd,* 162. Cf. Maqdisī, *Aḥsan,* 360–61: "Their king was a Jew who had Muslim, Jewish, Christian, and pagan customs and judges."

800. Maqdisī, *Aḥsan,* 361.

Epilogue

1. Peter Brown, *The World of Late Antiquity A.D. 150–750* (London, 1971), 196.

2. Claude Cahen, "Movements populaires et autonomisme urbain dans l'Asie musulmane du moyen âge," *Arabica* 6 (1959): 259.

Glossary of Foreign Terms (Mainly Arabic)

Terms are arranged according to the roman alphabet and disregarding the significance of both diacritical symbols and the Arabic letters hamzah (ʾ) and ʿayn (ʿ).

The meanings ascribed to terms in this list relate primarily to the centuries covered by the text: numerous words had somewhat different meanings both before and after that period, as also in different parts of the Islamic world.

A denotes Aramaic; *G*, Greek; *L*, Latin; *P*, Persian; and *S*, Sanskrit.

abāʾī: a class of finely textured garments.

ʿabd, pl. ʿabīd: devotee, slave.

adab, ādāb: belles-lettres with an emphasis on mores and etiquette; courtesy; urbanity; humanitas.

adhān: call to prayer.

adīb, pl. udabāʾ: cultured, refined, urbane person.

afrīqī, pl. afāriqah: indigenous peoples of the Ifrīqiyah (Tunisia and western Libya) other than those Berbers who had adopted a Greco-Latin lifestyle.

ahl, pl. ahlūn, ahālin: a man's kin, family.

ahl al-aswāq: market community.

ahl al-bayt: dominant lineage.

ahl al-dhimmah: community of the covenant; in other words, members of officially tolerated religions.

ahl al-mihan: artisan class.

ājurr: baked brick.

akhbārīyūn: literati; authors providing information not pertaining to the Prophet in particular.

ālāt-ha-yi mad-hūn (P): glazed ware.

ʿālim, pl. ʿulamāʾ: specialist in religious law; the plural signifies the Muslim ecclesiastical class.

ʿallāfīn: provender suppliers, fodder merchants.

ʿamal: government post.

ʿamal, pl. aʿmāl: administrative district, province.

ʿamām: paternal blood relationship.

ʿamāmah, pl. ʿamāʾim: turban.

ʿāmil, pl. ʿummāl, ʿumalāʾ: representative, agent, overseer, minister.

ʿāmil-i sulṭān (P): tax collector.

amīn, pl. umanāʾ: head of a unit in the hierarchical disbursement of civilian stipends in al-Kūfah.

amīr, pl. umarāʾ: commander, ruler, prince.

amīr al-umarāʾ: commander of commanders, commander-in-chief of the army, generalissimo; title adopted from ʿAbbāsid times by many virtually independent rulers under the nominal suzerainty of the caliphs.

ʿanbar: ambergris, a solid, fatty, inflammable substance that occurs as a biliary concretion in the intestine of the sperm whale *(Physeter macrocephalus,* Linn.); in the Islamic world used as a cosmetic, a spice for food, and in the preparation of incense.

ʿaqd, pl. ʿuqūd: contract, pact, transaction.

aqṭaʿah: the granting of a tract of land to a specific individual by a duly constituted authority.

ʿarab, pl. aʿrāḅ: dweller in a portable tent.

arbāb al-ṣanāʾiʿ: master craftsmen.

arg (P): fortress.

ʿarif: head of an *ʿirāfah* (= stipend unit).

ariq: irrigation canal in Turkestān.

ʿaṣabīyah: tribal solidarity.

asākifah: shoemakers.

ʿasb: striped cloth manufactured in Marv and Hārāt.

aṣḥāb al-fākihah: fruit vendors.

aṣḥab al-rāyāt: tribal chiefs leading contingents in battle and responsible for arranging the military payroll.

ashrāf al-qabāʾil: tribal leaders.

ʿaṣīdah: a pudding of heated wheat flour moistened with clarified butter and sometimes honey.

ʿāṣimah, pl. ʿawāṣim: "inviolable one"; in the plural, denoted the system of northern frontier strongholds as consolidated by Hārūn al-Rashīd in 786.

ʿaṭāʾ: state pension.

aṭlas, pl. aṭālis: satin.

ʿattabī: silk-and-cotton striped cloth woven in the ʿAttābīyah quarter of Baghdād.

ʿaṭṭārīn: perfumers, perfume vendors.

Ayyām al-Aʿrāb: intertribal conflicts in the time of the ***Jāhilīyah.***

ʿayyār, pl. ʿayyarūn: rascal, vagabond, member of an urban faction / brotherhood.

ʿazab, pl. ʿuzzāb, aʿzāb: bachelor, single soldier.

bāb, pl. abwāb: door, entrance, gate, pass.

badal, pl. abdāl: a member of one of the degrees in the *Ṣūfī* hierarchical order of saints, generally accepted as the fifth rank.

badawī, pl. badū: desert dweller, nomad of Arab speech.

bādiyah: desert, steppe.

balad, pl. bilād: place, community, village, town, locale.

ballūrīyīn: manufacturers of glass and crystal.

banbūzī: an unidentified cloth, the name perhaps derived from Persian *panba* = cotton.

banū-sāsān: vagabonds, vagrants, beggars, mountebanks organized in loose associations in the urban underworld of the Eastern Caliphate.

barakah: divine blessing.

bāranj: a strain of melon peculiar to Khwarizm (perhaps < Pers. *bā rang* = colored).

bardhaʿ, pl. barādhiʿīd: cushion, saddlecloth.

bārgah (P): emporium.

barīd: post stage; variable, but al-Maqdīsī posited it at six Arab miles on the journey from Baghdād to al-Nahrawān.

bār-kadha (P): emporium.

baybāf: an unidentified textile product, but the name is perhaps derived from Persian *pai-bāf* = weaver.

bayt al-māl, pl. buyūt al-amwāl: treasury.

bāzār (P): market.

bazz, pl. buzūz: cloth, dry goods.

bazzāzīn: cloth makers, clothes makers.

beth maqdeʿshā (A): sanctuary, temple.

bidʿah: innovation, heretical doctrine.

bīmaristān: infirmary, hospital.

bīrūn (P): extension of a town beyond its actual or metaphorical walls, outskirts; often rendered as "suburb."

bisāṭ, pl. busuṭ: carpet.

biṭānah, pl. baṭāʾin: lining for a garment.

biṭrīq al-baṭāriqah: chief prince in the Province of Armīniyah.

buḥayrah, pl. buḥayrāt, baḥāʾir: green vegetable; in the plural, a vegetable garden.

būqalamūn: an iridescent cloth in which violet thread was crossed with red and green; in the tenth century it was manufactured exclusively in Tinnīs, although it seems to have been introduced originally from the Greek world.

burd, pl. burūd, abrād: a wrap of striped woollen cloth manufactured in the Yaman.

burj, pl. burūj, abrāj: square or round tower or redoubt, attached to a rampart or isolated.

buzyūn: a kind of brocade.

cardo, pl. cardines (L): principal street running north–south in a Roman city.

civitas, pl. civitates (L): the second-highest ranking settlement in the urban hierarchy in Roman North Africa.

colonia, pl. coloniae (L): the highest-ranking settlement in the urban hierarchy in Roman North Africa; a provincial capital.

dabbāghīn: leather workers.

dabīqī: a type of linen cloth originally manufactured in Dabīq but subsequently produced widely.

dāʿī, pl. duʿāt: chief propagandist among several dissenting Muslim groups; especially important in Ismāʿīlī movements.

dalīl, pl. adillah, dalāʾil, adillāʾ: caravan master and guide.

dānishūmand (< P *dānishmend*): sage.

dār, pl. dūr, diyār: house, habitation, compound; among the Āl Murra, a *ḥayy.*

Dār al-Ḥarb: "The Abode of War," countries of the infidels; the non-Muslim world.

dār al-hijrah: Islamic refuge providing opportunity for full participation in the life of the ***Ummah.***

dār al-imārah: building housing governmental offices and sometimes a gubernatorial residence.

dār al-malʿab: theater.

dār al-mulk: seat of government.

dār al-nadwah: council chamber.

dār al-ṣināʿah: an industrial establishment, workshop, shipyard; in Umayyad Spain, a workshop for the production of gold and silver objects intended for the sovereign and the manufacture of weapons of war.

darb, pl. durūb: alley, lane, street, track.

dasht (P): arid expanse of gravel or gravelly silt.

daskarah, pl. dasākir: Arabicized rendering of Pahlavi *dastkart* = settlement.

dastār: cloth, kerchief, turban cloth.

daʿwā/daʿwah: summons, missionary activity, propaganda, tribal rallying cry.

ḍayf, pl. ḍuyūf, aḍyāf: guest.

decumanus, pl. decumani (L): principal street running east–west.

dhibāb: purveyors of gazelle skins.

dhimmat Allāh: "those under the protection of Allāh"; in other words, the Muslim community.

dhimmī: a member of one of the "protected" religions tolerated by the Islamic state on payment of certain taxes and acceptance of inferior social status.

dhirāʿ, pl. adhruʿ, dhurʿān: cubit, basic measure of length, originally the length of the arm from the elbow to the tip of the middle finger; but a considerable number of different cubits were in common use in the Islamic world.

dhurrah: great sorghum, also called Indian millet (*Sorghum vulgare,* Pers.).

dība/dībaj: brocade.

dīdabān (P): scout.

dihqān, pl. dahāqīn (P): aristocrat of pre-Islamic Persia, subsequently integrated as minor officials into the Islamic administration and ultimately merged into the peasantry.

dīn, pl. adyān: religion, faith, creed.

dīnār: unit of gold currency under the Caliphate with a standard weight of one ***mithqāl*** = sixty-six grams.

dirham: unit of silver currency current in the eastern provinces of the Caliphate; standard weight about 2.97 grams.

dīwān, pl. dawāwīn: governmental or administrative office, bureau, secretariat, chancellery; a collection of poems.

dīwān al-kharaj: revenue office.

ḍiyāfah: hospitality.

dukkān, pl. dakākīn: shop.

dūr al-ṭuruz: *ṭirāz* factories.

dūshāb (P): grape/raisin syrup.

eparchos (G): governor of a province of the Byzantine Empire.

faḍīlah, pl. faḍā'il: a genre of literature lauding the excellences of things.

fāmiyīn: food sellers, corn dealers.

fanak: desert fox *(Vulpes rueppelli).*

faqīh, pl. fuqahā': legist, canon lawyer, jurisprudent.

farā'iḍi (*nisbah* < pl. of farīḍah): specialist in inheritance law.

farsakh, pl. farāsikh: measure of distance used in provinces of the Caliphate lying east of the Euphrates (al-Furāt) River; usually explicated as three Arab miles.

farsh, pl. furāsh: furniture, furnishings, upholstery, anything spread on the floor as bedding.

faṣīl, pl. fiṣāl: interval.

fidā': ransoming of Muslims from Christian captors.

finā', pl. afnīyah: special holding reserved for members of a small tribe or subtribal group unable to sustain a ***khiṭṭah*** of its own.

fiqh: Islamic jurisprudence.

funduq, pl. fanādiq: combined hostelry/inn and warehouse; depot.

fusṭāṭ, pl. fasāṭīṭ: pavilion, large, marquee-style tent; as a proper noun, a military cantonment established in Egypt in 641.

fūṭah, pl. fuwaṭ: cloth, napkin, shawl, wrapper.

futūḥ: conquest.

fuwwah: madder; bright red dye obtained from the plant *Rubia tinctorum,* Linn.

gabr/gabrakān (P): Zoroastrians.

ghallatun: cereal harvest (but see de Goeje, *BGA,* 4:310).

ghanam, pl. aghnām: sheep and/or goats, small livestock.

gharīb, pl. ghurabā': stranger, foreigner.

ghayḍah: scrub thickets.

ghāzī, pl. ghuzāt: originally, one who led or undertook a raid; subsequently, a frontier fighter, especially one who distinguished himself in battle.

ghazū, pl. ghizwān: raid, usually of limited scope and with the aim of acquiring plunder.

ghishā', pl. aghshiyah: awning, covering.

ghulām, pl. ghilmān: youthful slave warrior.

ghusl, pl. aghsāl: major ritual ablution.

gilīm (P): figured tapestry carpets.

ḥabbālīn: rope makers.

ḥabs, pl. ḥubūs: prison.

ḥaḍarī: inhabitants of permanent houses, settled populations, dwellers in a ***ḥāḍir.***

ḥaddādīn: ironworkers.

ḥaḍḍā'īn: sandal makers.

hadhdhā'īyīn: shoemakers.

ḥadīd mulabbas: iron plating.

ḥadīd muṣmat: solid iron.

ḥāḍir, pl. ḥuḍḍar: more or less permanent encampments, probably the same as ***parembole.***

ḥadīth, pl. aḥādīth: record of an action, utterance, or decision of the Prophet and his Companions, commonly rendered as "tradition"; the second source of Islamic law (after the Qur'ān).

ḥaffī: a kind of cloth made with the aid of a tool known as a *ḥaff;* specially associated with Nīshāpūr.

hajar: sanctified enclave.

ḥajar al-fatīlah: "wick stone"; in other words, asbestos.

ḥājib, pl. ḥujjāb, ḥajabah: chamberlain, superintendent of the palace, chief minister.

Ḥajj, pl. Ḥajjāt, Ḥijaj: official Muslim pilgrimage to Makkah (Mecca).

ḥakam, pl. ḥukkām: judge-arbiter.

ḥakīm, pl. ḥukamā': sage, physician, headman.

ḥallāj, pl. ḥallājūn: cotton carder/ginner.

ḥammām, pl. ḥammāmāt: bathhouse.

ḥanīf, pl. ḥunafā': professor of "the pure religion of Ibrāhīm," presumably a form of monotheism.

ḥānūt, pl. ḥawānīt: shop, factory, hostelry.

ḥaqība (P): saddlebag.

ḥaqq al-banī-ʿamm: blood relationship.

ḥaram, pl. aḥrām: sacred precinct.

ḥarīm, pl. ḥurum: women's quarters.

ḥarīr, pl. ḥarā'ir: silk, silk stuffs.

harīsah, pl. harā'is: a potage of boiled wheat flavored with meat, butter, cinnamon, and herbs.

ḥarrah, pl. ḥirār: volcanic terrain.

ḥashīsh: a narcotic product of *Cannabis sativa,* Linn.; sometimes used more generally for similar plants and others used in dyeing.

ḥaṣīr, pl. ḥuṣur: mat.

ḥaṣṣārīn: mat makers.

ḥawṭah: Ḥaḍramī *ḥaram.*

ḥayy, pl. aḥyā': camping cluster.

ḥērthā (A): encampment.

ḥijābah: guardianship of the **Kaʿbah.**

Hijrah*:** journey, especially the migration of the Prophet from Makkah (Mecca) to Yathrib (Medina) in 622; migration to a city where participation in the social and religious ambience of the ***Ummah was most accessible.

ḥimā': sanctified grazing reserve.

ḥiṣn, pl. ḥuṣūn: a term of considerable variability implying some sort of fortification: fort, stronghold, redoubt.

ḥujrah, pl. ḥujarāt, ḥujar: room, chamber.

ḥullah, pl. ḥulal: cloak, mantle, clothing.

ḥums: an alliance, focused on the **Kaʿbah,** of tribes involved in Quraysh trade.

hūrī: granary.

ḥūrīyah, pl. ḥūrīyāt, ḥūr: houri, virgin of paradise.

ʿibādah: service of God, worship.

ʿibrah: assessed value of revenue on an estate, calculated on the basis of the average annual value of crops over a number (usually three) of years.

ibrism: finely spun silk thread producing a cloth of heavy weight.

ʿīd, pl. aʿyād: festival, feast day.

īghār: an exemption with respect to taxes, the land covered by this privilege.

ikhādhah: occupation and management of a holding.

'ilf, ilāf, īlāf: security pact guaranteeing the safe passage of Quraysh caravans.

imām, pl. a'immah: prayer leader, extended to denote leader of the ***Ummah*** and a caliphal title; among **Shīʿī,** a title of their pretenders to the Caliphate.

ʿimārah, pl. ʿimārāt, ʿamā'ir: a number of camping clusters.

ʿimmah/ʿimamah, pl. ʿamā'im: turban.

iqlīm, pl. aqālīm: Arabic rendering of Greek *klima* = "climate"; also used to denote the Persian ***kishwar;*** in al-Maqdisī's technical vocabulary it signified a domain of autonomous political power modified only minimally by physiographic constraints.

iqṭāʿ, pl. iqṭāʿah: a territorial allotment granted to an individual by a duly constituted authority.

ʿirāfah: a unit designed to facilitate stipend disbursement; although a unit of ten or fifteen men in the time of Muḥammad, it evolved into a unit of variable size.

ishtiyam, pl. ashātimah: supercargo.

islām: originally, exclusive service of Allāh; later, submission to the will of Allāh.

isnād: uninterrupted chain of authorities.

isrā': Muḥammad's nocturnal journey to Jerusalem, whence he ascended to Heaven.

istabraqāt: brocade.

istaghnā: pride in wealth.

istiḥsan: discretionary/arbitrary personal opinion.

iṭr, pl. ʿuṭūr, ʿuṭūrāt: perfume.

iwān (P): hall open at one end; palace or official building.

ʿiyān: personal observation.

izār: probably bolts of cloth for the making of loincloths, women's cloaks, men's trousers, and veils for women, with all of which this word has at different times been identified.

jabbānah, pl. jabbanāt: originally, military muster ground-cum-tribal assembly venue; subsequently, cemetery, burial ground.

***Jahilīyah*:** the period when Arabia lacked a prophet and which could consequently be designated an Age of Ignorance; customarily restricted to the century prior to the lifetime of the Prophet; pre-Muslim.

jalīl, pl. ajillā', jalā'il: ashlar.

jāma-yi ibrishum (P): silk textiles.

jār, pl. jiwār: protection, neighborhood; usually the person protected but occasionally the protector.

jarīb: measure of capacity for grain, etc.; subsequently, a measure of surface area; in other words, the area of land that could be sown with a *jarīb* of seed: approximately sixteen hundred square meters.

jaushan (P): coat of mail.

jazīrah, pl. jazā'ir, juzur: island, peninsula, territory between large rivers.

jazzārīn: slaughterers.

jifā': boorishness, uselessness.

jihād: holy war for **Islam** against infidel states, a collaborative duty imposed on the Muslim community by the ***Sharīʿah.***

jinn: bodies, composed of vapor or flame, imperceptible to human senses but capable of appearing in a variety of forms. In pre-Islamic Arabia they were the nymphs and satyrs of the desert, representing aspects of nature unsubdued by humans.

jisr, pl. ajsur, jusūr: pontoon bridge, wooden bridge.

jiss: plaster.

jizyah: originally, a general term for tribute; subsequently, the poll tax paid by ***dhimmī***s.

julandā': originally, style of an Arab chieftain exercising control over part of ʿUmān in Sāsānian times, an authority that survived under Muslim hegemony.

jund, pl. ajnād, junūd: in early Islamic times, an administrative area occupied by an army in the period of the conquests and corresponding to a Byzantine *theme;* an army.

jurūm(īyah): hot coastal lowlands of Kirmān.

Kaʿbah: cube-shaped structure, within the great mosque at Makkah (Mecca), housing the sacred Black Stone.

kābulī: the big myrobalan; in other words, the dried, astringent fruit of *Terminalia chebula,* Retz.

kāfir, pl. kāfirūn, kuffār, kafarah, kifār: infidel, unbeliever.

kāhin, pl. kuhhān, kahanah: diviner, soothsayer.

kāmil, pl. kamalah: the exemplary man.

kanīsah, pl. kanā'is: (1) a litter; (2) church, synagogue, temple.

karī: lodger in the precincts of an endowment.

kārīz (P): term used in southeastern Īrān, Afghānistān, and Balūchistān to designate a system of water supply by means of gently sloping underground tunnels; ***qanāt.***

kashtībānān (P): boatmen.

kātib, pl. kuttāb: "secretary"; in other words, an official whose primary responsibility was the drafting of letters and administrative documents.

kattān: flax, linen.

kavīr (P): salt-encrusted depression.

khabar, pl. akhbar, akhābir: report, snippet of information, especially of a historical, biographical, or anecdotal nature.

khafīr, pl. khufarā': person of substance who, in return for shares in the profits of a trading venture, acted as a guarantor of its safety.

khalanj: fine-grained hardwood, *Acer* species, from the forests of Ṭabaristān.

khalīfah, pl. khulafā', khalā'if: vicegerent, deputy, successor; supreme ruler of the *Ummah;* caliph.

khallālīn: pickle vendors.

khān, pl. khānāt: (1) inn, hostelry; (2) (P) a term applied to various rulers of subordinate status, apparently of Turkish origin.

khānbārāt (P): warehouses.

khandaq, pl. khanādiq: ditch, trench, moat.

khānqāh/khāniqāh, pl. khawāniq, khanqāhāt (P): center of combined worship, teaching, and evangelism of certain Ṣūfī sects, particularly in Khurāsān and Transoxania (Mā Warā' al-Nahr).

kharābah, pl. kharābāt, kharā'ib: ruin, disintegrating structure.

kharāj: originally, a general term for tribute; subsequently, under the Caliphate, restricted to mean land tax.

kharkāhāt: tents, pavilions.

kharrāzīn: cobblers.

khaṭīb, pl. khuṭaba': spokesman for a tribe; preacher.

khawī: companion.

khawr: creek, inlet.

khayf: mountain shoulder overlooking a valley.

khaysh, pl. khuyūsh, akhyāsh: coarse, loosely woven linen made from poor-quality flax and used in the manufacture of sacks, wrappings, and tents.

khazz: silk.

khazz al-sakb: a thin silk material originally manufactured in al-Kūfah.

khazz raqm: striped silk.

khilʿah, pl. khilaʿ: robe of honor.

khiṭṭah, pl. khiṭāṭ: a plot of land marked on the ground and claimed with official authoritative approval, with the intention of continuing occupancy.

khizānah, pl. khizānāt, khazā'in: trade emporium, treasure-house, official archive.

khuldī, pl. khalādī: taffeta.

khums, pl. akhmās: one of the five tribal aggregations comprising early al-Buṣrah.

khuṭbah: sermon at the Friday prayer service in the mosque given by the sovereign or administrative head of a jurisdiction and constituting a political statement.

kirbās, pl. karābīs: white cotton cloth, muslin.

kisā', pl. aksiyah: robe, garment, dress.

kishwar (P kishvar): one of the seven earth regions recognized in Sāsānian Īrān.

klimata (G): "climates"; portions of the earth lying between two parallels of latitude and delimited by successive changes in the lengths of days and nights; *segmenta mundi,* in Pliny's phrase.

kundakī/kundajī: coarsely woven garments.

kūrah, pl. kuwar: district, locale, small- or medium-sized town.

labin: sun-dried brick.

lafūrajī: cloth manufactured in the town of Lapūr in Ṭabaristān.

laqab, pl. alqab: an honorific or descriptive element in an Arabo-Islamic name; sometimes a nickname, often a title.

lashkargāh (P): military cantonment.

libd, pl. lubūd, labad: felt.

libn/labin: unburnt brick, sun-dried brick, adobe.

libs muṭarraz: embroidered garments.

liwā': tribal standard.

lubūd thalāthīnīyah: "thirty-felts," high-quality felt furnishings woven specially for a ruler in al-Andalus (Islamic Spain).

madhhab, pl. madhāhib: any of the four orthodox schools of Islamic law.

madīnah, pl. mudun, madā'in: originally, seat of government; subsequently, an inner, usually walled, city; in al-Maqdisī's technical terminology, a district capital, usually in a politically and/or ecologically marginal situation.

madīnat al-dākhilah: inner city, ***shahristān.***

madrasah, pl. madāris: school as both institution and place of learning.

maḥallah, pl. maḥallāt: urban quarter, section, locality.

maḥfūr: deep pile (applied to carpets).

maḥram, pl. maḥārim: sacred precinct, same as ***ḥaram.***

maḥras, pl. maḥāris: small fortified structure, guardhouse, watchtower.

majlis, pl. majālis: council of elders made up of heads of families and representatives of clans.

maʿjūn (P): electuaries.

mā khalūq: perfumed water.

malban: sweetmeat of fig paste pressed into the shape of small bricks.

malbās, pl. malbūs, malābis: clothing.

malik, pl. mulūk: king, sovereign.

mamlakat al-Islam: the Islamic world, the idealized domain of the Caliphate.

manār/manārah: in pre-Islamic Arabia, an elevated site for the sending of fire or smoke signals; subsequently, a watchtower; later, minaret = tower attached to a mosque from which the ***mu'adhdhin*** uttered the call to prayer.

mandīl/mindīl, pl. manādil: napkin, kerchief.

manhaj/minhaj, pl. manāhij: main street.

manṣab: guardian of a Ḥaḍramī **ḥawṭah;** a recognized arbiter.

manzil, pl. manāzil: dwelling, way station, halting place.

manzil gāh (P): caravanserai.

maqʿad/miqʿad, pl. maqāʿid: cushion, pillow.

maqāniʿ qazzīyāt: long silk veils.

maqbar, pl. maqābir: tomb, cemetery, graveyard.

maqṣūrah, pl. maqṣūrāt, maqāṣīr: compartment or box near the ***miḥrāb*** in a mosque, reserved for the ruler.

maradd: tribal custom.

marawī: used widely by the Arabs to denote any closely woven garment from Khūrāsān.

marʿazzāʾ/marʿizzāʾ: mohair.

marghzār (P): pasturelands.

marḥalah, pl. marāḥil: a stage on a journey, normally the distance a traveller could cover in one day and consequently highly variable; al-Maqdisī specifically assumed it to be six or seven ***farsakh****s*.

maʿrifah: gnosis; knowledge, cognition.

marzbān/marzubān (P): governor of a Sāsānian province and consequently an important magnate at the royal court; district administrator exercising both civil and military authority.

masāliḥ: garrison.

mā sanḍal: sandalwood-scented water.

mashhad, pl. mashāhid: shrine, mausoleum.

masjid, pl. masājid: mosque.

masjid al-jāmiʿ: congregational mosque where Friday prayers were offered and the ***khuṭbah*** preached.

maslak, pl. masālik: road, path, way.

maʿṣūr/maqṣūr: closely woven.

mavīz (P): raisins.

mawāt: "dead land"; uncultivated land with no claimants to ownership.

mawlā, pl. mawālī: client of a kin group; in the early Islamic centuries, a non-Arab convert adopted into the Arab tribal system.

mawsim: in the Maghrib, a fair; festival, generally with religious overtones.

maydān, pl. mayādīn: a large, open, demarcated area, generally roughly rectangular and designed for equestrian activity.

maysānī: high-quality cloth from Maysān in southeastern ʿIrāq.

mā zaʿfarān: saffron-scented water.

miḥrāb, pl. maḥārīb: recess in the wall of a mosque indicating the direction of the ***qiblah.***

milk, pl. amlāk: landed property held in fee simple.

minbar, pl. manābir: pulpit of a mosque from which the ***khuṭbah*** was delivered.

mirʾāʾ: observation post.

mirbaḍ: originally, floor for the drying of dates; subsequently, horse stall, thoroughfare; in al-Baṣrah, the great market on the western edge of the city.

miṣr, pl. amṣār: this word for long preserved the implication of border warfare inherent in its ancient Semitic root. As such it denoted the military cantonments established as bases for the Arab armies during the conquests, a meaning retained by lexicographers as late as the tenth century: a city lying on the boundary between two countries. At the same time, lawyers defined it as a large urban settlement with a resident governor in which legal punishments were administered, having a tax base adequate for its needs, and overseeing a supportive rural district. In popular speech *miṣr* denoted any large and important city. In al-Maqdisī's technical terminology it signified the locale where the supreme ruler of a territory resided, where fiscal administration was situated, and which exerted a dominant influence over all other urban centers in an ***iqlīm.*** As a proper name, it denoted (1) Egypt; (2) the Egyptian conurbation of al-Fusṭāṭ-al-Qāhirah.

mithqāl: a unit of weight based on the Byzantine *solidus;* the weight of one ***dīnār.***

miʾzar, pl. maʾāzir: length of cloth usable for various types of wraparound garments.

muʾadhdhin: announcer of the hour of prayer.

muʿallim, pl. muʿallimūn: master navigator/pilot.

muʿaskar, pl. muʿaskarāt: military encampment.

mubram, pl. mabārim: a type of silk stuff.

mudhakkir, pl. mudhakkirūn: public preacher, reciter, singer.

mughrah: red ochre.

muhājir, pl. muhājirūn: one who accompanied Muḥammad on the ***Hijrah*** to Yathrib (Medina).

muḥashshāt: cloths with borders, hems, or selvages.

muḥtasib: magistrate overseeing markets, weights, measures, and public morality.

mujallid, pl. mujallidūn: bookbinder.

mulḥam: stuff having a warp of silk and a weft of some other material.

mumarjal: a red-colored cloth manufactured in Samarqand.

mūmiyāʾ: a bituminous vulnerary mined near Dārābjird.

munāfiq, pl. munāfiqūn: subversive (but usually rendered as "hypocrite").

munayyar: silken cloth of double warp or weft.

municipium, pl. municipia (L): a town in Roman North Africa in which most of the inhabitants were Roman citizens but were governed by their own magistrates and ordinances.

munkhal: sieve cloth.

munyāt: estates, often urban owned in al-Andalus (Islamic Spain).

muqāsamah: sharing of the annual yield.

muqāṭaʿah: the sum paid by a tax farmer for the right to collect and manage the revenue from a particular district.

muqātil, coll. muqātilah: fighter, warrior, combatant.

murābiṭ, pl. murābiṭūn: originally, a warrior who gave his life in the holy war against the infidel; subsequently, a warrior-monk inhabiting a ***ribāṭ.***

murayyash: striped cloth.
muṣallāʾ, pl. muṣallayāt: prayer mat, prayer ground.
muṣallabah: intersection, cruciform distribution.
mushammaʿ: wax cloth.
mushtī: apparently a fabric in some way associated with *musht* = a type of weavers' card; manufactured in Nīshāpūr.
mutaʾaddib, pl. mutaʾaddibūn: neophyte scholar.
mutaʿallim, pl. mutaʿallimūn: savant.
mutaʿāraf: conventional usage.
muwallad, pl. muwalladūn: non-Arab Muslim.
naddāfīn: cotton carders.
nadwah: council, assembly.
nāḥiyah, pl. nawāḥin: distinctive territory within a province.
nāʾibah, pl. nawāʾib, nāʾibāt: calamity, misfortune, impost.
najjārīn: carpenters.
nakhkh, pl. nakhākh, nikhākh, ankhākh: carpet runners.
namad, pl. anmād: felt; saddlecloth.
namak (P): salt crust, salt lake.
namaṭ, pl. anmāṭ: carpet, mat.
naqīb, pl. nuqabāʾ: head of a unit in the hierarchical disbursement of civilian stipends in al-Kūfah.
nāqūs, pl. nawāqīs: piece of wood or metal struck with a rod to summon a Christian congregation to divine service.
nasaj: woven stuff; for example, *muhalhal al-nasaj* = material of a light, delicate weave.
nasīʾ: intercalary month.
nāṣir, pl. anṣār, nāṣirūn, nuṣṣār: a resident of Yathrib (Medina) who supported Muḥammad after the ***Hijrah.***
naṭʿ, pl. anṭāʿ: leather mat.
naṭrūn: hydrated sodium carbonate found in solution in the soda lakes of Egypt.
nīl: indigo *(Indigo tinctoria,* Linn).
nisbah: an adjectival element in the Arabo-Islamic name usually derived from a person's place of birth, origin, or residence; sometimes from his sect, tribe, or family; and occasionally from his tribe or profession.
nishāstah: man of learning.
oppidum, pl. oppida (L): town, the lowest-ranking settlement in the urban hierarchy in Roman North Africa.
págarchos, pl. págarchoi (G): administrator of a district within a city territory under the Byzantines.
palās (P): woollen garments worn by the poor, manufactured in Gūzgānān.
parda (P): curtains.
parembole, pl. parembolai (G): seminomadic encampment.
pīshavar (P): artisans.
qabālah: lease; farming of special revenues; procedure for guaranteeing by a notable the payment of land tax.
qabīlah, pl. qabāʾil: tribe.
qaddāḥīn: vendors of drinking cups.
qāḍī, pl. quḍāt: judge in a court administering the ***Sharīʿah.***
qaflāʿyīn: marine wreckers and repairers.
qāʾid, pl. quwād: military officer.
qalʿah, pl. qilāʾ, qulūʿ: fortress, citadel, stronghold.
qallāʾīn: vendors of fried foods.
qamīṣ, pl. qumuṣ, aqmiṣah: shirt, blouse, gown.
qanāt, pl. qanawāt: canal irrigation, especially by means of underground tunnels.
qanṭarah, pl. qanāṭir: masonry bridge.
qarwanī, pl. qarawīyūn: *ḥaḍarī* pasturing close to established dwellings.
qaryah, pl. quran: village, hamlet, settlement.
qaṣab: loosely woven, gauzelike linen material.
qaṣabah, pl. qaṣabāt: in al-Maqdisī's technical terminology, a provincial capital.
qāshī: lustrous blue-and-green tiles (so named after Qāshān, their place of manufacture).
qaṣīr, pl. qiṣār: neighbor.
qaṣr, pl. quṣūr: a term of protean implications ranging from fortress to palace to villa.
qāṣṣ, pl. quṣṣās: originally, a tracker interpreting spoor and other signs on the ground; in this work, a popular storyteller.
qaṣṣābīn: butchers.
qaṭīʿah, pl. qaṭāʾiʿ: fief, land grant bestowed by ruler.
qaṭṭān, pl. qaṭṭānūn: cotton merchant, cotton manufacturer.
qawārīrīyīn: glaziers.
qawm, pl. aqwām: a number of camping clusters; often rendered into English as "clan."
qayrawān: garrison cantonment.
qaysarīyah: enclosed, often roofed, market and/or warehouse.
qayyārīn: asphalt purveyors.
qazhāgand (P): quilted garment.
qazz, pl. quzūz: silk.
qiblah: direction to which Muslims turn in prayer toward the **Kaʿbah.**
qindīl, pl. qanādīl: lamp.
qirmiz: crimson dye extracted from the insect *Kermococcus vermilis,* Planchon.
qishr, pl. qushūr: wrapping, covering.
qiṭʿah, pl. qiṭaʿ: piece of cloth.
qiyās: analogical deduction, judicial reasoning by analogy.
qubāṭī: cloth manufactured in Coptic workshops or areas of predominantly Coptic population.
qubbah, pl. qibāb, qubab: dome, cupola.
quhandiz (P): citadel, keep.
qūhī: popular name for a figured cloth manufactured in Qūhistān.
quṭn/quṭun, pl. aqṭān: raw cotton.
rabaḍ, pl. arbāḍ: extension of a town beyond its actual or metaphorical walls; outskirts; often rendered as "suburb."
rabīʾah, pl. rabāyāʾ: a companion acting as a guarantor in hostile territory.
rādifah, pl. rawādif: = "those who come after"; a specific level of entitlement to state stipends paid to soldiers and officials; ear-

lier migrants to al-Kūfah received amounts higher than did those who arrived later.

rāfiḍī: originally, sectarians who rejected the legitimacy of the caliphs Abū Bakr and ʿUmar; by the tenth century, signified little more than **Shīʿī.**

raḥbah, pl. raḥbāt: public square, courtyard.

raḥim/riḥm, pl. arḥām: kinship.

rāʿi, also rāʿu, pl. rāʿīyah: *ḥaḍirī* agriculturalists who follow their flocks of sheep and goats into the steppe during the winter.

raʾīs/rayyis: officer, official.

raqīb, pl. ruqabāʾ: courier, guardian, one of the names of God.

raqīq, pl. ariqqāʾ, riqāq: slave/slaves (sing. and coll.).

rasm, pl. rusūm: official fee, rate, tax.

rasūl, pl. rusul: envoy, messenger, apostle.

rawāsīn: vendors of sheeps' heads.

rayḥān: dispenser of aromatics.

ribāṭ, pl. ribāṭāt, rubuṭ: originally, a mustering of hobbled cavalry mounts; by late in Umayyad or early in ʿAbbāsid times, some type of fortified edifice, usually in a frontier situation and incorporating overtones of a hospice for *ghazīs* or even travellers. The implications of this term lie in its functions rather than in any particular architectural feature.

riddah: apostasy from **Islam.**

rifādah: provisioning of pilgrims to the Makkan *ḥaram.*

rīq-ravān (P): moving sands.

riḥlah, pl. riḥlāt: journey.

riwāq, pl. arwiqah: covered colonnade.

riyāḍī, pl. riyāḍīna: a word of uncertain implication but probably tallyman.

rizq, pl. arzāk: payment in kind to troops registered in the *dīwān.*

rubʿ, pl. arbāʿ: one of the four wards (lit., "quarters") into which Ziyād ibn Abīhi divided al-Kufah for administrative purposes in 670; one of the four principal administrative divisions of Khurāsān under the ʿAbbāsids.

rubāʿi, pl. rubāʿiyyāt: in Persian prosody, a four-line verse, quatrain; used by Ibn Ḥawqal as a measure for cloth, presumably involving the integer four or a multiple of it.

rukn, pl. arkān: pillar, principle.

rustaq, pl. rusātiq: a tract of country exhibiting a significant degree of uniformity in terrain and land use; sometimes rendered as "canton."

rūyānī: textiles manufactured in Rūyān district in Ṭabaristān.

sabbāghīn: dyers.

sābiqah: principles of Arabo-Islamic precedence.

sabkhah (P): salt swamp.

ṣadaqah, pl. ṣadaqāt: voluntary alms.

sādhij: plain cloth.

safaṭ, pl. asfāṭ: frail, basket.

ṣaffārīn: coppersmiths.

ṣāghah: goldsmiths.

ṣaḥābī, pl. ṣaḥābah: Companion of the Prophet (dating from the first conversions to the death of Anas ibn Mālik in 710 or 712).

ṣāḥib, pl. aṣḥāb, ṣaḥabah: counsellor, representative.

ṣāḥib al-kharāj: chief revenue officer.

ṣāḥib al-madīnah: town prefect.

ṣāḥib al-shurṭah: chief of police.

sāḥil: the eastern, coastal, cultivable fringe of the North African latitudinal steppe zone as it appears in central Tunisia.

ṣaḥn, pl. ṣuḥūn: courtyard, cleared open space.

saʿīdī: striped stuffs manufactured at Ṣanʿāʾ in the Yaman.

saʾifah, pl. ṣawāif: summer expeditions, raids, or forays.

ṣalāh, pl. ṣalawāt: official Islamic prayer ritual.

ṣalāt al-jumʿah: Friday noon service.

samūm: a powerful flow of hot, dry air drawn in from the south in advance of a depression.

ṣāniʿ, pl. ṣunnāʿ: artisan, craftsman, artificer.

saqaṭ, pl. asqāṭ: junk, trash, rubbish.

sāruq (< P *srk/srwk*): fortress.

sawīq: a syrup of barley and honey drunk ritually by pilgrims to Makkah.

sawwāqīn: flour merchants.

ṣaydallānīn: apothecaries.

sayyaḥ: pilgrim.

ṣayyārifah: money changers.

sayyid: in early **Islam,** a person exercising spiritual power; subsequently, a widely used term for a distinguished personality, especially for a descendant of the Prophet in the Ḥusaynid line.

shabb: alum, potash, found in the desert of Upper Egypt.

shāhijānī (< P *shāhgān* = *royal*): a general term used by the Arabs to denote any finely woven garment from Khurāsān.

shāh-rāh (P): royal road (from Bukhārā to Samarqand).

shahristān (P): administrative center, inner sector of a Mashriqī city.

shaʿr/shaʿar, pl. ashʿār, shuʿūr, shiʿār: mohair.

sharābīyah: a type of linen cloth.

sharb/sharāb, pl. shurūb: linen stuff.

***Sharīʿah*:** sacred law of **Islam.**

sharīf, pl. ashrāf, shurafāʾ: notable, distinguished, noble; in some contexts, denoted a descendant of the Prophet in the Ḥasanid line; used by Arab historians for a subordinate Ḥimyarite ruler.

shaṭāwī: linen cloth manufactured in Shaṭāʾ in the Nile Delta.

shatt, pl. ashtāt: a mud-filled saline depression; in the plural, a system of such features extending from southern Tunisia westward into Algeria; transcribed in French as *chott.*

shaṭṭ, pl. shuṭūṭ (P): channel of salty, viscous mud occurring in *kavīrs;* more generally (Arabic), shore, beach, strand, river.

shaykh, pl. shuyūkh, mashāyikh, mashāʾikh: a tribal or religious leader.

shibr, pl. ashbār: span of the hand, from the thumb to the little finger, and consequently variable.

Shīʿī: a follower of the Shīʿah, an Islamic sect that began by promoting the claim of ʿAlī, the Prophet's son-in-law, to the caliphate. Subsequently it split into a number of subsects, including the Ithnāʿasharī, Zaydī, and Ismāʿīlī.

shiqqah, pl. shiqaq, shiqāq: piece, length (of cloth).

shūristān (P): salt swamp.
shurrāfah, pl. shurrāfāt: crenelle.
shwāyah, also shūyān: *a'rāb* of the desert border.
sikkah, pl. sikak: side street, lane, path.
sipāhsālār (P): title of the governor of Khurāsān under the Sāmānids; rendered in Arabic as *ṣāḥib al-jaysh;* title given to senior military officers in many states of the eastern medieval Islamic world.
siqāyah: office charged with supplying water to Makkan pilgrims.
ṣiqlātūn: a heavy, figured silk stuff.
sitārah, pl. satā'ir: veil, screen.
sitr, pl. sutūr, astār: screen, curtain, drape.
stadium, pl. stadia (L): a Roman (originally Greek) measure of distance, usually taken as 606 feet.
stupa: a mound or architectural structure often containing a relic of the Buddha.
sub', pl. asbā': one of the seven sections into which Sa'd ibn Abī-Waqqās divided al-Kūfah.
ṣūf, pl. aṣwāf: wool.
ṣūf al-bahr: "sea wool," a fabric manufactured from the fine, silky hairs of the byssus of the mollusk *Pinna nobilis,* Linn.
ṣuffah: shelter, portico.
Ṣūfī: a Muslim mystic, usually a member of a brotherhood or order.
ṣulḥ: peace covenant.
Sunnī: member of the dominant Muslim majority group.
sūq, pl. aswāq: market.
sūqah: habitués of the *sūq.*
sūq al-harīr: silk market.
sūrah, pl. suwar: section of the Qur'ān, a unit of revelation.
surmāhī: sturgeon.
ṣurrat al-arḍ: navel of the earth; *axis mundi.*
sūsanjird/sūzan-kard (P): a textile that was a product of both weaving (woollen and silk bases) and silk embroidery.
suwayqah, pl. suwayqāt: small market.
ta'āruf: conventional usage.
tabbanīn: straw sellers.
tābi', pl. tābi'ūn: follower of the Prophet's Companions.
tābūt, pl. tawābit: coffin, casket, sarcophagus.
ṭaghā: presumption.
ṭāhirī: perhaps cloth made to order of Ṭāhirid governors in Nīshāpūr or manufactured in the town of Ṭāhirīyah in Khwarizm.
tājir, pl. tujjār, tijār: merchant, trader.
takbīr: the exclamation "*Allāhu akbar!*"
tākhtanj/rākhtanj: probably a type of tightly spun silk produced exclusively in Nīshāpūr.
takhṭīṭ: the laying out of a *khiṭṭah.*
tall, pl. tilāl, atlāl, tulūl: hill, elevation; as a proper noun, denotes the upland spine of northern and central Tunisia, itself an eastward extension of the Atlas Mountain system of Morocco and Algeria.
tamṣīr: originally, the transformation of the mechanical solidarity of an army cantonment into the organic solidarity of a developed city; the urbanization process that accompanied the diffusion of **Islam.**
ṭang-i asp (P): saddle girth.
tanzīl (< nazala): the occupation of a *khiṭṭah.*
ṭāqāt al-kubrā/al-ṣughrā': large/small arcades.
taqīyah: dissimulation of religious belief under duress.
ta'rīf: enactment of the *Wuqūf* ritual at 'Arafāt in certain provincial cities, with the aim of allowing Muslims whose duties in distant lands prevented them from undertaking the Greater Pilgrimage to participate in some rites of the *Ḥajj.*
ṭarīq al-āḥād: authority of an individual.
tawwajī/tawwazī/tūzī: generic term for cloth of exceptionally delicate weave manufactured throughout northwest Fārs; named for Tawwaj, its original place of manufacture.
ṭaylasān, pl. ṭayālisah: a shawl-like garment worn over the head and shoulders, particularly by religious scholars and notables in the Mashriq.
thaghr, pl. thughūr: fortress; in the plural, denoted a system of defensive positions stretching from Ṭarsūs northeastward to Qālīqala' and beyond.
tharīdah, pl. tharā'id: dumplings of crumbled bread and meat soaked in broth.
thawb, pl. thiyāb, athwāb: garment, fabric, material, cloth.
tikkah: trouserbands or cords.
ṭīn, pl. aṭyān: unfired brick.
ṭirāz, pl. ṭuruz: material used for the robes of rulers and ceremonial costumes bestowed as marks of honor on high officials, both civil and military; the workshop producing such materials or clothing.
ṭirrīkh: a kind of salted herring.
tubba', pl. tabābi'ah: Ḥimyarite royal title as preserved in Arabic literature.
turbah, pl. turab: tomb surmounted by a dome.
tūtiyā': tutty (an impure oxide of zinc).
***Ummah*:** in pre-Islamic usage, a religious community; in the Qur'ān it denoted groups (not exclusively Muslim) to whom a messenger had been sent; by the Madīnan period it had come to signify a totally Islamic community.
'ushb, pl. a'shāb: grass, plants, thatch.
'ushr, pl. a'shār, 'ushūr: canonical tax of one-tenth levied on Muslims, more or less equivalent to **zakāt.**
ustādh, pl. asātidhah: teacher.
'utb: cotton.
uṭūm, pl. āṭām: tower house.
vāspuhr (P): prince of the blood.
vihāra (S): monastery.
viqāyah (P): long veils; Ar. *wiqāyah* = belt, band to hold hair in place.
wadhārī: a saffron-colored cloth manufactured in Wadhār in the Samarqand oasis, soft and light to the touch but very durable.
wādī, pl. widyān: stream, channel, often a watercourse carrying water only at certain seasons of the year.

wāfid, pl. wufūd, awfād, wuffād: tribal delegation.
wakīl, wukalā': agent, factor.
walī: in mystical discourse, friend of God, saint.
wālī: governor of a province.
waqf, pl. awqāf: a pious endowment, usually of land, the revenues from which are assigned to a specific purpose.
warraq, pl. warraqīn: paper seller, copyist of manuscripts.
washī: a figured cloth.
wazīr, pl. wuzarā': an official who first appeared under the early ʿAbbāsids as chief executive of the administration under the caliph.
wazzānīn: makers of scales.
wilāyah, pl. wilāyāt: administrative district, usually headed by a **wālī.**
Wuqūf: the ritual standing (before God) at ʿArafah during the *Ḥajj.* It lasts from high noon on the ninth day of Dhū al-Ḥijjah until sunset, encompassing the supreme hours of the *Ḥajj.*
zaʿfarān: saffron (*Crocus sativus,* Linn.).
zaʿfurī: a type of silk cloth produced preeminently in Astarābād.
zāhid, pl. zuhhad: ascetic; pious person who has renounced worldly goods.
zakāt: canonical alms tax of one-tenth, one of the five basic obligations of a Muslim.
zanabīl: a particular type of date basket made and used in Sijistān.
zandanījī: muslin originally manufactured in the village of Zandanah, near Bukhārā, and used as a uniform for the Sāmānid household guard.
ẓarā'ifī: an unidentified fabric.
zarbaft: gold brocades.
zarībah, pl. zarā'ib: stockade, cattle pen, fold.
zāwiyah, pl. zawāyā': prayer room, small mosque, retreat.
zīlū: rug.
zirah: cumin *(Cuminum cyminum,* Linn.).
zirih (P): armor.
ẓullah: roofed portico.
zullīyah, pl. zalālī: large rug.
zuqāq, pl. aziqqah: lane, alley.

Bibliography

Primary Sources: Texts and Translations

This list, with very few exceptions, is restricted to sources cited in the text. It is ordered alphabetically by author with the exceptions that *al-* and *ibn* in Islamic names are disregarded, as are *ʿayn* (ʿ) and *hamzah* (ʾ), the diacritics, denoting velarized alveolars (*ṭ, ṣ, ẓ, ḍ*), and the voiceless pharyngeal fricative *ḥ*. Arab authors are listed under what are judged to be the names by which they are best known, whether denoting descent *(kunyah)*, origin or profession *(nisbah)* distinguishing characteristic *(laqab)*, or personal name *(ism)* (e.g., al-Ṭabarī rather than Muḥammad ibn Jarīr). Only editions of texts available to me have been listed; no attempt has been made to provide a comprehensive bibliography of all editions of the texts used.

Abū ʿAbdullah Muḥammad ibn al-Abbār. *Kitāb al-Ḥullah al-Siyarāʾ*. Edited in part by R. Dozy under the title *Notices sur Quelques Manuscrits Arabes.* Leyden, 1847–51. Complete editing by H. Muʾnis, 2 vols. (al-Qāhirah, A.H. 1383); critical analysis by ʿAbd Allāh al-Ṭabbāʿ (Bayrūt, A.H. 1382).

Ibn ʿAbd-Rabbihi. *Al-ʿIqd al-Farīd.* Al-Qāhirah, A.H. 1303/A.D. 1913.

ʿImād al-Dīn Abū al-Fidāʾ. *Mukhtaṣar Taʾrikh al-Bashar.* 2 vols. Istanbul, A.H. 1286.

———. *Taqwīn al-Buldān.* Edited by J. T. Reinaud and MacGuckin de Slane. Paris, 1840. French translations by Reinaud (Paris, 1848) and Stanislas Guyard (Paris, 1883).

Abū al-Fidāʾ al-Tadmurī, *Muthir al-Gharam.* Edited by C. D. Matthews under the title "The Muṯir al-Gharām of Abū-l-Fidāʾ of Hebron," *Journal of the Palestine Oriental Society* 17 (1937): 108–37, 149–208. Translation by Matthews under the title *Palestine–Mohammedan Holy Land* (New Haven, Conn., 1949).

Abū Nuʿaym Aḥmad al-Iṣfahānī. *Kitāb Dhikr Akhbār Iṣbahān.* Edited by S. Dedering. 2 vols. Leiden, 1931–34.

———. *Ḥilyat al-Awliyāʾ.* 10 vols. Al-Qāhirah, A.H. 1351–57.

Habīb ibn Aws Abū Tammām. *Dīwān al-Ḥamāsah.* Edited with commentary of al-Tibrīzī by G. Freytag under the title *Hamasae Carmina cum Tebrisii Scholiis, Ashʿār al-Ḥamāsah.* Bonn, 1828.

Abū ʿUbayd al-Qāsim ibn Sallām. *Kitāb al-Amwāl.* Edited by Muḥammad Khalīl Harrās. Al-Qāhirah, A.H. 1388.

Yaḥyā ibn Ādam. *Kitāb al-Kharāj.* Edited, translated, and annotated by A. Ben Shemesh under the title *Taxation in Islam,* vol. 1. Rev. ed., Leiden and London, 1965.

Kamāl al-Dīn Abū al-Qāsim ʿUmar ibn al-ʿAdīm. *Bughyat al-Ṭalab fī Taʾrīkh Ḥalab.* 10 Ms. volumes in Istanbul, others in Paris and Mawṣil (Mosul); partial publication by Iḥsan ʿAbbās in *Shadharāt min Kutub Mafqūdah fī Taʾrīkh* (Bayrūt, A.H. 1408).

———. *Zubdat al-ḥalab min Taʾrīkh Ḥalab.* Critical edition by Sāmī Dahhān: vol. 1, 1–457 (Dimashq, 1370); vol. 2, 457–569 (Dimashq, 1373); vol. 3, 569–641 (Dimashq, 1388).

Aḥmad Fuʾad Ahwānī. Al-Taʿlim fī Raʾy al-Qābisi. Al-Qāhirah, A.H. 1364/A.D. 1945.

Akhbār al-Ṣīn wa-l-Hind. Edited and translated by Jean Sauvaget under the title *Relation de la Chine et de l'Inde.* Paris, 1948.

Akhbār Majmūʿah fī Fatḥ al-Andalus. Edited by Emilio Lafuente y Alcántara. Madrid, 1867.

Sharaf al-Dīn ʿAlī Yazdī. *Ẓafar-Nāmah.* Published in *Bibliotheca Indica.* Calcutta, 1887. French translation by Petis de la Croix under the title *Histoire de Timour Bec* (Paris, 1722).

Maḥmud Alūsī-Zādā. *Bulūgh al-ʿArab fī Maʿrifat Aḥwāl al-ʿArab.* 2 vols. Al-Qāhirah, A.H. 1341/A.D. 1923–24.

Michele Amari, ed. *Biblioteca Arabo-Sicula.* 2 vols. Arabic text, Lipsia (Leipzig); Italian translation, Torino/Roma, 1881–82.

Abū al-ʿArab al-Tamīmī. *Ṭabaqāt. Ulamāʿ Ifrīqiyah.* Published with a French translation by Mohammed Ben Cheneb under the title *Classes des Savants de l'Ifrîqiyah (Tabaqât ʻUlamâʼ Ifrîqiyah).* Publication de la Faculté des Lettres d'Alger, vol. 51. Alger, 1915.

Muḥyi al-Dīn ibn al-ʿArabī. *Muḥāḍarat al-Abrār wa Musāmarāt al-Akhyār.* 2 vols. Al-Qāhirah, A.H. 1324/A.D. 1906.

Arculf. *Relatio de Locis Sanctis.* Edited by T. Tobler under the title *Itinera et Descriptiones,* vol. 1, 195 et seq.

ʿArrām ibn al-Aṣbagh. *Kitāb Asmāʾ Jibāl al-Tihāmah wa Makā-*

nihā. Edited by ʿAbd al-Salām Hārūn in *Nawādir al-Makhṭūṭāt.* Vol. 2. Al-Qāhirah, A.H. 1374/A.D. 1954.

Thiqat al-Dīn Abū al-Qāsim ibn ʿAsākir al-Dimashqī. *Ta'rīkh Madīnat Dimashq.* Edited by Ṣalāḥ al-Dīn al-Munajjid. 2 vols. Dimashq, 1951–54. French translation of vol. 2 (the section on the historical topography of al-Dimashq) by Nikita Elisséef under the title *La Description de Damas d'Ibn ʿAsākir* (Damas, 1959).

Abū Dā'ūd Sulaymān ibn al-Ashʿath (d. 888). *Kitāb al-Sunan.* Al-Qāhirah, A.H. 1280.

ʿIzz al-Dīn ibn al-Athīr. *Al-Kāmil fī al-Ta'rīkh.* Edited by C. J. Tornberg under the title *Ibn al-Athiri Chronicon quod Perfectissimum Inscribitur . . .* 14 vols. Uppsala, 1851–53; Lugduni Batavorum, 1867–76.

Majd al-Dīn ibn al-Athīr. *Al-Jāmiʿ al-Uṣūl.* 10 vols. Al-Qāhirah, A.H. 1369/A.D. 1949.

Abū Zakarīyā' Yazīd ibn Muḥammad al-Azdī. *Ta'rīkh al-Mawṣil.* Edited by ʿAlī Ḥabībah. Al-Qāhirah, A.H. 1387/A.D. 1967.

Ibn al-Azraq al-Fāriqī. *Ta'rīkh Mayyāfāriqīn wa-Āmid.* Edited by B. A. L. ʿAwaḍ. Al-Qāhirah, A.H. 1379/A.D. 1959.

Abū al-Walīd Muḥammad al-Azraqī. *Kitāb Akhbār Makkah.* In *Die Chroniken der Stadt Mekka,* edited by Ferdinand Wüstenfeld. 4 vols. Leipzig, 185–61. Reprint, Hildesheim, 1981, 2 vols.

ʿAbd al-Qāhir ibn Ṭāhir al-Baghdādī. Kitāh al-Farq bayn al-Firāq. Edited by M. Badr. Al-Qāhirah, A.H. 1328. Translated by Philip K. Hitti under the title *al-Baghdādī's Characteristics of Muslim Sects* (Cairo, 1924) and by K. Seelye and A. Halkin, *Moslem Schisms and Sects,* vol. 1 (New York, 1920) and vol. 2 (Tel-Aviv, 1935).

Baḥshāl al-Wāsiṭī. *Tārīkh Wāsiṭ.* Published by Kurkīs ʿAwwād. Baghdād, A.H. 1387/A.D. 1967.

Abū ʿUbayd ʿAbd Allāh ibn ʿAbd al-ʿAziz al-Bakrī. *Muʿjam Mā Istaʿjama al Bakri.* In *Das Geographische Wörterbuch des al-Bekrī,* edited by Ferdinand Wüstenfeld. Göttingen and Paris, 1876–77. 4 vols., Cairo, 1945–51.

———. *Kitāb al-Masālik wa-l-Mamālik.* Edited and translated by Baron Mac Guckin de Slane under the title *Description de l'Afrique Septentrionale par Abou-Obeïd-el-Bekri.* Alger, 1857–58. 2d ed., Alger, 1911–13; reprint, Paris, 1965.

Aḥmad ibn Yaḥyā al-Balādhurī. *Kitāb Futūḥ al-Buldān.* Edited by M. J. de Goeje under the title *Liber Expugnationis Regionum . . .* Lugduni Batavorum, 1906. Translated under the title *The Origins of the Islamic State* by Philip K. Hitti, pt. 1 and Francis C. Murgotten, pt. 2, Columbia University Studies in History, Economics and Public Law, vol. 68. New York, 1916, 1924.

———. *Ansāb al-Ashrāf.* Vol. 1 edited by Muḥammad Ḥamīdullāh. Al-Qāhirah, A.H. 1379/A.D. 1959. Vol. 4A edited by Max Schloessinger and M. J. Kister (Jerusalem, 1971); vol. 4B by Max Schloessinger (Jerusalem, 1938); vol. 5 by S. D. F. Goiten (Jerusalem, 1936); and vol. 11 by W. Ahlwart (Greifswald, Germany, 1883).

Abū Muḥammad ʿAbd Allāh al-Balawī. *Kitāb Sīrat Āl Ṭūlūn.* Edited with commentary by Muḥammad Kurd ʿAlī. Dimashq, A.H. 1358.

Shams al-Dīn Abū ʿAbd Allāh Muḥammad ibn Baṭṭuṭah. *Tuḥfat al-Nuẓẓār fī Gharā'ib al-Amṣār wa-ʿAjā'ib al-Asfār.* Edited by C. Defrémery and B. R. Sanguinetti. 4 vols. Third impression, Paris, 1879–93. Translation by H. A. R. [Sir Hamilton] Gibb under the title *The Travels of Ibn Baṭṭūṭa,* 4 vols. (continuing): Hakluyt Society, 2d ser., nos. 110, 117, 141 (Cambridge, 1958–).

ʿAbd Allāh ibn ʿUmar al-Bayḍāwī. *Anwār al-Tanzīl wa-Asrār al-Ta'wīl.* Edited by H. O. Fleischer. 2 vols. Leipzig, 1846–48. Indices by W. Fell (Leipzig, 1878).

Ẓahīr al-Dīn Abū al-Ḥasan al-Bayhaqī. *Tarīkh-ī Bayhaq.* Edited by A. Bahmanyār. Ṭihrān, A.H. 1317/A.D. 1968.

Muḥammad ibn ʿAbd Allāh al-Ḥākim al-Nīsābūrī/al-Bayyiʿ. *Ta'rīkh Naysābūr.* Extant only in excerpts from a Persian translation. An Arabic work based on the *Ta'rīkh* was compiled by ʿAbd al-Ghāfir ibn Ismāʿīl al-Fārisī (d. 1134) under the title *Kitāb al-Siyāqli-Ta'rīkh Nīsābūr,* of which only the second part survives. However, the entire work was epitomized by Ibrāhīm ibn Muḥammad al-Sarīfīnī (d. 1243). The so-called Persian recension, the second part of al-Fārisī's version, and al-Sarīfīnī's epitome have been reproduced in facsimile by Richard N. Frye, *The Histories of Nishapur* (The Hague, 1965). An index of personal and place names in al-Fārisī's text has been compiled by Habib Jaouiche, *The Histories of Nishapur* (Wiesbaden, 1984).

Benjamin ben Jonah of Tudela. *Safer ha-Massaot.* English translation by Marcus Nathan Adler. 1907, reprint, New York, 1983.

Muḥammad ibn Ismāʿīl al-Bukhārī. Al-Jāmiʿ al-Ṣaḥīḥ. Būlāq, Egypt, A.H. 1295. French translation by O. Houdas and W. Marçais under the title *El-Bokhâri, Les Traditions Islamiques,* 4 vols. (Paris, 1903–14; reprint, Paris, 1984).

Darband-nāma. Edited and translated by Mirza A. Kazem-Beg under the title *Derbend-nâmeh, or the History of Derbend . . . Translated from a Select Turkish Version . . . and with Notes. Mémoires des Savants Étrangers Publiés par l'Académie des Sciences,* vol. 6 (St. Petersburg, 1851). Russian translation under the supervision of [subsequently General] Alikhanov-Avarsky (Tiflis, 1898).

ʿAbd al-Raḥmān ibn ʿAlī ibn al-Daybaʿ. Cambridge University MS 2894. Edited by Muḥammad al-Akwaʿ under the title *Qurrat al-ʿUyūn fī Akhbār al-Yaman al-Maymūn.* Al-Qāhirah, A.H. 1397/A.D. 1977.

Dïgenes Akrites. Edited and translated by J. Mavrogordato. Oxford, 1956.

Jaʿfar ibn ʿAlī al-Dimashqī. *Al-Ishārah ilā Maḥāsin al-Tijārah.* Al-Qāhirah, A.H. 1318/A.D. 1900.

Shams al-Dīn al-Dimashqī. *Nukhbāt al-Dahr fī ʿAjā'ib al-Barr wa-l-Baḥr.* Edited by A. F. Mehren under the title *Cosmographie de Chems-el-Din Abou Abdallah Mohammed el-Dimichqui.* Arabic text, St. Petersburg, 1866. French translation by Mehren under the title *Manuel de la Cosmographie du Moyen Âge* (Copenhagen, 1874).

Mujīr al-Dīn al-ʿUlaymī. *Al-Uns al-Jalīl fī-Ta'rīkh al-Quds wa-l-Khalīl.* Cairo, A.H. 1283/A.D. 1866; An Najaf, Iraq, A.H. 1388; and Ammān, A.H. 1393. Partial French translation of the Qāhirah edition by H. Sauvaire under the title *Histoire de Jérusalem et d'Hébron* (Paris, 1876).

Sharaf al-Dīn, Amīr of Baleš (Bidlīs). *Sharaf-Nāma.* Published by V. Veliaminov-Zernov under the title *Scheref-Nameh ou His-*

toire des Kourdes par Scheref Prince de Bidlis. 2 vols. St. Petersbourg, 1862. French translation by B. F. Charmoy under the title *Chéref-Nâmeh ou Fastes de la Nation Kourde par Cháref-ou'd-Dine Prince de Bidlis dans l'líâlet d'Arzeroûme,* 4 vols. (St. Petersbourg, 1868–75).

Dionysios of Tell Mahré. *La Chronique de Denys de Tell Mahré.* Translated by J. B. Chabot. Paris, 1895.

Ḥusayn ibn Muḥammad al-Diyārbakrī. *Taʾrīkh al-Khamīs fī Aḥwāl Anfas Nafīs.* Al-Qāhirah, A.H. 1302/A.D. 1884. Reprint, Bayrūt, A.H. 1390.

Abū Dulaf Misʿar ibn Muhalhil al-Khazrajī al-Yanbūʿī. *Risālah.* Translated by V. Minorsky under the title "La deuxième risala d'Abu-Dulaf," *Oriens* 5 (1952): 23–27. Minorsky's *Abū Dulaf Misʿar ibn al-Muhalhil's Travels in Iran (circa A.D. 950)* (Cairo, 1955) reproduces the Mashhad text (discovered in 1923) of the second *risālah,* together with an English translation and a detailed commentary.

Ṣārim al-Dīn ibn Duqmāq. *Kitāb al-Intiṣār li-Wāsiṭat ʿIqd al-Amṣār.* Parts 4 *(al-Qāhirah)* and 5 *(al-Iskandarīyah),* all that remain extant of an original 10 vols., published by Vollers under the title *Description de l'Égypte par Ibn Doukmak.* Būlāq, Egypt, A.H. 1308/A.D. 1890–91.

Abū Bakr Muḥammad ibn al-Ḥasan ibn Durayd. *Kitāb al-Ishtiqāq.* Edited by Ferdinand Wüstenfeld. Göttingen, Germany, 1854.

———. *Al-Jamharat al-Lughah.* 4 vols. Baghdād, A.H. 1392.

Pirkê de Rabbi Eliezer (The chapters of Rabbi Eliezer the Great). Translated by Gerald Friedlander. London, 1916.

Abū ʿAbd Allāh Muḥammad al-Fākihī. *Kitāb Akhbār Makkah.* Only the second half is extant, of which part has been edited by Ferdinand Wüstenfeld under the title *Die Chroniken der Stadt Mekka,* 4 vols. (Leipzig, 1857–61).

Ibn al-Faqīh al-Hamadhānī. *Kitāb al-Buldān.* In *Compendium Libri Kitâb al-Boldân,* vol. 5 of *Bibliotheca Geographorum Arabicorum,* edited by M. J. de Goeje. Lugduni Batavorum, 1885.

Farid al-Dīn ʿAṭṭār. Tadhkirat al-Awliyā. Edited by R. A. Nicholson. 2 vols. London and Leiden, 1905–7.

Ibn al-Azraq al-Fāriqī. *Taʾrīkh Mayyātāriqīn wa-Āmid.* British Library *Ms. Or. 5803;* Marwānid sections edited by B. A. L. ʿAwad (al-Qāhirah, A.H. 1379/A.D. 1959).

ʿAbd al-Ghāfir ibn Ismāʿīl al-Fārisī. See al-Bayyiʿ.

Fārs-Nāmah. Edited by Guy Le Strange and R. A. Nicholson. E. J. W. Gibb Memorial Series, n.s., 1. London, 1921. English translation by Guy Le Strange under the title *Description of the Province of Fars, in Persia, at the Beginning of the Twelfth Century A.D.* ... Asiatic Society Monographs, vol. XIV (London, 1912). Originally published in *Journal of the Royal Asiatic Society* (1912): 1–30, 311–39, 865–89.

ʿAlī ibn Abī Zarʿ al-Fāsī. *Al-Anīs al-Muṭrib bi-Rawḍ al-Qirṭās fī Akhbār Mulūk al-Maghrib wa-Taʾrīkh Madīnat Fās.* Rabāṭ, Morocco, A.H. 1355. Edited with a German translation by Dombay under the title *Geschichte de mauritanischen Könige* (Agram, Croatia, 1794–97). Edited with a Spanish translation by Moura under the title *Historia dos Soberanos Mahometanos* (Lisboā, 1824); edited with a Latin translation by C. J. Tornberg, *Annales Regum Mauritaniae* (Uppsala, 1843–46); French translation by A. Beaumier, *Histoire des Souverains du Maghreb (Espagne et Maroc) et Annales de la Ville de Fès* ... (Paris, 1860); and a Spanish translation by Ambrosio Huici Miranda, *Rawd al-Qirtas,* 2d ed. (Valencia, 1964).

Shāh Ḥusayn ibn Malik Ghiyāth al-Dīn. *Iḥyāʾ al-Mulūk.* Edited by Manūchihr Sitūda. Tehran, A.H. 1344.

Muḥammad ibn Ḥabīb. *Kitāb al-Muḥabbar.* Edited by Ilse Lichtenstädter. Haydarābād, India, 1942.

Abū ʿAbd Allāh ibn al-Ḥājj al-Fāsī. *Mudkhal al-Sharʿ al-Sharīf.* 3 vols. Al-Qāhirah, A.D. 1929/A.H. 1348.

Muslim ibn al-Hajjāj al-Qushayrī al-Jāmiʿ al-ṣaḥīḥ. *Masājid.* In *Concordance et indices de la Tradition musulmane,* edited by A. J. Wensinck. Leiden, 1936–64.

Ibn ʿAbd al-Ḥakam. *Kitāb Futūḥ Miṣr wa-l-Ifrīqiya.* Arabic text and a French translation published by Albert Gateau under the title *Conquête de L'Afrique du Nord et de l'Espagne (Futūhʾ Ifrīqiya wa'l-Andalus).* 2d ed., Alger, 1947. The text reproduced by Gateau is essentially that established by Charles C. Torrey under the title *The History of the Conquest of Egypt, North Africa and Spain Known as the Futūḥ Miṣr* (New Haven, Conn., 1922).

ʿAlī ibn Burhān al-Dīn al Ḥalabī. *Al-Sīrat al-Ḥalabīyah.* 2 vols. Al-Qāhirah, A.H. 1329/A.D. 1911.

———. *Insān al-ʿUyūn.* 2 vols. Al-Qāhirah, A.H. 1351.

Al-Ḥasan ibn Aḥmad al-Hamdānī/Ibn al-Ḥāʾik. *Al-Iklīl min Akhbār al-Yaman,* of which only four (of ten) volumes are extant. A facsimile of vols. 1 and 2 was published in Berlin, 1943. Bk. 1 edited by O. Löfgren in *Bibliotheca Ekmaniana,* vol. 58 (Uppsala, 1954, 1965) and by Muḥammad ibn ʿAlī al-Akwaʿ al-Ḥiwālī (al-Qāhirah, A.H. 1383/A.D. 1963). The final section of bk. 2 edited by Löfgren, *Südarabisches Muštabih,* in *Bibl. Ekmaniana,* vol. 57 (Uppsala, 1954). Bk. 8 edited and translated by Nabih Amin Faris under the title *The Antiquities of South Arabia* (Princeton, N.J., 1938; reprint, Westport, Conn., 1981). Bk. 10 edited by Muḥibb al-Dīn al-Khaṭīb (al-Qāhirah, A.H. 1368/A.D. 1948).

———. *Ṣifat Jazīrat al-ʿArab.* 2 vols. Edited by D. H. Müller under the title *Sifa: al-Hamdânî's Geographie der Arabischen Halbinsel.* Leyden, 1884–91; reprint, 1968. 2d ed. by Muḥammad ibn ʿAlī al-Akwaʿ al-Ḥiwālī (Riyāḍ, Saudi Arabia, A.H. 1394).

Abū ʿAbd Allāh Ibn Ḥammād. *Akhbār Mulūk Bani-ʿUbayd.* Edited and translated by M. Vonderheyden under the title *Histoire des Rois Obaïdites.* Alger, 1927.

Ḥamzah al-Iṣfahīnī. *Taʾrīkh Sinī Mulūk al-Arḍ wa-l-Anbiyāʾ.* Edited by I. M. E. Gottwaldt. Lipsiae (Leipzig), 1844. Translated into Latin by Gottwaldt (Lipsiae, 1848).

Aḥmad ibn Ḥanbal. *Al-Musnad.* Edited by Aḥmad Muḥammad Shākir. Al-Qāhirah, A.H. 1368–.

Abū al-Hasan ʿAlī ibn Abī Bakr al-Harawī. *Kitāb al-Ishārāt ilā Maʿrifat al-Ziyārāt.* Edited by Janine Sourdel-Thomine under the title *Guide des Lieux de Pèlerinage.* 2 vols. Damas, 1953, 1957.

Sayf al-Harawī. *Taʾrīkh Nāma-i Harát.* Edited by Muḥammad aṣ-Siddíqí. Calcutta, 1944.

Abū al-Qāsim ibn ʿAlī al-Nasībī ibn Ḥawqal. *Kitāb Ṣūrat al-Arḍ/Kitāb al-Masālik wa-l-Mamālik.* In *Opus Geographicum Auctore Ibn Haukal.* Volume 2 of *Bibliotheca Geographorum Arabicorum,* edited by Johannes Henrik Kramers. Lugduni Batavorum, 1938–39. French translation by J. H. Kramers and

G. Wiet under the title *Configuration de la Terre* (Beyrouth and Paris, 1964).

The Chronography of Gregory Abū'l Faraj . . . Bar Hebraeus. Translated by E. A. Wallis Budge. 2 vols. Oxford, 1932; reprint, Amsterdam, 1976.

Ibn ʿAbd al-Munʿim al-Himyarī, comp. *Al-Rawḍ al-Miʿṭār.* Edited and translated into French by Évariste Lévi-Provençal under the title *La Péninsule Ibérique au Moyen Âge d'après le Kitāb al-Rawḍ al-Miʿṭār fī Ḥabar al-Akṭār.* Leiden, 1938.

Ḥudūd al-ʿĀlam. Published under the posthumous editorship of V. V. Barthold in 1930 and again by Manūchihr Sutūdah in 1962. English translation by V. Minorsky under the title *Ḥudud al-ʿĀlam* (E. J. W. Gibb Memorial Series, n.s., 11 [London, 1937]; 2d ed. by C. E. Bosworth [London, 1970]).

Jarwal ibn Aws al-Ḥuṭay'ah. *Dīwān.* Edited by Nuʿmān Amīn Ṭāhā. Al-Qāhirah, A.H. 1378/A.D. 1958.

Ibn ʿIdhārī al-Marrākushī. *Al-Bayān al-Maghrib fī (Ikhtiṣar)* Akhbār Mulūk al-Andalus wa-l-Maghrib. Vols. 1 and 2 edited by G. S. Colin and E. Lévi-Provençal under the title *Histoire de l'Afrique du Nord et de l'Espagne Musulmane, Intitulé Kitab al-Bayan al-Mughrib.* Leiden, 1948–51. Vol. 3 edited by Lévi-Provençal (Paris, 1930).

ʿAdud al-Dīn ibn Rukn al-Dīn al-Ījī. *Sharḥ ʿalā Mukhtaṣar al-Muntahā li-Ibn al-Ḥājib.* Constantinople, 1889.

Abū al-Faraj al-Iṣfahānī. *Kitāb al-Aghānī.* 20 vols. Būlāq, Egypt, A.H. 1285. An additional volume was published by R. Brünnow (Leiden, 1888).

Muḥammad ibn Ḥasan Ibn Isfandiyār. *Tārīkh-i Ṭabaristān.* Edited by ʿAbbās Iqbāl. 2 vols. Tehran, A.H. 1320. Abridged English translation by E. G. Browne (Leiden and London, 1905).

Muʿin al-Dīn al-Zamčī al-Isfizārī. *Rawḍat al-Jannāt fī Awṣāf Madīnat Harāt.* Edited by Sayyid Muḥammad Kāẓim Imām. Tehran, 1959.

Muḥammad ibn Isḥāq. *Sīrat Sayyidinā Muḥammad Rasūli'llāh.* In *Das Leben Muhammeds nach Muhammed ibn Ishâk, Bearbeit von Abd al-Malik ibn Hischâm,* edited by Ferdinand Wüstenfeld. 2 vols. Göttingen, Germany, 1858–60. Edited by Mustafā al-Saqqā, Ibrāhīm al-Abyarī, and ʿAbd al-Ḥafīẓ Shalabī (Qāhirah, A.H. 1355/A.D. 1937); English translation by Alfred Guillaume under the title *The Life of Mohammad* (Oxford, 1955).

Muḥammad ibn Ismāʿīl al-Jāmiʿal-ṣaḥīḥ. *Ṣalat.* In *Concordance et indices de la Tradition musulmane,* edited by A. J. Wensinck. Leiden, 1936–64.

Abū Isḥāq al-Iṣṭakhrī. *Al-Masālik wa-l-Mamālik.* In *Viae Regnorum Descriptio Ditionis Moslemicae,* vol. 1 of *Bibliotheca Geographorum Arabicorum,* edited by M. J. de Goeje. Lugduni Batavorum, 1870.

ʿIyāḍ ibn Musaʿ. *Tartīb al-Madārik.* Edited by M. Talbi. Bayrūt, 1965.

Abū ʿUthmān ʿAmr ibn Baḥr al-Jāḥiẓ (attrib.). "Al-Tabaṣṣur bi-l-Tijārah," edited by Hasan H. ʿAbd al-Wahhāb. *Revue de l'Académie de Damas* 12 (1932): 337, 345.

———. *Kitāb al-Ḥayawān.* Edited by ʿAbd al-Salām Muḥammad Hārūn. 7 vols. Al-Qāhirah, A.H. 1357/A.D. 1938–45.

———. *Kitāb al-Bayān wa-l-Tabyīn.* Edited by ʿAbd al-Salām Muḥammad Hārūn. 4 vols. Al-Qāhirah, A.H. 1367.

———. *Kitāb al-Bukhalā'.* Edited by Ḥājirī. Al-Qāhirah, A.H. 1368.

Abū ʿAbd Allāh al-Jahshiyārī. *Kitāb al-Wuzarā' wa-l-Kuttāb.* Only the first part, dealing with the period prior to al-Ma'mūn's caliphate, is extant. A facsimile edition of this part was published by Hans von Mžik (Leipzig, 1926) and edited by Mustafā al-Saqqā' et al. (al-Qāhirah, A.H. 1357/A.D. 1938).

ʿAbd al-Raḥman ibn ʿAlī ibn al-Jawzī. *Al-Muntaẓam fī-l-Ta'rīkh al-Mulūk wa-l-Umam.* Vols. 5–10 edited by F. Krenkow. Hyderabad, India, 1938–39.

———. *Manāqib Baghdād.* Edited by M. M. al-Atharī. Baghdād, A.H. 1341. Partially translated by George Makdisi in *Arabica* 6 (1959) : 185–95.

Abū al-Ḥasan ʿAlī al-Jaznaʿī. *Zahrat al-Ās.* Edited and translated by A. Bel under the title *Zahrat al-Ās (La Fleur du Myrte) Traitant de la Fondation de la Ville de Fès.* Alger, 1923.

John, Bishop of Nikiu. *The Chronicle of. . . .* Edited and translated by R. H. Charles. London, 1916.

Abū al-Ḥusayn ibn Jubayr. *Riḥlah.* Edited by William Wright (Leiden, 1852); subsequently by M. J. de Goeje as vol. 5 of the Gibb Memorial Series (Leyden and London, 1907) and by H. Nassar (al-Qāhirah, A.H. 1374/A.D. 1955). Italian translation by C. Schiaparelli under the title *Viaggio in Ispagna, Sicilia . . .* (Roma, 1906); English translation by R. J. C. Broadhurst under the title *The Travels of Ibn Jubayr* (1952); French translation by M. Gaudefroy-Demombynes in *Documents Relatifs à l'Histoire des Croisades,* 3 fascs. (Paris, 1949–56).

ʿAla al-Dīn ʿAṭā Malik Juwaynī. *Tarīkh-i Jahān Gushā.* Edited by Mirzā Muḥammad Qazvīnī. E. J. W. Gibb Memorial Series, no. 16. 3 vols. London, 1912, 1916, 1937.

Minhāj al-Dīn ibn Sirāj Jūzjānī. *Ṭabaqāt-i Nāṣirī.* Edited by W. Nassau Lees. Calcutta, 1863. Edited by Abd al-Hayy Habībī, 2 vols. (Kābul, Afghanistan, A.H. 1342–43).

Ibn Sālim al-Kalāʿī. *Kitāb al-Iktifā' fī Maghāzī al-Mustafā wa-l-Thalātha al-Khulafā.* Vol. 1 of *Bibliotheca Arabica* no. 6, edited by H. Massé. Alger and Paris, 1931.

Hishām ibn al-Kalbī. *Kitāb al-Aṣnām.* Edited by Aḥmad Zakī Pasha. Al-Qāhirah, A.H. 1330. German translation by Rosa K. Rosenberger (Leipzig, 1941); English translation by N. A. Faris (Princeton, N.J., 1952); partial French translation by M. S. Marmardji, *Revue Biblique* 35 (1926) : 397–420; revised edition of the text with annotated French translation by W. Atallah (Paris, 1969).

K'artlis Cχovreba. Published with French translation by M. Brosset under the title *Histoire de la Géorgie.* 5 vols. St. Petersbourg, 1849–58.

Maḥmud ibn al-Ḥusayn al-Kāshgharī. *Dīwān Lughāt al-Turk.* Edited by Kilisli Muʿallim Rifʿat Bey. 2 vols. Istanbul, A.H. 1333–35/A.D. 1917.

Imād al-Dīn Ismāʿīl Ibn Kathīr. *Al-Bidayah wa-l-Nihāyah fī-l-Ta'rīkh.* Al-Qāhirah, A.H. 1351–58.

Katib Čelebī Ḥājjī Khalīfah. *Kitāb Kashf al-Ẓunūn ʿan Asāmī al-Kutub wa-l-Funūn.* Edited by Gustav Flügel in *Lexicon Bibliographicum et Encyclopaedicum . . .* (Arabic text with Latin translation and indexes). 7 vols. Leipzig, 1835–58.

Abd al-Rahmān ibn Khaldūn. *Kitāb al-ʿIbar wa Dīwān al-Mubtada' wa-l-Khabar fi Ayyām al-ʿArab wa-l-ʿAjam wa-l-Barbar.* Edited by Naṣr al-Hūrīnī. 7 vols. Būlāq, Egypt, A.H. 1284/A.D. 1867. Partially edited by William MacGuckin de Slane (Alger, 1847–51); partial French translation by de Slane under the title *Ibn Khaldoun: Histoire des Berbères et des Dynasties Musulmanes de l'Afrique Septentrionale,* 4 vols. (Alger, 1852–56); commercial edition with indexes (Bayrūt, A.H. 1375–78).

Shams al-Dīn Ibn Khallikān. *Wafāyāt al-A'yān wa-Anba Abnā' al-Zamān.* Al-Qāhirah, A.H. 1299. English translation by MacGuckin de Slane under the title *Ibn Khallikān's Biographical Dictionary,* 4 vols. (Paris, 1842–71). Edited by I. Abbās (Bayrūt, A.H. 1388–92/A.D. 1968–72) and by Muḥammad Muḥyī al-Dīn 'Abd al-Ḥamīd, 6 vols. (al-Qāhirah, A.H. 1367/A.D. 1948).

Abu Bakr Ahmad ibn 'Alī al-Khaṭīb al-Baghdādī. *Ta'rīkh Baghdād.* 14 vols. Al-Qāhirah, A.H. 1349. Introduction edited and translated into French by G. Salmon under the title *L'Introduction Topographique à l'Histoire de Bagdâdh . . .* (Paris, 1904). See also J.-P. Pascual, *Index Schématique du Ta'rīḫ Baġdād* (Paris, 1971).

Lisān al-Dīn ibn al-Khaṭīb. *Al-Iḥāṭah fī Akhbār Gharnāṭah.* Abbreviated ed. 2 vols. Al-Qāhirah, A.H. 1319/A.D. 1901. Incomplete ed. by Abd Allāh Inān (al-Qāhirah, A.H. 1374).

Abū al-Qāsim 'Ubayd Allāh ibn 'Abd Allāh ibn Khurradādhbih. *Kitāb al-Masālik wa-l-Mamālik.* In *Bibliotheca Geographorum Arabicorum.* Pars Sexta, *Kitāb al-Masālik wa'l-Mamālik (Liber viarum et regnorum) auctore Abu'l-Kâsim Obaidallah ibn Abdallah ibn Khordâdhbeh . . . ,* edited by M. J. de Goeje. Lugduni Batavorum, 1889.

Abū 'Abd Allāh al-Khushanī, *Ṭabaqāt 'Ulamā' Ifrīqiyah.* Published with a French translation by Mohammed Ben Cheneb under the title *Classes des Savants de l'Ifrîqiya (Tabaqât 'Ulamâ' Ifrîqiyah).* Publication de la Faculté des Lettres d'Alger, vol. 52. Alger, 1920.

Abū 'Abd Allāh Muḥammad ibn Mūsā al-Khwārizmī. *Mafātīḥ al-'Ulūm.* Edited by G. van Vloten. Leiden, 1895.

———. *Kitāb Sūrat al-Ard.* Edited by H. von Mžik. Wien, 1926.

'Umar al-Kindī. *Faḍā'il Miṣr.* Edited and translated by J. Østrup in *Oversigt over det Kongelige Danske Videnskabernes Selskab Forhandlinger* (Kobenhavn, 1896), 173–245. Edited by I. A. al-'Adawī and 'Alī M. 'Umar (al-Qāhirah, A.H. 1391).

Abū 'Umar Muḥammad ibn Yusuf al-Kindī. *Kitāb al-Umarā (al-Wulāt)* and *Kitāb al-Qudāt.* Edited by Rhuvon Guest and published together under the title *The Governors and Judges of Egypt or Kitâb El Umarā (El Wulâh) wa Kitâb El Qudâh of El Kindî.* E. J. W. Gibb Memorial Series, vol. 19. Leyden and London, 1908–12. Re-edition of *Kitāb al-Wulāt* by Husayn Nassār (Bayrūt, A.H. 1379/A.D. 1959).

Afḍal al-Dīn Aḥmad ibn Ḥāmid Kirmānī. *'Iqd al-'Ulā li-l-Mawqif al-A'lā.* Edited by 'Alī Muḥammad 'Āmirī Na'inī. Tehrān, A.H. 1311.

Kitāb al-Uyūn wa-l-Ḥadā'iq fi akhbar al-haga'iq. Edited by 'Umar Sa'idi. Dimashq, 1972.

Mufaḍḍal ibn Sa'd al-Māfarrūkhī. *Risālat Maḥāsin Iṣfahān.* Edited by Jalāl al-Dīn Ṭihrānī. Ṭihrān, A.H. 1312. A fourteenth-century Persian translation by al-'Alawī, with numerous interpolations postdating al-Māfarrūkhī, has been edited by 'Abbās Iqbal under the title *Tarjuma-yi Maḥasin-i Iṣfahān* (Ṭihrān, A.H. 1328).

Muḥammad Bāqir ibn Muḥammad Taqī Majlisī. *Biḥār al-Anwār.* Tehrān, A.H. 1379.

Abū Bakr 'Abd Allāh ibn Muḥammad al-Mālikī. *Kitāb Riyāḍ al-Nufūs fī Ṭabaqāt 'Ulamā' al-Qayrawān wa-Ifrīqiyah.* Edited by H. Mu'nis. 2 vols. Al-Qāhirah, A.H. 1370/A.D. 1949).

Al-As'ad ibn Mammātī. *Qawānīn al-Dawānīn.* Edited by A. S. Aṭiyah. Al-Qāhirah, A.H. 1362.

Muḥammad ibn Mukarram ibn Manẓūr. *Lisān al-'Arab.* Edited by Y. Khayyat and N. Mar'ashlī. 3 vols. Bayrūt, n.d.

Shams al-Dīn al-Maqdisī [also known as al-Bashshārī]. *Aḥsan al-Taqāsīm fī Ma'rifat al-Aqālīm.* In *Descriptio Imperii Moslemici Auctore al-Moqaddassi.* Vol. 3 of *Bibliotheca Geographorum Arabicorum,* edited by M. J. Goeje. 1st ed., Lugduni Batavorum, 1877; rev. ed., 1906. Partial translation by G. S. A. Ranking and R. F. Azoo in vol. 1 of *Bibliotheca Indica, Asiatic Society of Bengal* (Calcutta, 1897, 1910), fasc. 1–4. German translation of most of section on al-Shām in *Zeitschrift des Deutschen Palästinavereins* 7 (1884) : 143–72 and 215–30; English translation of the same section in its entirety by Guy Le Strange, *Palestine Pilgrims' Text Society* 3 (1886) : i–xvi and 1–116; French translation of the introduction and section on al-Shām by André Miquel, *Aḥsan at-Taqāsīm fī Ma'rifat al-Aqālim* (Damas, 1963), and of the section on Miṣr by the same author: "L'Égypte vue par un géographe arabe du IVe / Xe siècle: al-Muqaddasī," *Annales Islamologiques* 11 (1972) : 109–39. French translation of the sections on the Maghrib by Charles Pellat, *Description de l'Occident Musulman au IVe Siècle,* Bibliothèque Arabe-Française no. 9 (Alger, 1950). Complete English translation by Basil Anthony Collins under the title *Al-Muqaddasī. The Best Divisions for Knowledge of the Regions* (Reading, England, 1994).

Shihāb al-Dīn ibn Muḥammad al-Maqqarī. *Nafḥ al-Ṭīb.* Printed at Būlāq, Egypt, A.H. 1279; in 4 vols. at al-Qāhirah, 1302 and 1304; 10 vols. at al-Qāhirah, A.H. 1367; 8 vols. edited by Iḥsān 'Abbās at Bayrūt, A.H. 1388; part 1 of 2 translated into French and published by R. Dozy, G. Dugat, L. Krehl, and W. Wright under the title *Analectes sur l'Histoire et la Littérature des Arabes d'Espagne,* 2 vols. (Leyden, 1855–61); English translation by D. Pascual de Gayangos under the title *The History of the Mohammedan Dynasties in Spain,* 2 vols. (London, 1840–43).

———. *Azhār al-Riyāḍ fī Akhbār 'Iyāḍ.* Edition begun in Tūnis, A.H. 1322; 3 vols. in al-Qāhirah, A.H. 1359–61; and vols. 4 and 5 at al-Muḥammadīyah, A.H. 1398–1400.

Taqī al-Dīn Aḥmad al-Maqrīzī. *Al-Mawā'iẓ wa-l-I'tibār fī Dhikr al-Khiṭāṭ wa-l-Āthār.* 2 vols. Būlāq, A.H. 1270/A.D. 1853. Edited by Gaston Wiet, 2 vols. (LeCaire [Cairo]), 1911.

———. *Itti'āz al-Ḥunafā bi-akhbar al-a'immah al-Fatimiyin al-khulata.* Edited by Jamal al-Din Shayyal. Al-Qahīrah, 1967.

Ibn 'Idhārī al-Marrākushī. *Al-Bayān al-Maghrib fī (Ikhtiṣar) Akhbār Mulūk al-Andalus wa-l-Maghrib.* Vols. 1 and 2 edited by G. S. Colin and E. Lévi-Provençal under the title *Histoire de l'Afrique du Nord et de l'Espagne Musulmane, Intitulé Kitab al-Bayan al-Mughrib.* (Leiden, 1948–51); vol. 3 edited by Lévi-Provençal (Paris, 1930). French translation of an edition of pts. 1 and 2 prepared by R. Dozy in 1848–51 made by E. Fagnan under the title *Histoire de l'Afrique et de L'Espagne Intitulée Al-Bayano l-Mogrib,* 2 vols. (Alger, 1901–4).

'Alī ibn Muḥammad ibn Ḥabīb al-Māwardī. *Kitāb al-Aḥkam al-Sulṭānīyah.* Al-Qāhirah, A.H. 1380. Translated by E. Fagnan under the title *Les Statuts Gouvernementaux* (Alger, 1915; new ed., Paris, 1982).

Abū ʿAlī Aḥmad ibn Muḥammad al-Marzūqī. *Kitāb al-Azminah wa-l-Amkinah.* 2 vols. Haydarābād, India, A.H. 1332/A.D. 1913.

Abū al-Ḥasan ʿAlī al-Masʿūdī. *Murūj al-Dhahab wa-Maʿādin al-Jawhar.* Edited and translated by C. Barbier de Meynard and Pavet de Courteille under the title *Les Prairies d'Or et les Mines de Pierres Précieuses,* 9 vols. Paris, 1861–77. Revised and translated by Charles Pellat: 5 vols. of text, Publications de l'Université Libanaise, Section des Etudes Historiques, vol. 11 (Beirut, 1966–74); 2 vols. of Arabic indexes; and 3 vols. of translations (Beirut, 1962–).

———. *Kitāb al-Tanbīh wa-l-Ishrāf.* Volume 8 of *Bibliotheca Geographorum Arabicorum,* edited by M. J. de Goeje. Leyden, 1893–94. Reprint, Beirut, 1965.

Michael Syrus. *La Chronique de Michel le Syrien, Patriarche Jacobite d'Antioche.* Edited and translated by J.-B. Chabot. 4 vols. Paris, 1899–1924; reprint, 1963.

Abū Muḥammad ibn Yaʿqūb Miskawayh. *Tajārib al-Umam wa Taʿāqib al-Humam.* Edited and translated into English by H. F. Amedroz and D. S. Margoliouth, with the continuations of Abū Shujāʿ al-Rūdhrāwarī and Hilāl ibn al-Muḥassin, in *The Experience of Nations,* 7 vols., in the series *The Eclipse of the ʿAbbāsid Caliphate.* 3 vols. text, 3 vols. translation, plus index. Oxford and London, 1921.

Movsēs Kalankatwacʿi [Dasχuranҫi]. *Patmutʿiwn Alwanic ʿAšχarhi.* Translated by C. J. F. Dowsett under the title *The History of the Caucasian Albanians.* London, 1961.

Movsēs Xorenacʿi. *Patmutʿiwn Hayocʿ.* Edited and translated by P. E. Le Vaillant de Florival, Venice, 1841. Edited by M. Abelean and S. Yarutʿiwnean (Tiflis, 1913); Russian translation by J.-B. Emin (Moscow, 1958).

Al-Mubarrad. *Al-Kāmil fī-l-Lughah.* Edited by William Wright (Leipzig, 1864) and by Z. Mubārak and A. M. Shākir (al-Qāhirah, A.H. 1356).

Al-Mufaḍḍal al-Ḍabbī. *Al-Mufaḍḍalīyāt.* Translated and annotated by C. J. Lyall. Oxford, 1918.

Abū al-Ḥusayn al-Ḥasan ibn Aḥmad al-Miṣrī al-Muhallabī. *Kitāb al-Masālik wa-l-Mamālik* (usually known as *al-ʿAzīzī).* Now lost except for 14 folios dealing mainly with Jerusalem and Damascus which Ṣalāḥ al-Dīn al-Munajjid has edited in *Revue de l'Institut des Manuscrits Arabes* 4 (1958) : 43–72. The passage on Damascus was reprinted in the same author's *Madīnat Dimashq ʿind al-Jughrāfīyīn wa-l-Raḥḥālīn al-Muslimīn* (Bayrūt, A.H. 1378), 80–86. Extracts from the lost parts of al-Muhallabī's book have been preserved in Yāqūt (*Muʿjam al-Buldān,* 57 citations), Abū al-Fidāʾ (*Taqwīm al-Buldān,* 135 citations), and al-Qalqashandī (*Ṣubḥ al-Aʿshā,* 69 citations).

Yūsuf ibn Yaʿqūb ibn al-Mujāwir (attrib.). *Tarīkh al-Mustabṣir.* Edited by Oscar Löfgren under the title *Descriptio Arabiae Meridionalis. Taʾrīḫ al-Mustabṣir.* 2 vols. Leiden, 1951–54.

Sāwīrus ibn al-Muqaffaʿ [Severus of al-Ushmunayn]. *Historia Patriarchorum Alexandrinorum.* Edited by C. F. Seybold in *Corpus Scriptorum Christianorum Orientalium,* Scr. Ar. Ser. III, tome 9, fascs. 1, 2. Beirut, 1904–10. English translation by B. Evetts, *History of the Patriarchs of the Coptic Church of Alexandria,* in *Patrologia Orientalis:* vols. 5, 1–215; and 10, 357–55) (Paris, 1904–15).

Ḥamd-Allāh Mustawfī. *Nuzhat al-Qulūb.* Lithograph edition by Mīrzā Muḥammad Shīrāzī. Bombay, A.H. 1311/A.D. 1894. A variorum edition of the third part was published by Guy Le Strange (E. J. W. Gibb Memorial Series, vol. 23 [Leyden and London, 1915]).

———. *Tarīkh-i Guzīdeh.* Edited by Edward G. Browne under the title *The Taʾríkh-i-guzída; or, "select history" of Hamdaʾlláh Mustawfí-i-Qazwíní.* Leiden, 1910–13.

Ziyād ibn Muʿāwiyah al-Nābighah. *Diwān al-Nābighah al-Dhubyānī.* Edited by Shukrī Fayṣal. Bayrūt, A.H. 1388/A.D. 1968.

Abū al-Faraj ibn al-Nadīm. *Kitāb al-Fihrist.* Edited by Gustav Flügel. 2 vols. Leipzig, 1871–2. Persian translation by R. Tajadod (Tehran, A.H. 1385). English translation by Bayard Dodge under the title *The Fihrist of al-Nadim. A Tenth-Century Survey of Muslim Culture,* 2 vols. (New York, 1970).

Ibn Nājī. *Maʿālim al-Īmān.* Tūnis, A.H. 1320/A.D. 1902/3.

Abū Yaʿqūb al-Najīramī. *Aymān al-ʿArab fī al-Jāhilīyah.* Edited by Muhibb al-Dīn al-Khatīb. Al-Qāhirah, A.H. 1346/A.D. 1928.

Abū Bakr Muḥammad ibn Jaʿfar ibn Zakarīyā al-Narshakhī. *Taʾrīkh Bukhārā.* Persian translation by Abū Naṣr Aḥmad al-Qubāvī in 1128 (with additional materials); abridgment of this latter work by Muḥammad ibn Zufar ibn ʿUmar in 1178–79; edited by Charles Schéfer under the title *Description Topograpique [sic] et Historique de Boukhara . . . par Mohammed Nerchaky, 943 (332 H.)* (Paris, 1892; reimpression, Amsterdam, 1975) and by Mudarris Razavī [Riḍawī] (Tehrān, n.d. but probably about 1939); Russian translation by G. V. Lykoshin under the title *Istoriya Bukhary* (Tashkent, 1897); annotated English translation by Richard N. Frye under the title *The History of Bukhara* (Cambridge, Mass., 1954).

Nāṣir-i Khusraw. *Safar Nāmah.* Annotated French translation by Charles Schéfer under the title *Sefer Nameh. Relation du Voyage de Nassiri Khosrau . . .* Ecole des Langues Orientales Vivantes. Paris, 1881. Edited by Muḥammad Dabīr-Siyāqī (Tehrān, A.H. 1335/A.D. 1956) and translated into English by W. M. Thackston Jr. under the title *Nāser-e Khosraw's Book of Travels (Safarhāma)* (New York, 1986).

Aḥmed Nedīm. *Ṣaḥāʾif al-Akhbār.* 3 vols. Istanbul, A.H. 1285. This is an epitomized Turkish translation of Aḥmad ibn Luṭfullāh Münejjim-Bashī, *Jāmīʿ al-Duwal,* a general history written in Arabic that still exists only in manuscript in several Turkish libraries.

Shihāb al-Dīn Aḥmad al-Nuwayrī. *Nihāyat al-Arab fī Funūn al-Adab.* Al-Qāhirah, 1955–.

Marco Polo. *Le Devisement dou Monde.* Variorum edition and translation by A. C. Moule and Paul Pelliot under the title *Marco Polo: The Description of the World.* 2 vols. London, 1938.

Procopius. *History of the Wars.* Edited and translated by H. B. Dewing. London, 1904.

Pseudo-Methodios. *Apokalypse.* Syriac text edited and translated by Francisco Javier Martinez. Ph.D. diss., Catholic University, 1985. Greek text edited and translated by A. Lolos under the title *Die Apokalypse des Ps.-Methodios, Beiträge zur klassischen Philologie,* vol. 83 (Meisenheim am Glan, 1976).

Abū ʿAlī Ismāʿil al-Qālī. *Dhayl al-Amālī wa-l-Nawādir.* 3 vols. Bayrūt, A.H. 1384/A.D. 1964.

Abū al-ʿAbbās Aḥmad al-Qalqashandī. *Kitāb Ṣubḥ al-Aʿshā fī*

Ṣinā'at al-Inshā'. 14 vols. Al-Qāhirah, A.H. 1331–40/A.D. 1913–19.

Ibn Abī Dīnār al-Qayrawānī. *Al-Mu'nis fī Akhbār Ifrīqiyah wa-Tūnis.* Tūnis, A.H. 1286/A.D. 1869. French translation by Pellissier and Remusat (Paris, 1845).

Zakarīyā ibn Muḥammad al-Qazwīnī. *Kitāb 'Ajā'ib al-Makhlūqāt wa-Gharā'ib al-Mawjūdāt.* In *Zakarija ben Muhammed ben Mahmud al-Cazwini's Kosmographie,* edited by Ferdinand Wüstenfeld. 2 vols. Göttingen, Germany, 1847–49.

———. *Āthār al-Bilād wa Akhbār al-'Ibād.* Edited by F. Wüstenfeld. Göttingen, Germany, 1848; reprint, Bayrūt, A.H. 1380/A.D. 1960–61.

'Alī ibn Yūsuf al-Qifṭī. *Ikhbār al-'Ulamā' bi Akhbār al-Ḥukamā.* Edited by Julius Lippert. Leipzig, 1903.

Qudāmah ibn Ja'far. *Kitāb al-Kharāj.* Partial translation by A. Ben Shemesh under the title *Taxation in Islam.* Rev. ed., vol. 2. Leiden and London, 1965.

Ḥasan ibn Muḥammad ibn Ḥasan Qummī, *Tārīkh-i Qumm.* Persian translation by Ḥasan ibn 'Alī ibn Ḥasan ibn 'Abd al-Malik Qummī in A.H. 805/A.D. 1403. Edited by Sayyid Jalāl al-Dīn Ṭihrānī (Ṭihrān, A.H. 1313/A.D. 1895).

Abū 'Abd Allāh Muḥammad al-Qurṭubī. *Al-Jāmi' li-Aḥkām al-Qur'ān wa-l-Mubayyin li-mā Tadammana min al-Sunnah wa-Ayāt al-Furqān.* 10 vols. Al-Qāhirah, A.H. 1387/A.D. 1967.

'Abd Allāh ibn Muslim ibn Qutaybah. *Kitāb al-Ma'ārif.* Edited by Ferdinand Wüstenfeld. Göttingen, Germany, 1850.

———. *Al-Shi'r wa-l-Shu'arā'.* Edited by M. J. de Goeje. Leyden, 1904.

[Pseudo-] Ibn al-Raqiq. *Ta'rikh.* Tunis, A.H. 1388.

Aḥmad ibn 'Abdullāh al-Rāzī. *Ta'rīkh Madīnat Ṣan'ā'.* Edited by Ḥusayn ibn 'Abdullāh al-'Amri and 'Abd al-Jabbār Zakkār. Dimashq, A.H. 1395/A.D. 1975.

Abū Bakr Aḥmad ibn Muḥammad ibn Mūsā al-Rāzī. A Castilian version of this author's preface to his now-lost history of Islamic Spain was published by Pascual de Gayangos under the title *Memoria sobre la Autenticidad de la Crónica Denominada de Moro Rasis. Memorias de la Real Academia de la Historia,* vol. 8. Madrid, 1852. The original of this text was a rendering by Gil Peres of a lost Portuguese translation dating from about the turn of the fourteenth century. A Portuguese version, derived from Gil Peres's translation, was published in *Crónica Geral de Espanha de 1334,* edited by L. E. Lindley Cintra (Lisboā, 1952). A French translation and reconstructed Arabic text of the Castilian version have been prepared by Évariste Lévi-Provençal under the title "La 'Description de l'Espagne' d'Aḥmad al-Rāzī," *Andalus,* 18 (1953) : 51–108.

Abū 'Alī Aḥmad ibn 'Umār ibn Rustah. *Kitāb al-A'lāq al-Nafīsah.* The seventh, and only surviving, part has been edited by M. J. de Goeje in *Bibliotheca Geographorum Arabicorum,* vol. 7. Lugduni Batavorum, 1892. French translation by Gaston Wiet under the title *Les Atours Précieux* (Le Caire, 1955).

Hilāl al-Ṣābi'. *Rusūm Dār al-Khilāfah.* Edited by M. 'Awād. Al-Qāhirah, A.H. 1383.

Muḥammad ibn Sa'd. *Kitāb al-Ṭabaqāt al-Kabīr.* 9 vols. Edited by Eduard Sachau et al. Leyden and Berlin, 1904–28.

Ibn al-Saghīr. (An anecdotal chronicle). Edited with a French translation by A. de C. Motylinski under the title "Chronique d'Ibn Saghīr sur les imams rostémides de Tahert." *Actes du XIVe Congrès International des Orientalistes* (Alger, 1905; third part, Paris, 1908), 3–132.

Ḥamzah al-Sahmī. *Ta'rīkh Jurjān aw Kitāb Ma'rifat 'Ulamā' Ahl Jurjān.* Ḥaydarābād, India, A.H. 1387.

Muḥammad ibn Sa'īd al-Kushayrī. *Ta'rīkh al-Raqqah.* Edited by Ṭāhir al-Na'sānī. Ḥamā, Syria, A.H. 1378.

Ibn Samā'ah. *Al-Iktisāb fī-l-Rizq al-Mustaṭab.* Al-Qāhirah, A.H. 1357.

'Abd al-Karīm al-Sam'ānī. *Kitāb al-Ansāb.* Facsimile text published by D. S. Margoliouth. E. J. W. Gibb Memorial Series, vol. 20. London, 1913. Partial edition by 'Abd al-Raḥmān ibn Yaḥyā al-Yamānī and Muḥammad 'Abd al-Mu'īd Khīd Khān, 6 vols. (Ḥaydarābād, India, A.H. 1382–86).

'Alī ibn Aḥmad al-Samhūdī. *Wafā' al-Wafāh bi-Akhbār Dār al-Muṣṭafā.* Edited by Muḥammad Muḥyī al-Dīn 'Abd al-Ḥamīd. Al-Qāhirah, A.H. 1374.

Sebēos. *Sébéos. Histoire d'Héraclius.* Translated by F. Macler. Paris, 1904.

'Izz al-Dīn ibn Shaddād al-Ḥalabī. *Al-A'lāq al-Khaṭīrah fī Dhikr Umarā' al-Shām wa-l-Jazīrah.* Edited by Ch. Ledit. *Al-Mashriq* 30 (1935) : 179–223. Section on al-Dimashq published by Sāmī Dahhān (al-Dimashq, A.H. 1382); on Ḥalab by Dominique Sourdel (Bayrūt, A.H. 1372); on Lebanon, Jordan, and Palestine by Sāmī Dahhān (al-Dimashq, A.H. 1383); and on the Jazīrah by Claude Cahen, "La Djazīra au milieu du XIIIe siècle d'après 'Izz al-Dīn ibn Chaddād," *Revue des Etudes Islamiques* 8 (1934) : 109–28.

Abū al-'Abbās Aḥmad al-Shammākhī. *Kitāb al-Siyar.* Al-Qāhirah, A.H. 1301. Extracts translated into French by E. Masqueray in *Chronique d'Abou Zakaria* (Alger, 1878), 342–90.

'Abd al-Karīm al-Sharastānī. *Kitāb al-Milal wa-l-Nihal.* Edited by W. Cureton. London, 1842–46.

Muḥammad Shaybānī. *Kitāb al Kasb.* Now lost, but substantial portions have survived in Ibn Samā'ah, *al-Iktisāb,* q.v.

Nisterot Rabbi Shim'on Ben Yokhay. In *Beth ha-Midrash. Sammlung kleiner Midraschim und vermischter Abhandlungen aus der älteren jüdischen Literatur,* edited by A. Jellinek. 2d ed. Jerusalem, 1938.

Ibn Zarkūb Shīrāzī. *Shīrāz-Nāmah.* Edited by Bahman Karīmī. Tehrān, A.H. 1310/A.D. 1931.

Abū 'Alī al-Ḥusayn ibn Sīnā. *Kunūz al-Mu'azzimīn.* Edited by Jalāl al-Dīn Homā'ī. Tehran, A.H. 1331/A.D. 1912.

———. An opuscula, edited by A. F. von Mehren under the title *Traités Mystiques.* Leyden, 1889–94.

———. *Fi Bayân al-Mu'jizât wa-l-Karâmât.* Edited by G. N. Atiyeh under the title "Avicenna's Conception of Miracles." Ph.D. diss., University of Chicago, 1954.

Tāj al-Dīn al-Subki. *Ṭabaqāt al-Shāfi'īyah.* Edited by Maḥmūd Muḥammad al-Tanāḥī and Muḥammad 'Abd al-Fattaḥ al-Ḥilw. 10 vols. Al-Qāhirah, A.H. 1383–96.

Jalāl al-Dīn al-Suyūṭī. *Ḥusn al-Muḥāḍarah fī Akhbār Miṣr wa-l-Qāhirah.* 2 vols. Al-Qāhirah, A.H. 1321/A.D. 1903.

———. *Bughyat al-Wu'āh.* Al-Qāhirah, A.H. 1326/A.D. 1908.

———. *Al-Durr al-Manthūr.* 2 vols. Tehran, A.H. 1377/A.D. 1957.

———. *Ta'rīkh al-Khulafā'.* Edited by S. Lee and Mawlawī 'Abdalḥaqq. Calcutta, 1857. Translated by H. S. Jarret (Calcutta, 1881).

Synodicon Orientale. Edited by J. B. Chabot. Notices et Extraits des Manuscrits, vol. 37. Paris, 1902.

Abū Jaʿfar Muḥammad ibn Jarīr al-Ṭabarī. *Taʾrīkh al-Rusul wa-l-Mulūk.* Edited by M. J. de Goeje et al., 15 vols. (Leiden, 1879–1901), and by Muḥammad al-Faḍl Ibrāhīm, 10 vols. (al-Qāhirah, A.H. 1388).

———. *Jāmiʿ al-Bayān fī Tafsīr al-Qurʾān.* 30 pts. Būlāq, Egypt, A.H. 1323–30. Edited by Maḥmūd and Muḥammad Shākir, 16 vols. (al-Qāhirah, A.H. 1374).

Al-Faḍl ibn al-Ḥasan al-Ṭabarsī/al-Tabrisī. *Majmaʿ al-Bayān fī Tafsīr al-Qurʾān.* 10 vols. Bayrūt, A.H. 1380/A.D. 1961.

Abū al-Maḥāsin ibn Taghrībirdī. *Al-Nujūm al-Zāhirah fī Mulūk Miṣr wa-l-Qāhirah.* Edited by F. G. Juynboll and B. F. Matthes under the title *Abū ʾl-Mahasin ibn Tagri Bardii Annales.* Leyden, 1855–61.

Taʾrīkh Sīstān. Written ca. 1062 but continued to 1325 by a second author. Edited by Malek al-Shoʿarā Bahār under the title *Tārikh-i Sistān.* Tehran, A.H. 1314. English translation by Milton Gold under the title *The Tārikh-e Sistān* (Persian Heritage Series, no. 20 [Roma, 1976]).

Abū ʿAmr al-Tarsūsī. *Siyar al-Thughūr.* Lost but cited extensively by Ibn al-ʿAdīm, *Bughyat al-Ṭalab fī Taʾrīkh Ḥalab,* q.v.

Taqī al-Dīn ibn Taymīyah. *Qāʿidah fī Ziyārat Bayt al-Maqdis.* Edited by Ch. D. Matthews, "A Muslim iconoclast (Ibn Taymiyyah on the 'merits' of Jerusalem and Palestine)." *Journal of the American Oriental Society* 56 (1936) : 1–21.

Abū Manṣūr ʿAbd al-Malik ibn Muḥammad al-Thaʿālibī. *Thimar al-Qulūb fī al-Muḍaf wa-l-Mansūb.* Al-Qāhirah, A.H. 1326/A.D. 1908.

———. *Al-Laṭāʾif al-Maʿārif.* Edited by P. de Jong (Leyden, 1867) and by Ibrāhīm al-Abyārī and Ḥasan Kāmil al-Sayrafī (al-Qāhirah, A.H. 1380/A.D. 1960). English translation by C. E. Bosworth under the title *The Book of Curious and Entertaining Information.* The Laṭaʾif al-Maʿārarif of Thaʿālibī (Edinburgh, 1968); translation of chap. 10 by O. Rescher, "Das Kapitel X aus eth-Thaʿâlibî's Laṭâʾif el-Maʿârif: über die Eigentumlichkeiten der Länder und Städte," in *Orientalistische Miszellen,* vol. 1 (Istanbul, 1925), 194–228.

———. *Taʾrīkh Ghurar Akhbār Mulūk al-Furs.* Edited and translated by H. Zotenberg under the title *Histoire des Rois des Perses.* Paris, 1900.

Thābit ibn Sinān. *Tārīkh Akhbār al-Qarāmitah.* Edited by Suhayl Zakkār. Bayrūt, A.H. 1391/A.D. 1971.

Al-Khaṭīb al-Tibrīzi. *Mishkāt al-Naṣābīh.* 10 vols. St. Petersburg, 1898.

Al-Tijānī. *Riḥlah.* Ms. Bibl. Universitaire d'Alger no. 2014. Translated by Alphonse Rousseau under the title "Voyage du Scheikh el-Tidjani dans la Régence de Tunis, pendant les années 706, 707 et 708 de l'Hégire (1306–1309)." *Journal Asiatique,* 4th ser., vol. 20 (1852).

Aḥmad ibn ʿUmar ibn Anas al-ʿUdhrī. Al-Masālik ilā Jamīʿ al-Masālik. Edited by ʿAbd al-ʿAzīz al-Ahwānī. Madrid, 1965.

Najm al-Dīn ʿUmārah al-Ḥakamī. *Taʾrīkh al-Yaman.* English translation by Henry Cassells Kay under the title *Yaman, Its Early Medieval History.* London, 1892; reprint, Farnborough, Hampshire, 1968.

Abū Naṣr ʿAbd al-Jabbār al-ʿUtbī. *Al-Taʾrikh al-Yamīnī.* Al-Qāhirah, A.H. 1286/A.D. 1869.

Vardan. *Mecin Vardanay Barjrberdcʿoy Patmutʿiwn Tiezerakan.* Edited by J.-B. Emin. Moscow, 1861. Edited with partial French translation by J. Muyldermans under the title *La Domination Arabe en Arménie. Extrait de l'Histoire Universelle de Vardan* (Louvain and Paris, 1927).

Aḥmad ʿAlī Khān Vazīrī. *Taʾrikh-i Kirmān (Taʾrikh-i Sālārīyah).* Annotated edition by Muḥammad Ibrāhīm Bāstānī-i Pārīzī. Publications of the Farmān-Farmāyān Memorial Library, no. 1. Tehran, A.H. 1340/A.D. 1961.

Al-Wāḥidī. *Asbāb al-Nuzūl.* Al-Qāhirah, A.H. 1388/A.D. 1968. Published by Fr. Dieterici in his edition of al-Mutannabī's *Diwān* (Berlin, 1858–61).

Abū Bakr Aḥmad ibn ʿAlī al-Ṣūfī al-Qussaynī/al-Kasdanī al-Waḥshīyah. *Kitāb al-Filāḥatal-Nabaṭīyah.* Edited by Toufic Fahd under the title *L'Agriculture Nabatéenne. Traduction en Arabe Attribuée à Abū Bakr Aḥmad b. ʿAlī al-Kasdānī Connu sous le Nom d'Ibn Waḥšiyya.* 2 vols. Institut Français de Damas. Damascus, 1993–95. Arabic text with French preliminaries.

Muḥammad ibn ʿUmar al-Wāqidī. *Kitāb al-Maghāzī.* Edited by Alfred von Kremer (Calcutta, 1855–56), ʿAbbas al-Shirbīnī (al-Qāhirah, A.H. 1366), and Marsden Jones, 3 vols. (Oxford, 1966). Abridged translation by Julius Wellhausen under the title *Muhammed in Medina; das ist Vakidis Kitab al-Mahghazi in verkürzter deutscher Wiedergabe* (Berlin, 1882).

Abū Zakarīyā al-Warjalānī. *Al-Sīrah wa-Akhbār al-Aʾimmah.* Edited and translated into French by Roger Le Tourneau under the title "'La Chronique' d'Abū Zakariyyā al-Wargalānī (m. 471 H = 1078 J.-C.)." *Revue Africaine* 105 (1961) : 117–76. French translation by Emile Masqueray under the title *Chronique d'Abou Zakaria* (Alger, 1878).

Al-Washshā. *Kitāb al-Muwashshā.* Edited by R. E. Brünnow. Leyden, 1886.

Ibrahīm ibn Waṣīf Shah. *Muktaṣar al-ʿAjāʾib.* French translation by Carra de Vaux under the title *L'Abrégé des Merveilles.* Paris, 1898.

Ṣāliḥ ibn Yaḥyā. *Tārīkh Bayrūt.* Edited by Francis Hours, S. J., and Kamal Salībī. Beirut, A.H. 1389/A.D. 1969.

Aḥmad ibn Abī Yaʿqūb al-Yaʿqūbī. *Taʾrīkh.* In *Historiae,* 2 vols., edited by M. Th. Houtsma. Leyden, 1883; Bayrūt, A.H. 1380.

———. *Kitāb al-Buldān.* Edited by T. G. J. Juynboll (1861). Edited by M. J. de Goeje under the title *Kitâb al-Boldân Auctore Ahmed ibn Abî Jaʿkūb ibn Wâdhih al-Kâtib al-Jaʿkûbî.* Vol. 7 of *Bibliotheca Geographorum Arabicorum,* edited by de Goeje. Lugduni Batavorum, 1892. French translation by Gaston Wiet under the title *Yaʿkūbī. Les Pays* (Le Caire [Cairo], 1937).

———. *Mushākalat al-Nās li-Zamānihim wa-mā Yaghlibu ʿalayhim fī Kulli ʿAṣrin.* Translated by William G. Millward under the title "The adaptation of men to their time: an historical essay by al-Yaʿqūbī," *Journal of the American Oriental Society* 84 (1964), 339–40.

Yāqūt al-Rūmī/al-Ḥamawī. *Kitāb Muʿjam al-Buldān.* Published by Ferdinand Wüstenfeld under the title *Jacut's geographisches Wörterbuch,* 6 vols. (Leipzig, 1866–73); by Amīn al-Khānojī, 10 vols. with a supplement (al-Qāhirah, A.H. 1324/A.D. 1906–7; and in an edition of 5 vols. (Bayrūt, A.H. 1374–76/A.D. 1955–57). An abridged version of the *Muʿjam, al-Marāṣid al-Iṭṭilāʿ ʿalā Asmāʾ al-Amkinah wa-l-Biqāʿ*, by ʿAbd al-Muʿmin ibn ʿAbd al-Ḥaqq al-Baghdādī, has been edited by T. G. J. Juynboll, *Lexicon Geographicum cui Titulus est Marāṣid al-Iṭṭilā ʿalā Asmā al-Amkina wa-l-Biqā*, 6 vols. (Leyden, 1851–64). An abridged version was also prepared by Jalāl al-Dīn al-Suyūṭī (second half of the fifteenth century) under the title *Mukhtaṣar Muʿjam al-Buldān*. Index to Wüstenfeld's edition by Oskar Rescher, *Sachindex zu Wüstenfeld's Ausgabe von Jacut's "Muʿǧam al-Buldān"* (Stuttgart, 1928). Extracts translated into French by C. Barbier de Meynard under the title *Dictionnaire Géographique, Historique et Littéraire de la Perse et des Contrées Adjacentes. Extrait du Modjem el-Bouldan de Yaqout* (Paris, 1861); English translation of chapters 1–5 by Wadie Jwaideh under the title *The Introductory Chapters of Yāqūt's Muʿjam al-Buldān* (Leiden, 1959). *Al-Mushtarik Waḍʿan wa-l-Mukhtalif Ṣaqʿan* (an abridged version of the *Muʿjam* executed by Yaqūt himself) was edited by Ferdinand Wüstenfeld (Göttingen, Germany, 1846).

———. *Muʾjam al-Udabā*. Edited by D. S. Margoliouth (Leyden, 1907–26).

Ibn al-Zabayr. *Al-Dhakhāʾir wa al-Taḥaf.* Edited by Salāḥ al-Dīn al-Manajjid. Bayrūt, A.H. 1379.

Al-Muṣʿab al-Zubayrī. *Nasab Quraysh*. Edited by E. Lévi-Provençal. Al-Qāhirah, A.H. 1372.

Secondary Sources, Commentary, and Explication

The numerous articles relevant to this work in *The Encyclopaedia of Islam*, with rare exceptions, are not listed in this bibliography. The reader is advised to consult the *Encyclopaedia* whenever additional information is required on a particular topic.

Al-Sayyid ʿAbd al-ʿAzīz Sālim, Aḥmad Mukhtār al-ʿAbbādī, *Taʾrīkh al-Baḥrīyah al-Islamīyah fī Miṣr wa-l-Shām*. Bayrūt, A.H. 1401/A.D. 1981.

Iḥsān ʿAbbās. *Al-ʿArab fī Ṣiqillīyah*. Al-Qāhirah, A.H. 1379.

———. *Taʾrīkh Bilād al-Shām fī al-ʿAṣr al-ʿAbbāsī, 132-255 h./750–870 m.* Ammān, 1992.

———. "Al-ʿAlāqāt al-tijarīyah bayna Makka wa-l-Shām ḥattā bidāyat al-Fatḥ al-Islāmī." *Al-Abḥāth* 38 (A.H. 1410) : 3–40.

Abū Naṣr Muḥammad ibn ʿAbd al-Jabbār al-ʿUtbī. *Al-Taʾrīkh al-Yamīnī*. Al-Qāhirah, A.H. 1286/A.D. 1869.

A. Abdussaid. "Barqa, modern El-Merj." *Libya Antiqua* 8 (1971) : 121–28.

Jamil M. Abun-Nasr. *A History of the Maghrib*. Cambridge, 1971.

———. *A History of the Maghrib in the Islamic Period*. Cambridge, 1987.

Robert McC. Adams. *Land Behind Baghdad. A History of Settlement on the Diyala Plains*. Chicago and London, 1965.

Robert McC. Adams and Donald P. Hansen. "Archaeological reconnaissance and soundings in Jundī Shāhpūr"; appendix by Nabia Abbott, "Jundī Shāhpūr: a preliminary historical sketch." *Ars Orientalis* 7 (1968) : 53–73.

Chahryār Adle. "Contribution à la géographie historique du Damghan." *Le Monde Iranien et l'Islam* 1 (1971) : 69–104.

Saʾīd al-Afghānī. *Aswāq al-ʿArab fi-l-Jāhilīyah wa-l-Islam*. Dimashq, A.H. 1380.

ʿAzīz Aḥmad. *A History of Islamic Sicily*. Edinburgh, 1975.

J. F. Ade and Ajayi and Ian Espie, eds. *A Thousand Years of West African History*. Ibadan, 1965.

———. *Crisis in the Built Environment: The Case of the Muslim City*. Singapore, 1988.

Jamel Akbar. "Khaṭṭa and the territorial structure of early Muslim towns." *Muqarnas. An Annual of Islamic Art and Architecture* 6 (1989) : 22–32.

Nurudeen Alao, Michael F. Dacey, Omar Davies, Kenneth G. Denike, James Huff, John B. Parr, and M. J. Webber. *Christaller Central Place Structures: An Introductory Statement*. Northwestern University Studies in Geography, no. 22. Evanston, Ill., 1977.

Ṣāliḥ ibn Ḥāmid al-ʿAlawī. *Taʾrīkh Ḥaḍramawt*. Juddah, A.H. 1388.

W. F. Albright. "The chronology of ancient south Arabia in light of the first campaign of excavation in Qataban." *Bulletin of the American Schools of Oriental Research* 119 (1950): 5–15.

———. "The chronology of the Minaean kings of Arabia." *Bulletin of the American Schools of Oriental Research* 129 (1953) : 20–24.

Jawād ʿAlī. *Taʾrīkh al-ʿArab qabla al-Islam*. 4 vols. Baghdād, A.H. 1370–76.

Maḥmūd ʿAlī. "Tanqībāt fī al-Ḥīrah." *Sumer* 2 (1946) : 29–32.

Ṣāliḥ Aḥmad al-ʿAlī (Saleh A. el-Ali). "Khiṭaṭ al-Basrah." *Sumer* 8 (1952) : 72–83, 281–302.

———. *Al-Tanẓīmāt al-Ijtimāʿīyah wa-l-Iqtiṣādīyah fī-l-Baṣrah fī-l-Qarn al-ʾAwwal al-Hijrī*. Baghdād, 1953.

———. "Aḥkam al-Rasūl fī-l-Arādhil." *Bulletin of the College of Arts and Science* (Baghdād) 1 (1955) : 1–21.

———. "Muslim estates in Hidjaz in the first century A.H." *Journal of the Social and Economic History of the Orient* 2 (1959) : 247–61.

———. "Studies in the topography of Medina (during the first century A.H.)." *Islamic Culture* 35, no. 1 (1961) : 65–92.

———. "Minṭaqat al-Ḥīrah." *Majallat Kullīyat al-Ādāb* 5 (1962) : 17–44.

———. "Al-Madāʾin fī al-Maṣādir al-ʿArabīyah." *Sumer* 23 (1967) : 47–65.

———. "Maṣadīr dirāsat tārikh al-Kūfah fī-l-qurūn al-Islamīyah al-ūlā." *Majallat al-Majmaʿ al-ʿIlmī al-ʿIrāqī* 24 (A.H. 1394) : 137–71.

———. "The Foundation of Baghdād." In *The Islamic City: A Colloquium*, edited by Albert Hourani and S. M. Stern. Oxford, 1970.

G. R. Allen. "The 'Courbes des Populations': a further analysis." *Bulletin of the Oxford University Institute of Statistics* 16 (1954) : 179–89.

M. Almagro, L. Caballero, J. Zozaya, and A. Almagro. *Qusayr ʿAmra. Residencia y Baños Omeyas en el Deserto de Jordania*. Madrid, 1975.

Nezar AlSayyad. *Cities and Caliphs. On the Genesis of Arab Muslim Urbanism*. New York, 1991.

Albrecht Alt. "Aila und Adroa im spätrömischen Grenzschutzsystem." *Zeitschrift der Deutschen Morgenländischen Gesellschaft* 59 (1936) : 92–111.

———. "Das Territorium von Bostra." *Zeitschrift des Deutschen Palästina-Vereins* 68 (1951) : 235–45.

Franz Altheim. *Aus Spätantike und Christentum*. Tübingen, 1951.

Michele Amari. *Bibliotheca Arabo-Sicula*. 2 vols. Arabic text, Lipsia; Italian translation, Torino/Roma, 1881–82.

———. *Storia dei Musulmani di Sicilia.* 2d ed. by C. A. Nallino. 3 vols. Catania, Italy, 1933–39.

H. F. Amedroz. "Three Arabic MSS. on the history of the city of Mayyāfāriqīn." *Journal of the Royal Asiatic Society* (1902) : 785–812.

———. "The Marwānid dynasty at Mayyāfāriqīn in the tenth and eleventh centuries A.D." *Journal of the Royal Asiatic Society* (1903) : 123–54.

Ardavan Amirshahi. "Le développement de la ville de Qazwīn jusqu'au milieu du VIIIe/XIVe siècle." *Revue des Etudes Islamiques* 49 (1990) : 1–20.

Awliyā' Allāh Muḥammad ibn Ḥasan Āmulī. *Ta'rīkh-i Rūyān.* Tehran, A.H. 1313.

Nels Anderson, ed. *Urbanism and Urbanization.* Leiden, 1964.

Tor Andrae. *Mohammed, sein Leben und sein Glaube.* Göttingen, 1932.

ʿAbd al-Qaddūs al-Anṣārī. *Āthār al-Madīnah al-Munawwarah.* Dimashq, A.H. 1353.

Shaykh Ḥasan Jābirī Anṣārī. *Tā'rīkh-i Iṣfahān va Rayy.* Tehran, A.H. 1321/A.D. 1944.

A. R. al-Ansary. *Qaryat al-Fau. A Portrait of Pre-Islamic Civilisation in Saudi Arabia.* Al-Riyādh, 1982.

Arthur J. Arberry. *Shiraz. Persian City of Saints and Poets.* Norman, Okla., 1960.

———. "Muslim Cordoba." In *Cities of Destiny,* edited by Arnold Toynbee. London, 1967.

C. van Arendonk. *Les Débuts de l'Imāmat Zaidite au Yemen.* Leyden, 1960.

Rachel Arié. *España Musulmana (Siglos VIII–XV).* Barcelona, 1982.

ʿĀrif al-ʿĀrif. *Al-Mufaṣṣal fī Ta'rīkh al-Quds.* Al-Quds, A.H. 1380.

T. W. Arnold and R. A. Nicholson, eds. *Ajabnáma, a Volume of Oriental Studies Presented to Edward G. Browne.* Cambridge, 1922.

Eliyahu Ashtor. "The number of Jews in mediaeval Egypt." *Journal of Jewish Studies* 19 (1968) : 8–12.

———. *Histoire des Prix et des Salaires dans l'Orient Médiéval.* Paris, 1969.

———. *A Social and Economic History of the Near East in the Middle Ages.* Berkeley, Calif., 1976.

E. Ashtor-Strauss. "L'administration urbaine en Syrie médiévale." *Rivista degli Studi Orientali* 31 (1956) : 81–82.

Aziz S. Atiya, ed. *The Coptic Encyclopedia.* 8 vols. New York, 1991.

G. N. Atiyeh. "Avicenna's Conception of Miracles." Ph.D. diss., University of Chicago, 1954.

J. Aubin. "La ruine de Sīrāf et les routes du Golfe Persique aux Xie et XIIe siècles." *Cahiers de Civilisation Médiévale* 2 (1959) : 295–301.

———. "L'aristocratie urbaine dans l'Iran seldjukide: l'example de Sabzavār." In *Mélanges Offerts à René Crozet,* edited by P. Gallais and Y. J. Rion. Poitiers, France, 1966.

———. "La question de Sīrğan aux XIIIe siècle." *Studia Iranica* 6 (1977) : 285–90.

F. Auerbach. "Das Gesetz der Bevölkerungskonzentration." *Petermanns Geographische Mitteilungen* 59 (1913) : 74–76.

J. L. Austin. *How to Do Things with Words.* Oxford, 1962.

Michael Avi-Yonah. "The foundation of Tiberias." *Israel Exploration Journal* 1 (1950–51) : 160–69.

———. *The Madaba Mosaic Map.* Jerusalem, 1954.

———. "Scythopolis." *Israel Exploration Journal* 12 (1962) : 123–34.

———. *The Holy Land from the Persian to the Arab Conquest (536 B.C. to A.D. 640): A Historical Geography.* Grand Rapids, Mich., 1966.

Gideon Avni. *Nomads, Farmers, and Town-Dwellers: Pastoralist-Sedentist Interaction in the Negev Highlands, Sixth–Eighth Centuries CE.* Jerusalem, 1996.

G. ʿAwaḍ. "Mā ṭubiʿah ʿan buldān al-ʿIrāq bi al-lughat al-ʿArabīyah." *Sumer* 10 (1954) : 40–72.

Bolanle Awe. "Empires of the Western Sudan." In *A Thousand Years of West African History,* edited by J. F. Ade and Ajayi and Ian Espie. Ibadan, Nigeria, 1965.

ʿAwwād Mājid al-Aʿzamī. *Ta'rīkh Madīnat al-Quds.* Baghdād, A.H. 1392.

Nazih Muḥammad al-ʿAẓm. *Riḥlah fī Bilād al-ʿArab al-Saʿīdah.* Al-Qāhirah, n.d.

Jere L. Bacharach. "The Court-Citadel: An Islamic Urban Symbol of Power." In *Urbanism in Islam,* vol. 3, edited by Yukawa Takeshi. Tokyo, 1989.

———. "Administrative Complexes, Palaces, and Citadels. Changes in the Loci of Medieval Muslim Rule." In *The Ottoman City and Its Parts. Urban Structure and Social Order,* edited by Irene A. Bierman, Rifa'at A. Abou-el-Haj, and Donald Preziosi. New Rochelle, N.Y., 1991.

———. "Marwanid Umayyad building activities: speculations on patronage." *Muqarnas* 13 (1996) : 27–44.

Elizabeth E. Bacon. "Types of pastoral nomadism in Central and Southwest Asia." *Southwestern Journal of Anthropology* 10 (1954) : 44–68.

George Percy Badger. *History of the Imams and Seyyids of 'Omân, by Salîl-ibn-Razîk, from A.D.* 661–1856. Hakluyt Society, 1st ser., no. 44. London, 1871.

Leo Bagrow. "The origin of Ptolemy's Geographia." *Geografiska Annaler* 27, pts. 3–4 (1945) : 318–87.

———. *History of Cartography.* Rev. and enl. by R. A. Skelton. London, 1964.

Muḥammad ʿAdnān al-Bakhīt and Muḥammad Aṣfūr [Asfour], eds. *Proceedings of the Symposium on Bilād al-Shām during the Byzantine Period (1983),* vol. 1: *Bilād al-Shām fī al-ʿAhd al-Bīzanṭī* (in Arabic); vol. 2: *Proceedings . . .* (in English). Ammān, 1986.

M. Bakhīt and R. Schick, eds. *The Fourth International Conference on the History of Bilad al-Shām during the Umayyad Period.* English Section, vol. 2. Ammān, 1989.

———. *The Fifth International Conference on the History of Bilad al-Shām during the ʿAbbāsid Period.* English Section, vol. 2. Ammān, 1992.

L. Torres Balbás. "Notas sobre Sevila en la época musulmana." *Al-Andalus* 10 (1945) : 177–96.

J. M. S. Baljon. *Modern Muslim Interpretation (1880–1960).* Leiden, 1961.

D. Z. H. Baneth. "What did Muḥammad mean when he called his religion 'Islam'? The original meaning of aslama and its derivatives." *Israel Oriental Studies* 1 (1971) : 183–90.

Michael Banton, ed. *The Relevance of Models for Social Anthropol-*

ogy. Monographs of the Association of Social Anthropologists no. 1. London and New York, 1965.

C. Barbier de Meynard. *Dictionnaire Geographique, Historique et Littéraire de la Perse et des Contrées Adjacentes. Extrait du Modjem el-Bouldan de Yaqout.* Paris, 1861.

———. "Le livre des routes et des provinces par Ibn-Khordadbeh." *Journal Asiatique* 5 (1865) : 5–127, 227–96.

Julio Caro Baroja. "Sobre la historia de la noria de tiro." *Revista de Dialectología y Tradiciones Populares* 11 (1955) : 15–79.

Vasili Vladimirovich Barthol'd [Wilhelm Barthold/Bartold]. "Otchot o poyezdke v Sred'uyu Aziyu, 1893–4." *Mémoires de l'Académie des Sciences de St. Pétersbourg,* VIIIe série, vol. 1, no. 4 (1897).

———. "Merverrūd." *Zapiski Vostochnogo Otdeleniya Imperatorskago Russkogo Arkheologicheskogo Obshchestva* 14 (1901) : 023–032.

———. *Istoriko-Geograficheskii obzor Irana.* St. Petersburg, 1903. Collected works *(Sochineniia),* vol. 7 (Moscow, 1971), 31–225. English translation by Svat Soucek and edited by C. E. Bosworth under the title *An Historical Geography of Iran* (Princeton, N.J., 1984).

———. Nachrichten über den Aral-See und den Unteren Lauf des Amu-Darja. Leipzig, 1910; Russian original, 1902.

———. "Musaylima." *Bulletin de l'Académie des Sciences de Russie* 19 (1925).

———. *Mussulman Culture.* Translated from the Russian by Shahid Suhrawardy. Calcutta, 1934.

———. *Histoire des Turcs d'Asie Centrale.* Paris, 1945.

———. *Turkestan down to the Mongol Invasion.* E. J. W. Gibb Memorial Series, n.s., no. 5. 3d ed. London, 1968.

Karin Bartl and Stefan R. Hauser, eds. *Continuity and Change in Northern Mesopotamia from the Hellenistic to the Early Islamic Period.* Berliner Beiträge zum Vorderen Orient 17. Berlin, 1996.

Suliman Bashear. "Yemen in early Islam: an examination of nontribal traditions." *Arabica* 36 (1989) : 327–61.

John Bastin and R. Roolvink, eds. *Malayan and Indonesian Studies. Essays Presented to Sir Richard Winstedt on His Eighty-fifth Birthday.* Oxford, 1964.

G. Bawden. "Continuity and disruption in the ancient Hejaz: an assessment of current archaeological strategies." *Arabian Archaeology and Epigraphy* 3 (1992) : 1–22.

S. Beal. *Si-yu-ki, Buddhist Records of the Western World.* London, 1906.

Joëlle Beaucamp. "Rawwafa et les Thamoudéens." *Supplemént au Dictionnaire de la Bible,* no. 9 (1979), 1467–75.

Keith S. O. Beavon. *Central Place Theory: A Reinterpretation.* London, 1977.

Carl Heinrich Becker. *Vom Werden und Wesen der islamischen Welt, Islamstudien.* Leipzig, 1924.

M. J. Beckmann. "City hierarchies and the distribution of city size." *Economic Development and Cultural Change* 6 (1958) : 243–48.

Charles I. Beckwith. "The plan of the City of Peace: Central Asian Iranian Factors in early ʿAbbāsid design." *Acta Orientalia Academiae Scientiarum Hungaricae* 38 (1984).

A. F. L. Beeston. "A Sabean penal law." *Le Muséon* 64 (1951).

———. "The so-called harlots of Ḥaḍramaut." *Oriens* 5 (1952) : 16–22.

———. *Epigraphic South Arabian Calendars and Datings.* London, 1956.

———. "Functional Significance of the Old South Arabian 'Town.'" In *Proceedings of the Seminar for Arabian Studies* 1 (1971) : 26–31.

———. "Kingship in ancient South Arabia." *Journal of the Economic and Social History of the Orient* 15 (1972) : 256–68.

A. F. L. Beeston, et al. *Sabaic Dictionary (English-French-Arabic).* Beirut, 1982.

A. F. L. Beeston, T. M. Johnstone, R. B. Serjeant, and G. R. Smith, eds. *Arabic Literature to the End of the Umayyad Period.* Cambridge, 1983.

Chaikh Békhri. "Le Kharijisme berbère: quelques aspects du royaume rustumide." *Annales de l'Institut d'Etudes Orientales de l'Université d'Alger* 15 (1957) : 55–108.

H. I. Bell. "The administration of Egypt under the Umayyads." *Byzantinische Zeitschrift* 28 (1928) : 278–86.

Richard Bell. "Who were the Ḥanīfs?" *Moslem World* 20 (1930) : 120–24.

E. A. Belyaev. *Araby, Islam i Arabskii Khalifat v Rannee Srednevekov'e,* 2d ed. Moscow, 1966.

M. Benabbud. *Al-Tārīkh al-Siyāsī wa-l-Ijtimāʿī lī-Ishbīliyah fī ʿAhd Duwal al-Ṭawāʾif.* Tétouan, Morocco, 1983.

E. Benveniste. "Le nom de la ville de Ghazna." *Journal Asiatique* 221 (1935) : 141–43.

Max van Berchem. *Matériaux pour un Corpus Inscriptionum Arabicarum: Égypte.* Paris, 1894.

———. *Amida: Matériaux pour l'Épigraphie et l'Histoire Musulmanes du Diyar-bekr.* Heidelberg, 1910.

L. Bercher. *Etudes sur le Ḥadīth.* Alger, 1952.

V. Bernard and J-F. Salles. "Discovery of a Christian Church at al-Qusur, Failaka (Kuwait)." In *Proceedings of the Seminar for Arabian Studies* 21 (1991) : 7–21.

Brian J. L. Berry. "Ribbon developments in the urban business pattern." *Annals of the Association of American Geographers* 49 (1959) : 145–55.

———. "City size distributions and economic development." *Economic Development and Cultural Change* 9 (1961) : 573–88.

———. "Cities as Systems within Systems of Cities." In *Papers and Proceedings of the Regional Science Association* 13 (1964) : 147–63.

B. J. L. Berry, H. G. Barnum, and R. J. Tennant. "Retail Location and Consumer Behavior." In *Papers and Proceedings of the Regional Science Association* 9 (1962) : 65–106.

Brian J. L. Berry and William L. Garrison. "Recent Developments of Central Place Theory." In *Papers and Proceedings of the Regional Science Association* 4 (1958) : 107–20.

———. "Alternate [*sic*] explanations of urban rank-size relationships." *Annals of the Association of American Geographers* 48 (1958) : 83–91.

René Berthelot. *La Pensée de l'Asie et l'Astrobiologie.* Paris, 1949.

Ahmad Issa Bey. *Histoire des Bimaristans à l'Époque Islamique.* Le Caire (Cairo), 1928; Arab translation, Damas, 1939.

Aly Bahgat Bey and Albert Gabriel. *Fouilles d'al-Fousṭâṭ.* Paris, 1921.

Thierry Bianquis. "La prise du pouvoir par les Fatimides en Egypte (357–363/968–974)." *Annales Islamogiques* 11 (1972):49–108.

J. C. Biella. *Dictionary of Old South Arabic. Sabaean Dialect.* Chico, Calif., 1982.

Irene A. Bierman. *Writing Signs: The Fatimid Public Text.* Berkeley, Calif., 1998.

Irene A. Bierman, Rifa'at A. Abou-el-Haj, and Donald Preziosi, eds. *The Ottoman City and its Parts. Urban Structure and Social Order.* New Rochelle, N.Y., 1991.

H. Bieteñhård. "Die Dekapolis von Pompeius bis Trainan: ein Kapitel aus der neutestamentlichen Zeitgeschichte." *Zeitschrift des Deutschen Palästina-Vereins* 79 (1963) : 24–58.

———. *Die Dekapolis von Pompeius bis Trajan.* Frankfurt, 1963.

Ramzi Jibran Bihazi. "*The Ḥamdānid Dynasty of Mesopotamia and North Syria.*" Ph.D. diss., University of Michigan, 1981.

Harris Birkeland. *The Lord Guideth. Studies on Primitive Islam.* Oslo, 1956.

Ghazi Izzeddin Bisheh. "The Mosque of the Prophet at Madīnah throughout the First-Century A.H. with Special Emphasis on the Umayyad Mosque." Ph.D. diss., University of Michigan, 1979.

———. "Qaṣr al-Hallabat: An Umayyad Desert Retreat or Farm-Land?" In *Studies in the History and Archeology of Jordan,* edited by Adnan Hadidi. Vol. 2. London, 1985.

W. Björkman. "Jerusalem im Corpus Inscriptionum Arabicarum." *Der Islam* 15 (1926).

Régis Blachère. "Fès chez les géographes arabes du moyen âge." *Hespéris* 18 (1934) : 41–48.

———. *Le Coran: Traduction selon un Essai de Reclassement des Sourates.* 3 vols. Paris, 1947–51. 2d ed., 1966; reprint, 1973.

———. *Histoire de la Littérature Arabe des Origines à la Fin du XVe Siècle de J.C.* Paris, 1952.

———. *Le Problème de Mahomet: Essai de Biographie Critique du Fondateur de l'Islam.* Paris, 1952.

———. "L'agglomération du Caire vue par quatre voyageurs arabes du moyen âge." *Annales Islamologiques* 8 (1969) : 2–4.

R. Blachère and H. Darmaun. *Extraits des Principaux Géographes Arabes du Moyen Age.* Paris, 1957.

Richard E. Blanton. *Prehispanic Settlement Patterns in the Irtapalapa Peninsula Region, Mexico.* Occasional Paper in Anthropology no. 6, Department of Anthropology, The Pennsylvania State University. University Park, 1972.

———. "Anthropological studies of cities." *Annual Review of Anthropology* 5 (1976) : 249–64.

Richard E. Blanton, Stephen A. Kowalewski, Gary Feinman, and Jill Appel. *Ancient Mesoamerica: A Comparison of Change in Three Regions.* Cambridge, 1981.

Jonathan Bloom. *Minaret, Symbol of Islam.* Oxford, 1989.

C. A. de Bode. *Travels in Luristan.* London, 1845.

R. V. C. Bodley. *The Messenger: The Life of Mohammed.* Garden City, N.Y., 1946.

D. J. Bogue. *The Structure of the Metropolitan Community: A Study of Dominance and Subordinance.* Ann Arbor, Mich., 1949.

Pons Boigues. *Ensayo Bio-Bibliográfico sobre los Historiadores y Geógrafos Arábigo-Españoles.* Madrid, 1898.

Michael E. Bonine. "The morphogenesis of Iranian cities." *Annals of the Association of American Geographers* 69, no. 2 (1979) : 208–24.

Michael E. Bonine, Eckart Ehlers, Thomas Krafft, and George Stöber, eds. *The Middle Eastern City and Islamic Urbanism: An Annotated Bibliography of Western Literature.* Bonn, 1994.

Michael D. Bonner. "The Emergence of the Thughūr: The Arab-Byzantine Frontier in the Early ʿAbbāsid Age." Ph.D. diss., Princeton University, 1987.

———. "Some observations concerning the early development of Jihad on the Arab-Byzantine frontier." *Studia Islamica* 75 (1992) : 12–21.

———. "The naming of the frontier: ʿawāṣim, thughūr, and the Arab geographers." *Bulletin of the School of Oriental and African Studies* 57 (1994) : 17–24.

———. *Aristocratic Violence and Holy War: Studies in the Jihad and the Arab-Byzantine Frontier.* New Haven, Conn., 1996.

James L. Boone and Charles L. Redman. "Alternate pathways to urbanism in the medieval Maghrib." *Comparative Urban Research* 9 (1982) : 28–38.

———. "Comparative urbanism in the Islamic Far West." *World Archaeology* 14 (1982–83) : 355–77.

James L. Boone, J. Emlen Myers, and Charles L. Redman. "Archeological and historical approaches to complex societies: the Islamic states of medieval Morocco." *American Anthropologist* 92, no. 3 (1990) : 630–46.

J. Bosch. *La Sevilla Islámica, 712–1248.* 2d ed. Sevilla, 1988.

Clifford Edmund Bosworth. "The rise of the Karāmīyah in Khurāsān." *Muslim World* 50 (1960) : 5–14.

———. "The early Islamic history of Ghūr." *Central Asiatic Journal* 6 (1961) : 116–33.

———. *The Ghaznavids: Their Empire in Afghanistan and Eastern Iran.* Edinburgh, 1963.

———. *The Islamic Dynasties: A Chronological and Genealogical Handbook.* Edinburgh, 1967.

———. *Sīstān under the Arabs, from the Islamic Conquest to the Rise of the Saffarids (30–250/651–864).* Rome, 1968.

———. "Abū ʿAbdallāh al-Khwārazmī on the technical terms of the secretary's art." *Journal of the Economic and Social History of the Orient* 12 (1969) : 113–64.

———. "The Banū Ilyās of Kirmān (320–57/932–68)." In *Iran and Islam: In Memory of the Late Vladimir Minorsky,* edited by C. E. Bosworth, Edinburgh, 1971.

———. "ʿUbaidallah b. Abī Bakra and the 'Army of Destruction' in Zābulistān (79/698)." *Der Islam* 50 (1973) : 268–83.

———. "The Kūfichīs or Qufs in Persian history." *Iran, Journal of the British Institute of Persian Studies* 14 (1976) : 9–17.

———. "The city of Tarsus and the Arab-Byzantine frontiers in Early and Middle ʿAbbāsid times." *Oriens* 33 (1992) : 268–86.

———. "Abū ʿAmr "Uthmān al-Tarsusī's *Siyar al-Thughūr* and the last years of Arab rule in Tarsus (Fourth / Tenth century)." *Graeco-Arabica* 5 (1993) : 183–95.

———. *The History of the Saffarids of the Sistan and the Maliks of Nimruz (247/861 to 949/1542–3).* Costa Mesa, Calif., 1994.

———, ed. *Iran and Islam. In Memory of the Late Vladimir Minorsky.* Edinburgh, 1971.

G. H. Bousquet. "Observations sociologiques sur les origines de l'Islam." *Studia Islamica* 11 (1954) : 61–87.

———. "Observations sur la nature et les causes de la conquête arabe." *Studia Islamica* 6 (1956) : 37–52.

———. "Quelques remarques critiques et sociologiques sur la conquête arabe et les théories émises à ce sujet." In *Studi Orientalistici in Onore de Giorgio Levi della Vida,* Vol. 1. Roma, 1956.

———. *Les Berbères (Histoire et Institutions).* Paris, 1957.

Edwin von Boventer. "Towards a unified theory of spatial economic structure." *Papers of the Regional Science Association* 10 (1962): 163–87.

Richard LeBaron Bowen Jr. and Frank P. Albright. *Archaeological Discoveries in South Arabia.* Baltimore, 1958.

Glen W. Bowersock. *Roman Arabia.* Cambridge, Mass., 1983.

Alan K. Bowman. *Egypt after the Pharoahs, 332 B.C.–A.D.642.* Berkeley and Los Angeles, 1989.

Albertus van den Branden. *Histoire de Thamoud.* Publications de l'Université Libanaise, Section des Etudes Historiques. No. 6. Beyrouth, 1960.

Erich Bräunlich. Bistām ibn Qais. Ein vorislamischer Beduinenfürst und Held. Leipzig, 1923.

———. "Beiträge zur Gesellschaftsordnung der arabischen Beduinenstämme." *Islamica* 6 (1934) : 68–111, 182–229.

M. M. Bravmann. *The Spiritual Background of Early Islam: Studies in Ancient Arab Concepts.* Leiden, 1972.

Michael Brett. "The Arab Conquest and the Rise of Islam in North Africa." In *The Cambridge History of Africa,* vol. 2, edited by J. D. Fage and Roland Oliver. Cambridge, 1978.

S. P. Brock. "Syriac sources for seventh-century history." *Byzantine and Modern Greek Studies* 2 (1976) : 17–36.

———. "Syriac Views of Emergent Islam." In *Studies on the First Century of Islamic Society,* edited by G. H. A. Juynboll. Carbondale, Ill., 1982.

Carl Brockelmann. *Geschichte der Arabischen Literatur.* 2d ed., 2 vols. Leiden, 1943–49; *Supplement,* 3 vols. (Leiden, 1937–42).

M. Brosset. *Collection d'Historiens Arméniens.* St. Pétersbourg, 1874.

Edward G. Browne. "Some account of the Arabic work entitled 'Niháyatu'l-irab fi akbāri' l-Furs wa'l-'Arab' . . ." *Journal of the Royal Asiatic Society* (1900) : 195–204.

———. "Account of a rare manuscript History of Iṣfahán." *Journal of the Royal Asiatic Society* (1901) : 411–46, 661–704.

Iain Browning. *Petra.* London, 1973.

———. *Palmyra.* Park Ridge, N.J., 1979.

———. *Jerash and the Decapolis.* London, 1982.

R. E. Brünnow and A. von Domaszewski. *Die Provincia Arabia.* Strassburg, 1905.

Robert Brunschvig. "Un aspect de la littérature historico-géographique de l'Islam." In *Mélanges Gaudefroy-Demombynes.* Series of the Institut Français d'Archéologie Orientale du Caire (Le Caire [Cairo], 1935–45), 147–58.

———. "Ibn 'Abdalh'akam et la conquête de l'Afrique du Nord par les Arabes." *Annales de l'Istitut des Etudes Orientales* 6 (1942–47): 108–55.

———. "Urbanisme médiéval et droit musulman." *Revue des Études Islamiques* 15 (1947).

John E. Brush. "The hierarchy of central places in southwestern Wisconsin." *Geographical Review* 43 (1953): 380–402.

J. E. Brush and H. E. Bracey. "Rural service centers in southwestern Wisconsin and southern England: *The Geographical Review* 45 (1955): 559–69.

Frants (P. W.) Buhl. *Muhammeds Livs.* N.p., 1903. German translation by Hans Heinrich Schaeder under the title *Das Leben Muhammeds* (Leipzig, 1930).

Richard W. Bulliet. *The Patricians of Nishapur. A Study in Medieval Islamic Social History.* Cambridge, Mass., 1972.

———. *The Camel and the Wheel.* Cambridge, Mass., 1975.

———. "Medieval Nishapur: a topographic and demographic reconstruction." *Studia Iranica* 5 (1976): 67–91.

———. *Conversion to Islam in the Medieval Period: An Essay in Quantitative History.* Cambridge, Mass., 1979.

———. "Sedentarization of Nomads in the Seventh Century: The Arabs in Baṣra and Kūfa." In *When Nomads Settle,* edited by Philip C. Salzman, 35–47. Brooklyn, N.Y., 1980.

———. *Islam: The View from the Edge.* New York, 1994.

John Lewis [Johann Ludwig] Burckhardt. *Travels in Arabia, Comprehending an Account of those Territories in Hedjaz which the Mohammedans Regard as Sacred.* London, 1829.

Heribert Busse. *Chalif und Grosskönig. Die Buyiden in Iraq (945–1055).* Beirut, 1969.

———. "The Revival of Persian Kingship under the Būyids." In *Islamic Civilisation, 950–1150,* edited by D. S. Richards. Oxford, 1973.

Alfred J. Butler. *The Arab Conquest of Egypt and the Last Thirty Years of the Roman Dominion.* Oxford, 1902. Reissued by P. M. Fraser in 1978 with additional documentation and a critical bibliography.

Karl W. Butzer. "Der Umweltfaktor in der grossen arabischen Expansion." *Saeculum* 8 (1957): 359–71.

Leone Caetani. *Annali dell'Islam.* 10 vols. Milano, 1905–26.

———. *Studi di Storia Orientale.* Milano, 1911.

Claude Cahen. "Fiscalité, propriété, antagonismes sociaux en Haute-Mésopotamie au temps des premiers 'Abbāsides d'après Denys de Tell-Mahré." *Arabica* 1 (1954): 136–52.

———. "Mouvements populaires et autonomisme urbain dans l'Asie musulmane du Moyen Âge." *Arabica* 5 (1958): 225–50; vol. 6 (1959): 25–56, 233–65.

———. *Vom Ursprung bis zu den Anfängen des Osmanenreiches.* Vol. 1 of *Der Islam.* Frankfurt-am-Main, 1968. French version under the title *L'Islam des Origines au Début de l'Empire Ottomane* (Paris, 1970).

Giovanna Calasso. "I nomi delle prime città di fondazione Islamica nel *Buldān* di Yāqūt: etimologie e racconti di origine." In *Studi in Onore di Franceso Gabrieli nel suo Ottantesimo Compleanno,* edited by R. Traini. Vol. 1. Roma, 1984.

Averil Cameron. *The Mediterranean World in Late Antiquity A.D. 359–600.* London, 1993.

Averil Cameron and Lawrence I. Conrad, eds. *The Byzantine and Early Islamic Near East.* Vol. 1: *Problems in the Literary Source Material.* Studies in Late Antiquity and Early Islam, I. Princeton, N.J., 1993.

Marius Canard. "L'impérialisme des Fatimides et leur propagande." *Annales des Etudes Orientales* 4 (1942–47).

———. "Les H'amdanides et l'Arménie." In *Annales de l'Institut d'Études Orientales,* vol. 7. Alger, 1948.

———. *Histoire de la Dynastie des H'amdanides de Jazîra et de Syrie.* Publications de la Faculté des Lettres d'Alger, 2d ser., 21 (Paris, 1953).

———. "Quelques observations sur l'introduction géographique

de la Bughyat at'-T'alab de Kamâl ad-Dîn ibn al-ʿAdîm d'Alep." *Annales d'Etudes Orientales d'Alger* 15 (1957): 41–53.

———. "Le riz dans le Proche-Orient aux premiers siècles de l'Islam." *Arabica* 6 (1959): 113–31.

———. "Baghdād au IVe siècle de l'hégire." *Arabica* 9 (1964): 268–87.

———. "L'expansion arabe: le problème militaire." In *L'Occidente e l'Islam nell'Alto Medioevo,* vol. 1: *Settimane di Studio del Centro Italiano di Studi sull'Alto Medioevo,* XII, 2–8, aprile 1964. Spoleto, Italy, 1965.

Pierre Canivet and Jean-Paul Rey-Coquais, eds. *La Syrie de Byzance à l'Islam: VIIe-VIIIe Siècles.* Damas, 1992.

J. Cantineau. *Le Nabatéen.* 2 vols. Paris, 1930–32.

Pauline Carlier. "Qastal: Château Ommeyade?" 2 vols. Ph.D. diss., University Aix-Marseilles, 1984.

Thomas Francis Carter. *The Invention of Printing in China and Its Spread Westward.* 2d ed. revised by L. Carrington Goodrich. New York, 1955.

Paul Casanova. "Les noms coptes du Caire." *Bulletin de l'Institut Français d'Archéologie Orientale du Caire* 1 (1901): 193–97.

———. *Essai de Reconstitution Topographique de la Ville d'al-Fousṭâṭ ou Miṣr.* 3 vols. together constituting vol. 35 of *Mémoires Publiés par les Membres de l'Istitut Français d'Archéologie Orientale du Caire.* Le Caire, 1913–19.

———. "Les Ispehbeds de Firīm." In *ʿAjabnáma, a Volume of Oriental Studies Presented to Edward G. Browne,* edited by T. W. Arnold and R. A. Nicholson, 117–22. Cambridge, 1922.

Werner Caskel. *Das altarabische Königreich Lihjan.* Krefeld, 1950.

———. *Die Bedeutung der Beduinen in der Geschichte der Araber.* Köln and Opladen, 1953.

———. *Lihyan und Lihyanisch.* Köln and Opladen, 1954.

———. "Der arabische Stamm vor dem Islam und seine gesellschaftliche und juristiche Organisation." In *Atti del Convegno Internazionale sul Tema: Dalla Tribu allo Stato (Roma, 13–16 aprile 1961).* Roma, 1962.

———. *Ǧamharat an-Nasab: das geneaologische Werk des Hišām ibn Muḥammad al-Kalbī.* 2 vols. Leiden, 1966.

Ernst Cassirer. *Philosophie der Symbolischen Formen, II: Das Mythische Denken.* Berlin, 1925.

Diaz Cassou. "Ordenanzas y costumbres de la huerta de Murcia." In *Historia de Murcia Musulmana,* by M. Caspar Remiro. Zaragoza, Spain, 1905.

Gertrude Caton-Thompson and Elinor Wight Gardner. "Climate, irrigation, and early man in the Hadramawt." *The Geographical Journal* 93 (1939): 18–38.

M. Caudel. *Les Premières Invasions Arabes dans l'Afrique du Nord et l'Orient au Moyen Âge.* Paris, 1900.

J. B. Chabot. *Incerti Auctoris Chronicon Pseudo-Dionysianum Vulgo Dictum (CSCO 91, 104, Ser. syri 43, 53).* 1952–53.

———. *Anonymi Auctoris Chronicon ad Annum Christi 1234 Pertinens (CSCO 81-2, Ser. syri 36-7).* 1953.

———. ed. *Synodicon Orientale, Notices et Extraits des Manuscrits,* Vol. 37. Paris, 1902.

Victor Chapot. *La Frontière de l'Euphrate de Pompée à la Conquête Arabe.* Paris, 1907.

Henri Charles. *Le Christianisme des Arabes Nomades sur le Limes et dans le Désert Syro-Mésopotamien aux Alentours de l'Hégire.* Paris, 1936.

Maurice Chehab. "The Umayyad palace at ʿAnjar." *Ars Orientalis* 5 (1963): 17–27.

Joseph Chelhod. *Les Structures du Sacré chez les Arabes.* Paris, 1964.

———. *Le Droit dans la Société Bédouine.* Paris, 1971.

———. "Introduction à l'histoire sociale et urbaine de Zabīd." *Arabica* 25, pt. 1 (1978): 48–88.

H. Neville Chittick and Robert I. Rotberg, eds. *East Africa and the Orient: Cultural Syntheses in Pre-Colonial Times.* New York, 1975.

Walter Christaller. *Die zentralen Orte in Süddeutschland: eine ökonomisch-geographische Untersuchung über die Gesetzmässigkeit der Verbreitung und Entwicklung der Siedlungen mit Städtischen Funktionen.* Jena, Germany, 1933.

G. P. E. Clarkson, *The Theory of Consumer Demand: A Critical Appraisal.* Englewood Cliffs, N.J., 1963.

Dietrich Claude. *Die Byzantinische Stadt im 6. Jahrhundert.* München, 1969.

Paul M. Cobb. "Al-Amṣar: Civic and Semantic Development in the Early Islamic Period." Typescript, 1991.

———. "The Missing *Amṣar* of Syria: Alternative Urbanization at Ḥimṣ." Typescript, 1993.

———. "A note on ʿUmar's visit to Ayla in 17/638." *Der Islam* 71, pt. 2 (1994): 283–88.

Donald P. Cole. *Nomads of the Nomads. The Āl Murrah Bedouin of the Empty Quarter.* Chicago, 1975.

Basil A. Collins. *Al-Muqaddasi: The Man and His Work.* Michigan Geographical Publication no. 10. Ann Arbor, 1974.

Lawrence I. Conrad. "The *quṣūr* of medieval Islam. Some implications for the social history of the Near East." *Al-Abhāth* 29 (1981): 7–23.

———. "The plague in Bilād al-Shām in Pre-Islamic times." *Bilād al-Shām* 2 (1986): 143–63.

———. "Abraha and Muḥammad: some observations apropos of chronology and literary topoi in the early Arabic historical tradition." *Bulletin of the School of Oriental and African Studies* 50, pt. 2 (1987): 225–40.

———. "Seven and the *tasbīʿ*: on the implications of numerical symbolism for the study of medieval Islamic history." *Journal of the Economic and Social History of the Orient* 31 (1988): 42–73.

———. "The Conquest of Arwād: A Source-Critical Study in the Historiography of the Early Medieval Near East." In *The Byzantine and Early Islamic Near East,* Vol. 1, *Problems in the Literary Source Material,* edited by Averil Cameron and Lawrence I. Conrad, 317–401. Princeton, N.J., 1992.

Michael Cook. *Muhammad.* Oxford and New York, 1983.

G. A. Cooke. *A Text-Book of North-Semitic Inscriptions.* Oxford, 1903.

Georgette Cornu et al. *Atlas du Monde Arabo-Islamique à l'Epoque Classique. IXe-Xe Siècles.* Leiden, 1985.

P. M. Costa and T. J. Wilkinson, eds. "The hinterland of Sohar. archaeological surveys and excavations within the region of an Omani seafaring city." *The Journal of Oman Studies* 9 (Muscat, Oman, 1987).

Christian Courtois. *Les Vandales et l'Afrique.* Paris, 1955.

K. A. C. Creswell. *Early Muslim Architecture.* 2d ed. Oxford, 1969.

———. *A Short Account of Early Muslim Architecture.* Harmondsworth, Middlesex, England, 1958. Rev. ed. by James W. Allan (Cairo, 1989).

Patricia Crone. *Slaves on Horses: The Evolution of the Islamic Polity.* Cambridge, 1980.

———. *Meccan Trade and the Rise of Islam.* Princeton, N.J., 1987.

Patricia Crone and Michael Cook. *Hagarism: The Making of the Islamic World.* Cambridge, 1977.

Patricia Crone and Martin Hinds. *God's Caliph. Religious Authority in the First Centuries of Islam.* Cambridge, 1986.

Slobodan Ćurčić. "Late antique palaces: the meaning of context." *Ars Orientalis* 23 (1993):67–90.

Michael F. Dacey. "Analysis of Central Place and Point Patterns by a Nearest Neighbor Method." In *Human Geography.* Vol. 24 of Lund Studies in Geography, Series B. Lund, Sweden, 1962.

———. "A probability model for central place location." *Annals of the Association of American Geographers* 56 (1966):550–68.

Elton L. Daniel. *The Political and Social History of Khurasan under Abbasid Rule 747–820.* Minneapolis and Chicago, 1979.

Dānishjū. *Khūzistān va Khūzistāniyān.* Tehran, A.H. 1326.

Ṣalāḥ Daradkah. "Lamaḥāt min taʾrīkh Aylat al-ʿAqabah." *Dirāsāt Taʾrīkhīyah* 15–16 (1984):67–110.

Saʿīd al-Daywajī/al-Dewuchī/al-Dīwuhjī. "Khiṭāṭ al-Mawṣil fī al-ʿahd al-Umawī." *Sumer* 7, no. 1 (1951):88–98.

———. *Taʾrīkh al-Mawṣil.* Vol. 1. Baghdād, A.H. 1402.

Christian Decobert. *Le Mendiant et le Combattant.* Paris, 1991.

Emilienne Demougeot. "Le chameau et l'Afrique du nord romaine." *Annales: Economies, Sociétés, Civilisations* 15 (1960): 209–47.

D. C. Dennett. *Conversion and the Poll Tax in Early Islam.* Cambridge, 1950.

Frederick Mathewson Denny. "The meaning of *ummah* in the Qurʾan." *History of Religions* 15 (1975):34–69.

———. "*Ummah* in the Constitution of Medina." *Journal of Near Eastern Studies* 36 (1977):39–47.

Sylvie Denoix. *Décrire Le Caire. Fusṭāṭ-Miṣr d'après Ibn Duqmāq et Maqrīzī.* Le Caire (Cairo), 1992.

J.-M. Dentzer, ed. *Hauran I: Recherches Archéologiques sur la Syrie du Sud à l'Époque Hellénistique et Romaine.* Paris, 1985.

J. Deny. *Principes de Grammaire Turque ('Türk' de Turquie).* Paris, 1955.

D. Derenk. *Leben und Dichtung des Omaiyadenkalifen al-Walīd ibn Yazīd. Ein Quellenkritischer Beitrag.* Freiburg im Bresgau, 1974.

Emile Dermenghem. *Mohamet.* 2d ed. Paris, 1950.

Jean Despois. "L'emplacement et les origines de Kairouan." *Revue Tunisienne* 33 (1927).

———. "Kairouan: origine et évolution d'une ancienne capitale musulmane." *Annales de Géographie* 39 (1930):159–77.

———. *La Tunisie Orientale. Sahel et Basse Steppe.* Paris, 1955.

L. Dillemann. *Haute Mésopotamie Orientale et Pays Adjacents.* Paris, 1962.

Hicham (Hichem) Djaït. "Le Wilāya d'Ifrīqiya au IIe/VIIIe siècle: étude institutionnelle." *Studia Islamica* 27 (1967):77–121 and 28 (1968):79–107.

———. "L'Afrique arabe au VIIIe siècle (86–184 H./705–800)." *Annales: Économies, Sociétés, Civilisations* (1973):601–21.

———. "Les Yamanites à Kūfa au Ier siècle de l'Hégire." *Journal of the Economic and Social History of the Orient* 19 (1976): 148–81.

———. *Al-Kūfa: Naissance de la Ville Islamique.* Paris, 1986.

Brian Doe. *Monuments in South Arabia.* Naples and Cambridge, 1983.

R. A. Donkin. "The insect dyes of western and west-central Asia." *Anthropos* 72 (1977):849–53, 859–63.

———. "Spanish Red: An Ethnogeographical Study of Cochineal and the Opuntia Cactus." In *Transactions of the American Philosophical Society* 67, pt. 5 (1977).

Fred McGraw Donner. "Mecca's food supplies and Muḥammad's boycott." *Journal of the Economic and Social History of the Orient* 20, pt. 2 (1977):249–66.

———. "Muḥammad's political consolidation in Arabia up to the conquest of Mecca: a reassessment." *The Muslim World* 69 (1979):229–47.

———. *The Early Islamic Conquests.* Princeton, N.J., 1981.

———. "The formation of the Islamic state." *Journal of the American Oriental Society* 106 (1986):283–96.

———. *Narratives of Islamic Origins. The Beginnings of Islamic Historical Writing.* Princeton, N.J., 1998.

Glanville Downey. *Gaza in the Early Sixth Century.* Norman, Okla., 1963.

Reinhardt Dozy. *Histoire des Musulmans d'Espagne: jusquʾ á la conquê te de l'Andalousie par les almovarides (711–1110).* Leyden, 1861. 2d ed. by Évariste Lévi-Provençal, 3 vols. (Leiden, 1932). English translation under the title *Spanish Islam* (London, 1913).

———. *Corrections sur les Textes du Bayáno'l-Mogrib.* Leiden, 1883.

———. *Supplément aux Dictionnaires Arabes.* 2d ed. 2 vols. Paris, 1927.

Reinhardt Dozy and M. J. de Goeje, eds. *Description de l'Afrique et de l'Espagne.* Leyden, 1866.

A. Ducellier, M. Kaplan, and B. Martin. *Le Proche-Orient Médiéval.* Paris, 1978.

James S. Duncan. *The City as Text: The Politics of Landscape Interpretation in the Kandyan Kingdom.* Cambridge, 1990.

Michael Collins Dunn. "The Struggle for ʿAbbasid Egypt." Ph.D. diss., Georgetown University, 1975.

ʿAbd al-ʿAzīz al-Dūrī. "Al-Zuhrī: a study on the beginnings of history writing in Islam." *Bulletin of the School of Oriental and African Studies* 19 (1957):1–12.

———. "Al-Islām wa-intishār al-lughat al-ʿArabīyah wa-l-tuʿrīb." In *al-Qawmīyat al-ʿArabīyah wa-l-Islām.* Centre d'Études pour l'Unité Arabe (Beyrouth, 1981), 70–74.

Émile Durkheim. *De la Division du Travail Social: Étude sur l'Organisation des Sociétés Supérieures.* Paris, 1893.

René Dussaud. *Les Arabes en Syrie avant l'Islam.* Paris, 1907.

———. *Topographie Historique de la Syria Antique et Médiévale.* Paris, 1927.

Noël Duval. "Observations sur l'urbanisme tardif de Sufetula (Tunisie)." *Cahiers de Tunisie* 45–46 (1964).

Dale F. Eickelman. "Musaylima: an approach to the social anthropology of seventh century Arabia." *Journal of the Economic and Social History of the Orient* 10 (1967):17–52.

Amikam Elad. "Why Did ʿAbd al-Malik Build the Dome of the Rock? A Re-examination of the Muslim Sources." In *Bayt al-Maqdis: ʿAbd al-Malik's Jerusalem,* pt. 1, edited by Julian Raby and Jeremy Johns. Oxford, 1992.

———. *Medieval Jerusalem and Islamic Worship. Holy Places, Ceremonies, Pilgrimage* (Leiden, 1993).

Mircea Eliade. *Comentarii la legenda Meşterului Manole.* Bucharest, 1943.

———. *Traité d'Histoire des Religions.* Paris, 1948. English translation under the title *Patterns in Comparative Religion* (New York, 1958).

———. *Le Mythe de l'Éternel Retour: Archétypes et Répétition.* Paris, 1949. English translation under the titles *The Myth of Eternal Return* (New York, 1954) and *Cosmos and History* (New York, 1959).

———. "Centre du monde, temple, maison." In *Le Symbolisme Cosmique des Monuments Religieux,* Serie Orientale Roma XIV. Roma, 1957.

———. *Das Heilige und das Profane.* Hamburg, 1957. English translation under the title *The Sacred and the Profane* (New York, 1959).

Nikita Elisséeff. "Damas à la lumière de theories de Jean Sauvaget." In *The Islamic City. A Colloquium.* Edited by Albert Hourani and S. M. Stern. Oxford, 1970.

Kazuo Enoki. "On the nationality of the Ephthalites." *Memoirs of the Research Department of the Toyo Bunko* 18 (1959): 1–58.

I. Epstein. *The Response of Rabbi Simon ben Ẓemaḥ.* London, 1930.

Daniel Eustache. "El-Baṣra, capitale idrissite et son port." *Hesperīs* 42 (1955): 217–38.

E. E. Evans-Pritchard. *Nuer Religion.* Oxford, 1956.

B. T. Evetts, ed. *The Churches and Monasteries of Egypt.* Oxford, 1894–95.

Toufic Fahd. *Le Panthéon de l'Arabie Centrale à la Veille de l'Hégire.* Paris, 1968.

Rizwi S. Faizer. "The issue of authenticity regarding the traditions of al-Wāqidī as established in his *Kitāb al-Maghāzī.*" *Journal of Near Eastern Studies* 58, no. 2 (1999): 97–106.

Ahmed Fakhry. *An Archaeological Journey to Yemen.* 2 vols. Cairo, 1952.

O. von Falke. *Decorative Silks.* 3d ed. London, 1936.

N. A. Faris and H. W. Glidden. "The development of the meaning of the Koranic Ḥanīf." *Journal of the Palestine Oriental Society* 19 (1939): 1–13.

Sayyid Qadratallah Fatimi. "In quest of Kalah." *Journal [of] Southeast Asian History* 1, no. 2 (1960): 62–101.

———. *Islam Comes to Malaysia.* Singapore, 1963.

C. Féraud. *Histoire des Villes de la Province de Constantine: La Calle.* Alger, 1877.

Gabriel Ferrand. *Voyage du Marchand Arabe Sulaymān . . . suivi de Remarques par Abū Zayd Ḥasan.* Paris, 1922.

———. *Instructions Nautiques et Routiers Arabes et Portugais.* Paris, 1928.

A. J. Festugière. *Antioche Paienne et Chrétienne.* Paris, 1959.

J. G. Février. *Essai sur l'Histoire Politique et Économique de Palmyre.* Paris, 1931.

J. M. Fiey. "Topography of al-Madā'in." *Sumer* 23 (1967): 3–38.

———. "The Iraqi section of the Abbassid road Mosul—Nisibin," *Iraq* 26 (1964): 107–17.

B. Finster. *Frühe Iranische Moscheen.* Berlin, 1994.

Walter J. Fischel. "The Jews of Central Asia (Korasan) in medieval Hebrew and Islamic literature." *Historia Judaica* 7 (1945): 29–50.

———. "Isfahan. The Story of a Jewish Community in Persia." In *Joshua Starr Memorial Volume.* New York, 1953.

A. Fischer. "Al-Maqdisi und al-Muqaddasi." *Zeitschrift der Deutschen Morgenländischen Gesellschaft* 60 (1906): 404–10.

K. Fischer. "'Ἀλεξανδρόπολις μητρόπολις Ἀραχωσίας: zur Lage von Kandahar an Landesverbindungen zwischen Iran und Indien." *Bonner Jahrbücher* 167 (1967): 129–232.

W. Fischer, ed. *Aufsätze zur Arabischen Wissenschaftsgeschichte.* Hildesheim, 1970.

Gustav Flügel. *Concordantiae Corani Arabicae.* Leipzig, 1842.

C. Fontinoy. "Les noms de l'Égypte en hébreu et leur étymologie," *Chronique d'Egypte* 64 (1989): 90–97.

Paul G. Forand. "The governors of Mosul according to al-Azdī's *Ta'rīkh al-Mawṣil.*" *Journal of the American Oriental Society* 89 (1969): 88–105.

Henri and H. A. Frankfort, John Wilson, and Thorkild Jacobsen. *The Intellectual Adventure of Ancient Man.* Chicago, 1946. Reprinted under the title *Before Philosophy* (Harmondsworth, Middlesex, England, 1949).

Anis Frayḥā. *Muʿjam Asmā' al-Mudun wa-l-Qurā al-Lubnānīyah.* Bayrut, A.H. 1392.

P. W. M. Freeman and D. L. Kennedy. *The Defence of the Roman Empire and Byzantine East.* Oxford, 1986.

Richard N. Frye. "Notes on the history of Transoxiana." *Harvard Journal of Asiatic Studies* 19 (1956): 106–19.

———. "Remarks on Baluchi history." *Central Asiatic Journal* 5–6 (1959–61): 44–50.

———. "Biyābānak: the oases of Central Iran." *Central Asiatic Journal* 5–6 (1959–61): 182–97.

———. *Bukhara, the Medieval Achievement.* Norman, Okla., 1965.

———. *The Histories of Nishapur.* Cambridge, Mass., 1965.

———. "The Sasanian System of Walls for Defense." In *Studies in Memory of Gaston Wiet,* edited by Myriem Rosen-Ayalon. Jerusalem, 1977.

———, ed. *The Cambridge History of Iran.* Vol. 4, *The Period from the Arab Invasion to the Saljuqs.* Cambridge, 1975.

J. Fück. *Muḥammad ibn Isḥāq.* Frankfurt-am-Main, 1925.

Gideon Fuks. *Greece in the Land of Israel—Beth Shean (Scythopolis) in the Graeco-Roman Period.* Jerusalem, 1983.

Michael Jeffrey Fuller. "Abila of the Decapolis: A Roman-Byzantine City in Transjordan." Ph.D. diss., Washington University, 1987.

———, ed. *Abila Reports.* St. Louis Community College, Florissant Valley, 1986.

Alfons Gabriel. "Recherches archéologiques à Palmyre." *Syrie* 7 (1926).

———. *Voyages Archéologiques dans la Turquie Orientale.* Vol. 1. Paris, 1940, 241–51.

Francesco Gabrieli. *Geschichte der Araber.* Stuttgart, 1963.

———. *Muhammad and the Conquests of Islam.* New York and Toronto, 1968.

———. "Ibn Hawqal e gli Arabi di Sicilia." *Revista degli Studi Orientali* 37 (19??): 245–53.

———, ed. "Histoire et culture de la Sicile arabe." *Revue de la Méditerranée* (Paris-Alger, mai-jun 1957): 241–59.

———, ed. *L'Antica Società Beduina.* Roma, 1959.

P. Gallais and Y. J. Rion, eds. *Mélanges Offerts à René Crozet.* Poitiers, France, 1966.

Micheline Galley and David R. Marshall, eds. *Proceedings of the First Congress of Mediterranean Studies of Arab-Berber Influence.* Algiers, 1973.

C. J. Galpin. *The Social Anatomy of an Agricultural Community.* Research Bulletin no. 34, Agricultural Experiment Station of the University of Wisconsin. Madison, 1915.

J.-C. Garcin. "Pour un recours à l'histoire de l'espace vécu dans l'étude de l'Egypte arabe." *Annales—Économies, Sociétés, Civilisations* 35 (1980): 436–51.

Louis Gardet. *La Cité Musulmane: Vie Sociale et Politique,* 3d ed. Paris, 1969.

J. Gascou. "Les grands domaines, la cité et l'état en Égypte byzantine." *Travaux et Mémoires* 9 (1985): 1–90.

Th. H. Gaster. "Myth and story." *Numen* 1 (1954): 184–212.

Heinz Gaube. *Die Südpersische Provinz Arrağān/Kūh-Gīlūyeh von der Arabischen Eroberung bis zur Safawidenzeit.* Wien, 1973.

———. *Iranian Cities.* New York, 1979.

———. "Die syrischen Wüstenschlösser: einige wirtschaftliche und politische Gesichtspunkte zu ihrer Enstehung." *Zeitschrift des Deutschen Palästina-Vereins* 95 (1979): 182–209.

———. "Khirbat al-Bayda: A Reconsideration." Paper presented to the Workshop on Late Antiquity and Early Islam, University of London, 25–27 April 1991.

M. Gaudefroy-Demombynes. *Le Pèlerinage à la Mekke.* Paris, 1923.

———. *L'Afrique Moins l'Égypte.* Paris, 1927.

———. *Mahomet.* Paris, 1957.

Émile Félix Gautier. *L'Islamisation de l'Afrique du Nord. Les Siècles Obscurs du Maghreb.* Paris, 1927. 2d ed. published under the title *Le Passé de l'Afrique du Nord. Les Siécles Obscurs* (Paris, 1952).

Michal Gawlikowski. "The Oriental City and the Advent of Islam." In *Die Orientalische Stadt,* edited by G. Wilhelm, 339–50. Berlin, 1997.

Roland-Pierre Gayraud, ed. *Colloque International d'Archéologie Islamique.* Le Caire (Cairo), 1998.

Charles L. Geddes. "The Yuʿfirid Dynasty of Ṣanʿāʾ." Ph.D. diss., University of London, 1959.

Pedro Chalmeta Gendrón. *El Señor del Zoco en España.* Madrid, 1973.

R. Génier. *Vie de Saint Euthyme le Grand.* Paris, 1909.

Yūsuf Ghawanmah. *Aylah (al-ʿAqabah) wa-l-Baḥr al-Aḥmar.* Irbid, Jordan, A.H. 1406/A.D. 1984.

M. Ghazarian. *Armenien unter der arabischen Herrschaft.* Marburg, 1903.

Ghévond: Histoire des Guerres et des Conquêtes des Arabes en Arménie. Edited and translated by G. Chahnazarian. Paris, 1856. Translated by Zaven Arzoumanian under the title *History of Lewond the Eminent Vardapet of the Armenians* (Philadelphia, 1982).

R. Ghirshman. "Une mosquée de Suse au début de l'Hégire." *Bulletin des Études Orientales* 12 (1947–48): 77–91.

———. *Les Chionites-Hephthalites.* Le Caire (Cairo), 1948.

———. *Bichapour.* Paris, 1971.

H. A. R. [later Sir Hamilton] Gibb. *The Arab Conquests in Central Asia.* London, 1923.

Moshe Gil. "The Constitution of Medina: a reconsideration." *Israel Oriental Studies* 4 (1974): 44–66.

———. *A History of Palestine, 634–1099.* Cambridge, 1992. Previously published in Hebrew, Tel Aviv, 1983.

Moshe Gil and Shaul Shaked. "Review of M. B. Morony, *Iraq after the Muslim Conquest.*" *Journal of the American Oriental Society* 106 (1986): 819–23.

J. Gildemeister. "Beiträge zur Palästinakunde aus arabischen Quellen." *Zeitschrift des Deutschen Palästinavereins* 7 (1884).

———. "Über den Titel des Masudischen Werkes *Murūj al-Dhahab.*" *Zeitschrift für die Kunde* 9: 202–204.

Eduard Glaser. *Skizze der Geschichte und Geographie Arabiens.* Berlin, 1890.

Thomas F. Glick. *Irrigation and Society in Medieval Valencia.* Cambridge, Mass., 1970.

———. *Islamic and Christian Spain in the Early Middle Ages.* Princeton, N.J., 1979.

Carol A. M. Glucker. *The City of Gaza in the Roman and Byzantine Periods.* British Archeological Reports, International Series 325 (Oxford, 1987).

Nelson Glueck. *The Other Side of the Jordan.* New Haven, Conn., 1940.

S. Godlund. "Bus Service in Sweden." In *Human Geography.* Vol. 17 of Lund Studies in Geography, Series B. Lund, Sweden, 1956.

M. J. de Goeje. *Bibliotheca Geographorum Arabicorum.* 8 vols. Lugduni Batavorum, 1870–1906.

———. "Mémoire sur les Migrations des Tsiganes à travers l'Asie." *Zeitschrift der Deutschen Morgenlandischen Gesellschaft,* 1871.

———. *Mémoire sur les Carmathes du Bahraïn et les Fatimides.* Leyden, 1886.

S. D. Goitein. "A Muslim iconoclast (Ibn Taymiyyah on the 'merits' of Jerusalem and Palestine)." *Journal of the American Oriental Society* 56 (1936): 1–21.

———. "The Sanctity of Jerusalem and Palestine in Early Islam." In *Studies in Islamic History and Institutions.* Leiden, 1966.

———. *A Mediterranean Society: The Jewish Communities of the Arab World as Portrayed in the Documents of the Cairo Geniza.* 5 vols. Berkeley and Los Angeles, 1967–83.

———. *Studies in Islamic History and Institutions.* Leiden, 1968.

———. "Cairo: An Islamic City in the Light of the Geniza Documents." In *Middle Eastern Cities. A Symposium on Ancient, Islamic, and Contemporary Middle Eastern Urbanism,* edited by Ira M. Lapidus. Berkeley, 1969.

Ignaz Goldziher. *Muhammedanische Studien.* Halle, 1889–90; English translation by C. R. Barber and S. M. Stern under the title *Muslim Studies* (London, 1966 and Chicago, 1967).

———. *Abhandlungen zur Arabischen Philologie.* Leiden, 1896.

———. *Vorlesungen über den Islam.* Heidelberg, 1910. 2d ed., 1925.

———. *Die Richtungen der islamischen Koranauslegung.* Leiden, 1920, 1952.

Lisa Golombek. "Urban Patterns in Pre-Safavid Iran." In "Studies on Isfahan," edited by Renata Holod. *Iranian Studies* 7, nos. 1–2 (1974): 18–44.

———. "The Draped Universe of Islam." In *Content and Context of Visual Arts in the Islamic World: Papers from a Colloquium in Memory of Richard Ettinghausen,* edited by Priscilla Soucek. University Park, Pa., and London, 1988.

Lucien Golvin. *Le Maghrib Central à l'Epoque des Zirides: Recherches d'Archéologie et d'Histoire.* Paris, 1957.

P. Goubert. "Le problème Ghassanid à la veille d'Islam." In *Congrès des Etudes Byzantines* 1 (1950): 103–18.

Oleg Grabar. "Al-Mushatta, Baghdād, and Wāsiṭ." In *Essays in Honour of Philip K. Hitti,* edited by J. Kritzeck and R. Bayly Winder, 99–108. London, 1959.

———. *The Formation of Islamic Art.* Rev. ed. New Haven, Conn., 1987.

———. *The Shape of the Holy: Early Islamic Jerusalem.* Princeton, N.J., 1996.

Oleg Grabar, Renata Holod, James Knustad, and William Trousdale. *City in the Desert: Qasral-Hayr East.* 2 vols. Harvard Middle Eastern Monographs 23/24. Cambridge, Mass., 1978.

Hubert Grimme. *Mohammed.* Münster i. W., 1892.

Adolf Grohmann. *Studien zur Historischen Geographie und Verwaltung des Frühmittelalterlichen Äygypten.* Vol. 77 of *Österreichisehe Akademie der Wissenschaften.* Wien, 1959.

———. *Arabien.* München, 1963.

H. Grotzfeld. *Das Bad im Arabisch-Islamischen Mittelalter: Eine Kulturgeschichte Studie.* Wiesbaden, 1970.

René Grousset. *Histoire de l'Arménie des Origines à 1071.* Paris, 1947.

Gustave von Grunebaum, ed. "Review of Matthews' *Palestine.*" *Journal of Near Eastern Studies* 11 (1952): 230–32.

———, ed. *Studies in Islamic Cultural History. Memoir no. 76 of the American Anthropological Association.* Menasha, Wis., 1954.

———. "Die islamische Stadt." *Saeculum* 6 (1955): 138–53.

———. *Islam. Essays in the Nature and Growth of a Cultural Tradition.* 2d ed. London, 1961.

———. "The Sacred Character of Islamic Cities." In *Mélanges Ṭāhā Ḥusain: Offerts par ses Amis et ses Disciples a l'Occasion de son 70ième Anniversaire.* Le Caire (Cairo), 1962.

———. *Classical Islam: A History, 600 A.D.–1258 A.D.* Chicago, 1970.

Irene Grütter. "Arabische Bestattungsbräuche im frühislamischer Zeit." *Der Islam* 32 (1957).

S. Gsell. *Histoire Ancienne de l'Afrique du Nord.* Paris, 1913.

A. Rhuvon Guest. "The foundation of Fustat and the khittahs of that town." *The Journal of the Royal Asiatic Society of Great Britain and Ireland* (1907): 49–83.

———. "The Delta in the Middle Ages. A note on the branches of the Nile and the kurahs of Lower Egypt. . . ." *The Journal of the Royal Asiatic Society of Great Britain and Ireland* (1912): 941–80.

M. Guidi. *Storia e Cultura Degli Arabi Fino alla Morte di Maometto.* Florence, 1951.

Alfred Guillaume. *The Traditions of Islam. An Introduction to the Study of the Hadith Literature.* Oxford, 1924.

C. Haas. *Alexandria in Late Antiquity: Topography and Social Conflict.* Baltimore, 1997.

Claus-Peter Haase. *Untersuchungen zur Landschaftsgeschichte Nord syriens in der Umayyedenzeit. Zeitschrift des Deutschen Morgenlündīschen Gesellschaft,* suppl. 3/1. Leipzig and Wiesbaden, 1977.

———. "Bilād al-Shām during the ʿAbbāsid Period." In *Proceedings of the Fifth International Conference on the History of Bilād al-Shām,* edited by Muḥammad ʿAdnān al-Bakhīt and R. Schick. Ammān, 1991.

M. Hadj-Sadok [Muḥammad Ḥajj-Sadūk]. *Description du Maghreb et de l'Europe du IIIe au IVe Siècle.* Bibliothèque Arabe-Française, vol. 6. Alger, 1949.

John F. Haldon. *Byzantium in the Seventh Century.* Cambridge, 1990.

John F. Haldon and Hugh Kennedy. "The Arab-Byzantine frontier in the eighth and ninth centuries." *Recueil des Travaux de l'Institut d'Études Byzantines* (Belgrade) 19 (1980): 79–116.

Muḥammad Maher Ḥamadeh. "Muḥammad the Prophet: A Selected Bibliography." Ph.D. diss., University of Michigan, 1965.

S. Hamarnah. "Zirāʿat qaṣab al-sukkar wa ṣināʿatuhu ʿinda al-ʿArab al-Muslimīn." *Annual of the Department of Antiquities [of Jordan]* 22 (1977–78): 12–19.

Muḥammad Ḥamīdullāh. "Al-īlāf ou les rapports économico-diplomatiques de La Mecque préislamique." In *Mélanges Louis Massignon.* Damas, 1957.

———. *Le Prophète de l'Islam: sa vie, son Oeuvre.* 2 vols. Paris, 1959.

———. *Majmūʿāt al-Wathāʾiq al-Siyāsīyah.* Bayrūt, A.H. 1389/A.D. 1969).

R. W. Hamilton. *Khirbat al-Mafjar. An Arabian Palace in the Jordan Valley.* Oxford, 1959.

Philip Hammond. *The Nabataeans: Their History, Culture and Archaeology.* Studies in Mediterranean Archaeology, no. 37. Gothenburg, Sweden, 1973.

Oscar Handlin and John Burchard, eds. *The Historian and the City.* Cambridge, Mass., 1963.

Masashi Haneda and Toru Miura. *Islamic Urban Studies: Historical Review and Perspectives.* London and New York, 1994.

Muḥammad Ḥannānī. "Al-Asbāb wa al-asāṭir al-murtabiṭah bi-taʾsīs al-mudun al-Islāmīyah bi al-Maghrib." In *Madīnah fī Taʾrīkh al-Maghrib al-ʿArabī.* Casablanca, A.H. 1411.

J. Hansman. "The problem of Qūmis." *Journal of the Royal Asiatic Society* (1968): 111–39.

Michael J. L. Hardy. *Blood Feuds and the Payment of Blood Money in the Middle East.* Leiden, 1963.

Claire Hardy-Guilbert. "Contribution à l'analyse du tissu urbain de Suse à partir du IXe siècle." *Paléorient* 11, no. 2 (1985): 101–13.

Claire Hardy-Guilbert and Axelle Rougeulle. "Ports islamiques du Yémen. Prospections archéologiques sur les côtes yéménites (1993–1995)." *Archéologie Islamique* 7 (1997): 147–96.

J. B. Harley and David Woodward, eds. *The History of Cartography.* 2 vols. to date. Chicago, 1992–.

Chauncy D. Harris and Edward L. Ullman. "The nature of cities." *The Annals of the American Academy of Political Science* 242 (1945): 7–17.

J. R. Harris, ed. *The Legacy of Egypt.* 2d ed. Oxford, 1971.

Timothy P. Harrison. "The early Umayyad settlement at Ṭabariyah: a case of yet another *miṣr*?" *Journal of Near Eastern Studies* 51 (1992): 51–59.

M. Hartmann. *Der Islamische Orient.* Bd. 2: *Die Arabische Frage, mit einem Versuche der Archäologie Jemens.* Leipzig, 1909.

ʿAlī Ibrāhīm Ḥasan. *Al-Tarīkh al-Islāmī al-ʿĀmm.* Al-Qāhirah, A.H. 1383/A.D. 1963.

Zaky Mohamed Hassan. *Les Tulunides. Études de l'Égypte Musulmane à la Fin du IXe Siècle 868-905.* Paris, 1933.

Saleh al-Hathloul. "Tradition, Continuity, and Change in the Physical Environment." Ph.D. diss., Massachusetts Institute of Technology, 1981.

G. R. Hawting. "The disappearance and re-discovery of Zamzam and the 'well of the Kaʿba.'" *Bulletin of the School of Oriental and African Studies* 43 (1980): 44–54.

———. "The Origins of the Muslim Sanctuary at Mecca." In *Studies on the First Century of Islamic Society,* edited by G. H. A. Juynboll. Carbondale, Ill., 1982.

———. "The origin of Jedda and the problem of al-Shuʿaybah." *Arabica* 31 (1984): 318–26.

———. "Al-Hudaybiyya and the conquest of Mecca: a reconsideration of the tradition about the Muslim takeover of the sanctuary." *Jerusalem Studies in Arabic and Islam* 8 (1986): 1–23.

———. *The First Dynasty of Islam.* Beckenham, England, 1987.

H. S. Helaisi. "Bedouins and tribal life in Saudi Arabia." *International Social Science Journal* 11, no. 4 (1959): 532–38.

Joseph Hell. *Neue Huḍailiten-Diwane.* Leipzig, 1933.

S. W. Helms. "Kandahar of the Arab Conquest." *World Archaeology* 14 (1983): 342–54.

W. B. Henning. "Argi and the 'Tokharians.'" *Bulletin of the School of Oriental and African Studies* 9 (1938).

———. "Gabae." *Asia Major,* n.s., vol. 2. 1952.

J. Henninger. "Das Opfer in den altssüdarabischen Hochkulturen." *Anthropos* 37–40 (1942–45): 779–810.

Albert Herrmann. "Die Hephthaliten und ihre Beziehungen zu China." *Asia Major* 2 (1925): 564–80.

———. "Die alteste turkische Weltkarte." *Imago Mundi* 1 (1935): 21–28.

Georgina Herrmann, K. Kurbansakhatov, St. John Simpson, et al. "The international Merv project. Preliminary report on the fifth season (1996)." *Iran* 35 (1997): 1–33. For previous reports see *Iran* 31 (1992): 39–62; 32 (1993): 53–75; 33 (1994): 31–60; 34 (1995): 1–22.

E. Herzfeld. *Samarra, Aufnahmen und Untersuchungen zur Islamischen Archäologie.* Berlin, 1907.

———. "Mitteilungen über die Arbeiten der Zweiten Kampagne von Samarra." *Der Islam* 5 (1914): 196–204.

———. "Khorasan. Denmalsgeographische Studein sur Kulturgeschichte des Islam in Iran." *Der Islam* 11 (1921): 107–74.

———. *Der Wandschmuck der Bauten von Samarra.* Berlin, 1923.

———. "Geschichte der Stadt Samarra." *Ausgrabungen von Samarra* 6 (1948).

J.-Chr. Heusch and M. Meinecke. "Grabungen im Abbāsidischen Palastareal von ar-Raqqa/ar-Rāfiqa 1982–1983." *Damaszener Mitteilungen* 2 (1985): 85–105.

R. H. Hewsen. "Introduction to the Study of Armenian Historical Geography." Ph.D. diss., Georgetown University, 1967.

Carole Hillenbrand. "The History of the Jazīra 1100–1150: The Contribution of Ibn al-Azraq al-Fāriqī." Ph.D. diss., University of Edinburgh, 1979.

Robert Hillenbrand. "*La dolce vita* in early Islamic Syria: the evidence of later Umayyad palaces." *Art History* 5 (1982): 1–35.

———. "'The Ornament of the World': Medieval Córdoba as a Cultural Centre." In *The Legacy of Muslim Spain,* edited by Salma Khadra Jayyusi. Leiden, 1992.

———. *Islamic Architecture: Form, Function and Meaning.* New York, 1994.

Martin Hinds. "Kûfan political alignments and their backgrounds in the mid-seventh century A.D." *International Journal of Middle East Studies* 2 (1971): 346–67.

Maria Höfner. "Die Kultur des vorislamischen Südarabien." *Zeitschrift der Deutschen Morgenländischen Gesellschaft* 99 (1945–49): 15–28.

———. "War der sabäische Mukarrib ein 'Priesterfürst'?" *Wiener Zeitschrift für die Kunde des Morgenlandes* 54 (1957): 77–85.

M. Höfner, K. Mlaker, and Nikolaus Rhodokanakis. *Zur südarabische Epigraphik und Archäologie II. Wiener Zeitschrift für die Kunde des Morgenlandes* 41 (Wien, 1934): 67–106.

Paul M. Hohenberg and Lynn Hollen Lees. *The Making of Urban Europe 1000–1950.* Cambridge, Mass., 1985.

Renata Holod. "Comments." *Iranian Studies* 7 (1974): 45–48.

P. M. Holt, Ann K. S. Lambton, and Bernard Lewis, eds. *The Cambridge History of Islam.* Vol. 2. Cambridge, 1970.

Kenneth G. Holum and Robert L. Hohlfelder, eds. *King Herod's Dream: Caesarea on the Sea.* New York, 1988.

Denise Homès-Fredericq and J. Basil Hennessy, eds. *Archaeology of Jordan.* 2 vols. Leuven, 1986–89, continuing.

F. Hommel. *Südarabische Chrestomathie.* München, 1893.

———. "Ethnologie und Geographie des alten Orients." Vol. 3, pt. 1, sect. 1 of *Handbuch der Klass. Altertumswiss.* München, 1926.

Ernst Honigman. *Die Ostgrenze des Byzantinischen Reiches von 363 bis 1071.* Bruxelles, 1935.

———. *Le Synekdémos d'Hiéroklès et l'Opuscule Géographique de Georges de Chypre.* Bruxelles, 1939.

J. F. P. Hopkins. *Medieval Muslim Government in Barbary until the Sixth Century of the Hijra.* London, 1958.

Josef Horovitz [Horowitz]. "Alter und Ursprung des Isnad." *Der Islam* 8 (1918).

———. *Koranische Untersuchungen.* Berlin and Leipzig, 1926.

———. "The earliest biographies of the Prophet and their authors." *Islamic Culture* 1 (1927): 535–59.

Albert Hourani and S. M. Stern, eds. *The Islamic City: A Colloquium.* Oxford, 1970.

George F. Hourani. *Arab Seafaring in the Indian Ocean in Ancient and Early Medieval Times.* Princeton Oriental Studies no. 13. Princeton, N.J., 1951.

Th. Houtsma. *Recueil de Textes Relatifs à l'Histoire des Seldjoukides.* Leiden, 1886.

A. Houtum-Schindler. *Eastern Persian Irak.* London, 1896.

Robert G. Hoyland. *Seeing Islam as Others Saw It. A Survey and Evaluation of Christian, Jewish and Zoroastrian Writings on Early Islam.* Princeton, N.J., 1997.

Charles Huart. "Les Ziyārides." In *Mémoires de l'Institut National de France.* Académie des Inscriptions et Belles-Lettres 42 (1922).

———. *Les Musafirides de l'Azerbaidjan.* Paris, 1922.

Clément Imbault Huart. *Littérature Arabe.* Paris, 1923.

H. Hübschmann. *Armenische Grammatik.* Leipzig, 1897.

———. "Die altarmenischen Ortsnamen." *Indo-Germanen Forschungen* 16 (1904): 197–479. Armenian translation (Wien, 1907).

Jean-Baptiste Humbert and Alain Desreumaux. "Huit campagnes de fouilles au Khirbet es-Samra (1981–1989)." *Revue Biblique* 97 (1990): 252–69.

R. S. Humphreys. "Urban Topography and Urban Society: Damascus under the Ayyubids and Mamluhs." In *Islamic History: A Framework for Inquiry.* Princeton, N.J., 1991.

C. Snouck Hurgronje. *Mekka in the Latter Part of the Nineteenth Century.* Leiden, 1931.

Mir Hussein. "Merve Rud." *Afghanistan* 9, no. 3 (1954): 8–17, no. 4 (1955): 19–25.

Mahmood Ibrahim. *Merchant Capital and Islam.* Austin, Tex., 1990.

Moawiyah M. Ibrahīm, ed. *Arabian Studies in Honor of Mahmoud Ghul.* Wiesbaden, 1989.

Saad E. Ibrahim and Donald P. Cole. "Saudi Arabian Bedouin." In *Cairo Papers in Social Science.* Vol. 1. Cairo, 1978.

Hady Roger Idris. "Contribution à l'histoire de l'Ifriqiya. Tableau de la vie intellectuelle et administrative à Kairouan sous les Aglabites et les Fatimites . . . d'après le Riyād En Nufūs de Abū Bakr el-Mālakī." *Revue des Etudes Islamiques* 9 (1935): 105–78, 273–305; 10 (1936): 45–104.

———. "Deux juristes kairouanais de l'époque zīrīde: Ibn Abī Zayd et al-Qābisī." *Annales de l'Institut d'Etudes Orientales de l'Université d'Alger* 12 (1954): 121–98.

———. *La Berbérie Orientale sous les Zirides, Xe-XIIe Siècles.* 2 vols. Paris, 1962.

S. M. Imamuddin [Imām al-Dīn]. *Muslim Spain 711–1492 A.D.: A Sociological Study.* Leiden, 1981.

Iqbāl Yaghmār-ī. *Jughrāfiyā-yi Ta'rīkh-yi Dāmghān.* Tehran, A.H. 1377.

ʿIrāq Government Department of Antiquities. *Excavations at Samarra 1936–1939.* Baghdād, 1940.

Washington Irving. *Mahomet and his Successors.* New York, 1849.

Muṭahhar al-Iryānī. *Fī Ta'rīkh al-Yaman.* Ṣanʿā', A.H. 1393.

W. Ivanow. "Ismailis and Qarmatians." *Journal of the Bombay Branch of the Royal Asiatic Society* 16 (1940): 43–85.

Jibrail S. Jabbur. *The Bedouins and the Desert. Aspects of Nomadic Life in the Arab East.* Albany, N.Y., 1995. Translated by Lawrence I. Conrad from Jabbur's *Badu wa-l-Badiyah.*

Georg Jacob. *Altarabisches Beduinenleben.* Berlin, 1897. Reprint, Hildesheim, 1967.

D. Jacques-Meunié. *Le Maroc Saharien des Origines à 1670.* Paris, 1982.

Makkī al-Jamīl. *Al-Badawah wa-l-Badū fī-l-Bilād al-ʿArabīyah.* Al-Qāhirah, A.H. 1382/A.D. 1962.

Albert Jamme. "Le panthéon sud-arabe préislamique d'après les sources épigraphiques." *Le Muséon* 60 (1947): 55–147.

———. "On a drastic current reduction of South Arabian chronology." *Bulletin of the American Society for Oriental Research* 145 (1957): 28 et seq.

———. *Sabaean Inscriptions from Mahram Bilqīs (Marib).* Publications of the American Foundation for the Study of Man, vol. 3. Baltimore, 1962.

Kaẓim al-Janābī. *Takhṭīṭ Madīnat al-Kūfah ʿan al-Maṣādir al-Tarīkhīyah wa-l-Athārīyah.* Baghdād, 1967.

D. al-Habīb al-Janḥānī. *Al-Maghrib al-Islāmī: al-Ḥayāt al-Iqdtiṣādīyah wa-l-Ijtimāʿīyah.* Tūnis, A.H. 1398.

J. J. G. Jansen. *The Interpretation of the Koran in Modern Egypt.* Leiden, 1974.

Caroline Janssen. *Bābil, the City of Witchcraft and Wine: The Name and Fame of Babylon in Medieval Arabic Geographical Texts.* Ghent, 1995.

A. Janzūrī. *Al-Thughūr al-Barrīyat al-Islāmīyah.* Al-Qāhirah, A.H. 1399.

J. Jarry. "L'Égypte et l'invasion musulmane." *Annales Islamologiques* 6 (1966).

Ḥamad al-Jāsir. *Fī Shamāl Gharb al-Jazīrah.* Riyāḍ, A.H. 1390.

A. Jaubert, trans. *Géographie d'Edrisi.* 2 vols. Paris, 1836–40.

A. Jaussen and R. Savignac. *Mission Archaéologique en Arabie.* Paris, 1909.

———. *Les Châteaux Arabes de Qeseir ʿAmra, Harāneh et Tūba.* 2 vols. Paris, 1922.

Bendelī Jawzī. *Min Ta'rīkh al-Harakāt al-Fikrīyah fī-l-Islām.* Jerusalem, n.d., but preface dated A.H. 1347/A.D. 1928.

Salma Khadra Jayyusi, ed. *The Legacy of Muslim Spain.* Leiden, 1992.

Raḍī al-Dīn Sayyid ʿAbd Allāh Jaza'irī. "Faqīr." In *Tā'rīkh-i Shushtar.* Calcutta, A.H. 1342/A.D. 1924.

Mark Jefferson. "Distribution of the world's city folks." *The Geographical Review* 21 (1931).

———. "The law of the primate city." *The Geographical Review* 29, no. 2 (1939): 226–32.

Arthur Jeffery. *The Foreign Vocabulary of the Qur'ān.* Gaekwad Oriental Series, no. 74. Baroda, India, 1938.

N. Jidejian. *Beirut through the Ages.* Beirut, 1973.

F. H. Jimenez. "El almimbar movil del siglo $\bar{x}$ de la mezquita de Cordoba." *Al-Andalus* 24 (1959): 381–99.

A. H. Johns. "Sufism as a category in Indonesian literature and history." *Journal of Southeast Asian History* 2 (1961): 10–23.

Jeremy Johns. "The Greek Church and the conversion of Muslims in Norman Sicily." *Byzantinische Forschungen* 21 (1995): 133–57.

Douglas L. Johnson. *The Nature of Nomadism: A Comparative Study of Pastoral Migrations in Southwestern Asia and Northern Africa.* University of Chicago, Department of Geography Research Paper no. 118. Chicago, 1947.

Gregory A. Johnson. *Local Exchange and Early State Development in Southwest Iran.* Anthropological Paper no. 51 of the Museum of Anthropology, University of Michigan. Ann Arbor, 1973.

Michael Join-Lambert. *Jérusalem Israélite, Chrétienne, Musulmane.* Paris, 1956.

Jacques Jomier. *Le Commentaire Coranique du Manâr: Tendances Modernes de l'Exégèse Coranique en Egypte.* Paris, 1954.

A. H. M. Jones. *The Greek City from Alexander to Justinian.* Oxford, 1940.

A. H. M. Jones et al. *The Cities of the Eastern Roman Provinces.* 2d ed. Oxford, 1971.

Marsden Jones. "Al-Sīra al-Nabawiyya as a Source for the Economic History of Western Arabia at the Time of the Rise of Islam." In *Proceedings of the First International Symposium on the History of Arabia, 22rd–28th April, 1977* (1977), 15–23.

Charles-André Julien. *Histoire de l'Afrique du Nord: Tunisie, Algérie, Maroc.* Paris, 1931. 2d ed. rev. by Roger Le Tourneau (Paris, 1952); rev. 2d ed., Paris, 1966; English translation under the title *History of North Africa: Tunisia, Algeria, Morocco* (London, 1970).

Al-Ḥabīb al-Junḥāhī. "Tahart: ʿAṣimah al-Dawlah al-Rustamīyah." *Revue Tunisienne de Sciences Sociales* 40–43 (1975).

Ferdinand Justi. *Iranisches Namenbuch.* Marburg, 1895.

G. H. A. Juynboll. *The Authenticity of the Tradition Literature: Discussions in Modern Egypt.* Leiden, 1969.

———, ed. *Studies on the First Century of Islamic Society.* Carbondale, Ill., 1982.

T. G. J. Juynboll. *Lexicon Geographicum cui Titulus est Marāṣid al-Iṭṭilā ʿala Asmā al-Amkina wal-l-Biqā.* 6 vols. Leyden, 1851–64.

M. Kably. *Société, Pouvoir et Religion au Maroc à la fin du Moyen Âge.* Paris, 1986.

Walter E. Kaegi. "Some seventh-century sources on Caesarea." *Israel Exploration Journal* 28 (1978):177–81.

———. *Byzantium and the Early Islamic Conquests.* Cambridge, 1992.

———. "Egypt on the Eve of the Muslim Conquest." In *The Cambridge History of Egypt,* vol. 1, *Islamic Egypt: 640–1517,* edited by Carl F. Petry. Cambridge, 1998.

Umar Rīḍā Kaḥḥālah. *Muʿjam Qabāʾil al-ʿArab.* 3 vols. Bayrūt, A.H. 1388/A.D. 1968.

Paul Kahle. "Zur Geschichte des mittelalterlichen Alexandria." *Der Islam* 12 (1921):29–84.

ʿAlī Jawāhir Kalām. *Zanda-rūd yā Jughrāfiyā-i Tāʾrīkhī-yi Iṣfahan va Julfā.* Tehran, A.H. 1390–91/A.D. 1970–71.

J. von Karabaček. *Die Persische Nadelmalerei Susanschird.* Leipzig, 1881.

———. *Zur Orientalischen Altertumskunde, I. Die Arabischen Papyrusprotokolle: Sitzungsb. Phil.-Hist. Kl., Akademie, Wien.* Vol. 161, 1909.

Bahman Karīmī. *Jughrāfiyā-yi Tāʾrīkhī-yi Mufaṣṣal-i Gharbi-i Īrān.* Tehran, A.H. 1317/A.D. 1938.

Sayyidah Ismāʿīl Kāshif. *Miṣr fī ʿAṣr al-Wulāt.* Al-Qāhirah, n.d.

Sayyid Ahmad Kasravī. *Pādshāhān-i Gumnām-i Īrān.* Fascs. 1–3. Tehran, A.H. 1347–49.

Irfan Kawar [Irfan Shahīd]. "Arethas, son of Jabalah." *Journal of the American Oriental Society* 75 (1955):205–16.

———. "The Arabs in the peace treaty of A.D. 561." *Arabica* 3 (1957):181–213.

———. "Procopius on the Ghassānids." *Journal of the American Oriental Society* 77 (1957):79–87.

———. "Ghassān and Byzantium: a new terminus a quo." *Der Islam* 33 (1958):145–58.

———. "The last days of Salīḥ." *Arabica* 5 (1958):145–58.

———. "The Etymology of Ḥîra." In *Linguistic Studies in Memory of Richard Slade Harrell,* edited by Don Graham Stuart. Washington, D.C., 1967.

———. *Rome and the Arabs: A Prolegomenon to the Study of Byzantium and the Arabs.* Washington, D.C., 1984.

———. *Byzantium and the Arabs in the Fifth Century.* Washington, D.C., 1989.

———. *Byzantium and the Arabs in the Sixth Century.* Washington, D.C., 1995.

Henry Cassels Kay. *Yaman, Its Early Medaeval History.* London, 1892. Reprint, Farnborough, Hampshire, England, 1968.

Edward J. Keall. "The dynamics of Zabid and its hinterland: the survey of a town on the Tihamah plain of North Yemen." *World Archaeology* 14, no. 3 (1983):378–92.

Benjamin Z. Kedar. "The Arab conquests and agriculture: a seventh-century apocalypse, satellite imagery, and palynology." *Asian and African Studies* 19 (1985):1–15.

Hugh Kennedy. "The last century of Byzantine Syria: a reinterpretation." *Byzantinisches Forschungen* 10 (1985):141–83.

———. "From polis to *madīna:* urban change in late antique and early Islamic Syria." *Past and Present,* no. 106 (1985):3–27.

———. "The Towns of Bilād al-Shām and the Arab Conquest." In *Proceedings of the Symposium on Bilād al-Shām during the Byzantine Period, Muḥarram 9–13, 1404 A.H./November 15–19, 1983,* edited by M. A. Bakhīt and M. Asfour. ʿAmmān, 1986.

———. *The Prophet and the Age of the Caliphates. The Islamic Near East from the Sixth to the Eleventh Century.* London and New York, 1986.

———. "Egypt as a Province in the Islamic Caliphate, 641–868." In *The Cambridge History of Egypt,* vol. 1, *Islamic Egypt, 640–1517,* edited by Carl F. Petry. Cambridge, 1998.

Hugh Kennedy and John F. Haldon. "The Arab-Byzantine frontier in the eighth and ninth centuries." *Recueil des Travaux de l'Institut d'Études Byzantines* (Belgrade) 19 (1980):79–116.

Hugh Kennedy and J. H. W. G. Liebeschuetz. "Antioch and the villages of Northern Syria in the fifth and sixth centuries A.D.: trends and problems." *Nottingham Medieval Studies* 32 (1989):65–90.

Monique Kervran. "Transformations de la ville de Suse et de son économie de l'époque sasanide à l'époque abbaside." *Paléorient* 11, no. 2 (1985):91–100.

Monique Kervran and Axelle Rougelle. "Recherche sur les niveaux islamiques de la ville des Artisans." In *Cahiers de la Délégation Française en Iran.* Paris, 1984.

B. Khalateantz. *Textes Arabes Relatifs à l'Arménie.* Vienne, 1919.

Ismāʿīl R. Khālidi. "The Arab kingdom of Ghassan: its origins, rise, and fall." *Moslem World* 46 (1956):193–206.

Tarif Khalidi. *Islamic Historiography: The Histories of Masʿūdī.* Albany, N.Y., 1975.

———. "Some Classical Islamic Views of the City." In *Studia Arabica: Festschrift for Ihsān ʿAbbās on His Sixtieth Birthday,* edited by Wadād al-Qāḍī. Beirut, 1981.

Rami G. Khouri. *Jerash: A Frontier City of the Roman East.* London, 1986.

———. *Amman: A Brief Guide to the Antiquities.* Amman, 1988.

———. *The Antiquities of the Jordan Rift Valley.* Amman, 1988.

Nuha N. N. Khoury. "The Dome of the rock, the Kaʿba, and Ghumdan: Arab myths and Umayyad monuments." *Muqarnas* 10 (1993): 57–65.

———. "The mihrab: from text to form." *International Journal of Middle East Studies* 30 (1998): 1–27.

Raif Georges Khoury. *Abd Allāh ibn Lahiʿa (97–174/715–790): Juge et Grand Maître de l'École Égptienne.* In *Codices Arabici Antiqui,* vol. 4. Wiesbaden, 1986.

Muḥammad Jaʿfar al-Ḥusaynī Khurmūjī. *Tāʾrīkh-i Shīrāz.* Tehran, A.H. 1276/A.D. 1860.

Alastair C. Killick, ed. *Udruh: Caravan City and Desert Oasis.* Romsey, England, 1987.

David A. King. "The earliest Islāmic mathematical methods and tables for finding the direction of Mecca." *Zeitschrift für Geschichte der Arabisch-Islamischen Wissenshaften* 3 (1986): 82–149.

———. "The orientation of medieval Islamic architecture and cities." *Journal for the History of Astronomy* 26 (1995): 253–74.

David A. King and Richard P. Lorch. "Qibla Charts, Qibla Maps, and Related Instruments." In *The History of Cartography,* vol. 2, bk. 1, *Cartography in the Traditional Islamic and South Asian Societies,* edited by J. B. Harley and David Woodward, Chicago, 1992–.

G. R. D. King. "Islamic archaeology in Libya, 1969–1989." *Libyan Studies* 20 (1989): 193–207.

G. R. D. King and Averil Cameron, eds. *The Byzantine and Early Islamic Near East,* vol. 2: *Land Use and Settlement Patterns.* Princeton, N.J., 1994.

Leslie J. King. "A multivariate analysis of the spacing of urban settlements in the United States." *Annals of the Association of American Geographers* 51 (1961): 222–23.

———. "A quantitative expression of the pattern of urban settlements in selected areas of the United States." *Tijdschrift vóór Economische en Sociale Geographie* 53 (1962): 1–7.

———. *Central Place Theory.* Beverly Hills, Calif., 1984.

Paul Kirchhoff. "The principles of clanship in human society." *Davidson Journal of Anthropology* 1 (1955): 1–10.

Meir J. Kister. "Mecca and Tamīm (aspects of their relations)." *Journal of the Economic and Social History of the Orient* 8 (1965): 113–63.

———. "Al-Ḥîra: some notes on its relations with Arabia." *Arabica* 15 (1968): 143–69.

———. "'You shall only set out for three mosques': a study of an early tradition." *Le Muséon* (1969): 173–96.

———. "A bag of meat." *Bulletin of the School of Oriental and African Studies* 33 (1970): 267–75.

———. "Some reports concerning Mecca from Jāhiliyya to Islam." *Journal of the Economic and Social History of the Orient* 15 (1972): 61–93.

———. "Labbayka, Allāhumma, labbayka . . .: on a monotheistic aspect of a Jāhiliyya practice." *Jerusalem Studies in Arabic and Islam* 8 (1986): 47–48.

———. "'Do not assimilate yourselves . . .': *lā tashabbahū* (with appendix)." *Jerusalem Studies in Arabic and Islam* 12 (1989): 321–71.

S. Klein. "Asya." In *J. Freimann Jubilee Volume* (Berlin, 1937), 116ff.

Ernst Axel Knauf. "Umm el-Jimāl: an Arab town in late Antiquity." *Revue Biblique* 91 (1984): 578–86.

J. H. Kolb. *Service Relations of Town and Country.* Research Bulletin no. 58, Agricultural Experiment Station of the University of Wisconsin. Madison, 1923.

J. H. Kolb and E. de S. Brunner. *A Study of Human Society.* 2d ed. Boston, 1940.

J. Koren and Y. D. Nevo. "Methodological approaches to Islamic studies." *Der Islam* 68 (1991): 87–107.

I. Yu Kračkoviskiy. *Arabskaya Geografičeskaya Literatura.* Moscow-Leningrad, 1957.

———. *Izbrannîe sočineniya.* Moscow-Leningrad, 1957.

C. H. Kraeling, ed. *Gerasa, City of the Decapolis.* New Haven, 1938.

Johannes Henrik Kramers. "La question Balḫî-Iṣṭaḫrî-Ibn Ḥauqal et l'atlas de l'Islam." *Acta Orientalia* 10 (1932): 9–30.

F. Krenkow. "The annual fairs of the pagan Arabs." *Islamic Culture* 21 (1946): 111–13.

J. Kritzeck and R. Bayly Winder, eds. *The World of Islam: Studies in Honour of Philip K. Hitti.* London, 1959.

John R. Krueger. "A note on Alexander's Arabic epithet." *Journal of the American Oriental Society* 81, no. 4 (1961): 426–27.

Doğan Kuban. *Muslim Religious Architecture.* Part 1 of *The Mosque and Its Early Development.* Leiden, 1974.

Ḥamdān ʿAbd al-Majīd al-Kubaysī. *Aswaq Baghdād ḥattā Bidāyah al-ʿAṣr al-Buwayhī.* Baghdād, A.H. 1399.

Władysław B. Kubiak. *Al-Fustat: Its Foundation and Early Urban Development.* Cairo, 1987.

Władysław Kubiak and George T. Scanlon. *Fusṭāṭ Expedition Final Report.* Volume 2. Winona Lake, Ind., 1989.

Ernst Kühnel. "Mschatta." In *Bilderhefte der Islamischen Kustabteilung.* Pt. 2. Berlin, 1933.

Muḥammad Kurd ʿAlī. *Khiṭaṭ al-Shām.* 6 vols. Dimashq, A.H. 1343–47, A.D. 1925–28.

Kuwabara Jitsuzō. "On Pʿu Shou-keng, a man of the western regions. . . ." *Memoir of the Research Department of the Tōyō Bunkō,* vol. 2 (1928): 1–79; vol. 7 (1935): 1–104 [This is an English translation of an article that was originally published in *Shigaku Zasshi,* vols. 26–29 (1915–18).]

Z. van Laer. "La ville de Carthage dans le sourat es arabes des XIe–XIIIe secles." In *Studia Phoenicia,* vol. 6, *Carthago* (Leuven, 1988), 245–58.

Léon Lalanne. "Essai d'une théorie des réseaux de chemin de fer, fondée sur l'observation des faits et sur les lois primordiales qui président au groupement des populations." *Comptes Rendus Hebdomadaires des Séances de l'Academie des Sciences* 42 (1863): 206–10.

Alistair Lamb. "A visit to Siraf, an ancient port on the Persian Gulf." *Journal of the Malayan Branch of the Royal Asiatic Society* 37, pt. 1 (1964): 1–19.

Ann K. S. Lambton. "An account of the *Tārīkh-i Qumm.*" *Bulletin of the School of Oriental and African Studies* 12 (1948): 585–96.

Henri Lammens. "La 'bādia' et le 'ḥīra' sous les Omayyades: le problème de Mśattā." *Mélanges de la Faculté Orientale [de Beyrouth]* 4 (1910).

———. "La république marchande de la Mecque vers l'an 600 de

notre ère." *Bulletin de l'Institut Egyptien,* 5th ser., 4 (1910): 23–54.

———. "Ziad ibn Abihi vice-roi de l'Iraq." *Rivista degli Studi Orientali* 4 (1911–12): 1–145, 199–250, 653–93.

———. *Le Berceau de l'Islam. L'Arabie Occidentale à la Vielle de l'Hégire.* Vol. 1, *Le Climat—les Bédouins.* Rome, 1914.

———. "Le culte des bétyles." *Bulletin de l'Institut Français d'Archéologie Orientale* 17 (Cairo, 1919).

———. "La cité arabe de Ṭaif à la veille de l'hégire." *Mélanges de l'Université Saint-Joseph, Beyrouth (Syrie)* 8, fasc. 4 (1922): 132[20]–134[22].

———. "La Mecque à la veille de l'Hegire." *Mélanges de l'Université Saint-Joseph, Beyrouth (Syrie)* 9 (1924): 180 et seq.

———. "Les sanctuaires préislamites dans l'Arabie occidentale." *Mélanges de l'Université Saint-Joseph, Beyrouth (Syrie),* 11 (1926): 39–173.

———. *Etudes sur le Siècle des Omayyades.* Beyrouth, 1930.

William Lancaster. *The Rwala Bedouin Today.* Cambridge, 1981.

Ella Landau-Tasseron. "Sayf ibn ʿUmar in medieval and modern scholarship." *Der Islam,* band 67 (1990): 1–26.

H. Laoust. "La vie et la Philosophie d'Abū al-ʿAlā al-Maʿrrī." *Bulletin d'Etudes Orientales d'Institut Français des Etudes Arabes de Damas,* vol. 10.

Ira M. Lapidus. "The conversion of Egypt to Islam." *Israel Oriental Studies* 2 (1972): 248–62.

———. "The early evolution of Muslim urban institutions." *Comparative Studies in Society and History* 15, no. 1 (1973): 21–50.

———. "Traditional Muslim Cities: Structure and Change." In *From Madina to Metropolis. Heritage and Change in the Near Eastern City,* edited by L. Carl Brown, 51–72. Princeton, N.J., 1973.

———. "The separation of state and religion in the development of early Islamic society." *International Journal of Middle East Studies* 5 (1975): 363–85.

———. "Arab Settlement and Economic Development of Iraq and Iran in the Age of the Umayyad and Early Abbasid Caliphs." In *The Islamic Middle East, 700–1900: Studies in Economic and Social History,* edited by A. L. Udovitch. Princeton, N.J., 1981.

———. "The Arab conquests and the formation of Islamic society." In *Studies on the First Century of Islamic Society,* edited by G. H. A. Juynboll, 49–72. Carbondale, Ill., 1982.

———. *A History of Islamic Societies* (Cambridge, 1988).

———, ed. *Middle Eastern Cities. A Symposium on Ancient, Islamic, and Contemporary Middle Eastern Urbanism.* Berkeley and Los Angeles, 1969.

Abdallah Laroui. *L'Histoire du Maghreb: un Essai de Synthèse.* Paris, 1970. English translation under the title *The History of the Maghrib* (Princeton, N.J., 1977).

Jacob Lassner. "The *ḥabl* of Baghdād and the dimensions of the city: a metrological note." *Journal of the Economic and Social History of the Orient* 6 (1963): 228–29.

———. *The Topography of Baghdād in the Early Middle Ages. Text and Studies.* Detroit, 1970.

———. *The Shaping of ʿAbbāsid Rule.* Princeton, N.J., 1980.

———. *Khutat Baghdād fi al-ʾuhud al-ʾAbbasiyah al-ulʾa.* Baghdād, 1984.

Curtis E. Larsen. *Life and Land Use on the Bahrain Islands.* Chicago, 1983.

Harold D. Lasswell and Abraham Kaplan. *Power and Society. A Framework for Political Inquiry.* New Haven, Conn., 1950.

Berthold Laufer. *Sino-Iranica. Chinese Contributions to the History of Civilization in Ancient Iran.* Field Museum of Natural History Publication 201: Anthropological Series vol. 15, no. 3. Chicago, 1919.

J. Laurent. *L'Arménie entre Byzance et l'Islam depuis la Conquête Arabe Jusqʼen 886.* Paris, 1919.

Pierre Lavedan. *Histoire de l'Urbanisme.* 3 vols. Paris, 1926–52.

———. *Géographie des Villes.* Paris, 1936.

Michael Lecker. "The estates of ʿAmr b. al-ʿAṣ in Palestine: notes on a new Negev Arabic inscription." *Bulletin of the School of Oriental and African Studies* 52 (1989): 24–37.

———. *Judaism among Kinda and the Ridda* of Kinda." *Journal of the American Oriental Society* 115, no. 4 (1995): 635–50.

———. *Muslims, Jews and Pagans. Studies on Early Islamic Medina.* Leiden, 1995.

Stefan Leder. "Authorship and transmission in unauthored literature: the Axbār attributed to al-Haitam ibn ʿAdī." *Oriens* 31 (1988).

Anthony Leeds and Andrew P. Vayda, eds. *Man, Culture and Animals. The Role of Animals in Human Ecological Adjustment.* Washington, 1965.

Karl Lehmann. "The Dome of Heaven." *Art Bulletin* 14, no. 1 (1945).

W. Leibeschuetz. *Antioch in the Age of Libanius.* Oxford, 1972.

C. J. Lenzen. "Beit Ras excavations: 1988 and 1989." *Syria* 67 (1990): 474–76.

C. J. Lenzen and E. A. Knauf. "Beit Ras/Capitolias: a preliminary evaluation of the archaeological and textual evidence." *Syria* 64 (1987): 21–46.

Guy Le Strange. "Description of Syria, including Palestine. By Mukaddasi (circa 985 A.D.)." *Palestine Pilgrims' Text Society* 3 (1886): i–xvi, 1–116. Reprint, New York, 1971.

———. *Palestine under the Moslems.* London, 1890.

———. "Description of Mesopotamia and Baghdād written about the year 900 A.D. by Ibn Serapion . . . ," *Journal of the Royal Asiatic Society* (1895): 1–76, 255–315.

———. "On the medieval castle and sanctuary of Abrīk, the modern Arabkir; with some further notes on Mesopotamia as described by Ibn Serapion." *Journal of the Royal Asiatic Society* (1895): 739–49.

———. "The cities of Kirman in the time of Ḥamd Allah . . . Mustawfī and Marco Polo." *Journal of the Royal Asiatic Society* (1901): 281–90.

———. *The Lands of the Eastern Caliphate.* Cambridge, 1905.

Roger Le Tourneau. "North Africa to the Sixteenth Century." In *The Cambridge History of Islam,* vol. 2, edited by P. M. Holt, Ann K. S. Lambton, and Bernard Lewis. Cambridge, 1970.

Yaacov Lev. "The Faṭimid vizier Yaʿqūb ibn Killis and the beginning of the Faṭimid administration in Egypt." *Der Islam* 58 (1981): 237–49.

G. Levi della Vida. "Pre-Islamic Arabia." In *The Arab Heritage,* edited by N. A. Farris. Princeton, N.J., 1944.

Évariste Lévi-Provençal. *L'Espagne Musulmane au Xième Siècle.* Paris, 1932.

———. *La Péninsule Ibérique au Moyen Age d'après la "Kitab ar-Rawd al-Miʿṭar."* Leyden, 1938.

———. *Histoire de l'Espagne Musulmane.* 3 vols. Paris, 1944–53.

———. *Islam d'Occident.* Paris, 1948.

———. "Un nouveau récit de la conquête de l'Afrique du Nord par les Arabes." *Arabica* 1 (1954): 17–43.

L. I. Levine. *Caesaria under Roman Rule.* Leiden, 1975.

Nehemia Levtzion. "Ibn Ḥawqal, the cheque, and Awdaghost." *Journal of African History* 9 (1968): 223–33.

———. *Ancient Ghana and Mali.* London, 1973.

T. E. Levy, ed. *The Archaeology of Society in the Holy Land.* London, 1995.

Lucien Lévy-Bruhl. *L'Âme Primitive.* Paris, 1927.

Ronald Lewcock. *The Old Walled City of Ṣanʿāʾ.* Paris, 1986.

———. *Wadī Ḥaḍramawt and the Walled City of Shibām.* Paris, 1986.

Tadeusz Lewicki. "Les premiers commerçants arabes en Chine." *Rocznik Orientalistyczny* 11 (1935): 176–81.

———. "Une langue romane oubliée de l'Afrique du Nord." *Rocznik Orientalistyczny* 17 (1951–52): 417–19.

———. "La répartition géographique des groupements ibāḍites dans l'Afrique du Nord au moyen-âge." *Rocznik Orientalistyczny* 21 (1957): 301–43.

———. "Les subdivisions de l'Ibadiyya." *Studia Islamica* 9 (1958).

———. "Les historiens, biographes et traditionistes ibādites-wahbites de l'afrique du Nord du VIIIe au XVIe siècle." *Folia Orientalia* 3 (1961–62): 105–6.

———. "L'état nord-africain de Tāhert et ses relations avec le Soudan occidental à la fin d VIIIe et au IXe siècle." *Cahiers d'Etudes Africaines* 2 (1962): 513–35.

Bernard Lewis. *The Arabs in History.* New York, 1960.

Naphtali Lewis. *Life in Egypt under Roman Rule.* Oxford, 1983.

Alexandre Lézine. *Mahdia.* Paris, 1965.

———. *Deux Villes d'Ifriqiya, Sousse, Tunis.* Paris, 1971.

Baruch Lifschitz. "Scythopolis: l'histoire, les institutions et les cultes de la ville à l'époque hellénistique et impériale." *Aufstieg und Niedergang der Römischen Welt* 2 (1978): 262–92.

Ralph-Johannes Lilie. *Die Byzantinische Reaktion auf die Ausbreitung der Araber.* Miscellanea Byzantina Monacensis XXII. München, 1976.

M. Lindner. *Petra und das Königreich der Nabatäer.* 3d ed. München, 1968.

Arnold S. Linsky. "Some generalizations concerning primate cities." *Annals of the Association of American Geographers* 55, no. 3 (1965): 506–13.

E. O. von Lippmann. *Geschichte des Zuckers.* Leipzig, 1890.

E. Littmann. *Thamūd und Safa.* Leipzig, 1940.

H. V. Livermore. *The Origins of Spain and Portugal.* London, 1971.

Laurence Lockhart. *Persian Cities.* London, 1960.

Frede Loekkegaard. *Islamic Taxation in the Classical Period.* Copenhagen, 1950.

August Lösch. *Die räumliche Ordnung der Wirtschaft.* Jena, Germany, 1944.

Otto Loth. "Die Vulkanregionen (Ḥarra's) von Arabien nach Jaḳut." *Zeitschrift der Deutschen Morgenländischen Gesellschaft* 22 (1868): 365–82.

A. J. Lotka. "The law of urban concentration." *Science* 94 (1941).

A. G. Loundine [Lundin] and Jacques Ryckmans. "Nouvelles données sur la chronologie des rois de Sabaʾ et Ḏū-Raydān." *Le Muséon* 77 (1964): 407–27. *See also* A. G. Lundin.

Nicholas M. Lowick. *Siraf XV. The Coins and Monumental Inscriptions.* London, 1985.

D. D. Luckenbill. *Ancient Records of Assyria and Babylonia.* 2 vols. Chicago, 1927.

ʿA. ʿA. al-Lumaylim. *Nufūdh al-Atrāk fī al-Khilāfah al-ʿAbbasīyah.* Riyad, A.H. 1404.

A. Lumpe. "Zur Kulturgeschichte des Bades in der Byzantinischen Ära." *Byzantinische Forschungen* 6 (1979): 151–66.

A. G. Lundin. "Južnaja Aravija v VI. veke." *Palestinskij Sbornik* 8 (1961): 17 et seq.

———. "Eponymat sabéen et chronologie sabéenne." In *XXVI Congrès International des Orientalistes, Conf. Pres. par la Delegation de l'USSR.* Moscow, 1963.

———. "Le régime citadin de l'Arabie du Sud aux IIe–IIIe siècles de notre ère." In *Proceedings of the Sixth Seminar for Arabian Studies* (London, 1973), 26–28. First published in Russian in *Pis'mennye Pamjatniki i Problemy Istorii Kul'tury Narodov Azii* 5 (1969): 55–57.

Nimrod Luz. "The construction of an Islamic city in Palestine. The case of Umayyad al-Ramlah." *Journal of the Royal Asiatic Society,* ser. 3, vol. 7 (1997): 27–54.

ʿAbd al-Qādir Sulaymān al-Maʿādīdī. *Wāsiṭ fī al-ʿAṣr al-Umawī.* Baghdād, A.H. 1396.

———. *Wāsiṭ fī al-ʿAṣr al-ʿAbbāsī.* Baghdād, A.H. 1403.

Henry Innes MacAdam. "Boston Gloriosa." *Berytus* 34 (1986): 169–92.

———. "Settlements and Settlement Patterns in Northern and Central Transjordania, ca. 550–ca. 750." In *Land Use and Settlement Patterns,* vol. 2 of *The Byzantine and Early Islamic Near East,* edited by G. R. D. King and Averil Cameron. Princeton, N.J., 1994.

Burton MacDonald, ed. *The Southern Ghors and Northeast ʿArabah Archaeological Survey.* Sheffield, England, 1992.

James Rose MacPherson. "Pilgrimage of Arculfus in the Holy Land (about the year A.D. 670)." In *Palestine Pilgrims' Text Society.* London, 1889.

ʿAbd al-Muhsin al-Madʿaj. *The Yemen in Early Islam, 9–233; 630–847: A Political History.* University of Durham Middle East Monograph 3 (Durham, England, 1988).

ʿUbayd al-Madanī. "Uṭūm al-Madīnah al-Munawwarah." *Journal of the College of Arts at the King Saud University* 3 (1973–74): 213–26.

Wilferd Madelung. "Fatimiden und Bahrainqarmaten." *Der Islam* 34 (1959): 34–88.

———. *Der Imam al-Qāsim b. Ibrāhīm und die Glaubenslehre der Zaiditen.* Berlin, 1966.

———. "The ʿAlid Rulers of Ṭabaristān, Daylamān and Gīlān." In *Atti de III Congresso di Studi Arabi e Islamici.* Napoli, 1967.

———. "The Minor Dynasties of Northern Iran." In *The Cam-*

bridge History of Iran, Vol. 4: *The Period from the Arab Invasion to the Saluqs,* edited by R. N. Frye, 198–249. Cambridge, 1975.

———. "Apocalyptic prophecies in Ḥimṣ in the Umayyad age." *Journal of Semitic Studies* 31 (1986): 141–85.

———. *The Succession to Muḥammad. A Study of the Early Caliphate.* Cambridge, 1997.

O. Maenchen. "Huns and Hsiung-nu." *Byzantion* 17 (1945): 225–31.

S. Mahlī. *Ḥimṣ: Umm al-Hijār al-Sūd.* Dimashq, ?A.H. 1383.

George Makdisī. "Notes on Ḥilla and the Mazyadids in medieval Islam." *Journal of the American Oriental Society* 74 (1954): 249–62.

———. "The topography of eleventh century Baghdād: materials and notes." *Arabica* 6 (1959): 178–97, 281–309.

A. Makkī. *Qudāma b. Ǧaʿfar et Son Oeuvre.* Paris, 1955.

Joannes Malalas. *Chronographia.* Edited by L. Dindorf. Bonn, 1831.

Prince P. H. Mamour. *Polemics on the Origin of the Fatimi Caliphs.* London, 1934.

Hakob A. Manandian. "Les invasions arabes en Arménie." *Byzantion* 18 (1946–48), 163–92.

Cyril Mango. "The Temple Mount A.D. 614–638." In *Bayt al-Maqdis: ʿAbd al-Malik's Jerusalem,* pt. 1, edited by Julian Raby and Jeremy Johns. Oxford, 1992.

Mohammad Abd el-Maqsoud. "Excavations at Tell el-Farama (Pelusium)." *Annales de la Service des Antiquités de l'Égypte* 70 (1984–85): 3–8.

Georges Marçais. "Achir (Recherches d'Archéologie Musulmane)." *Revue Africaine* (1922): 21–38.

———. "Note sur les ribaṭs en Berbérie." In *Mélanges René Basset,* vol. 2 (Paris, 1925), 395–430.

———. "La Berbérie au IXe siècle d'après el-Yaʿqoûbî." *Revue Africaine* (1941): 40–61.

———. "La conception de villes dans l'Islâm." *Revue d'Alger* 2, no. 10 (1945): 517–33.

———. *La Berbérie Musulmane et l'Orient au Moyen Âge.* Paris, 1946.

William Marçais. "Les siècles obscurs du Maghreb." *Revue Critique d'Histoire et de Littérature* (1929): 255–70.

———. "Comment l'Afrique du nord a été arabisée." *Annales de l'Institut d'Etudes Orientales de l'Université d'Alger* 17 (1938): 1–22.

———. *Articles et Conferences: Publications de l'Institut d'Etudes Orientales, Faculté des Lettres d'Alger* 21. Paris, 1961.

W. Harold Mare. "Quwailiba: Abila of the Decapolis." *Archiv für Orientforschung* 33 (1986): 206–209.

J. Margat. "Note sur la morphologie du site de Sijilmassa (Tafilalt)." *Hespéris* 3–4 (1959): 254–60.

D. S. Margoliouth. "The Russian seizure of Bardhaʿah in 943 A.D." *Bulletin of the School of Oriental and African Studies* 3 (1918): 82–95.

———. *Mohammed.* London, 1939.

Josef Markwart [Marquart]. *Ērānšahr nach der Geographie des Ps. Moses Xorenacʿi. Mit Historisch-Kritischen Kommentar und Historischen und Topographischen Excursen.* Abhandlungen der Königlichen Gesellschaft der Wissenschaften zu Göttingen, Phil.-Hist. Kl., n.s., vol. 3. Berlin, 1901.

———. *Osteuropäische und ostasiatische Streifzüge.* Leipzig, 1903.

———. *Südarmenien und die Tigrisquellen nach Griechischen und Arabischen Geographen.* Wien, 1930.

———. *A Catalogue of the Principal Capitals of Ērānšahr.* Edited by G. Messina. Rome, 1931.

———. *Wehrot und Arang. Untersuchungen zur Mythischen und Geschichtlichen Landeskunde von Ostiran.* Edited by H. H. Schaeder. Leiden, 1938.

J. Marquart and J. J. M. de Groot. "Das Reich Zābul und der Gott Žūn vom 6–9 Jahrhundert." In *Festschrift Eduard Sachau.* Berlin, 1915.

A.-S. Marmardji. *Textes Géographiques Arabes sur la Palestine, Recueillis, Mis en Ordre Alphabétique et Traduits en Français.* Paris, 1951.

A. Masmoudi. "Les Fonctions Urbaines de Mahdia." Doctoral thesis, University of Paris, published at Tūnis, 1985.

Jean Maspero and Gaston Wiet. *Matériaux pour Servir à la Géographie de l'Égypte.* Vol. 36 of *Memoires Publiés par les Membres de l'Institut Français de l'Archéologie Orientale du Caire.* Le Caire (Cairo), 1919.

Louis Massignon. *Lexique Technique de la Mystique Musulmane.* Paris, 1922.

———. "Salmân Pâk et les prémices spirituelles de l'Islam iranien." *Publications de la Société des Etudes Iraniennes,* no. 7 (1934).

———. "Explication du plan de Kûfa (Irak)." In *Mélanges Maspéro.* Vol. 3. Le Caire, 1940.

———. "L'Umma et ses synonymes: notion de 'communauté sociale' en Islam." *Revue des Etudes Islamiques* 15, pt. 1 (1941–46, but published in 1947): 151–57.

———. "Explication du plan de Baṣra (Irak)." In *Westöstliche Abhandlungen: Rudolf Tschudi zum Siebzigsten Geburtstag überrecht von Freunden und Schülern,* edited by Fritz Meier. Wiesbaden, 1954.

V. M. Masson and V. A. Romodin. *Istoriia Afghanistana.* Moscow, 1964.

C. D. Matthews. "The Muṯir al-Gharām of Abū-l-Fidāʾ of Hebron." *Journal of the Palestine Oriental Society* 17 (1937): 108–137, 149–208.

Philip Mayerson. "The First Muslim Attacks on Southern Palestine (A.D. 633–634)." In *Transactions and Proceedings of the American Philological Association* 95 (1964): 155–99.

Aly Mazahéri. *La Vie Quotidienne des Musulmans au Moyen Âge Xe au XIIIe siècle.* Paris, 1951.

R. D. McChesney, ed. *A Way Prepared. Essays on Islamic Culture in Honor of Richard Bayly Winder.* New York, 1988.

A. W. McNicoll and A. Walmsley. "Pella/Fahl in Jordan during the early Islamic Period." In *Studies in the History and Archaeology of Jordan,* no. 1, edited by Adnan Hadidi. Amman, 1982.

Alison McQuitty. "Bait Ras." *Archiv für Orientforschung* 33 (1986): 153–55.

Surinder K. Mehta. "Some demographic and economic correlates of primate cities: a case for reevaluation." *Demography* 1, no. 2 (1964): 136–47.

Fritz Meier, ed. *Westöstliche Abhandlungen: Rudolf Tschudi zum Siebzigsten Geburtstag überreicht von Freunden und Schülern.* Wiesbaden, 1954.

Richard L. Meier. "The Organization of Technological Innovation in Urban Environments." In *The Historian and the City,* edited by Oscar Handlin and John Burchard. Cambridge, Mass., 1963.

A. S. Melikian-Chirvani. "L'évocation littéraire du Bouddhisme dans l'Iran musulman." *Le Monde Iranian et l'Islam,* 2 (1974): 1–72.

Birgit Mershen and Ernst Axel Knauf. "From Gadar to Umm Qais." *Zeitschrift des Deutschen Palästina-Vereins* 104 (1988): 128–45.

Ronald A. Messier. "Local economy and long distance trade in medieval Sijilmasa." *Al-ʿUṣūr al-Wusṭā* 5, no. 1 (1993): 1–6.

M. A. Meyer. *A History of the City of Gaza.* New York, 1907.

Adam Mez. *Die Renaissance des Islâms.* Heidelberg, 1922. English translation by Salahuddin Khuda-Bakhsh and D. S. Margoliouth under the title *The Renaissance of Islam* (Patna, India, 1937).

George C. Miles. "Some New Light on the History of Kirmān in the First Century of the Hijrah." In *The World of Islam: Studies in Honour of Philip K. Hitti,* edited by James Kritzeck and R. Bayly Winder. London, 1959.

J. Innes Miller. *The Spice Trade of the Roman Empire, 29 B.C. to A.D. 641.* Oxford, 1969.

Konrad Miller. *Mappae Arabicae: Arabische Welt- und Länderkarten des 9.–13. Jahrhunderts.* 6 vols. Stuttgart, 1926–31. Extracts and index arranged by Heinz Gaube under the title *Beihefte zum Tübinger Atlas des vorderen Orients,* Reihe B, Geisteswissenschaften no. 65, 2 vols. (Wiesbaden, 1986).

Roy Andrew Miller. *Accounts of Western Nations in the History of the Northern Chou Dynasty.* Chinese Dynastic Histories Translations no. 6. Berkeley, 1959.

William G. Millward. "A Study of al-Yaʿqūbī with Special Reference to His Alleged Shi'ah Bias." Ph.D. diss., Princeton University, 1961.

V. Minorsky. "Transcaucasica." *Journal Asiatique* (1930): 41–56.

———. *La Domination des Dailamites.* Publications de la Société des Etudes Iraniennes, no. 3. Paris, 1932.

———. "A false Jayhānī." *Bulletin of the School of Oriental and African Studies* 13 (1949): 89–96.

———. "La deuxième risala d'Abu-Dulaf." *Oriens* 5 (1952): 23–27.

———. *Studies in Caucasian History.* London, 1952.

———. *A History of Sharvān and Darband in the 10th and 11th Centuries.* Cambridge, 1953.

———. *Abū-Dulaf Misʿar ibn al-Muhalhil's Travels in Iran (circa A.D. 950).* Cairo, 1955.

———. "Ibn Farīghūn and the Ḥudud al-ʿAlam." In *A Locust's Leg. Studies in Honour of S. H. Taqizadeh.* London, 1962.

André Miquel. *Aḥsan at-Tāqasīm fī Maʿrifat al-Aqālīm.* Damas, 1963.

———. *La Géographie Humaine du Monde Musulman jusqu'au Milieu du IIe Siècle.* Paris and La Haye, 1967.

———. "L'Egypte vue par un géographe arabe du IVe/Xe siècle: al-Muqaddasī." *Annales Islamologiques* 11 (1972): 109–39.

K. Mlaker. *Die Hierodulenlisten von Maʿīn.* Leipzig, 1943.

———. "Chronologisches." In *Zur südarabische Epigrafik und Archäologie II. Wienen Zeitschrift für die Kunde des Morgenlandes,* by M. Höfner, K. Mlaker, and Nikolaus Rhodokanakis. Wien, 1934.

Ugo Monneret de Villard. "Ricerche sulla topografia di Qasr eš-Šam." *Bulletin de la Société Géographique d'Égypte* 12 (1923–24): 205–32; 13 (1924–25): 73–94.

Robert Montagne. *La Civilisation du Désert. Nomades d'Orient et d'Afrique.* Paris, 1947.

———. *The Berbers: Their Social and Political Organization.* English translation of the original French by David Seddon. London, 1973.

Albert Morabia. "Recherches sur quelques noms de couleur en arabe classique." *Studia Islamica* 21 (1964).

A. D. Mordtmann. "Hekatompylos. Ein Beitrag zur vergleichenden Geographie Persiens." *Sitzungsberichte der Königlichen Akademie der Wissenschaften zu München,* Phil.-Hist. Kl. 1 (1869): 497–536.

———. "Zur südarabischen Altertumskunde." *Zeitschrift der Deutschen Morgenländischen Gesellschaft* 46 (1892): 320–23; 47 (1893): 397–417.

Kōsei Morimoto. *The Fiscal Administration of Egypt in the Early Islamic Period.* Kyōtō, 1981.

Michael G. Morony. *Iraq after the Muslim Conquest.* Princeton, N.J., 1984.

———. "Conquerors and Conquered: Iran." In *Studies on the First Century of Islamic Society,* edited by G. H. A. Juynboll. Carbondale, Ill., 1982.

Sabatino Moscati, ed. *Le Antiche Divinità Semitiche.* Roma, 1958.

Roy P. Mottahedeh. *Loyalty and Leadership in an Early Islamic Society.* Princeton, N.J., 1980.

Sulaiman Mougdad. *Bosra: Historical and Archaeological Guide.* Translated by Henry Innes MacAdam. Damascus, 1978.

Khaleel Ibrahim al-Muaikel. *Study of the Archaeology of the Jawf Region, Saudi Arabia.* Riyadh, 1994 A.D./1414 A.H.

Sir William Muir. *The Life of Mohamet; with Introductory Chapters on the Original Sources . . .* 4 vols. London, 1858–61. Rev. abridged ed., Edinburgh, 1923.

———. *The Caliphate: Its Rise, Decline and Fall.* 1898. Reprint, Beirut, 1963.

D. H. Müller. "Die Burgen und Schlösser Südarabiens nach dem Iklîl des Hamdânî." *Sitzungsberichte der Akademie der Wissenschaften in Wien,* Phil.-Hist. Kl., Bd. 94 (1879): 335–423; Bd. 97 (1881): 955–1050.

Werner Müller. *Die Heilige Stadt.* Stuttgart, 1961.

Dieter Müller-Wodarg. "Die Landwirtschaft Ägyptens in der frühen ʿAbbāsidenzeit. . . ." *Der Islam* 31 (1954): 174–227.

Alois Musil. "Ḳuṣejr ʿAmra und andere Schlösser östlich von Moab." *Sitzungs-Berichte der Philos.-Hist. Klasse der K. Akad. der Wissenschaften* 144, pt. 7 (Wien, 1902): 5ff.

———. *Ḳuṣejr ʿAmra: I, Textband.* Wien, 1907.

———. *The Northern Ḥeǧâz.* New York, 1926.

———. *The Manners and Customs of the Rwala Bedouin.* New York, 1928.

Muḥammad ʿAlī Muṣṭafā. "Preliminary report on the excavations in Kūfa during the Third Season." *Sumer* 19 (1963): 36–64.

J. Muyldermans. *La Domination Arabe en Arménie: Extrait de l'Histoire Universelle de Vardan Traduit de l'Arménien et Annoté.* Louvain and Paris, 1927.

A. A. Naimi. "Un regard sur Ghor. Préambule: la géographie, l'histoire et les sites historiques." *Afghanistan* 4 (1949): 1–23.

ʿAbd al-Jabbār Nājī. *Al-Imārah al-Mazyadīyah, Dirāsah fī Waḍʿihā al-Siyāsī wa-l-Iqtiṣādī wa-l-Ijtimāʿī 387-558h.* Al-Baṣrah, n.d. (1971?).

C. A. Nallino. "Sulla costituzione delle tribù arabe prima dell'-islamismo." In *Raccolta di Scritti Editi e Inediti.* No. 3: Istituto per l'Oriente. Roma, 1941. Reprint of a paper written in 1893.

Naval Intelligence Division. *Persia.* Geographical Handbook Series, (British) Naval Intelligence Division. Oxford, 1945.

———. *Western Arabia and the Red Sea.* (British) Naval Intelligence Division. Oxford, 1946.

Cynthia Nelson, ed. *The Desert and the Sown: Nomads in the Wider Society.* University of California, Institute of International Studies Research Series no. 21. Berkeley, 1973.

Angelika Neuwirth. *Studien zur Komposition der mekkanischen Suren.* Studien zur Sprache, Geschichte, und Kultur des islamischen Orients, n.s., vol. 10. Berlin, 1981.

Jehuda D. Nevo and Judith Koren. "The origins of the Muslim descriptions of the Jāhilī Meccan sanctuary." *Journal of Near Eastern Studies* 49, no. 1 (1990):23–44.

Gordon D. Newby. "Abraha and Sennacherib: a Talmudic parallel to the tafsīr on Sūrat al-Fīl." *Journal of the American Oriental Society* 94, no. 4 (1974):431–37.

David Nicolle. "Arms manufacture and the arms trade in South-Eastern Arabia in the Early Muslim period." *The Journal of Oman Studies* 6 (1983):231–38.

Ditlef Nielsen, ed. *Handbuch der altarabischen Altertumskunde.* Vol. 1, *Die altarabische Kultur.* Copenhagen, 1927.

C. A. O. van Nieuwenhuijze. "The *ummah*—an analytic approach." *Studia Islamica* 70 (1959):5–22.

Theodor Nöldeke. "Zur Topographie und Geschichte des Damascenischen Gebietes und der Haurângegend." *Zeitschrift der Deutschen Morgenländischen Gesellschaft* 29 (1875):419–44.

———. *Geschichte der Perser und Araber sur Zeit der Sasaniden.* Leyden, 1879.

———. *Die Ghassânischen Fürsten aus dem Hause Gafna's. Abhandlungen der Königlichen Akademie der Wissenschaften zu Berlin.* Berlin, 1887. Arabic translation by Pendali Jousé and Costi Zurayk under the title *ʿUmarā Banī-Ghassān* (Bayrūt, 1933).

Theodor Nöldeke, Friedrich Schwally, Gotthelf Bergsträsser, and Otto Pretzl. *Geschichte des Qorāns.* 2d ed. 3 vols. Leipzig, 1909–38.

Alastair Northedge. "The Racecourses at Sāmarrā." *Bulletin of the School of Oriental and African Studies* 53 (1990):31–56.

———. *Samarra: Residenz der ʿAbbasidenkalifen 836–892 v. Chr. (221–279 Higri).* Eberhard-Karls-Universität Tübingen, Orientalisches Seminar, 1990.

———. "The palace at Iṣṭabulāt, Sāmarrā." *Archéologie Islamique* 3 (1992):61–86.

———. *Studies on Roman and Islamic Amman.* Oxford, 1992.

———. "Archaeology and New Urban Settlement in Early Islamic Syria and Iraq." In *The Byzantine and Early Islamic Near East,* edited by G. R. D. King and Averil Cameron. Princeton, N.J., 1994.

———. "Analyse du plan du palais du Caliphe al-Muʿtasim à Sāmarrāʾ." In *Colloque International d'Archéologie Islamique.* Le Caire (Cairo), 1998.

Albrecht Noth. "Iṣfahān-Nihāwand. Eine quellenkritische Studie zur frühislamischen Historiographie." *Zeitschrift der Deutschen Morgenländischen Gesellschaft,* 118 (1968):274–96.

———. *Quellenkritische Studien zu Themen, Formen und Tendenzen frühislamischer Geschichtsüberlieferung:* I, *Themen und Formen.* Bonn, 1973. Revised and expanded with the collaboration of Lawrence Conrad, under the title *The Early Arabic Historical Tradition: A Source Critical Study,* translated by Michael Bonner (Princeton, N.J., 1994).

Kalervo Oberg. "Types of social structure among the lowland tribes of South and Central America." *American Anthropologist* 57, no. 3 (1957):472–87.

Ignacio Olangüe. *La Revolución Islámica en Occidente.* Barcelona, 1974.

Gunnar Olinder. *The Kings of Kinda of the Family of Ākil al Murār.* Lunds Universitets Årsskrift, Ny Fôljd, Fôrsta Avdelningen. Lund, Sweden, 1927.

G. Olsson and A. Persson. "The Spacing of Central Places in Sweden." In *Papers and Proceedings of the Regional Science Association* 12 (1964):87–93.

A. Leo Oppenheim. *Ancient Mesopotamia. Portrait of a Dead Civilization.* Chicago, 1964.

———. "Mesopotamia—Land of Many Cities." In *Middle Eastern Cities. A Symposium on Ancient, Islamic, and Contemporary Middle Eastern Urbanism,* edited by Ira M. Lapidus. Berkeley and Los Angeles, 1969.

Max A. S. von Oppenheim. *Die Beduinen.* Vols. 1 and 2. Leipzig, 1939, 1943. Vols. 3 and 4 edited by Werner Caskel (Wiesbaden, 1952, 1968).

F. Osman. *Al-Ḥudūd al-Islāmīyah al-Bīzanṭīyah.* Al-Qāhirah, A.H. 1387–88.

G. Ostrogorsky. "Byzantine Cities in the Early Middle Ages." In *Dumbarton Oaks Papers,* vol. 13 (Cambridge, Mass., and Washington, D.C., 1959), 47–66.

Rudolf Otto. *Das Heilige.* New ed. München, 1947.

Walter F. Otto. *Die Götter Griechenlands: Das Bild des Göttlichen in Spiegel des Griechischen Geistes.* 2 vols. Frankfurt-am-Main, 1947. English translation by Moses Hadas under the title *The Homeric Gods: The Spiritual Significance of Greek Religion* (New York, 1954).

Roger Paret. "Les villes de Syrie du Sud et les routes commerciales d'Arabie à la fin du VIe siècle." *Akten des XI. Internationalen Byzantinisten-Kongresses, München 1958* (München, 1960), 438–44.

Rudi Paret. "Note sur un passage de Malalas concernant les phylarques arabes." *Arabica* 5 (1958):251–62.

———. *Mohammed und der Koran: Geschichte und Verkündigung des arabischen Propheten.* 2d ed. Stuttgart, 1966.

S. Thomas Parker. "The Decapolis reviewed." *Journal of Biblical Literature* 94 (1975):437–41.

———. *Romans and Saracens: A History of the Arabian Frontier.* Winona Lake, 1986.

J. B. Parr. "Frequency distributions of central places in southern Germany: a further analysis." *Economic Geography* 56 (1980):141–54.

Jeffrey R. Parsons. *Prehistoric Settlement Patterns in the Texcoco Region, Mexico.* Memoir no. 3 of the Museum of Anthropology, University of Michigan. Ann Arbor, Mich., 1971.

Talcott Parsons and Neil J. Smelser. *Economy and Society. A Study in the Integration of Economic and Social Theory.* London, 1956.

Walter M. Patton. "Blood revenge in Arabia and Israel." *American Journal of Theology* 5 (1901): 703–31.

Edmond Pauty. "Villes spontanées et villes créées en Islam." *Annales de l'Institut d'Études Orientales* 9 (1951): 52–75.

Johannes Pedersen. *Den Arabiske Bog.* English translation by Geoffrey French under the title *The Arabic Book* (Princeton, N.J., 1984).

Charles Pellat. *Description de l'Occident Musulman au IVe-Xe Siècle.* Bibliothèque Arabe-Française no. 9. Alger, 1950.

———. *Le Milieu Baṣrien et la Formation de Ǧāḥiẓ.* Paris, 1953.

Paul Pelliot. "Des artisans chinois à la capitale Abbasside en 751–762." *T'oung Pao* 26 (1928): 110–12.

———. *Notes on Marco Polo.* 3 vols. Paris, 1959–73.

Peter Pentz. *The Invisible Conquest. The Ontogenesis of Sixth and Seventh Century Syria.* Copenhagen, 1992.

———. *Hama: Fouilles et Recherches de la Fondation Carlsberg 1931–1938: IV 1-Text, The Medieval Citadel and Its Architecture.* København, 1997.

P. G. N. Peppelenbosch. "Nomadism on the Arabian Peninsula—a general appraisal." *Tijdschrift voor Economische en Sociale Geografie* 59 (1969): 335–46.

A. Pesce. *Jiddah: Portrait of an Arabian City.* London, 1974.

Carl F. Petry, ed., *Islamic Egypt, 640–1517.* Vol. 1 of *The Cambridge History of Egypt.* Cambridge, 1998.

Harry St. J. B. [subsequently ʿAbdullāh] Philby. *Arabia.* London, 1930.

Wendell Phillips. *Qatabān and Sheba.* New York, 1955.

Nina Viktorovna Pigulevskaja. "Efiopiya i Khimyar v ikh Vzaimootnojeniyakh s Vostotchnorimskoy Imperiei." In *Vestnik Drevnei Istorii,* vol. 1 (Moscow, 1948), 87–97.

———. *Goroda Irana v Rannem Sredievekov'e.* Moscow and Leningrad, 1956. French translation by the author under the title *Les Villes de l'État Iranien aux Époques Parthe et Sassanide: Contribution à l'Histoire Sociale de la Passé Antiquité* (Paris and La Haye, 1963).

———. "Les rapports sociaux à Nedjrān au début du VIe siècle de l'ère chrétienne." *Journal of the Economic and Social History of the Orient* 4 (1961): 1–14.

———. *Araby u granic Vizantii i Irana v IV-VI vv.* Moscow and Lenigrad, 1964.

O. Pinto. "The libraries of the Arabs during the time of the Abbasids." *Islamic Culture* 3 (1929): 525–37.

Jacqueline Pirenne. *Le royaume Sud-Arabe de Qatabān et sa Datation.* Louvain, Belgium, 1961.

Xavier de Planhol. *Le monde Islamique: Essai de Géographie Religieuse.* Paris, 1957. English translation under the title *The World of Islam* (Ithaca, N.Y., 1959).

Karl Polanyi, Conrad M. Arensberg, and Harry W. Pearson, eds. *Trade and Market in the Early Empires.* Glencoe, Ill., 1957.

Jean Poncet. "L'évolution des genres de vie en Tunisie (autour d'une phrase d'Ibn Khaldoun)." *Les Cahiers de Tunisie,* nos. 7–8 (1954): 315–23.

Arthur Upham Pope. "Persepolis as a ritual city." *Archaeology* 10 (1957): 123–30.

———. *Persian Architecture.* New York, 1965.

Nadine F. Posner. "The Muslim Conquest of Northern Mesopotamia: An Introductory Essay into Its Historical Background and Historiography." Ph.D. diss., New York University, 1985.

———. "Whence the Muslim Conquest of Northern Mesopotamia." In *A Way Prepared. Essays on Islamic Culture in Honor of Richard Bayly Winder,* edited by Farhad Kazemi and R. D. McChesney, 27–52. New York, 1988.

Otto Procksch. *Über die Blutrache bei den vorislamischen Arabern und Mohammeds Stellung zu Ihr.* Leipziger Studien aus dem Gebiete der Geschichte. Leipzig, 1899.

Procopius. *Procopii Caesariensis Opera Omnia.* Edited by J. Haury. Leipzig, 1905–13. Rev. ed. by G. Wirth (Leipzig, 1962–64).

M.-A. Prost. *Hierarchie des Villes.* Paris, 1965.

G.-R. Puin. *Der Diwân von ʿUmar ibn al-Ḫaṭṭâb.* Bonn, 1970.

Wadad al-Qāḍī. "Madkhal ilā dirāsat ʿuhūd al-ṣulḥ al-Islāmīyah zaman al-futūh." In *The Fourth International Conference on the History of Bilād al-Shām,* Arabic Papers, vol. 2, edited by Muḥammad ʿAdnān al-Bakhīt and Iḥsān ʿAbbas (Amman, 1987), 193–269.

Ibn Abī Dīnār al-Qayrawānī. *Al-Muʾnis fī Akhbār Ifrīqiyah wa Tūnis.* Tūnis, A.H. 1387.

H. L. Rabino (di Borgomale). "Les dynasties alaouides du Mazandéran." *Journal Asiatique* 210 (1927): 253–77.

———. *Mázandarán and Astarábád.* E. J. W. Gibb Memorial Publications, n.s., no. 7. London, 1928.

———. "Les dynasties du Māzandarān de l'an 50 avant l'hégire à l'an 1066 de l'hégire (572 à 1597–98) après les chroniques locales." *Journal Asiatique* 228 (1936): 397–474.

———. "L'Histoire du Māzandarān." *Journal Asiatique* 234 (1943–45): 211–43.

Julian Raby and Jeremy Johns, eds. *Bayt al-Maqdis: ʿAbd al-Malik's Jerusalem.* Part 1. Oxford, 1992.

Friedrich Ragette. *Baalbeck.* Park Ridge, N.J., 1980.

Yūsuf Rāġib. *Marchands d'Étoffes du Fayyoum au IIIe/IXe Siècle d'après leurs Archives (Actes et Lettres). Supplément aux Annales Islamologiques:* vol. 1, *Les Actes des Banū ʿAbd al-Muʾmin* (Le Caire [Cairo], 1982); vol. 2, *La Correspondance Administrative et Privée des Banū ʿAbd al-Muʾmin* (Le Caire, 1985).

Fazlur Rahman. *Islam.* 2d ed. Chicago, 1979.

Roy A. Rappaport. "The sacred in human evolution." *Annual Review of Ecology and Systematics* 2 (1971): 23–44.

———. *Ecology, Meaning, and Religion.* Richmond, Calif., 1979.

Saʿd A. al-Rāshīd. *Darb Zubaydah. The Pilgrim Road from Kufa to Mecca.* Al-Riyāḍ, A.H. 1399.

———. *Al-Rabadhah. A Portrait of Early Islamic Civilisation in Saudi Arabia.* Al-Riyāḍ, 1986.

Carl Raswan. "Tribal areas and migration lines of the North-Arabian bedouins." *Geographical Review* 20 (1930): 494–502.

———. *Black Tents of Arabia.* New York, 1935. Reprint, New York, 1971.

Carl Ratjens. "Kulturelle Einflüsse in Südwest-Arabien von den ältesten Zeiten bis zum Islam, unter besonderer Berücksichtigung des Hellenismus." *Jahrbuch für Kleinasiatische Forschung* 1 (1950–51): 1–42.

Charles L. Redman. "Comparative urbanism in the Islamic Far West." *World Archaeology* 14 (1982–83): 355–77.

A. Reifenberg. "Caesarea: a study in the decline of a town," *Israel Exploration Journal* 1 (1950–51): 20–32.

W. J. Reilly. *The Law of Retail Gravitation.* New York, 1931.

J. T. Reinaud. *Relations des Voyages Faits par les Arabes et les Per-*

sans dans l'Inde et à la Chine dans le IXe Siècle de l'Ère Chrétienne. Paris, 1845.

Else Reitemeyer. *Die Städtegründungen der Araber im Islam nach dem Arabischen Historikern und Geographen.* München, 1912.

Mohamed Rekaya. "Māzyār, résistance ou intégration d'une province iranienne au monde musulman au milieu du IXe siècle après J.C." *Studia Iranica* 2 (1973): 143–92.

———. "La place des provinces sud-caspienne dans l'histoire de l'Iran de la conquête arabe à l'avènement des Zaydites (16–250 H./637–864 J.C): particularisme régional ou rôle 'national'?" *Revista degli Studi Orientali* 48 (1974): 117–52.

M. Gaspar Remiro. *Historia de Murcia Musulmana.* Zaragoza, Spain, 1905.

Nikolaus Rhodokanakis. "Die Bodenwirtschaft im alten Südarabien." *Anzeiger der Kaiserlichen Akademie der Wissenschaften in Wien,* Philologische-Historische Klasse 53 (1916): 173–204.

D. Talbot Rice. "The Oxford excavations at Ḥīra." *Ars Islamica* 1 (1934): 51–73.

John Rich, ed. *The City in Late Antiquity.* London, 1992.

D. S. Richards, ed. *Islam and the Trade of Asia: A Colloquium.* Oxford, 1970.

———. *Islamic Civilisation, 950–1150.* Oxford, 1973.

Ibrāhīm Rif'at. *Mir'āt al-Ḥarāmayn.* 2 vols. Al-Qāhirah, A.H. 1345/A.D. 1925.

Abdul-Kader Rihaoui. "Aperçu sur la civilisation de al-Jazira et de la vallée de l'Euphrate à l'époque arabe-musulmane." *Les Annales Archéologiques Arabes Syriennes,* vol. 9 (Damas, 1969), Arabic pp. 56–59; French pp. 84–87.

Helmer Ringgren. *Islam, 'Aslama and Muslim.* Horae Soederblomianae no. 2. Uppsala, 1949.

Carl Ritter. *Geschichte der Erdkunde.* Berlin, 1861.

H. Ritter. "Ein Arabisches Handbuch der Handelswissenschaft." *Islam* (1916): 28–31.

———. "Das Proömium des Matnawī-i Maulawī." *Zeitschrift der Deutschen Morgenländischen Gesellschaft* 93 (1939).

M. C. Robic. "Cent ans avant Christaller. Une théorie des lieux centraux." *L'Espace Géographique* 11 (1982): 5–12.

Maxime Rodinson. "Recherches sur les documents arabes relatifs à la cuisine." *Revue des Etudes Islamiques* (1949), 95–165.

———. "Comment est né l'Islam?" *Le Courier Rationaliste* (Paris, 23 September 1956), 136–41.

———. "The life of Muhammad and the sociological problem of the beginnings of Islam." *Diogenes,* no. 20 (1957): 28–51.

———. *Mahomet.* Paris, 1961. English translation under the title *Muhammad* (New York, 1971).

Mieczylslaw Rodziewicz. "Graeco-Islamic elements at Kom el Dikka in the light of the new discoveries: remarks on early medieval Alexandria." *Graeco-Arabica* 1 (1982): 35–49.

———. "Alexandria and district of Mareotis." *Graeco-Arabica* 2 (1983): 199–216.

———. "Transformation of Ancient Alexandria into a Medieval City." In *Colloque International d'Archéologie Islamique,* edited by Roland-Pierre Gayraud. Le Caire (Cairo), 1998.

J. M. Rogers. "Sāmarrā. A Study in Medieval Town Planning." In *The Islamic City: A Colloquium,* edited by Albert Hourani and S. M. Stern. Oxford, 1970.

W. H. Roscher. "Neue Omphalosstudien." *Abhandlungen der Königlich Sächsischen Gesellschaft der Wissenschaft,* Phil.-Hist. Klasse, vol. 31, pt. 1 (1915).

Myriam Rosen-Ayalon. *The Early Islamic Monuments of al-Ḥaram al-Sharīf: An Iconographic Study.* Monographs of the Institute of Archaeology, vol. 28 (Jerusalem, 1989).

———, ed. *Studies in Memory of Gaston Wiet.* Jerusalem, 1977.

Franz Rosenthal. *A History of Muslim Historiography.* Leiden, 1952.

Gustav Rothstein. *Die Dynastie der Laḥmiden in al-Ḥîra. Ein Versuch zur arabisch-persischen Geschicte zur Zeit der Sasaniden.* Berlin, 1899.

A. Rowe. *The Topography and History of Beth-Shan.* Philadelphia, 1930.

M. B. Rowton. "Urban autonomy in a nomadic environment." *Journal of Near Eastern Studies* 32 (1973): 201–15.

James E. Royster. "A study of Muḥammad: a survey of approaches from the perspective of the history and phenomenology of religion." *The Muslim World* 82 (1972): 49–70.

Uri Rubin. "The Ka'ba. Aspects of its ritual, functions and position in pre-Islamic and early Islamic times." *Jerusalem Studies in Arabic and Islam* 8 (1986): 97–131.

———. *The Eye of the Beholder. The Life of Muḥammad as Viewed by the Early Muslims.* Princeton, N.J., 1995.

Gerard Rushton. "Postulates of Central-Place Theory and the properties of central-place systems." *Geographical Analysis* 3 (1971): 140–56.

K. W. Russell. "The earthquake chronology of Palestine and Northwest Arabia from the 2nd through the mid 8th century A.D." *Bulletin of the American Schools of Oriental Research* 260 (1985): 47–49.

Eldon Rutter. "The habitability of the Arabian desert." *The Geographical Journal* 76 (1930): 512–15.

Gonzague Ryckmans. *Les Religions Arabes Préislamiques.* 2d ed. Louvain, Belgium, 1951.

———. "On some problems of South Arabian epigraphy and archaeology." *Bulletin of the School of Oriental and African Studies* 14 (1952): 1–10.

Jacques Ryckmans. *L'institution Monarchique en Arabie Méridionale avant l'Islam (Ma'īn et Saba).* Louvain, Belgium, 1951.

———. "La Chronologie des Rois de Saba' et ḏū-Raydān." In *Nederlands Historisch-archaeologisch Instituut in het Nabije Oosten.* Vol. 16. Istanbul, 1964.

Simha Sabari. *Mouvements Populaires à Bagdād à l'Époque 'Abbasside, IXe–XIe Siècles.* Paris, 1981.

Eduard Sachau. "Zur Geschichte und Chronologie von Khwārazm." *Sitzungsberichte der Wiener Akademie der Wissenschaften.* Phil.-Hist. Klasse, 73 (1873): 491(20)–495(24).

Dorothée Sack. *Die Grosse Moschee von Resafa—Ruṣafāt Hišām.* Mainz, Germany, 1996.

P. Saey. "Three fallacies in the literature on central place theory." *Tijdschrift vóór Economische en Sociale Geografie* 64 (1973): 181–94.

Mohammad el-Saghir. *Le Camp Romain de Louqsour.* Le Caire (Cairo), 1986.

Marshall D. Sahlins. *Tribesmen.* Englewood Cliffs, N.J., 1968.

Al-Sahmī. *Tārikh Jurjān* (Hyderabad, India, 1950).

Kamal S. Salibi. *Syria under Islam: Empire on Trial 634–1097.* Delmar, N.Y., 1977.

———. *A History of Arabia.* Beirut, 1980.

Muḥammad Amīn Ṣāliḥ. *Ta'rīkh al-Yaman al-Islāmī.* Al-Qāhirah, A.H. 1395.

G. Salmon. "Études sur la topographie du Caire." *Mémoires Publiés par les Membres de l'Istitut Français d'Archéologie Orientale du Caire* 7 (1902).

Philip C. Salzman, ed. *When Nomads Settle.* Brooklyn, N.Y., 1980.

Yūnis Ibrāhīm al-Sāmarrā'ī. *Tārīkh Madīnat al-Sāmarrā'.* 3 vols. Baghdād, A.H. 1388.

Claudio Sanchez-Albornoz. "Rasis fuente de Aben Alatir." *Bulletin Hispanique* 41 (1939): 5–59.

———. *La España Musulmana.* 3d ed. Madrid, 1973.

Paula Sanders. *Ritual, Politics, and the City in Fatimid Cairo.* Albany, N.Y., 1994.

William T. Sanders and Barbara J. Price. *Mesoamerica: The Evolution of a Civilization.* New York, 1968.

Avedis Sanjian. "Anastas Vardapet's list of Armenian monasteries in seventh-century Jerusalem: a critical examination." *Le Muséon* 82 (1969): 265–92.

F. Sarre and E. Herzfeld. *Archäologische Reise im Euphrat- und Tigrisgebiet.* 2 vols. Berlin, 1911–20.

Maurice Sartre. *Bostra, des Origines à l'Islam.* Paris, 1985.

"Le peuplement et le développement du Hauran antique à la lumière des inscriptions grecques et latines." In *Hauran I: Recherches Archéologiques sur la Syrie du Sud à l'Époque Hellénistique et Romaine,* pt. 1, edited by J.-M. Dentzer. Paris, 1985.

Sato Tsugitaka. "Isuramu Shakaishi eno Shiten." In *Rekishigaku,* edited by K. Kabayama, Tōkyō, 1977.

John J. Saunders. "The nomad as empire builder: a comparison of the Arab and Mongol conquests." *Diogenes,* no. 52 (1965): 79–103.

Jean Sauvaget. "Esquisse d'une histoire de la ville de Damas." *Revue des Études Islamiques* 8 (1934): 421–80.

———. *Alep. Essai sur le Développement d'une Grande Ville Syrienne, des Origines au Milieu du XIXe Siècle.* Bibliothèque Archéologique et Historique. Vol. 36. Paris, 1941.

———. *Historiens Arabes.* Paris, 1946.

———. *La Mosquée Omeyyade de Médine.* Paris, 1947.

———. *'Ahbar as-Sīn wa-l-Hind: Relation de la Chine et de l'Inde Rédigée en 851.* Paris, 1948.

———. "Châteaux umayyades de Syrie. Contribution à l'étude de la colonisation arabe aux ler et IIe siècles de l'Hégire." *Revue des Etudes Islamiques* 35 (1967): 1–49.

H. Sauvaire. *Histoire de Jérusalem et d'Hebron . . . par Moudjir ed-Dyn.* Paris, 1876.

Elizabeth Savage. "Berbers and Blacks, Ibadi slave traffic in eighth-century North Africa." *Journal of African History* 33 (1992): 351–68.

———. *A Gateway to Hell, a Gateway to Paradise: The North African Response to the Arab Conquest.* Princeton, N.J., 1997.

Ibn Sbayyil. *Dīwān al-Naba'ṭ.* Published by Kh. M. al-Faraj in 2 vols. Dimashq, A.H. 1371. Translated by Saad Abdullah Sowayan under the title *Nabaṭi Poetry* (Berkeley and Los Angeles, 1985).

George T. Scanlon. "Housing and Sanitation: Some Aspects of Medieval Islamic Public Service." In *The Islamic City: A Colloquium,* edited by Albert Hourani and S. M. Stern. Oxford, 1970.

———. "Fustat: Archaeological Reconsiderations." In *Colloque Internationale sur l'Histoire du Caire, 1969* (Le Caire, [Cairo], 1972), 415–22.

Joseph Schacht. *Origins of Muhammadan Jurisprudence.* 4th ed. Oxford, 1967.

Charles Schéfer. *Chrestomathie Persane.* Paris, 1883.

Ph. Schertl. "Ela-'Aḳaba." *Orientalia Christiana Periodica* 2 (1936): 33–77.

Robert Schick. "The Settlement Pattern of Southern Jordan: The Nature of the Evidence." In *The Byzantine and Early Islamic Near East,* vol. 2, *Land Use and Settlement Patterns,* edited by G. R. D. King and Averil Cameron. Princeton, N.J., 1994.

———. *The Christian Communities of Palestine from Byzantine to Islamic Rule. A Historical and Archaeological Study.* Princeton, N.J., 1995.

Thorkild Schiøler. *Roman and Islamic Water-Lifting Wheels.* Copenhagen, 1973.

Kurd de Schloezer. *Abu Dolaf Misaris ben Mohalhal de Itinere Suo Asiatico.* Berlin, 1845.

D. Schlumberger. *La Palmyrène du Nord-Ouest.* Paris, 1951.

Erich F. Schmidt. *Persepolis.* Publications of the Oriental Institute, vols. 68, 69. Chicago, 1953, 1957.

Andreas Schmidt-Colinet. *Palmyra: Kulturbegegnung im Grenzbereich.* Mainz am Rhein, 1985.

Karl Schmitt-Korte. *Die Nabatäer: Spuren einer arabischen Kultur der Antike.* Hannover, 1976.

B. Schulz and J. Strzgowski. "Mschatta." *Jahrbuch der Königlich-Preussischen Kunstsammlungen* 25 (1904): 105–76.

G. Schumacher. *Pella of the Decapolis.* London, 1888.

———. *Abila of the Decapolis.* London, 1889.

E. Schürer. *The History of the Jewish People in the Age of Jesus Christ.* 2 vols. Edinburgh, 1979.

Joshua J. Schwartz. *Lod (Lydda), Israel. From Its Origins through the Byzantine Period 5600 BCE–640 CE. British Archaeological Report 571.* Oxford, 1991.

Paul Schwarz. *Iran im Mittelalter nach der Arabischen Geographen.* 9 vols. Leipzig, Zwikau, Stuttgart, Berlin, 1896–1936. Reissued Hildesheim, 1969.

———. "Die Zuckerpresser von Ahwāz." *Der Islam* 6 (1916): 269–79.

———. "Bemerkungen zu den Arabischen Nachrichten über Balkh." In *Oriental Studies in Honour of Cursetji Erachji Pavry.* London, 1933.

A. V. Sedov. "New archaeological and epigraphic material from Qana (South Arabia)." *Arabian Archaeology and Epigraphy* 3 (1992).

J. B. Segal. *Edessa, "The Blessed City."* Oxford. 1970.

Robert B. Serjeant. "Two tribal law cases (documents): (Wāhidī Sultanate, South-West Arabia)." *Journal of the Royal Asiatic Society* (1951): 167–68.

———. "Ḥūd and other pre-Islamic prophets of Ḥaḍramawt." *Le Muséon* 67 (1954): 121–78.

———. *The Saiyids of Ḥaḍramawt. An Inaugural Lecture delivered on 5 June 1956.* School of Oriental and African Studies, University of London, 1957.

———. "Professor A. Guillaume's translation of the Sīrah." *Bulletin of the School of Oriental and African Studies* 21 (1958): 7.

———. Review of *Muhammad at Medina,* by W. Montgomery

Watt. *Bulletin of the School of Oriental and African Studies* 21 (1958): 187–88.

———. "Ḥaram and Ḥawṭah, the Sacred Enclave in Arabia." In *Mélanges Ṭāhā Ḥusain: Offerts par ses Amis et ses Disciples à l'Occasion de son 70ième Anniversaire* (Le Caire, 1962), 41–58.

———. "The 'Constitution of Medina.'" *The Islamic Quarterly* 8 (1964): 3–16.

———. *Islamic Textiles. Material for a History up to the Mongol Conquest.* Beirut, 1972. Originally published serially in *Ars Islamica,* vols. 9–16 (1942–51).

———. "The *Sunnah Jāmiʿah,* pacts with the Yathrib Jews, and the *taḥrīm* of Yathrib: an analysis and translation of the documents comprised in the so-called 'Constitution of Medina.'" *Bulletin of the School of Oriental and African Studies* 41, pt. 1 (1978): 1–42.

———. "Early Arabic Prose." In *Arabic Literature to the End of the Umayyad Period,* edited by A. F. L. Beeston, T. M. Johnston, R. B. Serjeant, and G. R. Smith. Cambridge, 1983.

———. "Meccan trade and the rise of Islam: misconceptions and flawed polemics." *Journal of the American Oriental Society* 110, no. 3 (1990): 472–86.

Robert B. Serjeant and Ronald Lewcock, eds. *Ṣanʿāʾ. An Arabian Islamic City.* London, 1983.

Elman Service. *Primitive Social Organization: An Evolutionary Perspective.* New York, 1962.

———. *Origins of the State and Civilization. The Process of Cultural Evolution.* New York, 1975.

Fuat Sezgin. *Geschichte des arabischen Schrifttums.* Leiden, 1967–.

Muḥammad Abdulhayy Shaban. *The ʿAbbasid Revolution.* Cambridge, 1970.

———. *Islamic History,* A.D. *600–750* (A.H. *132*). A New Interpretation. Cambridge, 1971.

———. "Khurāsān at the Time of the Arab Conquest." In *Iran and Islam: In Memory of the Late Vladimir Minorsky,* edited by C. E. Bosworth. Edinburgh, 1971.

ʿUmar ibn Shabbah. *Taʾrīkh al-Madīnah al-Munawwarah.* Edited by Fahīm Muḥammad Shaltut. Makkah, A.H. 1399.

Mir Husain Shah. "Panjwayee-Fanjuwai." *Afghanistan* 17 (1962): 23–27.

Irfan Shahīd. *See* Irfan Kawar.

S. Shaked. *A Tentative Bibliography of the Geniza Documents.* Paris and The Hague, 1964.

Aḥmad Shalabī. *Al-Taʾrīkh al-Islāmī wal-l Hadārah al-Islāmīyah.* Al-Qāhirah, A.H. 1378/A.D. 1959.

Ṣabbāh Ibrāhīm Saʿīd al-Shaykhlī. *Al-Aṣnāt fī al-ʿAṣr al-ʿAbbāsī: Nashʾahā wa Taṭawwurhā.* Baghdād, A.H. 1396.

Ahmad M. H. Shboul. *Al-Masʿūdī and His World: A Muslim Humanist and His Interest in Non-Muslims.* London, 1979.

Dorothy G. Shepard and W. B. Henning. "Zandanījī Identified?," In *Aus der Welt der islamischen Kunst: Festschrift für Ernst Kühnel zum 75 Geburtstag,* edited by Richard Ettinghausen. Berlin, 1959.

Shimuzu Kosuke. "Iranshī no naka no toshizo: 10–11 seiki no Nishapuru." *Shicho,* n.s., vol. 28 (1990).

Kurakichi Shiratori. *A Study on Su-tʿe, or Sogdiana. Memoirs of the Research Department of the Tōyō Bunkō,* no. 2. Tōkyō, 1928.

Muʿīn al-Dīn Junayd Shīrazī. *Shadd al-Izār fī Khaṭṭ al-Awzār ʿan Zuwwar al-Mazār.* Tehrān, A.H. 1338/A.D. 1940.

Elias Shoufani. *Al-Riddah and the Muslim Conquest of Arabia.* Toronto, 1973.

Muḥammad ʿAlī Imām Shushtarī. *Taʾrīkh wa Jughrafiyā-yi Khūzistān.* Tehrān, A.H. 1331/A.D. 1952.

H. A. Simon. "On a class of skew distribution functions." *Biometrica* 42 (1955): 425–40.

Robert Simon. "L'inscription Ry 506 et la préhistoire de La Mecque." *Acta Orientalia Academiae Scientiarum Hungaricae* 20 (1967): 325–37.

———. "Ḥums et īlāf, ou commerce sans guerre (sur la genèse et le caractère du commerce de la Mecque)." *Acta Orientalia Academiae Scientiarum Hungaricae* 23 (1970): 205–32.

———. *Meccan Trade and Islam: Problems of Origin and Structure.* Bibliotheca Orientalis Hungarica, vol. 32. Budapest, 1989.

Peter von Sivers. "Military, merchants and nomads: the social evolution of the Syrian cities and countryside during the Classical period, 780–969/164–358." *Der Islam* 56 (1979): 213–44.

———. "Taxation and trade in the ʿAbbasid thughūr, 750–962/133–351." *Journal of the Economic and Social History of the Orient* 25, pt. 1 (1982): 71–99.

Bogdan Składanek. "Settlements in Gharchistān during the early Islamic period (up to the 11th century A.D.)." *Rocznik Orientalistyczny* 34 (1971): 57–71.

Neil J. Smelser. "A comparative view of exchange systems." *Economic Development and Cultural Change* 7 (1959): 173–82.

Bruce D. Smith, ed. *Mississippian Settlement Patterns.* New York, 1978.

Dennis Mack Smith. *A History of Sicily: Medieval Sicily 800–1713.* London, 1968.

E. Baldwin Smith. *The Dome.* Princeton, N.J., 1950.

Robert Houston Smith. "Pella of the Decapolis." *Arts and the Islamic World* (Spring, 1984): 58–60.

———. "Trade in the Life of Pella of the Decapolis." In *Studies in the History and Archeology of Jordan,* no. 3 (1987), 53–58.

———. *Pella of the Decapolis.* Vol. 1, Wooster, Ohio, 1973; vol. 2, 1989.

Sidney Smith. "Events in Arabia in the 6th century A.D." *Bulletin of the School of Oriental and African Studies* 16 (1954): 425–68.

William Robertson Smith. *Kinship and Marriage in Early Arabia.* London, 1903. Reprint, Boston, n.d.

Dominique Sourdel. *Les Cultes du Hauran à l'Époque Romaine.* Paris, 1952.

———. "Nouvelles recherches sur la deuxième partie du *Livre des Viziers* d'al-Ǧahšiyari." *Mélanges Louis Massignon* 3 (1957): 287–89.

———. "La fondation umayyade d'al-Ramla." In *Studien zur Geschichte und Kultur des Vorderen Orients: Festschrift für Bertold Spuler,* edited by H. Roester and A. Noth. Leiden, 1981.

Dominique Sourdel and Janine Sourdel. *La Civilisation de l'Islam Classique.* Paris, 1968.

Robert F. Spencer. "The Arabian matriarchate: an old controversy." *Southwestern Journal of Anthropology* 8 (1952): 478–502.

A. Spijkerman. *The Coins of the Decapolis and Provincia Arabia.* Studii Biblici Franciscani Collectio Maior, no. 25. Jerusalem, 1978.

Brian Spooner. *The Cultural Ecology of Pastoral Nomads.* Reading, Mass., 1975.

Aloys Sprenger. *Die Post- und Reiserouten des Orients. Abhandlungen für die Kunde des Morgenländes.* Leipzig, 1864.

———. *Das Leben und die Lehre des Moḥammed.* 3 vols. Berlin, 1869.

———. *Die alte Geographie Arabiens als Grundlage der Entwicklungsgeschichte des Semitismus.* N.p., 1875.

Bertold Spuler. *Iran in Früh-Islamischer Zeit: Politik, Kultur, Verwaltung und Öffentliches Leben Zwischen der Arabischen und der Seldschukischen Eroberung 633 bis 1055.* Wiesbaden, 1952.

H. Stern. "Les origines de l'architecture de la mosquée omeyyade." *Syria* 28 (1951), 269–79.

S. M. Stern. "The early Ismāʿīlī missionaries in north-west Persia and in Khurāsān and Transoxania." *Bulletin of the School of Oriental and African Studies* 23 (1960): 62–63.

———. "Rāmisht of Sīrāf, a merchant millionaire of the twelfth century." *Journal of the Royal Asiatic Society* (1967): 10–14.

Julian H. Steward and Louis C. Faron. *Native Peoples of South America.* New York, 1959.

C. T. Stewart. "The size and spacing of cities." *Geographical Review* 48 (1958): 222–45.

Maximilian Streck. *Die Alte Landschaft Babylonien nach den Arabischen Geographen.* 2 vols. Leiden, 1900–1901.

———. "Seleucia und Ktesiphon." *Der Alte Orient* 16 (1917).

D. Sturm. "Bedeutung der Syrischen Stadt ar-Raqqa von der Arabischen Eroberung bis zur Gegenwart." *Hallesche Beiträge zur Orientwissenschaft* 1 (1979): 35–72.

ʿAbd al-Mājūd Aḥmad al-Sulaymān. *Al-Mawṣil fī al-ʿAhdayn al-Rashidī wa-l-Umawī.* Al-Mawṣil, Iraq, A.H. 1405.

W. M. Sumner. "Cultural Development in the Kur River Basin, Iran: An Archaeological Analysis of Settlement Patterns." Ph.D. diss., University of Pennsylvania, 1972.

Husayn Qūlī Sutūdah. "Tārīkh-i Qazwīn." In *Barrasīhā-yi Tārīkhī.* Vol. 4. 1969–70.

Louise Sweet, ed. *Peoples and Cultures of the Middle East.* Garden City, N.Y., 1970.

Sir Percy Sykes. *Ten Thousand Miles in Persia.* London, 1902.

ʿAbd al-Jalīl al-Ṭāhir. *Al-Badū w-al-ʿAshāʾir fi-l-Bilād al-ʿArabīyah.* Al-Qāhirah, A.H. 1373/A.D. 1954.

Yukawa Takeshi, ed. *Urbanism in Islam.* Vol. 3. Tokyo, 1989.

Mohamed Talbi. *L'Emirat Aghlabide, Histoire Politique.* Paris, 1966.

———. "Hérésie, acculturation et nationalisme des Berbères Bargawata." In *Proceedings of the First Congress of Mediterranean Studies of Arab-Berber Influence,* edited by Micheline Galley and David R. Marshall, Algiers, 1973.

Moira Tampoe. *Maritime Trade between China and the West. An Archaeological Study of the Ceramics from Siraf (Persian Gulf), 8th to 15th Centuries A.D.* British Archaeological Reports, International Series, 555. Oxford, 1989.

Georges Tate. "Les villes syriennes aux époques hellénistique, romaine et byzantine." In *Die Orientalische Stadt,* edited by G. Wilhelm, 351–58. Berlin, 1997.

G. P. Tate. *Seistan, a Memoir on the History, Topography, Ruins, and People of the Country.* Pts. 1–4. Calcutta, 1910–12.

Donna Taylor. "Some Locational Aspects of Middle-Range Hierarchical Societies." Ph.D. diss., the City University of New York, 1975.

Pedro Teixeira. *Relacion de Persia.* Amberes, 1610.

Aram Ter-Ghewondyan [Ter-Ghévondian]. *The Arab Emirates in Bagratid Armenia.* Translated by Nina Garsoïan. Lisbon, 1976. Originally published in Armenian under the title *Arabakan Amirayutʿyunnere Bagratunyacʿ Hayastanum* (Erevan, Armenia, 1965).

———. "L'Arménie et la conquête arabe." In *Armenian Studies/Etudes Arméniennes in Memoriam Haig Berbérian,* edited by Dikran Kouymjian, 773–92. Lisbon, 1986.

Henri Terrasse. "Notes sur les ruines di Sijilmassa." In *Deuxième Congrès de la Fédération des Sociétes Savantes.* Alger, 1936.

———. *Histoire de Maroc des Origines à l'Establissement du Protectorat Français.* Casablanca, 1949.

———. *Islam d'Espagne: une Rencontre de l'Orient et de l'Occident.* Paris, 1958.

Wilfred Thesiger. "The badu of southern Arabia." *Journal of the Royal Central Asian Society* 37 (1950): 53–61.

———. *Arabian Sands.* London, 1959. Penguin edition, Harmondsworth, Middlesex, England, 1964.

E. N. Thomas. "Towards an expanded central place model." *Geographical Review* 51 (1961): 400–11.

———. "The Stability of Distance-Population-Size Relationships for Iowa Towns from 1900–1950." In *Human Geography.* Vol. 24 of *Lund Studies in Geography.* Series B. Lund, Sweden, 1962.

———. "The Spatial Behavior of a Dispersed Non-Farm Population." In *Papers and Proceedings of the Regional Science Association* 8 (1962): 107–33.

Alton C. Thompson. "Some comments on Lösch." *Geographical Analysis* 2 (1970): 397–400.

Gerald R. R. Tibbetts. "The Malay Peninsula as known to the Arab geographers." *The Malayan Journal of Tropical Geography* 7 (1955): 24–33.

———. *A Study of the Arabic Texts Containing Material on South-East Asia.* Oriental Translation Fund, n.s., 10. Leiden, 1979.

———. "The Balkhī School of Geographers." In *The History of Cartography,* vol. 2, bk. 1, edited by J. B. Harley and David Woodward, 108–36. Chicago, 1992–.

J. Tinbergen. "The spatial dispersion of production: an hypothesis." *Schweizerische Zeitschrift für Volkwirtschaft und Statistik* 97 (1961): 412–19.

———. "Sur un modèle de la dispersion géographique de l'activité économique." *Revue d'Economie Politique* 74 (1964): 30–44.

B. M. Tirmidhi. "Zoroastrians and their fire temples in Iran and adjoining countries from the 9th to the 14th centuries [*sic*] as gleaned from the Arabic geographical works." *Islamic Culture* 24 (1950): 271–84.

T. Tobler, ed. *Itinera et Descriptiones Terrae Sanctae Lingua Latina, Saec. IV-XI. Exarata, Sumptibus Societatis Illustrandis Orientis Latini Monumentis.* Genève, 1877.

T. Tobler and A. Molinier. *Itinera Hierosolymitana.* London, 1889.

Z. V. Togan. *See* A. Z. Validov.

H. Töllner. *Die Türkischen Garden am Kalifenhof von Samarra.* Bonn, 1971.

S. P. Tolstov. "Goroda Guzov." *Sovetskaya Ethnografiya* 3 (1947): 55–102.

———. *Auf den Spuren der Altchoresmischen Kultur.* Berlin, 1953.

Wilhelm Tomaschek. "Soghdiana." *Sitzungsberichte der Wiener Akademie der Wissenschaften* 87 (1887): 67–120.

———. "Über die ältesten Nachrichten über den Skythischen Norden." *Sitzungsberichte der Kaiserlichen Akademie der Wissenschaften zu Wien,* Phil.-Hist. Kl., vol. 116 (1888).

———. *Zur Historischen Topographie von Kleinasien im Mittelalter.* Wien, 1891.

S. Tomin. *Das christliche-kopitische Ägypten im arabischen Zeit.* Wiesbaden, 1984.

Ernst Topitsche. *Vom Ursprung und Ende der Metaphysik: Eine Studie zur Weltanschauungskritik.* Wien, 1958.

Charles C. Torrey. *The Commercial-Theological Terms in the Koran.* Leyden, 1892.

C. Toumanoff. "The Bagratids of Iberia from the eighth to the eleventh century." *Le Muséon* 74 (1961): 5–42, 233–316.

J. Toutain. "Le progrès de la vie urbaine dans l'Afrique du Nord sous la domination romaine." In *Mélanges [R.] Cagnat.* Paris, 1912.

Arnold Toynbee, ed. *Cities of Destiny.* London, 1967.

R. Traini, ed. *Studi in Onore di Francesco Gabrieli nel suo Ottantesimo Compleanno.* Roma, 1984.

J. Spencer Trimingham. *A History of Islam in West Africa.* Oxford, 1970.

———. *Christianity among the Arabs in Pre-Islamic Times.* London and Beirut, 1979.

V. Tsaferis. *Excavations at Capernaum.* Vol. 1: *1978–1982.* Winona Lake, Ind., 1989.

Yoram Tsafrir. "From Scythopolis to Baysan—Changing Concepts of Urbanism." Paper presented at the Workshop on Late Antiquity and Early Islam, School of Oriental and African Studies, University of London, 25–27 April 1991.

Yoram Tsafrir and Gideon Forester. "The dating of the earthquake of the sabbatical year 749 C.E." *Tarbiz* 58 (1989): 357–62.

O. Tuominen. "Das Einflussgebiet der Stadt Turku im System der Einflussgebiete S.W. Finnlands." *Fennia* 71 (1949): 114–21.

K. S. Twitchell. *Saudi Arabia.* Princeton, N.J., 1947.

A. L. Udovitch, ed. *The Islamic Middle East, 700–1900: Studies in Economic and Social History.* Princeton, N.J., 1981.

Stephen Urice. *Qasr Kharana in the Transjordan.* Durham, N.C., 1987.

Dan Urman. *The Golan: A Profile of a Region during the Roman and Byzantine Periods.* British Archaeological Reports, International Series 269. Oxford, 1985.

S. Valavanis. "Lösch on location." *American Economist* 45 (1955): 637–44.

Rafael Valencia. "Islamic Seville: Its Political, Social and Cultural History." In *The Legacy of Muslim Spain,* edited by Salma Khadra Jayyusi, 136–48. Leiden, 1992.

A. Z. Validov [A. Z. Validi Toğan]. "Meshkhedskaya Rukopis Ibnu-l-Fakikha." *Izvestiya Russkoy Akad. Nauk.,* no. 1 (1924): 237–48.

———. "Azerbaycanîn tarihî cografyasî." *Azerbaycan Yurt Bilgisi* (1932), no. 1, 35–48; no. 2, 1–15; no. 3, 123–32; no. 4, 145–56.

———. *Ibn Faḍlans Reisebericht.* In *Abhandlungen für die kunde des Morgenlandes,* vol. 24. Leipzig, 1939.

———. "Azerbaycan ethnografisne dair." *Azerbaycan Yurt Bilgisi* (1953), no. 14, 49–56.

———. "The topography of Balkh down to the middle of the seventeenth century." *Central Asiatic Journal* 14 (1970): 277–88.

Joaquín Vallvé. "Sobre algunos problemas se la invasión musulmana." *Anuario de Estudios Medievales* 4 (1967): 361–63.

L. Vanden Berghe. *Archéologie de l'Iran Ancien.* Leiden, 1959.

R. Vasmer. "Beiträge zur muhammedanischen Münzkunde: I. Die Münzen der Abū Daʿudiden." *Numismatische Zeitschrift,* n.s., 18 (1925): 49–62.

———. "Die Eroberung Tabaristāns durch die Araber zur Zeit des Chalifen al-Manṣūr." *Islamica* 3 (1927): 86–150.

———. *Chronologie der Arabischen Statthalter von Armenien . . . (750–887).* Wien, 1931.

V. Velgus. "The countries of Mo-lin and Po-sa-lo (Lao-po-sa) in Chinese medieval reports on Africa." *Africana,* n.s., 90 (1966): 104–21.

Juan Vernet. *Los Musulmanes Españoles.* Barcelona, 1961.

L. H. Vincent, E. J. H. Mackay, and F. M. Abel. *Hébron, le Haram al-Khalil, Sépulture des Patriarches.* Paris, 1923.

R. Vining. "A description of certain spatial aspects of an economic system." *Economic Development and Cultural Change* 3 (1955): 147–95.

H. Viollet. "Description du Palais d'al-Moutasim . . . à Samarra. . . ." In *Mémoires de l'Academie des Inscriptions et Belles-Lettres* 12, pt. 2 (Paris, 1909): 577–94.

Giovanna Vitelli. *Islamic Carthage. The Archaeological, Historical and Ceramic Evidence.* Centra d'Études et de Documentation Archéologique de Carthage. Institut National d'Archéologie et d'Art de Tunisie. Carthage, Tunisia, 1981.

Jaime Vincens Vives. *An Economic History of Spain.* Princeton, N.J., 1969.

Gerlof van Vloten. *De Opkomst der Abbasiden in Chorasan.* Leiden, 1890.

———. *Recherches sur la Domination Arabe, le Chiitisme et les Croyances Messaniques sous le Khalifa des Omayades.* Amsterdam, 1894.

François-Marie Arouet de Voltaire. *Le Fanatisme ou Mahomet le Prophète.* Vol. 3, Œuvres Complètes, Théatre. Paris, 1877.

M. Vonderheyden. *La Berbérie Orientale sous la Dynastie des Benoû'l-Arlab (800–909).* Paris, 1927.

Bert de Vries. "The Umm el-Jimal project, 1972–77." *Bulletin of the American Schools of Oriental Research* 244 (1981): 53–72.

———. "Urbanization in the Basalt Region of North Jordan in Late Antiquity: The Case of Umm el-Jimal." In *Studies in the History and Archaeology of Jordan,* edited by Adnan Hadidi. Vol. 2. London, 1985.

———. "Umm al-Jimal in the Third Century." In *The Defence of the Roman and Byzantine East,* by P. W. M. Freeman and D. L. Kennedy. Oxford, 1986.

Jan de Vries. *European Urbanization 1500–1800.* Cambridge, Mass., 1984.

J. A. Vullers. *Lexicon Persico-Latinum Etymologicum.* Bonn, 1855–67.

Alan Walmsley. "The Administrative Structure and Urban Geography of the Jund of Filastin and the Jund of al-Urdunn." Ph.D. diss., University of Sydney, 1987.

———. "Pella/Fiḥl after the Islamic conquest (A.D. 635–c. 900): a convergence of literary and archaeological evidence." *Mediterranean Archaeology* 1 (1988): 142–59.

———. "Ceramics and the social history of early Islamic Jordan: the example of Pella (Tabaqat Fahl)." *Al-ʿUṣūr al-Wusṭā* 9, no. 1 (1997): 1–3, 12.

John Wansbrough. "Africa and the Arab Geographers." In *Language and History in Africa,* edited by J. Dalby, 89–101. New York, 1970.

———. *Quranic Studies: Sources and Methods of Scriptural Interpretation.* Oxford, 1977.

———. *The Secretarian Milieu: Content and Composition of Islamic Salvation History.* London, 1978.

Andrew M. Watson. "The Arab agricultural revolution and its diffusion, 700–1100." *The Journal of Economic History,* 34, no. 1 (1974): 8–35.

———. *Agricultural Innovation in the Early Islamic World. The Diffusion of Crops and Farming Techniques, 700–1100.* Cambridge, 1983.

W. Montgomery Watt. *Muhammad et Mecca.* Oxford, 1953.

———. "Economic and social aspects of the origin of Islam." *The Islamic Quarterly* 1–2 (1954–55): 90–103.

———. *Muhammad at Medina.* Oxford, 1956.

———. *Islam and the Integration of Society.* London, 1961.

———. *Muhammad, Prophet and Statesman.* Oxford, 1961.

———. *A History of Islamic Spain.* Edinburgh, 1965.

———. *Islamic political thought. The basic concepts.* Edinburgh, 1968.

Michael J. Webber. "Empirical verifiabiilty of classical Central Place Theory." *Geographical Analysis* 3 (1971): 15–28.

Thomas Weber and Rami G. Khouri. *Umm Qais: Gadara of the Decapolis.* Amman, 1989.

G. Weil, ed. *Festschrift Eduard Sachau.* Berlin, 1915.

Julius Wellhausen. *Skizzen und Vorarbeiten.* 6 vols. Berlin, 1884–99.

———. *Medina vor dem Islam.* Berlin, 1889.

———. *Reste arabischen Heidentums,* 2d ed., Berlin, 1897. Reprint, Berlin, 1927, 1961.

———. *Das arabische Reich und sein Sturz.* Berlin, 1902. English translation by Margaret Graham Weir under the title *The Arab Kingdom and Its Fall* (London and Calcutta, 1927; reprint, Khayats Oriental Reprint no. 6, Beirut, 1963).

———. "Die religiös-politischen Oppositionspartei im alten Islam." *Abhandlungen der Königlichen Gesellschaft der Wissenschaften zu Göttingen,* Phil.-Hist. Klasse, n.s., vol. 5, no. 2 (1901). Arabic translation by ʿA. Badawī (Kuwayt, A.H. 1398).

Charles Wendell. "Baghdād: *imago mundi,* and other foundation-lore." *International Journal of Middle East Studies* 2 (1971): 99–128.

Arent Jan Wensinck. *Mohammed en de Joden te Medina.* Leiden, 1908. English translation under the title *Muhammad and the Jews of Medina* (Freiburg, Germany, 1975).

———. "The ideas of the Western Semites concerning the navel of the earth." *Verhandelingen der Koninklijke Akademie van Wetenschappen te Amsterdam, Afdeeling Letterkunde,* n.s., vol. 17, no. 1 (1916).

Antoine Wessels. *A Modern Arabic Biography of Muḥammad: A Critical Study of Muḥammad Ḥusayn Haykal's 'Ḥayāt Muḥammad'.* Leiden, 1972.

Paul Wheatley. "Geographical notes on some commodities involved in Sung maritime trade." *Journal of the Malayan Branch of the Royal Asiatic Society* 32 (1959): 1–140.

———. *The Golden Khersonese.* Kuala Lumpur, 1961.

———. "Desultory Remarks on the Ancient History of the Malay Peninsula." In *Malayan and Indonesian Studies. Essays Presented to Sir Richard Winstedt on His Eighty-Fifth Birthday,* edited by John Bastin and R. Roolvink. Oxford, 1964.

———. *The Pivot of the Four Quarters. A Preliminary Enquiry into the Origins and Character of the Ancient Chinese City.* Edinburgh and Chicago, 1971.

———. "Analecta Sino-Africana Recensa." In *East Africa and the Orient: Cultural Syntheses in Pre-Colonial Times,* edited by H. Neville Chittick and Robert I. Rotberg. New York, 1975.

———. *La Città come Simbolo.* Brèscia, Italy, 1981.

———. *Nagara and Commandery. Origins of the Southeast Asian Urban Traditions.* University of Chicago, Department of Geography Research Papers no. 207–8. Chicago, 1983.

———. "A pioneer in the study of urban hierarchies: al-Maqdisī." *Al-ʿUṣūr al-Wusṭā* 5, no. 1 (1993): 4–6.

Donald S. Whitcomb. "The archaeology of Oman: a preliminary discussion of the Islamic periods." *Journal of Oman Studies* 1 (1975): 123–57.

———. "The archaeology of al-Hasa Oasis in the Islamic period." *Atlal, Journal of Saudi Arabian Studies* 2 (1978): 95–113.

———. "The City of Istakhr and the Marvdasht Plain." In *Akten des VII. Internationalen Kongresses für Iranische Kunst und Archäologie, München 7.-10, September 1976,* Berlin, 1979.

———. "Trade and Tradition in Medieval Southern Iran." Ph.D. diss., University of Chicago, 1979.

———. *Before the Roses and Nightingales: Excavations at Qasr-i Abu Nasr, Old Shiraz.* New York, 1985.

———. "Islamic archaeology at Susa." *Paléorient* 11, no. 2 (1985): 85–90.

———. "Excavations in Aqaba: first preliminary report." *Annual of the Department of Archaeology of Jordan* 31 (1987): 247–66.

———. *Aqaba—Port of Palestine on the China Sea.* Amman, 1988.

———. "Islamic Archaeology in Aden and the Hadhramaut." In *Araby the Blest: Studies in Arabian Archaeology,* edited by D. T. Potts, 176–263. Copenhagen, 1988.

———. "Khirbet al-Mafjar reconsidered: the ceramic evidence." *Bulletin of the American Schools of Oriental Research* 271 (1988): 51–67.

———. "Evidence of the Umayyad Period from the Aqaba Excavations." In *The Fourth International Conference on the History of Bilad al-Sham during the Umayyad Period,* vol. 2, edited by M. Bakhīt and R. Schick, 164–84. Amman, 1989.

———. "Diocletian's *miṣr* at Aqaba." *Zeitschrift des Deutschen Palästinavereins* 106 (1990): 156–61.

———. "The Islamic Period as Seen from Selected Sites." In *The Southern Ghors and Northeast ʿArabah Archaeological Survey,* edited by B. MacDonald, 232–42. Sheffield, England, 1992.

———. "Southern Ghors and Northeast ʿArabah Archaeological Survey." In *The Southern Ghors and Northeast ʿArabah*

Archaeological Survey, edited by B. MacDonald. Sheffield, England, 1992.
———. *Ayla: Art and Industry in the Islamic Port of Aqaba.* Chicago, 1994.
———. "The Miṣr of Ayla: Settlement at al-ʿAqaba in the Early Islamic Period." In *The Byzantine and Early Islamic Near East,* vol. 2, *Land Use and Settlement Patterns,* edited by G. R. D. King and Averil Cameron, 155–70. Princeton, N.J., 1994.
———. "Water and recent excavations at Aqaba." *The Oriental Institute News and Notes,* no. 141 (1994):4–5.
———. "Amṣār in Syria? Syrian cities after the conquest." *ARAM* 6 (1994):13–33.
———. "Islam and the Socio-Cultural Transition of Palestine—Early Islamic Period (638–1099 C.E.)." In *The Archaeology of Society in the Holy Land,* edited by T. E. Levy, 488–501. London, 1995.
———. "The Misr of Ayla: New Evidence for the Early Islamic City." In *Studies in the History and Archaeology of Jordan,* edited by G. Bisheh, 5:277–88. Amman, 1995.
———. "Urbanism in Arabia." *Arabian Archaeology and Epigraphy* 7 (1996):38–51.
———. "Out of Arabia: Early Islamic Aqaba in Its Regional Context." In *Colloque International d'Archéologie Islamique,* 403–18. Le Caire (Cairo), 1998.
David Whitehouse. "Excavations at Sīrāf. First interim report." *Iran* 6 (1968):10–22.
———. "Second interim report." *Iran* 7 (1969):39–62.
———. "Third interim report," *Iran* 8 (1970):1–18.
———. "Sīrāf: a medieval port on the Persian Gulf." *World Archaeology* 2, no. 2 (1970):141–58.
———. "The houses of Siraf, Iran." *Archaeology* 24 (1971): 255–62.
———. "Excavations at Siraf. Fourth interim report." *Iran* 9 (1971):1–17.
———. "Fifth interim report." *Iran* 10 (1972):63–87.
———. "Sixth interim report." *Iran* 12 (1974):1–30.
———. *Siraf III. The Congregational Mosque and Other Mosques from the Ninth to the Twelfth Centuries.* London, 1980.
E. Wiedemann. *Aufsätze zur arabischen Wissenschaftsgeschichte.* Vol. 1. Hildesheim, 1970.
Gaston Wiet. *L'Épigraphie Arabe de l'Exposition d'Art Persan du Caire. Memoires Présentés à l'Institut d'Égypte.* Le Caire (Cairo), 1935.
———. "Tapis égyptiens." *Arabica* 6 (1959):9–10.
———. "La vie de plaisir à la Mecque et à Médine au premier siècle de l'Islam." *Académie des Inscriptions et Belles-Lettres, Comptes Rendus des Séances de l'Année 1959.* Paris, 1960.
———. *Baghdād, Metropolis of the Abbasid Caliphate.* Norman, Okla., 1971.
G. J. Wightman. *The Walls of Jerusalem from the Canaanites to the Mamluks.* Sydney, 1993.
G. Wilhelm, ed. *Die Orientalische Stadt: Kontinuität, Wandel, Bruch.* Berlin, 1997.
Charles K. Wilkinson. "Life in early Nishapur." *Bulletin of the Metropolitan Museum of Art,* n.s., vol. 9, no. 2 (1950):60–72.
———. *Nishapur: Pottery of the Early Islamic Period.* New York, 1975.
———. *Nishapur: Some Early Islamic Buildings and Their Decoration.* New York, 1986.
J. C. Wilkinson. "A sketch of the historical geography of the Trucial Oman down to the beginning of the sixteenth century." *The Geographical Journal* 130 (1964):337–47.
———. "The Origins of the Omani State." In *The Arabian Peninsula: Society and Politics,* edited by Derek Hopwood. London, 1972.
———. "The Julanda of Oman." *The Journal of Oman Studies* 1 (1975):97–108.
———. *Jerusalem Pilgrims before the Crusades.* Jerusalem, 1977.
———. "Ṣuḥār (Sohar) in the Early Islamic Period: The Written Evidence." In *South Asian Archeology,* vol. 2, edited by M. Taddei. Naples, 1979.
"Ibādī Theological Literature." In *Religion, Learning and Science in the ʿAbbasid Period,* edited by M. J. L. Young, J. D. Latham, and R. B. Serjeant. Cambridge, 1990.
A. Williamson. *Sohar and Omani Seafaring in the Indian Ocean.* Oman, Muscat, 1973.
Hugo Winckler. "Arabisch-Semitisch-Orientalisch." *Mitteilungen der Vorderasiatischen Gesellschaft* no. 4 (1901):85–90.
A. J. van Windekens. "Huns blancs et ārçi. Essai sur les apellations du 'tokharien.'" *Le Muséon* 54 (1941):181–86.
F. R. Wingate. *Ten Years' Captivity in the Mahdi's Camp 1882–1892, from the Original Manuscripts of Father Joseph Ohrwalder.* 2d ed. London, 1892.
F. V. Winnett. *A Study of the Lihyanite and Thamudic Inscriptions.* Toronto, 1937.
———. "The place of the Minaeans in the history of Pre-Islamic Arabia." *Bulletin of the American Schools of Oriental Research* 73 (1939):3–9.
F. V. Winnett and W. L. Reed. *Ancient Records from North Arabia.* Toronto, 1970.
Eugen Wirth. "Die orientalische Stadt: ein Überblick aufgrund jüngerer Forschungen zur materiellen Kultur." *Saeculum* 26 (1975):45–94.
Hermann von Wissman. "Ḥimyar, ancient history." *Le Muséon* 77 (1964):429–99.
———. *Zur Archäologie und antiken Geographie von Südarabien. Ḥaḍramaut, Qatabān und das ʿAden-Gebiet in der Antike,* Nederlands Historisch-Archaeologisch Instituut te Istanbul, publication no. 24. Istanbul, 1968.
Hermann von Wissmann and Maria Höfner. *Beiträge zur historischen Geographie des Vorislamischen Südarabiens.* Mainz, 1953.
Abdullah al-Wohaibi. *The Northern Hijaz in the Writings of the Arab Geographers 800–1150.* Beirut, 1973.
Eric R. Wolf. "The social organization of Mecca and the origins of Islam." *Southwestern Journal of Anthropology* 7, no. 4 (1951):329–56.
———. *Peasants.* Englewood Cliffs, N.J., 1966.
Ferdinand Wüstenfeld. *Die Chroniken Der Stadt Mecca.* 4 vols. Leipzig, 1858–61; reissued at Hildesheim, 1981.
Werner Wycichl. "Al-Andalus (Sobre la Historia de un Nombre)." *Al-Andalus* 17 (1952):449–50.
M. J. L. Young, J. D. Latham, and R. B. Sergeant, eds. *Religion, Learning, and Science in the ʿAbbāsid Period.* Cambridge, 1990.

Sir Henry Yule. *The Book of Ser Marco Polo the Venetian concerning the Kingdoms and Marvels of the East.* 2 vols. London, 1903.

Eduard von Zambaur. *Manuel de Généalogie et de Chronologie pour l'Histoire de l'Islam.* Hanover, 1927.

Juris Zarins and Awad Zahrani. "Recent archaeological investigations in the Southern Tihama Plain (the sites of Athar, and Sihi, 1404/1984)." *ATLAL* 9 (1985):65–107.

Jūrjī Zaydān. *Ta'rīkh al-Tamaddun al-Islāmīyah.* 3 vols. Al-Qāhirah, A.H. 1322.

Slimane Mostfa Zbiss. "Mahdia et Ṣabra-Manṣoûriya." *Journal Asiatique* 244 (1956):79–93.

———. Al-Munastīr: Maʿālimuhā al-Āthārīyah. Tunis, n.d.

Alī Zeyadeh. "An Archaeological Assessment of Six Cities in al-Urdunn: From the Fourth Century to the Mid-Eighth Century A.D." In *The Fifth International Conference on the History of Bilād al-Shām during the ʿAbbāsid Period,* Arabic section, edited by Muḥammad ʿAdnān Bakhīt and Muḥammad Yūnus al-ʿAbbādī. Ammān, 1992.

———. "Baysan: A City from the Ninth Century A.D." In *Bilād al-Shām during the ʿAbbāsid Period,* English Section, edited by Muḥammad ʿAdnān Bakhīt and R. Schick, 2:114–34. Ammān, 1992.

V. A. Zhukovskii. *Razvaliny Starogo Merva (The Ruins of Old Marv).* N.p., 1894.

H. Ziegert and A. Abdussalam. "The White Mosque of Old Zuila." *Libya Antiqua* 9 and 10 (1973):221–22.

G. K. Zipf. *Human Behavior and the Principle of Least Effort.* New York, 1949.

M. H. al-Zubaydī. *Al-Ḥayāt al-Ijtimā ʿīyah wa-l-Iqtiṣādīya fī al-Kūfah fī-al-Qarn al-Awwal al-Hijrī.* Baghdād, A.H. 1379; al-Qāhirah, A.H. 1390.

INDEX